Electronic Commerce
2004

A Managerial Perspective

Electronic Commerce 2004

A Managerial Perspective

Efraim Turban
City University of Hong Kong

David King
Geac Computer Corporation Ltd.

Jae Lee
Korea Advanced Institute of Science and Technology

Dennis Viehland
Massey University, New Zealand

PEARSON
Prentice Hall

Pearson Education International

Executive Editor: Robert Horan
VP/Publisher: Natalie E. Anderson
Development Editor: Ann Torbert
Project Manager (Editorial): Lori Cerreto
Editorial Assistant: Robyn Goldenberg
Media Project Manager: Joan Waxman
Senior Marketing Manager: Sharon Koch
Marketing Assistant: Danielle Torio
Managing Editor (Production): John Roberts
Production Editor: Renata Butera
Production Assistant: Joe DeProspero
Permissions Supervisor: Suzanne Grappi
Manufacturing Buyer: Arnold Vila
Design Manager: Maria Lange
Interior Design: Jill Little
Cover Design: Pat Smythe/Jill Little
Cover Illustration: John Bleck
Manager, Print Production: Christy Mahon
Composition/Full-Service Project Management: BookMasters, Inc.
Printer/Binder: Courier-Kendallville

Credits and acknowledgments borrowed from other sources and reproduced, with permission, in this textbook appear on appropriate pages within the text.

Pearson Education LTD.
Pearson Education (Singapore), Pte. Ltd
Pearson Education, Canada, Ltd
Pearson Education–Japan
Pearson Education of Australia PTY. Limited

Pearson Education North Asia Ltd
Pearson Educación de Mexico, S.A. de C.V.
Pearson Education Malaysia, Pte. Ltd
Pearson Education, Upper Saddle River, New Jersey

10 9 8 7 6 5 4 3 2 1

ISBN 0-13-123015-8

Dedicated to all those who are interested in learning about electronic commerce.

Contents in Brief

www.prenhall.com/turban

Contents

Part 2 Internet Consumer Retailing   80

Part 6 EC Strategy and Implementation 563

Online Chapter

Online Appendix

Online Technical Appendixes

Online Tutorials

As we enter the third millennium, we are experiencing one of the most important changes to our daily lives—the move to an Internet-based society. The U.S. Department of Commerce reported that in January 2002 more than 55 percent of all Americans (141 million) surfed the Internet. More interesting is the fact that over 90 percent of people 5 to 17 years old surf the Internet on a regular basis. It is clear that this percentage will continue to increase. Similar trends exist in most other countries. As a result, much has changed at home, school, work, and in the government—and even in our leisure activities. Some changes are already here and are spreading around the globe. Others are just beginning. One of the most significant changes is in how we conduct business, especially in how we manage marketplaces and trading. For example, the senior author of this book pays all his bills online, trades stock online, buys airline and event tickets online, purchased his computer, printer, and memory sticks online, buys books online, and much more.

Electronic commerce (EC), also known as e-business, describes the manner in which transactions take place over networks, mostly the Internet. It is the process of electronically buying and selling goods, services, and information. Certain EC applications, such as buying and selling stocks on the Internet, are growing very rapidly. But electronic commerce is not just about buying and selling; it is also about electronically communicating, collaborating, and discovering information. It is about e-learning, e-government, and much more. Electronic commerce will impact a significant portion of the world, affecting businesses, professions, and, of course, people.

The impact of EC is not just in the creation of Web-based corporations; it is the building of a new industrial order. Such a revolution brings a myriad of opportunities as well as risks. Bill Gates is aware of this, as the company he founded, Microsoft, is continually developing Internet and EC products and services. Yet, Gates has stated that Microsoft is always two years away from failure—that somewhere out there is an unknown competitor who could render their business model obsolete. Bill Gates knows that competition today is not among products or services, but among business models. What is true for Microsoft is true for just about every other company. The hottest and most dangerous new business models out there are on the Web.

The purpose of this book is to describe the essentials of EC—how it is being conducted and managed as well as assessing its major opportunities, limitations, issues, and risks. As electronic commerce is an interdisciplinary topic, it should be of interest to managers and professional people in any functional area of the business world. People in government, education, health services, and other areas will benefit from learning about EC.

Today, EC is going through a period of consolidation in which enthusiasm for new technologies and ideas is now being accompanied by careful attention to strategy, implementation, and profitability. Most of all, people recognize that e-business has two parts; it is not just about technology, it is also about business.

This book is written by experienced authors who share academic as well as real-world practices. It is a comprehensive text that can be used in one-quarter, one-semester, or two-semester courses. It also can be used to supplement a text on Internet fundamentals, MIS, or marketing.

FEATURES OF THIS BOOK

Several features are unique to this book.

MANAGERIAL ORIENTATION

Electronic commerce (e-commerce) can be approached from two major aspects: technological and managerial. This text uses the second approach. Most of the presentations are about EC applications and implementation. However, we do recognize the importance of the technology; therefore, we present the essentials of security in Chapter 12 and the essentials of infrastructure and system development in Online Chapter 18, which is located on the book's Web site (www.prenhall.com/turban). We also provide some detailed technology material in the appendices and tutorials on the book's Web site.

INTERDISCIPLINARY APPROACH

E-commerce is interdisciplinary, and we illustrate this throughout the book. Major related disciplines include accounting, finance, information systems, marketing, management, and human resources management. In addition, some nonbusiness disciplines are related, especially public administration, computer science, engineering, psychology, political science, and law. Finally, economics plays a major role in the understanding of EC.

REAL-WORLD ORIENTATION

Extensive, vivid examples from large corporations, small businesses, and government and not-for-profit agencies from all over the world make concepts come alive. These examples show students the capabilities of EC, its cost and justification, and the innovative ways real corporations are using EC in their operations.

SOLID THEORETICAL BACKGROUND

Throughout the book we present the theoretical foundations necessary for understanding EC, ranging from consumer behavior to economic theory of competition. Furthermore, we provide Web site addresses, many exercises, and extensive references to supplement the theoretical presentations. Lists of additional readings are also available on the book's Web site. Finally, the Online Research Appendix offers topics, discussion, and resources relating to emerging research issues in e-commerce.

CURRENT EC TOPICS

The book presents the most current topics of EC, as evidenced by the many 2001, 2002, and 2003 citations. Topics such as e-learning, e-government, e-strategy, Web-based supply chain systems, collaborative commerce, mobile commerce, pervasive computing, and EC economics are presented both from the theoretical point of view and from the application side.

INTEGRATED SYSTEMS

In contrast to other books that highlight isolated Internet-based systems, we emphasize those systems that support the enterprise and supply chain management. Intra- and interorganizational systems are particularly highlighted, including the latest innovations in global EC and in Web-based applications.

GLOBAL PERSPECTIVE

The importance of global competition, partnerships, and trade is rapidly increasing. E-commerce facilitates export and import, the management of multinational companies, and electronic trading around the globe. International examples are provided throughout the book.

EC FAILURES AND LESSONS LEARNED

In addition to EC success stories, we also present EC failures, and, where possible, analyze the causes of those failures.

USER-FRIENDLINESS

While covering all major EC topics, this book is clear, simple, and well organized. It provides all the basic definitions of terms as well as logical conceptual support. Furthermore, the book is easy to understand and is full of interesting real-world examples and "war stories" that keep the reader's interest at a high level. Relevant review questions are provided at the end of each section so the reader can pause and digest the new material.

ORGANIZATION OF THE BOOK

The book is divided into 17 chapters grouped into six parts. One additional chapter, four technology appendixes, a research appendix, and tutorials are available as online supplements.

PART 1—INTRODUCTION TO E-COMMERCE AND E-MARKETPLACES

In Part 1 we provide an overview of the entire book as well as the fundamentals of EC and some of its terminology (Chapter 1) and a discussion of electronic markets and their mechanisms (Chapter 2).

PART 2—INTERNET CONSUMER RETAILING

In Part 2 we describe EC B2C applications in three chapters. Chapter 3 addresses e-tailing and electronic service industries. Chapter 4 deals with consumer behavior online and market research. Chapter 5 covers online advertising. A tutorial on building a B2C store front is available online (T2).

PART 3—BUSINESS-TO-BUSINESS E-COMMERCE

In Part 3 we examine the one-to-many B2B models (Chapter 6), including auctions, and the many-to-many models (Chapter 7), including exchanges. Chapter 8 describes the e-supply chain, intrabusiness EC, and collaborative commerce. An appendix to Chapter 6 provides discussion of the transition from traditional EDI to Internet-based EDI; an appendix to Chapter 7 provides additional material on extranets; and an appendix to Chapter 8 provides additional materials on intranets. Online tutorial T3 deals with the supply chain and its management.

PART 4—OTHER EC MODELS AND APPLICATIONS

Part 4 begins with several interesting applications such as e-government, e-learning, and consumer-to-consumer EC, as presented in Chapter 9. Chapter 10 explores the developing applications in the world of wireless EC (m-commerce, l-commerce, and pervasive computing).

PART 5—EC SUPPORT SERVICES

Chapter 11, the first chapter of Part 5, provides an overview of electronic auctions and bartering. Chapter 12 begins with a discussion of the need to protect privacy and intellectual property. It also describes various types of computer fraud and crime and discusses how to minimize these risks through appropriate security programs. Chapter 13 describes a major EC support service: electronic payments. Chapter 14 concentrates on order fulfillment and on content generation, delivery, and management.

PART 6—EC STRATEGY AND IMPLEMENTATION

Chapter 15 discusses strategic issues in implementing and deploying EC. The chapter also presents global EC and EC for small businesses. Chapter 16 is unique in any EC text; it describes how to build an Internet company from scratch. It takes you through all the necessary steps and provides you with guidelines for success. Chapter 17 deals with legal, ethical, and societal issues, and it concludes the book with an overview of future EC directions. An interactive online tutorial (T1) deals with creation of a business plan for Internet companies and a business case for EC applications. Finally, online Chapter 18 deals with EC applications development including the upcoming wave of Web services.

LEARNING AIDS

The text offers a number of learning aids to help the student.

- **Chapter outlines.** A listing of the main headings ("Content") at the beginning of each chapter provides a quick overview of the major topics covered.
- **Learning objectives.** Learning objectives at the beginning of each chapter help students focus their efforts and alert them to the important concepts to be discussed.
- **Opening vignettes.** Each chapter opens with a real-world example that illustrates the importance of EC to modern corporations. These cases were carefully chosen to call attention to the major topics covered in the chapters. Following each vignette, a short section titled "What We Can Learn . . ." links the important issues in the vignette to the subject matter of the chapter.
- **EC Application Cases.** In-chapter cases highlight real-world problems encountered by organizations as they develop and implement EC. Questions follow each case to help direct the student's attention to the implications of the case material.
- **Insights and Additions.** Topics sometimes require additional elaboration or demonstration. Insights and Additions boxes provide an eye-catching repository for such content.
- **Exhibits.** Numerous attractive exhibits (both illustrations and tables) extend and supplement the text discussion.
- **Review questions.** Each section ends with a series of review questions about that section. These questions are intended to help students summarize the concepts introduced and to digest the essentials of each section before moving on to another topic.
- **Marginal glossary and key terms.** Each bolded key term is defined in the margin when it first appears. In addition, an alphabetical list of key terms appears at the end of each chapter with a page reference to the location in the chapter where the term is discussed.
- **Managerial Issues.** The final section of every chapter explores some of the special concerns managers face as they adapt to doing business in cyberspace. These issues are framed as questions to maximize readers' active engagement with them.

▶ **Chapter summary.** The chapter summary is linked one-to-one to the learning objectives introduced at the beginning of each chapter.

▶ **End-of-chapter exercises.** Different types of questions measure students' comprehension and their ability to apply knowledge. Discussion Questions are intended to promote class discussion and develop critical thinking skills. Internet Exercises are challenging assignments that require students to surf the Internet and apply what they have learned. Over 250 hands-on exercises send students to interesting Web sites to conduct research, investigate an application, download demos, or learn about state-of-the-art technology. The Team Assignment and Role Playing exercises are challenging group projects designed to foster teamwork.

▶ **Real-World Cases.** Each chapter ends with a real-world case, which is presented in somewhat more depth than the in-chapter EC Application Cases. Questions follow each case.

SUPPLEMENTARY MATERIALS

The following support materials are also available.

INSTRUCTOR'S RESOURCE CD-ROM

This convenient *Instructor's CD-ROM* includes all of the supplements: Instructor's Manual, Test Item File, TestGen, PowerPoint Lecture Notes, and Image Library (text art).

The Instructor's Manual, written by Professor Jon C. Outland of National American University, includes answers to all review and discussion questions, exercises, and case questions. The Test Item File (Test Bank), written by Professor James Steele of Chattanooga State Technical Community College, includes multiple-choice, true-false, and essay questions for each chapter.

The Test Bank is provided in Microsoft Word, as well as in the form of TestGen.

The PowerPoint Lecture Notes, by Judy Lang, are oriented toward text learning objectives. They are also available at the book's Web site at www.prenhall.com/turban.

MYCOMPANION WEB SITE (WWW.PRENHALL.COM/TURBAN)

The book is supported by a MyCompanion web site that includes:

▶ An online chapter (Chapter 18 on EC applications and infrastructure).

▶ Bonus EC Application Cases and Insights and Additions features.

▶ An online appendix that focuses on the latest research topics in e-commerce. This unique appendix identifies 10 to 15 research issues per chapter, briefly discusses the issue, and provides a supportive literative review, including research-related URLs.

▶ Four technology appendices (on the topics of EC infrastructure, Web page design, Web programming, and software agents).

▶ Three interactive tutorials, two on storefront development and one on preparation of an EC business plan.

▶ A password-protected faculty area where instructors can download the Instructor's Manual and Test Item File.

▶ PowerPoint Lecture Notes.

▶ Interactive Study Guide, by Professor Jon C. Outland of National American University, includes multiple-choice, true-false, and essay questions for each chapter. Each question includes a hint and coaching tip for students' reference. Students receive automatic feedback upon submitting each quiz.

- All of the Internet Exercises from the end of each chapter in the text are provided on the Web site for convenient student use.
- EC case studies, some with teaching notes.
- Links to a large number of case studies, including customer success stories and academically oriented cases.
- Links to many EC vendors' sites.

WEB STRATEGY PRO

Prentice Hall is pleased to offer this powerful educational version of Web Strategy Pro software. This Windows-based, easy-to-use program allows you to bring the entire process of planning an Internet strategy alive in your classroom in seven easy steps. Web Strategy Pro is not available as a stand-alone item but can be packaged with the Turban text at an additional charge. Contact your local Prentice Hall representative for more details.

ONLINE COURSE SUPPORT

- **WebCT** (www.prenhall.com/webct). Gold Level Customer Support, available exclusively to adopters of Prentice Hall courses, is provided free of charge upon adoption and provides you with priority assistance, training discounts, and dedicated technical support.

- **BlackBoard** (www.prenhall.com/blackboard). Prentice Hall's abundant online content combined with BlackBoard's popular tools and interface result in robust Web-based courses that are easy to implement, manage, and use—taking your courses to new heights in student interaction and learning.

- **CourseCompass** (www.prenhall.com/coursecompass). CourseCompass is a dynamic, interactive online course management tool powered exclusively for Pearson Education by BlackBoard. This exciting product allows you to teach market-leading Pearson Education content in an easy-to-use customizable format.

ACKNOWLEDGMENTS

Many individuals helped us create this text. Faculty feedback was solicited via reviews and through a focus group. We are grateful to the following faculty for their contributions.

CONTENT CONTRIBUTORS

The following individuals contributed material for previous editions, some of which has been used in this edition as well:

- Judy Lang, Eastern Illinois University, contributed several of the cases and conducted much of the online research that supports this book, especially the current edition.
- Matthew Lee, City University of Hong Kong, an Internet lawyer and IS professor, contributed to Chapter 17.
- Merrill Warkentin of Mississippi State University contributed to Chapter 3. Merrill is a co-author of our *Electronic Commerce 2002*.
- Mohamed Khalifa, City University of Hong Kong, contributed to online Chapter 18.

REVIEWERS

We wish to thank the faculty who participated in reviews of this text and our other EC titles.

David Ambrosini, Cabrillo College

Deborah Ballou, University of Notre Dame

Martin Barriff, Illinois Institute of Technology

Stefan Brandle, Taylor University

Joseph Brooks, University of Hawaii

Clifford Brozo, Monroe College–New Rochelle

Stanley Buchin, Boston University

John Bugado, National University

Ernest Capozzolli, Troy State University

Jack Cook, State University of New York at Geneseo

Larry Corman, Fort Lewis College

Mary Culnan, Georgetown University

Ted Ferretti, Northeastern University

Ken Griggs, California Polytechnic University

Varun Grover, University of South Carolina

James Henson, Barry University

Paul Hu, University of Utah

Jim Im, Sacred Heart University

Jeffrey Johnson, Utah State University

Morgan Jones, University of North Carolina

Douglas Kline, Sam Houston State University

Mary Beth Klinger, College of Southern Maryland

Byungtae Lee, University of Illinois at Chicago

Lakshmi Lyer, University of North Carolina

Michael McLeod, East Carolina University

Susan McNamara, Northeastern University

Mohon Menon, University of South Alabama

Ajay Mishra, SUNY–Binghamton

Bud Mishra, New York University

William Nance, San Jose State University

Lewis Neisner, University of Maryland

Katherine Olson, Northern Virginia Community College

Craig Peterson, Utah State University

Dien Phan, University of Vermont

H. R. Rao, SUNY–Buffalo

Catherine Roche, Rockland Community College

Greg Rose, California State University, Chico

Linda Salchenberger, Loyola University of Chicago

George Schell, University of North Carolina at Wilmington

Sri Sharma, Oakland University

Sumit Sircar, University of Texas at Arlington

Kan Sugandh, DeVry Institute of Technology

Linda Volonino, Canisius College

Ken Williamson, James Madison University

Gregory Wood, Canisius College

James Zemanek, East Carolina University

Several individuals helped us with the administrative work. Special mention goes to Judy Lang of Eastern Illinois University who helped in editing, typing, URL verification, and more. We also thank the many students of City University of Hong Kong for their help in library searches, typing, and diagramming. Most of the work was done by Christy Cheung and Mavis Chan. We thank Daphne Turban and all these people for their dedication and superb performance shown throughout the project.

The Information System Department of City University of Hong Kong was extremely supportive in providing all the necessary assistance. Many faculty members provided advice and support material. Special thanks go to Kwok-Kee Wei, the department head, and to Doug Vogel, Matthew Lee, Chris Wagner, and Louis Ma.

We also recognize the various organizations and corporations that provided us with permission to reproduce material.

Thanks also to the Prentice Hall team that helped us from the inception of the project to its completion under the leadership of Executive Editor Bob Horan and Publisher and Vice President Natalie Anderson. The dedicated staff includes Project Manager–Editorial Lori Cerreto, Production Managers John Roberts and Gail Steier de Acevedo, Project Managers–Production Renata Butera and April Montana, Art Directors Maria Lange and Pat Smythe, Editorial Assistant Robyn Goldenberg, Senior Marketing Manager Sharon Koch, Marketing Assistant Danielle Torio, and Media Project Manager Joan Waxman.

Last, but not least, we thank Ann Torbert, the book's developmental editor, who spent long hours in contributing innovative ideas and providing the necessary editing.

OVERVIEW OF ELECTRONIC COMMERCE

Content

Learning objectives

Upon completion of this chapter, you will be able to:

1. Define electronic commerce (EC) and describe its various categories.

2. Describe and discuss the content and framework of EC.

3. Describe the major types of EC transactions.

4. Describe some EC business models.

5. Describe the benefits of EC to organizations, consumers, and society.

6. Describe the limitations of EC.

7. Describe the role of the digital revolution in EC.

8. Describe the contribution of EC to organizations responding to environmental pressures.

MARKS & SPENCER—A NEW WAY TO COMPETE

The Problem

Marks & Spencer (*marksandspencer.com*) is a UK-based, upscale, global retailer known for its high-quality, high-priced merchandise. Operating in more than 30 countries, the company faces stiff competition, especially since the beginning of the economic slowdown that started in 1999. Customer service became a critical success factor for Marks & Spencer. Other critical success factors included an appropriate store inventory system and efficient supply chain activities. To attract shoppers, the company had to reduce prices at its stores, which drastically reduced profit. Several other big retailers were wrestling with similar problems, including Kmart, which had to file for bankruptcy. Will Marks & Spencer (M & S), a world-class retailer, be able to survive?

The Solution

M & S realized that in the digital era survival depends on the use of information technology in general and *electronic commerce* in particular. Electronic commerce (EC, e-commerce) is a process of buying, selling, transferring, or exchanging products, services, and/or information via electronic networks and computers. M & S initiated several EC initiatives, including the following.

- **Selling online.** Like many other retailers, M & S sells some of its merchandise online. Shoppers can collect their merchandise in a "shopping basket," pay online, and receive the merchandise the next day (in the UK). Online shoppers are encouraged to provide a UPC code in order to get the same product they see at a physical store, frequently at a lower price.

- **Security.** A security system tracks transaction data in real time, looking for fraudulent events. If any fraudulent events are discovered, the system alerts the in-store security staff in the affected store by sending them a short text message via cell phone.

- **Warehouse management.** A mainframe-based warehouse management system, known as the Multi-User Warehouse System (MUWS), was installed first at M & S's Hardwick distribution center near Birmingham, United Kingdom. Using Microsoft.Net infrastructure, store sales are reported to a *data warehouse* (a repository of corporate data), almost in real time. The data are then available for decision making on inventory replenishment (when and how much to ship to each store). The data are also available

to the company's third-party logistics service providers, who run the warehouse operation and deliveries.

- **Merchandise receiving.** The process of matching orders and invoices is automated, making it faster and free of errors. Information about arriving goods is passed automatically to both the warehouse and the stores. This way MUWS can do a real-time check of arriving and available stock. Also, the system enables M & S to pay suppliers more quickly, which makes them happier and more cooperative.

- **Inventory control.** The warehouse management and the merchandise receiving system, in addition to the real-time data reporting, improve customer relationships. Customers can find what they want because replenishment is accomplished quickly (sometimes within one-half hour).

- **Speeding up the supply of fashion garments.** Using special software, merchandisers can access and change allocation plans from any computing device (PC, laptop, pocket PC) anywhere and at any time in response to changing demand patterns. This is especially important for fashion garments, where meeting ever-changing demand is critical for competitiveness.

- **Collaborative commerce.** M & S can now pass more accurate forecast demands to its suppliers for fast delivery of goods, often directly to the M & S retail stores. The new information system enables M & S to work with suppliers to reroute merchandise to different depots and change allocations to where they are needed.

The Results

M & S's CEO, in a message to the shareholders (summer 2002), indicated that a turnaround is underway. He sees M & S as a leader and example setter in retailing, resulting in increased profitability and growth.

Sources: Compiled from *marksandspencer.com*; various news reports during 2002; Penelope (2002); and *Financial Times* news items, 2002.

WHAT WE CAN LEARN . . .

As the story about M & S demonstrates, traditional brick-and-mortar companies are facing increasing pressures in a competitive marketing environment. A possible response to these pressures is to introduce a variety of e-commerce initiatives that can reduce costs, improve the supply chain operation (the flow of materials, information, and money from raw materials through factories and warehouses to the end customer), increase customer service, and open up markets to more customers. The implementation of such e-commerce initiatives and the issues involved will be explored in this chapter and throughout this textbook.

Chapter 1 defines e-commerce and discusses the content of the field and the various business models used. It illustrates the benefits and limitations of e-commerce. It also describes the digital economy and the role EC plays in enabling companies to survive and even prosper in it. Finally, the chapter demonstrates the "drivers" of EC that make it so attractive.

1.1 ELECTRONIC COMMERCE: DEFINITIONS AND CONCEPTS

Let's begin by looking at what a management guru, Peter Drucker, has to say about EC.

> The truly revolutionary impact of the Internet Revolution is just beginning to be felt. But it is not "information" that fuels this impact. It is not "artificial intelligence." It is not the effect of computers and data processing on decision making, policymaking, or strategy. It is something that practically no one foresaw or, indeed even talked about 10 or 15 years ago; e-commerce—that is, the explosive emergence of the Internet as a major, perhaps eventually *the* major, worldwide distribution channel for goods, for services, and, surprisingly, for managerial and professional jobs. This is profoundly changing economics, markets and industry structure, products and services and their flow; consumer segmentation, consumer values and consumer behavior; jobs and labor markets. But the impact may be even greater on societies and politics, and above all, on the way we see the world and ourselves in it. (Drucker 2002, pp. 3–4)

DEFINING EC

Electronic commerce (EC) describes the process of buying, selling, transferring, or exchanging products, services, and/or information via computer networks, including the Internet. EC can be defined from the following perspectives:

> ▸ **Communications.** From a communications perspective, EC is the delivery of goods, services, information, or payments over computer networks or by any other electronic means.
>
> ▸ **Commercial (trading).** From a commercial perspective, EC provides the capability of buying and selling products, services, and information on the Internet and via other online services.
>
> ▸ **Business process.** From a business process perspective, EC is doing business electronically by completing business processes over electronic networks, thereby substituting information for physical business processes (Weill and Vitale 2001, p. 13).
>
> ▸ **Service.** From a service perspective, EC is a tool that addresses the desire of governments, firms, consumers, and management to cut service costs while improving the quality of customer service and increasing the speed of service delivery.
>
> ▸ **Learning.** From a learning perspective, EC is an enabler of online training and education in schools, universities, and other organizations, including businesses.
>
> ▸ **Collaborative.** From a collaborative perspective, EC is the framework for inter- and intraorganizational collaboration.
>
> ▸ **Community.** From a community perspective, EC provides a gathering place for community members to learn, transact, and collaborate.

electronic commerce (EC)
The process of buying, selling, or exchanging products, services, and information via computer networks.

DEFINING E-BUSINESS

Some people view the term *commerce* only as describing transactions conducted between business partners. When this definition of commerce is used, the term *electronic commerce* would be fairly narrow. Thus, many use the term e-business instead. E-business refers to a broader definition of EC, not just the buying and selling of goods and services, but also servicing customers, collaborating with business partners, conducting e-learning, and conducting electronic transactions *within* an organization. However, some view e-business as the "other than buying and selling" activities on the Internet, such as collaboration and intrabusiness activities (online activities between and within businesses). In this book we use the broadest meaning of electronic commerce, which is basically equivalent to e-business. The two terms will be used interchangeably throughout the text.

e-business
A broader definition of EC, which includes not just the buying and selling of goods and services, but also servicing customers, collaborating with business partners, and conducting electronic transactions within an organization.

PURE VERSUS PARTIAL EC

Electronic commerce can take several forms depending on the *degree of digitization* (the transformation from physical to digital) of (1) the *product* (service) sold, (2) the *process,* and (3) the *delivery agent* (or intermediary). Choi et al. (1997) created a framework, shown in

Exhibit 1.1, that explains the possible configurations of these three dimensions. A product can be physical or digital, the process can be physical or digital, and the delivery agent can be physical or digital. These alternatives create eight cubes, each of which has three dimensions. In traditional commerce, all three dimensions are physical (lower-left cube), and in pure EC all dimensions are digital (upper-right cube). All other cubes include a mix of digital and physical dimensions.

If there is at least one digital dimension, we consider the situation EC, but only *partial EC*. For example, buying a shirt at Marks & Spencer online or a book from Amazon.com is partial EC, because the merchandise is physically delivered. However, buying an e-book from Amazon.com or a software product from Buy.com is *pure EC*, because the product, its delivery, payment, and transfer agent are all digital.

EC organizations. Pure physical organizations (corporations) are referred to as **brick-and-mortar** (or old-economy) **organizations**, whereas companies that are engaged only in EC are considered **virtual** or **pure-play organizations. Click-and-mortar** (or *click-and-brick*) **organizations** are those that conduct some e-commerce activities, yet their primary business is done in the physical world. Gradually, many brick-and-mortar companies are changing to click-and-mortar ones (e.g., Marks & Spencer).

INTERNET VERSUS NON-INTERNET EC

Most EC is done over the Internet, but EC can also be conducted on private networks, such as *value-added networks* (VANs, networks that add communications services to existing common carriers), on *local area networks* (LANs), or even on a single computerized machine. For example, buying food from a vending machine that you pay with a smart card or a cell phone can be viewed as EC activity.

An example of non-Internet EC would be field employees (such as sales reps) who are equipped with mobile handwriting-recognition computers so they can write their notes in the field; for instance, immediately after a sales call. (For a more in-depth example, see the Maybelline Real-World Case at the end of this chapter.)

brick-and-mortar organizations
Old-economy organizations (corporations) that perform most of their business off-line, selling physical products by means of physical agents.

virtual (pure-play) organizations
Organizations that conduct their business activities solely online.

click-and-mortar organizations
Organizations that conduct some e-commerce activities, but do their primary business in the physical world.

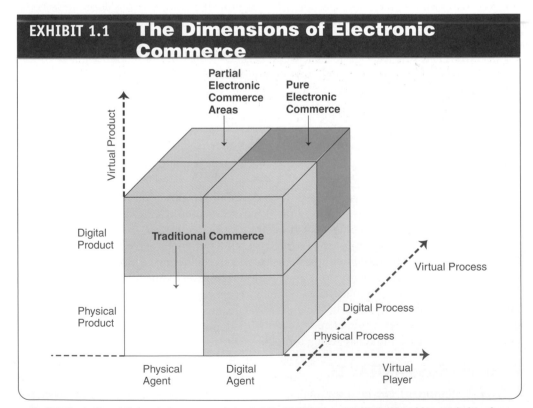

EXHIBIT 1.1 The Dimensions of Electronic Commerce

Source: *Economics of Electronic Commerce,* 1/E by Choi/Stahl/Whinston, ©1997. Reprinted by permission of Pearson Education, Inc., Upper Saddle River, NJ.

ELECTRONIC MARKETS AND INTERORGANIZATIONAL AND INTRAORGANIZATIONAL INFORMATION SYSTEMS

E-commerce can be conducted in an **electronic market** where buyers and sellers meet online to exchange goods, services, money, or information. Electronic markets may be supplemented by interorganizational or intraorganizational information systems. **Interorganizational information systems (IOSs)** are those where only routine transaction processing and information flow take place between two or more organizations. E-commerce activities that take place *within* individual organizations are facilitated by **intraorganizational information systems**. These systems are also known as *intrabusiness EC.*

Section 1.1 ▶ REVIEW

1. Define EC and e-business.
2. Distinguish between pure and partial EC.
3. Define click-and-mortar organizations.
4. Define electronic markets, IOSs, and intraorganizational information systems.

1.2 THE EC FRAMEWORK, CLASSIFICATION, AND CONTENT

The opening case illustrates a new way of conducting business—electronically, using networks and the Internet. The case demonstrates the many ways that businesses can use e-commerce to improve the bottom line. In general, there are two major types of e-commerce: *business-to-consumer (B2C)* and *business-to-business (B2B)*. In B2C transactions, online transactions are made between businesses and individual consumers, such as the selling of merchandise at Marks & Spencer's Web site. In B2B transactions, businesses make online transactions with other businesses, such as M & S electronically buying merchandise from its suppliers. M & S also conducts EC inside its own organization (*intrabusiness* EC), including services to its own employees (*business-to-employees*, or *B2E*). Several other types of EC will be described soon.

With only a few products and services that are now sold globally (e.g., financial services), EC is not yet a significant global economic element. Predictions are that it could become globally significant within 10 to 20 years (Drucker 2002). Networked computing is the infrastructure for EC, and it is rapidly emerging as the standard computing environment for business, home, and government applications. *Networked computing* connects multiple computers and other electronic devices that are located in several different locations by telecommunications networks, including *wireless* ones. This connection allows users to access information stored in several different physical locations and to communicate and collaborate with people separated by great geographic distances.

Although some people still use a stand-alone computer exclusively, the vast majority of people use computers connected to a global networked environment known as the *Internet* or to its counterpart within organizations, an intranet. An **intranet** is a corporate or government network that uses Internet tools, such as Web browsers, and Internet protocols. Another computer environment is an **extranet**, a network that uses the Internet to link multiple intranets (see Fingar et al. 2000).

Networked computing is enabling large numbers of organizations, both private and public, in manufacturing, agriculture, and services not only to excel, but also in many cases simply to survive.

AN EC FRAMEWORK

The EC field is a diversified one, involving many activities, organizational units, and technologies (e.g., see Shaw et al. 2000). Therefore, a framework that describes its content is useful. Exhibit 1.2 (page 6) introduces one such framework.

As can be seen in the exhibit, there are many EC applications (top of exhibit), some of which were illustrated in the opening case about Marks & Spencer; others will be shown throughout the book. (Also see Huff et al. 2001 and Farhoomand and Lovelock 2001.) To execute these applications, companies need the right information, infrastructure, and support

---

electronic market (e-marketplace)
An online marketplace where buyers and sellers meet to exchange goods, services, money, or information.

interorganizational information systems (IOSs)
Communications system that allows routine transaction processing and information flow between two or more organizations.

intraorganizational information systems
Communication systems that enable e-commerce activities to go on *within* individual organizations.

intranet
An internal corporate or government network that uses Internet tools, such as Web browsers, and Internet protocols.

extranet
A network that uses the Internet to link multiple intranets.

EXHIBIT 1.2   A Framework for Electronic Commerce

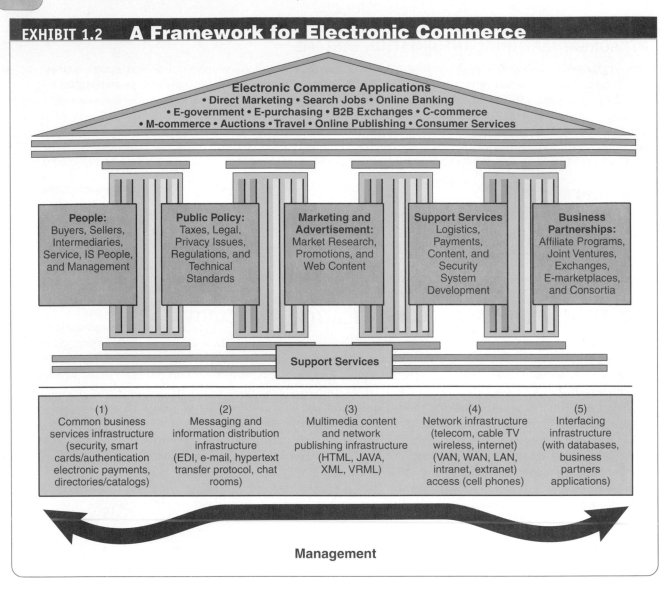

services. Exhibit 1.2 shows that the EC applications are supported by infrastructure and by five support areas (shown as supporting pillars). These pillars are:

- **People.** Sellers, buyers, intermediaries, information systems specialists, other employees, and any other participants comprise an important support area.
- **Public policy.** Legal and other policy and regulating issues, such as privacy protection and taxation, which are determined by governments. Included as part of public policy is the issue of technical standards, which are established by government-mandated policy-making groups.
- **Marketing and advertising.** Like any other business, EC usually requires the support of marketing and advertising. This is especially important in B2C online transactions where the buyers and sellers usually not know each other.
- **Support services.** Many services are needed to support EC. These range from content creation to payments to order delivery.
- **Business partnerships.** Joint ventures, exchanges, and business partnerships of various sorts are common in EC. These occur frequently throughout the *supply chain* (i.e., the interactions between a company and its suppliers, customers, and other partners).

At the bottom of Exhibit 1.2 is the infrastructure for EC. The infrastructure support describes the hardware, software, and networks used in EC, ranging from browsers to multimedia. All of these infrastructure components require good *management practices*. This means that companies need to plan, organize, motivate, devise strategy, and reengineer processes as needed to optimize their business using EC tools and strategies. Management also deals with strategic and operational decisions (see Chapter 15 and examples throughout the book.)

Exhibit 1.2 can be viewed as a framework for understanding the relationships among the EC applications and other EC components and for conducting research in the EC field. In this text, we will provide details on most of the components of the framework. The infrastructures of EC are described in online Technical Appendixes A through D on the book's Web site and in the online Chapter 18.

CLASSIFICATION OF EC BY THE NATURE OF THE TRANSACTIONS OR INTERACTIONS

A common classification of EC is by the nature of the transaction or the relationship among participants. The following types are commonly distinguished.

Business-to-business (B2B). All of the participants in **business-to-business (B2B)** e-commerce are businesses or other organizations (see Chapters 6–8). For example, several of Marks & Spencer's applications involve B2B with its suppliers. Today, over 85 percent of EC volume is B2B (Cunningham 2001).

Business-to-Consumer (B2C). **Business-to-consumer (B2C)** EC includes retail transactions of products or services from businesses to individual shoppers. The typical shopper at Marks & Spencer online or at Amazon.com is a *consumer* or *customer*. This EC type is also called **e-tailing** (see Chapter 3).

Business-to-business-to-consumer (B2B2C). In **business-to-business-to-consumer (B2B2C)** EC, a business provides some product or service to a client business. The client business maintains its own customers, which can be its own employees, to whom the product or service is provided without adding any value to it. One example is that of a company that pays AOL to provide its employees with Internet access (rather than having each employee pay an access fee directly to AOL). Another example is wholesaler-to-retailer-to-consumer merchandising, such as Qantas' Pan Pacific, which provides travel services such as airline tickets and hotel rooms to business partners such as travel agencies, who sell the services to customers. (For more, see the book's Web site, Chapter 18). The term B2B frequently includes B2B2C as well.

Consumer-to-business (C2B). The **consumer-to-business (C2B)** category includes individuals who use the Internet to sell products or services to organizations, as well as individuals who seek sellers to bid on products or services they need (see Chapter 2). Priceline.com is a well-known C2B organizer of such transactions.

Consumer-to-consumer (C2C). In the **consumer-to-consumer (C2C)** category (see Chapter 3), consumers sell directly to other consumers. Examples include individuals selling residential property, cars, and so on, in online classified ads. The advertisement of personal services over the Internet and the selling of knowledge and expertise online are other examples of C2C. In addition, many auction sites allow individuals to place items up for auction.

Peer-to-peer applications. **Peer-to-peer** technology can be used in C2C, B2B, and B2C (see Chapter 9). This technology enables networked peer computers to share data and processing with each other directly. For example, in a C2C peer application, people can exchange (swap) music, videos, software, and other digitizable goods electronically.

Mobile commerce. E-commerce transactions and activities conducted in full or in part in a *wireless environment* are referred to as **mobile commerce**, or **m-commerce** (see Chapter 10). For example, from some suitably equipped cell phones, a person can do their banking or order a book from Amazon.com. Many m-commerce applications involve Internet-enabled mobile devices. If such transactions are targeted to individuals in specific locations, at specific times, they are referred to as **location-based commerce**, or **l-commerce**, transactions. Some people define m-commerce as transactions conducted with people who are away from their home or office; such transactions can be done both on wireless or wireline systems. (See the Maybelline case at the end of this chapter.)

Intrabusiness EC. The **intrabusiness EC** category includes all internal organizational activities that involve the exchange of goods, services, or information among various units

---

business-to-business (B2B)
E-commerce model in which all of the participants are businesses or other organizations.

business-to-consumer (B2C)
E-commerce model in which businesses sell to individual shoppers.

e-tailing
Online retailing, usually B2C.

business-to-business-to-consumer (B2B2C)
E-commerce model in which a business provides some product or service to a client business that maintains its own customers.

consumer-to-business (C2B)
E-commerce model in which individuals use the Internet to sell products or services to organizations or individuals seek sellers to bid on products or services they need.

consumer-to-consumer (C2C)
E-commerce model in which consumers sell directly to other consumers.

peer-to-peer
Technology that enables networked peer computers to share data and processing with each other directly; can be used in C2C, B2B, and B2C e-commerce.

mobile commerce (m-commerce)
E-commerce transactions and activities conducted in a wireless environment.

location-based commerce (l-commerce)
M-commerce transactions targeted to individuals in specific locations, at specific times.

intrabusiness EC
E-commerce category that includes all internal organizational activities that involve the exchange of goods, services, or information among various units and individuals in an organization.

business-to-employees (B2E)
E-commerce model in which an organization delivers services, information, or products to its individual employees.

collaborative commerce (c-commerce)
E-commerce model in which individuals or groups communicate or collaborate online.

e-learning
The online delivery of information for purposes of training or education.

exchange (electronic)
A public electronic market with many buyers and sellers.

exchange-to-exchange (E2E)
E-commerce model in which electronic exchanges formally connect to one another for the purpose of exchanging information.

e-government
E-commerce model is which a government entity buys or provides goods, services, or information to businesses or individual citizens.

and individuals in that organization. Activities can range from selling corporate products to one's employees to online training and collaborative design efforts (see Chapter 8). Intrabusiness EC is usually performed on intranets or *corporate portals* (in general, gateways to the Web).

Business-to-employees (B2E). The **business-to-employees (B2E)** category is a subset of the intrabusiness category, in which the organization delivers services, information, or products to individual employees, as Maybelline is doing (see the Real-World Case at the end of this chapter). A major category of employees are *mobile employees,* such as field representatives. EC support to such employees is called *B2ME (business-to-mobile employees).*

Collaborative commerce. When individuals or groups communicate or collaborate online, they may be engaged in **collaborative commerce,** or **c-commerce** (see Chapter 8). For example, business partners in different locations may design a product together, using screen sharing, or they may jointly forecast product demand, as Marks & Spencer does with its suppliers.

Nonbusiness EC. An increased number of nonbusiness institutions such as academic institutions, not-for-profit organizations, religious organizations, social organizations, and government agencies are using EC to reduce their expenses or to improve their general operations and customer service. (Note that in the previous categories one can usually replace the word *business* with *organization.*)

E-Learning. In **e-learning,** training or education is provided online (see Chapter 9). E-learning is used heavily by organizations for training employees (called *e-training*). It is also practiced at virtual universities.

Exchange-to-exchange (E2E). An **exchange** describes a *public electronic market* with many buyers and sellers (see Chapter 7). As B2B exchanges proliferate, it is logical for exchanges to connect to one another. **Exchange-to-exchange (E2E) EC** is a formal system that connects exchanges.

E-Government. In **e-government** EC, a government entity buys or provides goods, services, or information to businesses (G2B) or to individual citizens (G2C). An example of e-government initiative is provided in EC Application Case 1.1.

We will provide many examples of these various types of EC transactions throughout this book.

THE INTERDISCIPLINARY NATURE OF EC

Because EC is a new field, it is just now developing its theoretical and scientific foundations. From just a brief overview of the EC framework and classification, you can probably see that EC is related to several different disciplines. The major EC disciplines include the following: *computer science, marketing, consumer behavior, finance, economics, management information systems, accounting, management, business law, robotics, public administration,* and *engineering.*

A BRIEF HISTORY OF EC

EC applications were first developed in the early 1970s with innovations such as *electronic funds transfer* (EFT) (see Chapter 13) in which funds could be routed electronically from one organization to another. However, the extent of the applications was limited to large corporations, financial institutions, and a few other daring businesses. Then came *electronic data interchange* (EDI), a technology used to electronically transfer routine documents, which expanded electronic transfers from financial transactions to other types of transaction processing (such as ordering). (See Chapter 6 for more on EDI.) This new application enlarged the pool of participating companies from financial institutions to manufacturers, retailers, services, and many other types of businesses. More new EC applications followed, ranging from travel reservation systems to stock trading. Such systems were called *interorganizational system* (IOS) applications, and their strategic value to businesses has been widely recognized.

The Internet began life as an experiment by the U.S. government in 1969, and its initial users were a largely technical audience of government agencies and academic researchers and scientists. When the Internet commercialized and users began flocking to participate in the World Wide Web in the early 1990s, the term *electronic commerce* was coined. EC applications rapidly expanded. A large number of so-called *dot-coms,* or *Internet start-ups,* also

CASE 1.1
EC Application
VOICE-BASED 511 TRAVELER INFORMATION LINE

Tellme Networks, Inc. (*tellme.com*) developed the first voice-activated 511 traveler information line in Utah, setting a national example for future 511 services to be launched by Department of Transportation (DOT) agencies on a state-by-state basis in the United States. The 511 service debuted on December 18, 2001. Simply by using their voices, callers on regular or cell phones within the state of Utah are now able to request and get real-time information on traffic, road conditions, public transportation, and so on. The answers are generated from the Internet and participating databases. During the February 2002 Olympic Winter Games, callers were able to request event schedules, driving directions, up-to-the-minute news and announcements, and tips for avoiding traffic congestion.

In July 2000, the U.S. Federal Communications Commission (FCC) officially allocated 511 as the single nationwide number for traveler information, in the same way callers can dial 411 for directory assistance and 911 for emergency services. Previously, state governments and local transportation agencies used more than 300 local telephone numbers nationwide to provide traffic and traveler information. This marks the first time one number has been accessible for people to access travel information whether they are touring the country or simply driving home from work. The Utah 511 travel information line is provided as a free service by the Utah DOT.

The 511 application is a special use of voice portals (see Chapters 2, 8, and 10), in which callers can access the Web from any telephone by voice. Martin Knopp, Director of Intelligent Transportation Systems, Utah DOT, said, "As the national 511 working group has stipulated, voice recognition is the way for callers to access information on 511. . . . In addition, there was no up-front capital cost and we were able to leverage the same information and investment we had made in our regular Web infrastructure" (quoted by Singer 2001).

Tellme Networks is revolutionizing how people and businesses use the telephone by fundamentally improving the caller's experience with Internet and voice technologies. Tellme enables businesses and governments to empower their callers while slashing costs and complexity.

Source: Condensed from *tellme.com* (accessed May 2002).

Questions

1. Enter *tellme.com* and find more information about this case. Summarize the benefits to the users.

2. What is the role of Tellme? What Internet technology is used?

3. Can this application be classified as m-commerce? As l-commerce? Why or why not?

---

appeared (see Cassidy 2002). One reason for this rapid expansion was the development of new networks, protocols, and EC software. The other reason was the increase in competition and other business pressures (see discussion in Section 1.5).

Since 1995, Internet users have witnessed the development of many innovative applications, ranging from online direct sales to e-learning experiences. Almost every medium- and large-sized organization in the world now has a Web site, and most large U.S. corporations have comprehensive portals through which employees, business partners, and the public can access corporate information. Many of these sites contain tens of thousand of pages and links. In 1999, the emphasis of EC shifted from B2C to B2B, and in 2001 from B2B to B2E, c-commerce, e-government, e-learning, and m-commerce. Given the nature of technology and the Internet, EC will undoubtedly continue to shift and change. Lately, we are seeing more and more EC successes (see Athitakis 2003).

EC Successes

During the last few years we have seen extremely successful virtual EC companies such as eBay, VeriSign, AOL, and Checkpoint. We also have witnessed major successes in click-and-mortar companies such as Cisco, General Electric, IBM, Intel, and Schwab (see Carton 2002; Farhoomand and Lovelock 2001; Saloner 2001; and Huff et al. 2001). There are many success stories of start-up companies such as Alloy.com (a young adults–oriented portal), Drugstore.com, FTD.com, PTSweb.com, and Campusfood.com (see EC Application Case 1.2 on page 10).

EC Failures

Starting in 1999, a large number of EC-dedicated companies, especially e-tailing ones, began to fail (see startupfailures.com; disobey.com/ghostsites; Useem 2000; Carton 2002; Perkins and Perkins 2001; and Kaplan 2002). Well-known B2C failures are eToys, Xpeditor, MarchFirst,

CASE 1.2

EC Application

THE SUCCESS STORY OF CAMPUSFOOD.COM

Campusfood's recipe for success was a simple one: Provide interactive menus to college students, using the power of the Internet to replace and/or facilitate the traditional telephone ordering of meals. Launched at the University of Pennsylvania (Penn), the company is taking thousands of orders each month for local restaurants, bringing pizzas, hoagies, and wings to the Penn community and to dozens of other universities.

Founder Michael Saunders began developing the site (*campusfood.com*) in 1997 while he was a junior at Penn. With the help of some classmates, Saunders launched the site in 1998. After graduation, he began building the company's customer base. This involved expanding to other universities, attracting students, and generating a list of restaurants from which students could order food for delivery. Currently, some of these activities are outsourced to a marketing firm, enabling the addition of dozens of schools nationwide.

Financed through private investors, friends, and family members, the site was built on an investment of less than $1 million. (For comparison, another company with services also reaching the college-student market invested $100 million.) Campusfood.com's revenue is generated through *transaction fees*—the site takes a 5 percent commission on each order from the sellers (the restaurants).

When you visit *campusfood.com*, you can:

▸ Navigate through a list of local restaurants, their hours of operation, addresses, phone numbers, and other information.
▸ Browse an interactive menu. The company takes a restaurant's standard print menu and converts it to an electronic menu that lists every topping, every special, and every drink offered, along with the latest prices.
▸ Bypass "busy" telephone signals to place an order online, and in so doing, avoid miscommunications.
▸ Get access to special foods, promotions, and restaurant giveaways. The company is working to set up meal deals that are available online exclusively for Campusfood.com customers.
▸ Arrange electronic payment of your order.

Sources: Compiled from Prince (2000) and *campusfood.com* (2002).

Questions

1. Classify this application by EC transaction type.
2. Explain the benefits of Campusfood.com for its student customers and for the restaurants it represents.
3. Trace the flow of digitized information in this venture.
4. How does the outsourcing of the marketing activities contribute to the business?

Drkoop.com, Webvan.com, and Boo.com. Well-known B2B failures are Chemdex.com, Ventro.com, and Verticalnet.com. (Incidentally, the history of these pioneering companies is documented in a special project by David Kirch at the Business School, University of Maryland.) We will discuss reasons for these and other EC failures in detail in Chapters 3 and 15.

Does the large number of failures mean that EC's days are numbered? Absolutely not! First, the dot-com failure rate is declining sharply. Second, the EC field is basically experiencing consolidation, as companies test different business models and organizational structures. Third, most pure EC companies, including giants such as Amazon.com, are not yet making a profit or are making only small profits, but they *are* expanding operations and generating increasing sales. (Amazon.com posted its first quarterly profit in the fourth quarter of 2001, largely on the strength of holiday sales, though it still lost money for the year.) Some analysts predict that by 2004 many of the major pure EC companies will begin to generate profits.

THE FUTURE OF EC

In 1996, Forrester Research Institute (forrester.com), a major EC-industry analyst, predicted that B2C would be a $6.6 billion business in 2000, up from $518 million in 1996. In 2000, B2C sales in the United States actually were about $18 billion, or 1 percent of total retail sales. Today's predictions about the future size of EC, provided by respected analysts such as AMR Research, Emarketer.com, and Forrester, vary (also see Plunkett 2001). For example, for 2004, total online shopping and B2B transactions in the United States are estimated to be in the range of $3 to $7 trillion. The number of Internet users worldwide is predicted to reach 750 million by 2008. Experts predict that as many as 50 percent of all Internet users will shop online by that time. EC growth will come not only from B2C, but also from B2B and from newer applications such as e-government, e-learning, B2E, and c-commerce. Overall, the growth of the field will continue into the foreseeable future. (See Chapter 17 for further discussion about the EC future.) Despite the failures of individual companies and initiatives, the total volume of EC is continuously growing.

Section 1.2 ▶ REVIEW

1. List the major components of the EC framework.
2. List the major transactional types of EC.
3. Describe the major landmarks in EC history.
4. List some EC successes and failures.

1.3   E-COMMERCE BUSINESS PLANS, CASES, AND MODELS

One of the major characteristics of EC is that it enables the creation of new business models. A **business model** is a method of doing business by which a company can generate revenue to sustain itself. The model also spells out where the company is positioned in the value chain—that is, by what activities the company adds value to the product or service it supplies. (The *value chain* is the series of value-adding activities that an organization performs to achieve its goals at various stages of the production process.) Some models are very simple. For example, Marks & Spencer buys merchandise, sells it, and generates a profit. In contrast, a TV station provides free broadcasting to its viewers. The station's survival depends on a complex model involving advertisers and content providers. Public Internet portals, such as Yahoo, also use a complex business model. One company may have several business models.

> Business models are a subset of a business plan or a business case. Frequently these concepts are mixed up. (In other words, some equate a business model to a business plan.) However, as the next section explains, business plans and cases are different from business models.

business model
A method of doing business by which a company can generate revenue to sustain itself.

BUSINESS PLANS AND BUSINESS CASES

A **business plan** is a written document that identifies the business goals and outlines the organization's plan of how to achieve them. Business plans are used for various purposes. Entrepreneurs use business plans to get funding from investors, such as *venture capitalists.* Or, a business plan can be used for the purposes of restructuring or reengineering an organization. The term is a very broad one, its meaning varies with the type, purpose, and size of the plan and the amount of money involved. The content of a typical business plan is shown in Exhibit 1.3. An interactive example is provided in online tutorial T1. Several software packages are available for the creation of business plans (e.g., see bplans.com and planware.org).

business plan
A written document that identifies the business goals and outlines the plan of how to achieve them.

EXHIBIT 1.3   The Content of a Business Plan: Suggested Structure for a Dot-Com Business Plan

- **Mission statement and company description.**
- **The management team:** Who they are, their experience, etc.
- **The market and the customers:** Who the potential customers are (demographics, location, etc). The size of the market and how the market will be served by the proposed company and product. What the perceived value proposition is.
- **The industry and competition:** What companies and products the proposed business is going to compete with. The competitive advantage of the proposal.
- **The product or service:** The specifics of the products and/or services to be offered and how they will be developed.
- **Marketing and sales plans and strategies:** How marketing and sales will be done. Advertising and promotion plans. How customer service will be provided. Is there a need for a market research? If so, how will it be done?
- **Operations:** How the business will be run. What operations will be done in house and what will be outsourced.
- **Financial projections and plans:** The revenue generation model, cash flow, cost of financing, and so on.
- **Risk analysis:** How risky is the venture? What are the contingencies?
- **Technology analysis:** What technology is necessary and how it is going to be obtained.
- **Organization structure:** What organizational structure is necessary to support the business plan.

Source: Based on Eglash (2001).

business case
A written document that is used by managers to garner funding for specific applications or projects; its major emphasis is the justification for a specific investment.

A **business case** is a written document that is used by managers to garner funding for one or more specific applications or projects. It is narrower than a business plan: Its major emphasis is the justification for a specific required investment. A business case is usually conducted in *existing organizations* that want to embark on new EC projects, for example, an e-procurement project. The business case provides the bridge between the initial plan and its execution. Its purpose is not only to get approval and funding, but also to provide the foundation for tactical decision making and technology risk management. The business case helps to clarify how the organization will use its resources in the best way to accomplish the e-strategy. (A complete coverage of business cases for e-commerce is provided by Kalakota and Robinson 2001 and in online tutorial T1 on the book's Web site.) Software for preparing a business case for e-commerce is commercially available (e.g., from paloalto.com and from bplans.com).

Note that a business plan concentrates on the *viability* of a company, whereas a business case concentrates on justification, risk management, and fit of an EC project or initiative with the organization's mission. One business plan or business case may contain one or several business models.

THE STRUCTURE OF BUSINESS MODELS

The structure of business models varies because the methods used by companies to generate revenue to sustain themselves vary widely. Similarly, there are several different structures of EC business models, depending on the company, the industry, and so on.

Weill and Vitale (2001) developed a framework for evaluating the viability of e-business initiatives. According to this methodology, there are eight elementary, or "atomic," e-business models, which can be combined in different ways to create operational e-business initiatives. The eight atomic business models are direct marketing, intermediary, content provider, full-service provider, shared infrastructure, value net integrator, virtual community, and consolidator of services for large organizations. For example, the Amazon.com business model combines direct marketing, the intermediary role, virtual community, and content provider. Each atomic model can be described by four characteristics: strategic objectives, sources of revenue, critical success factors, and core competencies required. The authors show how to combine the atomic business models into initiatives and how to evaluate them properly. We will return to this issue in Chapter 15.

All business models must specify their *revenue model* and a *value proposition*.

Revenue Models

revenue model
Description of how the company or an EC project will earn revenue.

A **revenue model** outlines how the organization or the EC project will earn revenue. For example, in our opening case, the revenue model for M & S's EC project showed revenue from online sales. The major revenue models are:

▶ **Sales.** Companies generate revenue from selling merchandise on their Web sites or from providing a service. An example is when Walmart.com or M & S sells a product online.

▶ **Transaction fees.** A company receives a commission based on the volume of transactions made. For example, when you sell a house, you typically pay a transaction fee to the broker. The higher the value of the sale, the higher the total transaction fee. Alternatively, transaction fees can be levied *per transaction*. In trading stocks electronically, for example, you pay a fixed fee per trade, regardless of the volume.

▶ **Subscription fees.** Customers pay a fixed amount, usually monthly, to get some type of service. An example would be the access fee to AOL. Thus, AOL's primary revenue model is subscription (fixed monthly payments).

▶ **Advertising fees.** Companies charge others for allowing them to place a banner on their sites (see Chapter 4).

▶ **Affiliate fees.** Companies receive commissions for referring customers to other Web sites.

▶ **Other revenue sources.** Some companies allow you to play games for a fee or to watch a sports competition in real time for a fee (e.g., see msn.espn.go.com). Another revenue source is licensing fees (e.g., datadirect-technologies.com). Licensing fees can be assessed as an annual fee or a per usage fee. Microsoft takes fees from each workstation that uses Windows, for example.

A company uses its revenue model to describe how it will earn income and its business model to describe the *process* it will use to earn revenue. Exhibit 1.4 summarizes five common revenue models. For example, the revenue model of 7-Eleven stores in Japan is the sales model. Its business model would show that customers can order products online (using a PC or a cell phone) or at 7-Eleven stores, where they can pay the cashier. The customers can pick up the merchandise at 7-Eleven stores (only in Japan in 2002) or, for an extra charge, can have it shipped to their homes. The revenue comes from sales, which take place both off-line and online.

The revenue model can be part of the value proposition or it may complement it.

Value Proposition

Business plans also include a value proposition statement in their business model. A **value proposition** refers to the benefits, including the intangible, nonquantitative ones, that a company can derive from conducting operations (such as from using EC). In B2C e-commerce, for example, a value proposition defines how a company product or service fulfills the needs of customers. The value proposition is an important part of the marketing plan of any product or service.

value proposition
The benefits a company can derive from using EC.

Specifically, how do e-marketplaces create value? Amit and Zott (2001) identify four sets of values being created by e-business: *search and transaction cost efficiency, complementarities, lock-in,* and *novelty. Search and transaction cost efficiency* enables faster and more informed decision making, wider product and service selection, and greater economies of scale (cost savings per unit as greater quantities are produced) through demand and supply aggregation for small buyers and sellers. *Complementarities* involve bundling some goods and services together to provide more value than offering them separately. *Lock-in* is attributable to the high switching cost that ties customers to particular suppliers. *Novelty* creates value through innovative ways for structuring transactions, connecting partners, and fostering new markets.

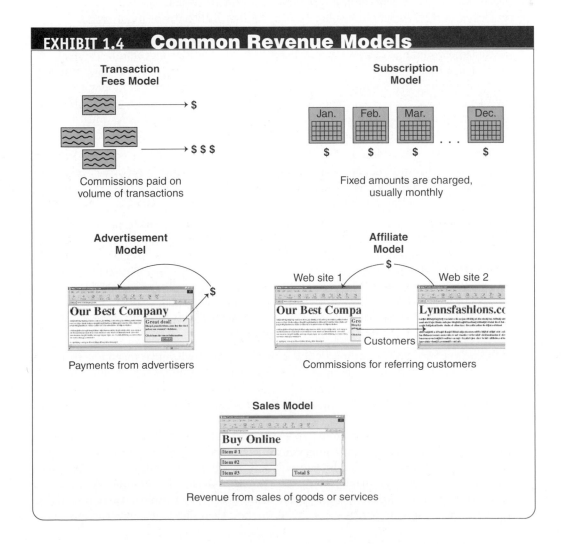

EXHIBIT 1.4   Common Revenue Models

Transaction Fees Model
Commissions paid on volume of transactions

Subscription Model
Jan. Feb. Mar. Dec.
Fixed amounts are charged, usually monthly

Advertisement Model
Our Best Company
Great deal!
Payments from advertisers

Affiliate Model
Web site 1   Web site 2
Our Best Compa   Lynnsfashlons.co
Customers
Commissions for referring customers

Sales Model
Buy Online
Item #1
Item #2
Item #3   Total $
Revenue from sales of goods or services

Bakos (1991) identifies similar values: reduced search cost, significant switching cost, economies of scale and scope, and network externality (the tendency for consumers to place more value on a good or service as more of the market uses that good or service). Bakos regards *search cost reduction* as the single attribute most specific to e-marketplaces. It is the subject of analysis in many studies on e-marketplaces.

Other value propositions have not received the same level of attention, though they are not necessarily less significant. Overall, they fall along two dimensions: demand (and/or supply) *aggregation* and *interfirm collaboration*. Aggregation overcomes market fragmentation, affording suppliers with wider market access, buyers with more choices, and both with price transparency (meaning that the price they see is the price they get). Collaboration enables market participants to build and deepen their business relationships for the purposes of improving individual business processes and overall supply chain performance. For further details on aggregation and collaboration, see Le (2002).

TYPICAL BUSINESS MODELS IN EC

There are many types of EC business models. Examples and details can be found throughout this text (and also in Weill and Vitale 2001; Timmers 1999; Applegate 2000; and Afuah and Tucci 2003). The following list describes some of the most common or visible models. Details are provided throughout the text.

tendering (reverse auction)
Model in which a buyer requests would-be sellers to submit bids, and the lowest bidder wins.

name-your-own-price model
Model in which a buyer sets the price he or she is willing to pay and invites sellers to supply the good or service at that price.

affiliate marketing
An arrangement whereby a marketing partner (a business, an organization, or even an individual) refers consumers to the selling company's Web site.

1. **Online direct marketing.** The most obvious model is that of selling online, from a manufacturer to a customer (eliminating intermediaries), or such as in the case of Marks & Spencer, from retailers to consumers (making distribution more efficient). Such a model is especially efficient for digitizable products and services (those that can be delivered electronically). There are several variations to this model (see Chapters 2, 3, and 6). It is practiced in B2C (where it is called *e-tailing*) and in B2B types of EC.

2. **Electronic tendering systems.** Large organizational buyers, private or public, usually make large-volume or large-value purchases through a **tendering** (bidding) system, also known as a *reverse auction*. The buyer requests would-be sellers to submit bids, the lowest bidder wins. Such a tendering can be done online, saving time and money. Pioneered by General Electric Corp, e-tendering systems are gaining popularity. Indeed, several government agencies mandate that most procurement by the agencies must be done through e-tendering (see Chapter 6).

3. **Name your own price.** Pioneered by Priceline.com, the **name-your-own-price** model allows a buyer to set the price they are willing to pay for a specific product or service. Priceline.com will try to match the customer's request with a supplier willing to sell the product or service at that price. This model is also known as a "demand collection model" (see Chapters 2 and 11).

4. **Find the best price.** According to the this model, also known as a "search engine model" (see Bandyopadhyay et al. 2001), a customer specifies his or her need and then an intermediate company, such as Hotwire.com, matches the customer's need against a database, locates the lowest price, and submits it to the consumer. The potential buyer then has 30 to 60 minutes to accept or reject the offer. Many companies employ similar models to find the lowest price. For example, consumers can go to eloan.com to find the best interest rate for auto or home loans and to insweb.com for insurance rates. A well-known company in this area is Dealtime.com, which is discussed with similar companies in Chapter 3.

5. **Affiliate marketing.** **Affiliate marketing** is an arrangement whereby a marketing partner (a business, an organization, or even an individual) refers consumers to a selling company's Web site (see Chapter 5). The referral is done by placing a banner ad or the logo of the selling company on the affiliated company's Web site. Whenever a customer that was referred to the selling company's Web site makes a purchase there, the affiliated partner receives a commission (which may range from 3 to 15 percent) of the purchase price. In other words, by using affiliate marketing, a selling company creates a *virtual commissioned sales force*. Pioneered by CDNow (see Hoffman and Novak 2000), the concept is now employed by thousands of retailers and manufacturers (see *affiliateworld.com*). For example, Amazon.com has close to 500,000 affiliates, and even tiny Cattoys.com offers individuals and organizations the opportunity to put its logo and link on their Web sites to generate commissions.

6. **Viral marketing.** According to the **viral marketing** model (see Chapter 5), an organization can increase brand awareness or even generate sales by inducing people to send messages to other people or to recruit friends to join certain programs. It is basically a Web-based word-of-mouth marketing.

7. **Group purchasing.** In the off-line world of commerce, discounts are usually available for purchasing large quantities. So, too, EC has spawned the concept of *demand aggregation*, wherein a third party finds individuals or **SMEs** (small-to-medium enterprises), aggregates their orders to get a large quantity, and then negotiates (or conducts a tender) for the best deal. Thus, using the concept of **group purchasing**, a small business or even an individual can get a discount. This model, also known as a "volume-buying model," is described in Chapter 6. Some leading aggregators are Letsbuyit.com and Shop2gether.com. (Also see Rugullis 2000.)

   There are several variations of group purchasing, also known as **e-co-ops**. For example, Accompany.com lists the suggested price of a product and a prenegotiated discounted price. Then it invites consumers to place an order and *name a price* that is lower than the discounted price (but not ridiculously low). The more people who place orders, the lower the posted price moves due to the increased volume generated during a preset purchasing period. Thus, a buyer may pay a price even lower than their initial bid. If a person participates in such a purchase, they should e-mail or call their friends to buy too (a form of viral marketing), and thus lower the price of the product.

8. **Online auctions.** Almost everyone has heard about eBay.com, the world's largest online auction site. Several hundred other companies, including Amazon.com and Yahoo.com, also conduct online auctions. In the most popular type of auctions, online shoppers make consecutive bids for various goods and services, and the highest bidders get the items auctioned.

9. **Product and service customization. Customization** of products or services means creating a product or service according to the buyer's specifications. Customization is not a new model, but what *is* new is the ability to quickly customize products online for consumers at prices not much higher than their noncustomized counterparts (see Chapters 2 and 3). Dell Computer is a good example of a company that customizes PCs for its customers.

   Many other companies are following Dell's lead: The automobile industry is customizing its products and expects to save billions of dollars in inventory reduction alone every year by producing cars made-to-order (see Wiegram and Koth 2000). Mattel's My Design lets fashion-doll fans custom-build a friend for Barbie at Mattel's Web site; the doll's image is displayed on the screen before the person places an order. Nike allows customers to customize shoes, which can be delivered in a week. De Beers allows customers to design their own engagement rings.

   Configuring the details of the customized products, even designing, ordering, and paying for them, is done online. Also known as "build-to-order," customization can be done on a large scale, in which case it is called *mass customization*. For a historical discussion of the development of the idea of mass customization, see Appendix 2A at the end of Chapter 2 (page 78).

10. **Electronic marketplaces and exchanges.** Electronic marketplaces existed in isolated applications for decades (e.g., stock and commodities exchanges). But as of 1999, thousands of e-marketplaces have introduced new efficiencies to the trading process by going to the Internet (see Chapters 6 and 7). If they are well organized and managed, e-marketplaces can provide significant benefits to both buyers and sellers. Of special interest are *vertical* marketplaces, which concentrate on one industry (e.g., NewView.com for the steel industry and Chemconnect.com for the chemical industry).

11. **Value-chain integrators.** Similar to the previous one, this model offers complementary goals and services that aggregate information-rich products into a more complete package for customers, thus adding value. For example, Carpoint.com provides several car-buying–related services, including insurance (see Chapters 2, 3, and online Tutorial T3 on the supply chain).

12. **Value-chain service providers.** These providers specialize in a supply chain function such as logistics (UPS.com) or payments (PayPal.com, now part of eBay) (see Chapters 13 and 14).

13. **Information brokers.** Information brokers (see Chapters 2 through 4) provide privacy, trust, matching, search, content, and other services (e.g., Bizrate.com, Google.com).

viral marketing
Word-of-mouth marketing in which customers promote a product or service to friends or other people.

SMEs
Small to medium enterprises.

group purchasing
Quantity purchasing that enables groups of purchasers to obtain a discount price on the products purchased.

e-co-ops
Another name for online group purchasing organizations.

customization
Creation of a product or service according to the buyer's specifications.

14. **Bartering.** Under this model (see Chapters 2 and 11), companies exchange surpluses they do not need for things that they do need. A market maker (e.g., BigVine.com) arranges such exchanges.

15. **Deep discounting.** Companies such as Half.com offer products and services at deep discounts, such as 50 percent off the retail price (see Chapters 2 and 3).

16. **Membership.** A popular off-line model, in which only members get a discount, is also being offered online (e.g., Netmarket.com and NYTimes.com). (For details, see Bandyopadhyay 2001.)

17. **Supply chain improvers.** One of the major contributions of EC is in the creation of new models that change or improve supply chain management, as shown in the opening case about Marks & Spencer. Most interesting is the conversion of a *linear* supply chain, which can be slow, expensive, and error prone, into a *hub*. An example of such an improvement is provided in EC Application Case 1.3.

In order to succeed in the fast-moving marketplace, business and revenue models often must change with changing market conditions. A good example is Amazon.com, which moved from selling only books to becoming a huge online store for products and services. Amazon.com also added auctions as a marketing channel. In addition, it provides order-fulfillment services as a subcontractor to others, and much more.

Another example is America Online (AOL), which is now part of AOL Time Warner. According to Pruitt (2002), AOL was struggling with its business and revenue model strategy in 2002 and considering reviving a revenue model that it had abandoned in 1997, one that would now be applied to broadband. In this model, AOL creates original, exclusive content, such as chats with celebrities or video footage of vacation spots, with the purpose of selling goods and services to AOL subscribers. In 1997, AOL virtually ceased creating content in favor of selling and leasing the space on its Web site to others, who wooed AOL's members.

However, this revenue source (advertising), which was booming until 2000, has plummeted, leaving AOL looking for new sources of revenue. Some question the viability of content creation, which may be too expensive. It may be much cheaper to use syndicators, but then AOL would not be able to distinguish itself from its competitors. Furthermore, content should also be adapted to take advantage of high-speed cable-line connections. Of course, AOL is making money from its low-speed, modem-based Internet access services. But the question being asked at the corporate level at AOL Time Warner is whether AOL should concentrate on this source or focus its energies on high-speed broadband connections (a competitive market in which AOL charges more than its competitors, struggling to justify that price to consumers). Choosing the right revenue model at this point in its life may well determine AOL's future existence.

Any of the preceding business models can be independent or they can be combined amongst themselves or with traditional business models. Examples are provided throughout the book. One company may use several different business models. The models can be used for B2C, B2B, and other forms of EC. Although some of the models are limited to B2C or B2B, others can be used in several types of transactions, as will be illustrated throughout the book.

Section 1.3 ▶ REVIEW

1. Define a business plan, business case, and business model.

2. Describe a revenue model and a value proposition.

3. Describe the following business models: name your own price, affiliate marketing, viral marketing, and product customization.

4. Identify business models related to buying and those related to selling.

5. Describe how a linear supply chain can be changed to a hub.

1.4   BENEFITS AND LIMITATIONS OF EC

Few innovations in human history encompass as many benefits as EC does. The global nature of the technology, the opportunity to reach hundreds of millions of people, the interactive nature of EC, the variety of possibilities for its use, and the resourcefulness and rapid growth of its supporting infrastructures, especially the Web, result in many potential benefits to organizations,

CASE 1.3
EC Application
ORBIS GROUP CHANGES A LINEAR PHYSICAL SUPPLY CHAIN TO AN ELECTRONIC HUB

Orbis Group (*orbisglobal.com*) is a small, Australian company that provides Internet and EC services. One of its services, ProductBank (*productbank.com.au*), revolutionized the flow of information and products in the B2B advertising field. To put together a retail catalog or brochure, someone must gather pictures of the many products to be advertised and consult with an ad agency on how to present them. These pictures are obtained from each manufacturer, such as Sony or Nokia. The traditional process is linear, as shown in the following figure.

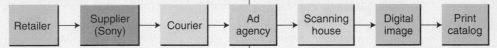

The traditional process works like this: When retailers need a photo of a product for a new brochure, they contact the manufacturers, who send the photos via a courier to a designated ad agency. The agency then sends out the photos to be scanned and converted into digital images, which are transferred to a print house, where the brochures are printed. The cycle time for each photo is 4 to 6 weeks, and the total transaction cost of preparing one picture for a brochure is about $150 AU.

ProductBank simplifies this lengthy process. It has changed the linear flow of products and information to a digitized hub, as shown in the next figure.

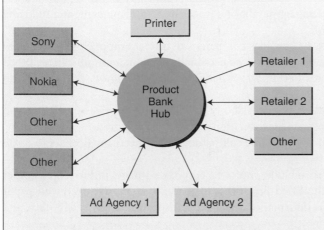

With the new process, manufacturers send digitized photos to Orbis, and Orbis enters and organizes the photos in a database. When retailers need pictures, they can view the digitized images in the database, decide which they want to include in their catalog, and communicate that information electronically to their ad agency, which views the photos in the Orbis database. When the ad agency completes its design, the pictures can be downloaded by the printer into the printing press. The transaction cost per picture (usually paid by the manufacturer) is 30 to 40 percent lower, and the cycle time 50 to 70 percent shorter than in the traditional catalog production method.

The Orbis case provides some tips for succeeding in the digital economy:

▶ Digitize as much as you can; eliminate paper and other physical transactions.
▶ Digitize as early as possible, at the beginning of the transaction process.
▶ Change the supply chain from a linear model to a hub-based model.
▶ Aggregate many business partners into one place, such as an information hub or an electronic marketplace.

Sources: Author's attendance at public lecture by Orbis, July 2001; *productbank.co.au*, September 2002; and *orbisglobal.com*, September 2002.

Questions

1. Identify the benefits of the ProductBank system to the supply chain participants.
2. Where does the cost reduction in the ProductBank process come from?
3. Where does the cycle time reduction come from?
4. Explain the benefits of electronic collaboration between the catalog owner and the ad agency.

individuals, and society. These benefits are just starting to materialize, but they will increase significantly as EC expands. It is not surprising that some maintain that the EC revolution is as profound as the change that accompanied the Industrial Revolution (Clinton and Gore 1997).

THE BENEFITS OF EC

Benefits to Organizations

EC's benefits to organizations are as follows.

Global reach. EC expands the marketplace to national and international markets. With minimal capital outlay, a company can easily and quickly locate the best suppliers, more customers, and the most suitable business partners worldwide. Expanding the base of customers and suppliers enables organizations to buy cheaper and sell more.

Cost reduction. EC decreases the cost of creating, processing, distributing, storing, and retrieving paper-based information. High printing and mailing costs are lowered or eliminated. Examples of potential cost reductions are provided in Exhibit W1.1 at the book's Web site.

Supply chain improvements. Supply chain inefficiencies, such as excessive inventories and delivery delays, can be minimized with EC. For example, by building autos to order instead of for dealers' showrooms, the automotive industry is expecting to save tens of billions of dollars annually just from inventory reduction.

Extended hours: 24/7/365. The business is always open on the Web, with no overtime or other extra costs.

Customization. Pull-type production (build-to-order) allows for inexpensive customization of products and services and provides a competitive advantage for companies who implement this strategy. A well-known example of pull-type production is that used by Dell Computer Corp.

New business models. EC allows for many innovative business models that provide strategic advantages and/or increase profits. Group purchasing (Chapter 6) combined with reverse auctions is one example of such an innovative business model.

Vendors' specialization. EC allows for a high degree of specialization that is not economically feasible in the physical world. For example, a store that sells only dog toys (Dogtoys.com) can operate in cyberspace, but in the physical world such a store would not have enough customers.

Rapid time-to-market. EC reduces the time between the inception of an idea and its commercialization (due to improved communication and collaboration).

Lower communication costs. EC lowers telecommunication costs—the Internet is much cheaper than VANs.

Efficient procurement. EC enables efficient e-procurement that can reduce administrative costs by 80 percent or more, reducing purchasing prices by 5 to 15 percent, and reducing cycle time by more than 50 percent.

Improved customer relations. EC enables companies to interact more closely with customers, even if through intermediaries. This allows personalization of communication, products, and services, which promotes better *customer relationship management* (CRM) and increases customer loyalty.

Up-to-date company material. Any material on the Web, such as prices in catalog, can be correct up to the minute. All company information can always be current.

No city business permits and fees. Online companies do not need any licenses to operate nor do they pay license fees.

Other benefits. Other benefits include improved corporate image, improved customer service, new business partners, simplified processes, increased productivity, reduced paper and paperwork, increased access to information, reduced transportation costs, and increased operation and trading flexibility.

Benefits to Consumers

The benefits of EC to consumers are as follows.

Ubiquity. EC allows consumers to shop or perform other transactions year round, 24 hours a day, from almost any location.

More products and services. EC provides consumers with more choices; they can select from many vendors and from more products.

Cheaper products and services. EC frequently provides consumers with less expensive products and services by allowing them to shop in many places and conduct quick comparisons.

Instant delivery. In the cases of digitized products, EC allows for quick delivery.

Information availability. Consumers can locate relevant and detailed product information in seconds, rather than days or weeks. Also, multimedia support is cheaper and better.

Participation in auctions. EC makes it possible for consumers to participate in virtual auctions. These allow sellers to sell things quickly and buyers to locate collectors' items and bargains.

Electronic communities. EC allows customers to interact with other customers in electronic communities and exchange ideas as well as compare experiences.

"Get it your way." EC facilitates customization and personalization of products and services.

No sales tax. In many countries, online business is exempt from sales tax.

Benefits to Society

The benefits of EC to society are as follows.

Telecommuting. More individuals work at home and do less traveling for work or shopping, resulting in less traffic on the roads and reduced air pollution.

Higher standard of living. Some merchandise can be sold at lower prices, allowing less affluent people to buy more and increase their standard of living.

Hope for the poor. People in Third World countries and rural areas are now able to enjoy products and services that were unavailable in the past. These include opportunities to learn skilled professions or earn a college degree.

Availability of public services. Public services, such as health care, education, and distribution of government social services, can be done at a reduced cost and/or improved quality. For example, EC provides rural doctors and nurses access to information and technologies with which they can better treat their patients.

THE LIMITATIONS AND BARRIERS OF EC

The limitations of EC can be classified as technological and nontechnological. The major limitations are summarized in Exhibit 1.5.

According to a 2000 study conducted by CommerceNet (commerce.net), the top 10 barriers to EC in the United States by declining order of their importance are security, trust and risk, lack of qualified personnel, lack of business models, culture, user authentication and lack of public key infrastructure, organization, fraud, slow navigation on the Internet, and legal issues. In global EC, culture, organization, B2B interfaces, international trade barriers, and lack of standards were placed at the top of the barriers list.

Despite these limitations, EC is expanding rapidly. For example, the number of people in the United States who buy and sell stocks electronically increased from 300,000 at the beginning of 1996 to over 25 million by the spring of 2002 (emarketer.com June 2002). In Korea, about 51 percent of all stock market transactions took place over the Internet in the spring of 2002 (versus 2 percent in 1998) (*Korean Times*, news item, August 22, 2002). According to IDC Research (2000), the number of online brokerage customers worldwide

EXHIBIT 1.5 **Limitations of Electronic Commerce**	
Technological Limitations	**Nontechnological Limitations**
1. There is a lack of universally accepted standards for quality, security, and reliability.	1. Security and privacy concerns deter customers from buying.
2. The telecommunications bandwidth is insufficient, especially for m-commerce.	2. Lack of trust in EC and in unknown sellers hinders buying.
3. Software development tools are still evolving.	3. Many legal and public policy issues, including taxation, are as yet unresolved.
4. There are difficulties in integrating the Internet and EC software with some existing (especially legacy) applications and databases.	4. National and international government regulations sometimes get in the way.
5. Special Web servers are needed in addition to the network servers (added cost).	5. It is difficult to measure some benefits of EC, such as advertising. There is a lack of mature measurement methodology.
6. Internet accessibility is still expensive and/or inconvenient.	6. Some customers like to feel and touch products. Also, customers are resistant to the change from a real to a virtual store.
7. Order fulfillment of large-scale B2C requires special automated warehouses.	7. People do not yet sufficiently trust paperless, faceless transactions.
	8. In most case, there is an insufficient number (critical mass) of sellers and buyers which are needed for profitable EC operations.
	9. There is an increasing amount of fraud on the Internet.
	10. It is difficult to obtain venture capital due to the dot-com disaster (failure of many dot-coms).

will reach 122.3 million in 2004, compared with 76.7 million in 2002 (as reported by Plunkett Research 2003). As experience accumulates and technology improves, the cost-benefit ratio of EC will increase, resulting in greater rates of EC adoption.

The benefits presented here may not be convincing enough reasons for a business to implement EC. Much more compelling, perhaps, are the omnipresence of the digital revolution and the influence of the business environment discussed in the next section.

Section 1.4 ❱ REVIEW

1. Describe some EC benefits to organizations, individuals, and society.
2. List the major technological and nontechnological limitations of EC.

1.5 THE DIGITAL REVOLUTION, ITS BUSINESS ENVIRONMENT, AND ORGANIZATIONAL RESPONSES

THE DIGITAL REVOLUTION

digital economy

An economy that is based on digital technologies, including digital communication networks, computers, software, and other related information technologies; also called the *Internet economy,* the *new economy,* or the *Web economy.*

The **digital economy** refers to an economy that is based on digital technologies, including digital communication networks (the Internet, intranets, extranets, and VANs), computers, software, and other related information technologies. The digital economy is also sometimes called the *Internet economy,* the *new economy,* or the *Web economy.* In this new economy, digital networking and communications infrastructures provide a global platform over which people and organizations interact, communicate, collaborate, and search for information. According to Choi and Whinston (2000), this platform includes the following characteristics:

❱ A vast array of digitizable products—databases, news and information, books, magazines, TV and radio programming, movies, electronic games, musical CDs, and software—that are delivered over a digital infrastructure any time, anywhere in the world.

❱ Consumers and firms conducting financial transactions digitally through digital currencies or financial tokens that are carried via networked computers and mobile devices.

❱ Microprocessors and networking capabilities embedded in physical goods such as home appliances and automobiles.

The term *digital economy* also refers to the convergence of computing and communications technologies on the Internet and other networks and the resulting flow of information and technology that is stimulating e-commerce and vast organizational changes. This convergence enables all types of information (data, audio, video, etc.) to be stored, processed, and transmitted over networks to many destinations worldwide.

The digital economy is creating an economic revolution, which, according to the *Emerging Digital Economy II* (esa.doc.gov/TheEmergingDigitalEconomyII.cfm) is evidenced by unprecedented economic performance and the longest period of uninterrupted economic expansion in U.S. history (1991–2000) combined with low inflation.

Web-based EC systems are accelerating the digital revolution by providing competitive advantage to organizations. In a study conducted by Lederer et al. (1998), "enhancing competitiveness or creating strategic advantage" was ranked as the number-one benefit of Web-based systems. Let's examine how such enhancement works in the business environment.

THE NEW BUSINESS ENVIRONMENT

To understand the contribution of EC and its impacts on organizations, it is worthwhile to examine today's business environment, the pressures it creates on organizations, the organizational responses to those pressures, and the potential role of EC in supporting those responses.

Economic, legal, societal, and technological factors have created a highly competitive *business environment* in which customers are becoming more powerful. These environmental factors can change quickly, sometimes in an unpredictable manner. For example, James Strong, the CEO of Qantas Airways, once said (*Business Review Weekly of Australia*, August 25, 2000), "The lesson we have learned is how quickly things can change. You have to be prepared to move fast when the situation demands." Companies need to react quickly to both the problems and the opportunities resulting from this new business environment. Because the pace of change and the level of uncertainty are expected to accelerate, organizations are operating under increasing pressures to produce more products, faster and with fewer resources.

According to Huber (2003), the new business environment has been created due to advances in science occurring at an accelerated rate. These advances create scientific knowledge that feeds on itself, resulting in more and more technology. The rapid growth in technology results in a large variety of more complex systems. As a result, we observe the following characteristics in the business environment: a more turbulent environment, with more business problems and opportunities; stronger competition; the need for organizations to make decisions more frequently, either by expediting the decision process or by having more decision makers; a larger scope for decisions because more factors (market, competitive, political, and global) need to be considered; and more information and/or knowledge needed for making decisions.

THE ENVIRONMENT-RESPONSE-SUPPORT MODEL

In order to succeed—and frequently, even to survive—in the face of this dramatic change and environmental pressures, companies must not only take traditional actions such as lowering cost and closing unprofitable facilities, but also introduce innovative actions such as customizing or creating new products or providing superb customer service (Carr 2001). We refer to both activities as *critical response activities*.

Critical response activities can take place in some or all organizational processes, from the daily processing of payroll and order entry to strategic activities such as the acquisition of a company. Responses can also occur in the supply chain, as demonstrated by the case of Marks & Spencer. A response activity can be a reaction to a specific pressure already in existence or it can be an initiative that will defend an organization against future pressures. It can also be an activity that exploits an opportunity created by changing conditions.

Many response activities can be greatly facilitated by EC. In some cases, EC is the *only* solution to these business pressures (Tapscott et al. 1998; Callon 1996; Turban et al. 2004). The relationship among business pressures, organizational responses, and EC is shown in Exhibit 1.6. The pressures are shown as the arrows pointing from the three business environments toward organizations (arrows pointing inward). The organizational responses are shown as the arrows pointing from organizations toward the business environment (arrows

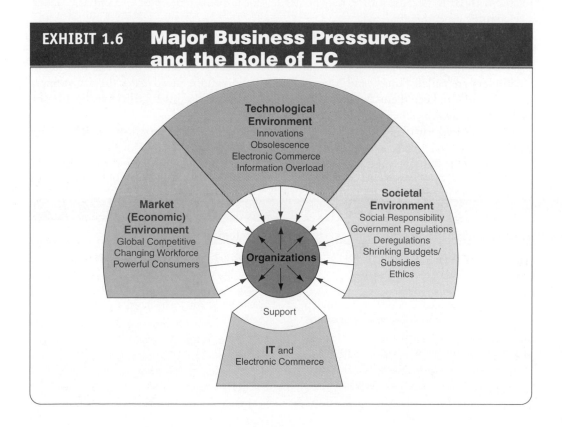

EXHIBIT 1.6   Major Business Pressures and the Role of EC

Technological Environment
Innovations
Obsolescence
Electronic Commerce
Information Overload

Market (Economic) Environment
Global Competitive
Changing Workforce
Powerful Consumers

Societal Environment
Social Responsibility
Government Regulations
Deregulations
Shrinking Budgets/Subsidies
Ethics

Organizations

Support

IT and Electronic Commerce

pointing outward). The organizational responses are supported by information technology (IT) and by EC. Now, let's examine the three components of this model in more detail.

BUSINESS PRESSURES

In this text, business pressures in the digital environment are divided into the following categories: market (economic), societal, and technological. The main types of business pressures in each category are listed in Exhibit 1.7.

ORGANIZATIONAL RESPONSES

Because some traditional response activities may not work in today's turbulent and competitive business environment, many of the old solutions need to be modified, supplemented, or discarded. Alternatively, new responses can be devised. Here we present some examples from among the many EC-supported response activities.

Strategic systems. *Strategic systems* provide organizations with strategic advantages, enabling them to increase their market share, better negotiate with their suppliers, or prevent competitors from entering into their territory (Callon 1996). There are a variety of EC-supported strategic systems. One example is FedEx's tracking system, which allows FedEx to identify the status of every individual package, anywhere in the system. Most of FedEx's competitors have already copied the FedEx system. In response, FedEx has introduced new Web-based initiatives (see EC Application Case W1.1).

Continuous improvement efforts and business process reengineering. Many companies continuously conduct programs to improve their productivity, quality, and customer service. Two examples of how EC can help are Dell Computer and Intel. Dell takes its orders electronically and immediately moves them via *enterprise resources planning* (ERP) software into the just-in-time assembly operation. Intel tracks the consumption of its products by a dozen of its largest customers, using an almost real-time extranet-based monitoring system, in order to plan production schedules and deliveries.

However, continuous improvement programs may not be a sufficient solution for some business problems. Strong business pressures may require a radical structural change. Such an effort is referred to as *business process reengineering* (BPR). E-commerce is frequently interrelated with BPR, because a BPR may be needed for implementation of EC initiatives such as electronic procurement.

Customer relationship management. One of the major symptoms of the digital revolution is that the bargaining power of customers is stronger than ever, and that power is growing continuously. Availability of information and comparisons online increases this trend. Customers are called "kings" and "queens," and organizations must make their customers happy in order to keep them. As discussed in Insights and Additions 1.1, this may be done by *customer relationship management* (CRM).

As indicated earlier, EC is not just about buying and selling. Supporting CRM, as we will see throughout the book and especially in Chapters 3 and 4 is a major function of EC. Such support is done by multiple technologies, ranging from computerized call centers to

EXHIBIT 1.7 **Major Business Pressures**		
Market and Economic Pressures	**Societal Pressures**	**Technological Pressures**
• Strong competition	• Changing nature of workforce	• Increasing innovations and new technologies
• Global economy	• Government deregulation—more	• Rapid technological obsolescence
• Regional trade agreements (e.g., NAFTA)	competition	• Increases in information overload
• Extremely low labor cost in some countries	• Shrinking government subsidies	• Rapid decline in technology cost versus performance ratio
• Frequent and significant changes in markets	• Increased importance of ethical and legal issues	
• Increased power of consumers	• Increased social responsibility of organizations	
	• Rapid political changes	

Insights and Additions 1.1 E-Commerce and CRM

The topic of *customer relationship management* (CRM) has been closely related to EC since 1997, when EC and CRM were put together for the first time. There are many definitions of CRM (Greenberg 2002). A panel of CRM experts, working with CRMGuru.com, defined CRM as follows:

> CRM is a business strategy to select and manage customers to optimize long-term value. CRM requires a customer-centric business philosophy and culture to support effective marketing, sales and service processes. CRM applications can enable effective Customer Relationship Management, provided that an enterprise has the right leadership, strategy, and culture. (*greaterchinacrm.org* 2003).

CRM is a very diversified field, which can be divided into the following areas (Greenberg 2002; *metagroup.com*, look for "delta"):

▶ **Operational CRM.** Operational CRM is used for typical business functions involving customer services, order management, invoice/billing, or sales and marketing automation and management. It involves integration with all the functional areas, frequently via ERP (enterprise resource planning). E-commerce transactions are closely related to operational CRM.

▶ **Analytical CRM.** Analytical CRM involves the capture, storage, extraction, processing, interpretation, and reporting of customer data to a user. Then, these data can be analyzed as needed. E-commerce can be closely related to analytical CRM. For example, personalization of data required for one-to-one advertisement, a part of CRM, is done with EC tools.

▶ **Collaborative CRM.** Collaborative CRM deals with all the necessary communication, coordination, and collaboration between vendors and customers. E-commerce tools, such as corporate portals, are very useful in supporting this type of CRM.

---

many types of intelligent agents. Some of the CRM/EC topics that we especially will highlight in this book are sales-force automation; call center tools and operations; personalization; empowerment of frontline employees; support of mobile employees; and partner relationship management.

Many vendors offer *CRM/EC* (or *eCRM*) methodologies and tools. These vendors offer valuable information at their Web sites (e.g., see peoplesoft.com, siebel.com, SAP.com, oracle.com, epiphany.com, saleslogix.com, and microsoft.com). For an overview of CRM/EC, see the special issue of *International Journal of Electronic Commerce*, Winter 2001/2002; Romano and Fjermestad (2001–2002); and Section 4.6 in Chapter 4 of this book.

Business alliances. Many companies realize that alliances with other companies, *even competitors*, can be beneficial. For example, General Motors, Ford, and others in the automotive industry created a huge B2B e-marketplace called Covisint (see Chapter 7). There are several other types of business alliances, such as resource-sharing partnerships, permanent supplier-company relationships, and joint research efforts.

One of the most interesting types of business alliances is the electronically supported temporary joint venture in which companies form a special organization for a specific, time-limited mission. This is an example of a major type of *virtual corporation*, which could be a common business organizational structure in the future. In a virtual corporation, an organization outsources most of its activities to business partners. A more *permanent* type of business alliance is known as *keiretsu* (a Japanese term meaning a permanent business alliance). This alliance links manufacturers, suppliers, and finance corporations on an ongoing basis. These various types of alliances are heavily supported by EC technologies ranging from electronic transmission of maps and drawings to use of real-time collaborative technologies.

Electronic markets. Electronic markets, private or public, can optimize trading efficiency, enabling their members to compete globally. Most electronic markets require the collaboration of different companies, sometimes even competitors, as will be shown in Chapters 7 and 8.

Reductions in cycle time and time-to-market. Cycle time reduction—shortening the time it takes for a business to complete a productive activity from its beginning to end—is extremely important for increasing productivity and competitiveness (Davis 2001; Wetherbe 1996). Similarly, reducing the time from the inception of an idea to its implementation (*time-to-market*) is important because those who are first on the market with a product or who can provide customers with a service faster than their competitors do enjoy a distinct competitive

cycle time reduction
Shortening the time it takes for a business to complete a productive activity from its beginning to end.

advantage. Extranet-based applications can expedite the various steps in the process of product or service development, testing, and implementation. An example of EC-supported cycle time reduction in bringing new drugs to the market is described in EC Application Case 1.4. (Also see EC Application Case 4.1 on Procter & Gamble in Chapter 4.)

Empowerment of employees. Giving employees the authority to act and make decisions on their own is a strategy used by many organizations as part of a productivity improvement program. Management delegates authority to individual or teams (see Lipnack and Stamps 2000) who can then execute the work faster and with fewer delays. Empowerment of employees may also be part of CRM. Empowered salespeople and customer service employees are given the authority to make customers happy and do it quickly, helping to increase customer loyalty. EC allows the decentralization of decision making and authority via empowerment and distributed systems, but simultaneously supports a centralized control.

Supply chain improvements. EC, as will be shown throughout the book and especially in Chapters 8 and 14, can help reduce supply chain delays, reduce inventories, and eliminate other inefficiencies. The Orbis case (EC Application Case 1.3, page 17) illustrated supply chain improvements. Another supply chain improvement was shown in the Marks & Spencer opening case.

Mass customization: make-to-order in large quantities in an efficient manner. As today's customers demand customized products and services, the business problem is how to provide customization and do it efficiently. This can be done, in part, by changing manufacturing processes from mass production to mass customization (Anderson 2002; Pine and

---

CASE 1.4
EC Application
THE INTERNET AND THE INTRANET SHORTEN TIME TO MARKET FOR NEW DRUGS

The Federal Drug Administration (FDA) must be extremely careful in approving new drugs. However, the FDA is under public pressure to approve new drugs quickly, especially those for cancer and HIV. The problem is that to ensure quality, the FDA requires companies to conduct extensive research and clinical testing. The development programs of such research and testing cover 300,000 to 500,000 pages of documentation for each new drug. The subsequent results and analyses are reported on 100,000 to 200,000 additional pages. These pages then are reviewed by the FDA prior to approval of a new drug. Manual processing of this information significantly slows the work of the FDA, so that the total approval process takes 6 to 10 years.

A software program called Computer-Aided Drug Application Systems (by Research Data Corporation, New Jersey) offered a computerized solution. The software used a network-distributed document-processing system that enabled the pharmaceutical company to scan all related documents into a database. The documents were indexed, and full-text search and retrieval software was attached to the system. Using keywords, corporate employees could search the database via their company's intranet. The database was also accessible, via the Internet, to FDA employees, who no longer had to spend hours looking for a specific piece of data. Information could be processed or printed at the user's desktop computer. These functions enabled the U.S. government to offer an electronic submission and online review process for approval of new drugs (*fda.gov/cder*).

This system helped not only the FDA, but also the companies' researchers, who suddenly had every piece of required information at their fingertips. Remote corporate and business partners could also access the system. The overall result was that the time-to-market of a new drug could be reduced by up to a year. Each week saved translates into the saving of many lives and also yields up to $1 million profit. The system also reduced the time it took to patent a new drug.

An interesting use of this technology is the case of ISIS Pharmaceuticals, Inc. (*isispharm.com*), which developed an extranet-based system similar to the one described here. The company uses CD-ROMs to submit reports to the FDA and opens its intranet to FDA personnel. This step alone could save 6 to 12 months from the average 15-month review time. Simply by submitting an FDA report electronically, the company can save one month of review time. To cut time even further, SmithKline Beecham Corporation is using electronic publishing and hypertext links to enable FDA reviewers to quickly navigate its submissions.

Sources: Compiled from Folio (2002) and Macht (1997).

Questions

1. How does the computerized drug application system facilitate collaboration?

2. How is cycle time reduced?

Gilmore 1997). In mass production, a company produces a large quantity of identical items. In **mass customization**, items are produced in a large quantity but are customized to fit the desires of each customer. EC is an ideal facilitator of mass customization, for example, by enabling interactive communication between buyers and designers so customers can quickly and correctly configure the products they want. Also, electronic ordering reaches the production facility in minutes. Note that mass customization is not easy to achieve (e.g., see Zipkin 2001); however, EC can help.

Intrabusiness: from sales force automation to inventory control. One area where EC made major progress in supporting organizational responses is applications inside the business. As seen in the opening case and in the Real-World Case at the end of this chapter, support can be provided to field representatives, warehouse employees, designers, researchers, and office workers. The improvements in productivity for these kinds of employees were fairly slow until the introduction of EC.

Knowledge management. Knowledge management (KM) refers to the process of creating or capturing knowledge, storing and protecting it, updating and maintaining it constantly, and using it whenever necessary. Knowledge management programs and software are frequently associated with EC. For example, knowledge is delivered via corporate portals to assist users or to teach employees. Also, EC implementation requires knowledge, and EC activities like market research create knowledge. For more on the EC/KM connection, see Chapters 4 and 9.

mass customization
Production of large quantities of customized items.

knowledge management (KM)
The process of creating or capturing knowledge, storing and protecting it, updating and maintaining it, and using it.

Section 1.5 ▶ REVIEW

1. Define the digital economy.
2. List the three characteristics of the digital revolution cited by Choi and Whinston.
3. List the major business pressures faced by organizations today.
4. List the major organizational responses to business pressures.
5. Describe how EC supports organizational responses to business pressures.

1.6 PUTTING IT ALL TOGETHER

The task facing each organization is how to put together the components that will enable the organization to transform itself to the digital economy and gain competitive advantage by using EC (e.g., see Dutta and Biren 2001; Weill and Vitale 2001). The first step is to put in the right connective networks, as part of the needed infrastructure, upon which applications can be structured, as shown in the Marks & Spencer case. The vast majority of EC is done on computers connected to the *Internet* or to its counterpart within organizations, an intranet. Many companies employ a **corporate portal**, a gateway for customers, employees, and partners to reach corporate information and to communicate with the company. (For more detail, see Fingar et al. 2000 and Chapter 7.)

The major concern of many companies today is how to transform themselves in order to take part in the digital economy, where e-business is the norm. If the transformation is successfully completed, many companies will reach the status of our hypothetical company, Toys, Inc., shown in Exhibit 1.8 (page 26), which uses the Internet, intranets, and extranets in an integrated manner to conduct various EC activities.

It may take 5 to 10 years for companies to become fully digitized like the hypothetical Toys, Inc. Major companies like Schwab, IBM, Intel, and General Electric are moving rapidly toward such a status (Slywotzky and Morrison 2001; Weill and Vitale 2001). The major characteristics of such a company are shown in Exhibit 1.9, where they are compared to those of a brick-and-mortar business.

corporate portal
A major gateway through which employees, business partners, and the public can enter a corporate Web site.

Section 1.6 ▶ REVIEW

1. Define intranets and extranets.
2. What is a corporate portal?
3. Identify EC transaction models (e.g., B2B) in Exhibit 1.9 (page 27).

EXHIBIT 1.8   The Networked Organization: How a Company Uses the Internet, Intranets, and Extranets

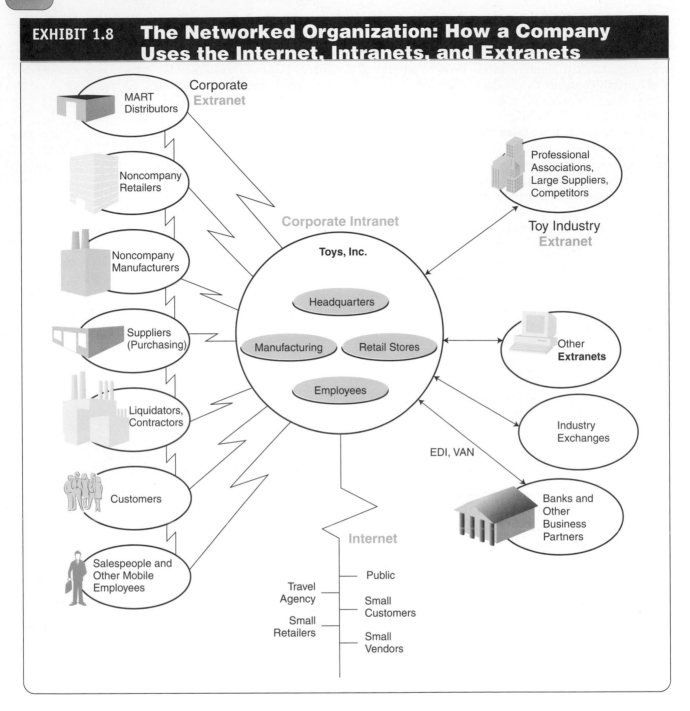

1.7 TEXT OVERVIEW

This book is composed of 17 chapters, divided into six parts, as shown in Exhibit 1.10 (page 28). In addition more content is available online at the book's Web site. There you will find a seventh part, with one additional chapter, plus an appendix, three tutorials, and four technical appendices that are available online.

The specific parts and chapters of this textbook are as follows.

PART 1: INTRODUCTION TO E-COMMERCE AND E-MARKETPLACES

This section of the book includes an overview of EC, its content, benefits, and limitations, and the impact of EC on the business environment, which are presented in Chapter 1. Chapter 2 presents electronic markets with their mechanisms, such as electronic catalogs.

EXHIBIT 1.9   The Digital Versus Brick-and-Mortar Company

Brick-and-Mortar Organizations	Digital Organizations
Selling in physical stores	Selling online
Selling tangible goods	Selling digital goods
Internal inventory/production planning	Online collaborative inventory forecasting
Paper catalogs	Smart electronic catalogs
Physical marketplace	Marketspace (electronic)
Use of VANs and traditional EDI	Use of the Internet and extranets
Physical and limited auctions	Online auctions, everywhere, any time
Broker-based services, transaction	Electronic infomediaries, value-added services
Paper-based billing	Electronic billing
Paper-based tendering	Electronic tendering (reverse auctions)
Push production, starting with demand forecast	Pull production, starting with an order
Mass production (standard products)	Mass customization, build-to-order
Physical-based commission marketing	Affiliated, virtual marketing
Word-of-mouth, slow and limited advertisement	Explosive viral marketing
Linear supply chains	Hub-based supply chains
Large amount of capital needed for mass production	Less capital needed for build-to-order; payments can flow in before production starts
Large fixed cost required for plant operation	Small fixed cost required for plant operation
Customers' value proposition is frequently a mismatch (cost > value)	Perfect match of customers' value proposition (cost = value)

Also, the economic and organizational impacts of EC on the functional areas of companies are presented there.

PART 2: INTERNET CONSUMER RETAILING

This section is composed of three chapters. Chapter 3 describes e-tailing (B2C), including some of its most innovative applications of selling products online. It also describes the delivery of services, such as online banking, travel, and insurance. Chapter 4 explains consumer behavior in cyberspace, online market research, and customer relationship management. Internet advertising is described in Chapter 5.

PART 3: BUSINESS-TO-BUSINESS AND E-COMMERCE

Part 3 is composed of three chapters. In Chapter 6, we introduce B2B EC and describe primarily company-centric models (one buyer-many sellers, one seller-many buyers). Electronic exchanges (many buyers and many sellers) are described in Chapter 7. Chapter 8 deals with e-supply chain topics and with collaborative commerce and corporate portals.

PART 4: OTHER EC MODELS AND APPLICATIONS

In Part 4 we present several other EC models and applications. E-government, e-learning, C2C, and knowledge management are the subjects of Chapter 9. In Chapter 10, we introduce the topics of m-commerce and pervasive computing.

PART 5: EC SUPPORT SERVICES

Part 5 examines issues involving the support of EC applications. Chapter 11 describes the use of e-auctions to conduct EC. Chapter 12 delves into EC security. Of the many diverse Web support activities, we concentrate on three: payments (Chapter 13), order fulfillment, and content creation and maintenance, which are presented in Chapter 14.

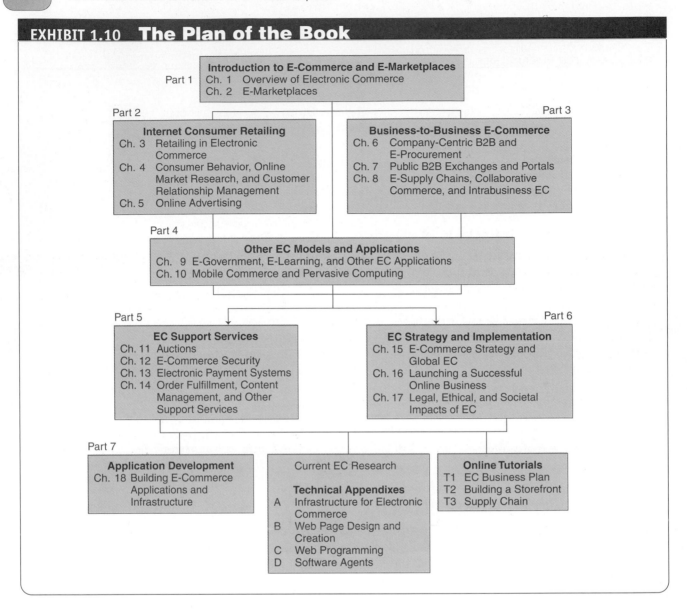

EXHIBIT 1.10   The Plan of the Book

Part 1 — Introduction to E-Commerce and E-Marketplaces
- Ch. 1 Overview of Electronic Commerce
- Ch. 2 E-Marketplaces

Part 2 — Internet Consumer Retailing
- Ch. 3 Retailing in Electronic Commerce
- Ch. 4 Consumer Behavior, Online Market Research, and Customer Relationship Management
- Ch. 5 Online Advertising

Part 3 — Business-to-Business E-Commerce
- Ch. 6 Company-Centric B2B and E-Procurement
- Ch. 7 Public B2B Exchanges and Portals
- Ch. 8 E-Supply Chains, Collaborative Commerce, and Intrabusiness EC

Part 4 — Other EC Models and Applications
- Ch. 9 E-Government, E-Learning, and Other EC Applications
- Ch. 10 Mobile Commerce and Pervasive Computing

Part 5 — EC Support Services
- Ch. 11 Auctions
- Ch. 12 E-Commerce Security
- Ch. 13 Electronic Payment Systems
- Ch. 14 Order Fulfillment, Content Management, and Other Support Services

Part 6 — EC Strategy and Implementation
- Ch. 15 E-Commerce Strategy and Global EC
- Ch. 16 Launching a Successful Online Business
- Ch. 17 Legal, Ethical, and Societal Impacts of EC

Part 7 — Application Development
- Ch. 18 Building E-Commerce Applications and Infrastructure

Current EC Research

Technical Appendixes
- A Infrastructure for Electronic Commerce
- B Web Page Design and Creation
- C Web Programming
- D Software Agents

Online Tutorials
- T1 EC Business Plan
- T2 Building a Storefront
- T3 Supply Chain

PART 6: EC STRATEGY AND IMPLEMENTATION

In this part of the text, Chapter 15 deals with e-strategy and planning, including going global and the impact of EC on small businesses. Chapter 16 deals with creating, operating, and maintaining an Internet company. Chapter 17 concludes the book with legal and societal issues in EC.

ONLINE PART 7: APPLICATION DEVELOPMENT

One additional complete chapter is online at the book's Web site (prenhall.com/turban). Chapter 18 addresses EC application development processes and methods.

ONLINE TUTORIALS

Three tutorials are available on the book's Web site (prenhall.com/turban):

- ▶ Tutorial T1: EC Business Plan
- ▶ Tutorial T2: Building a Storefront
- ▶ Tutorial T3: Supply Chain

ONLINE APPENDIXES

Five appendixes are available on the book's Web site (prenhall.com/turban). Four of these we call Technical Appendixes because of the technical nature of their content. The online appendixes are:

▶ Current EC Research

Technical Appendixes:

▶ Appendix A Infrastructure for Electronic Commerce
▶ Appendix B Web Page Design and Creation
▶ Appendix C Web Programming
▶ Appendix D Software Agents

MANAGERIAL ISSUES

Many managerial issues are related to EC. These issues are discussed throughout the book and also are summarized in a separate section (like this one) near the end of each chapter. Some managerial issues related to this introductory chapter are as follows.

1. **Is it real?** For those not involved in EC, the first question that comes to mind is, "Is it real?" We do believe that the answer is an emphatic "yes." Just ask anyone who has banked from home, purchased company stocks online, or bought a book from Amazon.com. Jack Welch, former Chief Executive Officer (CEO) of General Electric, has commented, "Any company, old or new, that doesn't see this technology literally as important as breathing could be on its last breath." (McGee 2000).

2. **How should we evaluate the magnitude of the business pressures?** A good approach is to solicit the expertise of research institutions, such as GartnerGroup or Forrester Research, which specialize in EC. The consulting arms of big certified public accounting companies may be of help too. (PricewaterhouseCoopers, Accenture, and others provide considerable EC information on their Web sites.) It is especially important for management to know what is going on in its own industry.

3. **Why is B2B e-commerce so attractive?** Several reasons: First, some B2B models are easier to implement. In contrast, B2C has several major problems, ranging from channel conflict with existing distributors to lack of a critical mass of buyers. Also the value of transactions is larger in B2B, and the potential savings are larger and easier to justify. Many companies can start B2B by simply buying from existing online stores or they can sell electronically by joining existing marketplaces or an auction house. The problem is determining where to buy or sell.

4. **There are so many EC failures—how can one avoid them?** Industry consolidation often occurs after a "gold rush." About 100 years ago, hundreds of companies tried to manufacture cars, following Ford's success in the United States; only three survived. The important thing is to learn from the success and failures of others. For lessons to be learned from EC successes and failures, see Chapters 3 and 15.

5. **What should be my company's strategy toward EC?** There are three basic strategies: lead, wait, or experiment. This issue is revisited in Chapter 15, together with related issues such as the cost-benefit tradeoffs of EC, integration of EC into the business, outsourcing, going global, and how a SME can use EC. Another strategic issue is the prioritization of the many initiatives and applications available to a company (see Rosen 1999).

6. **How do we transform our organization into a digital one?** Once a company determines its strategy and decides to move to EC, it is necessary to plan how to implement the strategy. The process is shown in Chapters 15 and 18 (online). (It also is discussed at length by Slywotzky and Morrison 2001; Weill and Vitale 2001; Willcocks and Plant 2001; and Dutta and Biren 2001).

7. **What are the top challenges of EC?** The top 10 *technical* issues for EC (by the order of their importance) are security, adequate infrastructure, data access, back-end system integration, bandwidth, network connectivity, uptime, data warehousing and mining, systems that do not scale, and content distribution. The ten *managerial* issues for the introduction of EC are budgets, project deadlines, keeping up with technology, privacy issues, high cost of capital expenditures, unrealistic management expectations, training, reaching new customers, improving customer ordering services, and employee hiring revision. Most of these issues are discussed throughout this book.

SUMMARY

In this chapter you learned about the following EC issues as they relate to the learning objectives.

1. **Definition of EC and description of its various categories.** EC involves conducting transactions electronically. Its major categories are pure versus partial EC, Internet-based versus non-Internet based, and electronic markets versus interorganizational systems and intraorganizational transactions.

2. **The content and framework of EC.** The applications of EC, and there are many, are based on infrastructures and supported by people; public policy and technical standards; marketing and advertising; support services such as logistics, security, and payment services; and business partners—all tied together by management.

3. **The major types of EC transactions.** The major types of EC transactions are B2B, B2C, C2B, C2C, m-commerce, intrabusiness commerce, B2E, c-commerce, e-government, and e-learning.

4. **The major business models.** The major business models include: online direct marketing, electronic tendering systems, name your own price, affiliate marketing, viral marketing, group purchasing, online auctions, mass customization (make-to-order), electronic exchanges, supply chain improvers, find the best price, value-chain integration, value-chain providers, information brokers, bartering, deep discounting, and membership.

5. **Benefits to organizations, consumers, and society.** EC offers numerous benefits. Because these benefits are substantial, it looks as though EC is here to stay, and cannot be ignored.

6. **Limitations of EC.** The limitations of EC can be categorized as technological and nontechnological. As time passes, and network capacity, security, and accessibility continues to improve through technological innovations, the barriers posed by technological limitations diminish. Nontechnological limitations will also diminish with time, but some of them, especially the behavioral ones, may persist for many years in some organizations, cultures, or countries.

7. **The role of the digital revolution.** EC is a major product of the digital revolution, which enables companies to simultaneously increase both growth and profit.

8. **The role of EC in combating pressures in the business environment.** The new business environment is rapidly changing mainly due to technological breakthroughs. Market (economic), technological, and societal pressures force organizations to respond. Traditional responses may not be sufficient because of the magnitude of the pressures and the pace of the changes involved. Therefore, organizations frequently must innovate and reengineer their operations. In many cases, EC is the major facilitator of such organizational responses.

KEY TERMS

Affiliate marketing	14	Cycle time reduction	23	Intraorganizational information systems	5
Brick-and-mortar organizations	4	Digital economy	20	Intranet	5
Business case	12	E-business	3	Knowledge management (KM)	25
Business model	11	E-co-ops	15	Location-based commerce (l-commerce)	8
Business plan	11	E-government	8	Mass customization	25
Business-to-business (B2B)	7	E-learning	8	Mobile commerce (m-commerce)	8
Business-to-business-to-consumer (B2B2C)	7	E-tailing	7	Name-your-own-price	14
Business-to-consumer (B2C)	7	Electronic commerce (EC)	3	Peer-to-peer	7
Business-to-employees (B2E)	8	Electronic market (e-marketplace)	5	Revenue model	12
Click-and-mortar organizations	4	Exchange (electronic)	8	SMEs	15
Collaborative commerce (c-commerce)	8	Exchange-to-exchange (E2E)	8	Tendering	14
Consumer-to-business (C2B)	7	Extranet	5	Value proposition	13
Consumer-to-consumer (C2C)	7	Group purchasing	15	Viral marketing	15
Corporate portal	25	Interorganizational information systems (IOSs)	5	Virtual (pure-play) organizations	4
Customization	15	Intrabusiness EC	8		

DISCUSSION QUESTIONS

1. Compare and contrast viral marketing with affiliate marketing.
2. Carefully examine the nontechnological limitations of EC. Which are company dependent and which are generic?
3. Compare brick-and-mortar and click-and-mortar organizations.
4. Why is it said that EC is a catalyst of fundamental changes in organizations?
5. Explain how EC is related to supply chain management.

6. Which of the EC limitations do you think will be more easily overcome—the technological or the non-technological limitations, and why?
7. Explain how EC can reduce cycle time, improve employees' empowerment, and facilitate customer support.
8. How does EC facilitate customization of products and services?
9. Why is buying with a smart card from a vending machine considered EC?
10. Why is distance learning considered EC?

INTERNET EXERCISES

1. Enter bigboxx.com and identify the services the company provides to its customers. What type of EC is this? What business model(s) does Big-boxx use?
2. Enter Amazon.com's site (amazon.com) and locate recent information in the following areas:
   a. Find the five top-selling books on EC.
   b. Find a review of one of these books.
   c. Review the customer services you can get from Amazon.com and describe the benefits you receive from shopping there.
   d. Review the products directory.
3. Enter priceline.com and identify the various business models it uses.
4. Go to ups.com and find information about recent EC projects that are related to logistics and supply chain management.
5. Go to mixonic.com and create a CD. Then go to nike.com and design your own shoes. Next visit

iprint.com and create your own business card. Finally, enter jaguar.com and configure the car of your dreams. What are the advantages of each activity? The disadvantages?

6. Enter chemconnect.com. What kind of EC does this site represent? What benefits can it provide to buyers? To sellers?
7. It is time to sell or buy on an online auction. You can try eBay.com, auction.yahoo.com, or an auction site of your choice. You can participate in an auction in almost any country. Prepare a short report describing your experiences.
8. Try to save on your next purchase by using group purchasing. Visit letsbuyit.com, shop2gether.com, and buyerzone.com. Which site do you prefer? Why?
9. Enter espn.com and identify all sources of revenue there.

TEAM ASSIGNMENTS AND ROLE PLAYING

1. Assign each team two failed or failing Internet companies (e.g., mixonic.com, comdex.com). Use startup failures.com to identify companies that are in distress. Fortune.com is a good source of details for particular business failures. Have each team prepare a report on why the companies failed or are failing.

2. Each team will research two EC success stories. Members of the group should examine companies that operate solely online and some that extensively utilize a click-and-mortar strategy. Each team should identify the critical success factors for its companies and present a report to the other teams.

REAL-WORLD CASE

E-COMMERCE SUPPORTS FIELD EMPLOYEES AT MAYBELLINE

The Problem

Maybelline is a leader in color cosmetics products (eye shadow, mascara, etc.), selling them in more than 70 countries worldwide. The company uses hundreds of salespeople (field merchandising representatives, or "reps"), who visit drugstores, discount stores, super-markets, and cosmetics specialty stores to close business deals. This method of selling has proved to be fairly effective, and it is used by hundreds of other manufac-turers in various industries (e.g., Kodak, Nabisco, and Procter & Gamble). In all cases of field selling, it is nec-essary for the selling company to know, as quickly as possible, when a deal is closed or if there is any problem with the customer.

Information technology has been used extensively to support field reps. Until 2000, Maybelline, as well as many other large consumer product manufacturers such as Kodak, equipped their reps with an *interactive voice response* (IVR) system that enabled reps to enter, every evening, information about their daily activities. This solution deployed hundreds of reps with paper-based sur-veys to complete for every store they visited each evening. For example, the reps noted how each product was displayed, how much stock was available, how items were promoted, and so on. In addition to their own com-pany's products, the reps surveyed the competitors' prod-ucts as well. In the evening, the reps translated the data collected into answers to the voice response system, which asked them routine questions, which the reps answered by pressing the appropriate telephone keys. The system had problems: Frequently, reps were late in reporting. Even if they were on time, information was inflexible, because the reports were all menu driven. The old system also consolidated information, bundling and delivering it to top management as hard copy. Unfortunately, these reports sometimes reached top man-agement days or weeks too late, missing important changes in trends and the opportunities to act on them in time.

Another problem was the inflexibility of the system. With the old voice system, the reps answered only the specific questions that applied to a situation. To do so, they had to wade through more than 50 questions, skip-ping the irrelevant ones. This was a waste of time. In addition, some of the material that needed to be reported had no matching menu questions. Considered a success in the 1990s, the IVR system was unable to meet the needs of the twenty-first century. It was too cumbersome to set up and operate and was also prone to input errors.

The Solution

Maybelline equipped its reps with a mobile system from Thinque Corp. (*thinque.com*), called Merchandising Sales

Portfolio (MSP). It runs on handheld, pen-based PDAs (from NEC), powered by Microsoft's CE operating system. The system enables the reps to enter their reports by handwriting, directly at the clients' sites. From the hand-held device, data can automatically upload to a Microsoft SQL Server database at the headquarters every evening by accessing the corporate intranet via a secured Internet connection (a synchronization process). It also enables district managers to electronically send daily schedules and other important information to each rep.

The system also replaced some of the function of the EDI system, a pride of the 1990s. For example, the reps reports include inventory-scanned data from retail stores. These are processed quickly by an *order manage-ment system* and passed whenever needed to the ship-ment department for inventory replenishment.

In addition to routine information, the new system is used for decision support. It is not enough to speed information along the supply chain; managers need to know the *reasons* why certain products are selling well, or not so well, in every location. They need to know the conditions at retail stores that affect the sales of each product, and they need to know it in a timely manner. The new system offers that capability.

The Results

The system provided Maybelline with an interactive link to the mobile field force. Corporate planners and decision makers can now respond much more quickly to situations that need attention. The solution is helping the company forge stronger ties with its retailers. It also considerably reduces the amount of after-hours time that the reps spend on data transfer to headquarters—from 30 to 50 minutes per day to mere seconds.

The new system also performs market analysis that enables managers to optimize merchandising and customer-service efforts. It also enables Maybelline to use a more sophisticated IVR unit to capture data for special situations. Moreover, it provides browser-based reporting tools that enable managers, regardless of where they are, to view retail information within hours of its capture. Thanks to the error checking and validation feature in the MSP system, there are significantly fewer data-entry errors (because no rekeying is needed).

Finally, the quality of life of Maybelline reps has been greatly improved. Not only do they save 30 to 40 minutes per day, but also their stress level and anxi-ety due to the possibility of making errors has been sig-nificantly reduced. As a result, employee turnover has declined appreciably, saving money for the company.

Source: Compiled from "Industry Solutions—Maybelline" at *thinque.com*, May 15, 2002.

Questions

1. IVR systems are still popular. What advantages do they have over a system in which the reps mail or fax reports?

2. Explain why the MSP application is an e-commerce application. Compare it to the definitions and classifications in the chapter.

3. The existing technology enables transmission of data any time an employee can access the Internet with a PC. Technically, the system can be enhanced so that the data can be sent *wirelessly* from any location as soon as they are entered. Would you recommend such a wireless system to Maybelline? Why or why not?

4. Summarize the advantages of the new MSP system over the IVR one.

REFERENCES

Afuah, A., and C. L. Tucci. *Internet Business Models and Strategies*, 2nd edition. New York: McGraw Hill, 2003.

Amit, R., and C. Zott. "Value Creation in E-Business." *Strategic Management Journal* 22, no. 6 (2001).

Anderson, D. *Build-to-Order and Mass Customization*. Los Angeles: CIM Press, 2002.

Applegate, L. M. "E-business Models." Chap. 3 in *Information Technology for the Future Enterprise: New Models for Managers*, edited by G. W. Dickson and G. DeSanctis, Upper Saddle River, NJ: Prentice Hall, 2000.

Athitakis, M. "How to Make Money on the Net." *Business 2.0*, May 2003.

Bakos, J. J. "A Strategic Analysis of Electronic Marketplaces." *MIS Quarterly* 15, no. 3 (1991).

Bandyopadhyay, S., et al. "A Critical Review of Pricing Strategies for Online Business Model." *Quarterly Journal of Electronic Commerce* 2, no. 1 (2001).

Callon, J. D. *Competitive Advantage Through Information Technology*. New York: McGraw-Hill, 1996.

campusfood.com (accessed October 2002).

Carr, N. G. (ed.). *The Digital Enterprise*. Boston: Harvard Business School Press, 2001.

Carton, S. *The Dot.Bomb Survival Guide*. New York: McGraw-Hill, 2002.

Cassidy, J. *Dot.com: The Greatest Story Ever Sold*. New York: Harper Collins Publication, 2002.

Choi, S. Y., and A. B. Whinston. *The Internet Economy, Technology, and Practice*. Austin, TX: Smartecon.com, 2000.

Choi, S. Y., A. B. Whinston, and D. O. Stahl. *The Economics of Electronic Commerce*. Indianapolis, IN: Macmillan Technical Pub., 1997.

Clinton, W. J., and A. Gore, Jr. "A Framework for Global Electronic Commerce." dcc.syr.edu/ford/course/e-commerce-framework.pdf, 1997 (accessed April 2003).

CommerceNet. "Barriers to Electronic Commerce: 2000 Study." *CommerceNet*, 2000. commerce.net/research/barriers-inhibitors/2000/Barriers2000study.html (accessed June 2003).

Cunningham, M. S. *B2B: How to Build a Profitable E-Commerce Strategy*. Cambridge: Perseus Pub., 2001.

Davis, B. *Speed Is Life*. New York: Doubleday/Currency, 2001.

Drucker, P. *Managing in the Next Society*. New York: Truman Talley Books, 2002.

Dutta, S., and B. Biren. "Business Transformation on the Internet." *European Management Journal* (October 2001).

Eglash, J. *How to Write a .com Business Plan*. New York: McGraw-Hill, 2001.

Emarketer.com. "Online Purchases in the U.S., by Category, 2002." emarketer.com, June 26, 2002.

Farhoomand, A., and P. Lovelock. *Global E-Commerce*. Singapore: Prentice Hall, 2001.

"FedEx to Acquire Certain Assets from Fritz, a UPS Company; Agreement Includes Customs Clearance Operations and Employees Dedicated to FedEx." *Business Wire,* January 31, 2002.

"FedEx Companies Compete Collectively to Simplify Shipping for North American Importers." *Business Wire,* February 1, 2002.

"FedEx Custom Critical Enhances Online Shipping Toolkit." *Business Wire*, March 6, 2002.

"FedEx InSight Now Provides FedEx Ground Visibility; Keeps 'Logistics Channels Running at Peak Efficiency.'" *Business Wire,* April 1, 2002.

"FedEx Now on Nextel Online Wireless Portal; Subscribers Have Easy Access to FedEx Tracking, Location Information." *Business Wire,* January 16, 2002.

Financial Times, news items, 2002.

Fingar, P., H. Kumar, and T. Sharma. *Enterprise E-Commerce*. Tampa, FL: Meghan Kiffer Press, 2000.

Folio. "SmithKline Beecham Streamlines its Drug Approval Process." folio.de/aktuell/IN300797.htm (accessed September 2002).

GreaterchinaCRM.org. "Definitions of CRM: Perspectives of CRMguru.com's Contributors." greaterchinacrm.org/eng/content_details.jsp?contentid=413&subjectid=9 (accessed April 2003).

Greenberg, P. *CRM at the Speed of Light: Capturing and Keeping Customers in Internet Real Time*, 2d ed. New York: McGraw-Hill, 2002.

Hoffman, K. L., and T. P. Novak. "How to Acquire Customers on the Web." *Harvard Business Review* (May/June 2000).

Huber, G. *The Business Environment in the Digital Economy*. New York: McGraw-Hill, 2003.

Huff, S. L., et al. *Cases in Electronic Commerce*. New York: McGraw-Hill, 2001.

Kalakota, R., and M. Robinson. *e-Business 2.0*. Boston: Addison-Wesley, 2001.

Kaplan, P. J. *F'd Companies: Spectacular Dot.com Flameouts*. New York: Simon and Schuster, 2002.

Korean Times, news item, August 22, 2002.

Le, T. T. "Pathways to Leadership for B2B Electronic Marketplaces." *Electronic Markets* 12, no. 2 (2002).

Lederer, A. L., et al. "Using Web-based Information Systems to Enhance Competitiveness." *Communication of the ACM* (July 1998).

Lipnack, J., and J. Stamps. *Virtual Teams—Reaching Across Space, Time, and Organizations with Technology*, 2d ed. New York: John Wiley & Sons, 2000.

Macht, J. D. "The Two Hundred Million Dollar Dash." Inc.com, September 15, 1997, inc.com/articles/it/computers_networks/collaborative/1432.html (accessed June 2003).

McGee, M. K. "Chiefs of the Year: Internet Call to Arms." *InformationWeek*, November 27, 2000, informationweek.com/814/chchall.htm (accessed June 2003).

metagroup.com (accessed June 2003).

Microsoft Corp. "Industry Solutions: Manufacturing—Maybelline." thinque.com/pdfs/ThinqueMaybellineCS.pdf (accessed October 2002).

Penelope, O. "An Enhanced Response to Customer Demands." *Financial Times*, June 19, 2002, 11.

Perkins A. B., and M. C. Perkins. *The Internet Bubble*, rev. ed. New York: Harper Business, 2001.

Pine, B. J., and J. Gilmore. "The Four Faces of Mass Customization." *Harvard Business Review* (January/February 1997).

Plunkett, J. W. *Plunkett's E-Commerce Business Trends and Statistics*. Aylesbury, UK: Plunkett Research Ltd., 2001.

Prince, M. "Easy Doesn't Do It." *Wall Street Journal*, July 17, 2000.

Pruitt, S. "AOL Set to Lay Out New Broadband, Content Strategy." *Infoworld* (November 25, 2002).

"Qantas: Turbulence Ahead." *Business Review Weekly of Australia* 23, no. 33, August 25, 2000.

Romano, W. C., and J. Fjermestad. "Electronic Commerce Relationship Management: An Assessment of Research." *International Journal of Electronic Commerce* (Winter 2001–2002).

Rosen, A. *The E-Commerce Q and A Book: A Survival Guide for Business Managers*. New York: AMACOM, 1999.

Rugullis, E. "Power to the Buyer with Group Buying Sites." *e-Business Advisor* (February 2000).

Saloner, G. *Creating and Capturing Value: Perspectives and Cases on E-Commerce*. New York: Wiley, 2001.

Shaw, M. J., et al. *Handbook on Electronic Commerce*. Berlin: Springer-Verlag, 2000.

Singer, M. "TellMe: The 511 in Utah." December 18, 2001, siliconvalley.internet.com/news/article.php/3531_942671 (accessed June 2003).

"State of Online Financial Services." *Plunkett Research*, plunkettresearch.com/finance/financial_overview.htm#6 (accessed April 2003).

Slywotzky, A. J., and D. J. Morrison. *How Digital Is Your Business?* London: Nicholas Brealy Pub., 2001.

Tapscott, D., A. Lowry and D. Ticoll eds. *Blueprint to the Digital Economy: Wealth Creation in the Era of E-Business*. New York: McGraw-Hill, 1998.

Timmers, P. *Electronic Commerce*. New York: Wiley, 1999.

Turban, E., et al. *Information Technology for Management*, 4th ed. New York: John Wiley & Sons, 2004.

U.S. Department of Commerce. "The Emerging Digital Economy II," June 1999. esa.doc.gov/TheEmergingDigitalEconomyII.cfm (accessed June 2003).

Useem, J. "Dot-coms: What Have We Learned?" *Fortune*, October 30, 2000.

Weill, P., and M. R. Vitale. *Place to Space: Migrating to eBusiness Models*. Boston: Harvard Business School Press, 2001.

Wetherbe, J. C. *The World on Time*. Santa Monica, CA: Knowledge Exchange, 1996.

Wiegram, G., and H. Koth. *Custom Enterprise.com*. Upper Saddle River, NJ: Financial Times/Prentice Hall, 2000.

Willcocks, L. P., and R. Plant. "Getting from Bricks to Clicks." *MIT Sloan Management Review* (Spring 2001).

Zipkin, P. "The Limits of Mass Customization." *MIT Sloan Management Review* (February 2001).

CHAPTER 2

E-MARKETPLACES: STRUCTURE, MECHANISMS, ECONOMICS, AND IMPACTS

Content

Learning objectives

Upon completion of this chapter, you will be able to:

1. Define e-marketplaces and list their components.

2. List the major types of electronic markets and describe their features.

3. Describe the types of intermediaries in EC and their roles.

4. Describe electronic catalogs, shopping carts, and search engines.

5. Describe the various types of auctions and list their characteristics.

6. Discuss the benefits, limitations, and impacts of auctions.

7. Describe bartering and negotiating online.

8. Define m-commerce and explain its role as a market mechanism.

9. Discuss liquidity, quality, and success factors in e-marketplaces.

10. Describe the economic impact of EC.

11. Discuss competition in the digital economy.

12. Describe the impact of e-marketplaces on organizations.

HOW RAFFLES HOTEL IS CONDUCTING E-COMMERCE

The Problem

Raffles Hotel, one of Singapore's colonial-era landmarks, is the flagship of Raffles Holding Ltd., which owns and manages luxury and business hotels worldwide. Raffles Hotel operates in a very competitive environment. To maintain its world-renowned reputation, the hotel spends lavishly on every facet of its operation. For example, it once stocked 12 different kinds of butter, at a high cost. The success of the company and each of its hotels depends on the company's ability to lure customers to its hotels and facilities and on its ability to contain costs.

The Solution

To maintain its image and contain costs, Raffles must address two types of issues—business-to-consumer and business-to-business. On the business-to-consumer side, Raffles maintains a diversified corporate portal (*raffles.com*), open to the public, that introduces customers to the company and its services. The portal includes information on the hotels, a reservation system, links to travelers' resources, a CRM program, and an online store for Raffles products.

On the business-to-business side, Raffles has interorganizational systems that enable efficient contacts with its suppliers. To do business with Raffles, each of the 5,000 potential vendors must log on to Raffles' private marketplace. As for purchasing, Raffles conducts e-procurement using *reverse auctions* among qualified suppliers, in which sellers bid for sales contracts, and the lowest bidder wins. With the reverse auction, the number of suppliers is reduced and the quantity purchased from each increases, which leads to lower purchasing prices. For example, butter is now purchased from only two suppliers. Procurement negotiations now take place online. Buyer-seller relationships have been strengthened by the private, online marketplace.

The e-marketplace also has a sell-side, allowing other hotels to buy Raffles-branded products, such as tiny shampoo bottles and bathrobes, from electronic catalogs. Even competitors buy Raffles-branded products because they are relatively inexpensive. Also, the luxury products make the hotel that purchases them look upscale.

The Results

The corporate portal helps in customer acquisition. Using promotions and direct sales, the hotel is able to maintain relatively high occupancy rates in difficult economic times. The private marketplace is strategically advantageous to Raffles in forcing suppliers to disclose their prices, thus increasing competition among suppliers. The company is saving about $1 million a year on procurement of eight high-volume supplies (toilet paper, detergents, etc.) alone. The success of the company is evidenced by its aggressive expansion in the Asian markets.

Source: Source to come

WHAT WE CAN LEARN . . .

For an old-economy hotel to transform itself into a click-and-mortar business, it had to create two separate electronic markets: a B2C market for selling its services to consumers and a B2B private market to buy from its suppliers and to sell products to other hotels. In addition, it had to use several e-commerce mechanisms: a corporate portal, electronic catalogs, and e-procurement using reverse auctions. Electronic markets and some of their supporting mechanisms are described in this chapter. We also will examine the economics of e-commerce and its impacts on organizations.

EXHIBIT 2.1 **Functions of a Market**		
Matching of Buyers and Sellers	**Facilitation of Transactions**	**Institutional Infrastructure**

• Determination of product offerings
  Product features offered by sellers
  Aggregation of different products
• Search (of buyers for sellers and of
  sellers for buyers)
  Price and product information
  Organizing bids and bartering
  Matching seller offerings with
    buyer preferences
• Price discovery
  Process and outcome in
    determination of prices
  Enabling price comparisons
	• Logistics
	  Delivery of information, goods,
	    or services to buyers
	• Settlement
	  Transfer of payments to sellers
	• Trust
	  Credit system, reputations, rating
	    agencies like Consumers Reports
	    and BBB. Special escrow and
	    trust online agencies
		• Legal
		  Commercial code, contract law,
		    dispute resolution, intellectual
		    property protection
		  Export and import law
		• Regulatory
		  Rules and regulations, monitoring,
		    enforcement

Source: "The Emerging Role of Electronic Marketplaces on the Internet," by Y. Bakos, in *Communications of the ACM*, ©1998 by ACM Inc.

2.1 ELECTRONIC MARKETPLACES

According to Bakos (1998), markets play a central role in the economy, facilitating the exchange of information, goods, services, and payments. In the process, they create economic value for buyers, sellers, market intermediaries, and for society at large.

Markets (electronic or otherwise) have three main functions: (1) matching buyers and sellers; (2) facilitating the exchange of information, goods, services, and payments associated with market transactions; and (3) providing an institutional infrastructure, such as a legal and regulatory framework, that enables the efficient functioning of the market.

In recent years, markets have seen a dramatic increase in the use of IT and EC (Turban et al. 2004). EC has increased market efficiencies by expediting or improving the functions listed in Exhibit 2.1. Furthermore, EC has been able to significantly decrease the cost of executing these functions.

The emergence of electronic marketplaces (also called *e-marketplaces* or *marketspaces*), especially Internet-based ones, changed several of the processes used in trading and supply chains. These changes, driven by IT, resulted in even greater economic efficiencies. EC leverages IT with increased effectiveness and lower transaction and distribution costs, leading to more efficient, "friction-free" markets. An example of such efficiency can be seen in the NTE case in EC Application Case 2.1 (page 38).

MARKETSPACE COMPONENTS

Similar to a physical marketplace, in a **marketspace** sellers and buyers exchange goods and services for money (or for other goods and services if bartering is used), but they do it electronically. A marketspace includes electronic transactions that bring about a new distribution of goods and services. The major components and players of a marketspace are customers, sellers, goods (physical or digital), infrastructure, a front end, a back end, intermediaries and other business partners, and support services. A brief description of each follows.

> **Customers.** The tens of millions of people worldwide that surf the Web are potential buyers of the goods and services offered or advertised on the Internet. These consumers are looking for bargains, customized items, collectors' items, entertainment, and more. They are in the driver's seat. They can search for detailed information, compare, bid, and sometimes negotiate. Organizations are the major consumers, accounting for over 85 percent of EC activities.

> **Sellers.** Millions of storefronts are on the Web, advertising and offering a huge variety of items. Every day it is possible to find new offerings of products and services. Sellers can sell direct from their Web site or from e-marketplaces.

marketspace
A marketplace in which sellers and buyers exchange goods and services for money (or for other goods and services), but do so electronically.

CASE 2.1
EC Application
NTE EVENS THE LOAD

The hauling industry is not very efficient. Though trucks are likely to be full on outbound journeys, they are often empty on the way back. (About 50 percent of the trucks on America's roads at any one time are not full.) National Transportation Exchange (NTE) has attempted to solve this problem.

NTE (*nte.com*) uses the Internet to connect shippers who have loads they want to move cheaply with fleet managers who have space to fill. NTE helps create what is called a *spot market* (a very short-term or one-time job market) by setting daily prices based on information from several hundred fleet managers about the destinations of their vehicles and the amount of space they have available. (Such a spot market differs from repetitive arrangements that are negotiated and secured by a long-term contract.) NTE also gets information from shippers about their needs and flexibility in dates. It then works out the best deals for the shippers and the haulers. When a deal is agreed upon, NTE issues the contract and handles payments. The entire process takes only a few minutes. NTE collects a commission based on the value of each deal, the fleet manager gets extra revenue that they would otherwise have missed out on, and the shipper gets a bargain price, at the cost of some loss of flexibility.

When NTE was first set up in 1995, it used a proprietary network that was expensive and that limited the number of buyers and sellers who could connect through it. By using the Internet, NTE has been able to extend its reach down to the level of individual truck drivers and provide a much wider range of services. Today, drivers can also use wireless Internet access devices to connect to the NTE Web site on the road.

In 2001, NTE expanded its services to improve inventory management, scheduling, and vendor compliance along the entire supply chain. NTE's software is integrated with its customers' operations and systems. The company also offers such value-added services as insurance, performance reporting, and customer care. NTE's business is currently limited to ground transportation within the United States. In Hong Kong, Arena.com (*arena.com.hk*) provides similar port services with its product called LINE (Logistics Information Network Enterprise).

Sources: Compiled from *The Economist,* June 26, 1999; Davidson (2001); *nte.com* (accessed 2003); and *arena.com.hk* (accessed 2001).

Questions

1. What type of transaction is done at NTE? What type of business model does NTE use?

2. What are the benefits of NTE's services to truckers? To shippers?

---

digital products
Goods that can be transformed to digital format and delivered over the Internet.

front end
The portion of an e-seller's business processes through which customers interact, including the seller's portal, electronic catalogs, a shopping cart, a search engine, and a payment gateway.

back end
The activities that support online order-taking. It includes fulfillment, inventory management, purchasing from suppliers, payment processing, packaging, and delivery.

▶ **Products.** One of the major differences between the marketplace and the marketspace is the possible digitization of products and services in a marketspace. Although both types of markets can sell physical products, the marketspace also can sell **digital products**, which are goods that can be transformed to digital format and delivered over the Internet. In addition to digitization of software and music, it is possible to digitize dozens of other products and services, as shown in Exhibit W2.1. Digital products have different cost curves than those of regular products. In digitization, most of the costs are fixed and the variable cost is very small. Thus, profit will increase very rapidly as volume increases, once the fixed costs are paid for. This is one of the major advantages of electronic markets.

▶ **Infrastructure.** An electronic market infrastructure includes hardware, software, networks, and more. (EC infrastructure was presented in Chapter 1, Exhibit 1.2; see also Chapter 18).

▶ **Front end.** Customers interact with a marketspace via a **front end**. The infrastructure in the front end includes the seller's portal, electronic catalogs, a shopping cart, a search engine, and a payment gateway.

▶ **Back end.** All the activities that are related to order aggregation and fulfillment, inventory management, purchasing from suppliers, accounting and finance, payment processing, packaging, and delivery are done in what is termed the **back end** of the business.

▶ **Intermediaries.** In marketing, an **intermediary** typically is a third party that operates between sellers and buyers. Intermediaries of all kinds offer their services on the Web. The role of these electronic intermediaries (as will be seen throughout the text and especially in Chapters 3, 6, and 10) is frequently different from that of regular intermediaries (such as wholesalers). Online intermediaries create and manage the online markets (such as in the NTE case). They help match buyers and sellers, provide some infrastructure services, and help customers and/or sellers to institute and complete transactions. Most of these online intermediaries operate as computerized systems.

▶ **Other business partners.** In addition to intermediaries, there are several types of partners, such as shippers, that collaborate on the Internet, mostly along the supply chain.

▶ **Support services.** Many different support services are available, ranging from certification and trust services, which ensure security, to knowledge providers. These services address implementation issues.

intermediary
A third party that operates between sellers and buyers.

Section 2.1 ▶ REVIEW

1. What is the difference between a physical marketplace and an e-marketplace (marketspace)?

2. List the components of a marketspace.

3. Define a digital product and provide five examples.

2.2 TYPES OF ELECTRONIC MARKETS: FROM STOREFRONTS TO PORTALS

There are several types of e-marketplaces. In B2C the major e-marketplaces are *storefronts* and *Internet malls*. In B2B we find private *sell-side* (one seller–many buyers) e-marketplaces, *buy-side* (one buyer–many sellers) e-marketplaces, and *exchanges*. Let's elaborate on these as well as on the gateways to the e-marketplaces—the portals.

ELECTRONIC STOREFRONTS

An electronic or Web **storefront** refers to a single company's Web site where products and services are sold. It is an electronic store. The storefront may belong to a manufacturer (e.g., geappliances.com, dell.com), to a retailer (e.g., walmart.com), to individuals selling from home, or to another type of business.

A storefront includes several mechanisms that are necessary for conducting the sale. The most common features are *electronic catalogs*, a *search engine* that helps the consumer to find products in the catalog; an *electronic cart* for holding items until checkout; *e-auction facilities*; a *payment gateway* where payment arrangements can be made; a *shipment court* where shipping arrangements are made; and *customer services*, including product information and a register for warranties. We will describe the first three mechanisms in Section 2.4; e-auction facilities are described in Section 2.5 and in Chapter 11; mechanisms for payments are described in Chapter 13; and shipments are discussed in Chapter 14. Customer services, which can be fairly elaborate, are covered in Chapter 4 and throughout the book.

storefront
A single company's Web site where products and services are sold.

ELECTRONIC MALLS

In addition to shopping in individual storefronts, consumers can shop in electronic malls (e-malls). Similar to malls in the physical world, an **e-mall** (online mall) is an online shopping location where many stores are located. For example, Hawaii.com (hawaii.com) is an e-mall that aggregates Hawaiian products and stores. It contains a directory of product categories and the stores in each category. When a consumer indicates the category they are interested in, they are transferred to the appropriate independent storefront to conduct their shopping. This kind of a mall does not provide any shared services. It is merely a directory. Other malls do provide shared services (e.g., choicemall.com). Some malls are actually large click-and-mortar retailers, and some (e.g., buy.com) are virtual retailers.

e-mall (online mall)
An online shopping center where many stores are located.

TYPES OF STORES AND MALLS

There are several types of stores and malls:

▶ **General stores/malls.** These are large marketspaces that sell all types of products. Examples are amazon.com, choicemall.com, shop4.com, spree.com, and the major public portals (yahoo.com, aol.com, and lycos.com). All major department and discount stores fall into this category.

▶ **Specialized stores/malls.** These sell only one or a few types of products, such as books, flowers, wine, cars, or pet toys. Amazon.com started as a specialized e-bookstore, but today is a generalized store. At buy.com you can purchase only computers and consumer electronic products; at 1800flowers.com you can buy flowers and related gifts; fashionmall. com/beautyjungle specializes in beauty products, tips, and trends; and uvine.com and vinyardsonline.com sell only wine.

▸ **Regional versus global stores.** Some stores, such as e-grocers or sellers of heavy furniture, serve customers that live nearby. For example, parknshop.com serves the Hong Kong community; it will not deliver groceries to New York. However, some local stores will sell to customers in other countries if the customer will pay the shipping, insurance, and other costs (e.g., see hothothot.com).

▸ **Pure online organizations versus click-and-mortar stores.** Stores can be pure online ("virtual" or "pure-play") organizations, such as Amazon.com, Buy.com, or Cattoys.com. They do not have physical stores. Others are physical ("brick-and-mortar") stores that also sell online (e.g., Walmart.com, 1800flowers.com, Marks & Spencer, or Woolworths.com.au). This second category is called *click-and-mortar*. Both categories will be described further in Chapter 3.

Marketplaces

In general conversation, the distinction between a mall and a marketplace is not always clear. In the physical world, we view a mall as a collection of stores (a shopping center) where the stores are isolated from each other and prices are generally fixed. In contrast, marketplaces, some of which are located outdoors ("open air"), imply a place where many vendors and shoppers are looking for bargains and are expected to negotiate prices.

On the Web, the term *marketplace* has a different and distinct meaning. If individual customers want to negotiate prices, they may be able to do so in some storefronts or malls. However, the term **e-marketplace** usually implies B2B, not B2C. We distinguish three types of such e-marketplaces: private, public, and consortia.

Private E-Marketplaces

Private e-marketplaces are those owned by a single company (see Chapter 6). As can be seen in the Raffles Hotel story, two types of such markets exist: sell-side and buy-side. In a **sell-side e-marketplace**, a company such as Cisco Systems will sell either standard or customized products to qualified companies. This is similar to a storefront in B2C. In a **buy-side e-marketplace**, a company conducts purchasing from invited suppliers. For example, Raffles Hotel buys its supplies from approved vendors that come to its market. Private marketplaces are open only to selected members and are not publicly regulated. We will return to the topic of private e-marketplaces in Chapter 6.

Public E-Marketplaces

Public e-marketplaces are B2B markets that are owned by a third party (not a seller or a buyer) and include markets with many sellers and many buyers. These markets are also known as *exchanges* (e.g., a stock exchange). They are open to the public and regulated by the government or the exchange's owners. We will look at public e-marketplaces in more detail in Chapter 7. An exchange may be owned by one company that may be either the seller or the buyer or in some cases they may be owned by a consortium.

Consortia

A small group of major buyers may create an e-marketplace to deal with suppliers, usually in their same industry. A group of sellers may also create an e-marketplace to deal with industry buyers. Such e-marketplaces are owned by and called **consortia** (singular, a *consortium*). They can be completely private, where only invited suppliers can participate, or they can be open to more suppliers, resembling a public e-marketplace. We will return to consortia in Chapter 7.

E-marketplaces can be *vertical*, meaning they are confined to one industry, or *horizontal*, meaning that different industries trade there.

---

e-marketplace
An online market, usually B2B, in which buyers and sellers exchange goods or services; the three types of e-marketplaces are private, public, and consortia.

private e-marketplaces
Online markets owned by a single company; can be either sell-side or buy-side marketplaces.

sell-side e-marketplace
A private e-market in which a company sells either standard or customized products to qualified companies.

buy-side e-marketplace
A private e-market in which a company makes purchases from invited suppliers.

public e-marketplaces
B2B markets, usually owned and/or managed by an independent third party, that include many sellers and many buyers; also known as *exchanges*.

consortia
E-marketplaces owned by a small group of large vendors, usually in a single industry.

INFORMATION PORTALS

With the growing use of intranets and the Internet, many organizations encounter information overload at a number of different levels. Information is scattered across numerous documents, e-mail messages, and databases at different locations and systems. Finding relevant and accurate information is often time-consuming and requires access to multiple systems.

As a consequence, organizations lose a lot of productive employee time. One solution to this problem is to use portals. A portal is an information gateway. It attempts to address information overload through an intranet-based environment in which to search and access relevant information from disparate IT systems and the Internet using advanced search and indexing techniques. An **information portal** is a single point of access through a Web browser to critical business information located inside and outside of an organization, and it can be personalized.

Portals appear under many descriptions and shapes. One way to distinguish among them is to look at their content, which can vary from narrow to broad, and their community or audience, which can also vary. We distinguish six types of portals:

information portal
A single point of access through a Web browser to business information inside and/or outside an organization.

1. **Commercial (public) portals.** These portals offer content for diverse communities and are the most popular portals on the Internet. Although they offer customization of the user interface, they are still intended for broad audiences and offer fairly routine content, some in real time (e.g., a stock ticker and news about a few preselected items). Examples of such sites are yahoo.com, lycos.com, and msn.com.

2. **Corporate portals.** As discussed earlier, corporate portals coordinate rich content within the relatively narrow corporate and partners' communities. They are also known as *enterprise portals* or *enterprise information portals*. Corporate portals are described in more detail in Chapter 8.

3. **Publishing portals.** These portals are intended for communities with specific interests. These portals involve relatively little customization of content, but they provide extensive online search and some interactive capabilities. Examples of such sites are techweb.com and zdnet.com.

4. **Personal portals.** These target specific filtered information for individuals. They offer relatively narrow content but are typically much more personalized, effectively having an audience of one.

5. **Mobile portals.** Mobile portals are portals that are accessible from mobile devices (see Chapter 10 for details). Although most of the other portals mentioned here are PC-based, increasing numbers of portals are accessible via mobile devices. One example of such a mobile portal is i-Mode, which we will describe in Section 2.7.

mobile portal
A portal accessible via a mobile device.

6. **Voice portals.** Voice portals are Web sites, usually portals, with audio interfaces. This means that they can be accessed by a standard or cell phone. AOLbyPhone is an example of a service that allows users to retrieve e-mail, news, and other content. It uses both speech recognition and text-to-speech technologies. Companies such as Tellme.com (see EC Application Case 1.1, page 9) and i3mobile.com (see Internet Exercise 11) offer such software.

voice portal
A portal accessed by telephone or cell phone.

Section 2.2 ❱ REVIEW QUESTIONS

1. Describe electronic storefronts and e-malls.
2. List the various types of stores and e-malls.
3. Differentiate between private and public e-marketplaces.
4. What are information portals?

2.3 INTERMEDIATION AND SYNDICATION IN E-COMMERCE

Intermediaries (brokers) play an important role in commerce by providing value-added activities and services to buyers and sellers. There are many types of intermediaries. The most well-known intermediaries in the physical world are wholesalers and retailers. In cyberspace there

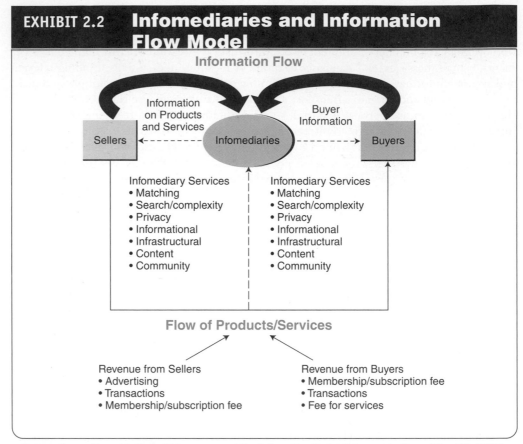

EXHIBIT 2.2   Infomediaries and Information Flow Model

Source: Grover, V., and J. Teng. "E-Commerce and the Information Market." *Communications of the ACM,* ©2001 by ACM Inc.

infomediaries
Electronic intermediaries that control information flow in cyberspace, often aggregating information and selling it to others.

are, in addition, intermediaries that control information flow. These electronic intermediaries are known as **infomediaries**. The information flows to and from buyers and sellers via infomediaries, as shown in Exhibit 2.2. Frequently, they aggregate information and sell it to others. As we continue our study of e-commerce market mechanisms, we need to examine the roles of intermediaries.

THE ROLES AND VALUE OF INTERMEDIARIES IN E-MARKETS

Producers and consumers may interact directly in an e-marketplace: Producers provide information to customers, who then select from among the available products. In general, producers set prices; sometimes prices are negotiated. However, direct interactions are sometimes undesirable or unfeasible. In that case, intermediation is needed. Intermediaries, whether human or electronic, can address the following five important *limitations* of direct interaction.

1. **Search costs.** It may be expensive for providers and consumers to find each other. In electronic marketplaces, thousands of products are exchanged among thousands of vendors and millions of people. Producers may have trouble accurately gauging consumer demand for new products; many desirable items may never be produced simply because no one recognizes the demand for them. Some intermediaries maintain databases of customer preferences, and they can predict demand and *reduce search costs* by selectively routing information from providers to consumers and by *matching* customers with products and/or services.

2. **Lack of privacy.** Either the buyer or seller may wish to remain anonymous or at least protect some information relevant to a trade. Intermediaries can relay messages and make pricing and allocation decisions without revealing the identity of one or both parties.

3. **Incomplete information.** The buyer may need more information than the seller is able or willing to provide, such as information about product quality, competing products, or customer satisfaction. An intermediary can gather product information from sources other than the product provider, including independent evaluators and other customers. Many third-party Web sites provide such information (e.g., bizrate.com, mysimon.com, and consumerguide.com).

4. **Contract risk.** A consumer may refuse to pay after receiving a product or a producer may provide inferior products or give inadequate postpurchase service. Intermediaries have a number of tools to reduce such risks. First, the broker can disseminate information about the behavior of providers and consumers. The threat of publicizing bad behavior or removing a seal of approval may encourage both producers and consumers to meet the broker's standard for fair dealing. Or, the broker may accept responsibility for the behavior of parties in transactions it arranges and act as a policeman on its own. Third, the broker can provide insurance against bad behavior. The credit card industry uses all three approaches to reduce providers' and consumers' exposure to risk.

  In the online auction area, there are companies that act as "escrow agencies," accepting and holding payment from the buyer while the seller completes delivery of the product or service to the escrow agency. Then, if the product is satisfactory, the agency releases payment to the seller and the product to the buyer.

5. **Pricing inefficiencies.** By jockeying to secure a desirable price for a product, providers and consumers may miss opportunities for mutually desirable trades. This is particularly likely in negotiations over unique or custom products, such as houses, and in markets for information products and other public goods where freeloading is a problem. Intermediaries can use pricing mechanisms that induce just the appropriate trades, for example, dealing with an imbalance of buy and sell orders in stock markets.

E-DISTRIBUTORS IN B2B

A special type of intermediary in e-commerce is the B2B **e-distributor**. These intermediaries connect manufacturers (suppliers) with buyers, such as retailers (or resellers in the computer industry). E-distributors basically aggregate the catalogs or the product information from many suppliers, sometimes thousands of them, in one place—the intermediary's Web site. In the past such intermediaries worked with paper catalogs.

For buyers, e-distributors offer a one-stop location from which to place an order. The items purchased are mostly **maintenance, repair, and operation items (MROs)**—that is, items that are usually not under regular contract with suppliers. E-distributors offer unbiased advice on a wide range of products; bundled products and services offer added value processing in small order fulfillment (Berryman and Heck 2001).

One of the most well-known distributors that moved aggressively online is W. W. Grainger (grainger.com), the largest U.S. distributor of MROs. Grainger actually buys products from manufacturers and, like a retailer in B2C, sells them, but to businesses. Another B2B e-distributor is Ingram Micro (ingrammicro.com), the largest global wholesale provider of technology products and supply chain management services. Of its many EC initiatives, one of the more interesting is IM-Logistics, which connects leading technology and consumer electronic manufacturers to more than 7,500 retailers in the United States. Ingram Micro is operating in a complex supply chain, which is shown in online Exhibit T7.3 (together with another intermediary, Solectron). The job of Solectron is to match customized orders collected from customers by Ingram and arrange for one or more suppliers to fulfill them.

Many e-distributors also provide support services, such as payments, deliveries, or escrow services. E-distributors aggregate buyers' and or sellers' orders, they provide valuable services such as security, payments, and escrows, and they may arrange delivery.

DISINTERMEDIATION AND REINTERMEDIATION

Intermediaries provide two types of services: (1) They provide relevant information about demand, supply, prices, and requirements, and in doing so, help match sellers and buyers; and

e-distributor
An e-commerce intermediary that connects manufacturers (suppliers) with buyers by aggregating the catalogs of many suppliers in one place—the intermediary's Web site.

maintenance, repair, and operation items (MROs)
Routine items that are usually not under regular contract with suppliers.

(2) they offer value-added services such as consulting or assistance in finding a business partner. The first type of service can be fully automated, and thus is likely to be assumed by e-marketplaces, infomediaries, and portals that provide free or low-commission services. The second type requires expertise, such as knowledge of the industry, the products, and technological trends, and it can only be partially automated.

Intermediaries who provide only (or mainly) the first type of service may be eliminated, a phenomena called disintermediation. For example, discount stockbrokers that only execute trades will disappear. On the other hand, brokers who provide the second type of service or who manage electronic intermediation are not only surviving, but may actually be prospering. This phenomenon, in which disintermediated organizations take on new intermediary roles, is called reintermediation.

The Web offers new opportunities for reintermediation. First, brokers are especially valuable when the number of market participants is enormous, as with the stock market, or when complex information products are exchanged. Second, many brokering services require information processing. Electronic versions of these services can offer more sophisticated features at a lower cost than is possible with human labor. Finally, for delicate negotiations, a computer mediator may be more predictable, and hence more trustworthy, than a human. For example, suppose a mediator's role is to inform a buyer and a seller whether a deal can be made without revealing either side's initial price to the other, as such a revelation would influence subsequent price negotiations. A software-based mediator will reveal only the information it is supposed to; a human mediator's fairness is less easily ensured. Intermediation and reintermediation are discussed further in Chapters 3, 7, and 15.

Disintermediation is more likely to occur in supply chains involving several intermediaries, as illustrated in the case of precious stones in EC Application Case 2.2 (page 45). The case also illustrates an intermediary that does both B2C and B2B (as do retailers Wal-Mart and Staples and manufacturer Dell).

SYNDICATION AS AN EC MECHANISM

disintermediation
Elimination of intermediaries between sellers and buyers.

reintermediation
Establishment of new intermediary roles for traditional intermediaries that were disintermediated.

syndication
The sale of the same good (e.g., digital content) to many customers, who then integrate it with other offerings and resell it or give it away free.

According to Werbach (2000), syndication involves the sale of the same good to many customers, who then integrate it with other offerings and resell it or give it away free. Syndication has long been extremely popular in the world of entertainment and publishing, but was rare elsewhere until the arrival of the Internet. The digitization of products and services, and the resulting ease with which information can flow, makes syndication a popular business model (e.g., see isyndicate.com and Chapter 14). Let's look at a few examples.

Virtual stockbrokers, such as E*TRADE, offer considerable information on their portals (e.g., financial news, stock quotes, research, etc.). Yahoo and other portals offer other types of information. These brokers and portals buy the information from information creators or originators, such as Reuters, who sell the same information to many portals or other users. Customers may buy directly from the information creators, but in many cases creators use a supply chain of syndicators and distributors, as shown in Exhibit 2.3, to move news and information to the end consumers. Content creators, such as Inktomi (see Carr 2000) and Reuters, make their money by selling the same information to many syndicators and/or distributors. The information distributors, such as E*TRADE, then distribute free information to the public (customers).

Syndication is especially popular with software and other digitizable items. For example, companies syndicate EC services such as payments and shopping-cart ordering systems used by e-tailers. Logistics, security, and systems integration tools are frequently syndicated.

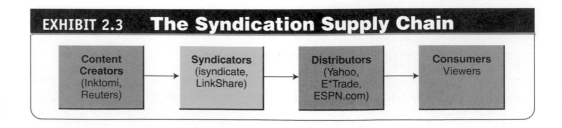

EXHIBIT 2.3   The Syndication Supply Chain

CASE 2.2
EC Application
DIAMONDS FOREVER—ONLINE

The gems market is a global one with hundreds of thousands traders buying about $40-billion worth of gems each year. The age-old business is very inefficient: Several layers of intermediaries can jack up the price of a gem 1,000 percent between wholesale and final retail prices.

Chanthaburi (Thailand) is one of the world's leading centers for processing gems. That is where an American, Don Kogen, landed at the age of 15 to search for his fortune. He found it in about 10 years. After failing to become a gem cutter, Kogen moved into gem sorting, and soon he learned to speak Thai. For 3 years, he observed how gem traders haggled over stones, and then he decided to try the business himself. He started by purchasing low-grade gems from sellers that arrived early in the morning and then selling them for a small profit to dealers from India and Pakistan who arrived late in the day. This quick turnover of inventory helped him build up his capital resources. Using advertising, he reached the U.S. gem market and soon had 800 potential overseas customers. Using faxes, he shortened the order time, which resulted in decreasing the entire time from order to delivery. These various business methods enabled Kogen to grow his mail-order business to $250,000 a year by 1997.

In 1998, Kogen decided to use the Internet. Within a month, he established a Web site (*thaigem.com*) and sold his first gem online. By 2001, the revenue from his online business reached $4.3 million, and it more than doubled (to $9.8 million) in 2002. Online sales account for 85 percent of the revenue. The buyers are mostly dealers or retailers such as Wal-Mart or QVC, although he also sells to small buyers. Kogen buys raw or refined gems from all over the world, some online, trying to cater to the demand of his customers. Payments are made safely, securely, and conveniently using either PayPal or Escrow.com.

Thaigem's competitive edge is low prices. The proximity to gem processing factories and the low labor cost enable Kogen to offer prices significantly lower than his online competitors (such as Tiffany's at *tiffany.com*). Kogen makes only 20 to 25 percent profit, about half the profit that other gem dealers make. Unsatisfied customers can return merchandise within 30 days, no questions asked. Delivery to any place in the world is made via Federal Express, at about $15 per shipment. To make his business even more competitive, Kogen is trying to reduce Thaigem's huge gems inventory, which in 2002 he turned over once in a year (his goal is to reduce it to 6 months).

No jewel is guaranteed, but Kogen's name is trusted by over 68,000 potential customers worldwide. Kogen enjoys a solid reputation on the Web. For example, he uses eBay to auction gems as an additional selling channel. Customers' comments on eBay are 99 percent positive versus 1 percent negative.

Sources: Compiled from *thaigem.com* (2002) and from Meredith (August 2002).

Questions

1. Describe Thaigem's business model, including the revenue model. How are logistics and payments organized? (Visit *thaigem.com* to find more details.)

2. Compare this entrepreneurial business to click-and-mortar gem businesses, such as Tiffany's online business (*tiffany.com*). Visit the two sites and comment on the differences.

3. During the 2000–2002 shakeout of dot-coms, Thaigem.com was prospering. Why do you think it was not affected by the dot-com downturn?

4. Of the $40 billion annual sales in the gem industry, only about 2 percent are done online. Do you think that selling gems online will grow to more than 2 percent? Why or why not?

5. Go to *gemcentral.com* and compare it with *thaigem.com*.

Syndication can be done in several ways. Therefore, there are a number of different revenue-sharing models along the supply chain in Exhibit 2.3. For example, the *affiliate* program discussed in Chapter 1, which is used by CDNow, Amazon.com, and many other e-tailers, is a variation of syndication (Helmstetter and Metivier 2000). For discussion of the organizational impacts of syndication, see Werbach (2000) and Carr (2000).

Section 2.3 ❱ REVIEW QUESTIONS

1. List the roles of intermediaries in e-markets.

2. Describe e-distributors.

3. What are disintermediation and reintermediation?

4. Explain how syndication works in e-commerce.

2.4 ELECTRONIC CATALOGS AND OTHER MARKET MECHANISMS

To enable selling online, one usually needs *EC merchant server software* (see Chapter 18 online). The basic functionality offered by such software includes electronic catalogs, search engines, and shopping carts.

ELECTRONIC CATALOGS

electronic catalogs

The presentation of product information in an electronic form; the backbone of most e-selling sites.

Catalogs have been printed on paper for generations. Recently, electronic catalogs on CD-ROM and the Internet have gained popularity. **Electronic catalogs** consist of a product database, directory and search capabilities, and a presentation function. They are the backbone of most e-commerce sites. For merchants, the objective of electronic catalogs is to advertise and promote products and services. For the customer, the purpose of such catalogs is as a source of information on products and services. Electronic catalogs can be searched quickly with the help of search engines.

The majority of early online catalogs were replications of text and pictures from printed catalogs. However, online catalogs have evolved to become more dynamic, customized, and integrated with selling and buying procedures. As the online catalog is integrated with shopping carts, order taking, and payment, the tools for building online catalogs are being integrated with merchant sites (e.g., see store.yahoo.com).

Electronic catalogs can be classified according to three dimensions:

1. **The dynamics of the information presentation.** Catalogs can be static or dynamic. In *static catalogs*, information is presented in text and static pictures. In *dynamic catalogs*, information is presented in motion pictures or animation, possibly with supplemental sound.

2. **The degree of customization.** Catalogs can be standard or customized. In *standard catalogs*, merchants offer the same catalog to any customer. In *customized catalogs*, content, pricing, and display are tailored to the characteristics of specific customers.

3. **Integration with business processes.** Catalogs can be classified according to the degree of integration with the following business processes or features: order taking and fulfillment; electronic payment systems; intranet workflow software and systems; inventory and accounting systems; suppliers' or customers' extranets; and paper catalogs. For example, when you place an order at amazon.com, your order will be transferred automatically to a computerized inventory check.

Although used occasionally in B2C commerce, customized catalogs are especially useful in B2B e-commerce. For example, e-catalogs can show only the items that the employees are allowed to purchase and can exclude items the buying company's managers do not want their employees to see or to buy. E-catalogs can be customized to show the same item to different customers at different prices, reflecting discounts or purchase-contract agreements. They can even show the buyer's ID for the item, model, or *stock-keeping unit* (SKU) numbers, rather than the seller's ID numbers. Extranets, especially, can deliver customized catalogs to different business customers.

For a comprehensive discussion of online catalogs see jcmax.com/advantages.html and purchasing.about.com.

Comparison of Online Catalogs with Paper Catalogs

The advantages and disadvantages of online catalogs are contrasted with those of paper catalogs in Exhibit 2.4. Although online catalogs have significant advantages, such as ease of updating, ability to integrate with the purchasing process, coverage of a wide spectrum of products, and a strong search capability, they do have disadvantages and limitations. To begin with, customers need computers and the Internet in order to access online catalogs. However, as computers and Internet access are spreading rapidly, we can expect a large portion of paper catalogs to be supplemented by, if not actually replaced by, electronic catalogs. On the other hand, considering the fact that printed newspapers and magazines have not diminished due

EXHIBIT 2.4	**Comparison of Online Catalogs with Paper Catalogs**	
Type	**Advantages**	**Disadvantages**
Paper Catalogs	• Easy to create without high technology • Reader is able to look at the catalog without computer system • More portable than electronic	• Difficult to update changed product information promptly • Only a limited number of products can be catalog displayed • Limited information through photographs and textual description is available • No possibility for advanced multimedia such as animation and voice
Online Catalogs	• Easy to update product information • Able to integrate with the purchasing process • Good search and comparison capabilities • Able to provide timely, up-to-date product information • Provision for globally broad range of product information • Possibility of adding on voice and animated pictures • Long-term cost savings • Easy to customize • More comparative shopping • Ease of connecting order processing, inventory processing, and payment processing to the system	• Difficult to develop catalogs, large fixed cost • There is a need for customer skill to deal with computers and browsers

to the online ones, we can guess that paper catalogs will not disappear. There seems to be room for both media, at least in the near future. However, in B2B, paper catalogs may disappear more quickly.

A representative tool for building online catalogs is Microsoft's Commerce Server 2002. BuyUSA.com builds and maintains electronic catalogs based on their customers' paper catalogs. The service includes search capabilities, the ability to feature large numbers of products, enhanced viewing capabilities, and ongoing support (see the enhanced catalogs demo at buyusa.com).

Customized Catalogs

A *customized catalog* is a catalog assembled specifically for a company, usually a customer of the catalog owner. It can also be tailored to loyal individual shoppers or to a segment of shoppers (e.g., frequent buyers). There are two approaches to customized catalogs.

The first approach is to let the customers identify the interesting parts out of the total catalog, as is done by software products such as One-to-One from Broadvision (broadvision. com). Customers then do not have to deal with topics that are irrelevant to them. Such software allows the creation of catalogs with branded value-added capabilities that make it easy for customers to find the products they want to purchase, locate the information they need, and quickly compose their order.

The second approach is to let the system automatically identify the characteristics of customers based on their transaction records. However, to generalize the relationship between the customer and items of interest, data-mining technology (Chapter 4) may be needed. This second approach can be effectively combined with the first one.

As an example of the second approach, consider this scenario, which uses Oracle's Internet Commerce Server (ICS):

Scenario: Joe Smith logs on to the Acme Shopping site, where he has the option to register as an account customer and record his preferences in terms of address details, interest areas, and preferred method of payment. Acme Shopping offers a wide range of products, including electronics, clothing, books, and sporting goods. Joe is interested only in clothing and electronics. He is neither a sportsman nor a great book lover. Joe also has some very distinct hobby areas—one is photography.

After Joe has recorded his preferences, each time he returns to Acme's electronic store, the first page will show him only the clothing and electronics departments. Furthermore, when Joe goes into the electronics department, he sees only products related to photography—cameras and accessories. Some of the products are out of Joe's price range, so Joe further can refine his preferences to indicate that he is interested only in electronics that relate to photography and cost $300 or less. Such personalization gives consumers a value-added experience and adds to their reasons for revisiting the site, thus building brand loyalty to that Internet store.

Against the backdrop of intense competition for Web time, personalization provides a valuable way to get consumers matched to the products and information in which they are most interested as quickly and painlessly as possible. An example of how corporations customize their catalogs for corporate clients is provided in EC Application Case 2.3.

Implementing E-Catalogs

Implementing e-catalogs on a small scale is fairly simple (e.g., see store.yahoo.com in online Tutorial T2). However, transforming a large-scale catalog to an e-catalog is not an easy task, because it is necessary to create a matching customer support system. See Kapp (2001) and Chapter 14 for a discussion of the topic, examples of successes and failures, and implementation of suggestions.

SEARCH ENGINES AND INTELLIGENT AGENTS

<div class="sidebar">

search engine
A computer program that can access a database of Internet resources, search for specific information or keywords, and report the results.

</div>

A **search engine** is a computer program that can access a database of Internet resources, search for specific information or keywords, and report the results. For example, customers tend to ask for information (e.g., requests for product information or pricing) in the same general manner. This type of request is repetitive, and answering such requests is costly when done by a human. Search engines deliver answers economically and efficiently by matching questions with FAQ (frequently asked question) templates, which include standard questions and "canned" answers to them.

Google, AltaVista, and Lycos are popular search engines. Portals such as AOL, Netscape, and MSN have their own search engines. Special search engines, organized to answer certain questions or search in specified areas, include AskJeeves, Northern Light, and Looksmart. Thousands of different public search engines are available (see searchengineguide.com). In addition, thousands of companies have search engines on their portals or storefronts.

<div class="sidebar">

software (intelligent) agent
Software that can perform routine tasks that require intelligence.

</div>

Unlike a search engine, a **software (intelligent) agent** can do more than just "search and match." It has capabilities that can be used to perform routine tasks that require intelligence. For example, it can monitor movements on a Web site to check whether a customer seems lost or ventures into areas that may not fit their profile. If it detects such confusion, the agent can notify the customer and provide assistance. Software agents can be used in e-commerce to support tasks such as comparing prices, interpreting information, monitoring activities, and working as an assistant. Users can even chat or collaborate with agents.

Users use both search engines and intelligent agents in e-commerce. If customers are inside a storefront or an e-mall, they can use the search engine to find a product or a service. They will also use Web search engines, such as *google.com*, to find general information about a product or service. Finally, they will use software agents that do comparisons (e.g., *mysimon.com*) and conduct other tasks. The essentials of software agents are provided in online Technical Appendix D. Applications of software agents are described in several chapters, especially in Chapters 3 through 7.

SHOPPING CARTS

<div class="sidebar">

electronic shopping cart
An order-processing technology that allows customers to accumulate items they wish to buy while they continue to shop.

</div>

An **electronic shopping cart** is an order-processing technology that allows customers to accumulate items they wish to buy while they continue to shop. In this respect, it is similar to

EC Application
ELECTRONIC CATALOGS AT BOISE CASCADE

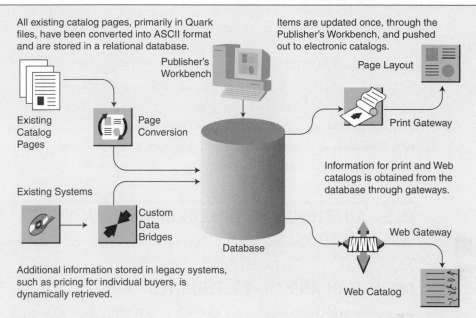

All existing catalog pages, primarily in Quark files, have been converted into ASCII format and are stored in a relational database.

Items are updated once, through the Publisher's Workbench, and pushed out to electronic catalogs.

Publisher's Workbench

Page Layout

Existing Catalog Pages

Page Conversion

Print Gateway

Existing Systems

Custom Data Bridges

Database

Information for print and Web catalogs is obtained from the database through gateways.

Web Gateway

Additional information stored in legacy systems, such as pricing for individual buyers, is dynamically retrieved.

Web Catalog

Source: Netscape Diagram ©2003 Netscape Communications Corporation. Diagram used with permission.

Boise Cascade Office Products is a $4-billion office products wholesaler. Its customer base includes over 100,000 large corporate customers and 1 million small ones. The company's 900-page paper catalog used to be mailed to customers once each year. Throughout the year, Boise also sent mini-catalogs tailored to customers' individual needs based on past buying habits and purchase patterns. The company sells over 200,000 different items and has a global reach, allowing them to serve multinational companies.

In 1996, the company placed its catalogs online. Customers view the catalog at *boiseoffice.com* and can order straight from the site or submit orders by e-mail. The orders are shipped the next day. Customers are then billed. In 1997, the company generated 20 percent of its sales through the Web site. In early 1999, the figure was over 30 percent. The company acknowledges that its Internet business is the fastest growing segment of its business. It expects the Internet business to generate 80 percent of its total sales by 2004.

Boise prepares thousands of individualized catalogs for its customers. As of 2002, the company has been sending paper catalogs only when specifically requested. As indicated earlier, the vast majority of customers use the online catalogs. It used to take about 6 weeks to produce a single paper customer catalog, primarily because of the time involved in pulling together all the data. Now the process of producing a Web catalog that is searchable, rich in content, and available in a variety of formats takes only 1 week.

One major advantage of customized catalogs is pricing. If everyone has the same catalog, you cannot show the customized price for each buyer, which is based on the contract the customer signed and on the volume of goods being purchased.

Boise estimates that electronic orders cost approximately 55 percent less to process than paper-based orders. The figure shows the process of working with the electronic catalogs.

Sources: *boiseoffice.com/about/ecommerce.shtml* (accessed April 2003) and "Boise Cascade Saves $1 Million in First Year of Web Catalog," *wp.netscape.com/solutions/business/profiles/boisecascade.html* (accessed April 2003).

Questions

1. What are the advantages of the electronic catalog to Boise Cascade? To its customers?

2. How are the customized catalogs created by Boise Cascade?

a physical-world shopping cart. The software program of an electronic shopping cart allows customers to select items, review what has been selected, make changes, and then finalize the list. Clicking on "buy" will trigger the actual purchase.

Shopping carts for B2C are fairly simple (visit amazon.com to see an example), but for B2B, a shopping cart may be more complex. A B2B shopping cart could enable a business customer to shop at several sites while keeping the cart on the buyer's Web site to integrate it with the buyer's e-procurement system. A special B2B cart was proposed for this purpose by Lim and Lee (2002) where, in addition to the cart offered at the seller's site, there is a buyers' cart ("b-cart") that resides on the buyers' sites and is sponsored by the participating sellers.

Shopping-cart software is sold or provided for free as an independent component (e.g., monstercommerce.com, edubiz.bizhosting.com, e-shopping-cart-software.com, and actinic.com). It also is embedded in merchants' servers, such as store.yahoo.com.

Section 2.4 ▶ REVIEW

1. List the dimensions by which electronic catalogs can be classified.
2. List the benefits of electronic catalogs.
3. Explain how customized catalogs are created and used.
4. Compare search engines with software agents.
5. Describe an electronic shopping cart.

2.5 AUCTIONS AS EC MARKET MECHANISMS

One of the most interesting market mechanisms in e-commerce is electronic auctions. They are used in B2C, B2B, C2C, G2B, G2C, and more.

DEFINITION AND CHARACTERISTICS

auction
A market mechanism by which a seller places an offer to sell a product and buyers make bids sequentially and competitively until a final price is reached.

An **auction** is a market mechanism by which a seller places an offer to sell a product and buyers make bids sequentially and competitively until a final price is reached. A wide variety of online markets qualify as auctions using this definition. Auctions, an established method of commerce for generations, deal with products and services for which conventional marketing channels are ineffective or inefficient, and they ensure prudent execution of sales. For example, auctions can expedite the disposal of items that need liquidation or a quick sale.

There are several types of auctions, each with its own motives and procedures. (For details, see Chapter 11.) Auctions can be done *online* or *off-line*. They can be conducted in *public* auction sites, such as at eBay. They can also be done by invitation to *private* auctions.

In this section we present the essential information about auctions that is necessary for understanding Chapters 3 through 10. An even fuller treatment of auctions is available in Chapter 11. (Also see Kambil and van Heck 2002.)

Limitations of Traditional Off-line Auctions

Traditional off-line auctions, regardless of their type, have the following limitations: They generally last only a few minutes, or even seconds, for each item sold. This rapid process may give potential buyers little time to make a decision, so they may decide not to bid. Therefore, sellers may not get the highest possible price; bidders may not get what they really want or they may pay too much for the item. Also, in many cases, the bidders do not have much time to examine the goods. As bidders must usually be physically present at auctions, many potential bidders are excluded.

Similarly, it may be difficult for sellers to move goods to an auction site. Commissions are fairly high, as a place must be rented, the auction needs to be advertised, and an auctioneer and other employees need to be paid. Electronic auctioning removes these deficiencies.

Electronic Auctions

The Internet provides an infrastructure for executing auctions electronically at lower cost, with a wide array of support services, and with many more sellers and buyers. Individual consumers and corporations both can participate in this rapidly growing and very convenient form of e-commerce. Forrester Research projected that the Internet auction industry would reach $54.3 billion in sales by 2007 (Johnson 2002).

electronic auctions (e-auctions)
Auctions conducted online.

Electronic auctions (e-auctions) are similar to off-line auctions except that they are done on a computer. E-auctions have been in existence for several years on local area networks and were started on the Internet in 1995. Host sites on the Internet serve as brokers, offering services for sellers to post their goods for sale and allowing buyers to bid on those items.

Major online auctions such as eBay offer consumer products, electronic parts, artwork, vacation packages, airline tickets, and collectibles, as well as excess supplies and inventories being auctioned off by B2B marketers. Another type of B2B online auction is increasingly used to trade special types of commodities, such as electricity transmission capacities and gas and energy options. Furthermore, conventional business practices that traditionally have relied on contracts and fixed prices are increasingly being converted into auctions with bidding for online procurements (e.g., Raffles Hotel).

Of course, many consumer goods are not suitable for auctions, and for these items, conventional selling—such as posted-price retailing—is more than adequate. Yet the flexibility offered by online auction trading offers innovative market processes for many other goods. For example, instead of searching for products and vendors by visiting sellers' Web sites, a buyer may solicit offers from all potential sellers. Such a buying mechanism is so innovative that it has the potential to be used in almost all types of consumer goods auctions (as will be shown later when we discuss reverse auctions and "name-your-own-price" auctions).

DYNAMIC PRICING AND TYPES OF AUCTIONS

A major characteristic of auctions is that they are based on dynamic pricing. **Dynamic pricing** refers to prices that change based on supply-and-demand relationships at any given time. That is, the prices are not fixed, but are allowed to change as supply and demand in a market change. In contrast, catalog prices are fixed, as are prices in department stores, supermarkets, and many electronic storefronts.

dynamic pricing
Prices that change based on supply and demand relationships at any given time.

Dynamic pricing appears in several forms. Perhaps the oldest ones are negotiation and bargaining, which have been practiced for many generations in open-air markets. It is customary to classify dynamic pricing into four major categories, depending on how many buyers and sellers are involved. These four categories are outlined in the following text and are discussed more fully in Chapter 11.

One Buyer, One Seller

In this configuration, one can use negotiation, bargaining, or bartering. The resulting price will be determined by each party's bargaining power, supply and demand in the item's market, and (possibly) business environment factors.

One Seller, Many Potential Buyers

In this configuration, the seller uses a **forward auction**, an auction in which a seller entertains bids from buyers. (Because forward auctions are the most common and traditional form, they are often simply called auctions.) There are four major types of forward auctions: *English* and *Yankee* auctions, in which bidding prices increase as the auction progresses, and *Dutch* and *free-fall* auctions, in which bidding prices decline as the auction progresses (see Chapter 11 for details).

forward auction
An auction in which a seller entertains bids from buyers.

One Buyer, Many Potential Sellers

There are two types of auctions in which there is one buyer and many potential sellers: reverse and "name-your-own-price." These are two of the most popular auction models on the Internet.

Reverse auctions. When there is one buyer and many potential sellers, a **reverse auction** (also called a **bidding** or **tendering system**) is effective. In a reverse auction, the buyer places an item for bid (or *tender*) on a *request for quote* (RFQ) system. Potential suppliers bid on the job, reducing the price sequentially (see Exhibit 2.5 on page 52). In electronic bidding in a reverse auction, several rounds of bidding may take place until the bidders do not further reduce the price. The winner is the one with the lowest bid (assuming that only price is considered). Reverse auctions are primarily a B2B or G2B mechanism. (For further discussion and examples, see Chapter 6.)

reverse auction (bidding or tendering system)
Auction in which the buyer places an item for bid (*tender*) on a request for quote (RFQ) system, potential suppliers bid on the job, with price reducing sequentially, and the lowest bid wins; primarily a B2B or G2B mechanism.

EXHIBIT 2.5   The Reverse Auction Process

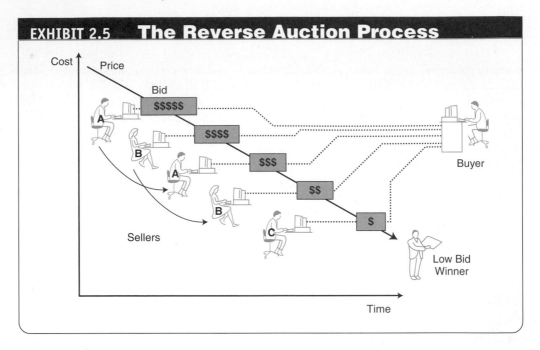

"name-your-own-price" model

Auction model in which a would-be buyer specifies the price (and other terms) they are willing to pay to any willing and able seller. It is a C2B model, pioneered by Priceline.com.

The name-your-own-price model. Priceline.com pioneered the "name-your-own-price" model. In this model, a would-be buyer specifies the price (and other terms) that they are willing to pay to any willing and able seller. For example, Priceline.com presents consumer requests to sellers, who fill as much of the guaranteed demand as they wish at prices and terms requested by buyers. Alternately, Priceline.com searches its own database that contains vendors' lowest prices and tries to match supply against requests. Priceline.com asks customers to guarantee acceptance of the offer if it is at or below the requested price by giving a credit card number. This is basically a C2B model, although some businesses use it too. (See Chapter 11 for details.)

Many Sellers, Many Buyers

When there are many sellers and many buyers, buyers and their bidding prices are matched with sellers and their asking prices considering the quantities on both sides. Stocks and commodities markets are typical examples of this configuration. Buyers and sellers can be individuals or businesses. Such an auction is called a **double auction**. (See Chapter 11 for details.)

double auction

Auctions in which multiple buyers and their bidding prices are matched with multiple sellers and their asking prices, considering the quantities on both sides.

BENEFITS, LIMITATIONS, AND IMPACTS OF E-AUCTIONS

Electronic auctions are becoming important selling and buying channels for many companies and individuals. E-auctions enable buyers to access goods and services anywhere auctions are conducted. Moreover, almost perfect market information is available about prices, products, current supply and demand, and so on. These characteristics provide benefits to all.

Benefits of E-Auctions

A listing of the benefits of e-auctions to sellers, buyers, and e-auctioneers is provided in Insights and Additions 2.1.

Limitations of E-Auctions

E-auctions have several limitations. The most significant limitations are the lack of security, the possibility of fraud, and limited participation.

Lack of security. Some of the C2C auctions conducted on the Internet are not secure because they are done in an unencrypted environment and credit card numbers could be stolen during the payment process. Recent payment methods such as PayPal (paypal.com) can solve the payment problem (see Chapter 13). (eBay purchased PayPal in summer 2002.) However, some B2B auctions are conducted on highly secure private lines.

Insights and Additions 2.1   Benefits of Electronic Auctions

Benefits to Sellers	Benefits to Buyers	Benefits to E-Auctioneers
• Increased revenues from broadening customer base and shortening cycle time. • Chance to bargain instead of buying at a fixed price. • Optimal price setting determined by the market (more buyers). • Sellers can gain more customer dollars by offering items directly (saves on the commission to intermediaries; also, physical auctions' fees are very expensive compared to e-auctions). • Can liquidate large quantities quickly. • Improved customer relationship and loyalty (in the case of specialized B2B auction sites and electronic exchanges).	• Opportunities to find unique items and collectibles. • Entertainment. Participation in e-auctions can be entertaining and exciting. • Anonymity. With the help of a third party, buyers can remain anonymous. • Convenience. Buyers can bid from anywhere, even with a cell phone; they do not have to travel to an auction place.	• Higher repeat purchases. Jupiter Media Metrix (*jmm.com*) found that auction sites, such as eBay, tend to garner higher repeat-purchase rates than the top e-commerce B2C sites, such as Amazon.com. • High "stickiness" to the Web site (the tendency of customers to stay at sites longer and come back more often). Auction sites are frequently "stickier" than fixed-priced sites. Stickier sites generate more ad revenue for the e-auctioneer. • Expansion of the auction business.

Possibility of fraud. Auction items are in many cases unique, used, or antique. Because the buyer cannot see the items, the buyer may get defective products. Also, buyers can commit fraud by receiving goods or services without paying for them. Thus, the fraud rate on e-auctions is very high. For a discussion of e-auction fraud and of fraud prevention, see Chapter 11.

Limited participation. Some auctions are by invitation only, whereas others are open to dealers only. Limited participation is a disadvantage to sellers, who usually benefit from as large a pool of buyers as possible.

Impacts of Auctions

Because the trade objects and contexts for auctions are very diverse, the rationale behind auctions and the motives of the different participants for setting up auctions are quite different. Representative impacts of e-auctions include the following.

Auctions as a coordination mechanism. Auctions are increasingly used as an efficient coordination mechanism for establishing an equilibrium in price. An example is auctions for the allocation of telecommunications bandwidth.

Auctions as a social mechanism to determine a price. For objects not being traded in traditional markets, such as unique or rare items, or for items that may be offered randomly or at long intervals, an auction creates a marketplace that attracts potential buyers, and often experts. By offering many of these special items at a single time, and by attracting considerable attention, auctions provide the requisite exposure of purchase and sale orders, and hence liquidity of the market in which an optimal price can be determined. Typical examples are auctions of fine arts or rare items, as well as auctions of communications frequencies, Web banners, and advertising space. For example, wine collectors can find a global wine auction at winebid.com.

Auctions as a highly visible distribution mechanism. Another type of auction is similar to the previous one, but deals with special offers. In this case, a supplier typically auctions off a limited amount of items, using the auction primarily as a mechanism to gain attention and to attract those customers who are bargain hunters or have a preference for the gambling dimension of the auction process. The airline-seat auctions by Cathay Pacific, American Airlines, and Lufthansa fall into this category. (See Kambil and van Heck 2002.)

CASE 2.4

EC Application

REVERSE MORTGAGE AUCTIONS IN SINGAPORE

Homebuyers like to get the lowest possible mortgage rates. In the United States, Priceline.com (*priceline.com*) will try to find you a mortgage if you "name your own price." However, a better deal may be available to homebuyers in Singapore, where reverse auctions are combined with "group purchasing," saving about $20,000 over the life of a mortgage for each homeowner, plus $1,200 in waived legal fees. Dollardex (*dollarDEX.com*, 2000) offers the service in Singapore, Hong Kong, and other countries.

Here is how Dollardex arranged its first project: The site invited potential buyers in three residential properties in Singapore to join the service. Applications, including financial credentials, were made on a secure Web site. Then, seven lending banks were invited to bid on the loans. In a secure "electronic room," borrowers and lenders negotiated. After 2 days of negotiations of interest rates and special conditions, the borrowers voted on one bank. In the first project, 18 borrowers agreed to give the job to United Overseas Bank (UOB), paying about 0.5 percent less than the regular mortgage interest rate. The borrowers negotiated the waiver of the legal fee as well. From this first project, UOB generated $10 million of business. Today, Dollardex allows customers to participate in an individual reverse auction if they do not want to join a group.

The banks involved in the auctions can see the offers made by competitors. Flexibility is high; in addition to inter-est rates, banks are willing to negotiate down payment size and the option of switching from a fixed-rate to variable-rate loan. On average, there are 2.6 bank bids per customer.

As of summer 2003, in addition to mortgages, Dollardex.com offers car loans, insurance policies, and travel services. It also alllows comparisons of mutual funds that have agreed to give lower front-end fees. They also offer insurance (including health, motor, home, home content, and SARS insurance). You can also choose one or more unit trusts in which you want to invest, set up a gift registry page for your wedding and invite your givers to place funds in them. Reports and advice are also available online as well as face-to-face.

Sources: Compiled from "DollarDEX Launches Reverse Auction on Mortgages" (2002) and from *dollarDEX.com* (2002 and 2003).

Questions

1. How is group purchasing organized at *dollardex.com*? What services are offered?
2. Why does a reverse auction take place?
3. Can this model exist without an intermediary?

Auctions as a component in e-commerce. Auctions can stand alone or they can be combined with other e-commerce activities. An example of the latter is the combination of group purchasing with reverse auctions, as described in EC Application Case 2.4.

Section 2.5 ▶ REVIEW

1. Define auctions and describe how they work.
2. Describe the benefits of electronic auctions over traditional (off-line) auctions.
3. List the four types of auctions.
4. Distinguish between forward and reverse auctions.
5. Describe the "name-your-own-price" auction model.
6. List the major benefits of auctions to buyers, sellers, and auctioneers.
7. What are the major limitations of auctions?
8. List the major impacts of auctions trading on markets.

2.6 BARTERING AND NEGOTIATING ONLINE

ONLINE BARTERING

bartering
An exchange of goods and services.

Bartering, an exchange of goods and services, is the oldest method of trade. Today, it is usually done primarily between organizations. The problem with bartering is that it is difficult to find trading partners. Businesses and individuals may use e-classified ads to advertise what they need and what they offer, but through such advertising they may not find what they want. Intermediaries may be helpful, but they are expensive (20 to 30 percent commission) and very slow.

E-bartering (electronic bartering)—bartering conducted online—can improve the matching process by attracting more partners to the barter. In addition, matching can be done faster, and as a result, better matches can be found. Items that are frequently bartered online include office space, storage, and factory space; idle facilities; and labor, products, and banner ads. (Note that e-bartering may have tax implications that need to be considered.)

E-bartering is usually done in a **bartering exchange**, a marketplace in which an intermediary arranges the transactions. These exchanges can be very effective. Representative bartering Web sites include allbusiness.com, intagio.com, bigvine.com, ubarter.com, and whosbartering.com. The process works like this: First, you tell the bartering exchange what you want to offer. The exchange then assesses the value of your products or services and offers you certain "points" or "bartering dollars." You use the "points" to buy the things you need from a participating member in the exchange.

Bartering sites must be financially secure. Otherwise users may not have a chance to use the points they accumulate. (For further details, see "virtual bartering 101" at fortune.com/smallbusiness and Lorek 2000).

ONLINE NEGOTIATING

Dynamic prices can also be determined by *negotiation*. Negotiated pricing commonly is used for expensive or specialized products. Negotiated prices also are popular when large quantities are purchased. Much like in auctions, negotiated prices result from interactions and bargaining among sellers and buyers. However, in contrast with auctions, negotiation also deals with nonpricing terms, such as payment method and credit. Negotiation is a well-known process in the off-line world (e.g., in real estate, automobile purchases, and contract work). In addition, in cases where there is no standard service or product to speak of, some digital products and services can be personalized and "bundled" at a standard price. Preferences for these bundled services differ among consumers, and thus they are frequently negotiated.

According to Choi and Whinston (2000), *online (electronic) negotiation* is easier than off-line negotiation. Due to customization and bundling of products and services, it often is necessary to negotiate both prices and terms for online sales. E-markets allow such online negotiations to be conducted for virtually all products and services. Three factors may facilitate online negotiation: (1) products and services that are bundled and customized, (2) computer technology that facilitates the negotiation process, and (3) software (intelligent) agents that perform searches and comparisons, thereby providing quality customer service and a base from which prices can be negotiated.

Section 2.6 ▶ REVIEW

1. Define bartering and describe the advantages of e-bartering.
2. Explain the role of online negotiation in EC.

2.7 E-COMMERCE IN THE WIRELESS ENVIRONMENT: M-COMMERCE

The widespread adoption of wireless and mobile networks, devices (handsets, PDAs, etc.), and *middleware* (software that links application modules from different computer languages and platforms) is creating exciting new opportunities. These new technologies are making **mobile computing** possible—meaning that when using wireless computing they permit *real-time* access to information, applications, and tools that, until recently, were accessible only from a desktop computer. **Mobile commerce (m-commerce)** refers to the conduct of e-commerce via

e-bartering
Bartering conducted online, usually by a bartering exchange.

bartering exchange
A marketplace in which an intermediary arranges barter transactions.

mobile computing
Permits real-time access to information, applications, and tools that, until recently, were accessible only from a desktop computer.

mobile commerce (m-commerce)
E-commerce conducted via wireless devices.

m-business
The broadest definition of
m-commerce, in which
e-business is conducted
in a wireless environment.

wireless devices or from portable devices (see Maybelline case, Chapter 1), including smart cards. It is also sometimes called **m-business** when reference is made to its broadest definition (Kalakota and Robinson 2001; Sadeh 2002), in which the e-business environment is wireless.

There is a reason for the strong interest in the topic of mobile commerce. According to the International Data Corporation (ITAsia One, September 2002), the number of mobile devices is projected to top 1.3 billion by 2004. These devices can be connected to the Internet, allowing users to conduct transactions from anywhere. The Gartner Group estimates that at least 40 percent of all B2C transactions, totaling over $200 billion by 2005, will be initiated from smart wireless devices. Others predict much higher figures because they believe that mobile devices will soon overtake PCs as the predominant Internet access device, creating a global market of over 500 million subscribers. However, others predict a much slower adoption rate (see Chapter 10).

THE PROMISE OF M-COMMERCE

Since 1999, m-commerce has become one of the hottest topics in IT in general and in EC in particular. Mobility significantly changes the manner in which people and trading partners interact, communicate, and collaborate, and mobile applications are expected to change the way we live, play, and do business. Much of the Internet culture, which is currently PC-based, may change to one based on mobile devices. As a result, m-commerce creates new business models for EC, notably location-based applications (which we cover in Chapter 10).

Although there are currently many hurdles to the widespread adoption of m-commerce, it is clear that many of these will be reduced or eliminated in the future. Many companies are already shifting their strategy to the mobile world. Many large corporations with huge marketing presence—Microsoft, Intel, Sony, AT&T, AOLTimeWarner, to name a few—are transforming their businesses to include m-commerce–based products and services. Nokia emerged as a world-class company not just because it sells more cell phones than anyone else, but also because it has become the major player in the mobile economy. Similarly, major telecommunications companies, from Verizon to Vodafone, are shifting their strategies to wireless products and services. In Europe alone, over 200 companies offer mobile portal services. In the United States, over 2 million subscribers used General Motors' OnStar in-vehicle mobile services in 2002 (see *onstar.com*). DoCoMo, the world's largest mobile portal, with more than 30 million customers in Japan, is investing billions of dollars to expand its services to other countries, via its i-Mode services.

i-MODE: A SUCCESSFUL MOBILE PORTAL

To illustrate the potential spread of m-commerce, let's examine DoCoMo's (nttdocomo.com) i-Mode, the pioneering wireless service that took Japan by storm in 1999 and 2000. With a few clicks on a handset, i-Mode users can conduct a large variety of m-commerce activities ranging from online stock trading and banking to purchasing travel tickets and booking karaoke rooms. Users can also utilize i-Mode to send and receive color images. Launched in February 1999, i-Mode went international in 2000 and had over 15 million users by the end of that year and 30 million by the end of 2002 (*Business Week* 2002). Here are some interesting applications of i-Mode:

▶ **Shopping guides.** Addresses and telephone numbers of the favorite shops in the major shopping malls in Tokyo and other cities are provided with a supporting search engine. Consumers can locate information about best-selling books and then buy them. Users can purchase music online to enjoy anywhere.

▶ **Maps and transportation.** Digital maps show detailed guides of local routes and stops of the major public transportation systems in all major cities. Users can access train and bus timetables, guides to shopping areas, and automatic notification of train delays.

▶ **Ticketing.** Airline tickets and movie tickets can be purchased online.

EC Application
WIRELESS PEPSI INCREASES PRODUCTIVITY

Pepsi Bottling Group (PBG), the largest manufacturer, seller, and distributor of Pepsi-Cola, has a mountainous job stocking and maintaining their Pepsi vending machines, including a huge amount of paperwork and frustrating searches for parts and equipment necessary to fix the machines. Any time one of the tens of thousands of machines is out of stock or not functioning, the company loses revenue and profits.

In 2002, the company began to equip its service technicians with handheld devices hooked into a wireless wide area network (WWAN). The handheld is the Melard Sidearm (from Melard Technologies), and it is designed to work with many wireless platforms. iAnywhere (from Sybase, Inc., *sybase.com*) provides the mobile database application that allows wireless communications around the country in real time. The database includes the repair parts inventory available on each service truck, so dispatchers know who to send for maintenance and where the truck is at any given moment. It also has a back-office system that maintains the overall inventory. In the near future, the company will be able to locate the whereabouts of each truck in real time, using global positioning systems (GPS). This will make scheduling and dispatching more effective.

In the summer of 2002, only about 700 technicians used the wireless system, but already the company was saving $7 million per year. Each of these technicians has been able to handle one more call each day than previously. PBG provided the wireless capability to about 300 more technicians in 20 more locations in late 2002 and will do so to many more in the future.

Source: Compiled from Rhey (2002).

Questions

1. What were the capabilities of the handheld devices used by the Pepsi Bottling Group technicians?
2. Relate the handheld to the mobile database.
3. This case deals with the maintenance issue. In what ways, if any, could wireless technologies help with stocking issues?

▶ **News and reports.** Fast access to global news, local updated traffic conditions, the air pollution index, and weather reports are provided continuously.

▶ **Personalized movie service.** Updates on the latest movies with related information, such as casting and show times, are provided. Also, subscribers can search for their own favorite movies by entering the name of the movie or the name of the movie theater.

▶ **Entertainment.** Up-to-date personalized entertainment, such as playing favorite games, can be searched easily. Online "chatting" is also provided, and users can send or receive photos. Also, users can subscribe to receive Tamagotchi's characters each day for only $1 a month.

▶ **Dining and reservations.** The exact location of a selected participating restaurant is shown on a digital map. Subscribers can also find a restaurant that provides a meal in a particular price range. Reservations can be made online. Discount coupons are also available online.

▶ **Additional services.** Additional services such as banking, stock trading, telephone directory searches, dictionary services, and a horoscope are available.

These applications are for individual users and are provided via a mobile portal. An even greater number of applications are available in the B2B area and in the intrabusiness area, as illustrated in EC Application Case 2.5. For more complete coverage of m-business applications, see Chapter 10 of this book, Kalakota and Robinson (2001), and Sadeh (2002).

Section 2.7 ▶ REVIEW

1. Define mobile computing and m-commerce.
2. How does m-commerce differ from EC?
3. What are some of the major services provided by i-Mode?

2.8 ISSUES IN E-MARKETS: LIQUIDITY, QUALITY, AND SUCCESS FACTORS

LIQUIDITY: THE NEED FOR A CRITICAL MASS OF BUYERS AND SELLERS

A critical mass of buyers is needed in order for an EC company or initiative to survive. As will be shown in Section 2.9, the fixed cost of deploying EC can be high, sometimes very high. Without a large number of buyers, sellers will not make money. In 2001, the number of Internet users worldwide was estimated by Nielsen NetRatings (Nua Internet Surveys, 2003) to be between 580 million, and many of them do not shop online. This number is a small figure compared with an estimated 2 *billion* television viewers worldwide. This situation will change, especially when TV/PC integration becomes widespread and wireless devices become a popular way to access the Internet (as described in Section 2.7).

At the global level, governments are assisting industry to achieve a critical mass of EC buyers. Canada, for example, has a goal to be recognized as an EC-friendly country in order to attract international investments and business. Hong Kong is developing a multibillion-dollar "cyberport" that will facilitate EC development and may position the country as a center for global EC in Southeast Asia. Korea supports nine major B2B exchanges that relate to the country's major industries (e.g., semiconductors). Finally, in 2001, the U.S. government introduced BuyUSA.com (buyusa.com) to facilitate global trade.

early liquidity
Achieving a critical mass of buyers and sellers as fast as possible, before a start-up company's cash disappears.

Having a critical mass of buyers and sellers is referred to as *liquidity*. One of the major success factors for a start-up B2B vendor is **early liquidity**—achieving a critical mass of buyers and sellers as fast as possible, before the company's cash disappears (see Ramsdell 2000 and Chapter 7). Finally, in addition to the issue of profitability, a critical mass of both buyers and sellers is needed for markets to be truly efficient, so that strong and fair competition can develop.

QUALITY UNCERTAINTY AND QUALITY ASSURANCE

Although price is a major factor for any buyer, quality is extremely important in many situations, especially when buyers cannot see and feel a product before they purchase it. When consumers buy a brand-name PC from Dell, IBM, or Compaq, they are fairly sure about the quality of the product or service being purchased. When a consumer buys from a not-so-well-known vendor, however, quality can become a major issue. The issue of quality is related to the issues of trust (discussed in Chapter 4) and consumer protection (Chapter 12). Quality assurance can be provided through a trusted third-party intermediary. For example, TRUSTe and the BBBOnLine provide a testimonial seal for participating vendors. BBBOnLine is known for its quality-assurance system and its physical testing of products.

quality uncertainty
The uncertainty of online buyers about the quality of non-commodity type products that they have never seen, especially from an unknown vendor.

The problem of quality is frequently referred to as **quality uncertainty**. Customers have cognitive difficulty accepting products that they have never seen, especially from an unknown vendor. The BBBOnLine and TRUSTe seals can convince some customers, but not all. Those who remain skeptical are not sure what they will get. There are several possible solutions to quality uncertainty, however. One is to provide *free samples*. This is a clear signal that the vendor is confident about the quality of its products. However, samples cost money. It is a sunk cost that will need to be recovered from future sales. The cost for digital samples, however, is minimal. Shareware-type software is based on this concept.

Another solution to quality uncertainty is to offer *returns* if the buyer is not satisfied. This policy is common in several countries and is used by most large retailers and manufacturers. This policy, which provides a guarantee or a full refund for dissatisfied customers, is helpful in facilitating trust in EC. Such a policy, however, might not be feasible for digital products for the following reasons: First, many digital products, such as information, knowledge, or music, are fully consumed when they are viewed by consumers. After they are consumed, returning the products has little meaning. Unlike physical products, returning a digital product does not prevent the consumer from using the product in the future. Also, the vendor cannot resell the returned product. Second, returning a product or refunding a purchase price may be impractical due to transaction costs. For example, a microproduct, a small digital product costing a few cents, must be transported twice over the network, so the cost of the refund may exceed the price. Therefore, for microproducts supported by *micropayments* (small payments, see Chapter 13), some companies do not offer a quality guarantee or a refund. (For further discussion of quality uncertainty, see Choi et al. 1997 and Choi and Whinston 2000.)

microproduct
A small digital product costing a few cents.

A third solution to quality uncertainty is to offer insurance, escrow, and other services. Many services, such as insurance and escrow, are available to ensure quality and prevent fraud. Of special interest are those offered by auction houses, such as eBay.com, as discussed in Chapter 11.

E-MARKET SUCCESS FACTORS

Based on an analysis of the EC examples presented in this chapter, it is apparent that EC will impact some industries more than others. The question is, "What are some of the factors that determine this level of impact?" Strader and Shaw (1997) have identified e-market success factors that fall within one of four categories: product, industry, seller, and consumer characteristics.

Product Characteristics

Digitizable products are particularly suited for e-markets because they can be electronically distributed to customers, resulting in very low distribution costs. Digitization also allows the order-fulfillment cycle time to be minimized.

A product's price may also be an important determinant to its success. The higher the product price, the greater the level of risk involved in the market transaction between buyers and sellers who are geographically separated and may have never dealt with each other before. Therefore, some of the most common items currently sold through e-markets are low-priced items such as CDs and books.

Finally, computers, electronic products, consumer products, and even cars can be sold electronically because the consumer knows exactly what they are buying. The more product information that is available, the better. The use of multimedia, for example, can dramatically facilitate product description. Products that sell very well online, both in B2C and B2B, are jewelry and gems (see EC Application Case 2.2 on page 45).

Industry Characteristics

Electronic markets are most useful when they are able to directly match buyers and sellers. However, some industries require transaction brokers, thus they may be affected less by e-markets than industries where no brokers are required. Stockbrokers, insurance agents, and travel agents may provide services that are still needed, but in some cases software may be able to reduce the need for these brokers. This is particularly true as intelligent systems become more available to assist consumers. Other important issues are: Who are the major players (corporations) in the industry? How many companies in the industry are well managed? How strong is the competition, including foreign companies?

Seller Characteristics

Electronic markets reduce search costs, allowing consumers to find sellers offering lower prices. In the long run, this may reduce profit margins for sellers that compete in e-markets, although it may also increase the number of transactions that take place. If sellers are unwilling to participate in this environment, then the impact of e-markets may be reduced. However, in highly competitive industries with low barriers to entry, sellers may not have a choice but to join in.

Consumer Characteristics

Consumers can be classified as impulse, patient, or analytical (as we will discuss further in Chapter 4). Electronic markets may have little impact on industries where a sizable percentage of purchases are made by impulse buyers. Because e-markets require a certain degree of effort on the part of the consumer, e-markets are more conducive to consumers who do some comparison and analysis before buying (the patient and analytical buyers). Analytical buyers can use the Internet to evaluate a wide range of information before deciding where to buy. On the other hand, m-commerce is banking on impulse buyers—on the customer being in the right place at the right time.

Section 2.8 ▶ REVIEW

1. What is early liquidity? Why is it important?
2. How can quality be assured in EC?
3. Describe some success factors for e-markets.

2.9 ECONOMICS OF E-MARKETPLACES

The economics of EC are based on principles that sometimes differ from those underlying traditional markets. These EC principles are drawn from the economic principles that apply to information and telecommunications networks. Consider the following examples.

PRODUCTS' COST CURVES

The average-cost (AVC) curve of many physical products and services is U-shaped (see Exhibit 2.6a). This curve indicates that, at first, as quantity increases, the average cost declines. As quantity increases still more, the cost goes back up due to increasing variable costs (especially administrative and marketing costs) in the short run.

In contrast, the variable cost per unit of digital products is very low (in most cases) and almost fixed, regardless of the quantity. Therefore, as illustrated in Exhibit 2.6b, total cost per unit will decline as quantity increases, as the fixed costs are spread (prorated) over more units. This relationship results in increasing returns with increased sales.

OTHER COST CURVES

EC has other economic advantages over traditional commerce. In Exhibit 2.7 we show three cost components—the production function, transaction costs, and agency/administration costs—and the effect of EC on each.

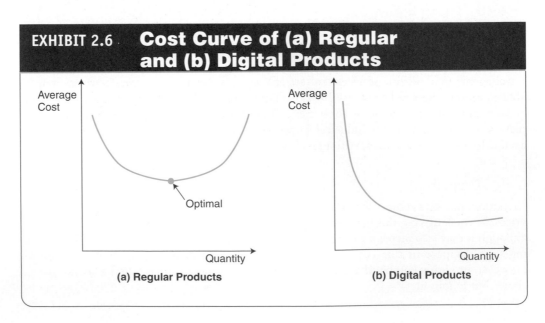

EXHIBIT 2.6 · Cost Curve of (a) Regular and (b) Digital Products

(a) Regular Products

(b) Digital Products

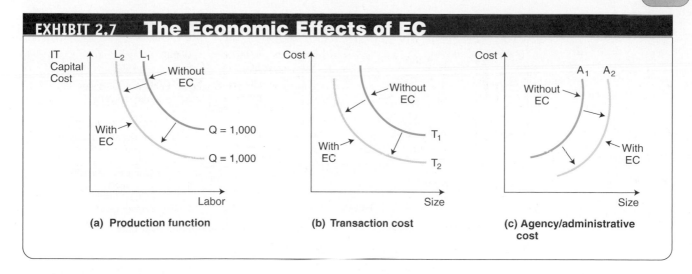

EXHIBIT 2.7   The Economic Effects of EC

(a) Production function

(b) Transaction cost

(c) Agency/administrative cost

Production Function

The production function is shown in Exhibit 2.7a. It indicates that for the same quantity of production, Q, companies either can use a certain amount of labor or invest in more automation (they can substitute IT capital for labor). For example, for a quantity $Q = 1,000$, the lower the amount of labor needed, the higher the required IT investment (capital costs). When EC enters the picture, it shifts the function inward (from L_1 to L_2), lowering the amount of labor and/or capital needed to produce the same $Q = 1,000$.

Transaction Costs

The economics of the firm's *transaction costs* (the costs associated with conducting a sale) are shown in Exhibit 2.7b. Traditionally, in order to reduce this cost, firms had to grow in size (as depicted in curve T_1). In the digital economy, the transaction cost is shifted inward, to position T_2. This means that EC makes it possible to have low transaction costs with smaller firm size or to enjoy much lower transaction costs when firm size increases.

Agency Costs

Exhibit 2.7c shows the economics of the firm's agency (administrative) costs. In the "old economy," agency costs (A_1) grew with the size (and complexity) of the firm, frequently preventing companies from growing to a very large size. In the digital economy, the agency costs curve is shifted outward, to A_2. This means that as a result of EC, companies can significantly expand their business without too much increase in administrative costs.

REACH VERSUS RICHNESS

Another economic impact of EC is the trade-off between the number of customers a company can reach (called "reach") and the amount of interactions and information services they can provide to customers (called "richness"). According to Evans and Wurster (2000), for a given level of cost (resources), there is a trade-off between reach and richness. The more customers a company wants to reach, the fewer services they can provide to them. This economic relationship is depicted in Exhibit 2.8a (page 62). Using EC, it is possible to shift the curve outward.

Exhibit 2.8b shows an implementation of the reach versus richness concept at Charles Schwab brokerage house. Initially, Schwab attempted to increase its reach. To do so, the company went downward along the curve, reducing its richness. However, with its Web site (schwab.com), Schwab was able to drastically increase its reach and at the same time provide richness in terms of customer service and financial information to customers. For example, Schwab's *Mutual Fund Screener* allows customers to design their own investment portfolios by selecting from an array of mutual funds. This service may be combined with other tools such as the *Asset Allocator* and the *Performance Monitor*. Providing such services (richness) allows Schwab to increase the number of its customers (larger reach), as well as to charge

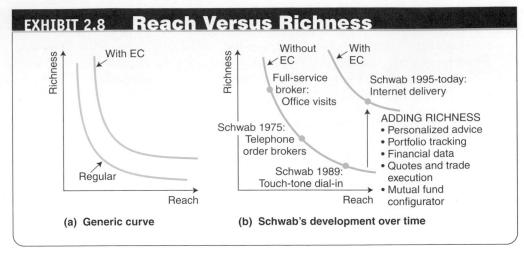

EXHIBIT 2.8   Reach Versus Richness

(a) Generic curve

(b) Schwab's development over time

Sources: Part (a) developed by the authors. Part (b) reprinted by permission of Harvard Business School Press. From *Blown to Bits: How the New Economics of Information Transforms Strategy* by P. Evans and T. S. Wurster. Boston, MA: 2000, fig. 5.2. Copyright ©2000 by Harvard Business School Publishing Corporation; all rights reserved.

higher fees than competitors that provide little or no value-added service. (For additional details, see Slywotzkty and Morrison 2001.)

Section 2.9 ▶ REVIEW

1. Describe how traditional economic relationships have changed in the digital era.
2. Describe the contribution of EC to the reach/richness relationship.

2.10   COMPETITION IN THE DIGITAL ECONOMY

THE INTERNET ECOSYSTEM

The prevailing model of competition in the Internet economy is more like a web of interrelationships than the hierarchical, command-and-control model of the industrial economy. Because of these interrelationships, the business model of the Internet economy has been called the Internet ecosystem. Just like an ecosystem in nature, activity in the Internet economy is self-organizing: The process of *natural selection* takes place around company profits and value to customers. The Internet economy has low barriers to entry, and so it is expanding rapidly. As the Internet ecosystem evolves, both technologically and in population, it will be even easier and likelier for countries, companies, and individuals to participate in the Internet economy. Already, there is $1 trillion in technical infrastructure in place, ready and available for anyone to use at any time—free of charge. New ideas and ways of doing things can come from anywhere at any time in the Internet economy. Some of the old competition rules no longer apply (see discussions at americasnetwork.com).

Internet ecosystem
The business model of the Internet economy.

Competitive Factors

EC competition is very intense because online transactions enable the following:

Lower search costs for buyers. E-markets reduce the cost of searching for product information, frequently to zero. This can significantly impact competition, enabling customers to find cheaper (or better) products and forcing sellers, in turn, to reduce prices and/or improve customer service. Sellers that provide information to buyers can exploit the Internet to gain a considerably larger market share.

Speedy comparisons. Not only can customers find inexpensive products online, but they also can find them quickly. For example, a customer does not have to go to several bookstores to quickly find the best price for a particular book. Using shopping search engines such as *allbookstores.com* or *bestwebbuys.com/books*, or *dealtime.com* for consumer products, customers can find what they want and compare prices. Companies that sell online and provide information to search engines will gain a competitive advantage.

Differentiation and personalization. Differentiation involves providing a product or service that is not available elsewhere. For example, Amazon.com differentiates itself from other book retailers by providing customers with information that is not available in a physical bookstore, such as communication with authors, almost real-time book reviews, and book recommendations.

In addition, EC provides for personalization or customization of products and services. Personalization refers to the ability to tailor a product, service, or Web content to specific user preferences. For example, Amazon.com will notify you by e-mail when new books on your favorite subject or by your favorite author are published.

Consumers like differentiation and personalization and are frequently willing to pay more for them. Differentiation reduces the substitutability between products, thus benefiting sellers who use this strategy. Also, price cutting in differentiated markets does not impact market share very much: Many customers are willing to pay a bit more for the personalized products or services.

Lower prices. Buy.com, Half.com, and other companies can offer low prices due to their low costs of operation (no physical facilities, minimum inventories, and so on). If volume is large enough, prices can be reduced by 40 percent or more.

Customer service. Amazon.com and Dell.com provide superior customer service. As will be shown in Chapters 3 and 4, such service is an extremely important competitive factor.

Certain other competitive factors have become less important as a result of EC. For example, the size of a company may no longer be a significant competitive advantage (as will be shown later). Similarly, location (geographical distance from the consumer) now plays a less significant role, and language is becoming less important as translation programs remove some language barriers (see Chapter 14). Finally, product condition is unimportant for digital products, which are not subject to normal wear and tear. (See discussion in Choi and Whinston 2000.)

All in all, EC supports efficient markets and could result in almost perfect competition. In such markets, a *commodity* (an undifferentiated product) is produced when the consumer's willingness to pay equals the marginal cost of producing the commodity and neither sellers nor buyers can influence supply or demand conditions individually. The characteristics necessary for *perfect competition* are the following:

- ▷ Many buyers and sellers must be able to enter the market at little or no entry cost (no barriers to entry).
- ▷ Large buyers or sellers are not able to individually influence the market.
- ▷ The products must be homogeneous (no product differentiation). (For customized products, therefore, there is no perfect competition.)
- ▷ Buyers and sellers must have comprehensive information about the products and about the market participants' demands, supplies, and conditions.

EC could provide, or come close to providing, these conditions. It is interesting to note that the ease of finding information benefits both buyers (finding information about products, vendors, prices, etc.) and sellers (finding information about customer demands, competitors, etc.).

It can be said that competition between companies is being replaced by competition between *networks*. The company with better networks, advertising capabilities, and relationships with other Web companies (e.g., having an affiliation with Amazon.com) has a strategic advantage. It can also be said that competition is between *business models*. The company with a better business model will win.

Porter's Competitive Analysis in an Industry

Porter's (2001b) competitive forces model views five major forces of competition that determine an industry's structural attractiveness. These forces, in combination, determine how the economic value created in an industry is divided among the players in the industry. Such an industry analysis helps companies develop their competitive strategy.

Because the five forces are affected by both the Internet and e-commerce, it is interesting to examine how the Internet influences the industry structure portrayed by Porter's model. Porter

---

differentiation
Providing a product or service that is unique.

personalization
The ability to tailor a product, service, or Web content to specific user preferences.

competitive forces model
Model, devised by Porter, that says that five major forces of competition determine industry structure and how economic value is divided among the industry players in the industry; analysis of these forces helps companies develop their competitive strategy.

divided the impacts of the Internet into either positive or negative for the industry. As shown in Exhibit 2.9, most of the impacts are negative (marked by a minus sign). (Of course, there are variations and exceptions to the impacts shown in the illustration, depending on the industry, its location, and its size.) A negative impact means that competition will intensify in most industries as the Internet is introduced. The competition is not only between online and off-line companies, but also among the online newcomers. This competition, which is especially strong in commodity-type products (toys, books, CDs), was a major contributor to the collapse of many dot-com companies in 2000 to 2001. To survive and prosper in such an environment, a company needs to use innovative strategies.

Section 2.10 ▶ REVIEW

1. Why is competition so intense online?
2. Describe Porter's competitive forces model as it applies to the Internet.

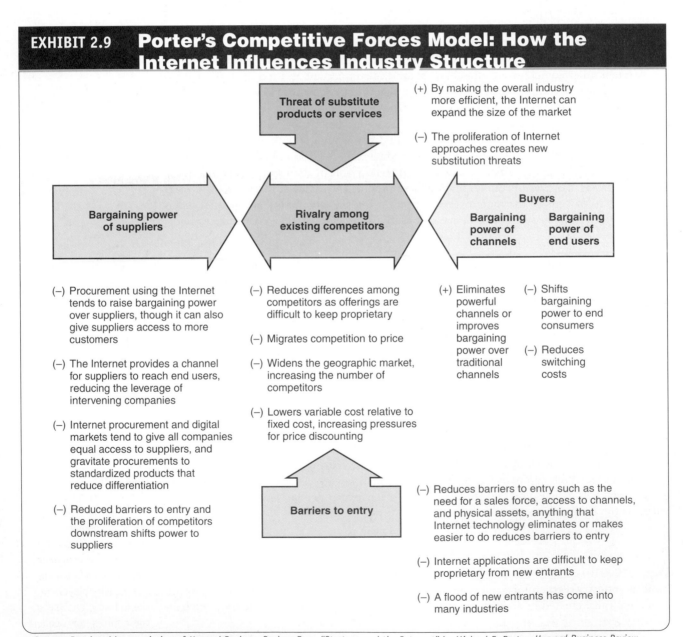

EXHIBIT 2.9   Porter's Competitive Forces Model: How the Internet Influences Industry Structure

Threat of substitute products or services

(+) By making the overall industry more efficient, the Internet can expand the size of the market

(−) The proliferation of Internet approaches creates new substitution threats

Bargaining power of suppliers

Rivalry among existing competitors

Buyers

Bargaining power of channels   **Bargaining power of end users**

(−) Procurement using the Internet tends to raise bargaining power over suppliers, though it can also give suppliers access to more customers

(−) The Internet provides a channel for suppliers to reach end users, reducing the leverage of intervening companies

(−) Internet procurement and digital markets tend to give all companies equal access to suppliers, and gravitate procurements to standardized products that reduce differentiation

(−) Reduced barriers to entry and the proliferation of competitors downstream shifts power to suppliers

(−) Reduces differences among competitors as offerings are difficult to keep proprietary

(−) Migrates competition to price

(−) Widens the geographic market, increasing the number of competitors

(−) Lowers variable cost relative to fixed cost, increasing pressures for price discounting

Barriers to entry

(+) Eliminates powerful channels or improves bargaining power over traditional channels

(−) Shifts bargaining power to end consumers

(−) Reduces switching costs

(−) Reduces barriers to entry such as the need for a sales force, access to channels, and physical assets, anything that Internet technology eliminates or makes easier to do reduces barriers to entry

(−) Internet applications are difficult to keep proprietary from new entrants

(−) A flood of new entrants has come into many industries

2.11 IMPACTS OF E-MARKETS ON BUSINESS PROCESSES AND ORGANIZATIONS

Little statistical data or empirical research on EC is available because of the relative newness of the field. Therefore, the discussion in this section is based primarily on experts' opinions, logic, and some actual data.

New Web technologies are offering organizations unprecedented opportunities to rethink strategic business models, processes, and relationships. Feeny (2001) called these *e-opportunities*, dividing them into three categories: e-marketing (Web-based initiatives that improve the marketing of existing products), e-operations (Web-based initiatives that improve the creation of existing products), and e-services (Web-based initiatives that improve customer services).

The discussion here is also based in part on the work of Bloch et al. (1996), who approached the impact of e-markets on organizations from a value-added point of view. Their model, which is shown in Exhibit 2.10, divides the impact of e-markets into three major categories: improving direct marketing, transforming organizations, and redefining organizations. We will look at each of these impacts, in turn, in this section.

IMPROVING DIRECT MARKETING

Traditional direct marketing was done by mail order (catalogs) and telephone (telemarketing). According to the U.S. Department of Commerce, in 2001 direct mail generated sales of over $110 billion in the United States, of which only $5 billion was via e-markets. This figure is small, but growing rapidly.

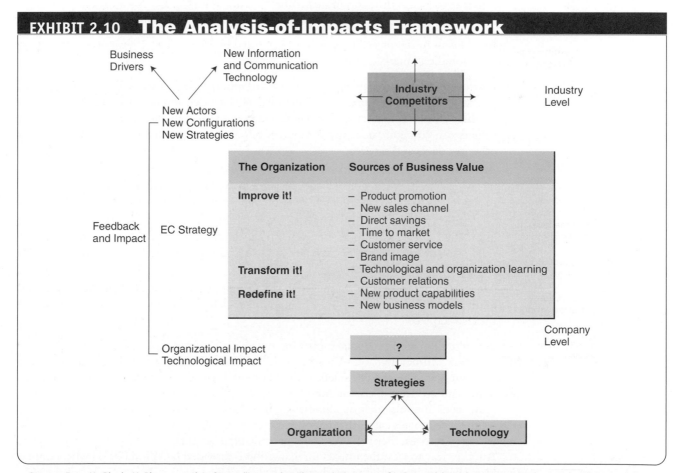

EXHIBIT 2.10 The Analysis-of-Impacts Framework

Source: From M. Bloch, Y. Pigneur, and A. Segev. "Leveraging Electronic Commerce for Competitive Advantage: A Business Value Framework." *Proceedings of the Ninth International Conference on EDI-IOS*, Bled, Slovenia, June 1996.

Bloch et al. (1996) suggested the following impacts of e-markets on B2C direct marketing:

▶ **Product promotion.** The existence of e-markets has increased the promotion of products and services through direct marketing. Contact with customers has become more information-rich and interactive.

▶ **New sales channel.** Because of the direct reach to customers and the bidirectional nature of communications in EC, a new distribution channel for existing products has been created.

▶ **Direct savings.** The cost of delivering information to customers over the Internet results in substantial savings to senders of messages. Major savings are also realized in delivering digitized products (such as music and software) versus delivery of physical products.

▶ **Reduced cycle time.** The delivery time of digitized products and services can be reduced to seconds. Also, the administrative work related to physical delivery, especially across international borders, can be reduced significantly, cutting the cycle time by more than 90 percent. One example of this is TradeNet in Singapore, which reduced the administrative time of port-related transactions from days to minutes. Cycle time can be reduced through improvements along the supply chain.

▶ **Improved customer service.** Customer service can be greatly enhanced by enabling customers to find detailed information online. For example, FedEx and other shippers allow customers to trace the status of their packages. Also, autoresponders (see Chapter 4) can answer standard e-mail questions in seconds. Finally, human experts' services can be expedited using help-desk software.

▶ **Brand or corporate image.** On the Web, newcomers can establish corporate images very quickly. What Amazon.com did in just 3 years took traditional companies generations to achieve. A good corporate image facilitates trust, which is necessary for direct sales. Traditional companies such as Intel, Disney, Wal-Mart, Dell, and Cisco use their Web activities to affirm their corporate identity and brand image. EC Application Case W2.1 demonstrates how one company uses personalization to bolster its image.

In addition to the preceding impacts (suggested by Bloch et al. 1996), other impacts of e-markets on direct marketing include the following:

▶ **Customization.** EC enables customization of products and services. Buying in a store or ordering from a television advertisement usually limits customers to a supply of standard products. Dell Computer is the classic example of customization success. Today, customers can configure not only computers but also cars, jewelry, gifts, and hundreds of other products and services.

▶ **Advertising.** With direct marketing and customization comes one-to-one, or direct, advertising, which can be much more effective than mass advertising. As will be shown in Chapter 5, the entire concept of advertising is going through a fundamental change due to EC.

▶ **Ordering systems.** Taking customer orders can be drastically improved if it is done online, reducing both processing time and mistakes. Electronic orders can be quickly routed to the appropriate order-processing site. This process reduces expenses and also saves time, freeing salespeople to sell products.

▶ **Market operations.** Direct e-marketing is changing traditional markets. Some physical markets may disappear, as will the need to make deliveries of goods to intermediaries in the marketplace.

For digitally based products—software, music, and information—the changes brought by e-markets will be dramatic. Already, small but powerful software packages are delivered over the Internet. The ability to deliver digitized products electronically affects (eliminates) packaging and greatly reduces the need for specialized distribution models.

New sales models such as shareware, freeware, and pay-as-you-use are emerging. Although these models currently exist only within particular sectors, such as the software and publishing industries, they will eventually pervade other sectors.

Another way to view the impact on marketing is provided by Wind (2001) who summarized the changes in marketing, as shown in Exhibit 2.11.

EXHIBIT 2.11 The Changing Face of Marketing

	Old Model—Mass and Segmented Marketing	New Model—Customization
Relationships with customers	Customer is a passive participant in the exchange	Customer is an active coproducer
Customer needs	Articulated	Articulated and unarticulated
Segmentation	Mass market and target segments	Segments looking for customized solutions and segmented targets.
Product and service offerings	Line extensions and modification	Customized products, services, and marketing.
New product development	Marketing and R&D drive new product development	R&D focuses on developing the platforms that allow consumers to customize
Pricing	Fixed prices and discounting	Customer determined pricing (e.g., Priceline.com; auctions); value-based pricing models
Communication	Advertising and PR	Integrated, interactive, and customized marketing communication, education, and entertainment
Distribution	Traditional retailing and direct marketing	Direct (online) distribution and rise of third-party logistics services.
Branding	Traditional branding and cobranding	The customer's name as the brand (e.g., My Brand or Brand 4 ME)
Basis of competitive advantage	Marketing power	Marketing finesse and "capturing" the customer as "partner" while integrating marketing, operations, R&D, and information

Source: Wind, Y., "The Challenge of Customization in Financial Services." *The Communications of the ACM.* ©2001 AMC, Inc.

All of these impacts of e-markets on direct marketing provide companies with a competitive advantage over the traditional direct-sales methods. Furthermore, because the competitive advantage is so large, e-markets are likely to replace many nondirect marketing channels. Some people predict the "fall of the shopping mall," and many retail stores and brokers of services (stocks, real estate, and insurance) are labeled by some as soon-to-be-endangered species.

TRANSFORMING ORGANIZATIONS

The second impact of e-markets suggested by Bloch et al. (1996) is the transformation of organizations. Here, we look at two key organizational transformations: organizational learning and the nature of work.

Technology and Organizational Learning

Rapid progress in EC will force a Darwinian struggle: To survive, companies will have to learn and adapt quickly to the new technologies. This struggle will offer them an opportunity to experiment with new products, services, and business models, which may lead to strategic and structural changes. These changes may transform the way in which business is done. Bloch et al. (1996) believe that as EC progresses, it will have a large and durable impact on the strategies of most organizations.

Thus, new technologies will require new organizational structures and approaches. For instance, the structure of the organizational unit dealing with e-marketspaces might have to be different from the conventional sales and marketing departments. Specifically, a company's e-commerce unit might report directly to the chief information officer (CIO) rather than to the sales and marketing vice president. To be more flexible and responsive to the market, new processes must be put in place. For a while, new measurements of success may be needed. For example, the measures—called "metrics"—used to gauge success of an EC project in its early stages might need to be different from the traditional revenue–expenses framework. However, in the long run, as many dot-coms have found out, no business can escape the traditional revenue–expenses framework.

In summary, corporate change must be planned and managed. Before getting it right, organizations may have to struggle with different experiments and learn from their mistakes.

The Changing Nature of Work

The nature of some work and employment will be transformed in the Digital Age; it is already happening before our eyes. For example, driven by increased competition in the global marketplace, firms are reducing the number of employees down to a core of essential staff and outsourcing whatever work they can to countries where wages are significantly less. The upheaval brought on by these changes is creating new opportunities and new risks and is forcing us into new ways of thinking about jobs, careers, and salaries.

Digital-Age workers will have to be very flexible. Few will have truly secure jobs in the traditional sense, and many will have to be willing and able to constantly learn, adapt, make decisions, and stand by them. Many will work from home.

The Digital-Age company will have to prize its core of essential workers as its most valuable asset. It will have to constantly nurture and empower them and provide them with every means possible to expand their knowledge and skill base.

REDEFINING ORGANIZATIONS

Some of the ways in which e-markets will redefine organizations are presented next.

New and Improved Product Capabilities

E-markets allow for new products to be created and for existing products to be customized in innovative ways. Such changes may redefine organizations' missions and the manner in which they operate. Customer profiles (see Chapter 4), as well as data on customer preferences, can be used as a source of information for improving products or designing new ones.

Mass customization, as described earlier, enables manufacturers to create specific products for each customer, based on the customer's exact needs. For example, Motorola gathers customer needs for a pager or a cellular phone, transmits the customer's specifications electronically to the manufacturing plant where the device is manufactured, and then sends the finished product to the customer within a day. Dell Computer and General Motors use the same approach in building their products. Customers can use the Web to design or configure products for themselves. For example, customers can use the Web to design T-shirts, furniture, cars, jewelry, Nike shoes, and even a Swatch watch. Using mass-customization methods, the cost of customized products is at or slightly above the comparable retail price of standard products. Exhibit 2.12 shows how customers can order customized Nike shoes.

New Business Models

E-markets affect not only individual companies and their products, but also entire industries. The wide availability of information and its direct distribution to consumers will lead to the use of new business models (e.g., the name-your-own-price model of Priceline.com). Another example of a new business model is that of Dandelion Moving & Storage Company (DM & S), which added an online bidding system. The system not only improved the company's operations, but also eventually expanded to be a matching e-marketplace for small trucking companies (see the Dickerabid.com case in Chapter 11 and *Inc.* 2000).

Improving the Supply Chain

One of the major benefits of e-markets is the potential improvement in supply chains. A major change is the creation of a hub-based chain, as shown in Exhibit 2.13 (page 70).

Impacts on Manufacturing

EC is changing manufacturing systems from mass production lines to demand-driven, just-in-time manufacturing. These new production systems are integrated with finance, market-

EXHIBIT 2.12   How Customization Is Done Online: The Case of Nike Shoes

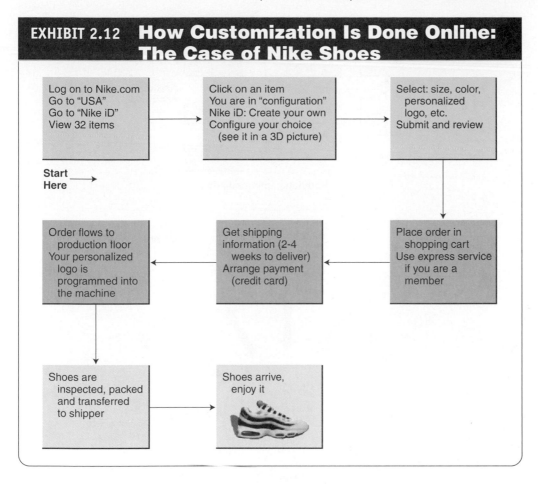

ing, and other functional systems, as well as with business partners and customers. Using Web-based enterprise resource planning (ERP) systems (supported by software such as SAP R/3), companies can direct customer orders to designers and/or to the production floor within seconds (see Norris et al. 2000). Production cycle time is cut by 50 percent or more in many cases, especially if production is done in a different country from where the designers and engineers are located.

An interesting organizational concept is that of *virtual manufacturing*—the ability to run multiple manufacturing plants as though they were at one location. A single company controls the entire manufacturing process, from the supply of components to shipment, while making it completely transparent to customers and employees. For example, Cisco System works with 34 plants globally, 32 of which are owned by other companies. Each of Cisco's products will look exactly alike, regardless of where it was manufactured. Up-to-the-minute information sharing is critical for the success of this mass-production approach (Pine 1999).

Companies such as IBM, General Motors, General Electric, and Boeing assemble products from components that are manufactured in many different locations, even different countries. Subassemblers gather materials and parts from their vendors, and they may use one or more tiers of manufacturers. Communication, collaboration, and coordination are critical in such multitier systems. Using electronic bidding, assemblers get subassemblies 15 to 20 percent cheaper than before and 80 percent faster (e.g., see the GE case in Chapter 6). Furthermore, such systems are flexible and adaptable, allowing for fast changes with minimum cost. Also, costly inventories that are part of mass-production systems can be minimized.

Build-to-order. The biggest change in manufacturing will be the move to build-to-order systems. In these systems, manufacturing or assembly will start only after an order is received. This will change not only the production planning and control, but also the entire supply chain and payment cycle. For more on build-to-order production, see Appendix 2A at the end of this chapter.

build-to-order
Production system in which manufacturing or assembly will start only after an order is received.

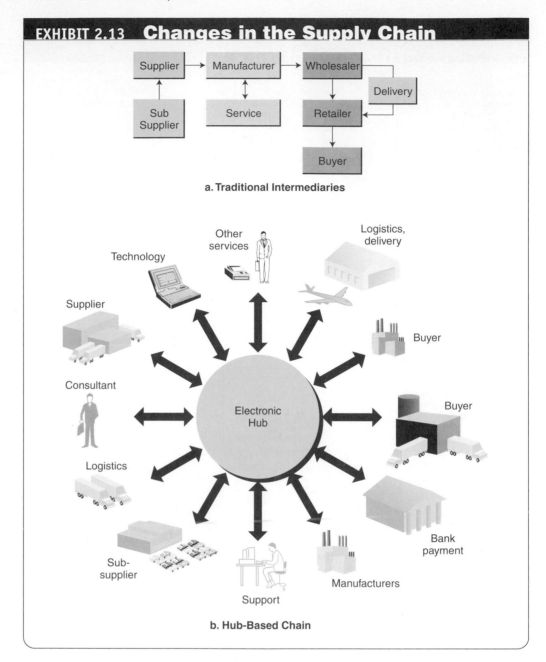

EXHIBIT 2.13   Changes in the Supply Chain

a. Traditional Intermediaries

b. Hub-Based Chain

Impacts on Finance and Accounting

E-markets require special finance and accounting systems. Most notable of these are electronic payment systems. Traditional payment systems are ineffective or inefficient for electronic trade. The use of new payment systems such as electronic cash is complicated because legal issues and agreements on international standards are involved. Nevertheless, electronic cash is certain to come soon, and it will change how payments are made. It could also change consumers' financial lives and shake the foundations of financial systems.

Executing an electronic order triggers an action in what is called the back office. *Back-office* transactions include buyers' credit checks, product availability checks, order confirmation, changes in accounts payable, receivables, billing, and much more. These activities must be efficient, synchronized, and fast so that the electronic trade will not be slowed down. An example of this is online stock trading. In most cases, orders are executed in less than 1 second, and the trader can find an online confirmation of the trade immediately.

One of the most innovative concepts in accounting and finance is the "virtual close," which would allow companies to close their accounting records within a day. This Cisco Systems project is described in EC Application Case W2.2.

Impact on Human Resources Management and Training

EC is changing how people are recruited (see Chapter 3), evaluated, promoted, and developed. EC also is changing the way training and education are offered to employees. Online distance learning is exploding, providing opportunities that never existed in the past. Companies are cutting training costs by 50 percent or more, and virtual courses and programs are mushrooming (see Chapter 9).

New e-learning systems offer two-way video, on-the-fly interaction, and application sharing. Such systems provide for interactive remote instruction systems, which link sites over a high-speed intranet. At the same time, corporations are finding that e-learning may be their ticket to survival as changing environments, new technologies, and continuously changing procedures make it necessary for employees to be trained and retrained constantly.

Section 2.11 ▶ REVIEW

1. List the major parts of Bloch et al.'s model.
2. Describe how EC improves direct marketing.
3. Describe how EC transforms organizations.
4. Describe how EC redefines organizations.
5. Describe the concept of build-to-order (customization).
6. Describe the concept of the virtual close.

2.12 E-REALITY

The overexpectations of what EC would accomplish ended with the failure of hundreds of dot-com companies. In place of the hype came the realization that the adoption of EC will be much slower than anticipated. Rosenbloom (2002) identified 10 myths about e-commerce that were heavily publicized during the 1998–2000 period of hype; he argues that these are merely *myths,* and that they are not contributing to the EC revolution. For example, Rosenbloom argues that the promise of lower costs through EC is a myth. The reality, he says, is that lower costs are not occurring, due to the costs of order fulfillment and customer acquisition, both of which are very high. Rosenbloom's argument is debatable: some agree with it, others disagree. A list of Rosenbloom's myths and the realities is presented at the book's Web site.

Whether one believes all of Rosenbloom's "myths" or the "realities," or believe some of each, these issues spark debate over the future of e-commerce. We do believe that the world will be strongly impacted by the Web and by EC. It is only a matter of time and of learning that are needed to implement EC correctly. As that occurs, organizations, individuals, and society will reap the full benefits of EC, including those that at present are myths. Also, as pointed out by Porter (2001b), the real value of EC is in exploiting the characteristics that by themselves may only be myths in such a way that one can use EC to complement the conventional ways of doing business. In order to reap the economic advantages of EC, one needs an EC strategy (see Chapter 15 and Porter 2001a and 2001b).

Section 2.12 ▶ REVIEW

1. In your opinion, based on your observations and experience, what are the biggest impacts EC is making on individuals? On business? On society?
2. Go to Rosenbloom's list of myths and realities at the book's Web site. List the five myths with which you most agree (those you think are most definitely myths).

MANAGERIAL ISSUES

Some managerial issues related to this chapter are as follows.

1. **How do we compete in the digital economy?** Although the basic theories of competition are unchanged, the rules are different. Of special interest are digital products and services, whose variable costs are very low. Competition involves both old-economy and new-economy companies. The speed of changes in competitive forces can be rapid, and the impact of new business models can be devastating. As Bill Gates once said, "Competition is not among companies, but among business models" (Financial Analysts Meeting, 1998).

2. **What about intermediaries?** Many EC applications will change the role of intermediation. This may create a conflict between a company and its distributors. It may also create opportunities. In many cases, the distributors will need to change their roles. This is a sensitive issue that needs to be planned for during the transformation to the e-business plan.

3. **What organizational changes will be needed?** Companies should expect organizational changes in all functional areas once e-commerce reaches momentum. At a minimum, purchasing will be done differently in many organizations; introducing models such as forward auctions and affiliate programs may also have a major impact on business operations.

4. **Should we auction?** A major strategic issue is whether or not to use auctions as a selling channel. Forward auctions may create conflicts with other distribution channels. If a company decides to auction, it needs to select an auction mechanism and determine a pricing strategy. These decisions determine the success of the auction and the ability to attract and retain visitors on the site. Auctions also require support services. Decisions about how to provide these services and to what extent to use business partners are critical to the success of repeated high-volume auctions.

5. **Should we barter?** Bartering can be an interesting strategy, especially for companies that need cash and have some surplus inventory. However, the valuation of what is bought or sold may be hard to determine, and the tax implications in some countries are not clear.

6. **What m-commerce opportunities are available?** A company should develop an m-commerce strategy if it is likely to be impacted by m-commerce. The opportunities presented by m-commerce are enormous, but so are the risks. However, doing nothing may be even riskier. (For further discussion, see Kalakota and Robinson 2001 and Sadeh 2002).

SUMMARY

In this chapter you learned about the following EC issues as they relate to the learning objectives.

1. **E-marketplaces and their components.** A marketspace or e-marketplace is a virtual market that does not suffer from limitations of space, time, or borders. As such, it can be very effective. Its major components include customers, sellers, products (some digital), infrastructure, front-end processes, back-end activities, electronic intermediaries, other business partners, and support services.

2. **The major types of e-markets.** In the B2C area there are storefronts and e-malls. In the B2B area there are private and public e-marketplaces, which can be vertical (within one industry) or horizontal (across different industries). Different types of portals provide access to e-marketplaces.

3. **The role of intermediaries.** The role of intermediaries will change as e-markets develop; some will be eliminated (disintermediation), others will change their roles and prosper (reintermediation). In the B2B area, for example, e-distributors connect manufacturers

with buyers by aggregating catalogs of many suppliers. New value-added services that range from content creation to syndication are mushrooming.

4. **Electronic catalogs, search engines, and shopping carts.** The major mechanisms in e-markets are electronic catalogs, search engines and software (intelligent) agents, and electronic shopping carts. These mechanisms facilitate EC by providing a user-friendly shopping environment.

5. **Types of auctions and their characteristics.** In forward auctions, bids from buyers are placed sequentially, either in increasing (English and Yankee) mode or in decreasing (Dutch and free-fall) mode. In reverse auctions, buyers place an RFQ and suppliers submit offers in one or several rounds. In "name-your-own-price" auctions, buyers specify how much they are willing to pay for a product or service, and an intermediary tries to find a supplier to fulfill the request.

6. **The benefits and limitations of auctions.** The major benefits for sellers are the ability to reach many buyers, to sell quickly, and to save on commissions to intermediaries. Buyers have a chance to obtain bargains and collectibles while shopping from their homes. The major limitation is the possibility of fraud.

7. **Bartering and negotiating.** Electronic bartering can greatly facilitate the swapping of goods and services among organizations, thanks to improved search and matching capabilities, which is done in bartering exchanges. Software agents can facilitate online negotiation.

8. **The role of m-commerce.** Mobile commerce is emerging as a phenomenon that can provide Internet access to millions of people. It also creates new location-related applications.

9. **Liquidity, quality, and success factors in e-markets.** Two major e-market issues are the need for a large number of participating sellers and buyers (liquidity) and the need for quality assurance. Factors that influence EC success are product, industry, seller, and consumer characteristics.

10. **Economic impact of EC.** E-commerce is a major product of the digital revolution, which enables companies to simultaneously increase growth and profit, "reach" and "richness," and more.

11. **Competition in the digital economy.** The competition in online markets is very intense due to the increased power of buyers, the ability to find the lowest price, and the ease of switching to another vendor. There is more global competition as well.

12. **The impact of e-markets on organizations.** All functional areas of an organization are affected by e-markets. Broadly, e-markets improve direct marketing and transform and redefine organizations. Direct marketing (manufacturers to customers) and one-to-one marketing and advertising are becoming the norm, and mass customization and personalization are taking off. Production is moving to a build-to-order model, changing supply chain relationships and reducing cycle time. Virtual manufacturing is on the rise. Financial systems are becoming more efficient as they become networked with other business functions, and the human resources activities of recruiting, evaluation, and training are being managed more efficiently due to employees' interactions with machines.

KEY TERMS

Auction	50	Early liquidity	58	Mobile computing	55
Back end	38	Electronic auction (e-auction)	50	Mobile portal	41
Bartering	54	Electronic catalog	46	"Name-your-own-price" model	52
Bartering exchange	55	Electronic shopping cart	48	Personalization	63
Build-to-order	69	Forward auction	51	Private e-marketplace	40
Buy-side e-marketplace	40	Front end	38	Public e-marketplace	40
Competitive forces model	63	Infomediary	42	Quality uncertainty	58
Consortia	40	Information portal	41	Reintermediation	44
Differentiation	63	Intermediary	39	Reverse auction (bidding or	
Digital product	38	Internet ecosystem	62	tendering system)	51
Disintermediation	44	M-business	56	Search engine	48
Double auction	52	Maintenance, repair, and		Sell-side e-marketplace	40
Dynamic pricing	51	operation item (MRO)	43	Software (intelligent) agent	48
E-bartering	55	Marketspace	37	Storefront	39
E-distributor	43	Microproduct	59	Syndication	44
E-Mall (online mall)	39	Mobile commerce		Voice portal	41
E-marketplace	40	(m-commerce)	55		

DISCUSSION QUESTIONS

1. Compare marketplaces with marketspaces. What are the advantages and limitations of each?

2. What are the major benefits of syndication to the various participants?

3. Compare and contrast competition in traditional markets with that in digital markets.

4. Explain how NTE provides real-time procurement services (EC Application Case 2.1).

5. Which type of e-marketplace is NTE (EC Application Case 2.1)? Why?

6. The "name-your-own-price" model is considered a reverse auction. However, this model does not include

RFQs or consecutive bidding. Why is it called a reverse auction?

7. Discuss the advantages of dynamic pricing over fixed pricing. What are the potential disadvantages of dynamic pricing?

8. Why are sell-side and buy-side markets in the same company usually separated, whereas in an exchange they are combined?

9. Discuss the advantages of m-commerce over e-commerce.

INTERNET EXERCISES

1. Enter arena.com.hk and examine the products and services provided. Which are similar to those offered by NTE? Examine the Global Cargo exchange and other initiatives. Classify the services according to the EC business models presented in Chapter 1.

2. Go to cisco.com, google.com, and cio.com and locate information about the status of the "virtual close." Write a report based on your findings.

3. Visit ticketmaster.com, ticketonline.com, and other sites that sell event tickets online. Assess the competition in online ticket selling. What services do the different sites provide?

4. Examine how bartering is conducted online at tradeaway.com, bigvine.com, abarter.com, and intagio.com. Compare the functionalities and ease of use of these sites.

5. Enter ebay.com/anywhere and investigate the use of "anywhere wireless." Review the wireless devices and find out how they work.

6. Enter imandi.com and review the process by which buyers can send RFQs to merchants of their choice.

Also, evaluate the services provided in the areas of marketing, staffing, and travel. Write a report based on your findings.

7. Enter bloomsburgcarpet.com. Explain how the site solves the problem of sending carpet sample books to representatives all over the country. What are the special features of the electronic catalogs here? (Hint: It might be useful to read Kapp 2001.)

8. Enter respond.com and send a request for a product or a service. Once you receive replies, select the best deal. You have no obligation to buy. Write a short report on your experience.

9. Enter onstar.com and review its services. Comment on the usability of each.

10. Compare the search engine at invisibleweb.com and at northernlight.com. Report on the unique capabilities of each.

11. Enter i3mobile.com, and examine the demo. What are the benefits of such a service?

TEAM ASSIGNMENTS AND ROLE PLAYING

1. Several competing exchanges operate in the steel industry (e.g., newview.com and isteelasia.com). Assign one group to each exchange. Look at its market structure, at the services it offers, and so on. The group then will make a presentation to convince buyers and sellers to join its exchange.

2. Have several teams each review Porter's (2001b) and Bakos's (1998) articles. Each team member will research one of the issues raised in the papers (such as competition, disintermediation, and Internet impacts) in light of recent developments in the economy and the e-commerce field.

ROSENBLUTH INTERNATIONAL— A NEW WAY TO COMPETE

The Problem

Rosenbluth International (*rosenbluth.com*) is a major international player in the competitive travel agency industry. The digital revolution introduced the following threats to Rosenbluth and the travel agent industry in general:

- Airlines, hotels, and other service providers are attempting to bypass travel agents by moving aggressively to direct electronic distribution systems, for example, electronic ticketing via online booking as in the Qantas case (see the online material for Chapter 1).

- Commissions caps have been reduced (from $50 to $10), and most major airlines decreased travel agents' commission percentages from 10 percent to 5 percent.

- Large numbers of new online companies (e.g., *expedia.com*) provide diversified travel services at bargain prices in an effort to attract individual travelers. However, these online services are now penetrating the corporate travel market as well.

- Competition among the major players is based on rebates. The travel agencies basically give part of their commission back to their customers by using the commission to subsidize lower prices.

- Innovative business models that were introduced by e-commerce, such as name-your-own-price auctions and reverse auctions, have been embraced by many companies in the travel industry (see the Qantas case in the online material for Chapter 1), adding competitive pressures.

The Solution

Rosenbluth International responded to theses new pressures with two strategies. First, the company decided to get out of the leisure travel business, becoming a pure corporate travel agency. Second, it decided to rebate customers with their entire commission. Instead of generating revenues by commission, Rosenbluth now bills customers according to the service provided. For example, fees are assessed for consultations on how to lower corporate travel costs, for the development of in-house travel policies for corporate clients, for negotiating for their clients with travel providers, and for travel-related calls answered by the Rosenbluth's staff.

To implement the second strategy, which completely changed the company's business model, Rosenbluth now uses several innovative e-commerce applications. The company uses a comprehensive Web-based business travel management solution that integrates travel planning technology, policy and profile management tools, proprietary travel management applications, and seamless front-line service/support. This browser-based service allows corporate travelers to book reservations any time, anywhere, within minutes. The specific tools in this system are:

- DACODA (Discount Analysis Containing Optimal Decision Algorithms) is a patented yield-management system that optimizes a corporation's travel savings, enabling travel managers to decipher complex airline pricing and identify the most favorable airline contracts.

- Electronic messaging services allow clients to manage their travel requests via e-mail. These services use a Web-based template that permits clients to submit reservation requests without picking up the phone. Additionally, a structured itinerary is returned to the traveler via e-mail.

- E-Ticket tracks, monitors, reports on, and collects the appropriate refund or exchange for unused e-tickets. As the amount of e-tickets usage grows, so does the amount of unused e-tickets that need to be refunded or exchanged.

- Res-Monitor, a patented low-fare search system, tracks a reservation up until departure time and finds additional savings for one out of every four reservations.

- Global distribution network electronically links the corporate locations and enables instant access to any traveler's itinerary, personal travel preferences, or corporate travel policy.

- Custom-Res is a global electronic reservation system that ensures policy compliance, consistent service, and accurate reservations.

- IntelliCenters are advanced reservations centers that use innovative telecommunications technology to manage calls from multiple accounts, resulting in cost savings and personal service for corporate clients.

- Network Operations Center (NOC) monitors the many factors impacting travel, including weather, current events, and air traffic. This information is disseminated to the company's front-line associates so they can inform their clients of potential changes to their travel plans. The NOC also tracks call volume at all offices and enables the swift rerouting of calls as needed.

In late 2002, Rosenbluth International opened a Web-based exchange where SMEs can post their travel needs. Airlines, hotel chains, and other suppliers can bid on the business. SMEs were, until then, shut out of the negotiated discount process; now, companies provide their needs, including travel policy and data on employees' historical travel patterns. They also post desired discounts. The negotiation can be completed online. First introduced in North America, the exchange moved to include Asia and Europe in 2003.

The Results

In 1979 the company had $40 million in sales, primarily from leisure-oriented travelers in the Philadelphia area. By 1997 that figure had grown to over $3 billion due mainly to several EC and IT innovations. Today, the company operates in 24 countries and has about 4,500 employees. Since the introduction of the Web-based solutions in 1997, sales increased to about $5 billion in 3 years (a 60 percent increase). The company not only survived the threats of elimination but also increased its market share and profitability.

Sources: Compiled from Clemons and Hann (1999) and from information at *rosenbluth.com* (2001).

Questions

1. Describe the strategy the company uses to counter disintermediation.

2. Explain how EC facilitated the strategy.

3. Analyze the competitive solution using Porter's five forces model.

4. Check *carlson.com* to find its EC initiatives. Compare these to Rosenbluth's.

REFERENCES

arena.com.hk (accessed 2001).

Bakos, Y. "The Emerging Role of Electronic Marketplaces on the Internet." *Communications of the ACM* (August 1998).

Beiser, D. "Cisco Chief Pushes 'Virtual Close': Intranets Allow Up-to-minute Look at Books." *USA Today*, October 12, 1999.

Berryman, K., and S. Heck. "Is the Third Time the Charm for B2B?" *The McKinsey Quarterly*, no. 2 (2001).

Bloch, M., et al. "Leveraging Electronic Commerce for Competitive Advantage: A Business Value Framework." *Proceedings of the Ninth International Conference on EDI-IOS*, Bled, Slovenia, June 1996.

"Boise Cascade Saves $1 Million in First Year of Web Catalog." wp.netscape.com/solutions/business/profiles/boisecascade.html (accessed April 2003).

boiseoffice.com/about/ecommerce.shtm (accessed April 2003).

bombaysapphire.com (accessed April 2003).

Business Week, "A Slow Climb from Wireless' Dark Ages." Business Week Special Report: Cell Phones at the Crossroads, February 15, 2002, businessweek.com/technology/content/feb2002/tc20020215_3636.htm (accessed June 2003).

Carr, N. G. "On the Edge." *Harvard Business Review* (May–June 2000).

Choi, S. Y., and A. B. Whinston. *The Internet Economy: Technology and Practice*. Austin, TX: Smartecon.com, 2000.

Choi, S. Y., et al. *The Economics of Electronic Commerce*. Indianapolis, IN: Macmillan Technical Publishing, 1997.

cisco.com (accessed 2000; 2003)

Clemons, E. K., and L. H. Hann, "Rosenbluth International: Strategic Transformation." *Journal of MIS* (Fall, 1999).

Davidson, J., "Driving Logistics Online Markets," nte.com/dynamic/articles/TW0401.pdf (accessed April 2001).

dollarDEX.com (accessed 2002 and April 2003).

"DollarDEX Launched Reverse Auction on Mortgages," *Hong Kong Economic Times* (E Times), April 4, 2000, http://hk.dollardex.com/press/index.cfm?show=i_hong kong.htm.

Evans, P., and T. S. Wurster. *Blown to Bits: How the New Economics of Information Transforms Strategy*. Boston: Harvard Business School Press, 2000.

Feeny, D. "Making Business Sense of the E-Opportunity." *MIT Sloan Management Review* (Winter, 2001): 41–51.

Financial Analysts Meeting, Seattle, WA, July 23, 1998.

Grover, V., and J. Teng. "E-commerce and the Information Market." *Communications of the ACM* 44, no. 4 (2001): 79–86.

Helmstetter, G., and P. Metivier. *Affiliate Selling: Building Revenue on the Web*. New York: John Wiley and Sons, 2000.

Hoffman, W., et al. "The Unexpected Return of B2B." *The McKinsey Quarterly*, no. 3 (2002): 97–106.

Holweg, M., and F. Pil. "Successful Build-to-order Strategies Start with the Customer." *MIT Sloan Management Journal* 43, no. 1 (2001): 74–83.

home.netscape.com, 2001 (accessed April 2003).

Inc. "Web Awards 2000: Innovation," inc.com/magazine/20001115/21019.html. November 15, 2000 (accessed April 2003).

ITAsia One, "Java Empowers M-commerce," it.asia1.com.sg/specials/issues20020911_003.html (accessed April 2003).

Johnson, C. et al., "Online Auctions Will Boom Through 2007," October 2002, forrester.com/ER/Research/Brief/Excerpt/0,1317,15776,00.html (accessed April 2003).

Kalakota, R., and M. Robinson. *M-Business: The Race to Mobility*. New York: McGraw-Hill, 2001.

Kambil, A., and E. van Heck. *Marking Markets*. Boston: Harvard Business School Press, 2002.

Kapp, K. "A Framework for Successful E-technology Implementation: Understand, Simplify, Automate." *Journal of Organizational Excellence* (Winter 2001): 57–64.

Lim, G. G., and J. K. Lee. "Buyer Carts for B2B EC: The B-cart Approach." *Proceedings of the International Conference on Electronic Commerce*, Seoul, Korea, August 21–24, 2000.

Lorek, L. "Trade Ya? E-barter Thrives." *InteractiveWeek*, August 14, 2000.

Meredith, R. "From Rocks to Riches." *Forbes Magazine*, August 8, 2002.

"Nielsen NetRatings: Global Net Population." *Nua Internet Surveys*, February 23, 2003, nua.ie/surveys/?f=VS&art_id=905358729&rel=true (accessed June 2003).

Norris, G., et al. *E-Business and ERP*. New York: John Wiley and Sons, 2000.

nte.com (accessed 2003).

Pine, J., II. *Mass Customization*. Boston: Harvard Business School Press, 1999.

Porter, M. E. *Competitive Advantage: Creating and Sustaining Superior Performance*, rev. ed. New York: The Free Press, 2001a.

Porter, M. E. "Strategy and the Internet." Harvard Business Review (March 2001b).

Pratt, P. S. *Business Valuation: Discounts and Premiums*. New York: John Wiley and Sons, 2001.

Ramsdell, M. "The Real Business of B2B." McKinsey Quarterly (Third Quarter 2000).

Rhey, E., "Pepsi Refreshes, Wirelessly." *PC Magazine*, September 17, 2002, pp. 4–5.

Rosenbloom, B. "The 10 Deadly Myths of E-commerce." *Business Horizons*, March–April 2002, pp. 61–66.

rosenbluth.com, 2001 (accessed April 2003).

Sadeh, N. *Mobile Commerce: New Technologies, Services and Business Models*. New York: John Wiley & Sons, April 2002.

Slywotzkty, A. J., and D. J. Morrison. *How Digital Is Your Business?* London: Nicholas Brealy Publishing, 2001.

Strader, T. J., and H. J. Shaw. "Characteristics of Electronic Markets." *Decision Support Systems*, no. 21 (1997).

thaigem.com/wel_about.php (accessed April 2003).

Turban, E., et al. *Information Technology for Management*, 4th ed. New York: Wiley, 2004.

Werbach, K. "Syndication—The Emerging Model for Business in the Internet Era." *Harvard Business Review* (May–June 2000).

Wind, Y., "The Challenge of Customization in Financial Services." *The Communications of the ACM* (2001): 41.

BUILD-TO-ORDER PRODUCTION

The concept of *build-to-order* means that a firm starts to make a product or service only after an order for it is placed. This concept is as old as commerce itself and was the only method of production until the Industrial Revolution. According to this concept, if a person needs a pair of shoes, they go to a shoemaker, who takes their measurements. The person negotiates quality, style, and price and pays a down payment. The shoemaker buys the materials and makes a customized product for the customer. Customized products were expensive, and it took a long time to finish them. The Industrial Revolution introduced a new way of thinking about production.

The Industrial Revolution started with the concept of dividing work into small parts. Such *division of labor* makes the work simpler, requiring less training for employees. It also allows for *specialization*. Different employees become experts in executing certain tasks. Because the work segments are simpler, it is easier to *automate* them. As machines were invented to make products, the concept of *build-to-market* developed. To implement build-to-market, it was necessary to design standard products, produce them, store them, and then sell them.

The creation of standard products by automation drove prices down, and demand accelerated. The solution to the problem of increased demand was *mass production*. In mass production, a company produces large amounts of standard products at a very low cost and then "pushes" them to consumers. Thus began the need for sales and marketing organizations. Specialized sales forces resulted in increased competition and the desire to sell in wider, and more remote, markets. This model also required the creation of large factories and specialized departments such as accounting and personnel to manage the activities in the factories. The workers do not know the customers personally, and frequently do not care about customers' needs or product quality. However, the products are inexpensive and good enough to fuel demand, and the concept became a dominant one. Mass production also required inventory systems at various places in the supply chain, which were based on forecasted demand. If the forecasted demand was wrong, the inventories were incorrect. Thus, companies were always trying to achieve the right balance between not having enough inventory to meet demand and having too much inventory on hand.

As society became more affluent, the demand for customized products increased. Manufacturers had to meet this kind of demand to satisfy customers. As long as the demand for customized product was small, it could be met. Cars, for example, have long been produced using this model. Customers were asked to pay a premium for customization and wait a long time to receive the customized product, and they were willing to do so.

Slowly, the demand for customized products and services increased. Burger King introduced the concept of "making it your way," and manufacturers were looking for solutions to providing customized products in large quantities, which is the essence of *mass customization*. Such solutions were usually enhanced by some kind of information technology (Pine and Gilmore 1997). The introduction of customized personal computers (PCs) by Dell Computer was so successful that many other industries wanted to try mass customization. However, they found that it is not so easy to do so (Zipkin 2001; Agrawal et al. 2001).

Using EC can facilitate the use of customization and even the use of mass customization (Holweg and Pil 2001). To understand the use of EC, let's look first at a comparison of mass production, also known as a *push system*, and mass customization, also known as a *pull system*, shown in Exhibit 2A.1.

Notice that one important area in the supply chain is ordering. Using EC, a customer can self-configure the desired product online. The order is received in seconds. Once the order is verified and payment arranged, the order is sent electronically to the production floor. This saves time and money. In complex products, customers may collaborate in real time with the manufacturer's designers, as is done at Cisco Systems. Again, time and money are saved and errors are reduced due to better communication and collaboration. Other contributions of EC are: the customers' needs are visible to all partners in the order fulfillment chain (fewer delays, faster response time), inventories are reduced due to rapid communication, and digitizable products and services can be delivered electronically.

A key issue in mass customization is understanding what the customers want. EC is very helpful in this area due to the use of online market research methods such as collaborative filtering (see Chapter 4 and Holweg and Pil 2001). Using collaborative filtering, a company can discover what each customer wants without asking him or her. Such market research is accomplished more cheaply by a machine than by human researchers.

From the production point of view, EC also can enable mass customization. In the factory, for example, IT in general and e-commerce in particular can help in expediting the production changeover from one item to another. Also, because most mass production is based on assembly of standard components, EC can help make the production configuration in minutes, including the identification of the needed components and their location. Furthermore, a production schedule can be automatically generated and

EXHIBIT 2A.1 Push Versus Pull Production Systems

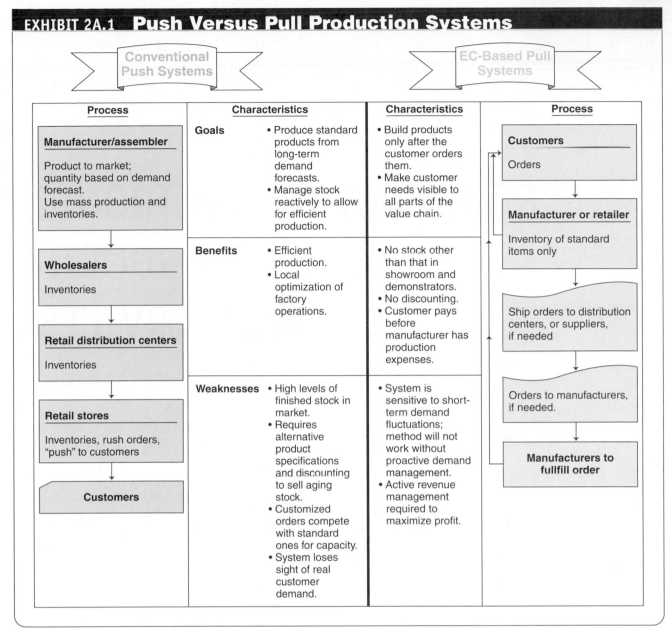

Conventional Push Systems

Process

Manufacturer/assembler

Product to market; quantity based on demand forecast.
Use mass production and inventories.

↓

Wholesalers

Inventories

↓

Retail distribution centers

Inventories

↓

Retail stores

Inventories, rush orders, "push" to customers

↓

Customers

Characteristics

Goals
- Produce standard products from long-term demand forecasts.
- Manage stock reactively to allow for efficient production.

Benefits
- Efficient production.
- Local optimization of factory operations.

Weaknesses
- High levels of finished stock in market.
- Requires alternative product specifications and discounting to sell aging stock.
- Customized orders compete with standard ones for capacity.
- System loses sight of real customer demand.

EC-Based Pull Systems

Characteristics
- Build products only after the customer orders them.
- Make customer needs visible to all parts of the value chain.

- No stock other than that in showroom and demonstrators.
- No discounting.
- Customer pays before manufacturer has production expenses.

- System is sensitive to short-term demand fluctuations; method will not work without proactive demand management.
- Active revenue management required to maximize profit.

Process

Customers

Orders

↓

Manufacturer or retailer

Inventory of standard items only

↓

Ship orders to distribution centers, or suppliers, if needed

↓

Orders to manufacturers, if needed.

↓

Manufacturers to fullfill order

Source: Drawn by authors with input from Holweg and Pil (2001), p. 81.

needed resources can be deployed, including money. This is why many industries, and particularly the auto manufacturers, are planning to move to build-to-order using EC. By doing so, they are expecting huge cost reductions, shorter order-to-delivery times, and lower inventory costs (see Agrawal et al. 2001, Exhibit 1; Holweg and Pil 2001).

Mass customization on a large scale is not easy to attain (Zipkin 2001; Agrawal et al. 2001), but if properly performed, it may become the dominant model in many industries.

REFERENCES

Agrawal, M., T. V. Kumaresh, and G. A. Mercer. "The False Promise of Mass Customization." *The McKinsey Quarterly* no. 3 (2001).

Holweg, M., and F. Pil. "Successful Build-to-Order Strategies Start with the Customer." *MIT Sloan Management Journal* 43, no. 1 (2001): 74–83.

Pine, B. J., and J. Gilmore. "The Four Faces of Mass Customization." *Harvard Business Review* 75, no. 1 (January–February 1997): 91–101.

Zipkin, P., "The Limits of Mass Customization," *MIT Sloan Management Review* (Spring 2001).

RETAILING IN ELECTRONIC COMMERCE: PRODUCTS AND SERVICES

Learning objectives

Upon completion of this chapter, you will be able to:

1. Describe e-tailing and its characteristics.
2. Define and describe the primary business models of electronic retailing ("e-tailing").
3. Describe how online travel and tourism services operate and their industry impact.
4. Discuss the online employment market, including its participants, benefits, and limitations.
5. Describe online real estate transactions.
6. Discuss online stock trading services.
7. Discuss cyberbanking and online personal finance.
8. Describe on-demand delivery by e-grocers.
9. Describe the delivery of digital products and online entertainment.
10. Discuss various e-tail consumer aids, including comparison-shopping aids.
11. Identify the critical success factors and failure avoidance tactics for direct online marketing and e-tailing.
12. Describe reintermediation, channel conflict, and personalization in e-tailing.

Content

AMAZON.COM: THE KING OF E-TAILING

The Opportunity

It was not a business problem but rather an opportunity that faced entrepreneur Jeff Bezos: He saw the huge potential for retail sales over the Internet and selected books as the most logical product for e-tailing. In July 1995, Bezos started Amazon.com, an e-tailing pioneer, offering books via an electronic catalog from its Web site (*amazon.com*). Over the years, the company has recognized that it must continually enhance its business models and electronic store by expanding product selection, improving the customer's experience, and adding services and alliances. Also, the company recognized the importance of order fulfillment and warehousing. It invested hundreds of millions of dollars in building physical warehouses designed for shipping small packages to hundreds of thousands of customers. Amazon.com's challenge was, and remains, how to succeed where many have failed—namely, how to compete in selling consumer products online, showing profit and a reasonable rate of return on the huge investment it has made.

The Technology Used

In addition to its initial electronic bookstore, Amazon.com has expanded in a variety of directions: It now offers specialty stores, such as its professional and technical store. It has expanded its editorial content through partnerships with experts in certain fields. It has increased product selection with the addition of millions of used and out-of-print titles. It also is expanding its offerings beyond books. For example, in June 2002 it became an authorized dealer of Sony Corp. for selling Sony products online. Key features of the Amazon.com superstore are easy browsing, searching, and ordering; useful product information, reviews, recommendations, and personalization; broad selection; low prices; secure payment systems; and efficient order fulfillment.

The Amazon.com Web site has a number of features that make the online shopping experience more enjoyable. Its "Gift Ideas" section features seasonally appropriate gift ideas and services. Its "Community" section provides product information and recommendations shared by customers. Through its "E-Cards" section, customers can send free animated electronic greeting cards to friends and family, and much, much more.

Amazon.com also offers various marketplace services. Amazon Auctions hosts and operates auctions on behalf of individuals and small businesses throughout the world. The zShops service hosts electronic storefronts for a monthly fee, offering small businesses the opportunity to have customized storefronts supported by the richness of Amazon.com's order-fulfillment processing.

Amazon.com is recognized as an online leader in creating sales through customer intimacy and CRM, which are cultivated by informative marketing front ends and one-to-one advertisements. For example, to support CRM, in May 2002 Amazon started posting—at no cost—restaurant menus from thousands of restaurants. In addition, sales are supported by highly automated, efficient back-end systems. When a customer makes a return visit to Amazon.com, a cookie file (see Chapter 4) identifies the user and says, for example, "Welcome back, Sarah Shopper," and then proceeds to recommend new books from the same genre of previous customer purchases. The company tracks customer purchase histories and sends purchase recommendations via e-mail to cultivate repeat buyers. It also provides detailed product descriptions and ratings to help consumers make informed purchase decisions. These efforts usually result in satisfactory shopping experiences and encourage customers to return. The site has an efficient search engine and other shopping aids.

Customers can personalize their accounts and manage orders online with the patented "One-Click" order feature. This personalized service includes an *electronic wallet* (see Chapter 13), which enables shoppers to place an order in a secure manner without the need to enter their address, credit card number, and other information each time they shop. One-Click also allows customers to view their order status, cancel or combine orders that have not yet entered the shipping process, edit the shipping options and addresses on unshipped orders, modify the payment method for unshipped orders, and more.

In 1997, Amazon.com started an extensive affiliates program. By 2002, the company had more than 500,000 partners that refer customers to Amazon.com. Amazon pays a 3 to 5 percent commission on any resulting sale. Starting in 2000, Amazon.com has undertaken alliances with major "trusted partners" that provide knowledgeable entry into new markets. For example, Amazon.com's alliance with Cardsdirect.com allows it to sell cars online. Clicking "Health and Beauty" on the Amazon.com Web site takes the visitor to a site Amazon.com operates jointly with Drugstore.com; clicking on "Wireless Phones" will suggest a service plan from an Amazon.com partner in that market. (Later in this chapter, we discuss the special alliance between Amazon.com and Toys R Us.) In yet another extension of its services, in September 2001 Amazon signed an agreement with Borders Group Inc., providing Amazon.com's users with the option of picking up books, CDs, and other merchandise at Borders' physical bookstores. Amazon.com also is becoming a Web fulfillment contractor for national chains such as Target and Circuit City.

The Results

According to Retail Forward's study, *Top E-Retail 2001* (Retail Forward 2002), Amazon.com was the number one e-tailer in 2001, generating $3.12 billion. This level of sales represented 22 percent of the total online sales for all 50 companies in the study. According to Bayers (2002), Amazon is becoming very successful in reducing its costs and increasing its profitability.

Annual sales for Amazon.com have trended upward, from $15.7 million in 1996 to $600 million in 1998 to about $4 billion by 2002. This pioneer e-tailer now offers over 17 million book, music, and DVD/video titles to some 20 million customers. Amazon.com also offers several features for international customers, including over 1 million Japanese-language titles.

In January 2002, Amazon.com declared its *first* profit—for the 2001 fourth quarter. This was followed by a profitable first quarter of 2002, two more unprofitable quarters, and a solidly profitable fourth quarter. However, the company's financial suc-

cess is by no means assured. Like all businesses—and especially all e-tailing businesses—Amazon.com, the king of e-tailers, will continue to walk the fine line of profitability, at least in the short run.

Sources: Compiled from Bayers (2002), Daisey (2002), Sandoval (2002), and press releases from Amazon.com (2001–2003.)

WHAT WE CAN LEARN . . .

The case of Amazon.com, the most recognized e-tailer worldwide, demonstrates some of the features and managerial issues related to e-tailing. It demonstrates the evolution of e-tailing, some of the problems encountered by e-tailers, and the solutions employed by Amazon.com to expand its business. In this chapter, we will look at the delivery of both products and services online to individual customers. We also will discuss e-tailing successes and failures.

3.1 INTERNET MARKETING AND ELECTRONIC RETAILING (E-TAILING)

The Amazon.com case illustrates how marketing can be done on the Internet. Indeed, the amount and percentage of goods and services sold on the Internet is increasing rapidly, despite the failure of many dot-com companies. As discussed in Chapters 1 and 2, there are many reasons to market online. While initially companies were using the Internet as a cyberbrochure, there is evidence of the increasing use of innovative marketing strategies online. In this chapter, we present an overview of Internet retailing, its diversity, prospects, and limitations. (For more detailed analysis, see Wang et al. 2002). Retailing, especially when done in a new frontier, must be supported by an understanding of consumer buying behavior, market research, and advertisement, topics that will be presented in Chapters 4 and 5. Let us begin our discussion of EC products and services with an overview of electronic retailing.

OVERVIEW OF E-TAILING

A retailer is a sales *intermediary*, a seller that operates between manufacturers and customers. Even though many manufacturers sell directly to consumers, they supplement their sales through wholesalers and retailers (a *multichannel approach*). In the physical world, retailing is done in stores (or factory outlets) that customers must visit in order to make a purchase. Companies that produce a large number of products, such as Procter & Gamble, must use retailers for efficient distribution (e.g., see the opening case in Chapter 5). However, even if you sell only a relatively few products (e.g., Kodak), you still may need retailers in order to reach a large number of customers.

Catalog sales offer companies and customers a respite from the restraints of space and time: Catalogs free a retailer from the need for a physical store from which to distribute products, and customers can browse catalogs on their own time. With the ubiquity of the Internet, the next logical step was for retailing to move online. Online retail sales are called electronic retailing, or e-tailing, and those who conduct retail business online are called e-tailers. E-tailing also can be conducted through auctions. E-tailing makes it easier for a manufacturer to sell directly to the customer, cutting out the intermediary. In this chapter, we will deal with the various types of e-tailing and related issues.

The concept of retailing and e-tailing implies sales of goods and/or services to *individual customers*—that is, B2C e-commerce. However, the distinction between B2C and B2B e-commerce is not always clear cut. For example, Amazon.com sells books mostly to individuals (B2C), but it also sells to corporations (B2B). Amazon.com's chief rival, Barnes & Noble (barnesandnoble.com), has a special division that caters only to business customers.

electronic retailing (e-tailing)
Retailing conducted online, over the Internet.

e-tailers
Those who conduct retail business over the internet.

Walmart.com sells to both individuals and businesses (via Sam's Club). Dell sells its computers to both consumers and businesses from dell.com, Staples sells to both markets at staples.com, and insurance sites sell to both to individuals and corporations.

SIZE AND GROWTH OF THE B2C MARKET

The statistics for the volume of B2C EC sales, including forecasts for future sales, come from many sources. The following sites provide statistics on e-tailing:

- amrresearch.com
- business2.com
- cyberatlas.com
- cyberdialogue.com
- emarketer.com
- forrester.com
- gomez.com
- idc.com
- jmm.com
- statmarket.com

More resources are listed in Chapter 4.

Reported amounts of online sales deviate substantially due to how the numbers are derived. Some of the variation stems from the use of different definitions and classifications of EC. For example, when tallying the financial data, some analysts include the investment costs in Internet infrastructure, whereas others include only the amount of the actual transactions conducted via the Internet. Another issue is how the items for sale are categorized. Some sources combine certain products and services, others do not. Here are some general statistics about online sales: According to a *Forbes/eMarketer* white paper (2002), the number of U.S. online buyers will increase as a share of all Internet users from 53.2 percent in 2001 to just shy of 60 percent by 2004, when there will be 90 million people purchasing online. Total U. S. revenues from online B2C buying are predicted to go from $73 billion in 2001 to $190 billion in 2004.

The U.S. Census Bureau publishes periodic reports on retail e-commerce sales (census.gov/mrts/www/mrtshist.html). For example, in May 2002 the bureau reported sales of $9.8 billion in the first quarter of 2002 (up 19.3 percent from the first quarter of 2001). The Census Bureau also estimates e-commerce sales each quarter. The annual 2002 sales were estimated to be over $40 billion, close to 1.4 percent of total retail sales, up from 1.1 percent in 2001 (census.gov/mrts/www/current.html). The average online shopper spent over $300 per quarter.

WHAT SELLS WELL ON THE INTERNET

Hundreds of thousands of items are available on the Web, from numerous vendors. The most recognizable categories are the following.

Computer hardware and software. Dell and Gateway are the major online vendors of computer hardware and software, with more than $15 billion in sales in 2002. Hardware is most popular, but more and more people buy software online as well. For example, the computer used for preparing this book was purchased at Dell.com together with Microsoft Office and other software.

Consumer electronics. According to Cox (2003), consumer electronics are the second biggest product category sold online. Digital cameras, printers, scanners, wireless devices (including personal digital assistants [PDAs] and cell phones) are some of the consumer electronics bought online.

Sporting goods. Sporting goods sell very well on the Internet. However, it is difficult to measure the exact figure as there are only a few e-tailers that sell sporting goods exclusively online (e.g., fogdog.com).

Office supplies. Sales of office supplies at officedepot.com alone reached over $2.3 billion in 2002 (officedepot.com 2003). Both B2C and B2B sales of office supplies are increasing rapidly, all over the world.

Books and music. Amazon.com and Barnesandnoble.com are the major sellers of books (over $5 billion in 2001). However, hundreds of other e-tailers sell books on the Internet, especially specialized books (e.g., technical books, children's books).

Toys. After two rocky Christmas seasons in which toy e-tailers had problems delivering ordered toys, toy sales are now moving successfully to the click-and-mortar mode. With the Toys R Us/Amazon alliance leading the pack, and Kbkids.com following, consumers can buy their favorite toys online at discount stores (e.g., Target and Wal-Mart), department stores, or direct from some manufacturers (e.g., mattel.com, lego.com).

Health and beauty. A large variety of health and beauty products, from vitamins to cosmetics to jewelry, are sold online by most large retailers and by specialty stores.

Entertainment. This is another area where dozens of products, ranging from tickets to events (e.g., ticketmaster.com) to paid fantasy games (e.g., espn.com), are embraced by millions of shoppers worldwide.

Apparel. With the possibility of buying customized shirts, pants, and even shoes, the online sale of apparel is also growing.

Cars. The sale of cars over the Internet is just beginning (people still like to "kick the tires"), but cars could be one of the top sellers on the Internet by 2007. Already, car manufacturers, retailers, and intermediaries that provide related services, both click-and-mortar and pure-play companies, are participating. The business is a multibillion dollar one, involving new and used cars, fleets or rental car companies, and auto parts; the market includes B2B, B2C, C2C, G2B, and G2C. Customers like the build-to-order capabilities (see Section 3.2), but even selling used cars online has advantages and is increasing rapidly. Auctions of antique, used, or new cars are very popular too. Slater (1999) reviews the field and lists the major participants. Support services such as financing, warranties, and insurance also are selling well online.

Services. Sales in service industries, especially travel, stock trading, electronic banking, real estate, and insurance, are increasing, and more than doubling every year in some cases. According to Jupiter Research (2002), the most popular EC activity is online banking and bill paying, which is used by 35 percent of all U.S. Internet users. According to Forrester.com (Harteveldt 2002), airline tickets were the largest *single* B2C item sold on the Internet.

Others. Many other products, ranging from flowers to food to pet supplies, are offered on the Internet. As more and more retailers sell online, virtually every item that is available in a physical store may be sold online as well. Many of these items are specialized or niche products. The Internet offers an open and global market to shops that are trying to sell specialized products they would not be able to market in any other way (e.g., antique Coca-Cola bottles at antiquebottles.com, tea tree oil at teatree.co.uk).

CHARACTERISTICS OF SUCCESSFUL E-TAILING

Retail and e-tail success comes from offering quality merchandise at good prices, coupled with excellent service. In that sense, the online and traditional channels are not very different. However, e-tailers can offer expanded consumer services not offered by traditional retailers. These services will be discussed later in this and the following chapter. With all else being equal in the online environment, goods with the following characteristics are expected to facilitate higher sales volumes:

- High brand recognition (e.g., Lands' End, Dell, Sony)
- A guarantee provided by highly reliable or well-known vendors (e.g., Dell, L.L. Bean)
- Digitized format (e.g., software, music, or videos)
- Relatively inexpensive items (e.g., office supplies, vitamins)
- Frequently purchased items (e.g., groceries, prescription drugs)
- Commodities with standard specifications (e.g., books, CDs, airline tickets), making physical inspection unimportant
- Well-known packaged items that cannot be opened even in a traditional store (e.g., foods, vitamins)

In the next section we will look at the business models that have proved successful in e-tailing.

1. Describe the nature of B2C e-commerce.
2. What sells well in B2C?
3. What are the characteristics of high-volume products and services?

3.2 E-TAILING BUSINESS MODELS

In order to better understand e-tailing, let's view it from the point of view of a retailer or a manufacturer who sells to individual consumers. The seller has its own organizations and must also buy goods and services from others. As shown in Exhibit 3.1, e-tailing, which is basically B2C (right side of the exhibit), is done between the seller (a retailer or a manufacturer) and the buyer. The exhibit shows other EC transactions and related activities, because they may impact e-tailing. In this section, we will look at the various B2C models and their classifications.

E-tailing business models can be classified in several ways. For example, some classify e-tailers by the scope of items handled (general purpose versus specialty e-tailing) or by scope of the sales region covered (global versus regional), whereas others use classification by revenue models (see Chapter 1). Here we will classify the models by the distribution channel used.

CLASSIFICATION BY DISTRIBUTION CHANNEL

A common way of classifying e-tailing business models is to look at the distribution channel. Here we distinguish five categories.

1. **Mail-order retailers that go online.** Most traditional mail-order retailers, such as Sharper Image and Lands' End, simply added another distribution channel—the Internet. Several of these retailers also operate physical stores, but their main distribution channel is direct marketing.
2. **Direct marketing from manufacturers.** Manufacturers, such as Dell, Nike, Lego, or Sony, market directly online from company sites to individual customers. Most of these manufacturers are click-and-mortar, also selling in their own physical stores or via retailers.

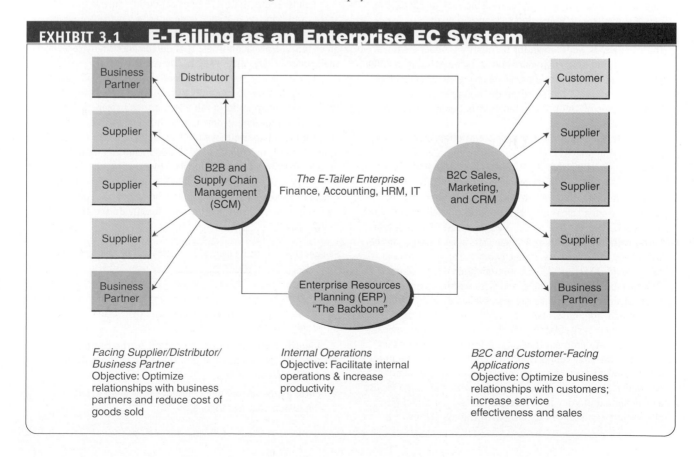

EXHIBIT 3.1   E-Tailing as an Enterprise EC System

Facing Supplier/Distributor/Business Partner
Objective: Optimize relationships with business partners and reduce cost of goods sold

Internal Operations
Objective: Facilitate internal operations & increase productivity

B2C and Customer-Facing Applications
Objective: Optimize business relationships with customers; increase service effectiveness and sales

3. **Pure-play e-tailers.** These e-tailers have no physical stores, only an online sales presence. Amazon.com is an example of a pure-play e-tailer.

4. **Click-and-mortar retailers.** These are traditional retailers with a supplementary Web site (e.g., walmart.com, homedepot.com, and sharperimage.com).

5. **Internet (online) malls.** As described in Chapter 2, these malls include large numbers of independent storefronts.

We'll look at each of these categories of distribution channels in the pages that follow.

direct marketing
Broadly, marketing that takes place without intermediaries between manufacturers and buyers; in the context of this book, marketing done online between any seller and buyer.

Direct Marketing by Mail-Order Companies

In a broad sense, direct marketing describes marketing that takes place without intermediaries. Direct marketers take orders directly from consumers, bypassing traditional wholesale or retail distribution.

An example of a successful mail-order company. Firms with established, mature mail-order businesses have a distinct advantage in online sales, given their existing payment processing, inventory management, and order fulfillment operations, as shown in EC Application Case 3.1.

CASE 3.1

EC Application

LANDS' END: HOW A MAIL-ORDER COMPANY MOVED ONLINE

Some of the most successful B2C e-tailers are mail-order companies that were once based solely on paper catalogs. One reason for their success was the logistics system such companies already had in place. Here we look at Lands' End, now a subsidiary of Sears, Roebuck and Company.

Lands' End is a successful direct-marketing company. The company is well-known for its quality products, casual-styled clothing, and customer service. Internet sales in 2000 (before it became a subsidiary of Sears) were 10 percent of the company's $1.3 billion total, doubling the 5 percent Internet sales of 1999. Projected Internet sales are 20 percent in 2003.

Lands' End's Web site (*landsend.com*) offers all of the company's catalog products. (To show how far the company has come with e-tailing, in 1995 it offered only 100 products online; as of 2002, all of its products are online.) Besides the product offerings, the Web site allows women customers to build and store a three-dimensional model of their body (called the Personal Model). The model then recommends outfits that flatter certain body profiles and suggests sizes based upon the customer's measurements. Male customers can use a feature called "Oxford Express" to sort through hundreds of fabrics, styles, collar and cuff options, and sizes within seconds. Personal shopping accounts are also available on the Web site.

In addition, customers can track their order status online and request catalogs using the Internet. The company has an affiliate program that pays a 5 percent commission for every sale that comes from a referral. It also maintains a B2B "store" at *landsend.com/corpsales*, where companies can customize clothing such as polo shirts with their logo for use as company uniforms, incentives, or gifts. Lands' End Live allows online customers to shop with the assistance of a

"real" personal shopper. Lands' End extends its presence globally by having localized sites in Japan, Germany, and the United Kingdom.

Lands' End operates 16 physical outlets in the United States and 3 in the United Kingdom. Orders made online are shipped from these distribution outlets. Because of their order fulfillment capabilities, U.S. customers usually receive their orders 2 days after they are placed.

Lands' End became a subsidiary of Sears in 2002, and it continues to offer its products through its catalogs and on its Web site. Beginning in fall 2002, an assortment of Lands' End clothing for men, women, and children, as well as products for the home, were available at a select group of Sears stores around the country; and in 2003 Lands' End products became featured items in all Sears stores.

As 88 percent of the company's customers are college graduates, most having computers, the company expects its online business to continue to grow rapidly during the next few years.

Source: Compiled from *landsend.com* October 2002 and April 2003.

Questions

1. Discuss the advantage of Lands' End over other online stores like Gap.

2. Identify the factors that are critical to the company's success. (In business jargon, these are called critical success factors [CSF].)

3. Enter *landsend.com* and configure your ideal outfit. Report on your experience.

Direct Sales by Manufacturers

Dell Computer has established itself as one of the world's most successful manufacturers, selling its computers directly to millions of consumers over the Internet (from dell.com). Besides the cost advantages, the parties in this type of direct marketing have a greater opportunity to influence each other. Sellers can understand their markets better because of the direct connection to consumers, and consumers gain greater information about the products through their direct connection to the manufacturers. Dell is primarily using a build-to-order approach. (See Appendix 2A for more on build-to-order.)

Direct sales by manufacturers are gaining popularity due to the ability to customize products or services, a concept championed by Dell. Customization is usually an *additional* marketing channel for most manufacturers (e.g., see nike.com, lego.com). Direct marketing can more effectively support the consumer's build-to-order requests. Insights and Additions 3.1 (page 88) describes the process by which customers can build cars to order online.

Pure-Play E-Tailers

Virtual (pure-play) e-tailers are firms that sell directly to consumers over the Internet without maintaining a physical sales channel. Amazon.com is a prime example of this type of e-tailer. Virtual e-tailers have the advantage of low overhead costs and streamlined processes. Virtual e-tailers may be general purpose or specialized.

Specialty e-tailers can operate in a very narrow market, as does CatToys.com, described in EC Application Case W3.1. Such a specialized business could not survive in the physical world because it would not have enough customers.

Click-and-Mortar Retailers

The fourth type of online retailer is a click-and-mortar retailer, a brick-and-mortar retailer with an added-on transactional Web site. Brick-and-mortar retailers are retailers that conduct business in the physical world, in traditional brick-and-mortar stores. Traditional retailing frequently involves a single distribution channel, the physical store. In some cases, traditional sellers may also operate a mail-order business. In today's new economy, click-and-mortar retailers sell via stores, through voice phone calls to human operators, via touch-tone phones, over the Internet through interactive Web sites, and by mobile devices. A firm that operates both physical stores and an online e-tail site is said to be a click-and-mortar business selling in a multichannel business model (see Reda 2002). Examples would be department stores such as Macy's (macys.com) or Sears (sears.com), as well as discount stores such as Wal-Mart (walmart.com). It also includes supermarkets and all other types of retailing.

Although there may be practical advantages to being a virtual seller, such as lower overhead costs, it has many drawbacks and barriers, which we will describe later. Therefore, many experts suggest that the ultimate winners in many market segments will be the companies that are able to leverage the best of both worlds using the click-and-mortar approach.

Retailing in Online Malls

Online malls, as described in Chapter 2, are of two types: referring directories and malls with shared services.

Referring directories. This type of mall is basically a directory organized by product type. Catalog listings or banner ads at the mall site advertise the products or stores. When a user clicks on the product and/or a specific store, they are transferred to the storefront of the seller, where they then complete the transaction. An example of a directory is hawaii.com. The stores listed in a directory either collectively own the site or they pay a subscription fee or a commission to the third party (e.g., a portal) that advertises their logos. This type of e-tailing is basically a kind of affiliate marketing. Interesting directories are internetplaza.com and delamez.com.

Malls with shared services. In online malls with shared services, a consumer can actually find the product, order and pay for it, and arrange for shipment. The hosting mall provides these services, but they are executed by each store independently. (To see the variety of services provided, consult both shopping.store.yahoo.com and Online Tutorial T2). The buyer must repeat the process in each store visited in the mall, but it is basically the same

virtual (pure-play) e-tailers
Firms that sell directly to consumers over the Internet without maintaining a physical sales channel.

click-and-mortar retailers
Brick-and-mortar retailers with a transactional Web site from which to conduct business.

brick-and-mortar retailers
Retailers who do business in the non-Internet, physical world in traditional brick-and-mortar stores.

multichannel business model
Describes a company that sells in multiple marketing channels simultaneously (e.g., both physical and online stores).

Insights and Additions 3.1   Buying Cars Online: Build to Order

The world's automobile manufacturers are complex enterprises with thousands of suppliers and millions of customers. Their traditional channel for distributing cars has been the automobile dealer, who orders cars and then sells them from the lot. When a customer wants a particular feature or color ("options"), the customer may have to wait weeks or months until the "pipeline" of vehicles has that particular car on the production line.

In the traditional system, the manufacturers conduct market research in order to estimate which features and options will sell well, and then they make the cars they wish to sell. In some cases, certain cars are ultimately sold from stock at a loss when the market exhibits insufficient demand for a particular vehicle. The carmakers have long operated under this "build-to-stock" environment where they build cars that are carried as inventory during the outbound logistics process (ships, trucks, trains, and dealers' lots). General Motors estimates that it holds as much as $40-billion worth of unsold vehicles in its distribution channels. Other automakers hold similar amounts.

Ford and GM, along with many other carmakers around the world, have announced plans to implement a "build-to-order" program much like the Dell approach to building computers. These auto giants intend to transform themselves from build-to-stock companies to build-to-order companies, thereby cutting inventory requirements in half (Simison 2000; Agrawal et al. 2001), while at the same time giving customers the vehicle they want, in a short period (e.g., 1 to 2 weeks).

As an example of this trend toward build-to-order mass customization in the new car market, Jaguar car buyers can build a dream car online. On Jaguar's Web site (*jaguar.com*), consumers are able to custom configure their car's features and components, see it online, price it, and have it delivered to a nearby dealer. Using a virtual car on the Web site, customers can view in real time more than 1,250 possible exterior combinations out of several million, rotate the image 360 degrees, and see the price updated automatically with each selection of trim or accessories. After storing the car in a virtual garage, the customer can decide on the purchase and select a dealer at which to pick up the completed car. (Thus conflicts with the established dealer network channel are avoided.) The Web site helps primarily with the research process—it is not a fully transactional site. The configuration, however, can be transmitted to the production floor, thereby reducing delivery time and contributing to increased customer satisfaction. Similar configuration systems are available from all the major car manufacturers. Customers can electronically track the progress of the car, including visualization of the production process in the factory.

Sources: Simison (2000), Agrawal et al. (2001), and jaguar.com

---

process. The storefront owners pay rent and/or transaction fees to the owner. ChoiceMall (choicemall.com) is another example of such a mall. Both manufacturers and retailers sell in such malls. As you will note from the online Cat Toys.com story, Yahoo hosts cattoys.com. When you go to Yahoo and click on "toys" and then on "cattoys," you will be directed to this store. Alternatively, you can go directly to cattoys.com; if you do so, you will not know that you are in the Yahoo environment until you are ready to purchase your items. Other malls with shared services are firststopshops.com and shopping.msn.com.

Ideally, the customer would like to go to different stores in the same mall, use one shopping cart, and pay only once. This arrangement is extremely rare.

OTHER B2C MODELS

Several other business models are used in B2C. They are discussed in various places throughout the book. Some of these models are also used in B2B, G2B, and other types of EC. A summary of these other models is provided in Exhibit 3.2.

In the following sections we will describe the delivery of services online.

Section 3.2 ▶ REVIEW

1. List the B2C distribution channel models.
2. Describe how mail-order houses are going online.
3. Describe the direct marketing model used by manufacturers.
4. Describe virtual e-tailing.
5. Describe the click-and-mortar approach.
6. Describe electronic malls.

EXHIBIT 3.2   Other B2C Business Models

Model Name	Description	Reference in Book
Transaction brokers	Electronically mediate between buyers and sellers. Popular in services, travel, job market, stocks, insurance.	Chapters 2, 3, 7, 9
Information portals	Besides information, most provide links to merchants, for which they are paid a commission (affiliate marketing). Some provide hosting and software (e.g., *store.yahoo.com*), some also sell.	Chapters 1, 2, 9
Communities portal	Combine community services with selling or affiliate marketing (e.g., *hometownconnections.com*)	Chapter 17
Content creator or disseminators	Provide content to the masses (news, stock data). Also participate in the syndication chain. (e.g., *espn.com*, *reuters.com*, *cnn.com*).	Chapters 2, 14
Viral marketing	Use e-mail or SMS to advertise. Also can sell direct or via affiliates (e.g., *blueskyfrog.com*).	Chapter 5
Market makers	Create and manage many-to-many markets (e.g., *chemconnect.com*); also auction sites (e.g., *ebay.com*, *dellauction.com*). Aggregate buyers and/or sellers (e.g., *ingrammicro.com*).	Chapters 6, 7
Make (build)-to-order	Manufacturers that customize their products and services via online orders (e.g., *dell.com*, *nike.com*, *jaguar.com*)	Chapters 1, 2, 3, 6
Service providers	Offer online payments, order fulfillment (delivery), and security (e.g., *paypal.com*, *netship.com*).	Chapters 3, 13, 14

3.3   TRAVEL AND TOURISM SERVICES ONLINE

The Internet is an ideal place to plan, explore, and arrange almost any trip. Convenience and potential savings are available through special sales and the elimination of travel agents by buying directly from service providers.

Some major travel-related Web sites are expedia.com, orbitz.com, travelocity.com, asiatravel.com, hotwire.com, travelweb.com, eurovacations.com, and priceline.com. Online travel services also are provided by all major airlines, vacation services, large conventional travel agencies, trains (e.g., amtrak.com), car rental agencies, hotels, commercial portals, and tour companies. Publishers of travel guides such as Fodors and Lonely Planet provide considerable amounts of travel-related information on their Web sites (fodors.com and lonelyplanet.com), as well as selling travel services there. Online ticket consolidator ebookers.com and travel information broker TIScover.com are linking up to create a comprehensive Web-travel resource. (For an overview of travel Web sites, see Keizer 2002.)

The revenue models of online travel services include direct revenues (commissions), revenue from advertising, consultancy fees, subscription or membership fees, revenue-sharing fees, and more. Other important considerations for the growth of online travel services are the value propositions such as increased customer trust, loyalty, and brand image (see Joo 2002).

SERVICES PROVIDED

Virtual travel agencies offer almost all the services delivered by conventional travel agencies, from providing general information to reserving and purchasing tickets, accommodations, and entertainment. In addition, they often provide services that most conventional travel agencies do not offer, such as travel tips provided by people who have experienced certain situations (e.g., a visa problem), electronic travel magazines, fare comparisons, currency conversion calculators, fare tracking (free e-mail alerts on low fares to and from a city and favorite destinations), worldwide business and place locators, an outlet for travel accessories and books, experts' opinions, major international and travel news, detailed driving maps and directions within the United States and several other countries (see biztravel.com), chat rooms and bulletin boards, and frequent-flier deals. In addition, some offer several other innovative services, such as online travel auctions.

SPECIAL SERVICES

Many online travel services offer travel bargains. Consumers can go to special sites, such as those offering stand-by tickets, to find bargain fares. Lastminute.com offers very low airfares and discounted accommodations prices to fill otherwise-empty seats and hotel rooms. Last-minute trips can also be booked on americanexpress.com, sometimes at a steep discount. Special vacation destinations can be found at priceline.com, tictactravel.com, stayfinder.com, and greatrentals.com. Flights.com offers cheap tickets and also Eurail passes. If a person needs to access the Internet while they are traveling, they can access cybercaptive.com for a list of about 5,000 Internet cafes around the world. Similar information is available via many portals such as Yahoo and MSN.

Also of interest are sites that offer medical advice and services for travelers. This type of information is available from the World Health Organization (who.int), governments (e.g., cdc.gov/travel), and private organizations (e.g., tripprep.com, medicalert.com, webmd.com).

Wireless Services

Several airlines (e.g., Cathay Pacific, Delta, Qantas) allow customers with WAP (Wireless Application Protocol) cell phones (cell phones with Internet access) to check their flight status, update frequent flyer miles, and book flights. In the summer of 2001, Singapore Airlines became the first airline to offer customers global flight alerts via short message service (SMS). Users register the flight for which they want to receive an alert at singaporeair.com and specify when they wish to receive the alert and provide their phone number. British Air offers a broadband Internet connection for passengers on board (initially for first and business classes). As of 2003, Lufthansa offers Wi-Fi Internet connections for laptops (for a fee).

Direct Marketing

Airlines sell electronic tickets over the Internet. When a person purchases an electronic ticket online (or by phone), all they have to do when they arrive at the airport is enter their credit card at an *electronic kiosk* and they will get their boarding pass. Alternatively, the traveler can get the boarding pass at the ticket counter.

Using direct marketing techniques, airlines are able to build customer profiles and target specific customers with tailored offers. Many airlines offer "specials" or "cyber offers" on their Web sites (e.g., cathaypacific.com). Airlines such as Scandinavian Airlines offer booking, seat selection, Web check-in, automated flight status service via SMSs; frequent-flyer point claiming, personalized services, and more (see sas.se).

Alliances and Consortia

Airlines and other travel companies are creating alliances to increase sales or reduce purchasing costs (see the Qantas case in Chapter 1 online). For example, some consortia aggregate participants' Internet-only fares. Several alliances exist in Europe, the United States, and Asia. For example, zuji.com is a travel portal dedicated to Asia-Pacific travelers. It is a consortium of regional airlines, Travelocity, some hotel chains, and car-rental providers. It specializes in tour packages in the region. The company also has a booking engine for travel agents who keep their customers (a B2B2C service).

BENEFITS AND LIMITATIONS OF ONLINE TRAVEL SERVICES

The benefits of online travel services to travelers are enormous. The amount of free information is tremendous, and it is accessible at any time from any place. Substantial discounts can be found, especially for those who have time and patience to search for them. Providers of travel services also benefit: Airlines, hotels, and cruise lines are selling otherwise-empty spaces. Also, direct selling saves the provider's commission and its processing.

Online travel services do have some limitations. First, many people do not use the Internet. Second, the amount of time and the difficulty of using virtual travel agencies may be significant, especially for inexperienced Internet surfers. Finally, complex trips or those that require stopovers may not be available online because they require specialized knowledge and arrangements, which may be better done by a knowledgeable, human travel agent. Therefore, the need for travel agents as intermediaries remains, at least for the immediate future. However, as we will show later, intelligent agents may lessen some of these limitations, further reducing the reliance on travel agents.

IMPACT OF EC ON THE TRAVEL INDUSTRY

Bloch and Segev (1997) predict that travel agencies as we know them today will disappear. Only the value-added activities of travel agencies will not be automated, and these activities will be performed by travel organizations that will serve certain targeted markets and customers (also see Van der Heijden 1996). Travel superstores, which will provide many products, services, and entertainment, may enter the industry, as will innovative individuals operating as travel agents from their homes. A more recent analysis on the impact of online travel services on the travel industry is provided by Standing and Vasudavan (2001).

With the increased popularity of online reservations, several service providers, such as the large hotel chains, have found that an additional intermediary has appeared between them and the consumers: Consumers who used to order accommodations directly from a hotel are now using the Internet to compare prices and frequently are buying from an intermediary (such as Hotwire.com) that provides them with the lowest price. The large hotel chains now offer similar services (e.g., see hilton.com). (For a comprehensive discussion, see Rich 2002.)

CORPORATE TRAVEL

The corporate travel market is huge and has been growing rapidly in recent years. Corporations can use all of the travel services mentioned earlier. However, many large corporations receive additional services from large travel agencies. To reduce corporate travel costs, companies can make arrangements that enable employees to plan and book their own trips. Using online optimization tools provided by travel companies (such as those offered at rosenbluth.com; see the Real-World Case at the end of Chapter 2), companies can try to reduce travel costs even further. Travel authorization software that checks availability of funds and compliance with corporate guidelines is usually provided by travel companies such as Rosenbluth International. Another vendor in the corporate travel market is Amadeus Global Travel Distribution (amadeus.com), via e-Travel.com, which provides marketing, distribution, and IT services to automate and manage online booking. Expedia Inc. (expedia.com), Travelocity (travelocity.com), and Orbitz (orbitz.com) also offer software tools for corporate planning and booking.

An example of how a major corporation uses online corporate travel services is described in EC Application Case W3.2.

INTELLIGENT AGENTS IN TRAVEL SERVICES

There is no doubt that EC will play an even greater role in the travel industry in the future. One area that is very promising is the use of software (intelligent) agents. The agents emulate the work and behavior of human agents in executing organizational processes, such as travel authorization (Bose 1996) or planning (Camacho et al. 2001). Each agent is capable of acting autonomously, cooperatively, and collectively to achieve the stated goal (see Online Technical Appendix D). The system increases organizational productivity by carrying out several tedious watchdog activities, thereby freeing humans to work on more challenging and creative tasks.

Intelligent agents could be involved in buyer-seller negotiations, as shown in the following scenario: You want to take a vacation in Hawaii. First you called a regular travel agent who gave you the impression he was too busy to help you. Finally, though, he gave you a plan and a price that you do not like. A friend suggested that you use a software agent instead. Here is how the process works: First you enter your desired travel destination, dates, available budget, special requirements, and desired entertainment to your online agent residing on your computer. The software agent then "shops around," entering the Internet and communicating electronically with the databases of airlines, hotels, and other vendors. The agent attempts to match your requirements against what is available, negotiating with the vendors' agents. These agents may activate other agents to make special arrangements, cooperate with each other, activate multimedia presentations, or make special inquiries. Within minutes the software agent returns to you with suitable alternatives. You have a few questions and you want modifications. No problem. Within a few minutes, the agent will provide replies. Then it is a done deal. No waiting for busy telephone operators and no human errors. Once you approve the deal, the intelligent agent will make the reservations, arrange for payments, and even report to you about any unforeseen delays in your departure. How do you communicate with your software agent? By voice, of course. This scenario is not as far off as it may seem. Such a scenario may be possible by 2005.

Section 3.3 ▶ REVIEW

1. What travel services are available online that are not available off-line?

2. List the benefits of online travel services to travelers and to service providers.

3. What role do software (intelligent) agents have in travel services?

3.4   EMPLOYMENT PLACEMENT AND THE JOB MARKET

The job market is very volatile, and supply and demand are frequently unbalanced. Traditionally, job matching has been done in several ways, ranging from ads in classified sections of newspapers to the use of corporate recruiters, commercial employment agencies, and headhunting companies. The job market has now also moved online. The online job market connects individuals who are looking for a job with employers who are looking for employees with specific skills. It is a very popular approach. For example, one study found that 50 million Americans have used the online job market (Pew Internet Project 2002). Advantages of the online job market over the traditional one are listed in Exhibit 3.3.

THE INTERNET JOB MARKET

The Internet offers a rich environment for job seekers and for companies searching for hard-to-find employees. The job market is especially effective for technology-oriented companies and jobs because these companies and workers use the Internet regularly. However, thousands of other types of companies advertise available positions, accept resumes, and take applications over the Internet (e.g., see Brice and Waung 2002). The following parties use the Internet job market:

▶ **Job seekers.** Job seekers can reply to employment ads. Or, they can take the initiative and place their resumes on their own homepages or on others' Web sites, send messages to members of newsgroups asking for referrals, and use the sites of recruiting firms such

EXHIBIT 3.3 Traditional Versus Online Job Markets		
Characteristic	**Traditional Job Market**	**Online Job Market**
Cost	Expensive, especially in prime space	Can be very inexpensive
Life cycle	Short	Long
Place	Usually local and limited if global	Global
Context updating	Can be complex, expensive	Fast, simple, inexpensive
Space for details	Limited	Large
Ease of search by applicant	Difficult, especially for out-of-town applicants	Quick and easy
Ability of employers to find applicants	May be very difficult, especially for out-of-town applicants	Easy
Matching of supply and demand	Difficult	Easy
Reliability	Material can be lost in mail	High
Communication speed between employees and employers	Can be slow	Fast
Ability of employees to compare jobs	Limited	Easy, fast

as headhunter.net, asiajobsearch.org, hotjobs.com, and monster.com (see Harrington 2002). For entry-level jobs and internships for newly minted graduates, job seekers can go to jobdirect.com. Job seekers can also assess their market value at different U.S. cities at wageweb.com.

▶ **Employers seeking employees.** Many organizations, including public institutions, advertise openings on their Web sites. Others advertise job openings on popular public portals, online newspapers, bulletin boards, and with recruiting firms. Employers can conduct interviews and administer tests on the Web. Some employers, such as Home Depot, have kiosks in their facilities on which they post job openings and allow applicants to complete an application electronically.

▶ **Job agencies.** Hundreds of job agencies are active on the Web. They use their own Web pages to post available job descriptions and advertise their services in e-mails and at other Web sites. Job agencies and/or employers use newsgroups, online forums, bulletin boards, Internet commercial resume services, and portals such as Yahoo and AOL.

An unsuccessful dot-com employment agency was Refer.com. The company listed vacancies of hard-to-fill positions. People and agencies were asked to find candidates. The finders received $1,000 or more for a successful match. The company folded in 2001 because employers were flooded with hundreds of unqualified candidates, and so those employers preferred to continue to work with their regular off-line agencies, who did better screening of potential employees (see Dixon 2001).

▶ **Government agencies and institutions.** Many government agencies advertise openings for government positions on their Web sites and on other sites; some are required by law to do so. In addition, some government agencies use the Internet to help job seekers find jobs elsewhere, as done in Hong Kong and the Philippines (see EC Application Case 3.2).

Consortium of Large Employers

Large employers such as GE, IBM, and Xerox spend hundreds of thousands of dollars annually on commissions to online job companies. To save money, those companies and others have joined a nonprofit consortium that created a career portal called directemployers.com. The site is used primarily to catalog job postings from the sites of the member employers. Having the job postings of a number of large employers in one place makes it easy for job searchers to explore available openings.

CASE 3.2

EC Application

MATCHING WORKERS WITH JOBS IN THE PHILIPPINES

The Philippines is a country with many skilled employees but few open jobs. In January 1999, the government created a special Web site that matches people with jobs. The site is part of a computerized project of the Department of Labor, and it is a free service.

For those people who do not have computers or Internet access, the government placed kiosks (computer terminals) in hundreds of locations throughout the country. The job placement system is also connected with Philippine embassies around the world, especially in countries where there are many overseas Filipino workers, so that they can find a job and return home. Government employees help those applicants who do not know how to use the system.

This system gives job seekers a chance to find a job that would best suit their qualifications. At the heart of the system are its matchmaking capabilities. For the matchmaking

process, a database stores all the job vacancies submitted by different employers. Another database stores the job applications fed into the system. The system matches qualified applicants with companies. It also automatically does a ranking based on the matches. This job-matching feature differentiates this site from other online job sites. Everything is done electronically, so job seekers can see the match results in seconds.

Source: *Computerworld Hong Kong* (1999).

Questions

1. What is the role of Internet kiosks in the Philippines' employment system?

2. How are jobs matched with applicants?

EXHIBIT 3.4   Advantages of the Electronic Job Market for Job Seekers and Employers

Advantages for Job Seekers	Advantages for Employers
• Can find information on a large number of jobs worldwide	• Can advertise to a large numbers of job seekers
• Can communicate quickly with potential employers	• Can save on advertisement costs
• Can market themselves directly to potential employers (e.g. *discoverme.com*)	• Can reduce application processing costs by using electronic application forms
• Can write and post resumes for large-volume distribution (e.g., Personal Search Engine at *careerbuilder.com*, *jobweb.com*, *brassring.com*).	• Can provide greater equal opportunity for job seekers
• Can search for jobs quickly from any location	• Increased chance of finding highly skilled employees
• Can obtain several support services at no cost (e.g., career planning is provided by *hotjobs.com* and *monster.com*)	
• Can assess their market value (e.g., *wageweb.com* and *rileyguide.org*; look for salary surveys).	
• Can learn how to use their voice effectively in an interview (*greatvoice.com*)	
• Can access newsgroups that are dedicated to finding jobs (and keeping them)	

BENEFITS AND LIMITATIONS OF THE ELECTRONIC JOB MARKET

As indicated earlier, the electronic job market offers a variety of benefits for both job seekers and employers. These advantages are shown in Exhibit 3.4.

Probably the biggest limitation of the online job market is the fact that many people do not use the Internet. This limitation is even more serious with non-technology–oriented jobs. To overcome this problem, companies may use both traditional advertising approaches and the Internet. However, the trend is clear: Over time, more and more of the job market will be on the Internet. One solution to the problem of limited access is the use of Internet kiosks, as described in EC Application Case 3.2 (page 93) and as used by companies such as Home Depot in their stores.

Security and privacy may be another limitation. For one thing, resumes and other online communications are usually not encrypted, so one's job-seeking activities may not be secure. For another, it is possible that someone at a job seeker's current place of employment (possibly even their boss) may find out that they are job hunting. The electronic job market may also create high turnover costs for employers by accelerating employees' movement to better jobs. Finally, finding candidates online is more complicated than most people think, mostly due to the large number of resumes available online. Some sites offer prescreening of candidates (e.g., jobtrak.com), which may alleviate this problem.

INTELLIGENT AGENTS IN THE ELECTRONIC JOB MARKET

The large number of available jobs and resumes online makes it difficult both for employers and employees to search the Internet for useful information. Intelligent agents can solve this problem by matching openings and jobs. Exhibit 3.5 shows how intelligent agents in the online job market work for both job seekers and recruiters.

Intelligent Agents for Job Seekers

A free service that uses intelligent agents to search the Internet's top job sites and databases for job postings based on users' profiles is offered at careershop.com. Users can create as many as five different profiles based on more than 100 different job categories, geographic regions, and key words. Users receive a daily e-mail containing job opportunities from over a dozen top job sites around the Internet (e.g., Personal Search Engine at careerbuilder.com), that match their career interests. This saves the users a tremendous amount of time.

EXHIBIT 3.5   Intelligent Agents Match Resumes with Available Jobs

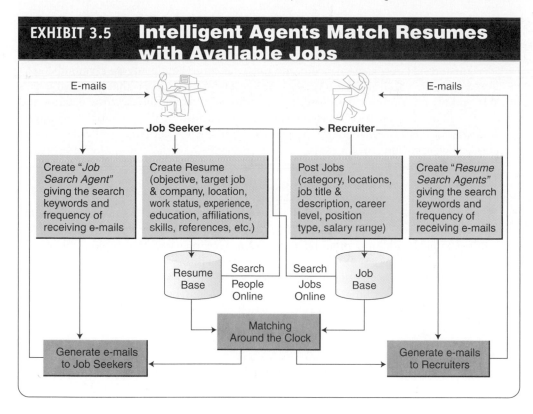

Intelligent Agents for Employers

A special search engine powered by an intelligent agent can help employers find resumes that match specific job descriptions. For example, here is how the search engine Resumix at enterprise.yahoo.com/resumix (now a subsidiary of Yahoo Enterprise Solutions) works: Hiring managers can view job applications; operators can scan resumes; and a recruiter can search for a candidate or identify existing employees for training programs, redeployment opportunities, or new initiatives. The core of this powerful system is Resumix's Knowledge Base, a computerized intelligent system. The Knowledge Base interprets a candidate's resume, determining skills based on context and matching those skills to the position criteria. For example, a potential employer might be looking for a product manager. Being a member of the AMA (American Marketing Association) might be one of the desirable properties for the job. However, if the potential employer used only a basic keyword search, they might get candidates who have listed AMA, but are really members of the American Medical Association or American Meatpackers Association. Those are not relevant to their search. Resumix Knowledge Base would select only the candidates who are members of the American Marketing Association and possess whatever other relevant skills the potential employer specifies.

Section 3.5 ❱ REVIEW

1. What are the driving forces of the electronic job market?
2. What are the major advantages of the electronic job market to the candidate? To employers?
3. Describe the role of intelligent agents in the electronic job market.

3.5 REAL ESTATE, INSURANCE, AND STOCK TRADING ONLINE

REAL ESTATE ONLINE

Real estate transactions are an ideal area for EC for a number of reasons. First, potential homebuyers can view many properties online, at any time and from anywhere, saving time for the buyer and the broker. For example, the real estate market in London is very active;

buyers from Hong Kong, Singapore, India, and many other countries are active in this market. To optimize their business with such international buyers, a number of developers that have real estate properties in London actively advertise on the Internet: galliard-homes.co.uk, berkeleyhomes.co.uk, weston-homes.com, and fpdsavills.com. (For details see Dymond 2002.)

A second reason for using the Internet for real estate transactions is that potential buyers can sort and organize properties according to specific criteria and preview the exterior and interior design of the properties, shortening the search process. Finally, potential homebuyers can find *detailed information* about the properties and frequently get larger real estate listings than brokers will provide.

In some locations, real estate databases are only available to realtors over private networks in their offices, but in many cities, this information is available to potential buyers from their personal Internet connections. For example, realtor.com allows Web surfers to search a database of over 1 million homes located all over the United States. The database is composed of local multiple listings of all available properties and of properties just sold in hundreds of locations. In addition, other realtors, such as Cushman and Wakefield of New York (cushwake.com), are using the Internet to sell commercial property (e.g., office buildings).

Builders, too, now use virtual reality technology on their Web sites to demonstrate three-dimensional floor plans to homebuyers. "Virtual models" enable buyers to "walk through" three-dimensional mock-ups of homes.

Real Estate Applications

The real estate industry is just starting to discover EC. Some real estate applications and services, with their representative Web addresses, are shown in the following list. More applications and services are sure to proliferate in the coming years.

▶ Advice to consumers on buying or selling a home is available at assist2sell.com.
▶ International Real Estate Directory and News (ired.com) is a comprehensive real estate Web site.
▶ A national listing of properties for sale can be found at realtor.com and at land.net.
▶ Commercial real estate listings can be found at starboardnet.com.
▶ Listings of residential real estate in multiple databases can be viewed at homescout.com and realestate.yahoo.com.
▶ The National Association of Realtors (realtor.com) has links to house listings in all major cities.
▶ Maps are available on mapquest.com and realestate.yahoo.com.
▶ Information on current mortgage rates is available at bankrate.com, eloan.com, and quickenloans.quicken.com.
▶ Mortgage brokers can pass loan applications over the Internet and receive bids from lenders who want to issue mortgages (e.g., eloan.com).
▶ Online lenders such as arcsystems.com can tentatively approve loans online.
▶ To automate the closing of real estate transactions, which are notorious for the paperwork involved, see closeyourdeal.com.
▶ Property management companies (residential, commercial, and industrial) are using the Internet for many applications ranging from security to communication with tenants. For an example see superhome.net in Hong Kong.
▶ Sites for home sellers such as owners.com provide a place for persons who want to sell their homes privately, without using a real estate agent.
▶ Decided not to buy? Rental properties are listed on homestore.net. Several services are available, including a virtual walk-through of some listings.

In general, online real estate is supporting rather than replacing existing agents. Due to the complexity of the process, real estate agents are still charging high commissions. However, several Web sites have started to offer services at lower commissions (e.g., see assist2sell.com).

Real Estate Mortgages

Large numbers of companies compete in the residential mortgage market. Several online companies are active in this area (e.g., see lendingtree.com and eloan.com). Many sites offer loan calculators (e.g., eloan.com and quickenloans.quicken.com. Mortgage brokers can pass loan applications over the Internet and receive bids from lenders who want to issue mortgages. Priceline.com (priceline.com) offers its "name your own price" model for obtaining residential loans. In another case, a Singaporean company aggregates loan seekers and then places the package for bid on the Internet. Some institutions approve loans online in 10 minutes and settle in 5 days (e.g., homeside.com.au). Large numbers of independent brokers are active on the Internet, sending unsolicited e-mails to millions of people in the United States, promising low rates for refinancing and new homes (an activity that some recipients see as "spam"; see Chapters 5 and 17).

INSURANCE ONLINE

An increasing number of companies use the Internet to offer standard insurance policies, such as auto, home, life, or health, at a substantial discount. Furthermore, third-party aggregators offer free comparisons of available policies. Several large insurance and risk-management companies offer comprehensive insurance contracts online. Although many people do not trust the faceless insurance agent, others are eager to take advantage of the reduced premiums. For example, a visit to insurerate.com will show a variety of different policies. At order.com customers and businesses can compare car insurance offerings and then make a purchase online. Some other popular insurance sites include quotesmith.com, insweb.com, insurance.com, ebix.com, and quicken.com. Many insurance companies use a dual strategy (MacSweeney 2000), keeping human agents but also selling online. Like the real estate brokers, insurance brokers send unsolicited e-mails to millions of people.

ONLINE STOCK TRADING

Although U.S. stock traders were among the first to embrace the Internet, traders in Korea really love it. By 2003, more than 55 percent of all stock trades in Korea were transacted online (versus about 30 percent in the United States). Why trade securities (stocks and bonds) online? Because it makes a lot of "dollars and sense" (Schonfeld 1998).

The commission for an online trade is between $4 and $19 (these fees tend to go down with time), compared to an average fee of $100 from a full-service broker or $25 from a discount broker. With online trading, there are no busy telephone lines, and the chance for error is small, as there is no oral communication in a frequently noisy environment. Orders can be placed from anywhere, at any time day or night, and there is no biased broker to push a sale. Furthermore, investors can find a considerable amount of free information about specific companies or mutual funds.

Several discount brokerage houses initiated extensive online stock trading, notably Charles Schwab in 1995. Full-service brokerage companies such as Merrill Lynch followed in 1998–1999. By 2002, most brokerage firms in the United States offered online trading, and the volume of trading has increased significantly in the last 5 years. In 2002, Charles Schwab opened cybertrader.com, charging only $9.95 per trade.

How does online trading work? Let's say an investor has an account with Schwab. The investor accesses Schwab's Web site (schwab.com), enters their account number and password, and clicks on stock trading. Using a menu, the investor enters the details of the order (buy, sell, margin or cash, price limit, or market order). The computer tells the investor the current "ask" and "bid" prices, much as a broker would do over the telephone, and the investor can approve or reject the transaction. The flow chart of this process is shown in Exhibit 3.6 (page 98). However, companies such as Schwab are now also licensed as exchanges. This allows them to match the selling and buying orders of their own customers for many securities in about 1 to 2 seconds.

Some well-known companies that offer online trading are E*TRADE, Ameritrade, TD Waterhouse, Suretrade, Discover, and Lombard. E*TRADE offers many finance-related

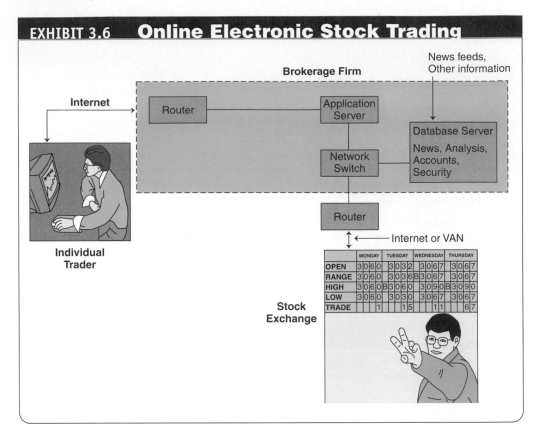

EXHIBIT 3.6   Online Electronic Stock Trading

services (e.g., see Lee 2000). It also challenges investors to participate in a simulated investment game.

Of the many brokers online, of special interest are ameritrade.com and datek.com. These two brokers have now combined as one company and offer customers extremely fast executions or their commission money back. The most innovative collection of online brokerage services is that of E*TRADE. In 1999, E*TRADE broadened its services by starting its own portfolio of mutual funds. E*TRADE is expanding rapidly into several countries, enabling global stock trading. (For further details on brokers and services provided online, see Gilbert et al. 2000.)

Investment Information

There is an almost unlimited amount of investment-related information available online, mostly free (usually in exchange for a registration). Here are some examples:

- Current financial news is available at CNN Financial (money.cnn.com). This portal also has large amounts of company information, all free. Similar information is available at Hoover's (hoovers.com) and Bloomberg (bloomberg.com).
- Municipal bond prices are available at bloomberg.com.
- Many tools are available to help investors in the bond market. For example, "how to invest manuals," free research reports, and charts and tables of foreign currencies all are available.
- A good source of overall market information, with many links to other financial sites, is investorguide.com.
- Free "guru" (expert) advice is available from thestreet.com.
- Stock screening and evaluation tools are available at MultexInvestor (marketguide.com) and money.cnn.com.
- Articles from the *Journal of the American Association of Individual Investors* can be read at investware.com/aaii.stm.
- The latest on funding and pricing of initial public offerings (IPOs) is available at hoovers.com/ipo and at ipodata.com.

- Chart lovers will enjoy bigcharts.com. Charts are also available on many other sites.
- Mutual fund evaluation tools and other interesting investment information are available from Morningstar (morningstar.com).
- Earnings estimates and much more are available at firstcall.com.
- Almost anything that anyone would need to know about finance and stocks can be found at finance.yahoo.com.
- A comprehensive site that tries to educate, amuse, and enrich is The Motley Fool (fool.com). A portal for individual investors, the site has gained considerable popularity. It acts as a community and is managed by two brothers who also author books and write a nationally syndicated column in newspapers.

Most of these services are free. Many other services relating to global investing, portfolio tracking, and investor education are also available. For example, a number of free Web sites allow investors to scan mutual-fund offerings to find a suitable investment sector, country to invest in, and risk profile. For instance, Morningstar (morningstar.com) not only rates mutual funds, but also provides a search engine to help users narrow their search. Investors can use the "Fund selector" option and go to "Morningstar category." If investors want to invest in, say, Southeast Asia, they can find funds operating not only from the United States, but also from Hong Kong, Singapore, or Malaysia. Once the investor has picked a market, they can segment it by the size of the fund, by return on investment during the last 5 or 10 years, and by other criteria. They also can consider the fund's risk level and even the fund-manager's tenure. The site has news and chat rooms for each fund. It also lets investors look at the top-10 holdings of most funds. Other evaluation sites similar to Morningstar, such as lipperweb.com, also rank funds by volatility. Investors can get their fund details and charts showing past performance against a relevant index for each fund.

Related Financial Markets

In addition to stocks, online trading is expanding to include commodities, financial derivatives, and more. Futures exchanges around the world are moving to electronic trading. For example, the Chicago Board of Trade, the world's largest futures exchange, is offering full-range electronic trading. Of special interest is *mortgage banking online* (see Stanford 2002).

The Risk of Having an Online Stock Account

The major risk of online trading is security. Although all trading sites require users to have an ID and password, problems still may occur, as illustrated in EC Application Case 3.3 (page 100).

Problems of this nature may occur in conducting similar online trading, especially in banking, our next topic.

Section 3.5 ▶ REVIEW

1. List the major online real estate applications.
2. What are the advantages of online stock tracking?
3. What investment information is available online?
4. What are some of the risks of trading stocks online?

3.6 BANKING AND PERSONAL FINANCE ONLINE

Electronic banking (e-banking), also known as cyberbanking, virtual banking, online banking, and home banking, includes various banking activities conducted from home, business, or on the road instead of at a physical bank location. Consumers can use e-banking to pay bills online or to secure a loan electronically.

Electronic banking saves time and money for users. For banks, it offers an inexpensive alternative to branch banking and a chance to enlist remote customers. Many physical banks now offer home banking services, and some use EC as a major competitive strategy. One such U.S. bank is Wells Fargo (wellsfargo.com). In Hong Kong, a leading bank is the Bank of East Asia (hkbea-cyberbanking.com). Overall, 15 million online bank accounts were active in 2002

electronic banking (e-banking)
Various banking activities conducted from home or the road using an Internet connection; also known as *cyberbanking, virtual banking, online banking,* and *home banking.*

CASE 3.3

EC Application

THE DANGERS OF ONLINE TRADING

Koreans hold several Internet usage records, including the fact that almost 55 percent of stock trading in Korea is done online. However, on Friday, August 23, 2002, Koreans were shocked to learn how easy it was to conduct a U.S. $20.7 million (25 billion in Korean *won*) fraudulent online stock trade.

A criminal used a PC in an Internet cafe to place a buy order at a fairly high price for 5 millions shares of Delta Information and Communication in the name of a well-known buyer, Hyundai Investment Trust Management, using the trust company's correct account number and password, which he stole. Over 100 people sold more than 10,000 shares each for a total of 2.7 million shares, all in 90 seconds, pushing the price of the shares way up. Then, the hacker stopped buying and disappeared. Because there were no more buyers, the price of Delta's shares started to decline, and by the time the fraud was announced publicly the following Monday, the shares had lost 12 percent (the daily limit on Korea's stock exchange) on each of two trading days, August 23 and 26. The Hyundai account is managed by a large brokerage firm, Daewoo Securities, which suffered U.S.$5 million paper losses in 2 days.

The police speculated that some of Delta's shareholders, who sold shares on August 23, may have been involved in the scheme, but stated that it would be difficult to prove who conspired with the unknown hacker. Daewoo Securities suffered the losses because they had to take the 2.7 million shares into their account. Besides the $5 million in paper losses in the 2 days, shares of Daewoo Securities dropped considerably.

Sources: Compiled from television and newspaper stories in Korea, August 24–27, 2002 and BBC News 2002.

Questions

1. Most online trading systems in the world accept an account number and a password as sufficient to conduct a trade. Therefore, a similar incident could have occurred elsewhere. How one can prevent this type of fraud? (See Chapters 12 and 13 for some ideas).

2. In this case, the buyer's account was managed by Daewoo, therefore Daewoo will pay the damage. If the hacker had selected a "buyer" whose account was not managed by a brokerage firm, who would pay the damage? How would you feel if someone bought shares into your account, and then they plunged 12 percent in a day?

---

in the United States; 25 million are projected by 2004 (Torris 2002). Also, many traditional banks around the world offer diversified e-banking services (e.g., see main.hangseng.com). Many banks offer wireless services (see Chapter 10). According to *eMarketer Daily* (2002), banking online is becoming popular even with small businesses. In 2002, about 25 percent of small businesses banked online versus 18 percent in 2001 and only 6 percent in 1998.

HOME BANKING CAPABILITIES

The major capabilities of home banking include the following:

▶ **View current account balances and history at anytime.** Consumers can easily check the status of their checking, savings, credit card, and money market accounts. Also, historical data can be viewed.

▶ **Obtain charge and credit card statements.** Users can even set up their account to pay off cards automatically every month.

▶ **Pay bills.** Electronic payments from accounts are normally credited the same day or the next. The cost of paying bills electronically may be less than the postage involved in sending out a large number of payments each month.

▶ **Download account transactions.** Account transactions can easily be imported into money management software such as Quicken.

▶ **Transfer money between accounts.** No more waiting in lines or filling out deposit slips. Money can be transferred between a consumer's accounts or between a consumer's account and those belonging to others.

▶ **Balance accounts.** For people who forget to record ATM withdrawals, online banking may help them get organized. Users can download transactions and import them into their check registers.

- **Send e-mail to the bank.** Got a problem with an account? Users can send a quick note to their online bank representative.
- **Expand the meaning of "banker's hours."** Consumers can manage their money and bills on their own schedules.
- **Handle finances when traveling.** Consumers can access accounts when they are on the road and even arrange for bill payments to be made in their absence.
- **Use additional services.** Customers of some banks receive phone banking with their online banking service, all for free or for a $5 to $7 monthly fee. Union Bank of California, for example, throws in free checking, ATM withdrawals, and bill paying (for 1 year). Several banks, such as Bank of America, waive regular checking charges if consumers sign up for online banking.

Electronic banking offers several of the EC benefits listed in Chapter 1, both to the bank and to its customers, such as expanding the bank's customer base and saving on the cost of paper transactions (Gosling 2000).

VIRTUAL BANKS

In addition to regular banks adding online services, *virtual banks* have emerged; these have no physical location, but only conduct online transactions. Security First Network Bank (SFNB) was the first such bank to offer secure banking transactions on the Web. Amidst the consolidation that has taken place in the banking industry, SFNB has since been purchased and now is a part of RBC Centura (centura.com). Other representative virtual banks in the United States, from about 40 in total (see Loizos 2000), are NetBank (netbank.com) and First Internet Bank (firstib.com). Virtual banks exist in many other countries (e.g., bankdirect.co.nz). In some countries, virtual banks are involved in stock trading (e.g., see Bank One at oneinvest.com), and stockbrokers are doing some banking (e.g., see etrade.com).

A word of caution about virtual banking: Before sending money to any cyberbank, especially those that promise high interest rates for your deposits, make sure that the bank is a legitimate one. Several cases of fraud have already occurred.

INTERNATIONAL AND MULTIPLE-CURRENCY BANKING

International banking and the ability to handle trades in multiple currencies are critical for international trading. Although some international retail purchasing can be done by providing a credit card number, other transactions may require international banking support. Examples of such cross-border support include the following.

- Hong Kong Bank developed a special system called HEXAGON to provide electronic banking in Asia. Using this system, the bank has leveraged its reputation and infrastructure in the developing economies of Asia to become a major international bank rapidly, without developing an extensive new branch network (Peffers and Tunnainen 1998). For details of this system, see the HEXAGON case on the book's Web site (prenhall.com/turban).
- Tradecard and MasterCard have developed a multiple-currency system for global transactions (see tradecard.com). This system is described in Chapter 13.
- Bank of America and most other major banks offer international capital raising, cash management, trades and services, foreign exchange, risk management investments, merchant services, and special services for international traders.
- *Fxall.com* is a multidealer foreign exchange service that enables faster and cheaper foreign exchange transactions (e.g., see Sales 2000). Special services are being established for stock market traders who need to pay for foreign stocks (e.g., at Charles Schwab).

IMPLEMENTATION ISSUES IN ONLINE FINANCIAL TRANSACTIONS

As you might expect, the implementation of online banking and online stock trading can be interrelated. In many instances, one financial institution offers both services. The following are some implementation issues for online financial transactions. (For an in-depth analysis, see Dewan and Seidmann 2001.)

Securing Financial Transactions

Financial transactions such as home banking and online trading must be very secure. In Chapter 13, we discuss the details of secure EC payment systems. In EC Application Case 3.4, we give an example of how Bank of America provides security and privacy to its customers.

Access to Banks' Intranets by Outsiders

Many banks provide their large business customers with personalized service by allowing them access to the bank's intranet. For example, Bank of America allows its business customers access to accounts, historical transactions, and other data, including intranet-based decision-support applications, which may be of interest to large-business customers. Bank of America also allows its small-business customers to apply for loans through its Web site.

Using Imaging Systems

Several financial institutions (e.g., Bank of America and Citibank) allow customers to view images of all of their incoming checks, invoices, and other related online correspondence. Image access can be simplified with the help of a search engine.

CASE 3.4

EC Application

ONLINE SECURITY AT BANK OF AMERICA

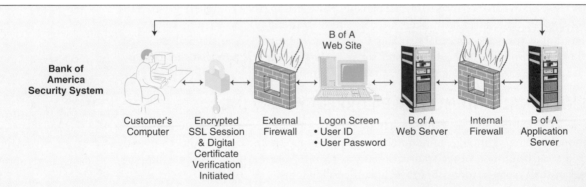

Bank of America (B of A) provides extensive security to its customers. Here are some of the safeguards it provides:

- Customers accessing the B of A system from the outside must go through encryption provided by SSL (Secure Socket Layer) and digital certification verification (see Chapters 12 and 13). The certification process assures users that each time customers sign on that they are indeed connected to the Bank of America. Then the customer inquiry message goes through an external firewall. Once the log-on screen is reached, a user ID and a password are required. This information flows through a direct Web server, and then goes through an internal firewall to the application server. (See figure.)
- The bank maintains accurate information. Corrections are made quickly.
- Information is shared among the company's family of partners only for legitimate business purposes. Sharing information with outside companies is done with extreme care.
- The bank does not capture information provided by customers when they conduct "what-if" scenarios using the bank's planning tools.

- The company uses cookies to learn about its customers. However, customers can control both the collection and use of the information.
- The bank provides suggestions on how users can increase security (e.g., "Use a browser with 128-bit encryption.")

Sources: Compiled from press releases and information on security from Bank of America's Web site (*bankofamerica.com* 2000–2003).

Questions

1. Why is security so important for the bank?
2. Why is there a need for two firewalls?
3. Who is protected by the bank's security system—the customer, the bank, or both? Elaborate.
4. What might be the limitations of such a system? (Hint: Refer to EC Application Case 3.3.)

Pricing Online Versus Off-Line Services

Computer-based banking services are offered free by some banks, whereas others charge $5 to $10 a month. Also, some banks charge fees for individual transactions (e.g., fee per check, per transfer, and so on). Financial institutions must carefully think through the pricing of online and off-line services. Pricing issues must take into account the costs of providing the different types of services, the organization's desire to attract new customers, and the prices offered by competitors. (For further discussion, see Baker et al. 2001.)

Risks

Online banks, as well as click-and-mortar banks, may carry some risks and problems, especially in international banking. The first risk that most people think of is the risk of hackers getting into their account. In addition, some believe that virtual banks carry *liquidity* risk (the risk of not having sufficient funds to pay obligations as they come due) and could be more susceptible to panic withdrawals. Regulators are grappling with the safeguards that need to be imposed on e-banking.

PERSONAL FINANCE ONLINE

Individuals often combine electronic banking with personal finance and portfolio management. Also, brokerage firms such as Schwab offer personal finance services such as retirement planning. However, vendors of specialized personal finance software offer more diversified services (Tyson 2000). For example, both Quicken (from Intuit) and Microsoft's Money offer the following capabilities: bill paying and electronic check writing; tracking of bank accounts, expenditures, and credit cards; portfolio management, including reports and capital gains (losses) computations; investment tracking and monitoring of securities; stock quotes and past and current prices of stocks; personal budget organization; record keeping of cash flow and profit and loss computations; tax computations and preparations (also see riahome.com and taxlogic.com); and retirement goals, planning, and budgeting.

Although Quicken is the most popular personal finance software, more sophisticated packages such as Prosper (from Ernst & Young) and CAPTOOL (captools.com) are available. All of these products are available as independent software programs for use with the Internet or are coupled with other services, such as those offered by AOL.

Online Billing and Bill Paying

In a recent study, 90 percent of people surveyed in the Bay Area of California indicated a desire to pay their bills on the Internet (from *Internet Times*, 1998). People prefer to pay monthly bills, such as telephone, utilities, credit cards, cable television, and so on, online. The recipients of such payments are equally eager to receive money online, because online payments are received much more regularly and quickly and have lower processing costs.

The following are representative payment systems:

▷ **Automatic transfer of mortgage payments.** This method has existed since the late 1980s. The payer authorizes their bank to pay the mortgage directly from their bank account, including escrow for tax payments.

▷ **Automatic transfer of funds to pay monthly utility bills.** Since fall 1998, the city of Long Beach has allowed its customers to pay their gas and water bills automatically from their bank accounts. Many other utilities worldwide provide such an option today.

▷ **Paying bills from online banking accounts.** Payments from your bank account can be made into any other bank account. Many people pay their monthly rent and other bills directly into the payees' bank accounts.

▷ **Merchant-to-customer direct billing.** Under this model, a merchant such as American Express posts bills on its Web site, where customers can then view and pay them. (This approach is called presentment and payment; see Chapter 13.) Several utilities in Los Angeles allow customers to pay bills on the utilities' Web sites, charging customers 20 cents per transaction, which is less than the price of a stamp. However, this means that customers have to go to many different Web sites to pay all their bills.

▶ **Using an intermediary for bill consolidation.** In this model, a third party such as Transpoint (from Microsoft, Citibank, and First Data Corporation) consolidates all of a customer's bills at one site and in a standard format. Collecting a commission on each transaction, the intermediary makes it convenient both to the payee and payer to complete transactions. This latest model is of interest to many vendors, including E*TRADE and Intuit.

▶ **Person-to-person direct payment.** An example of this service is PayPal (paypal.com), which enables a person to send funds to another individual over the Internet by opening an account with PayPal (now part of eBay.com) and charging on a credit card or bank account the amount they want to send. PayPal alerts by e-mail the person to whom the user wants to send the funds, and the recipient accesses the account and transfers the funds to a credit card or bank account (see Chapter 13). PayPal is being followed in the market by a number of competitors.

Online billing and bill paying can be classified into B2C, B2B, or C2C. In this section, we have focused largely on B2C services, which help consumers to save time and payees to save on processing costs. However, large opportunities also exist in B2B services, which can save businesses about 50 percent of billing costs. In Hong Kong, for example, CitiCorp links suppliers, buyers, and banks on one platform, enabling automatic payments.

Taxes

One important area in personal finance is advice about and computation of taxes. Dozens of sites are available to help people in their federal tax preparations. Many sites will help people legally cut their taxes. The following list offers some sites worth checking.

▶ irs.gov: The most extensive tax-related site, run by the U.S. government

▶ wwwebtax.com: The second most extensive site, this is a massive directory of tax-related information, research, and services

▶ fairmark.com: A tax guide for investors

▶ moneycentral.msn.com/tax/workshop: A useful reference and educational site

▶ quicken.com/taxes: Emphasizes tax planning

▶ taxcut.com/taxtips and smartmoney.com/ac/tax: Offer advice on ways to minimize taxes

▶ taxprophet.com: Provides tax advice in an entertaining manner

▶ bankrate.com/brm/itax: Contains informative articles about taxation

▶ 1040.com: Teaches about deduction rules

▶ unclefed.com: Offers advice on audits

Section 3.6 ▶ REVIEW

1. List the capabilities of online banking. Which of these capabilities would be most beneficial to you?

2. Discuss some implementation issues of financial services.

3. List the major personal finance services available online.

4. Explain online bill paying.

3.7 ON-DEMAND DELIVERY SERVICES AND E-GROCERS

Most e-tailers use common carriers to deliver products to customers. They may use the postal system within their country or they may use private shippers such as UPS, FedEx, Airborne Express, or Tiger. Delivery can be made within days or overnight if the customer is willing to pay for the expedited shipment.

Some e-tailers and direct marketing manufacturers own a fleet of delivery vehicles and incorporate the delivery function into their business plan in order to provide greater value to the consumer. These firms will either provide regular deliveries on a daily or other regular schedule or they will deliver items within very short periods of time, usually 1 hour. They may also provide additional services to increase the value proposition for the buyers. An example is Bigboxx.com (bigboxx.com), presented in Chapter 6 (page 224). An online grocer, or e-grocer, is a typical example of businesses in this category. Home delivery of food from restaurants is another example. In addition, another class of firms (groceries, office supplies, repair parts, and pharmaceutical products) promise virtually instantaneous or at least same-day delivery of goods to consumers.

Whether the delivery is made by company-owned vehicles or is outsourced to a carrier, an express delivery model is referred to as an **on-demand delivery service** (see Warkentin and Bajaj 2001). In such a model, the delivery must be done fairly quickly after an order is received. (For more on this topic, see Chapter 14.) A variation of this model is *same-day delivery*. According to this model, delivery is done faster than "overnight" but slower than the 30 to 60 minutes expected in on-demand delivery. E-grocers often deliver using the same-day delivery model.

THE CASE OF E-GROCERS

The U.S. grocery market is valued at over $300 billion annually. It is a very competitive market, and therefore margins are very thin. Online grocery sales exceeded $5 billion in 2002, and Andersen Consulting projected in 1998 (Nichols 1998) that the market would top out at $85 billion by 2007, capturing about 15 percent of U.S. households. (Jupiter Media Matrix projects only $35 billion by 2007.) Most e-grocers are click-and-mortar retailers that operate in the countries where they have physical stores, such as Woolworths in Australia (woolworths. com.au). (For statistics on the grocery industry, see retailindustry.about.com/library.)

All e-grocers offer consumers the ability to order items online and have them delivered to their houses. Some e-grocers offer free regular "unattended" weekly delivery (e.g., to your garage), based on a monthly subscription model. Others offer on-demand deliveries (if you are at home), with a surcharge added to the grocery bill and sometimes an additional delivery charge. One e-grocer sells only nonperishable items shipped via common carrier. Many offer additional services, such as dry-cleaning pickup and delivery. Other add-on features include "don't run out" automatic reordering of routine foods or home office supplies, as well as fresh flower delivery, movie rentals, meal planning, recipe tips, multimedia features, and nutritional information.

Recently, it became possible to shop for groceries from cell phones and PDAs (see Chapter 10 and Lawrence et al. 2001).

Who Are the E-Grocery Shoppers?

An extensive survey conducted by the Consumer Direct Cooperative in 2000 (Cude and Morganosky 2000) pointed to the following groups of potential online grocery shoppers: *Shopping avoiders* are willing to shop online because they dislike going to the grocery store; *necessity users* would do so because they are limited in their ability to shop (e.g., disabled and elderly people, shoppers without cars). "*New technologists,*" those who are young and comfortable with technology, represent another group of online grocery shoppers. Extremely busy, *time-starved consumers* may be willing to shop online in order to free up time in their schedules. Finally, some consumers gain a sense of self-worth from online shopping from being on the "leading edge" of what may be a new trend.

Online grocery customers are generally repeat customers who order week after week in a tight ongoing relationship with the grocer. The user interaction with the Web site is much more substantial than with other B2C Web sites, and user feedback is also more prevalent. Shopping for groceries online is a very sophisticated purchase compared to most EC shopping transactions. As an example, in a typical shopping experience at amazon.com a person might buy one to four items. In an e-grocery purchase, the average order has 54 different items in different food categories (Kruger 2000).

Around the world, many e-grocers are targeting the busy consumer with the promise of home delivery of groceries. For example, Parknshop (parknshop.com), the largest supermarket chain in Hong Kong, offers a "personal shopping list" that helps customers easily order repetitive items on each visit. (The Web site also uses advertising as an additional source of revenue to make the business model a bit more solid.) The Tesco chain in the United Kingdom (tesco.com) is another successful e-grocer. (For discussion of the success factors of e-grocers, see Keh and Shieh 2001.) So far, online sales are usually not as profitable as sales in physical grocery stores due to the delivery costs and low volume of online sales. However, this additional channel allows grocers to increase their sales volume and serve customers who

e-grocer
A grocer that will take orders online and provide deliveries on a daily or other regular schedule or will deliver items within a very short period of time.

on-demand delivery service
Express delivery made fairly quickly after an online order is received.

are unable to visit their physical stores. In addition, they can increase their brand recognition by maintaining an Internet presence.

However, despite the promise that on-demand delivery seems to hold, virtual e-grocers have not been successful in this competitive market. (For an analysis, see Keh and Shieh 2001.) For example, StreamLine.com and ShopLink.com folded in 2000. HomeGrocer.com and Kozmo.com folded in 2001 (see Chapters 1 and 14). Other virtual e-grocers, such as Peapod.com and NetGrocer.com, were struggling as of spring 2002. Preliminary data from fourth quarter 2002 rankings of e-grocer performance found leading firms continuing to improve in areas that make most sense in the e-grocery market—such as ease of use of Web sites, convenience, personal interface between buyer and seller, and service after the sale (Ernst and Hooker 2003).

One of the most interesting stories of e-grocers that failed is that of Webvan.com, a company that raised many expectations but finally folded in 2001 after "burning" $1 billion. Webvan was founded in 1999 with a goal of delivering anything (particularly groceries), any time and anywhere in an efficient manner. Webvan designed and started to build sophisticated automated warehouses—each the size of seven football fields and equipped with more than 4 miles of conveyor belts (see Steinert-Therlkeld 2000). In 2001, Webvan purchased Homegrocer.com, a smaller rival, but was unable to merge the two companies properly. Furthermore, the company was unable to secure more funds due to the accumulating failures of dot-com companies, which led to a loss of investor confidence, and declining demands due to economic conditions contributed to staggering losses. Finally, in 2001, Webvan folded. Overall, it lost more than $1 billion, the largest of any dot-com failure. (For more details, see Helft 2001.)

A similar company, Groceryworks.com, was purchased by Safeway, a successful click-and-mortar grocer. The results have been quite different from those of Webvan, as EC Application Case 3.5 details.

Section 3.7 ▶ REVIEW

1. Explain on-demand delivery service.

2. Describe e-grocers and how they operate.

3. Who are the typical e-grocery shoppers? (Would you shop online for groceries?)

3.8 ONLINE DELIVERY OF DIGITAL PRODUCTS, ENTERTAINMENT, AND MEDIA

Certain goods, such as software, music, or news stories, may be distributed in a physical form (such as CD-ROM, DVD, and newsprint) or they may be digitized and delivered over the Internet. For example, a consumer may purchase a shrink-wrapped CD-ROM containing software (along with the owner's manual and a warranty card) or they may pay for the software at a Web site and immediately download it onto their computer (usually through File Transfer Protocol [FTP], a fast way to download large files).

As described in Chapter 2, products that can be transformed to digital format and delivered over the Internet are called *digital products*. Exhibit 3.7 shows some digital products that may be distributed either physically or digitally. Each delivery method has advantages and disadvantages for both sellers and buyers. Customers, for example, may prefer the formats available through physical distribution. They perceive value in holding a physical CD-ROM or music CD as opposed to a downloaded file. In addition, the related packaging of a physical product may be significant. Current technology makes a standard music CD more versatile for use in cars and portable devices than a downloaded MP3 file. In some cases, customers enjoy the "liner notes" that accompany a music CD. Paper-based software user manuals and other materials also have value, and may be preferred over online help features. On the other hand, customers may have to wait days for physical products to be delivered.

For sellers, the costs associated with the manufacture, storage, and distribution of physical products (DVDs, CD-ROMs, paper magazines, etc.) can be enormous. Inventory management also becomes a critical cost issue, and so does delivery and distribution. The need for retail intermediaries requires the establishment of relationships with channel partners and revenue-sharing plans. Direct sales of digital content through digital download, however,

CASE 3.5
EC Application
GROCERY SHOPPING IN THE PALM OF YOUR HAND

Safeway Stores, a grocery chain with $14 billion in sales per year, has implemented its Easi-Order services using a Palm handheld device (PDA) to allow customers to point and click their grocery lists and send them to Safeway via phone. The program is part of the company's "Collect & Go" service. Valued customers are given handheld devices that are loaded with an application that contains a list of thousands of grocery items, including descriptions and prices. The Palm PDA that customers are given is a fully functional unit that can be used for contacts, note taking, e-mail, to-do lists, calendaring and scheduling, and so on.

Customers can review the items and make their grocery lists off-line when time permits. (The estimated time savings is 60 to 90 minutes each week.) When the customer is ready to place the order, the device is plugged into a standard phone socket, and it dials up the Collect & Go server. The shopping list is downloaded to the server, and next week's suggested list along with suggestions and promotions are uploaded to the device. The complete transaction takes about 60 to 90 seconds. The data collected by Safeway allow the company to offer outstanding customer service on a very personal basis to each individual customer by evaluating the individual customer's purchases and buying habits.

The order is picked and packed by the store and set aside for the customer to pick up at their specified, convenient time. Items that customers prefer to select for themselves are easily added to the order at the time of collection by scanning the bar code of the additional items with the same handheld device. Collection is done at dedicated check-out counters. Some Safeway stores are implementing Easi-Pay terminals, which allow customers to avoid check-out lines altogether.

In certain areas, delivery to customers' homes also is available. To make delivery possible, Safeway purchased Groceryworks.com, which developed an innovative order fulfillment model for the e-grocery industry (see Chapter 14 online for details).

Safeway and IBM collaborated on the Easi-Order project to develop the Java-based server. Safeway was able to contact customers in its loyalty-card database, and the customer orders are downloaded to the same database. Easi-Order takes advantage of the Internet by making it possible for customers to download their orders directly to the Collect & Go intranet.

In the future, Safeway's plan is to have screen phones, digital TV, and speech processing devices assist grocery shoppers in making their shopping experiences, as easy as verbally telling the program what they want.

Sources: Compiled from IBM (2002), *safeway.com* (2002), and *Business Times Online* (2003).

Questions

1. What are the benefits of Safeway's Easi-Order and Collect & Go programs for customers?
2. Why is this an EC application?
3. What is the role of mobile devices?
4. Compare order fulfillment done at stores versus that for home delivery.

allow a producer of digital content to bypass the traditional retail channel, thereby reducing overall costs and capturing greater profits. However, retailers are often crucial in creating demand for a product through in-store displays, advertising, and human sales efforts, all of which are lost when the producer "disintermediates" the traditional channel.

THE NAPSTER EXPERIENCE: ITS RISE AND COLLAPSE

With improvements in Internet technologies, the possibility exists for widespread distribution of digital content from businesses to consumers and from consumers to consumers. The rise in importance of Napster, a Web site that allows individuals to find and share music files,

EXHIBIT 3.7	**Distribution of Digital Versus Physical Products**	
Type of Product	**Physical Distribution**	**Digital Distribution**
Software	Boxed, shrink-wrapped	FTP, direct download, e-mail
Newspapers, magazines	Home delivery, postal mail	Display on Web, "e-zines"
Greeting cards	Retail stores	E-mail, URL link to recipient
Images (e.g., clip-art, graphics)	CD-ROM, magazines	Web site display, downloadable
Movies	DVD, VHS, NTSB, PAL	MPEG3, streaming video: RealNetwork, AVI, QuickTime, etc.
Music	CD, cassette tape	MP3, WAV, RealAudio downloads, wireless devices

coincided with the near universality of computer availability on college campuses and the widespread adoption of MP3 as a music file compression standard. MP3 files are much smaller than earlier file alternatives and allow individuals to download a standard song in far less time. The Napster network does not require the use of a standard Web browser such as Netscape or Internet Explorer. Nor does the user's client machine actually download the MP3 files from Napster's servers. Rather, Napster only shares "libraries," or lists of songs, and then enables a *peer-to-peer* file-sharing environment (see Chapter 9) in which the individual users literally download the music from each others' machines (called *peers*). The growth of the "Napster community"—with over 60 million registered users by the end of 2002 and as many as 1.3 million using the service at the same time—was nothing short of phenomenal (Borland 2002). It is said to have grown faster than any other community in history.

Because of the potential challenge to their revenue sources, the Recording Industry Association of America (RIAA) and five major record labels engaged in a legal battle with Napster, suing it for copyright infringement (see Chapter 17). Napster argued that its file sharing never actually published music that could be "pirated" or copied illegally in violation of internationally recognized copyright and licensing laws. However, the court ruled that as a manager of file exchanges, Napster must observe copyright. Thus, free file sharing is no longer allowed; Napster was forced to charge customers for use of its file-sharing service. The users of the free services were not happy with the charge and abandoned the service, driving Napster into bankruptcy.

Napster surprised everyone when it entered into an agreement with Bertelsmann AG, the large global music label based in Germany and now a major shareholder in Napster. As part of the deal, Bertelsmann's BMG music unit, which participated in the lawsuit against Napster, agreed to withdraw from the complaint. The latest version of Napster's file-swapping software features a "buy button" that links to CDNow (cdnow.com), a Bertelsmann-owned Web site that sells traditional, physical music CDs. (Napster's assets have since been acquired by Roxio Inc.)

The future of this consumer environment is clearly in doubt, though it is clear that technological developments will probably continue to outpace the ability of the market and legal structures to react and adapt. After the collapse of Napster, other peer-to-peer tools have emerged, including Kazaa, Freenet, and Gnutella, which have continued to offer variations of file sharing (see Chapter 9 for details).

ONLINE ENTERTAINMENT

Online entertainment is growing rapidly. A survey by Knowledge Networks/Statistical Research Inc., (Castex 2002), shows that entertainment online is already the most popular medium in the United States among youngsters between the ages of 8 and 17. Thirty-three percent of these respondents prefer to be entertained online, whereas only 26 percent prefer to watch television. There are many kinds of Internet entertainment. Basically, forms of Internet entertainment can be broadly categorized into two types: interactive and noninteractive.

Interactive Entertainment

Interactive entertainment is online entertainment in which the user is involved by making decisions or suggestions or by exchanging information. The major forms of interactive entertainment are the following.

> **Web browsing.** This category includes Web sites that require more than the usual user input as part of the process of using the Web site. It is likely in the future that the Web itself will transform into an environment where the user can move through the Web in a virtual reality world.

> **Internet gaming.** This includes all forms of gaming, including lotteries, casino gaming, promotional incentives, and so on.

> **Single and multiplayer games.** This includes online games where multiple users log on to a Web site to participate in a game as well as games that require downloading from the Web site and installation on the PC.

> **Adult entertainment.** Adult entertainment has exploded onto the Internet. This is one industry that seems certain to find a most lucrative home on the Internet. Indeed, adult entertainment has been called the Net's most profitable business model (See Chapter 9.)

▶ **Participatory Web sites.** Participatory Web sites include clubs, user groups, and "info-tainment" sites (a site that provides information on all aspects of a topic and provides mechanisms for the user to interact with other people interested in the topic, for example, a Web site about sports).

▶ **Reading.** E-books are now published on the Web (see Chapter 9). Web versions of print media, including magazines and newspapers, are now available.

Noninteractive Entertainment

Noninteractive entertainment refers to Internet activities that are related to entertainment but in which users are not being entertained. The major forms of noninteractive entertainment are the following.

▶ **Event ticketing.** The click-and-mortar giant TicketMaster (ticketmaster.com) is the most popular place for getting tickets to many types of off-line entertainment. However, tickets also can be obtained from the vendors directly. An example of ticketing in Asia is cityline.com.hk, which offers tickets to events and movie theaters. Tickets are also sold via cell phones (see Chapter 10).

▶ **Restaurants.** Many restaurants allow online reservations. Some do deliveries as well. Examples are pizza places and Chinese restaurants. This kind of service is done frequently via cell phones, telephones, or the Internet (e.g., dialadinner.com.hk).

▶ **Information retrieval.** Many portals offer entertainment-related information for retrieval by users. The Internet has quickly become the greatest source of information available.

▶ **Retrieval of audio and video entertainment.** Users can download audio, music, video, and movies from Internet servers for non-real-time playback.

Both interactive and noninteractive entertainment are available in many countries via cell phones (e.g., i-Mode in Japan).

DEVELOPMENTS IN THE DELIVERY OF DIGITAL PRODUCTS

An interesting development in music distribution is the availability of custom CD sites (e.g., see angelfire.com and grabware.com). These sites enable consumers to collect their favorite songs from various artists and then create a "personal favorites" compilation CD, which is shipped to the consumer. The CD mastering sites pay royalties to the various artists through established channels.

Another trend is the disintermediation of traditional print media. Several journals and magazines ceased publishing "dead paper" versions and have become strictly online distributors of digital content (e.g., pcai.com), generating revenues through advertising or by online subscriptions. (Some of these transformations were subsequently reversed due to lack of financial success of the online version.) Other prominent publications, including the *Wall Street Journal*, now offer either a paper-only subscription, an online-only subscription (at a lower subscription price), or a dual-mode subscription for consumers who want to access their business news through both methods so that they can use search engines to find archived information or read information not available in the paper version.

Similarly, Egghead Software closed all of its brick-and-mortar stores and became a pure-play software store called egghead.com. In doing so, the company dramatically cut operating costs and streamlined its inventory requirements but lost certain advantages offered by a physical presence. Unfortunately, Egghead.com went out of business due to strong online competition in 2001, and its assets were picked up by Amazon.com. Time will tell if digital delivery replaces or enhances traditional delivery methods for various types of digital content.

Section 3.8 ▶ REVIEW

1. Describe digital goods and their delivery.
2. Explain the Napster business model.
3. What are the benefits and the limitations of digital delivery?

3.9 ONLINE PURCHASE DECISION AIDS

Many sites and tools are available to help consumers with online purchasing decisions. Consumers must decide which product or service to purchase, which site to use for the purchase (a manufacturer site, a general purpose e-tailer, a niche intermediary, or some other site), and what other services to employ. Some sites offer price comparisons as their primary tool, others evaluate services, trust, quality, and other factors. Shopping portals, shopping robots ("shopbots"), business ratings sites, trust verification sites, and other shopping aids also are available.

SHOPPING PORTALS

shopping portals
Gateways to storefronts and malls; may be comprehensive or niche oriented.

Shopping portals are gateways to storefronts and e-malls. Like any other portal, they may be comprehensive or niche oriented. Comprehensive or general-purpose portals have links to many different sellers that evaluate a broad range of products. Comprehensive portals include Gomez Advisors (gomez.com) and activebuyersguide.com. Several public portals also offer shopping opportunities and comparison aids. Examples are dealtime.com, shopping.yahoo.com, eshop.msn.com, and webcenter.shop.aol.com. These all have clear shopping links from the main page of the portal, and they generate revenues by directing consumers to their affiliates' sites. Some of these portals even offer comparison tools to help identify the best price for a particular item. Several of these evaluation companies have purchased shopbots (see following discussion) or other, smaller shopping aids and incorporated them into their portals.

Shopping portals may also offer specialized niche aids, with information and links for purchasers of automobiles, toys, computers, travel, or some other narrow area. Such portals also help customers conduct research. Examples include bsilly.com for kid's products and zdnetshopper.cnet.com and shopper.com for computer equipment. The advantage of niche shopping portals is their ability to specialize in a certain line of products and carefully track consumer tastes within a specific and relevant market segment. Some of these portals seek only to collect the referral fee from their affiliation with sites they recommend. Others have no formal relationship with the sellers; instead, they sell banner ad space to advertisers who wish to reach the communities who regularly visit these specialized sites. In other cases, shopping portals act as intermediaries by selling directly to consumers, though this may harm their reputation for independence and objectivity.

SHOPBOTS AND SOFTWARE AGENTS

shopping robots
(also **shopping agents** or **shopbots**)
Tools that scout the Web on behalf of consumers who specify search criteria.

Savvy Internet shoppers may bookmark their favorite shopping sites, but what if they want to find other stores with good service and policies that sell similar items at lower prices? Shopping robots (also called shopping agents or shopbots) are tools that scout the Web for consumers who specify search criteria. Different shopbots use different search methods. For example, MySimon (mysimon.com) searches the Web to find the best prices and availability for thousands of popular items. This is not a simple task. The shopbot may have to evaluate different SKU (stock-keeping unit) numbers for the same item, because each e-tailer may have a different SKU rather than a standardized data-representation code.

Some agents specialize in certain product categories or niches. For example, consumers can get help shopping for cars at autobytel.com, autovantage.com, and carpoint.com. Zdnet.com/computershopper searches for information on computers, software, and peripherals. A shopping agent at office.com helps consumers find the best price for office supplies. A shopping agent for books is isbn.nu. In addition, agents such as pricegrabber.com are able to identify customers' preferences. Dealtime.com allows consumers to compare over 1,000 different merchant sites and keeps seeking lower prices on their behalf. There are even negotiation agents and agents that assist auction bidders (e.g., auctionbid.com) by automating the bid process using the bidder's instructions.

"Spy" Services

"Spy" services in this context are not the CIA or MI5. Rather, they are services that visit Web sites for you, at your direction, and notify you of their findings. Web surfers and shoppers constantly monitor sites for new information, special sales, ending time of auctions, stock updates, and so on, but visiting sites to monitor them is time-consuming. Several sites will track stock prices or airline special sales and send you e-mails accordingly. For example, cnn.com, pcworld.com, and expedia.com will send you personalized alerts. For other cases you can use spyonit.com, which lets you create a list of "spies" that visit Web sites for you and send you an e-mail when they find something of interest. You can choose predesigned spies or create your own (see Internet Exercise 15). Special searches are provided by web2mail.com, which responds to e-mail queries. Of special interest is Yahoo Alerts alerts.yahoo.com, an index of e-mail alerts for many different things, including job listings, real estate, travel specials, and auctions. You set up alerts to hit your in-box periodically or whenever new information is available. The alerts are then e-mailed to you (with commercial ads).

Wireless Shopping Comparisons

Users of Mysimon.com (all regular services) and AT&T Digital PocketNet service have access to wireless shopping comparisons. Users who are equipped with an AT&T Internet-ready telephone find the service appearing on the main menu of AT&T; it enables shoppers to compare prices any time from anywhere, including from any physical store.

BUSINESS RATINGS SITES

Many Web sites rate various e-tailers and online products based on multiple criteria. Bizrate.com, Consumer Reports Online (consumerreports.org), Forrester Research (forrester.com), and Gomez Advisors (gomez.com) are such well-known sites. At gomez.com, the consumer can actually specify the relative importance of different criteria when comparing online banks, toy sellers, e-grocers, or others. Bizrate.com has a network of shoppers that report on various sellers and uses the compiled results in its evaluations. Note that different raters may provide different rankings.

TRUST VERIFICATION SITES

With so many sellers online, many consumers are not sure whom they should trust. A number of companies purport to evaluate and verify the trustworthiness of various e-tailers. The TRUSTe seal appears at the bottom of each TRUSTe-approved e-tailer's Web site. E-tailers pay TRUSTe for use of the seal (which they call a "trustmark"). TRUSTe's 1,300-plus members hope that consumers will use the seal as an assurance and as a proxy for actual research into their privacy policy and personal information protection. However, even TRUSTe is not foolproof. It has been criticized for its lax verification processes, and a number of high-profile privacy violations and other problems with TRUSTe members have led to publication of a study that investigated a TRUSTe "Hall of Shame" (Rafter 2000).

The most comprehensive trust verification sites are VeriSign, BBBOnline, and WebTrust (cpawebtrust.org). VeriSign (verisign.com) tends to be the most widely used. Other sources of trust verification include Secure Assure (secureassure.com), which charges yearly license fees based on a company's annual revenue. In addition, Ernst and Young, the global public accounting firm, has created its own service for auditing e-tailers in order to offer some guarantee of the integrity of their business practices.

OTHER SHOPPER TOOLS

Other digital intermediaries assist buyers or sellers, or both, with the research and purchase processes. For example, escrow services (e.g., tradenable.com, escrow.com) assist buyers and sellers in the exchange of items and money. As buyers and sellers do not see or know each other, a trusted third party frequently is needed to facilitate the proper exchange of money and goods. Escrow sites may also provide payment-processing support, as well as letters of credit (see Chapter 13).

Other decision aids include communities of consumers who offer advice and opinions on products and e-tailers. One such site is epinions.com, which has searchable recommendations on thousands of products. Pricescan.com is a price comparison engine, and pricegrabber.com is a comparison shopping tool that covers over 1 million products. Dealtime.com specializes in electronics, and iwon.com specializes in apparel, health and beauty, and other categories. Other software agents and comparison sites are presented in Exhibit 3.8.

Another shopper's tool is a *wallet*—in this case, an *electronic wallet*, which is a program that contains the shopper's information. To expedite online shopping, a consumer can use an electronic wallet so that they do not need to reenter the information each time they shop. Although sites such as Amazon.com offer their own specialized wallets, Microsoft has a universal wallet in its Passport program (see Chapters 13 and 17 for details).

EXHIBIT 3.8	**Representative Software Agents and Comparison Sites**	
Agent Classification	**Product (URL)**	**Description**
Learning agents	Empirical (*empirical.com*)	Surveys user's reading interests and uses machine learning to find Web pages using neural-network-based collaborative filtering technology.
Comparison shopping agents	MySimon (*mysimon.com*)	Using VLA (virtual learning agent) technology, shops for the best price from merchants in hundreds of product categories with a real-time interface.
	CompareNet (*compare.net*)	Interactive buyer's guide that educates shoppers and allows them to make direct comparisons between brands and products.
AI/Logic-supported approaches	Cnetshopper (*shopper.cnet.com*)	Makes price comparisons.
Computer-related shopping guide	Netbuyer (*netbuyer.co.uk*)	Supplies sales and marketing solutions to technology companies, by delivering information about computer and communications industry trends, products developments, and buyer activity.
Car-related shopping guide	Auto-by-Tel (*autobytel.com*)	A low-cost, no-haggle car-buying system used by leading search engines and online programs such as Excite, NetCenter, Lycos, and AT&T WorldNet Services.
	Autovantage (*cendant.com*)	Provides the Web's premier savings site for great deals on autos. (Also offers travel, shopping, dining, and other services.)
	CarPoint (*carpoint.msn.com*)	A one-stop shopping place for searching and purchasing automobiles.
Microsoft-related agent technology	Agentmart (*microsoft.com/products/msagent*)	Provides Microsoft's agent infospace and agent directory. First Web site with animated conversational characters such as Genie, Merlin, and so on.
Aggregator portal	Pricing Central (*pricingcentral.com*)	Aggregates information from other shopping agents and search engines. Comparison shopping is done in real time (latest pricing information).
Real-time agents	Kanndu (*kanndu.com*)	Allows users to surf over to a single mobile Internet portal and click around to multiple e-shopping sites to make purchases with only a few keystrokes.
	UShop (*ushop.co.jp*)	Compares prices; saves you time and money by giving key information right at the moment you shop online.

1. Define shopping portals and provide two examples.
2. What are shopbots?
3. Explain the role of business rating and site verification tools in the purchase decision process.
4. Why are escrow services and electronic wallets useful for online purchases?

3.10 SUCCESSFUL CLICK-AND-MORTAR STRATEGIES

Although thousands of companies have evolved their online strategies into mature Web sites with extensive interactive features that add value to the consumer purchase process, many sites remain simple "brochureware" sites with limited interactivity. Many traditional companies are in a transitional stage. International Data Corp. (idc.com) predicted in 2002 that by 2003, 32 percent of companies that have Web sites will fully support interactive online transactions.

Mature transactional systems include features for payment processing, order fulfillment, logistics, inventory management, and a host of other services. In most cases, a company must replicate each of its physical business processes and design many more that can only be performed online. Today's environment includes sophisticated access to order information, shipping information, product information, and more through Web pages, touch-tone phones, Web-enabled cellular phones, and PDAs over wireless networks. Faced with all of these variables, the challenges to implementing EC can be daunting.

The real gains for traditional retailers will come from leveraging the benefits of their physical presence and the benefits of their online presence. Web sites frequently offer better prices and selection, whereas physical stores offer a trustworthy staff and opportunities for customers to examine items before purchasing. (Physical examination often is critical for clothing and ergonomic devices, for example, but not for commodities, music, or software.) Large, efficient established retailers, such as Wal-Mart (walmart.com), Marks & Spencer (marksandspencer.com), Takashimaya (takashimaya.co.jp) and Nordstrom (nordstrom.com) are able to create the optimum value proposition for their customers by providing a complete offering of services.

A traditional brick-and-mortar store with a mature Web site uses a click-and-mortar strategy to do the following:

❱ **Speak with one voice.** A firm can link all of its back-end systems to create an integrated customer experience. Regardless of how a customer interfaces with a company, the information received and service provided should be consistent.

❱ **Empower the customer.** The seller needs to create a powerful 24/7 channel for service and information. Through various technologies (see Chapter 4), sellers can give customers the opportunity to perform various functions interactively, at any time. Such functions include the ability to find store locations, product information, and inventory availability online. Circuit City's Web site (circuitcity.com), for example, allows customers to receive rich product comparisons between various models of consumer electronics products, as we will explain in the following section.

❱ **Leverage the multichannels.** The innovative retailer will offer the advantages of each marketing channel to customers from all channels. Whether the purchase is made online or at the store, the customer should benefit from the presence of both channels. For example, customers who purchase from the Web site should be allowed to return items to the physical store (Eddie Bauer's policy). In addition, many physical stores, such as BestBuy, now have terminals in the store for ordering items from the Web site if they are not available in the store. Needless to say, prices should be consistent in both channels to avoid "channel conflict" (discussed in Section 3.12).

Here we provide examples of two click-and-mortar strategies as used by some well-known companies: the transformation to click-and-mortar accomplished by retailer Circuit City and the alliance of virtual and traditional retailers Amazon.com and Toys R Us.

TRANSFORMATION TO CLICK-AND-MORTAR OPERATIONS: CIRCUIT CITY

Circuit City is the second-largest U.S. retailer of consumer electronics (behind BestBuy), operating about 650 stores located across the United States. Prior to the summer of 1999, Circuit City's Web site was largely a brochureware site, capable only of selling gift certificates. When Circuit City launched the new circuitcity.com in 1999, it already had some of the needed EC systems in place—the credit card authorization and inventory-management systems at its brick-and-mortar stores. However, linking the company's brick-and-mortar systems with the EC system was neither cheap nor easy. "It's safe to say that millions of dollars need to be spent to have a *Fortune* 500 kind of presence on the Web in a transactional way," indicated George Barr, Circuit City's director of Web development. "It's just not something you could do for $100,000" (Calem 2000).

A few features of the circuitcity.com site deserve special attention. First, the site educates customers about the various features and capabilities of different products, cutting through the jargon to help the customer understand why these features may be desirable and what the trade-offs are. In this personal and nonthreatening way, customers can gain valuable knowledge to assist them in the purchase decision. (Some consumers find shopping in the traditional brick-and-mortar Circuit City store to be intimidating because they do not understand the terms and product features discussed by store personnel.) Second, at the Web site, customers can perform powerful searches on a product database to help find the appropriate models to consider. Third, the site offers an extensive amount of information about electronics and other products, organized in a very flexible way. This assists buyers as they gather information before a purchase is made, whether or not they eventually buy from circuitcity.com. Visitors can select several product models and compare them by viewing a dynamically created table of purchase criteria, displayed side-by-side, with drill-down details if necessary.

Circuit City has engineered the online purchase to be smooth, secure, and seamless. Poor process design will scare off many customers. It has been reported that in other stores only 17 percent of all online purchase processes are completed, versus over 50 percent for Circuit City. Customers who abandon the purchase typically do so because of confusion and complexity, surprises (such as shipping costs), concerns about security and privacy of personal information, system errors, slow transmission speeds, and other factors.

Finally, the site's order fulfillment method is flexible. The customer is given three choices: (1) receive the purchase via common carrier with no sales tax but with a small shipping charge for 3-day delivery, (2) pay a larger shipping charge for overnight delivery, or (3) pick up the item at the nearby brick-and-mortar store and pay sales tax but no shipping, and thus have the item almost immediately. If the customer chooses the self-pickup, the customer prints a confirmation page and takes it to the front desk of the store, along with a picture ID. The customer can pick up a new purchase, such as a DVD player, in under 2 minutes.

ALLIANCE OF VIRTUAL AND TRADITIONAL RETAILERS: AMAZON.COM AND TOYS R US

In online toy retailing, eToys was the pioneer. However, as electronic orders increased, particularly during the peak holiday season, eToys was unable to meet its delivery requirements due to its limited logistics capability and poor demand forecasting. Price wars and high customer acquisition costs also caused problems for this e-tailer. Eventually, eToys closed, and its assets were sold to KB Toys and its Web channel, kbtoys.com.

Meanwhile, giant toy retailer Toys R Us, a competitor of KB Toys, had been unsuccessful in creating an independent e-tailing business. One solution seemed promising: an alliance between Toys R Us and Amazon.com. Amazon.com is known as a premier site for creating customer loyalty and for driving sales through its execution of CRM with efficient back-office order fulfillment systems. Toys R Us, backed by 40 years of toy-industry experience, is known for its broad product offerings and a deep understanding of the toys market, customer tastes, and suppliers. It has strong B2B supplier relationships and a well-developed inventory system.

Before the alliance with Toys R Us, Amazon.com had failed in the toy business because it lacked the strong B2B supplier relationships with toy manufacturers. It could not get the best toys from manufacturers and did not know how to manage inventory against product demand (Karpinski 2000). Toys R Us also had problems. It could not figure out how to effectively manage a direct-to-consumer distribution center or how to balance its retail-store business with its online business (Karpinski 2000).

During the 1999 Christmas season, before their alliance, both companies failed to profitably deliver toys on time. Amazon.com miscalculated inventory requirements and was left with millions of toys it had to write off. ToysRUs.com badly bungled the operations side by creating a Web site that was unable to handle large amounts of traffic and order shipping. ToysRUs.com could not execute its Web business effectively due to a lack of experience with both the front-end design and the back-end order fulfillment processes. As a result, that year 1 in 20 children failed to get presents from ToysRUs.com in time for Christmas. The company compensated customers with $100 customer discount coupons.

After bad press, lost business, and rebates to customers, these two companies decided to combine their efforts for 10 years, commencing with the 2000 Christmas season. They have pooled their expertise to form a single online toy store. The alliance allows the partners to leverage each other's core strengths (Schwartz 2000). Under the 10-year agreement, ToysRUs.com identifies, purchases, and manages inventory, using the parent company's clout to get the best lineup of toys. Because Amazon.com has a distribution network with plenty of excess capacity and a solid infrastructure, it is responsible for order fulfillment and customer service. Amazon.com applies its expertise in front-end site design, offering a powerful customer-support environment. Revenues are split between the two companies; the risks also are equally shared.

This is an innovative model. The two companies must coordinate disparate systems—operational, technological, and financial—as they merge their corporate cultures. If they succeed and execute this strategy successfully, this kind of partnership could be a prime model for the future of e-tailing. In the alliance's first Christmas season, things went "so-so"; in the second season, business was even better. E-commerce alliances are becoming very popular, and their usability is increasing (see Ernst et al. 2001).

Section 3.10 ▶ REVIEW

1. What motivates a brick-and-mortar company to offer Web services?
2. What customer services are provided by Circuit City on its Web site?
3. Describe the logic of the alliance between Amazon.com and ToysRUs.com.

3.11 PROBLEMS WITH E-TAILING AND LESSONS LEARNED

As the experiences of eToys and others indicate, e-tailing is no panacea. Some companies do not even try e-tailing. Reasons that retailers give for not going online include: product is not appropriate for Web sales, 47 percent; lack of significant opportunity, 24 percent; too expensive, 17 percent; technology not ready, 9 percent; online sales conflict with core business, 3 percent (Diorio 2002). Others try e-tailing but do not succeed. E-tailing offers some serious challenges and tremendous risks for those who fail to provide value to the consumer, who fail to establish a profitable business model, or who fail to execute the model they establish. The road to e-tail success is littered with dead companies that could not deliver on their promises. The shakeout from mid-2000 to early-2002 caused many companies to fail; others learned and adapted.

In Insights and Additions 3.2 (page 116) we provide a sample of failed B2C companies. Some enduring principles can be distilled from the failures, and these "lessons learned" are discussed next, following the Insights and Additions box. (Also, see Chapter 15 for further discussion.)

Insights and Additions 3.2   Failures of B2C Dot-Coms

During 2000–2001, more than 600 dot-coms folded in the United States and more than 1,000 folded worldwide. Here are some examples.

Kozmo.com. Kozmo.com was a creative idea for on-demand deliveries of movie rentals (and related items) to customer's doors. The problem was how to return the movies. Drop boxes for the returns were vandalized, volume was insufficient, competitors entered the market, and even an alliance with Starbucks (to host the drop boxes) and a large porn selection did not help. In addition, the company was sued for refusal to deliver to low-income neighborhoods. The company failed in 2001 after "burning" $250 million. (See Chapter 14 for the full story.)

Furniture.com. Selling furniture on the Internet may sound great. Furniture.com even paid $2.5 million for its domain name. Delivering the furniture was the problem. A number of manufacturers were not able to meet the delivery dates for the most popular items. In addition, many pieces of furniture cannot be delivered by UPS because of their size and weight. The cost of special deliveries was $200 to $300 per shipment, resulting in a loss. The company folded in 2001 after "burning" $75 million.

eRegister.com. Registering online for classes via an intermediary may sound interesting to investors, but not to customers. If a person wants to register to take a class at the YMCA or Weight Watchers, why not do it directly? The business model simply did not work, and the company folded in 2001.

Go.com. Go.com was a Disney portal site that was formed to manage Disney's Web sites and generate revenue from advertising. The business model did not work. To cover the salaries of its 400 employees, it was necessary for Go.com to sell 2 *billion* paid ad impressions per year. The company was able to sell only 1.6 million impressions. After losing $790 million in write-offs and $50 million in expenses, the site closed in February 2000. No amount of Disney magic helped.

Pets.com. Pets.com, a Web site devoted to selling pet food, pet toys, and pet supplies, operated in a very competitive market. This market competition forced Pets.com to advertise extensively and to sell goods below cost. The cost of acquiring customers mounted to $240 per new customer. Yet, being one of the early dot-com companies, it was able to buy a rival, Petstore.com, in 2000. After spending $147 million in less than 2 years, Pets.com had a lot of brand recognition, but not a real brand. After collapsing, its assets were sold to Petsmart.com, a click-and-mortar pet supplies retailer. At the same time, click-and-mortar Petco.com purchased Petopia.com, another B2C failure in the pet area.

Source: Compiled from Kaplan (2002).

WHAT LESSONS CAN WE LEARN FROM THESE FAILURES?

Painful as failures are, at least they can point out some valuable lessons. The following lessons can be drawn from the B2C dot-com failures in Insights and Additions 3.2.

Don't Ignore Profitability

One fundamental lesson is that each marginal sale should lead to a marginal profit. It has been said that in business, "If it doesn't make cents, it doesn't make sense." The trouble with most virtual e-tailers is that they lose money on every sale as they try to grow to a profitable size and scale. Amazon.com may generate about $5 per book order, but it still loses about $5.50 per sale on nonbook sales. Some e-tailers will have to adjust prices or refocus their market targets to concentrate on profitable sales.

Many pure-play e-tailers were initially funded by venture capital firms that provided enough financing to get the e-tailers started and growing. However, in many cases, the funding ran out before the e-tailer achieved sufficient size and maturity to break even and become self-sufficient. In some cases, the underlying cost and revenue models were not sound—the firms would never be profitable without major changes in their funding sources, revenue model, and controlled costs. Long-run success requires financial viability.

Manage New Risk Exposure

The Internet creates new connectivity with customers and offers the opportunity to expand markets. However, it also has the potential to expose a retailer to more sources of risk. Local companies have to contend only with local customers and local regulations, whereas national firms have more constituents with which to interact. Global firms have to contend with numerous cultural, financial, and other perspectives: Will they offend potential customers because of a lack of awareness of other cultures? Global Internet firms also have to manage their exposure to risk from the mosaic of international legal structures, laws, and regulations. For example, they can be sued in other countries for their business practices. (For further details, see Chapter 15.)

Groups of disgruntled employees or customers can band together to contact the news media, file a class action lawsuit, or launch their own Web site to publicize their concerns. One example of this is the walmartsucks.com, which was created by a customer who felt he was mistreated at one Wal-Mart store. He created a repository of all the negative news stories he could find about Wal-Mart and anecdotal accounts from fired employees and unhappy customers. Similar information about other corporations and government agencies is available at sucks500.com. When disgruntled individuals used to tell 50 to 100 friends and coworkers about their frustration, it may have resulted in a few lost sales; with the Internet, these people can now reach thousands or even millions of potential customers.

Watch the Cost of Branding

Branding has always been considered a key to retail success. Consumers are thought to be more willing to search out products with strong brand recognition, as well as pay a bit more for them. According to Dayal et al. (2000), Internet sites such as Amazon.com are putting established brands (e.g., traditional brick-and-mortar booksellers) at risk by creating quick brand recognition. However, in e-tailing, the drive to establish brand recognition quickly often leads to excessive spending. In one case, an upstart e-tailer (*epidemic.com*) spent over 25 percent of its venture capital funding on one 30-second television advertisement during the Super Bowl! The company folded a few months later (Carton and Locke 2001). In other cases, e-tailers offered extravagant promotions and loss-leading offers to drive traffic to their sites, and then lost money on every sale. The huge volume of site traffic merely served to increase their losses. The lesson from success stories is that most customers, especially long-term loyal customers, come to a Web site from affiliate links, search engines, or personal recommendations—not from Super Bowl ads.

Do Not Start with Insufficient Funds

It may seem obvious that a venture will not succeed if it lacks enough funds at the start, but many people are so excited about their business idea that they decide to try anyway. An example of this is the failure of Garden.com. Garden.com was a Web site that provided rich, dynamic gardening content (how to plant bulbs, tips on gardening, an "ask the expert" feature, etc.) and a powerful landscape design tool, which allowed a visitor to lay out an entire garden and then purchase all the necessary materials with one click. Garden.com also hosted various "community" features with discussions about various gardening-related topics. Gardeners are often passionate about their hobby and like to learn more about new plants and gardening techniques. The business idea sounded good. However, the site failed due to the company's inability to raise sufficient venture capital necessary to cover losses until enough business volume was reached.

The Web Site Must Be Effective

Today's savvy Internet shoppers expect Web sites to offer superior technical performance—fast page loads, quick database searches, streamlined graphics, and so forth. Web sites that delay or frustrate consumers will not experience a high sales volume because of a high percentage of abandoned purchases. We will see what functionalities are needed for effective sites in Online Chapter 18.

Keep It Interesting

Web sites without dynamic content will bore returning visitors. Static design is a turnoff. Today, most e-tailers offer valuable tips and information for consumers, who often come back just for that content and may purchase something in the process. L. L. Bean, for example, offers a rich database of information about parks and recreational facilities as well as its buying guides. Visitors who visit the site to find a campground or a weekend event may also purchase a tent or a raincoat.

Although there have been many e-tailing failures (mostly pure-play e-tailers, but some click-and-mortar companies or EC initiatives, too), there are many success stories. Many are described throughout this book and in Taylor and Terhune (2002). The successful case of a floral business is presented in EC Application Case W3.3. In general, whereas pure-play online retailing is risky and its future is not clear, online retailing is growing very rapidly as a complementary distribution channel to physical stores and mail-order catalogs. In other words, the click-and-mortar model appears to be winning.

Section 3.11 ▶ REVIEW

1. Why are virtual e-tailers usually not profitable?
2. Relate branding to profitability.
3. Why are technical performance and dynamic site content important?

3.12 ISSUES IN E-TAILING

DISINTERMEDIATION AND REINTERMEDIATION

In the traditional distribution channel, intermediating layers exist between the manufacturer and consumer, such as wholesalers, distributors, and retailers, as shown in part (a) of Exhibit 3.9. In some countries, such as Japan, one may find inefficient distribution networks with as many as 10 layers of intermediaries. These extra layers can add as much as a 500 percent markup to the

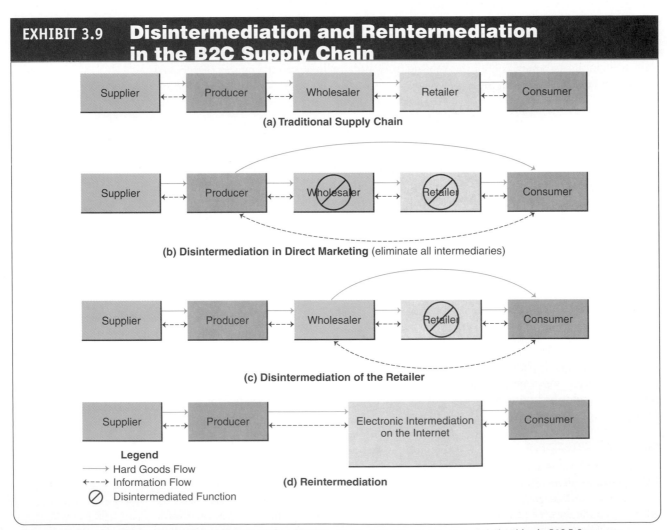

EXHIBIT 3.9   Disintermediation and Reintermediation in the B2C Supply Chain

(a) Traditional Supply Chain

(b) Disintermediation in Direct Marketing (eliminate all intermediaries)

(c) Disintermediation of the Retailer

(d) Reintermediation

Legend
→ Hard Goods Flow
←--→ Information Flow
⊘ Disintermediated Function

Source: Modified from Warkentin, M., et al. "The Role of Mass Customization in Enhancing Supply Chain Relationships in B2C E-Commerce Markets." *Journal of Electronic Commerce Research* 1, no. 2 (2000): 1–17.

manufacturers' prices. Intermediaries traditionally have provided trading infrastructure (such as a sales network), and they manage the complexity of matching buyers' and sellers' needs. However, the introduction of EC has resulted in the automation of many tasks provided by intermediaries. Does this mean that travel agents, real estate brokers (e.g., see Grant and Rich 2000), job agency employees, insurance agents, and other such jobs will disappear?

Using the Internet, manufacturers can sell directly to customers and provide customer support online. In this sense, the traditional intermediaries are eliminated, or disintermediated. Disintermediation refers to the removal of organizations or business process layers responsible for certain intermediary steps in a given supply chain. As shown in parts (b) and (c) of Exhibit 3.9, the manufacturer can bypass the wholesalers and retailers, selling directly to consumers.

However, consumers may have a problem of how to select the online vendors, vendors may have a problem of delivery to customers, and both may need an escrow service to ensure the transaction. Thus, new online assistance may be needed, and it may be provided by new or by the traditional intermediaries. In such cases, the traditional intermediaries fill new roles, providing *added value* and assistance. This process is referred to as reintermediation. It is pictured in part (d) of Exhibit 3.9. Thus, for the intermediary, the Internet offers new ways to reach new customers, new ways to bring value to customers, and perhaps new ways to generate revenues.

An example of reintermediation is that of Rosenbluth International (see the Real-World Case in Chapter 2). This travel company completely changed its business model by providing value-added services to its business customers. At a time when many travel agencies were losing their role as intermediaries, Rosenbluth was able to survive, and even prosper, by using EC-based reintermediation business models.

Bloch et al. (1996) think that the intermediary's role will shift to one that emphasizes value-added services such as assisting customers in comparison shopping from multiple sources, providing total solutions by combining services from several vendors, and providing certifications and trusted third-party control and evaluation systems. For instance, in the world of online new and used car sales, electronic intermediaries assist buyers and/or sellers. These are new *reintermediaries*, namely intermediaries that have restructured their role in the purchase process.

As an example of reintermediation, certain intermediaries are selling cars to consumers without the involvement of traditional car dealers. Some of these sites include Kelly Blue Book (kbb.com), which offers pricing information for consumers, Edmunds (edmunds.com), which gives consumers information about the dealer's true costs, Carfax (carfax.com), which will research a specific used car and tell you if it has ever been in an accident or had an odometer rollback, and iMotors (imotors.com), which gives members discounts on insurance, gas, and repairs. Additionally, "lead services" direct buyers to member dealers and, in some cases, also offer direct sales of new cars. The leading site in this category is autobytel.com, others include carsdirect.com (Amazon.com's partner), autoweb.com, and cars.com.

Some reintermediaries are newcomers, rivaling the traditional retail stores, whereas others are additional operations established by the traditional retailers or intermediaries, such as Edmunds, who do both the old and the new intermediation (like click-and-mortar). Some reintermediaries cooperate with manufacturers or retailers to provide a needed service to the seller or distributor in the online environment. Other reintermediaries are virtual e-tailers that fill a unique niche. Intermediaries such as online retailers (e.g., amazon.com) and shopping portals can also act as reintermediaries. The evolution and operation of these companies is critical to the success of e-commerce.

Cybermediation

In addition to reintermediation, there is a completely new role in EC called cybermediation, or electronic intermediation. These terms describe special Web sites that use intelligent agents to facilitate intermediation. Cybermediators can perform many roles in EC. To illustrate the diversity of such roles, Giaglis et al. (1999) examined the market functions listed in Exhibit 3.10 (page 120) and found that cybermediation can affect most market functions. For example, intelligent agents can find when and where an item that a consumer wants will be auctioned. The matching services described in this chapter are done by *cybermediator*

disintermediation
The removal of organizations or business process layers responsible for certain intermediary steps in a given supply chain.

reintermediation
The process whereby intermediaries (either new ones or those that had been disintermediated) take on new intermediary roles.

cybermediation (electronic intermediation)
The use of software (intelligent) agents to facilitate intermediation.

EXHIBIT 3.10 Opportunities and Threats to Intermediaries in Electronic Markets

Market Function	Electronic Market Influence	Likely Effects on Intermediation
Determination of product offerings	Personalization of products Aggregation Disaggregation	Disintermediation (especially in digital products) Cybermediation (aggregators) Disintermediation (pay-per-use)
Searching	Lower search costs More complex search requirements Lower barriers to entry	Disintermediation Cybermediation Cybermediation/Reintermediation
Price discovery	Redistribution of mechanisms New markets	Cybermediation/Reintermediation Cybermediation
Logistics	Lower logistical costs Economics of scale	Disintermediation Reintermediation
Settlement	New cost structures New payment mechanisms	Reintermediation Cybermediation/Reintermediation
Trust	Increased protection requirements	Cybermediation/Reintermediation
Legal and regulatory	Institutional support for electronic markets	Reintermediation

Source: Compiled from Giaglis, G. M., Klein, S., and O'Keefe, R. M. "The Role of Intermediaries in Electronic Marketplaces: Developing a Contingency Model," *Information Systems Journal* 12:3 (2002): pp. 231–246. Courtesy of Blackwell Publishing.

agents. Cybermediator agents also conduct price comparisons of insurance policies, long-distance calls, and other services. Cybermediation services are spreading rapidly around the globe (Vandermerwe 1999; Berghel 2000; Kauffman et al. 2000).

Hypermediation

hypermediation
Extensive use of both human and electronic intermediation to provide assistance in all phases of an e-commerce venture.

In some cases, EC transactions require extensive human and electronic intermediation. Many EC applications require content providers, security services, affiliate sites, search engines, portals, ISPs, software makers, escrow services, and more. A large e-tailer, such as Amazon.com, for example, uses all of these services, and also employs auction services, payments services, logistics support, and more. This phenomenon is called **hypermediation**, meaning extensive use of new types of intermediation. According to Carr (2000), hypermediation runs opposite to disintermediation, providing intermediaries with a chance to profit from EC.

Unbundling

An EC application may have another impact that is related to disintermediation and reintermediation. Bauer and Colgan (2002) call this impact *unbundling*. According to this concept, old economy processes will be broken into specialized segments that can be delivered by specialized intermediaries. For example, in the financial services industry, buying a stock may be done in five separate segments: information gathering, trade ordering, execution, settlement, and account keeping. As a result of unbundling the processes, the specialized services that are offered can be executed in small segments better, faster, and more efficiently. This trend for specialization also was described by Hagel and Singer (1999.)

CHANNEL CONFLICT

Many traditional retailers establish a new marketing channel when they start selling online. Similarly, some manufacturers have instituted direct marketing initiatives in parallel with their established channels of distribution, such as retailers or dealers. In such cases, channel conflict may occur. **Channel conflict** refers to any situation in which the online marketing channel upsets the traditional channels due to real or perceived damage from competition.

Another type of marketing conflict may occur between the online and off-line departments of the same company. For example, the online department may want to offer lower prices and have more online advertising than the off-line department offers. The off-line department wants the opposite. Because the two departments are competing in different markets, they need different strategies. The conflict occurs when corporate resources are limited and an action by one department may be at the expense of another. Staff conflict also may occur, as staff members want to join the new, future-oriented, online department, and those in the off-line department feel left behind. Finally, a price conflict may occur.

channel conflict
Situation in which an online marketing channel upsets the traditional channels due to real or perceived damage from competition.

DETERMINING THE RIGHT PRICE

Pricing a product or service on the Internet, especially by a click-and-mortar company, is complicated. On one hand, prices need to be competitive on the Internet. Today's comparison engines will show the consumer the prices at many stores, for almost all commodity products. On the other hand, prices should be in line with the corporate policy on profitability, and in a click-and-mortar company, in line with the off-line channel's pricing strategy. To avoid price conflict, some companies created independent online subsidiaries.

Baker et al. (2001) maintain that EC offers companies new opportunities to test prices, segment customers, and adjust to changes in supply and demand. The authors argue that companies are not taking advantage of these opportunities. Companies can make prices more precise (optimal prices), they can be more adaptable to changes in the environment, and they can be more creative and accurate regarding different prices to different segments. In addition, in one-to-one marketing (Chapter 4), a company can have personalized prices. (For more on pricing strategies as they relate to different business models, see Bandyopadhyay et al. 2001.)

PERSONALIZATION

One significant characteristic of many online marketing business models is the ability of the seller to create an element of *personalization* for each individual consumer. For example, an e-tailer can use cookie files and other technologies to track the specific browsing and buying behavior of each consumer. With that information, the e-tailer can create a marketing plan tailored to that consumer's pattern by showing items of interest, offering incentives that appeal to that consumer's sense of value, or providing certain services that will attract that consumer back to the Web site. The Internet also allows for easy self-configuration ("design it your way"). This creates a large demand for personalized products and services. Manufacturers can meet that demand by using a *mass customization* strategy. As indicated earlier, many companies offer customized products from their Web sites.

Although pure-play e-tailing is risky, and its future is unclear, e-tailing is growing rapidly as a complementary distribution channel to traditional stores and catalogs. In other words, the *click-and-mortar model currently is winning*.

Section 3.12 ▶ REVIEW

1. Define disintermediation.
2. Describe mediation issues, including disintermediation, reintermediation, cybermediation, hypermediation, and unbundling.
3. Describe channel and other conflicts that may appear in e-tailing.
4. Describe price determination in e-tailing.
5. Explain personalization and mass customization opportunities in e-tailing.

MANAGERIAL ISSUES

Some managerial issues related to this chapter are as follows.

1. **Should we grab a first-mover advantage or wait and learn?** It has often been suggested that the first firm to enter a new marketspace and sell products online in that category will be able to dominate that niche by establishing its brand and becoming the recognized seller. This is known as the "first-mover advantage," and it does seem to apply in certain categories. For example, Amazon.com was the first major online bookseller, and despite strong competition, it remains the most recognized Web site for online consumer purchases of books. However, in many cases, the "first-to-market" firms make many mistakes, and if they are not agile enough to adapt to the market or other conditions, they may fail, leaving room for the "second-to-market" firms to rush in and attract the online customers who leave the first mover.

   In many cases, the second-mover firm or firms can learn from the initial company's mistakes and avoid the expense and losses associated with those mistakes. If the first mover makes a strategic mistake that upsets buyers, such as failure to ship items in a timely way or violation of their customers' privacy, the buyers will look for another, similar e-tailer. (See Chapter 15 for further discussion.)

2. **What should our strategic position be?** The most important decision for retailers and e-tailers is the overall *strategic position* they establish within their market. What niche will they fill? What business functions will they execute internally and which functions will be outsourced? What partners will they use? How will they integrate brick-and-mortar facilities with their online presence? What are their revenue sources in the short and long run, and what are their fixed and marginal costs? An e-business is still a business and must establish solid business practices in the long run in order to ensure profitability and viability.

3. **Are we financially viable?** The collapse of the dot-com bubble that started in early 2000 provided a wake-up call to many e-tailers. Some pursued a return to business fundamentals, whereas others sought to redefine their business plan in terms of click-and-mortar strategies or alliances with traditional retailers (as Amazon.com did with Toys R Us). Because most easy sources of funding have dried up and revenue models are being scrutinized, many e-tailers are also pursuing new partners, and consolidation will continue until there is greater stability within the e-tail segment. Ultimately, there will likely be a smaller number of larger sellers with comprehensive sites and many smaller, specialized niche sites.

4. **Should we recruit out of town?** Out-of-town recruitment can be an important source of skilled workers. Using video teleconferencing, recruiters can interview potential employees from a distance. Aptitude tests also can be taken from a distance. Furthermore, for many jobs, companies can use telecommuters. This could be a major strategy in the twenty-first century. However, online recruiting may result in too many irrelevant resumes and wasted time.

5. **Are there international legal issues regarding online recruiting?** Various international legal issues must be considered with online recruiting. For example, online recruitment of people from other countries may be complicated. The validity of contracts signed in different countries must be checked by legal experts.

6. **Do we have ethics and privacy guidelines?** Ethical issues are extremely important in an agentless system. In traditional systems, human agents play an important role in assuring the ethical behavior of buyers and sellers. Will ethics and the rules of etiquette be sufficient to guide behavior on the Internet? Only time will tell. For example, as job-applicant information travels over the Internet, security and privacy become even more important. It is management's job to make sure that information from applicants is secure. Also, e-tailers need to establish guidelines for protecting the privacy of customers who visit their Web sites.

7. **How will intermediaries act in cyberspace?** It will take a few years before the new roles of Internet intermediaries will be stabilized, as well as their fees. Also, the emergence of support services, such as escrow services in global EC, will have an impact on intermediaries and their role.

8. **Should we set up alliances?** Alliances for online initiatives are spreading rapidly. For example, in Hong Kong, four banks created a joint online e-bank (to save on capital costs and share the risk). Some online trading brokers are teaming up with banks. Banks are teaming up with telecommunications companies, software companies, and even airlines. Finally, six of the largest music retailers created a joint company (named Echo) to sell music that can be downloaded from the Web (Patsuris 2003).

SUMMARY

In this chapter, you learned about the following EC issues as they relate to the learning objectives.

1. **The scope of e-tailing.** E-tailing, the online selling of products and services, is growing rapidly. Computers, software, and electronics are the major items sold online. Books, CDs, toys, office supplies, and other standard commodities also sell well. More successful are services sold online, such as airline tickets and travel services, stocks, and insurance.

2. **E-tailing business models.** The major e-tailing business models can be classified by distribution channel—a manufacturer or mail-order company selling direct to consumers, pure-play (virtual) e-tailing, a click-and-mortar strategy with both online and traditional channels, and online malls that provide either referring directories or shared services.

3. **How online travel/tourism services operate.** Most services available through a physical travel agency are also available online. In addition, customers get much more information, much more quickly through online resources. Customers can even receive bids from travel providers. Finally, travelers can compare prices, participate in auctions and chat rooms, and view videos and maps.

4. **The online job market and its benefits.** The online job market is growing rapidly, with thousands and thousands of jobs matched with job seekers each year. The major benefits of online job markets are the ability to reach a large number of job seekers at low cost, to provide detailed information online, to take applications, and even to conduct tests. Also, using intelligent agents, resumes can be checked and matches made more quickly. Millions of job offers posted on the Internet help job seekers, who also can post their resumes for recruiters.

5. **The electronic real estate market.** The online real estate market is basically supporting rather than replacing existing agents. However, both buyers and sellers can save time and effort in the electronic market. Buyers can purchase distant properties much more easily and in some places have access to less expensive services. Eventually, commissions on regular transactions are expected to decline as a result of the electronic market for real estate, and more sales "by owner" will materialize.

6. **Online trading of stocks and bonds.** One of the fastest growing online businesses is the online trading of securities. It is inexpensive, convenient, and supported by a tremendous amount of financial and advisory information. Trading is very fast and efficient, almost fully automated, and moving toward 24/7 global trading. However, security breaches could occur, so tight protection is a must.

7. **Cyberbanking and personal finance.** Branch banking is on the decline due to less expensive, more convenient online banking. The world is moving toward online banking; today, most routine banking services can be done from home. Banks can reach customers in remote places, and customers can bank with faraway institutions. This makes the financial markets more efficient. Online personal finance applications, such as bill paying, tracking of accounts, and tax preparation, also are very popular.

8. **On-demand delivery service.** On-demand delivery service is needed when items are perishable or when delivering medicine, express documents, or urgently needed supplies. One example of on-demand delivery is e-groceries; these may be ordered online and are shipped or ready for store pickup within 24 hours or even less.

9. **Delivery of digital products.** Anything that can be digitized can be successfully delivered online. Delivery of digital products such as music, software, movies, and other entertainment online has been a success. Some print media, such as electronic versions of magazines or electronic books (see Chapter 9), also are having success when digitized and delivered electronically.

10. **Aiding consumer purchase decisions.** Purchase decision aids include shopping portals, shopbots and comparison agents, business rating sites, trust verification sites, and other tools.

11. **Critical success factors.** Critical success factors for direct online sales to consumers and e-tailing are managing risk properly; using correct business models; creating a profitable; effective, and interesting site; and watching operating costs. Also, sufficient cash flow is critical, as is appropriate customer acquisition.

12. **Disintermediation and reintermediation.** Direct electronic marketing by manufacturers results in disintermediation by removing wholesalers and retailers. However, online reintermediaries provide additional value, such as helping consumers make selections among multiple products and vendors. Traditional retailers may feel threatened or pressured when manufacturers decide to sell online; such direct selling can cause channel conflict. Pricing of online and off-line products and services is one issue that always needs to be addressed.

KEY TERMS

DISCUSSION QUESTIONS

1. What are the success factors of Amazon.com? Is its decision not to limit its sales to books, music, and movies, but to offer a much broader selection of items, a good marketing strategy? With the broader selection, do you think the company will dilute its brand or extend the value proposition to its customers? (Read Bayers 2002; available online at business2.com.)

2. Compare the major e-tail business models.

3. Will direct marketing of automobiles be a successful strategy? How should the dealers' inventory and the automakers' inventory and manufacturing scheduling be coordinated to meet a specific order with a quick due date?

4. Discuss the advantages of established click-and-mortar companies such as Wal-Mart over pure-play e-tailers such as Amazon.com. What are the disadvantages of click-and-brick retailers as compared with pure-play e-tailers?

5. Discuss the advantages of an online partnership such as that of Amazon.com and Toys R Us. Are there any disadvantages?

6. Discuss the advantages of shopping aids to the consumer. Should a vendor provide a comparison tool on its site that will show that a competitor is cheaper? Why or why not?

7. Discuss the advantages of a specialized e-tailer, such as dogtoys.com. Can such a store survive in the physical world? Why or why not?

8. Discuss the benefits of build-to-order to buyers and sellers. Are there any disadvantages?

9. Why are online travel services a popular Internet application? Why do so many Web sites provide free travel information?

10. Compare the advantages and disadvantages of online stock trading with off-line trading.

11. It is said that the service Zuji.com provides to travel agents will lead to their reintermediation. Discuss.

12. Intelligent agents read resumes and forward them to potential employers without the knowledge of the candidates. What are the benefits of this use of intelligent agents? Do they violate the privacy of job seekers?

13. Online employment services make it easy to change jobs; therefore, turnover rates may increase. This could result in total higher costs for employers because of increased costs for recruiting and training new employees and the need to pay higher salaries and wages to attract or keep employees. What can companies do to ease this problem?

14. How can brokerage houses offer very low commissions for online stock purchases (as low as $4 per trade, with some even offering no commission for certain trades)? Why would they choose to offer such low commissions? Over the long run, do you expect commissions to increase or continue to decrease?

15. Explain what is meant by the statement, "Intermediaries will become knowledge providers rather than transaction providers."

16. Compare the advantages and disadvantages of distributing digitizable products electronically versus physically.

INTERNET EXERCISES

1. Visit peapod.com (now at stopandshop.com) and netgrocer.com. Compare the products and services offered by the two companies and evaluate their chances for success. Why do you think "unattended delivery" e-grocers such as shoplink.com failed?

2. Many consumer portals offer advice and ratings of products or e-tailers. Identify and examine two separate general-consumer portals that look at other sites and

compare prices or other purchase criteria. Try to find and compare prices for a digital camera, a microwave oven, and an MP3 player. Summarize your experience. Comment on the strong and weak points of such shopping tools.

3. Design a trip to Kerala, India (use stayfinder.com). Find accommodations, restaurants, health clubs, festival information, and art. Arrange a tour for two people for 7 days. How much will it cost?

4. Almost all car manufacturers allow consumers to configure their car online. Visit a major automaker's Web site and configure a car of your choice (e.g., jaguar.com). Also visit one electronic intermediary (e.g., autobytel.com). After you decide what car you want, examine the payment options and figure your monthly payments. Print your results. How does this process compare to visiting an auto dealer? Do you think you found a better price online? Would you consider buying a car this way?

5. Visit amazon.com and identify at least three specific elements of its personalization and customization features. Browse specific books on one particular subject, leave the site, and then go back and revisit the site. What do you see? Are these features likely to encourage you to purchase more books in the future from Amazon.com? List the features and discuss how they may lead to increased sales. Now visit Amazon zShops (go to amazon.com and click on zShops) to identify and compare three sellers of food and beverages. Can you find items not normally available in your local grocery store?

6. Use a statistics source (e.g., jmm.com, emarketer.com, or cyberatlas.com) and look for recent statistics about the growth of Internet-based consumer-oriented EC in your country and in three other countries. Where is the greatest growth occurring? Which countries have the largest total e-tail sales? Which countries have the highest per-capita participation (the "penetration rate")? What are the forecasts for continued growth in the coming years?

7. Visit landsend.com and prepare a customized order for a piece of clothing. Describe the process. Do you think this will result in better-fitting clothing? Do you think this personalization feature will lead to greater sales volume for Lands' End?

8. Make your resume accessible to millions of people. Consult asktheheadhunter.com for help in rewriting your resume. See jobweb.com for ideas about planning your career. Get prepared for a job interview (hotjobs.com). Also, use wageweb.com to determine what salary you can get in the city of your choice in the United States.

9. Visit homeowner.com, decisionaide.com, or a similar site and compute the monthly mortgage payment on a 30-year loan at 7.5 percent fixed interest. Also check current interest rates. Estimate your closing costs on a $200,000 loan. Compare the monthly payments of the fixed rate with that of an adjustable rate for the first year. Finally, compute your total payments if you take the loan for 15 years at the going rate. Compare it to a 30-year mortgage. Comment on the difference.

10. Access the Virtual Trader game at citycomment.co.uk and register for the Internet stock game. You will be bankrolled with £100,000 in a trading account every month. You can also play investment games at investorsleague.com, fantasystockmarket.com, and etrade.com.

11. Enter etrade.com and boom.com and find out how you can trade stocks in countries other than the one you live in. Prepare a report based on your findings.

12. Enter wellsfargo.com and examine its global and B2B services. For each service that is offered, comment on the advantages of conducting it online versus off-line.

13. Examine the consolidated billing process. Start with e-billingonline.com, and intuit.com. Identify other contenders in the field. What standard capabilities do they all offer? What capabilities are unique to certain sites?

14. Compare the price of a Sony digital camera at dealtime.com, mysimon.com, bottomdollar.com, and pricescan.com. Which site locates the best deal?

15. Enter spyonit.com and create three "spies" for areas of your interest. Also, use two of the existing spies. Prepare a report on your experience. Then create a Yahoo alert. Compare the two services.

TEAM ASSIGNMENTS AND ROLE PLAYING

1. Each team will investigate the services of the online car selling sites in the following list. When teams have finished, they should bring their research together and discuss their findings.
   a. Buying new cars through an intermediary (autobytel.com, carsdirect.com, autoweb.com, or amazon.com).
   b. Buying used cars (autotrader.com).
   c. Buying used cars for auto dealers (manheim.com).
   d. Automobile ratings sites (carsdirect.com, auto invoices.com, and fueleconomy.gov).
   e. Car-buying portals (thecarportal.com and cars.com).
   f. Sites where antique cars can be purchased (classic cars.com and antiquecars.com).

2. Each team will represent a broker-based area (e.g., real estate, insurance, stocks, job finding). Each team will find a new development that has occurred in the assigned area over the most recent 3 months. Look for the site vendor's announcement and search for more information on the development with google.com or another search engine. Examine the business news at bloomberg.

com. After completing your research, as a team, prepare a report on disintermediation in your assigned area.

3. Airline sites (e.g., aa.com) and consortia (e.g., orbitz. com) are competing with Travelocity, Expedia, and other online travel agents. Research several of these sites (each team will examine one) and analyze the competitive advantage of the airlines over the online agents. Prepare a report based on your findings. Make a presentation that will predict a winner from among the following: airline sites, travel agencies, consortia, or online sites such as Expedia.

REAL-WORLD CASE

WAL-MART GOES ONLINE

Wal-Mart is the largest retailer in the world with over 2,700 stores in the United States and about 750 stores in other countries. Its standard company cheer ends with, "Who's number one? The customer." Wal-Mart has established itself as a master of the retail process by streamlining its supply chain process and undercutting competitors with low prices. However, one problem with its strategy for growing online sales is the demographics of its primary customer base. Wal-Mart's target demographic is households with $25,000 in annual income, whereas the median income of online consumers is perhaps $60,000.

Despite these demographics, online sales (primarily in music, travel, and electronics) through *walmart.com* already account for about 10 percent of Wal-Mart's U.S. sales. One way that its long-time chief rival, Kmart, Inc., tried to attract its demographic audience to its Web site *kmart.com* was to offer free Internet access. This appealed to its cost-conscious, lower-income constituency, and also provided the opportunity for those customers to access the site to conduct purchases. However, this move decreased company profits in the short run and was one of the factors that led Kmart to file for bankruptcy in 2002.

Wal-Mart also has concerns about cannibalizing its in-store sales. Its 2001 alliance with AOL was designed to provide cobranded $9.94/month Internet access to dwellers in both very rural and very urban areas, where there are no nearby Wal-Mart stores. The intent is to lure new market segments and thus cancel the effect of cannibalization. Ultimately, a hybrid e-tailer that can offer a combination of huge selection with the click-and-mortar advantages of nearby stores (e.g., merchandise pickup or returns) may prove to be the 800-pound gorilla of online consumer sales.

In 2002, *walmart.com* matured, offering order status and tracking, a help desk, a clear return policy and mechanisms, a store locator, and information on special sales and liquidations. Also, community services such as photo sharing are provided.

Sources: Maguire 2002 and walmart.com 2002–2003.

Questions

1. Compare *walmart.com* with *amazon.com*. What features do the sites have in common? Which are unique to Wal-Mart.com? To Amazon.com?

2. Will Wal-Mart.com become the dominant e-tailer in the world, replacing Amazon.com? What factors would contribute to its success in the online marketplace? What factors would detract from its ability to dominate online sales the way it has been able to dominate physical retail sales in many markets?

3. Perform a strategic analysis of *walmart.com*. Who are its competitors, customers, and suppliers? What is its relative strength or power in each of these relationships? What is its distinctive competence? How much of its strength is borrowed from its knowledge of physical stores?

4. Visit *walmart.com*, *target.com*, *marksandspencer. com*, and *sears.com*. Identify the common features of their online marketing and at least one unique feature evident at each site. Do these sites have to distinguish themselves primarily in terms of price, product selection, or Web site features?

REFERENCES

Agrawal, M., et al. "The False Promise of Mass Customization." *The McKinsey Quarterly* no. 3 (2001).

Baker, W. L., et al. "Getting Prices Right on the Web." *The McKinsey Quarterly* no. 2 (2001).

Bandyopadhyay, S., et al. "A Critical Review of Pricing Strategies for Online Business Models." *Quarterly Journal of Electronic Commerce* 2, no. 1 (2001).

Bank of America. free-online-banking-internet-checking. com/security.html (accessed April 2003).

Bauer, C., and J. Colgan. "The Internet As a Driver for Unbundling: A Transaction Perspective from the Stockbroking Industry." *Electronic Markets* 12, no. 2 (2002): 130–134.

Bayers, C. "The Last Laugh (of Amazon's CEO)." *Business 2.0*, September 2002.

BBC News. "South Korea Probes Online Dealing Fraud." August 26, 2002, news.bbc.co.uk/2/hi/business/2217584. stm (accessed April 2003).

Berghel, H. "Predatory Disintermediation." *Communications of the ACM* 43, no. 5 (2000): 23–29.

Bloch, M., and A. Segev. "The Impact of Electronic Commerce on the Travel Industry." *Proceedings 30th Annual HICSS*, Maui, HI, January 1997.

Bloch, M., et al. "Leveraging Electronic Commerce for Competitive Advantage: A Business Value Framework." *Proceedings of the Ninth International EC Conference*, Bled, Slovenia, June 1996.

Borland, J., "Napster CEO Touts New Swapping Service." *News.com*, January 9, 2002, news.com.com/ 2100-1023-806886.html (accessed April 2003).

Bose, K. "Intelligent Agents Framework for Developing Knowledge-Based DSS for Collaborative Organizational Processes." *Expert Systems with Applications* 11, no. 3 (1996).

Brice, T., and M. Waung. "Web Site Recruitment Characteristics: America's Best Versus America's Biggest." *SAM Advanced Management Journal* 67, no. 1 (2002).

Business Times Online. "Infinite Possibilities." January 16, 2003, business-times.asia1.com.sg/sub/supplement/ story/0,4574,64197,00.html (accessed April 2003).

Calem, R. E. "Deal Clinchers: How to Get from Brochureware to Online Business." *Industry Standard*, February 14, 2000.

Camacho, D., et al. "Intelligent Travel Planning: A MultiAgent Planning System to Solve Web Problems in the e-Tourism Domain." *Autonomous Agents and Multi-Agent Systems* no. 4 (2001).

Carr, N. G. "Hypermediation: Commerce as Clickstream." *Harvard Business Review* (January–February 2000).

Carton, W., and C. Locke. *Dot.Bomb.* New York: McGraw-Hill, 2001.

Castex, S. "Trends and News." *Promotional Products Business*, July 2002, ppai.org/Publications/PPB/Article.asp? NewsID=1436 (accessed April 2003).

cattoys.com (accessed October 2002).

Computerworld Hong Kong, January 14, 1999.

Cude, B. J., and M. A. Morganosky. "Online Grocery Shopping: An Analysis of Current Opportunities and Future Potential." *Consumer Interests* 46, 2000, consumerinterests.org/public/articles/online.PDF (accessed April 2003).

Daisey, M. *21 Dog Years: Doing Time @ Amazon.com.* New York: Free Press, 2002.

Dayal, S., et al. "Building Digital Brands." *The McKinsey Quarterly* no. 2 (2000).

Dewan, R., and A. Seidmann (eds.). "Current Issues in E-Banking." *Communications of the ACM* 44, no. 6 (2001): 31–32.

Diorio, S. *Beyond "e."* New York: McGraw-Hill, 2002.

Dixon, P. *Job Searching Online for Dummies.* Foster City, CA: IDG Books, 2001.

Dymond, C. "High-Tech Spin on Sales." *Financial Times*, June 29–30, 2002.

Economics and Statistics Administration. "U.S. Department of Commerce News." *U.S. Census Bureau*, revised February 24, 2003, census.gov/mrts/www/current.html (accessed April 2003).

eMarketer Daily. October 2, 2002.

Ernst, D., et al. "A Future for E-alliances." *McKinsey Quarterly* no. 2 (2001).

Ernst, S., and N. H. Hooker. "E-Grocery: Emerging Trend or Just Another Case Study?" The Ohio State University Outlook Policy Program, 2003, agecon.ag.ohio-state.edu/ programs/e-agbiz/Papers&Presentations/2003% 20Outlook.E-Grocery.pdf (accessed June 2003).

Forbes/eMarketer. "Online Advertising Update." white paper, March 2002, forbes.com/fdc/emarketer.pdf (accessed April 2003).

Giaglis, G. M., et al. "Disintermediation, Reintermediation, or Cybermediation." *Proceedings of the Twelfth International EC Conference*, Bled, Slovenia, June 1999.

Gilbert, J., et al. *Online Investment Bible.* Berkeley, CA: Hungry Minds, Inc., 2000.

Gosling, P. *Changing Money: How the Digital Age Is Transforming Financial Services.* Dulles, VA: Capital Books, Inc., 2000.

Grant, P., and M. Rich. "Goldman's Real-Estate Web Site Bypasses Traditional Brokers." *The Asia Wall Street Journal*, April 14–15, 2000.

Hagel, J. I., and M. Singer. "Unbundling the Corporation." *Harvard Business Review* (March–April 1999).

Harrington, A. "Can Anyone Build a Better Monster?" *Fortune*, May 13, 2002.

Harteveldt, H. H. et al. "Travel October 2002 Data Overview: Covers U.S. Leisure Forecasts, Web Travel Winners, Brand Loyalty, and Channel Use." *Consumer Technographics Report Forrester.com*, October 2002, forrester.com/ER/Research/DataOverview/Summary/ 0,2740,14530,00.html (accessed April 2003).

Helft, M. "What a Long, Strange Trip It's Been for Webvan." *The Industry Standard*, July 23, 2001. thestandard. com/article/0,1902,27911,00.html?body_page=3 (accessed April 2003).

IBM. "Safeway Stores Puts Grocery Shopping in the Palm of Your Hands with IBM Built, Java-Based Easi-Order Solution." *IBM Success Story*, www-3.ibm.com/ software/ success/cssdb.nsf/CS/KLKR-4BB3R3?Open Document&Site=default (accessed October 2002).

Internet Times. "Survey: Nine Out of Ten Want to Pay Bills on Internet." November 15, 1998. investor.officedepot.com/ireye/ir_site.zhtml?ticker=odp&script=411&layout=;7&item_id=382135 (accessed April 2003).

Joo, J. "A Business Model and Its Development Strategies for Electronic Tourism Markets." *Information System Management* (Summer 2002): 58–62.

Jupiter Research. "Jupiter Consumer Survey." *Jupiter Research*, September 30, 2002, jupiterresearch.com/jupres_onlineshopper.html (accessed April 2003).

Kaplan, P. J. *The F'd Companies: Spectacular Dot.Com Flameouts.* New York: Simon & Schuster, 2002.

Karpinski, R. "E-Business Risk Worth Taking on Path to Success." *B to B 85*, August 28, 2000.

Kauffman, R., et al. "Analyzing Information Intermediaries in Electronic Brokerage." *Proceedings of the Thirty-third HICSS*, Maui, HI, January 2000.

Keh, H., and E. Shieh. "Online Grocery Retailing: Success Factors and Potential Pitfalls." *Business Horizons*, July–August 2001, 73–83.

Keizer, G. "Travel Web Sites: Just the Ticket?" *PC World*, July 2002.

Kruger, J. Interview by Merrill Warkentin, September 13, 2000.

landsend.com (accessed October 2002 and April 2003).

Lawrence, R. B., et al. "Alternative Channels of Distribution E-Commerce Strategies for Industrial Manufacturers." *Production and Inventory Management Journal* (Third/Fourth Quarter 2001).

Lee, L. "Tricks of E*Trade." *Business Week*, February 7, 2000, 36–45.

Lee, M. K. O. *Internet Retailing in Hong Kong China.* City University of Hong Kong, 2001.

Loizos, C. "Card Sharks." *Business 2.0*, November 28, 2000, 197–207

MacSweeney, G. "Dual Strategy." *Insurance and Technology* (July 2000).

Maguire, J. "Case Study: Walmart.com." *Internet.com*, November 15, 2002, ecommerce.internet.com/news/insights/trends/article/0,,10417_1501651,00.html (accessed June 2003).

Nichols, P. "Study Predicts Boom in Online Grocery Shopping." *Internet.com*, January 21, 1998, www.internetnews.com/ec-news/article.php/25251 (accessed April 2003).

Patsuris, P. "Music Chains Raise the Volume on Downloads." *Forbes.com*, January 27, 2003, forbes.com/2003/01/27/cx_pp_0127music.html. (accessed June 2003).

Peffers, K., and V. K. Tunnainen. "Expectations and Impacts of a Global Information System: The Case of a Global Bank from Hong Kong." *Journal of Global Information Technology Management* 1, no. 4 (1998).

Pew Internet Project. "Online Job Hunting: A Pew Internet Project Data Memo." July 17, 2002, pewinternet.org/releases/release.asp?id=46 (accessed April 2003).

Rafter, M. V. "Trust or Bust?" *Industry Standard*, March 6, 2000.

Reda, S. "On-Line Retail Grows Up." *Stores*, February 2002, 30–34.

Retail Forward. "Top 50 E-Retailers." *E-Retail Intelligence Program*, July 2002, retailforward.com/freecontent/pressreleases/press48.asp (accessed April 2003).

Rich, M. "Your Reservation Has Been Cancelled." *Wall Street Journal Europe*, June 14–16, 2002.

Sales, R. "Electronic FX: Reality or Just a Smoke Screen?" *Wall Street and Technology*, April 2002, 16–17.

Sandoval, G. "Amazon: How Big Can It Get?" *CNET News.com*, June 25, 2002, news.com.com/2100-1017-823319.html (accessed April 2003).

Schonfeld, E. "Schwab—Put It All Online." *Fortune*, December 7, 1998.

Schwartz, E. "Amazon, Toys R Us in E-Commerce Tie-Up." *InfoWorld* 22 (August 14, 2000).

Simison, R. L. "GM Retools to Sell Custom Cars Online." *Wall Street Journal*, February 22, 2000.

Slater, D. "Car Wars." *CIO Magazine*, September 15, 1999, cio.com/archive/091599_auto_content.html (accessed April 2003).

Stanford, M. "Mortgage Banking: Internet and Integration Are Key." *IEEE IT Professional* 4, no. 2 (2002): 47–52.

Standing, C., and T. Vasudavan. "The Impact of Electronic Commerce on the Travel Agency Sector." *Journal of Information Technology Cases and Applications* 3, no. 1 (2001).

Steinert-Therlkeld, T. "GroceryWorks: The Low Touch Alternative." *Interactive Week*, January 31, 2000.

Taylor, D., and A. D. Terhune. *Doing E-Business.* New York: John Wiley & Sons, 2002.

Torris, T. et al. "Executive Overview: Net Banking at a Crossroads." *Forrester Brief*, July 2, 2002, forrester.com/ER/Research/Brief/Excerpt/0,1317,15276,00.html (accessed April 2003).

Tyson, E. *Personal Finance for Dummies*, 3d ed. San Francisco: Hungry Minds, Inc., 2000.

Van der Heijden, J. G. M. "The Changing Value of Travel Agents in Tourism Networks: Towards a Network Design Perspective." In Stefan Klein, et al. (ed.), *Information and Communication Technologies in Tourism.* New York: Springer-Verlag, 1996: 151–159.

Vandermerwe, S. "The Electronic 'Go-Between Service Provider': A New Middle Role Taking Center." *European Management Journal* (December 1999).

walmart.com (accessed 2002–2003).

Wang, F., et al. "E-Tailing: An Analysis of Web Impacts on the Retail Market." *Journal of Business Strategies* 19, no. 1 (2002): 73–92.

Warkentin, M., and A. Bajaj. "The On-Demand Delivery Services Model for E-Commerce." In A. Gangopadhay (ed.), *Managing Business with Electronic Commerce: Issues and Trends.* Hershey, PA: Idea Group Publishing, 2001.

Warkentin, M., et al. "The Role of Mass Customization in Enhancing Supply Chain Relationships in B2C E-Commerce Markets." *Journal of Electronic Commerce Research* 1, no. 2 (2000): 1–17.

CHAPTER 4

CONSUMER BEHAVIOR, ONLINE MARKET RESEARCH, AND CUSTOMER RELATIONSHIP MANAGEMENT

Content

Learning objectives

Upon completion of this chapter, you will be able to:

1. Describe the factors that influence consumer behavior online.

2. Understand the decision-making process of consumer purchasing online.

3. Describe how companies are building one-to-one relationships with customers.

4. Explain how personalization is accomplished online.

5. Discuss the issues of e-loyalty and e-trust in EC.

6. Describe consumer market research in EC.

7. Describe CRM, its methods, and its relationship with EC.

8. Explain the implementation of customer service online and describe its tools.

9. Describe Internet marketing in B2B, including organizational buyer behavior.

RITCHEY DESIGN LEARNS ABOUT CUSTOMERS

The Problem

Ritchey Design, Inc. of Redwood City, California, is a relatively small ($15 million sales per year) designer and manufacturer of mountain-bike components. The company sells its products to distributors and/or retailers, who then sell them to individual consumers. The company opened a Web site in 1995 (*ritcheylogic.com*), but like so many companies' Web sites, Ritchey's was more a status symbol than a business tool. Most of the site's visitors came to get information on Team Ritchey (now Ritchey Yahoo Team), the company's world-class mountain-bike team, or to find out where Ritchey products were sold, but that was where the site's usefulness ended. It did not give customers all the information they wanted nor did it enable the company to gain insight into its customers' wants and needs.

The Solution

In late 1995, Philip Ellinwood, Ritchey's chief operating officer and IS director, decided to rework the Web site so that the company could hear from its customers directly. First, Ellinwood set up customer surveys on the site. To induce visitors to participate, the company offers visitors who answer the surveys a chance to win free Ritchey products. Visitors are asked to enter their names and addresses and then to answer questions about the company's products.

A special software program, Web Trader, automatically organizes and saves the answers in a database. The information is later used to help make marketing and advertising decisions.

Ellinwood can easily change the questions to learn customers' opinions about any of about 15 new products Ritchey develops each year. In the past, the company knew little about how consumers might react to a new product until it was in the stores. Ellinwood says, "The process could save us as much as $100,000 a year on product development."

To educate retailers and consumers about the technological advantages of Ritchey's high-end components over competitors' parts, Ellinwood created an electronic catalog, accessible through the Web site. Visitors can browse through the product catalog, which includes detailed descriptions and graphics of Ritchey's products.

The Results

As of this writing, Ritchey has a Web site (*ritcheylogic.com*) where the company sells only team items such as t-shirts, bags, water bottles, and other gear directly to individuals online. The company does not sell bike parts directly online because it wants to maintain its existing distribution system. However, dealers can place orders on the site, and they can learn about new products quickly, so they no longer push only those products about which they know the most. The site is basically used in B2C EC for communicating with customers, conducting market research, and delivering advertising, which are basic activities in Internet marketing (Catalano and Smith 2001).

Source: Compiled from *ritcheylogic.com* (accessed 2000–2003).

WHAT WE CAN LEARN . . .

This case illustrates the benefits a company can derive from changing its Web site from a passive one (just having a presence on the Web) to one with interactivity. Ritchey can now hear from its customers directly, even though it uses intermediaries for its sales. The new interactive Web site allows the company to learn more about its customers while educating customers at the same time. The company also uses the site for customer service. These topics are the subjects of this chapter. In addition, the company uses the site for advertisement (the topic of Chapter 5), and it is a companion site for collaboration with its business partners (Chapters 6 through 8).

4.1 LEARNING ABOUT CONSUMER BEHAVIOR ONLINE

Companies today operate in an increasingly competitive environment. Therefore, they treat customers like royalty as they try to lure them to buy their goods and services. Finding and retaining customers is a major critical success factor for most businesses, off-line and online. One of the keys to building effective customer relationships is an understanding of consumer behavior online.

A MODEL OF CONSUMER BEHAVIOR ONLINE

For decades, market researchers have tried to understand consumer behavior, and they have summarized their findings in various models. The purpose of a consumer behavior model is to help vendors understand how a consumer makes a purchasing decision. If a firm understands the decision process, it may be able to influence the buyer's decision, for example, through advertising or special promotions.

Exhibit 4.1 (page 132) shows the basics of the consumer behavior model, adjusted to fit the EC environment. The model is composed of the following parts:

- *Independent* (or uncontrollable) *variables,* which are shown at the top of Exhibit 4.1, can be categorized as personal characteristics and environmental characteristics.

- *Intervening* or *moderating* variables are variables within the vendors' control. They are divided into market stimuli (on the left) and EC systems (at the bottom) in Exhibit 4.1.

- The *decision-making process*, which is shown in the center of the exhibit, is influenced by the independent and intervening variables. This process ends with the buyers' decisions (shown on the right) resulting from the decision-making process.

- The *dependent variables* describe decisions made by buyers (in the box at the right).

Exhibit 4.1 identifies some of the variables in each category. In this chapter, we deal mainly with the following model-related issues: the decision process, seller–customer relationship building, and customer service. Advertising is the topic of Chapter 5. Discussions of other issues can be found in Internet marketing books, such as Strauss and Frost (2001).

Before we discuss some of the consumer behavior model's variables, let us examine who the EC consumers are. Online consumers can be divided into two types: *individual consumers,* who get much of the media attention, and *organizational buyers,* who do most of the actual shopping in cyberspace in terms of dollar volume of sales. Organizational buyers include governments, private corporations, resellers, and public organizations. Purchases by organizational buyers are generally used to create other products (services) by adding value to the products. Also, organizational buyers may purchase products for resale without any further modifications. We will briefly discuss organizational purchasing in Section 4.7 and describe it in detail in Chapter 6.

The Independent Variables

Two types of independent variables are distinguished: personal characteristics and environmental variables.

Personal characteristics. Personal characteristics, which are shown in the top-left portion of Exhibit 4.1, include age, gender, and other demographic variables. Several Web sites provide information on customer buying habits online (e.g., emarketer.com, jmm.com). The major demographics that such sites track are gender, age, marital status, educational level, ethnicity, occupation, and household income, which can be correlated with Internet and EC data. For example, higher education and/or income levels are associated with more online shopping. Exhibit 4.2 (page 132) provides the major sources and types of these and other Internet and EC statistics.

It is interesting to note that the more experience people have with Internet shopping, the more likely they are to spend more money online. We can learn from Internet statistics not only what people buy, but also why they *do not* buy. The two most-cited reasons for *not* making purchases are shipping charges (51 percent) and the difficulty in judging the quality of the product (44 percent). (People were asked to cite the two or three most important reasons; thus, the answers total to more than 100 percent.) Some users, about 32 percent, do not make

EXHIBIT 4.1   EC Consumer Behavior Model

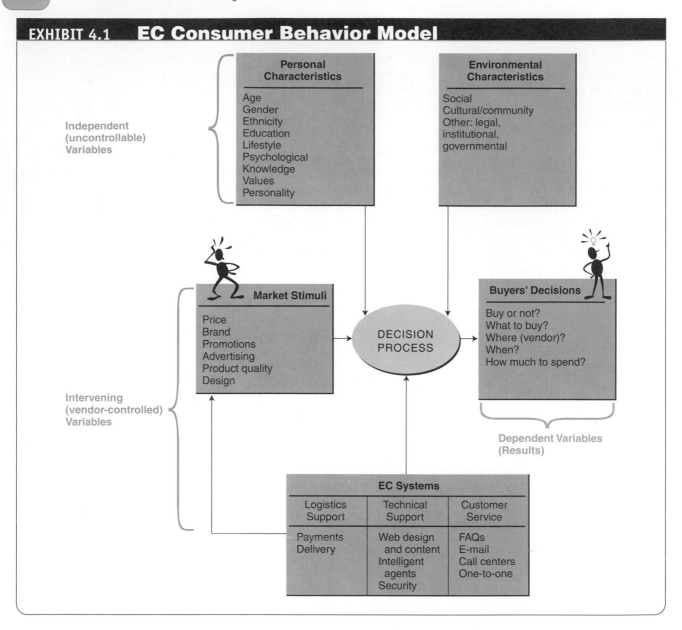

purchases because they cannot return items easily. Twenty-four percent are worried about credit card safety. An additional 23 percent of users do not purchase online because they cannot ask questions; 16 percent say they do not buy when it takes too long to download the screen; 15 percent are concerned about delivery time; and 10 percent enjoy shopping off-line. However, according to Forrester Research only 1.9 percent of online consumers have actually had an unfavorable experience (the least-cited reason for not making more purchases on the

EXHIBIT 4.2	Sources and Types of Internet and EC Statistics
Data sources	*ecominfocenter.com*, AMR Research *amrresearch.com, cyberdialogue.com, forrester.com, gartner.com, lionbridge.com, idc.com, jup.com, jmm.com, nua.ie/surveys, statmarket.com, yankeegroup.com*
Available data	Age, buying patterns (items, price), country of residence, educational level, ethnicity, gender, household income, Internet access options, Internet usage patterns, occupation, length and frequency of use, marital status

Web) (Temkin 2002). Psychological variables are another personal characteristic studied by marketers. Such variables include personality and lifestyle characteristics. These variables are briefly mentioned in several places throughout the text. The reader who is interested in the details of psychological variables on e-marketing should see Solomon (2002).

Environmental variables. As shown in the box in the top-right portion of the figure, the *environmental variables* can be grouped into the following categories:

▶ **Social variables.** These variables play an important role in EC purchasing. People are influenced by family members, friends, coworkers, and "what's in fashion this year." Of special importance in EC are Internet communities (covered in Chapter 17) and discussion groups, in which people communicate via chat rooms, electronic bulletin boards, and newsgroups. These topics are discussed in various places in the text.

▶ **Cultural/community variables.** It makes a big difference in what people buy if a consumer lives near Silicon Valley in California or in the mountains in Nepal. Chinese shoppers differ from French shoppers, and rural shoppers differ from urban ones. For further discussion of the impact of these variables, see Hasan and Ditsa (1999).

▶ **Other environmental variables.** These include things such as the available information, government regulations, legal constraints, and situational factors.

The Intervening (Moderating) Variables

The intervening (moderating) variables are those that can be controlled by vendors. In the off-line environment, these include pricing, advertising and promotions, and branding (the products themselves and their quality). The physical environment (e.g., display in stores), logistics support, technical support, and customer services also are important. Customer service is described in this chapter; the other intervening variables (logistics and technical support) will be described in various chapters of the book.

The Dependent Variables: The Buying Decisions

With the dependent variables, the customer is making several decisions, such as "to buy or not to buy?" "what to buy?" and "where, when, and how much to buy?" (see Bhatnagar et al. 2000). These decisions *depend* on the independent and intervening variables. The objective of learning about customers and conducting market research is to know enough so that the vendors who provide some of the market stimuli and/or control the EC systems can make decisions on the intervening variables.

The structure of the consumer behavior model in Exhibit 4.1 is a simplified version of what actually goes on in the decision-making process. In reality, consumer decision making can be complicated, especially when new products or procedures need to be purchased. For example, for online buying, a customer may go through the following five adoption stages: awareness, interest, evaluation, trial, and adoption. See McDaniel and Gates (2001) and Solomon (2002) for details.

Section 4.1 ▶ REVIEW

1. Describe the major components and structure of the consumer online purchasing behavior model.

2. List some major personal characteristics that influence consumer behavior.

3. List the major environmental variables of the purchasing environment.

4. List and describe the major vendor-controlled variables.

4.2 THE CONSUMER DECISION-MAKING PROCESS

Returning to the central part of Exhibit 4.1, where consumers make purchasing decisions, let's clarify the roles people play in the decision-making process. The major roles are as follows (Kotler and Armstrong 2002):

▶ **Initiator.** The person who first suggests or thinks of the idea of buying a particular product or service.

> **Influencer.** A person whose advice or view carries some weight in making a final purchasing decision.
> **Decider.** The person who ultimately makes a buying decision or any part of it—whether to buy, what to buy, how to buy, or where to buy.
> **Buyer.** The person who makes an actual purchase.
> **User.** The person who consumes or uses a product or service.

If one individual plays all of these roles, the marketer needs to understand and target that individual. When more than one individual plays these different roles, it becomes more difficult to properly target advertising and marketing. How marketers deal with the issue of multiple people in decision-making roles is beyond the scope of this book.

Several models have been developed in an effort to describe the details of the decision-making process that lead up to and culminate in a purchase. These models provide a framework for learning about the process in order to predict, improve, or influence consumer decisions. Here we introduce three relevant models.

A GENERIC PURCHASING-DECISION MODEL

A general purchasing-decision model consists of five major phases. In each phase we can distinguish several activities and, in some of them, one or more decisions. The five phases are: (1) need identification, (2) information search, (3) evaluation of alternatives, (4) purchase and delivery, and (5) after-purchase evaluation. Although these phases offer a general guide to the consumer decision-making process, do not assume that all consumers' decision making will necessarily proceed in this order. In fact, some consumers may proceed to a point and then revert back to a previous phase or they may skip a phase altogether.

The first phase, *need identification*, occurs when a consumer is faced with an imbalance between the actual and the desired states of a need. A marketer's goal is to get the consumer to recognize such imbalance and then convince them that the product or service the seller offers will fill this gap.

product brokering
Deciding what product to buy.

merchant brokering
Deciding from whom (from what merchant) to buy a product.

After identifying the need, the consumer *searches for information* (phase 2) on the various alternatives available to satisfy the need. Here, we differentiate between two decisions: what product to buy (**product brokering**) and from whom to buy it (**merchant brokering**). These two decisions can be separate or combined. In the consumer's search for information, catalogs, advertising, promotions, and reference groups influence decision making. During this phase, online product search and comparison engines, such as can be found at compare.com and mysimon.com, can be very helpful.

The consumer's information search will eventually generate a smaller set of preferred alternatives. From this set, the would-be buyer will further *evaluate the alternatives* (phase 3) and, if possible, will negotiate terms. In this phase, a consumer will use the collected information to develop a set of criteria. These criteria will help the consumer evaluate and compare alternatives. In phase 4, the consumer will make the *purchasing decision*, arrange payment and delivery, purchase warranties, and so on.

The final phase is a *postpurchase* phase (phase 5), which consists of customer service and evaluation of the usefulness of the product (e.g., "This product is really great!" or "We really received good service when we had problems").

A CUSTOMER DECISION MODEL IN WEB PURCHASING

The preceding generic purchasing-decision model was used by O'Keefe and McEachern (1998) to build a framework for a Web purchasing model, which they called the Consumer Decision Support System (CDSS). According to their framework, shown in Exhibit 4.3, each of the phases of the purchasing model can be supported by both CDSS facilities and Internet and Web facilities. The CDSS facilities support the specific decisions in the process. Generic EC technologies provide the necessary mechanisms, and they enhance communication and collaboration. Specific implementation of this framework is demonstrated throughout the text.

EXHIBIT 4.3	Purchase Decision-Making Process and Support System	
Steps in the Decision-Making Process	**CDSS Support Facilities**	**Generic Internet and Web Support Facilities**
Need recognition	Agents and event notification	Banner advertising on Web sites URL on physical material Discussions in newsgroups
Information search	Virtual catalogs Structured interaction and question/answer sessions Links to (and guidance on) external sources	Web directories and classifiers Internal search on Web site External search engines Focused directories and information brokers
Evaluation, negotiation, selection	FAQs and other summaries Samples and trials Models that evaluate consumer behavior Pointers to and information about existing customers	Discussions in newsgroups Cross-site comparisons Generic models
Purchase, payment, and delivery	Ordering of product or service Arrangement of delivery	Electronic cash and virtual banking Logistics providers and package tracking
After-purchase service and evaluation	Customer support via e-mail and newsgroups	Discussions in newsgroups

Source: O'Keefe, R. M., and T. McEachern. "Web-Based Customer Decision Support System." *The Communications of the ACM.* ©1998 ACM, Inc.

Others have developed similar models. The point here is that the planner of B2C marketing needs to consider the Web purchasing models in order to better influence the customer's decision making (c.g., by effective one-to-one advertising and marketing).

ONLINE BUYER DECISION SUPPORT MODEL

Silverman et al. (2001) developed a model for a Web site that supports buyer decision making and searching. This model revises the generic model by describing the purchasing framework that is shown in Exhibit 4.4 (page 136). The model is divided into three parts. The first is based on Miles et al. (2000), and it includes three stages of buyer behavior (see top of exhibit): identify and manage buying criteria, search for products and merchants, and compare alternatives. Below these activities are seven boxes with decision support system (DSS) design options (such as product representation), the options to support searching, and the options to compare alternatives.

The second part (on the right), which is based on Guttman et al. (1998), has three boxes: price, shipping, and finance. These become relevant when alternatives are compared. The third part, at the bottom of the exhibit, is composed of three boxes. The model demonstrates the flow of data and the decisions that support EC.

OTHER MODELS

Several other purchasing-decision models have been proposed. Some are referenced in Online Research Appendix "Current EC Research". Of special interest is a model proposed by Chaudhury et al. (2001). In this model, the buying decision is influenced by how much time is available and the locale (space) where the purchasing is done. In this context, *space* is the equivalent to shelf space in a physical store—namely how well a product is presented online and where it is presented in the Web site. Space also can refer to whether products are sold via wireline or wireless devices. The model distinguishes four scenarios: "less time and more space," "more time and less space," "more time and more space," and "less time

EXHIBIT 4.4   Overview of Design Space for Online Buyer Decision Support

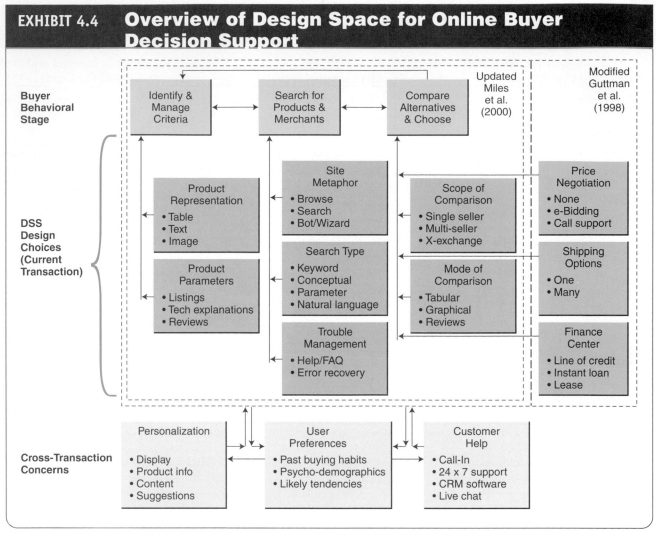

Source: Guttman et al. (1998). Silverman, B. G., et al. "Implications of Buyer Decision Theory for Design of E-Commerce Web Sites." *International Journal of Human Computer Studies* 55, 2001, with permission from Elsevier.

and less space." For example, the space on a small banner ad is more limited than the space on a large pop-up ad. For each scenario the vendors can develop different Web sites.

Section 4.2 ▶ REVIEW

1. List the roles people play in purchasing.
2. List the five stages in the generic purchasing-decision model.
3. Describe the Web-based purchasing-decision model.
4. Describe the architecture of the online buyer decision support model.

4.3   ONE-TO-ONE MARKETING AND PERSONALIZATION IN EC

one-to-one marketing
Marketing that treats each customer in a unique way.

One of the greatest benefits of EC is its ability to match products and services with individual consumers. Such a match is a part of **one-to-one marketing**, which treats each customer in a unique way to fit marketing and advertising with the customer's needs. The ability of EC to match individuals with products/services and/or with advertising includes *personalization* or *customization* of products/services ("make it your way"). Let's first look at the one-to-one relationship in EC in general.

HOW ONE-TO-ONE RELATIONSHIPS ARE PRACTICED

Although some companies have had one-to-one marketing programs for years, it may be much more beneficial to institute a corporatewide policy of building one-to-one relationships around the Web. This can be done in several ways. For example, the Gartner Group, an IT consulting company, proposed what it calls "the new marketing cycle of relationship building" (see Marcus 2001). This proposal, illustrated in Exhibit 4.5, views relationships as a two-way street: The process can start at any place in the cycle. Usually, though, it starts with "Customer receives marketing exposure" (at the top of the figure). The customer then decides how to respond to the marketing exposure (e.g., whether to buy the product online or offline; if online, whether to buy as individual or to use group purchasing). When a sale is made, customer information is collected (lower-right corner) and then is placed in a database. Then, a customer's profile is developed and the so-called *"Four P's"* of marketing (product, place, price, and promotion) are generated on a one-to-one basis. Based on this individualized profile, appropriate advertisements are prepared that will hopefully lead to another purchase by the customer. Once a purchase is made, the detailed transaction is added to the database, and the cycle is repeated. All of this can, and should, be done in the Web environment.

One of the benefits of doing business over the Internet is that it enables companies to better communicate with customers and better understand customers' needs and buying habits. These improvements, in turn, enable companies to enhance and frequently customize their future marketing efforts. For example, Amazon.com can e-mail customers announcements of books published in their areas of interest as soon as they are published; Expedia.com will ask consumers where they like to fly and then e-mail them information about special discounts to their desired destination.

Here we will address the key issues related to one-to-one marketing: personalization, collaborative filtering, customer loyalty, and trust. (For details on these and other issues related to implementing EC-based one-to-one marketing, see Peppers et al. 1999; Sindell 2000; and Todor and Todor 2001.) For discussion of how one-to-one marketing is related to CRM, see Section 4.6.

PERSONALIZATION

As discussed in Chapter 2, personalization refers to the matching of services, products, and advertising content to individuals. The matching process is based on what a company knows about the individual user. This knowledge is usually referred to as a user profile. The user profile defines customer preferences, behaviors, and demographics.

personalization
The matching of services, products, and advertising content to individual consumers.

user profile
The requirements, preferences, behaviors, and demographic traits of a particular customer.

EXHIBIT 4.5   The New Marketing Model

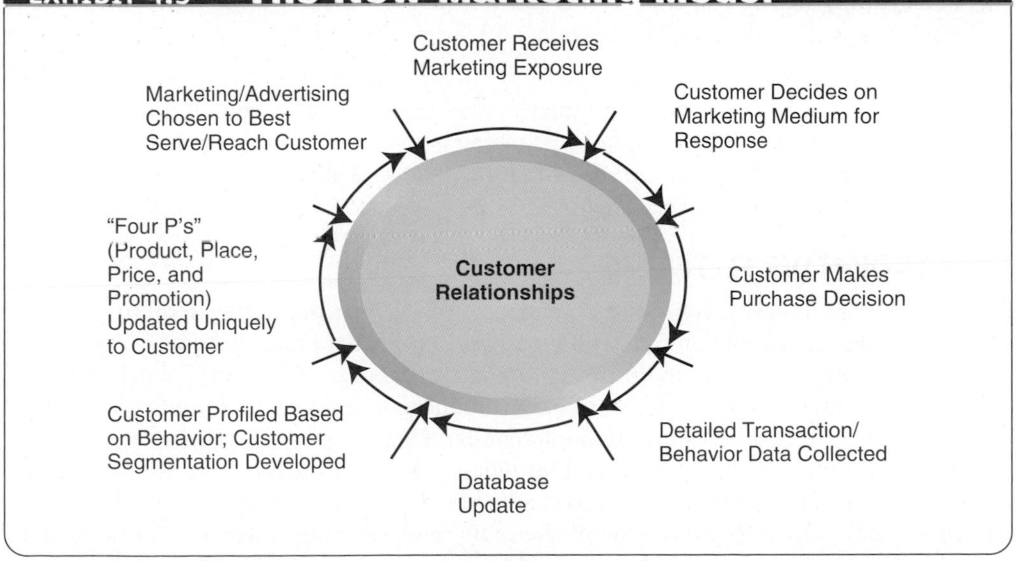

Customer Receives Marketing Exposure

Marketing/Advertising Chosen to Best Serve/Reach Customer

Customer Decides on Marketing Medium for Response

"Four P's" (Product, Place, Price, and Promotion) Updated Uniquely to Customer

Customer Relationships

Customer Makes Purchase Decision

Customer Profiled Based on Behavior; Customer Segmentation Developed

Detailed Transaction/ Behavior Data Collected

Database Update

Source: Linden, A. *Management Update: Data Mining Trends Enterprises Should Know About.* Gartner Group, October 9, 2002. © Gartner Group. All rights reserved.

Insights and Additions 4.1 Cookies in E-Commerce

Are cookies bad or good? The answer is "both." When a user revisits Amazon.com or other sites, they are greeted by their first name. How does Amazon.com know the user's identity? Through the use of cookies! Vendors can provide consumers with considerable personalized information if they use cookies that signal a consumer's return to a site. A variation of cookies is known as *e-sugging* ("SUG-ing," which means selling under the guise of research). For example, if a consumer visits several travel sites, they may get more and more unsolicited e-mails and pop-ups related to travel.

Cookies can provide a wealth of information to marketers, which then can be used to target ads to consumers. Thus, marketers get higher rates of "click-throughs" and customers can view the most relevant information. Cookies can also prevent repetitive ads because vendors can arrange for a consumer not to see the same ad twice. Finally, advanced data mining companies, such as NCR and Sift, can analyze information in the cookie files and better meet the customers' needs.

However, some people object to cookies because they do not like the idea that "someone" is watching their activity on the Internet. If a consumer does not like cookies, they can *disable* them in many cases. However, some consumers may want to keep the friendly cookies. For example, many sites recognize a person as a subscriber, so that they do not need to reregister. Netscape 6 and higher allows users to block third-party cookies. Internet Explorer (IE) 6.09 and higher also gives users control over third-party cookies. (Go to "Internet Options" under "Tools" and select "Private tab," click on "Advanced" and put a check mark next to "Override automatic cookie handling." Then, direct the IE to accept first-party cookies.) See *pcworld.com/resource/browse/0,cat,1384,sortIdx,1,00.asp* for more on cookies.

Profiles can be generated in several ways. The major strategies used to compile user profiles include the following:

▶ **Solicit information directly from the user.** This is usually done by asking the user to fill in a questionnaire or by conducting an interview with the user.

▶ **Observe what people are doing online.** A common way to observe what people are doing online is through use of a cookie—a data file that is stored on the user's hard drive, frequently without disclosure or the user's consent. Sent by a Web server over the Internet, the information stored will surface when the user's browser again accesses the specific Web server, and the cookie will collect information about the user's activities at the site (see cookiecentral.com). The use of cookies is one of the most controversial issues in EC, as discussed in Insights and Additions 4.1.

▶ **Build from previous purchase patterns.** For example, Amazon.com builds customer profiles to recommend books and CDs based on what customers purchased before, rather than asking customers, using cookies, or doing market research.

▶ **Perform marketing research.** Firms can research the market using tools such as data mining, as will be described in Appendix 4A (page 171).

Once a customer profile is constructed, a company matches the profile with a database of products, services, or contents. The actual matching process is usually done by software agents, as will be described later. Manual matching is too time-consuming and expensive.

One-to-one matching can be applied through several different methods. One well-known method is *collaborative filtering*.

cookie
A data file that is placed on a user's hard drive by a Web server, frequently without disclosure or the user's consent, that collects information about the user's activities at a site.

COLLABORATIVE FILTERING

Once a company knows a consumer's preferences (e.g., what music they like), it would be useful if the company could predict, without asking, what other products or services this consumer might enjoy. One way to do this is through collaborative filtering, which uses customer data to infer customer interest in other products or services. This prediction is based on special formulas derived from behavioral sciences. (See sins.berkeley.edu/resources.collab/ for details. For more on the methods and formulas used to execute collaborative filtering, see Ridell et al. [2002]). The prediction also can be based on what marketers know about other customers with similar profiles. One of the pioneering filtering systems was Firefly (now embedded in Microsoft's Passport System). Many personalization systems are based on collaborative filtering (e.g., backflip.com, c5corp.com, and blink.com).

collaborative filtering
A personalization method that uses customer data to predict, based on formulas derived from behavioral sciences, what other products or services a customer may enjoy; predictions can be extended to other customers with similar profiles.

The following are some variations of collaborative filtering:

▶ **Rule-based filtering.** A company asks consumers a series of yes/no or multiple-choice questions. The questions may range from personal information to the specific information the customer is looking for on a specific Web site. Certain behavioral patterns are predicted using the collected information. From this information, the collaborative filtering system derives behavioral and demographic rules such as, "If customer age is greater than 35, and customer income is above $100,000, show Jeep Cherokee ad. Otherwise, show Mazda Protégé ad."

▶ **Content-based filtering.** With this technique, vendors ask users to specify certain favorite products. Based on these user preferences, the vendor's system will recommend additional products to the user. This technique is fairly complex because mapping among different product categories must be completed in advance.

▶ **Activity-based filtering.** Filtering rules can also be built by watching the user's activities on the Web.

For more about personalization and filtering, see personalization.com and cio.com.

Legal and Ethical Issues in Collaborative Filtering

Information is frequently collected from users without their knowledge or permission. This raises several ethical and legal questions, including invasion-of-privacy issues. Several vendors offer *permission-based* personalization tools. With these, companies request the customer's permission to receive questionnaires and ads (e.g., see knowledgestorm.com). See Chapter 17 for more on privacy issues.

CUSTOMER LOYALTY

One of the major objectives of one-to-one marketing is to increase customer loyalty. *Customer loyalty* is the degree to which a customer will stay with a specific vendor or brand. Customer loyalty is expected to produce more sales and increased profits over time. Also, it costs a company between five to eight times more to *acquire* a new customer than to *keep* an existing one. Increased customer loyalty can bring cost savings to a company in various ways: lower marketing costs, lower transaction costs, lower customer turnover expenses, lower failure costs such as warranty claims, and so on. Customer loyalty also strengthens a company's market position because loyal customers are kept away from the competition.

Loyalty is a multidimensional concept. Coyles and Gokey (2002) distinguish six degrees of loyalty. Three of the levels identify customers as loyalists; that is, the customers are maintaining or increasing their expenditures with the company. These customers are loyal because they are emotionally attached to their current provider, have rationally chosen it as their best option, or do not regard switching as worth the trouble. The remaining segments—the downward migrators in terms of loyalty—have one of three reasons for spending less: their lifestyle has changed (as a result, say, of moving or having a child), so they have developed new needs that the company is not meeting; they continually reassess their options and have found a better one; or they are actively dissatisfied, often because of a single bad experience (e.g., a rude salesperson). Understanding customers' feelings and logic in these six levels enables sellers to solidify loyalty.

The introduction of EC decreases loyalty in general because customers' ability to shop, compare, and switch to different vendors becomes easier, faster, and less expensive given the aid of search engines and other technologies. On the other hand, companies have found that loyal customers end up buying more when they have a Web site to shop from. For example, W.W. Grainger, a large industrial-supply company, found that loyal B2B customers increased their purchases substantially when they began using Grainger's Web site (grainger.com). (See Grainger, Inc. [1998] for more information.) Also, loyal customers may refer other customers to a site. Therefore, any company's goal is to increase customer loyalty. The Web offers ample opportunities to increase loyalty (PR Newswire 2002).

E-Loyalty

E-loyalty refers to customers' loyalty to an e-tailer. Customer acquisition and retention is a critical success factor in e-tailing. The expense of acquiring a new customer can be over $100;

e-loyalty
Customer loyalty to an e-tailer.

even for Amazon.com, which has a huge reach, it is more than $15. In contrast, the cost of maintaining an existing customer at Amazon.com is $2 to $4.

Companies can foster e-loyalty by learning about their customers' needs; interacting with customers, as Ritchey Design did (see opening case); and providing superb customer service. A major source of information about e-loyalty is e-loyaltyresource.com. One of its major services is an online journal, the *e-Loyalty Resource Newsletter*, which offers numerous articles describing the relationships among e-loyalty, customer service, personalization, CRM, and Web-based tools. Another source of information is colloquy.com, which concentrates on loyalty marketing. Comprehensive reviews of the use of the Web and the Internet to foster e-loyalty are provided by Reichheld (2001) and Reichheld and Schefter (2000).

In addition, e-loyalty is a major barrier that customers must cross when deciding to exit to a competitor. See Insights and Additions W4.1 at the book's Web site for more on customer exit barriers.

TRUST IN EC

trust
The psychological status of involved parties who are willing to pursue further interaction to achieve a planned goal.

Trust is the psychological status of involved parties who are willing to pursue further interactions to achieve a planned goal. When people trust each other, they have confidence that as transaction partners they will keep their promises. However, both parties in a transaction assume some risk. In the marketspace, sellers and buyers do not meet face to face. The buyer can see a picture of the product but not the product itself. Promises of quality and delivery can be easily made—but will they be kept? To deal with these issues, EC vendors need to establish high levels of trust with current and potential customers. Trust is particularly important in global EC transactions due to the difficulty in taking legal action in cases of a dispute or fraud and the potential for conflicts caused by differences in culture and business environments.

In addition to sellers and buyers trusting each other, both must have trust in the EC computing environment and in the EC infrastructure. If people do not trust the security of the EC infrastructure, they will not feel comfortable about using credit cards to make EC purchases.

EC Trust Models

Several models have been put forth that try to explain the EC–trust relationship. For example, Lee and Turban (2001) examined the various aspects of EC trust and developed the model shown in Exhibit 4.6. According to this model, the level of trust is determined by numerous variables (factors) shown on the left side and in the middle of the figure. The exhibit illustrates the complexity of trust relationships, especially in B2C EC.

Birkhofer et al. (2000) developed a model that relates sellers' strategies to trust, and McKnight and Chervany (2001–2002) developed a model for developing and validating trust measures in EC.

How to Increase Trust in EC

How does one establish the necessary level of trust for EC? It depends on the type of trust. For example, in trust between buyers and sellers, the desired level of trust is determined by the following factors: the degree of initial success that each party experienced with EC and with each other, well-defined roles and procedures for all parties involved, and realistic expectations as to outcomes from EC (Shapiro et al. 1992). Conversely, trust can be decreased by any user uncertainty regarding the technology (uncertainty about the EC computing environment), by lack of initial face-to-face interactions, and by lack of enthusiasm among the trading parties.

Brand recognition is very important in EC trust. For example, when a consumer buys online from Dell or Wal-Mart, the consumer probably will have a great deal of trust. Obviously, the consumer needs to be assured that Dell is the actual seller. Therefore, EC security mechanisms can help solidify trust. In addition, it is necessary for EC vendors to disclose and update their latest business status and practices to potential customers and to build transaction integrity into the system. They must also guarantee information and protection privacy through various communication channels.

Several third-party vendors operate services that aim to increase trust. Notable are companies such as TRUSTe (truste.com; see Benassi 1999) and BBBOnLine (the online version of the Better Business Bureau). Also useful are escrow providers and reputation finders (see Wagner 2002 and

EXHIBIT 4.6   The EC Trust Model

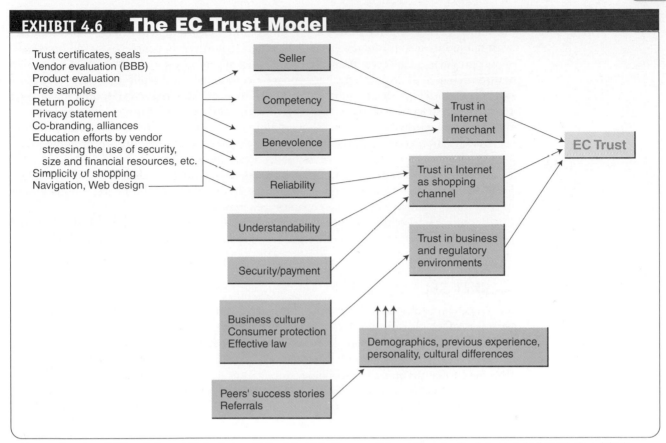

Source: From Lee, Matthew K. O., and Efraim Turban. "A Trust Model for Consumer Internet Shopping," vol. 6, no. 1 (Fall 2001). Copyright © 2001 M.E. Sharpe, Inc. Reprinted with permission.

sites such as cyberalert.com and cymfony.com), which provide business-critical intelligence on how brands are being used on the Internet as well as research about spying on businesses. Working against EC trust are stories of a considerable amount of fraud on the Internet, especially when unknown parties are involved. In Chapters 12 and 17, we describe measures that are being taken to reduce fraud and increase trust. (For a more comprehensive treatment of EC trust, see Camp 2000; Keen et al. 2000; Atif 2002; Luo 2002; and Computer Associates International 2002).

Section 4.3 ▶ REVIEW

1. Describe one-to-one marketing.
2. Explain how personalization (matching people with goods/services) is done.
3. Define loyalty and describe e-loyalty.
4. Describe the issue of trust in EC and how to increase it.

4.4 MARKET RESEARCH FOR EC

The goal of market research is to find information and knowledge that describes the relationships among consumers, products, marketing methods, and marketers. Its aim is to discover marketing opportunities and issues, to establish marketing plans, to better understand the purchasing process, and to evaluate marketing performance. On the Web, the objective is to turn browsers into buyers. Market research includes gathering information about topics such as the economy, industry, firms, products, pricing, distribution, competition, promotion, and consumer purchasing behavior. Here we focus on the latter. In Chapter 15, we will look at some other market research topics: the need to research the market, the competition (e.g., see rivalwatch.com), the technology, the business environment, and much more.

Businesses, educational institutions, and even governments use various tools to conduct consumer market research both off-line and online. For example, business representatives with questionnaires in shopping malls collect information from people about clothing, consumer products, or Internet usage. Surveyors may appear just about anywhere there is high traffic, such as supermarkets, theaters, and airport terminals, and replicating a survey in various cities can yield fairly generalized results. Another conventional way of conducting market research is by telephone surveys, where an interviewer calls current or prospective customers or a randomly selected sample of customers and asks questions regarding a specific product or service. Questionnaires may also be sent to specific individuals in a company or household.

In addition, *focus groups* can be useful. In these, groups of selected individuals are asked to discuss products or services in order for marketers to identify differences in attributes, benefits, and values of various potential markets. Analyzing these differences among groups of consumers is important when companies seek new target markets.

Because EC also has to identify an appropriate customer group for specific products and services, it is important first to understand how groups of consumers are classified. This classification is called segmentation.

MARKET SEGMENTATION

For years, companies used direct mail to contact customers. However, they frequently did so regardless of whether the products or services were appropriate for the specific individuals on the company's mailing list. For example, ABC Company sends out four mailings of 1,000,000 pieces each year. The cost of the direct mailings was $1.25 per customer, and only 1 percent responded. This meant that the cost per responding customer was $125. Obviously, this type of direct marketing was frequently not cost-effective (techmorrow.com 2003).

market segmentation

The process of dividing a consumer market into logical groups for conducting marketing research, advertising, and sales.

Markets can be segmented in order to formulate effective marketing strategies that appeal to specific consumer groups. Market segmentation is the process of dividing a consumer market into logical groups for conducting marketing research, advertising, and sales. A consumer market can be segmented in several ways—for example, by geography, demographics, psychographics, and benefits sought, as shown in Exhibit 4.7. A company can separate even millions of customers into smaller segments and tailor its campaigns to each of those segments. For example, advertisers may try to find people interested in travel and then send them travel information.

Segmentation is done with the aid of tools such as data modeling and data warehousing (e.g., see Levinson 2000). Using data mining (Berry and Linoff 2002) and Web mining (see Appendix 4A), businesses can look at consumer buying patterns to slice segments even finer. This is not an easy process, and it requires considerable resources and computer support. Most of the segmentation success stories involve large companies. For example, Royal Bank of Canada segments its 10 million customers at least once a month to determine credit risk, profitability, and so on. This segmentation has been very successful: The response to Royal Bank of Canada advertising campaigns has increased from 3 to 30 percent (Gold 2001). Segmentation can be very effective in the Web environment. For example, Hutt et al. (2001) found that segmentation by age, employment status, family role, and household structure

EXHIBIT 4.7	Consumer Market Segmentation in the United States (a partial list)
Segmentation	**Bases/Descriptors**
Geographic	Region; size of city, county, or Standard Metropolitan Statistical Area (SMSA); population density; climate
Demographic	Age, occupation, gender, education, family size, religion, race, income, nationality
Psychosocial	Social class, lifestyle, personality
Cognitive, affective, behavioral	Attitudes, benefits sought, loyalty status, readiness stage, usage rate, perceived risk, user status, innovativeness, usage situation, involvement

produces the best results for customer acquisition. See Lochridge (2001) for more on segmentation and its relationship to personalization.

CONDUCTING MARKET RESEARCH ONLINE

EC market research can be conducted by conventional methods, such as those described earlier, or it can be done with the assistance of the Internet. Although telephone or shopping mall surveys will continue, interest in Internet research methods is on the rise. Market research that utilizes the Internet is frequently faster and more efficient and allows the researcher to access a more geographically diverse audience than those found in off-line surveys (see FAQs at casro.org and accutips.com). Also, on the Web, market researchers can conduct a very large study much more cheaply than with other methods. The larger the sample size, the larger the accuracy and the predictive capabilities of the results. Telephone surveys can cost as much as $50 per respondent. This may be too expensive for a small company that needs several hundred respondents. An online survey will cost a fraction of a similarly sized telephone survey and can expedite research considerably, as shown in EC Application Case 4.1. Miller and Dickson (2001) provide a comprehensive review of online market research technologies, methods, tools, and issues, including ethical ones.

What Are We Looking for in EC Market Research?

By looking at a personal profile that includes observed behaviors on the Web, it is possible for marketers to explain and predict online buying behavior. For example, companies want to know why some customers are online shoppers whereas others are not (see Bhatnagar et al. 2000). Major factors that are used for prediction are (in descending order of importance): product information requested, number of related e-mails, number of orders made, what products/services are ordered, and gender.

Typical questions that online market research attempts to answer are: What are the purchase patterns for individuals and groups (segmentation)? What factors encourage online purchasing? How can we identify those who are real buyers from those who are just browsing?

CASE 4.1
EC Application

INTERNET MARKET RESEARCH EXPEDITES TIME-TO-MARKET AT PROCTER & GAMBLE

For decades, Procter & Gamble (P&G) and Colgate-Palmolive have been competitors in the market for personal care products. Developing a major new product, from concept to market launch, used to take over 5 years. First, a concept test was done (step 1); the companies sent product photos and descriptions to potential customers, asking whether they might buy it. If the feedback was negative, they tried to improve the product concept and then repeated step 1. Once positive response was achieved, sample products were mailed out, and the customers were asked to fill out detailed questionnaires. When customers' responses met the companies' internal hurdles, the company would start with mass TV advertising.

However, thanks to the Internet, it took P&G only 3 and one-half years to get Whitestrips, the teeth-brightening product, onto the market and to a sales level of $200 million a year—considerably quicker than other oral care products. In September 2000, P&G threw out the old marketing test model and instead introduced Whitestrips on the Internet, offering the product for sale on P&G's Web site. The company spent several months studying who was coming to the site and buying the product and collecting responses to online questionnaires, which was much faster than the old mail-outs.

The online research, which was facilitated by data mining conducted on P&G's huge historical data (stored in a data warehouse) and the new Internet data, revealed the most enthusiastic groups. These included teenage girls, brides-to-be, and young Hispanic Americans. Immediately, the company started to target these segments with appropriate advertising. The Internet created a product awareness of 35 percent, even before any shipments were made to stores. This "buzz" created a huge demand for the product by the time it hit the shelves.

From this experience, P&G learned important lessons about flexible and creative ways to approach product innovation and marketing. The whole process of studying the product concept, segmenting the market, and expediting product development has been revolutionized.

Sources: Compiled from Buckley 2002, p. 5, and from *pg.com* (February–December 2002).

How does an individual navigate—does the consumer check information first or do they go directly to ordering? What is the optimal Web page design? Knowing the answers to questions such as these helps a vendor to advertise properly, to price items, to design the Web site, and to provide appropriate customer service. Online market research can provide such data about individuals, about groups, and even about the entire Internet.

An example of what market research looks at is provided by Ranganathan and Grandon (2002), who explored the factors affecting online sales. They looked at content, design, security, and privacy factors. Using a survey, they found that the most significant factors are frequent update of content, information on a company, provision for having individual accounts and passwords, tight site security, and availability of good privacy statements. This study targeted the general Internet population, but a similar study could be conducted on a segment population regarding a specific product.

Internet-based market research is often done in an interactive manner, allowing personal contact with customers, and it provides marketing organizations with greater ability to understand the customer, the market, and the competition. For example, it can identify early shifts in product and customer trends, enabling marketers to identify products and marketing opportunities and to develop those products that customers really want to buy. It also tells management when a product or a service is no longer popular. To learn more about market research on the Web, see the tutorials at webmonkey.com.

The following discussion describes some online market research methods.

Online Market Research Methods

Online research methods range from one-to-one communication with specific customers, usually by e-mail, to moderated focus groups conducted in chat rooms to questionnaires placed on Web sites to tracking of customers' movements on the Web. Professional pollsters and marketing research companies frequently conduct online voting polls (e.g., see cnn.com, acnielsen.com). For an overview of online market research methods, see "Market Research on the Internet" at Online Chapter 4 of the book's Web site and Miller and Dickson (2001). A typical Internet-based market research process is shown in Exhibit 4.8.

Companies offer incentives such as games, prizes, or free software to draw customers. Then, using questionnaires, the companies collect information from customers before they are allowed to play the games, win prizes (see opening case study), or download the free software. However, according to recent surveys conducted by the Georgia Institute of Technology, more than 40 percent of the information people place on such questionnaires is incorrect (1998; 1999). Therefore, appropriate design of Web questionnaires and incentives for true completion are critical for the validity of the results.

Online market researchers have to address numerous issues. For example, customers may refuse to answer certain questions. Also, the analysis of questionnaires can be lengthy and costly. Furthermore, researchers risk losing respondents to online questionnaires because the respondents may not have the latest computers or a fast Internet connection.

Web-based surveys. Web-based surveys are becoming popular among companies and researchers. For example, Mazda North America used a Web-based survey to help design its Miata line. Web surveys can be passive (only fill in a questionnaire) or interactive (respondents download questionnaires, add comments, ask questions, and discuss issues). For more information and additional software tools, see supersurvey.com, surveymonkey.com, websurveyor.com, clearlearning.com, and tucows.com/webforms. For an introduction on how to conduct Web-based surveys, see Lazar and Preece (1999), and for some hands-on experiences, see Compton (1999).

A major vendor that provides services online is Zoomerang (zoomerang.com). At Zoomerang, one can select survey templates, edit them, send them to preselected recipients, or use the company's consumer panels. The basic service is free.

The limitations of Web surveys are difficulties in getting a representative sample, the quality of the collected data, the lack of experience of those conducting the research, and the fact that people need to sit by a computer to answer the questions.

Online focus groups. Several research firms create panels of qualified Web regulars to participate in online focus groups. For example, NPD's panel (npd.com) consists of 15,000 consumers recruited online and verified by telephone; Greenfield Online (greenfieldonline.com) picks users

EXHIBIT 4.8   Online Market Research Process

Steps in Collecting Market Research Data

1. Define the research issue and the target market.
2. Identify newsgroups and Internet communities to study.
3. Identify specific topics for discussion.
4. Subscribe to the pertinent groups; register in communities.
5. Search discussion group topic and content lists to find the target market.
6. Search e-mail discussion group lists.
7. Subscribe to filtering services that monitor groups.
8. Read FAQs and other instructions.
9. Visit chat rooms.

Content of the Research Instrument

1. Post strategic queries to groups.
2. Post surveys on a Web site.
3. Offer rewards for participation.
4. Post strategic queries on a Web site.
5. Post relevant content to groups, with a pointer to a Web site survey.
6. Post a detailed survey in special e-mail questionnaires.
7. Create a chat room and try to build a community of consumers.

Target Audience of the Study

1. Compare audience with the target population.
2. Determine editorial focus.
3. Determine content.
4. Determine what Web services to create for each type of audience.

Source: Based on Vassos (1996), pp. 66–68.

from its own database, then calls them periodically to verify that they are who they say they are. Another online research firm, Research Connections (researchconnections.com), recruits in advance by telephone, and takes the time to help new users connect to the Internet, if necessary. Use of these preselected focus group participants helps overcome some of the problems (e.g., sample size and partial responses) that sometimes limit the effectiveness of Web-based surveys.

Hearing directly from customers. Instead of using focus groups, which are costly and may be slow, one can ask customers directly what they think about a product or service. Nikitas (2002), who advocates such an approach, cites an example of toy maker Lego, who used a market research vendor to establish a survey on an electronic bulletin board where millions of visitors read each other's comments and shared opinions about Lego toys. The research vendor analyzed the responses daily and submitted the information to Lego. In addition to bulletin boards, it is possible to use chat rooms, newsgroups, and electronic consumer forums. For details, see Gelb and Sundaram (2002).

Software tools that can be used to hear directly from customers include C-Feedback Suite from informative.com (used by Lego), Betasphere (betasphere.com), InsightExpress (insightexpress.com), and survey.com.

Customer scenarios. According to Seybold (2001), companies often concentrate on their own offerings, failing to see how those products and services fit into the real lives of their customers. To correct this deficiency, Seybold suggests the use of *customer scenarios*, situations that describe the customer's needs and the manner in which the product fulfills the needs. For example, one customer may buy a refrigerator because they need an "emergency replacement," whereas another customer may buy a similar refrigerator because they are "furnishing a home." The information gathered is used to design products and advertising. Seybold describes the case of National Semiconductor's customer scenario, in which they offer Web tools to help engineers design electronic devices. Another user of this approach is Tesco (tesco.co.uk).

Tracking customer movements. To avoid some of the problems of online surveys, especially the giving of false information, some marketers choose to learn about customers by observing their behavior rather than by asking them questions. Many marketers keep track of consumers' Web movements using methods such as transaction logs or cookie files.

transaction log

A record of user activities at a company's Web site.

Transaction Logs. A transaction log records user activities at a company's Web site. A transaction log is created by a log file, which is a file that lists actions that have occurred. With log file analysis tools, it is possible to get a good idea of where visitors are coming from, how often they return, and how they navigate through a site. The transaction log approach is especially useful if the visitors' names are known (e.g., when they have registered with the site). Also, one can combine actual shopping data from the shopping-cart database.

clickstream behavior

Customer movements on the Internet; and, what the customer is doing there.

Note that as customers move on the Net, they establish their clickstream behavior, a pattern of their movements on the Internet, which can be seen in their transaction logs. Both ISPs and individual Web sites are capable of tracking a user's clickstream.

An example of the use of transaction logs is Internet Profile Corporation (IPC) (ipro.com), which collects data from a company's client/server logs and provides the company with periodic reports that include demographic data such as where customers come from or how many customers have gone straight from the homepage to placing an order. IPC also translates the Internet domain names of visitors into real company names. This way, a company can know where their customers are coming from.

Web bugs

Tiny graphics files embedded on e-mail messages and in Web sites that transmit information about the user and their movements to a Web server.

Cookies, Web Bugs, and Spyware. Cookies and Web bugs can supplement transaction-log methods. As discussed earlier, cookies allow a Web site to store data on the user's PC; when the customer returns to the site, the cookies can be used to find what the customer did in the past. Cookies are frequently combined with Web bugs, tiny graphics files embedded on e-mail messages and on Web sites. Web bugs transmit information about the user and their movements to a monitoring site (see Harding et al. 2001).

spyware

Software that gathers user information, through an Internet connection, without the user's knowledge.

Spyware is software that gathers user information through an Internet connection without the user's knowledge. Originally designed to allow freeware authors to make money on their products, spyware applications are typically bundled together with freeware for download onto users' machines. Many users do not realize they are downloading spyware with the freeware they want. Sometimes this may be indirectly dealt with in the licensing agreement (e.g., "may include software that occasionally notifies users of important news"). Spyware stays on the user's hard drive and continually tracks the user's actions, periodically sending information to its instigator concerning the user's activities. It is typically used to gather information for advertising purposes. Users cannot control what data is sent via the spyware, and unless using special tools, cannot uninstall the spyware, even if the software it was bundled with is removed from the system (Lang 2002).

Representative vendors that provide tools for tracking customers' movements are Tealeaf Technology, Inc. (tealeaf.com, log files), Acxiom Corp. (acxiom.com, data warehousing), and Net IQ (netiq.com/webtrends, real-time tracking). For details, see Tedeschi (2000).

The use of both cookies and Web bugs stirs controversy about whether their use invades customer privacy (see privacyfoundation.org). Tracking customers' activities *without their knowledge or permission* may be unethical or even illegal.

Analysis of B2C clickstream data. Large and ever-increasing amounts of B2C data can be collected on consumers, products, and so on. Such data come from several sources: internal data (e.g., sales data, payroll data, etc.), external data (e.g., government and industry reports), and clickstream data. *Clickstream data* are those that occur inside the Web environment; they provide a trail of the user's activities (the user's clickstream behavior) in the Web site. These data include a record of the user's browsing patterns: every Web site and every page of every Web site the user visits, how long the user remains on a page or site, in what order the pages were visited, and even the e-mail addresses of mail that the user sends and receives. By analyzing clickstream data, a firm can find out, for example, which promotions are effective and which population segments are interested in specific products.

According to Inmon (2001), B2C clickstream data can reveal information such as the following:

▶ What goods the customer has looked at and has not looked at
▶ What goods the customer purchased
▶ What goods the customer examined but did not purchase
▶ What items the customer bought in conjunction with other items

- ▶ What items the customer looked at in conjunction with other items but did not purchase
- ▶ What ads and promotions are effective and which are not effective at generating sales
- ▶ What ads generate a lot of attention but few sales
- ▶ Whether certain products are too hard to find and/or too expensive
- ▶ Whether there is a substitute product that the customer finds first
- ▶ Whether there are too many products for the customer to wade through
- ▶ Whether certain products are not being promoted
- ▶ Whether the products have adequate descriptions

In addition, the clickstream data can be maintained in a clickstream data warehouse for further analysis (see Sweiger et al. 2002). However, it is fairly difficult to analyze transaction logs or clickstream data (e.g., see webtrends.com).

LIMITATIONS OF ONLINE MARKET RESEARCH

One problem with online market research is that too much data may be available. To use data properly, one needs to organize, edit, condense, and summarize it. However, such a task may be expensive and time-consuming. The solution to this problem is to automate the process by using data warehousing and data mining. The essentials of this process, known as *business intelligence*, are provided in Appendix 4A.

Some of the limitations of online research methods are accuracy of responses, loss of respondents because of equipment problems, and the ethics and legality of Web tracking. In addition, focus group responses can lose something in the translation from an in-person group to an online group. A researcher may get people online to talk to each other and play off of each other's comments, but eye contact and body language are two interactions of traditional focus group research that are lost in the online world. On the other hand, just as it hinders the two-way assessment of visual cues, Web research can actually permit some participants the anonymity necessary to elicit an unguarded response. Finally, a major limitation is the difficulty to have truly representative samples, because the researcher does not know who is going to participate in the surveys.

Concerns have been expressed over the potential lack of representativeness in samples composed of online users. Online shoppers tend to be wealthy, employed, and well educated. Although this may be a desirable audience for some products and services, the research results may not be extendable to other markets. Although the Web-user demographic is rapidly diversifying, it is still skewed toward certain population groups, such as those with Internet access. Another important issue concerns the lack of clear understanding of the online communication process and how online respondents think and interact in cyberspace.

It is important that a company verifies the target audience or demographic it wants so that it can perform the right kind of sampling. For audience recruiting methods, see Cheyne and Ritter (2001). Web-based surveys typically have a lower response rate than e-mail surveys, and there is no respondent control for public surveys. If target respondents are allowed to be anonymous, it may encourage them to be more truthful in their opinions. However, anonymity may result in the loss of valuable information about the demographics and characteristics of the respondents. Finally, there are still concerns about the security of the information transmitted, which may also have an impact on the truthfulness of the respondents.

Some researchers are wildly optimistic about the prospects for market research on the Internet; others are more cautious. One expert predicts that in the next few years, 50 percent of all market research will be done on the Internet and that 10 years from now, national telephone surveys will be the subject of research methodology folklore. Others believe that this outcome won't happen that soon, but will take place within 20 years. To overcome some of the limitations, a company can outsource its market research needs. Only large companies have specialized market research departments. Most other companies use third-party research companies such as AC Nielsen.

Section 4.4 ▶ REVIEW

1. Describe the objectives of market research.
2. Define and describe segmentation.

3. Describe how market research is done online and the major market research methods.

4. Describe the role of Web logs and clickstream data.

5. Relate cookies, Web bugs, and spyware to market research.

6. Describe the limitations of online market research.

4.5   CRM AND ITS RELATIONSHIP WITH EC

customer relationship management (CRM)
A customer service approach that focuses on building long-term and sustainable customer relationships that add value both for the customer and the company.

Customer relationship management (CRM) (see Chapter 1) recognizes that customers are the core of a business and that a company's success depends on effectively managing its relationship with them (see Greenberg 2002). CRM focuses on building long-term and sustainable customer relationships that add value both for the customer and the company (Romano and Fjermestad 2001; Kalakota and Robinson 2001). (See also crm-forum.com and crmassist.com.)

WHAT IS CRM?

In Chapter 1, we provided some definitions of CRM. Greenberg (2002) provides more than 10 definitions, several made by CEOs of CRM providers or users. The Patricia Seybold Group (2002) provides several additional definitions, as do Tan et al. (2002). Why are there so many definitions? The reason is that CRM is new and still evolving. Also, it is an interdisciplinary field, so each discipline (e.g., marketing, MIS, management) defines CRM differently. We will repeat part of the definition from Chapter 1 here.

> CRM is a business strategy to select and manage customers to optimize long-term value. CRM requires a customer-centric business philosophy and culture to support effective marketing, sales, and service processes. (crmguru.com 2003)

TYPES OF CRM

In Chapter 1, we distinguished three types of CRM activities: operational, analytical, and collaborative. Operational CRM related to typical business functions involving customer services, order management, invoice/billing, or sales and marketing automation and management. Analytical CRM involves activities that capture, store, extract, process, interpret, and report customer data to a user, who then analyzes them as needed. Collaborative CRM deals with all the necessary communication, coordination, and collaboration between vendors and customers.

Classification of CRM Programs

Tan et al. (2002) distinguishes the following classifications of CRM programs:

▶ **Loyalty program.** These programs are aimed at increasing customer loyalty. An example is the frequent-flyer points given by airlines (see Section 4.4).

▶ **Prospecting.** These programs are intended to win new, first-time customers (see Chapter 5).

▶ **Save or win back.** These are programs that try to convince customers not to leave or, if they have left, to rejoin (see Section 4.4). When one of the authors of this book left AOL, for example, the company's representative offered many incentives to stay.

▶ **Cross-sell/up-sell.** By offering complementary products (cross-sell) or enhanced products (up-sell) that customers would like, companies make customers happy and increase their own revenue.

Another classification of CRM programs divides them by the service or product they offer (e.g., self-configuration, account tracking, call centers). These programs are presented in Section 4.6.

eCRM

Managing customer relationships is a business activity that has been practiced by corporations for generations. As evidenced by the many successful businesses that existed before the computer, computers are not required in order to manage one's customers well. However, since the mid-1990s, CRM has been enhanced by various types of information technologies. CRM technology is an evolutionary response to environmental changes, making use of new

IT devices and tools. The term **eCRM** was coined in the mid-1990s when customers started using Web browsers, the Internet, and other electronic touch points (e-mail, POS terminals, call centers, and direct sales). eCRM also includes online process applications such as segmentation and personalization. The use of the Internet, intranets, and extranets made customer services, as well as services to partners (see partner relationship management [PRM] in Chapter 7), much more effective and efficient than it was before the Internet.

eCRM
Customer relationship management conducted electronically.

Through Internet technologies, data generated about customers can be easily fed into marketing, sales, and customer service applications and analysis. The success or failure of these efforts can now be measured and modified in real time, further elevating customer expectations. In the world connected by the Internet, eCRM has become a requirement for survival, not just a competitive advantage. eCRM covers a broad range of topics, tools, and methods, ranging from the proper design of digital products and services to pricing and loyalty programs (e.g., see e-sj.org, *Journal of Service Research* (sagepub.co.uk/journals/details/j0229.html), and ecrmguide.com).

Note that eCRM is sometimes referred to as *e-service* (see Rust and Lemon 2001). However, the term e-service has several meanings. For example, some define e-service as EC in service industries such as banking, hospitals, and government, whereas others confine its use to e-self-service. To avoid confusion, we prefer to use the term eCRM rather than e-service. Note that people use the terms eCRM and CRM interchangeably. Most vendors use just CRM, and that term is also most often used in the accounting-profession literature. Therefore, from now on, we use only the term CRM.

THE SCOPE OF CRM

For online transactions, CRM often provides help features (e.g., see searchhp.com). In addition, if a product is purchased off-line, customer service may be offered online. For example, if a consumer purchases a product off-line and needs expert advice on how to use it, they may find detailed instructions online (e.g., livemanuals.com).

According to Voss (2000), there are three levels of CRM:

1. **Foundation of service.** This includes the *minimum necessary* services, such as site responsiveness (e.g., how quickly and accurately the service is provided), site effectiveness, and order fulfillment.

2. **Customer-centered services.** These services include order tracing, configuration and customization, and security/trust. These are the services that *matter the most* to customers.

3. **Value-added services.** These are *extra services,* such as dynamic brokering, online auctions, and online training and education. An example of how value-added services helped a B2C company to succeed is provided in EC Application Case 4.2 (page 150).

The Extent of Service

Customer service should be provided throughout the entire product life cycle. The value chain for CRM is composed of four parts (Plant 2000):

1. **Customer acquisition (prepurchase support).** A service strategy that reflects and reinforces the company's brand and provides information to potential customers to encourage them to buy.

2. **Customer support during purchase.** This service strategy provides a shopping environment that the consumer sees as efficient, informative, and productive.

3. **Customer fulfillment (purchase dispatch).** This involves timely delivery; including keeping the customer informed about the fulfillment process, especially if there are any delays.

4. **Customer continuance support (postpurchase).** Information and support help maintain the customer relationship between purchases.

BENEFITS AND LIMITATIONS OF CRM

The major benefit of CRM is the provision of superior customer care through the use of the Internet and IT technologies. In other words, CRM makes customers happy by providing choices of products and services, fast problem resolution and response, easy and quick access

CASE 4.2
EC Application
ONLINE WEEKEND IN FLORENCE: A CUSTOMER SERVICE SUCCESS STORY

Outstanding customer service and building customer relationships are the secret to the success of Alessandro Naldi's Web site, Weekend in Florence (*waf.it*). The site, based in Florence, Italy, sells high-quality, bona fide Italian merchandise made in the many small factories located in Tuscany and Florence, as well as services available in the area.

Naldi's dream of making the superb goods of his native area available to the world became possible with the advent of the Internet. His company does not maintain an inventory, traditional shippers, warehouses, distribution points, transportation hubs, or methods of mass production. Rather, he has secured the loyalty of customers, service providers, and suppliers that produce customized or standard products once orders are received. A number of factors are key to his success:

▶ **Exceptional merchandise.** The company offers authentic, high-quality local goods.
▶ **Relationships with suppliers.** Naldi has established close business relationships with local artisans and owners of small local factories.
▶ **Exclusive offers.** The Web site offers services such as advanced reservations to Florence's many art museums.
▶ **Near-zero marketing budget.** Naldi uses no banner ads or other advertising but instead uses what would have been spent on advertising to provide better customer service. Advertising is done by word-of-mouth from satisfied customers.
▶ **Customer service.** Customer needs are of foremost importance to the company. For example, Naldi even opened

cybercafes to make the Web site available to travelers who may have forgotten their reservation numbers.
▶ **Ability to change direction.** Merchandising was the beginning; now the site includes travel and event booking services.
▶ **Service providers network.** Naldi relies on a supportive network of contractors as service providers; each provider is responsible for their own area of expertise.
▶ **Customer bonding.** Opt-in e-mail marketing has formed loyalty bonds with many customers.

Although the success of Weekend in Florence may not be traditional in the sense of most Internet success stories, it does point out that what the majority of consumers want from a shopping experience is personal treatment and reliance on quality. For these simple considerations, they give their loyal support.

Sources: Compiled from Cross (2001) and from *waf.it* (2002).

Questions

1. List the site's critical success factors.
2. Relate the case to e-loyalty and trust.
3. How can this business grow and contend with competitors without any advertising budget?
4. Enter *waf.it* and identify additional customer service features.

---

to information, and much more (see Section 4.6). Companies try to gain competitive advantage over their competitors by providing better CRM.

The major limitation of CRM is that it requires integration with a company's other information systems, which may not be an easy task. Also, as will be discussed later in this section, justifying the expense of CRM is not easy. Finally, the mobility of certain employees makes it difficult to support them. It is only in the last few years that m-commerce is finally creating exciting CRM applications.

CRM IMPLEMENTATION ISSUES

Seybold and Marshak (1998) highlight some important steps in building an EC strategy that is centered on the customer. These steps include a focus on the end customer; systems and business processes that are designed for ease of use and from the end customer's point of view; and efforts to foster customer loyalty (the key to profitability in EC). To successfully make these steps, businesses must take the following actions:

▶ Deliver personalized services (e.g., dowjones.com)
▶ Target the right customers (e.g., aa.com, nsc.com)
▶ Help the customers do their jobs (e.g., boeing.com)
▶ Let customers help themselves (e.g., iprint.com)
▶ Streamline business processes that impact the customers (e.g., ups.com, amazon.com)

▶ "Own" the customer's total experience by providing every possible customer contact (e.g., amazon.com, hertz.com).

▶ Provide a 360-degree view of the customer relationship (e.g., wellsfargo.com, verizon.com)

Many of these steps are valid both for B2C and for B2B EC. In B2B, CRM is known as PRM (see Chapter 7).

Large-scale CRM implementation is neither easy nor cheap. Tan et al. (2002) suggest the following five factors that are required to implement a CRM program effectively:

1. **Customer-centric strategy.** A customer-centric strategy should be established first on the corporate level. This strategy must be based on and consistent with the overall corporate strategy and must be communicated across the whole organization.

2. **Commitments from people.** The more commitments from people across the corporation to the transformation of business strategy, the more likely the CRM implementation will succeed. Employees should be willing to learn the necessary technological skills.

3. **Improved or redesigned processes.** It is inherently difficult to identify the processes that need to be involved and frequently redesigned when implementing CRM.

4. **Software technology.** CRM software can record business transactions, create operations-focused databases, facilitate data warehousing and data mining, and provide decision-making support and marketing campaign management tools. Companies should select the appropriate CRM packages to meet specific corporate CRM needs as well as to enable integration with legacy enterprise applications such as the ERP system. Major CRM vendors are Siebel, Oracle, PeopleSoft, SAP, IBM, and Nortel/Clarify. Smaller players are Vignettee, BroadVision, Onyx, Microstrategy, E.piphany, Roundarch, and KANA. Major CRM consultants are KMPG Consultants, Deloitte Consultants, and the Patricia Seybold Groups (see Greenberg 2002).

5. **Infrastructure.** Effective CRM implementation requires suitable corporate infrastructure. This infrastructure includes network setup, storage, and data backup, computing platforms, and Web servers. However, only effective corporate infrastructure *integration* can provide solid support for the CRM implementation.

See Deck (2001) and Ling and Yen (2001) for additional tips on CRM implementation.

INTEGRATING CRM INTO THE ENTERPRISE

Some CRM applications are independent of enterprise systems. However, many CRM applications must be integrated with other information systems. To understand why, let us examine Exhibit 3.1 (page 85 in Chapter 3).

As can be seen in the exhibit, CRM lies primarily between the customers and the enterprise. The communication between the two is done via the Internet, regular telephone, snail mail, and so on. However, to answer customer queries it is necessary to access files and databases. In medium and large corporations, these are usually part of a legacy system and/or ERP system. Companies may check data relevant to a customer order with their manufacturing plants, transportation vendors, suppliers, or other business partners. Therefore, CRM needs to interface with the supply chain, and do so easily and quickly. In addition, CRM must be integrated with the data warehouse because, as will be shown in Appendix 4A, it is easier to build applications using data in the warehouse than using data residing in several internal and external databases. Finally, CRM itself collects customer and product data, including clickstream data. These need to be prepared for data mining and other types of analysis.

The integration of ERP and CRM must include low-level data synchronization as well as business process integration so that the integrity of business roles can be maintained across systems and workflow tasks can pass between the systems. Such integration also ensures that organizations can perform *business intelligence* across systems.

JUSTIFYING CUSTOMER SERVICE AND CRM PROGRAMS

Two major problems arise when companies try to justify expenditures for customer service and CRM programs. The first problem is the fact that most of the benefits of CRM are intangible, and the second is that substantial benefits can usually be reaped only from loyal customers. This, of course, is true for both off-line and online organizations. In a 1990 study published in *Harvard Business Review* titled, "Zero Defections: Quality Comes to Services" (see details at Reichheld and Schefter 2000), researchers demonstrated that the high cost of acquiring customers renders many customer relationship programs unprofitable during their early years. Only in later years, when the cost of retaining loyal customers falls and the volume of their purchases rises, do CRMs generate big returns (Reichheld and Schefer 2000). Therefore, companies are very careful about determining how much customer service to provide (see Petersen 1999).

Metrics in Customer Service and CRM

metrics
Standards of performance; may be quantitative or qualitative.

One way to determine how much service to provide is to compare a company against a set of standards known as **metrics**. Metrics can be either quantitative or qualitative standards. (See Jagannathan et al. 2001 and Sterne 2002.) Here are some Web-related metrics a company can use to determine the appropriate level of customer support:

- **Response time.** Many companies have a target response time of 24 to 48 hours. If a company uses intelligent agents, a response can be made in real time or the system can provide an acknowledgement that the customer's message has been received and a response will be forthcoming.
- **Site availability.** Customers should be able to reach the company Web site at any time (24 hours a day). This means that downtime should be as close to zero as possible.
- **Download time.** Users usually will not tolerate downloads that last more than 10 to 20 seconds.
- **Timeliness.** Information on the company site must be up-to-date. The company sets an interval (say, every month) at which information must be revised. If a set interval is not used, companies may have new products in stores but not on the Web or vice versa. In either case, potential sales may be lost.
- **Security and privacy.** Web sites must provide sufficient privacy statements and an explanation of security measures. (This metric is measurable as "yes" or "no"—either the statement and explanation are there or they are not.)
- **On-time order fulfillment.** Order fulfillment must be fast and when promised to the customer. For example, a company can measure the time it takes to fulfill orders, and it can count the number of times it fails to meet its fulfillment promises.
- **Return policy.** In the United States and several other countries, return policies are a standard service. Having a return policy increases customer trust and loyalty. The ease by which customers can make returns is important to customer satisfaction.
- **Navigability.** A Web site must be easy to navigate. To gauge navigability, companies might measure the number of customers who get part way into an order and then "bail out."

Providing CRM can be done through a large number of applications, as will be illustrated in Section 4.6.

Section 4.5 ▶ REVIEW

1. Define CRM. What is eCRM?
2. Describe the benefits and limitations of CRM.
3. Describe some implementation issues relating to CRM, including integration with the enterprise.
4. Discuss the issue of justifying CRM service.
5. Describe metrics related to CRM and customer service.

4.6 DELIVERING CUSTOMER SERVICE IN CYBERSPACE: CRM APPLICATIONS AND TOOLS

CRM applications are *customer service* activities designed to enhance customer satisfaction (the feeling that a product or service has met the customer's expectations). CRM applications improve upon traditional customer service by means of easier communications and speedier resolution of customer problems, frequently by automatic responses to questions or by customer self-service. Today, in order to satisfy the increased customer expectations, EC marketers must respond by providing the best, most powerful, and innovative systems and software. As a matter of fact, they must create customer-centric EC systems (Focazio 2001).

Customer service (or support) is the final link in the chain between providers and customers. It adds value to products and services, and it is an integral part of a successful business. Almost all medium and large companies today use the Web as a customer support channel (Chaudhury et al. 2001). CRM applications on the Web can take many forms, ranging from providing search and comparison capabilities (Chapter 3) to allowing customers to track the status of their orders.

CLASSIFICATIONS OF CRM APPLICATIONS

The Patricia Seybold Group (2002) distinguishes among *customer-facing*, *customer-touching*, and *customer-centric intelligence* CRM applications. These three categories of applications are described below and are shown in Exhibit 4.9 (page 154). The exhibit also shows how customers interact with these applications.

- **Customer-facing applications.** These include all the areas where customers interact with the company: call centers, including help desks; sales force automation; and field service automation. Such CRM applications basically automate the information flow or they support employees in these areas.
- **Customer-touching applications.** In this category, customers interact directly with the applications. Notable are self-service, campaign management, and general purpose e-commerce applications.
- **Customer-centric intelligence applications.** These are applications that are intended to analyze the results of operational processing and use the results of the analysis to improve CRM applications. Data reporting and warehousing and data mining are the prime topics here.

To this classification of CRM applications we add the following fourth category:

- **Online networking and other applications.** Online networking refers to methods that provide the opportunity to build personal relationships with a wide range of people in business. These include chat rooms and discussion lists.

We use these four categories of applications to organize our presentation of CRM applications in the remainder of this section. (Further details on the first three categories can be found at psgroup.com, in the free download of *An Executive's Guide to CRM*.)

CUSTOMER-FACING APPLICATIONS

Customer-facing applications are those where customers interact with a company. The primary application is *Web-based call centers*, otherwise known as customer interaction centers.

Customer Interaction Centers

A **customer interaction center (CIC)** is a comprehensive customer service entity in which EC vendors take care of customer service issues communicated through various contact channels. It allows customers to communicate and interact with a company in whatever way they choose. Providing well-trained customer service representatives who have access to data such as customer history, purchases, and previous contacts is one way to improve customer service (see Adria and Chaudhury 2002). New products are extending the functionality of the conventional call center to e-mail, fax, voice, and Web interactivity (e.g., Web chat), integrating them into one product.

A multichannel CIC works like this: (1) The customer makes a contact via one or more channels. (2) The system collects information and integrates it with a database, then determines a service response. (3) The customer is routed to self-service or a human agent. (4) The service is provided to the customers (e.g., their problem is resolved or question is answered).

An example of a well-managed integrated call center is that of Bell Advanced Communication in Canada, whose subscribers can submit customer service queries over the

customer interaction center (CIC)
A comprehensive service entity in which EC vendors address customer-service issues communicated through various contact channels.

EXHIBIT 4.9   CRM Applications

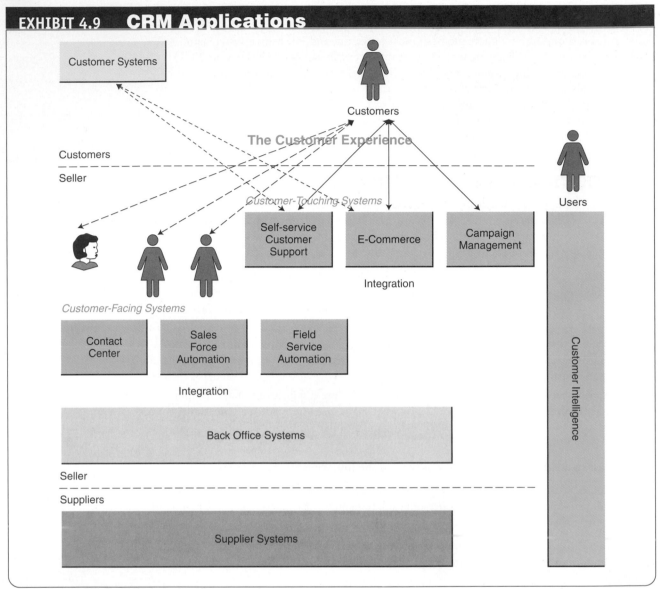

Source: Patricia Seybold Group. *An Executive's Guide to CRM*, March 21, 2002.

Web. From the Bell Advanced Web site, a customer can fill out an e-mail form with drop-down menus that help pinpoint the customer's problem. The e-mail then is picked up by the call center, which either answers the question immediately or tries to have a human response within 1 hour. Another example is a product called eFrontOffice (e.epicor.com/efrontoffice), which combines Web channels such as automated e-mail reply, Web knowledge bases, and portal-like self-service with call center agents or field service personnel. Such centers are sometimes called **telewebs**, and their capabilities are listed in Online Exhibit W4.1. An example of a teleweb is provided in EC Application Case W4.1.

For another example of a Web-based call center, see EC Application Case W4.2 about Canadian Tire's integrated call center at the book's Web site. A comprehensive description of Web-based call centers, including a tutorial, articles, and information on leading vendors is available at call-centers.org. For more examples of CICs and call centers, see callcenterops.com.

Intelligent agents in customer service and call centers. To ease information overload related to several CRM activities, companies can use intelligent agents (see Chapter 5). Of special interest is a suite of five agents ("SmartBots") from Artificial-Life, Inc. (artificial-life.com). The system is shown schematically in Exhibit 4.10. As can be seen, an agent called Web Guide can interactively assist customers to navigate a Web site using plain English (or

EXHIBIT 4.10 Intelligent Agents in Call Centers

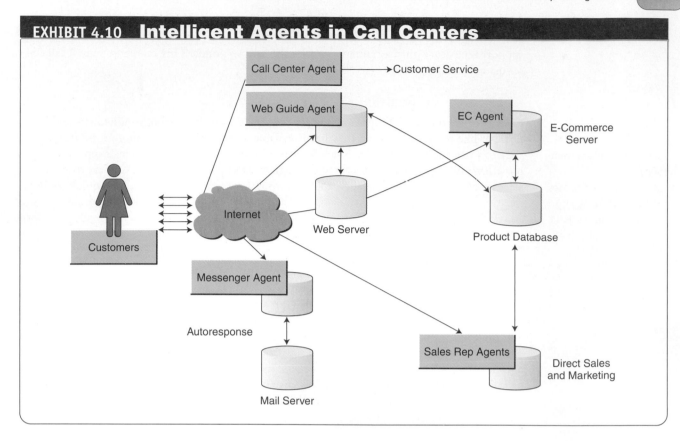

another language). An agent called Messenger evaluates incoming e-mail and generates autoresponses. The Call Center agent provides a problem resolution component to the conversations between the Web Guide and customers. It also refers the customer to a real person if necessary. The EC agent executes tasks related to EC, such as providing real-time information on account status. Finally, the Sales Rep agent can create a user profile based on information collected from the other agents. For further details on agents, see agentland.com and Barker (1999).

Automated Response to E-Mail (Autoresponder)

The most popular online customer service tool is e-mail. Inexpensive and fast, e-mail is used to disseminate information and to conduct correspondence on many topics, including responses to customer inquiries.

The ease of sending e-mail messages has resulted in a flood of customer e-mail. Some companies receive tens of thousands of e-mails a week, or even a day. Answering these e-mails manually would be expensive and time-consuming. Customers want quick answers, usually within 24 hours (a policy of many organizations). Several vendors offer automated e-mail reply systems known as **autoresponders**, which provide answers to commonly asked questions. Autoresponders, also called "infobots" and "e-mail on demand," are text files that are returned via e-mail, automatically on demand. They can relay standard information for support of customer service, marketing, and promotions. (See egain.com, aweber.com, firepond.com, brightware.com, and quark.com.) The eGain system (egain.com), for example, looks for certain phrases or key words such as "complaint" or "information on a product," and then taps into a knowledge base to generate a canned, matching response. For messages that require human attention, the query is assigned an ID number and passed along to a customer agent for a reply.

Severina Publications is a full-service Internet publishing and marketing company that offers autoresponders as a service to clients as well as a library of autoresponders as part of its Internet marketing strategy. Examples of the company's responders are:

autoresponders
Automated e-mail reply systems (text files returned via e-mail), which provide answers to commonly asked questions.

▶ 12steps@severina.co.uk, which retrieves a list of 12 ways to promote a Web site off-line.

▶ Classified@severina.co.uk, which retrieves a list of classified ad sites on the Internet.

▶ Ezines@severina.co.uk, which retrieves a list of e-zines on the Web.

Many companies do not provide actual answers in their automatic responses, but only acknowledgement that a query has been received. Customer queries are classified in a decision-support repository until a human agent logs in and responds. This can be done in a call center using intelligent agents (see Barker 1999).

Sales Force Automation

sales force automation (SFA)
Software that automates the tasks performed by sales people in the field, such as data collection and its transmission.

Sales people constitute the major contact point with customers (both individuals and businesses). The more automation they have available, the better (quicker, more accurate) service they can provide to customers. Sales force automation (SFA) applications support the selling efforts of a company's sales force, managing leads, prospects, and customers through the sales pipeline. An example of such applications is a wireless device that allows quick communication with the corporate intranet (see Chapter 10). Another example was provided in the Maybelline case in Chapter 1 (page 32); that company implemented a reporting system involving mobile devices. For further discussion, see B2E in Chapter 8.

Field Service Automation

Field service employees, such as sales representatives, are on the move, and they interact directly with the customers. Field service representatives include repair people from the telephone or electric company who go to customers' homes. Providing service employees with automation can increase customer service. Field service automation applications support the customer service efforts of field service reps and service managers. These applications manage customer service requests, service orders, service contracts, service schedules, and service calls. They provide planning, scheduling, dispatching, and reporting features to field service representatives. Examples are wireless devices, such as provided in SFA. Some of these are *wearable devices* (see Chapter 10).

CUSTOMER-TOUCHING APPLICATIONS

Customer-touching applications are those where customers use computer programs rather than interacting with people. The following are popular customer-touching applications.

Personalized Web Pages

Many companies provide customers with tools to create their own individual Web pages (e.g., MyYahoo). Companies can efficiently deliver customized information such as product information and warranty information when the customer logs on to the personalized page. Not only can a customer pull information from the vendor's site, but the vendor can also push information to the consumer. In addition, these Web pages can be used to record customer purchases and preferences. Typical personalized Web pages include those for banking accounts, stock portfolio accounts, credit card accounts, and so on. On such sites, users can see their balances, records of all current and historical transactions, and more.

Vendors can use customer information collected from customized Web sites to facilitate customer service. Information that in the past may have been provided to the customer 1 to 3 months after a transaction was completed is now provided in real or almost-real time, and it can be traced and analyzed for an immediate response or action. Companies now use customer information to help market additional products by matching valuable information about product performance and consumer behavior. Companies use personalized Web pages for other benefits as well. For example, by tracking the status of an order, a customer does not need to call the company about it, saving the customer time, and at the same time saving the company the cost of having an employee answer the call. American Airlines is an example of one company that uses personalized Web sites to help increase the bottom line, as shown in EC Application Case 4.3.

E-Commerce Applications

As described in Chapter 1, e-commerce applications implement marketing, sales, and service functions through online touch points, most typically the Web. These applications let customers shop for products through a virtual-shopping-cart metaphor and purchase the prod-

AMERICAN AIRLINES OFFERS PERSONALIZED WEB SITES

In late 1998, American Airlines (AA) unveiled a number of features on its Web site (*aa.com*) that some thought made the site the most advanced (at that time) for personalized, one-to-one interactions and transactions on the Web. The most innovative feature of this site was its ability to generate personalized Web pages for each of about 1 million registered, travel-planning customers. How can AA handle such a large amount of information and provide real-time customized Web pages for each customer? The answer—intelligent agents.

The AA site was developed by BroadVision (*broadvision.com*), a major developer of one-to-one marketing applications, using a complex software called One-to-One Application. One of the core components needed to generate personalized Web pages is intelligent agents, which dynamically match customer profiles (built on information supplied by the customer, observed by the system, or derived from existing customer databases) to the database of contents. The output of the matching process triggers the creation of a real-time customized Web page, which for AA can contain information on the consumer's home airport and preferred destinations.

By using intelligent agent technology, AA built a considerable edge over its competitors. Personalizing Web pages offered the potential to increase customer loyalty and cement relationships with customers. The Web site also fostered the community of AA frequent flyers.

In May 2002, AA launched the new and improved Web site using the flexibility of Art Technology Group's (ATG) Relationship Management platform. The new site offers more value and convenience and greater personalization with its platform upgrade, new booking engine, and improved navigation.

Sources: Compiled from *aa.com* (2002), *broadvision.com* (2002), Yoon (2002), and *PR Newswire* (2002).

Questions

1. What are the benefits of the personalized pages to American Airlines?
2. What role do intelligent agents play in the personalization process?

ucts in their shopping carts through a virtual-check-out metaphor. Customers may also perform self-service support tasks such as order status and history inquiry, returns processing, and customer information management. This provides convenience to many customers and also saves them money, thus increasing their satisfaction. Details on EC applications were provided in Chapter 3 and throughout the book.

Campaign Management

Campaign management applications automate marketing campaign activities such as online ad planning and analysis. They present offers to targeted leads, prospects, and customers on demand, on a schedule, or in response to business events through direct mail, e-mail, a contact center, field sales, and Web touch points. Ideally, these applications should be able to record responses to offers. Campaign management applications were presented in Sections 4.3 and 4.4 and will also be covered in Chapter 5. For further details see Greenberg (2002).

Web Self-Service

The Web environment provides an opportunity for customers to serve themselves. Known as Web self-service, this strategy provides tools for users to execute activities previously done by corporate customer service personnel. Personalized Web pages, for example, are one tool that may support Web self-service. Self-service applications can be used with customers (e.g., to support CRM; see rightnow.com) and with employees, suppliers, and any other business partners.

A well-known example is FedEx's tracking system. Previously, if a customer wanted information about the whereabouts of a package, they had to call a representative, give the information about their shipment, and wait for an answer. Today, customers go to fedex.com, insert their airbill number, and view the status of their package shipment. Many other examples exist, ranging from checking the arrival time of an airplane to finding the balance of a checking account. Initially, self-service was done in voice-based customer response systems

Web self-service

Activities conducted by users on the Web to provide answers to their questions (e.g., tracking) or for product configuration.

(known as voice activated response [VAR]; e.g., netbytel.com). Today, these systems are integrated and complementary to Web-based systems.

Some self-service applications are done only online. Examples are using FAQs at a Web site and self-diagnosis of computers online. On the other hand, updating an address with a personnel department can be done online or via VAR.

The benefits of Web self-service for customers are quick response time; consistent, and sometimes more accurate, replies or data; the possibility of getting more details; and less frustration and more satisfaction. The benefits for organizations are lower expenses of providing service (up to 95 percent savings), ability to scale service without adding more staff, strengthening business partnerships, and improved quality of service.

It is not easy to implement large-scale self-service systems. They require a complex blend of work processes and technology understanding. Also, only well-defined and repeatable procedures are well-suited for such systems. For further details and implementation tips, see Cunningham (2001).

Of the various self-service tools available, two are of special interest: self-tracking and self-configuration.

Self-tracking. Self-tracking refers to systems, like that of FedEx, where customers can find the status of an order or service in real (or close to real) time. Most large delivery services provide such services as do direct marketers such as Dell, Amazon.com, or Staples. Some auto manufacturers (e.g., Ford) allow customers to track the progress of the production of a customized car. Some employers, universities, and public agencies will let job applicants track the status of their job application.

Self-configuration and customization. Many build-to-order vendors, from Dell to Mattel, provide customers with tools to self-configure their product or service. One of the best ways to satisfy customers is provide them with the ability to customize products and services (see Chapters 1 and 2). Holweg and Pil (2001) assert that in order to have an effective build-to-order system, companies and their suppliers must first understand what customers want. This can be done by finding the customers' requirements (e.g., via self-configuration) and then linking the configured order directly to production, so that production decisions are based on real customer demand. In addition, customers should be linked interactively to the company and *if necessary* to product designers at the company. (see Chapter 8). According to Berry (2001), the superior "new retailer" provides for customization, offers superb customer services, and saves the customer time.

CUSTOMER-CENTRIC APPLICATIONS

Customer-centric applications support customer data collection, processing, and analysis. The major applications are as follows.

Data Reporting and Warehousing

CRM data need to be collected, processed, and stored. The general business intelligence process is described in Appendix 4A. Here we present two elements of the process: reports and data warehouses.

Data reports. Data reporting presents raw or processed CRM-related information, which managers and analysts can view and analyze. Reports provide a range of tabular and graphical presentation formats. Analysts can interact with the report presentation, changing its visual format, "drilling up" into summary information, or "drilling down" into additional detail.

data warehouse
A single, server-based data repository that allows centralized analysis, security, and control over the data.

Data warehouse. Medium and large corporations organize and store data in a central repository called a **data warehouse** so that it will be easy to analyze later on, when needed. The process is described in Appendix 4A. Data warehouses contain both CRM and non-CRM data. According to the Patricia Seybold Group (2002), data warehouses can be effective CRM tools if they contain the following information: customer information used by all operational CRM applications and by possible analytic applications (such as customer scores); information about the company's products and services and the channels through which it offers them; information about the company's marketing, sales, and services initiatives and customers' responses to them; information about customer requests and the company's responses; and information about customer transactions.

Data Analysis and Mining

Analytic applications automate the processing and analysis of CRM data. Many statistical, management science, and decision support tools can be used for this purpose (e.g., see Aronson and Turban 2004; Patricia Seybold Group 2002). Analytic applications process a warehouse's data, whereas reports merely present that information. Analytic applications are tools that can be used to analyze the performance, efficiency, and effectiveness of an operation's CRM applications. Their output should enable a company to improve the operational applications that deliver customer experience in order to achieve the CRM objectives of customer acquisition and retention. For example, analytic applications may be designed to provide insight into customer behavior, requests, and transactions, as well as into customer responses to the corporation's marketing, sales, and service initiatives. Analytic applications also create statistical models of customer behavior, values of customer relationships over time, and forecasts of customer acquisition, retention, and desertion, as described in Sections 4.1 through 4.4. See SAS (2000) for additional information and examples.

Data mining is another analytic activity that involves sifting through an immense amount of data to discover previously unknown patterns. In some cases, the data are consolidated in a data warehouse and data marts; in others, they are kept on the Internet and in intranet servers. For more on data analysis and data mining, see Appendix 4A.

Online Networking and Other Applications

Online networking and other applications support communication and collaboration among customers, business partners, and company employees. Representative technologies are discussed here.

Online networking. Representative online networking tools and methods include the following:

- ▶ **Forums.** Available from Internet services such as AOL, forums offer users the opportunity to participate in discussions as well as to lead forums on a "niche" topic.
- ▶ **Chat rooms.** Found on a variety of Web sites, they offer one-to-one or many-to-many real-time conversations.
- ▶ **Usenet groups.** These are collections of online discussions, grouped into communities. (See usenet2.org for details.)
- ▶ **E-mail newsletters.** These newsletters usually offer the opportunity for readers to write in, particularly in "Let us hear from you" sections. Users can find newsletters of interest by browsing a topic in a search engine. Many newsletter services (e.g., e-marketer.com) invite you to sign in. Others (e.g., aberdeen.com) only allow access to articles to users who register. Usually registration is an opt-in option (i.e., a person can remove themselves from the list at any time).
- ▶ **Discussion lists.** A discussion list is a redistribution tool through which an e-mail is sent to one address and then is automatically forwarded to all the people who subscribe to the list.

These last two networking tools are discussed in more detail in the following text.

E-Mail newsletters. The goal of an e-mail newsletter, according to Kinnard (2002), is to build a relationship with the subscribers. The best beginning is to focus on service by providing valuable information about an industry, which might range from tips ("tip of the day") to a full-blown newsletter consisting of columns of text and including graphics.

Because of the current bulk of e-mail advertising and marketing, customers may initially be distrustful of e-mail marketing. Therefore, newsletter articles, commentary, special offers, tips, quotes, and other pieces of information e-mailed to people must be presented in a professional and attractive manner. As customers find that they can trust the information provided, they will supply a company with more demographic and personal information that can be added to the company's customer database.

Sample resources for information on newsletters are list-universe.com and new-list.com.

Discussion lists. Discussion lists automatically forward an e-mail to all the people who subscribe to the list so that they can react to it. Discussion lists are distributed *post-by-post* (each recipient gets each e-mail from other members individually) or *digested* (all e-mails are compiled and sent out according to a schedule, e.g., once per day).

The three main reasons to use these lists is for a company to learn more about customers in a particular industry (assuming customers will react to the e-mail), to market the company's products and services, and to gather and share information with a community of individuals with similar interests. If a company hosts a discussion list, it can define the subject matter to be discussed, determine the frequency of the publication, and even make it a revenue-gathering tool. Sources for more information on discussion lists are listz.com and everythingemail.net/email_discussion.html.

Additional information about networking online can be found at The Creative Enterprises Network at creativethought.com, About.com's chat site at chatting.miningco.com, and Usenet 2 at usenet2.org.

Mobile CRM

Mobile CRM refers to the delivery of CRM applications to any user, whenever and wherever needed. This is done by use of the wireless infrastructure and/or mobile and wearable devices.

Many wireless and mobile m-commerce tools can be used to provide customer service. As we will see in Chapter 10, services such as finding a bank balance, stock trading, and finding airline arrival times are available with wireless devices. The major objective is to provide customer service faster and more conveniently. Furthermore, companies can use a "push" rather than a "pull" approach to giving customers needed information (e.g., by sending SMSs). As was shown in the 511 case in Chapter 1 (page 9), the government is also going wireless with some of its public services. As we will see in Chapter 8, many employees' and partners' services are provided in a wireless environment. The advantages of mobile CRM over traditional CRM are shown in Exhibit 4.11.

Giving mobile workforces the same power to interact with customers as they have on the desktop significantly expands a company's ability to build successful customer relationships. Mobile CRM can be provided both to sales representatives and service employees (B2E, Chapters 8 and 10) and directly to customers (Chapter 10). For a comprehensive presentation, see PeopleSoft (2002).

Voice Communication

The most natural way of communicating is by voice. Given the opportunity to do so, many customers prefer to connect to the Internet via voice. During the 1990s, VAR systems became popular. Today, Web-based voice systems are taking their place. One solution for accessing the Internet by voice is provided by companies such as i3 Mobile (i3mobile.com) and TellMe (tellme.com). It involves converting voice to text, processing and transmitting the text message, and then converting text to voice. Such systems excel in finding information on the Internet (e.g., see the demo at i3mobile.com). Even more advanced systems will be available in the near future.

Imagine this scenario. A person is on their way to the airport and gets stuck in traffic. The person calls the airport on their cell phone and hears "All agents are busy. You are important to us; please stay on the line." With Visual Text to Speech technology from AT&T, the person can click on "talk to agent" on their Internet-enabled smartphone. A smiling face of a virtual agent appears. The person tells the agent their problem and asks to reschedule their flight. A voice confirmation is provided in seconds.

Most people are more comfortable talking with a person, even a virtual one, than they are interacting with machines. The smile and the clear pronunciation of the agent's voice increases shoppers' confidence and trust. For details, see Lohr et al. (2002).

Language Translation

Some people prefer customer service to be in their native or selected language. Web site translation is most helpful in serving tourists. A device called InfoScope (from IBM) can read signs, restaurant menus, and other text written in one language and translate them into several other languages. Currently, these translators are available only for short messages. For more on this topic, see Chapter 14.

EXHIBIT 4.11 Traditional Versus Mobile CRM

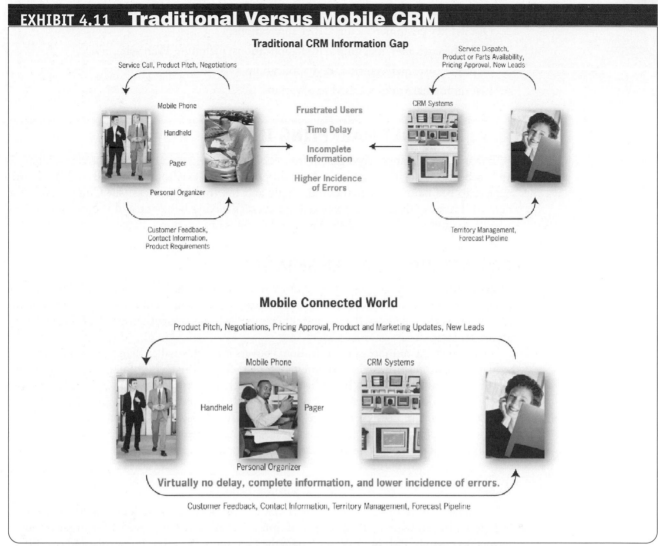

Source: *The Business Case for Mobile CRM: Opportunities, Pitfalls, and Solutions.* Pleasanton, CA: PeopleSoft Press, 2002.

The Role of Knowledge Management and Intelligent Agents in CRM

Automating inquiry routing and answering queries requires *knowledge,* which can be generated from historical data and from human expertise and stored in knowledge bases for use whenever needed (see Appendix 4A). Examples would be the answers to FAQs or the detailed product information requested by customers. Companies need to automate the provision of such knowledge in order to contain costs. *Intelligent agents* support the mechanics of inquiry routing, autoresponders, and so on. Some autoresponders, for example, use agents that use keyword recognition to guess what the query is about. The answer may be correct in only 80 percent of the cases, but the savings to the company and the instant reply may justify such an answer. Of course, in such a case, the customer needs to be aware that this is a machine-generated response (and that it might be wrong). Smarter agents are coming that know what they can or cannot answer. In the latter case, they will refer you to a human. However, they are not 100 percent correct either. (Their accuracy increases with time.)

Kwok et al. (2001) developed a much more intelligent system that can answer less structured and nonroutine questions. This is done via intelligent information retrieval systems, using a technology called natural language processing. A similar system that "understands" incoming customer e-mail queries is SelectResponse from ehnc.com. It is based on neural computing. For more on intelligent agents in CRM, see Chapter 5. A summary of some of the applications presented in this chapter, as well as some additional applications, is provided in Exhibit W4.2 at the book's Web site.

Section 4.6 ▶ REVIEW

1. Discuss key customer-facing CRM applications.
2. Describe customer-touching CRM applications, including Web self-service.
3. Describe customer-centric CRM applications.
4. List online networking CRM applications

4.7 INTERNET MARKETING IN B2B

B2B marketing is completely different from B2C marketing, which we introduced in Chapter 3 and in Sections 4.1 through 4.6. Major differences also exist between B2B and B2C with respect to the nature of demand and supply and the trading process (see Coupey 2001 for details). Here we discuss the corporate purchaser's buying behavior and the marketing and advertising methods used in B2B. More discussion is provided in Chapter 6 through 8.

ORGANIZATIONAL BUYER BEHAVIOR

Organizations buy large quantities of *direct materials* that they consume or use in the production of goods and services and in the company's operations. They also buy *indirect materials* (such as PCs, delivery trucks, and office supplies) to support their production and operations processes.

Although the number of organizational buyers is much smaller than the number of individual buyers, their transaction volumes are far larger, and the terms of negotiations and purchasing are more complex. In addition, the purchasing process itself, as will be seen in Chapter 6, is usually more complex than the purchasing process of an individual customer. Also, the organization's buyer may be a group. In fact, decisions to purchase expensive items are usually decided by a group. Therefore, factors that affect individual consumer behavior and organizational buying behavior are quite different.

A Behavioral Model of Organizational Buyers

The behavior of an organizational buyer can be described by a model similar to that of an individual buyer, which was shown in Exhibit 4.1. A behavioral model for organizational buyers is shown in Exhibit 4.12. Compare the two, and notice the similarities and the differences. Note that some independent variables differ; for example, the family and Internet communities may have no influence. Also, an *organizational influences module* is added to the B2B model. This module includes the organization's purchasing guidelines and constraints (e.g., contracts with certain suppliers) and the purchasing system used. Also, interpersonal influences such as authority are added. Finally, the possibility of group decision making must be considered. (For a detailed discussion of organizational buyers, see Kotler and Armstrong 2002. For Internet procurement by purchasing agents, see Martin and Hafer 2002.)

THE MARKETING AND ADVERTISING PROCESSES IN B2B

The marketing and advertising processes for businesses differ considerably from those used for selling to individual consumers. For example, traditional (off-line) B2B marketers use the following methods: trade shows at which they exhibit products, advertisements in industry magazines, e-mail and paper catalogs, and salespeople who call on existing customers and potential buyers.

In the digital world, these approaches may not be effective, feasible, or economical. Therefore, organizations are using a variety of online methods to reach business customers. Popular methods are online directory services, use of matching services to find business partners, use of the marketing and advertising services of exchanges (Chapter 7), co-branding or alliances (Chapter 15), affiliate programs, online marketing services (e.g., see digitalcement.com), or use of e-communities (see Chapter 17 and b2bcommunities.com). Several of these methods are discussed next.

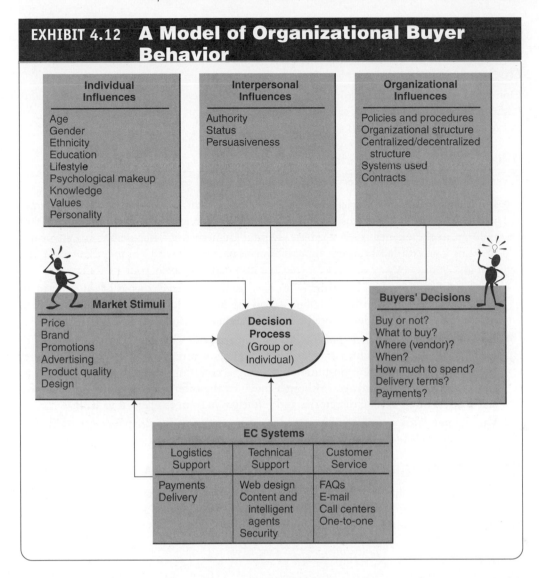

EXHIBIT 4.12 A Model of Organizational Buyer Behavior

METHODS FOR B2B ONLINE MARKETING

When a B2C niche e-tailer seeks to attract its audience of skiers or musicians or cosmetic customers, it may advertise in traditional media targeted to those audiences, such as magazines or television shows. The same is true in B2B when trade magazines and directories are used. But when a B2B vendor wants to grow by adding new customers or products, it may not have a reliable, known advertising channel. How will it reach its potential customers?

Targeting Customers

A B2B company, whether a provider of goods or services, an operator of a trading exchange, or a provider of digital real-time services, can contact all of its targeted customers individually when they are part of a well-defined group. For example, to attract companies to an exchange for auto supplies, one might use information from industry trade association records or industry magazines to identify potential customers.

Another method of bringing new customers to a B2B site is through an affiliation service, which operates just as a B2C affiliate programs does. A company pays a small commission every time the affiliation company "drives traffic" to its site. For more on online B2B marketing, see Coupey (2001) and b2business.net.

An important part of any marketing effort is advertising. Several of the advertising methods that will be presented in Chapter 5 are applicable to B2B. For example, the concept of an *ad server network provider*, such as that from DoubleClick (doubleclick.com), is a method used to target customers in B2B2C e-commerce.

Electronic Wholesalers

One of the interesting B2B ventures is the e-wholesaler. Like click-and-mortar e-tailer Sam's Club, this kind of intermediary sells directly to businesses, but does so exclusively online. An example is Bigboxx.com, described in Chapter 6 (page 224).

Other B2B Marketing Services

Several other B2B marketing services exist. Here are several examples:

- **Digital Cement.** This service provides corporate marketing portals that help companies market their products to business customers. In essence, this company provides content tailored to the client's customer base. Digital Cement (digitalcement.com) advocates utilizing a private-label content approach versus partnering with a branded dot-com that will give your company content for free, but also may take away your customers.
- **National Systems.** This company (nationalsystems.com) tracks what is going on in an industry. It does competitive intelligence on pricing, product mix, promotions, and ad content, and then provides tailored marketing and advertising services.
- **BusinessTown.** This firm (businesstown.com) provides information and services to small businesses, including start-ups. It includes a directory of businesses in over 20 industries, information on functional areas (accounting, finance, legal, marketing), and business planning advice. Although much of the offering deals with intrabusiness and B2C, it offers several directories and information sources relevant to B2B.
- **Vantagenet.** This vendor (vantagenet.com) offers free tools that help increase traffic to a company's Web site. These tools range from horoscopes to guest books.

AFFILIATE PROGRAMS, INFOMEDIARIES, AND DATA MINING

Many more methods and approaches can be used in B2B marketing and advertising (e.g., see Sharma 2002; Minnett 2001). Here we examine three popular methods: affiliate programs, infomediaries, and online data mining services.

Affiliate Programs

The concept of B2C affiliation services was introduced in Chapter 1. There are several types of affiliate programs. In the simplest one, which is used extensively in B2C, affiliates put a banner of another vendor, such as Amazon.com or CDNow, on their sites. Whenever a consumer clicks on the vendor's banner, the consumer brings up that company's EC site, and a commission is paid to the affiliate if the customer makes a purchase. The same method works for B2B.

With B2B, there are additional types of affiliate programs. Schaeffer Research (schaeffersresearch.com), for example, offers financial institutions a *content* alliance program in which content is exchanged so that all can obtain some free content. For more on B2B affiliate programs see Gary and Gary (1999).

Infomediaries and Online Data Mining Services

Marketing managers need to understand their customers' shopping behavior in order to optimally advertise or approach customers in the future. Traditional B2C retailers evaluate point-of-sale (POS) data (e.g., grocery scanner data) and other available data in order to generate valuable marketing information. In today's online environment, more relevant information is available than ever before. However, the potential of the information can only be realized if the clickstream data can be analyzed and mined to produce useful knowledge that can be used to improve services and marketing efforts. A new intermediary is emerging to provide such services to Web site owners who do not have the specialized knowledge and systems to perform such data mining on their own. As described in Chapter 2, these B2C and B2B intermediaries are called *infomediaries*.

Infomediaries start by processing existing information until new, useful information is extracted from it. This new information is sold to B2B customers or exchanged for more information, which is manipulated yet again, until even more valuable information can be extracted. B2B vendors use the information from infomediaries to identify likely buyers with much greater precision than ever before—leading to increased sales and drastically reduced marketing expenses. Representative infomediaries and data mining specialists are SAS Institute (sas.com), NetTracker, WebTrends, NetIntellect, HitList, and SurfReport. For a discussion of data mining and an example of its use in B2B, see Appendix 4A.

Section 4.7 ▶ REVIEW

1. Distinguish between organizational buyers and individual consumers.
2. Describe B2B marketing and advertising methods.
3. Explain how affiliate programs and data mining work in B2B.

MANAGERIAL ISSUES

Some managerial issues related to this chapter are as follows.

1. **Do we understand our customers?** Understanding the customers, specifically what the customer needs and how to respond to those needs, is the most critical part of consumer-centered marketing. To excel, companies need to satisfy and retain customers, and management must monitor the entire process of marketing, sales, maintenance, and follow-up service.

2. **What do customers want from technology?** Complex lifestyles, a more diverse and fragmented population, and the power of technology all contribute to changing consumer needs and expectations in the digital age. In certain societies, EC has become more and more popular because it saves time, not because it saves money. Technology also provides consumers the ability to get customized products quickly. Vendors should understand these relationships and take advantage of them in their marketing efforts.

3. **How is our response time?** Acceptable standards for response in customer service must be set. For example, customers want acknowledgment of their query within 24 hours. Many companies seek to provide this response time and do so at a minimum cost.

4. **How do we measure and improve customer service?** The Internet provides an excellent platform for delivery of superb customer service via a variety of tools. The problem is that the returns are mostly intangible and may only be realized in the distant future.

5. **Is CRM for real?** CRM is a necessity; most companies must have some CRM in order to survive. The issue is how much to provide. However, it is difficult to justify CRM, and there are many CRM programs from which to choose. Therefore, a careful analysis must be done.

6. **Do we have to use electronically supported CRM?** For a large company, it is a must. It is not economically feasible to provide effective CRM otherwise. Some CRM programs, such as e-mail, are inexpensive. However, large computerized call centers are expensive to install and operate.

7. **Should we use intelligent agents?** Any company engaged in EC must examine the possibility of using intelligent agents to enhance customer service, and possibly to support market research. Commercial agents are available on the market at a reasonable cost. For heavy usage, companies may develop customized agents.

8. **Who will conduct the market research?** B2C requires extensive market research. This research is not easy to do, nor is it inexpensive. Deciding whether to outsource to a market research firm or maintain an in-house market research staff is a major management issue.

9. **Are customers satisfied with our Web site?** This is a key question, and it can be answered in several ways. Many vendors are available to assist you; some provide free software. For discussion on how to improve customer satisfaction, see webhelp.com and e-satisfy.com. For Web site improvements see futurenowinc.com.

10. **Can we use B2C marketing methods and research in B2B?** Some methods can be used with adjustments; others cannot. B2B marketing and marketing research require special methods.

SUMMARY

In this chapter, you learned about the following EC issues as they relate to the learning objectives.

1. **Essentials of consumer behavior.** Consumer behavior in EC is similar to that of any consumer behavior. It is described in a stimuli-based decision model that is influenced by independent variables (personal characteristics and environmental characteristics). The model also contains a significant vendor-controlled component that includes both market stimuli and EC systems (logistics, technology, and customer service). All of these characteristics and systems interact to influence the decision-making process and produce an eventual buyer decision.

2. **The online consumer decision-making process.** The goal of marketing research efforts is to understand the consumers' online decision-making process and formulate an appropriate strategy to influence their behavior. For each step in the process, sellers can develop appropriate strategies.

3. **Building one-to-one relationships with customers.** EC offers companies the opportunity to build one-to-one relationships with customers that are not possible in other marketing systems. Product customization, personalized service, and getting the customer involved interactively (e.g., in feedback, order tracking, and so on) are all practical in cyberspace. In addition, advertising can be matched with customer profiles so that ads can be presented on a one-to-one basis.

4. **Online personalization.** Using personal Web pages, customers can interact with a company, learn about products or services in real time, or get customized products or services. Companies can allow customers to self-configure the products or services they want. Customization can also be done by matching products with customers' profiles.

5. **Increasing loyalty and trust.** Customers can switch loyalty online easily and quickly. Therefore, enhancing e-loyalty (e.g., through e-loyalty programs) is a must. Similarly, trust is a critical success factor that must be nourished.

6. **EC customer market research.** Several fast and economical methods of online market research are available. The two major approaches to data collection are soliciting voluntary information from the customers and using cookies, transaction logs, or clicksteam data to track customers' movements on the Internet. Understanding market segmentation by grouping consumers into categories is also an effective EC market research method. However, online market research has several limitations, including data accuracy and representation of the population by a sample.

7. **CRM, its technologies, and EC connection.** CRM is becoming a necessity for doing business, and it is facilitated by IT. Its major categories are customer-facing applications, customer-touching applications, and customer-centric intelligent applications. Using CRM methods, customers can order online more easily, check their orders and accounts, and communicate and collaborate with the company better.

8. **Implementing customer service online.** Retaining customers by satisfying their needs is the core of customer service. Customer service on the Web is provided by e-mail, on the corporate Web site, at customer interaction (call) centers, by automated responses, in personalized Web pages, by the use of data warehousing and data mining, by online networking, and by intelligent agents. Online customer service is media rich, effective, and usually less expensive than off-line services.

9. **B2B Internet marketing and organizational buyers.** Marketing methods and marketing research in B2B differ from those of B2C. A major reason for this is that the buyers must observe organizational buying policies and frequently conduct buying activities as a committee. Organizations use modified B2C methods such as affiliate marketing.

KEY TERMS

Autoresponders	155	eCRM	149	Sales force automation (SFA)	156
Clickstream behavior	146	E-loyalty	139	Spyware	146
Collaborative filtering	138	Market segmentation	142	Telewebs	154
Cookie	138	Merchant brokering	134	Transaction log	146
Customer relationship		Metrics	152	Trust	140
management (CRM)	148	One-to-one marketing	136	User profile	137
Customer interaction		Personalization	137	Web bugs	146
center (CIC)	153	Product brokering	134	Web self-service	157
Data warehouse	158				

DISCUSSION QUESTIONS

1. What would you tell an executive officer of a bank about the critical success factors for increasing loyalty of banking customers by using the Internet?

2. Why is data mining becoming an important element in EC? How is it used to learn about consumer behavior? How can it be used to facilitate customer service?

3. Discuss the contribution of a CICs to CRM.

4. Explain why online trust is more difficult to achieve than off-line trust.

5. Discuss the similarities and differences between data mining and Web mining. (*Hint:* To answer this question, you will need to read Appendix 4A.)

6. Many question the short-term return on investment of CRM tools. Explain why.

7. How would you convince a CEO to invest in Web self-services? With what issues could the CEO counter your advice?

8. Discuss the importance of trust in EC. How can market research contribute to improved trust?

9. Discuss why B2C marketing and advertising methods may not fit B2B.

INTERNET EXERCISES

1. Survey two department store Web sites, such as JCPenney (jcpenney.com), Marks & Spencer (marksandspencer.com), or Sears (sears.com). Write a report that highlights the different ways they provide customer service online.

2. Surf the Home Depot Web site (homedepot.com) and check whether (and how) the company provides service to customers with different skill levels. Particularly, check the "kitchen and bath design center" and other self-configuration assistance.

3. Examine a market research Web site (e.g., acnielsen.com). Discuss what might motivate a consumer to provide answers to market research questions.

4. Enter mysimon.com and share your experiences about how the information you provide might be used by the company for marketing in a specific industry (e.g., the clothing market).

5. Go to reflect.com. Examine how this company provides a personalized service. Examine ecommerceandmarketing.com and personalization.com and identify new developments in product and service personalization.

6. Enter marketingterms.com and conduct a search by key words as well as by category. Check the definitions of 10 key terms in this chapter.

7. Enter dell.com and attempt to buy a PC online. Fill in the forms and examine all options available. What CRM is provided to you? (You do not have to buy the computer you configured.)

8. Enter dell.com/us/en/pub/misc/segmenter_ccare.htm and examine all the services available. Examine the tracking services they provide to their customers. Finally, examine their association with bizrate.com. Write a report about customer service at Dell.

9. Enter intellifact.com and identify areas for market research about consumers.

10. Enter ford.com. Find out how Ford develops relationships with the actual drivers of cars (not dealers). Why do they do this?

11. Enter nielsenmedia.com and view the demos on e-market research. Then go to clickz.com and find their offerings. Summarize your findings.

TEAM ASSIGNMENTS AND ROLE PLAYING

1. Each team should select an overnight delivery service company (FedEx, DHL, UPS, U.S. Postal Service, and so on). The team will then identify all of the online customer service features offered by their company. Each team then will try to convince the class that its company provides the best customer service.

2. Go to webmonkey.com and find the market research tutorial. Then enter surveymonkey.com and, using the free version, design a survey instrument that will measure user satisfaction with the customer service given at your local supermarket. Submit the survey instrument to the instructor.

3. Enter willmaster.com. Have each team member examine the free marketing tools and related tutorials and demos. Each team will try to find a similar site and compare the two. Write a report discussing the team's findings.

REAL-WORLD CASE

CRM INITIATIVES AT NEW PIPER AIRCRAFT

Today, New Piper Aircraft is the only general aviation manufacturer offering a complete line of aircraft, from trainers and high-performance aircraft for personal and business use to turbine-powered business aircraft. However, in 1992, the company (then Piper Aircraft) was making fewer than 50 planes per year and had only $1,000 in cash. By 2001, the company delivered 441 planes and took in $243 million in revenue.

The fundamental reason for the company's success is its new ownership and management that introduced computer-based customer service. Piper realized that its ability to provide assistance needed to be completely overhauled. The company purchased Siebel Systems' MidMarket, a CRM software tool, and customized it. The result was the Piper Unlimited Liaison via Standards of Excellence (PULSE) Center. The system tracks all contacts and communications between New Piper and its dealers and customers. It also helps meet the growing needs of a complete customer-care program.

The installation of the software was not trouble free, but in less than 1 year the Web-based call center increased productivity 50 percent, the number of lost leads was reduced 25 percent, and sales representatives handled 45 percent more sales. Before the system was instituted, an 11-person call center used spiral notebooks crammed into numerous cabinets to store data and contacts; it took 30 minutes to locate a contact. Today, the call center tracks 70,000 customers among 17 dealers, and contact information is available in less than a minute.

In January 2003, development of the PULSE Center was still in progress. The first three phases had been completed: Phase 1, loading current aircraft owners, dealers,

fleet customers aircraft, and new customer service employees into the system to develop the organization infrastructure; Phase 2, enabling the Customer Service Center to process activities; and Phase 3, enabling dealers to access sales opportunities pertinent to their territory.

Phase 4, the opening of the Dealer Web Portal, began in winter 2003. It allows dealers access to particular areas of PULSE and provides the technology to make service requests online. Phase 5 will streamline entry of warranty claims. Phase 6, the Partner Web Portal, will allow key suppliers access to areas of the PULSE system and assist in communication with those suppliers. Phase 7 will provide for ordering parts online, and Phase 8 will be the Customer Web Portal, giving customers access to open service requests, online logbooks, and product and survey information.

Piper's Vice President, Customers, Dan Snell says, "New Piper's goal is to lead the industry with respect to quality, excellence, and customer care. It is a challenging mission, but certainly not daunting, and will be achieved through initiatives such as PULSE."

Sources: Compiled from Galante (2002), pp. 2–3; New Piper (2002); and *newpiper.com* (2002).

Questions

1. Describe the major features of the CRM program.

2. Why does the company need such an elaborate CRM program? How would you justify it?

3. How can one system serve both individual customers and business customers, including dealers?

REFERENCES

aa.com (accessed October 2002).

Adria, M., and S. D. Chaudhury. "Making Room for the Call Center." *Information Systems Management* (2002).

agentland.com (accessed September 2002).

Aronson, J., and E. Turban. *Decision Support Systems and Intelligent Systems*, 7th ed. Upper Saddle River, NJ: Prentice Hall, 2004.

Atif, Y. "Building Trust in E-Commerce." *IEEE Internet Computing* (January/February 2002).

Barker, D. "The Secret Agent Man: Agents Working Together." *BotSpot.com*, 1999, www.botspot.com/pcai/article11.htm (accessed September 2002).

Benassi, P. "TRUSTe: An Online Privacy Seal Program." *Communications of the ACM* 42, no. 2 (1999).

Berry, L. L. "The Old Pillars of New Retailing." *Harvard Business Review* (April 2001).

Berry, M. J. A., and G. S. Linoff. *Mining the Web: Transforming Customer Data.* New York: John Wiley & Sons, 2002.

Bhatnagar, A., et al. "On Risk, Convenience, and Internet Shopping Behavior." *Communications of the ACM* 43, no. 11 (2000).

Birkhofer, B., et al. "Transaction- and Trust-Based Strategies in E-Commerce—A Conceptual Approach." *Electronic Markets* 10, no. 3 (2000): 169–175.

broadvision.com (accessed October 2002).

Buckley, N. "E-Route to Whiter Smile." *Financial Times*, August 26, 2002.

Camp, L. J. *Trust and Risk in Internet Commerce.* Cambridge, MA: MIT Press, 2000.

Catalano, F., and B. Smith. *Internet Marketing for Dummies*. Foster City, CA: IDG Books, 2001.

Chaudhury, A., et al. "Web Channels in E-Commerce." *Communications of the ACM* (January 2001).

Cheyne, T. L., and F. E. Ritter. "Targeting Audiences on the Internet." *Communications of the ACM* 44, no. 4 (2001): 94–98.

Compton, J. "Instant Customer Feedback." *PC Computing*, December 1999.

Computer Associates International, Inc. "eTrust Audit." *Computer Associates* white paper, 2002, ca.com/solutions/ enterprise/etrust/whitepapers.htm (accessed January 2003).

Coupey, E. *Marketing and the Internet*. Upper Saddle River, NJ: Prentice Hall, 2001.

Coyles, S., and T. C. Gokey. "Customer Retention Is Not Enough." *The McKinsey Quarterly* no. 2 (2002).

crmguru.com (accessed June 2003).

Cross, R. "Spend a Weekend in Florence—Online!" *Direct Marketing*, September 2001, 53–54.

Cunningham, M. J. "Ten Steps to Successful Web Self-Service." *e-Business Advisor*, July–August 2001, 34–39.

Deck, S. "CRM Made Simple." *CIO Magazine*, September 15, 2001.

Emarketer.com. "First Comes Privacy, Then Trust." E-Marketer Research, February 19, 2003, emarketer.com/ products/database.php?PHPSESSID=940008704f4bde d8717bf13aa0473d0e&f_search_type=Basic&f_arg_ 0=online+shopping+experience (accessed April 2003).

Focazio, M. T. *The e-Factor (Customer-Centric EC)*. New York: Amacom, 2001.

Galante, D. "Case Studies: Digital Do-Overs." *Forbes*, October 7, 2002.

Gary, D., and D. Gary. *The Complete Guide to Associate and Affiliate Programs on the Net*. New York: McGraw-Hill, 1999.

Gelb, B. D., and S. Sundaram. "Adapting to 'Word of Mouse.'" *Business Horizons*, July–August 2002.

Georgia Institute of Technology, Graphics, Visualization, and Usability (GVU) Center. *Eighth WWW User Survey*, 1998, gvu.gatech.edu/user_surveys/survey-1997-10/ (accessed April 2003).

Georgia Institute of Technology, Graphics, Visualization, and Usability (GVU) Center. *Ninth WWW User Survey*, 1999, gvu.gatech.edu/user_surveys/survey-1998-04 (accessed April 2003).

Gold, R. Y. "Segmenting Strategically: Building Customer Piece of Mind." March 5, 2001, royalbank.com/sme/ articles/segmenting.html (accessed April 2003).

Grainger, Inc. "E-Commerce Gaining Loyalty Among Businesses Buying Operating Supplies Online." December 10, 1998, prnewswire.com/cgi-bin/stories. pl?ACCT=105&STORY=/www/story/12-10-1998/ 0000822471 (accessed April 2003).

Greenberg, P. *CRM at the Speed of Light: Capturing and Keeping Customers in Internet Real Time*, 2d ed. New York: McGraw-Hill, 2002.

Guttman, R., et al. "Agent-Mediated Electronic Commerce: A Survey." *Knowledge Engineering Review* 13, no. 3, 1998.

Harding, W. T., et al. "Cookies and Web Bugs: What They Are and How They Work Together." *Information Systems Management* (Summer 2001).

Hasan, H., and G. Ditsa. "The Impact of Culture on the Adoption of IT: An Interpretive Study." *Journal of Global Information Management* (January/February 1999).

Holweg, M., and F. Pil. "Successful Build-to-Order Strategies." *MIT Sloan Management Review* (Fall 2001).

Hutt, E., et al. "Simplifying Web Segmentation." *The McKinsey Quarterly* no. 3 (2001).

ibm.com (accessed December 2002).

Inmon, B. "Why Clickstream Data Counts." *e-Business Advisor*, April 2001.

Jagannathan, S., et al. *Internet Commerce Metrics*. Upper Saddle River, NJ: Prentice Hall, 2001.

Kalakota, R., and M. Robinson. *E-Businesses: Roadmap for Success*. Reading, MA: Addison Wesley, 2001.

Keen, P., et al. *Electronic Commerce Relationships: Trust by Design*. Upper Saddle River, NJ: Prentice Hall, 2000.

Kinnard, S. *Marketing with E-Mail*. Gulf Breeze, FL: Maximum Press, 2002.

Kotler, P., and G. Armstrong. *Principles of Marketing*, 9th ed. Upper Saddle River, NJ: Prentice Hall, 2002.

Kwok, C., et al. "Scaling Question Answering to the Web." *ACM Transactions on Information Systems* 19, no. 3 (2001).

Lang, T. "Cookies and Web Bugs and Spyware, Oh My!" *Infosecurity Opinion*, July 31, 2002, infosecnews.com/ opinion/2002/07/31_04.htm (accessed September 2002).

Lazar, J., and J. Preece. "Designing and Implementing Web-Based Surveys." *Journal of Computer Information Systems* (April 1999).

Lee, M., and E. Turban. "Trust in B2C Electronic Commerce: A Proposed Research Model and its Application." *International Journal of Electronic Commerce* 6, no. 1 (2001).

Levinson, M. "Customer Segmentation: Slices of Lives." *CIO Magazine*, August 15, 2000.

Linden, A. "Management Update: Data Mining Trends Enterprises Should Know About." Gartner Group, October 9, 2002.

Ling, R., and D. C. Yen. "Customer Relationship Management: An Analysis Framework." *Journal of Computer Information Systems* (Spring 2001).

Lochridge, S. "Do You Really Know Your Customers?" *e-Business Advisor*, April 2001, 28–30.

Lohr, S., et al. "The Future in Gear." *PC Magazine*, September 3, 2002.

Luo, X. "Trust Production and Privacy Concerns on the Internet: A Framework Based on Relationship Marketing and Social Exchange Theory." *Industrial Marketing Management* 31 (2002): botspot.com (accessed May 2003).

Marcus, C. "Loyal Customers Can't Be Strangers." *Microsoft Executive Circle* 1, no. 2, May 2001, microsoft.com/misc/

external/executivecircle/2001_q2/loyal_customers.asp (accessed April 2003).

Martin, T. N., and J. C. Hafer. "Internet Procurement by Corporate Purchasing Agents: Is It All Hype?" *SAM Advanced Management Journal* (Winter 2002).

McDaniel, C., and R. H. Gates. *Marketing Research: The Impact of the Internet*. Cincinnati, OH: South-Western Publishing, 2001.

McKnight, D. H., and N. L. Chervany. "What Trust Means in E-Commerce Customer Relationships: An Interdisciplinary Conceptual Typology." *International Journal of Electronic Commerce* (Winter 2001–2002).

Miles, G. E., et al. "A Framework for Understanding Human Factors in Web-Based E-Commerce." *International Journal of Human Computer Studies* 52 (2000).

Miller, T. W., and P. R. Dickson. "On-line Market Research." *International Journal of Electronic Commerce* 5, no. 3 (2001).

Minnett, S. *B2B Marketing: Radically Different Approach for Business-to-Business Marketers*. Upper Saddle River, NJ: Prentice Hall, 2001.

New Piper. "Piper Rolls Out Further Customer Relations Initiatives." New Piper news release, July 22, 2002.

Nikitas, T. "Your Customers Are Talking. Are You Listening?" *Smart Business*, February 1, 2002, informative.com/news/newsArticles_smartBusiness_020102.html (accessed September 2002).

O'Keefe, R. M., and T. McEachern. "Web-Based Customer Decision Support System." *Communications of the ACM* (March 1998).

Patricia Seybold Group. *An Executive's Guide to CRM*. Boston, MA: Patricia Seybold Group, 2002, psgroup.com/freereport/imedia/resport/asp (accessed April 2003).

PeopleSoft. *The Business Case for Mobile CRM: Opportunities, Pitfalls, and Solutions*. Pleasanton, CA: PeopleSoft Press, 2002.

Peppers, D., M. Rogers, and B. Dorf. *The One-to-One Fieldbook*. New York: Currency and Doubleday, 1999.

Petersen, G. S. *Customer Relationship Management Systems: ROI and Results Measurement*. New York: Strategic Sales Performance, 1999.

pg.com (accessed February–December 2002).

Plant, R. T. *E-Commerce: Foundation of Strategy*. Upper Saddle River, NJ: Prentice Hall, 2000.

PR Newswire. "American Airlines Web Site Features ATG Online CRM Offering." *ScreamingMedia*, May 15, 2002, industry.java.sun.com/javanews/stories/story2/0,1072,45470,00.html (accessed April 2003).

Ranganathan, C., and E. Grandon. "An Exploratory Examination of Factors Affecting Online Sales." *Journal of Computer Information Systems* 42, no. 3 (2002).

Reichheld, F. *Building Loyalty in the Age of the Internet*. Boston: Harvard Business School Press, 2001.

Reichheld, F., and P. Schefter. "E-Loyalty—Your Secret Weapon on the Web." *Harvard Business Review* (July–August 2000).

Ridell, J., et al. *Word of Mouse: The Marketing Power of Collaborative Filtering*. New York: Warner Books, 2002.

ritcheylogic.com (accessed 2000–2003).

Romano, N. C., Jr., and J. Fjermestad (eds.). "Introduction to the Special Section: Electronic Commerce Customer Relationship Management (ECCRM)." *International Journal of Electronic Commerce* (Winter 2001–2002).

Rust, R. T., and K. N. Lemon. "E-Service and the Consumer." *International Journal of Electronic Commerce* 5, no. 3 (2001): 85–101.

SAS. "The SAS Solution for CRM." SAS Institute, 2000, sas.com/offices/europe/uk/press_office/press_kits/seugi_2000/crm.pdf (accessed September 2002).

Seybold, P. B. "Get Inside the Lives of Your Customers." *Harvard Business Review* (May 2001): 81–89.

Seybold, P. B., and R. Marshak. *Customer.com: How to Create a Profitable Business Strategy for the Internet and Beyond*. New York: Times Books, 1998.

Shapiro, D., et al. "Business on a Handshake." *The Negotiation Journal*, October 1992.

Sharma, A. "Trends in Internet-based B2B Marketing." *Industrial Marketing Management* 31, no. 1 (2002).

Silverman, B. G., et al. "Implications of Buyer Decision Theory for Design of E-Commerce Web Sites." *International Journal of Human Computer Studies* 55, no. 5 (2001).

Sindell, K. *Loyalty Marketing for the Internet Age*. Chicago: Dearborn Trade, 2000.

Solomon, M. R. *Consumer Behavior*. Upper Saddle River, NJ: Prentice Hall, 2002.

Sterne, J. *Web Metrics: Proven Methods for Measuring Web Site Success*. New York: Wiley, 2002.

Strauss, J., and R. Frost. *Internet Marketing*, 2d ed. Upper Saddle River, NJ: Prentice Hall, 2001.

Sweiger, M., et al. *Clickstream Data Warehousing*. New York: Wiley, 2002.

Tan, X., et al. "Internet Integrated Customer Relationship Management." *Journal of Computer Information Systems* (Spring 2002).

Techmorrow.com. "Increased Profits Via Customer Relationship Marketing (CRM/ECRM)." techmorrow.com, techmorrow.com/article_3.htm (accessed April 2003).

Tedeschi, B. "A Fresh Spin on 'Affinity Portals' to the Internet." *New York Times*, April 17, 2000.

Todor, J. I., and W. D. Todor. *Winning Mindshare: The Psychology of Personalization and One to One Marketing*. Marion, IA: Whetstone Group, 2001.

Temkin, B. C. "Focus on Customer Experience, Not CRM." *Forrester Research*, September 2002, forrester.com/ER/Research/Report/Summary/0,1338,14798,FF.html (accessed April 2003).

Vassos, J. *Strategic Internet Marketing*. Indianapolis, IN: Que Publishing, 1996.

Voss, C. "Developing an eService Strategy." *Business Strategy Review* 11, no. 11 (2000).

waf.it (accessed September 2002).

Wagner, M. "Standing Watch over Corporate Reputations." *B2B*, June 10, 2002.

Yoon, S. "Brand Names Are at the Virtual Mall." *Wall Street Journal Europe*, June 13, 2002.

BUSINESS INTELLIGENCE: FROM DATA COLLECTION TO DATA MINING AND ANALYSIS

Data for EC organizations can be viewed as either transactional or analytical. Transactional data are those pieces of information that are collected in traditional transactions processing systems (TPSs), are organized mainly in a hierarchical structure, and are centrally processed. Newer systems that contain transactional data may be Web-based and in medium to large organizations may be part of an ERP system. These are known as *operational systems*, and the results of the processing are mainly summaries and reports.

Today, the most successful companies are those that can respond quickly and flexibly to market changes and opportunities, and the key to this response is the effective and efficient use of data and information. EC transactions must be done online in real time. This is done not only via transaction processing, but also through the supplementary activity of *analytical processing*, which involves analysis of accumulated data, mainly by end users. Analytical processing includes Web applications, market research, data mining, CRM activities, and decision support systems. Placing strategic information in the hands of decision makers aids productivity, empowers users to make better decisions, and improves customer service, leading to greater competitive advantage.

COLLECTING, ORGANIZING, AND STORING DATA FOR ANALYTICAL PROCESSING

Analytical processing can basically be done in two ways. One is to work directly with the operational systems (the "let's use what we have" approach), using software tools and components known as front-end tools and middleware. This option can be optimal for companies that do not have a large number of end users running queries and conducting analyses against the operating systems. Since the mid-1990s, a wave of front-end tools that allow end users to directly conduct queries and report on data stored in *operational databases* have become available. The problem with this approach, however, is that the tools are effective only with end users who have a medium- to high-degree of knowledge about databases.

These limitations call for a second, improved option of analytical processing, which involves three concepts:

1. A business representation of data for end users
2. A user-friendly Web-based environment that gives the customers and corporate employees query and reporting capabilities
3. A single, server-based data repository, called the **data warehouse (DW)**, that allows centralized analysis, security, and control over the data

DATA WAREHOUSES

The purpose of a data warehouse is to establish a repository that makes operational data accessible in a form readily acceptable for analytical processing activities such as EC applications, decision support, and other end-user applications. As part of this accessibility, detail-level operational data must be transformed to a *relational* form, which makes them more amenable to analytical processing. Thus, data warehousing is not a concept by itself, but is interrelated with data access, retrieval, analysis, and visualization (see Gray and Watson 1998).

The process of building and using a data warehouse is shown in Exhibit 4A.1. The organization's data are stored in operational systems (left side of the figure). Not all data are transferred to the data warehouse, and frequently only a summary of the data is transferred in a process of extraction, transformation, and load (ETL). The data that are transferred are organized within the warehouse as a relational database so that it is easy for end users to access. Also, the data are organized by subject, such as by product, customer segment, or business partner. EC data may also be organized according to a business process, such as ordering, shipping, or available inventory. The data then can be optionally replicated in data marts (explained later). Data access is provided through Web browsers via middleware software. On the right side of the figure are various applications that may use the data.

The activities conducted during much of the process described in Figure 4A.1 (page 172) are generally referred to as **business intelligence**. The major reason for the name is that these activities not only collect and process data, but they enable analysis that results in useful—intelligent—solutions to business

data warehouse (DW)
A single, server-based data repository that allows centralized analysis, security, and control over the data.

business intelligence
Activities that not only collect and process data, but also make possible analysis that results in useful—intelligent—solutions to business problems.

171

EXHIBIT 4A.1   Data Warehouse Framework and Views

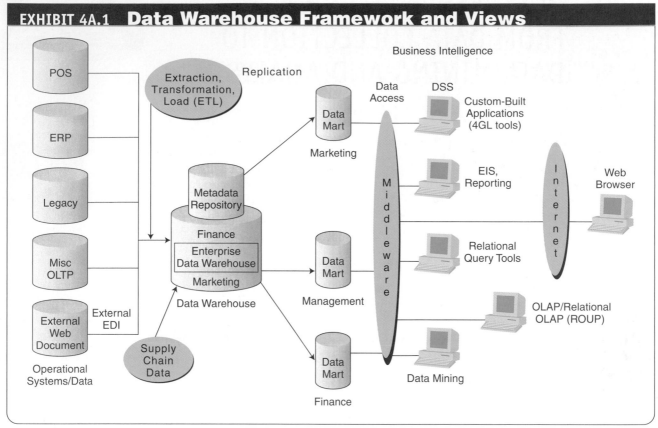

Source: Turban, Efraim, R. Kelly Rainer, Jr., and Richard E. Potter. *Introduction to Information Technology*, 2nd Edition. © 2002 by John Wiley & Sons, Inc.; This material is used by permission of John Wiley & Sons, Inc.

problems. The concept of business intelligence originated from executive information system (EIS) activities, but it is used today to describe online analytical processing and data mining activities as well.

Data warehouses provide for the storage of metadata, which are data about data. Metadata include software programs about data, rules for organizing data, and data summaries that are easier to index and search, especially with Web tools.

metadata

Data about data, including software programs about data, rules for organizing data, and data summaries.

Characteristics of Data Warehousing

The major characteristics of data warehousing include the following:

▶ **Organization.** Data are organized by detailed subject (e.g., by customer, vendor, product, price level, and region) and only contain information relevant for decision support.

▶ **Consistency.** Data in different operational databases may be encoded differently. For example, gender data may be encoded 0 and 1 in one operational system and "m" and "f" in another. Within each warehouse they will be coded in a *consistent* manner.

▶ **Time variant.** The data are kept for 5 to 10 years so that they can be used for trends, forecasting, and comparisons over time.

▶ **Nonvolatile.** Once entered into the warehouse, data are not updated (but new related data may replace or supplement old data).

▶ **Relational.** The data warehouse typically uses a relational structure (organized into tables of rows and columns).

Benefits of Data Warehouses

The major benefits of data warehouses are (1) the ability of users to reach data quickly, because data are located in one place and organized properly, and (2) the ability to reach data easily, frequently by end users themselves, using Web browsers. Another benefit is that a data warehouse provides a consolidated view of corporate data, which is better than providing many smaller (and differently formatted) views. For example, separate production systems may track sales and coupon mailings. Combining data from these different systems may yield insights into the cost efficiency of coupon sales promotions that would not be immediately evident from the output data of either system alone. Integrated within a data warehouse, however, such information can be easily extracted.

Data warehouses allow information processing to be off-loaded from expensive operational systems onto low-cost servers (or processed by application service providers, ASPs). Once this is done, end-user tools can handle a significant number of end-user information requests. Furthermore, some operational system reporting requirements can be moved to Web-based decision support systems, thus freeing up production processing.

In addition, accessibility to data warehouse content by decision makers is provided throughout the enterprise via an intranet. Users can view, query, and analyze the data and produce reports using Web browsers. This is an extremely economical and effective method of delivering data.

The various benefits offered by data warehouses can improve business knowledge, provide competitive advantage, enhance customer service and satisfaction, facilitate decision making, and help in streamlining business processes.

Suitability

Data warehousing is most appropriate for organizations in which some of the following apply:

▶ Large amounts of data need to be accessed by end users.

▶ The operational data are stored in different systems.

▶ An information-based approach to management is in use.

▶ The company has a large, diverse *customer base* (such as in a utility company or a bank).

▶ The same data are represented differently in different systems.

▶ Data are stored in highly technical formats that are difficult to decipher.

▶ Extensive end-user computing is performed (many end users performing many activities).

Hundreds of successful applications have been reported (e.g., see client success stories and case studies at Web sites of vendors such as MicroStrategy, Brio Technology Inc., Business Objects, Cognos Corp., Information Builders, NCR Corp., Platinum Technology, Software A&G, Comshare Inc., and Pilot Software). For further discussion see McFadden and Watson (1996), Barquin and Edelstein (1997), Gray and Watson (1998), and Inmon et al. (2000). Also visit the Data Warehouse Institute (dw-institute.org).

Although data warehouses offer some substantial benefits, the cost of a data warehouse can be very high, both to build and to maintain. Furthermore, it may difficult and expensive to incorporate data from obsolete legacy systems. Finally, there may be a lack of incentive among departments within a company to share data. Therefore, a careful feasibility study must be undertaken before a commitment is made to data warehousing. Alternatively, one or more data marts can be used.

DATA MARTS

The high cost of data warehouses confines their use mostly to large companies. An alternative used by many other firms is the creation of a lower-cost, scaled-down version of a data warehouse called a **data mart**. A data mart is a small warehouse designed for a strategic business unit (SBU) or a department. A data mart can be fully dedicated to EC.

data mart
A small data warehouse designed for a strategic business unit (SBU) or a department.

The advantages of data marts over data warehouses include the following:

▶ The cost is low (prices under $100,000 versus $1 million or more for large data warehouses).

▶ The lead time for implementation is significantly shorter, often less than 90 days.

▶ They are controlled locally rather than centrally, conferring power on the using group.

▶ They contain less information than the data warehouse. Hence, they have more rapid response and are more easily understood and navigated than an enterprisewide data warehouse.

▶ They allow an EC department to build its own decision support systems without relying on a centralized IS department.

There are two major types of data marts: replicated (dependent) and stand-alone. *Replicated (dependent) data marts* are those in which functional subsets of the data warehouse have been replicated (copied) into smaller data marts. The reason for using replicated data marts is that sometimes it is easier to work with a small subset of the data warehouse. Each of these replicated data marts is dedicated to a certain area, as shown in Exhibit 4A.1. The replicated data mart is *an addition to* the data warehouse. (This is why it is also termed *dependent*—its existence depends on the data warehouse.) Alternatively, a company can have one or more *independent* (*stand-alone*) data marts without having a data warehouse. Stand-alone data marts are typically used for marketing, finance, and engineering applications.

OPERATIONAL DATA STORES

operational data store
A database for use in trans-action processing (opera-tional) systems that uses data warehouse concepts to provide clean data.

An operational data store is a database for transaction processing systems that uses data warehouse concepts to provide clean data. That is, it brings the concepts and benefits of the data warehouse to the operational portions of the business, at a lower cost. It is used for short-term decisions involving mission-critical applications rather than for the medium- and long-term decisions associated with the regular data warehouse. These decisions depend on much more current information. For example, a bank needs to know about all the accounts quickly for a given customer who has sent an e-mail inquiry. The operational data store can be viewed as situated between the operational data (legacy systems) and the data warehouse. A comparison between the two is provided by Gray and Watson (1998).

SUCCESSES AND FAILURES OF DATA WAREHOUSING

Since their early inception, data warehouses have produced many success stories. However, there have also been many failures. Carbone (1999) defined several types of warehouse failures:

▶ Warehouse did not meet the expectations of those involved.
▶ Warehouse was completed, but went severely over budget in relation to time, money, or both.
▶ Warehouse failed one or more times but eventually was completed.
▶ Warehouse failed and no effort was made to revive it.

Carbone identified a number of reasons for failures (which are typical for many other large information systems):

Data Problems: **Not enough summarization of data**

▶ Failure to align data marts and data warehouses
▶ Lack of data quality (e.g., omitted information)
▶ Lack of user input
▶ Using data marts instead of data warehouses (and vice versa)
▶ Insecure access to data manipulation (users should not have the ability to change any data)
▶ Poor upkeep of information (e.g., failure to keep information current)

Technology Problems: **Inappropriate architecture**

▶ Using the warehouse only for operational, not informational, purposes
▶ Poor upkeep of technology
▶ Inappropriate format of information—a single, standard format was not used

Other Problems: **Training and Management Issues**

▶ Vendors overselling capabilities of products
▶ Lack of training and support for users
▶ Inexperienced/untrained/inadequate number of personnel
▶ Unrealistic expectations—overly optimistic time schedule or underestimation of cost
▶ Lack of coordination (or requires too much coordination)
▶ Cultural issues were ignored
▶ Improperly managing multiple users with various needs
▶ Unclear business objectives; not knowing the information requirements
▶ Lack of effective project sponsorship
▶ Interfering corporate politics

Suggestions on how to avoid data warehouse failure are provided by Griffin at datawarehouse.com (2000) and by Ferranti.

DATA ANALYSIS AND KNOWLEDGE DISCOVERY

Once the data are in the data warehouse and/or data marts they can be accessed by end users. Users can then conduct several types of analytical activities with the data, ranging from decision support and execu-tive support analyses to ad-hoc queries, online analytical processing (OLAP), and data mining.

AD-HOC QUERY

Ad-hoc queries allow users to request real-time information from the computer that is not available in periodic reports. Such answers are needed to expedite decision making. The system must be intelligent enough to understand what the user wants. Simple ad-hoc query systems are based on menus. More intelligent systems use SQL (structured query language) and query-by-example approaches or Web-based applications.

Web-Based Ad-Hoc Query Tools

Web-based ad-hoc query tools allow users to access, navigate, and explore relational data to make key business decisions in real time. For instance, users can gauge the success of a Web marketing campaign according to the number of Web hits received last month, last week, or even yesterday, in relation to products or services purchased. This insight helps companies better target marketing efforts and forge closer, more responsive relationships with customers. Several vendors offer such tools. For example, Cognos Corp. (see cognos.com/products/query.html) offers Web users powerful ad-hoc exploration of corporate data assets, with little or no user training needed.

Advanced query tools can be connected to intranets and extranets for B2B and CRM querying. Also, a drill-down from multidimensional analysis to DSS and other tools are available. Answers to queries can be delivered to visualization tools.

ONLINE ANALYTICAL PROCESSING

Online analytical processing (OLAP) refers to such end-user activities as DSS modeling using spreadsheets and graphics, which are done online. OLAP is an information system that enables the user to query the system, conduct an analysis, and so on, while the user is at his or her PC. The result is generated in seconds. Unlike *online transaction processing (OLTP)* applications, OLAP involves many data items (frequently many thousands or even millions) in complex relationships. One objective of OLAP is to analyze these relationships and look for patterns, trends, and exceptions. Another objective is to answer users' queries.

A typical OLAP query might access a multigigabyte, multiyear sales database in order to find all product sales in each customer segment (female, male, young people, etc.). After reviewing the results, an analyst might further refine the query to find sales volume for each sales channel by hours of the day or by product type. As a last step, the analyst might want to perform year-to-year or quarter-to-quarter comparisons for each sales channel. This whole process must be carried out online with rapid response time.

Thus, OLAP queries are able to analyze the relationships between many types of business elements (e.g., sales, products, regions, and channels) involving aggregated data over time (e.g., sales volumes, budgeted dollars, and dollars spent, on a monthly, quarterly, or yearly basis). The ability to present data in different perspectives involving complex calculations between data elements (e.g., expected profit as calculated as a function of sales revenue for each type of sales channel in a particular region) enables users to pursue an analytical thought process without being stymied by the system.

Many vendors provide ready-made analytical tools, mostly in finance, marketing, and operations (e.g., productivity analyses, profitability analyses). Such packages include built-in Web-based DSSs. For example, *Cognos Finance* (from cognos.com) is an enterprisewide financial application for monitoring the financial performance of a business organization. It provides a framework for completing financial processes in a timely manner: monthly and quarterly closes, the budget process, and integration of the latest actual data with user-supplied forecasts. Users can also integrate Web information for a single view of the organization.

However, although OLAP is very useful in many cases, it is retrospective in nature and cannot provide the automated and *prospective* knowledge discovery that is done by advanced *data mining* techniques.

online analytical processing (OLAP)
End-user analytical activities, such as DSS modeling using spreadsheets and graphics, that are done online.

KNOWLEDGE DISCOVERY

The process of extracting useful knowledge from volumes of data is known as knowledge discovery in databases (KDD), or just knowledge discovery. KDD's objective is to identify valid, novel, potentially useful, and ultimately understandable patterns in data. KDD is useful because it is supported by three technologies that are now sufficiently mature: massive data collection, powerful multiprocessor computers, and data mining algorithms.

Formal computer-based knowledge discovery has been done since the 1960s. However, the enabling techniques have been expanded and improved over time. KDD processes have appeared under various names and have shown different characteristics. KDD tools have evolved over time. As time has passed, KDD has become able to answer more complex business questions. For details see Fayyad (1996).

knowledge discovery in databases (KDD)/ knowledge discover (KD)
The process of extracting useful knowledge from volumes of data.

DATA MINING

Data mining derives its name from the similarities between searching for valuable business information in a large database and mining a mountain for a vein of valuable ore. Both processes require either sifting through an immense amount of material or intelligently probing it to find exactly where the value resides. In some cases the data are consolidated in a data warehouse and data marts; in others they are kept on the Internet and intranet servers.

Given databases of sufficient size and quality, data mining technology can generate new business opportunities by providing these capabilities:

▶ **Automated prediction of trends and behaviors.** Data mining automates the process of finding predictive information in large databases. Questions that traditionally required extensive hands-on analysis can now be answered directly and quickly from the data. A typical example of a predictive problem is targeted marketing. Data mining can use data on past promotional mailings to identify the targets most likely to respond favorably to future mailings. Other predictive examples include forecasting bankruptcy and other forms of default and identifying segments of a population likely to respond similarly to given events.

▶ **Automated discovery of previously unknown patterns.** Data mining tools identify previously hidden patterns in one step. An example of pattern discovery is the analysis of retail sales data to identify seemingly unrelated products that are often purchased together, such as baby diapers and beer. Other pattern discovery problems include detecting fraudulent credit card transactions and identifying *invalid (anomalous) data* that may represent data entry keying errors.

When data mining tools are implemented on high-performance, parallel-processing systems, they can analyze massive databases in minutes. Often, these databases will contain data stored for several years. Faster processing means that users can experiment with more models to understand complex data. High speed makes it practical for users to analyze huge quantities of data. Larger databases, in turn, yield improved predictions.

Data mining also can be conducted by nonprogrammers. The "miner" is often an end user, empowered by "data drills" and other power query tools to ask ad-hoc questions and get answers quickly, with little or no programming skill. Data mining tools can be combined with spreadsheets and other end-user software development tools, making it relatively easy to analyze and process the mined data. Data mining appears under different names, such as knowledge extraction, data dipping, data archeology, data exploration, data pattern processing, data dredging, and information harvesting. "Striking it rich" in data mining often involves finding unexpected, valuable results.

Data mining yields five types of information:

1. **Association.** Relationships between events that occur at one time (e.g., the contents of a shopping cart, such as orange juice and cough medicine)

2. **Sequences.** Relationships that exist over a period of time (e.g., repeat visits to a supermarket)

3. **Classifications.** The defining characteristics of a certain group (e.g., customers who have been lost to competitors)

4. **Clusters.** Groups of items that share a particular characteristic that was not known in advance of the data mining

5. **Forecasting.** Future values based on patterns within large sets of data (e.g., demand forecasting)

Data miners use several tools and techniques: case-based reasoning (using historical cases to recognize patterns); neural computing (a machine learning approach by which historical data can be examined for patterns through massive parallel processing); association analysis (using a specialized set of algorithms to sort through data sets and express statistical rules among items); and intelligent agents (expert or knowledge-based software embedded in information systems).

A Sampler of Data Mining Applications

According to a 2000 Gartner Group report (see Linden 2002), more than half of all the *Fortune* 1000 companies worldwide are using data mining technology. Data mining can be very helpful, as shown by the representative examples that follow. Note that the intent of most of these examples is to identify a business opportunity in order to create a sustainable competitive advantage.

▶ **Retailing and sales distribution.** Predicting sales, determining correct inventory levels and distribution schedules among outlets

▶ **Banking.** Forecasting levels of bad loans and fraudulent credit card use, predicting credit card spending by new customers, predicting which kinds of customers will best respond to (and qualify for) new loan offers

- ▶ **Manufacturing and production.** Predicting machinery failures, finding key factors that control optimization of manufacturing capacity
- ▶ **Brokerage and securities trading.** Predicting when bond prices will change, forecasting the range of stock fluctuations for particular issues and the overall market, determining when to buy or sell stocks
- ▶ **Insurance.** Forecasting claim amounts and medical coverage costs, classifying the most important elements that affect medical coverage, predicting which customers will buy new policies
- ▶ **Computer hardware and software.** Predicting disk-drive failures, forecasting how long it will take to create new chips, predicting potential security violations
- ▶ **Police work.** Tracking crime patterns, locations, and criminal behavior, identifying attributes to assist in solving criminal cases
- ▶ **Government and defense.** Forecasting the cost of moving military equipment, testing strategies for potential military engagements, predicting resource consumption
- ▶ **Airlines.** Capturing data on where customers are flying and the ultimate destination of passengers who change carriers in hub cities so that airlines can identify popular locations that they do not service, checking the feasibility of adding routes to capture lost business
- ▶ **Health care.** Correlating demographics of patients with critical illnesses, developing better insights on symptoms and their causes and how to provide proper treatments
- ▶ **Broadcasting.** Predicting the most popular programming to air during prime time, predicting how to maximize returns by interjecting advertisements
- ▶ **Marketing.** Classifying customer demographics that can be used to predict which customers will respond to a mailing or buy a particular product

TEXT MINING

Text mining is the application of data mining to nonstructured or less-structured text files. Data mining takes advantage of the infrastructure of stored data to extract predictive information. For example, by mining a customer database, an analyst might discover that everyone who buys product A also buys products B and C, but does so 6 months later. Text mining, however, operates with less-structured information. Documents rarely have strong internal infrastructure, and when they do, it is frequently focused on document *format* rather than document content.

Text mining helps organizations find the "hidden" content of documents, as well as additional useful relationships. It also helps them group documents by common themes (e.g., identify all the customers of an insurance firm who have similar complaints).

text mining
The application of data mining to nonstructured or less-structured text files.

Web Mining

The previous discussion of data mining refers to data that are stored usually in a data warehouse. However, to analyze a large amount of data on the Web, one needs somewhat different mining tools. Web mining is the application of data mining techniques to discover meaningful patterns, profiles, and trends from Web sites. The term Web mining is used to describe two different types of information mining. The first, Web *content mining* is the process of discovering information from millions of Web documents. The second, Web *usage mining*, is the process of analyzing what customers are doing on the Web—that is, analyzing clickstream data.

In Web mining, the data are clickstream data, usually stored in a special clickstream data warehouse (see Sweiger et al. 2002) or in a data mart. The strategies used may be the same in both. Several companies provide tools for Web mining (e.g., Iopus.com, kdnuggets.com, megaputer.com, and spss.com).

Web mining
The application of data mining techniques to discover meaningful patterns, profiles, and trends from both the content and usage of Web sites.

KEY TERMS

REFERENCES

Barquin, R., and H. Edelstein. *Building, Using, and Managing the Data Warehouse.* Upper Saddle River, NJ: Prentice Hall, 1997.

Carbone, P. L. "Data Warehousing: Many of the Common Failures." May 3, 1999, presentation,mitre.org/support/papers/tech . . . 9_00/d-arehoulse_presentation.htm (accessed April 2003).

Fayyad, U. M. *Advances in Knowledge Discovery.* Boston: MIT Press, 1996.

Ferranti, M. "Data Warehouse World: Checking Out Success, Failure, and Myth." *Sunworld*, August 1998, sunsite.uakom.sk/sunworldonline/swol-08-1998/swol-08-datawarehouse.html (accessed April 2003).

Gray, P., and H. J. Watson. *Decision Support in the Data Warehouse.* Upper Saddle River, NJ: Prentice Hall, 1998.

Griffin, J. "Fundamental Pitfalls to Avoid in Your Data Warehouse." datawarehouse.com, July 18, 2000, datawarehouse.com/iknowledge/articles/article.cfm?ContentID=218 (accessed April 2003).

Inmon, W. H., et al. *Corporate Information Factory*, 2d ed. New York: Wiley, 2000.

Linden, A. "Management Update: Data Mining Trends Enterprises Should Know About." Gartner Group, October 9, 2002, gartner.com/Init (accessed April 2003).

McFadden, F., and H. J. Watson. "The World of Data Warehousing: Issues and Opportunities." *Data Warehousing* 1, no. 1 (1996).

Sweiger, M. *Clickstream Warehousing.* New York: John Wiley & Sons, 2002.

Turban, E., et al, *Electronic Commerce: A Managerial Perspective.* Upper Saddle River, NJ: Prentice Hall, 2004.

CHAPTER 5

ONLINE ADVERTISING

Content

Web Advertising Strategy Helps P&G Compete

Learning objectives

Upon completion of this chapter, you will be able to:

1. Describe the objectives of Web advertising and its characteristics.

2. Describe the major advertising methods used on the Web.

3. Describe various online advertising strategies and types of promotions.

4. Describe the issues involved in measuring the success of Web advertising as it relates to different pricing methods.

5. Describe permission marketing, ad management, localization, and other advertising-related issues.

6. Understand the role of intelligent agents in consumer issues and advertising applications.

7. Understand the problem of unsolicited ads and possible solutions.

WEB ADVERTISING STRATEGY HELPS P&G COMPETE

The Problem

The consumer goods market is a global one and extremely competitive. Giant corporations such as Procter & Gamble, Colgate Palmolive, Unilever, Nestlé, and The Coca-Cola Company are competing on hundreds of products, ranging from toothpaste to baby diapers to beverages. To survive, these companies must constantly research the markets, develop new products, and advertise, advertise, advertise. Market research and advertising budgets can amount to as much as 20 percent of sales, thus reducing profits. However, failure to advertise sufficiently and properly results in smaller revenue, loss of market share, and possibly going out of business. Thus, the proper advertising strategy, including Web advertising, is critical to the welfare of any company in the consumer goods industry.

Procter & Gamble (P&G) is the largest packaged-goods company in the United States, with over 300 brands (ranging from Crest to Tide to Pampers) and annual sales of over $50 billion. P&G spends more money on advertising than any other company, about $4 billion a year. P&G's business problem is how to best use its advertising budget to get the most marketing "bang for its bucks."

The Solution

P&G started to advertise on the Internet in the late 1990s, both on major portals (using pop-up and banner ads for Scope and Tide) and on its own Web sites. By 2000, it had 72 active sites, mostly one site for each product (e.g., *pampers.com*, *tide.com*, and *crest.com*). Several of the sites were general (e.g., *being girl.com*, where teens find answers to questions about their bodies as well as advice about boys; *pantene.com*, where consumers can get personalized hair consultations; and *reflect.com*, where consumers can get customized beauty products). Today, P&G is considered by many (e.g., Bulik 2000) to be "pushing the envelope on the Web" by experimenting with many Web projects, mostly related to market research online and online advertising.

P&G's major objective is to build around each major product a community of users on the Web. The company has the following objectives in building and maintaining these sites: developing brand awareness and recognition (brand equity); collecting valuable data from consumers; cutting down on advertising costs; conducting one-to-one advertisement; experimenting with direct sales of commodity-type products; and selling customized beauty products to individuals (through *reflect.com*).

P&G's off-line approach has always included research, development, and investment in hundreds of products simultaneously. Thus, the company's broad online approach is no surprise. Other aspects of its online advertising strategy include developing marketing partnerships (e.g., with iVillage.com), investing in promising start-ups (e.g., Plumtree Software), and joining

Transora.com, a B2B marketplace consortium (other partners include Unilever, Coca-Cola, and Hershey Foods). P&G's advertising approach is in itself experimental in nature: The company believes that its Internet strategy could lead to a comprehensive e-commerce position in the market. However, P&G also recognizes that the strategy could be just branding and result in a waste of money.

P&G's key reason for branching out from the laundry-tip types of sites (e.g., *tide.com*) to the more interactive sites (e.g., *being-me.com*) is so that it can conduct data mining on Web data. Interactive sites not only build brand equity and test the waters for direct sales to customers, they also collect valuable data from consumers. This information helps curtail marketing and advertising expenses by enabling the company to target consumers more precisely and economically. It lets the company gather more information about both the customers and the products and permits more one-to-one advertising. Examples of sites developed for research purposes are:

- *being-me.com*: Users take a quiz to determine what feminine products best fit their individual needs and then can purchase the products.
- *reflect.com*: Beauty products are customized based on the user's preferences.
- *physique.com*: A site for a hair styling product registered 600,000 consumers in its "club" before the brand was even launched.

The Results

As Robert Rubin of Netquity (a joint venture between Forrester Research and Information Resources) says, "P&G is the leading consumer packaged-goods company on the Net because they're willing to try everything" (Bulik 2000). Although most of the improvements achieved by its Web advertising strategy were qualitative, P&G was also doing extremely well during the economic downturn of 2000–2003. As an indication of its success, its stock price climbed about 50 percent, whereas the average stock price on the New York Stock Exchange dropped over 30 percent.

Sources: Compiled from Bulik (2000), pp. 48–53, and from *tide.com*, *crest.com*, *pantene.com*, *beinggirl.com*, *being-me.com*, *reflect.com*, and *physique.com*.

WHAT WE CAN LEARN . . .

The case of P&G points to several issues related to online advertising. First, advertising can be conducted in several different ways (e.g., pop-ups, banners). Second, there are many options of where and how to use such methods. Therefore, it is necessary to develop a Web advertising strategy, which is difficult due to the fact that everything is very new and changing rapidly on the Web. Also, the case illustrates the difficulty in measuring quantitative results of online advertising as well as the relationship of advertising to market research online. The case also points to the possibilities of one-to-one advertisement and product customization. Finally, the possibility of relating advertising to direct sales online, not only of customized products but also of commodity-type products, is highlighted. These and other topics will be addressed in this chapter.

5.1 WEB ADVERTISING

Advertising on the Web by all types of organizations, and especially by purely online ones, plays an extremely important role in e-commerce. According to *PC Magazine* (2002), expenditures on Web ads in the United States increased from $7.9 billion in 2001 to $11.4 billion in 2002, and they are forecasted to reach $18.8 billion by 2005.

OVERVIEW OF WEB ADVERTISING

Advertising is an attempt to disseminate information in order to affect buyer-seller transactions. In *traditional* marketing, advertising was impersonal, one-way mass communication that was paid for by sponsors. Telemarketing and direct mail ads were attempts to personalize advertising in order to make it more effective. These *direct marketing* approaches worked fairly well but were expensive and slow and seldom truly one-to-one interactive. For example, a direct mail campaign costs about $1 per person, with a response rate of only 1 to 3 percent. This makes the cost per responding person in the range of $33 to $100. Such an expense can be justified only for high-ticket items (e.g., cars).

One of the problems with direct mail advertising was that the advertisers knew very little about the recipients. Segmentation of markets by various characteristics (e.g., age, income, gender) helped a bit, but did not solve the problem. The Internet introduces the concept of **interactive marketing,** which has enabled advertisers to interact directly with customers. In interactive marketing, a consumer can click on an ad in order to obtain more information or send an e-mail to ask a question. Besides the two-way communication and e-mail capabilities provided by the Internet, vendors also can target specific groups and individuals on which they want to spend their advertising dollars. Finally, the Internet enables truly one-to-one advertising. A comparison of mass advertising, direct mail advertising, and interactive online advertising is shown in Exhibit 5.1 (page 182).

Companies use Internet advertising as *one* of their advertising channels. At the same time, they may use also TV, newspapers, or other channels. In this respect, the Web competes with the other channels. There are two major business models for advertising online: (1) using the Web as a channel to advertise a firm's own products and services, and (2) making a firm's site a public portal site and using captive audiences to advertise products offered by other firms. For example, the audience might come to a P&G Web site learn about Tide, but they might also get additional ads for products made by companies other than P&G.

In this chapter, we deal with Internet advertising in general. (For additional resources on Internet advertising, see adage.com and hotwired.com/webmonkey.)

SOME INTERNET ADVERTISING TERMINOLOGY

The following glossary of terms will be of use as you read about Web advertising.

▸ **Ad views. Ad views** are the number of times users call up a page that has a banner on it during a specific time period (e.g., "ad views per day"). They are also known as *impressions* or *page views*.

interactive marketing
Online marketing, enabled by the Internet, in which advertisers can interact directly with customers and consumers can interact with advertisers/ vendors.

ad views
The number of times users call up a page that has a banner on it during a specific time period; known as *impressions* or *page views*.

click (click-through or ad click)
A count made each time a visitor clicks on an advertising banner to access the advertiser's Web site.

CPM (cost per thousand impressions)
The fee an advertiser pays for each 1,000 times a page with a banner ad is shown.

hit
A request for data from a Web page or file.

visit
A series of requests during one navigation of a Web site; a pause of request for a certain length of time ends a visit.

unique visit
A count of the number of visitors to a site, regardless of how many pages are viewed per visit.

stickiness
Characteristic that influences the average length of time a visitor stays in a site.

▶ **Button.** A *button* is a small banner that is linked to a Web site. It may contain downloadable software.

▶ **Page.** A *page* is an HTML (Hypertext Markup Language) document that may contain text, images, and other online elements, such as Java applets and multimedia files. It may be statically or dynamically generated.

▶ **Click.** A click (click-through or ad click) is counted each time a visitor clicks on an advertising banner to access the advertiser's Web site.

▶ **CPM.** The CPM is the cost per thousand impressions. This is the fee the advertiser pays for each 1,000 times a page with a banner ad is shown.

▶ **Hit.** A hit refers to any request for data from a Web page or file. Hits are often used to determine the popularity/traffic of a site in the context of getting so many "hits" during a given period.

▶ **Visit.** A user may make a sequence of requests during one navigation, or visit, to a site. Once the visitor stops making requests from a site for a given period of time, called a *time-out* (usually 15 or 30 minutes), the next hit by this visitor is considered a new visit.

▶ **Unique visit.** A unique visit is a count of the number of visitors to a site, regardless of how many pages they view per visit.

▶ **Stickiness.** The characteristic that influences the average length of time a visitor stays in a site is termed stickiness. The longer visitors stay at a site, the stickier it is considered to be.

WHY INTERNET ADVERTISING?

The major traditional advertising media are television (about 36 percent), newspapers (about 35 percent), magazines (about 14 percent), and radio (about 10 percent) (Boswell 2002). Although Internet advertisement is a small percentage of the $120-billion-a-year advertising industry (about 4 percent in 2002) (Boswell 2002), it is growing rapidly. For example, according to Jupiter Media Mix (as reported in Boswell 2002), Internet advertising expenditures in 2000 were about $5 billion (this amount grew to over $6 billion in 2002), and are projected to reach $15 billion in 2006 (Boswell 2002).

Companies advertise on the Internet for several reasons. To begin with, television viewers are migrating to the Internet. Forrester Research found that over three-quarters of PC users

EXHIBIT 5.1   From Mass Advertising to Interactive Advertising

	Mass Advertising	Direct Mail Advertising	Interactive Advertising
Desired outcomes	Volume sales	Targeted reach, more sales, customer data	Volume sales, CRM, customer feedback
Consumer activities	Passive	Passive	Active
Leading products	Food, personal care products, beer, autos, cameras, computers, appliances	Credit cards, travel, autos, some appliances	Upscale apparel, banking, books, travel, insurance, computers, autos, jewelry, office supplies
Market strategy	High-volume products	Targeted goods to segments	Targeted individual or groups
Nerve centers (command centers)	Madison Avenue (advertisers)	Postal distribution centers, warehouses	Cyberspace, logistics companies
Preferred media vehicle	Television, newspapers, magazines	Mailing lists	Online services, e-commerce, banners
Preferred technology	Storyboards, TV	Databases	Servers, on-screen navigators, the Web
Worst outcome	Channel surfing	Recycling bins	Log off

Source: Based on *InformationWeek*, October 3, 1994, p. 26.

are giving up some television time to spend more time on their computers (Legmanila 2003). A November 2001 study conducted at UCLA confirms this trade-off: According to an Arbitron Internet Information and Edison Media Research survey (McDonald 2001), people between the ages of 12 and 24 clearly prefer the Internet (47 percent) to TV (26 percent), and one-third of all Internet users would give up their televisions before giving up their Internet access. This gap will grow in the future, especially with the new technology coming to cell phones that offer Internet access. In addition, many Internet users are well educated and have high incomes. Therefore, many Internet surfers are a desired target for advertisers.

Finally, an ad in a print publication or on TV will not offer statistics tracking the number of people who actually saw the ad or even opened the page featuring an ad. Print ads cannot be rotated based on the number of times someone opens the same page; that is, ad number one appears the first time someone opens the page, and ad number two appears the next time. Print ads cannot be filtered only to female readers who earn over $50,000, own a home, and work in a university. Of the people who look at the ad, the advertiser cannot even record the time consumers spent looking at it. The only piece of hard data available for traditional advertising is the total number of printed copies sold or the estimated viewing audience of the TV program. Everything else is guesswork. The world of online advertising offers much more information and feedback. Special tracking and ad management programs offered for ads on portals, online magazines, and almost every type of Web site in existence enable advertisers to do all the things mentioned here and more (see Sections 5.3 and 5.5).

Meeker (1997) examined the length of time it took for each ad media to reach 50 million U.S. users. Meeker found that it took radio 38 years, television 13 years, and cable television 10 years to reach 50 million viewers. Remarkably, it took only about 5 years for the Internet to reach 50 million users! Exhibit 5.2 extends the study to the year 2000, at which time more than 300 million people were using the Internet. Since then, the rate of adoption of the Internet has been growing even faster. It is estimated that more than 500 million people will use the Internet in 2004. According to these statistics, the Internet is by far the fastest growing communication medium. Of course, advertisers are interested in a medium with such potential reach, both locally and globally.

Other reasons why Web advertising is growing rapidly include:

▶ **Cost.** Online ads are sometimes cheaper than those in other media. In addition, ads can be updated at any time with minimal cost.

▶ **Richness of format.** Web ads can effectively use the convergence of text, audio, graphics, and animation. In addition, games, entertainment, and promotions can easily be

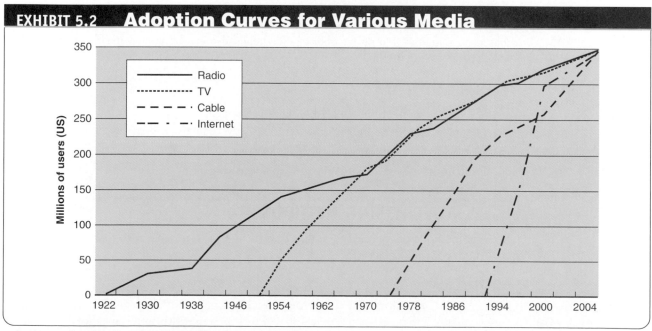

EXHIBIT 5.2   Adoption Curves for Various Media

Millions of users (US)

Radio
TV
Cable
Internet

Source: Developed by the authors, based, in part, on Meeker (1997).

combined in online advertisements. Also, wireless services such as MySimon.com enable customers to compare ads at any time from anywhere.

▶ **Personalization.** Web ads can be interactive and targeted to specific interest groups and/or individuals. That is, the Web is a much more focused medium.

▶ **Timeliness.** Internet ads can be fresh and up-to-the-minute.

▶ **Participation.** The Web is a participatory tool. Many people can communicate with each other in the context of an online community.

▶ **Location-basis.** Using wireless technology, Web advertising can be location based; Internet ads can be sent to consumers whenever they are in a specific location (e.g., near a restaurant or a theater).

▶ **Digital branding.** Even the most price-conscious online shoppers are willing to pay premiums for brands they trust. These brands may be click-and-mortar brands (e.g., P&G), or dot-coms such as Amazon.com. British Airways places many Internet banner ads. However, these ads are not for clicking on to buy—they are all about branding, or establishing British Airways as a brand.

As of 1998, these factors began to convince large, consumer-products companies, such as P&G, to shift an increasing share of their advertising dollars away from traditional media to Web advertising.

Of course, each advertising medium, including the Internet, has its advantages and limitations. Exhibit 5.3 compares the advantages and limitations of Internet advertising against traditional advertising media. For a comprehensive comparison of the effectiveness of Internet ads versus traditional methods, see Yoon and Kim (2001).

ADVERTISING NETWORKS

advertising networks
Specialized firms that offer customized Web advertising, such as brokering ads and helping target ads to selected groups of consumers.

One of the major advantages of Internet advertising is the ability to customize ads to fit individual viewers. Specialized firms have sprung up to offer this service to companies that wish to locate customers through targeted advertising. Called advertising networks (or *ad server networks*), these firms offer special services such as brokering banner ads for sale, bringing together online advertisers and providers of online ad space, and helping target ads to consumers who are presumed to be interested in categories of advertisements based on technology-based consumer profiling. DoubleClick is the premier company in this area. DoubleClick created an advertising network for several hundred companies. It prepares thousands of ads for its clients every week, following the process shown in EC Application Case 5.1 (page 186).

One-to-one targeted advertising and marketing can be expensive, but it can also be very rewarding. According to Taylor (1997), for example, successful targeted online ads proved very effective for selling Lexus cars, at a cost of $169 per car sold. Targeting ads to groups based on segmentation rather than to individuals also can be very cost-effective depending on the advertising method used.

Section 5.1 ▶ REVIEW

1. Define Web advertising and the major terms associated with it.
2. Describe the reasons for the growth in Web advertising.
3. List the major characteristics of Web advertising.
4. Explain the role of ad networks in Web advertising.

5.2 ADVERTISING METHODS

Several methods can be used for online advertising. Most notable are banners, pop-ups (and pop-unders), and e-mails.

BANNERS

banner
On a Web page, a graphic advertising display linked to the advertiser's Web page.

A **banner** is a graphic display that is used for advertising on a Web page. The size of the banner is usually 5 to 6.250 inches in length, 0.5 to 1 inch in width, and is measured in pixels. A banner ad is linked to an advertiser's Web page. When users "click" on the banner, they are

EXHIBIT 5.3   Advantages and Limitations of Internet Advertising Compared to Traditional Media

Medium	Advantages	Limitations
TV	• Intrusive impact—high attention getter • Ability to demonstrate product and to feature "slice of life" situations • Very "merchandisable" with media buyers	• Fragmented ratings, rising costs, "clutter" • Heavy "downscale" audience skew • Time is sold in multiprogram packages. Networks often require major up-front commitments. Both limit the advertiser's flexibility.
Radio	• Highly selective by station format • Allows advertisers to choose the time of day or the day of the week to exploit timing factors • Copy can rely on the listener's mood or imagination.	• Audience surveys are limited in scope, do not provide socioeconomic demographics. • Difficult to buy with so many stations to consider • Testing of copy is difficult because there are few statistical guidelines
Magazines	• Offer unique opportunities to segment markets, both demographically and psychographically • Ads can be studied and reviewed at leisure • High impact can be attained with good graphics and literate, informative copy	• Reader controls ad exposure, can ignore campaign • Difficult to exploit "timing" aspects
Newspapers	• High single-day reach opportunity • Reader often shops for specific information when ready to buy • Portable format	• Lack of creative opportunities for "emotional" selling campaigns • High cost for large-size ads • Lack of demographic selectivity; despite increased zoning, many markets have only one paper. • Low-quality reproduction, lack of color
Internet	• Internet advertisements are available 24 hours a day, 365 days a year • Costs are the same regardless of audience location • Accessed primarily because of interest in the content, so market segmentation opportunity is large • Opportunity to create one-to-one direct marketing relationship with consumer • Multimedia will increasingly create more attractive and compelling ads • Distribution costs are low (just technology costs), so reaching millions of consumers costs the same as reaching one • Advertising and content can be updated, supplemented, or changed at any time, and can therefore always be up-to-date. • Response (click-through rate) and results (page views) are immediately measurable. • Logical navigation—you click when and where you want, and you can spend as much time as you want at the site	• No clear standard or language of measurement • Immature measurement tools and metrics • Although the variety of ad content format and style that the Internet allows can be considered a positive in some respects, it also makes apples-to-apples comparisons difficult for media buyers • Difficult to measure size of market, therefore it is difficult to estimate rating, share, or reach and frequency • Audience is still small

Source: Based on Meeker (1997), pp. 1–10.

EC Application
TARGETED ADVERTISING: THE DOUBLECLICK APPROACH

One-to-one targeted advertising can take many forms. Assume that 3M Corp. wants to advertise its multimedia projectors that cost $10,000. It knows that potential buyers are people who work in advertising agencies, in information systems departments of large corporations, or in companies that use UNIX as their operating system. 3M approaches DoubleClick and asks the firm to identify such potential customers. How does DoubleClick find them? The answer is both clever and simple.

As of 1997, DoubleClick (*doubleclick.com/us*) monitors people browsing the Web sites of several hundred cooperating companies such as Quicken (*quicken.com*) and Travelocity (*travelocity.com*). By inspecting the Internet addresses of the visitors to these companies' Web sites and matching them against a database with about 100,000 Internet domain names that include a line-of-business code (code that tells the classification of each industry), DoubleClick can find those people working for advertising agencies. By checking the users' browsers, it also can find out which visitors are using UNIX. Although DoubleClick cannot find out a visitor's name, it can build a dossier on the visitor that is attached to an ID number that was assigned during the visitor's first visit to any of the cooperating sites. As the visitor continues to visit the sites, an intelligent (software) agent builds a relatively complete dossier on the visitor that includes the sites they visit, the pages they

looked at, the Internet address from which they came, and so on. This process is done with a cookie, so the Web site can "remember" a visitor's past behavior on the Internet.

DoubleClick then prepares an ad about 3M projectors. The ad is targeted to people whose profiles match the criteria listed earlier. If a visitor is a UNIX user or if they work for an advertising agency, on their next browsing trip to *any* of the participating Web sites, they will be greeted with an ad that 3M hopes will be of interest to them—an ad for the multimedia projector.

How is this activity financed? DoubleClick charges 3M for the ad. The fee is then split with the participating Web sites that carry the 3M ads, based on how many times the ad is matched with visitors.

In 1998, DoubleClick expanded the service, called Dynamic Advertising Reporting and Targeting (DART), from pinpoint target and ad design to advertising control, ad frequency determination, and providing verifiable measures of success. DoubleClick brings the right advertisement to the right person at the right time. DART works with 22 criteria that it tries to find on each consumer (e.g., location, time of day, etc.). A schematic view of the process is shown in the following figure.

(continued)

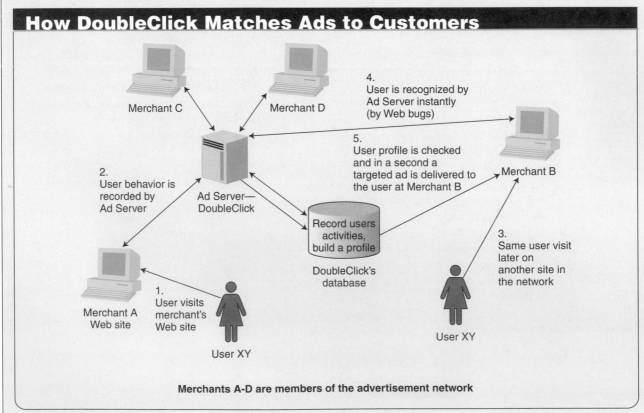

How DoubleClick Matches Ads to Customers

Merchants A-D are members of the advertisement network

Source: Based on information collected at *doubleclick.com* (2003).

CASE 5.1   (continued)

In June 1999, DoubleClick announced the purchase of Abacus Direct, whose database contains the buying habits of 88 million U.S. households. DoubleClick wanted to tie its online consumer data with that of Abacus to collect personal information online. This way, names and addresses would be in DoubleClick's database. Privacy-protection groups opposed the merger, asking the FTC to open an investigation. Under pressure, DoubleClick agreed to limit the connection.

Sources: Compiled from Rothenberg (1999); *doubleclick.com* (2001–2003); and Brown (2002).

Questions

1. How does DoubleClick build dossiers on people?
2. How are ads matched with individual viewers?
3. Why is an advertising network needed?
4. What role do the "participating sites" play in the DART system?

transferred to the advertiser's site. Advertisers go to great lengths to design a banner that catches consumers' attention. Banners often include video clips and sound. Banner advertising is the most commonly used form of advertising on the Internet.

There are several types of banners. **Keyword banners** appear when a predetermined word is queried from a search engine. They are effective for companies that want to narrow their target audience. **Random banners** appear randomly, not as a result of some action by the viewer. Companies that want to introduce new products (e.g., a new movie or CD) use random banners. *Static banners* are always on the Web page. Finally, *pop-up banners* appear when least expected, as will be described later.

If an advertiser knows something about a visitor, such as the visitor's user profile, it is possible to *match* a specific banner to that customer. Obviously, such targeted, personalized banners are the most effective.

keyword banners
Banner ads that appear when a predetermined word is queried from a search engine.

random banners
Banner ads that appear at random, not as the result of the viewer's action.

Benefits and Limitations of Banner Ads

The major benefit of banner ads is that by clicking on them users are transferred to an advertiser's site, and frequently directly to the shopping page of that site. Another advantage of using banners is the ability to customize some of them to the targeted individual surfer or market segment of surfers. Also, viewing of banners is fairly high because, in many cases, customers are forced to see banner ads while waiting for a page to load or before they can get the free information or entertainment that they want to see (a strategy called "forced advertising"). Finally, banners may include attention-grabbing multimedia.

The major disadvantage of banners is their cost. If a company demands a successful marketing campaign, it will need to allocate a large percentage of the advertising budget to place banners on high-volume Web sites. Another drawback is that a limited amount of information can be placed on the banner. Hence, advertisers need to think of a creative but short message to attract viewers.

Additionally, it seems that viewers have become somewhat immune to banners and simply do not notice them as they once did. The **click ratio**, which measures the success of a banner in attracting visitors to click on it, has been declining over time. For example, if a page received 1,000 views and there are 30 "clicks" on a banner, the click ratio is 3 percent. The University of Michigan found the average click ratio, which was 3 percent in the mid-1990s, to be less than 1 percent today, and it is declining with time (Doyle et al. 1997; Meskauskas 2001).

Because of these drawbacks, it is important to decide where to place banners. For example, a study of Web ads conducted by the University of Michigan showed that ads placed in the lower-right-hand corner of the screen, next to the scrollbar, generate 228 percent higher click-through than ads at the top of the page (Doyle et al. 1997). The study also found that ads placed one-third of the way down the page and centered increased click-through 77 percent over ads at the top of the page, where ads are frequently positioned. For this reason, the price of the banner should depend on where it is located on the page.

click ratio
The ratio between the number of clicks on a banner ad and the number of times it is seen by viewers; measures the success of a banner in attracting visitors to click on the ad.

Banner Swapping

banner swapping
An agreement between two companies to each display the other's banner ad on its Web site.

Banner swapping means that company A agrees to display a banner of company B in exchange for company B displaying company A's banner. This is probably the least expensive form of banner advertising, but it is also difficult to arrange. A company must locate a site that could generate a sufficient amount of relevant traffic. Then, the company must contact the owner/Webmaster of the site and inquire if they would be interested in a reciprocal banner swap. Because individual swaps are difficult to arrange, many companies use banner exchanges.

Banner Exchanges

banner exchanges
Markets in which companies can trade or exchange placement of banner ads on each other's Web sites.

Banner exchanges are markets where companies can trade or exchange placement of banner ads on each other's Web sites. A multicompany banner match may be easier to arrange than a two-company swap. For example, company A can display B's banner to good advantage, but B cannot display A's banner optimally. However, B can display C's banner, and C can display A's banner. Such bartering may involve many companies. Banner exchange organizers arrange the trading, which works much like an off-line bartering exchange. Firms that are willing to display others' banners join the exchange. Each time a participant displays a banner for one of the exchange's other members, it receives a credit. After a participant has "earned" enough credits, its own banner is displayed on another member's site. Most exchanges offer members the opportunity to purchase additional display credits.

Bcentral.com, via its Link Exchange, acts as a banner-ad clearinghouse for thousands of small Web sites. The site (bcentral.com) is organized into more than 1,600 categories. Bcentral.com also monitors the content of the ads of all its members.

Banner exchanges are not without their disadvantages. To begin with, they are not free, charging members either money or ad space, or both. Second, some banner exchanges will not allow certain types of banners. In addition, there are tax implications for companies that barter banners.

Overall, banner advertising was very valuable as an early form of Web advertising. Its share of the market is declining, however, because Web users are increasingly ignoring banner ads, which are now being replaced by pop-ups.

POP-UP AND SIMILAR ADS

pop-up ad
An ad that appears before, after, or during Internet surfing or when reading e-mail.

pop-under ad
An ad that appears underneath the current browser window, so when the user closes the active window, they see the ad.

One of the most annoying phenomena in Web surfing is the increased use of pop-up, pop-under, and similar ads. A **pop-up ad**, also known as *ad spawning*, is the automatic launching of new browser windows with an ad when a visitor enters or exits a site, on delay, or on other triggers. A pop-up ad appears in front of the active window (Martin and Ryan 2002). A **pop-under ad** is an ad that appears underneath (in back of) the current browser window; when users close the active window, they see the ad. (There also are pop-under exchanges that function much like banner exchanges. They cover your current screen and may be difficult to close. See popunder.com.) Pop-up and pop-under ads are controversial: Many users strongly object to this advertising method, which they consider intrusive.

Several related tactics, some of which are very aggressive, are used by advertisers, and their use is increasing. Here are a few examples according to cyveillance.com (2003).

Mouse-trapping. Disables the user's ability to go back, exit, or close while viewing the page.

Typo-piracy and cyber-squatting. Uses misspellings and derivations of a popular brand to divert traffic to an unintended site.

Unauthorized software downloads. Leaves behind software that can contain embedded advertising or tracking capabilities. Sometimes coupled with mislabeling of buttons so download occurs regardless of whether "yes" or "no" is selected.

Visible seeding. Visibly places popular brands, slogans, and proprietary content into a site to optimize search-engine rankings.

Invisible seeding. Hides content to optimize search service rankings.

Changing homepage or favorites. Substitutes a new homepage setting or makes changes to the user's "favorites" list.

Framing. Keeps customer on the original site while the customer views content of another site through the original site's window; can then use higher visit time statistics to attract advertisers.

Spoof or magnet pages. Seeds site content with select words, brands, slogans, and personalities to draw traffic.

Mislabeling links. Falsely labels hyperlinks that send the shopper to an unintended destination.

Some of these tactics are accompanied by music, voice, and other rich multimedia. To read about how customers can protect themselves against these aggressive ads, see the discussion on how to deal with unsolicited ads and Section 5.7.

INTERSTITIALS

An **interstitial**, a type of pop-up ad, is a page or box that appears after a user clicks on a link. These ads remain while content is loading. (The word *interstitial* comes from *interstice*, which means a small space between things.) An interstitial may be an initial Web page or a portion of one that is used to capture the user's attention for a short time, either as a promotion or a lead-in to the site's homepage or to advertise a product or a service. They pop onto the PC screen much like a TV commercial.

interstitial
An initial Web page or a portion of it that is used to capture the user's attention for a short time while other content is loading.

How to Deal with Unsolicited Pop-Ups, Pop-Unders, and Interstitials

The major advantage of pop-ups and similar methods over any other online advertising method is that viewers tend to look at them while they wait for the requested content to appear. To promote viewing of these ads, advertisers can create innovative multimedia effects and provide sufficient information for delivery in one visit. However, if viewers do not want to see these ads, they can remove them by simply closing them or by installing software to block them. Several software packages are available on the market to assist users in blocking these types of ads (see Section 5.7 for details).

E-MAIL ADVERTISING

A popular way to advertise on the Internet is to send company or product information to people or companies listed in mailing lists via electronic mail—e-mail. According to Schibsted (2000), e-mail marketing is increasing rapidly, and e-mail marketing expenditures are expected to reach $7.3 billion by 2005. E-mail messages may be combined with brief audio or video clips promoting a product and with on-screen links that users can click on to make a purchase. E-mail is also exploding because it is now available in a wireless environment as well as on interactive TV (e.g., in France).

The advantages of the e-mail advertising approach are its low cost and the ability to reach a wide variety of targeted audiences. Also, e-mail is an *interactive* medium, and it can combine advertising and customer service. Most companies have a database of customers to which they can send e-mail messages. However, using e-mail to send ads (sometimes floods of ads) without the receivers' permission is considered *spamming* (see Section 5.7 and Chapter 17).

Undoubtedly, the quantity of e-mail that consumers receive is exploding. In light of this, marketers employing e-mail must take a long-term view and work toward motivating consumers to continue to read the messages they receive. As the volume of e-mail increases, consumers' tendency to screen messages will rise as well. Many e-mail services (e.g., see hotmail.com) permit users to block messages from specific sources.

A list of e-mail addresses can be a very powerful tool with which a company can target a group of people it knows something about. For information on how to create a mailing list, consult groups.yahoo.com (the service is free), emailfactory.com, or topica.com. E-mail also can be sent to PDA devices and to mobile phones. Mobile phones offer advertisers a real chance to advertise interactively and on a one-to-one basis with consumers. In the future, e-mail ads will be targeted to individuals based not only on their user profiles, but also on their physical location at any point in time. See Chapter 10 for a description of this concept, known as *l-commerce*.

E-Mail Advertising Management

Although sending e-mail ads sounds simple, it really is not. Preparing mailing lists, deciding on content, and measuring the results are some of the activities that are part of e-mail advertising management. One important area is getting mailing lists. Companies such as Worldata.com can help supply lists for both B2C and B2B e-commerce. They also provide ad management services. (See the demo of the e-mail tracking system at worldata.com.) The free services at emailresults.com include free newsletters, suggestions, and leads for e-mail advertising.

E-Mail Advertising Methods and Successes

E-mail advertising can be done in a number of different ways (see Gordon-Lewis 2002), as shown in the following examples.

E-mail promotions. E-Greetings Network (egreetings.com) produces digital postcards and animations to its customers, who are both individuals and corporations. For a modest membership fee ($13.95 annually), members have access to over 5,000 e-greeting cards, plus designs for flyers, fax covers, and envelopes. Through its free membership trial and its members list, E-Greetings Network has compiled a database of millions of recipients. According to Kinnard (2002), E-Greetings Network's goals for its e-mail promotion campaign include bringing value to its customers, driving traffic and transactions at the customer's site, stimulating involvement with the site, expanding customer relationships, offering added means of sponsorship, and supporting brand affinity. E-Greetings' main relationship-building tool is their newsletter "What's Up @ E-greetings!" Key factors in its success are the fact that the mailing list is totally opt-in (called permission advertising); newsletters are distributed on a regular, biweekly schedule; the content is relevant; and they handle unsubscribe difficulties and customer service in a timely manner.

Discussion lists. Internet Security Systems (ISS), with $1 billion in sales per year, provides software that detects weaknesses in systems and gives detailed corrective measures for fixing security holes. Its success began when its founder, Chris Klaus, posted a notice about his security software at a newsgroup. He then offered a shareware version of the program to the newsgroup members and received 200 e-mail responses the following day. His company's discussion list program includes approximately 80 specialized e-mail lists reaching over 100,000 people through discussions, partner lists, customer lists, and product announcement lists (Kinnard 2002). Sponsorship of discussion groups, communities, and newsletters is becoming quite popular on the Web (see sponsorship.com).

E-mail list management. L-Soft's Listserv, the leader in software for e-mail list management and marketing, is known for its electronic newsletters, discussion groups, and direct e-mail messaging. According to Kinnard (2002), the company understands that 9 out of 10 customer interactions are not transactions, so it offers database integration, mail merges, and customizable Web interfaces that allow companies to send pertinent information, such as product details or advertising, to specific customers. Listserv delivers 30 million messages each weekday and 1 million messages per hour from a single server.

NEWSPAPER-LIKE STANDARDIZED ADS

The Internet Advertising Bureau, an industry trade group, in 2001 adopted five standard ad sizes for the Internet. These standardized ads are larger and more noticeable than banner ads. They look like the ads in a newspaper or magazine, so advertisers like them. Tests found that users read these ads four times more frequently than banners (Tedeschi 2001). The ads appear on Web sites in columns or boxes. One of the most popular of the standardized ads is a full-column-deep ad called a *skyscraper ad*. Publishers, such as the *New York Times* (nytimes.com), publish these standardized ads, sometimes as many as four on one Web page. Some of these ads are interactive; users can click on a link inside the ad for more information about a product or service. These sizes also are used in pop-up ads, in fixed banners, or in classified ads. (To find out how much an Internet ad currently costs, see webconnect.com/wise.)

Classified Ads

Another newspaper-like ad is the *classified* ad. These ads can be found on special sites (e.g., infospace.com/info.cl2k/?ran=8769), as well as on online newspapers, exchanges, portals, and so on. In many cases, posting regular-size classified ads is free, but placing them in a larger size or with some noticeable features is done for a fee.

URLs

Most search engines allow companies to submit their Internet addresses, called URLs (Universal Resource Locators), for free so that these URLs can be searched electronically. Search engine spider crawls through the submitted site, indexing its content and links. The site is then included in future searches. Because there are several thousand search engines, advertisers who use this method should register URLs with as many search engines as possible.

The major advantage of using URLs as an advertising tool is that it is free. Anyone can submit a URL to a search engine and be listed. By using URLs, it is likely that searchers for a company's products will receive a list of sites that mention the products, including the company's own site.

However, the URL method has several drawbacks. The major one has to do with location: The chance that a specific site will be placed at the top of a search engine's display list (say, in the first 10 sites) is very slim. Furthermore, even if a company's URL makes it to the top, others can quickly displace the URL from the top slot. Second, different search engines index their listings differently, therefore it is difficult to make the top of several lists. The searcher may have the correct keywords, but if the search engine indexed the site listing using the "title" or "content description" in the meta tag, then the effort could be fruitless.

Improving a Company's Search-Engine Ranking

By simply adding, removing, or changing a few sentences, a Web designer may alter the way a search engine's spider ranks its findings (see Nobles and O'Neil 2000), and therefore improve a company's ranking on the search engine's list. Several companies have services that optimize Web content so that a site has a better chance of being discovered by a search engine (e.g., keywordcount.com or webpositiongold.com). More tips for improving a site's listing in various search engines can be found at searchenginewatch.com.

Paid Search-Engine Inclusion

Several search engines charge fees for including URLs at or near the top of the search results. For example, Overture (overture.com) charges firms for placement of "sponsor matching" on eight popular search engines. The more the company pays, the closer it will be to the top. Overture works with AltaVista, Lycos, and other search engines. Many major search engines allow for paid inclusion. A debatable issue is the *ethics* of this strategy. Basically, promotion is given to those who pay more. Although this is a fact of advertising in general (a company pays more for a TV ad in the Super Bowl than for one during the late-night news), it is a fact that may not be known to customers who use the search engines.

ADVERTISING IN CHAT ROOMS

A chat room can be used to build a community, to promote a political or environmental cause, to support people with medical problems, or to let hobbyists share their interest. It can be used for advertising as well (e.g., see Gelb and Sundaram 2002).

Vendors frequently sponsor chat rooms. The sponsoring vendor places a chat link on its site, and the chat vendor does the rest (e.g., talkcity.com), including placing the advertising that pays for the session. The advertising in a chat room merges with the activity in the room, and the user is conscious of what is being presented.

The main difference between an advertisement that appears on a static Web page and one that comes through a chat room is that the latter allows advertisers to cycle through messages and target the chatters again and again. Also, advertising can become more thematic in a chat room. An advertiser can start with one message and build upon it to a climax, just as an author does with a good story. For example, a toy maker may have a chat room dedicated to electronic toys. The advertiser can use the chat room to post a query such as, "Can anyone tell me about the new Electoy R3D3?" In addition, a company can go to their competitors' chat rooms and observe the conversations there.

Chat rooms also are used as one-to-one connections between a company and its customers. For example, Mattel (mattel.com) sells about one-third of its Barbie dolls to collectors. These collectors use the chat room to make comments or ask questions that are then answered by Mattel's staff.

OTHER FORMS OF ADVERTISING

advertorial

An advertisement "disguised" to look like an editorial or general information.

Online advertising can be done in several other ways, ranging from ads in newsgroups to ads in computer kiosks. Advertising on *Internet radio* is just beginning, and soon advertising on *Internet television* will commence. Some use an **advertorial**, which is material that looks like editorial content or general information but is really an advertisement. Others advertise to members of Internet communities (Chapter 17). Community sites, such as geocities.com, offer direct advertising opportunities and usually offer discounts to members on the advertised products. There are also ads that link users to other sites that might be of interest to community members and targeted ads that can also go to the members' portals. In addition, the *domain name* itself can be used for brand recognition. This is why some companies are willing to pay millions of dollars to keep certain domain names in their own control (see alldomains.com) or to buy popular names. Finally, advertisement on cell phones and other mobile devices is expected to grow very rapidly, especially after 2007, as will be shown in Chapter 10.

Section 5.2 ▶ REVIEW

1. Define banner ads and describe their benefits and limitations.
2. Describe banner swapping and banner exchanges.
3. Describe the issues surrounding pop-ups and similar ads.
4. Explain how e-mail is used for advertising.
5. Describe advertising via standardized and newspaper-like ads.
6. Discuss advertising via URLs and in chat rooms.

5.3   ADVERTISING STRATEGIES AND PROMOTIONS

Several advertising strategies can be used over the Internet. In this section, we will present the major strategies used.

ASSOCIATED AD DISPLAY

associated ad display (text links)

An advertising strategy that displays a banner ad related to a term entered in a search engine.

Sometimes it is possible to associate the content of a Web page with a related ad. Suppose a person is interested in finding material on e-loyalty. If they use Yahoo to search for e-loyalty, they will receive a list of sources and a banner ad that will say, "Search Books! Barnes and Noble, E-Loyalty." The same banner ad will appear when they click on the top sites that deal with e-loyalty. This strategy of displaying a banner ad related to a term entered in a search engine is called **associated ad display** or **text links**. For example, when using MapQuest (mapquest.com), which supports hotel reservations, the user may select an indexed category such as "lodging" within a city, and an associated ad for a Radisson hotel may be displayed.

Another example of associated ad display can be found at amazon.com. When a customer reads about a book, a list of books is displayed under the heading "Customers who bought this book also bought. . . ." To support this kind of service, Amazon.com uses data mining capabilities. The associated ads appear only as a reaction to user actions.

Companies usually implement the associated ad display strategy through their *affiliates programs* (e.g., see Helmstetter and Metivier 2000), as is done by Yahoo.

AFFILIATE MARKETING AND ADVERTISING

affiliate marketing

A marketing arrangement by which an organization refers consumers to the selling company's Web site.

In Chapters 1 through 3 we introduced the concept of **affiliate marketing**, the arrangement by which an organization refers consumers to the selling company's Web site. Affiliate marketing is used mainly as a marketing tool (a referral system), but the fact that a company's logo is placed on many other Web sites provides free advertising as well. Consider Amazon.com, whose logo can be seen on about 500,000 affiliate sites! For a comprehensive directory of affiliate programs, see cashpile.com. In addition, Hoffman and Novak (2000) provide an example of how CDNow is using affiliate marketing.

ADS AS A COMMODITY

With the *ads-as-a-commodity* approach, people are paid for the time that is spent viewing an ad. This approach is used at mypoints.com, clickrewards.com, and others. At mypoints.com, interested consumers read ads in exchange for payments made by the advertisers. Consumers fill out data on personal interests, and then they receive targeted banners based on their personal profiles. Each banner is labeled with the amount of payment that will be paid if the consumer reads the ad. If interested, the consumer clicks the banner to read it, and after passing some tests as to its content, is paid for the effort. Readers can sort and choose what they read, and the advertisers can vary the payment level reflecting the frequency and desirability of readers. Payments can be cash (e.g., $0.50 per banner) or discounts on products.

VIRAL MARKETING

Viral marketing refers to word-of-mouth marketing in which customers promote a product or service by telling others about it. This can be done by e-mail, in conversations facilitated in chat rooms, by posting messages in newsgroups, and in electronic consumer forums. Having people forward messages to friends, asking them, for example, to "check out this product," is an example of viral marketing. This marketing approach has been used for generations, but now its speed and reach are multiplied by the Internet. This ad model can be used to build brand awareness at a minimal cost (Helm 2000; Gelb and Sundaram 2002), as the people who pass on the messages are paid very little or nothing for their efforts.

viral marketing
Word-of-mouth marketing by which customers promote a product or service by telling others about it.

Viral marketing has long been a favorite strategy of online advertisers pushing youth-oriented products. For example, advertisers might distribute, embedded within a sponsor's e-mail, a small game program that is easy to forward. By releasing a few thousand copies of the game to some consumers, vendors hope to reach hundreds of thousands of other consumers. Viral marketing also was used by the founder of Hotmail, a free e-mail service, which grew from zero to 12 million subscribers in its 18 initial months and to over 50 million in about 4 years. Each e-mail sent via Hotmail carried an invitation for free Hotmail service. Also known as *advocacy marketing*, this innovative approach, if properly used, can be effective, efficient, and relatively inexpensive.

One of the downsides of this strategy is that several e-mail hoaxes have been spread this way (see find.pcworld.com/22021). Another danger of viral advertising is that a destructive virus can be added to an innocent advertisement-related game or message. Fraud is also a danger. A person may get an e-mail that tells them that their credit card number is invalid and that their AOL service or newspaper delivery will be terminated unless they send another credit card number as a reply to the e-mail. Do not do it! For defense (protection) strategies, see emailfactory.com.

CUSTOMIZING ADS

The Internet has too much information for customers to view. Filtering irrelevant information by providing consumers with customized ads can reduce this information overload. BroadVision (broadvision.com) provides a customized ad service platform called One-to-One. The heart of One-to-One is a customer database, which includes registration data and information gleaned from site visits. The companies that advertise via One-to-One use the database to send customized ads to consumers. Using this feature, a marketing manager can customize display ads based on users' profiles.

Another model of personalization can be found in Webcasting, a free Internet news service that broadcasts personalized news and information. A user signs into the Webcasting system and selects the information they would like to receive, such as sports, news, headlines, stock quotes, or desired product promotions. The user then receives the information they requested, along with personalized ads based on their expressed interests and general ads based on their profile.

Webcasting
A free Internet news service that broadcasts personalized news and information in categories selected by the user.

ONLINE EVENTS, PROMOTIONS, AND ATTRACTIONS

In the winter of 1994, the term EC was hardly known, and people were just starting to discover the Internet. One company, DealerNet, which was selling new and used cars from physical lots, demonstrated a new way of doing business: It started a virtual car showroom on the Internet. It let people "visit" dozens of dealerships and compare prices and features. At the time, this was a revolutionary way of selling cars. To get people's attention, DealerNet gave away a car over the Internet.

This promotion, unique at the time, received a lot of off-line media attention and was a total success. Today, such promotions are regular events on thousands of Web sites. Contests, quizzes, coupons, and giveaways designed to attract visitors are as much a part of online marketing as they are of off-line commerce (see Sterne 2001; O'Keefe 2002). Some innovative ideas used to encourage people to pay attention to online advertising are provided in Insights and Additions 5.1.

Insights and Additions 5.1   How to Attract Web Surfers

Advertisers use dozens of innovative techniques to lure consumers into viewing online ads. The following list is only a sample of the many interesting ideas companies have used to attract Web surfers. For more on promotions, visit *promomagazine.com*.

▶ Retailers can provide online shoppers with special offers while they are purchasing or "checking out." If a shopper's profile or shopping history is known, the ads can be targeted.

▶ Netstakes runs sweepstakes that require no skill. Users register only once and win prizes at random (*webstakes.com*). The sponsors pay Netstakes to send them traffic. Netstakes also runs online ads, both on the Web and through e-mail lists that people subscribe to.

▶ Cydoor (*cydoor.com*) places ads, news, and other items on software applications. Consumers who download the software receive a reward each time they use the software (and presumably read the ads).

▶ CBS Marketwatch (*cbsmarketwatch.com*) uses animated beer bottles and interactive charts to attract viewers to its free financial site.

▶ Sometimes a catchy name draws Web surfers. For example, an old-economy seller of hard-to-find light bulbs changed its name to *topbulb.com* and created an online catalog, called the Bulbguy, through which it sells light bulbs online at a discount. The Web site is advertised both online and off-line, and business is booming!

▶ *Promotionbase.com* is a magazine-format site dedicated to Web site promotions. Users can find rich resources and promotions on how to increase Web traffic.

▶ To promote its sport utility vehicle, the 4Runner, Toyota wanted to reach as many Internet users as possible. The company displayed Toyota banners on the search engine AltaVista (*altavista.com*). Whenever someone used AltaVista to search for anything related to automotives, they would see the Toyota banner. Also, Kelly Blue Book's new-car pricing catalog (*kbb.com*) had links to Toyota's car. In the first 2 months of the campaign, over 10,000 potential car buyers clicked on the banner ads looking for more detailed information about the Toyota 4Runner.

▶ Web surfers can play games, win prizes, and see "e-tractions" at *uproar.com*. Special promotion campaigns are also featured.

▶ To promote its job-recruiting visits on U.S. college campuses, IBM created over 75,000 college-specific banners such as, "There is life after Boston College: click to see why." The students clicked on the banners at a very high rate (5 to 30 percent). As a result of this success rate, IBM restructured its traditional media plans using the "Club Cyberblue" scheme.

▶ Each year, almost 500,000 brides-to-be use *theknot.com* to plan their wedding. A "Knot Box" with insert folders is sent to users by regular mail. Each insert is linked to a corresponding page at *theknot.com*. Advertisers underwrite the mail campaign. The Web site provides brides with information and help in planning the wedding and selecting vendors. Orders can be placed by phone or online (not all products can be ordered online). *Weddings411.com* is a similar service, operating primarily online.

Bargain hunters can find lots of bargains on the Internet. Special sales, auctions, and downloading of coupons are frequently combined with ads. Of special interest are sites such as *coolsavings.com*, *hotcoupons.com*, *supercoups.com*, *clickrewards.com*, *mypoints.com*, and *windough.com*. A popular lottery site is *world-widelotto.com*. In addition to lotteries and coupons, free samples are of interest to many consumers, and "try-before-you buy" gives consumers confidence in what they are buying. *Freesamples.com* began to offer free samples in June 2000.

Live Web Events

Live Web events (concerts, shows, interviews, debates, videos), if properly done, can generate tremendous public excitement and bring huge crowds to a Web site. According to Akamai Technologies, Inc. (2000a), the best practices for successful live Web events are:

▶ Careful planning of content, audience, interactivity level, preproduction, and schedule
▶ Executing the production with rich media if possible
▶ Conducting appropriate promotion via e-mails, affinity sites, and streaming media directories, as well as conducting proper off-line and online advertisement
▶ Preparing for quality delivery
▶ Capturing data and analyzing audience response so that improvements can be made

For further details, see Akamai Technologies, Inc. (2000a).

Admediation

Conducting promotions, especially large-scale ones, may require the help of vendors who specialize in promotions such as those listed in Insights and Additions 5.1. Gopal et al. (2001) researched this area and developed a model that shows the role of third-party vendors (such as mypoints.com), which they call **admediaries**. Their model is shown in Exhibit 5.4. The exhibit concentrates on e-mail and shows the role of the admediaries (in the box between the customers and sellers). Examples of admediaries, the services they provide both to consumers and sellers, and the value-added issues are shown in the online supplement to Chapter 5.

admediaries
Third-party vendors that conduct promotions, especially large scale ones.

Running promotions on the Internet is similar to running off-line promotions. According to Chase (1998) and Clow and Baack (2002), some of the major considerations when implementing an online ad campaign include the following:

▶ The target audience needs to be clearly understood and should be online surfers.
▶ The traffic to the site should be estimated, and a powerful enough server must be prepared to handle the expected volume of traffic.
▶ Assuming that the promotion is successful, what will the result be? This assessment is needed to evaluate the budget and promotion strategy.
▶ Consider cobranding; many promotions succeed because they bring together two or more powerful partners.

For more information about promotions and ad strategies, see Clow and Baack (2002).

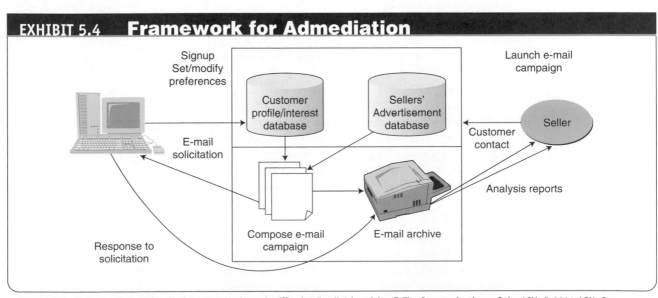

EXHIBIT 5.4   Framework for Admediation

Source: Gopal, R. D., et al. "Admediation: New Horizons in Effective Email Advertising." *The Communications of the ACM.* © 2001 ACM, Inc.

Section 5.3 ▶ REVIEW

1. Describe the associated ad (text links) strategy.
2. Discuss the process and value of affiliate marketing.
3. How does the ads-as-a-commodity strategy work?
4. Describe viral marketing.
5. How are ads customized?
6. List some typical Internet promotions.
7. Define admediaries and describe their roles.

5.4 ECONOMICS OF ADVERTISING

One of the major issues in advertising is its *cost-benefit* (the relationship of its cost to the benefits it provides) to the advertisers. The cost depends mostly on the method of payment.

PRICING OF ADVERTISING

Justifying the cost of Internet advertising is more difficult than doing so for conventional advertising for two reasons: (1) the difficulty in measuring the effectiveness of online advertising and (2) disagreements on pricing methods. Several methods are available for measuring advertising effectiveness, conducting cost-benefit analyses, and pricing ads. Four representative methods are discussed in the following sections. Before proceeding, it might be a good idea to flip back to pages 181 and 182 and review the advertising terminology used there.

Pricing Based on Ad Views, Using CPM

Traditional ad pricing is based on exposure or circulation. So far, this model has been the standard advertising rate-pricing tool for Web sites as well, usually using *ad views* to measure circulation. Because advertisers pay an agreed-upon multiple of the number of "guaranteed" ad views using a CPM formula, it is very important that ad views are measured accurately in the context of the advertising business model. Generally, CPMs seem to average on the order of $40 (per 1,000 ad viewers), resulting in a cost of $0.04 per impression viewed (per ad view).

Some companies, such as USA Today Online, charge their clients according to the number of *hits* (about $0.03 per hit in 2003). However, hits are not an accurate measure of visitation, because one ad view may have several hits.

Pricing Based on Click-Through

Ad pricing based on click-through is an attempt to develop a more accountable way of charging for Web advertising. In this model, the payment for a banner ad is based on the number of times visitors actually click on the banner. Payment based on click-through guarantees not only that the visitor was *exposed to* the banner ad, but also that the visitor was sufficiently interested to click on the banner and view the target ad (Hoffman and Novak 2000).

However, a relatively small proportion of those exposed to a banner ad (about 1 to 3 percent of viewers) actually click on the banner. Therefore, space providers usually object to this method, claiming that simply viewing a banner ad may lead to a purchase later or to an offline purchase, much as newspaper or TV ads do. Advertisers, on the other hand, do not like to pay for ad views; they prefer the click-through method, which they feel is more accurate. Only large advertisers such as Procter & Gamble can pressure space sellers to accept click-through payment methods, or even better, interactivity.

Payment Based on Interactivity

Although payment based on click-through guarantees exposure to target ads, it does not guarantee that the visitor liked the ad or even spent a substantial time viewing it. The *interactivity model* (Hoffman and Novak 1996) suggests basing ad pricing on how the visitor interacts with the target ad. Such an interactivity measure could be based on the duration of time spent viewing the ad, the number of pages of the target ad accessed, the number of additional clicks generated, or the number of repeat visits to the target ad. Obviously, this method is more complex to administer than the previous methods.

Payment Based on Actual Purchase: Affiliate Programs

Many advertisers prefer to pay for ads only if an actual purchase has been made. Such arrangements usually take place through *affiliate programs*. Merchants ask partners, known as *affiliates*, to place the merchant's logo on the affiliate's Web site. The merchants promise to pay the affiliate a *commission* of 5 to 15 percent whenever a customer clicks on the merchants' logo (banner) on the affiliate's Web site and eventually moves to the merchant site and makes a purchase. For example, if a customer saw Amazon.com's banner at AOL's Web site, clicked on it, moved to amazon.com, and completed the purchase, AOL would receive a referral fee of say 5 percent of the purchase price of the book. This method can work only at sites where actual purchases can be made (e.g., see cdnow.com and cattoys.com). At the Ritchey Design or Coca-Cola (cocacola.com) sites, users only get information and brand awareness, thus this method would be inappropriate for these types of merchants.

Which Is the Most Appropriate Pricing Method?

In addition to the four major methods just described, still other methods can be used to pay for ads. For example, some space providers charge a fixed monthly fee to host a banner, regardless of the traffic. Others use a hybrid approach, a combination of some of the previous methods. The question is, which is the most appropriate method?

Web space providers, such as Yahoo, push for CPM. They argue that the problem with activity-based measures, such as click-through or interactivity, is that the Web space provider cannot be held responsible for activity related to an advertisement. (If the customer sees an ad, but it is a poor ad that does not inspire further activity, it is not the fault of the Web space provider.) They also argue that traditional media, such as newspapers or television, charge for ads whether or not they lead to sales. So why should the interactive condition be applied on the Web?

Advertisers and their agencies, on the other hand, argue that because the Web medium allows for accountability, models can and should be developed that measure actual consumer activities. The answer to the question of the most appropriate method has not been settled.

ADVERTISEMENT AS A REVENUE MODEL

Many of the dot-com failures in 2000 to 2002 were caused by a revenue model that contained advertising income as the major or the only revenue source (e.g., see the story of go.com in Chapter 3). Many small portals failed, but three large ones are dominating the field: AOL, Yahoo, and MSN. However, even these heavy-traffic sites reported only small revenue growth in 2001 and 2002. There are simply too many Web sites competing for advertising money. For these reasons, almost all portals are adding other sources of revenue.

However, if careful, a small site can survive by concentrating on a niche area. For example, playfootball.com is doing well. It pulls millions of dollars in advertising and sponsorship by concentrating on NFL fans. The site provides comprehensive and interactive content, attracting millions of visitors.

MEASURING ADVERTISING EFFECTIVENESS

Determining the cost of advertising is easier than assessing its benefits. Most of the benefits of advertising are intangible. However, more and more companies are requiring that some measure be made of the effectiveness of advertising. One financial measure is the return on investment. Another way to measure advertising effectiveness is to measure and analyze Web traffic.

Return on Investment

An increasing number of companies are requiring that the rate of *return on investment (ROI)* be used to measure the benefits received from their online advertising campaigns. ROI can be calculated in several ways. One popular formula for ROI is the net benefit (the total benefits minus the total cost) divided by the required investment. Obviously, the difficult part is to put a dollar amount on the total benefits. Nevertheless, Forrester Research (forrester.com) has developed an interactive ROI model (see Scheirer et al. 2001) for the "word-of-mouth" ad approach. Also, ad management companies such as Worldata.com generate reports that can help an organization to calculate the ROI of its e-mail ads (see the demo at worldata.com). Many other vendors offer ROI support services. For example, Advertising.com offers optimization services that analyze campaign data in real time, helping the advertising team make necessary adjustments to the campaign.

The cost of advertising is perhaps the key component of ROI. (It certainly is the one that companies and advertisers have the most control over.) One of the ways to improve ROI is to lower advertising costs. Various vendors offer services to help do that. To reduce expenses, a company can negotiate ad purchasing at valueclick.com. In addition, companies can use reverse auctions to solicit bids from space providers.

Measuring, Auditing, and Analyzing Web Traffic

Before a company decides to advertise on someone's Web site, it should verify the number of ad views, hits, clicks-through, or other data reported by the space sellers. A *site audit* validates the data claimed by the site, assuring advertisers that they are getting their money's worth. An impartial, external analysis is crucial to advertisers to verify the accuracy of any counts claimed by sites.

The Audit Bureau of Circulation (ABC) (see abc.org.uk) is a nonprofit association created by advertisers, advertising agencies, and publishers, who came together to establish advertising standards and rules. The ABC verifies circulation reports by auditing circulation figures of newspapers, TV, radio, and now the Internet. It provides credible and objective information to the buyers and sellers of advertising. Several other independent third-party Internet auditing companies also are in operation, such as BPA International (bpai.com), the Internet Advertisement Bureau (iab.net), and Audit (ipro.com).

Related to auditing is the rating of sites. This is done by companies such as Accure, Accipiter, Ipro, Netcount, Interse, Hotstats, and CNET. Rating is done by looking at multiple criteria such as content, attractiveness, ease of navigation, and privacy protection. Sites with higher ratings can command higher prices for advertising placed on their sites. In addition to outside independent monitoring, several vendors sell software that allows Webmasters to self-monitor traffic on their own Web sites. Examples are worldata.com, webtrends.com, siteguage.com, and netratings.com. Additionally, Webmasters can measure who is coming to a site and from where (e.g., see leadspinner.com). Using such software, companies can assess if placing ads really increases traffic to their sites.

Audience tracking. Advertisers are interested in gathering as much as information as possible about the acceptance of ads, both online and off-line. Arbitron Corporation has developed a portable, wearable meter (beeperlike) device. The device logs programming (including TV, radio, and streaming media Internet broadcasts) seen or heard anytime, anywhere, by whoever is wearing it. A motion detector on the device verifies that a person is wearing it (and does not just set it in front of the TV or computer screen). Each night the device is placed in a docking station in the wearer's home from which it transmits the day's data to Arbitron (arbitron.com).

Section 5.4 ▶ REVIEW

1. List the various methods of pricing Internet ads.
2. Describe the reasons for using payment methods other than CPM payments.
3. Describe the issues related to advertising as a revenue model.
4. Discuss how Web traffic is measured and audited.

5.5 SPECIAL ADVERTISING TOPICS

PERMISSION ADVERTISING

One of the major issues of one-to-one advertising is the flooding of users with unwanted (junk) e-mail, banners, pop-up ads, and so on. One of the authors of this book experienced a flood of X-rated ads. Each time such an ad arrived, he blocked receipt of further ads from this source. That helped for a day or two, but then the same ads arrived from another e-mail address. His e-mail service provider, Hotmail (hotmail.com), was very helpful in providing several options to minimize this problem. Hotmail can place software agents to identify and block such junk mail. This problem, the flooding of users with unsolicited e-mails, is called *spamming* (see Section 5.7). Spamming typically upsets users, which may keep useful advertising from reaching them in the future.

One solution used by advertisers is called **permission advertising** (**permission marketing** or the *opt-in approach*), in which users register with advertisers and *agree* to accept advertising (see netcreations.com). For example, the authors of this book agreed to receive large numbers of e-commerce newsletters, knowing that some would include ads. This way we can keep abreast of what is happening in the field. We also agree to accept e-mail from research companies, newspapers, travel agencies, and more. These vendors push, for free, very valuable information to us. The accompanying ads pay for such service. One way to conduct permission advertisement is to provide incentives, as shown in Section 5.3.

permission advertising (permission marketing) Advertising (marketing) strategy in which customers agree to accept advertising and marketing materials.

AD MANAGEMENT

The activities involved in Web advertising, which range from tracking viewers to rotating ads, require a special methodology and software known as **ad management**. Ad management software lets an advertiser send very specific ads on a schedule and target ads to certain population segments, which can be very small. For example, an advertiser can send an ad to all male residents of Los Angeles County between the ages of 26 and 39 whose income level is above $30,000. The advertiser can even refine the segment further by using ethnic origin, type of employment, or whether they own their home.

ad management Methodology and software that enable organizations to perform a variety of activities involved in Web advertising (e.g., tracking viewers, rotating ads).

When selecting ad management software, a company should look for the following features, which will optimize their ability to advertise online:

▸ **The ability to match ads to specific content.** Being able to match ads to Web content would allow an advertiser, for example, to run an ad from a car company to an article about the Indy 500.

▸ **Tracking.** Of course, the advertiser will need to deliver detailed metrics (performance measures) to their customers, showing impression rates, click-through rates, and other metrics. Tracking of viewing activity is essential in providing such metrics.

▸ **Rotation.** Advertisers may want to rotate different ads in the same space.

▸ **Spacing impressions.** If an advertiser buys a given number of impressions over a period of time, the software should be able to adjust the delivery schedule so that they are spread out evenly over time.

A variety of ad management software packages are available; including some from application service providers (ASPs) and some freeware. A comprehensive package is AdManager from Engage (engage.com), which delivers all the features just discussed.

One topic in ad management is campaign management; that is, management of an entire marketing and advertising campaign. Campaign management tools fall into two categories: those that are folded into CRM, which consist mainly of marketing automation, and those that are targeted, stand-alone campaign management products. Companies such as DoubleClick provide partial management. More comprehensive management is provided by Atlas DMT's Digital Marketing suite. For details, see Bannan (2002).

Another topic in ad management is measuring the effectiveness of Web advertising, which was discussed earlier.

LOCALIZATION

localization The process of converting media products developed in one country to a form culturally and linguistically acceptable in countries outside the original target market.

Localization is the process of converting media products developed in one country to a form culturally and linguistically acceptable in countries outside the original target market. It is usually done by a set of *internationalization* guidelines. Web-page translation (Chapters 14 and 15) is one aspect of internationalization. There are also several more aspects. For example, a U.S. jewelry manufacturer that displayed its products on a white background was astonished to find that this display might not appeal to customers in some countries where a blue background is preferred.

If a company aims at the global market (and there are millions of potential customers out there), it must make an effort to localize its Web pages. This may not be a simple task because of the following factors:

▶ Many countries use English, but the English used may differ in terminology, culture, and even spelling (e.g., United States vs. United Kingdom vs. Australia).

▶ Some languages use accented characters. If text includes an accented character, the accent will disappear when converted into English, which may result in an incorrect translation.

▶ Hard-coded text and fonts cannot be changed, so they remain in their original format in the translated material.

▶ Graphics and icons look different to viewers in different countries. For example, a U.S. mailbox resembles a European trashcan.

▶ When translating into Asian languages, significant cultural issues must be addressed, for example, how to address the elderly in a culturally correct manner.

▶ Dates that are written mm/dd/yy (e.g., June 8, 2002) in the United States are written dd/mm/yy (e.g., 8 June 2002) in many other countries. Therefore, "6/8" would have two meanings (June 8 or August 6), depending on the location of the writer.

▶ Consistent translation over several documents can be very difficult to achieve. (For free translation in six languages, see freetranslation.com.)

Automatic Versus Manual Web Page Translation

Certain localization difficulties result in a need for experienced human translators, who are rare, expensive, and slow. Therefore, companies are using automatic translation software, at least as an initial step to expedite the work of human translators. (See Chapter 14 for further discussion and references.)

Using Internet Radio for Localization

Internet radio
A Web site that provides music, talk, and other entertainment, both live and stored, from a variety of radio stations.

Internet radio is a Web site that provides music, talk, and other entertainment, both live and stored, from a variety of radio stations. The big advantage of Internet radio is that there are few limits on the type or number of programs it can offer, as compared to traditional radio stations. It is especially useful in presenting programming from local communities. For example, kiisfm.com is a Los Angeles site that features music from up-and-coming L.A. bands, live concerts, interviews with movie stars, and so forth. About 40 percent of the site's traffic comes from listeners in California, and the rest from listeners around the world. The company that powers kiisfm.com also operates sites focused on country music, Latin music, and so forth. Advertisers can reach fairly narrow audience segments by advertising on Internet radio.

WIRELESS ADVERTISING

As will be seen in Chapter 10, the number of applications of m-commerce in marketing and advertising is growing quickly. One area is that of *pervasive computing*—the idea that almost any device (clothing, tools, appliances, homes, and so on) can be imbedded with computer chips and connected to a network of other devices (see Chapter 10). An interesting application is digital ads atop taxis in Boston. The ads also include public service announcements. The technology comes from VERT Inc. (vert.net).

The VERT system is linked to the Internet via a wireless modem, as well as to databases and a global positioning system (GPS) that uses satellites to identify a taxi's location. Two of the ads were created specifically for VERT to take advantage of the system's real-time capabilities. One has the "Top 10" stock quotes from NASDAQ, and the other reports the weather. Leonid Fridman, president of VERT, based in Somerville, Massachusetts, said that the technology could eventually be used to vary the ads according to the neighborhood the taxi is driving through, the weather, or any other changing condition.

VERT Intelligent Displays: Advertising Used Atop Taxi Cabs

Source: Courtesy of Vert Incorporated.

AD CONTENT

The content of ads is extremely important, and companies use ad agencies to help in content creation for the Web just as they do for other advertising media. A major player in this area is Akamai Technologies, Inc. (akamai.com). In a white paper (Akamai Technologies, Inc. 2000b), the company points out how the right content can drive traffic to a site. The paper also suggests how to evaluate third-party vendors and what content-related services are important.

Content is especially important to increase *stickiness*. Customers are expensive to acquire, therefore it is important that they remain at a site, read its content carefully, and eventually make a purchase. The writing of the advertising content itself (copywriting) is of course important (see ebookeditingservices.com). Finding a good ad agency to write content and shape the advertising message is one of the key factors in any advertising campaign, online or off-line. Yet, matching ad agencies and advertising clients can be complex. Agencyfinder.com maintains a huge database that can be tapped for a perfect match.

Section 5.5 ▶ REVIEW

1. Describe permission advertising.
2. What is localization? What are the major issues in localizing Web pages?
3. How is wireless advertising practiced?
4. What is the importance of ad content?

5.6 SOFTWARE AGENTS IN CUSTOMER-RELATED AND ADVERTISING APPLICATIONS

As the volume of customers, products, vendors, and information increases, it becomes uneconomical, or even impossible, for customers to consider all relevant information and to manually match their interests with available products and services. The practical solution to handling such information overload is to use software (intelligent) agents. In Chapter 3, we demonstrated how intelligent agents help online shoppers find and compare products, resulting in significant time savings.

In this section, we will concentrate on how software agents can assist customers in the online purchasing decision-making process as well as in advertisement. Depending on their level of intelligence, agents can do many things (see Thompson 1999 and Technical Appendix D on the book's Web site).

A FRAMEWORK FOR CLASSIFYING EC AGENTS

Exhibit 4.3 (Chapter 4) detailed the customer's purchase decision-making process. A logical way to classify EC agents is by relating them to this decision-making process (in a slightly expanded form), as shown in Exhibit 5.5 (page 202). In the decision-making model in Exhibit 4.3, the second step was information search. Because of the vast quantity of information that software (intelligent) agents can supply, the step has been split into two types of agents: those that first answer the question, "What to buy?" and those that answer the next question, "From whom?" Let's see how agents support each of the phases of the decision-making process.

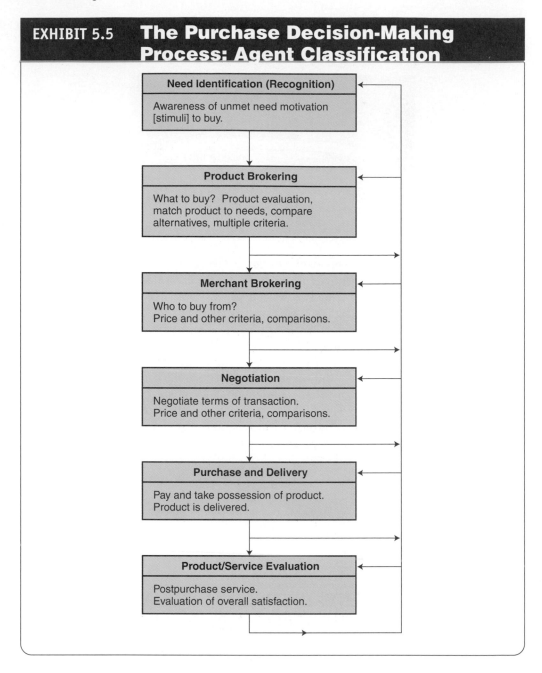

EXHIBIT 5.5   The Purchase Decision-Making Process: Agent Classification

Need Identification (Recognition)

Awareness of unmet need motivation [stimuli] to buy.

Product Brokering

What to buy? Product evaluation, match product to needs, compare alternatives, multiple criteria.

Merchant Brokering

Who to buy from?
Price and other criteria, comparisons.

Negotiation

Negotiate terms of transaction.
Price and other criteria, comparisons.

Purchase and Delivery

Pay and take possession of product.
Product is delivered.

Product/Service Evaluation

Postpurchase service.
Evaluation of overall satisfaction.

Agents That Support Need Identification (What to Buy)

Agents can help buyers recognize their need for products or services by providing product information and stimuli. For example, expedia.com notifies customers about low airfares to a customer's desired destination whenever they become available.

Several commercial agents can facilitate need recognition directly or indirectly. For example, salesmountain.com helps people find certain items when they are put "on sale." If customers specify what they want, salesmountain.com will send notification when the item is discounted. Similarly, findgift.com asks customers questions about the person they are buying a gift for and helps them hunt down the perfect gift.

Agents That Support Product Brokering (From Whom to Buy)

Once a need is established, customers search for a product (or service) that will satisfy the need. Several agents are available to assist customers with this task. The comparison agents cited in Chapter 3 belong to this category. Exhibit 5.6 shows the product-comparison screen from a search engine. Other examples of product brokering would be the software agents

EXHIBIT 5.6   A Sample Product Comparison Screen

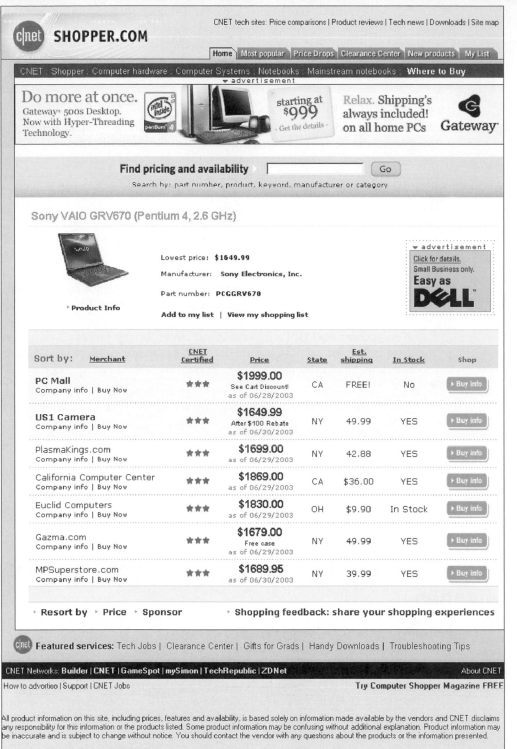

used by Fastparts (fastparts.com) and classifieds2000.com. An example of how these agents are used in advertising is provided in EC Application Case 5.2

Some agents can match people that have similar interest profiles. Even more ambitious agents try to predict which brands of computers, cars, and other goods will appeal to customers based on market segmentation preferences in a variety of different product categories such as wine, music, or breakfast cereal. (See the earlier discussion on *collaborative filtering*.) For a discussion on agents that do both product and merchant brokering, see Pedersen (2000).

Agents That Support Merchant Brokering and Comparisons

Once a customer has a specific product in mind, they need to find a place to buy it. BargainFinder (from Andersen Consulting) was the pioneering agent in this category. When used for online CD shopping, for example, this agent queried the price of a specific CD from a number of online vendors and returned a list of prices. However, this system encountered problems because vendors who did not want to compete on price managed to block out the agent's requests. (Today's version is at cdrom-guide.pricegrabber.com.) The blocking problem has been solved by agents such as Inktomi Shopping Agent, My Simon (mysimon.com), and Junglee (of amazon.com). These agents originate the requests from whatever computer the user is accessing at the time. This way, vendors have no way of determining whether the request comes direct from a real customer or from the comparison agent.

Fraud is of major concern to buyers, because buyers cannot see the products or the sellers. Several vendors offer agent-based fraud detection systems. One such system is Risk Suite (fairisaac.com). It is based on pattern recognition driven by neural computing.

Comparison agents. Part of the merchant brokering process is determining price and other purchase criteria. Large numbers of agents enable consumers to perform all kinds of comparisons, as was shown in Chapter 3. Here are some additional examples:

▶ Allbookstores.com and bestbookbuys.com are two of several agents that help consumers find the lowest prices of books available online.

▶ Bottomdollar.com, compare.net, pricewonders.com, shopper.com, roboshopper.com, and bargainvillage.com are examples of agents (out of several dozen) that suggest brands and compare prices once consumers specify what they want to buy.

▶ Pricescan.com guides consumers to the best prices on thousands of computer hardware and software products.

▶ Buyerzone.com is a B2B portal at which businesses can find the best prices on many products and services.

CASE 5.2

EC Application

FUJITSU USES AGENTS FOR TARGETED ADVERTISING IN JAPAN

Fujitsu (*fujitsu.com*) is a Japanese-based global provider of Internet-focused information technology solutions. Since the end of 1996, Fujitsu has been using an agent-based technology called the Interactive Marketing Interface (iMi). The system allows advertisers to interact directly with specific segments of the consumer market through the use of software agents, while ensuring that consumers remain anonymous to advertisers. Consumers submit a personal profile to iMi, indicating such characteristics as product categories of interests, hobbies, travel habits, and the maximum number of e-mail messages per week that they are willing to receive. In turn, customers receive product announcements, advertisements, and marketing surveys by e-mail from advertisers based on their personal profile information. By answering the marketing surveys or acknowledging receipt of advertisements, consumers earn iMi points, redeemable for gift certificates and phone cards. Many other companies in Japan (e.g., *nifty.com* and *lifemedia.co.jp*) also use this technology.

Source: Compiled from *fujitsu.com* (1999).

Questions

1. Why would customers agree to have a personal profile built on them?

2. What is the role of the software agent in this case?

Agents That Support Buyer–Seller Negotiation

The traditional concept of "market" implies negotiation, mostly about price. Whereas many large retail stores engage in fixed-price selling, many small retail stores and most markets use negotiation extensively. In several cultures (e.g., Chinese), negotiation is very common. In many B2B transactions, negotiation is common, too. The benefit of dynamically negotiating a price is that the pricing decision is shifted from the seller to the marketplace. In a fixed-price situation, if the seller fixes a price that is too high, sales volume will suffer. If the price is set too low, profits will be lower.

Negotiations, however, are time-consuming and often disliked by individual customers who cannot negotiate properly because they lack information about the marketplace and prices or they have not learned to negotiate. Many vendors do not like to negotiate either. Therefore, electronic support of negotiation can be extremely useful.

Agents can negotiate in pairs or one agent can negotiate for a buyer with several sellers' agents. In the latter case, the contact is done with each seller's agent individually, and the buyer's agent can conduct comparisons (Yan et al. 2000). Also, customers can negotiate with sellers' agents. One system automates the bargaining on a seller's side. The system can bargain with customers based on their bargaining behavior. For example, if the customer starts very low, the system helps the seller know how to respond. For details, see Lin and Chang (2001).

Agents That Support Purchase and Delivery

Agents are used extensively during the actual purchase, often arranging payment and delivery. For example, if a customer makes a mistake when completing an electronic order form, an agent will point it out immediately. When a customer buys stocks, for example, the pricing agent will tell the customer when a stock they want to buy on margin is not marginable or when the customer does not have sufficient funds. Similarly, delivery options are posted by agents at amazon.com, and the total cost of the transaction is calculated in real time.

Agents That Support After-Sale Service and Evaluation

Agents also can be used to facilitate after-sale service. For example, the automatic e-mail answering agents described in Chapter 4 are usually effective in answering customer queries. A non-Internet agent can monitor automobile usage and notify an owner when it is time to take their car in for periodic maintenance. Agents that facilitate feedback from customers also are useful.

CHARACTER-BASED ANIMATED INTERACTIVE AGENTS

Several agents enhance customer service by interacting with customers via animated characters. Other agents are used to facilitate advertising. Animated characters are software agents with personalities. They are versatile and employ friendly front ends to communicate with users. They are not necessarily intelligent. These animated agents are also called avatars. **Avatars** are animated computer representations of humanlike movements and behaviors in a computer-generated three-dimensional world. Advanced avatars can "speak" and exhibit behaviors such as gestures and facial expressions. They can be fully automated to act like robots. The purpose of avatars is to introduce believable emotions so that the agents gain credibility with users. Insights and Additions 5.2 (page 206) describes the use of avatars at a virtual mall in Korea.

avatars
Animated computer characters that exhibit humanlike movements and behaviors.

Avatars are considered a part of **social computing**, an approach aimed at making the human–computer interface more natural. Studies conducted by Extempo (extempo.com 1999) showed that interactive characters can improve customer satisfaction and retention by offering personalized, one-to-one service. They also can help companies get to know their customers and support advertising (see the Real-World Case at the end of this chapter).

social computing
An approach aimed at making the human–computer interface more natural.

Chatterbots

A special category of animation characters is characters that can chat, known as **chatterbots**. A chatterbot is a program that attempts to simulate a conversation, with the aim of at least temporarily fooling a customer into thinking they are conversing with a human. The concept started with Eliza, created by Joseph Weizenbaum at MIT in 1957. In his program, users

chatterbots
Animation characters that can talk (chat).

Insights and Additions 5.2   Brand Names at a Korean Virtual Mall

Avatars are big business in Korea. Internet users express themselves by putting clothes, shoes, and accessories on their avatars. The clothes are really pixels on the computer screen designed for avatars that represent the users and are moved around a virtual chat room. Clothing the avatars in attire bought in virtual malls is part of the fun. Sayclub, operated by NeoWiz, was the first to introduce avatar services there in 2000. The company had more than 15 million members in 2002 who spent a total of $1.6 million a month on their avatars, dressing them in the over 30,000 outfits from the virtual shopping mall (*saymall.sayclub.com*).

"It is an unusual strategy, but avatars can be very effective marketing tools," says Chung Jae Hyung, chief executive officer at DKIMS Communications, an online marketing agency. "They are so popular with young people these days that they can get you a lot of exposure very quickly. An avatar is a given; just like everyone has a cell phone, everyone has an avatar," says Chung. Samsung Economic Research Institute estimates that the avatar industry generated $16 million in revenue last year (Yoon 2002).

As competition grew from the top portals, such as Yahoo, Sayclub responded by offering more items, including hair dyes, accessories, and brands. "We needed something to differentiate ourselves and improve our brand image," says Chang Hyun Guk, manager of the business-planning team at Sayclub. "The best way to do that was to bring real-life brands to our virtual mall." Therefore, to improve its own brand image, Sayclub sought to offer well-known consumer brands as products one could buy for one's avatar from the Sayclub site. In addition to improving the Sayclub brand, these products would generate money from additional sales.

However, convincing top brands to go virtual was not easy. For example, because Mattel, the maker of Barbie, did not have any idea what the avatar market was all about, it needed to be educated before it would sign a licensing agreement allowing outfits from the Barbie Fashion Avenue line of doll dresses to be "avatarized" for a percentage of total sales. Numerous Barbie outfits have gone on sale at prices ranging from $4 to $5.35. That may not sound like much, but as of June 2002, avatar outfits made up almost 15 percent of Barbie's licensing business in Korea. By exposing Sayclub's users (mostly people in their teens and 20s) to Barbie paraphernalia, Mattel has been able to extend her popularity beyond children the ages of 8 or 9. Jisun Lee, a 23-year-old student, had not owned anything "Barbie" in over a decade, but spent more than $85 in 2002 dressing her avatar.

During the Korean World Cup games in June 2002, Sayclub formed a partnership with Nike Korea and introduced avatars based on real images of Korean soccer players. They provided various soccer-related avatar items, including uniforms and Nike products. Sayclub granted uniform numbers of national soccer players to all users who bought Nike soccer items, including soccer player avatars or national team uniforms. They also gave away gifts to users with uniform numbers (selected by lottery) if the players their avatars represented scored during the games.

Sources: Yoon (2002); *sayclub.com* (2002); and *neowiz.com* (2002).

---

conversed with a psychoanalyst. Today's version is very powerful (try eceeliza.cjb.net). The major differences are that today the programs are on the Web and they include a static or moving character. The technology is based on *natural language programming* (NLP), an applied artificial intelligence program that can recognize typed or spoken key words and short sentences.

A major use of character-based interactive agents is in customer service and CRM. The following sites offer demos and the opportunity to converse with virtual representatives:

▶ artificial-life.com. This site offers CRM and other agents. The site can be accessed by cell phones as well as traditional Web connections. (In Chapter 4, we illustrated the CRM agents of this company; see Exhibit 4.11.)

▶ nativeminds.com. This site offers "v-reps" (virtual representatives) that can answer customer questions and provide potential solutions.

▶ extempo.com. This site offers agents for various purposes, including CRM.

▶ zabaware.com. This site provides desktop assistance for answering customers' queries.

For an inventory of chatterbots and other resources, visit Simon Laven (spaceports.com).

Chatterbots can do many things to enhance customer service, such as greeting a consumer when they enter a site or giving the consumer a guided tour of the site. For example, consider the following chatterbot agents: Mr. Clean (mrclean.com) guides consumers to cleaning-related Procter & Gamble products. "Katie" is an interactive agent that provides personalized and interactive information about Dove's skincare products (dove.com). The Personal Job Search Agent at monster.com helps users find a job. "Ed, Harmony, and Nina" are virtual guides that help visitors who wish to learn more about products and tools available at extempo.com (which specializes in avatars). For additional information on interactive characters, see Hayes-Roth et al. (1999), microsoft.com/msagent/, extempo.com, and nativeminds.com.

AGENTS THAT SUPPORT AUCTIONS

Several agents support auction-related activities. Agents often act as auction aggregators, which tell consumers where and when certain items will be auctioned. Examples can be found at bidxs.com, rubylane.com, auctionwatch.com, and bidfind.com. Some aggregators provide real-time access to auctions.

Almost all auctions require users to personally execute the bidding. However, AuctionBot allows users to create intelligent agents that will take care of the bidding process for them. With AuctionBot, users create auction agents by specifying a number of parameters that vary depending on the type of the auction selected. After that, it is up to the agent to manage the auction until a final price is met or the auction deadline is reached. At yahoo.com, a bidding agent places bids on the user's behalf at the lowest possible increments. The user enters the highest amount they will pay, and the agent will try to win the bid at a lower price. For further details, see Chapter 11.

OTHER EC AGENTS

Other agents support consumer behavior, customer service, and advertising activities. For example, resumix.com (now at enterprise.yahoo.com/resumix) is an application that wanders the Web looking for Web pages containing resume information. If it identifies a page as being a resume, it tries to extract pertinent information from the page, such as the person's e-mail address, phone number, skill description, and location. The resulting database is used to connect job seekers with recruiters. For current lists of various EC agents, see botspot.com, agentland.com, and agents.umbc.edu (look at Agents 101 Tutorial). For a comprehensive guide to EC agents, see Fingar (1998).

Section 5.6 ▶ REVIEW

1. List the major types of software (intelligent) agents used in customer-related and advertising applications.
2. What role do software agents play in need identification?
3. How do software agents support product brokering and merchant brokering?
4. What are avatars and chatterbots? Why are they used on Web sites?
5. What type of support do software agents provide to online auctions?

5.7 UNSOLICITED ELECTRONIC ADS: THE PROBLEM AND SOLUTIONS

As the diversity and innovation of Internet advertising increase, so does the quantity of unsolicited ads. Such ads are not only an invasion of privacy, but they also are aggravating. The flood of unsolicited ads clogs the networks of ISPs, sometimes to the point of paralysis, and may prevent legitimate messages from getting through. The problem is reaching epidemic proportion in two areas: e-mail spamming and pop-ups.

E-MAIL SPAMMING

E-mail spamming, also known as unsolicited commercial e-mail or UCE (unsolicited commercial e-mail), involves using e-mail to send unwanted ads or correspondence. It has been part of the Internet for years. Unfortunately, the situation is getting worse with time. Let's look at some of the drivers of spamming and then at some of the potential solutions.

spamming
Using e-mail to send unwanted ads (sometimes floods of ads).

What Drives UCE?

Although many people think that spamming is mostly the result of legitimate commercial activities, the fact is different. According to the Coalition Against Unsolicited Commercial E-mail (cauce.org 2002), 80 percent of spammers are just trying to get people's financial information—credit card or bank account numbers—to defraud them. The pornography industry is another major source of spamming. The major drivers of increased UCEs are that the "postage" is free, the time and energy entailed in mass mailings is minimal, and it is easy to get a mailing list. Because the entry hurdles are relatively low compared to the potential payoffs, spammers have an incentive to find new ways to circumvent protective software, and they are succeeding: The total number of spammers and/or the quantity of e-mails delivered by each spammer is increasing.

Why It Is Difficult to Control Spamming

Let's look at one of the most well-known spammers, Al Ralsky. According to Stone and Lin (2002), Ralsky sends out more than 30 million e-mails each day, using 120 servers. Verizon is suing Ralsky, alleging that he crashed its servers. Ralsky (and others) buy bulk mailing lists, which can be purchased for as little as $2,000 for a list of 100 million addresses. Ralsky works with content providers that craft "pitches." He claims that he helps millions of people to buy cars, earn money, and so on, and that he helps small businesses to advertise. By some estimates, spam generates about 25 sales for every 1 million e-mails (Stone and Lin 2002).

Spammers send millions of e-mails, shifting Internet accounts to avoid detection. Using cloaking, they strip away clues (name and address) about where spam originates, and the server substitutes fake addresses. Many spam messages get sent undetected through unregulated Asian e-mail routes and back to the United States.

Spammers use different methods to find their victims. For example, they scour Web sites and chat rooms for addresses and they send e-mails to common names at mail servers, hoping to find a match. They also use computer programs that randomly generate thousands of addresses. In addition to regular commercial spammers that push products (e.g., ink for your printer) and services (e.g., home loans and insurance), the major spammers are the pornography sites.

Solutions to Spamming

Although antispam legislation is underway in many countries, its implementation may not be simple. Therefore, others must take action. The ISPs and e-mail providers such as Yahoo, MSN, AOL provide several options, ranging from junk-mail filters and automatic junk-mail deleters to blockers of certain URLs and e-mail addresses (e.g., see hotmail.com). AOL, Verizon, and others are especially keen on fighting the problem in their most recent editions (e.g., AOL version 8 has porn spam control).

In addition, many software packages are available to help users deal with the problem. For example, mailwasher.net can eliminate spam by reviewing e-mails before they are downloaded. Junkbusters.com will help users with free information and ideas for fighting spam. Other antispam tools are available from junkspy.com, spamex.com, zeroads.com, mailshell.com, surfcontrol.com, mymailoasis.com, contactplus.com, mcafee.com, and many others. Filtering tips are provided by Tynan (2002). Tips include instructions on the use of Outlook Express and Netscape Mail filters, how to opt out of permission-based e-mails, as well as how to surf smart, block cookies, deal with viruses, block hackers, encryption, and more (see find.pcworld.com/26702). The problem with spam-blocking software is that spammers find ways to circumvent the programs. For more information, see the Coalition Against Unsolicited Commercial E-Mail (cauce.org).

The problem of spam also exists in Internet-based wireless devices and is exploding. DoCoMo, the mobile portal, is taking several defensive measures, including imposing a fee on calls returned by unsuspected users who return calls to the spammers (Asahi Shimbun News Service 2002).

Users can complain about spam at abuse.com. That agency will transfer the complaint to the appropriate authority. Users can also contact mail-abuse.org.

Spam-filtering site for a country. According to Ki-tae (2002), Korean people are able to effectively block unsolicited e-mail by registering their e-mail addresses and telephone numbers on a government-run Web site. This service frees them from unwanted commercial e-messages and telephone calls to regular or mobile phones. To register, people enter nospam.go.kr or antispam.go.kr. Vendors are banned from sending unsolicited messages to the registered individuals. Offenders may lose their business license for up to a year or may be subject to criminal punishment.

Unfortunately, the system covers only registered businesses. Small, unregistered businesses can easily evade regulatory monitoring. However, the Korean government plans to make it compulsory for all businesses to refer to the antispam list. The government also plans to require all senders of promotional materials to identify them as commercials. Monitoring is done in collaboration with consumer protection groups.

A similar do-not-call list has been proposed to stop unwanted phone calls from telemarketers in the United States. However, it is being opposed by marketers who say that it violates their constitutional rights to advertise freely ("Do Not Call List Advances . . . ," 2003 Proposed legislation in both Canada and the United States (CAN. ACT S.630 and H.R. 3888) may address and curb e-mail spam.

POP-UPS

As discussed earlier, use of pop-ups and similar advertising programs is exploding. Sometimes it is even difficult to close these ads when they appear. Some may be part of a consumer's permission marketing agreement, but most are unsolicited. What can a user do about the unsolicited ones?

Tools for Stopping Pop-Ups

Several software packages offer pop-up stoppers. Some are free (e.g., panicware.com); others are available for fee (e.g. adsubtract.com). For tips and other products see find.pcworld.com/27401 (also 28221, 27424, and 27426). According to Luhn and Spanbauer (2002), users should consider the following ad blockers: Adsubtract Pro (adsubtract.com, guidescope.com), Norton Internet Security (symantec.com), and webwasher.com. These programs will block banners, flash ads, and cookies. Also, some cookie tools (e.g., Cookie Cop) are adding pop-up window killers. Finally, as in e-mail blocking, all major ISPs are providing pop-up protection.

Section 5.8 ▶ REVIEW

1. Why is e-mail spamming spreading so rapidly?
2. Why is it difficult to control spamming?
3. How can users fight e-mail spamming?
4. Describe the Korean solution to spamming.
5. Describe solutions to pop-ups.

MANAGERIAL ISSUES

Some managerial issues related to this chapter are as follows.

1. **Should we advertise anywhere but our own site?** Web advertising is a complex undertaking, and outsourcing should be seriously considered. Some outsourcers specialize in certain industries (e.g., ebizautos.com for auto dealers). Companies should examine the adage.com site, which contains an index of Web sites, their advertising rates, and reported traffic counts, before selecting a site on which to advertise. Companies also should consult third-party audits.

2. **What is our commitment to Web advertising, and how will we coordinate Web and traditional advertising?** Once a company is committed to advertising on

the Web, it must remember that a successful program is multifaceted. It requires input and vision from marketing, cooperation from the legal department, and strong technical leadership from the corporate information systems (IS) department. A successful Web advertising program also requires coordination with non-Internet advertising and top management support.

3. **Should we integrate our Internet and non-Internet marketing campaigns?** Many companies are integrating their TV and Internet marketing campaigns. For example, a company's TV or newspaper ads direct the viewers/readers to the Web site, where short videos

and sound ads, known as *rich media*, are used. With click-through ratios of banner ads down to less than 0.5 percent at many sites, innovations such as the integration of off-line and online marketing are certainly needed to increase the click-throughs.

4. **What ethical issues should we consider?** Several ethical issues relate to online advertising. One issue that receives a great deal of attention is spamming, which is now subject to pending legislation. Another issue is the selling of mailing lists and customer information. Some people believe not only that a company needs the consent of the customers before selling a list, but also that the company should share with customers the profits derived from the sale of such lists. Using cookies without an individual's consent is another ethical issue.

5. **Have we integrated advertising with ordering and other business processes?** This is an important requirement. For example, when customers go to amazon.com, they are directed to the shopping cart, then to the catalog, then to ordering and paying. Next, inventory availability is checked, and delivery is arranged. For maximum effectiveness, such integration of business processes should be seamless.

6. **How important is branding?** Market research attempts to find out how important a brand name is on the Internet. Obviously, a strong brand helps to increase trust. However, many online shoppers are more concerned with low prices than with purchasing a particular brand. Each company must decide its optimal balance of advertising its brand versus promotion based on low price. Also, it is important for newcomers in a market to know how much to invest in a brand name.

7. **What is the right amount of advertising?** At a minimum, companies these days need an Internet presence, such as a company Web site and an online brochure. A better idea is to have an interactive Web site, where customer service can be provided as well. The use of affiliate marketing is also highly recommended.

8. **Are any metrics available to guide advertisers?** A large amount of information has been developed to guide advertisers as to where to advertise, how to design ads, and so on. Specific metrics may be used to assess the effectiveness of advertising and to calculate the ROI from an organization's online advertising campaign.

SUMMARY

In this chapter, you learned about the following EC issues as they relate to the learning objectives.

1. **Objectives and characteristics of Web advertising.** Web advertising attempts to attract surfers to an advertiser's site. Once at the advertiser's site, consumers can receive information, interact with the seller, and in many cases, immediately place an order. With Web advertising, ads can be customized to fit groups of people with similar interests or even individuals. In addition, Web advertising can be interactive, is easily updated, can reach millions at a reasonable cost, and offers dynamic presentation by rich multimedia.

2. **Major online advertising methods.** Banners are the most popular online advertising method. Other frequently used methods are pop-up and similar ads (including interstitials), e-mail (including e-mail to mobile devices), classified ads, registration of URLs with search engines, and advertising in chat rooms.

3. **Various advertising strategies and types of promotions.** The major advertising strategies are ads associated with search results (text links), affiliate marketing, pay incentives for customers to view ads, viral marketing, ads customized on a one-to-one basis, and online events and promotions. Web promotions are similar to off-line promotions. They include giveaways, contests, quizzes, entertainment, coupons, and so on. Customization and interactivity distinguish Internet promotions from conventional ones.

4. **Measuring advertising success and pricing ads.** The traditional concept of paying for ads by exposure (by CPM) is also used on the Internet, but this is being challenged. Although space sellers prefer the CPM approach, advertisers prefer to pay for actions such as click-throughs. Paying commissions for electronic referrals is becoming a popular method.

5. **Permission marketing, ad management, and localization.** In permission marketing, customers are willing to accept ads in exchange for special (personalized) information or monetary incentives. Ad management deals with planning, organizing, and controlling ad campaigns and ad use. Finally, in localization, attempts are made to fit ads to a local environment.

6. **Intelligent agents.** Intelligent agents can gather and interpret data about consumer-purchasing behavior. Advanced agents can even learn about customer behavior and needs by observing their Web movements. Agents can facilitate or support all aspects of the purchasing process, including product brokering, merchant brokering, product comparison, buyer–seller negotiation, purchase and delivery, and after-sale customer service. Character-based interactive agents such as avatars and chatterbots "put a face" on the computing experience, making it more natural.

7. **Stopping unsolicited ads.** The amount of unsolicited e-mails and pop-ups is increasing very rapidly. Little legal relief is available. ISPs are trying to provide protection, but frequently it is necessary to use special software to do the job, and it is far from a perfect solution. Only legal action may help, but it is resisted by many.

KEY TERMS

DISCUSSION QUESTIONS

1. Compare banner swapping with a banner exchange.

2. Explain why third-party audits of Web site traffic are needed.

3. Discuss why banners are popular in Internet advertising.

4. Compare and contrast Internet and television advertising.

5. Discuss the advantages and limitations of listing a company's URL with various search engines.

6. How might a chat room be used for advertising?

7. Compare the use of the click-through pricing method with more interactive approaches to ad pricing.

8. Is it ethical for a vendor to enter a chat room operated by a competitor and pose queries?

9. Relate Web ads to market research.

10. Explain why online ad management is critical.

11. Examine some Web avatars and try to interact with them. Discuss the potential benefits and drawbacks of using avatars as an advertising media.

12. Explain the advantages of using chatterbots. Are there any disadvantages?

13. Discuss the advantages and disadvantages of spamming. Should antispamming legislation be developed? How can it be enforced?

14. Discuss the benefits of using software agents in marketing and advertising.

INTERNET EXERCISES

1. Enter selfpromotion.com and find some interesting promotion ideas for the Web.

2. Enter nativeminds.com and extempo.com. Find information about the "virtual representative" and check demos and customers' stories. Prepare a report that compares the two sites.

3. Enter the Web sites of ipro.com and selfpromotion.com. What Internet traffic management, Web results, and auditing services are provided? What are the benefits of each service? Find at least one competitor in each category (e.g., netratings.com; observe the "demo"). Compare the services provided and the prices.

4. Investigate the tools available to self-monitor Web sites. What are the major capabilities of these tools? Start with webarrange.com, webtrends.com, and doubleclick.com.

5. Enter hotwired.com and espn.com. Identify all of the advertising methods used on each site. Can you find those that are targeted advertisements? What revenue sources can you find on the ESPN site? (Try to find at least seven.)

6. Compare the advertisements and promotions at thestreet.com and marketwatch.com. Write a report.

7. Enter nameprotect.com and find out if your competitor or a company you know purchased a specific brand name. Summarize your findings.

8. Enter adweek.com, newroads.com, wdfm.com, adtech.com, iab.com, and adage.com and find new developments in Internet advertisement. Write a report based on your findings.

9. Enter clairol.com to determine your best hair color. You can upload your own photo to the studio and see how different shades look on you. You can also try different hairstyles. It is also for men. How can these activities increase branding? How can they increase sales?

10. Enter positionagent.com (part of Microsoft's "bCentral") and ask the Position Agent to rank your Web site or a site with which you are familiar. Assess the benefits versus the costs.

11. What resources do you find to be most useful at targetonline.com, clickz.com, admedia.org, i-m.com, and wdfm.com?

12. Enter eat.com. What advertising methods does the site use? How do these methods increase customer loyalty?

13. Enter doubleclick.com and examine all of the company's products. Prepare a report.

TEAM ASSIGNMENTS AND ROLE PLAYING

1. As a team, examine the various advertising options offered by m-commerce companies. Start with i-Mode at nttdocomo.com. Move on to nokia.com, motorola.com, and ericsson.com. Also check adage.com and any other sources you might find. Prepare a report based on your findings.

2. Each team will choose one advertising method and conduct an in-depth investigation of the major players in that part of the ad industry. For example, direct e-mail is relatively inexpensive. Visit the-dma.org to learn about direct mail. Then visit bulletmail.com, ezinemanager.com, permissiondirect.com, and venturedirect.com. Each team will prepare and present an argument as to why its method is superior.

3. In this exercise, each team member will enter uproar.com to play games and win prizes. What could be better? This site is the destination of choice for game and sweepstakes junkies and for those who wish to reach a mass audience of fun-loving people. Currently, Uproar and Reese's have partnered to create a "Fun Center" where you can win a year's supply of candy and other sweet things.

   After a brief registration process (and offers to enter about a "gazillion" other sweepstakes), you will receive 100 iCoins, the Uproar currency. Move through the site and spend your iCoins to play. Win more iCoins in return, as well as many other great prizes. Hang out in Reese's Land or move on to other channels for lottery, games, and game shows galore. Enter a sweepstakes (you must click on an ad banner to confirm your entry). Follow the instructions. Then compare experiences. Write a report.

4. Let the team try the services of constantcontact.com. Constant Contact offers a turnkey e-mail marketing package solution. In less than 5 minutes, you can set up an e-mail sign-up box on your Web site. As visitors fill in their names and e-mail addresses, they can be asked to check off topics of interest (as defined by you) to create targeted groups.

   Constant Contact then provides a system to create template e-mail newsletter layouts, by subject, that can be managed as separate campaigns and sent to your target users on a predetermined schedule. The site manages your mailings and provides reports that help you assess the success of your efforts. Pricing is based on the number of subscribers; less than 50 and the service is free. Write a report summarizing your experiences.

REAL-WORLD CASE

CHEVRON'S WORLD OF CAR CHARACTERS

To make its brand more easily recognized, especially among children, Chevron Corp. (now ChevronTexaco), a major oil and gas company, ran a promotional campaign that featured an animated toy car and was centered on the Web site *chevroncars.com*. Chevron built one of the freshest, most innovative corporate sites on the Web. Within 3 months, traffic at the site increased from about 1,500 hits per day to over 150,000 hits per day. The site won the 1997 Best of the Internet (BOTI) Award and generated about 100 suggestions per day from viewers, mostly children, ranging from ideas for new Claymation characters to new product designs. The site, which now includes games, is still very popular.

Among the highlights at *chevroncars.com* are a question-and-answer section of frequently asked questions (FAQs), the ability to customize toy cars ("My Cars"), free stuff (e.g., a car-themed screen saver), and a knowledge base about cars. A squirrel points out commercial messages and tasks for which children may need adult permission. At the Kid Shop, users can grab a shopping cart and buy a plastic version of one of Chevron's animated vehicles or other Chevron items. Finally, a "playground" with games such as crossword puzzles, connect the dots, and a concentration-like activity is available. The game that allows users to check how they did against players nationwide seems to be the hands-down favorite. If the user provides an incorrect response to any question in any game at the site, the site provides an empathetic "bummer" response.

The site has a definite commercial and branding message: Chevron is a responsible, necessary, and even fun type of business, and the company is ecologically aware, doing things such as protecting baby owls nesting in pumps. The company is thinking of ways to use the site to promote Chevron's math and science awards and to help teachers locate videos and other educational materials. In addition, the site lets users find out how a company like Chevron operates.

So what is the most popular part of the Chevron site? Shopping for the toy cars of course. The largest buying group tends to be the parents of children between ages 3 and 9. Next is the 18-to-21-year-old demographic, followed by "kids" 35 years and older.

For a national gasoline company that operated in just 26 markets (before its merger with Texaco), the real success of Chevron's site was in the brand recognition it afforded for both existing and future customers. The fun message also reflects the changing nature of the gasoline business—pumps giving way to service complexes including commercial markets, car washes, fast-food chains, and even hotels. The company believes that the site's success has had as much to do with listening to what people want as any static master plan it could have dreamed up at corporate headquarters.

Sources: Compiled from *chevroncars.com/wocc/index.jhtml* (2003); Hudgins-Bonafield (2002); and *polyweb.com/danno/toycars_awards/chevroncars_com_awards.html* (1999).

Questions

1. Explain the logic of using Claymation cars to advertise the Chevron brand. How would you compare the Web advertising with TV ads?

2. Why would Chevron want to target the 5 to 12-year-old demographic? They certainly do not buy gasoline, and by the time they drive cars, the market for gasoline sales may be completely different.

3. From what you have learned in this chapter, what factors do you think contributed to the site's success?

REFERENCES

Akamai Technologies, Inc. "Best Practices for Successful Live Web Event." Akamai Technologies, Inc., report, 2000a.

Akamai Technologies, Inc. "Delivering the Profits: How the Right Content Delivery Provider Can Drive Traffic, Sales, and Profits Through Your Web Site." Akamai Technologies, Inc., white paper, 2000b.

Asahi Shimbun News Service, News item, August 30, 2002.

Bannan, K. J. "Campaign Management." *Manage*, June 10, 2002, btobonline.com/cgi-bin/article.pl?id=9256 (accessed November 2002).

beinggirl.com (accessed September 2002).

being-me.com (accessed September 2002).

Boswell, K. "Digital Marketing vs. Online Advertising Breaking Waves for Marketers to Catch," *The Marketleap Report* 2, no. 5, March 19, 2002, marketleap.com/report/ml_report_24.htm (accessed April 2003).

Brown, J. "Click, Two." *Business Week*, February 18, 2002.

Bulik, B. S. "Procter & Gamble's Great Web Experiment." *Business 2.0*, November 28, 2000, 48–53.

cauce.org (accessed October 2002).

Chase, L. *Essential Business Tactics on the Net.* New York: John Wiley & Sons, 1998.

chevroncars.com/wocc/index.jhtml (accessed April 2003).

Clow, K., and D. Baack. *Integrated Advertising, Promotion, and Marketing Communication.* Upper Saddle River, NJ: Prentice Hall, 2002.

crest.com (accessed September 2002).

cyveillance.com (accessed January 2003).

"Do-Not-Call List Advances a Step Closer to Reality." *Wall Street Journal*, January 31, 2003, D2.

doubleclick.com (accessed January 2003).

Doyle, K., et al. "Banner Ad Placement Study." University of Michigan, 1997, webreference.com/dev/banners (accessed April 2003).

Extempo Systems, Inc. "Smart Interactive Characters: Automating One-To-One Customer Service." September 1999, extempo.com/company_info/press/webtechniques.shtml (accessed September 2002).

Fingar, P. "A CEO's Guide to E-Commerce Using Intergalactic Object-Oriented Intelligent Agents." July 1998, home1.gte.net/pfingar/eba.htm (accessed April 2003).

fujitsu.com (accessed October 1999).

Gelb, B., and S. Sundaram. "Adapting to 'Work of Mouse.'" *Business Horizons*, July–August 2002, 21–22.

Gopal, R. D., et al. "Admediation: New Horizons in Effective Email Advertising." *Communications of the ACM* 44, no. 12 (2001): 91–95.

Gordon-Lewis, H. *Effective E-Mail Marketing*. New York: Amacom, 2002.

Hayes-Roth, B., et al. "Web Guides." *IEEE Intelligent Systems* (March–April 1999).

Helm, S. "Viral Marketing." *Electronic Markets* 10, no. 3 (2000).

Helmstetter, G., and P. Metivier. *Affiliate Selling: Building Revenue on the Web*. New York: Wiley, 2000.

Hoffman, D. L., and T. P. Novak. "How to Acquire Customers on the Web." *Harvard Business Review* (May–June 2000).

Hoffman, D. L., and T. P. Novak. "Marketing in Hypermedia Computer Mediated Environments: Conceptual Foundations." *Journal of Marketing* (July 1996).

Hudgins-Bonafield, C. "Chevron's World of Car Characters: BOTI Awards: Most Innovative Site—chevroncars.com," www.chevroncars.com/wocc/abt/index.jhtml?mediaUrl=pages/awards.html (accessed October 2002).

InformationWeek, October 3, 1994, 26.

Kinnard, S. *Marketing with E-Mail*, 3d ed. Gulf Breeze, FL: Maximum Press, 2002.

Ki-tae, Kim. "Spam-Filtering Site to Open Today." *Korean Times*, August 22, 2002.

Legmanila.com. "Online Advertising Works," *Legmanila.com*, legmanila.com/info/advertise (accessed April 2003).

Lin, F., and K. Chang. "A Multiagent Framework for Automated Online Bargaining." *IEEE Intelligent Systems* 16, no. 4 (2001): 41–47.

Luhn, R., and S. Spanbauer. "AdSubtract 2.5," *PC World*, September 27, 2002, pcworld.com/downloads/file_description/0,fid,21340,00.asp (accessed April 2003).

Martin, D., and M. Ryan. "Pop-ups Abound but Most Advertisers Remain Inline." *NetRatings*, 2002, adrelevance.com/intelligence/intel_snapshot.jsp?pr=020829 (accessed October 2002).

McDonald, T., "Web Surfers: Take the TV, Give Me My Internet," *NewsFactor Network*, February 8, 2001, newsfactor.com/perl/story/7354.html (accessed June 2003).

Meeker, N. *The Internet Advertising Report*. New York: Morgan Stanley Corporation, 1997.

Meskauskas, J. "Are Click-through Rates Really Declining?" *Clicz.com*, January 16, 2001, clickz.com/media/plan_buy/article.php/835391 (accessed April 2003).

neowiz.com (accessed October 2002).

Nobles, R., and S. O'Neil. *Streetwise Maximize Web Site Traffic: Build Web Site Traffic Fast and Free by Optimizing Search Engine Placement*. Holbrook, MA: Adams Media Corporation, 2000.

O'Keefe, S. *Complete Guide to Internet Publicity*. New York: Wiley, 2002.

PC Magazine, March 12, 2002, 29.

pantene.com (accessed September 2002).

Pederson, P. E. "Behavioral Effects of Using Software Agents for Product and Merchant Brokering: An Experimental Study of Consumer Decision Making." *International Journal of Electronic Commerce* vol. 5, no. 1 (2000).

polyweb.com/danno/toycars_awards/chevroncars_com_awards.html (accessed February 1999).

physique.com (accessed September 2002).

reflect.com (accessed September 2002).

Rothenberg, R. "An Advertising Power, but Just What Does DoubleClick Do?" *New York Times*, September 22, 1999.

sayclub.com (accessed October 2002).

Schibsted, E. "Email Takes Center Stage." *Business 2.0*, December 26, 2000, 64–71.

Scheirer, E., et al. "Bigger Hits with Net Marketing." *Forrester Research*, August 2001, 1–20.

shopper.cnet.com/shopping/resellers/0-205442-311-5185337-0.html?fl=4&tag=shop (accessed July 2001).

Sterne, J. *WWW Marketing*, 3d ed. New York: Wiley, 2001.

Stone, B., and J. Lin. "Spamming the World." *Newsweek*, August 19, 2002, stacks.msnbc.com/news/792491.asp (accessed April 2003).

Taylor, C. P. "Is One-to-One the Way to Market?" *Interactive Week*, May 12, 1997.

Tedeschi, B. "E-Commerce Report: New Alternatives to Banner Ads." *New York Times*, February 20, 2001.

Thompson, C. "Agents and E-Commerce." *ROB Magazine*, September 1999, robmagzaine.com/archive/99ROBseptember/html/ft_agents_ecommerce.html (accessed October 2002).

tide.com (accessed September 2002).

Tynan, D. "How to Take Back Your Privacy: Keep Spammers and Online Snoops at Bay." *PCWorld*, June 2002.

UCLA Center for Communication Policy. "UCLA Internet Report 2001: Surveying the Digital Future." November 2001, ccp.ucla.edu/pdf/UCLA-Internet-Report-2001.pdf (accessed January 2003).

vert.net (accessed January 2003).

Yan, Y., et al. "A Multi-Agent Based Negotiated Support System." *Proceedings 33rd HICSS*, Maui, HI, January 2000.

Yoon, S. "Brand Names Are at the Virtual Mall." *Wall Street Journal Europe*, June 13, 2002.

Yoon, S. J., and J. H. Kim. "Is the Internet More Effective Than Traditional Media? Factors Affecting the Choice of Media." *Journal of Advertising Research* (November–December 2001).

COMPANY-CENTRIC B2B AND E-PROCUREMENT

Content

Learning objectives

Upon completion of this chapter, you will be able to:

1. Describe the B2B field.
2. Describe the major types of B2B models.
3. Discuss the characteristics of the sell-side marketplace, including auctions.
4. Describe the sell-side intermediary models.
5. Describe the characteristics of the buy-side marketplace and e-procurement.
6. Explain how reverse auctions work in B2B.
7. Describe B2B aggregation and group purchasing models.
8. Describe infrastructure and standards requirements for B2B.
9. Describe Web EDI, XML, and Web services.

GENERAL MOTORS' B2B INITIATIVES

The Problem

General Motors (GM) is the world's largest vehicle manufacturer. The company sells cars in 190 countries and has manufacturing plants in about 50. Because the automotive industry is very competitive, GM is always looking for ways to improve its effectiveness. Its most publicized new initiative is a futuristic project with which GM expects to custom-build the majority of its cars by 2005. The company hopes to use the system to save billions of dollars by reducing its inventory of finished cars.

In the meantime, GM sells custom-designed cars online through its dealers' sites. This way, online sales are not considered direct marketing to final consumers, avoiding channel conflict. This collaboration requires sharing information with dealers for online marketing and service on cars and warranties. Both GM and its many dealers also need to collaborate with GM's many suppliers. These suppliers work with other automakers as well. Therefore, a good communications system is needed.

Besides the need for effective communication, GM faces many operational problems that are typical of large companies. One of these is an ongoing financial challenge of what to do with manufacturing machines that are no longer sufficiently productive. These capital assets depreciate (lose value) over time and eventually must be replaced. GM traditionally has sold these assets through intermediaries at physical auctions. The problem was that these auctions took weeks, even months. Furthermore, the prices obtained in the auctions seemed to be too low, and a 20 percent commission had to be paid to the third-party auctioneer.

Anther operational problem for GM relates to procurement of commodity products, which can be either *direct* materials that go into the vehicles or *indirect* materials such as light bulbs or office supplies. GM buys about 200,000 different products from 20,000 suppliers, spending close to $100 billion annually. It was using a manual bidding process to negotiate contracts with potential suppliers. Specifications of the needed materials were sent by mail to the potential suppliers, the suppliers would then submit a bid, and GM would select a winner if a supplier offered a low enough price. If all the bids were too high, second and third rounds of bidding were conducted. In some cases, the process took weeks, even months, before GM was confident that the best deal, from both price and quality standpoints, had been achieved. The submission preparation costs involved in this process kept some bidders from submitting bids, so a less than optimal number of suppliers participated, resulting in higher prices paid by GM.

The Solution

To solve the problem of *connecting dealers and suppliers*, GM established an extranet infrastructure called *ANX* (Automotive Network eXchange). The ANX, which was supported by other automakers, has evolved into the consortium exchange *covisint.com* (described in more detail in EC Application Case 7.2, on page 274). To address the *capital assets problem*, in early 2000 GM implemented its own electronic market, which is now part of *covisint.com*, from which *forward auctions* are conducted. The first items put up for bid were eight 75–ton stamping presses. GM invited 140 certified bidders to view the pictures and service records of the presses online. After only 1 week of preparation, the auction went live online, and the presses were sold in less than 2 hours.

For the *resource procurement problem*, GM automated the bidding process using *reverse auctions* on its e-procurement site. Qualified suppliers use the Internet to bid on each item GM needs to purchase. Bids are "open," meaning that all bidders can see the bids of their competitors. GM is able to accept bids from many suppliers concurrently, and using predetermined criteria, such as price, delivery date, and payment terms, can award jobs quickly to the most suitable bidder.

The Results

Within just 89 minutes after the first *forward auction* opened, eight stamping presses were sold for $1.8 million. With the old off-line method, a similar item would have sold for less than half of its online price, and the process would have taken 4 to 6 weeks. In 2001, GM conducted over 150 other electronic auctions. Other sellers were encouraged to put their items up for sale at the site as well, paying GM a commission on the final sales price.

In the first online *reverse auction*, GM purchased a large volume of rubber sealing packages for vehicle production. The price GM paid was significantly lower than the price the company had been paying for the same items previously negotiated by manual tendering. Now, many similar bids are conducted on the site every week. The administrative costs per order have been reduced by 40 percent or more.

Finally, most GM dealers and thousands of GM's suppliers are connected on a common extranet platform, and 15 leading automakers have joined Covisint. On the exchange, both types of auctions have produced significant savings. Although Covisint and its infrastructure are still evolving, significant benefits have already materialized.

Sources: Miscellaneous press releases at *gm.com* (2002) and *tradexchange.com* (2000–2002).

WHAT WE CAN LEARN . . .

The GM case demonstrates the involvement of a large company in three EC activities: (1) connecting with dealers and suppliers through an extranet, (2) electronically auctioning used equipment to customers, and (3) conducting purchasing via electronic bidding. The auctioning and purchasing activities were conducted from GM's *private e-marketplace* that is implemented on Covisint, and the transactions were B2B. In B2B transactions, the company can be a seller, offering goods or services to many corporate buyers, or it can be a buyer, seeking goods or services from many corporate sellers (suppliers). When conducting such trades, a company can employ auctions, as GM did, or it can use electronic catalogs or other market mechanisms. These mechanisms and methods are the subject of this chapter.

6.1   CONCEPTS, CHARACTERISTICS, AND MODELS OF B2B EC

BASIC B2B CONCEPTS

Business-to-business e-commerce (B2B EC), also known as *eB2B* (*electronic B2B*) or just *B2B*, refers to transactions between businesses conducted electronically over the Internet, extranets, intranets, or private networks. Such transactions may take place between a business and its supply chain members, as well as between a business and any other business. In this context, a business refers to any organization, private or public, for profit or nonprofit. The major characteristic of B2B is that companies attempt to electronically automate the trading process in order to improve it. Note that B2B commerce can also be done without the Internet, but in this book we use the term B2B to mean B2B EC.

Key business drivers for B2B are the availability of a secure broadband Internet platform, private and public B2B marketplaces, the need for collaborations between suppliers and buyers, and technologies for intra- and interorganizational integration. (For details, see Warkentin 2002.)

business-to-business e-commerce (B2B EC)
Transactions between businesses conducted electronically over the Internet, extranets, intranets, or private networks; also known as *eB2B* (*electronic B2B*) or just *B2B*.

MARKET SIZE AND CONTENT OF B2B

First let's look at the B2B market. Market forecasters estimate that by 2005 the global B2B market may reach $7 to $10 trillion, continuing to be the major component of the EC market (Retter and Calyniuk 1998; Black 2001; Forrester Research 2001). The percentage of Internet-based B2B as a proportion of total non-Internet B2B commerce increased from 0.2 percent in 1997 to 2.1 percent in 2000 and is expected to grow to 10 percent by 2005 (Goldman Sachs Group 2001). Chemicals, computer electronics, utilities, agriculture, shipping and warehousing, motor vehicles, petrochemicals, paper and office products, and food are the leading items in B2B. According to *eMarketer* (2003), the dollar value of B2B comprises at least 85 percent of the total transaction value of e-commerce.

According to Berryman and Heck (2001), Lengel (2000), and Dai and Kauffman (2002), the B2B market, which went through major consolidation in 2000–2001, is again starting to grow. Different B2B market forecasters use different definitions and methodologies. Because of this, predictions frequently change and statistical data often differ. Therefore, we will not provide any specific data here. Data sources that can be checked for the latest information on the B2B market are provided in Exhibit 4.2 (page 132).

According to the Gartner Group, B2B EC is now entering its fifth dimension (or generation), as shown in Exhibit 6.1 (page 218). This dimension includes collaboration with suppliers and buyers (see Chapter 8), internal and external supply chain improvements (Chapter 8), and expert (intelligent) sales systems. In this chapter, we describe topics from the second, third, and fourth dimensions—namely online ordering (procurement) and e-marketplaces, customer management service, and multichannels. In Chapter 7, we deal with some topics of the third and fifth dimensions.

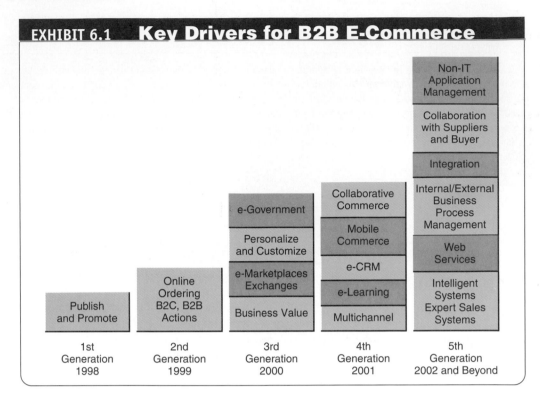

EXHIBIT 6.1   Key Drivers for B2B E-Commerce

				Non-IT Application Management
				Collaboration with Suppliers and Buyer
				Integration
			Collaborative Commerce	Internal/External Business Process Management
		e-Government	Mobile Commerce	Web Services
		Personalize and Customize	e-CRM	Intelligent Systems Expert Sales Systems
	Online Ordering B2C, B2B Actions	e-Marketplaces Exchanges	e-Learning	
Publish and Promote		Business Value	Multichannel	
1st Generation 1998	2nd Generation 1999	3rd Generation 2000	4th Generation 2001	5th Generation 2002 and Beyond

online intermediary
An online third party that brokers a transaction online between a buyer and a seller; can be virtual or click-and-mortar.

spot buying
The purchase of goods and services as they are needed, usually at prevailing market prices.

strategic sourcing
Purchases involving long-term contracts that are usually based on private negotiations between sellers and buyers.

direct materials
Materials used in the production of a product (e.g., steel in a car or paper in a book).

indirect materials
Materials used to support production (e.g., office supplies or light bulbs).

MROs (maintenance, repairs, and operations)
Indirect materials used in activities that support production.

B2B CHARACTERISTICS

Similar to the classic story of the blind men trying to describe an elephant, B2B can be described in a variety of ways, depending on what characteristic one is focusing on. Here we examine various qualities by which B2B transactions can be characterized.

Parties to the Transaction

B2B commerce can be conducted *directly* between a buyer and a seller or it can be conducted via an **online intermediary**. The intermediary is an online third party that brokers the transaction between the buyer and seller; it can be a virtual intermediary or a click-and-mortar intermediary. The electronic intermediaries for consumers mentioned in Chapter 3 can also be referenced for B2B by replacing the individual consumers with business customers.

Types of Transactions

B2B transactions are of two basic types: spot buying and strategic sourcing. **Spot buying** refers to the purchasing of goods and services as they are needed, usually at prevailing market prices, which are determined dynamically by supply and demand. The buyers and the sellers may not even know each other. Stock exchanges and commodity exchanges (oil, sugar, corn, etc.) are examples of spot buying. In contrast, **strategic sourcing** involves purchases made in long-term contracts that are usually based on private negotiation between sellers and buyers.

Spot buying may be conducted most economically on the public exchanges. Strategic purchases can be supported more effectively and efficiently through direct buyer–seller negotiations, which can be done in private exchanges or private trading rooms in public exchanges.

Types of Materials

Two types of materials and supplies are traded in B2B: direct and indirect. **Direct materials** are materials used in making the products, such as steel in a car or paper in a book. The characteristics of direct materials are that their use is scheduled and planned for. They are usually not shelf items, and they are usually purchased in large quantities and after negotiation and contracting.

Indirect materials are items, such as office supplies or light bulbs, that support production. They are usually used in **maintenance, repairs, and operations** activities, and are known collectively as MROs or nonproduction materials.

Direction of Trade

B2B marketplaces can be classified as either vertical or horizontal. **Vertical marketplaces** are those that deal with one industry or industry segment. Examples include marketplaces specializing in electronics, cars, steel, or chemicals. **Horizontal marketplaces** are those that concentrate on a service or a product that is used in all types of industries. Examples are office supplies, PCs, or travel services.

The various characteristics of B2B transactions are presented in summary form in Insights and Additions 6.1. (The final two categories are discussed in the next section.)

THE BASIC B2B TRANSACTION TYPES

The number of sellers and buyers and the form of participation used in B2B determine the basic B2B transaction types:

- **Sell-side.** One seller to many buyers (covered in Chapter 6)
- **Buy-side.** One buyer from many sellers (covered in Chapter 6)
- **Exchanges.** Many sellers to many buyers (covered in Chapter 7)
- **Collaborative commerce.** Communication and sharing of information, design, and planning among business partners (covered in Chapter 8)

Exhibit 6.2 (page 220) shows these B2B types.

One-to-Many and Many-to-One: Company-Centric Transactions

In one-to-many and many-to-one markets, one company does either all of the selling (*sell-side market*) or all of the buying (*buy-side market*). Because EC is focused on a single company's buying or selling needs in these transactions, it is referred to as **company-centric EC**. Company-centric marketplaces—both sell-side and buy-side—are the topic of this chapter. Several selling and buying methods are used in company-centric marketplaces, as will be demonstrated throughout the chapter.

vertical marketplaces
Markets that deal with one industry or industry segment (e.g., steel, chemicals).

horizontal marketplaces
Markets that concentrate on a service, materials, or a product that is used in all types of industries (e.g., office supplies, PCs).

company-centric EC
E-commerce that focuses on a single company's buying needs (many-to-one, or buy-side) or selling needs (one-to-many, or sell-side).

Insights and Additions 6.1 Summary of B2B Characteristics

PARTIES TO TRANSACTIONS	TYPES OF TRANSACTIONS
Direct, seller to buyer or buyer to seller	Spot buying
Via intermediaries	Strategic sourcing

TYPES OF MATERIALS SOLD	DIRECTION OF TRADE
Direct	Vertical
Indirect (MROs)	Horizontal

NUMBER AND FORM OF PARTICIPATION	DEGREE OF OPENNESS
One-to-many: Sell-side	Private
Many-to-one: Buy-side	Public
Many-to-many: Exchanges	
Many, connected: Collaborative	

EXHIBIT 6.2   Types of B2B E-Commerce

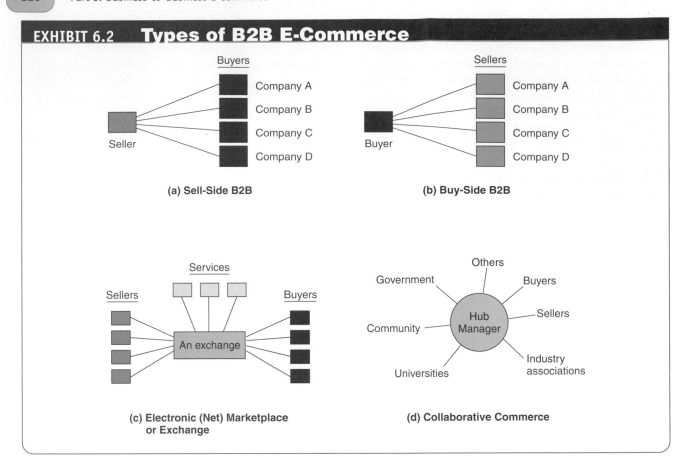

(a) Sell-Side B2B

(b) Buy-Side B2B

(c) Electronic (Net) Marketplace or Exchange

(d) Collaborative Commerce

private e-marketplaces
Markets in which the individual sell-side or buy-side company has complete control over participation in the selling or buying transaction.

exchanges (trading communities or trading exchanges)
Many-to-many e-marketplaces, usually owned and run by a third party or a consortium, in which many buyers and many sellers meet electronically to trade with each other; also called *trading communities* or *trading exchanges*.

public e-marketplaces
Third-party exchanges that are open to all interested parties (sellers and buyers).

In company-centric marketplaces, the individual sell-side or buy-side company has complete control over who participates in the selling or buying transaction and the supporting information systems. Thus, these transactions are essentially private. Therefore, sell-side and buy-side markets are considered **private e-marketplaces** (or exchanges).

Intermediaries. Most company-centric markets are conducted without the help of intermediaries. However, when it comes to auctions or to aggregating small buyers, an intermediary is frequently used. (Even when an intermediary is used, the market is still considered private, because the single buyer or seller that hires the intermediary maintains control of who is invited to participate in the market.)

Many-to-Many: Exchanges

In many-to-many e-marketplaces, many buyers and many sellers meet electronically for the purpose of trading with each other. There are different types of such e-marketplaces, which are also known as **exchanges**, **trading communities**, or **trading exchanges**. We will use the term *exchanges* in this book. Exchanges are usually owned and run by a third party or by a consortium. They are described in more detail in Chapter 7. Exchanges are open to all interested parties (sellers and buyers), and thus are considered **public e-marketplaces**.

Collaborative Commerce

Businesses deal with other businesses for purposes beyond just selling or buying. One example is that of *collaborative commerce*, which is communication, design, planning, and information sharing among business partners. To qualify as collaborative commerce, the activities that are shared must represent far more than just financial transactions. For example, they may include activities related to design, manufacture, or management. Collaborative commerce is described in Chapter 8.

SUPPLY CHAIN RELATIONSHIPS IN B2B

In the various B2B transaction types, business activities are usually conducted along the supply chain of a company. The supply chain process consists of a number of interrelated sub-processes and roles. These extend from the acquisition of materials from suppliers to the processing of a product or service to packaging it and moving it to distributors and retailers. The process ends with the eventual purchase of a product by the end consumer. B2B can make supply chains more efficient and effective or it can change the supply chain completely, eliminating one or more intermediaries (as will be shown in Chapter 8).

Historically, many of the segments and processes in the supply chain have been managed through paper transactions (e.g., purchase orders, invoices, and so forth). B2B applications are offered online so that they can serve as supply chain enablers that offer distinct competitive advantages. Supply chain management also encompasses the coordination of order generation, order taking, and order fulfillment and distribution. (See Chapters 8, 14, and Tutorial T3 for more discussion of supply chain management.)

Hoffman et al. (2002) looked at the effect of various B2B types on supply chain relationships. They found, for example, that a B2B private e-marketplace provides a company with high supply chain power and high capabilities for online interactions. This is basically how much bargaining and control power a company has. Joining a public e-marketplace, on the other hand, provides a business with high buying and selling capabilities, but will result in low supply chain power. Companies that choose an intermediary to do their buying and selling will be low on both supply chain power and buying/selling capabilities. Hoffman et al. recommend private e-marketplaces as most likely to result in effective supply chain relationships.

VIRTUAL SERVICE INDUSTRIES IN B2B

In addition to trading products between businesses along the supply chain, services can also be provided in B2B. Just as service industries such as banking, insurance, real estate, job matching, and stock trading can be conducted electronically for individuals, as described in Chapter 3, so too can they be supplied electronically to businesses. The major B2B services are:

▶ **Travel services.** Many large corporations arrange special travel discounts through corporate travel agents. To further reduce costs, companies can make special arrangements that enable employees to plan and book their own trips online. For instance, Rosenbluth International (rosenbluth.com) provides an agentless service to corporate clients.

▶ **Real estate.** Commercial real estate transactions can be very large and complex. Therefore, the Web may not be able to completely replace existing human agents. Instead, the Web can help businesses find the right properties, compare properties, and assist in negotiations. Some government-run foreclosed real estate auctions are open only to real estate dealers (companies) and are conducted online.

▶ **Financial services.** Internet banking is an economical way of making business payments, transferring funds, or performing other financial transactions. For example, electronic funds transfer (EFT) is popular with businesses. Transaction fees over the Internet are less costly than any other alternative method. To see how these work in B2B, see Chapter 13.

▶ **Online stock trading.** Some corporations are important stock investors. Online trading services are very attractive to institutional investors because fees for online trading are very low (as low as $3 per transaction) and flat, regardless of the trading amount.

▶ **Online financing.** Business loans can be solicited online from lenders. Bank of America, for example, offers its commercial customers a matching service on IntraLoan, which uses an extranet to match business loan applicants with potential lending corporations. Several sites, such as garage.com, provide information about venture capital.

▶ **Other online services.** Consulting services, law firms, health organizations, and others sell knowledge online. Many other online services, such as the purchase of electronic stamps (similar to metered postage, but generated on a computer), are available online (see stamps.com).

THE BENEFITS OF B2B

The benefits of B2B depend on which model is used. In general, though, the major benefits of B2B are that it:

- ▶ Eliminates paper and reduces administrative costs.
- ▶ Expedites cycle time.
- ▶ Lowers search costs and time for buyers.
- ▶ Increases productivity of employees dealing with buying and/or selling.
- ▶ Reduces errors and improves quality of services.
- ▶ Reduces inventory levels and costs.
- ▶ Increases production flexibility, permitting just-in-time delivery.
- ▶ Facilitates mass customization.
- ▶ Increases opportunities for collaboration.

The introduction of B2B may eliminate the distributor or the retailer, which may be a benefit to the seller and the buyer (though not a benefit to the distributor or retailer). In previous chapters, such a phenomenon was referred to as *disintermediation*.

In the remainder of the chapter, we will look in more depth at the company-centric B2B models and topics introduced in this opening section.

Section 6.1 ▶ REVIEW

1. Define B2B.
2. Discuss the following: spot buying versus strategic sourcing, direct materials versus indirect materials, and vertical markets versus horizontal markets.
3. What are buy-side and sell-side transactions? How are they different?
4. What are company-centric marketplaces? Are they public or private?
5. Define B2B exchanges.
6. Relate the supply chain to B2B transactions.
7. List the B2B service industries.
8. Summarize the benefits of B2B.

6.2 ONE-TO-MANY: SELL-SIDE MARKETPLACES

SELL-SIDE MODELS AND ACTIVITIES

sell-side e-marketplace
A Web-based marketplace in which one company sells to many business buyers from e-catalogs or auctions, frequently over an extranet.

In Chapter 3, we introduced the direct-selling model in which a manufacturer or a retailer sells electronically directly to consumers. The **sell-side e-marketplace** is the analogous model for business buyers. That is, the sell-side e-marketplace delivers to business customers a Web-based private sales channel, frequently over an extranet. The seller can be a manufacturer selling to a wholesaler, to a retailer, or to a business. Intel, Cisco, and Dell are examples of such sellers. Or, the seller can be a distributor selling to wholesalers, to retailers, or to businesses. In either case, sell-side involves one seller and many potential buyers. In this model, both individual consumers and business buyers may use the same sell-side marketplace, as shown in Exhibit 6.3, or they may use different marketplaces.

The architecture of this B2B model is similar to that of B2C EC. The major differences are in the process. For example, in B2B, large customers may receive customized catalogs and prices. Usually, companies will separate B2C orders from B2B orders. One reason for the separation is the different *order-fulfillment process* (see Chapter 14).

The one-to-many model has three major direct sales methods: (1) selling from *electronic catalogs*; (2) selling via *forward auctions* (as GM does with its old equipment); and (3) *one-to-one* selling, usually under a negotiated long-term contract. Such one-to-one negotiating is familiar: The buying company negotiates price, quantity, and quality terms with the selling company. We describe the other two methods in this chapter—the first method in this section and the second in Section 6.3.

EXHIBIT 6.3   Sell-Side B2B Marketplace Architecture

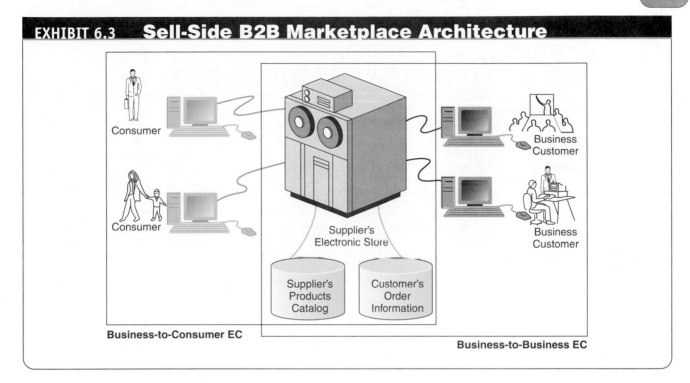

Business-to-Consumer EC

Business-to-Business EC

B2B Sellers

Sellers in the sell-side marketplace can be click-and-mortar manufacturers or intermediaries, usually distributors or wholesalers. The intermediaries may even be virtual, as in the case of Bigboxx.com, described in EC Application Case 6.1 (page 224).

Customer Service

Online sellers can provide sophisticated customer services. For example, General Electric receives 20 million calls a year regarding appliances. Although most of these calls come from individuals, many come from businesses. By using the Internet and automatic-response software agents (autoresponders), GE has reduced the cost of handling calls from $5 per call when done by phone to $0.20 per call.

Another example of B2B customer service is that of Milacron, Inc., which produces consumable industrial products for metalworking. The company launched an award-winning EC site aimed at its more than 100,000 SME customers. The site provides an easy-to-use and secure way of selecting, purchasing, and applying Milacron's 55,000 products. From this site, the SMEs also can access a level of technical service beyond that provided previously to even Milacron's largest customers (see milacron.com).

We now turn our attention to the first of the sell-side methods: selling from electronic catalogs.

DIRECT SALES FROM CATALOGS

Companies can use the Internet to sell directly from their online catalogs. A company may offer one catalog for all customers or a customized catalog for each customer.

In Chapter 2, we presented the advantages of e-catalogs over paper catalogs and showed how Boise Cascade uses e-catalogs for B2B sales. However, this model may not be convenient for large and repetitive business buyers because the buyer's order information is stored in the supplier's server and is not easily integrated with the buyer's corporate information system. In order to facilitate B2B direct sales, the seller can provide the buyer with a buyer-customized shopping cart (such as Bigboxx.com offers), which can store order information that can be integrated with the buyer's information system. This is particularly important when buyers have to visit several sites in one or several shopping malls (see Lim and Lee 2003).

CASE 6.1
EC Application
BUYING FROM VIRTUAL SELLER BIGBOXX

Bigboxx.com (*bigboxx.com*), based in Hong Kong, is a B2B retailer of office supplies. It has no physical stores and sells products through its online catalog, thus it is an online intermediary. The company has three types of customers: large corporate clients, medium-sized corporate clients, and small office/home offices (SOHO). It offers more than 10,000 items from 300 suppliers. Bigboxx.com's goal is to sell its products in various countries in Southeast Asia.

The company's portal is attractive and easy to use. The company also has a tutorial that instructs users on how to use the Web site. Once registered, the user can start shopping using the online shopping cart. Users can look for items by browsing through the online catalog or by searching the site with a search engine.

Users can pay by cash or by check (upon delivery), via automatic bank drafts, by credit card, or by purchasing card. Soon users will be able to pay through Internet-based direct debit, by electronic bill presentation and payment, or by Internet banking.

Using its own trucks and warehouses, Bigboxx.com makes deliveries within 24 hours or even on the same day. Delivery is scheduled online. The ordering system is integrated with an SAP-based back-office system.

Bigboxx.com provides numerous value-added services for customers. Among these are the ability to check item availability in real time; the ability to track the status of each item in an order; promotions and suggested items based on customers' user profiles; customized prices, for every product, for every customer; control and central-approval features; automatic activation at desired time intervals of standing orders for repeat purchasing; and a large number of Excel reports and data, including comparative management reports.

Bigboxx.com began operations in spring 2000. By the beginning of 2003, it had over 7,600 registered customers.

Sources: Compiled from Chan et al. (2001) and *bigboxx.com* (2002).

Questions

1. Enter *bigboxx.com* and *staples.com* and compare their offerings and purchase processes. (Take the tutorial at *bigboxx.com*.) What support services are provided?

2. One day, customers may be used to buying office supplies online. They may then try to buy directly from the manufacturers. Will Bigboxx.com then be disintermediated?

Many sellers provide separate pages and catalogs to their major buyers. For example, Staples.com, an office supply vendor, offers its business customers personalized catalogs and pricing at *stapleslink.com*.

Another example of B2B direct sales from catalogs is Microsoft, which uses an extranet to sell $5.5 billion of software annually to its channel partners. Using Microsoft's order-entry tool, MOET, customer partners can check inventory, make transactions, and look up the status of orders. The online orders are automatically fed into the customer's SAP applications. MOET was started in Europe in 1997 and has since been rolled out worldwide. The extranet handles about 500,000 transactions per year. The system reduces the number of phone calls, e-mails, and incorrect products shipped (Wagner 2000).

Configuration and Customization

As with B2C EC, B2B direct sales offer an opportunity for efficient customization. As we will see in the case of Cisco (described in detail later in the chapter), manufacturers can provide online tools for self-configuration. Business customers can customize products, get price quotes, and submit orders, all online.

Most click-and-mortar companies use a *multichannel distribution system*, in which the Internet is a new channel that enables greater efficiency in the ordering process, as shown in the case of Whirlpool in EC Application Case 6.2.

Benefits and Limitations of Direct Sales from Catalogs

Successful examples of the B2B direct sales model include manufacturers such as Dell, Intel, IBM, and Cisco, and distributors such as Ingram Micro (which sells to value-added retailers—the retailer adds some service along with the product). Sellers that use this model may be successful as long as they have a superb reputation in the market and a large enough group of loyal customers.

CASE 6.2
EC Application
WHIRLPOOL B2B TRADING PORTAL

Whirlpool is a $10.5-billion corporation based in Benton Harbor, Michigan. The 61,000–employee company competes in the $70-billion global industry of major home appliances. It is in the company's best interest to operate as efficiently and with as much customer service for the members of its selling chain as possible. However, the middle-tier partners, who comprise 25 percent of the total partner base and 10 percent of Whirlpool's annual revenue, were submitting their orders by phone or fax because they were not large enough to have system-to-system computer connections direct to Whirlpool.

In order to improve the service to these dealers, Whirlpool developed a B2B trading partner portal (Whirlpool Web World), using IBM e-business solutions. The technologies enable fast, easy Web self-service ordering processes that cut costs per order to under $5-a savings of 80 percent.

The company tested ordering via the Web by developing a portal for low-level products. It was so successful (resulting in a 100 percent ROI during the first 8 months of use) that Whirlpool went to a second-generation portal, which services the middle-tier partners. The Whirlpool Web World allows middle-tier trade partners to place orders and track their status through a password-protected site.

Simultaneously, the company was implementing SAP R/3 for order entry. The second-generation portal for middle-tier partners is integrated with the SAP R/3. The company is also committed to IBM, using its Application Framework for e-business, taking advantage of its rapid development cycles and associated cost reductions.

Using the same platform, Whirlpool launched a B2C site for U.S. customers for ordering small appliances and accessories. This site was so successful that the company realized a 100 percent ROI in 5 months.

Sources: Compiled from IBM (2000) and *whirlpool.com* (2002).

Questions

1. How do Whirlpool's customers benefit from the portal?
2. What are the benefits of the trading portal to Whirlpool?
3. Relate the B2B sell-side to a B2C storefront.

The major benefits of direct sales are:

▶ Lower order-processing costs (including commissions) and less paperwork
▶ A faster ordering cycle
▶ Fewer errors in ordering and product configuration
▶ Lower search costs of products for buyers, who can more easily compare prices among sellers
▶ For sellers, lower search costs of finding buyers; sellers can advertise and communicate online
▶ Lower logistics costs (due to less inventory, fewer shipments, and less handling)
▶ The ability to offer different catalogs and prices to different customers (personalization, customization) and to customize products and services efficiently

In terms of limitations, one of the major issues facing smaller direct sellers is how to find buyers. Many small companies know how to advertise in traditional channels but are still learning how to contact would-be buyers online. Also, B2B sellers may experience channel conflicts with their existing distribution systems. Another limitation is that if traditional EDI (the computer-to-computer direct transfer of business documents) is used, the cost to the customers can be high, and they will be reluctant to go online. The solution to this problem is the transfer of documents over the Internet or extranets (see Appendix 6A). Finally, the number of business partners online must be large enough to justify the system infrastructure and operation and maintenance expenses.

Section 6.2 ▶ REVIEW

1. List the types of sell-side B2B transaction models.
2. Distinguish between use and nonuse of intermediaries in B2B sell-side transactions.
3. Describe customer service in B2B systems.
4. Describe direct sales from catalogs.
5. Discuss the benefits and limitations of direct sales from catalogs.

6.3 SELLING VIA AUCTIONS

Auctions are gaining popularity as a B2B selling channel. Some major B2B auction issues are discussed in this section.

USING AUCTIONS ON THE SELL SIDE

As you read in the opening case study, GM uses *forward auctions* to sell its unneeded capital assets. In such a situation, items are displayed on an auction site (private or public) for quick disposal. Forward auctions offer a number of benefits to B2B sellers:

▶ **Revenue generation.** Forward auctions as a new sales channel support and expand online and overall sales. For example, Weirton Steel Corp. doubled its customer base when it started auctions (Fickel 1999). Forward auctions also offer businesses a new venue for quickly and easily disposing of excess, obsolete, and returned products.

▶ **Cost savings.** In addition to generating new revenue, conducting auctions electronically reduces the costs of selling auction items. These savings also help increase the seller's profits.

▶ **Increased page views.** Forward auctions give Web sites "stickiness." As discussed in Chapter 5, *stickiness* is a characteristic describing customer loyalty to a site, demonstrated by the number and length of visits to a site. Stickiness at an auction site, for example, means that auction users spend more time on a site, generate more page views than other users, and trade more.

▶ **Member acquisition and retention.** All bidding transactions result in additional registered members, who are future business contacts. In addition, auction software enables sellers to search and report on virtually every relevant auction activity for future analysis and use.

Forward auctions can be conducted in two ways. A company may conduct its forward auctions from its own Web site or it can sell from an intermediary auction site, such as ebay.com or freemarkets.com. Let's examine these options.

SELLING FROM THE COMPANY'S OWN SITE

For large and well-known companies that conduct auctions frequently, such as GM, it makes sense to build an auction mechanism on the company's own site. Why should a company pay a commission to an intermediary if the intermediary cannot provide the company with much added value? Of course, if a company decides to auction from its own site, the company will have to pay for infrastructure and operate and maintain the auction site. However, if the company already has an electronic marketplace for selling from e-catalogs, the additional cost for conducting auctions may not be too high.

USING INTERMEDIARIES

Large numbers of intermediaries offer B2B auction sites (e.g., see freemarkets.com and others discussed in Chapter 11). An intermediary may conduct private auctions for a seller, either from the intermediary's or the seller's site. Or, a company may choose to conduct auctions in a public marketplace, using a third-party hosting company (e.g., eBay, which has a special "business exchange" for small companies).

Using a third-party hosting company for conducting auctions has many benefits. The first is that no additional resources (e.g., hardware, bandwidth, engineering resources, or IT personnel) are required. Nor are there any hiring costs or opportunity costs associated with the redeployment of corporate resources. B2B auctions also offer fast "time-to-market": They enable a company to have a robust, customized auction up and running immediately. Without the intermediary, it may take a company weeks to prepare an auction site in-house.

A second benefit of using an intermediary relates to who owns and controls the auction information. In the case of an intermediary-conducted private auction, the intermediary sets up the auction to show the branding (company name) of the merchant rather than the intermediary's name. (For example, if an intermediary prepares a private auction for Blue Devils Company, customers see the Blue Devils name and logo.) Yet the intermediary does the work of controlling data on Web traffic, page views, and member registration; setting all the auction parameters (transaction fee structure, user interface, and reports); and integrating the information flow and logistics. Of course, if a company wants to dispose of unwanted assets without advertising to the public that it is doing so, an intermediary-conducted public auction would be the logical choice. If an intermediary does the auction, they don't have to provide answers regarding the quality of the product. If a manufacturer is selling off products, buyers get suspicious of the quality of the items. Another benefit of using intermediaries to run auction sites relates to billing and collection efforts, which are handled by the intermediary rather than the company. For example, intermediaries calculate merchant-specific shipping weights and charge customers for shipping of auctioned items. All credit card data are encrypted for secure transmission and storage, and all billing information can be easily downloaded by the merchant company for integration with existing systems. These services are not free of course. They are provided as part of the merchant's commission to the intermediary, a cost often deemed worth paying in exchange for the ease of the service.

Section 6.3 ▶ REVIEW

1. List the benefits of using B2B auctions for selling.
2. List the benefits of using auction intermediaries.

6.4 SELL-SIDE CASES

In this section, we look in some detail at three examples of successful sell-side marketplaces: a direct-sales model, used by Cisco Systems, and at two B2B intermediaries, used by Marshall Industries and Boeing.

DIRECT SALES: CISCO SYSTEMS

Cisco Systems (cisco.com) is the world's leading producer of routers, switches, and network interconnection services. Cisco's portal has evolved over several years, beginning with technical support for customers and developing into one of the world's largest direct sales EC sites. Today, Cisco offers about a dozen Internet-based applications to both end-user businesses and reseller partners (see Slater 2003).

Customer Service

Cisco began providing electronic support in 1991 using value-added networks (VANs). The first applications offered were software downloads, defect tracking, and technical advice. In spring 1994, Cisco placed its system on the Web and named its site Cisco Connection Online (CCO). By 2001, Cisco's customers and reseller partners were logging onto Cisco's Web site about 1.3 million times a month to receive technical assistance, place and check orders, or download software. The online service has been so well received that nearly 85 percent of all customer service inquiries and 95 percent of software updates are delivered online. The service is delivered globally in 14 languages. The CCO is considered a model for B2B success, and several books have been written about it (e.g., Bunnel and Brate 2000; Slater 2003; Waters 2002).

Online Ordering by Customers

Cisco builds virtually all its products made-to-order, thus it has very few off-the-shelf products. Before the CCO, ordering a product was a lengthy, complicated, and error-prone process because it was done by fax or by "snail mail." Cisco began deploying Web-based commerce tools in July 1995, and within a year, its Internet Product Center allowed users to purchase any Cisco product over the Web. Today, a business customer's engineer can sit down at a PC, configure a product, and find out immediately if there are any errors in the configuration (some feedback is given by intelligent agents).

By providing online pricing and configuration tools to customers, almost all orders (about 98 percent) are now placed through CCO, saving time for both Cisco and its customers. In the first 5 months of online ordering operations in 1996, Cisco booked over

$100 million in online sales. This figure grew to $4 billion in 1998 and to over $8 billion in 2002 (Cisco Annual Report 2002).

Order Status

Each month Cisco used to receive over 150,000 order-status inquiries such as, "When will my order be ready?" "How should the order be classified for customs?" "Is the product eligible for NAFTA agreement?" "What export control issues apply?" Cisco provides self-tracking and FAQ tools so that customers can find the answers to many of their questions by themselves. In addition, the company's primary domestic and international freight forwarders update Cisco's database electronically about the status of each shipment. CCO can record the shipping date, the method of shipment, and the current location of each product. All new information is made available to customers immediately. As soon as an order ships, Cisco sends the customer a notification by e-mail (see Waters 2002).

Benefits

Cisco reaps many benefits from the CCO system. The most important benefits include the following (Interwoven 2001):

▸ **Reduced operating costs for order taking.** By automating its order process online in 1998, Cisco has saved $363 million per year, or approximately 17.5 percent of its total operating costs. This is due primarily to increased productivity of the employees who take and process orders.

▸ **Enhanced technical support and customer service.** With more than 85 percent of its technical support and customer service calls handled online, Cisco's technical support productivity has increased by 250 percent per year.

▸ **Reduced technical support staff cost.** Online technical support reduced technical support staff costs by roughly $125 million each year.

▸ **Reduced software distribution costs.** Customers download new software releases directly from Cisco's site, saving the company $180 million in distribution, packaging, and duplicating costs each year. Having product and pricing information on the Web and Web-based CD-ROMs saves Cisco an additional $50 million annually in printing and distributing catalogs and marketing materials to customers.

▸ **Faster service.** Lead times were reduced from 4 to 10 days to 2 to 3 days.

The CCO system also benefits customers. Cisco customers can configure orders more quickly, immediately determine costs, and collaborate much more rapidly and effectively with Cisco's staff. Also, customer service and technical support are faster.

SALES THROUGH AN INTERMEDIARY: MARSHALL INDUSTRIES

Marshall Industries, now part of Avnet Electronics Marketing (avnet.com), is a large distributor of electronics components. It buys electronics components from manufacturers and sells them to businesses. Prior to its merger with Avnet in 1999, Marshall posted $1.7 billion in sales in fiscal year 1999 and served over 30,000 business customers, many of which are small in size. Marshall distributed over 130,000 different products worldwide. Avnet was a competitor. Now, together, they have sales of over $10 billion a year.

The electronics industry is very competitive. Distributors compete against each other and against direct marketing by the manufacturers, and they may face disintermediation. Thus, providing value-added services is key to a distributor's survival. Marshall added value to its customers through IT support. The company was known for its innovative use of information technologies and the Web (e.g., see Wilson 1998): It won a first prize in the 1997 SIM International awards competition (simnet.org) for the best paper describing how the company uses IT and EC (El-Sawy et al. 1999). In 1999, Marshall was the first ever to use the XML-based interoperable solution for B2B integration. (XML stands for eXtensible Markup Language, a standard for defining data elements on a Web page and B2B documents.) Marshall pioneered the use of the Internet and IT applications with a view to reengineer its business and create new competitive strengths. Its major Web-based initiatives,

EXHIBIT 6.4   Marshall Industries' EC Initiatives

Initiative	Description
MarshallNet	An intranet that supports salespeople in the field via wireless devices and portable PCs. Offers real-time access to the corporate database, DSS applications, and workflow and collaboration software.
Marshall on the Internet (portal)	A B2B portal for customers that offers information, ordering, and tracking (using UPS software) capabilities. Discussion group, chat room, connection to call centers. Offers special pages for value-added resellers and troubleshooting capabilities.
Strategic European Internet	A strategic partner in Europe that offers MarshallNet in 17 languages, as well as additional local information.
Electronic Design Center	Includes an online configuration tool. Provides technical specifications. Offers simulation capabilities for making virtual components. The company can produce sample products designed by customers.
PartnerNet	Customized Web pages for major customers and suppliers. Offers access to the company's intranet. Enables electronic payments and access to historical data and records. Also offers planning tools online.
NetSeminar	An online training tool; brings suppliers and customers together for live interactions.
Education and News Portal	Offers education, news, and entertainment services, including consulting, sales training, and interactive public product announcements.

which were interconnected, are listed in Exhibit 6.4. Most of these initiatives still remain in the systems offered by Avnet.

In addition to the physical distribution of components, distributors such as Marshall (and now Avnet) have increasingly taken on value-added tasks such as technical support, logistics, payment processing and accounts receivable, credit services, logistics, and more. The semiconductor industry, for example, is cyclical, causing major delivery and inventory problems that distributors seek to solve. In addition, large customers are global and require global sourcing. Time-to-market competition and customization at the customer end require a fast and flexible response from distributors. Just-in-time and supplier-managed inventories are increasingly required from distributors. These demands require tight integration of information and provision of value-added services along the value chain. Marshall (and now Avnet) met these demands in its e-commerce initiative by providing value-added services that enabled the company to survive as an intermediary.

Marshall's Survival Strategy

Marshall's use of e-commerce was combined with other innovations and with *business process reengineering* (BPR), the introduction of a fundamental change in the way a company does business. For example, Marshall made various business process changes: The company moved to a team-based organization with a flat hierarchy; decentralizing decision making; provided continuous improvement innovations jointly with its business partners; changed the salesperson's compensation from commission-based to profit sharing; promoted the use of CRM; provided new Web-based services to create value between suppliers and customers; and changed the internal organizational structure and procedures to fully support e-commerce initiatives.

Marshall was both very successful and profitable. Its EC initiatives are now practiced at Avnet Electronics Marketing as well. For additional information, see Timmers (1999), El-Sawy et al. (1999), and avnet.com (2003).

B2B INTERMEDIARY: BOEING'S PARTS MARKETPLACE

Boeing (boeing.com) is the world's largest maker of airplanes for commercial and military customers. It also plays the role of intermediary in supplying replacement and maintenance parts to airlines. Unlike other online B2B intermediaries, revenue from its intermediary activities may be a minor concern to Boeing, which makes most of its revenue from selling airplanes. The major goal of Boeing's intermediary parts market, called PART (Part Analysis and Requirement Tracking), is supporting customers' maintenance needs as a customer service.

The objective of PART is to link airlines that need maintenance parts with suppliers who are producing the parts for Boeing aircraft (see boeing.com/assocproducts/bpart/partpage). Boeing's online strategy is to provide a single point of online access through which airlines (the buyers of Boeing's aircraft) and the maintenance and parts providers (Boeing's suppliers) can access data about the parts they need. These data might come from the airframe builder, the component supplier, the engine manufacturer, or the airline itself. Thus, Boeing is acting as an intermediary between the airlines and the parts suppliers. With data from 300 key suppliers of Boeing's airplane parts, Boeing's goal is to provide its customers with one-stop shopping for online maintenance information and ordering.

The Spare Parts Business Using Traditional EDI

Ordering spare parts had been a multistep process for many of Boeing's customers. For example, an airline's mechanic informed the purchasing department of his company that a specific part was needed; the purchasing department approved the purchase order and sent it to Boeing by phone or fax. The mechanic did not need to know who produced the part, because the aircraft was purchased from Boeing as one body. However, Boeing had to find out who produced the part and then ask the producer to deliver the part to the customer (unless Boeing happened to keep an inventory of that part).

The largest airlines began to streamline the ordering process about 20 years ago. Because of the volume and regularity of their orders, they established EDI connections with Boeing over VANs. Not all airlines were quick to follow suit, however. It took until 1992 to induce 10 percent of the largest customers, representing 60 percent of the volume, to order through EDI. The numbers did not change much until 1996 due to the cost and complexity of VAN-based EDI.

Debut of PART on the Internet

Boeing viewed the Internet as an opportunity to encourage more of its customers to order parts electronically. With the initial investment now limited to a standard PC and basic Internet access, even its smallest customers can now participate in PART. Because of its interactive capabilities, many customer service functions that were handled over the telephone are now handled over the Internet.

In November 1996, Boeing introduced its PART page on the Internet, giving its customers around the world the ability to check parts availability and pricing, order parts, and track order status, all online. Less than a year later, about 50 percent of Boeing's customers used PART for parts orders and customer service inquiries. In its first year of operation, the Boeing PART portal handled over half a million inquiries and transactions from customers around the world. Boeing's spare parts business processed about 20 percent more shipments per month in 1997 than it did in 1996 with the same number of data entry people. In addition, as many as 600 phone calls a day to customer service staff were eliminated because customers had access to information about pricing, availability, and order status online. The use of PART online resulted in fewer parts being returned due to administrative errors. Furthermore, the service may encourage airlines to buy Boeing aircraft the next time they make an aircraft purchase. (For a demo of PART, visit boeing.com.)

As a result of PART's success, Boeing started a complementary EC initiative called Boeing OnLine Data (BOLD), which enables mechanics and technicians at the airport to access the technical manuals they need for repairs. These manuals are now available in digital form, and mechanics and technicians can access them via wireline or wireless devices. In May 2000, Boeing also launched a new e-business site for airline customers based on PART and BOLD (*Journal of Aerospace and Defense Industry News* 2000).

Section 6.4 ▶ REVIEW

1. Describe the online services that CCO offers.
2. What are the benefits of CCO to Cisco? To Cisco's customers?
3. Draw Marshall's supply chain.

4. Being an intermediary, how does Marshall (Avent) protect its existence?

5. Draw Boeing's PART supply chain.

6. What activities in Boeing's supply chain are improved by its online initiatives?

7. What are the similarities between CCO and PART?

6.5 ONE-FROM-MANY: BUY-SIDE MARKETPLACES AND E-PROCUREMENT

When a buyer goes to a sell-side marketplace, such as Cisco's, the buyer's purchasing department sometimes has to manually enter the order information into its own corporate information system. Furthermore, searching e-stores and e-malls to find and compare suppliers and products can be very slow and costly. As a solution, large buyers can open their own marketplaces called **buy-side e-marketplaces** and invite buyers to browse there and shop. The term *procurement* is used to refer to the purchase of goods and services for organizations. It is usually done by *purchasing agents*, also known as *corporate buyers*, (see Martin et al. 2001).

buy-side e-marketplace
A corporate-based acquisition site that uses reverse auctions, negotiations, group purchasing, or any other e-procurement method.

PROCUREMENT METHODS

Companies use different methods to procure goods and services depending on what and where they buy, the quantities needed, how much money is involved, and more. The major procurement methods include the following:

▶ Buy from manufacturers, wholesalers, or retailers from their catalogs, and possibly by negotiation.

▶ Buy from the catalog of an intermediary that aggregates sellers' catalogs or buy at industrial malls.

▶ Buy from an internal buyer's catalog in which company-approved vendors' catalogs, including agreed upon prices, are aggregated. This approach is used for the implementation of *desktop purchasing*, which allows the requisitioners to order directly from vendors, bypassing the procurement department. (See Section 6.7 for details.)

▶ Conduct bidding or tendering (a reverse auction) in a system where suppliers compete against each other. This method is used for large-ticket items or large quantities.

▶ Buy at private or public auction sites in which the organization participates as one of the buyers.

▶ Join a group-purchasing system that aggregates participants' demand, creating a large volume. Then the group may negotiate prices or initiate a tendering process.

▶ Collaborate with suppliers to share information about sales and inventory, so as to reduce inventory and stock-outs and enhance just-in-time delivery. (See Chapter 8 on collaborative commerce.)

Some of these activities are done in private marketplaces, others in public exchanges. A comparison of these major methods is provided on the book's Web site in Exhibit W6.1.

INEFFICIENCIES IN TRADITIONAL PROCUREMENT MANAGEMENT

Procurement management refers to the coordination of all the activities pertaining to the purchasing of the goods and services necessary to accomplish the mission of an enterprise. Approximately 80 percent of an organization's purchased items, mostly MROs, constitute 20 to 25 percent of the total purchase value. Furthermore, a large portion of corporate buyers' time is spent on non-value-added activities such as data entry, correcting errors in paperwork, expediting delivery, or solving quality problems.

For the high-value items, purchasing personnel need to spend a lot of time and effort on procurement activities. These activities include qualifying suppliers, negotiating prices and terms, building rapport with strategic suppliers, and carrying out supplier evaluation and certification. If buyers are busy with the details of the smaller items (usually the MROs), they do not have enough time to properly deal with the purchase of the high-value items.

procurement management
The coordination of all the activities relating to purchasing goods and services needed to accomplish the mission of an organization.

maverick buying
Unplanned purchases of
items needed quickly,
often at non-pre-negoti-
ated, higher prices.

Many other potential inefficiencies occur in procurement. These range from delays to paying too much for rush orders. Another procurement inefficiency is **maverick buying**. This is when a buyer makes unplanned purchases of items needed quickly, which results in buying at non-pre-negotiated higher prices. The traditional procurement process, shown in Exhibit 6.5, is often inefficient. To correct the situation, companies reengineer their procurement systems, implement new purchasing models, and in particular, introduce e-procurement.

THE GOALS AND BENEFITS OF E-PROCUREMENT

e-procurement
The electronic acquisition
of goods and services for
organizations.

Improvements to procurement have been attempted for decades, usually by using new information technologies. The real opportunity for improvement lies in the use of **e-procurement**, the electronic acquisition of goods and services for organizations. The general e-procurement process (with the exception of tendering) is shown in Exhibit 6.6.

By automating and streamlining the laborious routines of the purchasing function, purchasing professionals can focus on more strategic purchases, achieving the following goals:

▶ Increasing the productivity of purchasing agents (providing them with more time and reducing job pressure)

▶ Lowering purchase prices through product standardization and consolidation of purchases

▶ Improving information flow and management (e.g., supplier's information and pricing information)

▶ Minimizing the purchases made from noncontract vendors (eliminating maverick buying)

▶ Improving the payment process

▶ Establishing efficient, collaborative supplier relations

▶ Ensuring delivery on time, every time

▶ Reducing the skill requirements and training needs of purchasing agents

▶ Reducing the number of suppliers

▶ Streamlining the purchasing process, making it simple and fast (Sometimes this involves authorizing requisitioners to perform purchases from their desktops, bypassing the procurement department.)

▶ Reducing the administrative processing cost per order by as much as 90 percent (e.g., GM achieved a reduction from $100 to $10)

▶ Finding new suppliers and vendors that can provide goods and services faster and/or cheaper (improved sourcing)

▶ Integrating the procurement process with budgetary control in an efficient and effective way

▶ Minimizing human errors in the buying or shipping process

▶ Monitoring and regulating buying behavior.

An example of the actual benefits realized by IBM and GE through e-procurement initiatives is provided in Exhibit W6.2 on the book's Web site.

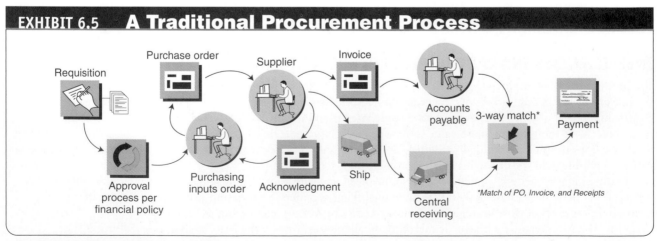

EXHIBIT 6.5   A Traditional Procurement Process

Requisition — Purchase order — Supplier — Invoice — Accounts payable — 3-way match* — Payment

Approval process per financial policy — Purchasing inputs order — Acknowledgment — Ship — Central receiving

*Match of PO, Invoice, and Receipts

Source: From *ariba.com* (2001). Used with permission.

EXHIBIT 6.6   The E-Procurement Process: A Buyer's View

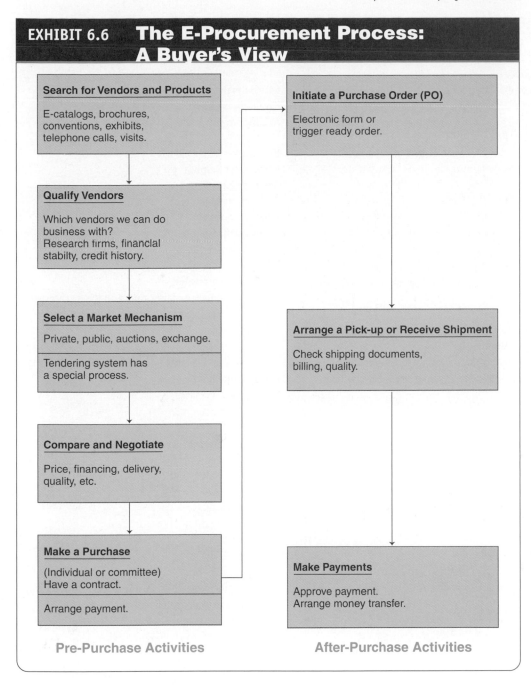

Search for Vendors and Products

E-catalogs, brochures, conventions, exhibits, telephone calls, visits.

Qualify Vendors

Which vendors we can do business with?
Research firms, financial stabilty, credit history.

Select a Market Mechanism

Private, public, auctions, exchange.

Tendering system has a special process.

Compare and Negotiate

Price, financing, delivery, quality, etc.

Make a Purchase

(Individual or committee)
Have a contract.

Arrange payment.

Initiate a Purchase Order (PO)

Electronic form or trigger ready order.

Arrange a Pick-up or Receive Shipment

Check shipping documents, billing, quality.

Make Payments

Approve payment.
Arrange money transfer.

Pre-Purchase Activities   After-Purchase Activities

E-procurement is relatively easy to implement (see Metz 2002). Channel conflict usually does not occur, and the resistance to change is minimal. Also, a wide selection of e-procurement software packages and other infrastructure are available at a reasonable cost.

MROs are often the initial target for e-procurement. However, improvement can be made in purchasing of direct materials as well. All existing manual processes of requisition creation, requests for quotation, invitation to tender, purchase order issuance, receiving goods, and making payment can be streamlined and automated. However, to most effectively implement such automated support, the people involved in procurement must collaborate with the suppliers along the supply chain, as described in Chapter 8.

IMPLEMENTING E-PROCUREMENT

Putting the buying department on the Internet may be the easy part of e-procurement. The more difficult part is implementing it. The potential components that can be found in e-procurement systems are shown in Exhibit 6.7 (page 234).

EXHIBIT 6.7   Potential E-Procurement Components

Module	Components
Catalog Management Module • Facilitates the creation of products, subassemblies, and components in a hierarchical manner.	• Catalog manager • Catalog exchanger • AVL (Approved Vendor List) editor
Collaborative Planning Module • Supports collaborative planning between buyers and suppliers.	• Request for Quote (RFQ) • Request for Proposal (RFP) • Demand forecaster • Contract manager • Inventory manager • Information flow controller
Online Purchase Module • Supports both systematic and spot procurement for direct and indirect materials and for contracts (for both goods and services).	• Purchase via contracts • Purchase from catalog • Reverse auction service for direct/indirect materials • Reverse auction service for contracts • Auction service
Purchase-Order Handling Module • Enables buyers to place purchase orders via on/off item master, reverse auction, contract purchasing, and spot market requisition.	• Purchase order manager • Demand aggregator • Consignment manager • Just-in-time order manager
Document Service Module • Facilitates a broad range of services for procurement documentation such as RFQ, RFP, PO, goods receipt, and accounts payable.	• Document indexing • SML exchanger • Document version controller
Historical Performance Service Module • Provides easy access to historical statistics of all transactions.	• Periodical reports • Customized reports • Statistical analysis
Information Service Module • Provides a unified information and message service that allows users to receive/send e-mails and view status of procurement activities.	• Message/task center • Status of procurement operations • Customized exceptional alerts • Smart search engine • Online negotiation/discussion service
System Administration Module • Provides tools that enable the company to control procurement activities.	• Company master data organizer • Product group builder • Workflow designer • Authorization matrix • Look and feel designer • User/department profile organizer

Source: www.e-jing.net-A supply chain management solution provider.

Major implementation issues for companies to consider as they plan e-procurement initiatives include the following:

▶ Fitting e-procurement into the company EC strategy. For example, matching the procurement method with the strategy of "use others' site," or do auctions yourself because the strategy is to build a strong information systems department.

▶ Reviewing and changing the procurement process itself. E-procurement may affect how many purchasing agents exist in the company, where they are located, and how purchases are being approved. Also important is the degree of purchasing centralization.

▶ Providing interfaces between e-procurement with integrated enterprisewide information systems such as ERP or supply chain management (SCM). If the company does not have such systems, it maybe beneficial to do some restructuring or a BPR prior to the installation of e-procurement.

▶ Coordinating the buyer's information system with that of the sellers. Sellers have many potential buyers. For this reason, some major suppliers, such as SKF (a Swedish automotive parts maker; see skf.com), developed an integration-oriented procurement system for its buyers. The SKF information system is designed to make it easier for the procurement systems of others (notably the distributors in other countries) that buy the company's bearings and seals to interface with the SKF system. The SKF system allows distributors to gain real-time technical information on the products, as well as details on product availability, delivery times, and commercial terms and conditions.

▶ Consolidating the number of regular suppliers to a minimum and assuring integration with their information systems, and if possible, with their business processes. Having fewer suppliers generally will minimize the number of connectivitiy issues that need to be solved and will lower expenses. Also, with fewer suppliers you will buy more from each supplier and develop better collaboration.

Meeting these challenges, many companies that have implemented e-procurement have been extremely satisfied with the payoffs. One such example is described in EC Application Case 6.3 (page 236).

Section 6.5 ▶ REVIEW

1. Define procurement and list the major procurement methods.
2. Describe the inefficiencies of traditional procurement.
3. Define e-procurement and its goals.
4. Differentiate direct materials from MROs. Why are MROs good candidates for e-procurement?
5. Describe the implementation of e-procurement.

6.6 BUY-SIDE E-MARKETPLACES: REVERSE AUCTIONS

One of the major methods of e-procurement is through reverse auctions. Recall from our discussions in Chapters 1 and 2 that a *reverse auction* is a tendering system in which suppliers are invited to bid on the fulfillment of an order, and the lowest bid wins. In B2B usage of a reverse auction, a buyer may open an electronic market on its own server and invite potential suppliers to bid on the items the buyer needs. The "invitation" to such reverse auctions is a form or document called a RFQ (request for quote). The reverse auction is referred to as the *tendering* or *bidding model*. Traditional tendering usually implied sealed bidding (see Chapter 11), whereas the reverse auction opens the bids to competing bidders. See Smeltzer and Carr (2002) for a comprehensive overview of reverse auctions.

request for quote (RFQ)
The "invitation" to participate in a tendering (bidding) system.

The reverse auction method is the most common model for large MRO purchases. Governments and large corporations frequently mandate this approach, which may provide considerable savings. To understand why this is so, study Insights and Additions 6.2 (page 237), which compares the pre-Internet tendering process with the Web-based reverse auction process. The electronic process is faster and administratively much less expensive. It also can result in locating the cheapest possible products or projects.

EC Application

DESKTOP E-PROCUREMENT AT SCHLUMBERGER

Schlumberger is the world's largest oil service company, with 60,000 employees in 100 countries and annual sales of $8.5 billion. In 2000, the company installed a Web-based automated procurement system in Oilfield Services, its largest division. With this system, the employees can buy office supplies and equipment as well as computers straight from their desktops.

The system replaced a number of older systems, including automated and paper-based ones. The single desktop system streamlined and sped up the purchasing operation, reducing costs as well as the number of people involved in the process. It also enables the company to consolidate purchases for volume discounts from vendors.

The system has two parts:

1. The internal portion uses Commerce One's BuySite procurement software and runs on the company's intranet. Using it is like shopping at an online store: Once the employee selects the item, the system generates the requisition, routes it electronically to the proper people for approval, and turns it into a purchase order.
2. Commerce One's MarketSite and BuySite are used to get the purchase order to the suppliers. The B2B Internet marketplace connects Schlumberger with hundreds of suppliers with a single, low-cost, many-to-many system.

Negotiation of exclusive prices is accomplished with individual vendors before their items are put into Schlumberger's system. For example, Office Depot's entire catalog is posted on the MarketSite, but the Schlumberger employees see only the subset of previously negotiated products and prices. In the future, the company plans to negotiate prices in real time through auctions and other bidding systems.

The benefits of the procurement system are evident in both cost and processes. The cost of goods has been reduced, and transaction costs have also fallen. Employees spend much less time in the ordering process, thus giving them more time for their core work. The system is also much more cost-efficient for the suppliers, who can then pass along savings to their customers. By using one system worldwide, Schlumberger saves time for employees who are transferred because they do not have to learn a new system at their new location. Procurement effectiveness can be increased because it is now possible to trace the overall procurement activity.

Getting the system up and running was easy because it was implemented in stages and ran at the same time as existing systems. Employees did not have to deal with implementation issues—once the system was in place, the old system was disabled, and there were no complaints with regard to the old system being shut down because it was no longer in use.

Sources: Compiled from Ovans (2000) and from *schlumberger.com* (2002).

Questions

1. Describe the benefits of the new systems over the old system.
2. Describe how the e-procurement system operates.
3. Summarize the benefits of e-procurement to the company.

CONDUCTING REVERSE AUCTIONS

Thousands of companies use the reverse auction model. Reverse auctions may be administered from a company's Web site, as with GM in the opening case, or from an intermediary's site. The bidding process conducted by large companies may last a day or more. In some cases, the bidders bid only once, but bidders can usually view the lowest bid and rebid several times.

As the number of reverse auction sites increases, suppliers will not be able to manually monitor all such tendering sites. This problem has been addressed with the introduction of *online directories* that list open RFQs. Another way to solve this problem is through the use of software agents (see Chapter 11). Other software agents can reduce the human burden in the bidding process. Typical agents that support the bidding process include AuctionBot (from the University of Michigan).

Alternatively, a third-party intermediary may run the electronic bidding, as they do for forward auctions. General Electric's GXS (now an independent company, described in detail later) is open to any buyer. Auction sites such as A-Z Used Computers (a-zuc.com) and FreeMarkets (freemarkets.com) also belong to this category. Conducting reverse auctions in B2B can be a fairly complex process, and this is why an intermediary may be essential, as demonstrated in the case of United Technologies in EC Application Case 6.4 (page 238). (Other examples of bidding managed by an intermediary are shown in Chapter 11.)

Insights and Additions 6.2 — Comparison of Pre-Internet and Web-Based Reverse Auction Processes

The Pre-Internet Tendering System Process	The Web-Based Reverse Auction Process
The buyer prepares a paper-based description of the product (project) that needs to be produced. The description includes specifications, blueprints, quality standards, delivery date, and required payment method.	The buyer gathers product information automatically from online sources.
The buyer announces the RFQ via newspaper ads, direct mail, fax, or telephone.	The buyer posts the RFQ on its secured corporate portal or sends e-mail to selected vendors.
Bidders (suppliers) that express interest receive detailed information (sometimes for a fee), usually by postal mail or a courier.	The buyer identifies potential suppliers from among those who responded to the online RFQ and invites suppliers to bid on the project. Bidders download the project information from the Web.
Bidders prepare proposals. They may call the company for additional information. Sometimes changes in the specs are made, which must be disseminated to all interested bidders.	Bidders conduct real-time or open-time reverse auctions. Requests for more information can be made online. Changes in specs can be disseminated electronically.
Bidders submit proposals, usually several copies of the same documents, by a preestablished deadline.	Bidders submit proposals in electronic format.
Proposals are evaluated, usually by several departments at the buyer's organization. Communication and clarification may take place via letters or phone/fax.	The buyer evaluates the suppliers' bids. Communications, clarifications, and negotiations to achieve the "best deal" take place electronically.
Buyer awards a contract to the bidder(s) that best meets its requirements. Notification is usually done via postal mail.	Buyer awards a contract to the bidder(s) that best meets its requirements. Notification is done online.

The reverse auction process is demonstrated in Exhibit 6.8 (page 239). As the exhibit shows, the first step is for the would-be buyer to post bid invitations. When bids arrive, contract and purchasing personnel for the buyer evaluate the bids and decides which one(s) to accept. The details of this process are explained in the General Electric case that follows.

The Procurement Revolution at General Electric

General Electric's material costs increased 16 percent between 1982 and 1992 (gxs.com 1999). During those same years, GE's product prices remained flat or for some products even declined. In response to the cost increases, GE began an all-out effort to improve its purchasing system. The company analyzed its procurement process and discovered that its purchasing was inefficient, involved too many transactions, and did not leverage GE's large volumes to get the best prices. In addition, more than one-quarter of its 1.25 million invoices per year had to be reworked because the purchase orders, receipts, and invoices did not match.

TPN at GE's Lighting Division. Of a number of steps GE took to improve its procurement, one of the most innovative was the introduction of an electronic tendering system that started in GE's Lighting Division.

Factories at GE Lighting used to send hundreds of RFQs to the corporate sourcing department each day, many for low-value machine parts. For each requisition, the accompanying blueprints had to be requested from storage, retrieved from the vault, transported to the processing site, photocopied, folded, attached to paper requisition forms with quote sheets, stuffed into envelopes, and mailed out to bidders. This process took at least 7 days and was so complex and time-consuming that the sourcing department normally sent out bid packages for each part to only two or three suppliers.

CASE 6.4

EC Application

BIDDING THROUGH A THIRD-PARTY AUCTIONEER: FREEMARKETS

Imagine this scenario: United Technologies Corp. needs suppliers to make $24-million worth of circuit boards. Twenty-five hundred suppliers, whose names were found in electronic registries and directories, were identified as possible contractors. The list of possible suppliers was submitted to FreeMarkets (*freemarkets.com*), a third-party auctioneer. Experts at FreeMarkets reduced the list to 1,000 based on considerations ranging from plant location to the size of the supplier. After further analysis of plant capacity and customer feedback, the list was further reduced to 100. A detailed evaluation of the potential candidates resulted in 50 qualified suppliers, who were then invited to bid. Those 50 suppliers received a password to review the circuit board specifications online.

A 3-hour auction of online competitive bidding was conducted. FreeMarkets divided the job into 12 lots, each of which was put up for bid. At 8:00 A.M., the first lot, valued at $2.25 million, was placed online. The first bid was $2.25 million, which was seen by all bidders. Minutes later, another bidder placed a $2.0 million bid. Using the reverse auction approach, the bidders further reduced their bids. Minutes before the bid closed, at 8:45 A.M., the 42nd bid, which was for $1.1 million, was received. No other bids were received. When the bidding ended, the bids for all 12 lots totaled $18 million (about a 35 percent savings to United Technologies).

To finalize the process, FreeMarkets conducted a comprehensive analysis of several of the lowest bidders of each lot, attempting to look at other criteria in addition to cost. Based on the bid amount as well as other factors, FreeMarkets then recommended the winners and collected its commission fees. (Additional FreeMarkets cases can also be found in Chapter 11. For more on e-procurement at United Technologies, see Britton 2000.)

Sources: Compiled from Jahnke (1998); FreeMarkets (1999); and Britton (2000).

Questions

1. What type of auction is this?
2. What role does FreeMarkets play in the procurement process?
3. Why would a large company such as United Technologies need an intermediary?

In 1996, GE Lighting piloted the company's first e-procurement system, called the Trading Process Network (TPN) Post. With this online system, the sourcing department received the requisitions electronically from its internal customers and sent off a bid package to suppliers around the world via the Internet. The system automatically pulled the correct drawings and attached them to the electronic requisition forms. Within 2 hours from the time the corporate sourcing department started the process, suppliers were notified of incoming RFQs by e-mail, fax, or EDI. They were given 7 days to prepare a bid and return it electronically to GE Lighting. Then the bid was transferred internally, over the corporate intranet, to the appropriate evaluators, and a contract could be awarded that same day.

Benefits of TPN. As a result of implementing TPN, GE realized a number of benefits:

- ▶ Labor involved in the procurement process declined by 30 percent. At the same time, material costs declined 5 to 50 percent due to the procurement department's ability to reach a wider base of competing suppliers online.

- ▶ GE was able to cut by 50 percent the number of staff involved in the procurement process and redeployed those workers into other jobs. As a result, the sourcing department had at least 6 to 8 free days a month to concentrate on strategic activities rather than on paperwork, photocopying, and envelope stuffing.

- ▶ It used to take 18 to 23 days to identify suppliers, prepare a request for bid, negotiate a price, and award the contract to a supplier. After implementation of the TPN, it took 9 to 11 days.

- ▶ With the transaction handled electronically from beginning to end, invoices could be automatically reconciled with purchase orders, reflecting any modifications that happen along the way.

- ▶ GE procurement departments around the world were able to share information about their best suppliers. In February 1997 alone, GE Lighting found seven new suppliers through the Internet, including one that charged 20 percent less than the second-lowest bid.

EXHIBIT 6.8   The Reverse Auction Process

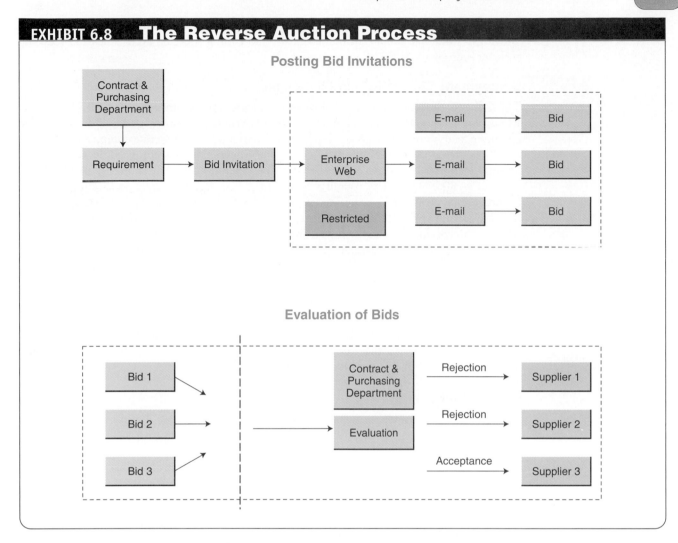

By 2001, 12 of GE's divisions were purchasing their nonproduction and MRO materials over the Internet for an annual total of $6 billion (35 percent of their total procurement). General Electric estimates that streamlining these purchases alone has saved the company $500 to $700 million annually.

The inception of GXS. Due to the success of TPN, GE expanded the system, making it a public posting place for other buyers. In 2001, TPN was acquired by GXS Express Marketplaces, which was operated by GE Global Exchange Services (gxs.com). GXS is now operated as a public marketplace on which many other companies place RFQs. GXS has over 100,000 trading partners in 58 countries, and in 2002 it processed over $1.2 billion in transactions valued at over $1 trillion. It is one of the few profitable dot-com companies. In June 2002, it was sold to Francisco Partners under whose control it continues to operate under the name GXS (gxs.com).

Benefits of GXS. Suppliers in the GXS system can gain instant access to global buyers (including GE) with billions of dollars in purchasing power. In addition, they may dramatically improve the productivity of their own bidding and sales activities. Other benefits are increased sales volume, expanded market reach and ability to find new buyers, lower administration costs for sales and marketing activities, shorter requisition cycle time, improved sales staff productivity, and a streamlined bidding process.

General Electric reports that the benefits of GXS extend beyond its own walls. As an example, computer reseller Hartford Computer Group reports that since joining GXS, it has increased its exposure to different GE business units so that its business with GE has grown by over 250 percent. In addition, GXS has introduced Hartford Computer Group to other potential customers.

More generally, the benefits of GXS to purchasing departments include the following: streamlining sourcing processes with current business partners; finding and building partnerships with new suppliers worldwide; rapidly distributing information, specifications, and electronic drawings to multiple suppliers simultaneously; and cutting sourcing cycle times and reducing costs for sourced goods.

Deployment Strategies and Challenges

The GE case demonstrates two deployment strategies for EC initiatives. The first is to start EC in one division (GE started in its Lighting Division) and slowly go to all divisions. The second is to also use the site as a public bidding marketplace to generate commission income.

Even though GE was successful with its e-procurement system, it could not reach its original plan of 100 percent e-procurement due to connectivity difficulties with SMEs. By 2001, of its 30,000 suppliers, roughly 25 percent (7,500 suppliers) were performing the critical procurement missions on the Web. Another 7,500 or so were connected to GE using the dated EDI networks. That left another 15,000 suppliers that relied mainly on manual processes to conduct business with GE (Moozakis 2001). (Connecting with SMEs is a common challenge in B2B implementation.)

GROUP REVERSE AUCTIONS

Group purchasing usually involves negotiated contracts. However, occasionally B2B reverse auctions are done in a private exchange for a group of partnering companies. Such *group reverse auctions* are popular in Korea and usually involve large conglomerates. For example, the LG Group operated the LG MRO auction for its members, and the Samsung Group operates iMarketKorea, as described in EC Application Case W6.1.

Section 6.6 ▶ REVIEW

1. Describe a manual tendering system.
2. How do online reverse auctions work?
3. List the benefits of Web-based reverse auctions.
4. Describe the business drivers of GE's TPN (GXS) and its evolution over time.
5. What was a primary challenge to GE in implementing its e-procurement system?

6.7   OTHER E-PROCUREMENT METHODS

Companies implement other innovative e-procurement methods as well. The most common ones are described in this section.

AN INTERNAL MARKETPLACE: AGGREGATING SUPPLIERS' CATALOGS

Large organizations have many corporate buyers or purchasing agents that are usually located in different places. For example, Bristol-Myers Squibb Corporation has more than 30,000 corporate buyers that are located all over the world. These agents buy from a large number of suppliers. The problem is that even if all purchases are made from approved suppliers, it is difficult to plan and control procurement. In many cases, in order to save time, buyers engage in *maverick buying*. In addition, an organization needs to control the purchasing budget. This situation is especially serious in government agencies and multinational entities where many buyers and large numbers of purchases are involved.

One effective solution to the procurement problem in large organizations is to aggregate the catalogs of all approved suppliers, combining them into a single *internal* electronic catalog. Prices can be negotiated in advance or determined by a tendering, so that the buyers do not have to negotiate each time they place an order. By aggregating the suppliers' catalogs on the organization's server, it is also easier to centralize and control all procurement. Such an aggregation is called an **internal marketplace**.

internal marketplace
The aggregated catalogs of all approved suppliers combined into a single *internal* electronic catalog.

Benefits of Internal Marketplaces

Using a search engine to look through the internal marketplace, corporate buyers can quickly find what they want, check availability and delivery times, and complete an electronic requisition form. Another advantage of such aggregation is that a company can reduce the number of its regular suppliers. For example, Caltex, a multinational oil company, reduced the number of its suppliers from over 3,000 to 800. Such reduction is possible because the central catalog enables buyers at multiple corporate locations to buy from remote but fewer sellers. Buying from fewer sellers typically increases the quantities bought and lowers the per unit price. Another example of a successful aggregation of suppliers' catalogs is that of MasterCard International, which aggregates more than 10,000 items from the catalogs of approved suppliers into an internal electronic catalog. The goal of this project is to consolidate buying activities from multiple corporate sites, improve processing costs, and reduce the supplier base. Payments are made with MasterCard's corporate procurement card. By 2002, the system was being used by more than 2,500 buyers. MasterCard is continually adding suppliers and catalog content to the system, which can be updated manually or by software agents.

Finally, internal marketplaces allow for easy financial controls. As buyers make purchases, their account balances are displayed. Once the budget is depleted, the system will not allow new purchase orders to go through. Therefore, this model is popular in public institutions and government entities.

Desktop Purchasing

The implementation (application) of internal marketplaces is frequently done via desktop catalog purchasing. **Desktop purchasing** implies purchasing directly from internal marketplaces without the approval of supervisors and without intervention of a procurement department. This is usually done by using a *purchasing card* (*P-card*) (see Chapter 13). This approach reduces the administrative cost and cycle time involved in purchasing urgently needed or highly frequent items of small dollar value. This approach is effective for MRO purchases. Thus, service industries, such as financial institutions, that do not need to purchase direct materials can adopt this approach effectively.

> **desktop purchasing**
> Direct purchasing from internal marketplaces without the approval of supervisors and without intervention of a procurement department.

Desktop purchasing can be implemented using internal marketplaces. For instance, Microsoft built its internal marketplace, named MS Market, for the procurement of small items, which occupy 70 percent of total purchase transactions yet account for only 3 percent in dollar value (Neef 2001). The aggregated catalog that is part of MS Market is used by Microsoft employees worldwide, whose purchasing totals $3 billion annually. The system has drastically reduced the role and size of the procurement department. For more on desktop purchasing at Microsoft, see EC Application Case W6.2. Another example is aeronautics company Lockheed Martin Corp., which adopted desktop purchasing to procure items that cost less than $10,000; such items constitutes 30 to 35 percent of purchase decisions by Lockheed Martin end users.

The desktop purchasing approach also can be implemented by partnering with external private exchanges. For instance, Samsung Electronics of Korea, a huge global manufacturer and its subsidiaries, has tightly integrated its iMarketKorea exchange (see EC Application Case W6.1) with the e-procurement systems of its buying agents. This platform can be easily linked with *group purchasing*, which is described later in this section.

Desktop purchasing systems. An extension of desktop purchasing using internal marketplaces (aggregated catalogs) is a desktop purchasing system. **Desktop purchasing systems** automate and support purchasing operations such as product and supplier selection, requisitions, catalog search, approval process, purchase order processing, catalog update and content management, and reporting of spending patterns and supplier performance. These systems are designed to support the nonpurchasing professional (employees whose job is other than purchasing agent) and casual end users. A schematic overview of such a system is shown in Exhibit 6.9 (page 242). It displays the key functionalities and connectivity options of such systems. In addition to end-user support, the system features administrative modules to support the central purchasing group and the IT features and activities (e.g., connectivity, integration, communication, security). For details, see Segev and Gebauer (2001). A major vendor of such systems is Oracle (oracle.com, see system 9i).

> **desktop purchasing systems**
> Software that automates and supports purchasing operations for nonpurchasing professionals and casual end users.

INDUSTRIAL MALLS AND INTERMEDIARIES' CATALOGS

Buying special materials and products and purchasing in small quantities (as is the case in small companies) are activities that are not conveniently done in reverse auctions. In such cases, e-procurement can be done via *industrial malls*—distributors that aggregate, in

EXHIBIT 6.9   Desktop Purchasing: Key Functionality and Connectivity

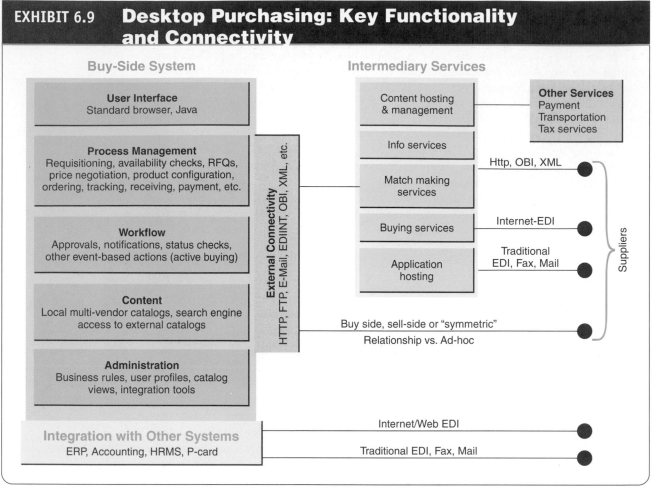

Source: Segev, A., and J. Gebauer. "B2B Procurement and Marketplace Transformation." *Information Technology and Management* (2001).

one place, products from hundreds or thousands of suppliers. These malls can be *horizontal*, carrying MRO (nonproduction) materials for use in a variety of industries, or they can be *vertical*, carrying products used by one industry but at various segments of the supply chain. Purchases from such malls are usually at catalog prices, although companies may negotiate a quantity discount. To understand how e-purchasing is done in these cases, let's see how Goodrich Corporation buys its MROs at W. W. Grainger, as described in EC Application Case 6.5.

BUYING AT E-AUCTIONS

Another popular approach to procurement is e-auctions. As described in Section 6.3, sellers are increasingly motivated to sell surpluses and even regular products via auctions. In some cases, e-auctions provide an opportunity to buyers to find inexpensive or unique items fairly quickly. A prudent corporate buyer should certainly look both at those manufacturers and distributors that conduct auctions periodically (e.g., GM or Dell) and at third-party auctioneers (e.g., eBay or auctions.yahoo.com). As will be shown in Chapter 11, auction aggregators can help purchasers find where and when auctions of needed items are conducted.

group purchasing
The aggregation of orders from several buyers into volume purchases so that better prices can be negotiated.

GROUP PURCHASING

Many companies are moving to group purchasing. With **group purchasing**, orders from several buyers are aggregated into volume purchases so that better prices can be negotiated. Two models are in use: *internal aggregation* and *external* (third-party) *aggregation*.

CASE 6.5
EC Application
W. W. GRAINGER AND GOODRICH CORPORATION

W. W. Grainger has a number of Web sites, but *grainger.com* is its flagship. In 2001, of Grainger's over $5 billion in annual sales, more than $150 million was done over the Web, with the majority of those sales placed through *grainger.com*.

More than 600,000 brand-name MRO supplies are offered at *grainger.com*, and a growing number of Grainger's 2 million customers are actively ordering online. The Web site continues the same kind of customer service and wide range of industrial products provided by Grainger's traditional off-line business, with the additional convenience of 24/7 ordering, use of search engines, and additional services.

This convenience is what first attracted BFGoodrich Aerospace (now called Goodrich Corporation) in Pueblo, Colorado. They found it to be one of the most convenient and easy purchasing sites to use. The purchasing agent of this small Goodrich plant of approximately 250 employees used to call in an order to a supplier, give the salesperson a part number, and wait until the price could be pulled up. There was also the chance that numbers could be transposed. Goodrich's purchaser now can place orders online in a matter of minutes, and the purchaser's display has Goodrich's negotiated pricing built in.

Goodrich can get just about anything it needs from *grainger.com*. Grainger interfaces with other suppliers, so if Goodrich needs something specific that Grainger does not normally carry, Grainger will research and find the items through its *findmro.com* site. With Grainger's buying power, it can get better prices than Goodrich can.

Goodrich has achieved additional savings from the tremendous decrease in paperwork that has resulted from buying through *grainger.com*. Individuals in each department now have access to purchasing cards, which allow them to do some of their own ordering. Before, the central purchasing department had to issue purchase orders for every single item. Now, employees with P-cards and passwords can place orders according to the spending limits that have been set up for their positions.

In 2002, the Goodrich Pueblo operation made $200,000 in purchases from *grainger.com*, which reflected a 10 to 15 percent savings on its purchases. Goodrich has now signed a companywide enterprise agreement that allows every Goodrich facility in the country to order through *grainger.com*, with an expected savings of at least 10 percent.

Sources: Compiled from *Fortune* (2003) and *grainger.com* (2003).

Questions

1. Enter *grainger.com* and review all of the services offered to buyers. Prepare a list of these services.
2. Explain how Goodrich's buyers save time and money.
3. What other benefits does Goodrich enjoy by using *grainger.com*?
4. How is desktop purchasing implemented at Goodrich Corporation?

Internal Aggregation

Large companies, such as GE, buy billions of dollars of MROs every year. Companywide orders for such items are aggregated, using the Web, and are replenished automatically. Besides economies of scale (lower prices for large purchases) on many items, GE saves on the administrative cost of the transactions, reducing transaction costs from $50 to $100 per transaction to $5 to $10 (Rudnitsky 2000). With 4 million transactions annually at GE, this is a substantial savings.

External Aggregation

Many SMEs would like to enjoy quantity discounts but have difficulty finding others to join them to increase the procurement volume. Such matching can be accomplished by an external third party such as buyerzone.com or allbusiness.com. The idea is to provide SMEs with better prices, selection, and services by aggregating demand online and then either negotiating with suppliers or conducting reverse auctions. The external aggregation group purchasing process is shown in Exhibit 6.10 (page 244).

One can appreciate the importance of this market by taking into consideration some data about small businesses: In the United States, according to the U.S. Department of Commerce , 90 percent of all businesses have fewer than 100 employees, yet they account for over 35 percent of all MRO business volume (Small Business Administration 2002). Therefore, the potential for external aggregators is huge.

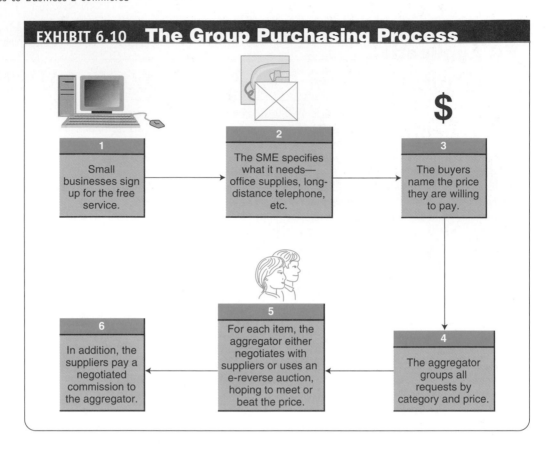

EXHIBIT 6.10   The Group Purchasing Process

Several large companies, including large CPA firms, EDS, and Ariba, are providing similar aggregation services, mainly to their regular customers. Yahoo and AOL offer such services too. A key to the success of these companies is a critical mass of buyers. An interesting strategy is for a company to outsource aggregation to a third party. For example, energy solutions.com provides group buying for community site partners in the energy industry.

Group purchasing, which started with commodity items such as MROs and consumer electronic devices, has now moved to services ranging from travel to payroll processing and Web hosting. Some aggregators use Priceline's "name-your-own-price" approach. Others try to find the lowest possible price. Similar approaches are used in B2C, and several vendors serve both markets (e.g., buy2gether.com).

PURCHASING DIRECT GOODS

Until 2001, most B2B e-procurement implementations took place in the sell-side of large vendors (Cisco, Intel, IBM) and in the procurement of MROs. In general, MROs comprise 20 to 50 percent of the purchasing budgets of companies. The remaining 50 to 80 percent of corporate purchases are for *direct materials* and *services*. Therefore, it is probable that greater benefits could come from introducing e-purchasing to direct goods so that buyers can get them faster, reduce the unit cost, reduce inventories, avoid shortages of materials, and expedite their own production processes. Sourcing direct materials typically involves more complex transactions requiring *collaboration* between the seller and buyer and greater information exchange. This leads us to collaborative commerce, which we will discuss in Chapter 8.

ELECTRONIC BARTERING

Bartering is the exchange of goods or services without the use of money. As described Chapters 2 and 11, the basic idea is for a company to exchange its surplus for something that it needs. Companies can advertise their surpluses in a classified area and may find a partner to make an exchange, but usually a company will have little success in finding an exact match. Therefore, companies ask an intermediary to help.

The intermediary can use a manual search-and-match approach or it can create an electronic bartering exchange. With a **bartering exchange,** a company submits its surplus to the exchange and receives points of credit, which can be used to buy items that the company needs. Popular bartering items are office space, idle facilities and labor, products, and even banner ads. In Chapter 2, we explained how this process works electronically and provided the names of some electronic bartering exchanges.

Section 6.7 ❱ REVIEW

1. Describe an internal marketplace and list its benefits.
2. Describe the benefits of desktop purchasing.
3. Discuss the relationship of desktop purchasing with internal marketplaces and group purchasing.
4. Describe how industrial malls operate and discuss their appeal to buyers.
5. Explain the logic of group purchasing and how it is organized.
6. How does B2B bartering work?

6.8 INFRASTRUCTURE, INTEGRATION, AND SOFTWARE AGENTS IN B2B EC

INFRASTRUCTURE FOR B2B

Large numbers of vendors, including Ariba, Oracle, Microsoft, and IBM, offer all the necessary B2B tools. The major infrastructures needed for B2B marketplaces include the following:

- ❱ Telecommunications networks and protocols (including EDI, extranets, and XML)
- ❱ Server(s) for hosting the databases and the applications
- ❱ Software for various activities, such as for executing the sell-side activities, including electronic catalogs; for conducting direct sale and auctions; for e-procurement (buy side), including reverse auctions; for PRM, such as using a call center; and for building a storefront or other applications
- ❱ Security for hardware and software

B2B software products are sold independently as components or integrated as suites. Most companies use vendors to build their B2B applications, as shown in the Real-World Case at the end of this chapter. The vendor sells or leases all of the necessary software to create the e-marketplace. The major vendors are IBM, Microsoft, Ariba, Oracle, and HP. (See Online Chapter 18 for a description of vendors' offerings.)

Extranets and EDI

In order for business partners to communicate online, companies must implement some type of secure interorganizational network, such as an extranet, and a common protocol, such as EDI. Briefly, *extranets* ("extended intranets") are secured networks, usually Internet-based, that allow business partners to access portions of each other's intranets. Extranets and their core technology are explained more fully in Chapters 7 and 12.

Electronic data interchange (EDI) is the electronic transfer of specially formatted standard business documents, such as bills, orders, and confirmations sent between business partners. Traditional EDI systems, which have been around for about 30 years, were implemented in **value-added networks (VANs),** which are private, third-party-managed common carriers that also provide communications services and security. However, VANs are relatively expensive and inflexible, and so SMEs found EDI over VANs to be unaffordable.

Internet-based (Web) EDI, on the other hand, is affordable to many companies. It can be used to replace or supplement traditional EDI. Downing (2002) discovered that companies that use Web-based EDI experience superior performance, both internally and externally. Web-based EDI can be easily implemented on the Internet by posting the sender's files on its own Web site. Senders can inform receivers about the posting by e-mail, and receivers can download the EDI files without special software. Thus, Web-based EDI can be flexibly

---

bartering exchange
An intermediary that links parties in a barter; a company submits its surplus to the exchange and receives points of credit, which can be used to buy the items that the company needs from other exchange participants.

electronic data interchange (EDI)
The electronic transfer of specially formatted standard business documents, such as bills, orders, and confirmations sent between business partners.

value-added networks (VANs)
Private, third-party-managed networks that add communications services and security to existing common carriers; used to implement traditional EDI systems.

Internet-based (Web) EDI
EDI that runs on the Internet and is widely accessible to most companies, including SMEs.

implemented among a small group of users without severe arguments about which standards to use. However, a potential limitation is that the received file may not be compatible with the input format of the receiver's system (though standards such as AS2 for data transmission may solve this problem). See Appendix 6A for more on the evolution of traditional EDI to Internet-based EDI.

According to Boucher-Ferguson (2002), all major retailers, from Home Depot to Wal-Mart, and many manufacturers, such as Sara Lee Corp., are *requiring* their suppliers to conduct business via Web-based EDI.

INTEGRATION

Integration with Existing Internal Infrastructure and Applications

EC applications of any kind need to be connected to the existing internal information systems. For example, an ordering system in sell-side B2B is usually connected to a payment verification system and to an inventory management application. Systems that must be integrated with EC applications include marketing databases and databases from other departments; legacy systems and their applications; ERP software, which may include e-procurement functions; catalog (product) information; the payment system; CRM software; logistics and inventory systems; workflow systems; sales statistics; SCM systems; and DSS applications. All major EC software vendors, including Ariba, IBM, Microsoft, Oracle, Commerce One, and SAP, provide for such integration.

Two competing approaches are used for integrating B2B with exchanges. The first is ERP II, or Extended ERP solutions. ERP II is provided by traditional ERP solution providers by expanding the B2B functions (such as SCM, SRM, and CRM) to ERP. The other is the ECM (Electronic Commerce Management) approach, which provides a multivendor open architecture for the integration of B2B and ERP. ERP (see Tutorial T3) integrates all the back office operations (accounting, inventory, finance, etc.). It must be integrated with EC since when an order is received in the front office, fulfillment starts by checking payment credibility, inventory on-hand, etc. Later billing and insurance need to be arranged. For more on this topic, see Chapters 7 and 8 and especially Online Chapter 18.

Integration with Business Partners

EC can be integrated more easily with internal systems than with external ones. For instance, in the sell-side e-marketplace, it is not easy for the many buying companies to connect to each seller. Similarly, a buy-side e-marketplace needs to be connected to hundreds or even thousands of suppliers for each buyer. One solution is to go to exchanges, where each buyer or seller needs to be connected only once. Another solution is a buyer-owned shopping cart (Lim and Lee 2003). The interface with back-end information systems allows the customer to put items from different sellers in a single cart. This makes shopping much more convenient because the customer pays only one time even though they made purchases from multiple sites locations.

Systems integrators and middleware vendors (such as tibco.com) provide many solutions for both internal integration (called Enterprise Application Integration, EAI) and external integration (called B2Bi, the *i* standing for integration). Details on systems integration are provided in Online Chapter 18 and in Linthicum (2001).

THE ROLE OF STANDARDS AND XML IN B2B INTEGRATION

For B2B companies to interact with each other easily and effectively, they must be able to connect their servers, applications, and databases. For this to happen, standard protocols and data representation schemes are needed. EDI is one such standard, but it has several limitations and is not structured for the Internet.

The Web is based on the standard communication protocols of *TCP/IP* (Transmission Control Protocol/Internet Protocol) and *HTTP* (Hypertext Transfer Protocol). Further, Web pages are written in the universally recognized standard notation of *HTML* (Hypertext Markup Language). However, this standard environment is useful only for displaying static, visual Web pages. To further extend the functionality of EC sites, one can use JavaScript and other Java and ActiveX programs. These tools allow for human interaction, but they still do not address the need to interconnect back-end database systems and applications. For that purpose, the industry is pursuing several alternatives for standardized data representation.

XML

One of the most promising standards is **XML (eXtensible Markup Language)** and its variants (see Raisinghani 2001; Linthicum 2000). XML is a simplified version of a general data description language known as SGML (Standard Generalized Markup Language). XML is promoted as a new platform for B2B and sometimes as a replacement for EDI systems. XML is used to improve compatibility between the disparate systems of business partners by defining the meaning of data in business documents.

XML differs from HTML. The purpose of HTML is to help build Web pages and display data on Web pages. The purpose of XML is to describe data and information. It does not say how the data will be displayed (which HTML does). XML can be used to send complex messages that include different files.

XML was created in an attempt at overcoming barriers to EDI implementation (which are discussed in Appendix 6A). XML can overcome EDI barriers for three reasons:

1. XML is a flexible language, therefore new requirements and changes can be incorporated into messages. This expands the rigid ranges of EDI.

2. Message content can be easily read and understood by people using standard browsers. Thus, receivers do not need EDI translators. This enables SMEs to receive, understand, and act on XML-based messages.

3. In order to implement EDI, it is necessary to have highly specialized knowledge of EDI methodology. Implementation of XML-based technologies requires less-specialized skills.

See Online Technical Appendix B and xml.org for more details on XML.

An example of an XML variant is voice XML, which is used to increase interactivity and accessibility with speech recognition systems. For an example of how XML works, see EC Application Case W6.3.

XML and other related standards require national and international agreements and cooperation. Several organizations are devoted to these topics. For example, ebXML, developed by UN/EDIFACT (EDI For Administration Commerce and Transport), is a popular standard, and most B2B XML protocols support it. See the book's Web site (Technical Appendix B) for a list of some important standards organizations and links to their Web sites.

WEB SERVICES

Web services is a general-purpose architecture that enables distributed applications to be assembled from a web of software services in the same way that Web sites are assembled from a web of HTML pages. It is one of the most talked-about topics in e-commerce and IT (see Glass 2002). The major technologies behind Web services include XML, SOAP, UDDI, and WDSL (see Online Chapter 18). Using these standards, Web services allow different applications from different organizations to communicate data without custom coding. Because all communication is in XML, Web services are not tied to any one operating system or programming language.

Web services are viewed as building blocks for distributed systems. Many believe that Web services will trigger a fundamental shift in the way that most distributed systems are created. Thus, Web services will play a major role in facilitating B2B because they make it easier to meet business customers' and channel partners' demands. See Online Chapter 18 for more about Web services.

THE ROLE OF SOFTWARE AGENTS IN B2B EC

Software (intelligent) agents play multiple roles in B2B. Chapter 3 discussed how software agents are used to aid customers in the comparison-shopping process. The major role of software agents in that case (the sell-side marketplace) was collecting data from multiple sellers' sites. Similarly, in B2B, software agents collect information from business sellers' sites for the benefit of business buyers.

XML (eXtensible Markup Language)
Standard (and its variants) used to improve compatibility between the disparate systems of business partners by defining the meaning of data in business documents.

Web services
An architecture enabling assembly of distributed applications from software services and tying them together.

Software agents play a similar role in the B2B buy-side marketplace. Suppose that a large number of buyers need to request quotes from multiple potential suppliers. Doing so manually would be slow, physically impossible, or uneconomical. Therefore, software agents are needed to assist both buyers and sellers. Also, agents are very useful in reverse auctions (see Chapter 11). Implementation of software agents in B2B will be discussed in Section 7.8 in Chapter 7.

Section 6.8 ▶ REVIEW

1. List the major infrastructures required for B2B EC.
2. Describe the difficulties of integration with business partners.
3. Describe the roles of extranets and EDI in interorganizational networks.
4. Distinguish traditional EDI from Web-based EDI.
5. Describe the purpose of XML.
6. Describe Web services and their role in integration.
7. What role do software agents play in B2B?

MANAGERIAL ISSUES

Some managerial issues related to this chapter are as follows.

1. **Can we justify the cost of B2B applications?** Because there are several B2B models, each of which can be implemented in different ways, it becomes critical to conduct a cost-benefit analysis of the proposed applications (projects). Such an analysis should include organizational impacts such as possible channel conflicts and how to deal with resistance to change within the organization. Also, implementation difficulties may increase costs (see Jap and Mohr 2002). One way to justify B2B is to look at the experiences of successful companies and at guidelines for success (see Cronin 2001).

2. **Which vendor(s) should we select?** Vendors normally develop B2B applications. Two basic approaches to vendor selection exist: (1) Select a primary vendor such as IBM, Ariba, or Oracle. This vendor will use its software and procedures and add partners as needed. Or, (2) use an integrator that will mix and match existing products and vendors to create "the best of breed" for your needs. See Online Chapter 18 for details.

3. **Which B2B model(s) should we use?** The availability of so many B2B models means that companies need to develop selection strategies based on preferred criteria. In addition to the company-centric models, several other types of exchanges should be considered.

4. **Should we restructure our procurement system?** If volume is heavy enough to attract the attention of major vendors, the company that is doing the purchasing might decide to restructure the procurement process by establishing a buy-side marketplace on its server. Or, the buying company could join a third-party intermediary-based marketplace (see Scacchi 2001).

5. **What restructuring will be required for the shift to e-procurement?** Many organizations fail to understand that a fundamental change in their internal processes must be implemented to realize the full benefits of e-procurement. The two critical success factors that many organizations overlook are the need to cut down the number of routine tasks and the reduction of the overall procurement cycle through the use of appropriate information technologies such as workflow, groupware, and ERP software. For example, IBM completely restructured its procurement processes prior to moving them online.

6. **What integration would be useful?** Trading in e-marketplaces is interrelated with logistics. Although this is particularly true in many-to-many exchanges, it is beneficial to consider the benefits of integration with logistics and other support services in company-centric marketplaces.

7. **What are the ethical issues in B2B?** Because B2B EC requires the sharing of proprietary information, business ethics are a must. Employees should not be able to access unauthorized areas in the trading system, and the privacy of trading partners should be protected both technically and legally.

8. **Will there be *massive* disintermediation?** With the increased use of private e-marketplaces there will be disintermediation as well as channel conflicts. However, reintermediation might occur with those vendors that can adapt to EC (see Chircu and Kauffman 2000; Klein and Teubner 2000).

SUMMARY

In this chapter, you learned about the following EC issues as they relate to the learning objectives.

1. **The B2B field.** The B2B field comprises e-commerce activities between businesses. B2B activities account for about 85 percent of all EC. B2B e-commerce can be done using different models.

2. **The major B2B models.** The B2B field is very diversified. It can be divided into the following segments: sell-side marketplaces (one seller to many buyers), buy-side marketplaces (one buyer from many sellers), trading exchanges (many sellers to many buyers), and collaborative commerce. Intermediaries play an important role in some B2B models.

3. **The characteristics of sell-side marketplaces.** Sell-side B2B EC is the online direct sale by one seller (a manufacturer or an intermediary) to many buyers. The major technology used is electronic catalogs, which allow for efficient customization, configuration, and purchase by customers. In addition, forward auctions are becoming popular, especially for selling surplus inventory. Sell-side auctions can be conducted from the seller's own site or from an intermediary's auction site. Sell-side activities can include extensive customer service.

4. **Sell-side intermediaries.** Intermediaries use B2B primarily to provide value-added services to manufacturers and business customers. They can also aggregate buyers and conduct auctions.

5. **The characteristics of buy-side marketplaces and e-procurement.** Today, companies are moving to e-procurement to expedite purchasing, save on item and administrative costs, and gain better control over the purchasing process. Major procurement methods are reverse auctions (bidding system); buying from storefronts and from catalogs; negotiation; buying from an intermediary that aggregates sellers' catalogs; internal marketplaces and group purchasing; desktop purchasing; buying in industrial malls; and bartering. E-procurement offers the opportunity to achieve real cost and time savings.

6. **B2B reverse auctions.** A reverse auction is a tendering system used by buyers to collect bids electronically from suppliers. Auctions can be done on a company's Web site or on a third-party auction site. Reverse auctions can dramatically lower buyer's costs, both product costs and the time and cost of the tendering process.

7. **B2B aggregation and group purchasing.** Increasing the exposure and the bargaining power of companies can be done by aggregating either the buyers or the sellers. Aggregating suppliers' catalogs into an internal marketplace gives buying companies better control of purchasing costs. In desktop purchasing, buyers are empowered to buy from their desktops up to a set limit without the need for approvals. They accomplish this by viewing internal catalogs with pre-agreed upon prices with the suppliers. Industrial malls specialize in one industry (e.g., computers) or in industrial MROs. They aggregate the catalogs of thousands of suppliers. You place an order at the mall, and shipping is arranged directly from the supplier or from the mall owner. Buyer aggregation through group purchasing is very popular because it allows SMEs to get better prices on their purchases. In addition to direct purchasing, items can be acquired via bartering.

8. **Infrastructure and standards in B2B.** To implement B2B, one may need a comprehensive set of hardware and software that includes networks and protocols, multiple servers, application software, and security. Of special utility are extranets and EDI (both traditional and Web based).

9. **Web-based EDI, XML, and Web services.** Traditional EDI systems were implemented over VANs, making EDI inaccessible to most small companies. Web-based EDI can replace traditional EDI or supplement it. To improve compatibility between business partners' systems, standards organizations are pursuing XML, a standard for defining data elements. The connectivity of B2B can be facilitated by Web services.

KEY TERMS

Bartering exchange	245	Direct materials	218	Horizontal marketplaces	219
Business-to-business e-commerce (B2B EC)	217	E-procurement	232	Indirect materials	218
		Electronic data interchange		Internal marketplace	240
Buy-side e-marketplace	231	(EDI)	245	Internet-based (Web) EDI	245
Company-centric EC	219	Exchanges (trading exchanges and		MROs (maintenance, repairs,	
Desktop purchasing	241	trading communities	220	and operations)	218
Desktop purchasing systems	241	Group purchasing	242	Maverick buying	232

DISCUSSION QUESTIONS

1. Explain how a catalog-based sell-side e-marketplace works and discuss its benefits.

2. Distinguish sell-side e-marketplaces from buy-side e-marketplaces.

3. Discuss the advantages of selling through online auctions over selling from catalogs.

4. Discuss the role of intermediaries in B2B.

5. How can companies buying from a sell-side e-marketplace integrate order information with their corporation's procurement system?

6. Discuss and compare all the mechanisms that aggregators of group purchasing can use.

7. Build a portfolio of e-procurement alternatives for a company that you are familiar with.

8. Should desktop purchasing be implemented only through an internal marketplace?

9. How do companies eliminate the potential limitations and risks associated with Web-based EDI? (To answer this, first see Appendix 6A.)

10. How can software agents work for multiple sellers and buyers?

11. Discuss the role of XML in B2B. Why is it so important?

12. Discuss the importance of Web services to B2B integration.

INTERNET EXERCISES

1. Visit milacron.com and its milpro.com site. Examine the sites from the buyer's perspective. Find out how to place an order. Check the "machinery flea market" link, click on the "search database." Report on your experiences.

2. Enter gxs.com and review GSX Express's bidding process. Describe the preparations your company would make in order to bid on GE jobs.

3. Enter commerceone.com and review the capabilities of BuySite and MarketSite. Find out how Commerce One supports the integration of many sellers' electronic catalogs for a specific buyer.

4. Visit allsystem.com to review All-System Aerospace International, Inc., a company that handles aircraft parts from several vendors. From an aircraft repair technician's point of view, evaluate whether this site can compete with Boeing's PART system.

5. Visit eventory.com, shop2gether.com, and escout.com. Compare the services offered by these businesses.

6. Examine the sites fastparts.com, ariba.com, trilogy.com, freemarkets.com, electricnet.com, peregrine.com, and ecweb.com. Match a B2B business model with each site.

7. Visit supplyworks.com and examine how the company streamlines the purchase process. How does this company differ from ariba.com?

8. Enter soho.org and onlinesoho.com and locate EC applications for SOHOs. Also, check the business services for small businesses provided by officedepot.com.

9. Visit ebay.com and identify all activities related to its small business auctions (business eXchange). What services are provided by eBay?

10. Visit avnet.com and find how its supply chain is structured. Draw the chain, showing Marshall's role. (Hint: See Timmers 1999 and Kalakota and Robinson 2001.)

11. Review the Cisco Connection Online (CCO) case (page 227).

    a. What is the CCO business model?

    b. Where are the success factors of CCO?

    c. What kinds of inquiries are supported when customers check their order status?

    d. What are the major benefits of CCO to Cisco and its customers?

TEAM ASSIGNMENTS AND ROLE PLAYING

1. Predictions about the future magnitude of B2B and statistics on its actual volume in various countries keep changing. In this activity, each team will locate current B2B predictions and statistics for different world regions (e.g., Asia, Europe, North America). Using at least five sources, each team will find the predicted B2B volume (in dollars) for the next 5 years in their assigned region. Possible sources are listed in Exhibit 4.2 (page 132).

2. Your goal in this assignment is to investigate the major B2B vendors. Each team should investigate a major vendor (e.g., Ariba, Microsoft, HP, Commerce One, Oracle, or IBM) or an application type (buy-side, sell-side, or auction). Find the major products and services offered, and examine customer success stories. Write a report of your findings. Convince the class that your vendor is the best.

REAL-WORLD CASE

EASTMAN CHEMICAL MAKES PROCUREMENT A STRATEGIC ADVANTAGE

Eastman Chemical (ECM), a multibillion-dollar, multinational corporation, operates in an extremely competitive environment (*eastman.com*). In response to competitive pressures, management decided to improve on the procurement of MRO items. In its effort to do so, the company embarked on two interrelated activities: integrating the supply chain and introducing e-procurement. The objectives of the project, which started in late 1999, were:

▶ To increase compliance with purchasing policies (reduce maverick buying)

▶ To support frontline employees while maintaining existing rules

▶ To reduce procurement transaction costs via elimination of non-value-added and redundant processes

▶ To leverage corporate spending to negotiate favorable trading terms with channel supply partners

Each year, the company purchases over $900 million in MROs from over 3,500 suppliers. The company used an SAP R/3 ERP system, part of the legacy system that interfaced with the e-procurement application. The system provided good control, but at a cost of $115 per order when a purchasing card (see Chapter 13) was used. The ERP helped to reduce the workload on accounts payable and procurement personnel. However, purchasing from noncontracted suppliers increased. (The card made such purchasing easy.) This maverick buying reduced purchase volumes with the primary suppliers, thus reducing the company's negotiating power and increasing costs.

As part of its initiative to improve the MRO procurement process, Eastman Chemical established channel partnership relationships with its largest MRO suppliers. This increased the company's buying leverage and reduced costs and delays. Inventories and service levels were improved. In addition, Eastman Chemical introduced two new EC applications to its procurement sys-

tem: Commerce One's BuySite e-procurement software for dealing with the suppliers and MarketSite for transaction management and value-added services.

Using BuySite, Eastman Chemical has created an *internal catalog* of all MRO products located in Eastman's storerooms. The e-commerce software checks availability and prevents redundant purchases. The software also supplies catalog-management features that ensure that all vendors' changes and updates are entered into the internal catalog.

The MarketSite application supported the creation of a portal that enables:

▶ Use of a common Web browser by all of Eastman Chemical's 16,000 employees

▶ Different types of employees to use the system without need for additional training

▶ The ability to integrate the SAP R/3 with EC and the procurement card

▶ An effective and efficient catalog management strategy

▶ Maintenance of the existing systems infrastructure

▶ Simplification of business processes

▶ Flexibility and empowerment of frontline employees

The overall effect of the new portal is to reduce costs and to increase profitability and competitiveness.

Eastman Chemical has a large sell-side as well. Here customers order plastics, resins, and fibers online and track their purchases and transaction history, even down to the level of a part of a shipment. Eastman Chemical also auctions its surplus materials in the marketplace.

Overall, Eastman Chemical's e-business logged 11 percent of the company's revenue in 2001 (*Forbes* 2002).

Sources: Compiled from *eastman.com* (2002); *aberdeen.com* (2002); *Forbes* (2002); *computerworld.com*; Page (2000); and *commerceone.com/news/releases/Eastman.html* (2002).

Questions	
1. Enter *commerceone.com* and find information about the capabilities of BuySite and MarketSite. How do the two applications differ? 2. Why did Eastman Chemical start first with e-procurement rather than with the sell-side? You may want to visit *eastman.com* to learn more about the company. 3. In July 2000, Eastman Chemical introduced an EC project that enables buyers to participate in its	private online price negotiations using LiveExchange from Moai (*moai.com*). Explain how the software works and why it is referred to as "dynamic commerce." 4. Which of the problems cited in this case can be solved by other EC applications? Relate your answer to Commerce One products.

REFERENCES

aberdeen.com (accessed December 2002).

ariba.com (accessed October 2001).

avnet.com. "Avnet Enterprise Solutions Storage Initiative Delivers Coast-to-Coast Expertise." March 24, 2003, avnet.com/pressroom/news/cm/2003_03_24a.html (accessed April 2003).

Berryman K., and S. Heck. "Is the Third Time the Charm for B2B?" *The McKinsey Quarterly* no. 2 (2001).

bigboxx.com (accessed October 2002).

Black, M. "Offshore E-Commerce." Biba.org, Spring 2001, biba.org/documents/articles/shore.pdf (accessed April 2003).

"Boeing Launches New E-Business Web Site." *Journal of Aerospace and Defense Industry News*, May 12, 2000.

Boucher-Ferguson, R. "Writing the Playbook for B2B." *Wilson Internet*, January 29, 2002.

Britton, K. "E-Procurement at United Technologies." *Business 2.com*, November 14, 2000.

Bunnell, D., and A. Brate. *Making the Cisco Connection.* New York: John Wiley & Sons, 2000.

Chan, W. C., et al. "Thinking Out of the Box." *The McKinsey Quarterly* no. 2 (2001).

Chircu, A. M., and R. J. Kauffman. "Reintermediation Strategies in B2B E-Commerce." *International Journal of Electronic Commerce* 14, no. 4 (2000).

Cisco Systems. "Cisco Annual Report 2002." cisco.com/warp/public/749/ar2002/online/financial_review/mda.html (accessed April 2003).

commerceone.com/news/releases/Eastman.html (accessed December 2002).

computerworld.com (accessed December 2002).

Cronin, C. "Five Success Factors for Private Trading Exchanges." *e-Business Advisor.com*, July–August 2001.

Dai, Q., and R. J. Kauffman. "B2B E-Commerce Revisited: Revolution or Evolution?" *Electronic Markets* 12, no. 2 (2002).

Downing, C. E. "Performance of Traditional and Web-Based EDI." *Information Systems Management* (2002).

eastman.com (accessed December 2002).

e-jing.net/products/products_procurement.htm#2 (accessed January 2003).

El-Sawy, O., et al. "Intensive Value Innovation in the Electronic Economy: Insight from Marshall Industries." *MIS Quarterly* (September 1999).

eMarketer. "Has B2B E-commerce Stagnated?" *Emarketer.com*, February 3, 2003, emarketer.com/products/database.php?f_arg_0=B2B+85+percent+of+e-commerce+2002&f_arg_0_b=B2B+85+percent+of+e-commerce+2002&f_num_args_changed=1&f_num_articles_found=2&f_num_charts_found=2&f_num_reports_found=0&f_reports_found=&f_request=&f_search_type=Basic&Image81.x=0&Image81.y=0 (accessed April 2003).

Fickel, L. "Online Auctions: Bid Business." *CIO Web Business Magazine*, June 1, 1999.

forbes.com, October 8, 2002 (accessed December 2002).

Forrester Research. "Estimates of the B2B Market." forrester.com, March 7, 2001 (accessed January 2003).

Fortune. "E-Procurement: Unleashing Corporate Purchasing Power." fortune.com/sections/eprocurement2000, 2000 (accessed April 2003).

FreeMarkets. freemarkets.com, 1999 (accessed October 2002).

Glass, G. *Web Services.* Upper Saddle River, NJ: Prentice Hall, 2002.

gm.com (accessed August 2002).

Goldman Sachs Group. Special report, gs.com, February 15, 2001 (accessed July 2001).

grainger.com (accessed January 2003).

gxs.com (accessed September 1999).

Hoffman, W., et al. "The Unexpected Return of B2B." *The McKinsey Quarterly* no. 3 (2002).

IBM. "Whirlpool's B2B Trading Portal Cuts per Order Cost Significantly." White Plains, NY: IBM Corporation Software Group, Pub. # G325-6693-00, 2000.

Interwoven, Inc. "Interwoven Solutions Power Cisco Connection Online." Case Study, 2001, interwoven.com/documents/casestudies/cisco_august.pdf (accessed April 2003).

Jahnke, A. "How Bazaar." *CIO Magazine*, August 1, 1998.

Jap, S. D., and J. J. Mohr. "Leveraging Internet Technologies in B2B Relationships." *California Management Review* (Summer 2002).

Kalakota, R., and M. Robinson. *E-Business 2.0*. Reading, MA: Addison-Wesley, 2001.

Klein, S., and A. Teubner. "Web-Based Procurement: New Roles for Intermediaries." *Information Systems Frontiers 2*, no. 1 (2000).

Lengel, K. "B2B: Back to Basics." *CIO Magazine*, August 1, 2000.

Lim, G., and J. K. Lee. "Buyer-Carts for B2B EC: The B-Cart Approach." *Organizational Computing and Electronic Commerce* (July–September 2003).

Linthicum, D. S. *B2B Application Integration*. Boston: Addison-Wesley, 2001.

Linthicum, D. S. "Applications with XML." *e-Business Advisor*, May 2000.

Martin, T. N., et al. "Purchasing Agents: Use of the Internet as a Procurement Tool." *Quarterly Journal of Electronic Commerce 2*, no. 1 (2001).

Metz, C. "Purchasing Power." *PC Magazine*, November 21, 2002.

Moozakis, C. "GE Scales Back." *Internet Week*, May 10, 2001, internetweek.com/newslead01/lead051001.htm (accessed January 2003).

Neef, D. *E-Procurement: From Strategy to Implementation*. Upper Saddle River, NJ: Prentice Hall, 2001.

Ovans, A. "E-Procurement at Schlumberger." *Harvard Business Review* (May–June 2000).

Page, E. "The Case for Procurement." *Business 2.0*, November 14, 2000.

Raisinghani, M. S. "Extensible Markup Language: Synthesis of Key Ideas and Perspectives for Management." *Information Management* 14, no. 3, 4 (2001).

Retter, T., and M. Calyniuk. *Technology Forecast: 1998*. Menlo Park, CA: Price Waterhouse, 1998.

Rudnitsky, H. "Changing the Corporate DNA." *Forbes Global*, July 24, 2000, forbes.com/global/2000/0724/0314099a.html (accessed August 2000).

Scacchi, W. "Redesigning Contracted Service Procurement for Internet-Based E-commerce: A Case Study." *Information Technology and Management* (July 2001).

schlumberger.com (accessed April 2002).

Segev, A., and J. Gebauer. "B2B Procurement and Marketplace Transformation." *Information Technology and Management*. (July 2001).

Slater, R. *The Eye of the Storm: How John Chambers Steered Cisco Through the Technology Collapse*. New York: HarperCollins, 2003.

Small Business Administration, sba.gov/advo/stats (accessed February 2002).

Smeltzer, L. R., and A. Carr. "Reverse Auctions in Industrial Marketing and Buying." *Business Horizons*, March–April 2002.

Timmers, P. *Electronic Commerce: Strategies and Models for B2B Trading*. Chichester, UK: John Wiley & Sons, 1999.

tradexchange.com (accessed July 2000–June 2002).

Trading Process Network. "Extending the Enterprise: TPN Post Case Study—GE Lighting." Trading Process Network, 1999, tpn.geis.com/tpn/resource_center/casestud.html (accessed January 2000).

tradevan.com.tx (accessed January 2001).

University of Michigan. "AuctionBot." Computer Science Department, 2002, tac.eecs.umich.edu/auction (accessed April 2003).

U.S. Department of Commerce. "The Emerging Digital Economy." ta.doc.gov/digeconomy/emerging.htm, 1998 (accessed November 2001).

Wagner, M. "Web Helps Microsoft Automate Its Business." *Internet Week*, 2000, internetweek.com/100/tech.htm (accessed April 2003).

Warkentin, M. (ed.). *Business to Business Electronic Commerce: Challenges and Solutions*. Hershey, PA: Idea Group Publishing, 2002.

Waters, J. K. *John Chambers and the Cisco Way*. New York: Wiley, 2002.

whirlpool.com, news item (accessed September 2002).

Wilson, T. "Marshall Industries: Wholesale Shift to the Web." *Internet Week*, July 20, 1998.

6A

FROM TRADITIONAL TO INTERNET-BASED EDI

As discussed in Chapter 6, the majority of B2B transactions are supported by EDI, XML, and extranets. In this appendix, we describe EDI and its transition to the Internet platform. Extranets are covered in Appendix 7A.

TRADITIONAL EDI

As defined in Chapter 6, EDI is a communication standard that enables the electronic transfer of routine documents, such as purchasing orders, between business partners. It formats these documents according to agreed-upon standards. An EDI implementation is a process in which two or more organizations determine how to work together more effectively through the use of EDI. For other organizations, it is an internal decision spurred by the desire for competitive advantage.

EDI often serves as a catalyst and a stimulus to improve the business processes that flow between organizations. It reduces costs, delays, and errors inherent in a manual document-delivery system. EDI has the following special characteristics that differentiate it from e-mail (see Exhibit 6A.1):

▶ **Business transaction messages.** EDI is used primarily to electronically transfer repetitive business transactions. These include purchase orders, invoices, credit approvals, shipping notices, confirmations, and so on.

▶ **Data formatting standards.** Because EDI messages are repetitive, it makes sense to use formatting (coding) standards. Standards can shorten the length of the messages and eliminate data entry errors, because data entry occurs only once. EDI deals with standard transactions while e-mail is open. EDI is converted to a special standard language and it is secured, while e-mail is not. You enter data once and the data is automatically converted to EDI language. If there is missing or wrong data, the EDI converter assists you. EDI fosters collaborative relationships and strategic partnerships. In the United States and Canada, data are formatted according to the ANSI X.12 standard. An international standard developed by the United Nations is called EDIFACT.

▶ **EDI translators.** An EDI translator converts data into a standard format.

EDI has been around for about 30 years in the non-Internet environment. To distinguish it from Internet-based EDI, we call EDI on the non-Internet platform traditional EDI.

APPLICATIONS OF TRADITIONAL EDI

Traditional EDI has changed the business landscape, triggering new definitions of entire industries. It is used extensively by large corporations; sometimes in a global network such as the one operated by General Electric Information System (which has over 100,000 corporate users). Well-known retailers such as Home Depot, Toys R Us, and Wal-Mart would operate very differently without EDI, because it is an integral and essential element of their business strategies. Thousands of global manufacturers, including Procter & Gamble, Levi Strauss, Toyota, and Unilever, have used EDI to redefine relationships with their customers through such practices as quick-response retailing and just-in-time (JIT) manufacturing. These highly visible, high-impact applications of EDI by large companies have been extremely successful. The benefits of EDI are listed in Exhibit 6A.2.

LIMITATIONS OF TRADITIONAL EDI

However, despite the tremendous impact of traditional EDI among industry leaders, the set of adopters represented only a small fraction of potential EDI users. In the United States, where several million businesses participate in commerce every day, fewer than 100,000 companies have adopted traditional EDI. Furthermore, most of these companies have had only a small number of their business partners on EDI, mainly due to its high cost. Therefore, in reality, few businesses have benefited from EDI. The major factors that held back more universal implementation of traditional EDI include the following:

▶ Significant initial investment is needed, and ongoing operating costs are high.

▶ Business processes must be restructured to fit EDI requirements.

EXHIBIT 6A.1   Traditional and Web-Based EDI

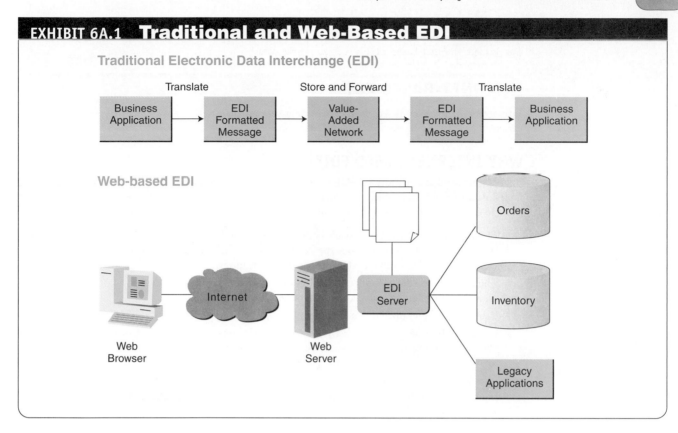

Traditional Electronic Data Interchange (EDI)

Web-based EDI

- A long start-up period is needed.
- EDI requires use of expensive, private VANs.
- EDI has a high operating cost.
- Multiple EDI standards exist, so one company may have to use several standards in order to communicate with different business partners.
- The system is difficult to use.
- A converter is required to translate business transactions to EDI code.
- The system is inflexible; it is difficult to make quick changes, such as adding business partners.

EXHIBIT 6A.2   The Benefits of EDI

- EDI enables companies to send and receive large amounts of routine transaction information quickly around the globe.
- Computer-to-computer data transfer reduces the number of errors.
- Information can flow among several trading partners consistently and freely.
- Companies can access partners' databases to retrieve and store standard transactions.
- EDI fosters true (and strategic) partnership relationships because it involves a commitment to a long-term investment and the refinement of the system over time.
- EDI creates a complete paperless TPS (transaction processing system) environment, saving money and increasing efficiency.
- Payment collection can be shortened by several weeks.
- Data may be entered off-line, in a batch mode, without tying up ports to the mainframe.
- When an EDI document is received, the data may be used immediately.
- Sales information is delivered to manufactures, shippers, and warehouses almost in real time.
- EDI can save companies a considerable amount of money.

These factors suggest that traditional EDI—relying on formal transaction sets, translation software, and VANs—is not suitable as a long-term solution for most corporations. Therefore, a better infrastructure was needed; Internet-based EDI is such an infrastructure.

INTERNET-BASED EDI

Internet-based (or Web-based) EDI is becoming very popular. Let's see why this is the case, review the various types of Web-based EDI, and review its prospects.

WHY INTERNET-BASED EDI?

When considered as a channel for EDI, the Internet appears to be the most feasible alternative for putting online B2B trading within reach of virtually any organization, large or small. There are several reasons for firms to create EDI ability over the Internet.

  ▶ The Internet is a publicly accessible network with few geographical constraints. Its largest attribute, large-scale connectivity (without the need for any special company networking architecture), is a seedbed for growth of a vast range of business applications.
  ▶ The Internet's global network connections offer the potential to reach the widest possible number of trading partners of any viable alternative currently available.
  ▶ Using the Internet instead of a VAN can cut communication costs by over 50 percent.
  ▶ Using the Internet to exchange EDI transactions is consistent with the growing interest of business in delivering an ever-increasing variety of products and services electronically, particularly via the Web.
  ▶ Internet-based EDI can complement or replace many current EDI applications.
  ▶ Internet tools such as browsers and search engines are very user-friendly, and most employees today know how to use them.
  ▶ Internet-based EDI has several functionalities not provided by traditional EDI, which include collaboration, workflow, and search engine capabilities (see Boucher-Ferguson 2002).

TYPES OF INTERNET-BASED EDI

The Internet can support EDI in a variety of ways.

  ▶ Internet e-mail can be used to transport EDI messages in place of a VAN. To this end, standards for encapsulating the messages within Secure Internet Mail Extension (S/MIME) were established.
  ▶ A company can create an extranet that enables its trading partners to enter information into a Web form, the fields of which correspond to the fields in an EDI message or document.
  ▶ Companies can use a Web-based EDI hosting service in much the same way that companies rely on third parties to host their EC sites. Netscape Enterprise is an example of the type of Web-based EDI software that enables a company to provide their own EDI services over the Internet. Harbinger Express is an example of those companies that provide third-party hosting services.

THE PROSPECTS OF INTERNET-BASED EDI

Companies that used traditional EDI in the past have had a positive response to Internet-based EDI. With traditional EDI, companies have to pay for network transport, translation, and routing of EDI messages into their legacy processing systems. The Internet simply serves as a cheaper alternative transport mechanism. The combination of the Web, XML, and Java makes EDI worthwhile even for small, infrequent transactions. Whereas EDI is not interactive, the Web and Java were designed specifically for interactivity as well as ease of use.

The following examples demonstrate the benefits of Internet-based EDI.

  ▶ Compucom Systems was averaging 5,000 transactions per month with traditional EDI. In just a short time after the transition to Web-based EDI, the company was able to average 35,000 transactions. The system helped the company to grow rapidly.
  ▶ Tradelink of Hong Kong was successful in recruiting only several hundred of the potential 70,000 companies to a traditional EDI that communicated with government agencies regarding export/import transactions. In 2001, Tradelink's Internet-based system had thousands of companies registered, and hundreds were being added monthly.
  ▶ Atkins Carlyle Corp., which buys from 6,000 suppliers and has 12,000 customers in Australia, is a wholesaler of industrial, electrical, and automotive parts. The large suppliers were using three differ-

ent EDI platforms. By moving to an Internet-based EDI, the company is able to collaborate with many more business partners, reducing the transaction cost by about $2 per message.

▶ Procter & Gamble replaced a traditional EDI system that had 4,000 business partners with an Internet-based system that has tens of thousands suppliers.

Note that many companies no longer refer to their collaborative systems as EDI, and the term may even disappear altogether. However, the *properties* of EDI are embedded in new e-commerce initiatives such as collaborative commerce and electronic exchanges.

REFERENCE

Boucher-Ferguson, R. "A New Shipping Rout (Web-EDI)." *eWeek*, September 23, 2002.

CHAPTER 7

PUBLIC B2B EXCHANGES AND PORTALS

Learning objectives

Upon completion of this chapter, you will be able to:

1. Define e-marketplaces and exchanges and describe their major types.
2. Describe the various ownership and revenue models of exchanges.
3. Describe B2B portals.
4. Describe third-party exchanges.
5. Distinguish between purchasing (procurement) and selling consortia.
6. Define dynamic trading and describe B2B auctions.
7. Discuss integration issues of e-marketplaces and exchanges.
8. Describe the major support services of B2B.
9. Discuss exchange networks and exchange management.
10. Describe the critical success factors of exchanges.

Content

ChemConnect: The World Chemical Exchange

CHEMCONNECT: THE WORLD CHEMICAL EXCHANGE

The Problem

The trading of raw and partially processed chemicals, plastics, and related materials is done daily by thousands of companies in almost every country in the world. Before the Internet, the trading process was slow, fragmented, ineffective, and costly. As a result, buyers paid too much, sellers had high expenses, and intermediaries were needed to smooth the trading process.

The Solution

Today, buyers and sellers of chemicals and plastics can meet electronically in a large Internet marketplace called ChemConnect (*chemconnect.com*). Global chemical industry leaders, such as British Petroleum, Dow Chemical, BASF, Hyundai, Sumitomo, and many more, make transactions over ChemConnect every day in real time. They save on transaction costs, reduce cycle time, and find new markets and trading partners around the globe.

ChemConnect provides a trading marketplace and an information portal to over 7,500 members in 135 countries. Members are producers, consumers, distributors, traders, and intermediaries involved in the chemical industry. In 2002, over 60,000 products were traded in this public e-marketplace, which was founded in 1995.

ChemConnect offers its members a Trading Center with three trading places:

1. **Marketplace for buyers.** In this marketplace buyers can find suppliers all over the world. They can post RFQs with reverse auctions, they can negotiate, and more.

2. **Marketplace for sellers.** This marketplace provides sellers with exposure to many potential new customers. It provides automated tools for quick liquidation.

3. **Commodity market platform.** This platform provides a powerful connection to the global spot marketplaces for chemicals, plastics, etc. Members can trade at market prices, access real-time market intelligence, and effectively manage risk. Traders can exchange bids and offers quickly, confidently, and with anonymity, until the deal is complete.

ChemConnect members can use the Trading Center to streamline sales and sourcing processes by automating requests for quotes, proposals, and new suppliers. The center enables a member to negotiate more efficiently with existing business partners as well as with new companies the member may invite to the table—all in complete privacy. With over 7,500 companies, the Trading Center is a highly effective way to get the best prices and terms available on the worldwide market. In addition, members can access a database containing more than 60,000 chemicals and plastics—virtually any product members are ever likely to look for.

ChemConnect is an independent, third-party intermediary, thus it works within certain rules and guidelines that ensure an unbiased approach to trades. All legal requirements, payments, trading rules, and other guidelines are fully disclosed. (Click on "Legal and privacy issues" on the site for more information on disclosure policies.) The revenue model includes members' annual transaction fees, subscription fees (for trading and for auctions), and fulfillment service fees.

All three trading locations provide up-to-the-minute market information that can be translated into 30 different languages. Members pay transaction fees only for successfully completed transactions. Business partners provide several support services. For example, Citigroup and ChemConnect jointly offer several financial services for exchange members. ChemConnect also offers systems for connecting companies' back-end systems with their business partners and with ChemConnect itself.

The Results

The overall benefits of ChemConnect to its members are more efficient business processes, lower overall transaction costs, and time saved during negotiations and biddings. For example, conducting a reverse auction in a trading room allows buyers to save up to 15 percent of a product's cost in just 30 minutes. The same process using manual bidding methods would take several weeks or months. One company that placed an RFQ for 100 metric tons of a certain acid to be delivered in Uruguay with a starting price of $1.10 per kilogram reduced the price to $0.95 in only six consecutive bids offered in 30 minutes. In addition, sellers can reach more buyers and liquidate surpluses rapidly.

ChemConnect is growing rapidly, adding members and increasing its trading volume each year. (Transaction volume in 2001 was over $4 billion.) The company hopes to become profitable in 2003.

Source: Based on information from *chemconnect.com* (March 2002).

WHAT WE CAN LEARN . . .

The ChemConnect story demonstrates an e-marketplace with many buyers and many sellers, all in one industry. These buyers and sellers, as well as other business partners, congregate electronically to conduct business. This type of a marketplace is an *electronic exchange* that is owned and operated by a third-party intermediary. As will be seen later in the chapter, ownership of an exchange has some major implications for B2B marketplaces.

In contrast with the company-centric models that were the focus of Chapter 6, the models in this chapter include *many buyers* and *many sellers*. They are *public* e-marketplaces, known by a variety of names and having a variety of functions. For now, we will simply call them *exchanges*.

7.1 B2B ELECTRONIC EXCHANGES—AN OVERVIEW

public e-marketplaces (public exchanges)
Trading venues open to all interested parties (sellers and buyers) and usually run by third parties.

exchange
A many-to-many e-marketplace. Also known as *e-marketplaces, e-markets,* and *trading exchanges*.

market maker
The third-party that operates an exchange (and in many cases, also owns the exchange).

As defined in Chapter 2, public e-marketplaces, or public exchanges, are trading venues that use a common technology platform open to all interested parties (many sellers and many buyers) and that are usually run by third parties or industry consortia (see Kambil and van Heck 2002). The term exchange is often used to describe many-to-many e-marketplaces. According to *The New Shorter Oxford English Dictionary*, an "exchange" is a building, office, or other area used for the transaction of business or for monetary exchange (e.g., a stock exchange). In the context of e-commerce, exchanges are *virtual* (online) trading venues, not physical locales, and they are electronically operated. Many exchanges support community activities, such as distributing industry news, sponsoring online discussion groups, and providing research. They also provide support services such as payments and logistics (see *Darwin Magazine* 2001).

Exchanges are known by a variety of names: *e-marketplaces, e-markets,* and *trading exchanges*. Other terms include *trading communities, exchange hubs, Internet exchanges, Net marketplaces,* and *B2B portals*. We will use the term *exchange* in this book to describe the general many-to-many e-marketplaces, but we will use some of the other terms in more specific contexts (e.g., see Sharma 2002).

The various types of e-marketplaces include B2B portals, third-party trading exchanges, consortium trading exchanges, and dynamic trading floors for matching. Auctions can be part of any of these types of exchanges. As discussed in the next section ("Classification of Exchanges"), exchanges can be vertical (industry oriented) or horizontal, and they can be used for long-term buying relationships or for fulfilling a short-term need. Despite their variety, all exchanges share one major characteristic: Exchanges are electronic trading-community meeting places for many sellers and many buyers, and possibly for other business partners, as shown in Exhibit 7.1. In the center of every exchange is a market maker, the third party that operates an exchange (and in many cases, also owns the exchange).

In an exchange, just as in a traditional open-air marketplace, buyers and sellers can interact and negotiate prices and quantities. Generally, free-market economics rule the exchange trade community, as demonstrated by ChemConnect.

According to Forrester Research (as reported by Shetty 2001), 2,500 exchanges worldwide, at several stages of operation, were in operation in the spring of 2001. Since then, more than 50 percent have folded due to a lack of customers, cash, or both (e.g., Chemdex and MetalSite). However, the companies that use exchanges, both as sellers and buyers, are generally pleased with them and plan to increase the number of exchanges they are participating in (from 1.7 to 4.1, on average), within 2 years (Dolinoy et al. 2001). The traders expect to more than double the value of transactions that they do through the exchanges.

CLASSIFICATION OF EXCHANGES

Exchanges can be classified in several ways. We will use the approach suggested by Kaplan and Sawhney (2000) and by Durlacher Research (2000). According to this classi-

EXHIBIT 7.1   Trading Communities: Information Flow and Access to Information

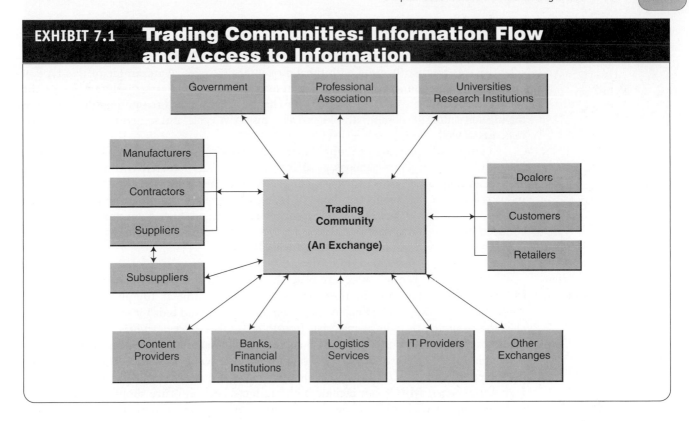

fication, an exchange can be classified into one of four cells of a matrix, as shown in Exhibit 7.2. The matrix is composed of two dimensions. Across the top, two types of materials are traded, either *direct* or *indirect* (MRO), as defined in Chapter 2. Down the left side are two possible sourcing strategies: *systematic* or *spot* sourcing. Systematic sourcing deals with purchases made in long-term supplier–buyer relationships. Spot sourcing refers to unplanned purchasing; that is, purchases made as the need arises. The intersection of these characteristics results in four exchange classifications (the four cells of Exhibit 7.2).

systematic sourcing
Purchasing done in long-term supplier–buyer relationships.

spot sourcing
Unplanned purchases made as the need arises.

EXHIBIT 7.2   Classification of B2B Exchanges

	Direct	Indirect (MRO)
Systematic Sourcing	(1) Vertical Distributors *plastics.com* *epapertrade.com* Methods: Aggregation, fixed/negotiated prices	(2) Horizontal Distributors *mro.com* Methods: Aggregation, fixed/negotiated prices
Spot Sourcing	(3) Vertical Exchanges *isteelasia.com* *chemconnect.com* Methods: Matching, dynamic pricing	(4) Horizontal Exchanges *employease.com* Methods: Matching, dynamic pricing

If systematic sourcing is used for direct materials, the market maker aggregates the buyers, the sellers, or both, and provides the platform for *negotiated* prices and contracted terms (first cell). Systematic sourcing of direct materials, which are usually traded in large quantities, is frequently done with the aid of intermediaries. An example of this type of exchange can be found at plastics.com, an exchange for the plastics industry. Using the speed, access, and ease of the Internet, the exchange simplifies and streamlines the process of buying and selling at substantially reduced administrative costs, and sometimes reduced product costs as well.

In systematic sourcing of indirect materials (MROs) (second cell), the market maker basically aggregates sellers' catalogs, as MRO.com (mro.com) does. MRO.com provides tools and technology in a hosted environment that enables manufacturers and distributors of industrial parts—the "supply" of the industrial supply chain—to participate in EC quickly and affordably. MRO.com creates one catalog containing products from multiple suppliers, connects the catalog to an order processing system, and offers different types of industrial buyers a single source from which to buy their MROs.

Spot sourcing of *direct materials* (third cell) takes place in vertical exchanges, which are considered vertical because sales take place in one industry or industry segment. Examples of a vertical exchange are the trading rooms of ChemConnect and an exchange called ISteelAsia (isteelasia.com), which conducts online auctions and bids for steel.

Spot sourcing of indirect materials (fourth cell) takes places in horizontal exchanges. These exchanges are considered horizontal because they handle materials traded for use by companies from different industries. For example, light bulbs and office supplies might be purchased in a horizontal exchange by both an automaker and a steelmaker. (In these horizontal exchanges, MROs can include both products, such as office supplies, and services, such as temporary labor.) Horizontal exchanges offer a variety of mechanisms, as shown in Exhibit 7.3.

vertical exchanges

An exchange whose members are in one industry or industry segment.

horizontal exchanges

Exchanges that handle materials used by companies in different industries.

DYNAMIC PRICING

The market makers in both vertical and horizontal exchanges match supply and demand in their exchanges, and this matching determines prices. In spot sourcing, the prices are *dynamic* and are based on changes in supply and demand. Dynamic pricing refers to a rapid movement of prices over time, and possibly across customers, as a result of supply and demand at any given time. Stock exchanges are the prime example of dynamic pricing. Prices on stock exchanges sometimes change second by second, depending at any moment on how much buyers are willing to pay for a stock and how many sellers of that stock are willing to sell at various prices. Another good example of dynamic pricing occurs in *auctions*, where prices vary all the time. The result of dynamic pricing may be that exactly the same product or service is sold to different customers at different prices.

Dynamic pricing is based on market information being available to buyers and sellers. One of the reasons the U.S. stock exchanges are thought to work as well as they do is the amount of financial information generally available to the traders. The Internet and certain market mechanisms (such as auctions) provide a large amount of product information, sometimes in real time. Therefore, the Internet facilitates many of the dynamic pricing models for both B2B and B2C. For example, Priceline.com uses a reverse auction process that results in dynamic pricing.

The typical process that results in dynamic pricing in most exchanges includes the following steps:

dynamic pricing

A rapid movement of prices over time, and possibly across customers, as a result of supply and demand.

1. A company posts a bid to buy a product or an offer to sell one.
2. Buyers and sellers can see the bids and offers but may not always see who is making them. Anonymity is often a key ingredient of dynamic pricing.
3. Buyers and sellers interact with bids and offers in real time. Sometimes buyers join together to obtain a volume discount price (group purchasing).

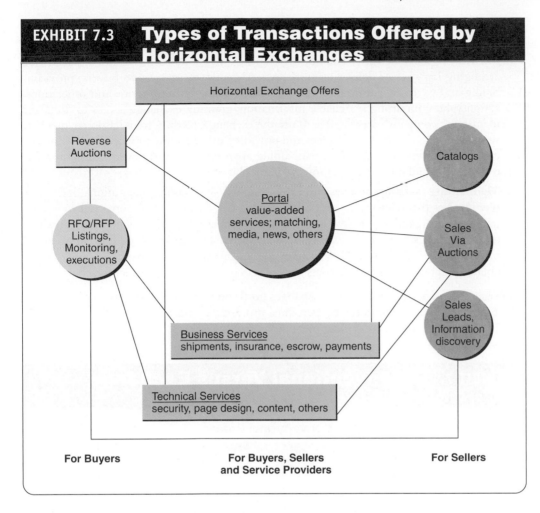

EXHIBIT 7.3   Types of Transactions Offered by Horizontal Exchanges

4. A deal is struck when there is an exact match between a buyer and a seller on price, volume, and other variables such as location or quality.

5. The deal is consummated, and payment and delivery are arranged.

Third-party companies outside the exchange provide supporting services such as credit verification, quality assurance, escrow service, insurance, and order fulfillment. They ensure that the buyer has the money and that the product is in good condition. They also coordinate product delivery (see Chapter 14).

In Chapter 6, we described group purchasing and forward auctions, which also employ dynamic pricing. When dynamic pricing is used with methods such as auctions, the process is referred to as *dynamic trading*. For example, IBM's WebSphere commerce suite (see Online Chapter 18) includes a dynamic trading module that enables reverse auctions, exchanges, and contract negotiations.

FUNCTIONS OF EXCHANGES

According to brint.com (2002), exchanges have three major functions:

1. **Matching buyers and sellers.** The matching of buyers and sellers includes such activities as establishing product offerings; aggregating and posting different products for sale; providing price and product information, including recommendations; organizing bids, bartering, and auctions; matching supplier offerings with buyer preferences; enabling

price and product comparisons; supporting negotiations and agreements between buyers and suppliers; and providing directories of buyers and sellers.

2. **Facilitating transactions.** Facilitating transactions includes the following activities: arranging logistics of delivering information, goods, or services to buyers; providing billing and payment information, including addresses; defining terms and other transaction values; inputting searchable information; granting exchange access to users and identifying company users eligible to use the exchange; settling transaction payments to suppliers, collecting transaction fees and providing other escrow services; registering and qualifying buyers and suppliers; maintaining appropriate security over information and transactions; and arranging for group (volume) buying.

3. **Maintaining exchange policies and infrastructure.** Maintaining institutional infrastructure involves the following activities: ascertaining compliance with commercial code, contract law, export and import laws, and intellectual property law for transactions made within the exchange; maintaining technological infrastructure to support volume and complexity of transactions; providing interface capability to standard systems of buyers and suppliers; and obtaining appropriate site advertisers and collecting advertising and other fees.

To execute these various functions, exchanges go through a process shown in Exhibit 7.4. The top of the exhibit shows the conventional process. The bottom shows the EC process. As can be seen, the EC process is simpler (and quicker).

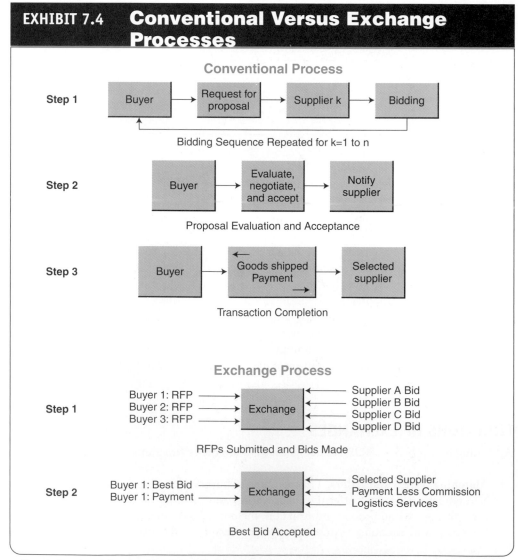

EXHIBIT 7.4 Conventional Versus Exchange Processes

OWNERSHIP, GOVERNANCE, AND ORGANIZATION OF EXCHANGES

Before we conclude our overview of exchanges and move on to detailed discussions of each type of exchange, we should pause to look at issues related to the ownership and organization of exchanges.

Ownership of Exchanges

Ownership models for Internet exchanges are of three basic types: industry giant, neutral entrepreneur, and a consortium.

▶ **An industry giant.** One manufacturer, distributor, or broker sets up the exchange and runs it. An example is IBM, which established an exchange for the purpose of selling patents (delphion.com). Initially, in 1999, IBM placed 25,000 of its own patents up for sale and invited others to sell their patents as well. This model is an extension of the sell-side model described in Chapter 6. General Electric's TPN is another classic example of a buy-side exchange controlled by an industry giant. It led to the creation of the GXS exchange, which is now owned by a group of investors. In the past, Samsung of Korea manually brokered various commodities; in 2002 it had several online exchanges, including one for fish. The major potential problem for this type of exchange is whether the giant's large competitors will be willing to use it.

▶ **A neutral entrepreneur.** A *third-party* intermediary sets up an exchange and promises to run an efficient and unbiased exchange. ChemConnect, for example, is one such neutral exchange. (This type of exchange is discussed in Section 7.3.) The potential problem for such exchanges is whether buyers and sellers will use the exchange.

▶ **The consortia (or co-op).** With this type of exchange, several industry players get together and decide to set up an exchange so that all can benefit. Covisint is an example of such as exchange. (Consortia are discussed in Section 7.4.) A major potential problem with this model is determining who is in charge of the exchange.

Revenue Models

Exchanges, like all organizations, require revenue to survive. Therefore, an exchange's owners, whoever they are, must decide how they will earn revenue. The following are potential sources of revenue for exchanges.

▶ **Transaction fees.** Transaction fees are basically a commission paid *by sellers* for each transaction they make (see Chapter 1). However, sellers may object to transaction fees, especially when their regular customers are involved. Exchanges charge relatively low transaction fees per order in order to attract sellers. Therefore, to cover its expenses, the exchange must generate sufficient volume (or be forced to raise its transaction fees).

▶ **Fee for service.** Some exchanges have successfully changed their revenue model from commission (transaction fee) to "fee for service." Sellers are more willing to pay for value-added services than they are to pay commissions. Sometimes buyers will also pay some service charges.

▶ **Membership fees.** A membership fee is usually a fixed annual or monthly fee. It usually entitles the exchange member to get some services free or at a discount. In some countries, such as China, the government may ask members to pay annual membership fees, and then provide the participating sellers with free services and no transaction fees. This encourages members to use the exchange. The problem is that low membership fees may result in insufficient revenue to the exchange. On the other hand, high membership fees discourage participants from joining.

▶ **Advertising fees.** Exchanges can also derive income from fees for advertising on the information-portal part of the exchange. For example, some sellers may want to increase their exposure and will pay for special advertisements on the portal (like boxed ads in the yellow pages of telephone books).

▶ **Other revenue sources.** If the company is doing auctions, it can charge auction fees. License fees can be collected on patented information or software. Finally, market makers can collect fees for their services.

Governance and Organization

Exchanges have their own board of directors and are governed by guidelines and rules, some of which are required by law. These rules and guidelines must be very specific regarding how the exchange operates, what the requirements are to join the exchange, what fees are involved, and what rules need to be followed. Furthermore, the governance document needs to specify security and privacy arrangements, what will happen in case of disputes, and so forth. The contract terms between an exchange and buyers and sellers are also critical, as are assurances that the exchange is fair.

Regardless of their ownership, revenue model, and governance structure, exchanges may include the following organizational elements.

Membership. Membership refers to the community in the exchange, which depends to some extent on the revenue model. For example, exchanges that do not charge members a fee to join (e.g., alibaba.com) may collect transaction or service fees. For exchanges that charge registration fees and annual membership fees (e.g., chemconnect.com), varying levels of membership may be offered. For example, members may be either *observing members*, who can only view what is going on but not trade, or *trading members*, who can make offers and bid, pay, and arrange deliveries. Trading members usually need to go through a qualification process with the market maker. In some cases a cash deposit is required. There may be other categories of members (e.g., associate members). Some exchanges set limits on how much each member can trade.

Site access and security. Exchanges must be secure. Because members' activities can be very strategic and competitors frequently congregate in the same exchange, information should be carefully protected. In addition to the regular EC security measures, special attention should be made to prevent illegal offers and bids. Several exchanges have a list of individuals that are authorized to represent the participating companies.

Services provided by exchanges. Exchanges provide many services to buyers and sellers. The types of services offered depend on the nature of the exchange. For example, the services provided by a stock exchange are completely different from those provided by a steel or food exchange or by an intellectual property or patent exchange. However, there are some services that most exchanges provide. These are shown in Exhibit 7.5.

ADVANTAGES AND LIMITATIONS OF EXCHANGES

Exchanges have several benefits, including making markets more efficient, providing opportunities for sellers and buyers to find new business partners, cutting the administrative costs of ordering MROs, and expediting processes. They also facilitate global trade and create communities of informed buyers and sellers.

Despite these benefits, beginning in 2001, exchanges started to collapse, and both buyers and sellers realized that they faced the risk of exchange failure or deterioration. In the case

EXHIBIT 7.5   Services in Exchanges

The Exchange

Sellers
A
B
C
D
•
•
•

- Buyer-seller registration, qualification, coordination
- Catalog management (conversion, integration, maintenance)
- Communication / protocol translation (EDI, XML, CORBA)
- Sourcing—RFQ, bid coordination (product configuration, negotiation)
- Security, anonymity
- Software: groupware, workflow
- Integration with members' back-office systems
- Auction management
- News, information, industry analysis
- Support services (financing, payment, insurance, logistics, tax, escrow, order tracking)
- Administration—profiles, statistics, etc.

Buyers
X
Y
Z
•
•
•

EXHIBIT 7.6	**Gains and Risks in B2B Exchanges**	
	For Buyers	**For Sellers**
Potential gains	• One-stop shopping, huge variety • Search and comparison shopping • Volume discounts • 24/7 ordering from any location • Make one order from several suppliers • Unlimited, detailed information • Access to new suppliers • Status review and easy reordering • Fast delivery • Less maverick buying	• New sales channel • No physical store is needed • Reduced ordering errors • Sell 24/7 • Reach new customers at little extra cost • Promote the business via the exchange • An outlet for surplus inventory • Can go global more easily
Potential risks	• Unknown vendors; may not be reliable • Loss of customer service quality (inability to compare all services)	• Loss of direct CRM and PRM • Price wars • Competition for value-added services • Transaction fees (including on seller's existing customers) • Possible loss of customers to competitors

of exchange failure, the risk is primarily a financial one—of suddenly losing the market in which one has been buying and selling, and therefore having to scramble to find a new exchange or to find buyers and sellers on one's own. In addition, finding a new place to trade is an operational risk. Buyers also risk potentially poor product performance and receipt of incomplete information from degraded exchanges, which is a risk the seller may face too.

The potential gains and risks of B2B exchanges for buyers and for sellers are summarized in Exhibit 7.6. As the exhibit shows, the gains outnumber the risks.

Section 7.1 ▌ REVIEW

1. Define B2B exchanges and list the various types of public e-marketplaces.
2. Define systematic sourcing and spot sourcing.
3. Differentiate between a vertical exchange and a horizontal exchange.
4. What is dynamic pricing? How does it work?
5. Describe the types of ownership and the possible revenue models of exchanges.
6. List the potential advantages, gains, limitations, and risks of exchanges.

7.2 B2B PORTALS

As you may recall, selling in B2C can be conducted in various types of public or private Web sites. Some of these public sites are *information portals* (often called just *portals*), such as Yahoo, where information (such as Yahoo's shopping directory) is targeted at individual customers or businesses. Orders can be placed from some portals; but in most cases the buyer is transferred to a seller's storefront to complete the transaction. Some portals provide order-taking and order-fulfillment services, making them e-marketplaces.

Similar situations exist in B2B. B2B portals are information portals for businesses. Some exchanges act as pure information portals. They usually include *directories* of products offered by each seller, lists of buyers and what they want, and other industry or general information. Buyers can then hyperlink to sellers' sites to complete trades. However, information portals may have a difficult time generating revenues, and so they are starting to offer, for a fee, additional services that support trading. This brings them closer to being trading communities or *exchanges*. An example B2B portal is MyBoeingFleet.com (myboeingfleet.com), which is a Web portal for airplane owners, operators, and MRO operators. Developed by

B2B portals

Information portals for businesses.

Boeing Commercial Aviation Services, MyBoeingFleet.com provides customers (primarily businesses) direct and personalized access to information essential to the operation of Boeing aircraft.

Like exchanges, information portals can be horizontal (e.g., Alibaba.com, described later), offering a wide range of products to different industries. Or, they can be vertical, focusing on a single industry or industry segment. Vertical portals are often referred to as **vortals**.

vortals
B2B portals that focus on a single industry or industry segment; "vertical portals."

Some use the word portal as equivalent to an exchange. The reason is that many B2B portals are adding capabilities that make them look like a full exchange. Also, many exchanges include their own information portals.

The two examples that follow illustrate some of the differences between *portals* and *exchanges*.

THOMAS REGISTER

Thomas Register of America (thomasregister.com), an information portal, publishes a directory of millions of manufacturing companies. In 1998, it teamed up with General Electric to create the TPN Register (now embedded in GXS), a portal that facilitates business transactions for MROs. TPN Register worked with buyers and sellers to build electronic trading communities. Sellers can distribute information on what they have to sell; buyers can find what they need and purchase over a comprehensive and secure procurement channel that helps them reduce costs, shrink cycle times, and improve productivity. For-fee services are also available. However, the Thomas Register is basically an information portal because it does not offer any opportunity for transactions on its site. For example, it does not offer a list of products with quantities needed (offers to buy) or offered (want to sell). A similar information-only service is provided by Manufacturing.Net (manufacturing.net).

ALIBABA.COM

Another intermediary that started as a pure information portal and is moving toward becoming a trading exchange is Alibaba.com (alibaba.com). Launched in 1999, Alibaba.com initially concentrated on China; in March 2003, it had over 1.6 registered traders in 216 countries. It includes a large, robust community of international buyers and sellers who are interested in direct trade without an intermediary. Initially, the site was a huge posting place for classified ads. Alibaba.com is a portal in transition, showing some characteristics of an information portal plus some services of an exchange. To understand the capabilities of Alibaba.com, we need to explore its marketplace capabilities and offerings.

The Database

The center of Alibaba.com is its huge database, which is basically a horizontal information portal with offerings in a wide variety of product categories. The portal is organized into 27 major product categories (as of 2003), including agriculture, apparel and fashion, automobiles, and toys. Each product category is further divided into subcategories (over 700 in total). For example, the toy category includes items such as dolls, electrical pets, and wooden toys. Each subcategory includes classified ads organized into four groups: sellers, buyers, agents, and cooperation. Each group may include many companies. The ads are fairly short. Note that in all cases a user can click on an ad for details. Currently, all ads are posted for free. Some categories have thousands of postings; therefore, a search engine is provided. The search engine works by country, type of advertiser, and age of the postings.

Reverse Auctions

Alibaba.com also allows buyers to post an RFQ. Would-be sellers can then send bids to the buyer, conduct negotiations, and accept a purchase order when one is offered. As of March 2003, the process was not fully automated. (To see how the process works, go to "My trade activity" and take the tour, initiate a negotiation, and issue a purchase order.)

Features and Services

In fall 2002, the following features were provided: free e-mail, free e-mail alerts, a China club membership, news (basically related to importing and exporting), legal information, arbitration, and forums and discussion groups. In addition, a member can create a company Web page, as well as a "sample house" (for showing their products); members can also post their own marketing leads (where to buy and sell). As of 2003, the site offers its services in English, Chinese, and Korean.

Certain other services are available for a fee. For-fee services include, for example, business credit reports, export/import reports, and a quote center for shipping services. In the future, additional services will be added to increase the company's revenue stream.

Alibaba.com also has a subsidiary, china.alibaba.com, a marketplace for China's domestic trade.

Revenue Model

As of fall 2002, the site's revenue stream was limited to advertisement and fees for special services. Alibaba.com competes with several global exchanges that provide similar services (e.g., see chinatradeworld.com and globalsources.com). The advantage of Alibaba.com is its low operational cost. Therefore, it will be able to sustain losses much longer than its competitors. Someday in the future, Alibaba.com may be in a position that will enable it to make a great deal of money. Possible sources of future revenue are one-time registration fees, annual maintenance fees, transaction fees, and fees for services. Will Alibaba.com be strong enough to sustain losses until that day? According to experts (see Section 7.7), there is a good chance it will. By then, with its added capabilities, Alibaba.com may have evolved into a trading exchange.

Section 7.2 ❱ REVIEW

1. Define B2B portals.
2. Distinguish a vortal from a horizontal portal.
3. List the major services provided by Alibaba.com.

7.3 THIRD-PARTY (TRADING) EXCHANGES

The opening vignette introduced us to ChemConnect, a neutral, public, third-party market maker. ChemConnect's initial success was well publicized, and dozens of similar third-party exchanges, mostly in specific industries, have been developed since. A thriving example of a third-party exchange is Rawmart.com, described in EC Application Case 7.1 (page 270).

Some other successful exchanges are RetailExchange (retailexchange.com), which links manufacturers and retailers to buy and sell excess inventory (5,000 members and $306 billion in goods in 2002); Neoforma Inc. (neoforma.com), which sells medical supplies; Globalnetxchange (gnx.com), which specializes in auctions, mostly to retailers; Global Healthcare Exchange (ghx.com), which specializes in hospital supplies; i-MARK (imark.com), which sells surpluses; Winery Exchange (wineryexchange.com), which specializes in wines; and ChemConnect (chemconnect.com), which offers chemicals and plastics.

Third-party exchanges are characterized by two contradicting properties. On one hand, they are *neutral*, not favoring either sellers or buyers. On the other hand, because they do not have a built-in constituency of sellers or buyers, they sometimes have a problem attracting enough buyers and sellers to attain financial viability. Therefore, to increase their financial viability, these exchanges try to team up with partners such as large sellers or buyers, financial institutions that provide payment schemes (as ChemConnect did with Citigroup), and logistics companies that fulfill orders. The goal of such partnerships and alliances is to increase liquidity. **Market liquidity** is the degree to which something can be bought or sold in a marketplace without affecting its price (e.g., without having

market liquidity
The degree to which something can be bought or sold in a marketplace without affecting its price.

CASE 7.1
EC Application
GLOBAL TRADING OF RAW MATERIALS AT RAWMART.COM

The Noble Group Limited (*thisisnoble.com*) supplies industry with the raw materials and transport resources that drive economic growth worldwide. It created Rawmart.com as an e-commerce initiative that integrates the sourcing, marketing, processing, financing, insuring, and transporting of industrial and agricultural commodities on a global basis.

Created by traders for traders, the Rawmart site (*rawmart.com*) is a multilingual (seven languages) online information and trading tool for producers, traders, and consumers of raw materials and commodities. Over 650 product categories are available. This information hub connects buyers and sellers in seven major industries, including agribusiness, chemicals, energy, metals, minerals, plastics, and pulp and paper, 24 hours a day.

Rawmart.com permits the entire procurement cycle of raw materials to be carried out in an environment customized to any company's needs. Decision makers can find more than 3,000 daily news items, 191 commodities prices and equity indices, and five detailed reports on 14 commodities. The site also offers weekly commodities reports, 32 weekly online newsletters, links to industry associations, a glossary and library with over 2,000 definitions and entries, more than 300 listings of industry events and conferences, and a world business holiday calendar for 63 countries. Each user can view and incorporate the rates of exchange, weather, and global time displays as needed into their transactions.

Site registration is free. The exchange offers eDeals—a free 60–day, buy-or-sell product listing. Registered members can browse and reply to the eDeal listings. For a low one-time fixed fee, users can build a personalized company profile, in which the company's name is listed in its chosen product or service categories. Rawmart.com customers can contact each other by clicking on the company profiles. Requests for Information (RFIs) and RFQs are then forwarded by Rawmart.com customer services. All members have unlimited free access to all product listings. Members can contact suppliers or buyers directly via an instant response box. All negotiations are private and take place solely between the buyer and supplier (within the infrastructure that Rawmart provides).

Source: Compiled from *rawmart.com* (2002).

Questions

1. Enter *rawmart.com*. Read any recent developments. What is the site's current revenue model?

2. Why is third-party ownership suited for this exchange?

3. Examine Exhibit 7.3. Which of the transactions listed there is offered by Rawmart.com?

---

to discount the price). In order to achieve liquidity in a market, there must be a sufficient number of participants in the marketplace as well as a sufficient volume of transactions (see Section 7.7).

However, not all partnerships bring the desired results. In a partnership that did not work, Chemdex, a pioneering exchange that closed in late 2000, allied itself with VWR Scientific Products, a large brick-and-mortar intermediary. In the case of Chemdex, its liquidity was not large enough, despite the alliance.

Third-party exchanges are electronic intermediaries. In contrast with a portal, such as Alibaba.com, the intermediary not only presents catalogs (which the portal does), but also tries to *match* buyers and sellers and encourage them to make transactions by providing electronic trading floors and rooms (which portals, in general, do not). Let's see how this is done by looking at two models of third-party exchanges: supplier aggregation and buyer aggregation.

THE SUPPLIER AGGREGATION MODEL

In the *supplier aggregation model*, virtual distributors standardize, index, and aggregate suppliers' catalogs or content and make this content available to buyers in a centralized location. The hosting can be done by an ISP or by a large telecommunications company such as NTT, Deutsche Telecom, or MCI.

An example is Commerce One's catalog of MRO suppliers at commerceone.net. As shown in Exhibit 7.7, Commerce One aggregates suppliers' catalogs and presents them to potential buyers. (This model is similar to the sell-side e-marketplace described in Chapter 6, but with *many* sellers.)

EXHIBIT 7.7 Supplier Aggregation Model

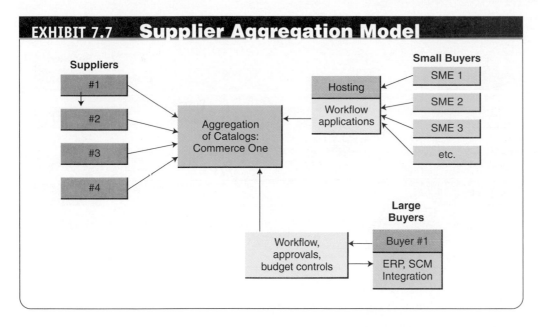

Notice that Exhibit 7.7 shows two types of buyers: large and small (SMEs). Large buyers need software to support the purchase-approval process (e.g., workflow software, see Chapter 8), budgeting, and the tracking of purchases across the buying organization. This requires system integration with existing company regulations, contracts, pricing, and so forth. Such integration may be provided by an ERP architecture. As you may recall from Chapter 6, Bigboxx.com provided such a service to its large buyers using SAP software (see EC Application Case 6.1 on page 224). (For more on ERP integration, see Norris et al. 2000 and Chapter 8.) For smaller buyers, hosted workflow and applications are available from ASPs, which team up with aggregators such as Ariba and Commerce One.

The major problems encountered in the supplier aggregation model are in recruiting suppliers and introducing the system to buyers. Solving these problems requires a strategic plan (see Cunningham 2000).

THE BUYER AGGREGATION MODEL

In the *buyer aggregation model*, buyers' RFQs are aggregated and then linked to a pool of suppliers that are automatically notified of the RFQs. The suppliers can then make bids. (This is similar to the buy-side e-marketplace described in Chapter 6). The buyers (usually small businesses) can benefit from volume discounts, especially if they use a group purchasing approach. The sellers benefit from the new source of pooled buyers. Exhibit 7.8 (page 272) shows the buyer aggregation model.

SUITABILITY OF THIRD-PARTY EXCHANGES

The aggregation models work best with MROs and services that are well defined, that have stable prices, and where the supplier or buyer base is fragmented. Buyers save on search and transaction costs and are exposed to more sellers. Sellers benefit from lower transaction costs as well as from an increase in their customer base.

As in other types of e-marketplaces, the most important key to the success of any third-party exchange is the critical mass of buyers and sellers (the liquidity). Fram (2002) believes that third-party exchanges, if properly planned and built, will be one of the prominent EC pillars of the future.

Section 7.3 ▶ REVIEW

1. What is a third-party exchange?
2. Define liquidity.

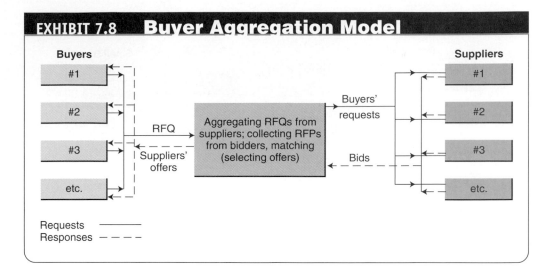

EXHIBIT 7.8   Buyer Aggregation Model

3. Describe the supplier aggregation exchange.

4. Describe the buyer aggregation exchange.

5. List the market characteristics that are most suitable for third-party exchanges.

7.4 CONSORTIUM TRADING EXCHANGES

consortium trading exchange (CTE)
An exchange formed and operated by a group of major companies to provide industrywide transaction services.

A subset of third-party exchanges is a **consortium trading exchange (CTE)**, an exchange formed and operated by a group of major companies. The major declared goal of CTEs (also called *consortia*) is to provide industrywide transaction services that support buying and selling. These services include links to the participants' back-end processing systems, as well as collaborative planning and design services.

Markets operate in three basic types of environments, shown in the following list. The type of environment indicates which third-party exchange is the most appropriate to use.

1. **Fragmented markets.** These markets have large numbers of both buyers and sellers. Examples include the life sciences and food industries. Where a large percentage of the market is fragmented, third-party–managed exchanges are most appropriate.

2. **Seller-concentrated markets.** In this type of market, several large companies sell to a very large number of buyers. Examples are the plastics and transportation industries. In this type of market, consortia may be most appropriate.

3. **Buyer-concentrated markets.** In this type of market, several large companies do most of the buying from a large number of suppliers. Examples are the automotive, airline, and electronics industries. Here, again, consortia may be most appropriate.

According to Karpinski (2001), CTEs fared much better than third-party independent exchanges during the dot-com shake-out that took place in 2000–2001. Yet, of the hundreds of CTEs that existed all over the world in 2000, by 2002 many had folded or were inactive.

There are four types of CTEs, defined by two main criteria: (1) whether they focus on buying or selling, and (2) whether they are vertical or horizontal. The four types of consortia are:

1. Purchasing oriented, vertical
2. Purchasing oriented, horizontal
3. Selling oriented, vertical
4. Selling oriented, horizontal

In addition to these categories, some CTEs (such as global transportation network (GTN), described in the Real-World Case at the end of the chapter) focus on providing services. The following sections describe the characteristics of each type of CTE, offer examples of each of type, and examine several issues related to consortia.

PURCHASING-ORIENTED CONSORTIA

Purchasing-oriented (procurement) consortia are by far the most popular B2B consortium model. The basic idea is that a group of companies join together in order to streamline the purchasing processes. Some claim that another goal of procurement consortia is to pressure suppliers to cut prices. This model can be either vertical or horizontal.

Vertical Purchasing-Oriented CTEs

Most CTEs are *vertical*, meaning that all the players are in the same industry. One example is Covisint, discussed in EC Application Case 7.2 (page 274) (also see Baker and Baker 2000).

Although the declared objective of vertical procurement CTEs is to support buying *and* selling, it is obvious that in a market owned and operated by large buyers the orientation is toward purchasing. Many of the consortia in Exhibit 7.9 (page 275) are vertical exchanges (e.g., aerospace, airlines, hospitality, mining, retailers). Each exchange may have tens of thousands of suppliers.

Horizontal Purchasing-Oriented CTEs

In a *horizontal* purchasing-oriented CTE, the owner-operators are large companies from different industries that unite for the purpose of improving the supply chain of MROs used by most industries. An example of this kind of CTE is Corprocure in Australia (corprocure.com). Fourteen of the largest companies in Australia (Qantas, Telstra Communications, the Post Office, ANZ Banking Group, Coles Myer, Coca-Cola, etc.) created the Corprocure exchange in 2001 to buy MROs.

SELLING-ORIENTED CONSORTIA

Selling-oriented consortia are less common than buying-oriented ones. Most selling-oriented consortia are vertical. Participating sellers have thousands of potential buyers within a particular industry. Here are some examples of selling-oriented consortia:

- Cargill, a producer of basic food ingredients, has a wide range of buyers and has major ownership in a food exchange (cargill.com).
- Several international airline consortia act like large travel agencies, selling tickets or travel packages to business buyers (e.g., lexres.com) and individuals (orbitz.com).
- Suppliers and distributors of health-care products (e.g., ghx.com).
- Plastics consortia (e.g., trplastics.com).

OTHER ISSUES FOR CONSORTIA

Consortia face a variety of other issues, including legal challenges. This section presents these challenges and also looks at the critical success factors for the success of consortia and the issue of combining consortia and third-party exchanges.

Legal Challenges for B2B Consortia

B2B exchanges and other e-marketplaces typically introduce some level of collaboration among both competitors and business partners. In both cases, antitrust and other competition laws must be considered. The concept of consortia itself may lead to antitrust scrutiny by governments, especially for industries in which either a few firms produce most or all of the output (oligopolies or monopolies) or in which there are only a few buyers (monopsonies). This could happen in many countries, especially in European countries, the United States, Australia, Japan, Korea, Hong Kong, and Canada.

CASE 7.2
EC Application
COVISINT: THE E-MARKET OF THE AUTOMOTIVE INDUSTRY

There are only several automakers, but they buy parts, materials, and supplies from tens of thousands of suppliers, who frequently buy parts and materials from thousands of subsuppliers. At times, the procurement process is slow, costly, and ineffective.

On February 25, 2000, General Motors Corporation, Ford Motor Company, and DaimlerChrysler launched a B2B integrated buy-side marketplace called Covisint. The goal was to eliminate redundancies from suppliers through integration and collaboration, with promises of lower costs, easier business practices, and marked increases in efficiencies for the entire industry.

The name Covisint (pronounced KO-vis-int) is a combination of the primary concepts of why the exchange was formed: The letters "Co" represent *connectivity, collaboration*, and *communication;* "vis" represents the *visibility* that the Internet provides and the *vision* of the future of supply chain management; and "int" represents the *integrated* solutions the venture offers as well as the *international* scope of the exchange.

The purpose of the marketplace's connectivity is to integrate buyers and sellers into a single network. Visibility would provide real-time information presented in a way that speeds decision making and enables communication through every level of a company's supply chain, anywhere in the world. By using the Web, a manufacturer's production schedule and any subsequent changes can be sent simultaneously and instantly throughout its entire supply chain. The result is less need for costly inventory at all levels of the supply chain and an increased ability to respond quickly to market changes.

To better understand the Covisint concept, examine the attached exhibit. The left side shows an automaker's traditional supply chain. Typically, an automaker would buy parts from one supplier, who in turn would buy from its suppliers (subsuppli-

ers), who would buy from other suppliers (sub-sub-suppliers). In this traditional linear supply chain, the automaker communicates only with its top-tier (tier 1) suppliers.

Imagine that the auto manufacturer has hundreds of similar supply chains, one for each supplier, and that many of the suppliers, in all tiers, produce for several manufacturers. The flow of information (as shown by the connecting lines in the drawing) will be very complex. This complexity introduces inefficiencies in communication as well as difficulties for the suppliers in planning their production schedules to meet demand, resulting in supply chain problems.

The Covisint process greatly changed supply chain communication in the automobile industry. Rather than being at the top point of a pyramid, as in the industry's traditional supply chain, the auto manufacturers now are at the center of a spoke-and-wheel arrangement. In 2001, there were six automakers in the Covisint marketplace—the three U.S. companies, Renault (France), Peugeot Citroen (France), and Nissan (Japan). Covisint has created a trading hub whereby any one of the automakers and the various suppliers and sub-suppliers can communicate directly with anyone else. Instead of an array of unorganized communication lines, it is all organized in one place. For an overview of the process, see Exhibit W7.1 at the book's Web site.

One of the major objectives of the exchange is to facilitate product design. Covisint offers its customers best-of-breed functionality; customers take the best aspects from multiple technical providers. The ability to integrate providers across the supply chain creates a unique environment for collaborative design and development (collaborative commerce), enables e-procurement, and provides a broad

(continued)

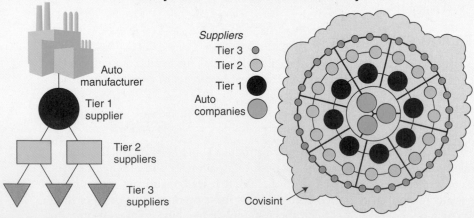

An Analysis of the Automotive Industry

a. Before Covisint: a linear supply chain

b. Covisint's hub concept

Source: Courtesy of Covisint, LCC.

CASE 7.2 (continued)

marketplace of buyers and suppliers. It makes accessible a wealth of supply chain expertise and experience, ranging from procurement to product development. Covisint's potential membership is about 30,000 suppliers.

Due to its huge size, the exchange is developing slowly. Nevertheless, Cleary (2001) reports that on May 8, 2001, DaimlerChrysler used Covisint to successfully conduct a $3-billion reverse auction for auto parts that lasted 4 days. By early 2003, a new CEO was trying to accelerate the progress of Covisint.

Sources: Compiled from *covisint.com*; Covisint press releases (2001a and b); and Cleary (2001).

Questions

1. Describe the concepts upon which Covisint is structured.
2. Describe how Covisint changed the supply chain in the automobile industry.

EXHIBIT 7.9   Representative Vertical Consortia

Consortium (CTE)	Industry Participants
Exostar (*exostar.com*)	Aerospace industry (Boeing, Lockheed Martin)
E-Markets (*e-markets.com*)	Agricultural commodities (Dow AgriSciences, Croplan Genetics)
Star Alliance (*staralliance.com*)	Airlines industry (Air Canada, Lufthansa)
Covisint (*covisint.com*)	Automotive industry (GM, Ford, DaimlerChrysler)
CorProcure (*corprocure.com*)	MRO procurement
GlobalNetXchange (*gnx.com*)	Packaged consumer products (Sears, Roebuck Co.; Karstadt Quelle; IBM Business Consulting)
Trade-Ranger (*trade-ranger.com*)	Energy industry (Royal/Dutch Shell, BP Amoco, Conoco)
Forest Express (*forestexpress.com*)	Paper and forest products (International Paper, Georgia-Pacific)
Transora (data collection) (*transora.com*)	Major consumer packaged goods manufacturers (57 members)
E2Open (*e2open.com*)	Personal computer manufacturers (Ariba, Hitachi, IBM, Netegrity, Oracle)
Amtrex Global Logistics (*amtrex.com*)	Global transport exchange (Bayer AG, Toshiba America, Newport Corp.)
World Wide Retail Exchange (*worldwideretailexchange.org*)	Major world retailers (Best Buy, Campbell's, J. C. Penney's, Kmart)
Global Healthcare Exchange (*ghx.com*)	Medical services and supplies (AmeriNet, Neoforma)
ElectronicFoodservice Network (*eFSNetwork.com*)	Food service industry (BiRite, McDonald's Company, Nestle)
Avendra (*avendra.com*)	Hospitality industry (Hyatt, Fairmont Hotels & Resorts, others)
MSA Metalsite (*metalsite.com*)	Metals and mining industry (Bethlehem Steel, Steel Dynamics)
Intercontinental Exchange (*intcx.com*)	Petroleum industry (British Petroleum, PG & E Energy Trading, Royal Bank of Canada,)
Plasticsnet (*plasticsnet.com*)	Plastics industry (Grand Effect Plastics, Strategic Systems International)
Constellation Real Technologies (*constellationllc.com*)	Real estate industry (Equity Office Properties Trust, Simon Property Group)
Rubber Network (*rubbernetwork.com*)	Rubber industry (Goodyear Tire & Rubber, Continental AG, Yokohama)
Transplace (*transplace.com*)	Transportation (air and land) industry (J. B. Hunt, U.S. Xpress, Werner)

GE Silicones (gesilicones.com) is an exchange for industrial sealants. GE Toshiba Silicone initiated this exchange and started discussions with other leading industrial sealant makers, such as Dow Corning, Wacker Chemical, and Shin-Etsu Chemical, about joining the marketplace. The initial group of participants controls over 80 percent of the world market of industrial sealants. The potential exists for the participants to deal with some sensitive business issues such as industry pricing policies, price levels, price changes, and price differentiations in ways that may violate antitrust laws. Similarly, many fear that buyers' consortia will "squeeze" the small suppliers in an unfair manner. Antitrust issues and investigations may slow the creation of CTEs, especially global ones. For example, the Covisint venture required government approval in the United Kingdom, the United States, and Germany. The German antitrust investigation was very slow and delayed the project by several months.

Critical Success Factors for Consortia

The critical success factors for consortia, according to Goldman Sachs (2000), include the following.

Appropriate business and revenue models. B2B exchanges exhibit a variety of business and revenue models. As discussed earlier in the chapter, revenue can come from *transaction fees* (platform fees, per unit fees), *auction fees* (advertisement fees and fees for services provided), *license revenue, market-maker fees,* and *subscription fees* (content and license fees). The strategy of which revenue model to use and how much to charge can make or break the exchange.

Size of the industry. The larger the size of the industry, the larger the addressable market, which in turn means a greater volume of transactions on the site. This leads to greater potential cost savings to the exchange participants and ultimately more profitability for the exchange itself. The danger here is that industry size may spawn several competing consortia, which has happened in the banking, mining, and airline industries.

Ability to drive user adoption. Consortia must have the ability to provide immediate liquidity to an exchange. The more oligopolistic the consortium is (the more it is controlled by a few players), the more accelerated the adoption can be.

elasticity

The measure of the incremental spending by buyers as a result of the savings generated.

Elasticity. A critical factor for any exchange is the degree of elasticity the exchange fosters. Elasticity is the measure of the incremental spending by buyers as a result of the savings generated. The consortium has the potential to reduce prices of individual products, thus enabling and encouraging consortium members to buy more.

Standardization of commodity-like products. The breadth of the suppliers brought in to transact with the buyers will help standardize near-commodity products due to content management and product-attribute description needs of online marketplaces. The more commodity-like the products are, the greater the market competition and the lower the prices.

Management of intensive information flow. A consortium has the ability to be a repository for the huge amounts of data that flow through supply chains in a given industry. It can also enable information-intensive collaboration between participants, including product collaboration, planning, scheduling, and forecasting. The more information the exchange has, the more added value the exchange provides the participants, and the more buyers will come to the exchange.

Smoothing of supply chain inefficiencies. It is important for the consortium-led exchange to help smooth inefficiencies in the supply chain, such as those in order fulfillment, logistics, and credit-related services.

Harmonized shared objectives. If the consortium cannot agree on shared objectives, the individual interests will be greater than the collective interests, and the exchange may fold.

Section 7.7 discusses critical success factors for exchanges in general, many of which also apply to consortia.

Combining Consortia and Third-Party Exchanges

Goldman Sachs (2000) suggested merging large consortia with a third-party owner (usually a dot-com) into what they call *dot-consortia.* Such a combination may bring about the advantage of both ownership and minimizing third-party limitations such as low liquidity. Indeed in many exchanges (e.g., newview.com), several industry leaders are shareholders, yet management is conducted by a third party.

According to Coia (2002a), consortia arrangements are common in the transportation industry. There, groups of shippers within an industry use a public exchange as a "semiprivate exchange" to leverage the amount of freight that they ship, allowing greater opportunities for competitive rates.

Section 7.4 ▶ REVIEW

1. Define CTEs.
2. Describe purchasing-oriented consortia and selling-oriented consortia.
3. Describe potential legal issues for consortia.
4. List the major critical success factors of consortia.

7.5 DYNAMIC TRADING: MATCHING AND AUCTIONS

Dynamic pricing, the rapid change in prices based on supply and demand, was discussed earlier. One of the major features of exchanges is dynamic trading. **Dynamic trading** is exchange trading that occurs in situations when prices are determined by supply and demand, therefore changing continuously. Two major mechanisms are used in dynamic trading in exchanges: matching and auctions.

MATCHING

An example of *matching* supply and demand is the stock market. When buyers place their bids and sellers list their asking prices, the market makers conduct the matching, sometimes by buying or selling stocks from their own accounts. The matching process may be more complex than buying and selling in regular auctions (discussed next) due to the need to match both prices and quantities. In other cases, quantity, delivery times, and locations also need to be matched. Today, matching in stock exchanges is fully computerized. Most commodity exchanges (e.g., wheat, oil, silver) are B2B, as are some financial markets.

AUCTIONS

As seen in the ChemConnect case, exchanges offer members the ability to conduct auctions or reverse auctions in *private trading rooms*. When this takes place, the one-to-many model is activated, as described in Chapter 6, with the hosting done *by the exchange*. The advantage of running an auction in an exchange is the ability to attract many buyers to a forward auction and many suppliers to a reverse auction. For SMEs that wish to buy or sell via auctions, finding auction participants can be a major problem. By going to an exchange, this problem may be solved.

Auctions can be arranged in several ways. Two options are as follows:

▶ An exchange offers auction services as one of its many activities, as ChemConnect does. Most vertical exchanges offer this option.
▶ An exchange is fully dedicated to auctions. Examples of this auctions-only arrangement are eBay for Businesses, GXS.com, and Ariba's Dynamic Trading.

An exchange can conduct many-to-many public auctions. These auctions may be vertical or horizontal and can run on the Internet or over private lines. Examples of auctions conducted over private lines are Aucnet in Japan, through which used cars are sold to dealers, and TFA, the Dutch flower market auction, described in EC Application Case W7.1.

Exhibit 7.10 (page 278) summarizes the major B2B, many-to-many models discussed thus far in the chapter.

dynamic trading
Exchange trading that occurs in situations when prices are being determined by supply and demand (e.g., in auctions).

EXHIBIT 7.10 Comparing the Major B2B Many-to-Many Models

Name	Major Characteristics	Types
B2B catalog-based exchanges	• A place for selling and buying • Fixed prices (updated as needed)	Vertical, horizontal • Shopping directory, usually with hyperlinks (only) • Shopping carts with services (payment, etc.)
B2B portals	• Community services • Communication tools • Classified ads • Employment markets • May sell, buy • Fixed prices • May do auctions	Vertical (vortals), horizontal • Shopping directory, usually with hyperlinks
B2B dynamic exchanges	• Matches buyer/seller orders at dynamic prices, auctions • Provides trading-related information and services (payment, logistics) • Highly regulated • May provide general information, news, etc. • May provide for negotiations	Vertical, horizontal • Auctions • Reverse auctions • Bid/ask exchanges

Section 7.5 ▶ REVIEW

1. Explain how matches are made in exchanges.

2. Explain how private and public auctions are conducted in public exchanges.

3. Compare fully dedicated and partially dedicated auction exchanges.

7.6 BUILDING AND INTEGRATING MARKETPLACES AND EXCHANGES

BUILDING E-MARKETPLACES

Building e-marketplaces and exchanges is a complex process. It is usually performed by a major B2B software company such as Commerce One, Ariba, Oracle, or IBM. In large exchanges, a management consulting company such as PriceWaterhouseCoopers, Gartner Group, or McKinsey usually participates. Also, technology companies such as IBM, Oracle, EDS, i2, Intel, Microsoft, and SAP have major roles in building large exchanges. Most exchanges are built jointly by several vendors.

Most large B2B software vendors have specially designed e-marketplace packages. For example, Oracle, Microsoft, Ariba, and Commerce One each has a set of e-marketplace solutions (see Online Chapter 18). A typical process for building a vertical e-marketplace is shown in online Exhibit W7.2.

THE INTEGRATION ISSUE

Seamless integration is needed between the third-party exchange and the participants' front- and back-office systems. Also, in private exchanges, one needs to integrate the seller's computing system with that of the customers (in a sell-side case) or integrate the buyer's system with that of the suppliers (in a buy-side case). This takes place through interfacing with applications and protocols. In addition, integration across multiple, frequently incompatible exchanges, each with its own XML scheme, is required. Tibco.com is the major infrastructure service provider for vertical exchanges.

The four most common elements of B2B integration solutions, which are discussed in the following sections, are external communications, process and information coordination, Web services, and system and information management.

External Communications

External communications require the following:

▶ **Web/client access.** Businesses can use a Web browser, such as Internet Explorer, to interact with a Web server application hosted by other businesses.

▶ **Data exchange.** Information is extracted from an application, converted into a neutral data format, and sent to other businesses. Examples of data exchange include EDI over VANs and Internet-based EDI.

▶ **Direct application integration.** Application integration often requires middleware technologies, such as distributed object technologies, message queuing, and publish/subscribe brokers, to coordinate information exchange between applications (see tibco.com and peregrine.com).

▶ **Shared procedures.** Businesses can agree to use the same procedures for certain processes. For example, a supplier and a buyer may agree to use the same order-management process.

Process and Information Coordination in Integration

Process and information coordination concerns how to coordinate *external communications* with *internal information systems*. This coordination includes external processes, internal processes, data transformation, and exception handling. For example, an online sales transaction must be processed directly to an internal accounting system.

Use of Web Services in Integration

Web Services (see details in Online Chapter 18) essentially enable different Web-based systems to communicate with each other using Internet-based protocols such as XML (see Chapter 6 and online Appendix B), SOAP (Simple Object Access Protocol), and UDDI (Universal Description Discovery and Integration). WSDL (Web Services Description Language) makes it expedient to use Web Services to connect different systems. For example, many companies still use legacy systems that are expensive to maintain and provide poor customer service. Also, large companies such as AT&T may have a mishmash of networks patched together over the years, some of which use proprietary languages and custom codes. Every time a change is made in one application, a Herculean effort is required to rewrite code in every connected application. It is very difficult to work under these kinds of conditions in B2B in general and in exchanges in particular.

By using Web Services, the time it takes to connect complex systems can be reduced by about 75 percent. Also, the development cost can be reduced by 10 percent (according to *Forbes* 2002).

System and Information Management in Integration

System and information management involves the management of software, hardware, and several information components, including partner-profile information, data and process definitions, communications and security settings, and users' information. Furthermore, because hardware and software change rapidly (i.e., upgrades or releases of new versions), the management of these changes is an essential element of B2B integration.

Section 7.6 ▶ REVIEW

1. List the steps in building a vertical exchange.
2. Describe the integration issues for third-party exchanges.

7.7 SUPPORT SERVICES FOR PUBLIC AND PRIVATE MARKETPLACES

In order to succeed in B2B, and particularly in exchanges, it is necessary to have support services. The Delphi Group (2001) (delphigroup.com) suggests that B2B services be organized into six major categories: e-infrastructure, e-processes, e-markets, e-content, e-communities, and e-services. E-processes (e.g., e-payments and fulfillment logistics) will be addressed in Chapter 14 and the topic of e-infrastructure in Online Chapter 18. This section will examine a few other support services.

DIRECTORY SERVICES AND SEARCH ENGINES

The B2B landscape is huge, with thousands of companies online. Directory services can help buyers and sellers manage the task of finding potential partners. Some popular directories are listed and described in Exhibit 7.11. Note that the last three entries in the exhibit are search engines, which can be used to discover information about B2B. Some of these are embedded in the directories.

EXHIBIT 7.11	**B2B Directory Services and Search Engines**
Directory Services	
b2business.net	A major resource for B2B professionals that provides listings of business resources in about 30 functional areas, company research resources (e.g., credit checks, customs research, financial reviews), and information on start-ups.
b2btoday.com	Contains listings of B2B services organized by type of service (e.g., Web site creation, B2B marketing, and B2B software) and product category (e.g., automotive, books).
communityb2b.com	Offers many B2B community services, such as news, a library, events calendar, job market, and resource directory.
a2zofb2b.com	Company directory organized in alphabetical order or industry order. Specifies the type and nature of the company, the venture capital (VC) sponsor, and the stock market ticker (if it is an IPO).
i-stores.co.uk	A UK-based directory of online stores; provides validation of secure Web sites.
dmoz.org/business/	A large business directory organized by location and by product or service. Also provides listings by industry and subindustry (according to SIC code).
thomasregister.com	Directory of more than 150,000 manufacturers of industrial products and services.
jupiterdirect.com	A comprehensive B2B guide for marketers that provides directories, news, auctions, and much more.
b2b.yahoo.com	Provides business directories that cover over 250,000 companies (as of 2003).
line56.com/directory	Provides information about B2B software, services, and marketplaces.
Search Engines	
moreover.com	In addition to locating information, also aggregates B2B (and other business) news.
google.com	In addition to its search tools, offers a directory of components for B2B and B2C Web sites (e.g., currency exchange calculators, server performance monitors, etc.).
Ientry.com	Provides B2B search engines, targeted "niche engines," and several industry-focused newsletters. Operates a network of Web sites and e-mail newsletters that reaches over 2,000,000 unique opt-in subscribers.

PARTNER RELATIONSHIP MANAGEMENT

Successful e-businesses carefully manage partners, prospects, and customers across the entire value chain, most often in a 24/7 environment. Therefore, one should examine the role of e-service solutions and technology, such as extranets, call centers, and collaboration tools, in creating an integrated online environment for engaging e-business customers and partners. The use of such solutions and technology appears under two names: CRM and PRM.

In Chapter 4, we introduced the concept of CRM in the B2C environment. Here our interest shifts to a situation where the customer is a business. Many of the customer service features of B2C are also used in B2B. For example, it may be beneficial to provide corporate customers with a chat room and a discussion board. A Web-based call center may also be useful for companies with many partners.

Corporate customers may require additional services. For example, customers need to have access to the supplier's inventory status report so they know what items can be delivered quickly. Customers may want to see their historical purchasing records, and they may need private showrooms and trade rooms. Large numbers of vendors are available for designing and building appropriate B2B CRM solutions. The strategy of providing such comprehensive, quality e-service for business partners is sometimes called **partner relationship management (PRM)**.

In the context of PRM, customers are only one category of business partner. Suppliers, partners in joint ventures, service providers, and others are also part of the B2B community in an exchange or company-centric B2B initiative. Companies with many suppliers, such as the automobile companies, may create special programs for them. Such programs are called *supplier relationship management (SRM)*.

Implementing PRM and SRM is different from implementing CRM with individual customers. For example, behavioral and psychological aspects of the relationships are less important in B2B than in CRM. However, trust, commitment, quality of services, and continuity are more important in B2B. For details see Coupey (2001).

> **partner relationship management (PRM)**
> Business strategy that focuses on providing comprehensive quality service to business partners.

E-COMMUNITIES AND PRM

B2B applications involve many participants: buyers and sellers, service providers, industry associations, and others. Thus, in many cases, the B2B application creates a *community*. Even in the case of a company-centric market (not an exchange), communities are likely to be formed. In such cases, the B2B application needs to provide community services such as chat rooms, bulletin boards, and possibly personalized Web pages. A detailed list of such services is provided in Online Chapter 18.

According to the Delphi Group (delphigroup.com, 2000), e-communities are connecting personnel, partners, customers, and any combination of the three. E-communities offer a powerful resource for e-businesses to leverage online discussions and interaction in order to maximize innovation and responsiveness. It is therefore beneficial to study the tools, methods, and best practices of building and managing e-communities. Although the technological support of B2B e-communities is basically the same as for any other online community (see Online Chapter 18), the nature of the community itself, and the information provided by the community, is different.

B2B e-communities are basically communities of transactions, and as such, the major interest of the members is trading. Most of the communities are associated with vertical exchanges; therefore, their needs may be fairly specific. However, it is common to find generic services such as classified ads, job vacancies, announcements, industry news, and so on. Service providers are also available for the design of exchange portals and their community services.

INTEGRATION

We conclude this section with two interesting issues: integration of service provision and hypermediation. This chapter has presented several value-added services such as content provision, matching of buyers and sellers, and order fulfillment. Other chapters will provide some more. These services need to interact with each other. In exchanges, the integration of such services becomes very important.

One model of such integration was proposed by the Keenan Report (2000). According to this model, business-to-exchange (B2X) hubs connect all of the Internet business services, the e-merchant services, the exchange infrastructure, buying and selling, member enterprises, and other B2X exchanges. Commerce One can be viewed as a type of exchange. A diagram of the model is shown in Exhibit W7.3 at the book's Web site.

Section 7.7 ❱ REVIEW

1. What type of information of use to B2B is provided by directory services and search engines?

2. How does PRM differ from CRM? From SRM?

3. List five other services for B2B.

4. Describe e-communities in B2B.

5. Describe the integration issue in exchanges.

7.8 IMPLEMENTATION ISSUES

Large exchanges are supposed to bring together entire industry sectors, creating supply chain efficiencies and reduced costs for buyers and sellers alike. However, despite the fact that more than 1,500 exchanges were created between January 1999 and December 2000, only a few hundred were active by the end of 2001, and less than half of these were conducting a high volume of transactions (AMR Research 2001). By 2003, signs of improvement appeared. Existing exchanges solidified, and a few new exchanges appeared. However, due to the worldwide economic slowdown, these changes were minor. Let's look at some of the implementation issues that might explain these numbers.

PRIVATE VERSUS PUBLIC EXCHANGES

private exchanges
E-marketplaces that are owned and operated by one company. Also known as *company-centric marketplaces.*

As described earlier, exchanges owned by a third party are referred to as *public exchanges.* In contrast, **private exchanges** are owned and operated by one company. They are essentially company-centric marketplaces (see Chapter 6). In October 2001, the Gartner Group (as reported by Konicki 2000) estimated that there were 30,000 active private exchanges and 600 public exchanges in the United States, and the numbers have not changed much since then. Both types of exchanges have implementation and viability problems (e.g., see Varon 2001).

Problems with Public Exchanges

Exchanges need to attract sellers and buyers. Attracting sellers, especially large businesses, to public exchanges is difficult for the following reasons.

Transaction fees. One of the major reasons that large and successful suppliers refuse to join third-party exchanges is that they are required to pay transaction fees even when they engage in transactions with their existing customers.

Sharing information. Many companies do not like to join public exchanges because they do not want to share key business data with their competitors.

Cost savings. Many of the first-generation exchanges were horizontal, concentrating on MROs. These are low-value items. Although administrative costs can be reduced by online ordering, the cost of the products to the buyers remains essentially the same. Thus, the monetary savings may not be attractive enough to buyers, especially SMEs.

Recruiting suppliers. One of the major difficulties facing public exchanges is the recruitment of large suppliers. For example, GE Plastics, a major vendor of plastic materials, said that the company was asked to join the public exchange Plasticsnet (plasticsnet.com), but it did not see any benefit in doing so. There was simply no business case for it. Instead, GE Plastics decided to develop e-purchasing capabilities for its customers. The company likes the *direct contact* with its customers, which it would lose if it were part of a public

exchange. Also, some suppliers just want to wait and see how exchanges will fare before they make a commitment to join.

Too many exchanges. When an exchange receives the publicity of being the *first mover*, as Chemdex did, it is sure to attract some competition. Competitors believe that they can do a better job than the first mover or that they have "deeper pockets" to sustain losses and survive. Two chemical exchanges competed against Chemdex, which closed in 2000.

Supply Chain Improvers

Public exchanges prepare the entire necessary infrastructure and ask suppliers to just "plug in" and start selling. However, companies are also interested in streamlining their internal supply chains, which requires integration with internal operations, not just plugging in. This is why companies such as i2 and Aspect, leaders in SCM, are partnering with some exchanges. According to *Business Review Weekly* of Australia (BRW Staff 2000), focusing on supply chain savings rather than on buy/sell savings can be very beneficial to exchanges. An example of an exchange that emphasizes supply chain improvement is Asite, as described in EC Application Case 7.3 (page 284).

Problems with Private Exchanges

Some (e.g., Young 2002) believe that public exchanges will not do as well as private exchanges. However, private exchanges have their problems, too. The primary problem is that they may not be trusted because they are run by one company, usually a large one. Such distrust can lead to liquidity issues. One way to ease liquidity problems is to combine private and public exchanges. Indeed, in 2001, some major manufacturers adopted private exchanges for their main supply chain (see Young 2002).

SOFTWARE AGENTS IN B2B EXCHANGES

The use of B2B exchanges has fostered a need within the B2B community for an efficient infrastructure to provide real-time, tighter integration between buyers and sellers and to facilitate management of multiple trading partners and their transactions across multiple virtual industry exchanges. Such capabilities can be provided by software agents.

One such software agent is AgentWare's Syndicator. This software enables customized syndication of content and services from multiple sources on the Internet to any device connected to the Internet. Thus, it allows access to real-time information on the exchange. (For details, see agentware.net.) Another software agent, Dotcom-Monitor (dotcom-monitor.com), monitors traffic on a B2B exchange and takes appropriate actions when needed, such as sending an alert to management when traffic is too heavy or routing traffic to other places. Some of the types of shopping agents cited in Chapters 3 through 5 (e.g., comparison and search agents) can also be used for B2B purposes.

DISINTERMEDIATION AND REINTERMEDIATION

Exchanges, especially consortia-like ones, could replace traditional B2B intermediaries (i.e., cause disintermediation). Let's look at some examples of exchanges that might replace (i.e., reintermediate) B2B intermediaries in certain industries.

- Sun Microsystems, after publicly announcing that there was no need for third-party exchanges because they waste time, joined a consortium, headed by IBM, that develops and smoothes lines in the computer maker's supply chain. This exchange competes with a similar exchange created by Compaq, HP, AMD, and NEC. Such exchanges may eliminate some distributors of computer components.
- Marriott, Hyatt, and several other competing hoteliers created an MRO exchange (avendra.com) that could eliminate wholesalers in that industry.

An analysis of reintermediation strategies in B2B, including exchanges, is provided by Chircu and Kauffman (2000).

EC Application

ASITE'S B2B E-MARKETPLACE FOR THE CONSTRUCTION INDUSTRY

Asite (*asite.com*) is a B2B e-marketplace for the construction industry in the United Kingdom. The construction industry is typified by a high degree of physical separation and fragmentation, and communication among the members of the supply chain (e.g., contractors, subcontractors, architects, supply stores, building inspectors) has long been a primary problem. Founded in February 2000 by leading players in the construction industry, the company understands two of the major advantages of the Internet: The ability it provides to communicate more effectively, and the increase in processing power that Internet technologies make possible. Taking advantage of the functions of an online portal as information broker and gateway to the services of technology partners, Asite developed a comprehensive portal for the construction industry.

Asite drew on employees from partner organizations with profound industry knowledge and expertise, and has benefited from having an anchor group of buyers participating at an early stage of its development. That combination has enabled Asite to rapidly build up the liquidity that online portals require. The company's goal is to be the leading information and transaction hub in the European construction industry.

Asite made the decision not to build its own technology, but to establish partnerships with technology vendors that have highly specialized products. It formed core partnerships with Commerce One (which provides the business solution for the portal); Microsoft (which provides the technology platform and core applications); and Attenda (the designer and manager of the Internet infrastructure).

Asite set up seven interconnected marketplaces within its portal to serve all the needs of the participants in the construction industry—building owners, developers, trade contractors, general contractors, engineers, architects, and materials suppliers—from design through procurement to materials delivery (see attached figure).

(*continued*)

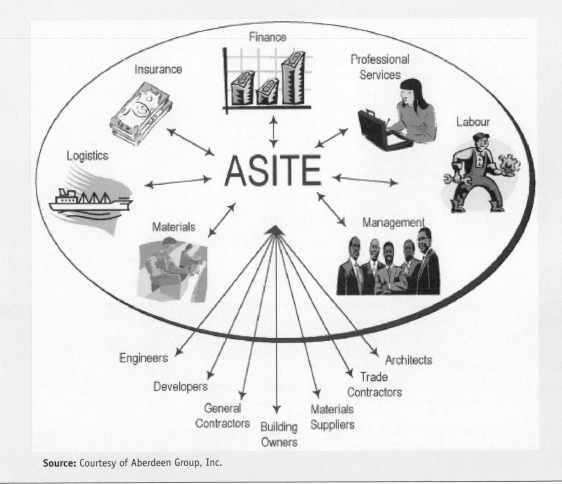

Source: Courtesy of Aberdeen Group, Inc.

CASE 7.3   (continued)

It began by addressing business problems, such as ineffective procurement processes and hit-or-miss information flows.

Asite is committed to strong partnerships that allow it to seamlessly interact with other e-marketplaces. The open standards espoused by these vendors also mean that the technology can be incorporated easily with participating firms' back-end technologies, allowing full visibility of the supply and demand chains. Participating firms need nothing more sophisticated than a browser to connect to Asite's portal. This ease of access makes it particularly well suited to an industry such as construction, which is distinguished by a high proportion of small, and even single-person, firms.

The combination of strong backing from industry participants, experienced management from the construction industry, and the commitment to working with best-of-breed technology infrastructure providers is helping construction firms streamline their supply chains.

Sources: Compiled from Aberdeen Group (2001) and *asite.com* (2002).

Questions

1. Identify the success factors of this company (see the list of success factors in Section 7.9).

2. How would you classify the ownership of this e-marketplace?

3. Examine the Webcor EC Application Case in Chapter 8. How does Webcor differ from Asite? How is it similar?

4. Enter *asite.com* and read about any new developments (within the last 6 months).

5. What is the exchange's revenue model?

6. Using the classification scheme presented in this chapter, is *asite.com* a portal or an exchange?

EVALUATING EXCHANGES

With the increased number of competing exchanges, companies need to carefully evaluate which ones will work best for them. Insights and Additions W7.1 offers some useful questions that buyers and sellers should ask in evaluating exchanges when deciding whether to join.

Section 7.8 ❱ REVIEW

1. List the problems of public exchanges.

2. List the problems of private exchanges.

3. How can exchanges cause disintermediation?

4. What are some of the questions one should ask when evaluating exchanges?

7.9   MANAGING EXCHANGES

The topic of managing exchanges is very broad. This section will describe a couple of major management issues. (For further details on exchange management, see Schully and Woods 2000). The section concludes with an examination of the critical success factors for exchanges (see also Diorio 2002).

NETWORKS OF EXCHANGES (E2E)

With the increasing number of vertical and horizontal exchanges, it is logical to think about connecting them. Large corporations may work with several exchanges, and they would like these exchanges to be connected in a seamless fashion. Today, most exchanges have different log-on procedures, separate sets of rules for fulfilling orders, and different business models for charging for their services.

At first, exchanges were created quickly so that they could be *first movers* in a market. The primary objective of these newly created exchanges has been the acquisition of buyers and sellers. Integration with other companies or with another exchange was a low priority. However, some exchanges have begun to integrate in order to better serve their customers.

Commerce One and Ariba have developed a strategy that allows them to plug a broad range of horizontal exchanges into their main networks (such as MarketSite from Commerce

One), as well as an increasing number of connected vertical marketplaces (such as ChemConnect). Corporations can plug into Ariba or Commerce One networks and reach thousands of suppliers. Each time a new customer signs up with Ariba or Commerce One, the customer can bring its business partners into the network. These business partners are then connected to any other company that plugs into the network. The network allows any customer to buy from any supplier connected to the network.

The joint network that combines the Commerce One and Ariba networks is expanding rapidly, and the two companies are launching horizontal exchanges in several countries. These exchanges range from a marketplace for governmental and educational institutions (buysense.com) to a New Zealand marketplace for businesses (supplynet.co.nz). Ariba and Commerce One also are partnering with vertical exchanges such as ChemConnect. Other large vendors, such as Oracle and SAP, may join the networks someday. (For further details, see Duvall 2000.)

Exchanges also can be connected in an industry supply chain, as shown in Exhibit 7.12. Each exchange serves different participants, but some are members of different exchanges.

CENTRALIZED MANAGEMENT

Managing exchanges and providing services to participants on an individual basis can be expensive. Therefore, it makes sense to have "families" of exchanges managed jointly. This way, one market builder can build and operate several exchanges from a unified, centralized place. The market maker manages all of the exchanges' catalogs, auction places, discussion forums, and so on, thus centralizing accounting, finance, human resources, and IT services. Furthermore, dealings with third-party vendors that provide logistic services and payment systems may be more efficient if a vendor is supplying services for many exchanges instead of just one.

Two such "families" of exchanges were those of VerticalNet (verticalnet.com) and Ventro. However, due to the large number of exchange failures in 2001, Ventro (now nexprise.com)

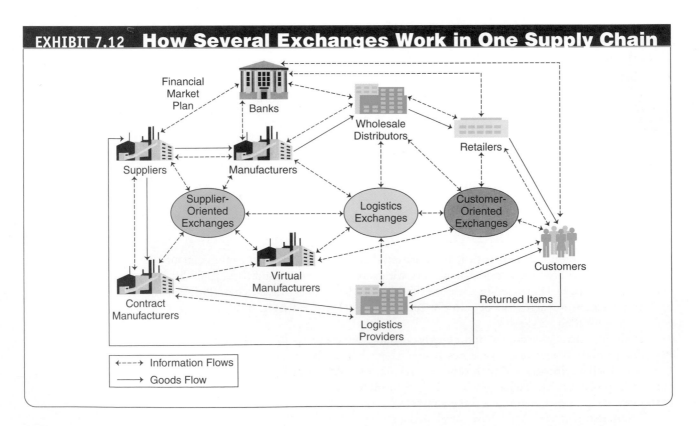

EXHIBIT 7.12   How Several Exchanges Work in One Supply Chain

changed its business model and became a software provider. VerticalNet (verticalnet.com) sold its exchanges and their management to Corry Publishing (corrypub.com) on July 15, 2002, which continues to operate the exchanges. In addition, other families of exchanges are also springing to life.

CRITICAL SUCCESS FACTORS FOR EXCHANGES

By early 2001, there were thousands of B2B exchanges. Since that time, as in the B2C area, many—perhaps 90 percent—folded or were failing. There were dozens of failures as early as 2000, including that of Chemdex.com. In certain areas or countries, there are too many competing exchanges. For example, Hong Kong probably does not have enough room for three toy exchanges (two failed by summer 2002). Therefore, B2B exchanges will continue to fail and consolidate. The question is, "What determines whether an exchange will survive?"

According to Ramsdell (2000) of McKinsey & Company, a major management consulting company, the following five factors are influencing the outcome of the B2B exchange shakeout.

1. **Early liquidity.** Recall that liquidity refers to the result of having a sufficient number of participants and amount of transaction volume. The *earlier* a business achieves the necessary liquidity level, the better its chances for survival. The more buyers that trade on an exchange, the more suppliers will come, which will lead to lower transaction fees, which in turn will increase liquidity even more.

2. **The right owners.** One way to increase liquidity is to partner with companies that can bring liquidity to the exchange. For example, Covisint was founded by the big automakers, which are committed to buying via the exchange. The desire to have suitable partners is why many vertical exchanges are of the consortia type. In a situation where both the sellers and buyers are fragmented, such as in the bioscience industry, the best owner may be an intermediary who can increase liquidity by pushing both the sellers and the buyers to use the exchange.

3. **The right governance.** Good management and effective operations and rules are critical to success. The governance provides the rules for the exchange, minimizes conflicts, and supports decision making. Furthermore, good management will try to induce the necessary liquidity. Also, good governance will minimize conflicts among the owners and the participants. Owners may try to favor some of their trading partners, a situation that may hurt the exchange if not checked by effective management. To succeed, good exchanges must be unbiased. In addition, good management of operations, resources, and people is mandatory for smooth operations and success. Finally, privacy must be protected.

4. **Openness.** Exchanges must be open to all, from both organizational and technological perspectives. Commitment to open standards is required, but there should be universal agreement on these standards. Using the wrong standards may hurt the exchange.

5. **A full range of services.** Although prices are important, buyers and sellers are interested in cutting their total costs. Therefore, exchanges that help cut inventory costs, spoilage, maverick buying, and so on, will attract participants. Many exchanges team up with banks, logistics services, and IT companies to provide support services. Furthermore, exchanges must be integrated with the information systems of their members—not a simple task (see the Real-World Case at the end of this chapter).

In addition to Ramsdell's five factors, a number of other factors are critical to the success of an exchange. These are presented and discussed in Insights and Additions 7.1 (page 288). In order to achieve these critical success factors, market makers must carefully select the vendors that design and build the exchanges.

For further discussion of critical success factors for exchanges, see Bryant (2002).

Insights and Additions 7.1   Other Critical Success Factors for Exchanges

▶ **Importance of domain expertise.** In order to meaningfully aggregate buyers and sellers in a community and subsequently enable transactions among them, operators should have knowledge of a given industry's structure and business processes, the nature of buyer and seller behavior in the industry and government, and policy stipulations that impact the sector.

▶ **Targeting inefficient industry processes.** The traditional business processes in most industries have many inefficiencies. These contribute to increased costs and delays for businesses transacting with one another. Addressing these inefficiencies can create significant opportunities for vertical exchanges to add value.

▶ **Targeting the right industries.** The most attractive vertical exchanges to target typically are characterized by (1) a large base of transactions; (2) many fragmented buyers and sellers; (3) difficulties in bringing buyers and sellers together; (4) high vendor and product search/comparison costs, which may be caused by information-intensive products with complex configurations and nonstandard specifications; (5) high process costs associated with manual processes based on paper catalogs, manual requisitioning, telephone- or fax-based ordering, the need for credit verification, and order tracking; (6) strong pressure to cut expenses; (7) a complex value chain, such as in the automotive industry; and (8) a climate of technological innovation. Targeting industries with some of these characteristics is desirable.

▶ **Brand building.** The low switching costs inherent in exchanges will make branding of exchanges of paramount importance to their long-term viability. Exchange operators must first invest in gaining brand awareness and getting businesses to use their exchange. For example, in Hong Kong, Bigboxx.com even advertises on buses. Exchange operators must then focus on customer retention. Adding valuable features and functionality is one way to increase switching costs (in this case, the services the customer would lose by switching).

▶ **Exploiting economies of scope.** Once a critical mass is reached, exchange operators must expand the services they provide to users. Value-added services, such as industry news, expert advice, or detailed product specification sheets, and so on, can make an exchange even more compelling. Expanding the range of services may also increase switching costs. Better-developed exchanges are now offering services such as systems integration, hosting, financial services (e.g., payment processing, receivables management, credit analysis), and logistics services (e.g., shipping, warehousing, and inspection), as well as risk-mitigation services.

▶ **Choice of business/revenue models.** To optimize the chances for success, exchange operators should generate multiple revenue streams, including software licensing, advertising, and sponsorship, and recurring revenues from transaction fees, subscription fees, and software subscription revenues. Other value-added services and applications, such as auctions, financial services, business reporting, and data mining services, may provide other sources of revenue.

▶ **Blending content, community, and commerce.** Exchanges differ in their approaches; some originate from a content/community perspective, whereas others have a focus on conducting EC transactions. Though content and community features have the advantage of stimulating traffic, the ability to conduct EC transactions is thought to create a higher level of customer "stickiness" and greater value for the exchanges. A successful exchange should combine rich content and community with the ability to conduct EC transactions.

▶ **Managing channel conflict.** The movement of buyers to interact directly with sellers and the consequent disintermediation of some portion of the supply chain intermediaries may be viewed as a hostile activity by existing fulfillment channels. The result is sometimes price erosion, which may affect a company's medium-term profitability. Exchanges are trying to minimize the conflict by using existing services of the major buyers and sellers.

▶ **Other factors.** Diorio (2002) added the following critical success factors for exchanges: value-added content, expertise, trust relationships, appropriate financing, first-mover advantage, and availability of resources. (For more on these factors, see Exhibit W7.4 at the book's Web site.)

NEW DIRECTIONS FOR B2B MARKETPLACES

The difficulties encountered by both third-party marketplaces and consortia have resulted in a search for new directions (such as the merger of the two). Berryman and Heck (2001) edited a special section in *The McKinsey Quarterly* in which they, with others, presented the *third wave of B2B exchanges.* (The first wave is dot-com-owned B2B exchanges; the second wave is consortia-owned exchanges.) After analyzing the problems of the first and second wave, they concurred with the view of Agrawal and Pak (2001) that many of the failures in the former waves were due mainly to the failure of these marketplaces to foster a broad-based sharing of information. The third wave contains both proven and potential success factors.

In the past, information flowed only between pairs of parties in a supply chain. The result was a multibillion-dollar version of the game of "telephone," in which small errors, magnified up and down the chain, led to incorrect forecasts and to either excessive or insufficient inventories. In contrast, marketplaces that became *information hubs* for distinct segments of the supply chain could instantaneously share data and insights gathered from each corporate participant. Such a hub-and-spoke model may be the way not only to save these B2Bs, but also to realize their value-creating potential.

Devine et al. (2001) explained why many consortia did not fare much better than third-party exchanges. In many cases, members of the consortium did not shift as much of their trading volume to the exchange as had been expected, thus the liquidity that their participation was supposed to guarantee did not materialize. Such consortia must recognize the more fundamental asset provided by their member base—its unique knowledge of the industry. Such recognition should enable consortia to become arenas for *sharing this knowledge,* and thereby make it possible to standardize products and processes, to spread risk, and to uncover new opportunities. Marketplaces that offer their members such benefits will have no shortage of liquidity.

Hansen et al. (2001) believe that one hallmark of third-wave B2B approaches is the idea of choosing a different model for each kind of transaction. Companies purchasing a commodity, for example, might value the liquidity, the transparency, and the price orientation of an online exchange (much like the benefits offered by commodity contracts already traded at the Chicago Mercantile Exchange and elsewhere). In contrast, companies making highly specialized purchases might value the possibilities for customization offered by the traditional bilateral relationship between buyers and sellers. As shown in Exhibit 7.13, each of the five basic categories of the stand-alone B2B marketplaces is suitable for a particular purpose. To know which category to choose, buyers must develop a deep and nuanced understanding of the cost structures of all their various purchases.

According to Baumgartner et al. (2001), sellers' reaction to B2B has ranged from skepticism to horror. Such negative reaction is based on the idea that these marketplaces serve a single overriding purpose—the promotion of price transparency—that entails a race to the profitless bottom. Of course, the authors note, certain buyers really are extremely price sensitive when they make certain purchases, and those buyers will naturally migrate to low-cost producers. However, many other purchases will continue to involve information-rich bilateral relationships.

A third model, which Berryman and Heck (2001) call *e-distributor*, lies between the two extremes of the stand-alone third-party exchange and the consortium. In this model, e-distributors, like distributors in the off-line world, take title to the goods they sell, aggregate those goods for the convenience of buyers, and (because they carry only certain products) in effect advise buyers which to choose. In addition, e-distributors perform a critical service for sellers by reaching hard-to-find buyers, such as small ones. The result, in many cases, is significant *extra value* for buyers and decent profits for sellers.

Another set of new directions is presented by Dai and Kauffman (2002) in a special section of the journal *Electronic Markets* in which six research papers were presented. Of special interest are interviews with leading scholars in the field. This special presentation deals with many of the topics presented in Chapters 6 through 8.

Section 7.9 ❯ REVIEW

1. Describe a network of exchanges.

2. List the five critical success factors for exchanges cited by Ramsdell.

3. Discuss other critical success factors for exchanges.

4. Review the new directions of B2B.

MANAGERIAL ISSUES

Some managerial issues related to this chapter are as follows.

1. **Have we "done our homework"?** Study the options and select the most secure and economical choice for exchange implementation. Consult the technical staff inside and outside of each partnering company. Planning is essential. This is true for exchange creators, operators, and users.

2. **Can we use the Internet?** Review the current proprietary or leased networks and determine if they can be replaced by intranets and extranets via the Internet (see Appendix 7A). Doing so may reduce costs and widen connectivity for customers and suppliers. In making this decision, also consider whether it is safe enough to switch to the Internet.

3. **Which exchange to join?** One of the major concerns of management is selecting exchanges in which to participate. At the moment, exchanges are not integrated, so there may be a substantial start-up effort and cost for joining an exchange. This is a multicriteria decision that should be analyzed carefully. A related issue is whether to join a third-party public exchange or a consortium or to create a private exchange.

4. **Will joining an exchange force restructuring?** Joining an exchange may require a restructuring of the internal supply chain, which may be expensive and time-consuming. Therefore, this possibility must be taken into consideration when deciding whether or not to join an exchange.

5. **Will we face channel conflicts?** Channel conflicts may arise when a company joins an exchange. You may anger your existing suppliers if you buy via an exchange. This issue must be considered, and an examination of its impact must be carried out.

6. **What are the benefits and risks of joining an exchange?** Companies must take very seriously the issues listed in Exhibit 7.6. The risks of joining an exchange must be carefully weighed against the expected benefits.

SUMMARY

In this chapter, you learned about the following EC issues as they relate to the learning objectives.

1. **E-marketplaces and exchanges defined and the major types of exchanges.** Exchanges are e-marketplaces that provide a trading platform for conducting business among many buyers, many sellers, and other business partners. Other names used are *trading portals* or *Net marketplaces*. Types of public e-marketplaces include B2B portals, third-party trading exchanges, consortium trading exchanges, and dynamic trading floors for matching. E-marketplaces may include auctions. They can be vertical (industry oriented) or horizontal. They can target systematic buying (long-term relationships) or spot buying (for fulfilling an immediate need).

2. **Ownership and revenue models.** Exchanges may be owned by one large company, an intermediary (a neutral third party), or a large group of buyers or sellers (a consortium). The major revenue models are transaction fees (flat or percentage), fees for value-added services, annual membership fees, and advertisement income.

3. **B2B portals.** These portals are similar to B2C portals such as Yahoo. B2B portals are gateways to B2B community-related information. They are usually of a vertical structure, in which case they are referred to as *vortals*. Some B2B portals offer product and vendor information and even tools for conducting trades, making it sometimes difficult to distinguish between B2B portals and trading exchanges.

4. **Third-party exchanges.** Third-party exchanges are owned by an independent company and usually operate in highly fragmented markets. They are open to anyone and therefore are considered public exchange. They try to maintain neutral relations with both buyers and sellers. Their major problem is acquiring enough customers to ensure liquidity. Two models of third-party exchanges are those that aggregate suppliers' catalogs and those that aggregate buyers' RFQs.

5. **Consortia and e-procurement.** A consortium trading exchange (CTE) is an exchange formed and operated by a group of major involved companies. Buying-oriented consortia are established by several large buyers (e.g., automakers). Their major objective is to smooth the procurement (purchasing) process. Selling-oriented consortia are owned and operated by several large sellers, usually in the same industry (e.g., plastics, airlines). Their major objective is to increase sales and smooth the supply chain to their customers. CTEs sometimes face antitrust scrutiny by governments.

6. **Dynamic pricing and trading.** Dynamic pricing occurs when prices are determined by supply and demand at any given moment. Dynamic trading refers to exchange trading in which prices are continuously changing. The two major dynamic pricing mechanisms

are matching of supply and demand (such as in stock markets) and auctions (forward and reverse).

7. **Integrating marketplaces and exchanges.** One of the major problems in building e-marketplaces is application integration, especially with business partners. In addition to application integration, there may also be problems of data and database integration as well as process integration. In the future, Web services will provide a universal open environment that will ease the integration problem.

8. **Major B2B support services.** Six categories of support services exist: e-infrastructure, e-processes, e-markets, e-content, e-communities, and e-services. Directory services and B2B search engines are examples of e-services. Partnership relationship management (PRM) is important in B2B, and it may be facilitated by various B2B support services.

9. **Exchange implementation issues.** The major implementation issues for exchanges are the choice between private and public exchanges (or their combination), evaluation of exchanges, identifying problem areas, and using software agents as a support mechanism.

10. **Exchange networks and management of exchanges.** It will benefit customers if exchanges are connected to one another. Such integration is complex and may take years to complete. Managing exchanges individually can be expensive; therefore, "families" of exchanges or networks of exchanges may emerge.

11. **Critical success factors for exchanges.** Some of the major critical success factors for exchanges are early liquidity, proper ownership, proper governance and management, openness (technological and organizational), and a full range of services.

KEY TERMS

B2B portals	267	Horizontal exchanges	262	Public e-marketplaces	
Consortium trading		Market liquidity	269	(public exchanges)	260
exchange (CTE)	272	Market maker	260	Spot sourcing	261
Dynamic pricing	262	Partner relationship		Systematic sourcing	261
Dynamic trading	277	management (PRM)	281	Vertical exchanges	262
Elasticity	276	Private exchanges	282	Vortals	268
Exchange	260				

DISCUSSION QUESTIONS

1. How does dynamic pricing differ from fixed pricing?

2. Suppose a manufacturer uses an outside shipping company. How can the manufacturer use an exchange to arrange for the best possible shipping? How can a shipment's status be tracked?

3. Explain the legal concerns regarding consortia.

4. Which types of exchanges are most suitable for third-party ownership and why?

5. Compare and contrast the supplier aggregation model with the buyer aggregation model in an industry of your choice.

6. Describe the various issues of integration related to B2B exchanges.

7. Explain the logic for networks of exchanges.

8. Discuss the need for auctions in exchanges and the types of auctions used.

9. Explain the importance of early liquidity and describe methods to achieve it.

10. How do exchanges affect disintermediation?

11. What questions should buyers and sellers ask when evaluating exchanges?

12. Compare the operation and viability of private exchanges versus public exchanges.

INTERNET EXERCISES

1. Visit ariba.com and commerceone.com. Find the software tools they have for building e-markets. Check the capabilities provided by each and comment on their differences.

2. Go to alibaba.com and sign up (free) as a member. Go to the site map and find the "sample house." Create a product and place it in the sample house. Tell your instructor how to view this product.

3. Compare the services offered by globalsources.com with those offered by alibaba.com and meetworldtrade.com. Assuming you are a toy seller, with which one would you register? Why? If you are a buyer of auto parts, which one would you join and why?

4. Enter chemconnect.com and view the demos for different trading alternatives. Examine the revenue model. Evaluate the services from both the buyer's and seller's points of view. Also, examine the site policies and legal guidelines. Are they fair? Compare chemconnect.com with chemicalonline.com, trade-ranger.com, and omnexus.com. Which of these do you think will survive? Explain your reasoning.

5. Most of the major exchanges use an ERP/SCM partner. Enter i2.com and view its solutions. What are the benefits of these solutions?

6. Enter fastparts.com and review the services offered there. Write a report based on your findings. Compare it to freemarkets.com.

7. Enter eBay's Business Industrial area (pages.ebay.com/catindex/business.html or ebay.com, select "wholesale"). What kind of e-marketplace is this? What are its major capabilities?

8. Visit converge.com. What kind of exchange is this? What services does it provide? How do its auctions work?

9. Enter bigyellow.com and netb2b.com. What services do they provide that are relevant to exchanges?

10. Enter communityb2b.com and find recent material on B2B exchanges (within the last 6 months). Prepare a report on developments not covered in this chapter.

11. Enter commerceone.com and review its composite Applications solution. Describe this system and its connection to UCCnet's global registry. Write a report.

TEAM ASSIGNMENTS AND ROLE PLAYING

1. Form two teams (A and B) of five or more members. On each team, person 1 plays the role of an assembly company that produces television monitors. Persons 2 and 3 are domestic parts suppliers to the assembling company, and persons 4 and 5 play foreign parts suppliers. Assume that the TV monitor company wants to sell televisions directly to business customers. Each team is to design an environment composed of membership in exchanges and present its results. A graphical display is recommended.

2. Investigate the status of Covisint, both in the United States and in Europe. What are the relationships between Covisint and the company-centered marketplaces of the large automakers? Have another team find similar industrywide exchanges and compare them with Covisint.

3. Enter isteelasia.com, metalworld.com, lme.co.uk, and newview.com. Compare their operations and services. These exchanges compete in global markets. Examine the trading platforms, portal capabilities, and support services (e.g., logistics, payments, etc.) offered by each. In what areas do these companies compete? In what areas do they not compete? What are the advantages of isteelasia.com in dealing with Asian companies? Are regional exchanges needed? If it is good for Asia to have a regional exchange, why not have a Western European exchange, an Eastern European exchange, a Central American exchange, and so on? If regional exchanges are needed, can they work together? How? If there are too many exchanges, which are likely to survive? Research this topic and prepare a report.

REAL-WORLD CASE

GLOBAL TRANSPORTATION NETWORK

Although much publicity is given to public exchanges that deal with materials and products, such as ChemConnect and Covisint, several service-oriented exchanges have been created, and some of them are growing rapidly. One such exchange is a global transportation exchange for ocean transportation named Global Transportation Network (GTN).

GTN was formed in 2001 by a consortium of 13 ocean carriers (lines) that collectively represent more than 40 percent of worldwide capacity and a software company, GT Nexus (*gtnexus.com*), that specializes in global logistics and supply chain products.

The objective of the exchange, which is primarily a portal type, is to serve the ocean-shipping industry. The industry is composed of carriers, shippers (such as Wal-Mart and others who import many goods from abroad), and service providers (such as banks, insurance brokers, freight forwarders, and logistics providers). The mission of the exchange is to fundamentally change the process of getting goods around the world by using the Internet to provide superior service that maintains complete security for customers and the carriers. GT Nexus and its CEO are the exchange managers.

To develop the portal, the management team worked with many customers to identify customer needs and determine how the portal could help meet them. Customers wanted a multi-EC model that could meet their diversified needs in a unified way. Existing B2B software products were too narrow; a custom portal had to be built.

The GNT e-commerce platform is much more than a portal. It supports core transactional capabilities such as booking, invoicing, payment, tracking and tracing, rate negotiation, container management, and scheduling. GTN offers standardized booking, documentation, and tracking systems and provides better and more efficient customer support. In addition, it provides customized capabilities tailored for specific customers and carriers, including rate and contract management, cargo forecasting, and resource allocation. The benefits of the system to the ocean-shipping industry include:

▶ **Significant efficiencies and cost savings.** A 2002 study conducted by Anderson Consulting estimated that cost savings from these process improvements and efficiencies alone resulted in savings of 5 to 10 percent for carriers and customers across a range of industries (Coia 2002b). GTN frees individual carriers from the huge capital costs associated with the advanced technologies and resources required to create proprietary technology methods.

▶ **Standardization and ease of use.** GTN automates core transactions and makes it easier for customers to conduct business with multiple providers using common standards.

▶ **Secure and confidential access.** GTN provides a secure and confidential environment for customers and carriers to conduct business over the Internet.

Industry experts have observed various improvements for the participants of the exchange (Goodman 2002). A single carrier cannot afford to offer as many EC applications as the exchange offers; therefore, the exchange has greatly expanded the number of applications available to carriers. The system also has enabled customers to do business electronically throughout every process in the shipment cycle. For example, contract negotiation, a very time-consuming process, has been speeded up by the exchange. In addition, because carriers now have access to many more shippers than they could have found on their own, the number of electronic transactions for carriers has doubled, even in the first year of operation in the exchange. Carriers have also been able to improve customer service, one of the major motivators for using the exchange.

The shipping industry is deregulated and very competitive. However, lots of cooperation, such as vessel sharing, still goes on. The GTN system helps to facilitate such collaboration. Several alliances among carriers also exist, and they are supported by the system. Information sharing via open-standards and Web-enabled systems is a primary objective of the portal.

The technology of the exchange has contributed to its effectiveness. Data fit the internal IT systems of all users. Standardized processes allow carriers to present their services to shippers in the same way. Clients are able to use one interface to retrieve any information, regardless of the carrier with which the booking was made. The system uses a secured Internet connection (with a VPN, virtual private network) and has an optional EDI for some transactions. It also allows for competitive tendering through reverse auctions (Chapter 5). The exchange was recognized by *InfoWorld Magazine* (Sanborn 2002) as one of top-three technology projects.

Sources: Compiled from Goodman (2002), *gtnexus.com* (2002), and Coia (2002b).

Questions

1. Identify the critical success factors of this exchange.

2. Is a consortium the best type of ownership for this kind of exchange?

3. Although there are thousands of shippers, some of them are very big (e.g., Wal-Mart). Does it make sense to have them create a shipper's exchange? Why or why not?

4. What motivates a carrier to participate in the exchange?

5. What motivates a shipper to participate in the exchange?

6. How was customer service improved by the exchange?

REFERENCES

Aberdeen Group Inc. "Asite Builds E-Marketplace Using Combined Strength of Commerce One, Microsoft, and Attenda." *Aberdeen Group Profile*, May 2001, p. 5, aberdeen.com/ab%5Fabstracts/2001/05/05012573.htm (accessed September 2002).

Agrawal, M. K., and M. H. Pak. "Getting Smart About Supply Chain Management." *The McKinsey Quarterly* no. 2 (2001).

alibaba.com (accessed October 2002).

AMR Research Staff. "B2B Marketplaces Report, 2000–2005." *AMR Research*, August 1, 2001, amrresearch.com/Content/view.asp?pmillid=14510&docid=600 (accessed January 2003).

asite.com (accessed October 2002).

Baker, S., and K. Baker. "Going Up! Vertical Marketing on the Web." *Journal of Business Strategy* (May–June 2000).

Baumgartner, T., et al. "A Seller's Guide to B2B Markets." *The McKinsey Quarterly* no. 2 (2001).

Berryman, K., and S. Heck. "Is the Third Time the Charm for B2B?" *The McKinsey Quarterly* no. 2 (2001).

brint.com/members/01040530/b2bexchanges, **p. 2**, February 2002 (accessed September 2002).

Bryant, G. "E-Markets Hit the Mark." *Businessonline*, businessonline.org, February 2002 (accessed June 2003).

BRW Staff. "B2B: The Rocky Road to Profits for Exchanges." *Business Review Weekly of Australia*, November 10, 2000.

chemconnect.com (accessed December 2002).

Chircu, A. M., and R. J. Kauffman. "Reintermediation Strategies in B2B Electronic Commerce." *International Journal of Electronic Commerce* (Summer 2000).

Cleary, M. "Covisint Talks Trash." *Interactive Week*, May 21, 2001.

Coia, A. "Going Online Brought Smooth Sailing to World of Ocean Shipping." supplychainbrain.com (accessed June 2002a).

Coia, A. "Evolving Transportation Exchanges." *World Trade*, July 2002b.

Coupey, E. *Marketing and the Internet*. Upper Saddle River, NJ: Prentice Hall, 2001.

Covisint. "Mercator Software Selected by Covisint to Integrate Best-of-Breed Applications." Covisint press release, February 7, 2001. covisint.com/about/pressroom/pr/2001/2001.FEB.07.shtml (accessed April 2001a).

Covisint. "Supply Chain Management: Supplyconnect." covisint.com/downloads/print/supplier_conn.pdf (accessed February 2001b).

Cunningham, M. J. *B2B: How to Build a Profitable E-Commerce Strategy*. Cambridge, MA: Perseus Book Group, 2000.

Dai, Q., and R. J. Kauffman. "B2B E-Commerce Revisited: Revolution or Evolution." *Electronic Markets* 12, no. 2 (2002).

Darwin Magazine. "Commerce Leads the Evolution of the E-Marketplace." White paper, darwinmag.com/read/whitepapers/041501_co.html (accessed August 2001).

Delphi Group. "Industry's Most Focused B2B e-Business Conference Now Accepting Case Study Submissions." January 13, 2000, delphigroup.com/about/pressreleases/2000–PR/20000113–summitpapercall.htm (accessed July 2001).

Devine, D. A., et al. "Building Enduring Consortia." *The McKinsey Quarterly* no. 1 (2001).

Diorio, S. *Beyond "e": 12 Ways Technology Is Transforming Sales and Marketing Strategy*. New York: McGraw-Hill, 2002.

Dolinoy, M., et al. "Customer Defined Networks." forrester.com/ER/Research/Report/Summary/0,1338,11071,FF.html (accessed April 2001).

Durlacher Research Ltd. "Business to Business E-Commerce Report: An Investment Perspective." durlacher.com/downloads/b2breports.pdf (accessed May 6, 2000).

Duvall, M. "E-Marketplaces Getting Connected." *Interactive Week*, January 10, 2000.

Fram, E. "E-Commerce Survivors: Finding Value Amid Broken Dreams." *Business Horizons*, July–August 2002, 15–20.

Forbes. "ASAP/Best of the Web Knowledge Management State of the Industry Report: Biotech/Web B2B Guide." *Forbes*, October 7, 2002.

Goldman Sachs, Inc. "Internet: B2B E-Commerce." gs.com (accessed May 8, 2000).

Goodman, R. "Going Online Brought Smooth Sailing to World of Ocean Shipping." *Supplychainbrain.com*, June 2002, supplychainbrain.com/archives/6.02.ocean.htm?adcode=90 (accessed January 2003).

GTNexus. "GT Nexus Names Jeff Lynch Vice President of Sales." *gtnexus.com press release*, October 2002, gtnexus.com/cgi-perl/press_releases.cgi?releaseID=45&lang=en (accessed April 2003).

Hansen, M. A., et al. "A Buyer's Guide to B2B Markets." *The McKinsey Quarterly* no. 2 (2001).

Kambil, A., and E. van Heck. *Making Markets*. Boston: Harvard Business School Press, 2002.

Kaplan, S., and M. Sawhney. "E-Hubs: The New B2B Market Places." *Harvard Business Review* (May–June 2000).

Karpinski, R. "Special Report: E-Marketplaces Come Full Circle." *BtoBOnline*, January 8, 2001.

Keenan Report. "Internet Exchange 2000." keenanvision.com/dt/document.asp?id=1000280 (accessed April 2000).

Konicki, S. "Exchanges Go Private." *InformationWeek*, June 12, 2000, informationweek.com/790/private.htm (accessed September 2001).

Norris, G., et al. *E-Business and ERP*. New York: John Wiley & Sons, 2000.

Ramsdell, G. "The Real Business of B2B: Five Factors for Success." McKinsey & Company, October 2, 2000.

rawmart.com (accessed October 2002).

Sanborn, S. "Sailing Online." *Inforworld Magazine*, October 18, 2002, archive.infoworld.com/articles/fe/xml/02/11/04/021104fegtn.xml (accessed December 2002).

Schully, A. B., and W. W. Woods. *B2B Exchanges*. New York: ISI Publications, 2000.

Sharma, A. "Trends in Internet B2B Marketing." *Industrial Marketing Management* 31, no. 1 (2002).

Shetty, B. "Forecast Online Sales by Exchange Type." *Forrester Research*, August 2001, forrester.com/search/ 1,6260,, 00.html?squery=2%2C500+exchanges+worldwide (accessed September 2002).

van Heck, E., et al. "New Entrants and the Role of IT— Case Study: The Tele-Flower Auction in the Netherlands." *Proceedings of the 30th Hawaiian International Conference on Systems Sciences*, Maui, HI, January 1997. Updated 2002.

Varon, E. "What You Need to Know About Public and Private Exchanges." *CIO Magazine*, September 1, 2001.

worldsteel.org (accessed October 2002).

Young, E. "Web Marketplaces that Really Work." *Fortune/CNET Tech Review*, Winter 2002.

7A APPENDIX

COMMUNICATION NETWORKS AND EXTRANETS FOR B2B

Chapter 6 pointed out the need for networks to support communication and collaboration among B2B business partners. It also described EDI and its supporting role in facilitating B2B communication and collaboration. This appendix looks at the networks needed for private e-marketplaces and public exchanges.

The major network structure used in e-marketplaces and exchanges is an *extranet*, or "extended intranet." It connects with both the Internet and individual companies' intranets. An extranet adds value to the Internet by increasing its security and expanding the available bandwidth. In order to better understand how an extranet interfaces with the Internet and intranets, we will first consider the basic concepts of the Internet and intranets and then turn our attention back to extranets.

THE INTERNET

Internet
A public, global communications network that provides direct connectivity to anyone over a LAN via an ISP or directly via an ISP.

The **Internet** is a public, global communications network that provides direct connectivity to anyone over a local area network (LAN) via an Internet service provider (ISP) or directly via an ISP. This public network is connected and routed over gateways. The ISPs are connected to Internet access providers, to network access providers, and eventually to the Internet backbone. Because access to the Internet is open to all, control and security are at a minimum.

INTRANETS

intranet
A corporate LAN or WAN that uses Internet technology and is secured behind a company's firewalls.

An **intranet** is a corporate LAN or wide area network (WAN) that uses Internet technology and is secured behind a company's firewalls. (Chapter 12 discusses firewalls.) An intranet links various servers, clients, databases, and application programs, such as ERP, within a company. Although intranets are based on the same TCP/IP protocol as the Internet, they operate as a private network with limited access. Only authorized employees are able to use them.

Intranets are limited to information pertinent to the company, and they contain exclusive, often proprietary, sensitive information. The intranet can be used to enhance communication and collaboration among authorized employees, customers, suppliers, and other business partners. Because an intranet allows access through the Internet, it does not require any additional implementation of leased networks. This open and flexible connectivity is a major capability and advantage of intranets. See Chapter 8 for more on intranets.

EXTRANETS

extranet
A network that uses a virtual private network to link intranets in different locations over the Internet; an "extended intranet."

An **extranet** uses the TCP/IP protocol to link intranets in different locations (as shown in Exhibit 7A.1). Extranet transmissions are usually conducted over the Internet, which offers little privacy or transmission security. Therefore, it is necessary to add security features. This is done by creating tunnels of secured data flows, using cryptography and authorization algorithms, to provide secure transport of private communications. An Internet with tunneling technology is known as a **virtual private network (VPN)** (see Chapter 12 for details).

virtual private network (VPN)
A network that creates tunnels of secured data flows, using cryptography and authorization algorithms, to provide secure transport of private communications over the public Internet.

Extranets provide secured connectivity between a corporation's intranets and the intranets of its business partners, materials suppliers, financial services, government, and customers. Access to an extranet is usually limited by agreements of the collaborating parties, is strictly controlled, and is available only to authorized personnel. The protected environment of an extranet allows partners to collaborate and share information and to perform these activities securely.

Because an extranet allows connectivity between businesses through the Internet, it is an open and flexible platform suitable for SCM. To increase security, many companies replicate the portions of their databases that they are willing to share with their business partners and separate them physically from their regular intranets. However, even separated data need to be secured. (See Chapter 12 for more on EC network security.)

According to Szuprowicz (1998), extranet benefits fall into five categories:

1. **Enhanced communications.** The extranet enables improved internal communications; improved business partnership channels; effective marketing, sales, and customer support; and facilitated collaborative activities support.
2. **Productivity enhancements.** The extranet enables just-in-time information delivery, reduction of information overload, productive collaboration between work groups, and training on demand.

EXHIBIT 7A.1   An Extranet

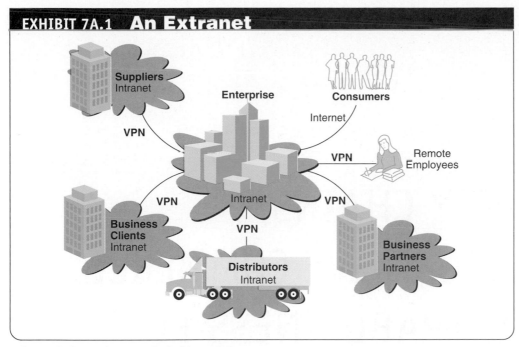

Source: B. Szuprowicz, 1998. Used with permission.

3. **Business enhancements.** The extranet enables faster time to market, potential for simultaneous engineering and collaboration, lower design and production costs, improved client relationships, and creation of new business opportunities.

4. **Cost reduction.** The extranet results in fewer errors, improved comparison shopping, reduced travel and meeting time and cost, reduced administrative and operational costs, and elimination of paper-publishing costs.

5. **Information delivery.** The extranet enables low-cost publishing, leveraging of legacy systems, standard delivery systems, ease of maintenance and implementation, and elimination of paper-based publishing and mailing costs.

Rihao-Ling and Yen (2001) reported additional advantages of extranets, such as ready access to information, ease of use, freedom of choice, moderate setup cost, simplified workflow, lower training cost, and better group dynamics. They also listed disadvantages, such as difficulty in justifying the investment (measuring benefits and costs), high user expectations, and drain on resources.

KEY TERMS

Extranet	296	Intranet	296	Virtual private network (VPN)	296
Internet	296				

REFERENCES

Rihao-Ling, R., and D. C. Yen. "Extranet: A New Wave of Internet." *SAM Advanced Management Journal* (Spring 2001).

Szuprowicz, B. *Extranet and Intranet: E-Commerce Business Strategies for the Future.* Charleston, SC: Computer Technology Research Corp., 1998.

E-SUPPLY CHAINS, COLLABORATIVE COMMERCE, AND INTRABUSINESS EC

Learning objectives

Upon completion of this chapter, you will be able to:

1. Define the e-supply chain and describe its characteristics and components.

2. List supply chain problems and their causes.

3. List solutions to supply chain problems provided by EC.

4. Define c-commerce and list its major types.

5. Describe collaborative planning and Collaboration, Planning, Forecasting, and Replenishing (CPFR), and list their benefits.

6. Define intrabusiness EC and describe its major activities.

7. Discuss integration along the supply chain.

8. Understand corporate portals and their types and roles.

9. Describe e-collaboration tools such as workflow and groupware.

Content

HOW GENERAL MOTORS IS COLLABORATING ONLINE

The Problem

Designing a car is a complex and lengthy process. Take, for example, just a small part of the process at General Motors (GM). Each model created needs to go through a frontal crash test. GM builds prototypes that cost about 1 million dollars each and tests how they react to a frontal crash. GM crashed these cars, made improvements, and then crashed them again. Even as late as the 1990s, GM crashed as many as 70 prototype versions of each new model.

The information regarding a new design collected from these crashes and other tests has to be shared among approximately 20,000 designers and engineers in hundreds of divisions and departments at 14 GM design labs, some of which are located in different countries. In addition, GM must communicate and collaborate with the design engineers of the more than 1,000 key suppliers. All of this communication and collaboration slowed the design process and increased its cost. It took over 4 years to get a new model to the market, and the new car often looked "stale" on arrival because public tastes had changed during the course of development.

The Solution

GM, like its competitors, has been transforming itself to an e-business. This gradual transformation has been going on since the mid-1990s, when Internet bandwidth increased sufficiently. GM's first task was to examine over 7,000 existing legacy IT systems, reducing that number to about 3,000 and making them Web enabled. GM's new EC system is centered on a computer-aided design (CAD) program from EDS (a large IT company, which is a subsidiary of GM). This system, known as Unigraphics, allows 3D design documents to be *shared online* by both the designers (internal and external) and engineers; all of whom are connected by the EDS software. In addition, collaborative and Web conferencing software tools, including Microsoft's NetMeeting and EDS's eVis, were added to enhance teamwork. These tools have radically changed the vehicle-review process.

To understand how GM now collaborates with a supplier, let's take as an example a needed cost reduction in a new seat frame made by Johnson Control. GM electronically sends its specifications for the seat to the vendor's product data system. Johnson Control's collaboration system (eMatrix) is integrated with EDS's Unigraphics. This collaboration allows joint searching, designing, tooling, and testing of the seat frame in real time, expediting the process and cutting costs by more than 10 percent. Finally, use of math-based modeling and a real-time, Web-based review process enables GM to electronically "crash" some of the cars during the design phases rather than doing it physically after each design change.

The Results

It now takes less than 18 months to bring a new car to market, compared to 4 or more years before, and the design cost is now much lower. For example, during the design phases, 60 cars are now "crashed" electronically, and only 10 prototype cars are crashed physically. The change has produced enormous savings. In addition, the shorter cycle time enables GM to bring out more new car models more quickly, providing the company with a competitive edge.

These changes have translated into profit. Despite the economic slowdown, GM's revenues increased more than 6 percent in 2002 and its earnings in the second quarter of 2002 doubled that of 2001.

Sources: Compiled from Sullivan (2002) and General Motors (2002).

WHAT WE CAN LEARN . . .

The process of designing cars involves many internal and external partners. The design process used to take a long time, and it was done at a very high cost. To improve the process, GM introduced several information systems that enabled electronic collaboration both internally and externally. The company also introduced information technology to expedite design, reduce problems along the supply and value chains of the design process, and drastically reduce costs. This case demonstrates several applications of EC that do not involve buying or selling: collaborative commerce, improvements along the supply chain, and B2E. These and related issues are the topics of Chapter 8.

8.1   E-SUPPLY CHAINS

Many people equate e-commerce with selling and buying on the Internet. However, although a company's success is clearly dependent on finding and retaining customers, its success may be far more dependent on what is *behind* the Web page than on what is *on* the Web page. In other words, the company's internal operations (the back end) and its relationships with suppliers and other business partners are as critical, and frequently much more critical, than customer-facing applications. This is of course true in the off-line business as well. In many cases, these "non-customer-facing applications" are related to the company's supply chain.

It has been well known for generations that the success of many organizations—private, public, and military—depends on their ability to manage the flow of materials, information, and money into, within, and out of the organization. Such a flow is referred to as a *supply chain*. Because supply chains may be long and complex and may involve many different business partners, we frequently see problems in the operation of the supply chains. These problems may result in delays, in customer dissatisfaction, in lost sales, and in high expenses from fixing the problems once they occur. World-class companies, such as Dell Computer, attribute much of their success to effective SCM, which is largely supported by IT and e-commerce technologies.

The essentials of supply chains and their management are described in Online Tutorial T3. This chapter focuses on supply chain issues related to e-commerce. In addition, it covers several related topics such as collaboration and integration along the supply chain. The topic of financial supply chains (payment systems) is covered in Chapter 13, and order fulfillment is covered in Chapter 14.

DEFINITIONS AND CONCEPTS

supply chain

The flow of materials, information, money, and services from raw material suppliers through factories and warehouses to the end customers.

To understand e-supply chains, one must first understand nonelectronic supply chains. A supply chain is the flow of materials, information, money, and services from raw material suppliers through factories and warehouses to the end customers. A supply chain also includes the *organizations* and *processes* that create and deliver products, information, and services to the end customers. The term supply chain comes from the concept of how the partnering organizations are *linked* together.

As shown in Exhibit 8.1, a simple linear supply chain links a company that manufactures or assembles a product (middle of the chain) with its suppliers (on the left) and distributors and customers (on the right). The upper part of the figure shows a generic supply chain. The bottom part shows a specific example of the toy-making process. The solid links in the figure show the flow of materials among the various partners. Not shown is the flow of returned goods (e.g., defective products) and money, which are flowing in the reverse direction. The broken links, which are shown only in the upper part of Exhibit 8.1, indicate the bidirectional flow of information.

A supply chain involves activities that take place during the entire product *life cycle*, "from dirt to dust," as some describe it. However, a supply chain is more than that, as it also includes the movement of information and money and the procedures that support the movement of a product or a service. Finally, the organizations and individuals involved are considered a part of the supply chain as well. Looked at very broadly, the supply chain actually ends when the product reaches its after-use disposal—presumably back to Mother Earth somewhere.

The supply chain shown in Exhibit 8.1 is fairly simple. As will be shown in Online Tutorial T3, supply chains can be much more complex, and they are of different types.

e-supply chain

A supply chain that is managed electronically, usually with Web technologies.

When a supply chain is managed electronically, usually with Web technologies, it is referred to as an **e-supply chain**. As will be shown throughout this chapter, improvements in e-supply chains are a major target for EC applications. However, before examining how e-supply chains are managed, it is necessary to better understand the composition of supply chains.

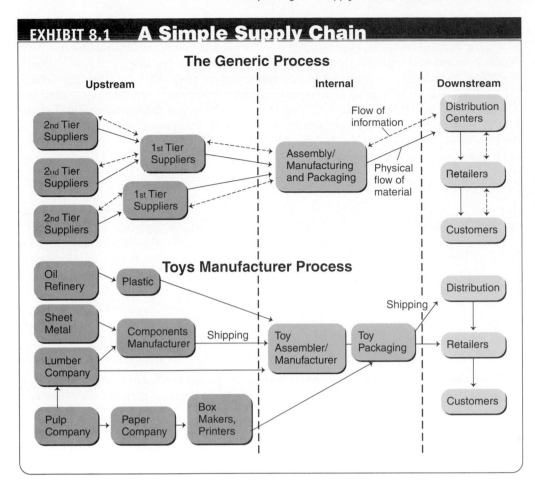

EXHIBIT 8.1   A Simple Supply Chain

The Generic Process

Upstream | Internal | Downstream

Toys Manufacturer Process

SUPPLY CHAIN PARTS

A supply chain can be broken into three major parts: upstream, internal, and downstream, as was shown in Exhibit 8.1.

▷ **Upstream supply chain.** The upstream part of the supply chain includes the activities of a manufacturing company with its suppliers (which can be manufacturers, assemblers, or both) and their connections to their suppliers (second-tier suppliers). The supplier relationship can be extended to the left in several tiers, all the way to the origin of the material (e.g., mining ores, growing crops). In the upstream supply chain, the major activity is *procurement*.

▷ **Internal supply chain.** The internal part of the supply chain includes all of the in-house processes used in transforming the inputs received from the suppliers into the organization's outputs. It extends from the time the inputs enter an organization to the time that the products go to distribution outside of the organization. In this part of the supply chain, the major concerns are production management, manufacturing, and inventory control.

▷ **Downstream supply chain.** The downstream part of the supply chain includes all the activities involved in delivering the products to the final customers. In the downstream supply chain, attention is directed at distribution, warehousing, transportation, and after-sale service.

A company's supply chain and its accompanying value chain (see Online Tutorial T3) encompass an array of business processes that create value by delivering goods or services to customers.

MANAGING SUPPLY CHAINS

Managing supply chains can be difficult due to the need to coordinate several business partners, several internal corporate departments, numerous business processes, and possibly many customers. Managing medium to large supply chains manually is almost impossible. Information technology provides two types of software solutions: (1) SCM and (2) ERP and its predecessors MRP and MRP II. (These types of software are defined in Online Tutorial T3.) A major requirement for any medium- to large-scale company that is moving to EC is the integration between the Web and the ERP/MRP/SCM solutions—in other words, creating an e-supply chain and managing it.

E-Supply Chains and Their Management

e-supply chain management (e-SCM)
The collaborative use of technology to improve the operations of supply chain activities as well as the management of supply chains.

As noted earlier, the term *e-supply chain* refers to the use of EC technologies in supporting supply chain operations. According to Norris et al. (2000), **e-supply chain management (e-SCM)** is the collaborative use of technology to enhance B2B processes and improve speed, agility, real-time control, and customer satisfaction. It involves the use of information technologies to improve the operations of supply chain activities (e.g., procurement) as well as the management of the supply chains (e.g., planning, coordination, and control). E-SCM is not about technology change alone; it also involves changes in management policies, organizational culture, performance metrics, business processes, and organizational structure across the supply chain.

The success of an e-supply chain depends on the following:

▶ **The ability of all supply chain partners to view partner collaboration as a strategic asset.** It is the tight integration and trust among the trading partners that generates speed, agility, and lower cost.

▶ **Information visibility along the entire supply chain.** Information about inventories at various segments of the chain, demand for products, delivery times, and any other relevant information must be visible to all members of the supply chain at any given time. Therefore, information must be managed properly—with strict policies, discipline, and daily monitoring.

▶ **Speed, cost, quality, and customer service.** These are the metrics by which supply chains are measured. Consequently, companies must clearly define the measurements for each of these four metrics together with the target levels to be achieved. The target levels should be attractive to the business partners.

▶ **Integrating the supply chain more tightly.** An e-supply chain will benefit from tighter integration, both within a company and across an extended enterprise made up of suppliers, trading partners, logistics providers, and the distribution channel.

Activities and Infrastructure of E-SCM

According to Norris et al. (2000), the e-supply chain consists of the following six processes:

Supply chain replenishment. Supply chain replenishment encompasses the integrated production and distribution processes. Companies can use replenishment information to reduce inventories, eliminate stocking points, and increase the velocity of replenishment by synchronizing supply and demand information across the extended enterprise. Real-time supply and demand information facilitates make-to-order and assemble-to-order manufacturing strategies across the extended enterprise. Supply-chain replenishment is a natural companion to Web-enabled customer orders. (For more on this topic, see Stevenson 2002.)

E-procurement. E-procurement, as described in Chapter 6, is the use of Web-based technology to support the key procurement processes, including requisitioning, sourcing, contracting, ordering, and payment. E-procurement supports the purchase of both direct and indirect materials and employs several Web-based functions such as online catalogs, contracts, purchase orders, and shipping notices. E-procurement can improve the operation of the supply chain in various ways: Online catalogs can be used to eliminate redesign of components in product development; visibility of available parts and their attributes enables quick decision making; online purchase orders expedite the ordering process; and advanced-shipping notifications and acknowledgments streamline delivery.

Collaborative planning. Collaborative planning requires buyers and sellers to develop a single shared forecast of demand and a plan of supply to support this demand, and to update it regularly, based on information shared over the Internet. It includes B2B workflow across multiple enterprises over the Internet, with data exchanged among them dynamically. This topic is discussed further in Section 8.4.

Collaborative design and product development. Collaborative product development involves the use of product design and development techniques across multiple companies to improve product launch success and reduce time to market (as demonstrated in the GM opening case). During product development, engineering and design drawings can be shared over a secure network among the contract house, testing facility, marketing firm, and downstream manufacturing and service companies. Other techniques include sharing specifications, test results, and design changes, and using online prototyping to obtain customer feedback. Development costs can also be reduced by tightly integrating and streamlining communication channels.

E-logistics. E-logistics is the use of Web-based technologies to support the warehouse and transportation processes. E-logistics enables distribution to couple routing optimization with inventory tracking information. For example, Internet-based freight auctions allow spot buying of trucking capacity. Third-party logistics providers offer virtual logistics services by integrating and optimizing distribution resources. This topic will be covered in Chapter 14. (For additional coverage, see Bayles 2001.)

Use of B2B exchanges and supply webs. The B2B exchanges introduced in Chapter 7 could play a critical role in e-supply chain management. Norris et al. (2000) view this role in what they call *supply webs*. Supply webs emerge as alternative configurations to the traditional supply chains. Information, transactions, products, and funds all flow to and from *multiple* nodes in a supply web. Supply webs that are formed as vertical exchanges (or vortals) and serve industry sectors by integrating the supply chain systems of various buyers and sellers create *virtual trading communities*.

The key activities just described use a variety of infrastructure and enabling tools. The following are the major infrastructure elements and tools of e-supply chains.

- **Extranets.** These were described in Chapter 7. Their major purpose is to support interorganizational communication and collaboration.
- **Intranets.** These are the corporate internal networks for communication and collaboration. They are described in the appendix to this chapter (Appendix 8A).
- **Corporate portals.** These provide a gateway for external and internal collaboration, communication, and information search. They are described in Section 8.7.
- **Workflow systems and tools.** These are systems that *manage* the flow of information in organizations. They are described in Section 8.8.
- **Groupware and other collaborative tools.** A large number of tools facilitate collaboration between two parties and among members of small as well as large groups. Various tools, some of which are collectively known as groupware, are available for purposes of collaboration, as described in Section 8.8.

Section 8.1 ❯ REVIEW

1. Define the e-supply chain and list its three major parts.
2. Describe success factors of e-supply chain management.
3. List the six processes of e-supply chains.
4. List the major e-supply chain management infrastructures and enabling tools.

8.2 SUPPLY CHAIN PROBLEMS AND SOLUTIONS

Supply chains have been plagued with problems, both in the military and in business operations, for generations. These problems have sometimes caused armies to lose wars and companies to go out of business. The problems are most apparent in complex or long supply chains and in cases where many business partners are involved. As this section will show, some remedies are finally available through the use of IT and EC.

TYPICAL PROBLEMS ALONG THE SUPPLY CHAIN

Supply chains can be very long, involving many internal and external partners located in different places. Both materials and information must flow among several entities, and these transfers, especially when manually handled, can be slow and error prone.

In the off-line world, there are many examples of companies that were unable to meet demand for certain products while having oversized and expensive inventories of other products. Similar situations exist online (see Chapter 14). One of the most publicized problems in EC was the supply-demand mismatch of toys during the holiday season of November–December 1999 (see Chapter 14). In this case, there was a shortage of toys due to incorrect demand forecasting. A demand forecast is influenced by a number of factors, including consumer behavior, economic conditions, competition, prices, weather conditions, technological developments, and more. Companies can improve their demand forecasting by using IT-supported forecasts, which are done in collaboration with business partners.

Another problem in the 1999 toy season was related to shipping. A lack of logistics infrastructure prevented the right toys from reaching their destinations on time. Various uncertainties exist in delivery times, which depend on many factors, ranging from vehicle failures to road conditions.

Quality problems with materials and parts can also contribute to deficiencies in the supply chain. The worst case is when quality problems create production delays, idling factories and workers and crimping inventories. Some companies grapple with quality problems due to general misunderstandings or to shipments of wrong materials and parts. Sometimes, the high cost of expediting operations or shipments is the unfortunate result.

Pure EC companies are likely to have more supply chain problems because they do not have a logistics infrastructure and are forced to use external logistics services. This can be expensive, plus it requires more coordination and dependence on outsiders. For this reason, some large virtual retailers, such as Amazon.com, are developing physical warehouses and logistics systems. Other virtual retailers are creating strategic alliances with logistics companies or with brick-and-mortar companies that have their own logistics systems. Other problems along the EC supply chain stem mainly from the need to coordinate several activities and internal units and business partners. (For more on supply chain problems, see Handfield et al. 2002 and Ayers 2000).

The Bullwhip Effect

bullwhip effect
Erratic shifts in orders up and down supply chains.

One additional supply chain problem, called the **bullwhip effect**, is worth noting here. The bullwhip effect refers to erratic shifts in orders up and down supply chains (see Lee et al. 1997). This effect was initially observed by P&G with their disposable diapers in off-line retail stores. Although actual sales in stores were fairly stable and predictable, orders from distributors had wild swings, creating production and inventory problems for P&G. An investigation revealed that distributors' orders were fluctuating because of poor demand forecasts, price fluctuations, order batching, and rationing within the supply chain. All of this resulted in unnecessary inventories in various places along the supply chain, fluctuations of P&G orders to its suppliers, and the flow of inaccurate information. Distorted or late information can lead to tremendous inefficiencies, excessive inventories, poor customer service, lost revenues, ineffective shipments, and missed production schedules.

The bullwhip effect is not unique to P&G. Firms from Hewlett-Packard in the computer industry to Bristol-Myers Squibb in the pharmaceutical field have experienced a similar phenomenon (Handfield et al. 2002). Basically, even slight demand uncertainties and variabilities become magnified when viewed through the eyes of managers at each link in the supply chain. If each distinct entity makes ordering and inventory decisions with an eye to its own interest above those of the chain, stockpiling may be occurring simultaneously at as many as seven or eight places across the supply chain. Such stockpiling can lead to as many as 100 days of inventory waiting "just in case." A 1998 industry study by the American Agricultural Economic Association (aaea.org, reported by Ricks et al. 1999) projected that $30 billion in savings could materialize in the grocery industry supply chains alone as a result of improved *information sharing*. Thus, companies may avoid the "sting of the bullwhip" if they take steps to share information along the supply chain. Such sharing is facilitated by EDI, extranets, and groupware technologies and is part of interorganizational EC and *collaborative commerce*, topics discussed elsewhere in this chapter and in Chapters 6 and 7.

THE NEED FOR INFORMATION SHARING ALONG THE SUPPLY CHAIN

By definition, a supply chain includes the flow of information to and from all participating entities. The information can be supportive of physical shipments or of shipments of digitized products (or services). It includes product pricing, inventory, shipping status, credit and financial information, and technology news. Many, if not most, of the supply chain problems that occur are the result of poor flow of information, inaccurate information, untimely information, and so on. Information must be managed properly in each supply chain segment.

Information systems are the links that enable communication and collaboration along the supply chain. According to Handfield and Nichols (1999), they represent one of the fundamental elements that link the organizations of the supply chain into a unified and coordinated system. In today's competitive business climate, information and information technology are one of the keys to the success, and perhaps even the survival, of any SCM initiative (Handfield and Nichols 1999).

Case studies of some world-class companies, such as Wal-Mart, Dell Computer, and FedEx, indicate that these companies created very sophisticated information systems, exploiting the latest technological developments and creating innovative solutions.

EC SOLUTIONS ALONG THE SUPPLY CHAIN

EC as a technology provides solutions along the supply chain, as has been shown throughout this book. Such solutions are beneficial both to brick-and-mortar operations and to online companies. Here is a representative list of the major solutions provided by an EC approach and technologies.

▶ *Order taking* can be done on the Internet, EDI, EDI/Internet, or an extranet, and it may be fully automated. For example, in B2B, orders are generated and transmitted automatically to suppliers when inventory levels fall below certain levels. The result is a fast, inexpensive, and more accurate (no need to rekey data) order-taking process. In B2C, Web-based ordering using electronic forms expedites the process, makes it more accurate (intelligent agents can check the input data and provide instant feedback), and reduces processing costs.

▶ *Order fulfillment* can become instant if the products can be digitized (e.g., software). In other cases, EC order taking interfaces with the company's back-office systems, including logistics. Such an interface, or even integration, shortens cycle time and eliminates errors. (See Chapter 14 for more on order fulfillment.)

▶ *Electronic payments* can expedite both the order fulfillment cycle and the payment delivery period. Payment processing can be significantly less expensive and fraud can be better controlled. (See Chapter 13 for more on electronic payments.)

▶ *Inventories can be minimized* both by introducing a make-to-order (pull) production process, as well as by providing fast and accurate information to suppliers. By allowing business partners to electronically track and monitor orders and production activities, inventory management can be improved and inventory levels and the expense of inventory management can be minimized.

▶ *Collaborative commerce* among members of the supply chain can be done in many areas ranging from product design to demand forecasting. The results are shorter cycle times, minimal delays and work interruptions, lower inventories, and less administrative cost.

EC Application

GLOBAL SUPPLY CHAIN SYNCHRONIZATION AT CORNING, INC.

Corning Inc., a glass manufacturer headquartered in upstate New York, makes optical fiber, cables and photonic components, LCD glass for flat panel displays and other products, as well as the glassware and cookware that were the company's original products. The company has multiple businesses and research, production, and distribution sites in 34 countries.

Although they share the direction and global focus of the organization, the company's 12 business units have been managing independently, since 1995, their own planning, order management, production, and other supply chain operations. Such decentralization empowers the units, but the company has experienced problems ranging from delivery delays to excessive inventory costs along its long and unsynchronized supply chains.

To ease these problems, Corning looked for solutions that would enable it to create and optimize truly global supply chains within its businesses. The Supply Chain Technology Strategy group, along with the process owners (the Corning managers who are responsible for the various processes), did wide-ranging analyses of each business unit. The group planned improvements in the supply chain process and tried to find the best SCM solutions to help carry out the improvements. Corning chose PeopleSoft as its ERP vendor. Using PeopleSoft technology, Corning was able to integrate the relevant activities of its manufacturers, suppliers, customer service organizations, sales organizations, and technology innovators.

To enable an optimized, real-time "virtual factory" environment, Corning Specialty Materials Group (manufacturer of semiconductors, photonics, and technical materials) combines PeopleSoft manufacturing, customer fulfillment management, and supply chain planning solutions to improve *collaboration* among the 14 factories and sales and research sites worldwide.

Rick Beers, Director of Supply Chain Technology at Corning, explains, "High performance at Corning means agility. We need to react quickly to opportunities or problems in our supply chains—to see snags coming and plan accordingly, or adjust production levels in response to demand. That requires real-time data and interoperability among applications. It all comes down to having the right information at the right place at the right time" (*peoplesoft.com* 2002).

The improved infrastructure, specifically a common database shared throughout Corning's organization, has made possible the flexibility to increase yield, decrease cycle time, and maintain low levels of inventory based on sales forecasts. The new process has transformed the supply chain by increasing or improving collaboration, workflow, planning, strategic analysis, and e-business initiatives. Corning is now experiencing significantly fewer problems along its supply chain.

Sources: Compiled from Springer (2002), *corning.com* (press releases 2002), and *peoplesoft.com/go/pt_scm* (2002).

Questions

1. What were the problems of Corning's old system?
2. What was the logic behind decentralizing operations?
3. How is integration of information done in the decentralized environment?
4. How is flexibility provided by the new system?

Supply chain problems may become more serious when the supply chain involves global segments. EC Application Case 8.1 reviews some of these problems and examines how they were solved by Corning Inc.

The next section examines supply chain solutions provided by collaborative commerce.

Section 8.2 ▶ REVIEW

1. Describe some typical problems along the supply chain.
2. Describe the reasons for supply-chain-related problems.
3. Describe the bullwhip effect.
4. Describe the benefits of information sharing along the supply chain.
5. List some EC solutions to supply chain problems.

8.3 COLLABORATIVE COMMERCE

Previous chapters introduced B2B activities related mainly to selling and buying. E-commerce can also be used to improve collaboration among organizations in the supply chain.

ESSENTIALS OF COLLABORATIVE COMMERCE

Collaborative commerce (c-commerce) refers to the use of digital technologies that enable companies to collaboratively plan, design, develop, manage, and research products, services, and innovative EC applications. These activities differ from selling and buying. An example would be a company that it is collaborating electronically with a vendor that designs a product or a part for the company, as was shown in the GM opening case. C-commerce implies communication, information sharing, and collaborative planning done electronically through tools such as groupware and specially designed EC collaboration tools.

Numerous studies (e.g., line56.com 2002) suggest that collaborative relationships result in significant impacts on organizations' performance. Major benefits cited are cost reduction, increased revenue, and better customer retention. These benefits are the results of fewer stock outs, less exception processing, reduced inventory throughout the supply chain, lower materials costs, increased sales volume, and increased competitive advantage.

C-commerce activities are usually conducted between and among supply chain partners. Chapter 1 (page 17) provided an example of Orbis, a small Australian company that uses a hub to communicate among all its business partners. A similar model is used by Webcor Builders, as shown in EC Application Case 8.2.

There are several varieties of c-commerce, ranging from joint design efforts to forecasting. Collaboration can be done both between and within organizations. For example, a collaborative platform can help in communication and collaboration between headquarters and subsidiaries or between franchisers and franchisees. The platform provides e-mail, message boards and chat rooms, and online corporate data access around the globe, no matter what the time zone. The following sections demonstrate some types and examples of c-commerce.

collaborative commerce (c-commerce)
The use of digital technologies that enable companies to collaboratively plan, design, develop, manage, and research products, services, and innovative EC applications.

CASE 8.2

EC Application

WEBCOR CONSTRUCTIONS GOES ONLINE WITH ITS PARTNERS

Webcor Builders (*webcor.com*) builds apartment buildings, hotels, and office parks and earns revenues of about $500 million a year. For years the company suffered from poor communication with its partners (architects, designers, building owners, subcontractors) and struggled with too much paperwork. Reams of documents were sent back and forth via "snail mail." In a very competitive industry, inefficiencies can be costly. Therefore, Webcor decided to introduce c-commerce into its operations. Webcor's goal was to turn its CAD drawings, memos, and other information into shared digital information.

To enable online collaboration, Webcor uses an application service provider (ASP) that hosts Webcor's projects using ProjectNet software on a secured extranet. The software is complex; it was difficult to get everyone to accept ProjectNet, and some user training was necessary. However, Webcor found itself in a strong enough market position to be able to say that in the near future, it would not partner with anyone who would not use ProjectNet.

With everyone on the ProjectNet system, Webcor's business partners can post, send, or edit complex CAD drawings, digital photos, memos, status reports, and project histories. ProjectNet provides a central meeting place where users can both download and transmit information to all parties. Everyone involved in a project is more accountable because there is a digital trail, and partners now get instant access to new building drawings.

One of the major benefits of ProjectNet is that employees now spend more time managing their work and less time on administrative paperwork. Several clerical workers were laid off, and the saved cost of their salaries is covering the software rental fees.

Sources: Compiled from press releases at *webcor.com* (2000–2002) and from DiCarlo (1999).

Questions

1. Draw the supply chain of Webcor before ProjectNet.
2. What B2B model is this (e.g., sell-side, buy-side, etc.)?
3. What are the benefits of this c-commerce project to Webcor?
4. What are the benefits of this c-commerce project to Webcor's clients?

COLLABORATIVE NETWORKS

Traditionally, collaboration took place among supply chain members, frequently those that were close to each other (e.g., a manufacturer and its distributor or a distributor and a retailer). Even if more partners were involved, the focus was on the optimization of information and product flow between existing nodes in the traditional supply chain. Advanced approaches such as the Collaboration, Planning, Forecasting and Replenishing (CPFR), which is described in the next section, do not change the basic structure.

Traditional collaboration results in a vertically integrated supply chain. However, as stated in Chapters 1 and 2, EC and Web technologies can *fundamentally change* the shape of the supply chain, the number of players within it, and their individual roles. The new supply chain can be a hub, as shown in the Orbis case (see Chapter 1), or even a network. A comparison between the traditional supply chain and the new one, which is made possible by Web technologies, is shown in Exhibit 8.2. Notice that the traditional chain in Part A (for the food industry) is basically linear. The *collaborative network* in Part B shows that partners at any point in the network can interact with each other, bypassing traditional partners. Interaction may occur among several manufacturers or distributors, as well as with new players such as software agents that act as aggregators, B2B exchanges, or logistics providers.

The collaborative network can take different shapes depending on the industry, the product (or service), the volume of information flow, and more. Examples of collaborative networks are provided by Poirier (2001) and by Walton and Princi (2000).

REPRESENTATIVE EXAMPLES OF E-COLLABORATION

Leading businesses are moving quickly to realize the benefits of c-commerce. For example, the real estate franchiser RE/MAX uses a c-commerce platform to improve communications and collaboration among its nationwide network of independently owned real estate

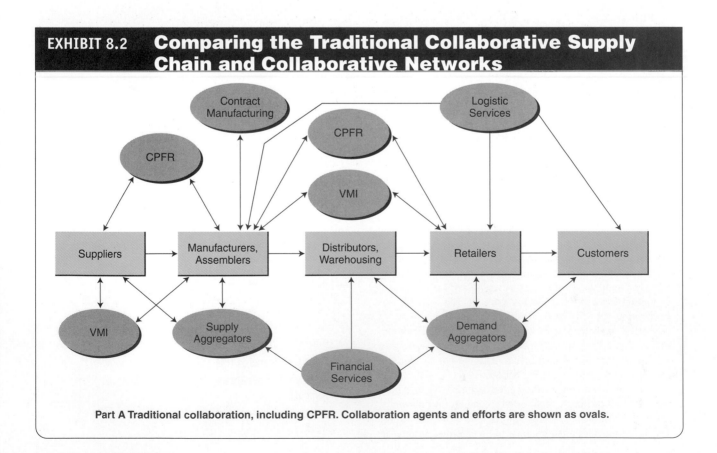

EXHIBIT 8.2 Comparing the Traditional Collaborative Supply Chain and Collaborative Networks

Part A Traditional collaboration, including CPFR. Collaboration agents and efforts are shown as ovals.

EXHIBIT 8.2   (continued)

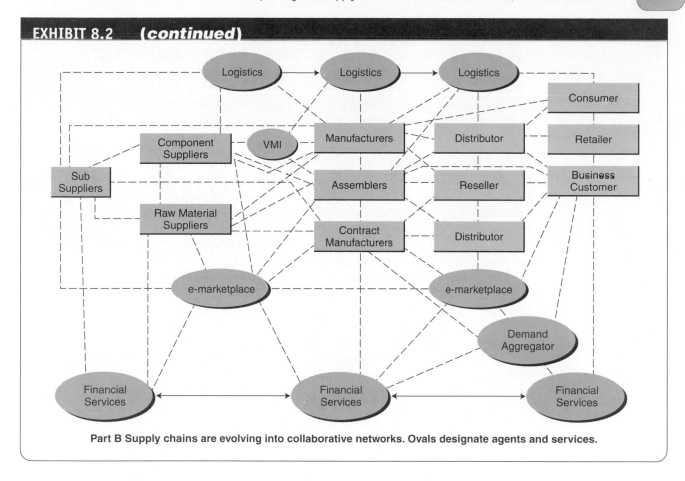

Part B Supply chains are evolving into collaborative networks. Ovals designate agents and services.

franchises, sales associates, and suppliers. Similarly, Marriott International, the world's largest hospitality company, started with an online brochure and then developed a c-commerce system that links corporations, franchisees, partners, suppliers, and customers, around the world. (See Intel 1999a and 1999b for details.) In addition, as described in EC Application Case W8.1, Nygard of Canada has developed a collaborative system along its entire supply chain.

There are many examples of e-collaboration. Here are some additional representative ones. For more, see Schram (2001) and Davison and de Vreede (2001).

Information Sharing Between Retailers and Suppliers: P&G and Wal-Mart

Information sharing among business partners, as well as among the various units inside each organization, is necessary for the success of SCM. Information systems must be designed so that sharing becomes easy. One of the most notable examples of information sharing is between P&G and Wal-Mart. Wal-Mart provides P&G access to sales information on every item P&G makes for Wal-Mart. The information is collected by P&G on a daily basis from every Wal-Mart store, and P&G uses the information to manage inventory replenishment for Wal-Mart. By monitoring the inventory level of each P&G item in every Wal-Mart store, P&G knows when the inventories fall below the threshold that triggers a shipment. All this is done electronically. The benefit for P&G is accurate demand information; the benefit for Wal-Mart is adequate inventory. P&G has similar agreements with other major retailers.

Retailer–Supplier Collaboration: Target Corporation

Target Corporation (targetcorp.com) is a large retail conglomerate (owner of Target Stores, Marshall Field's, Mervyn's, and Target Direct). It needs to conduct EC activities with about 20,000 trading partners. In 1998, then operating under the name Dayton-Hudson

Corporation, the company established an extranet-based system for those partners that were not connected to its VAN-based EDI. The extranet enabled the company not only to reach many more partners, but also to use many applications not available on the traditional EDI. The system (based on GE's InterBusiness Partner Extranet platform, geis.com) enabled the company to streamline its communications and collaboration with suppliers. It also allowed the company's business customers to create personalized Web pages that were accessible via either the Internet or GE's private VAN, as shown in Exhibit 8.3.

Reduction of Design Cycle Time: Adaptec, Inc.

Adaptec, Inc. (adaptec.com) is a large microchip manufacturer that supplies critical components to electronics-equipment makers. The company outsources manufacturing tasks, concentrating on product research and development. Outsourcing production, however, put the company at a disadvantage against competitors that have their own manufacturing facilities and can optimize their delivery schedules. It took Adaptec up to 15 weeks to deliver products to customers; competitors were able to deliver similar chips in only 8 weeks.

The longer delivery time was mainly caused by the need to coordinate design activities between Adaptec headquarters in California and its three principal fabrication factories in Hong Kong, Japan, and Taiwan. To solve this problem, the company introduced an extranet-based collaboration and enterprise-level supply chain integration software, which incorporates automated workflow and EC tools.

One initial benefit of the new system was a reduction in the time required to generate, transmit, and confirm purchase orders. Adaptec now uses e-mail to communicate with manufacturers across several time zones to automatically start the flow of raw materials, which in turn reduces invoicing and shipping times. In addition to business transaction documents, Adaptec can send chip design diagrams over the extranet, enabling the manufacturers

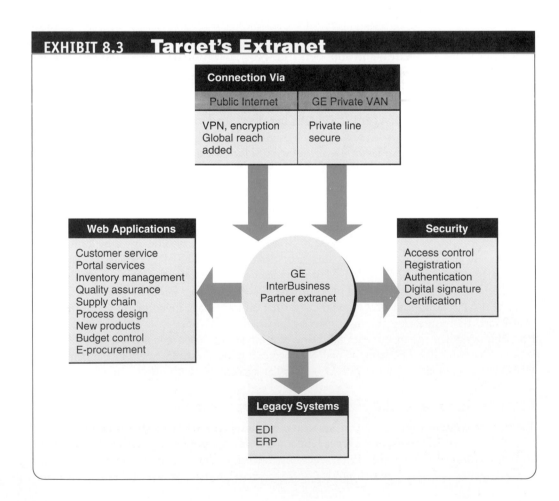

EXHIBIT 8.3 Target's Extranet

Connection Via

Public Internet	GE Private VAN
VPN, encryption Global reach added	Private line secure

Web Applications
Customer service
Portal services
Inventory management
Quality assurance
Supply chain
Process design
New products
Budget control
E-procurement

GE InterBusiness Partner extranet

Security
Access control
Registration
Authentication
Digital signature
Certification

Legacy Systems
EDI
ERP

to prepare for product changes and new designs. This faster communication method required Adaptec to adjust its decision-making processes that were based on the old assumption that at least 2 weeks were needed to put an order into production. The overall result was a reduction in its order-to-product-delivery time from 15 weeks to between 10 and 12 weeks.

See Ragusa and Bochenek (2001) for more on collaborative virtual design environments.

Reduction of Product Development Time: Caterpillar, Inc.

Caterpillar, Inc. (caterpillar.com) is a multinational heavy-machinery manufacturer. In the traditional mode of operation, cycle time along the supply chain was long because the process involved the transfer of paper documents among managers, salespeople, and technical staff. To solve the problem, Caterpillar connected its engineering and manufacturing divisions with its active suppliers, distributors, overseas factories, and customers through an extranet-based global collaboration system. By means of the collaboration system, a request for a customized tractor component, for example, can be transmitted from a customer to a Caterpillar dealer and on to designers and suppliers, all in a very short time. Customers also can use the extranet to retrieve and modify detailed order information while the vehicle is still on the assembly line.

Remote collaboration capabilities between the customer and product developers have decreased cycle time delays caused by rework time. Suppliers are also connected to the system so that they can deliver materials or parts directly to Caterpillar's shops or directly to the customer if appropriate. The system also is used for expediting maintenance and repairs.

COLLABORATIVE COMMERCE AND KNOWLEDGE MANAGEMENT

In Chapter 1, *knowledge management* was defined as the process of capturing or creating knowledge. According to Thuraisingham et al. (2002), collaborative commerce is essentially an integration of KM, EC, and collaboration tools and methodologies that are designed to carry out transactions and other activities within and across organizations. One can use various architectures to combine these ingredients. Therefore, c-commerce will differ in various industries and in B2B and B2C settings.

Knowledge and its management play a strategic role in collaboration For example, one function of knowledge management often is to gather and make available experts' opinions, and these opinions can be provided by one partner to others. Thus, one model of collaboration includes a knowledge provider with clients who want to acquire knowledge. Learning is also important in c-commerce, and it may be facilitated by KM. Creating a knowledge-sharing platform for collaboration can be facilitated by knowledge portals (see Kesner 2003 and Section 8.7). For further discussion of the integration of KM, EC, and collaborative tools, see Thuraisingham et al. (2002). Also, see the Amway case at the end of this chapter.

BARRIERS TO C-COMMERCE

Despite the many potential benefits, c-commerce is moving ahead fairly slowly. Reasons cited in various studies include technical reasons involving integration, standards, and networks; security and privacy concerns over who has access to and control of information stored in a partner's database; internal resistance to information sharing and to new approaches; and lack of internal skills to conduct collaborative commerce (Schram 2001).

A big stumbling block to the adoption of c-commerce is the lack of defined and universally agreed-on standards. Even early initiatives such as CPFR (see next section) are still in their infancy. New approaches such as the use of XML and its variants and the use of Web services could significantly lessen the problem of standards.

Sometimes collaboration is an organizational culture shock—people simply resist sharing. One reason for this is lack of trust. According to Gibson-Paul (2003), companies such as Boeing are grappling with the trust factor. Some techniques she suggests to increase trust include starting small (e.g., synchronizing one type of sales data); picking up projects that are likely to provide a quick return on investment for both sides; meeting face-to-face in the beginning of a collaboration; and showing the benefits of collaboration to all parties. Despite initial lack of trust, if potential collaborators judge the benefits of collaboration to be sufficient, and about equal among collaborators, they will be more eager to join in.

Finally, global collaboration involves all of these potential barriers, and more. Some of these additional barriers are described in Chapter 15. For more on c-commerce barriers, see Davison and de Vreede (2001).

Specialized software tools for c-commerce can be expected to break down some of the barriers to c-commerce (see Section 8.8). In addition, as companies hear more about the major benefits of c-commerce—benefits such as smoothing the supply chain, reducing inventories and operating costs, and increasing customer satisfaction and the competitive edge—it is expected that more will rush to jump on the c-commerce bandwagon.

Section 8.3 ▶ REVIEW

1. Define c-commerce.
2. List the major types of c-commerce.
3. Describe some examples of c-commerce.
4. Define collaborative networks and distinguish them from traditional supply chain collaboration.
5. Describe KM–collaboration relationships.
6. List some major barriers to c-commerce.

8.4 COLLABORATIVE PLANNING, CPFR, AND COLLABORATIVE DESIGN

In *collaborative planning*, business partners—manufacturers, suppliers, distribution partners, and other partners—all have real-time access to point-of-sale order information. Partners create initial forecasts, provide changes as necessary, and share forecasts. Thus, all parties work to a schedule aligned to a common view, and all have access to order and forecast performance that is globally visible through electronic links. Schedule, order, or product changes trigger immediate adjustments to all parties' schedules.

Collaborative planning is designed to synchronize production plans and product flows, optimize resource utilization over an expanded capacity base, increase customer responsiveness, and reduce inventories. Collaborative planning is a necessity in e-SCM (see Kalakota and Robinson 2001). The planning process is difficult because it involves multiple parties and activities, as shown in Exhibit 8.4.

This section examines several aspects of collaborative planning and collaborative design.

THE CPFR PROJECT

collaborative planning, forecasting, and replenishment (CPFR) Project in which suppliers and retailers collaborate in their planning and demand forecasting to optimize flow of materials along the supply chain.

Collaborative planning, forecasting, and replenishment (CPFR) is a project in which suppliers and retailers collaborate in their planning and demand forecasting in order to ensure that members of the supply chain will have the right amount of raw materials and finished goods when they need them. The collaborators agree on a standard process, shown in Exhibit 8.5 (page 314). The process starts with an agreement on a joint business plan and ends with an order forecast. CPFR provides a *standard framework* for collaborative planning. Retailers and vendors determine the "rules of engagement," such as how often and at what level information will be provided. Typically, they share greater amounts of more detailed information, such as promotion schedules and item point-of-sale history, and use store-level expectations as the basis of all forecasts.

The idea is to improve demand forecasting for all of the partners in the supply chain and then communicate forecasts using information-sharing applications (already developed by technology companies such as Manugistics, Oracle, PeopleSoft, and i2). For the retailer, collaborative forecasting means fewer out-of-stocks and resultant lost sales and less stored

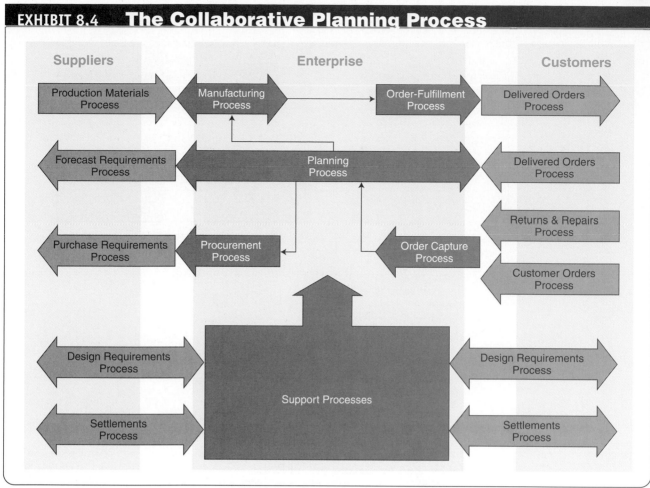

EXHIBIT 8.4   The Collaborative Planning Process

Source: *E-Business and ERP: Transforming the Enterprise* by Norris, G., et al., © 2000, John Wiley & Sons, Inc. This material is used by permission of John Wiley & Sons, Inc.

inventory. For the manufacturer, collaborative forecasting means fewer expedited shipments and optimally sized production runs.

Besides working together to develop production plans and forecasts for stock replenishment, suppliers and retailers also coordinate the related logistics activities (such as shipment or warehousing) using a common *language standard* and new information methodologies (Ireland and Bruce 2000).

A 2002 survey (Bradley 2002) found that 67 percent of 43 large food, beverage, and consumer products companies were researching, piloting, or implementing CPFR. About half of the respondents who were looking at CPFR said they planned to go ahead with their initiatives. Yet CPFR is not the answer for all trading partners or all types of stock-keeping units (SKUs). According to Tim Paydos, a vice president of markcting at Syncra Systems, CPFR has generated the highest payback on either highly promoted or seasonal goods, whose inventories historically have often been misaligned with demand. "If I'm going to make the investment in CPFR," notes Paydos, "I want to do it with the products with the greatest return" (Bradley 2002).

The CPFR strategy has been driven by Wal-Mart and various benchmaking partners. After a successful pilot between Wal-Mart and Warner-Lambert involving Listerine products, a VICS (Voluntary Interindustry Commerce Standards) subcommittee was established to develop the proposed CPFR standard for the participating retailing industries (Wal-Mart's suppliers). (For more, see EC Application Case W8.2 at the book's Web site.)

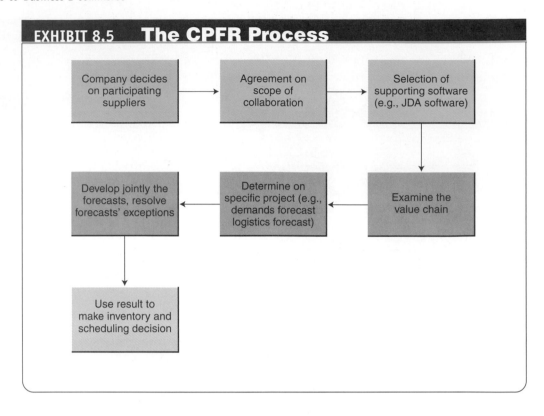

EXHIBIT 8.5 The CPFR Process

An interesting application of CPFR is that of Ace Hardware Corp., presented in EC Application Case 8.3.

CPFR can be used with a company-centric B2B and with sell-side or buy-side marketplaces. For more on the benefits of CPFR, see cpfr.org/cpfr_pdf/index.html. Also, for comprehensive coverage, see Industry Directions (2000).

CASE 8.3
EC Application
CPFR INITIATIVE AT ACE HARDWARE

Ace Hardware Corporation (*acehardware.com*), based in Oak Brook, Illinois, is a chain of 5,100 independently owned stores that sell everything from 10–penny nails to toasters. In 1999, Ace implemented a CPFR process, using its buy-side private exchange to achieve more intelligent relationships with its suppliers. This platform creates and executes a single, shared demand forecast, allowing Ace to increase revenue while reducing costs.

Ace began using CPFR with a single supplier, Henkel Consumer Adhesives, a manufacturer of duct tape, adhesives, and other do-it-yourself home and office products. During the first year of implementation, the two companies improved forecast accuracy by 10 percent, lowered distribution costs by 28 percent, lowered freight costs by 18 percent, increased annual sales by 9 percent, and increased employee productivity by more than 20 percent.

Since then, Ace has implemented CPFR initiatives with more than two dozen suppliers, including Black &

Decker, Rust-Oleum, Master Lock, and Sherwin-Williams. More accurate forecasts and seasonal profiles ensure that products are available when consumers want to buy them. Improved service levels, increased sales, and decreased supply chain costs have combined to make Ace Hardware more competitive.

Sources: Compiled from Buss (2002) and from press releases at *acehardware.com* (2002, 2003).

Questions

1. What motivated Ace to try CPFR?

2. Describe how Ace deployed the CPFR system.

3. Can you guess the common characteristics of the suppliers Ace used first?

ADVANCED PLANNING AND SCHEDULING

Advanced planning and scheduling (APS) systems are math-based programs that identify optimal solutions to complex planning problems that are bound by constraints, such as limited machine capacity or labor. Using algorithms (such as linear programming), these systems are able to solve a wide range of problems, from operational (e.g., daily schedule) to strategic (e.g., network optimization).

The role of APS in EC can be seen in Exhibit 8.6. Basically, it supplements ERP in revolutionizing a manufacturing or distribution firm's supply chain, providing a seamless flow of order fulfillment information from consumers to suppliers. It helps integrate ERP, CRM, SFA, KM, and more, enabling collaborative fulfillment and an integrated EC strategy. For additional details and discussion of ERP, SCM, and APS, see Online Tutorial T3.

advanced planning and scheduling (APS) systems
Programs that use algorithms to identify optimal solutions to complex planning problems that are bound by constraints.

PRODUCT LIFECYCLE MANAGEMENT

Product lifecycle management (PLM) is a business strategy that enables manufacturers to control and share product-related data as part of product design and development efforts and in support of supply chain operations (Day 2002; IBM 2003). Internet and other new technologies can automate the *collaborative aspects* of product development that even within one company can prove tedious and time-consuming if not automated. For example, by means of concurrent engineering and Web-based tools, companies simultaneously and interactively can design a product, its manufacturing process, and the supply chain that supports it. By overlapping these formerly disparate functions, a dynamic collaboration takes place among them, essentially forming a single large product team.

PLM can have a significant beneficial impact in engineering change, cycle time, design reuse, and engineering productivity. Studies have shown that electronic-based collaboration

product lifecycle management (PLM)
Business strategy that enables manufacturers to control and share product-related data as part of product design and development efforts.

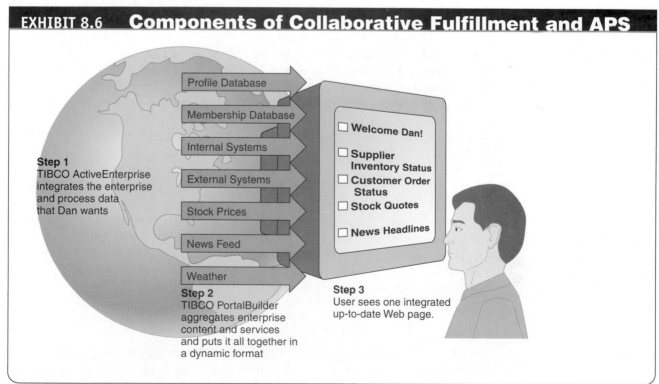

EXHIBIT 8.6 Components of Collaborative Fulfillment and APS

Profile Database
Membership Database
Internal Systems
External Systems
Stock Prices
News Feed
Weather

Step 1
TIBCO ActiveEnterprise integrates the enterprise and process data that Dan wants

Step 2
TIBCO PortalBuilder aggregates enterprise content and services and puts it all together in a dynamic format

- Welcome Dan!
- Supplier Inventory Status
- Customer Order Status
- Stock Quotes
- News Headlines

Step 3
User sees one integrated up-to-date Web page.

Source: Modified from *E-Procurement: From Strategy to Implementation* by Neef, Dale, © 2001. Reprinted by permission of Pearson Education, Inc., Upper Saddle River, NJ.

can reduce product costs by 20 percent and travel expenses by 80 percent, as well as significantly reduce costs associated with product-change management. Moreover, an explosion of new products that have minimal life cycles, as well as increasing complexity in supply chain management, are driving the need for PLM.

PLM is a big step for an organization, requiring it to integrate a number of different processes and systems. Ultimately, information must be moved through an organization as quickly as possible to reduce cycle time and increase profitability. The faster different groups know that a new component or design change is on its way, the faster they can react and get it manufactured or reengineered and out the door, and the sooner the organization can realize revenue from the customer. PLM tools are offered by SAP (MYSAP PLM), Matrix One, EDS, PTC, Dassault Systems, and IBM (IBM PLM).

Supporting joint design. Collaborative efforts are common in joint design, as illustrated in the GM opening case. This is one of the oldest areas of electronic collaboration, which is becoming even more popular due to EC tools, as discussed in EC Application Case W8.3 on the book's Web site.

Section 8.4 ▶ REVIEW

1. Define collaborative planning.
2. Define CPFR and describe its advantages.
3. Describe APS efforts.
4. Describe PLM.

8.5 INTERNAL SUPPLY CHAIN SOLUTIONS, INTRABUSINESS, AND B2E

The EC supply chain solutions presented thus far are mostly intended to rectify situations among business partners. This and the next section concentrate on solutions related to the corporate *internal* parts of the supply chain.

An internal supply chain can exist among the various departments in a manufacturing plant, between a warehouse and manufacturing facility, among several manufacturing plants, between warehouse and retail stores of a retailer, and so on. As in other parts of the supply chain, internal supply chains include flows of material, information, and sometimes funds.

One of the major areas of internal supply chain improvement is intrabusiness and B2E e-commerce.

INTRABUSINESS AND B2E EC

intrabusiness EC
E-commerce activities conducted *within* an organization.

As indicated in Chapter 1, e-commerce is conducted not only between business partners but also *within* organizations. Such within-the-company EC activity is referred to as **intrabusiness EC**, or, in short, *intrabusiness*. Intrabusiness can be done (1) between a business and its employees; (2) between units within the business; and (3) among employees in the same business. This section examines each of these forms of intrabusiness.

B2E EC

business-to-employee (B2E)
Intrabusiness EC in which an organization delivers products or services to its employees.

Intrabusiness in which an organization delivers products or services to its employees is termed **business-to-employee (B2E)**. B2E can be used either to increase employee productivity or for their personal use. According to Hansen and Deimler (2001), many companies (e.g. Cisco, Schwab, Coca-Cola, Delta Airlines) are setting up B2E systems that emulate B2B and B2C models; in many of these systems, employees are treated like the customers in B2C. In the process, the companies get a more satisfied, more productive workforce, while

CASE 8.4
EC Application
E-COMMERCE PROVIDES DECISION SUPPORT TO HI-LIFE

Hi-Life International Corp. owns and operates 720 convenience retail stores in Taiwan in which it sells over 3,000 different products. A major problem is keeping a proper level of inventory of each product in each store. Overstocking is expensive due to storage costs and tying money up to buy and maintain the inventory. Understocking reduces sales and could result in unhappy customers who may go to a competitor. To calculate the appropriate level of inventory, it is necessary to know exactly how many units of each product are in stock at specific times. This is known as *stock count*. A periodic stock count is needed because the actual amount in stock frequently differs from the theoretical one. The difference is due to "shrinkage" (e.g., theft, spoiled items, misplaced items, etc.).

Until 2002, the stock count was done manually. Employees counted the quantity of each product and recorded it on data collection sheets that were preprinted with the products' names. Then, the data were painstakingly keyed into each store's PC. The process took over 21 person hours in each store and was done on a weekly basis. This process was expensive and frequently delayed, causing problems along the entire supply chain due to delays in count and errors. Suppliers, customers, and employees were unhappy.

The first phase of improvement was introduced in spring 2002. Management included a Pocket PC (Jornada) from HP, that runs on Microsoft Windows (Chinese version). The Pocket PC enables employees to enter the inventory tallies directly on the forms on the screen by hand, using Chinese characters for additional notes. The Pocket PC has a synchronized cradle called ActiveSync. Once the Pocket PC is placed in the cradle, inventory information can be relayed instantly to Hi-Life's headquarters. The main menu of the Pocket PC contains an order-placing program, product information, and even weather reports in addition to the inventory module.

In the second phase, in 2003, a compact bar code scanner was added to the Pocket PC's expansion slot. Employees scan the products' bar codes and enter the quantity they find on the shelf. This expedites data entry and minimizes errors in product identification. The up-to-the second information enables headquarters to compute appropriate inventory levels, shipment schedules, and purchasing strategies using DSS formulas, all in minutes. The stores use the Internet (with a secured VPN) to upload data to the headquarters' intranet.

The results were astonishing. Inventory taking was reduced from 21 hours to less than 4 hours per store. Errors were down by more than 90 percent; order placing now is simple and quick, and administrative paperwork has been eliminated. Furthermore, quicker and more precise inventory count resulted in faster response times for changes in demand and in lower inventory levels. The entire product management process became more efficient and improved purchasing, stocking, selling, shelf-price audit and price checks, reticketing, discontinuance, and customer inquiries. The new EC-based system provides a total merchandise solution. The employees like the solution, too. It is very user friendly, both to learn and to operate, and the Pocket PC battery provides at least 24 hours of power, so charging can be done after hours. Finally, Hi-Life's employees now have more time to plan, manage, and chat with customers. More important, faster and better decisions are made possible at headquarters, contributing to greater competitiveness and profitability for Hi-Life.

Sources: Compiled from *hp.com/jornada* (2002) and from *microsoft.com/asia/Mobile* (2003).

Questions

1. How is corporate decision making improved by the new system?

2. Summarize the benefits of the Jornada system to the customers, suppliers, store management, and employees.

3. The data collected at ActiveSync can be uploaded to a PC and transmitted via regular telephone lines (or a DSL) to the corporate intranet via the Internet. It has also been suggested that transmission be done using a wireless system. Comment on the proposal.

---

enjoying major cost reductions. The decision support system described in EC Application Case 8.4 is an example of a B2E tool that increases productivity.

Some representative applications of B2E include the following:

▸ Providing field representatives and employees in yards, warehouses, and other nonoffice places with electronic communication tools

▸ Training and education provided over intranets

▸ Employee use of electronic catalogs and ordering forms to order supplies and material needed for their work (e.g., desktop purchasing)

▸ Employee use of the corporate intranet for both corporate and personal use to purchase discounted insurance, travel packages, and tickets to events

- ▶ Providing office employees with electronic tools for communication, collaboration, and information discovery
- ▶ Offering corporate stores on the intranet that sell the companies' products to employees, usually at a discount. Payment may be deducted from payroll or paid with the employee's personal credit card.
- ▶ Systems that disseminate information or allow employees to manage their fringe benefits via the intranet

Based on a survey they conducted, Hansen and Deimler (2001) found three types of B2E programs: online business processes, online people management, and online services to the workplace (see details in Online Exhibit W8.1). In each of these areas, the B2E program may result in significant cost reduction and productivity improvement.

Activities Between Business Units

Large corporations frequently consist of independent units, called *strategic business units* (SBUs), that "sell" or "buy" materials, products, and services from each other. (An SBU can be either a seller or a buyer.) Transactions of this type can be easily automated and performed over the organization's intranet.

Many large corporations also have a network of dealerships that are usually wholly or partially owned by the corporation. In such cases, a special network is constructed to support communication, collaboration, and execution of transactions between headquarters and the dealerships. For example, such intrabusiness commerce is conducted by auto manufacturers (e.g., Ford), equipment manufacturers (e.g., Caterpillar), oil companies (e.g., ExxonMobil), and many other large manufacturers. EC Application Case 8.5 describes intrabusiness commerce at a consumer-products company, Toshiba America.

Activities Among Corporate Employees

Many large organizations also provide a system by which employees can collaborate on an individual (sometimes nonbusiness) level. For example, some organizations allow employees to place classified ads on the intranet, through which they can buy and sell personal products and services from each other. Also, via classified ads, corporate equipment may be sold to employees for private use. Such ads are especially popular in universities and high-tech companies, where such advertisement was conducted even before the commercialization of the Internet.

Section 8.5 ▶ REVIEW

1. What is an internal supply chain?
2. List the major intrabusiness EC categories.
3. Describe B2E EC.
4. Describe EC activities among business units.
5. Describe EC among corporate employees. Can you think of additional activities among corporate employees that might be of interest?

8.6 INTEGRATION ALONG THE SUPPLY CHAIN

Previous chapters (Chapters 6 and 7) pointed out the need for systems integration in EC. For example, these chapters discussed the need for integrating systems between an exchange and its members, as well as between a company and its customers and suppliers. Such integration is usually done along the supply chain.

CASE 8.5
EC Application
INTRABUSINESS E-COMMERCE AT TOSHIBA AMERICA

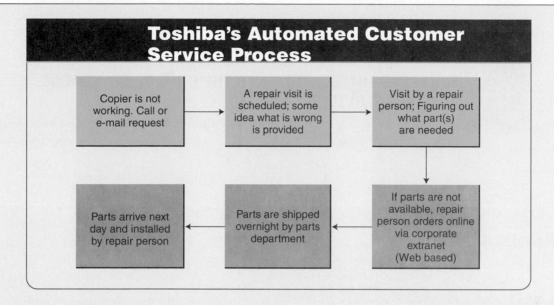

Toshiba's Automated Customer Service Process

Copier is not working. Call or e-mail request → A repair visit is scheduled; some idea what is wrong is provided → Visit by a repair person; Figuring out what part(s) are needed → If parts are not available, repair person orders online via corporate extranet (Web based) → Parts are shipped overnight by parts department → Parts arrive next day and installed by repair person

Toshiba America (*toshiba.com*) works with 300 dealers that sell its consumer-electronics products. Dealers who needed product parts used to place a daily telephone or fax order before 2:00 P.M. for next-day delivery. To handle other needs, express shipments had to be arranged at higher cost. For example, Toshiba's Electronic Imaging Division (EID), a maker of fax machines and copiers, had to spend $1.3 million annually on rush-order communication and deliveries, so it was charging $25 per express shipment to the dealers. A cumbersome electronic order-entry system was created in 1993, but no significant improvement was achieved.

In August 1997, Toshiba created a Web-based order-entry system for product parts using an extranet and intranets. Dealers can now place orders for parts until 5:00 P.M. for next-day delivery without extra charge. The company placed a physical warehouse in Memphis, Tennessee, near the FedEx headquarters to ensure quick delivery. Using this collaborative system, dealers can check accounts receivable balances and pricing arrangements and read service bulletins, press releases, and so on. The intranet also allows sales reps to interact more effectively with dealers. The dealers can be kept up-to-date about orders and inventory and can manage their volume-discount quotes online.

Once an order is submitted, a computer checks for the part's availability. If the part is available, the order is transferred automatically to Toshiba's warehouse in Memphis. Once at the warehouse site, the order pops up on a handheld wireless radio frequency (RF) monitor for quick fulfillment. Within a few hours, the part is packed, verified, and packaged for FedEx. See the attached exhibit for a summary of the process.

Using the intrabusiness system, Toshiba cut the cost per express order to about $10. EID's networking costs were reduced by more than 50 percent (to $600,000 a year). The low shipping cost resulted in overnight delivery of 98 percent of its orders, which has increased customer satisfaction. The site processed close to 90 percent of all dealers' orders in 2003.

Sources: Compiled from McCreary (1999) and *toshiba.com/US* (2003).

Questions

1. What are the benefits of Toshiba's intranet to the dealers?
2. What are the wireless devices used for?
3. What role does FedEx play in the order-fulfillment process?

HOW INFORMATION SYSTEMS ARE INTEGRATED

The integration issue can be divided into two parts: internal integration and integration with business partners. Internal integration includes connecting applications with databases and with each other and connecting customer-facing applications (front end) with order fulfillment and the functional information systems (back end). Integration with business partners connects an organization's systems with those of its external business partners, for example, a company's ordering system to its suppliers' fulfillment systems. Another example of integration with business partners would be connecting an organization's e-procurement system to the engineering departments of bidding companies.

In large corporations, it is necessary to connect the EC applications to the ERP system (see Siau and Messersmith 2002). An ERP system (see Online Tutorial T3) automates the flow of routine and repetitive information, such as submission of purchasing orders, billing, and inventory management. An example of the integration of EC applications with an ERP system is provided in EC Application Case 8.6.

ENABLING INTEGRATION AND THE ROLE OF STANDARDS AND WEB SERVICES

Integrating EC systems can be a complex task. As will be described in Online Chapter 18, integration involves connectivity, compatibility, security, and scalability. In addition, applications,

---

CASE 8.6
EC Application
INTEGRATING EC AND ERP AT CYBEX

In the late 1990s, Cybex International (*cybexintl.com*), a global maker of fitness machines, was having trouble meeting the soaring demand for its popular products. To maintain sales, the company had to work with rush orders from its close to 1,000 suppliers, at an extremely high cost. This was a result of poor demand forecasting for the machine's components that was caused by using three different legacy systems that Cybex inherited from merger partners.

After examining existing vendors' supply chain software, Cybex decided to install an ERP system (from PeopleSoft) for its supply chain planning and manufacturing applications. Together with the software installation, the company analyzed its business processes and made the necessary improvements. It also reduced the number of parts suppliers from 1,000 to 550.

Here is how the system works: Customer orders are accepted at the corporate Web site and are instantly forwarded to the appropriate manufacturing plant (the company has two specialized plants). The ERP uses its *planning module* to calculate which parts are needed for each model. Then, the ERP's *product configurator* constructs a component list and a bill-of-materials needed for each specific order. This takes seconds and expedites shipment.

The ERP system helps with other processes as well. For example, Cybex can e-mail a vendor detailed purchase orders with engineering changes clearly outlined. These changes are visible to everyone, so if one engineer leaves the company, their knowledge is in the system and is easy to find. Furthermore, dealers now know that they will get deliveries in less than 2 weeks instead of the previous 4 weeks, and they can now track the status of each order. The system also helps Cybex to better manage its 550 suppliers. For example, the planning engine looks at price variations across product lines, detecting opportunities to negotiate price reductions by showing suppliers that their competitors offer the same products at lower prices.

The new system gives Cybex's suppliers projected long-term and short-term production schedules. This helps suppliers with their own planning, and it helps Cybex ensure that all parts and materials are available when needed. More timely delivery of parts and materials also reduces the inventory level at Cybex. Furthermore, suppliers that cannot meet the required dates are replaced after quarterly reviews.

Some of the most impressive results included cutting Cybex's bill-of-material counts from 15,200 to 200; reducing the number of vendors from 1,000 to 550; cutting paperwork by two-thirds; and reducing build-to-order time from 4 to 2 weeks. Despite intense industry price cuts over the last few years, Cybex has remained very profitable, mainly due to its e-supply chain. Introducing the integrated ERP system cost money of course. In addition to the software, the technology staff has been increased from 3 to 12. However, the company feels that the investment has been more than justified, especially because it provided for much greater harmony between Cybex and its customers and suppliers.

Sources: Compiled from Gustke (2002) and from press releases at *cybexintl.com* (2002–2003).

Questions

1. Discuss the relationships between the EC applications and the ERP system. (Try to identify as many relationships as possible.)

2. What is the role of the planning module?

3. Summarize all of the activities needed for successful implementation of the ERP system at Cybex.

4. List some of the benefits of the ERP system to Cybex.

data, processes, and interfaces must be integrated. Finally, a major difficulty is the connection of Web-based systems to legacy systems.

To ease the task of integration, vendors have developed integration methodologies and special software called *middleware* (see Online Chapter 18). In addition, major efforts are being undertaken to develop standards and protocols that will facilitate integration, such as XML (described in Chapter 6). The topic of Web services, one of whose major goals is to facilitate seamless integration, will be further discussed in Online Chapter 18.

Section 8.6 ▶ REVIEW

1. Describe internal and external integration.
2. Explain the need to connect to an ERP system.
3. Describe the need for integrating standards and methodologies.

8.7 CORPORATE (ENTERPRISE) PORTALS

Portals and corporate portals were defined in Chapter 2. Corporate portals facilitate collaboration with suppliers, customers, employees, and others. Like workflow and groupwork tools (see Section 8.8), they support collaboration. This section provides in-depth coverage of corporate portals, including their support of B2E EC and c-commerce.

CORPORATE PORTALS: AN OVERVIEW

A **corporate (enterprise) portal** is a gateway to a corporate Web site that enables communication, collaboration, and access to company information. Kounadis (2000) more formally defines a corporate portal as a personalized, single point of access through a Web browser to critical business information located inside and outside of an organization. In contrast with commercial portals such as Yahoo and Lycos, which are gateways to general information on the Internet, corporate portals provide single-point access to information and applications available on the Internet, intranets, and extranets for a specific organization. Companies may have separate portals for outsiders and for insiders.

Corporate portals offer employees, business partners, and customers an organized focal point for their interactions with the firm. Through the portal, these people can have structured and personalized access to information across large, multiple, and disparate enterprise information systems, as well as the Internet. A schematic view of a corporate portal is provided in Exhibit 8.7 (page 322).

Many large organizations are already implementing corporate portals. The reasons for doing so are to cut costs, free up time for busy executives and managers, and add to the bottom line. (See ROI white papers and reports myKGN [2001] and plumtree.com [2002].) Corporate portals are popular in large corporations, as shown in Insights and Additions W8.1.

> **corporate (enterprise) portal**
> A gateway for entering a corporate Web site, enabling communication, collaboration, and access to company information.

TYPES OF CORPORATE PORTALS

Corporate portals can be of two types: generic and functional. Generic portals are defined by their audience (e.g., suppliers, employees). Functional portals are defined by the functionalities they offer.

Types of Generic Portals

The following generic types of portals can be found in organizations.

A portal for suppliers. Using such portals, suppliers can manage their own inventories online. They can view what they sold to the portal owner and for how much. They can see the inventory levels of the portal owner and send material and supplies when they see that a reorder level is reached, and they can collaborate with corporate buyers and other staff.

A portal for customers. Portals for customers can be used for businesses that are customers (the typical case) or for individual customers. Customers can use these *customer-facing portals* to view products and services and to place orders, which they can later track. They can

EXHIBIT 8.7   Corporate Portal As a Gateway to Information

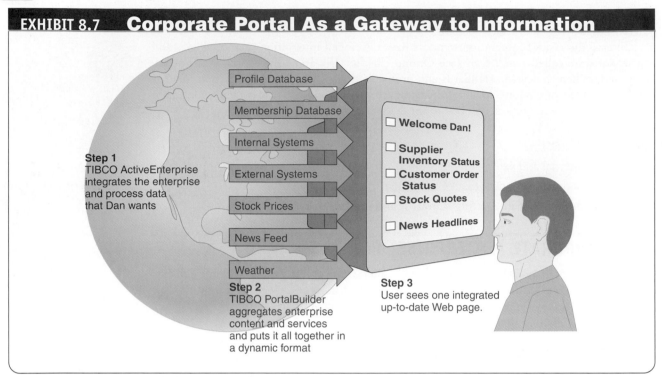

Step 1
TIBCO ActiveEnterprise integrates the enterprise and process data that Dan wants

Profile Database
Membership Database
Internal Systems
External Systems
Stock Prices
News Feed
Weather

Welcome Dan!
Supplier Inventory Status
Customer Order Status
Stock Quotes
News Headlines

Step 2
TIBCO PortalBuilder aggregates enterprise content and services and puts it all together in a dynamic format

Step 3
User sees one integrated up-to-date Web page.

Source: *tibco.com* (2001). Used with permission of Tibco Software Inc.

view their own accounts and see what is going on in almost real time. They can pay for products and services and arrange warranty and delivery.

At some portals, a repository of trending data enables a marketing manager to forecast whether a particular customer program would be useful based on usage patterns, transactional history, and data from similar customers. This enables marketing managers to push specific value-added programs to targeted customer segments at the customer portal.

In some applications, the relationship between the portal and its customers is completely transparent. A business customer, rather than calling, faxing, e-mailing, or using a catalog and creating a purchase order (PO), can go into their own system, create the PO, select the portal owner as their supplier, and commit a specific PO to their system. Then, their system takes that PO and sends an XML message to the portal vendor's SCM system, which accepts the message. In this case, the communication back and forth between a customer and the company using the portal is done largely at a system level. This creates a tighter integration between the portal owner and the customers. It gives both customers and suppliers more efficiencies, and it facilitates more of a partnership than a typical customer-vendor type of relationship.

A portal for employees. Such portals are used for training, dissemination of company news and information, discussion groups, and more. Employee portals are also used for self-service activities, mainly in the personnel area (e.g., change of address or tax withholding allowance, expense reports, register for classes, forms for tuition reimbursement). Employees' portals are sometimes bundled with supervisors' portals in what are known as *workforce portals* (e.g. EWM from Timera.com)

Supervisor portals. These portals enable managers and supervisors to control the entire workforce management process—from budgeting to workforce scheduling.

mobile portals

Portals accessible via mobile devices, especially cell phones and PDAs.

Mobile portals. Mobile portals are portals accessible via mobile devices, especially cell phones and PDAs. Most mobile portals are noncorporate information portals (i.e., they are commercial portals), such as DoCoMo's i-Mode. (See the description of i-Mode in Chapter 10 and in Bughin et al. 2001.) Eventually, large corporations will introduce mobile corporate portals. Alternatively, they will allow access to their regular portals from wireless devices.

Functional Portals

Whatever their audience, the functionalities of portals can vary from simple **information portals** that store data and enable users to navigate and query that data to sophisticated **collaborative portals** that enable collaboration.

Several types of functional portals exist: *Business intelligence portals* are used mostly by middle- and top-level executives and various analysts to conduct business analyses and decision support activities (Imhoff 2001; Ferguson 2001). For example, a business intelligence portal might be used to generate ad hoc reports or to conduct a risk analysis. *Intranet portals* are used mostly by employees for managing fringe benefits and for self-training (Ferguson 2001). *Knowledge portals* are used for collecting knowledge from employees and for disseminating collected knowledge. (For an example of a business intelligence and knowledge management portal, see the Amway case at the end of this chapter and Kesner 2003.)

CORPORATE PORTAL APPLICATIONS

According to a Delphi Group survey (Delphi Group 1999), the top portal applications, in decreasing order of importance, are as follows: knowledge bases and learning tools; business process support; customer-facing (front-line) sales, marketing, and services; collaboration and project support; access to data from disparate corporate systems; personalized pages for various users; effective search and indexing tools; security applications; best practices and lessons learned; directories and bulletin boards; identification of experts; news; and Internet access.

Exhibit 8.8 depicts a corporate portal framework. This framework illustrates the features and capabilities required to support various organizational applications.

information portals
Portals that store data and enable users to navigate and query these data.

collaborative portals
Portals that allow collaboration.

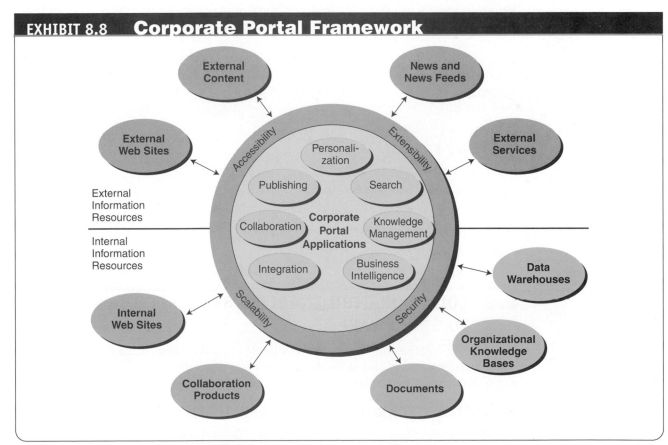

EXHIBIT 8.8   Corporate Portal Framework

Source: Compiled by N. Bolloju, City University of Hong Kong, from Aneja et al. (2000) and Kounadis (2000).

JUSTIFYING PORTALS

As for any IT project, management needs to be able to justify the development and use of a corporate portal by comparing its cost with its benefits. However, most of the benefits of portals are intangible. For example, Reda (2002) claims that employee portals have the potential to fundamentally change and improve employer–employee relationships—a desirable benefit, although somewhat difficult to measure. According to Ferguson (2001), portals offer the following additional benefits, which also are difficult to quantify:

▶ They offer a simple user interface for finding and navigating content via a browser.

▶ They improve access to business content and increase the number of business users who can access information, applications, and people.

▶ They offer access to common business applications from anywhere in a geographically distributed enterprise and beyond. Using Web-enabled mobile or wireless devices, content can be accessed from anywhere.

▶ They offer the opportunity to use platform-independent software (Java) and data (XML).

However, given that portals are relatively low-cost, low-risk devices (Cunningham 2002), it is not surprising that they are being adopted by thousands of organizations worldwide. A formal approach to justifying portals is offered by Plumtree (2002), which devised a framework for assessing the ROI of portals. The company offers several white papers and examples on this topic (e.g., see myKGN 2001) at its Web site (plumtree.com).

DEVELOPING PORTALS

Before a company can develop a corporate portal, it must decide what the purpose and content of the portal will be. For some practical guidelines for determining a corporate portal strategy, see Insights and Additions W8.2 at the book's Web site.

Many vendors offer tools for building corporate portals, as well as hosting services. Representative vendors are Tibco (Portal Builder at tibco.com), Computer Associates (Jasmine II Portal at ca.com), Sybase, PeopleSoft, and Plumtree. See Mendoza et al. (2002) for a case study.

Section 8.7 ▶ REVIEW

1. What is a corporate portal?
2. List the types of corporate portals.
3. List five applications of portals.
4. Discuss the issue of justifying enterprise portals.
5. List the benefits of corporate portals.

---

workflow

The movement of information as it flows through the sequence of steps that make up an organization's work procedures.

workflow systems

Business process automation tools that place system controls in the hands of user departments to automate information-processing tasks.

8.8 COLLABORATION-ENABLING TOOLS: FROM WORKFLOW TO GROUPWARE

As mentioned earlier, corporate portals facilitate e-collaboration. A large number of tools and methodologies are also available that facilitate e-collaboration. This section presents workflow technologies, groupware, and other collaboration-enabling tools.

WORKFLOW TECHNOLOGIES AND APPLICATIONS

Workflow is the movement of information as it flows through the sequence of steps that make up an organization's work procedures. Workflow systems are business process automation tools that place system controls in the hands of user departments. They employ a set of software programs that automate almost any information-processing task.

Workflow management is the automation of workflows so that documents, information, or tasks are passed from one participant to another in a way that is governed by the organization's rules or procedures. Workflow management involves all of the steps in a business process from start to finish, including all exception conditions. The key to workflow management is the tracking of process-related information and the status of each activity of the business process (see van der Aalst 2002). The major activities to be managed are job routing and monitoring, document imaging, document management, supply chain optimization, and control of work.

workflow management
The automation of workflows, so that documents, information, and tasks are passed from one participant to the next in the steps of an organization's business process.

Types of Workflow Applications

Workflow applications fall into three major categories: collaborative, production, and administrative workflow.

- **Collaborative workflow.** Collaborative workflow refers to those software products that address project-oriented and collaborative types of processes. They are administered centrally, yet are capable of being accessed and used by workers from different departments and even from different physical locations. The goal of collaborative workflow tools is to empower knowledge workers. The focus of an enterprise solution for collaborative workflow is on allowing workers to communicate, negotiate, and collaborate within a unified environment. Some leading vendors of collaborative workflow applications are Lotus, JetForm, FileNet, and Action Technologies.

- **Production workflow.** Production workflow tools address mission-critical, transaction-oriented, high-volume processes. They are often deployed only in a single department or to a certain set of users within a department. These applications often include document imaging and storage and retrieval capabilities. They also can include the use of intelligent forms, database access, and ad hoc capabilities. The goal is to improve productivity and quality of business processes. The leading vendors of workflow applications are FileNet, Staffware, IBM (MQ3), and Eastman WorkFlow. An example of production workflow that is mixed with collaborative workflow is presented in EC Application Case 8.7 (page 326).

- **Administrative workflow.** Administrative workflow can be considered as a cross between the previous two types of workflow. The flow is predefined (such as the steps required to approve an expense report), but it can be changed if needed. The goal of administrative workflow applications is to reduce clerical costs in systems with a low volume of complex transactions. The major vendors are Staffware, InTempo, and Metro.

In conclusion, the benefits of workflow management systems include the following:

- Improved control of business processes, with far less management intervention and fewer chances for delays or misplaced work than other systems.

- Improved quality of services through quicker response times with the best person available.

- Lower staff training costs because the work can be guided through complex procedures.

- Lower management costs, which enables managers to concentrate on nurturing employees and handling special cases rather than on routine reporting and distribution issues.

- Improved user satisfaction. Users typically have greater confidence that they are doing the best they can, and they enjoy greater satisfaction when completing their work with fewer conflicting requirements.

A major area for EC workflow applications is the aggregation of sellers or buyers, which was described in Chapters 6 and 7. When large suppliers or buyers are involved, a workflow system is needed for both the collaborative efforts and for supply chain and production improvements.

For information on workflow management, see Fischer (2002) and Basu and Kumar (2002). Additional information can be found at wfmc.org, aiim.org, waria.com, and omg.org. For discussion of the functionalities of workflow management systems, see the discussion online at the book's Web site.

Because workflow management systems support more than one individual, they are considered by some to be a subset of groupware, which is the next topic.

EC Application

USE OF A WORKFLOW SYSTEM TO MANAGE CURRENCY FLOWS AT A GERMAN BANK

Dresdner Bank in Germany has automated the way it handles the trading of currency orders. Whether they originate from within a single branch operation or across its trading rooms worldwide, it routes these orders using a workflow system called Limit Order Application (LORA). This workflow system, built on top of Microsoft Exchange, has replaced telephone and fax-based processes.

One of the main problems that Dresdner Bank sought to solve with the workflow system was the allocation and uptake of orders among different trading rooms around the world. Being able to route orders would allow more efficient trading across the different time zones, for instance, making it easier for traders to execute a Frankfurt order in New York after close of business in Germany.

Three types of bank staff—traders, controllers, and administrators—use this system, which works as follows: First, when an order is received, it is placed into an electronic folder by the controller. All order folders are held in a "public" file and can be viewed by the relevant staff. Next, when a trader accepts an order, the trader is responsible for that order from that moment on. Although the order can still be canceled or reversed at this stage, the details of price and order quantity cannot be changed. The status of the order is displayed, and the order is locked to prevent anyone from altering it. (Even small changes in the details of an order could result in huge profits or losses for the bank or its clients). Finally, when the order is executed, or if it is canceled or reversed or expires, it is sent to a subfolder to be archived.

The bank dropped an initial plan of implementing global common folders that could be accessed by any of its 1,000 traders from any location. It did so because of resistance from the traders, who did not like the idea of relinquishing local control and allowing other traders to process or execute

their orders. Instead, the bank has implemented a system of local folders that reside within the branch of origin; these can be read by, but cannot by processed by, traders elsewhere. Traders can decide whether orders are passed to other locations for processing.

With LORA, users can respond more quickly and accurately to customer queries because they are able to access and view on the computer screen the precise status of orders. Control has also been improved, with responsibility for any order always assigned to a specific staff member. The user interface was carefully designed to meet stringent requirements with respect to efficiency and ease of use.

LORA was built mainly with Visual Basic, with provisions to extend the system to allow reuse of existing components. The system was implemented in about 6 months to the bank's 500 dealers in Frankfurt. By 2003, it was implemented in all of the bank's branches.

Sources: Compiled from *microsoft.com/resources/casestudies/CaseStudy.asp?CaseStudyID=13324* (2000, 2003), and from *dresdner bank.com* (2003).

Questions

1. Identify the parties in this case that need to collaborate with each other.
2. Create a diagram that shows the flow of information in LORA.
3. How does the workflow system differ from typical transaction-oriented application?
4. Explain how the system facilitates collaboration.

GROUPWARE

groupware

Software products that support collaboration, over networks, among groups of people who share a common task or goal.

Groupware refers to software products that support groups of people who share a common task or goal and collaborate on its accomplishment. These products provide a way for groups to share resources and opinions. Groupware implies the use of networks to connect people, even if they are in the same room. Many groupware products are available on the Internet or an intranet, enhancing the collaboration of a large number of people worldwide. There are many different approaches and technologies for the support of groups on the Internet.

Groupware features that support collaboration and conferencing are listed in Exhibit 8.9.

Groupware products come either as a stand-alone product supporting one task (such as e-mail) or as an integrated kit that includes several tools (such as e-mail and screen sharing). In general, groupware technology products are fairly inexpensive and can be easily incorporated into existing information systems. The Internet, intranets, extranets, and private communication lines provide the infrastructure needed for the hardware and software of group-

EXHIBIT 8.9   Major Features in Collaboration and Conferencing Tools

General

- Built-in e-mail, messaging system, instant messaging
- Browser interface
- Joint Web-page creation
- Sharing of active hyperlinks
- File sharing (graphics, video, audio, or other)
- Built-in search functions (by topic or keyword)
- Workflow tools
- Use of corporate portals for communication, collaboration
- Shared screens
- Electronic decision rooms
- Peer-to-peer networks

Synchronous (same-time)

- Videoconferencing, multimedia conferencing
- Audioconferencing
- Shared whiteboard, smart whiteboard
- Text chart
- Brainstorming, polling (voting), and other decision support (consensus builder, scheduler)

Asynchronous (different times)

- Threaded discussions
- Users can receive/send e-mail, SMS
- Users can receive activity notification via e-mail
- Users can collapse/expand threads
- Users can sort messages (by date, author, or read/unread)
- Chat session logs
- Bulletin boards, discussion groups
- Use of blogs
- Collaborative planning and/or design tools

ware. Most of the software products are Web based. This section describes some of the most common groupware products.

Electronic Meeting Systems

An important area of virtual collaboration is electronic meetings. For decades, people have attempted to improve face-to-face meetings, which are known to have many potential dysfunctions. Initially, people attempted to better organize group meetings by using a facilitator and established procedures (known as *group dynamics*). More recently, there have been numerous attempts to use information technologies to improve meetings. The advancement of Web-based systems opens the door for electronically supported **virtual meetings**, where members are in different locations and frequently in different countries.

The events of September 11 and the economic slowdown of 2001–2003 have made virtual meetings more popular. It is hard for companies to ignore reported cost savings, such as the $4 million a month that IBM reported it saved just from cutting travel expenses to meetings (Callaghan 2002). In addition, improvements in supporting technology, reductions in the price of the technology, and the acceptance of virtual meetings as a respected way of doing business are fueling their growth (see Vinas 2002).

virtual meetings
Online meetings whose members are in different locations, frequently in different countries.

Virtual meetings can be supported by a variety of groupware tools, as will be shown in the remainder of this section. We begin our discussion with the support provided to decision making.

Group Decision Support Systems

A **group decision support system (GDSS)** is an interactive computer-based system that facilitates the solution of semistructured and unstructured problems by a group of decision makers. The goal of GDSSs is to improve the productivity of decision-making meetings, either by speeding up the decision-making process or by improving the quality of the resulting decisions, or both.

The major characteristics of a GDSS are as follows:

▶ Its goal is to support the process of group decision makers by providing automation of subprocesses using information technology tools.

▶ It is a specially designed information system, not merely a configuration of already-existing system components. It can be designed to address one type of problem or a variety of group-level organizational decisions.

▶ It encourages generation of ideas, resolution of conflicts, and freedom of expression. It contains built-in mechanisms that discourage development of negative group behaviors such as destructive conflict miscommunication and "groupthink."

The first generation of GDSSs was designed to support face-to-face meetings in what is called a *decision room*. Today, support is provided over the Web to virtual groups (group members may be in different locations). The group can meet at the same time or at different times by using e-mail, sending documents, and reading transaction logs. GDSS is especially useful when controversial decisions have to be made (such as resource allocation or which individuals to lay off). Its application requires a facilitator (when done in one room) or a coordinator or leader when done with virtual meetings.

GDSSs can improve the decision-making process in various ways. For one, GDSSs generally provide structure to the planning process, which keeps the group on track, although some permit the group to use unstructured techniques and methods for idea generation. In addition, GDSSs offer rapid and easy access to external information needed for decision making. GDSSs also support parallel processing of information and idea generation by participants and allow nonsynchronous computer discussion. They make possible larger meetings that would otherwise be unmanageable, and larger groups mean that more complete information, knowledge, and skills will be represented in the same meeting. Finally, voting can be anonymous, with instant results, and all information that passes through the system can be automatically recorded for future analysis (producing organizational memory).

GDSS products. More general GDSS products such as Microsoft NetMeeting, WebEx, and Lotus Notes/Domino provide for some of the functionalities just discussed. A more specialized GDSS product is GroupSystem, which is a complete suite of electronic meeting software (both for one room and virtual meetings). (Visit groupsystem.com and view the demo there.) Another specialized product is eRoom (now owned by Documentum.com). This is a comprehensive Web-based suite of tools that can support a variety of collaboration scenarios. (See Online Exhibit W8.2.) A third product is Team Expert Choice, which is an add-on product for Expert Choice (expertchoice.com). It has limited decision-support capabilities, mainly supporting one-room meetings.

Electronic Teleconferencing

Teleconferencing is the use of electronic communication that allows two or more people at different locations to have a simultaneous conference. Several types of teleconferencing are possible. The oldest and simplest is a telephone conference call, wherein several people talk to each other from three or more locations. The biggest disadvantage of this is that it does not allow for face-to-face communication. Also, participants in one location cannot see graphs, charts, and pictures at other locations. Although the latter disadvantage can be overcome by using a fax, this is a time-consuming, expensive, and frequently poor-quality process. One solution is *video teleconferencing*, in which participants can see each other as well as the documents.

Video teleconferencing. In a **video teleconference**, participants in one location can see participants at other locations. Dynamic pictures of the participants can appear on a large screen or on a desktop computer. Originally, video teleconferencing was the transmission of live, compressed TV sessions between two or more points. Today, video teleconferencing (or *videoconferencing*) is a digital technology capable of linking various types of computers across networks. Once conferences are digitized and transmitted over networks, they become a computer application.

With videoconferencing, participants can share data, voice, pictures, graphics, and animation. Data can also be sent along with voice and video. Such **data conferencing** makes it possible to work on documents and to exchange computer files during videoconferences. This allows several geographically dispersed groups to work on the same project and to communicate by video simultaneously.

Video teleconferencing offers various benefits. Two of them—providing the opportunity for face-to-face communication for individuals in different locations and supporting several types of media during conferencing—have already been discussed. Video teleconferencing also improves employee productivity, cuts travel costs, conserves the time and energy of key employees, and increases the speed of businesses processes (such as product development, contract negotiation, and customer service). It improves the efficiency and frequency of communications and saves an electronic record of a meeting, enabling specific parts of a meeting to be reconstructed for future purposes. Video teleconferencing also makes it possible to hold classes at different locations.

Web conferencing. *Web conferencing* is conducted on the Internet for as few as two and as many as thousands of people. It allows users to simultaneously view something, such as a sales presentation in Microsoft PowerPoint or a product drawing, on their computer screens; interaction takes place via messaging or a simultaneous phone teleconference. Web conferencing is much cheaper than videoconferencing because it runs on the Internet.

The latest technological innovations permit both B2B and B2C Web conferencing applications. For example, banks in Alaska use *video kiosks* in sparsely populated areas instead of building branches that will be underutilized. The video kiosks operate on the banks' intranet and provide videoconferencing equipment for face-to-face interactions. A variety of other communication tools such as online polls, whiteboards, and question-and-answer boards may also be used. Such innovations can be used to educate staff members about a new product line or technology, to amplify a meeting with investors, or to walk a prospective client though an introductory presentation.

Web conferencing is becoming very popular. Almost all Web conferencing products provide whiteboarding and polling features and allow users to give presentations and demos and share applications. Popular Web conferencing products are Centra EMeeting, Genesys Meeting Center, PlaceWare, and WebEx Meeting Center.

RTC Tools

The Internet, intranets, and extranets offer tremendous potential for real-time and synchronous interaction of people working in groups. *Real-time collaboration (RTC) tools* help companies bridge time and space to make decisions and collaborate on projects. RTC tools support synchronous communication of graphical and text-based information. These tools are being used in distance training, product demonstrations, customer support, e-commerce, and sales applications.

RTC tools can be purchased as stand-alone tools or used on a subscription basis. Many vendors offer these tools on a subscription basis. Exhibit 8.10 (page 330) shows a screen from one vendor of RTC tools, WebEx.

Interactive Whiteboards

Whiteboards are another type of groupware. Computer-based whiteboards work like "real-world" whiteboards with markers and erasers, except with one big difference: Instead of one person standing in front of a meeting room drawing on the whiteboard, all participants can

video teleconference
Virtual meeting in which participants in one location can see participants at other locations on a large screen or a desktop computer.

data conferencing
Virtual meeting in which geographically dispersed groups work on documents together and to exchange computer files during videoconferences.

join in. Throughout a meeting, each user can view and draw on a single document "pasted" onto the electronic whiteboard on a computer screen. Users can save digital whiteboarding sessions for future use. Some whiteboarding products let users insert graphics files that can be annotated by the group.

Take, for example, an advertisement that needs to be cleared by a senior manager. Once the proposed ad has been scanned into a PC, both parties can see it on their screens. If the senior manager does not like something, they can highlight what needs to be changed using a stylus pen. This tool makes communication between the two parties both easier and clearer. The two parties can also share applications. For example, if party A works with Excel, party B does not have to have Excel in order to work with it in the whiteboarding tool.

Besides being used to support people working on the same task, whiteboards are also used for training and learning. The following are two example whiteboarding products, Digital Wall Display and Intelligent Whiteboard.

▶ Digital Wall Display from 3M Corp. (3m.com) is a multifunction whiteboard. It shows whatever is written on it as well as anything—text, charts, still and moving pictures—that is stored in a computer and loaded onto the whiteboard. With a remote mouse, presenters or teachers can edit and move the material around on the touch-screen board. All of this, including audio, can be transmitted instantaneously to any connected board, anywhere in the world, making it useful for virtual, long-distance teaching or training. The system is also used for sharing research among colleagues.

▶ Intelligent Whiteboard from Smart Technologies Inc. (smarttech.com) was designed to support teaching. It has a "write" feature in electronic ink, a "touch" feature for controlling applications, and a "save" feature to save work to computer files. A model named Camfire is equipped with digital cameras that photograph what is written on the whiteboard. The images are then transferred to a Web site or e-mailed to students. The system also can connect to devices, such as a microscope, for presentation of hard-to-see information.

Screen Sharing

screen sharing
Software that enables group members, even in different locations, to work on the same document, which is shown on the PC screen of each participant.

In collaborative work, members are frequently in different locations. Using **screen sharing** software, group members can work on the same document, which is shown on the PC screen of each participant. For example, two authors can work on a single manuscript. One may sug-

EXHIBIT 8.10 WebEx

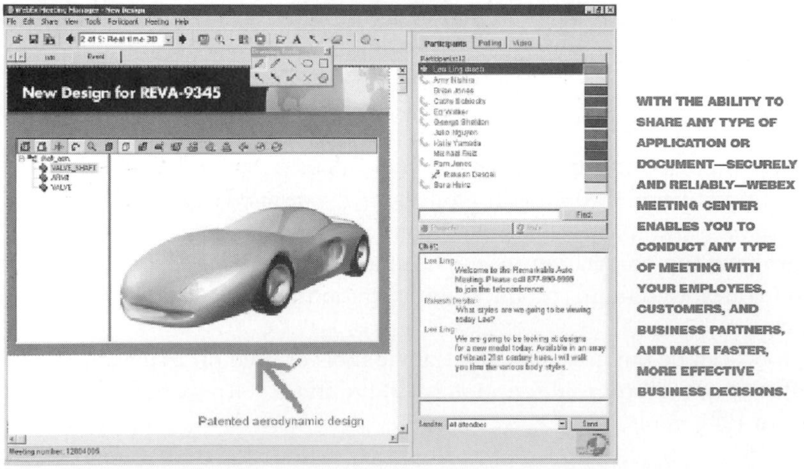

Source: Courtesy of WebEx Communications Inc.

gest a correction and execute it so that the other author can view the change. Collaborators can work together on the same spreadsheet or on the resultant graphics. Changes can be done by using the keyboard or by touching the screen. This capability can expedite the design of products, the preparation of reports and bids, and the resolution of conflicts.

A special screen-sharing capability is offered by Groove Inc. (groove.net). Its product enables the joint creation and editing of documents on a PC (see Team Assignment 1).

Instant Video

With the spread of instant messaging and Internet telephony has come the idea to link people via both voice and audio. Called *instant video*, the idea is for a kind of video chat room. It allows users to chat in real time, seeing the person they are communicating with. A simple way to do this is to add video cameras to the participants' computers. A more sophisticated and better-quality approach is to integrate an existing online videoconferencing service with instant messaging software, creating a service that offers the online equivalent of a videophone.

This idea is still in the early stages. One company that is attempting to develop instant video is Cuworld.com. Here is how its Cuworld software (which was in beta testing in January 2003) works: Users gets free software (Cuworld 6.0) that can compress and decompress video signals sent over an online connection. To start a conference, a user sends a request to an online buddy (via instant messenger). The Cuworld software goes to the directory of the instant messaging service to determine the Internet addresses of the users' connections, and, using the Web addresses, the computers of the video participants are linked directly via the Internet. A video conference can then begin.

Instant video sounds like a good product, but no one yet knows for sure how commercially viable it will be.

Integration and Groupware Suites

Because groupware technologies are computer based, it makes sense to integrate them with other computer-based or computer-controlled technologies. A *software suite* is created when several products are integrated into one system. Integrating several technologies can save time and money for users. For example, PictureTel Corporation (picturetel.com), in an alliance with software developer Lotus, developed an integrated desktop video teleconferencing product that uses Lotus Notes. Using this integrated system, publisher Reader's Digest has built several applications that have videoconferencing capabilities. A seamless integration is also provided in *groupware suites*. The following are some examples of popular groupware suites.

Lotus Notes/Domino. The Lotus Notes/Domino suite includes a document management system, a distributed client/server database, and a basis for intranet and e-commerce systems, as well as a communication-support tool. It enhances real-time communications with asynchronous electronic connections (e.g., e-mail and other forms of messaging).

Group members using Lotus Notes/Domino might store all their official memos, formal reports, and informal conversations related to particular projects in a shared, online data store, such as a database. Then, as individual members need to check on the contents, they can access the shared database to find the information they need.

Lotus Notes provides online collaboration capabilities, workgroup e-mail, distributed databases, bulletin whiteboards, text editing, (electronic) document management, workflow capabilities, instant virtual meetings, application sharing, instant messaging, consensus building, voting, ranking, and various application development tools. All these capabilities are integrated into one environment with a graphic-menu-based user interface. By the end of 2002, there were over 60 million Notes users worldwide (lotus.com 2003). For even more capabilities of Lotus Notes/Domino, see Internet Exercise 10 at the end of the chapter.

Microsoft NetMeeting. Microsoft's groupware suite NetMeeting is a real-time collaboration package that includes whiteboarding, application sharing (of any Microsoft Windows application document), remote desktop sharing, file transfer, text chat, data conferencing, desktop audio, and videoconferencing. The NetMeeting suite is included in Windows 98 and more recent versions.

Novell GroupWise. Novell's GroupWise offers a wide range of communication and collaboration capabilities integrated with document management capabilities including e-mail, calendaring, group scheduling, imaging, workflow, and electronic discussions, and more.

OTHER COLLABORATIVE TOOLS

Many different collaborative tools are available. A sampler of these tools is available at the book's Web site (Online Exhibit W8.3). Consult that resource for information about collaborative tools in addition to those already discussed. Before closing this discussion of collaborative tools, however, we need to mention virtual reality.

Virtual Reality

virtual reality (VR)
System that delivers interactive computer-generated 3D graphics to a user through a head-mounted display.

In order to facilitate virtual collaboration in product design, one can use the technology of virtual reality. **Virtual reality (VR)** is a system that delivers interactive computer-generated 3D graphics to a user through a head-mounted display. It is an environment that provides artificially generated sensory cues sufficient to engender in the user some willing suspension of disbelief. Kan et al. (2001) proposed the use of Internet-based VR for product design in a collaborative environment. This system, based on Java and VRML (Virtual Reality Modeling Language), is especially useful for product design by SMEs.

IMPLEMENTATION ISSUES FOR ONLINE COLLABORATION

This chapter has presented numerous issues of online collaboration of one sort or another. Here are a few implementation issues that must be addressed when planning online collaboration. First, to connect business partners, an organization needs an effective collaborative environment. Such an environment is provided by groupware suites such as Lotus Notes/Domino or eXcelon (exceloncorp.com). Another issue is the need to connect collaborative tools with file management products on an organization's intranet. Two such products that offer such connection capabilities are WiredRed server and client (wiredred.com) and eRoom's server (documentum.com).

In addition, throughout the book, the general trend of moving e-commerce applications onto the Web has been discussed. To change the read-only Web to a truly collaborative environment, one needs protocols. The protocols are needed for easy integration of different applications and for standardizing communication. One such protocol, which is relatively new, is WebDAV (Web Distributed Authoring and Versioning protocol) (see webdav.org).

Finally, note that online collaboration is not a panacea for all occasions or in all situations. Many times, a face-to-face meeting is a must. People sometimes need the facial cues and the physical closeness that no computer system can currently provide. (A technology called *pervasive computing* attempts to remove some of these limitations, e.g., by interpreting facial cues. For more, see Chapter 10.)

Section 8.8 ▶ REVIEW

1. Define workflow systems and management.

2. Explain the types and benefits of workflow systems.

3. List the major groupware tools.

4. Describe GDSSs and electronic meeting systems.

5. Describe the various types of electronic teleconferencing, including Web-based conferencing.
6. Describe whiteboards and screen sharing.

MANAGERIAL ISSUES

Some managerial issues related to this chapter are as follows.

1. **How difficult is it to introduce e-collaboration?** Dealing with the technology may be the easy part. Tackling the behavioral changes needed within an organization and its trading partners may be a greater challenge. Change management requires an understanding of the new interdependences being constructed and the new roles and responsibili-ties that must be adapted in order for the enterprise and its business partners to become more collaborative.

2. **How much can be shared with business partners? Can they be trusted?** Many companies are sharing forecast data and actual sales data. But when it comes to allowing real-time access to product design, inventory, and ERP systems, there may be some hesitation. It is basically a question of trust. The more information is shared, the better the collaboration. However, sharing information can also lead to the giving away of trade secrets. In some cases, there is a cultural resistance against sharing (some employees do not like to share information even within their own organization). The value of sharing needs to be carefully assessed against its risks.

3. **Who is in charge of our portal and intranet content?** Because content is created by many individuals, two potential risks exist. First, proprietary corporate information may not be secure enough, so unauthorized people may have access to it. Second, appropriate intranet "netiquette" must be maintained; otherwise unethical or even illegal behavior may develop. Therefore, managing content, including frequent updates, is a must.

4. **Who will design the corporate portal?** Corporate portals are the gateways to corporate information and knowledge. Appropriate portal design is a must, not only for easy and efficient navigation, but also because portals portray the corporate image to employees and to business partners who are allowed access to it. Design of the corporate portal must be carefully thought out and approved by management.

5. **Should we conduct virtual meetings?** Virtual meetings can save time and money and if properly planned can bring as good or even better results than face-to-face meetings. Although not all meetings can be conducted online, many can. The supporting technology is getting cheaper and better with time.

SUMMARY

In this chapter, you learned about the following EC issues as they relate to the learning objectives.

1. **The e-supply chain, its characteristics, and components.** Digitizing and automating the flow of information throughout the supply chain and managing it via the Web results in an entity called the e-supply chain. The major parts of the e-supply chain are upstream (to suppliers), internal (in-house processes), and downstream (to distributors and customers). Activities of e-supply chains include replenishment, procurement, collaborative planning, collaborative design/development, e-logistics, and use of exchanges or supply webs—all of which can be Internet based.

2. **Supply chain problems and their causes.** The major supply chain problems are access to inventories, lack of supplies when needed, need for rush orders, deliveries of wrong materials or to wrong locations, and poor customer service. These problems result from uncertainties in various segments of the chain (e.g., in transportation), from mistrust of partners and lack of collaboration and sharing, and from difficulties in forecasting demand (e.g., the bullwhip effect). Also, lack of appropriate logistics infrastructure can result in problems.

3. **Solutions to supply chains problem provided by EC.** EC technologies automate and expedite order taking, speed order fulfillment, provide e-payments, properly control inventories, provide for correct forecasting and

thus better scheduling, and improve collaboration among supply chain partners.

4. **C-commerce: Definitions and types.** Collaborative commerce refers to a planned use of digital technology by business partners. It includes planning, designing, researching, managing, and servicing various partners and tasks, frequently along the supply chain. Collaborative commerce can be between different pairs of business partners or among many partners participating in a collaborative network.

5. **Collaborative planning and CPFR.** Collaborative planning concentrates on demand forecasting and on resource and activity planning along the supply chain. Collaborative planning tries to synchronize partners' activities. CPFR is a business strategy that attempts to develop standard protocols and procedures for collaboration. Its goal is to improve demand forecasting by collaborative planning in order to ensure delivery of materials as needed. In addition to forecasting, collaboration in design is facilitated by IT, including groupware. Product lifecycle management (PLM) enables manufacturers to plan and control product-related information.

6. **Intrabusiness EC.** Intrabusiness EC refers to all EC initiatives conducted within an organization. These can be activities between an organization and its employees, between SBUs in the organization, and among the organization's employees.

7. **Integration along the supply chain.** Integration of various applications within companies and between business partners is critical to the success of companies. To simplify integration, one can use special software as well as employ standards such as XML. Web services are a most promising new approach for facilitating integration.

8. **Types and roles of corporate portals.** The major types of corporate portals are those for suppliers, customers, employees, and supervisors. There also are mobile portals (accessed by wireless devices). Functional portals such as knowledge portals and business intelligence portals provide the gateway to specialized knowledge and decision making. Corporate portals provide for easy information access, communication, and collaboration.

9. **Collaborative tools.** Hundreds of different collaboration tools are available. The major groups of tools are workflow and groupware. In addition, specialized tools ranging from group decision support systems (GDSSs) to devices that facilitate product design are also available.

KEY TERMS

DISCUSSION QUESTIONS

1. Discuss the benefits of e-supply chains.

2. Discuss the relationship between c-commerce and corporate portals.

3. Compare and contrast a commercial portal (such as Yahoo) with a corporate portal.

4. Explain the need for groupware to facilitate collaboration.

5. Discuss the need for workflow systems as a companion to e-commerce.

6. Discuss the relationship between portals and intranets at the same organization.

7. It is said that c-commerce signifies a move from a transaction focus to a relationship focus among supply chain members. Discuss.

8. Discuss the need for virtual meetings.

9. Discuss how CPFR can lead to more accurate forecasting and discuss how it can resolve the bullwhip effect.

10. Discuss the advantage of tools (suites) such as Lotus-Notes/Domino. Do these tools have any disadvantages?

11. Discuss the ways in which GDSS can facilitate the process of group decision making.

INTERNET EXERCISES

1. Enter ca.com/products and register. Then take the Clever Path Portal Test Drive (ca.com/Solutions/Collateral. asp?CID=33540&ID=305). (Flash Player from Macromedia is required.) Then enter peoplesoft.com and plumtree.com. Prepare a list of the major products available for building corporate portals.

2. Enter plumtree.com. Find the white papers about corporate portals and their justification. Prepare a report based on your findings.

3. Enter doublediamondsoftware.com/product_overview. htm and go to "products." Identify all potential B2B applications and prepare a report about them.

4. Investigate the status of CPFR. Start at cpfr.org/cpfr_pdf/index.html, vics.org, google.com, and yahoo.com. Also enter supply-chain.org and find information about CPFR. Write a report on the status of CPFR.

5. Enter mySAP.com and find the key capabilities of the Enterprise Portal there. List the benefits of five of its capabilities.

6. Enter nokia.com, mdsi.com, and symbolic.com. Identify the B2E products you find at these sites. Prepare a list of the different products.

7. Enter i2.com and review their products. Explain how some of the products facilitate collaboration.

8. Enter collaborate.com and read about recent issues related to collaboration. Prepare a report.

9. Enter smarterwork.com. Find out how collaboration is done. Summarize the benefits of this site to the participants.

10. Enter intraspect.com and read the company vision for Collaborative Commerce. Then view the demo. Explain in a report how the company facilitates c-commerce.

11. Enter lotus.com and find the collaboration-support products. How do these products support groups?

12. Enter i2.com and identify the collaborative tools for CRM, SCM, and SRM. Prepare a report that will show the major capabilities of each solution.

13. Enter supplyworks.com and worldchain.com. Examine the functionalities provided for supply chain improvements (the inventory management aspects).

14. Enter 3M.com and smartboard.com. Find infomation about their whiteboards. Compare the products.

TEAM ASSIGNMENTS AND ROLE PLAYING

1. Have each team download a free copy of Groove from groove.net. Install the software on the members' PCs and arrange collaborative sessions. What can the free software do for you? What are its limitations?

2. Each team is assigned to an organization. The team members will attempt to identify several supply chains, their components, and the partners involved. Draw the chains and show which parts can be treated as e-supply chain parts.

3. Each team is assigned to a major vendor of corporate portals, such as Plumtree, Tibero, Computer Associates, or PeopleSoft. Each team will check the capabilities of the corporate portal tools and try to persuade the class that its product is superior.

4. Each team is assigned to one area of collaborative commerce. The mission is to find recent applications and case studies in that area. Present the findings to the class.

REAL-WORLD CASE

PORTAL SPEEDS PRODUCT R&D AT AMWAY

Through thousands of independent agents all over the world, Amway sells more than 450 home, nutrition and wellness, and personal products. To be effective, the research and development (R&D) department at Amway must develop new products in a streamlined and cost-efficient manner. The R&D department consists of 550 engineers, scientists, and quality-assurance staff who have more than 1,000 projects in the works at any one time.

Fast and easy access to information such as product specifications, formulas, design criteria, production schedules, costs, and sales trends is required for supporting the design activity. Access to this information used to be difficult because the data sometimes resided in 15 to 20 disparate repositories. When scientists needed production or financial data, for instance, they had to request paper reports from each department, which could take days to be processed. Also the corporate knowledge and experience were scattered in a disorganized fashion over many different locations.

To meet the need for easier access to corporate knowledge, Amway developed a business intelligence and knowledge management portal called Artemis. Tailored to the R&D division, Artemis is a browser-based intranet application that enables R&D staff to quickly find the information and knowledge they require. It also includes features such as collaboration tools and a database for locating company experts. Using the Lotus Notes/Domino search agent, Artemis enables employees to pull data from disparate corporate sources and generate dynamic reports in response to user queries. This information is highly secured by Domino's superb security capabilities.

Artemis's collaborative features include a time-accounting function used to help the R&D staff calculate R&D tax credits. The Artemis event-reporting database also tracks project content and status.

After a staged rollout of Artemis, all employees now have access to the system. The time required to access information dropped from days to minutes or seconds, enabling fast "what-if" investigations by product developers. Initial user surveys indicated that 60 percent of the users were saving 30 minutes or more per week; that figure increased to 1 hour for most employees after additional links to more information sources were added and users gained comfort with the system. The target for the near future is a savings of 2 hours per employee each week. The system paid for itself ($250,000) in less than 6 months.

Sources: Abbott (2000) and *amway.com* press releases (2002).

Questions

1. Identify the KM elements in this case.
2. What activities related to decision making and support are evidenced in this case?
3. Relate this case to c-commerce.

REFERENCES

Abbott, C. "At Amway, BI Portal Speeds Product R&D." *DM Review*, October 2000.

acehardware.com (accessed September 2002 and January 2003).

amway.com (accessed September 2002).

Aneja, A., et al. "Corporate Portal Framework for Transforming Content Chaos on Intranets." *Intel Technology Journal*, Q1 (2000).

Ayers, J. "A Primer on Supply Chain Management." *Information Strategy: The Executive's Journal* (Winter 2000).

Basu, A., and A. Kumar. "Research Commentary: Workflow Management Issues in e-Business." *Information System Research* (March 2002).

Bayles, D. L. *E-Commerce Logistics and Fulfillment*. Upper Saddle River, NJ: Prentice Hall, 2001.

Bradley, P. "CPFR Gaining Converts." *Logistics*, April 2002.

bridgeton.com (accessed July 2002).

Bughin, J. R., et al. "Mobile Portals." *The McKinsey Quarterly* no. 2 (2001).

Buss, D. "CPFR Initiative Allows Ace to Boost Revenue While Cutting Costs." *Stores*, September 2002.

Callaghan, D. "IBM: E-Meetings Save $4 Million a Month." *eWeek*, June 26, 2002.

corning.com (accessed September 2002).

Cunningham, M. J. "Getting the Portal Payback." *e-Business Advisor*, March 2002.

cybexintl.com (accessed 2002 and June 2003)

Day, M. "What Is PLM?" *Cadserver*, April 15, 2002. tenlinks.com/NEWS/ARTICLES/cadserver/plm.htm (accessed September 2002).

Davison, R., and G. de Vreede. "The Global Application of Collaborative Technologies." *Communications of the ACM* (December 2001).

Delphi Group. "Business Portals: Applications & Architecture." delphigroup.com/research/reports/bus-portexcerpt.htm, 1999 (accessed April 2001).

DiCarlo, L. "Case Study: Webcor Builders." *PC Computing*, December 1999, 108–120.

Ferguson, M. "Corporate and E-Business Portals." *my ITadviser*, April 2001.

Fischer, L. *Workflow Handbook 2002.* Lighthouse Point, FL: Future Strategies, Inc., 2002.

General Motors. "2002 Product Information." gm.com, 2002, media.gm.com/news/presskits/technology/tech_overview.html (accessed June 2003).

Gibson-Paul, L. "Suspicious Minds." *CIO Magazine*, January 15, 2003.

Gustke, C. "No More Heavy Lifting at Cybex." *Forbes* (supplement), October 7, 2002.

Handfield, R. B., et al. *Supply Chain Redesign: Transforming Supply Chains into Integrated Value Systems.* Upper Saddle River, NJ: Financial Times Management/Prentice Hall, 2002.

Handfield, R. B., and E. L. Nichols, Jr. *Introduction to Supply Chain Management.* Upper Saddle River, NJ: Prentice Hall, 1999.

Hansen, U. T., and M. S. Deimler. "Cutting Costs While Improving Morale with B2E Management." *MIT Sloan Management Review* (Fall 2001).

hp.com/jornado (accessed May 2002).

IBM. "Product Lifecycle Management." ibm.com (accessed January 2003).

Imhoff, C. "Power Up Your Enterprise Portal." *e-Business Advisor*, May 2001.

Industry Directions. "The Next Wave of Supply Chain Advantage: CPFR." White paper, April 2000, industrydirections.com/pdf/CPFRPublicReport.pdf (accessed March 2002).

Intel Corp. "Franchising Meets the Internet." intel.com/ebusiness/ (go to Industry Solutions) (accessed March 1999a).

Intel Corp. "Marriott International Checks In." intel.com/ebusiness/ (go to Industry Solutions) (accessed March 1999b).

Ireland, R., and R. Bruce. "CPFR: Only the Beginning of Collaboration." *Supply Chain Management Review* (September/October 2000).

Jones, K. "Copier Strategy as Yet Unduplicated." *Interactive Week* (February 9, 1998).

Kalakota, R., and M. Robinson. *E-Business 2.0.* Reading MA: Addison-Wesley, 2001.

Kan, H. Y., et al. "An Internet Virtual Reality Collaborative Environment for Effective Product Design." *Computers in Industry* 45 (2001).

Kesner, R. M. "Building a Knowledge Portal: A Case Study in Web-Enabled Collaboration." *Information Strategy: The Executive Journal* (Winter 2003).

Kounadis, T. "How to Pick the Best Portal." *e-Business Advisor*, August 2000.

Lee H. L., et al. "The Bullwhip Effect in Supply Chains." *MIT Sloan Management Review* (Spring 1997).

line56.com. "Transportation and Warehousing Improving the Value of Your Supply Chain Through Integrated Logistics." May 1, 2002, elibrary.line56.com/data/detail?id= 1043954015_280&type=RES&x=1033897490 (accessed August 2002).

lotus.com (accessed January 2003).

McCreary, L. "Intranet Winners 1999." *CIO Web Magazine*, July 1, 1999.

Mendoza, L. E., et al. "Evaluation of Environments for Portals Development: A Case Study." *Information Systems Management* (Spring 2002).

microsoft.com/asia/Mobile (accessed January 2003).

microsoft.com/resources/casestudies/CaseStudy.asp?CaseStudyID=13324 , 2000 (accessed January 2003).

myKGN. "A Return-on-Investment Study: A META Group White Paper." plumtree.com/news_events/pressreleases/2001/press061901.htm (accessed June 2001).

Neef, D. *E-Procurement: From Strategy to Implementation.* Upper Saddle River, NJ: Prentice Hall, 2001.

Norris G., et al. *E-Business and ERP: Transforming the Enterprise.* New York: McGraw-Hill, 2000.

peoplesoft.com (accessed October 2002).

Plumtree. "A Framework for Assessing Return on Investment for a Corporate Portal Deployment: The Industry's First Comprehensive Overview of Corporate Portal ROI." plumtree.com/webforms/MoreInfo_FormActionTemplate.asp (updated April 2002).

Porirer, C. "Collaborative Commerce: Wave Two of the Cyber Revolution." *Computer Sciences Corporation Perspectives* (2001): 8.

Ragusa, J. M., and G. M. Bochenek. "Collaborative Virtual Design Environments." *Communications of the ACM* (December 2001).

Reda, S. "New Systems Foster Interaction with Store Employees." *Stores* (February 2002).

Ricks, D. et al. "Improving Vertical Coordination of Agricultural Industries Through Supply Chain Management." *American Agricultural Economic Association*, October 1999, agecon.lib.umn.edu/cgi-bin/pdf_view.pl?paperid=1780&ftype=.pdf (accessed July 2002).

Schram, P. *Collaborative Commerce: Going Private to Get Results.* New York: Deloitte Consulting, dc.com (accessed June 2001).

Siau, K., and J. Messersmith. "Enabling Technologies for E-Commerce and ERP Integration." *Quarterly Journal of Electronic Commerce* 3, no. 1 (2002).

Springer, A. "Corning Synchronizes its Global Supply Chain." *Peopletalk* 13, no. 3 (2002).

Stevenson, W. *Operations Management,* 7th ed. New York: McGraw-Hill, 2002.

Sullivan, M. "GM Moves into the Passing Lane." *Forbes* (*Best of the Web* supplement), October 7, 2002.

Toshiba.com/US (accessed September 2003).

tibco.com (accessed 2001).

Thuraisingham, B., et al. "Collaborative Commerce and Knowledge Management." *Knowledge and Process Management* 9, no. 1 (2002).

van der Aalst, W. M. P. *Workflow Management: Models, Methods and Systems.* Boston: MIT Press, 2002.

Vinas, T. "Meeting Makeover." *Industryweek*, February 2002.

Walton B., and M. Princi. "From Supply Chain to Collaborative Network." White paper, Andersen Consulting, 2000 (see ascet.com/documents.asp?d_ID=266) (accessed June 2003).

webcor.com (accessed March 2000–2002).

webex.com/pdf/MeetingCtr_brochure.pdf (accessed October 2002).

INTRANETS

As defined in Chapter 6, an **intranet** is a corporate LAN or WAN that uses Internet technology and is secured behind a company's firewall. This "internal network," or internal Web, is a network architecture designed to serve the internal informational needs of a company through the use of Web concepts and tools (e.g., easy and effective browsing, search engines, and tools for communication and collaboration).

intranet
A corporate LAN or WAN that uses Internet technology and is secured behind a company's firewall. This "internal network," or internal Web, is a network architecture designed to serve the internal informational needs of a company through the use of Web concepts and tools (e.g., easy and effective browsing, search engines, and tools for communication and collaboration).

OVERVIEW OF INTRANETS

Managers can use a Web browser to access the intranet to view employee resumes, business plans, and corporate procedures; they can retrieve sales data, review any desired document, and call a meeting. Employees can check availability of software for particular tasks and test the software from their workstations. Using screen sharing and other groupware tools, intranets can be used to facilitate the work of groups. Companies also publish newsletters and deliver news to their employees on intranets and conduct online training.

Intranets are fairly safe, operating within the company's firewalls (see Chapter 12). Employees can venture out onto the Internet, but unauthorized users cannot enter the intranet. However, intranets frequently have a secure connection to the Internet, enabling the company to conduct e-commerce activities, such as cooperating with suppliers and customers or checking a customer's inventory level before making shipments. Such activities are facilitated by *extranets*, as described in Chapter 7.

According to a Meta Group study (Stellin 2001), nearly 90 percent of all U.S. corporations have some type of intranet. Over 25 percent are using corporate portals that perform functions well beyond just publishing material on the intranet.

Intranet technology is mature enough for its applications to have become fairly standard. See case studies at vendors' sites for specific examples. Also look at whitepapers.earthweb.com and at google.com (search for "intranet case studies"). The material at this book's Web site, prenhall.com/turban (Chapter 18) and at cio.com/research/ec/cases.html also are good places to investigate.

INTRANET FUNCTIONALITIES

Intranets have some or all of the following functionalities:

- Web-based database access for ease of use
- Search engines, indexing engines, and directories that assist in keyword-based searches
- Interactive communication tools such as chatting, audio support, and videoconferencing
- Document distribution and workflow capabilities, including Web-based downloading and routing of documents
- Groupware, including enhanced e-mail, bulletin boards, screen sharing, and other group-support tools
- Conduit for a computer-based telephony system

In addition, intranets usually have the ability to integrate with EC applications and to interface with Internet-based electronic purchasing, payment, and delivery applications. They also can be part of extranets, so that geographically dispersed branches, customers, and suppliers can access certain portions of the intranets. These functions provide for numerous applications that increase productivity, reduce costs, reduce waste and cycle time, and improve customer service, as discussed in the following section.

INTRANET APPLICATIONS

According to a survey conducted by *InformationWeek* in 1998, with nearly a thousand responding managers, the information that is most frequently included in intranets is in the form of product catalogs (49 percent of all companies), corporate policies and procedures (35 percent), purchase ordering (42 percent), document sharing (39 percent), corporate phone directories (40 percent), and human resource forms (35 percent) (McGee 1998). Also included, in lower percentages, were training programs, customer databases, data warehouse and decision support access, image archives, and travel reservation services. These figures are probably much higher today, as intranets have matured over the past few years.

In addition to the many activities just discussed, intranets provide the following capabilities:

▶ **Search and access to documents.** The intranet provides access to information that can increase productivity and facilitate teamwork.

▶ **Personalized information.** The intranet can deliver personalized information via personalized Web pages and e-mail.

▶ **Enhanced knowledge sharing.** The Web-based intranet can encourage knowledge sharing among company employees.

▶ **Individual decision making.** Employees can make better decisions because they can easily access the right information and online expertise.

▶ **Software distribution.** Using the intranet server as the application warehouse helps eliminate many software maintenance and support problems.

▶ **Document management.** Employees can access pictures, photos, charts, maps, and other documents regardless of where they are stored or where the employees are located.

▶ **Project management.** Most project management activities are conducted over intranets.

▶ **Training.** A corporate Web page is a valuable source of information for employees. Employee training can be done through online classes over the intranet.

▶ **Enhanced transaction processing.** Data can be entered just one time into a database connected to an intranet, thus eliminating errors and increasing internal control.

▶ **Paperless information delivery.** Elimination of paper by disseminating information on the intranet can result in lower costs, easier accessibility to information, less paper to maintain, and increased security.

▶ **Employees control their own information.** Employees can check their annual vacation-day status or change their postal address, tax status, or retirement fund allocation.

When intranets are combined with an external connection (an extranet), these additional capabilities are possible:

▶ **Electronic commerce.** Intrabusiness marketing can be done online; selling to outsiders is done via the extranet, involving portions of the intranet.

▶ **Customer service.** An intranet-extranet combination is used by logistics companies such as UPS, FedEx, and others to enable customers to gather information about product shipment and availability. These companies have found that such applications increase customer satisfaction.

▶ **Enhanced group decision making and business processes.** Web-based groupware and workflow are becoming part of the standard intranet platform. They are delivered via the intranet and are included as a standard feature of intranet software. They can also be part of the internal supply chain operation.

▶ **Virtual organizations.** Web technology removes the barrier of incompatible technology between business partners.

▶ **Improved administrative processes.** The internal management of production, inventory, procurement, shipping, and distribution can be effectively supported by linking these functions in a single threaded environment (the intranet). These functions can also be seamlessly integrated with interorganizational extranets.

MORE INTRANET EXAMPLES

As noted, intranets can be used for a variety of business functions, as shown by the following examples.

▶ **Business intelligence.** In 2000, Financial Times (FT) Electronic Publishing implemented its online news and information service, FT Discovery, for 10,000 intranet users at KPMG Peat Marwick, one of the Big Five accounting firms. FT Discovery, which is integrated into the KPMG corporate intranet, provides immediate access to critical business intelligence from over 4,000 information sources. For example, Corporate Navigator from Story Street Partners is integrated into the intranet to provide in-depth advice on where to go for information on the issues and companies of interest to KPMG.

▶ **Public services.** The Hawaiian Islands are linked by a state educational, medical, and public services network (htdc.org). This ambitious intranet provides quality services to residents of all the Hawaiian Islands.

▶ **Corporate information.** Employees at IBM ranked the company's intranet as the most useful and credible source of corporate information. They use the intranet to order supplies, sign up for fringe benefits, take classes, track projects, and manage their retirement plans. IBM considers its intranet an extremely valuable source of information that helps increase productivity. For example, managers can post and read information about projects in progress without bothering other employees, making calls, or sending e-mails. IBM employees who telecommute can log onto the intranet from home and conduct work. In May 2001, IBM asked its employees to contribute ideas for solving some current problems. More than 6,000 suggestions were collected over the intranet in just 3 days.

▶ **Customer service.** At Charles Schwab, 25,000 employees use the intranet (Sch Web) regularly. It helps employees provide better customer service because it makes it easier to respond to customer inquiries. Using search engines, employees can quickly find the answers they need. It is now part of Schwab's culture to look at the intranet first to find answers. Schwab estimates tens of millions of dollars in savings due to its intranet (Hoffman 2001).

INDUSTRY-SPECIFIC INTRANET SOLUTIONS

Intranet solutions are frequently classified by industry instead of by technology. According to *InformationWeek Online* (InformationWeek 1998), the top 100 intranet and extranet solutions can be classified by industry as follows: financial services (banking, brokerages, other financial services, and insurance); information technology; manufacturing (chemicals and oil, consumer goods, food and beverage, general manufacturing, and pharmaceuticals); retail; and service providers (construction/engineering, education, environmental, health care, media, entertainment, telecommunications, transportation, and utilities). Internet applications are very diversified, as shown in the list of six industry-specific intranets in Online Appendix W8.1 (see prenhall.com/turban).

BUILDING INTRANETS

To build an intranet, a company needs Web servers, browsers, Web publishing tools, back-end databases, TCP/IP networks (LAN or WAN), and firewalls, as shown in Exhibit 8A.1. A *firewall* is software or hardware that allows only those external users with specific characteristics to access a protected network (see Chapter 12). Additional software may be necessary to support Web-based workflow, groupware, and ERP, depending upon the individual company's needs. Security schemes, which are similar for intranets and for the Internet, are described in Chapter 12.

A company may have one intranet composed of many LANs. Alternatively, a company may have several interconnected intranets, each composed of only a few LANs. The decision of how to structure the intranet depends on how dispersed the LANs are and what technologies are involved. In building an intranet, network architects need to consider and plan for the functionalities the network will need.

The cost of converting an existing client-server network to an intranet is relatively low, especially when a company is already using the Internet. Many computing facilities can be shared by both the Internet and intranets. An example of this is a client-server-based electronic conferencing software module from Pixion (pixion.com) that allows users to share documents, graphics, and video in real time. This capability can be combined with an electronic voice capability (e.g., Internet telephony).

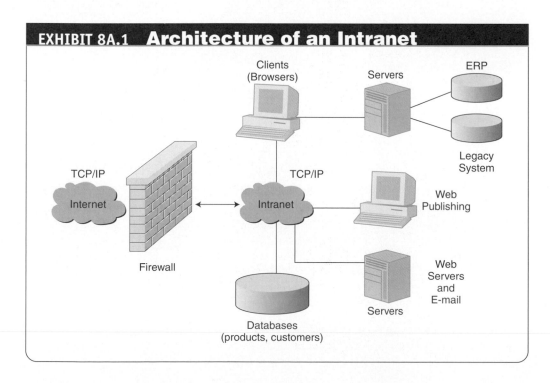

EXHIBIT 8A.1 Architecture of an Intranet

KEY TERM

Intranet   339

REFERENCES

Firstcall.com. "First Call Corp. Partners with Story Street to Develop Customized Intranet Solutions for Global Institutional Marketplace." February 1999, First Call press release, firstcall.com/press/news/1999/02_08.shtml?press%7Cnews%7Carticle (accessed April 2001).

Hoffman, T. "Intranet Helps Workers Navigate Corporate Maze." *Computerworld*, June 4, 2001, computerworld.com/managementtopics/management/helpdesk/story/0,10801,61019,00.html (accessed April 2002).

InformationWeek. "Solution Series: Intranet/Extranet 100." October 5, 1998, informationweek.com/657/intext.htm (accessed October 2000).

McGee, M. K. "Strategic Applications: Companies Are Forging a Unique Blend of Custom and Commercial Software to Gain a Competitive Advantage." November 23, 1998, informationweek.com/710/10prstr.htm (accessed September 2001).

Stellin, S. "Intranets Nurture Companies from the Inside." *New York Times*, January 29, 2001.

CHAPTER 9

E-GOVERNMENT, E-LEARNING, AND OTHER EC APPLICATIONS

Content

E-Learning at Cisco Systems

9.1 E-Government: An Overview

9.2 Implementing E-Government

9.3 Online Publishing, E-Books, and Blogging

9.4 E-Learning

9.5 Knowledge Management and E-Commerce

9.6 Customer-to-Customer E-Commerce

9.7 Peer-to-Peer Networks and Applications

9.8 Other EC Applications

Managerial Issues

Real-World Case: E-Government Initiatives in Hong Kong

Learning objectives

Upon completion of this chapter, you will be able to:

1. Describe e-government to citizens (G2C) and to business (G2B).

2. Describe various e-government initiatives.

3. Discuss online publishing and e-books.

4. Describe e-learning and virtual universities.

5. Describe knowledge management and dissemination.

6. Describe C2C activities.

7. Understand how peer-to-peer technology works in intrabusiness, in B2B, and in C2C.

8. Describe other EC applications.

E-LEARNING AT CISCO SYSTEMS

The Problem

Cisco Systems (*cisco.com*) is one of the fastest growing high-tech companies in the world, selling devices that connect computers and networks to the Internet and other networks. Cisco's products are continuously being upgraded or replaced; so extensive training of employees and customers is needed. Cisco recognizes that its employees, business partners, and independent students seeking professional certification all require training on a continuous basis. Traditional classroom training was flawed by its inability to scale rapidly enough. Cisco offered in-house classes 6 to 10 times a year, in many locations, but the rapid growth in the number of students, coupled with the fast pace of technological change, made the training both expensive and ineffective.

The Solution

Cisco believes that *e-learning* is a revolutionary way to empower its workforce and its partners with the skills and knowledge needed to turn technological change to an advantage. Therefore, Cisco implemented e-learning programs that enable students to learn new software, hardware, and procedures. Cisco believes that once people experience e-learning, they will recognize that it is the fastest, easiest way to get the information they need to be successful.

To implement e-learning, Cisco created the Delta Force, which was made up of its CEO John Chambers, the IT unit, and the Internet Learning Solution Group. The group's first project was to build two learning portals, one for 40 partner companies that sell Cisco products and one for 4,000 systems engineers who implement the products after the sale.

Cisco also wants to serve as a model of e-learning for its partners and customers, hoping to convince them to use its e-learning programs. To encourage its own employees to use e-learning, Cisco:

- Makes e-learning a mandatory part of employees' jobs.
- Offers easy access to e-learning tools via the Web.
- Makes e-learning nonthreatening through the use of an anonymous testing and scoring process that focuses on helping people improve rather than penalizing those who fail.
- Gives those who fail the tests precision learning targets (remedial work, modules, exercises, or written materials)

to help them pass and remove the fear associated with testing.

- Enables managers to track, manage, and ensure employee development, competency change, and, ultimately, performance change.
- Offers additional incentives and rewards such as stock grants, promotions, and bonuses to employees who pursue specialization and certification through e-learning.
- Adds e-learning as a strategic top-down metric for Cisco executives, who are measured on their deployment of IT in their departments.

For its employees, partners, and customers, Cisco operates E-Learning Centers for Excellence. These centers offer training at Cisco office sites as well as at customers' sites via intranets and the Internet. Some of the training requires the use of partnering vendors.

Cisco offers a variety of training programs supported by e-learning. For example, in 2001, Cisco converted a popular 4½–day, instructor-led training (ILT) course on Cisco's signature IOS (interorganizational information system) technologies into an e-learning program that blends both live and self-paced components. The goal was to teach seasoned systems engineers (SEs) how to sell, install, configure, and maintain those key IOS technologies, and to do so in a way that would train more people than the 25 employees the on-site ILT course could hold.

The Results

On the IOS course alone, Cisco calculated its ROI as follows:

- It cost $12,400 to develop the blended course.
- The course saved each SE 1 productivity day and 20 percent of the travel and lodging cost of a 1-week training course in San Jose. Estimating $750 for travel and lodging and $450 for the productivity day, the savings totaled $1,200 per SE.
- Seventeen SEs attended the course the first time it was offered, for a total savings of $20,400. Therefore, in the first offering of the course, Cisco recovered the development costs and saved $8,000 over and above those costs.

- Since March 2001, the IOS Learning Services team has presented two classes of 40 SEs per month. At that rate, Cisco saves $1,152,000 net for just this one course every 12 months.

In 2003, over 10,000 corporate salespeople, 150,000 employees of business partners, and 200,000 independent students were taking courses at Cisco learning centers, many using the e-learning courses. By 2003, Cisco had developed over 100 e-learning courses and was planning to develop many more. According to Galagan (2002), e-learning is a major underpinning of Cisco's economic health.

Sources: Compiled from *cisco.com* (2001), Galagan (2002), and Delahoussaye and Zemke (2001).

WHAT WE CAN LEARN . . .

This opening case demonstrates the application of e-learning as an efficient training tool, a topic that is gaining increasing attention in e-businesses. E-learning is also becoming popular in all levels and types of schools and universities. This chapter covers the topic of e-learning both in business and academic settings. It also will examine e-government, e-publishing and knowledge management, and consumer-to-consumer, peer-to-peer, and other EC applications.

9.1 E-GOVERNMENT: AN OVERVIEW

SCOPE AND DEFINITION

As e-commerce matures and its tools and applications improve, greater attention is being given to its use to improve the business of public institutions and governments (country, state, county, city, etc.). Several international conferences have been held in recent years to explore the potential of what is called e-government. E-government is the use of information technology in general, and e-commerce in particular, to provide citizens and organizations with more convenient access to government information and services and to provide delivery of public services to citizens, business partners, and those working in the public sector. It is also an efficient and effective way of conducting government business transactions with citizens and businesses and within the governments themselves.

E-government in the United States was especially driven by the 1998 Government Paperwork Elimination Act and by former President Clinton's December 17, 1999, Memorandum on E-Government, which ordered the top 500 forms used by citizens (such as tax forms) to be placed online by December 2000. The memorandum also directed agencies to construct a secure e-government infrastructure. Other drivers of e-government, according to Miller (2000), are increased computing power, the reduced cost of computing, the increased number of businesses and individuals on the Internet, and the need to make governments more efficient.

Some use the term e-government to mean an extension of e-commerce to government procurement. This use of the term views e-government only in the realm of B2G (business-to-government) transactions (International Trade Centre 2000). However, in this book, the term will be used in the broader context given earlier—the bringing together of governments, citizens, and businesses in a network of information, knowledge, and commerce.

In that broader view, e-government is both the advent of a new form of government and the birth of a new marketplace. It offers an opportunity to improve the efficiency and effectiveness of the functions of government and to make governments more transparent to citizens and businesses by providing access to more of the information generated by government.

Several major categories fit within this broad definition of e-government: government-to-citizens, government-to-business, government-to-government, and government-to-employees. Each of these, in turn, will be covered in the following sections. For a comprehensive listing of e-government resources, tutorials, and more, (see egov.gov). For a description of the range of e-government activities in the United States, see Dean (2000).

GOVERNMENT-TO-CITIZENS

The government-to-citizens (G2C) category includes all the interactions between a government and its citizens that can take place electronically. See Al-Kibsi et al. (2001) or Abramson and Means (2001) for an overview of G2C. As shown in the Real-World Case about Hong Kong at the end of the chapter, G2C can involve dozens of different initiatives. The basic idea is to enable citizens to interact with the government from their homes. G2C applications enable citizens to ask questions of government agencies and receive answers, pay taxes, receive payments and documents, and so forth. For example, citizens can renew driver's licenses, pay traffic tickets, and make appointments for vehicle emission inspections and driving tests. Governments also can disseminate information on the Web, conduct training,

e-government
The use of IT and e-commerce to provide access to government information and delivery of public services to citizens and business partners.

government-to-citizens (G2C)
E-government category that includes all the interactions between a government and its citizens.

help citizens find employment, and more. In California, for example, drivers' education classes are offered online and can be taken anytime, anywhere.

According to emarketer.com (2002b), the major features of government Web sites are phone and address information (96 percent), links to other sites (71 percent), publications (93 percent), and databases (57 percent). The major areas of G2C activities are tourism and recreation (77 percent), research and education (70 percent), downloadable forms (63 percent), discovery of government services (63 percent), information about public policy (62 percent), and advice about health and safety issues (49 percent).

An interesting area of application is the use of the Internet by politicians, especially during election periods. For example, during the 2000 presidential election in the United States, both major-party candidates used e-mail messages and had comprehensive information portals. In South Korea, politicians log onto the Internet to recruit voters, because many people who surf the Internet rarely read newspapers or watch TV. The target audience of these politicians is the 20- to 30-year-old age group, the vast majority of who surf the Internet. Pasdaq, the Seoul-based over-the-counter stock exchange of Korea, offers an Internet game that simulates the stock market and measures the popularity of some 300 politicians by allowing players to buy "stocks" in a politician. In one year, over 500,000 members signed up. It became a necessity in Korea for politicians to have a Web site. Involved citizens even make donations over the Internet using credit cards. Some politicians make decisions based on citizens' opinions collected on the Internet.

Another area of G2C activity is in solving constituents' problems. The government (or a politician) can use CRM-type software to assign inquiries and problem cases to the appropriate staff member. Workflow CRM software can then be used to track the problem's progress. For details and other applications, see "CRM for government" at peoplesoft.com.

Yet another common G2C use is the broadcasting of city council meetings, press conferences, and public addresses. In many municipalities, delivering training and educational courses, both to citizens and to employees, is a very popular Internet activity.

Government agencies and departments in many cities, counties, and countries are planning more and more diverse e-services. For example, many governments are now seriously considering electronic voting. In some countries, voters actually see their choice on the computer screen and are asked to confirm their vote, much as is done when purchasing a book online from Amazon.com, transferring funds, or selling stocks. (For further discussion of online voting and why it may take years to implement it in the United States, see Schwartz 2000 and Weiss 2001.)

Many believe that with the ever-increasing percentage of Net users who get information about government and politics online, also known as **Netizens**, the manner in which politics is conducted will change drastically in the not-so-distant future.

Netizen
A citizen surfing the Internet.

Electronic Benefits Transfer

One e-government application that is not new is *electronic benefits transfer* (EBT), which has been available since the early 1990s. The U.S. government, for example, transfers more than $600 billion in benefits annually to its citizens. In 1993, the U.S. government launched an initiative to develop a nationwide EBT system to deliver government benefits electronically. Initially, the attempt was made to deliver benefits to recipients' bank accounts. However, more than 20 percent of these transfers go to citizens who do not have bank accounts. To solve this problem, the government plans to use smart cards (see Chapter 13). Benefit recipients will be able to load electronic funds onto the cards and use the cards at automated teller machines (ATMs), point-of-sale locations, and grocery and other stores, just like other bank card users do. When the smart card systems are in place, recipients will either get electronic transfers to their bank accounts or be able to download money to their smart cards. The advantage is not only the reduction in processing costs (from about 50 cents per check to 2 cents), but also the reduction of fraud. With biometrics (see Chapter 12) coming to smart cards and PCs, officials expect fraud to be reduced substantially.

The smart card system is a part of a nationwide EBT system for miscellaneous payments, such as those for Social Security and welfare. Agencies at the federal, state, and local levels are expanding EBT programs into new areas, including health, nutrition, employment, and education. Also, many states operate EBT systems for state-provided benefits. Governments also use smart cards as purchasing media for G2B procurement. For more information on EBT in government, see fns.usda.gov.

GOVERNMENT-TO-BUSINESS

Governments seek to automate their interactions with businesses. Although we call this category **government-to-business (G2B)**, the relationship works two ways: government-to-business and business-to-government. Thus, G2B refers to e-commerce in which government sells to businesses or provides them with services, as well as to businesses selling products and services to government (see Schubert and Hausler 2001). Two key G2B areas are e-procurement and the auctioning of government surpluses.

Government E-Procurement

Governments buy large amounts of MROs and other materials direct from suppliers. In many cases, law mandates an RFQ or tendering system. For years, these tenderings were done manually; the systems are now moving online. These systems are basically *reverse auctions* (buy-side auction systems), such as those described in Chapter 6. An example of a reverse auction used for G2B procurement in Hong Kong is briefly described in the Real-World Case at the end of the chapter (and at info.gov.hk). For additional information about such reverse auctions, see gsa.gov. In the United States, the local housing agencies of HUD (Housing and Urban Development), which provides housing to low-income residents, are moving to e-procurement (see Corbeil 2002 and U.S. Department of Housing and Urban Development 2001). Governments provide all the support for such tendering systems, as shown in EC Application Case 9.1.

government-to-business (G2B)

E-government category that includes interactions between governments and businesses (government selling to businesses and providing them with services and businesses selling products and services to government).

CASE 9.1
EC Application
CONTRACT MANAGEMENT IN AUSTRALIA

The focus of the Western Australian (WA) government agency Contract and Management Services (CAMS) is to develop online contract management solutions for the public sector. CAMS Online allows government agencies to search existing contracts to discover the commonly used contracts. It also assists suppliers that want to sell to the government. Suppliers can view the current tenders (bids) on the Western Australia Government Contracting Information Bulletin Board and can download tender documents from this site.

CAMS Online also provides government departments and agencies with unbiased expert advice on e-commerce, Internet, and satellite services and how-to's on building a bridge between the technological needs of the public sector and the expertise of the private sector. The center offers various types of support for government procurement activities.

Support of E-Commerce Activities

WA's e-commerce activities include electronic markets for government buying. Government clients can purchase goods and services on the *CAMS Internet Marketplace,* which provides services ranging from sending a purchase order to receiving an invoice and paying for an item. The *WA Government Electronic Market* provides online supplier catalogs, electronic purchase orders, electronic invoicing, EFT, and check and credit card payments. The Victoria government and the New South Wales government in WA are spending over $500 million (U.S.) on e-procurement systems under the Government Electronic Market system (2002).

Other WA e-commerce functions are *ProcureLink,* a CAMS service that sends electronic purchase orders to suppliers via EDI, EDI Post (an online hybrid mail service), facsimile, and

the Internet; *SalesNet,* by which the government secures credit card payments for the sale of government goods and services across the Internet; and *DataLink,* which enables the transfer of data using a secure environment for message management. DataLink is an ideal solution for government agencies that need to exchange large volumes of operational information.

Training Online

In addition to G2B functions, the site also offers online training to citizens. A service called *Westlink* delivers adult training and educational programs to remote areas and schools, including rural and regional communities. A video-conferencing service offers two-way video and audio links, enabling government employees to meet together electronically from up to eight sites at any one time.

Access to the Online Services Centre is given to government employees and businesses that deal with the government via the CAMS Web site at *business.wa.gov.au.*

Source: Compiled from *business.wa.gov.au* (2002) and from *ecc.online.wa.gov.au/news* (2002).

Questions

1. How is contract management in WA facilitated by e-commerce tools?
2. What other e-commerce activities does the government perform?
3. Describe the WA online training program.

Group Purchasing

The concept of online group purchasing, introduced in Chapters 1 and 6, is practiced by the U.S. government as well. For example, the eFAST service conducts reverse auctions for aggregated orders (see gsa.gov). Suppliers post group purchasing offers, and the prices fall as more orders are placed. Alternatively, government buyers may post product requests, which other buyers may review and join in on. Pooled orders are then forwarded to suppliers for reverse auction bidding.

Forward E-Auctions

Many governments auction surplus or other goods, ranging from vehicles to foreclosed real estate. Such auctions used to be done manually, and then were done electronically over private networks. These auctions are now moving to the Internet. Governments can auction from a government Web site or they can use third-party auction sites such as eBay.com, bid4assets.com, or freemarkets.com for this purpose. In January 2001, the U.S. General Services Administration (GSA) launched a property auction site online (auctionrp.com) where real-time auctions for surpluses and seized goods are conducted. Some of these auctions are restricted to dealers; others are open to the public (see govexec.com).

Tax Collection and Management

Every year millions of individuals file tax reports. Similarly, hundreds of thousands of businesses do the same. Businesses in the United States must file quarterly reports. Electronic filing of taxes is now available in over 100 countries, from Thailand to Finland to the United States. In addition to personal and income tax, it is also possible to pay online sales tax and value-added tax. For a case study of successful online tax implementation in Thailand, see Hopfner (2002).

GOVERNMENT-TO-GOVERNMENT

government-to-government (G2G)
E-government category that includes activities within government units and those between governments.

The government-to-government (G2G) category consists of EC activities between units of government, including those within one governmental body and those between governments. Some examples of G2G in the United States include:

  ▶ **Intelink.** Intelink is an intranet that carries classified information shared by the numerous U.S. intelligence agencies.
  ▶ **Procurement at GSA.** The GSA's Web site, gsa.gov, uses technologies such as demand aggregation and reverse auctions to buy for various units of the federal government. This site seeks to apply innovative Web-based procurement methods to government buying. It offers many, many services (see gsa.gov/portal/buying/jsp).
  ▶ **Federal Case Registry (Department of Health and Human Services).** This service helps state governments locate information about child support, including data on paternity and enforcement. It is available at acf.dhhs.gov/programs/cse/newhire/fcr/fcr.htm.
  ▶ **Procurement Marketing and Access Network (Small Business Administration).** This service (pro-net.sba.gov) presents PRO-Net, a searchable database that contracting officers in various government units can use to find products and services sold by small, disadvantaged, or women-owned businesses.

For more examples of G2G services, see the Real-World Case at the end of the chapter and govexec.com.

GOVERNMENT-TO-EMPLOYEES

government-to-employees (G2E)
E-government category that includes activities and services between government units and their employees.

Governments employ large numbers of people. Therefore, governments are just as interested as private-sector organizations are in electronically providing services and information to their employees. Indeed, because employees of federal and state governments often work in a variety of geographic locations, government-to-employees (G2E) applications may be especially useful in enabling efficient communication. One example of G2E is the Lifelines service provided by the U.S. government to U.S. Navy employees and their families, described in EC Application Case 9.2.

CASE 9.2
EC Application
G2E IN THE U.S. NAVY

The U.S. Navy uses G2E to improve the flow of information to sailors and their families. Because long shipboard deployments cause strains on navy families, in 1995, the navy began seeking ways to ensure that quality-of-life information reaches navy personnel and their loved ones all over the world. Examples of quality-of-life information include self-help, deployment support, stress management, parenting advice, and relocation assistance.

Lifelines (*lifelines2000.org*) uses the Internet, simulcasting, teleconferencing, cable television, and satellite broadcasting to reach overseas personnel. The navy has found that certain media channels are more appropriate for different types of information. Lifelines regularly features live broadcasts, giving forward-deployed sailors and their families welcome information and, in some cases, a taste of home. On the Web, an average of 2,500 people access the Lifelines site each day.

The government provides several other e-services to navy personnel. Notable are online banking, personal finance services, and insurance. Education and training are also provided online. In 2001, the navy started issuing mobile computing devices to sailors while they are deployed at sea. The handheld devices offer both entertainment and information to navy personnel on active duty.

Sources: Compiled from online news items at GovExec.com (2000), Dean (2000), and *lifelines2000.org* (2001).

Questions

1. Why is the navy using multiple media channels?
2. Compare the G2E services provided by the navy with the B2E services discussed in Section 8.5.

Section 9.1 ▶ REVIEW

1. Define e-government.
2. What are the four categories of e-government services?
3. Describe G2C.
4. Describe how EBT works.
5. Describe the two main areas of G2B activities.

9.2 IMPLEMENTING E-GOVERNMENT

Like any other organization, government entities want to move into the digital era and become click-and-mortar organizations. Therefore, one can find large numbers of EC applications in government organizations. This section examines some of the issues involved in *implementing* e-government.

THE TRANSFORMATION PROCESS

The transformation from traditional delivery of government services to full implementation of online government services may be a lengthy process. The business consulting firm Deloitte and Touche conducted a study (see Wong 2000) that identified six stages in the transformation to e-government. These stages are shown in Exhibit 9.1 (page 350) and described in the following list.

▶ **Stage 1: Information publishing/dissemination.** Individual government departments set up their own Web sites. These provide the public with information about the department, the range of services it offers, and contacts for further assistance. In stage 1, governments may establish an electronic encyclopedia, the purpose of which is to reduce the number of phone calls customers need to make to reach the employee who can fulfill their service requests. These online resources also help to reduce paperwork and the number of help-line employees needed.

▶ **Stage 2: "Official" two-way transactions with one department at a time.** With the help of legally valid digital signatures and secure Web sites, customers are able to submit personal information to and conduct monetary transactions with single government departments. For example, the local government of Lewisham in the United Kingdome lets citizens claim income support and housing benefits by filing an electronic form. In

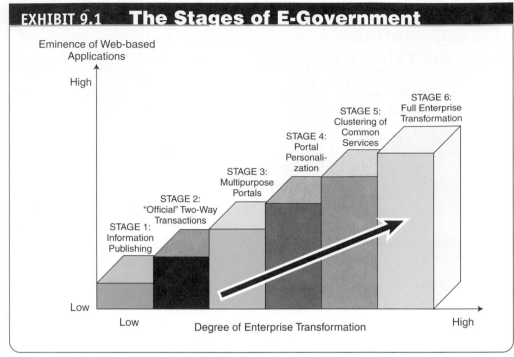

EXHIBIT 9.1   The Stages of E-Government

Source: Wong, W. Y. *At the Dawn of E-Government*. New York: Delioitte Research, Deloitte & Touche, 2000.

Singapore, payments to citizens and from citizens to various government agencies can be performed online. In many countries (e.g., United States, United Kingdom, Hong Kong), tax returns are filed online with attached payments, if needed. At this stage, customers must be convinced of the department's ability to keep their information private and free from piracy.

▌ **Stage 3: Multipurpose portals.** At this point, customer-centric governments make a big breakthrough in service delivery. Based on the fact that customer needs can cut across department boundaries; a portal allows customers to use a single point of entry to send and receive information and to process monetary transactions across multiple departments. For example, in addition to acting as a gateway to its agencies and related governments, the government of South Australia's portal (sa.gov.au) features a "business channel" and a link for citizens to pay bills (utilities, automotive), manage bank accounts, and conduct personal stock brokering. The Real-World Case at the end of this chapter is such a portal, as are Singapore's portals (ecitizen.gov.sg and gov.sg). The design of one-stop e-government sites is explored by Wimmer (2002), who developed a model for integrating multiple services in one location.

▌ **Stage 4: Portal personalization.** Through stage 3, customers can access a variety of services at a single Web site. In stage 4, government puts even more power into customers' hands by allowing them to customize portals with their desired features. To accomplish this, governments require much more sophisticated Web programming that permits interfaces to be manipulated by the users. The added benefit of portal personalization is that governments get a more accurate read on customer preferences for electronic versus nonelectronic service options. As in industry, this allows for true CRM in government. Such portals began in spring 2001, and many state and county governments in the United States, Australia, and several other countries have implemented them or are planning to do so no later than 2004. Examples include the U.S. Department of Education (ed.gov) and the Internal Revenue Service (irs.gov).

▌ **Stage 5: Clustering of common services.** Stage 5 is where real transformation of government structure takes shape. As customers now view once-disparate services as a unified package through the portal, their perception of departments as distinct entities will begin to blur. They will recognize groups of transactions rather than groups of agencies. To make this happen, governments will cluster services along common lines to accelerate the delivery of shared services. In other words, a business restructuring will take place. Initial stage 5 implementations are anticipated in Australia, Canada, New Zealand, the United Kingdom and the United States in 2005.

- **Stage 6: Full integration and enterprise transformation.** Stage 6 offers a full-service center, personalized to each customer's needs and preferences. At this stage, old walls defining silos of government services have been torn down, and technology is integrated across the new structure to bridge the shortened gap between the front and back offices. In some countries, new departments will have formed from the remains of predecessors. Others will have the same names, but their interiors will look nothing like they did before the e-government implementation.

IMPLEMENTATION ISSUES

The following implementation issues depend on which of the six stages of development a government is in and on its plan for moving to higher stages.

- **Transformation speed.** The speed at which a government moves from stage 1 to stage 6 varies, but usually the transformation is very slow. Some of the determining factors are the degree of resistance to change by government employees, the rate at which citizens adopt the new applications (see the following section), the available budget, and the legal environment. Deloitte and Touche found that in 2000, most governments were still in stage 1 (Wong 2000).

- **G2B implementation.** Implementation of G2B is easier than implementation of G2C. In some countries, such as Hong Kong, G2B implementation is outsourced to a private company that pays all of the start-up expenses in exchange for collecting future transaction fees. As G2B services have the potential for rapid cost savings, they can be a good way to begin an e-government initiative.

- **Security and privacy issues.** Governments are concerned about maintaining the security and privacy of citizens' data. According to emarketer.com (2002b), the number of U.S. government Web sites with *security policies* increased from 5 percent in 2000 to 34 percent in 2002. The percentage of those with *privacy policies* increased from 7 percent in 2000 to 43 percent in 2002. One area of particular concern is that of health care. From a medical point of view, it is necessary to have quick access to people's data, and the Internet and smart cards provide such capabilities; however, the protection of such data is very expensive. Deciding on how much security to provide is an important managerial issue.

- **Wireless applications.** Several wireless applications suitable for e-government will be presented in Chapter 10. Notable are B2E applications, especially for field employees, and B2C information discovery, such as the 511 system described in Chapter 1. Another example is the city of Bergen, Norway, which provides wireless tourist services. An interesting wireless application in the city of Manchester (United Kingdom) is provided by Davies et al. (2002). Many more applications are expected in the future. Therefore, such applications must be included in any transformation plan.

See Bacon et al. (2001) and Hart-Teeter (2001) for additional implementation issues.

CITIZEN ADOPTION OF E-GOVERNMENT

One of the most important issues in implementing e-government is its adoption and usage by citizens. Warkentin et al. (2002) constructed a model that attempts to explore this issue. They believe that the adoption rate depends on many variables, as shown in Exhibit 9.2 (page 352). One of the major variables is "trust in e-government," which is itself determined by several variables. Other variables, such as perceived ease of use and perceived usefulness, are generic to EC adoption. Moderating variables, such as culture, are also important.

NON-INTERNET E-GOVERNMENT

Today, e-government is associated with the Internet. However, governments have been using other networks, especially internal ones, to improve government operations for over 15 years.

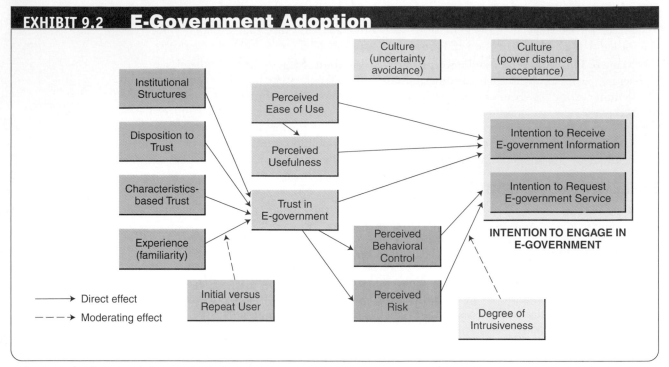

EXHIBIT 9.2   E-Government Adoption

Source: Warkentin, M., et al. "Encouraging Citizen Adoption of E-Government by Building Trust." *Electronic Markets 12*, no. 3 (2002). Courtesy of Taylor & Francis Ltd., tandf.eo.uk.journals.

For example, on January 17, 1994, a major earthquake shook Southern California. About 114,000 buildings were damaged, and more than 500,000 victims turned to the Federal Emergency Management Agency (FEMA) for help. Initially, tired and dazed citizens stood hours in lines to register and have in-person interviews. To expedite the process, an e-government application was installed to expedite the issuance of checks to citizens. Citizens called an 800-number, and operators entered the information collected directly into online electronic forms. Then the data traveled electronically to the mobile disaster inspectors. Once checked, data went electronically to financial management and finally to check writing. The data never touched paper, and the cycle time was reduced by more than 50 percent. Another example of non-Internet e-government is auctions conducted over private, secured telecommunication lines. Sooner or later, such non-Internet e-government initiatives will probably be converted to Internet-based ones.

Section 9.2 ▶ REVIEW

1. List and briefly describe the six stages of e-government development.

2. Describe some e-government implementation issues.

3. Provide an example of a non-Internet e-government service.

9.3   ONLINE PUBLISHING, E-BOOKS, AND BLOGGING

online publishing

The electronic delivery of newspapers, magazines, books, news, music, videos, and other digitizable information over the Internet.

Another major area of EC applications is online publishing and associated activities. Moving paper information to electronic form has created a revolution that impacts both dissemination of information and learning. **Online publishing** is the electronic delivery of newspapers, magazines, books, news, music, videos, and other digitizable information over the Internet (see Zhao and Resh 2001). Initiated in the late 1960s, online publishing was designed to provide online bibliographies and to sell knowledge that was stored in online commercial databases. Publicly funded online publishing was established for the purpose of disseminating medical, educational, and aerospace research information. It was all done on private communication lines.

Today, online publishing has additional purposes. It is related to e-learning, to entertainment, to the worldwide dissemination of knowledge, and to advertising (because it is sometimes provided free to attract people to sites where advertising is conducted). Publishers of traditional hard-copy media have expanded to add online operations. Magazine and newspaper publishers such as *Ad Week*, *PC Magazine*, the *Wall Street Journal*, and the *Los Angeles Times* all use online publishing to disseminate information online. Many magazines are offered only online; they are referred to as e-zines. Online publishing includes materials supplied for free or by subscription fee; sometimes such material may be customized for the recipient. The potential of new interactive technologies and other Internet applications are expected to aid the growth of online publishing.

e-zines
Electronic magazines.

ONLINE PUBLISHING APPROACHES AND METHODS

Several online publishing methods are in use. The following are several such methods.

▸ **Online-archive approach.** The online-archive approach is a digital archive. Such an archive may be a library catalog or a bibliographic database. With this approach, paper publications are converted to a digitized format, without any change, and are offered electronically.

▸ **New-medium approach.** The new-medium approach is used by publishers that seek to use the publication capabilities of the Web to create new material or add content and multimedia to paper publications. With this approach, publishers may provide extra analysis or additional information on any issue or topic online, offering more information than a traditional magazine or newspaper can offer. For example, chicagotribune.com (the online version of the *Chicago Tribune*) provides information from the paper's hard-copy issue plus additional news details, jobs and housing listings, and community service information. It also has an archive of past issues. One way of offering additional content is to offer integrated hypertext links to related stories, topics, and graphics. The Web medium also allows for easy customization or personalization, which old publishing media do not. Major journal publishers, such as Taylor and Francis Publishing Co., placed many of their journals online. The publisher provides, at no charge, abstracts, search engines, and more. Users that want the full-version article are asked to pay. Subscribers are provided with research services, hypertext links, summaries, and more. The new-medium approach also offers up-to-date material, including breaking news. Examples of the new-medium approach include HotWired (hotwired.lycos.com), which complements a paper version of *Wired* magazine, and the *Wall Street Journal* Online (wsj.com).

▸ **Publishing-intermediation approach.** The publishing-intermediation approach can be thought of as an online directory for news services. Publishing intermediation is an attempt to help people locate goods, services, and products online. Yahoo, Netscape and other portals provide publishing-intermediation services.

▸ **Dynamic approach.** The dynamic approach personalizes content *in real time* and transmits it on the fly in the format best suited to the user's location, tastes, and preferences. This approach is also referred to as the *just-in-time* approach, *print-on-demand*, or *point casting*.

CONTENT PROVIDERS AND DISTRIBUTORS

Content providers and distributors are, as their name implies, those who provide and distribute content online. These services are offered by several specialized companies (e.g., akamai.com, digisle.com, mirror-image.com), as well as by news services such as the Associated Press and ABC News. Due to the difficulty of presenting multimedia, especially in wireless systems, content providers face major challenges when operating in an environment of less-developed infrastructures. Also, the issue of intellectual property payments is critical to the success of content distribution. If authors do not receive payments for or recognition of their work, content providers may face legal problems. However, if payments *are* made, the providers' costs may be too high.

Since spring 2002, many online content providers were starting to charge for content, as advertising was insufficient to cover their expenses. In addition, more readers appeared willing to pay for online publications. For example, *The New York Times* and *South China Morning Post* started to charge for articles in 2002.

Of special interest in this area is Digimarc (digimarc.com), which provides a tool for linking print publications with the Web.

PUBLISHING OF MUSIC, VIDEOS, GAMES, AND ENTERTAINMENT

The Internet is an ideal medium for publishing music, videos, electronic games, and related entertainment. As with content providers, a major issue here is the payment of intellectual property fees (see Chapter 17).

One of the most interesting new capabilities in this area is peer-to-peer networks over which people swap digital files, such as music or video files (see Section 9.7). When such swapping is managed by a third-party exchange (e.g., Napster or Kazaa), the third party may be in violation of copyright law. (For more on the legal difficulties faced by Napster and its eventual collapse, see Chapters 3 and 17. For a comprehensive review of online music, see Drummond 2000.)

Webcasting

Webcasting
Live shows broadcast on the Web.

One way that new or obscure musicians promote their work on the Web is by using **Webcasting**, or "live Webcasting shows." For example, Digital Club Network (dcn.com) broadcasts on the Web—that is, Webcasts—live shows from a "virtual network" of night-clubs. Affiliate clubs and artists get royalty payments based on how many people purchase and download a performance. House of Blue's hob.com has been a pioneer, offering pay-per-view Webcasts.

Webcasting provides not only music but also public lectures. For example, DM Review (dmreview.com) offers Webcast Direct, a series of Webcast seminars, known as **Webinars**, on topics related to business intelligence, data warehousing and mining, and data quality.

Webinars
Seminars on the Web (Web-based seminars).

Edutainment

edutainment
The combination of education and entertainment, often through games.

Edutainment is a combination of education and entertainment, often through games. One of the main goals of edutainment is to encourage students to become active rather than passive learners. With active learning, a student is more involved in the learning process, which makes the learning experience richer and the knowledge gained more memorable. Edutainment embeds learning in entertainment to help students learn almost without their being aware of it.

Edutainment covers various subjects, including mathematics, reading, writing, history, and geography. It is targeted at varying age groups, ranging from preschoolers to adults, and it is also used in corporate training over intranets. Software Toolworks (toolworks.com, now a part of The Learning Company at broderbund.com) is a major vendor of edutainment products.

For over a decade, educational games have been delivered mostly on CD-ROMs. However, since 1998, increasing numbers of companies now offer online edutainment in a distance-learning format (e.g., Knowledge Adventure products at sunburst.com and education.com). One of the facilitators of edutainment is electronic books.

ELECTRONIC BOOKS

e-book
A book in digital form that can be read on a computer screen or on a special device.

An electronic book, or e-book, is a book in digital form that can be read on a computer screen, including handheld computers. A major event in electronic publishing occurred on March 24, 2000, when Stephen King's book *Riding the Bullet* was published exclusively online. For $2.50, readers could purchase the e-book at bn.com/ebook and other e-book providers. Several hundred thousand copies were sold in a few days. However, the publishing event did not go off without some problems. Hackers breached the security system and distributed free copies of the book.

Publishers of e-books have since become more sophisticated and the business of e-publishing more secure. E-books can be delivered and read in various ways:

▶ **Via a Web download.** Download the book to a PC.
▶ **Via a Web access.** Locate the book on the publisher's Web site and read it there. The book cannot be downloaded; it may be interactive, and typically includes links and rich multimedia.

) **Via a dedicated reader.** The book must be downloaded to a special device (an e-book reader).

) **Via a general-purpose reader.** The book can be downloaded to a general-purpose device such as a Palm Pilot.

) **Via a Web server.** The contents of a book are stored on a Web server and downloaded for print-on-demand (see later discussion).

Most e-books require some type of payment. Readers either pay when they download a book from a Web site or they pay when they order the special CD-ROM edition of the book.

Depending on the method by which the book is delivered, software and hardware may be needed to read the book. For example, e-book reader software such as Adobe Acrobat eBook Reader or Microsoft Reader may be required to read the e-book. These readers can be downloaded *for free* from Amazon.com or from other e-book sites. A portable hardware device such as Softbook or Rocket ebook may also be necessary. E-books can be loaded to some PDAs (e.g., to Palm devices) (see Boulton 2001). After installing the software, the user downloads the e-book itself and within minutes can enjoy reading it. The books may be portable (e.g., see Pocket PC store at amazon.com) and convenient to carry; 70 e-books (on average) can be loaded onto one CD-ROM; more can be loaded onto special memory sticks that (in 2003) could store over 100 Gigabytes. Books can also be read online, in which case no special hardware is needed.

Several aids are available to help readers who want to read large amounts of material online. For example, ClearType from Microsoft and CoolType from Adobe can be used to improve screen display, colors, and font sizes.

Types of e-Books

Several types of e-books are available.

) **Traditional book format.** Closely associated with a bookshelf, this type of e-book is a classic or new book that is presented in traditional linear format, usually without any special features such as hyperlink text or searching mechanisms. With the right reader (Adobe Portable Document Format), you can print the book.

) **Online bookshelf.** This is a *collection* of books (rather than just a single book) available for reading online or for download. They are simple in format and provide no hyperlink features.

) **The download.** This is an e-book in simple text files or HTML source documents or Adobe Acrobat files that *can be downloaded* once the viewer has paid a fee.

) **The Rubics-cube hyperlink book.** This is a truly multimedia, online-only book. It has hyperlinks and provides three-dimensional text and display, employing graphics, audio, and video in a dramatically supportive manner. It supports nonlinear exploration of topics.

) **The interactive, build-your-own (BYO) decision book.** This kind of book puts the reader "in the driver's seat." Combined with multimedia and VRML (a three-dimensional version of HTML, see Chapter 8), this e-book leads to dramatic engagement with content, plot, destiny, and responsibility. However, not many of these books have yet been developed; they are hard to find.

In addition to regular books, electronic *technical* documents and manuals are available from the eMatter division of Fatbrain (now a Barnesandnoble.com company). An increasing number of publishers produce e-books. In addition to all the major publishers that sell e-books directly from their Web sites, readers can also buy e-books at electronic bookstores. All major textbook publishers (e.g., Pearson Education, the publisher of this text) are creating electronic companion textbooks that feature audio, video, and other interactive elements (see Stellin 2001).

Advantages and Limitations of E-Books

In order for e-books to make an impact, they must offer advantages to both readers and publishers. Otherwise, there would be little incentive to change from the traditional format.

The major advantage of e-books to readers is portability. As noted earlier, a reader can carry as many as 70 books wherever they go (and more when attached memory drives are used). Other advantages are easy search capabilities and links; easy downloading; ability to quickly and inexpensively copy material, including figures; easy integration of content with other text; no wear and tear on a physical book; ability to find out-of-print books; and the books can be published and updated quickly, so they can be very up-to-date.

The primary advantage that e-books offer the publishers is lower production and distribution costs, which have a significant impact on the price of a book. Other advantages for publishers are lower updating and reproduction costs; ability to reach many readers; ease of combining several books, so professors can customize textbooks by combining materials from different books by the same publisher; and lower advertising costs.

Of course, e-books have some limitations: They require hardware and software that may be too expensive for some readers; some people have difficulty reading large amounts of material on a screen; batteries may run down; there are multiple, competing standards; and finally, only a few books are available as e-books.

E-Book Issues

The Association of American Publishers reported that sales of e-books grew from $211,000 in net sales in January 2002 to slightly more than $3.3 million in January 2003, an increase of 1,447.4 percent (Gwiazdowski 2003). Despite this growth and their advantages, e-books are generally not yet selling well, in relation to the overall size of the book market. Although e-books are easy to read, are generally platform independent, have high-resolution display, and can be read using long-lasting batteries, customers are still reluctant to change their habits. However, in Japan, where people ride trains daily for long periods of time, one sees hundreds of e-book readers.

However, the functionality of e-books is rapidly increasing. Software providers are supplying tools that make e-books easier to use—tools that search like search engines and that enable easy annotation and bookmarks that enable readers to expedite research of large volumes of information. Various other issues, when resolved, will contribute to the ease of use and popularity of e-books. These issues include:

- How to protect the publisher's/author's copyright.
- How to distribute and sell e-books.
- How much to charge for an e-book versus a hard copy, and how to collect payment for e-books.
- How to best support navigation in an e-book.
- Which standards to use (e.g., see the Online Information Exchange Standard [ONIX], and editeur.org/onix.html). These sites are concerned with standards for online publishing (see the special issue of Beat et al. 2001).
- How to increase reading speed. On the average screen, reading is 25 percent slower than hard-copy reading.
- How to transform readers from hard-copy books to e-books; how to deal with resistance to change.
- How to design an e-book (e.g., how to deal with fonts, typefaces, colors, etc., online).
- How publishers can justify e-books in terms of profit and market share.
- How to secure content (e.g., use encryption, Digital Rights Management [DRM]).

For more information on e-books, see ebookconnections.com and netlibrary.com.

PRINT-ON-DEMAND

A new trend in publishing is *print-on-demand*, which refers to customized printing jobs, usually in small quantities, and possibly only one document or book. The process is especially attractive for small print jobs because both the total fixed setup cost and the per unit setup cost are very low, whereas the per-unit variable cost is higher than in traditional publishing.

The print-on-demand process is composed of three steps:

1. A publisher creates a digital master, typically in Adobe Systems' Acrobat format, and sends it to a specialized print-on-demand company. The files are stored on the printing company's network, waiting for an order.

2. When an order is placed, a print-on-demand machine prints out the text of the document or book, then covers, binds, and trims it. The entire process can take about a minute for a 300-page book.

3. The books are packaged and shipped to the publisher or the consumer.

See Robinson (2001) for additional details on print-on-demand.

Online publishing is related to e-learning, the subject of the next section, and to knowledge management (see Zhao and Resh 2001 and Section 9.5).

WEBLOGGING

The Internet offers an opportunity for individuals to publish on the Web using a technology known as **Weblogging**, or **blogging**. A **blog** is a personal Web site, open to the public, in which the owner expresses his or her feelings or opinions. Blogs deal with many topics. People can write stories, tell news, and provide links to other articles and Web sites. Some blogs offer information that many Web surfers may have overlooked. People can read blogs to rapidly get up to speed on an issue of special interest. The number of blogs is growing rapidly, emarketer.com (2002) estimates that there are close to 1,000,000 of them on the Internet.

Blogs became very popular after the terrorist attacks of September 11, 2001. People were looking for as many sources of information as possible and for personal connections to the tragedy. Blogs comfort people in times of stress. They offer a place where people feel their ideas are noticed, and they can result in two-way communication and collaboration, group discussion, and so on.

An example blog is Instapundit (instapundit.com), created by Dr. Glenn Reynold of the University of Tennessee. Through the blog, Reynold provides commentary on current affairs. Launched in August 2001, this blog initially had about 1,500 hits per day. After September 11, 2001, traffic increased to an average of 4,800 hits, and on certain days it now reaches 80,000 hits. The blog enabled Reynold to trade e-mails with leading U.S. newspaper columnists who otherwise would probably never communicate with him. Two other good blogs are coldfury.com and samizdata.net.

Building blogs is becoming easier and easier. Programs downloadable from blogger.com, pitas.com, and others are very user-friendly. "Bloggers" (the people who create and maintain blogs) are handed a fresh space on their Web site to write in each day. They can easily edit, add entries, and broadcast whatever they want by simply clicking on the send key. Bloggers use a special terminology. (For a dictionary of blog terms, see samizdata.net.)

Blogs are criticized for their tendency to coalesce into self-referential cliques. Bloggers are noted for their mutual backslapping, endlessly praising and linking to one another's sites. Blogs are not yet used for commercial purposes, but they will probably be used for such activities in the future. For further discussion, see Phillips (2002).

Weblogging/blogging
Technology for personal publishing on the Internet.

blog
A personal Web site that is open to the public.

Section 9.3 ▶ REVIEW

1. Define online publishing and list some advantages it offers over traditional media.

2. List the major methods of online publishing.

3. What issues are involved in content creation and distribution?

4. Describe e-books and list their advantages.

5. Describe Weblogging (blogging).

9.4   E-LEARNING

The topic of e-learning is gaining much attention, especially because world-class universities such as MIT, Harvard, and Stanford in the United States and Oxford in the United Kingdom have started to implement it. Exhibit 9.3 shows the forces that are driving the transition from traditional education to online learning in the academic setting. E-learning is also growing as a delivery method for information in the business world and is becoming a major e-business activity. In this section, we will discuss several topics related to e-learning.

THE BASICS OF E-LEARNING

e-learning

The online delivery of information for purposes of education, training, or knowledge management.

E-learning is the online delivery of information for purposes of education, training, or knowledge management. It is a Web-enabled system that makes knowledge accessible to those who need it, when they need it, anytime, anywhere. E-learning can be useful both as an environment for facilitating learning at schools and as an environment for efficient and effective corporate training, as shown in the Cisco case at the beginning of the chapter.

Liaw and Huang (2002) describe how Web technologies can facilitate learning. For an overview and discussion of research issues related to e-learning, see Piccoli et al. (2001); this resource also compares e-learning with traditional classroom teaching.

EXHIBIT 9.3   The Effects of E-Commerce Forces on Education

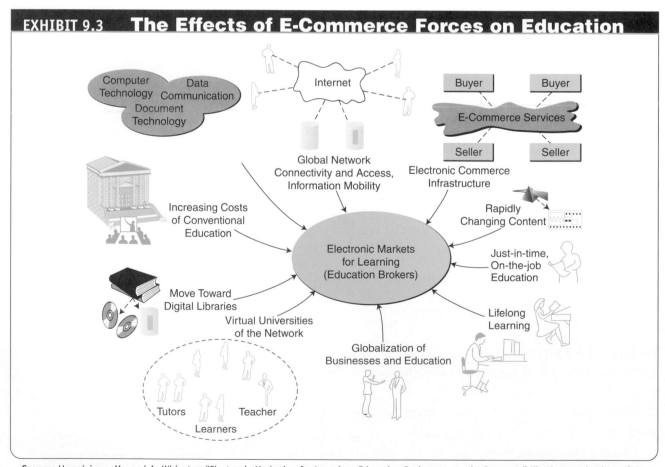

Source: Hamalainen, M., and A. Whinston."Electronic Marketing for Learning: Education Brokerages on the Internet," *The Communications of the ACM,* ©1996 ACM, Inc.

BENEFITS AND DRAWBACKS OF E-LEARNING

E-learning has many benefits. However, it has also many drawbacks, thus making it a controversial topic.

Benefits of E-Learning

E-learning can be a great equalizer: By eliminating barriers of time, distance, and socioeconomic status, it can enable individuals to take charge of their own lifelong learning. In the information age, skills and knowledge need to be *continually updated* and refreshed to keep up with today's fast-paced business environment. E-learning of new content will help organizations and countries adapt to the demands of the Internet economy by training their workers and educating their citizens. E-learning can save money, reduce travel time, increase access to experts, enable large number of students to take classes simultaneously, provide on-demand education, and enable self-paced learning. It also may make learning less frustrating by making it more interactive and engaging (e.g., see Delahoussaye and Zemke 2001 and Liaw and Huang 2002).

More specific benefits of e-learning are as follows:

▶ **Time reduction.** As shown in the Cisco case, e-learning can reduce training time by 50 percent.

▶ **Large volume and diversity.** E-learning can provide training to a large number of workers with diverse cultural backgrounds and educational levels even though they are at different locations in different time zones.

▶ **Cost reduction.** One study reported that the cost of providing a learning experience can be reduced by 50 to 70 percent when classroom lectures are replaced by e-learning sessions (see Urdan and Weggen 2000).

▶ **Higher content retention.** E-learning students are usually self-initiated and self-paced. Their motive for acquiring more knowledge may be to widen their scope of view or to develop career skills. Urdan and Weggen (2000) contend that such self-motivation results in content retention that could be 25 to 60 percent higher than that of lecturer-led training.

▶ **Flexibility.** E-learners are able to adjust the time, location, content, and speed of learning according to their own personal schedules. For example, if necessary, they can refer back to previous lectures without affecting the learning pace of other students.

▶ **Updated and consistent material.** It is almost impossible to update the information in textbooks more frequently than every 2 or 3 years; e-learning can offer just-in-time access to timely information. Urdan and Weggen (2000) report that e-learning has a 50 to 60 percent better consistency of material presented than traditional classroom learning because human variations (of the teachers) are eliminated.

▶ **Fear-free environment.** E-learning can facilitate learning for students who may not wish to join a face-to-face group discussion or participate in class. This kind of behavior is usually attributed to their reluctance to expose their lack of knowledge in public. E-learning can provide a fear-free and privacy-protected environment in which students can put forth any idea without fear of looking stupid if it is wrong.

E-learning provides a new set of tools that can add value to traditional learning modes. It does not usually replace the classroom setting, but instead enhances it, taking advantage of new content and delivery technologies. The better the match of content and delivery vehicle to an individual's learning style, the greater the content retention, and the better the learning results. Advanced e-learning support environments, such as Blackboard and WebCT, add value to traditional learning. See Insights and Additions 9.1 (page 360) for descriptions of these e-learning tools.

As the opening vignette about Cisco showed, e-learning also can be used in the business environment. Besides increasing access to learning and reducing costs, e-learning equips employees with the knowledge needed to help increase customer satisfaction, expand sales, and accelerate technology adoption. In short, e-learning enables companies to prepare their workforces for an increasingly competitive world marketplace.

Insights and Additions 9.1   Blackboard and WebCT

There is a good chance that you will use the Blackboard or WebCT frameworks when using this text. These competing products provide the Internet software needed for e-learning, serving one of the fastest-growing industry segments in the world. Eduventures.com, a leading independent e-learning industry analyst, projected that the higher education e-learning market will grow from $4 billion in 2001 to $11 billion by 2005 (*eduventures.com* 2001).

A publisher places a book's content, teaching notes, quizzes, and other materials on Blackboard or WebCT in a standardized format. Instructors can access modules and transfer them into their own specific Blackboard or WebCT sites, which can by accessed by their students.

Blackboard offers a complete suite of enterprise software products and services that power a total "e-education infrastructure" for schools, colleges, universities, and other education providers. Blackboard's two major lines of business are Course & Portal Solutions and Commerce & Access Solutions.

WebCT provides a similar set of tools, but with a different vision and strategy. It uses advanced pedagogical tools to help institutions of higher education make distance-learning courses possible. Such courses enable schools to expand campus boundaries, attract and retain students and faculty, and continually improve course and degree program quality.

Textbook publishers are embracing these tools by making their major textbooks Blackboard and/or WebCT enabled. Thus, a professor can easily incorporate a book's content into the software that is used by thousands of universities worldwide.

Sources: Compiled from *webct.com* (2002) and *blackboard.com* (2002 a and b).

For a classification of the dimensions of e-learning environments, see Piccoli et al. (2001) and Online Exhibit W9.1.

Drawbacks and Challenges of E-Learning

Despite the numerous benefits, e-learning does have some drawbacks. Issues cited as possible drawbacks of e-learning are as follows.

- **Need for instructor retraining.** Some instructors are not competent in teaching by electronic means and may require additional training. It costs money to provide such training.
- **Equipment needs and support services.** Additional funds are needed to purchase multimedia tools to provide support services for e-learning creation, use, and maintenance.
- **Lack of face-to-face interaction and campus life.** Many feel that the intellectual stimulation that takes places through instruction in a classroom with a "live" instructor cannot be fully replicated in e-learning.
- **Assessment.** In the environment of higher education, one criticism is that professors may not be able to adequately assess student work completed through e-learning. There is no guarantee, for example, of who actually completed the assignments or exams.
- **Maintenance and updating.** Although e-learning materials are easier to update than traditionally published materials, there are practical difficulties (e.g., cost, time of instructors) in keeping e-learning materials up-to-date. The content of e-learning material can be difficult to maintain due to the lack of ownership of and accountability for Web site material. In addition, no online course can deliver real-time information and knowledge in the way a "live" instructor can.
- **Protection of intellectual property.** It is difficult to control the transmission of copyrighted works downloaded from the e-learning platform.
- **Computer literacy.** E-learning cannot be extended to those students who are not computer literate.
- **Student retention.** Without some human feedback, it may be difficult to keep some students mentally engaged and enthusiastic about e-learning over a long period of time.

Some of these drawbacks can be reduced by advanced technology. For example, some online products have features that help stimulate student thinking. Offsetting the assessment drawback, biometric controls can be used to verify the identity of students who are taking examinations from home. However, these features add to the costs of e-learning.

In addition to these drawbacks, e-learning faces challenges that threaten its acceptance. From the learner's perspective, the challenge is simply to change the mindset of how learning typically takes place. Learners must be willing to give up the idea of traditional classroom training, and they must come to understand that continual, lifelong learning will be as much a part of normal work life, past the college years, as voice mail and e-mail. From the teaching perspective, all learning objects must be converted ("tagged") to a digital format. This task can be challenging. Finally, another challenge for e-learning systems is the updating of the knowledge in them—who will do it and how often? Also, how will the cost of the updating be covered?

Preventing E-Learning Failures

Many of those who have tried e-learning have been pleased with it. In many cases, self-selection ensures that those who are likely to benefit from e-learning choose e-learning opportunities. For example, students who live at a great distance from school or who have family responsibilities during traditional school hours will be motivated to put in the time to make e-learning work. Similarly, employees for whom a training course at a distant site is a problem, either because of budget or personal constraints, are likely to be enthusiastic about e-learning programs such as Cisco's.

E-learning does not work for everyone, though. Weaver (2002) believes that e-learning failures are due to the following issues:

- Believing that e-learning is always a cheaper learning or training alternative. E-learning can be less expensive than traditional instruction, depending on the number of students. However, if only a few students are to be served, e-learning can be very expensive because of the high fixed costs.
- Overestimating what e-learning can accomplish. People sometimes do not understand the limitations of e-learning and so may expect too much.
- Overlooking the shortcomings of self-study. Some people cannot do self-study or do not want to. Others may study incorrectly.
- Failing to look beyond the course paradigms. The instructor needs to look at the entire problem in the area of teaching and at the material creation and delivery as well.
- Viewing content as a commodity, which causes lack of attention to quality and delivery to individuals.
- Ignoring technology tools for e-learning or, on the other hand, fixating too much on technology as a solution.
- Assuming that learned knowledge will be applied.
- Believing that because e-learning has been implemented, employees and students will use it.

To prevent failure, companies and schools need to address these issues carefully and systematically. Balancing the benefits and the drawbacks of e-learning, many people remain enthusiastic about its potential.

VIRTUAL TEACHING AND ONLINE UNIVERSITIES

The term **distance learning** refers to formal education that takes place off campus, often from home. The concept is not new. Educational institutions have been offering correspondence courses and degrees for decades. What is new, however, is the application of IT in general and the Web in particular to expand the opportunities for distance learning to the online environment. Hofmann (2002) describes the role of the Internet in distance learning in

distance learning
Formal education that takes place off campus, usually, but not always, through online resources.

higher education, surveying implementation issues in terms of technology, course content, and pedagogy.

virtual university
An online university from which students take classes from home or other off-site locations usually via the Internet.

The concept of **virtual universities**, online universities from which students take classes from home or an off-site location via the Internet, is expanding rapidly. Hundreds of thousands of students in dozens of countries, from the United Kingdom to Israel to Thailand, are studying in such institutions. A large number of existing universities, including Stanford University and other top-tier institutions, offer online education of some form. Some universities, such as University of Phoenix (phoenix.edu), California Virtual Campus (cvc.edu), and the University of Maryland (umuc.edu/distance) offer hundreds of courses and dozens of degrees to students worldwide, all online. Other universities offer limited online courses and degrees but use innovative teaching methods and multimedia support in the traditional classroom, as described in Online Insights and Additions W9.1.

The virtual university concept allows universities to offer classes worldwide. Moreover, integrated degrees may soon appear, by which students can customize a degree that will best fit their needs and take courses at different universities. Several other new virtual schools include eschool-world.com, walden.com, and trainingzone.co.uk.

ONLINE CORPORATE TRAINING

Like educational institutions, a large number of business organizations are using e-learning on a large scale (e.g., see Kapp 2002). Many companies offer online training, as Cisco does. Some, like Barclays Bank, COX Industries, and Qantas Airways, call such learning centers "universities." New employees at IBM Taiwan Corp. are given Web-based "electronic training," and KPMG Peat Marwick offers e-learning to its customers.

Corporate training is often done via the intranet and corporate portals. However, in large corporations with multiple sites and for studies from home, the Internet is used to access the online material. For discussion of strategies for implementing corporate e-learning, see Delahoussaye and Zemke (2001). Vendors of online training and educational materials can be found at digitalthink.com, click2learn.com, deitel.com, and smartplanet.com.

THE DRIVERS OF E-LEARNING

The business forces that are driving the transition from traditional education to online learning are described next.

Technological change. Technological changes and global network connectivity have increased the complexity and velocity of the work environment. Today's workforce has to process more and more information in a shorter amount of time. New products and services are emerging with accelerating speed. As product life cycles and life spans shorten, today's knowledge will become obsolete. In the age of just-in-time production, just-in-time training becomes a critical element to organizational success.

Competition and cost pressures. Fierce competition in most industries leads to increasing cost pressure. In today's competitive environment, organizations can no longer afford to inflate training budgets with expensive travel and lodging. Time spent away from the job, traveling or sitting in a classroom, tremendously reduces per-employee productivity and revenue.

Globalization. Globalization of business is resulting in manifold challenges. Today's businesses have more locations in different time zones and employ larger numbers of workers with diverse cultural backgrounds and educational levels than ever before. Corporations worldwide are now seeking innovative and efficient ways to deliver training to their geographically dispersed workforce. E-learning is an effective way to achieve just this. Companies do not need to bring employees to a trainer or training facility (or even to send a trainer to the employees); online classes can run anywhere in the world.

Continual learning. In the new economy, corporations face major challenges in keeping their workforce current and competent. Learning has become a continual process rather than a distinct event. To retain their competitive edge, organizations have started to investigate which training techniques and delivery methods enhance motivation, performance, collaboration, innovation, and a commitment to lifelong learning.

Network connectivity. The Internet provides an ideal delivery vehicle for education. The emergence of online education relates not only to economic and social change, but also to access. Through its increasing penetration and simplicity of use, the Internet has opened the door to a global market where language and geographic barriers for many training products have been erased. Because of the popularity of the Internet, e-learning is perhaps the most effective way to deliver training electronically.

A study by Roberts and Stevenson (2001) on e-learning in business education (the point at which educational e-learning and business e-learning meet) identified three trends: (1) Traditional MBA programs are developing e-learning courses and programs, some in partnership with other universities, for a mostly international market. (2) Independent e-learning companies are developing course content on their own or in partnership with existing business schools. (3) The executive education marketplace is flooded with e-learning offerings.

Examples of top traditional MBA programs that are introducing e-learning are MIT, Kellogg (Northwestern), INSEAD, University of Chicago, Duke, Berkeley, Purdue, Wharton (University of Pennsylvania), and Cornell. Examples of joint ventures of MBA programs with industry can be seen at Duke, Darden (University of Virginia), UCLA, and INSEAD (partners with Pensure); Columbia, Stanford, and University of Chicago (partners with UNext), and Wharton (partners with FT Knowledge). Of special interest is the Harvard/Stanford Joint Venture in developing e-learning materials for executives. The materials are delivered in a combination of classroom teaching and e-learning known as Leading Change and Organizational Renewal. A similar venture is that of MIT (Sloan School) and IMD of Switzerland.

E-LEARNING TOOLS

Many e-learning tools are available. WebCT and Blackboard, described earlier, are two such tools. The following are several other examples.

- Learning Space from Lotus Corporation. lotus.com/products/learnspace.nsf/wdocs/homepage is a Web-based tool that can be customized to fit a company's training needs. The 5.0 and higher releases include self-paced learning and collaboration capabilities—all in real time. The product supports 22 languages.
- Computerprep.com offers close to 400 e-learning products, including a comprehensive library of Web-based classroom, distance learning, and self-study curricula. Students can even combine products from different categories to customize learning environments.
- Macromedia.com offers tools for wireless devices at macromedia.com/software/.
- Ecollege.com offers an e-learning platform that includes some free collaboration tools.

For more e-learning tools, see Online Exhibit W9.2 at the book's Web site.

IMPLEMENTING E-LEARNING IN LEARNING CENTERS

Most schools and industries use e-learning as a *supplementary* channel to traditional classrooms. One facility that is used in the integration of the two approaches is the learning center. A *learning center* is a focal point for all corporate training and learning activities, including online ones. Some companies have a dedicated online learning center, a learning center dedicated only to online training. However, most companies combine the online and off-line activities, as done by W. R. Grace and described in EC Application Case 9.3. (page 364)

Learning center facilities may be run by a third party rather than connected to any particular corporation, and they are referred to as electronic education malls (see Langenbach and Bodendorf 1999–2000). For example, Turbolinux.com (in collaboration with Hong Kong University) developed such a mall for primary and secondary schools in Hong Kong. For additional information about e-learning, see trainingmag.com, elearningmag.com, and learningcircuits.org.

E-learning content can be created with the aid of knowledge management, which is presented in the next section.

CASE 9.3

EC Application

ONLINE GLOBAL LEARNING CENTER AT W. R. GRACE

The newest concept for training and development is the *online learning center*. Online learning centers combine the Internet, intranets, and e-delivered courses with conventional learning media such as books, articles, instructor-led courses, and audio and videotapes.

W. R. Grace, a global specialty chemicals company, initiated its online learning center in 2001. The company's human resources leaders were looking for a solution that would provide fast and easy access to a wide selection of tools for developing employee skills. Surveys indicated a need for self-paced professional and personal training support for employees. Strategic Partners' learning center concept provided the solution. A pilot program was initiated in March 2001. Within 6 months, the center was available 24/7 to 6,000 employees worldwide.

The learning center is organized around the core competencies that characterize the knowledge, skills, and abilities all W. R. Grace employees are expected to achieve. It offers internal classroom training; external courses; CD-ROM courses; self-paced learning tools; streaming video; Internet learning conferences; e-learning courses; coaching tips for managers and mentors; audio and videotapes; books and articles; information about the corporate mission, values, and strategy; strategy guides suggesting specific development actions, on-the-job and in the community; and corporate and industry news. Employees can access resources on a particular topic; they can search a range of appropriate tools and action alternatives specific to their needs, including training sessions, recommended readings, a rental library, and a strategy guide.

The center's Global Steering Committee, made up of representatives from all the functional areas of the business from around the world, keeps the center in tune with the development needs of employees, and encourages the use of the center in all regions. The committee also provides human resources management with feedback on how the center is meeting identified needs.

Every 6 weeks, the center's electronic newsletter lands on each employee's desktop. The publication keeps employees up-to-date on the offerings of the center; reports on how employees are using the center; and encourages all employees to use the center as a source for learning and development. Corporate news is also included in the newsletter, keeping the company's initiatives and communications visible to all employees.

Based on its experience, W. R. Grace has the following suggestions for successful implementation of a learning center:

▶ Line up strong senior management support.
▶ Build gradually—start with a modest center, get it running smoothly, gather feedback from the users, make needed adjustments, and develop a more extensive center over time.
▶ Invite involvement—people support what they help to create.
▶ Provide a variety of learning tools, mixing in-house and external resources.
▶ Keep the learning center visible.
▶ Ensure the content is fresh and up-to-date.

W. R. Grace's Global Learning Center supports employee growth in a cost-effective manner while relating learning to performance and talent management, strategic communication, and individual development planning. It has proved to be a powerful learning and communications channel for the entire corporation.

Sources: Compiled from Boxer and Johnson (2002) and from press releases at *grace.com* (2002).

Questions

1. List the factors that drive e-learning at W. R. Grace.
2. How is e-learning integrated with other learning methods?
3. List the e-learning offerings of W. R. Grace's learning center.
4. Describe the critical success factors of e-learning offered by W. R. Grace.

Section 9.4 ▶ REVIEW

1. Define e-learning and describe its benefits.
2. List some of the major drawbacks of e-learning.
3. Describe virtual universities.
4. List some e-learning tools and describe WebCT and Blackboard.
5. Describe learning centers in industry.

9.5 KNOWLEDGE MANAGEMENT AND E-COMMERCE

The term *knowledge management* is frequently mentioned in discussions of e-learning. Why is this? To answer this question, one first needs to understand what knowledge management is.

Knowledge management and e-learning both use the same "coin of the realm"—knowledge. Whereas e-learning uses that "coin" for the sake of *individual* learning, knowledge management uses it to improve the functioning of an *organization*. Knowledge is one of the most important assets in any organization, and thus it is important to capture, store, and apply it. These are the major purposes of knowledge management. Thus, knowledge management (KM) refers to the process of capturing or creating knowledge, storing and protecting it, updating it constantly, and using it whenever necessary. (For a comprehensive coverage of KM, see Holsapple 2003).

Knowledge is collected from both external and internal sources. Then it is examined, interpreted, refined, and stored in what is called an organizational knowledge base, the repository for the enterprise's knowledge. A major purpose of an organizational knowledge base is to allow for *knowledge sharing*. Knowledge sharing among employees, with customers, and with business partners has a huge potential payoff in improved customer service, ability to solve difficult organizational problems, shorter delivery cycle times, and increased collaboration within the company and with business partners. Furthermore, some knowledge can be sold to others or traded for other knowledge.

KM promotes an *integrated* approach to the process of handling an enterprise's information assets, both those that are documented and the tacit expertise stored in individuals' heads. The integration of information resources is at the heart of KM. EC implementation involves a considerable amount of knowledge—about customers, suppliers, logistics, procurement, markets, and technology. The integration of that knowledge is required for successful EC applications. These applications are aimed at increasing organizational competitiveness (see Tiwana 2001 and Holsapple 2003).

The KM/EC connection will be described in more detail later in this section. First, though, let's examine KM types and activities.

KM TYPES AND ACTIVITIES

According to Lai and Chu (2002), organizational knowledge is embedded in the following resources: (1) *human capital*, which includes employee knowledge, competencies, and creativity; (2) *structured capital (organizational capital)*, which includes organizational structure and culture, processes, patents, and the capability to leverage knowledge through sharing and transferring; and (3) *customer capital*, which includes the relationship between organizations and their customers and other partners.

This organizational knowledge must be properly managed, and this is the purpose of KM. According to Davenport and Prusak (2000), KM has four tasks: (1) creating knowledge repositories where knowledge can be stored and retrieved easily; (2) enhancing a knowledge environment in order to conduct more effective knowledge creation, transfer, and use; (3) managing knowledge as an asset so as to increase the effective use of knowledge assets over time; and (4) improving knowledge access to facilitate its transfer between individuals. The knowledge access and transfer between individuals is part of knowledge usage and sharing.

Knowledge Sharing

Knowledge has a limited value if it is not shared. The ability to share knowledge decreases its cost and increases its effectiveness for greater competitive advantage. Thus, another major purpose of KM is to increase knowledge sharing. Song (2002) demonstrated that through effective knowledge sharing, organizations can reduce uncertainty and risk, improve efficiency, reduce training costs, and more. Roberts-Witt (2002) noted that KM used to be about sharing company databases, but that increasingly, it is also about sharing the information stored in people's heads.

Song (2002) proposed a framework for organizing and sharing knowledge gleaned from the Internet. According to this framework, organizations promote knowledge sharing via the use of rewards or incentives, through the use of different sharing mechanisms according to the type of knowledge, and by appropriately codifying knowledge. The proposed framework begins with the listing of strategic goals and objectives and the critical information

knowledge management (KM)
The process of capturing or creating knowledge, storing it, updating it constantly, interpreting it, and using it whenever necessary.

organizational knowledge base
The repository for an enterprise's accumulated knowledge.

needed for their attainment. Then, an analysis and storage mechanism is built as part of a business intelligence system (see Chapter 4). The framework also deals with knowledge collection (from internal and external sources) and its dissemination in support of attaining the goals. An example knowledge sharing system at Xerox is provided in EC Application Case 9.4.

The KM discussion thus far has been fairly generic. For additional material regarding major KM activities, see the discussion of KM activities online at the book's Web site. Let's now consider how KM relates to EC.

HOW IS KNOWLEDGE MANAGEMENT RELATED TO E-COMMERCE?

As seen throughout this book, EC has many external as well as internal applications, including both CRM and PRM. To better perform its EC tasks, organizations need knowledge, which is provided by KM. For example, according to Sugumaran (2002), who proposed a KM framework for EC organizations, strategic planning in traditional organizations needs considerable amounts of knowledge. To mitigate this problem, e-businesses can proactively incorporate KM processes to facilitate quick access to different types of knowledge.

In the EC marketspace, large amounts of data can be gathered easily, and by analyzing this data in a timely manner, organizations can learn about their clients and generate useful knowledge for planning and decision making. For example, in the B2B market, organizations can scan the environment to monitor changes in a vertical industry and can form strategic alliances or partnerships in response to business pressures. In order for these activities to be successful in both B2B and B2C, appropriate knowledge is needed to interpret information and to execute activities.

CASE 9.4
EC Application
ONLINE KNOWLEDGE SHARING AT XEROX

In the early 1990s, Xerox Corporation had a nationwide database that contained information that could be used to fix its copiers, fax machines, and high-speed printers. However, the information was not readily available to the 25,000 service and field employees and engineers whose job it is to repair the machines at customer sites. Satisfaction with customer service was low.

The engineers at Xerox's Palo Alto Research Center (PARC) spent 6 months observing repair personnel, watching how they worked, noting what their frustrations were, and identifying what kind of information they needed. They also determined that the repair personnel needed to share their knowledge with their peers. PARC engineers developed Eureka, an online knowledge-sharing system created to assist the service people with time-consuming and complicated repair problems.

Ray Everett, program manager for Eureka describes the powerful impact the program has had on service: "You went from not knowing how to fix something to being able to get the answer instantly. Even better, you could share any solutions you found with your peers around the globe within a day, as opposed to the several weeks it used to take."

Since its inception in 1996, Eureka has been implemented in 71 countries. It has helped solve 350,000 problems and has saved $3 to $4 million in parts and labor every year. The system is available to all of Xerox's service engineers via

notebook computers and is accessed through the Internet. Product fixes (50,000 of them), documentation updates, and product update bulletins are delivered over the Web. Individual service employees and engineers can enter possible new solutions to problems into the system. The solution will appear in Eureka, giving credit to the author and noting the service employee's country of origin. An alert about a new solution is sent to validators who test the solution; if it works consistently, it is sent to all engineers via Eureka updates.

The 2004 version is designed to work on wireless Internet connections. Eureka is a constantly evolving and growing system that connects and shares the collective knowledge of Xerox's service force.

Sources: Compiled from Roberts-Witt (2002) and *xerox.com* press releases (2002).

Questions

1. What knowledge is shared via Eureka, and how?
2. What EC technologies are described in this case? Classify the EC transactions.
3. What were the drivers of the program?
4. What advantages may be provided by the wireless system?

Core knowledge management activities for companies doing EC should include the following: identification, creation, capture and codification, classification, distribution, utilization, and evolution of the knowledge needed to develop products and partnerships. Knowledge creation involves using various tools and techniques to analyze transaction data and generate new trends. Knowledge capture and codification includes gathering new knowledge and storing it in a machine-readable form. Knowledge classification organizes knowledge using appropriate dimensions or how it was used in the past. Knowledge distribution is sharing relevant information with suppliers, consumers, and other stakeholders through electronic networks—both public and private. Knowledge utilization involves appropriate application of knowledge to problem solving. Knowledge evolution entails updating knowledge as time progresses.

Nah et al. (2002) investigated the specific relationship of KM and EC in B2C and auctions. Chen and Liou (2002) explored the relationship of the two from a theoretical point of view. Shaw et al. (2001) related KM and EC through data mining. Bose (2002) explored the relationship between KM and infrastructure for EC.

Fahey et al. (2001) believe that a major role of KM is linking e-business and operating processes. Specifically, knowledge generated in e-business contributes to the enhancement of three core operating processes: CRM, SCM, and product development management. For more on KM-enabling technologies and how they can be applied to business unit initiatives, see Online Exhibit W9.3.

KNOWLEDGE PORTALS

Knowledge portals are single point of access software systems intended to provide easy and timely access to information and knowledge and to support communities of knowledge workers who share common goals. Knowledge portals can be used for either external or internal use. A knowledge portal also can be defined as an information portal that will be used by knowledge workers.

Knowledge portals support various tasks performed by knowledge workers: gathering, organizing, searching, and analyzing information; synthesizing solutions with respect to specific task goals; and then sharing and distributing what has been learned with other knowledge workers. These tasks are illustrated in Exhibit 9.4 (page 368). In this example, Mack et al. (2001) illustrate how a knowledge portal was used to support the work of knowledge-work consultants at IBM and what technologies can be used to support each category of tasks. For further details on how knowledge portals are related to collaborative and intellectual capital management, see Mack et al. (2001) and Raisch (2001).

knowledge portal
A single point of access software system intended to provide timely access to information and to support communities of knowledge workers.

ONLINE ADVICE AND CONSULTING

Finally, another use of knowledge online can be to offer it in advice and consulting services. The online advice and consulting field is growing rapidly as tens of thousands of experts of all kinds sell their expertise on the Internet. The following are some examples.

▸ **Medical advice.** Companies such as WebMD and others (webmd.com, kasamba.com, and keen.com) provide health-advice consultations with top medical experts. Consumers can ask specific questions and get an answer from a specialist in a few days. Health sites also offer a considerable amount of advice and tips for travelers, as was shown in Chapter 3.

▸ **Management consulting.** Many consultants are selling their accumulated expertise from organizational knowledge bases. A pioneer in this area was Andersen Consulting (now Accenture at accenture.com). Another online management consultant is Aberdeen (aberdeen.com). Because of their high consultation fees, such services are used mainly by corporations.

▸ **Legal advice.** Delivery of legal advice to individuals and businesses by consultation services has considerable prospects. For example, Atlanta-based law firm Alston & Bird coordinates legal counseling with 12 law firms for a large health-care company and for many other clients. The company created an organizational knowledge base that contains

EXHIBIT 9.4   Knowledge Work Tasks with Examples of Supporting Technology

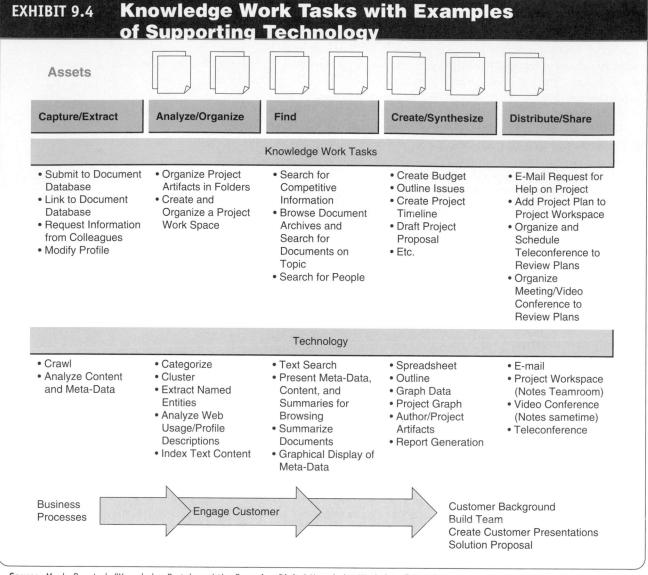

Source: Mack, R., et al. "Knowledge Portals and the Emerging Digital Knowledge Workplace." *IBM Systems Journal 40,* no. 4 (2001).

information from some of the best law firms in the country. This information is then made available to all 12 of the law firms in the consultation group. Also, many lawyers offer inexpensive consulting services online. Linklaters, a leading law firm in the United Kingdom, created a separate company (blueflag.com) to sell its legal services online. The company offers several products and also sells support technology to other law firms.

▶ **Gurus.** Several sites provide diversified expert services, some for free. One example is guru.com, which offers general advice and a job board for experts on legal, financial, tax, technical, lifestyle, and other issues. It aggregates over 200,000 professional "gurus." Expertise is sold at allexpert.com and elance.com, where one can post a required service for experts to bid on. Of special interest is sciam.com, which offers advice from science experts at *Scientific American.*

▶ **Financial advice.** Many companies offer extensive financial advice. For example, Merrill Lynch Online (askmerrill.ml.com) provides free access to some of the firm's research reports and analyses.

▶ **Other advisory services.** Many other advisory services are available online—some for free, and others for a fee. For example, guestfinder.com makes it easy for people who work in the media to find guests and interview sources.

One word of caution about advice: It is not wise to risk your health, your money, or your legal status on free or even for-fee online advice. Always seek more than one opinion, and carefully check the credentials of any advice provider.

Section 9.5 ▶ REVIEW

1. Define KM.
2. Discuss the relationship between KM and EC.
3. Describe knowledge portals.
4. Describe online advisory services.

9.6 CUSTOMER-TO-CUSTOMER E-COMMERCE

Previous chapters examined transactions between individuals and businesses (B2C, C2B) and among businesses (B2B). Another possible type of EC transaction is that between individual consumers. **Customer-to-customer (C2C)** e-commerce refers to e-commerce in which both the buyer and the seller are individuals (not businesses). C2C is conducted in several ways on the Internet; the best-known C2C activities are auctions. Millions of individuals are buying and selling on eBay and hundreds of other auction sites worldwide. In addition to the major C2C activity of auctions, other C2C activities include classified ads, personal services, exchanges, and support services.

customer-to-customer (C2C)
E-commerce in which both the buyer and the seller are individuals (not businesses); involves activities such as auctions and classified ads.

C2C AUCTIONS

In dozens of countries, selling and buying on auction sites is exploding. Most auctions are conducted by intermediaries (e.g., eBay). Consumers can select general sites such as eBay.com or auctionanything.com or they can use specialized sites such as buyit.com or bid2bid.com. In addition, many individuals are conducting their own auctions. For example, greatshop.com provides software to create C2C reverse auction communities online. See Chapter 11 for more on auctions.

CLASSIFIED ADS

People sell to other people every day through classified ads. Internet-based classified ads have several advantages over newspaper classified ads: They offer a national, rather than a local, audience. This greatly increases the supply of goods and services available and the number of potential buyers. For example, classifieds2000.com contains a list of about 500,000 cars, compared with the much smaller number one might find locally. Another example is freeclassified.com. Often, placing an ad on one Web site brings it automatically into the classified sections of numerous partners. This increases ad exposure, at no additional cost. To help narrow the search for a particular item, on some sites shoppers can use search engines. In addition, Internet-based classifieds often can be placed for free by private parties, can be edited or changed easily, and in many cases can display photos of the product offered for sale.

The major categories of classified ads are similar to those found in a newspaper: vehicles, real estate, employment, general merchandise, collectibles, computers, pets, tickets, and travel. Classified ads are available through most ISPs (AOL, MSN, etc.), in some portals (Yahoo, etc.), and from Internet directories, online newspapers, and more. Once a person finds an ad and gets the details, they can e-mail or call the other party to find out additional information or to make a purchase. Classified ad Web sites accept no responsibility for the content of any advertisement. Advertisers are identified by e-mail address. A password is used to authenticate the advertiser. Most classified ads are provided for free. Some classified ad sites generate revenue from advertisers who pay for larger ads, especially when the sellers are businesses.

PERSONAL SERVICES

Numerous personal services are available on the Internet (lawyers, handy helpers, tax preparers, investment clubs, dating services). Some are in the classified ads, but others are listed in specialized Web sites and directories. Some are free, some charge a fee. Be very careful before purchasing any personal services. Fraud or crime could be involved (e.g., a lawyer online may not be an expert in the area professed or may not deliver the service at all). Online advising and consulting, described in Section 9.5, also are examples of personal services.

C2C EXCHANGES

C2C exchanges are of several types. They may be *consumer-to-consumer bartering exchanges* (e.g., targetbarter.com) in which goods and services are exchanged without monetary transactions. Or, they may be *consumer exchanges* that help buyers and sellers find each other and negotiate deals. Another form of C2C exchange is one in which consumers exchange information about products (e.g., consumerdemocracy.com, epinions.com). For a complete list of such exchanges, see business2.com.

SUPPORT SERVICES FOR C2C

When individuals buy products or services from other individuals online, they usually buy from strangers. The issues of assuring quality, receiving payments, and preventing fraud are critical to the success of C2C. One service that helps C2C is payments by intermediary companies such as PayPal (paypal.com) (see Chapter 13). Other innovative services and technologies that support C2C are described in Chapters 12 through 15.

Section 9.6 ▶ REVIEW

1. List the major C2C applications.
2. Describe how C2C works in classified online ads.
3. Describe C2C personal services, exchanges, and other support services.

9.7 PEER-TO-PEER NETWORKS AND APPLICATIONS

peer-to-peer (P2P)
A network architecture in which workstations (or PCs) share data and processing with each other directly rather than through a central server.

Several C2C applications are based on a computer architecture known as peer-to-peer. **Peer-to-peer (P2P)** computer architecture is a type of network in which each client computer can share files or computer resources (such as processing power) *directly* with others rather than through a central server. This is in contrast with a *client/server* architecture in which some computers serve other computers via a central server. (Note that the acronym P2P also can stand for people-to-people, person-to-person, or point-to-point. Our discussion here refers to *peer-to-peer networks* over which files and other computing resources are shared.)

P2P technology is really two different things—the direct sharing of digital files and the sharing of different computers' processing power. The main benefit of P2P is that it can expand enormously the universe of information accessible from a personal computer or a mobile device (users are not confined to just Web pages). Additionally, some proponents claim that a well-designed P2P system can offer better security, reliability, and availability of content than the client/server model on which the Web is currently based. Other advantages over the client/server architecture include the following: no need for a network administrator, the network is fast and inexpensive to set up and maintain, and each PC can make a backup copy of its data to other PCs for security. The P2P technology is more productive than client/server because it enables direct connections between computers. However, P2P has some drawbacks that limit its usability, as can be seen from its characteristics.

Characteristics of P2P Systems

P2P systems have the following key characteristics: They provide for real-time access to other users through techniques such as instant messaging and multichannel collaboration applications. The user computers can act as both clients and servers. The overall system is easy to use and is well integrated, and it includes tools for easy creation of content or for adding functionalities. P2P systems maximize the use of physical attributes such as processor cycles, storage space, bandwidth, and location on the network. They employ user interfaces that load outside of a Web browser. They address the need to reach content resources located on the Internet periphery. They support "cross-networking" protocols such as SOAP or XML-RPC (remote procedure call, a protocol that enables a program on one computer to execute a program on a server computer). Finally, they often do something new or exciting, which creates popular interest.

As these characteristics of P2P computing indicate, devices can join the P2P network from any location with little effort. Instead of dedicated LANs, the Internet itself becomes the network of choice. Easier configuration and control over the applications enables people without network savvy to join the user community. In fact, P2P signifies a shift in peer-networking emphasis—from hardware to applications.

P2P networking connects people directly to other people. It provides an easy system for sharing, publishing, and interacting that does not require knowledge of system administration. The system wraps everything up into a user-friendly interface and lets people share or communicate with each other (for details, see Kwok et al. 2002). P2P networks overcome existing client/server inefficiencies and limitations. They will not replace the client/server architecture, but they can be used to create hybrid P2P-client/server networks that are faster, cheaper, and more powerful. According to Kini (2002), P2P networking improves upon the existing client/server hierarchy to efficiently use the processing power disk space and data available in a significant number of information sharing and knowledge management applications.

An example of a P2P network is illustrated in Exhibit 9.5. The PCs shown in the drawing perform computer-to-computer communication directly through their own operating systems; individual resources such as printers, CD-ROM drives, or disk drives are transformed into shared, collective resources that are accessible from any PC on the P2P network.

Models of P2P Applications

Four distinct models of P2P applications exist:

- **Collaboration.** This model allows real-time direct interactions between people, including instant messaging and videoconferencing applications.
- **Content distribution.** This model enables the file-sharing capability, made most famous by Napster and other music file-sharing services.
- **Business process automation.** This model is used to enhance existing business process applications. For example, users can control the type of data their e-mail client will accept.
- **Distributed search.** This model enables the sending of search requests in real time to multiple information repositories rather than searching a centralized index.

These characteristics and models allow for the various applications discussed next.

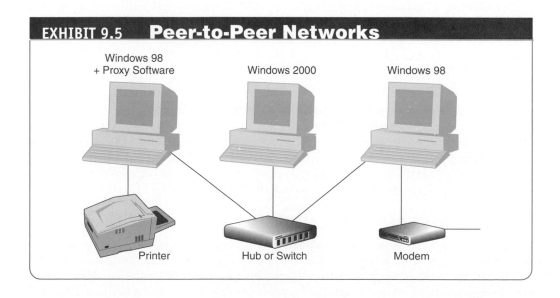

EXHIBIT 9.5   Peer-to-Peer Networks

Windows 98 + Proxy Software

Windows 2000

Windows 98

Printer

Hub or Switch

Modem

C2C P2P APPLICATIONS

The most publicized P2P applications are in the area of C2C. The most well known of these applications is the file sharing of music.

Napster—The File-Sharing Utility

In Chapter 3, Napster was presented as an example of C2C EC. By logging onto Napster, people could enter files that other people were willing to share. The network enabled users to search other members' hard drives for a particular file, including data files created by users or copied from elsewhere. Digital music and games were the most popular files accessed. Napster had more than 60 million members in 2002 before it went out of business.

The Napster server functioned as a directory that listed the files being shared by other users. Once logged into the server, users could search the directory for specific songs and locate the file owner. They could then directly access the owner's computer and download the songs they had chosen. Napster also included chat rooms to connect its millions of users.

However, a U.S. federal court found Napster to be in violation of copyright laws because it enabled people to obtain music files without paying the creators of the music for access to their material. Following this ruling, in March 2002, Napster closed its free services. Napster continued to operate, with users paying a fee for file sharing and Napster passing along part of the fee to copyright owners.

In December 2002, Roxio, a software maker specializing in CD-burning software, bought Napster's intellectual property assets, including its patents and brand name. (Roxio did not assume any of Napster's legal or financial liabilities.) Napster's remaining hardware—servers, routers, and miscellaneous computers—became part of the company's bankruptcy proceeding and were auctioned off December 11, 2002. Roxio plans to relaunch Napster by 2004. (For more on Napster, see Chapter 17.)

Other File-Sharing Programs

A number of free file-sharing programs still exist. For example, an even purer version of P2P is Gnutella (gnutella.com), a P2P program that dispenses with the central database altogether in connecting the peer computers. Similarly, Kazaa (for now) offers music file sharing. To access games over P2P networks, try fusiongames.com and battle.net. ICQ (the instant messenger-type chat room) can be considered a hybrid P2P technology because the chatters share the same screen. Attempts are being made to kill Kazaa (and others like it), but because Kazaa's servers are located in Denmark and users trade files using anonymous "supernodes," these attempts will take time.

A survey conducted by Ipsos-Reid in September 2002 reported that 49.7 percent of music files are downloaded by some P2P application without payment to their creators. The study found that 19.2 percent of people who use P2P file-sharing pay for downloading, and 24.8 percent buy music at e-tailers. Despite the temptation to get "something for nothing," remember that downloading copyrighted materials for free is against the law; violators are subject to penalties if caught.

Other Commercial P2P Applications in C2C

With P2P, users can sell digital goods directly from their computers rather than going through centralized servers. If users want to sell on eBay, for example, they are required to go through eBay's server, putting an item on eBay's site and uploading a photo. However, if an auction site uses *file sharing*, it can direct customers to the seller's Web site, where buyers can find an extensive amount of information, photos, and even videos about the items being sold. In this case, an auction site serves as an intermediary, making the P2P link between the sellers and buyers.

INTRABUSINESS P2P APPLICATIONS

Several companies are using P2P to facilitate internal collaboration. For example, in 1990, Intel wrote a file transfer program called NetBatch, which allows chip designers to use the additional processing power of colleagues' computers across sites in California, Arizona, and even foreign countries such as Israel. Intel saved more than $500 million between 1992 and

2001 (intel.com 2002). Under this arrangement, users were able to solve more complex problems that otherwise would have required the use of supercomputers.

B2B P2P APPLICATIONS

P2P could be a technology panacea for systems innovators building B2B exchanges. With P2P, people can share information, but they are not required to send it to an unknown server, as they do when using a regular exchange. Some companies fear that exchanges make it possible for unauthorized personnel to gain access to corporate data files. P2P applications enable such companies to store documents in-house instead of on an unknown, and possibly unsecured, server. According to McAffee (2000), P2P networks allow companies to avoid the fees charged by B2B exchanges and reduce the complexity and expense of the networking. Netrana Corporation's (netrana.com) software replaces the model of funneling all buyers and sellers into a central place with the ability of direct connection.

Several companies are using the P2P architecture as a basis for speeding up business transactions, as shown in the following examples.

- Groove Networks enables direct collaboration by small groups (see Kini 2002). Groove 2, which was introduced in April 2002, has many P2P-based capabilities.
- Hilgraeve of Monroe, Michigan, has a technology called DropChute that establishes a connection between two computers and allows users to transfer files. The company has won a U.S. patent for its P2P communication process that touts four levels of encryption and virus-scanning protection.
- Fort Knox Escrow Service in Atlanta, Georgia, which transmits legal and financial documents that must be highly secure, has leveraged DropChute to enable clients to deliver material electronically. "Instead of having to wait for an overnight package, we can do it all over the Internet," said Jeanna Israel, Fort Knox's director of operations (Lason Company 2000).
- Biz2Peer Technologies offers a trading platform that allows P2P product searches, cataloging, and order entry.
- Blue Tiger Networks makes a platform for P2P trading between businesses.
- Consilient creates "sitelets," which are mobile XML documents designed to manage themselves through built-in workflow rules. (For further explanation of this complex technology, see openp2p.com; search for Consilient.)

Peer networks effectively address some of the Web's B2B deficiencies. The model is a natural fit for the needs of business, as business relationships are intrinsically peer to peer. Peer networks allow businesses to communicate, interact, and transact with each other as never before by making business relationships interactive, dynamic, and balanced—both within and between enterprises.

However, the success of P2P in B2B is not guaranteed. It depends in part on the ability of the technology to address security and scalability issues. For additional information on P2P in B2B, see Gong (2002) and internetnews.com (2001).

B2C P2P APPLICATIONS

P2P has potential applications to marketing, advertising, and B2C payments. For example, Certapay (certapay.com) is a P2P e-mail payment platform that enables e-banking customers to send and receive money using only an e-mail address. Another company, Fandango (fandango.com), combines P2P with collaborative filtering (Chapter 4) for online ticket buying activities. Assuming a user is conducting a search for a ticket using Fandango's product, the user enters a search keyword, and the keyword is sent to 100 peers, which search local indexes of the Web pages they have visited. Those computers relay the query to 100 of their peers, and that group submits it to 100 of theirs, yielding, in theory, up to 1 million queries. The resulting URLs are returned to the user, weighted in favor of the most recently visited pages and peers with similar interests.

P2P is certain to enable new EC applications. Although sensitive information may require special security arrangements and many users may encounter scalability issues, P2P is indeed a very promising technology.

1. Define P2P networks and list their major characteristics.
2. List the major P2P models.
3. Describe P2P applications in C2C.
4. Describe P2P applications in B2B.

9.8 OTHER EC APPLICATIONS

The only limit to EC applications is the limit to human creativity. In fact, there are thousands of innovative EC applications, and the number is growing by leaps and bounds. This section presents only a few of these other applications.

SELLING PRESCRIPTION DRUGS ONLINE

The price consumers are asked to pay for prescription drugs in the United States is very high. In an effort to reduce costs, e-pharmacies are trying to sell prescription drugs online. By 2002, eMarketer projected that only about 2 percent of all prescription drugs were sold on the Net (Emarketer.com 2001) despite incentives offered by HMOs. Some of the more established sites offering this service are drugstore.com (partner of Rite Aid), cvs.com, more.com, cranespharmacy.com, and planetrx.com. These and other companies are experimenting with different strategies to capture a share in a market of over $125 billion (in 2002).

POSTAL SERVICES

One of the early applications of EC was online postal services with pioneering sites such as e-stamp.com. Today, Internet postage services are available in dozens of countries. For example, in China, customers can go to the post office and use computers there that offer online services to make remittances to sellers. (In China, the use of credit cards is very limited.) Another postal services example is postagebyphone.com, a system from Pitney Bowes (pb.com). It offers highly secure and reliable functions such as printing postage, as well as flexibility and convenience. The entire mailing process is done on the Internet (or via a telephone).

The U.S. Postal Service offers an integrated online postage meter, scale, and printer. The service allows (1) the downloading of postage via the Internet; (2) the weighing of a letter or package, calculating postage instantly; and (3) the printing of postage. With PC postage software, you can purchase postage over the Internet and use your standard desktop printer to print the PC postage indicia directly onto envelopes or labels for your mail or packages. See usps.com/postagesolutions for details. For $14.95 per month (in 2003), the U.S. Postal Service offers a system that enables customers to purchase and print postage around the clock, weigh packages up to 4.4 pounds, and prepare first class, priority, express, and international mail. Meters can be leased from commercial manufacturers in cooperation with the postal service that allow you to download postage directly into the machine and then print it as you need it. Customers can store frequent mailing addresses, print exact postage, track postage use, and more. The hardware is small enough that it fits in the palm of a hand.

SERVICES FOR ADULTS

The most profitable B2C model is that of selling sex on the Internet. There is nothing new about online pornography. According to a 1994 study conducted by Carnegie Mellon University (see McNeill 2000), 83.5 percent of all images posted on Usenet newsgroups were pornographic in nature. Today, over 100,000 pornographic Web sites are in operation worldwide. With little or no advertising effort to attract viewers, many of these sites are making money. As with any B2C business, attracting traffic is the key. According to reports by market research firms such as Forrester, IDC, DataMonitor, Jupiter, and NetRating that monitor the industry, viewers eagerly pay substantial subscription fees to view adult sites. One reason is that many customers may be hesitant to make a purchase at a local physical store but are comfortable making such purchases online because of the privacy afforded by such sites.

The sites also use innovative streaming video to attract customers. Adult entertainment sites also are well versed in the art of up-selling and cross-selling (e.g., adultshop.com). Many sites also collect fees from advertisers. Finally, adult entertainment sites cut costs by using banner exchanges, joint ventures, and affiliate programs.

A major problem for these sites is their ability to work within the regulatory framework of the local environment. As with any other successful business model, newcomers are continuously trying their luck. Increased competition drives down prices, and many porn sites may go out of business.

E-ALLIANCES

Doing business online may require several business partners. As will be discussed in Chapter 15, e-alliances can be formed in several ways. For example, for a large EC project, a company may join with a technology provider, a logistics provider, and a bank. According to Ernst et al. (2001), over 22,000 new business alliances were announced in 1999 and 37,000 in 2000. Of these, about 65 percent were e-alliances. However, many of these alliances never materialized because the dot-com companies that formed the e-alliances went out of business. Also, the business models used were not very conducive to staying in business.

E-alliances are popular in click-and-mortar situations. However, pure-play EC companies like Amazon.com also have many alliances (see Chapter 3). In 1999–2000 there were about twice as many B2C alliances as B2B ones. When going global, the need for e-alliances may become critical. According to Ernst et al. (2001), 75 percent of all cross-border alliances are successful versus 55 percent of domestic alliances.

WEDDING-RELATED SITES

"Domestic alliances" of another type—that is, weddings—are also a popular topic of online activity. Two of the most successful B2C areas are wedding channels and online gift registries.

Wedding Channels

Each year, almost 500,000 brides-to-be use "The Knot" to plan their weddings. A "Knot Box" with insert folders is sent to users by regular mail. Each insert is linked to a corresponding page on the theknot.com. Advertisers underwrite the mail campaign. The Web site provides brides with information and help in planning the wedding and selecting vendors. Orders can be placed by phone or online (although not all products can be ordered online). WeddingChannel (weddingchannel.com) is a similar service, but it operates primarily online. Both weddingchannel.com and theknot.com include promotions and ads from vendors.

Gift Registries

The U.S. bridal industry is estimated to have annual revenues of $30 to $50 billion. The gift registry part of the industry—where the lucky couple lists what presents they hope their guests will buy for them—is estimated to be about $17 billion (von Hoffman 2001). Gift registries are also used by people buying gifts for other occasions (anniversaries, birthdays, graduations, etc.).

From an IT point of view, a gift registry is a relatively complex set of database and supply chain interactions. Usually the gift registry is done jointly between the gift registry company and the department store (e.g., macys.com). The database has to present a secure environment to the person who is registering. That information is then displayed to those who are buying the gifts. When a specific gift is selected, it is removed from the list before anyone else orders the same thing. Meanwhile, the database has to interact with the selling company's inventory lists, showing what's in stock and, in the best of all possible worlds, alerting buyers and registrants when things are on back-order.

Section 9.8 ▶ REVIEW

1. Why are online sales of prescription drugs growing rapidly?
2. Why would one use online postal services?
3. Why are adult entertainment sites so successful?
4. Why are wedding-related sites successful?

MANAGERIAL ISSUES

Some managerial issues related to this chapter are as follows.

1. **Are there e-government opportunities?** If an organization is doing business with the government, they will eventually do some or all of it online. Organizations may find new online business opportunities with the government, because governments are getting serious about going online. Some even mandate it as the only way to conduct B2G and G2B.

2. **Are there e-learning opportunities?** Adding e-learning component to a company's activities is useful when employees need to retrain themselves and keep up with new knowledge. Organizations can cut retraining costs and shorten the learning period.

3. **Can we capitalize on C2C?** Businesses cannot capture much C2C activity unless they are providers of some innovative service such as paypal.com. Businesses may consider using P2P to support C2C.

4. **How well are we managing our knowledge?** Connecting e-commerce initiatives with a KM program, if one exists, is a very viable strategy. The knowledge is needed for the operation and implementation of EC projects.

5. **Are there P2P applications?** Watch for new developments in P2P tools and applications. Some experts say a major revolution is coming for faster and cheaper online communication and collaboration. As with any new innovation, it will take time to mature. This technology could be very helpful in B2B applications.

SUMMARY

In this chapter, you learned about the following EC issues as they relate to the learning objectives.

1. **E-government to citizens and businesses.** Governments worldwide are providing a large variety of services to citizens over the Internet. Such initiatives increase citizens' satisfaction and decrease government expenses in providing customer service applications. Governments are also active in electronically trading with businesses.

2. **Other e-government activities.** Governments, like any other organization, can use EC applications for great savings. Notable applications are e-procurement using reverse auctions, e-payments to and from citizens and businesses, auctioning of surplus goods, and electronic travel and expense management systems. Governments also conduct electronic business with other governments.

3. **Online publishing and e-books.** Online publishing of newspapers, magazines, and books is growing rapidly, as is the online publishing of other digitizable items such as software, music, games, movies, and other entertainment. Of special interest is blogging, the publishing by individuals on the Internet.

4. **E-learning, and virtual universities.** E-learning is the delivery of educational content via electronic media, including the Internet and intranets. Degree programs, lifelong learning topics, and corporate training are delivered by thousands of organizations worldwide. A growing area is distance learning via online university offerings. Some are virtual; others are delivered both online and off-line. Corporate online training is also increasing, sometimes at formal corporate learning centers.

5. **Knowledge management and dissemination.** Knowledge has been recognized as an important organizational asset. It needs to be properly captured, stored, managed, and shared. Knowledge is critical for many e-commerce tasks. Knowledge can be shared in different ways; expert knowledge is provided to nonexperts (for fee or free) via a knowledge portal or as a personal service.

6. **C2C activities.** C2C consists of consumers conducting e-commerce with other consumers, mainly in auctions (such as at eBay). Buying and selling of goods and personal services takes place through the use of online classified ads, exchanges, and support services to reach other individual consumers.

7. **Peer-to-peer technology and applications.** Peer-to-peer (P2P) technology enables direct communication among client computers. It enables file sharing among individuals and between organizations. The P2P technology has tremendous potential for increased effectiveness and reduced cost of communication and collaboration.

8. **Other innovative applications.** Many other applications exist on the Web but were not described in earlier chapters. Examples are sales of prescription drugs, online postal services, adult entertainment sites, e-alliances, and wedding sites.

KEY TERMS

DISCUSSION QUESTIONS

1. Some say that B2G is simply B2B. Explain.

2. Compare and contrast B2E with G2E.

3. Discuss the major properties of P2P.

4. Discuss some of the potential ethical and legal implications of people using P2P to download (i.e., file sharing) music, games, and so forth.

5. In what way can online publishing support a paper-based publication?

6. Discuss the advantages and disadvantages of e-books.

7. Will paper-based books and magazines be eliminated in the long run? Why or why not?

8. Describe the social phenomenon of blogging and speculate on its commercial possibilities.

9. Check an online version of a newspaper or magazine you are familiar with and discuss the differences between the print and online versions.

10. Discuss the advantages of e-learning for an undergraduate student.

11. Discuss the advantages of e-learning in the corporate training environment.

12. Discuss the relationship between KM and a portal.

13. In what ways does KM support e-commerce?

14. Which e-government EC activities are intrabusiness activities? Explain why they are intrabusiness.

15. Identify the benefits of G2C to citizens and to governments.

16. Discuss the relationship between P2P and KM. (Hint: See Kini 2002).

INTERNET EXERCISES

1. Enter whitehouse.gov/government and review the "Gateway to Government." Based on the stages presented in Exhibit 9.2, what stage does this site represent? Review the available tours. Suggest ways the government could improve this portal.

2. Enter oecd.org and identify the studies conducted by the Organization for Economic Cooperation and Development (OECD) on the topic of e-government. What are the organization's major concerns?

3. Enter fcw.com and read the latest news on e-government. Identify initiatives not covered in this chapter. Check the B2G corner. Then enter gcn.com. Finally, enter ec.fed.gov. Compare the information in the three Web sites.

4. Enter procurement.com and gov exec.com. Identify recent e-procurement initiatives and summarize their unique aspects.

5. Enter govhost.com/conyersga and find the specific G2C citizen's information provided.

6. Enter pcmag.com, fortune.com, or other e-zines. How would you compare reading the electronic magazine against the print version?

7. Enter webct.com and blackboard.com. Compare the capabilities of the two products.

8. Enter e-learningcentre.co.uk and evaluate its resources and activities.

9. Enter iguide.com, elearningmag.com, and online learningmag.com. Identify current issues and find articles related to the effectiveness of e-training. Write a report.

10. Identify a difficult business problem. Post the problem on elance.com. Summarize the offers to solve the problem.

11. Enter knowledgeleader.com. This knowledge base resides on Andersen's intranet. Sign up for the service for sample material. Why is such a system better when used on an intranet? Why not use a CD-ROM–based technology?

12. Enter xdegrees.com, centrata.com, and badblue.com and evaluate some of the solutions offered. Also, enter aberdeen.com to learn more about P2P operations. How can a search for a song be expedited at gnutella.co.uk?

13. Enter groove.net, netrana.com, and opencola.com and explore the latest developments in P2P.

TEAM ASSIGNMENTS AND ROLE PLAYING

1. Assign each team to a different country. Each team will then explore the e-government offerings of that country. Have each team make a presentation to convince the class that its country's offerings are the most comprehensive. (Exclude Hong Kong and Singapore.)

2. Create four teams, each representing one of the following: G2C, G2B, G2E, and G2G. Each team will prepare a plan of its major activities in a small country such as Denmark, Finland, or Singapore. A fifth team will deal with the coordination and collaboration of all e-government activities in each country. Prepare a report based on the activity.

3. Have teams search for virtual universities (e.g., the University of Phoenix, uophx.edu). Write a summary of the schools' e-learning offerings.

4. Have each team represent one of the following sites: netlibrary.com, ebooks.bn.com, ebooks.com, and zanderebooks.com. Each team will examine the technology, legal issues, prices, and business alliances associated with its site. Each team will then prepare a report answering the question, "Will e-books succeed?"

REAL-WORLD CASE

E-GOVERNMENT INITIATIVES IN HONG KONG

The Hong Kong (HK) Special Administrative Region (SAR) government initiated several e-government projects under the Digital 21 IT strategy (*info.gov.hk/digital21*). The major projects of this initiative were the electronic service delivery scheme (ESD), the interactive government services directory (IGSD), the electronic tendering system (ETS), the HKSAR Government Information Center, and the HK post office certification service (Post e-Cert). The highlights of some of these initiatives are provided here. Further information can be found at the specific URLs presented at *info.gov.hk*.

The Electronic Service Delivery Scheme (ESD)

The ESD project provides a major infrastructure through which the public can transact business electronically with 38 different public services provided by 11 government agencies, as demonstrated by the following examples.

1. **Transport Department.** Applications for driving and vehicle licenses, appointments for vehicle examinations and road tests, change-of-address reports, and so forth.

2. **Immigration.** Applications for birth/death/marriage certificates, appointments for ID card issuance, applications for foreign domestic helpers, communication on any other issue concerning immigration.

3. **HK Tourist Association.** Tourist information, maps, answers to queries.

4. **Labour Department.** List of job openings, job searches for job seekers, searches for applicants by employers, FAQs regarding legal issues, information on employee-compensation plans.

5. **Social Welfare Department.** Applications for senior citizen cards and special program participation, welfare information, registration for volunteer activities, requests for charitable fund-raising permits.

6. **Inland Revenue Department.** Electronic filing of tax returns, electronic payment program, change of address forms, interactive tax Q&A, applications for sole proprietor certificate, applications for business registrations, purchase of tax reserve certificates.
7. **Registration and Electoral Office.** Applications for voter registration, change of address forms, interactive Q&A.
8. **Trade and Industry Department.** Business license information and applications, SME information center.
9. **Treasury Department.** Electronic bill payment.
10. **Rating and Valuation Department.** Changes of rates and/or government rent payers' particulars, interactive Q&A.
11. **Innovation and Technology Commission.** Information on technology funding schemes, electronic applications for funding.

These services are provided in Chinese and English. The project is managed by ESD Services Limited (*esdlife.com*). For additional information, see *esd.gov.hk*.

In addition to these services, the Web site includes eight ESD clubs, or communities. The public can sign up for a club, get information, share experiences, or just chat. The eight clubs are ESDbaby (for new parents, family planning, etc.), ESDkids (how to raise kids), ESDteens (a meeting point for the teens on music, culture, learning, etc.), ESD1822 (lifestyle, education, jobs, and so on for adults aged 18 to 22), EDScouples (information on getting married and building a family), ESDprime (information on jobs, education, entertainment, investment, travel, for middle-aged adults, etc.), ESDsenior (health care, fitness, education, lifestyle), and ESDhospice (complete services for the end of life).

The Interactive Government Services Directory (IGSD)

IGSD is an interactive service that enables the public to access information and services not included in the ESD. For example, it includes:

▸ A telephone and Web site directory of public services containing information and links to hundreds of services.
▸ An interactive investment guide offered by the Industry Department (for investing in Hong Kong)
▸ Interactive employment services
▸ Interactive road traffic information

The Electronic Tendering System (ETS)

ETS is a G2B Web site that manages the reverse auctions conducted by the government supplies department. It includes supplier registration, notification of tenders, downloading of tendering documents, interactive Q&A, submission of tender offers, and more. The HK government conducts more than 5,000 tenders a year. For more information, see *ets.com.hk*.

The HKSAR Government Information Center

The HKSAR Government Information Center is the official government Web site (*info.gov.hk*). This site enables people to view news, government notices, guides to major government services, information on leisure and cultural activities, and more.

The HK Post E-Cert

HK Post e-Cert is the home of the Hong Kong Public Certification Authority (*hongkongpost.com*). The Hong Kong Post created a PKI system (see Chapter 12) and issues digital certificates (Post e-Cert) to individuals and organizations. It also maintains a certificate repository and directory of all certificates issued, so that the public can verify the validity of the certificates. The Post e-Cert also issues certificates to servers and to security systems.

Accessibility to the extensive Hong Kong e-government portal is available not only from PCs, but also from hundreds of kiosks placed in many public places in Hong Kong.

Sources: Student interview at *info.gov.hk/digital21* (2001 and 2002) and Art (2001).

Questions

1. Identify each of the five initiatives as G2C, G2B, C2G, or G2E.
2. Visit *info.gov.hk/digital21* and identify the goals of the five e-government initiatives.
3. How will the role of the HK government change when the initiatives mature and are fully utilized?
4. Compare the services offered by Hong Kong with those offered in Singapore (*ecitizen.gov.sg*). What are the major differences between the two?
5. What applications could the HK government add in the future?

REFERENCES

Abramson, M. A., and G. E. Means (eds). *E-Government 2001*. Lanham, MD: Rowman and Littlefield, 2001.

Al-Kibsi, G., et al. "Putting Citizens On-line, Not in Line." *The McKinsey Quarterly* no. 2 (March 2001).

Art, N. "Tendering Goes Online." *South China Morning Post*, March 30, 2001.

Bacon, K., et al. *E-Government: The Blue Print*. New York: John Wiley & Sons, 2001.

Beat, F. et al. "A Proposal for a Structured Database in the Complex World of Standards: What about a Structured Single Entry Point to the Standardization World?" *Electronic Markets* 11, no. 4, December 2001.

Blackboard.com. "Blackboard Learning and Community Portal System." blackboard.com/products/ps/index.htm (accessed June 2002a).

Blackboard.com. "Blackboard: Transaction System." blackboard.com/addons/b2/ts.htm (accessed June 2002b).

Bose, R. "Knowledge Management Capabilities and Infrastructure for E-Commerce." *Journal of Computer Information Systems* 42, no. 5, 2002.

Boulton, C. "Palm Unit to Dispense E-Books from HarperCollins." ecommercetimes.com, November 20, 2001 (accessed October 2002).

Boxer, K. M., and B. Johnson. "How to Build an Online Center." *Training and Development* (August 2002).

business.wa.gov.au (accessed October 2002).

Chen, M., and Y. I. Liou. "Building a Knowledge-Enabled EC Environment." *Journal of Computer Information Systems* 42, no. 5, 2002.

Cisco.com. "Partner E-Learning Connection—Celebrates One Year." Cisco Partner Summit, Las Vegas, NV, April 2001, cisco.com/warp/public/10/wwtraining/elearning/press/Final_PEC_release3_271.pdf (accessed August 2002).

Corbeil, P. "One-Stop Shopping." *Journal of Housing and Community Development* (March–April 2002).

Davenport, T. H., and L. Prusak. *Working Knowledge: How Organizations Manage What They Know*. Cambridge, MA: Harvard Business School Press, 2000.

Davies, N., et al. "Future Wireless Applications for a Networked City." *IEEE Wireless Communications* (February 2002).

Dean, J. "E-Gov in the Works." govexec.com, November 2000 (accessed October 2002).

Delahoussaye, M., and R. Zemke. "About Learning Online." *Training*, September 2001.

Drummond, M. "Big Music." *Business 2.0*, December 12, 2000.

ecc.online.wa.gov.au/main/site_index.htm (accessed April 2002).

ecc.online.wa.gov.au/news (accessed April 2002).

Eduventures.com. "Eduventures Releases Study of Higher Education E-Learning Market, a Subset of E-Education; Forecasts E-Education Market Growth from $4.5 billion in 2001 to $11 billion in 2005." December 18, 2001, eduventures.com/about/press_room/12_18_01.cfm (accessed December 2002).

Emarketer.com. "Blogging in Web's Footsteps." Emarketer.com, February 8, 2002a.

Emarketer.com. "U.S. Government Web Sites Concentrate on Security, Privacy." emarketer.com, October 2, 2002b.

Emarketer.com. "Online Drug Sales Getting Higher." May 9, 2001.

Ernst, D., et al. "A Future for E-Alliances." *The McKinsey Quarterly* no. 2 (2001).

Fahey, L., et al. "Linking E-Business and Operating Processes: The Role of KM." *IBM Systems Journal* 40, no. 4 (2001).

Galagan, P. A. "Delta Force at Cisco." *Training and Development* (July 2002).

Gong, L. (ed.). "Peer-to-Peer Networks in Action." Special issue (five papers), *IEEE Internet Computing* (January–February 2002).

GovExec.com. "Digital Government: Government to Employee." November 2000, govexec.com/features/1100/egov/g2e.htm (accessed June 2003).

grace.com (accessed December 2002).

Gwiazdowski, A. "E-Book Sales Lead Off 2003." *Association of American Publishers*, March 18, 2003, publishers.org/press/releases.cfm?PressReleaseArticleID=138 (accessed April 2003).

Hamalainen, M., et al. "Electronic Marketing for Learning: Education Brokerages on the Internet." *Communications of the ACM* (June 1996).

Hart-Teeter, R. *E-Government: The Next American Revolution*. Washington, DC: Council for Excellence in Government, 2001.

Hofmann, D. W. "Internet-Based Learning in Higher Education." *Techdirections*, August 2002.

Holsapple, C. W. (ed). *Handbook on Knowledge Management* (two volumes). Heidelberg, Germany: Springer Computer Science, 2003.

Hopfner, J. "A Revolution in (Tax) Revenue." *MIS Asia* (May 2002).

info.gov.hk/digital21, student interview, February 2001 and 2002.

Intel.com. "Peer-To-Peer: Spreading the Computing Power." intel.com/eBusiness/products/peertopeer/ar011102.htm (accessed June 2002).

International Trade Centre. "Export Development in the Digital Economy." *Executive Forum 2000*, September 2000, intracen.org/execforum/ef2000/eb200010.htm (accessed August 2002).

Internetnews.com. "CommerceNet and Peer Intelligence Research P2P for Business." August 2001, http://siliconvalley.internet.com/news/article.php/868511 (accessed July 2002).

Ipsos-Reid. "Digital Music Behavior Continues to Evolve." February 1, 2002, ipsos-reid.com/pdf/publicat/docs/

tempo_dldingprevalence.pdf (accessed December 2002).

Kapp, K. "Anytime E-Learning Takes Off in Manufacturing." *APICS* (June 2002).

Kini, R. B. "Peer-to-Peer Technology: A Technology Reborn." *Information Systems Management* (2002).

Kwok, S. H., et al. "Peer-to-Peer Technology Business and Service Models: Risks and Opportunities." *Electronic Markets* 12, no. 3 (2002).

Lai, H., and T. H. Chu. "Knowledge Management: A Review of Industrial Cases." *Journal of Computer Information System*, special issue 42, no. 5 (2002).

Langenbach, C., and F. Bodendorf. "The Electronic Mall: A Service Center for Distance Learning." *International Journal of Electronic Commerce* (Winter 1999–2000).

Lason Company. "Fort Knox Escrow Services—A Lason Company—Unveils Escrow Direct." press release lason.com, March 20, 2000, (accessed June 2003).

Liaw, S., and H. Huang. "How Web Technology Can Facilitate Learning." *Information Systems Management* (Winter 2002).

lifelines2000.org (accessed August 2001).

McAffee, A. "The Napsterization of B2B." *Harvard Business Review* (November–December 2000).

Mack, R., et al. "Knowledge Portals and the Emerging Digital Knowledge Workplace." *IBM Systems Journal* 40, no. 4 (2001).

McNeill, L. "The 'Net's Most Profitable B2C Business Model?" *e-Strategy*, November–December 2000.

Miller, J. R. "Technology, Digital Citizen, and E-Government: The E-Invention Revolution." 2000, wmrc.com/businessbriefing/pdf/wued2000/Publication/miller.pdf (accessed June 2002).

Nah, F., et al. "Knowledge Management Mechanisms in E-Commerce: A Study of Online Retailing and Auction Sites." *Journal of Computer Information Systems* 42, no. 5, 2002.

Phillips, S. "'Blogs' Has Moved into the Big Time." *Financial Times*, June 19, 2002.

Piccoli, G., et al. "Web-Based Virtual Learning Environments." *MIS Quarterly* (December 2001).

Raisch, W. D. *The eMarketplace*. New York: McGraw-Hill, 2001.

Roberts, M. J., and H. Stevenson. *Background Brief: The Evolving Market for Business Education (A Research Note)*. Boston: Harvard Business School Press, 2001.

Roberts-Witt, S. "A 'Eureka' Moment at Xerox." *PC Magazine*, March 26, 2002, pcmag.com/article2/0,4149,28792,00.asp (accessed August 2002).

Robinson, S. "Print-on-Demand Could Be Publishing's Future." *Interactive Week*, April 2, 2001.

Schubert, P., and U. Hausler. "E-Government Meets E-Business: A Portal Site for Start-up Companies in Switzerland." *Proceedings 34th HICSS*, Maui, HI, January 2001.

Schwartz, J. "E-Voting: Its Day Has Not Come Just Yet." *New York Times*, November 27, 2000.

Shaw, M. J., et al. "Knowledge Management and Data Mining for Marketing." *Decision Support Systems*, May 2001.

Song, S. "An Internet Knowledge Sharing System." *Journal of Computer Information Systems* (Spring 2002).

Stellin, S. "Textbook Publishers Try Online Education." *The New York Times*, March 7, 2001.

Sugumaran, V. *Intelligent Support Systems Technology: Knowledge Management*. Hershey, PA: Idea Publishing Group, 2002.

Tiwana, A. *The Essential Guide to Knowledge Management: E-Business and CRM Applications*. Upper Saddle River, NJ: Prentice Hall, 2001.

Urdan, T., and C. Weggen. "Corporate E-Learning: Exploring a New Frontier." W.R. Hambrecht & Co., March 2000, digitalpipe.com/pdf/dp/white_papers/e_learning/corporate_elearning_H_Q.pdf (accessed May 2003).

U.S. Department of Housing and Urban Development. "Electronic Government Strategic Plan: Fiscal Years 2001–2005." February 2001, hud.gov/offices/cio/egov/splan.pdf (accessed June 2003).

von Hoffman, C. "For Better or for Worse." *CIO Magazine*, June 1, 2001.

Warkentin, M., et al. "Encouraging Citizen Adoption of E Government by Building Trust." *Electronic Markets* 12, no. 3 (2002).

Weaver, P. "Preventing E-Learning Failure." *Training and Development* 56, no. 8 (2002): 45–50.

WebCT. "WebCT Learning Transformations." webct.com/transform (accessed June 2002a).

WebCT. "WebCT: About Us." webct.com/company (accessed June 2002b).

Weiss, A. "Click to Vote." *Communications of the ACM* 5, no. 1 (2001): 18–24.

Wimmer, M. A. "Integrated Service Modeling for Online One-Stop Government." *Electronic Markets* 12, no. 3 (2002).

Wong, W. Y. *At the Dawn of E-Government*. New York: Deloitte and Touche Study Report, Deloitte & Touche, 2000.

Xerox.com. "Eureka." parc.com/groups/spl/projects/commknowledge/eureka.html (accessed October 2002).

Zhao, J. L., and V. H. Resh. "Internet Publishing and Transformation of Knowledge Processes." *Communications of the ACM* (December 2001).

MOBILE COMMERCE AND PERVASIVE COMPUTING

Learning objectives

Upon completion of this chapter, you will be able to:

1. Discuss the characteristics and attributes of m-commerce.
2. Describe the drivers of m-commerce.
3. Understand the technologies that support m-commerce.
4. Describe wireless standards and transmission networks.
5. Discuss m-commerce applications in finance, advertising, and provision of content.
6. Describe the applications of m-commerce within organizations.
7. Understand B2B and supply chain applications of m-commerce.
8. Describe consumer and personal applications of m-commerce.
9. Describe some non-Internet m-commerce applications.
10. Describe location-based commerce.
11. Discuss the key characteristics and current uses of pervasive computing.
12. Describe the major inhibitors and barriers of m-commerce.

Content

NEXTBUS: A SUPERB CUSTOMER SERVICE

The Problem

Buses in certain parts of San Francisco have difficulty keeping up with the posted schedule, especially during rush hours. Buses are scheduled to arrive every 20 minutes, but at times passengers may have to wait 30 to 40 minutes. The scheduled times become meaningless.

The Solution

San Francisco implemented a system called NextBus (*nextbus.com*). The system tracks public transportation buses in *real time*. Knowing where each bus is and factoring in traffic patterns and weather reports, NextBus calculates the estimated arrival time of the bus to each bus stop on the route. San Francisco bus riders carrying an Internet-enabled wireless device, such as a cell phone or Palm or other PDA, can quickly find out when a bus is likely to arrive at a particular bus stop. The arrival times also are displayed in real time on the Internet and on a public screen at each bus stop.

The NextBus system has been used successfully in several other cities around the United States, in Finland, and in several other countries. Exhibit 10.1 (page 384) shows how the NextBus system works. The core of the NextBus system is the GPS satellites that let the NextBus information center know where a bus is located. Based on a bus's location, the scheduled arrival time at each stop can be calculated.

Currently, NextBus is an ad-free customer service, but in the near future advertising may be added. Because the system knows exactly where a rider is when they request information and how much time they have until their next bus, in the future, the system may send the rider to the nearest Starbucks for a cup of coffee, giving them an electronic $1 discount coupon.

The Results

Passengers in San Francisco are happy with the system; worries about missing the bus are diminished. Passengers may even discover they have time for a cup of coffee before the bus arrives! In rural areas in Finland, where buses are infrequent and the winters are very cold, passengers can stay in a warm coffeehouse not far from the bus stop rather than wait in the cold for a bus that may be an hour late. A bus company can also use the system to improve scheduling, arrange for extra buses when needed, and make its operations more efficient.

Sources: Compiled from Murphy (1999) and *nextbus.com* (2003).

WHAT WE CAN LEARN . . .

This opening vignette is an example of location-based e-commerce. This application is a major part of mobile commerce, in which EC services are provided to customers wherever they are located. This capability, which is not available in regular EC, may change many things in our lives. The vignette also exemplifies *pervasive computing*, in which services are seamlessly blended into the environment without the user being aware of the technology behind the scenes. The technologies, applications, and limitations of mobile commerce will be the main focus of this chapter. Later in the chapter, the technologies and EC applications of pervasive computing will be examined.

EXHIBIT 10.1   NextBus Operational Model

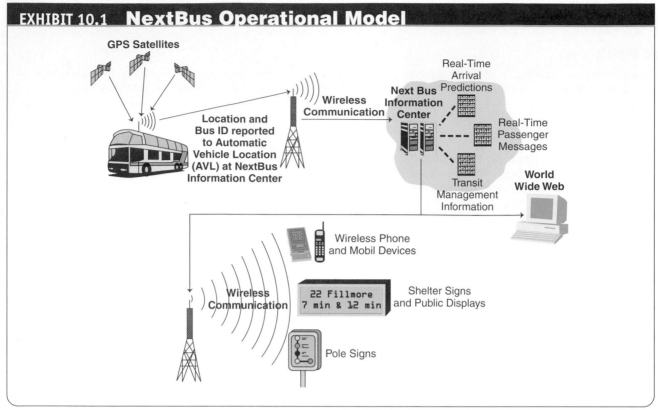

mobile commerce (m-commerce, m-business)
Any e-commerce done in a wireless environment, especially via the Internet.

1G
The first generation of wireless technology, which was analog based.

2G
The second generation of digital wireless technology; accommodates mainly text.

2.5G
Interim wireless technology that can accommodate limited graphics.

3G
The third generation of digital wireless technology; supports rich media such as video clips.

10.1   MOBILE COMMERCE: OVERVIEW, BENEFITS, AND DRIVERS

Mobile commerce, also known as m-commerce and m-business, is basically any e-commerce or e-business done in a wireless environment, especially via the Internet. Like regular EC applications, m-commerce can be done via the Internet, private communication lines, or other infrastructures.

M-commerce is not merely a variation on existing Internet services; it is a natural extension of e-business. Mobile devices create an opportunity to deliver new services to existing customers and to attract new ones. Varshney and Vetter (2001) classified the applications of m-commerce into 12 categories, as shown in Exhibit 10.2. This classification covers most of the applications that existed in 2001. (A classification by industry is provided at mobile.commerce.net. Also see mobiforum.org.)

M-COMMERCE TERMINOLOGY

Let's begin our discussion by defining some common m-commerce terms. Common m-commerce terms include the following:

▶ **1G.** The first generation of wireless technology. It was an analog-based technology in effect from 1979 to 1992.

▶ **2G.** The second generation of digital wireless technology. In existence today, 2G is based on digital radio technology and mainly accommodates text.

▶ **2.5G.** An interim technology based on GPRS (General Packet Radio Service, a new cell phone standard) and EDGE (Enhanced Data GSM Environment) (see Exhibit 10.6) that can accommodate limited graphics.

▶ **3G.** The third generation of digital wireless technology, which will support rich media such as video clips. It started in 2001 in Japan, reached Europe in 2002, and is expected

EXHIBIT 10.2 Classes of M-Commerce Applications

Class of Applications	Examples
Mobile financial applications (B2C, B2B)	Banking, brokerage, and payments for mobile users
Mobile advertising (B2C)	Sending user-specific and location-sensitive advertisements to users
Mobile inventory management (B2C, B2B)	Location tracking of goods, boxes, troops, and people
Proactive service management (B2C, B2B)	Transmission of information related to distributing components to vendors
Product locating and shopping (B2C, B2B)	Locating/ordering certain items from a mobile device
Wireless reengineering (B2C, B2B)	Improvement of business services
Mobile auction or reverse auction (B2C)	Services for customers to buy or sell certain items
Mobile entertainment services (B2C)	Video-on-demand and other services to a mobile user
Mobile office (B2C)	Working from traffic jams, airport, and conferences
Mobile distance education (B2C)	Taking a class using streaming audio and video
Wireless data center (B2C, B2B)	Information can be downloaded by mobile users/vendors
Mobile music/music-on-demand (B2C)	Downloading and playing music using a mobile device

Source: Varshney, U. and R. Vetter. "Recent Advances in Wireless Networking." *IEEE Computer 33*, no. 6 (2001): 100–103. © IEEE.

to reach the United States in 2003. As of 2003, the number of 3G cell phones in operation was around 130 million (a small percentage of the total number of cell phones in use today) (CellularOnline 2003a).

▶ **4G.** The expected next generation after 3G. The arrival of 4G, which will provide faster display of multimedia, is expected between 2006 and 2010.

▶ **Global positioning system (GPS).** This is a satellite-based tracking system that enables the determination of a GPS device's location. (See Section 10.9 for more on GPS.)

▶ **Personal digital assistant (PDA).** A small portable computer, such as the family of Palm handhelds, the offerings from Handspring, and the Pocket PC devices from companies such as HP.

▶ **Short Message Service (SMS).** A technology in existence since 1991 that allows for the sending of short text messages (up to 160 characters in 2002) on certain cell phones. Data are borne by the radio resources reserved in cellular networks for locating mobile devices and connecting calls. SMS messages can be sent or received concurrently, even during a voice or data call. Used by hundreds of millions of users, SMS is known as the e-mail of m-commerce.

▶ **Enhanced Messaging Service (EMS).** An extension of SMS that is capable of simple animation, tiny pictures, and short melodies.

▶ **Multimedia Messaging Service (MMS).** The next generation of wireless messaging; this technology will be able to deliver rich media.

▶ **Wireless Application Protocol (WAP).** A technology that offers Internet browsing from wireless devices (see Section 10.3).

▶ **Smartphones.** Internet-enabled cell phones that can support mobile applications. These "phones with a brain" are becoming standard devices. They include WAP microprocessors for Internet access.

THE ATTRIBUTES AND BENEFITS OF M-COMMERCE

Generally speaking, many of the EC applications described in this book can be done in m-commerce. For example, e-shopping, e-banking, e-stock trading, and e-gambling are gaining popularity in wireless B2C. Auctioning is just beginning to take place on cell phones, and wireless collaborative commerce in B2B is emerging. Wireless, non-Internet intrabusiness applications have been in use since the early 1990s. However, several new applications are

4G
The expected next generation of wireless technology.

personal digital assistant (PDA)
A handheld wireless computer.

Short Message Service (SMS)
Technology that allows for sending of short text messages on some cell phones.

Enhanced Messaging Service (EMS)
An extension of SMS capable of simple animation, tiny pictures, and short tunes.

Multimedia Messaging Service (MMS)
The next generation of wireless messaging; will be able to deliver rich media.

smartphone
Internet-enabled cell phones that can support mobile applications.

possible only in the mobile environment. To understand why this is so, let's examine the major attributes of m-commerce.

The Specific Attributes of M-Commerce

M-commerce has two major characteristics that differentiate it from other forms of e-commerce: mobility and broad reach.

▶ **Mobility.** M-commerce is based on the fact that users carry a cell phone or other mobile device everywhere they go. Mobility implies portability. Therefore, users can initiate a *real-time* contact with commercial and other systems from wherever they happen to be.

▶ **Broad reach.** With m-commerce, people can be reached at any time. Of course, users can block certain hours or certain messages, but when users carry an open mobile device, they can be reached instantly.

These two characteristics break the barriers of geography and time. As shown in Exhibit 10.3, they create five value-added attributes (discussed next). The benefits from these value-added attributes will drive the commercial development of m-commerce.

Ubiquity. Ubiquity refers to the attribute of being available at any location at any given time. A mobile terminal in the form of a smartphone or a PDA can fulfill the need both for *real-time information* and for communication independent of the user's location. It creates easier information access in a real-time environment.

Convenience. It is very convenient for users to operate in the wireless environment. All they need is a smartphone. The technology is making rapid progress. Soon, using GPRS, it will be easier and faster to access information on the Web without booting up a PC or placing a call via a modem.

Instant connectivity. Mobile devices enable users to connect easily and quickly to the Internet, intranets, other mobile devices, and databases. Thus, the new wireless devices could become the preferred way to access information.

Personalization. Product personalization enables the preparation of information for individual consumers. For example, a user who is identified as someone who likes to travel might be sent travel-related information and advertisements. Product personalization is still limited on mobile devices. However, the emerging need for conducting transactions electronically, combined with the availability of personalized information and transaction feasibility via mobile portals, will move personalization to new levels, leading ultimately to the mobile device becoming a major EC tool.

Localization of products and services. Knowing where a user is physically located at any particular moment is key to offering relevant services. Such services are known as location-based e-commerce, or l-commerce. Precise location information is known when a GPS is attached to a user's wireless device. GPS may be a standard feature in mobile devices by 2004. For example, a user might use their mobile device to find the nearest ATM or FedEx drop box. Localization can be general, to anyone in a certain location (e.g., all shoppers at a shopping mall). Or, even better, it can be targeted so that users get messages that depend both on where they are and what their preferences are, thus combining localization and personalization. For instance, if it is known that a person likes Italian food and they are strolling in a

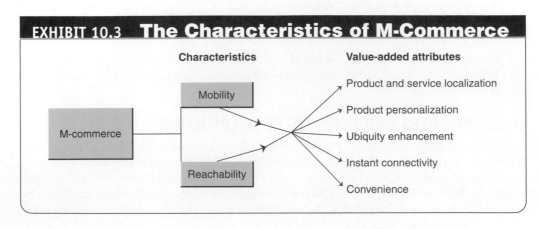

EXHIBIT 10.3   The Characteristics of M-Commerce

Characteristics

Value-added attributes

M-commerce

Mobility

Reachability

Product and service localization

Product personalization

Ubiquity enhancement

Instant connectivity

Convenience

mall that has an Italian restaurant, they might receive a SMS that tells them that restaurant's "special of the day" and offers a 10 percent discount.

Vendors and carriers can *differentiate* themselves in the competitive marketplace by offering new, exciting, and useful services based on these attributes. Such services will help vendors attract and keep customers and grow their revenues. In turn, the increasing number of value-added services will facilitate the use of m-commerce.

DRIVERS OF M-COMMERCE

In addition to the value-added attributes just discussed, m-commerce is driven by the following factors.

Widespread availability of devices. The number of cell phones throughout the world exceeds 1.3 billion (CellularOnline 2003b). Over the past few years, the growth rate in cell phone production has stagnated, although it has started to quicken over the last half of 2002. Over 35 percent of the new phones in production have color screens (Pilato 2002). It is estimated that within a few years, about 70 percent of cell phones will have Internet access (Dignan and Charny 2001). Thus, a potential mass market is available for conducting m-commerce. Cell phones are spreading quickly in developing countries. In 2002, for example, the number of cell phones in China exceeded 200 million, virtually equaling the number of fixed line phones in that country (CellularOnline 2003a).

No need for a PC. Because the Internet can be accessed via smartphone or other Internet-enabled wireless device, a PC is not needed to access the Internet. Even though the cost of a PC that is used primarily for Internet access can be as low as $500 (or even less), it is still a major expense for the vast majority of people in the world. Furthermore, one needs to learn how to operate a PC, service it, and replace it every few years to keep it up-to-date.

The handset culture. The widespread use of cell phones is becoming a social phenomenon, especially among the 15-to-25-year-old age group. These users will constitute a major force of online buyers once they begin to make and spend reasonable amounts of money. For example, the use of SMS has been spreading like wildfire in several European and Asian countries. In the Philippines, SMS is a national phenomenon in the youth market.

Vendors' push. Both mobile communication network operators and manufacturers of mobile devices are advertising the many potential applications of m-commerce so that they can push new technologies, products, and services to buyers.

Declining prices. With the passage of time, the price of wireless devices is declining, and the per-minute pricing of mobile services is expected to decline by 50 to 80 percent before 2005. At the same time, functionalities are increasing.

Improvement of bandwidth. To properly conduct m-commerce, it is necessary to have sufficient bandwidth for transmitting text; however, bandwidth is also required for voice, video, and multimedia. The 3G technology is expected to provide that, at a data rate of up to 2 mbps. This enables information to move seven times faster than when 56K modems are used.

M-COMMERCE VALUE CHAIN

Like EC, m-commerce is a complex process involving a number of operations and a number of players (customers, merchants, mobile operators, and the like). The key elements in the m-commerce value chain (the delivery of m-commerce content and applications to end users) are summarized in Exhibit 10.4 (page 388).

Section 10.1 ❱ REVIEW

1. Define m-commerce.
2. Define the following terms: 3G, PDA, WAP, SMS, GPS, and smartphone.
3. List the value-added attributes of m-commerce.
4. List at least five major drivers of m-commerce.
5. Briefly describe the key elements of the m-commerce value chain.

EXHIBIT 10.4   M-Commerce Value Chain

Link	Function	Provider
Transport	Maintenance and operation of the infrastructure supporting data communication between mobile users and application providers	Technology platform vendors
Enabling services	Server hosting, data backup, and system integration	Infrastructure equipment vendors
Transaction support	Mechanisms for assisting with transactions, security, and billing	Application platform vendor
Presentation services	Convert content of Web-based applications to applications suitable for mobile devices	Application developer
Personalization support	Gather users' preferences, information, and devices in order to provide individualized applications	Content developer
User applications	General and specialized applications for mobile users	Mobile service provider
Content aggregators	Design and operate portals that offer categorized information and search facilities	Mobile portal provider

Source: Siau, K., et al. "Mobile Commerce: Promises, Challenges, and Research Agenda." *Journal of Database Management 12*, no. 2 (2001). 4–13.

10.2   MOBILE COMPUTING INFRASTRUCTURE

Mobile computing requires hardware, software, and networks. The major components of mobile computing are described in this section.

M-COMMERCE HARDWARE

To conduct m-commerce, one needs devices for data entry and access to the Internet, applications, and other equipment. Several mobile computing devices are used in m-commerce. The major ones include the following:

- **Cellular (mobile) phones.** All major cell phone manufacturers are making or plan to make Internet-enabled cell phones. These cell phones are improving with time, adding more features, larger screens, keyboards, and more. Users can even play games and download music files. An example of an Internet-enabled cell phone is the Nokia 3510i. The Nokia 3510i includes Internet access, MMS, support for small Java applications (such as games), a calculator, scheduling tools, an address book, and more. Note that even phones without screen displays can be used to retrieve voice information from the Web (see tellme.com and the discussion of voice portals in Section 10.2).

- **Attachable keyboard.** Transactions can be executed with the regular handset entry keys, but it is fairly time-consuming to do so. An alternative is to use a larger cell phone such as the Nokia 9290 that contains a small-scale keyboard. Yet another solution is to plug an attachable keyboard into the cell phone. (Attachable keyboards are also available for other wireless devices, such as PDAs.)

- **PDAs.** PDAs with Internet access are now available from several vendors, and their capabilities are increasing. One example of an Internet-ready PDA is Palm's i705. Using special software, users can connect the PDA to the Internet via a wireless modem. PDAs for corporate users include additional capabilities, such as e-mail synchronization and exchange of data and backup files with corporate servers. (Examples of such PDAs are Jornada from HP, IPAQ from Compaq, and MobilePro from NEC.)

- **Interactive pagers.** Some two-way pagers can be used to conduct limited m-commerce activities on the Internet (mainly sending and receiving text messages, such as stock market orders).

- **Screenphones.** A telephone equipped with a color screen, possibly a keyboard, e-mail, and Internet capabilities is referred to as a screenphone. Initially, these were *wirelined*; that is, they were regular phones connected by wires to a network. Today, wireless screenphones are available. Some are portable. They are used mainly for e-mail.

- **E-mail handhelds.** To enhance wireless e-mail capabilities, one can use devices such as the BlackBerry Handheld (blackberry.net). This device includes a keypad, making it easy

screenphone

A telephone equipped with a color screen, possibly a keyboard, e-mail, and Internet capabilities.

to type messages. It is an integrated package, so there is no need to dial into an Internet provider for access. A variety of services for data communication are available, so users can receive and send messages from anywhere. A product demo is available at blackberry.net. Enterprise and home/personal solutions are available.

▶ **Other devices.** Notebooks, handhelds, and other mobile computers can be used in m-commerce. Many other wireless support devices are on the market. For example, with the Seiko SmartPad (siibusinessproducts.com), users can write from a notepad instantly to a cell phone or PDA screen, overcoming the device's small screen size. Portable PCs have been able to access the Internet since the early 1990s. Some new cell phones have built-in cameras; users can take a picture and e-mail it from their mobile location.

There is a clear trend toward the *convergence* of PDAs and cell phones. PDA manufacturers are providing PDAs with cellular or wireless capabilities. Handspring (handspring.com), for example, offers a series of PDA products (its TREOs line) that combine phone and Palm Organizer capabilities. Similarly, HP offers the Jornada 928 WDA that combines cellular capabilities with the PDA functions of an IPAQ Pocket PC. Cellular phone manufacturers and systems providers are offering phones with PDA capabilities. For example, the Nokia 9210 Communicator combines a cell phone with Internet browsing, calendaring, address book, word processing, and spreadsheet capabilities. Kyocera (kyrocera.com) also offers a state-of-the-art "smartphone" with wireless e-mail, Web surfing, PDA, and MP3 functionality.

In addition to the hardware described earlier, m-commerce also requires the following infrastructure hardware, most of which the user does not see or know about, but which is essential for wireless connectivity:

▶ A suitably configured wireline or wireless WAN modem, wireless LAN adapter, or wireless MAN (metro-area network) adapter.

▶ A Web server with wireless support, a WAP gateway, a communications server, and/or a mobile communications server switch (MCSS). Such a Web server provides communications functionality that enables the handheld device to communicate with the Internet or intranet infrastructure (see mobileinfo.com).

▶ An application or database server with application logic and a business application database providing e-commerce functionality.

▶ A GPS locator that is used to determine the location of the person carrying the mobile computing device. This is the basis for location-based applications, as described in Section 10.9. The GPS locator can be attached or inserted into a mobile device.

SOFTWARE

Developing software for wireless devices is challenging because, as of 2002, there was no widely accepted standard for wireless applications. Therefore, software applications need to be customized for each type of device with which the application may communicate. The major software products required for m-commerce include the following:

▶ **Microbrowsers.** Microbrowsers have limited bandwidth and limited memory requirements. They can access the Web via the wireless Internet.

▶ **Mobile-client operating system.** This is the operating system (OS) software that resides in the mobile device. It may be Windows 2000/2001/NT, PalmOS, Win CE (or Pocket PC), EPOC, a specialized OS such as BlackBerry, or a Web browser.

▶ **Bluetooth.** Bluetooth (named after a famous Viking king) is a chip technology that enables voice and data communications between many wireless devices (e.g., between a digital camera and a PC) through low-power, short-range, digital two-way radio frequency (RF). Bluetooth is a wireless personal area network (WPAN) standard backed by most wireless-industry corporations and employed by major corporate users. It is deployed by placing a radio chip and special software into the devices that the user wants to communicate with each other. As of 2003, it is effective only up to 30 meters. The technology enhances ubiquitous connectivity and enables easy data transfer. See bluetooth.com for details.

▶ **Mobile application user interface.** The interface is the application logic in a handheld PDA, smartphone, Palm, or Wintel notebook. In the Internet world, it is often under the control of a browser or microbrowser.

microbrowser
Wireless software designed with limited bandwidth and limited memory requirements.

Bluetooth
Chip technology that enables voice and data communications between many wireless devices through low-power, short-range, digital two-way radio frequencies.

▌ **Back-end legacy application software.** Legacy software that resides on large UNIX servers (from vendors such as Sun, IBM, and HP) or on mainframes is a major part of m-commerce software because it provides the back-end systems (e.g., accounting, inventory).

▌ **Application middleware.** Middleware is a piece of software that communicates with back-end legacy systems and Web-based application servers. IBM's WebSphere is one such example.

▌ **Wireless middleware.** Wireless middleware that links multiple wireless networks to application servers is also needed.

▌ **Wireless Application Protocol.** Wireless Application Protocol (WAP) is a set of communication protocols designed to enable different kinds of wireless devices (e.g., mobile phones, PDAs, pagers, etc.) to talk to a server installed on a mobile network so that users can access the Internet. It was designed especially for small screens and limited bandwidth. It enables the deployment of a microbrowser in mobile devices. WAP is being challenged by several competing standards, including Java-based applications (the J2ME platform), which offer better graphics and security (see wapforum.org).

▌ **Wireless Markup Language.** Wireless Markup Language (WML) is the scripting language used for creating content in the wireless Web environment. It is based on XML, and it removes unnecessary content, such as animation. This simplification increases speed. WML works with WAP to deliver content. WML does not require a keyboard or a mouse.

▌ **Voice XML.** Voice XML (VXML) is an extension of XML designed to accommodate voice.

MOBILE NETWORKS

At the core of most m-commerce applications are mobile networks. The global communications and cellular phone companies operate most of these networks. A very simple mobile system is shown in Exhibit 10.5. At the edge of the system are the mobile handsets. A *mobile handset* consists of two parts: terminal equipment that hosts the applications (e.g., a PDA) and a mobile terminal (e.g., a cell phone) that connects to the mobile network.

Some mobile handsets, especially in Europe, contain a Subscriber Identification Module (SIM) card. This is an extractable storage card that is used not only for identification, but also for providing customer location information, transaction processing, secure

---

Wireless Application Protocol (WAP)

A set of communications protocols designed to enable different kinds of wireless devices to talk to a server installed on a mobile network so users can access the Internet.

Wireless Markup Language (WML)

Scripting language used for creating content in the wireless Web environment; based on XML, minus unnecessary content to increase speed.

Voice XML (VXML)

An extension of XML designed to accommodate voice.

Subscriber Identification Module (SIM) card

An extractable storage card used for identification, transaction processing, and the like.

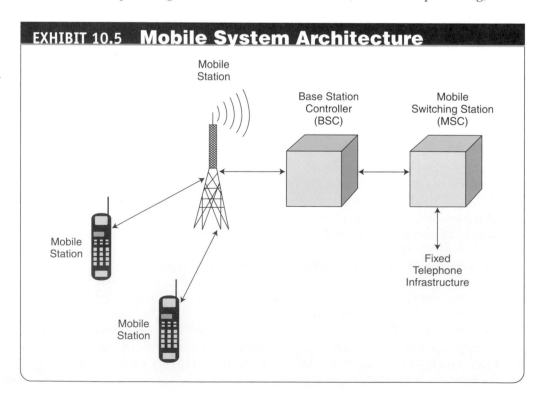

EXHIBIT 10.5   Mobile System Architecture

Mobile Station

Base Station Controller (BSC)

Mobile Switching Station (MSC)

Mobile Station

Mobile Station

Fixed Telephone Infrastructure

communications, and the like. A SIM card makes it possible for a handset to work with multiple phone numbers.

The mobile handset communicates with a *base transceiver station*. There are thousands of these throughout the world. A base transceiver station is connected to a *base station controller* that handles the handoff from one transceiver to next as the customer or user travels from one place to another. The various base station controllers are connected to *mobile switching centers* that connect the mobile network with the public wired phone network.

One of the major problems facing the mobile communication system providers is how to service extremely large numbers of users given limited communication bandwidth. This is done through multiplexing protocols. In today's mobile world, there are three main multiplexing protocols:

- **Frequency Division Multiple Access (FDMA).** Used by 1G systems, this protocol gives each user a different frequency to communicate on.
- **Time Division Multiple Access (TDMA).** Used with some of the more popular 2G systems, this protocol assigns different users different time slots on a given communications channel (e.g., every one-eighth time slot).
- **Code Division Multiple Access (CDMA).** Used with most 3G systems, this protocol separates different users by assigning different codes to the segments of each user's communications.

In today's mobile world, most of the networks rely on either TDMA or CDMA. The relationships between these two multiplexing methods and the major network standards are detailed in Exhibit 10.6, along with the evolution of these standards from today's 2G world to tomorrow's 3G world.

Wireless LANs

For the past few years, much of the discussion about m-commerce has revolved around cellular technologies. Slowly but surely, another technology, which has been around for at least a decade—wireless LANs—has been making its way to the forefront as the market factors

EXHIBIT 10.6 Evolution of Mobile Network Standards

Generation	TDMA		CDMA
2G	**Global System of Mobile Communication (GSM).** This standard has been in existence since 1992. Originally started in Europe, it is by far the most widely deployed standard in the world.	**Personal Digital Cellular (PDC).** Introduced by NTT DoCoMo in 1991, it is only used in Japan.	**CDMAone.** This is an interim wireless communication standard available commercially since October 2000. Considered a 2.75G technology, it is more advanced than 2.5G technologies.
2.5G	**General Packet Radio Services (GPRS).** The next phase of GSM, it provides "always-on," higher capacity, Internet-based content, and packet-based data services.		**CDMA2000 1X.** Provides CDMAone subscribers with enhanced services and speeds of 144 kbps.
3G	**Enhanced Data Rates for Global Evaluation (EDGE).** This is an extension of GSM that leverages GPRS infrastructures. It gives GSM communication speeds up to 384 kbps.	**Wideband-CDMA (W-CDMA).** An evolutionary step for PDC, this 3G technology will offer 2 mbps capacity. **3GSM.** Based on W-CDMA and GSM, it is a standard proposed by the European Technology Standards Institute (ETSI) for next-generation services.	**CDMA2000 1XEV.** The second phase of CDMA2000, providing speeds up to 2 mbps.

wireless LAN (WLAN)
LAN without the cables; used to transmit and receive data over the airwaves.

wireless access point
An antenna connecting a mobile device (laptop or PDA) to a wired LAN.

802.11b
Standard, developed by the IEEE, on which most of today's WLANs run; WLANs employing this standard have communication speeds of 11 mbps.

wireless fidelity (Wi-Fi)
Another name for the 802.11b standard on which most WLANs run.

impeding its growth are being addressed. (See Insights and Additions 10.1 for a discussion of these factors.) As the name implies, a **wireless LAN** or **WLAN** is like a wired LAN but without the cables. WLANs transmit and receive data over the airwaves.

In a typical configuration, a device with an antenna called a **wireless access point** connects to a wired LAN from a fixed location. A wireless access point provides service to a number of users within a small geographical perimeter (up to a couple hundred feet). Several wireless access points are needed to support larger numbers of users across a larger geographical area. End users can access a WLAN with their PCs or PDAs by adding a wireless network card. Recently, many PC manufacturers have begun to incorporate these cards directly in their PCs.

WLANs provide fast and easy Internet or intranet broadband access from public *hotspots* such as airports, hotels and conference centers. WLANs are also being used in universities and homes in place of the traditional wired LANs. This frees users to roam across the campus or throughout their homes.

Most of today's WLANs run on a standard known as **802.11b** that was developed by the IEEE (Institute of Electrical and Electronic Engineers). The standard is also called **Wi-Fi** (for **wireless fidelity**). WLANs employing this standard have communication speeds of 11 mbps. Although most wired networks run at 100 mbps, 11 mbps is sufficient for many applications. Two other new standards, 802.11a and 802.11g, support data transmissions at 54 mbps. The 802.11g standard is beginning to show up in commercial products because it is compatible with the 802.11b standard. PCs can take advantage of these speeds, but today's PDAs cannot because their expansion (network) cards are limited to the 11 mbps speeds.

M-COMMERCE SECURITY ISSUES

In 2001, a hacker sent an e-mail message to 13 million users of the i-Mode wireless data service in Japan. The message had the potential to take over the recipient's phone, causing it to dial Japan's emergency hotline (1-1-0). NTT DoCoMo, which provides the i-Mode service, rapidly fixed the problem so no damage was done. At the beginning of 2002, researchers in Holland discovered a bug in the operating system used by many Nokia phones that would enable a hacker to exploit the system by sending a malformed SMS message capable of crashing the system. Again, no real damage was done.

Today, most of the Internet-enabled cell phones in operation are incapable of storing applications and, in turn, incapable of propagating a virus, worm, or other rogue program from one phone to another. Most of these cell phones also have their operating systems and other functionality "burned" right into the hardware. This makes it difficult for a rogue program to permanently alter the operation of a cell phone. However, as the capabilities of cell phones increase and the functionality of PDAs and cell phones converge, the threat of attack from malicious code will certainly increase.

Just because a mobile device is less susceptible to attack by malicious code does not mean that m-commerce is more secure than e-commerce in the wired world. By their very nature, mobile devices and mobile transactions produce some unique security challenges. These include the following (Raina and Harsh 2002):

▶ **Physical security.** Because of their size, mobile devices are easily stolen. A stolen device can provide the thief with valuable data and digital credentials that can be used to compromise an m-commerce network.

▶ **Transactional issues.** Because transactions eventually get routed over a public network, security must be maintained not only by the mobile carriers, but all the way through to the m-commerce server. This means that m-commerce not only has its own security issues, but also is affected by many of the security issues facing the wired world.

▶ **Post-transaction issues.** Given the need to provide digital receipts or some other type of proof for problem resolution after a transaction has occurred, the overall system must provide some method of proving that a particular transaction has occurred (nonrepudiation).

Because m-commerce transactions eventually end up on the wired Internet, many of the processes, procedures, and technologies used to secure e-commerce transactions also can be applied in mobile environments. Of particular importance is the public key infrastructure

Insights and Additions 10.1   The Barriers to Commercial Wi-Fi Growth

The year 2003 may be a breakthrough year for wireless networking in offices, airports, hotels (see Section 10.8), and campuses around the United States.

Like a number of airports in the United States, the Minneapolis-St. Paul International airport is going Wi-Fi. The Northstar Crossing concession area, the Northwest Airlines' World Club lounge, the United Airlines' Red Carpet Club, and many of the main terminal concourses will provide wireless Internet access to anyone with a laptop or handheld device and a Wi-Fi network card. iPass is hosting the Internet service. The fee is $7.95 for unlimited daily access.

In 2002, T-Mobile installed Wi-Fi networks in approximately 2,000 Starbucks in the United States. Starbucks has plans to add Wi-Fi to 70 percent of its 6,000 locations worldwide over the next few years. T-Mobile is also installing Wi-Fi in hundreds of Borders Books & Music Stores. T-Mobile is charging $30 a month for unlimited access, with walk-in customers paying $2.99 for the first 15 minutes and 25 cents a minute thereafter. The Wi-Fi market got a boost at the end of 2002 when AT&T, Intel, and IBM, along with two global investment firms, joined forces to create Cometa Networks, Inc. Cometa (*cometa.com*) will work with major retail chains, hotels, universities, and real estate firms to deploy Wi-Fi hotspots throughout the top 50 metropolitan areas in the United States.

Two factors are standing in the way of rapid Wi-Fi market growth. First, some analysts question why anyone would pay $30 a month, $7.95 a day, or any other fee for Wi-Fi access when it is readily available in many locations for free. Because it is relatively inexpensive to set up a wireless access point that is connected to the Internet, a number of businesses offer their customers Wi-Fi access without charging them for the service. In fact, one organization, Freenetworks.org, is working toward the creation of free community wireless network projects around the globe. In areas such as San Francisco, where there is a solid core of high-tech professionals, many "gear heads" have set up their own wireless hotspots that give passersby free Internet connections. These Wi-Fi Internet hubs have been marked by symbols on sidewalks and walls to indicate nearby wireless access. This practice is called *war chalking*. It was inspired by the practice of hobos during the Great Depression who used chalk marks to indicate which homes were friendly.

A number of people have also made a hobby or sport out of war driving. *War driving* is the act of locating WLANs while driving around a city or elsewhere (see *wardriving.com*). To do war driving, a person needs a vehicle, a computer or PDA, a wireless card, and some kind of an antenna that can be mounted on top of or positioned inside the car. Because a WLAN may have a range that extends beyond the building in which it is located, an outside user may be able to intrude into the network, obtain a free Internet connection, and possibly gain access to important data and other resources. The term war driving was coined by computer security consultant Peter Shipley and derives from the term *war dialing*, a technique in which a hacker programs their system to call hundreds of phone numbers in search of poorly protected computer dial-ups. The term war dialing came from the movie *War Games*, which features Matthew Broderick performing the technique.

One of the primary aims of people engaged in war driving is to highlight the lax security of Wi-Fi hotspots. This is the second barrier to widespread acceptance of Wi-Fi. Wi-Fi has a built-in security system known as *wireless encryption protocol* (*WEP*), which encrypts the communications between a client machine (laptop or PDA) and a wireless access point. WEP provides weak encryption, meaning that it is secure against casual hacking as long as the person setting up the network remembers to turn it on. Unfortunately, many small businesses owners and homeowners with wireless LANs fail to do just that.

Although WEP offers a measure of security, the trade-off is inconvenience. In order to employ WEP, every Wi-Fi user must be educated in how it works, their computers must be reconfigured to connect to the network, and the encryption code must be changed frequently. Additionally, every authorized user must be given the encryption key, which means that a lot of people will be carrying around the keys to the network. In larger companies, if a hacker can gain access to the encryption key or can get through the WEP security in some other way—which is easily done with readily available software such as AirSnort (*airsnort.shmoo.com*) or WEPCrack (*wepcrack.sourceforge.net*)—the damage is often greater because companies have a habit of installing their wireless access points behind their firewalls (see Section 12.7).

Alternatives to WEP are available. If a company is concerned about the security of wireless data communications, it can use virtual private networking (VPN) technology (see Section 12.7) to create a secure connection over the wireless link. A new Wi-Fi security standard, *Wi-Fi Protective Access* (*WPA*), is under development. This standard has the backing of the Wireless Fidelity Alliance and the IEEE. WPA provides enhanced encryption and supports user authentication, something that was missing from WEP. The alliance has already begun certifying Wi-Fi products with WPA security. This enhanced security may encourage more business to experiment with Wi-Fi over the coming year.

Sources: Kellner (2003) and Fikes (2003).

(PKI; see Section 12.6). Because e-commerce security is detailed in Chapter 12, the discussion that follows will consider only some of the security approaches that apply directly to mobile devices and networks.

SIM-Based Authentication

GSM and its 2.5G and 3G counterparts all include SIM (see Section 10.2). This module is usually implemented as a smart card containing an authentication key along with other vital information about the subscriber. The authentication key also is stored on a "home-location registry," which can be thought of as a database that is part of the mobile (GSM) network. When the phone is turned on, the user is asked to enter a PIN number. This protects the cell phone against illegal use if it happens to be stolen or lost. If the PIN is correct, the cell phone and the network engage in a "challenge-response" process of authentication. A network authentication center sends a random number to the cell phone's SIM. The SIM computes a "signed response" by combining the random number with its authentication key. The signed response is sent over the network to the authentication center, which performs the same computation using a copy of the authentication key stored on the home-location registry. If the signed response matches the value computed by the authentication center, then the cell phone is authenticated. After that, communication takes place through symmetric encryption (see Section 12.6), using a key generated by both the authentication center and the SIM.

Although SIM cards protect against unauthorized use of a particular subscriber's account, they do not prevent the use of a stolen cell phone. If a thief steals a phone, the thief can simply replace the existing SIM card with another one and sell it on the open market. The police in Amsterdam employed an interesting method to thwart this practice (Evers 2001). Using a cell phone's International Mobile Equipment Identity number, the police were able to track down the mobile phone number being used on the stolen phone. Once the number was known, the police employed a special computer program to send out an SMS message to the stolen phone every 3 minutes. The message read, "This handset was nicked; buying or selling it is a crime. The police." Obviously, this made the stolen phone a lot less attractive to prospective buyers.

WTSL and WIM

Despite its shortcomings, WAP (see Section 10.1) has become the de facto standard for delivering Web content to mobile devices. The WAP Forum originated WAP. It was the joint effort of companies such as Ericsson, Nokia, and Motorola. Recently, the WAP Forum merged with Open Mobile Architecture Initiative to become the Open Mobile Alliance Ltd (openmobilealliance.org). This is the alliance that is responsible for specifying the WAP standards.

Exhibit 10.7 provides a high-level overview of the WAP architecture. In this architecture, there are two servers—a WAP gateway and a Web server. Basically, the *WAP gateway* receives a request from a mobile device via a communications tower, translates it into a form that is understandable by a Web server, and passes it on through the wired Internet to the appropriate Web server. In turn, the *Web server* passes the response back to the WAP gateway, which translates it into a form that is understandable by the mobile device. The translated communication is then sent to the communication tower and back to the mobile device.

The transmissions between the WAP gateway and the Web server can be secured through the wired Internet security protocols that will be discussed in Chapter 12 (e.g., PKI, SSL/TSL, the Secure Socket Layer and Transport Layer Security). These protocols cannot be used on the mobile side of the gateway. Instead, WAP relies on the Wireless Transport Layer Security (WTLS). Like its wired counterpart (TSL), WTLS enables encrypted communications between a mobile device and the WAP gateway. Additionally, WTLS supports the key elements of PKI—public and private encryption keys, digital certificates, digital signatures, and the like.

A *wireless identity module (WIM)* also can be used in combination with WTLS. A WIM is a smart card device much like a SIM (and in fact can be implemented on a SIM). It is designed to hold the security keys and digital certificates used by the gateway and the Web server to encrypt/decrypt communications. One of the advantages of a WIM is that it

Wireless Transport Layer Security (WTLS)
Communication protocols that enable encrypted communications between a mobile device and the WAP gateway and support the key elements of electronic payment systems.

EXHIBIT 10.7   WAP Architecture

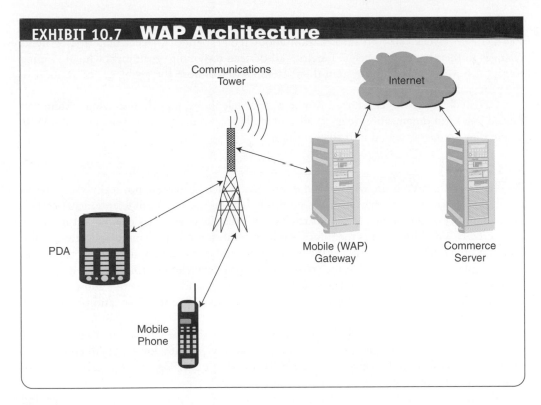

can be issued by a bank or other financial institution to handle m-commerce payments and transactions.

VOICE SYSTEMS FOR M-COMMERCE

The most natural mode of human communication is voice. When people need to communicate with each other from a distance, they use the telephone more frequently than any other communication device. Voice communication can now also be done on the computer using a microphone and a sound card.

Voice and data can work together to create useful applications. For example, operators of PBXs (private branch exchanges, which are basically the command center of intracompany phone systems) are letting callers give simple computer commands using interactive voice response (e.g., spelling the last name of the person one is calling). The number and type of voice technology applications are growing.

Voice technologies have the following advantages:

▶ Hand- and eyes-free operations increase the productivity, safety, and effectiveness of mobile computer users ranging from forklift drivers to military pilots.

▶ Disabled people can use voice commands to tell a computer to perform various tasks.

▶ Voice terminals are designed for portability; users do not have to go to the computer.

▶ Voice terminals are more rugged than keyboards; they operate better in dirty or moving environments.

▶ People can communicate about two-and-a-half times faster talking than typing.

▶ In most circumstances, speaking results in fewer data entry errors than does keyboard data entry, assuming a reliable voice recognition system is used.

One of the most popular conventional voice applications is interactive voice response.

Interactive Voice Response

Interactive voice response (IVR) systems enable users to interact with a computerized system to request and receive information and to enter and change data. These systems have been in use since the 1980s. The communication is conducted through regular telephone lines or through 1G cell phones. Examples of the application of this technology include the

interactive voice response (IVR)
A computer voice system that enables users to request and receive information and to enter and change data through regular telephone lines or through 1G cell phones.

following: Patients can schedule doctors' appointments. Users can request a pick-up from FedEx. Employees can find information about fringe benefits, select benefits, or make changes to their benefits package. Electric utilities can respond to customers who are calling to report power outages; the system then attempts to diagnose the problem and route it to the proper department.

Originally, IVR was conducted from a regular telephone, and the receiving system was hosted inside an organization (e.g., a call center). IVR systems are now moving to the Web, where they are incorporated into voice portals.

Voice Portals

voice portal

A Web site with an audio interface that can be accessed through a telephone call.

A **voice portal** is a Web site with an audio interface. Voice portals are not really Web sites in the normal sense because they are accessed through a standard or a cell telephone. A certain phone number connects the user to a participating Web site where they can request information verbally. The system finds the information, translates it into a computer-generated voice reply, and tells the user what they want to know. Several of these new sites are in operation. An example of this application is the voice-activated 511 traveler information line developed by Tellme.com (see Chapter 2). Sites such as tellme.com and bevocal.com allow callers to request information about the weather, local restaurants, current traffic, and other handy information.

In addition to retrieving information, some sites provide true interaction. One such site, iPing.com (iping.com) is a reminder and notification service that allows users to enter information via the Web and receive reminder calls. In addition, iPing.com can call a group of people to notify them of a meeting or conference call.

The real value for Internet marketers is that these voice portals can help businesses find new customers. Several of these sites are supported by ads; thus, the customer profile data they have available can deliver targeted advertising very precisely. For instance, a department-store chain with an existing brand image can use short audio commercials on these sites to deliver a message related to the topic of the call.

With the development of technical standards and the continuing growth of wireless technologies, the number of m-commerce applications is growing rapidly. Applications are derived from providing wireless access to existing B2C, intrabusiness, and CRM applications and from creating new location-based and SMS-based applications. The next six sections will examine m-commerce applications in a number of diverse categories.

Section 10.2 ▶ REVIEW

1. Describe the major hardware devices used for mobile computing.
2. List the major software items used for mobile computing.
3. Describe the major components of a mobile network.
4. Define FDMA, TDMA, and CDMA.
5. List the major standards used by mobile phone systems (e.g., GSM).
6. Describe the major components of a WLAN.
7. List some of the key security issues in an m-commerce transaction.
8. Describe the security issues and key solutions in m-commerce.
9. Describe IVR.
10. List some of the uses of voice portals.

10.3 MOBILE FINANCIAL APPLICATIONS

Mobile financial applications are likely to be a key driver for consumer-focused m-commerce. These applications include mobile banking, bill payment services, m-brokerage services, mobile money transfers, and mobile micropayments. Although many of these services are simply a subset of their online counterparts, they have the potential to turn a mobile device into a business tool, replacing banks, ATMs, and credit cards by letting a user conduct financial transactions with a mobile device.

MOBILE BANKING

Throughout Europe, the United States, and Asia, a large percentage of banks offer mobile access to financial and account information. For instance, Citibank has a diversified mobile banking service. Consumers can use their mobile handsets to access account balances, pay bills, and transfer funds using SMS. The Royal Bank of Scotland uses a mobile payment service provided by Magex (Lipset 2002). Many banks in Japan allow for all banking transactions to be done via cell phone. For example, one online bank, Japan Net Bank, allows customers to pay for goods and services from their cell phones, debiting their purchases from their accounts. In the same vein, a study of banks in Germany, Switzerland, and Austria found that over 60 percent offered some form of mobile financial service (Hornberger and Kehlenbeck 2002).

To date, the uptake of mobile banking has been minimal. Yet surveys indicate there is strong latent demand for these offerings that is waiting for the technology and transmission speeds to improve. The same picture holds true for other mobile financial applications such as mobile brokering.

WIRELESS ELECTRONIC PAYMENT SYSTEMS

Wireless payment systems transform mobile phones into secure, self-contained purchasing tools capable of instantly authorizing payments over the cellular network for goods and services. In Italy, for example, DPS-Promatic has designed and installed the first parking meter payable by mobile telephone (DPS-Promatic 2002). The service was developed in cooperation with Vodafone Omnitel and the local Park and Transport authority. In the United States, Cellbucks (cellbucks.com) offers a mobile payment service to participating sports stadiums that enables fans to purchase food, beverages, and merchandise by cell phone and have it delivered to their seats. The stadium supplies fans with a menu of choices. Any fan who is a member of the Cellbucks Network can dial a toll-free number provided on the menu, enter their pass code and seat location, and then select numbered items that correspond to desired menu selections. Once the fan's purchase has been validated and authorized, the order is passed on to the stadium and then the purchase is delivered to the fan's seat. An e-mail detailing the transaction is sent to the fan as further confirmation of the order.

MICROPAYMENTS

Micropayments are electronic payments for small-purchase amounts (generally less than $10). The demand for wireless micropayment systems is fairly high. An A.T. Kearney study (CyberAtlas 2002) found that more that 40 percent of the mobile phone users surveyed would like to use their mobile phone for small cash transactions such as transit fares or vending machines. The study noted that the desire for this sort of service was highest in Japan (50 percent) and lowest in the United States (38 percent). The percentage of mobile phone users who had actually used their phones for this purpose was only 2 percent, reflecting the fact that few systems offer micropayments.

micropayments
Electronic payments for small-purchase amounts (generally less than $10).

An Israeli firm, TeleVend, Inc. (televend.com), has pioneered a secure platform that allows subscribers to make payments using mobile phones of any type on any cellular infrastructure. A customer places a mobile phone call to a number stipulated by the merchant to authorize a vending device to dispense the service. Connecting to a TeleVend server, the user selects the appropriate transaction option to authorize payment. Billing can be made to the customer's bank or credit card account or to the mobile phone bill.

Micropayment technology has wide-ranging applications, such as making payments to parking garages, restaurants, grocery stores, and public utilities. The success of micropayment applications depends on the costs of the transactions. Transaction costs will be small only if there is a large volume of transactions. See Chapter 13 for more about micropayments.

WIRELESS WALLETS

Financial transactions can be made on the Web using what is called an *e-wallet*. As we will discuss in more detail in Chapter 13, an e-wallet is a piece of software that stores an online shopper's credit card numbers and other personal information so that the shopper does not have to reenter that information for every online purchase.

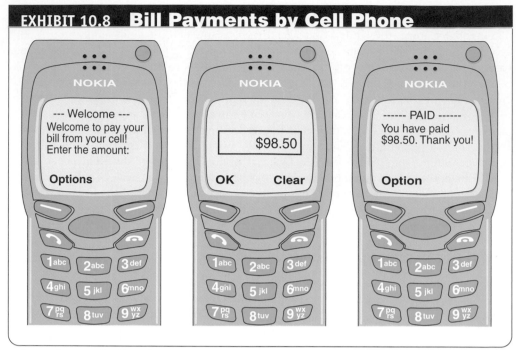

EXHIBIT 10.8   Bill Payments by Cell Phone

Source: Courtesy of Nokia, *nokia.com.*

m-wallet (mobile wallet)

A wireless wallet that enables cardholders to make purchases with a single click from their wireless device.

In the recent past, companies such as SNAZ offered m-wallet (mobile wallet) technologies that enabled cardholders to make purchases with a single click from their mobile devices. Although most of these companies are now defunct, some cell phone providers have incorporated m-wallets into their offerings. A good example is the Nokia wallet. This application provides users with a secure storage space in their phones for information (e.g., credit card numbers) to be used in mobile payments. The information can also be used to authenticate transactions by signing them digitally.

BILL PAYMENTS

In addition to paying bills with checks or through online banking, a number of companies are now providing their customers with the option of paying their bills directly from a cell phone (Lipset 2003). HDFC Bank of India (hdfcbank.com) provides customers with the means to pay their utility bills through SMS. Similarly, a number of mobile service and network providers such as Far EasTone of Taiwan allow their customers to pay their bills by phone. An example of how bill payments can be made using a mobile device is shown in Exhibit 10.8.

Section 10.3 ❱ REVIEW

1. Describe some of the services provided by mobile banking.
2. Discuss mobile micropayments.
3. Describe the m-wallet and wireless bill payments.

10.4   MOBILE SHOPPING, ADVERTISING, AND CONTENT-PROVIDING

Like EC, m-commerce B2C applications are concentrated in three areas—retail shopping, advertising, and providing content for a fee.

SHOPPING FROM WIRELESS DEVICES

Many vendors allow customers to shop from wireless devices. For example, customers who use Internet-ready cell phones can shop at certain sites such as mobile.yahoo.com or amazon.com. Shopping from wireless devices enables customers to perform quick searches, compare prices, order, and view the status of their order using their cell phones or wireless PDAs. Wireless shoppers are supported by services similar to those available for wireline shoppers. For example, users have access to shopping carts, as well as product search and price comparison tools.

Cell phone users also can participate in online auctions. For example, eBay offers "anywhere wireless" services. Account holders at eBay can access their accounts, browse, search, bid, and rebid on items from any Internet-enabled phone or PDA. The same is true for participants in Amazon.com auctions.

TARGETED ADVERTISING

Using demographic information collected by wireless services, Barnesandnoble.com, which launched its wireless service for mobile devices in 1999, now provides more personalization of services and an enhanced user interface for its wireless Web page. In one improvement, the company added music clips to its wireless Web page so that customers can download and listen to the clips on their cell phones.

Knowing the current location of mobile users (using GPS) and their preferences or surfing habits, marketers can send user-specific advertising messages. Advertisements can also be location sensitive, informing a user about various ongoing special sales in shops, malls, and restaurants close to where a potential buyer is. SMS messages or short paging messages can be used to deliver this type of advertising to cell phones and pagers, respectively. Many companies are capitalizing on targeted advertising, as shown in Insights and Additions W10.1 at the book's Web site.

As more wireless bandwidth becomes available, content-rich advertising involving audio, pictures, and video clips will be generated for individual users with specific needs, interests, and inclinations. Also, depending on the interests and personality types of individual mobile users, the network provider may consider using "push" or "pull" methods of mobile advertising on a per user basis or to a class of users (segmentation). The number of ads pushed to an individual customer should be limited to avoid overwhelming a user with too much information and also to avoid the possibility of congestion over the wireless networks. Wireless network managers may consider ad traffic to be of a lower priority compared with ordering or customer interaction. Finally, because ad pushers need to know a user's current location, a third-party vendor may be used to provide location services. This will require a sharing of revenues with a location service provider.

Getting Paid to Listen to Advertising

Would you be willing to listen to a 10-second ad when you dial your cell phone if you were paid 2 minutes of free long-distance time? It depends on which country you are in. In the United States, this service was a flop in most places and was discontinued. However, in Singapore, it works very well. Within a few months of offering the ads, thousands of people subscribed to the free minutes in exchange for listening to the ads offered by SingTel Mobile (Eklund 2001).

SingTel operates its program in partnership with Spotcast. In exchange for Spotcast's software platform, SingTel paid the Maryland-based company $600,000 and will continue to pay ongoing maintenance fees. Spotcast's technology enables SingTel to build increasingly accurate profiles of subscribers and target ads to them. SingTel recouped its initial investment from ad revenues in about a year.

Subscribers to SingTel's service fill out a personal questionnaire when they sign up. This information is fed into the Spotcast database and encrypted to shield subscribers' identities—Spotcast cannot match phone numbers to names, for example. To collect their free minutes—1 minute per call, up to 100 minutes a month—subscribers dial a four-digit code, then the phone number of the person they want to talk to. The code prompts SingTel to forward the call to Spotcast and, in an instant, Spotcast's software finds the best ad to send to the subscriber based on the subscriber's profile.

The Future of Wireless Advertising

In 2001, the Yankee Group concluded that the U.S. wireless advertising market would be worth only $10 million by 2004, substantially below earlier estimates that pegged the market at $130 million by that year (Yankee Group 2001). Although there is no way to verify their figures, it is certainly true that the wireless advertising initiatives to date have all been "trials." As the Yankee

Group noted, the most promising avenues of success for wireless advertising will incorporate it with other advertising media (e.g., hardcopy advertising that directs consumers to wireless or mobile ads offering incentives) or wireless ads directing users to Web sites or physical locations. According to the Yankee Group, many wireless advertising firms are betting their futures on the wide-scale acceptance of SMS, even in the United States, where its usage is small.

MOBILE PORTALS

mobile portal

A customer interaction channel that aggregates content and services for mobile users.

A mobile portal is a customer channel optimized for mobility that aggregates and provides content and services for mobile users. (See Chapter 2 for additional discussion.) Examples of pure mobile portals (those whose only business is to be a mobile portal) in Europe are Room 33 (room33.com) and Sonera Zed (zed.com). Increasingly, the field is being dominated by a few big companies (Global Mobile Suppliers Association 2002). In Europe, for instance, the big players are companies such as Vodafone, Orange, O2, and T-Mobile; in the United States, its companies such as Cingular, Verizon, and Sprint PCS. The services provided by these larger portals are virtually the same and include news, sports, e-mail, entertainment, travel information, restaurant and event information, leisure-related services (e.g. games, TV and movie listings), community services, and stock trading. A sizeable percentage of the portals also provide downloads and messaging, music-related services, and health, dating, and job information.

Mobile portals charge for their services. For example, a user may be asked to pay 50 cents to get a weather report over their mobile phone. Alternatively, users may pay a monthly fee for the portal service and get the report free any time they want it. In Japan, for example, i-Mode generates revenue mainly from subscription fees.

Section 10.4 ▶ REVIEW

1. Describe how mobile devices can be used to shop.
2. Explain targeted advertising in the wireless environment.
3. Describe mobile portals and the types of information they provide.

10.5 MOBILE INTRABUSINESS AND ENTERPRISE APPLICATIONS

Although B2C m-commerce is getting considerable publicity, most of today's applications are used within organizations. This section looks at how mobile devices and technologies can be used *within* organizations.

SUPPORT OF MOBILE EMPLOYEES

Roughly 165 million people worldwide are mobile workers. About 90 million use notebook computers, and 30 million use handheld computers known as PDAs (Takahashi 2002). Examples of mobile workers are salespeople in the field, traveling executives, telecommuters, people working in corporate yards and warehouses, and repair or installation employees who work at customers' sites or on utility lines. These mobile employees need the same corporate data available to employees working inside the company's offices. However, wireline devices may be inconvenient or impossible when employees are away from their offices.

The solution is a myriad of small, simple wireless devices—the smartphones and handheld companions carried by mobile workers and the in-vehicle information systems installed in cars.

Wearable Devices

wearable devices

Mobile wireless computing devices for employees who work on buildings and other difficult-to-climb places.

Employees who work on buildings, electrical poles, or other difficult-to-climb places may be equipped with a special form of mobile wireless computing devices called wearable devices. Examples of wearable devices include:

▶ **Cameras.** A camera is mounted on a safety hat. Workers can take digital photos and videos and transmit them instantly to a nearby portable computer. Photo transmission to a wearable device or computer is made possible via Bluetooth technology.

▶ **Screen.** A computer screen is mounted on a safety hat, in front of the worker's eyes, displaying information to the worker.

> **Keyboard.** A wrist-mounted keyboard enables typing by the other hand. It is an alternative to voice recognition systems, which are also wireless.

> **Touch-panel display.** In addition to the wrist-mounted keyboard, mobile employees can use a flat-panel screen, attached to the hand, that responds to the tap of a finger or stylus.

For an example of wearable devices used to support mobile employees, see EC Application Case W10.1 at the book's Web site and wearable.com.au.

Job Dispatch

Mobile devices are becoming an increasingly integral part of groupware and workflow applications. For example, nonvoice mobile services can be used to assign jobs to mobile employees, along with detailed information about the task. The target areas for mobile delivery and dispatch services include the following: transportation (delivery of food, oil, newspapers, cargo, courier services, tow trucks); taxis (already in use in Korea and Singapore); utilities (gas, electricity, phone, water); field services (computer, office equipment, home repair); health care (visiting nurses, doctors, social services); and security (patrols, alarm installation).

A dispatching solution enables improved response with reduced resources, real-time tracking of work orders, increased dispatcher efficiency, and a reduction in administrative work. AirIQ (edispatch.com) offers an interesting solution. AirIQ's OnLine system combines Internet, wireless, GPS, digital mapping, and intelligent information technologies. The system tracks vital information about a vehicle's direction, speed, and location which is provided by AirIQ's Onboard mobile application housed in each of the vehicles being tracked. Managers can view and access information about the fleet on digital maps, monitor vehicles on the Internet, and maintain top operating condition of their fleet. The company promises savings of about 30 percent in communication costs and increases in workforce efficiency of about 25 percent.

EC Application Case 10.1 (page 402) provides a detailed description of a job-dispatching system that U.S. Fleet has used to benefit both itself and its customers.

CUSTOMER SUPPORT

Supporting customers is the essence of CRM systems. Mobile access extends the reach of CRM—both inside and outside the company, to employees and partners alike on a 24/7 basis. According to Harte-Hanks, 12 percent of companies in the United States provided corporate users with mobile access to their CRMs (quoted in Eklund 2002).

Of the CRM functions available in the large software suites, such as Siebel's CRM, the two that have attracted the most interest are *sales force automation* and *field service* (see Insights and Additions 10.2 on page 403). For instance, a salesperson might be on a sales call and need to know the recent billing history for a particular customer. Or, a field service representative on a service call might need to know current availability of various parts in order to fix a piece of machinery. It is these sorts of situations where mobile access to customer and partner data is invaluable. Two of the more recent offerings in this arena are Salesforce.com's Airforce Wireless Edition (salesforce.com) and Upshot's Alerts (upshot.com) (Hill 2002).

Using Voice Portals in Marketing and Customer Service

Voice portal technology can be connected to legacy systems to provide enhanced customer service or to improve access to data for employees, as shown in the following examples. Customers who are away from the office could use a vendor's voice portal to check on the status of deliveries to a job site. Service technicians could be provided with diagnostic information, enabling them to diagnose more difficult problems. Salespeople could check on inventory status during a meeting to help close a sale.

A wide variety of CRM applications are available that use voice portal technology. The challenge is in learning how to create the navigation and other aspects of interaction that makes customers feel comfortable with voice-access technology.

U.S. FLEET SERVICES AND WIRELESS NETWORKING

Started in 1997, U.S. Fleet Services has grown to be the leading provider of mobile, onsite fueling in the United States with customers such as FedEx, Home Depot, Coca-Cola, Nabisco, Office Max, and more. Using trucks that resemble home fuel-delivery vehicles, U.S. Fleet travels to its customers, refueling the customers' vehicles onsite, usually during off-hours. Three years ago, U.S. Fleet considered building a wireless network for its drivers, but decided against it. Managers considered the project to be too hard and too expensive given the expected ROI. However, toward the end of 2001, they changed their minds.

Although a mobile wireless solution was the end goal, the first step in the project actually involved the implementation of an ERP system. This was followed by a Web-based application built on top of the ERP that provided customers with information about their fuel consumption and taxes, enabling them to do better fleet management. Finally, U.S. Fleet equipped its drivers with handheld devices that could communicate with the company's intranet using Wi-Fi.

The handheld device U.S. Fleet selected was the Intermec 710 (*intermec.com*). According to the architect of the U.S. Fleet system, this device was selected for a number of reasons. Besides having a built-in barcode scanner, it also runs Microsoft's Pocket PC operating system, supports Visual Basic programs, handles CompactFlash cards, and has an integrated wireless radio for short range Wi-Fi communications. The device is fairly lightweight with a drop resistant case that is sealed to protect against harsh weather conditions.

The system works as follows: Branch managers enter a delivery route and schedule for each driver into a centralized database via the company's intranet. Each driver starts their shift by downloading the route and schedule over the company's Wi-Fi network into a handheld. When the driver

reaches a customer stop, the handheld is used to scan a barcode attached to the customer's truck. This provides the driver with the type of fuel required by the truck. After the truck is fueled, a meter on the delivery truck sends a wireless signal to the handheld. The handheld then syncs with the meter, capturing the type and quantity of fuel delivered. The data are stored on the handheld's CompactFlash memory card. When the driver returns to the home base, the data are unloaded over the Wi-Fi network to the central database. At this point, the data are available for U.S. Fleet and its customers to analyze.

Before the handhelds were deployed, drivers would record the data manually. The data were then faxed from the branch offices to headquarters and entered by hand into the system. Not only were there delays, but the data were also subject to entry errors at both ends of the line. The company and its customers now have accurate data in a timely fashion, which provides the company with faster invoicing and cash flow. On average, the new system has also enabled drivers to service six to seven more stops per shift.

Source: Ludorf (2002).

Questions

1. What systems did U.S. Fleet have to put in place before implementing its wireless solution?

2. Why did U.S. Fleet select the Intermec 710 handheld device? How does the device communicate with the company's intranet?

3. What are the major benefits that U.S. Fleet has realized by combining handheld devices with Wi-Fi?

NON-INTERNET INTRABUSINESS APPLICATIONS

Wireless applications in the non-Internet enterprise environment have been around since the early 1990s. Examples of such applications include the following:

▶ Wireless networking, which is used to pick items out of inventory in warehouses via PCs mounted on forklifts, other vehicles, or carried by employees

▶ Delivery and order status updates, which are entered on PCs inside distribution trucks

▶ Online dispatching, online diagnosis support from remote locations, and parts ordering/inventory queries from service people in the field

▶ Mobile shop-floor quality control systems that enable voice reports by inspectors, data collection from facilities, and transmission to a central processor

▶ A corporate wireless network over which salespeople, using their PDAs, report sales, competitors' inventories in stores, orders from customers' sites, and charges to customers' credit cards

▶ Remote database queries regarding order status or product availability

The variety of possible wireless applications is shown in Exhibit 10.9 (page 404). Some of these are amenable to Web technologies and can be delivered on a wireless intranet.

Insights and Additions 10.2   Mobile Workplace Applications

The following are two scenarios of wireless applications for mobile employees.

SALES SUPPORT	CUSTOMER SERVICE SUPPORT
Linda is a member of the field sales team at Theru Tools (a fictitious company). Each day she drives out to her customers in a van stocked with products. For each sale, she has to note the customer, the number and type of products sold, and any special discounts made. This recordkeeping used to be done manually, and many errors were made, leading to customer complaints and lost sales. The company was reluctant to invest in laptops for such a limited application, but Linda and other sales reps wanted the speed and reliability of automation. With the help of SAP, Theru was able to implement a system using low-cost but powerful handheld wireless devices. Using Mobile Sales (an application for handhelds), accessed via the *mysap.com* Mobile Workplace, Linda and her coworkers in the field now have information at their fingertips, including updates on new products and special promotions. Linda can place orders without delay and get immediate feedback on product availability and delivery times. In addition, the system at headquarters can prompt Linda and make plausibility checks on the orders, eliminating many of the errors associated with the manual process. It can also check if she is giving the right discounts to the right customer and immediately trigger the invoicing process or print out a receipt on the spot.	Michael works for Euroblast, Inc. (another fictitious company) as a service engineer. It is his job to provide time-critical maintenance and support for the company's customers' electromechanical control systems. To do so, he needs to know immediately when a customer's system is faltering, what is malfunctioning, and what type of service contract is in effect for billing purposes. Using SAP's Mobile Service, Michael does not need to carry all of this information in his head, but instead has it in the palm of his hand. With only a few taps of the stylus, Michael accesses the *mysap.com* Mobile Workplace for all the data he requires, including the name and address of the next customer he should visit, equipment specifications, parts inventory data, and so forth. Once he has completed the job, he can report back on the time and materials he used, and these data can be employed for timely billing and service quality analysis. In addition, his company is able to keep track of his progress and monitor any major fluctuations in activities. As a result, both Michael and his supervisors are better informed and better able to serve the customer. **Source:** Compiled from SAP AG Corp. (2000).

For details on intrabusiness applications, see mdsi-advantex.com. The advantages offered by intrabusiness wireless solutions can be seen through an examination of workflow applications, shown in Exhibit 10.10 (page 405).

INTERNET-BASED INTRABUSINESS APPLICATIONS

A large number of Internet-based wireless applications have been implemented inside enterprises. Examples of such applications include the following:

- Employees at companies such as Telecom Italia Mobile (Republica IT 2001) get their monthly pay slips as SMS messages sent to their mobile phone. The money itself is transferred electronically to a designated bank account. The method is much cheaper for the company and results in less paperwork than the old method of mailing monthly pay slips.

- At Chicago's United Center—home of the NBA's Bulls and NHL's Blackhawks— manual inventory systems were replaced with procedures that take advantage of mobile computing. In November 1999, the concessionaire, Bismarck Enterprises, deployed throughout the United Center 25 handheld devices from Symbol Technologies that run the Palm OS and custom applications on an intranet with Web technology (McDougall 1999). Bismarck employees can now inventory a full warehouse of food items in about 3 hours. The company used to hand-count everything once a month, taking between 48 and 72 hours to do inventory. With the new system, employees can do reconciliation right on the spot. The system saves the company about $100,000 a year in labor (Palm Computing 2003).

- Express delivery companies, such as FedEx and UPS, have been employing handheld wireless devices for several years, but the units were usually connected to a private

EXHIBIT 10.9 Intrabusiness Workflow Applications

Before Wireless	With Wireless
Work orders are manually assigned by multiple supervisors and dispatchers.	Work orders are automatically assigned and routed within minutes for maximum efficiency.
Field service technicians commute to the dispatch center to pick up paper work orders.	Home-based field service technicians receive first work order via mobile terminal and proceed directly to first assignment.
Manual record keeping of time, work completed, and billing information.	Automated productivity tracking, record keeping, and billing updates.
Field service technicians call in for new assignments and often wait because of radio traffic or unavailable dispatcher.	Electronic transmittal of additional work orders with no waiting time.
Complete work orders dropped off at dispatch center at the end of the day for manual entry into the billing or tracking system. Uncompleted orders are manually distributed to available technicians. Overtime charges often result.	Technicians close completed work orders from the mobile terminals as they are completed. At the end of the shift, the technicians sign off and go home.

Source: Smith Advanced Technology, Inc. (2001).

network and generally designed to serve one vertical industry and transfer a specific type of data, say, the location of a package on the road. Today, a new generation of Web-enabled wireless devices provides their employees with this and a variety of other services. They also offer customers the ability to track packages and locate drop-off boxes through Web-enabled wireless devices.

▶ Kemper Insurance Company has piloted an application that lets property adjusters report from the scene of an accident. Kemper attached a wireless digital imaging system to a camera that lets property adjusters take pictures in the field and transmit them to a processing center (Henning 2002; Nelson 2000). The cameras are linked to Motorola's StarTac data-enabled cellular, which sends the information to a database. This application eliminates delays in obtaining information and in film processing that exist with conventional methods.

Section 10.5 ▶ REVIEW

1. Describe wireless job dispatch.
2. Discuss how wireless applications can be used to provide customer support.
3. List some of the major intrabusiness wireless applications.

10.6 MOBILE B2B AND SUPPLY CHAIN APPLICATIONS

Accurate and timely information is critical to business success. Companies must frequently respond in real time, and speedy response is especially important in managing the supply chain. Mobile computing solutions enable organizations to respond faster to supply chain disruptions by proactively adjusting plans or shifting resources related to critical supply chain events as they occur. With the increased interest in collaborative commerce comes the opportunity to use wireless communication to collaborate along the supply chain. For this to take place, integration is needed.

Integration of business processes along the supply chain is a key issue in wireless B2B EC. As these processes become increasingly time sensitive and participants become more mobile, mobile devices will be integrated into information exchanges. The integration of m-commerce is taking place on the buy-side as well as on the sell-side of B2B EC.

An integrated messaging system is at the center of B2B communications. By integrating the mobile terminal into the supply chain, it is possible to make mobile reservations of goods, check availability of a particular item in the warehouse, order a particular product from the manufacturing department, or provide security access to obtain confidential financial data from a management information system.

EXHIBIT 10.10 Automated Wireless Workflow Applications

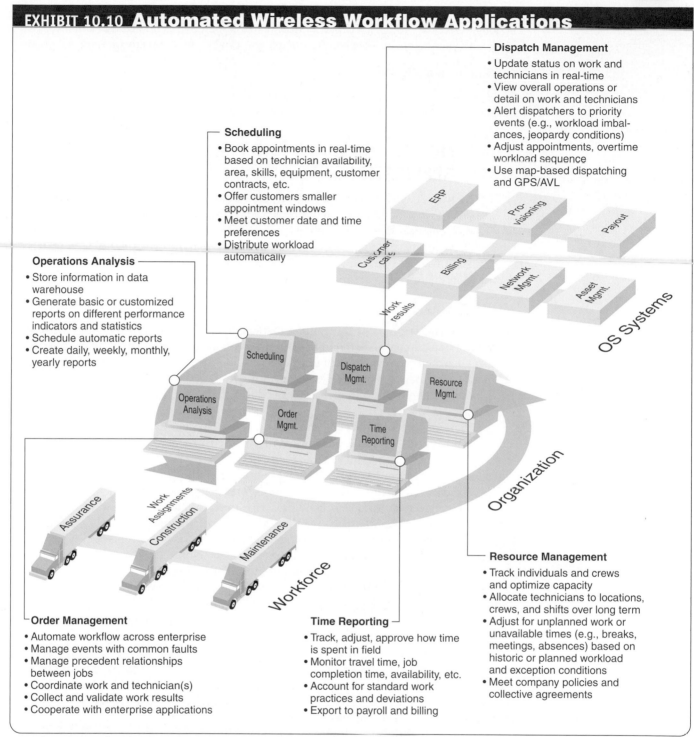

Dispatch Management
- Update status on work and technicians in real-time
- View overall operations or detail on work and technicians
- Alert dispatchers to priority events (e.g., workload imbalances, jeopardy conditions)
- Adjust appointments, overtime workload sequence
- Use map-based dispatching and GPS/AVL

Scheduling
- Book appointments in real-time based on technician availability, area, skills, equipment, customer contracts, etc.
- Offer customers smaller appointment windows
- Meet customer date and time preferences
- Distribute workload automatically

Operations Analysis
- Store information in data warehouse
- Generate basic or customized reports on different performance indicators and statistics
- Schedule automatic reports
- Create daily, weekly, monthly, yearly reports

Resource Management
- Track individuals and crews and optimize capacity
- Allocate technicians to locations, crews, and shifts over long term
- Adjust for unplanned work or unavailable times (e.g., breaks, meetings, absences) based on historic or planned workload and exception conditions
- Meet company policies and collective agreements

Order Management
- Automate workflow across enterprise
- Manage events with common faults
- Manage precedent relationships between jobs
- Coordinate work and technician(s)
- Collect and validate work results
- Cooperate with enterprise applications

Time Reporting
- Track, adjust, approve how time is spent in field
- Monitor travel time, job completion time, availability, etc.
- Account for standard work practices and deviations
- Export to payroll and billing

Source: Copyright © 2003 MDSI Mobile Data Solutions, Inc. Used with permission of MDSI.

One example of an integrated messaging system is wireless *telemetry,* which combines wireless communications, vehicle monitoring systems, and vehicle location devices. (See the opening case study; telemetry is described further in Section 10.9.) This technology makes possible large-scale automation of data capture, improved billing timeliness and accuracy, reduced overhead associated with the manual alternative, and increased customer satisfaction through service responsiveness. For example, vending machines can be kept replenished and in reliable operation by wirelessly polling inventory and service status continually to avert costly machine downtime.

Mobile devices can also facilitate collaboration among members of the supply chain. It is no longer necessary to call a partner company and ask someone to find certain employees who work with your company. Instead, these employees can be called directly on their cell phones.

Section 10.6 ▶ REVIEW

1. Describe wireless support along the supply chain.

2. How can telemetry improve supply chain operations?

10.7 MOBILE CONSUMER AND PERSONAL SERVICE APPLICATIONS

A large number of applications exist that support consumers and provide personal services. As an example, let's look at the situation of a person going to an international airport. Exhibit 10.11 lists 12 problem areas that can be solved using mobile devices. The capabilities shown in the table are now possible in some places and are expected to be more widely available by 2004.

Other consumer and personal service areas in which wireless devices can be used are described in the following sections. (See also attws.com.)

MOBILE GAMES

In the handheld segment of the gaming market, Nintendo has been the longtime leader. However, Nintendo has shown minimal interest in online or mobile games. In contrast, Sega has capitalized on the popularity of games such as Sonic the Hedgehog to garner 2.5 million Japanese subscribers for its mobile games and entertainment services (Becker 2002). In Japan, where millions of commuters kill time during long train rides, cell phone games have become a cultural fixture.

With more than 1 billion cell phones in use today (CellularOnline 2003b), the potential audience for mobile games is substantially larger than the market for other platforms—PlayStation and Game Boy included. Because of the market potential, Nokia has decided to enter the mobile gaming world, producing not only the phone/console, but also the games that will be delivered on memory cards. From Nokia's perspective, "Rich mobile games, combined with connected near distance multiplayer gaming over Bluetooth and wide area gaming using cellular networks, opens the door for totally new gaming concepts. Mobility will add a whole new dimension to innovative and creative games concepts and will provide opportunities for the games and telecom industry alike" (Nokia 2002).

A number of technologies are being used to deliver games on mobile phones. Some games are programmed directly into the phone's chipset and shipped with the phone. SMS games are played by sending messages to the phone number of the game provider's server, which in turn uses the message to perform some computations, and returns a message to the players with the results. WAP games are played by accessing the game provider's mobile or Web portal, downloading and viewing various pages, making various menu selections, submitting the selections to the server, and then viewing the resulting pages. A number of games are also being developed in Java 2 Micro Edition (J2ME), which has been optimized for mobile phones and PDAs. J2ME provides better control over the interface, allows simple animation, and can easily connect to remote servers.

In July 2001, Ericsson, Motorola, Nokia, and Siemens established the Mobile Games Interoperability Forum (MGIF) (mgif.org) to define a range of technical standards that will make it possible to deploy mobile games across multigame servers, wireless networks, and over different mobile devices. The forum includes a number of the top mobile game and entertainment providers, including Capcom, Codetoys, iFone, IN-FUSIO, Picofun, THQ, and Terraplay Systems.

MOBILE ENTERTAINMENT: MUSIC, PICTURES, AND VIDEO

The availability of portable MP3 players has lead to the development of music devices integrated with mobile phones. All of the major handset vendors offer MP3 phones, including Samsung (SPH-M100), Nokia (5510), Ericsson (MP3 Handsfree), and Audiovox (CMP3). All of these handsets enable music titles to be stored and played locally on the mobile device.

EXHIBIT 10.11 Traditional Versus Mobile Support at an Airport

Problem	Traditional Solution	Solution Enabled by the Local Mobile Network
Find a luggage cart.	The traveler searches for a cart; sooner or later they will find one.	The traveler's PDA/cell will inform them of where they are and where to find the closest available cart.
Find the right check-in desk.	Review all check-in desks and eventually find the right check-in desk. The traveler could also find a monitor which, with luck, is close to where they are.	The traveler's PDA/cell will, as soon as they have entered the departure hall, show the person the way to the right check-in desk and inform them of their estimated check-in time.
Get in line and wait at the check-in desk.	Visually try to find the quickest line.	The traveler's PDA/cell has already shown them which check-in desk to go to.
Find the way to customs.	Check the signs that lead to customs.	The traveler's PDA/cell will inform them of the way to customs.
Find the duty-free products of interest.	The traveler will wander through the duty-free stores and find the products they are looking for. Hopefully, they will get a good price.	When close to the shopping area, the traveler's PDA/cell will inform them of where to find the products they already preprogrammed their intent to buy. The traveler will also be informed about the price and "today's offering" for the product groups they are interested in.
Find a place to eat.	Review the different restaurants and their menus by walking through the airport.	The traveler types in what they want to eat and the PDA/cell informs them of where to find the food. The PDA/cell may also present alternative restaurants, their menu, prices, seat availability, and order time.
Find the closest washroom.	Walk around looking for signs with directions.	The PDA/cell will show the closest washroom.
Find out if there are any delays and when to board the aircraft	Find a monitor, which informs of any delays and/or gate changes.	The PDA/cell will beep and tell the traveler when they have to go to the gate depending on where they are in the airport building.
Find where to get luggage upon arrival.	Find a monitor, which informs the traveler of the baggage claim location.	The PDA/cell will inform the traveler of the baggage claim location to pick up their luggage.
Make taxi and hotel reservations while waiting for the luggage at the baggage-claim.	There are no options. The traveler must wait until they are in the arrival hall.	The local airport portal provides a number of services. While waiting for the luggage, the traveler can make taxi and hotel reservations and other arrangements from their PDA/cell.
The traveler's luggage never shows up.	The traveler has to find a place to report the missing luggage and make a loss report.	The luggage will be identified when leaving the cargo space. The PDA/cell will inform the traveler that the luggage has arrived and provide its estimated time to the baggage claim area. If the luggage is missing, the traveler will be informed and a loss report will be generated.
Finding information on where to find a connecting flight.	Find a monitor to find the connecting flight.	The PDA/cell will tell the traveler where to go after they have left the aircraft.

Source: Courtesy of AXIS Communications.

With higher bandwidth, music vendors will be able offer instant delivery of songs from their music libraries for online purchase. Location-based services can even be integrated to target subscribers with location-sensitive streaming content such as audio jingles promoting offers at retail outlets in the vicinity or movie trailers for films showing at the nearest theater.

The same handset vendors have also produced a new generation of cell phones that enable users to send pictures from one device to another. The Nokia 7650, Samsung A500, Sony Ericsson T300, and Sanyo SCP-5300 all have built-in digital cameras. These and a number of other cell phones can send and receive pictures through their MMP (multimedia messaging protocol capabilities.

As the 3G handsets hit the market, mobile devices will begin to support the downloading and real-time playback of audio and video clips. The U.S.-based Packet Video Corporation (packetvideo.com) is a pioneer in this area. The company has already demonstrated its new mobile-media software on Nokia's 3650 and 7650 phones. This software enables content to be captured by the mobile phone, viewed via streaming video, and shared via messaging and e-mail. Users can use the software to encode live video from the built-in device camera; stream favorite videos and other multimedia content across the wireless network to the handset; view news, sports, music videos, movie trailers, and other content; download content to the mobile device for forwarding to friends or storage for later retrieval; and view live cameras for travel, entertainment, security, and child or elderly monitoring (newstream.com 2002).

HOTELS

A number of hotels now offer their guests in-room, high-speed Internet connections. Some of these same hotels are beginning to offer Wi-Fi Internet access in public areas and meeting rooms. One such hotel is Marriott, which manages 2,500 hotels worldwide. After a 7-month test, Marriott has partnered with STSN (stsn.com), an ISP specializing in hotels, to provide Wi-Fi services in the 400 Marriott hotels that already have in-room broadband Internet access (Reuters 2002). In the same vein, AT&T has partnered with Wayport Inc. to offer Wi-Fi in 475 hotels throughout the United States. In India, the Taj Group is offering Wi-Fi access in its hotels (Taj Hotel 2002), and Megabeam (a wireless provider in England) is starting to offer the same service in select Holiday Inn and Crowne Plaza hotels in London.

Although Wi-Fi provides guests with Internet access, to date it has had minimal impact on other sorts of hotel services (e.g., check-in). This is where Bluetooth is coming into play. A small number of hotels are testing the use of this technology for check-in and check-out, for making purchases from hotel vending machines and stores, for tracking loyalty points (see tesalocks.com), and for opening room doors in place of keys (Mayor 2001). Guests are provided with Bluetooth-enabled phones that can communicate with Bluetooth access points located throughout the hotel. In 2001, Classwave signed a deal with Starwood Hotels & Resorts worldwide (which owns St. Regis, the Luxury Collection, Sheraton, Westin, Four Points by Sheraton, and W Brands hotels) to enable Bluetooth solutions within their hotels (Houck 2001).

See Exhibit 10.12 for a comparison of traditional and m-commerce hotel services. M-commerce capabilities are now available in some locations and are expected to be widely available by 2005.

WIRELESS TELEMEDICINE

Today, two different kinds of technology are used for telemedicine applications—the storage and forwarding of digital images from one location to another and videoconferencing used for real-time consultation with a patient in one location and a medical specialist in another. In most of the real-time consultations, the patient is in a rural area and the specialist is in an urban location.

A number of factors are impeding telemedicine. Some states do not allow physicians to provide medical advice across state lines. The threat of malpractice suits is another issue since there is no "hands-on" interaction between the physician and patient. In addition, from a technical standpoint, many telemedicine projects are hindered by poor telecommunications.

EXHIBIT 10.12 Traditional Versus Mobile Support at a Hotel

Problem	Traditional Solution	Solution Enabled by the Local Mobile Network
Arrive at the hotel for a check-in.	Line up at the check-in desk and sign in, hand over a credit card, and receive the room key.	Send personal information, preferences, and credit card details to the hotel system via a PDA/cell. The hotel system sends back the designated room number and the PIN-code to the room door.
Arriving at the room, the guest wants to know what restaurants and facilities exist at the hotel.	Look in the hotel binder, call reception, or find the info on the hotel TV broadcast.	Information on what facilities are available and different restaurants with menus is automatically transferred to the PDA/cell upon arrival.
Review menu and order food from room service.	Look in the hotel binder and call the room service telephone number to place an order.	The room service menu is downloaded to the PDA/cell and the guest may directly order the food of their choice. The next day's breakfast selection can also be ordered at the same time.
Access the Internet and the corporate intranet with a high-speed connection from the hotel room, lobby, and conference facilities.	Find the analog telephone plug, connect the laptop through a wire and make a remote dial-up. At some hotels, a specific device is required to be connected to the telephone.	As the guest enters the room, they will have instant broadband access available on their laptop, and their PDA/cell will automatically update the latest news headlines, private e-mail, and calendar information.
Make work-related telephone calls and call home from abroad.	Make the call on the available hotel phones and pay the local premium rates or use your mobile phone.	Specific discount telephony rates are offered by the hotel through Voice Over IP (VoIP) over the guest's mobile phone with Bluetooth wireless technology.
Book a rental car.	Ask the concierge to book a car or call the rental car companies directly.	Information is available on the PDA/cell. The guest may book a car directly with a simple click and send the required personal information at the same time.
Order transportation to the office or to the airport.	Ask the concierge or reception to book taxi or bus transportation.	A selection of transportation means is presented on the guest's PDA/cell. They may book and pay for their preference directly from their PDA/cell.

Source: Courtesy of AXIS Communications.

New wireless and mobile technologies, especially the next generation, not only offer the possibility of overcoming the hurdles imposed by remote locations, but also open a number of new and novel application opportunities:

▶ At the first warning signs of a heart attack, people are advised to contact emergency facilities as soon as possible. Manufacturers are working on wearable heart monitors linked to cell phones that can automatically contact doctors or family members at the first sign of trouble.

▶ The Swiss Federal Institute of Technology is designing portable devices that transmit the vital signs of avalanche victims up to 80 meters away (Baard 2002). Not only does the device provide location information, it also provides information about body orientation that helps reduce injuries as rescuers dig for the victims.

> In-flight medical emergencies occur much more frequently than one might think. Alaskan Airlines, for example, deals with about 10 medical emergencies per day (Conrad 2002). Mobile communications are already being used to attend to medical emergencies occurring on planes. MedLink, a service of MedAire in Phoenix, provides around-the-clock access to board-certified emergency physicians. These mobile services can also remotely control medical equipment, such as defibrillators, located onboard the plane.

> The military is involved in developing mobile telesurgery applications that enable surgeons in one location to remotely control robotic arms for surgery in another location. The technology could be particularly useful in battlefield situations.

OTHER SERVICES FOR CONSUMERS

Many other types of mobile computer services are available to consumers. Examples include services providing news, weather, and sports reports; online language translations; information about tourist attractions (hours, prices); and emergency services. Other services are listed in Exhibit W10.1 at the book's Web site. Also, see the case studies at mobileinfo.com.

NON-INTERNET CONSUMER APPLICATIONS

Non-Internet EC applications for consumers, mainly those using smart cards, have existed since the early 1990s. Active use of the cards is reported in transportation, where millions of "contactless" cards (also called *proximity cards*) are used to pay bus and subway fares and road tolls. Amplified remote-sensing cards that have an RF of up to 30 meters are used in several countries for toll collection. See EC Application Case 13.1 in Chapter 13 for more on the use of proximity cards for toll collection.

Section 10.7 ▶ REVIEW

1. Describe the application of wireless and mobile technologies to games and entertainment.
2. Discuss some of the potential applications of Wi-Fi and Bluetooth technologies in hotels.
3. Describe some potential uses of mobile and wireless technologies in providing medical care.

10.8 LOCATION-BASED COMMERCE

location-based commerce (l-commerce)
M-commerce transactions targeted to individuals in specific locations, at specific times

As discussed in Section 10.1, location-based commerce (l-commerce) refers to the localization of products and services. Location-based services are attractive to both consumers and businesses alike. L-commerce offers the following to consumers and businesses:

> **Safety.** A person can connect to an emergency service with a mobile device and have the service pinpoint their exact location.
> **Convenience.** People can locate what or who is nearby without have to consult a directory, pay phone, or map.
> **Productivity.** People can optimize their travel and time by determining points or people of interest that are within close proximity.

From a business supplier's point of view, l-commerce offers an opportunity to provide services that meet customers' needs. The basic services revolve around five key areas:

1. **Location.** Determining the basic position of a person or a thing (e.g. car or boat)
2. **Navigation.** Plotting a route from one location to another
3. **Tracking.** Monitoring the movement of a person or a thing (e.g., a package or vehicle)
4. **Mapping.** Creating maps of specific geographical locations
5. **Timing.** Determining the precise time at a specific location

L-COMMERCE TECHNOLOGIES

Providing location-based services requires the following location-based and network technologies:

▶ **Position-determining equipment (PDE).** This equipment identifies the location of the mobile device (either through GPS or by locating the nearest base station). The position information is sent to the mobile positioning center.

▶ **Mobile positioning center (MPC).** The MPC is a server that manages the location information sent from the PDE.

▶ **Location-based technology.** This technology consists of groups of servers that combine the position information with geographic- and location-specific content to provide an l-commerce service. For instance, location-based technology could present a list of addresses of nearby restaurants based on the position of the caller, local street maps, and an electronic database of businesses listed by location.

▶ **Geographic content.** Geographic content consists of streets, road maps, addresses, routes, landmarks, land usage, Zip codes, and the like. This information must be delivered in compressed form for fast distribution over wireless networks.

▶ **Location-specific content.** Location-specific content is used in conjunction with the geographic content to provide the location of particular services. Yellow-page directories showing the location of specific business and services exemplify this type of content. Exhibit 10.13 (page 412) shows how these technologies are used in conjunction with one another to deliver location-based services. Underlying these technologies are GPS and geographical information systems.

Global Positioning System

As indicated at the start of the chapter, a **global positioning system (GPS)** is a wireless system that uses satellites to enable users to determine their position anywhere on the earth. GPS equipment has been used extensively for navigation by commercial airlines and ships and for locating trucks and buses (as in the opening case study). GPS is supported by 24 U.S. government satellites that are shared worldwide. Each satellite orbits the earth once every 12 hours on a precise path at an altitude of 10,900 miles. At any point in time, the exact position of each satellite is known, because the satellite broadcasts its position and a time signal from its onboard atomic clock, which is accurate to one-billionth of a second. Receivers also have accurate clocks that are synchronized with those of the satellites.

Knowing the speed of the signals (186,272 miles per second), engineers can find the location of any receiving station (latitude and longitude) to within 50 feet by triangulation, using the distance from a GPS to three satellites to make the computation. GPS software then computes the latitude and longitude of the receiver. For an online tutorial on GPS, see trimble.com/gps.

GPS handsets. GPS handsets can be stand-alone units for applications such as tracking buses (NextBus case), tracking trucks on the roads, or finding a location in the outdoors. They also can be plugged into a mobile device or completely embedded in one.

global positioning system (GPS)
A wireless system that uses satellites to enable users to determine their position anywhere on the earth.

Geographical Information System

The location provided by GPS is expressed in terms of latitude and longitude. To make that information useful to businesses and consumers, it is necessary in many cases to relate those measures to a certain place or address. This is done by inserting the latitude and longitude onto an electronic map, which is the **geographical information system (GIS)**. The GIS data visualization technology integrates GPS data onto digitized map displays. (See Steede-Terry 2000 for an explanation of how this is done.) Companies such as mapinfo.com provide the GIS core spatial technology, maps, and other data content needed in order to power location-based GIS/GPS services, as shown in Exhibit 10.14 (page 413).

An interesting application of GPS/GIS is now available from several car manufacturers (e.g., Toyota, Cadillac) and car rental companies (e.g., Hertz, Avis). Some cars have a navigation system that indicates how far away the driver is from gas stations, restaurants, and other locations of interest. The GPS knows where the car is at any time, so the application can map the route for the driver to a particular destination.

geographical information system (GIS)
System that integrates GSP data onto digitized map displays.

EXHIBIT 10.13 Location-Based Services Involving Maps

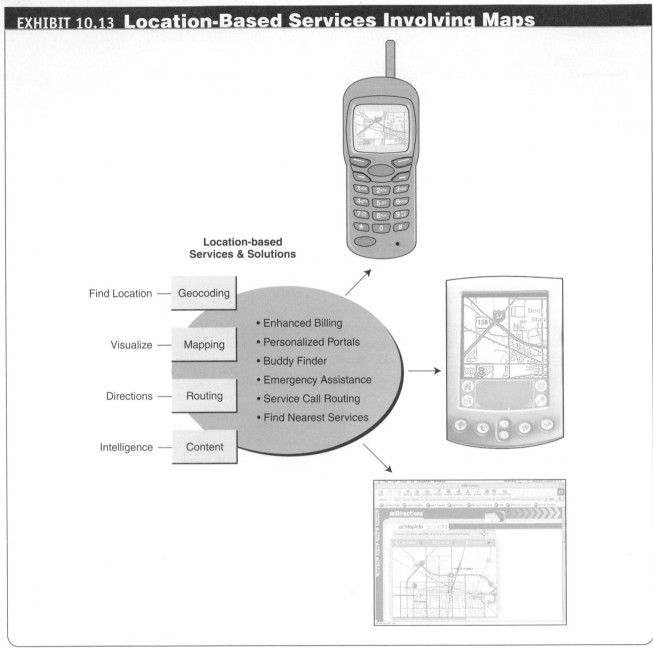

Location-based Services & Solutions

Find Location — Geocoding

Visualize — Mapping

Directions — Routing

Intelligence — Content

- Enhanced Billing
- Personalized Portals
- Buddy Finder
- Emergency Assistance
- Service Call Routing
- Find Nearest Services

Source: Based on Mapinfo.com (2003).

E-911 EMERGENCY CELL PHONE CALLS

wireless 911 (e-911)
Calls from cellular phones to providers of emergency services.

If someone dials 911 from regular wired phone, it is easy for the emergency service to pinpoint the location of the phone. But what happens if someone places a 911 call from a mobile phone? How can the emergency service locate the caller? A few years ago, the U.S. Federal Communication Commission issued a directive to wireless carriers to establish services to handle **wireless 911 (e-911)** calls. For an idea of the magnitude of this requirement, more than 55 million emergency calls were received on cell phones in the United States in 2001 (Monteith 2002).

The e-911 directive is to take effect in two phases, although the specifics of the phases vary from one wireless carrier (e.g., AT&T, Cingular, Sprint, etc.) to another. Phase 1 requires carriers, upon appropriate request by a local *Public Safety Answering Point (PSAP)*, to report the telephone number of a wireless 911 caller and the location of the cellular antenna that received the call. Phase 2, which is being rolled out over a 4-year period, from October 2001 to December 2005, requires wireless carriers to provide information that will enable the

EXHIBIT 10.14 GPS System

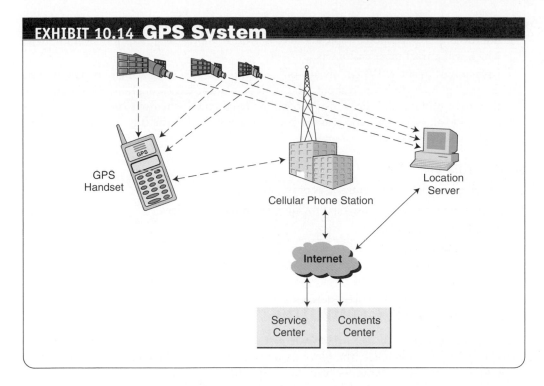

PSAP to locate a caller within 50 meters 67 percent of the time and within 150 meters 95 percent of the time. By the end of phase 2, 100 percent of the new cell phones and 95 percent of all cell phones will have these location capabilities. It is expected that many other countries will follow the example of the United States in providing e-911 service.

In the future, cars will have a device for **automatic crash notification (ACN)**. This still-experimental device will automatically notify the police of an accident involving an ACN-equipped car and its location.

TELEMATICS AND TELEMETRY APPLICATIONS

Telematics refers to the integration of computers and wireless communications in order to improve information flow. It uses the principles of *telemetry*, the science that measures physical remoteness by means of wireless transmission from a remote source (such as a vehicle) to a receiving station. The term *telematics* is often used to refer to vehicle monitoring systems and vehicle location devices. MobileAria (mobilearia.com) is a proposed standards-based telematics platform designed to bring multimedia services and m-commerce to automobiles.

General Motors Corporation popularized automotive telematics with its OnStar system. Nokia has set up a business unit, called Smart Traffic Products, that is focusing solely on telematics. Nokia believes that every vehicle will be equipped with at least one Internet Protocol (IP) address by the year 2010. Smart cars and traffic products are discussed in more detail in Section 10.9.

BARRIERS TO L-COMMERCE

What is holding back the widespread use of l-commerce? Several factors come into play, including the following:

▶ **Accuracy.** Some of the location technologies are not as accurate as people expect them to be. GPS provides a location that is accurate up to 15 meters. Less expensive but less accurate technologies can be used instead to find an approximate location (within about 500 meters).

▶ **The cost-benefit justification.** For many potential users, the benefits of l-commerce do not justify the price of the hardware or the inconvenience and time required to utilize the service.

automatic crash notification (ACN)
Device that automatically sends the police the location of a vehicle that has been involved in a crash.

telematics
The integration of computers and wireless communications to improve information flow using the principles of telemetry.

▶ **The bandwidth of GSM networks.** GSM bandwidth is currently limited; it will be improved as 3G technology spreads. As bandwidth improves, applications will improve, which will attract more customers.

▶ **Invasion of privacy.** When "always-on" cell phones are a reality, many people will be hesitant to have their whereabouts and movements tracked throughout the day, even if they have nothing to hide. This issue will be heightened when our cars, homes, appliances, and all sorts of other consumer goods are connected to the Internet. (For more, see Section 10.9 on pervasive computing.)

Section 10.8 ▶ REVIEW

1. Describe some of the potential uses of l-commerce.
2. Discuss the technologies used in providing l-commerce services.
3. Describe GPS and GIS.
4. Discuss telematics.
5. List some of the barriers to l-commerce.

10.9   PERVASIVE COMPUTING

Steven Spielberg's sci-fi thriller *Minority Report* depicts the world of 2054. Based on a 1956 short story by Philip K. Dick, the film immerses the viewer in the consumer-driven world of pervasive computing 50 years from now. Spielberg put together a 3-day think tank, headed by Peter Schwartz, president of Global Business Network (gbn.com), to produce a realistic view of the future (Mathieson 2002). The think tank projected out from today's marketing and media technologies—Web cookies, GPS, Bluetooth, personal video recorders, barcode scanners, and the like—to create a society where billboards beckon consumers by name, newspapers are delivered instantly over broadband wireless networks, holographic hosts greet shoppers at retail stores, and cereal boxes broadcast live commercials. Although the technologies in the film were beyond the leading edge, none was beyond the realm of the plausible.

pervasive computing
Invisible, everywhere computing that is embedded in the objects around us.

A world in which virtually every object has processing power with wireless or wired connections to a global network is the world of **pervasive computing**. Pervasive computing also goes by the names of *ubiquitous computing*, *embedded computing*, or *augmented computing*. The idea of pervasive computing has been around for years. However, the current version was first articulated by Mark Weiser in 1988 at the computer science lab of Xerox PARC. From Weiser's perspective, pervasive computing was the opposite of virtual reality. In virtual reality, the user is immersed in a computer-generated environment. In contrast, pervasive computing is invisible, "everywhere computing" that is embedded in the objects around us—the floor, the lights, our cars, the washing machine, our cell phones, our clothes, and so on (Weiser 1991).

INVISIBLE COMPUTING

By invisible, Weiser did not mean to imply that pervasive computing devices would not be seen, he meant that unlike a desktop computer, these embedded computers would not intrude on our consciousness. Think of a pair of eyeglasses. The wearer does not have to think about using them. The wearer simply puts on and they augment the wearer's ability to see. This is Weiser's vision for pervasive computing. The user does not have to think about how to use the processing power in the object; rather, the processing power automatically helps the user perform a task.

radio frequency identification (RFID)
Generic term for technologies that use radio waves to automatically identify individual items.

Invisible is how one would describe some of the new embedded technologies in use at Prada's "epicenter" stores in New York, San Francisco, and Los Angeles (Duan 2002). Prada is a high-end fashion retailer. In the company's epicenters, the items for sale have an RFID (radio frequency identification) tag attached. The tag contains a processor and an antenna. If a customer wants to know about a particular item, they can move with the item towards one of the many displays around the store. The display automatically detects the item and provides sketches, video clips of models wearing the item, and information about the item (color, cut, fabric, materials, and availability). If a customer takes a garment into one of the dressing rooms, the tags are automatically scanned and detected via an antenna embedded in the dressing room. Again, information about the item will be automatically displayed on an interactive touch screen in the dressing room. The dressing rooms also have a video-based "Magic Mirror." When the customer tries on the garment and turns around in front of the mirror, the images will be captured and played back in slow motion.

Invisible is also a term that characterizes an accelerometer device manufactured and sold by Fitsense Technology (fitsense.com), a Massachusetts developer of Internet sports and fitness monitors. With this 1–ounce device that is clipped to a shoelace, runners are able to capture their speed and the distance they have run. The device transmits the data via a radio signal to a wrist device that can capture and transmit the data wirelessly to a desktop computer for analysis. Along the same lines, Champion Chip (championchip.com), headquartered in the Netherlands, has developed a system that keeps track of the tens of thousands of participants in popular long-distance races. The tracking system includes miniature transponders attached to the runners' shoelaces or ankle bracelets and antenna mats at the finish line that use radio frequencies to capture start times, splits, and finish times as the runners cross them.

PROPERTIES OF PERVASIVE COMPUTING

Being invisible is only one of the properties of pervasive computing. A short list of its major characteristics (Amor 2001) follows.

- **Invisible devices.** Numerous and casually accessible, these devices are often invisible.
- **Embedded microchips.** Microchip intelligence is embedded into everyday devices and objects.
- **Always on.** Users have continuous access to information, entertainment, and communication with anyone, anytime, anywhere.
- **Ubiquitous network.** Everyone and everything is connected to an increasingly ubiquitous network structure.
- **Life-enhancing applications.** The technology will penetrate the mainstream mass market through a variety of life-enhancing applications.
- **Consumer-centric solutions.** The technology offers "gadgetry" for simple and practical consumer-centric solutions.
- **Increasing productivity.** The technology offers mainstream-market value propositions that enable consumers to save time or money and enhance leisure and entertainment.
- **Long-term vision.** In the long-term, the technology will enable people to work, live, and play more effectively.

THE TECHNICAL FOUNDATION OF PERVASIVE COMPUTING

As the preceding list suggests, three major technical requirements underlie pervasive computing. First, everyday objects will have to contain embedded microprocessors. Second, a ubiquitous network is needed to connect these microprocessors. Finally, the microprocessors must be able to communicate with the ubiquitous network. The day when these technical requirements all meet is not that far off.

According to Harbor Research (Edgington 2001), approximately 5 billion microprocessors were sold in 2000, and only 120 million of them (roughly 2.5 percent) were intended for PCs. It is estimated that in 5 years, the number of processors in the average home could grow from 40 to 280, the number of processors in the average car (now about 20) will increase substantially over the same time period, and the number of embedded chips sold to support increasingly intelligent devices could grow to over 9 billion (Edgington 2001). Intelligence and connectivity will be designed into almost every electronic device. The ubiquitous network environment over which these devices will communicate will, for the foreseeable future, be the Internet.

The way in which embedded devices will attach to or communicate with the Internet will vary. Some will be wired into the Internet—through broadband or dial-up—in the same way that the average desktop computer is connected. Others will connect through mobile or wireless networks in the same way that a cellular phone does. Finally, others, such as the

RFID tags used by Prada, will link in through small antennas that can send and receive messages in a wireless environment (e.g., Wi-Fi or Bluetooth).

Like a number of areas of EC or m-commerce, pervasive computing has been accompanied by a great deal of hype. In the last few years, people have talked about refrigerators that can tell a person when they need to order milk, TVs that provide entertainment on demand, gas pumps with Web connections, and a whole array of amazing gadgets. For instance, 3COM promoted Audrey, a small, wireless Internet appliance for the entire family. This tablet-like device offered e-mail, Web access, and calendaring. Despite a $20-million marketing campaign, Audrey was a resounding flop that was pulled from the market. The same has been true for most of the other ideas that cropped up during the dot-com heyday. Instead of looking at solutions to problems, many manufacturers have focused on connectivity as an end in itself, and so have not yet produced commercially successful products.

A number of pervasive computing initiatives are underway that do hold substantial promise for the future of EC and m-commerce and that have the substantial financial backing that will be needed for commercial success. This next part of this section will look at four of these initiatives: smart homes, smart appliances, smart cars, and smart things.

SMART HOMES

The concept of the smart or intelligent home is at least 30 years old. In a smart home, the home computer, television, lighting and heating controls, home security system, and many appliances within the home can "talk" to each other via the Internet or a home intranet. These linked systems can be controlled through various devices, including the home owner's pager, cellular phone, television, home computer, PDA, or even their automobile.

In the United States, tens of thousands of homes are already equipped with home-automation devices, and there are signs that Europe—which has much lower home Internet penetration levels—is also warming to the idea. For instance, a 2001 study by the United Kingdom's Consumers' Association found that almost half those surveyed were interested in having the functions a "smart home" could offer, if they were affordable (Edgington 2001).

Currently, home automation systems support a number of different tasks:

▶ **Lighting.** Users can program their lights to go on and off or dim them to match their moods and needs for comfort and security. Users can have bright lights when they are eating, dimmed lights for dessert, and "mood lights" for later.

▶ **Energy management.** A home's HVAC (heat, ventilation, and air conditioning) system can be programmed for maximum energy efficiency and controlled with a touch panel. When a home owner leaves in the morning, the automated system calibrates to the right temperature so that energy is not wasted when no one is home. Conversely, the home owner can get a head start in cranking up the heat or air conditioner before they get home by calling the automated system via their telephone or PDA. Today, numerous products are on the market that enable a home owner to remotely check their HVAC system.

▶ **Water control.** What if a home owner is on a trip and the water hose to the dishwasher bursts? Watercop (watercop.com), a device manufactured by DynaQuip Controls Corporation, can handle this situation. The device relies on a series of strategically placed moisture-detection sensors. When the moisture level rises in one of these sensors, it sends a wireless signal to the Watercop control unit, which turns off the main water supply to the house.

▶ **Home security and communications.** The window blinds, garage doors, front door, smoke detectors, and home security systems can all be automated from a network control panel. These can all be programmed to respond to scheduled events (e.g., when you go on vacation). Hidden surveillance cameras can be placed throughout a home so that the home owner can check on babysitters and the children via a computer and Internet connection at work.

▶ **Home theater.** Users can create a multisource audio and video center around their house that can be controlled with a touch pad or remote. For example, if a person has a DVD player in their bedroom but they want to see the same movie in a child's room, they can just click a remote to switch rooms. Ditto for piping music into different rooms.

The issue with the current generation of home automation devices is that the various systems are independent of one another and have their own proprietary methods of communication and control. In contrast, smart homes of the future will not only expand automation throughout the house, but will provide a single network of microprocessors and small computers that can be easily and conveniently controlled. These processors will either be used to turn devices and appliances on and off or to send and receive information. They will be linked together using either a dedicated cable, a wireless network, by sending a special signal through the main electricity cables, or some combination of these.

Analysts generally agree that the market opportunities for smart homes will take shape over the next 3 to 5 years. These opportunities are being driven by the increasing adoption of broadband (cable and DSL) services and the proliferation of LANs and WLANs within the home. As EC Application Case 10.2 shows, substantial opportunities exist for pervasive computing devices in other residential settings besides private homes.

SMART APPLIANCES

One of the key elements of a smart home is the smart appliance, an Internet-ready appliance that can be controlled by a small handheld device or desktop computer via a home intranet or the public Internet.

One organization that is focused on smart appliances is the Internet Home Alliance (internethomealliance.com). The alliance is made up of a number of appliance manufacturers

---

CASE 10.2

EC Application

EMPOWERING ASSISTED-LIVING PATIENTS

The elderly residents in assisted-living facilities have various needs that require differing levels of care. Some residents require minimal assistance, others have short-term memory problems and other health issues, and others have more severe problems such as Alzheimer's disease. At Elite Care's Estates Cluster Residential Care Facility in Milwaukie, Oregon, pervasive computing is being used to increase the autonomy of all of its residents, regardless of their individual needs.

Elite Care (*elite-care.com*) is a family owned business. It has been built from the ground up with the intent of providing "high tech, high touch" programs. Members of the facility's advisory committee, which includes representatives from the Mayo Clinic, Harvard University, the University of Michigan, the University of Wisconsin, and Sandia National Laboratory, have contributed a number of ideas that have been put into practice.

The entire facility is wired with a network of unobtrusive sensors that include biosensors (e.g., weight sensors) attached to each resident's bed; movement sensors embedded in badges worn by the residents and staff; panic buttons used to call for help; Internet access via touch screens in each room; and climate control, lights, and other regulated appliances. The biosensors and movement sensors enable the staff to determine the following conditions and activities in caring for patients:

▶ Weight loss (indicating conditions such as impending congestive heart failure)
▶ Restlessness at night (indicating conditions such as insufficient pain medication)
▶ Frequency of trips to the bathroom (indicating medical problems such as infection)
▶ Length of absence from bed (indicating that the patient may have fallen or be incapacitated in other ways)

▶ General location (indicating whether the resident is in an acceptable area of the facility)

One of the initial concerns with these monitors is that the privacy of the residents will be unnecessarily invaded. To alleviate this concern, residents and their families are given the choice of participating or not. Most of them choose to participate because the families believe that these monitors provide better tracking and care. The monitors also increase the autonomy of all the patients because it reduces the need for staff to constantly monitor residents in person, especially those with more acute care needs.

All of these sensors and systems are connected through a high-speed Ethernet. The data produced by the sensors and systems are stored in an SQL database and can be used to alert the staff in real-time if necessary. Although the data are not being used at the present time for analytical purposes or to develop individualized programs, the facility plans to work on these sorts of applications in the future.

Source: Stanford, J. "Using Technology to Empower Assisted Living Patients." *Healthcare Review*, July 2, 2002. Used with permission.

Questions

1. What are some of the pervasive devices used in the Elite Care facility? What types of data do these devices provide?

2. In what ways do these devices encroach upon the privacy of the residents?

(e.g., Whirlpool and Sunbeam), computer hardware companies (e.g., IBM and Cisco), retailers (e.g., Best Buy), and vendors specializing in home automation (e.g., Lutron Electronics). The mission of the alliance is to accelerate the process of researching, developing, and testing new home products and services that require a broadband or persistent connection to the Internet. Insights and Additions 10.3 exemplifies some of the types of smart appliances being developed by members of the alliance; in this case, however, the appliances are being used for commercial purposes, not in the home.

The appliance manufacturers are interested not only in the sale of appliances, but also in service. In most cases, when an appliance is purchased and taken home, the manufacturer loses touch with the appliance unless the customer registers the product for warranty purposes. Potentially, a networked appliance could provide a manufacturer, as well as the owner of the appliance, with information that could be used for (Pinto 2002):

▶ Capturing or reporting on the operation, performance, and usage of a device

▶ Diagnostic purposes—monitoring, troubleshooting, repairing, or maintaining the device

▶ Improving or augmenting the performance or features of a device

▶ Controlling and coordinating devices into a sequenced pattern of behavior

▶ Profiling and behavior tracking, such as tracking variations in geography, culture, performance, usage, and sale of a device

▶ Monitoring consumption in order to initiate a purchase order or actual transaction when levels of a consumable are low

▶ Tracking and optimizing the service support system for a device

Besides providing benefits to consumers and appliance manufacturers, Internet-enabled appliances can also benefit the larger society. Consider the electricity shortages that have

---

Insights and Additions 10.3   Washers and Dryers on the Web

Imagine hooking up your washer and dryer to the Internet. To most homeowners, this would make as much sense as networking their refrigerators or microwaves. But what about hooking up the washers and dryers in a laundromat? Would the payoff or acceptance be any greater? For IBM and USA Technologies the answer is yes, especially on college campuses.

USA Technologies (*usatech.com*) has created a system called eSuds.net. It is a comprehensive laundry system that combines payment and operating services and is wired to the Web. IBM hosts the associated Web sites and integrates the technology that handles inventory, payment authorization, and reports.

On a university campus, eSuds.net eliminates a number of the hassles and tedium associated with doing laundry by providing students with the following services:

▶ **Coin-free transaction options.** Washing and drying can be paid for with a student ID or PIN card and charged to one's student account.

▶ **E-mail or pager notification.** When the washing or drying is done, the system notifies the student via e-mail or a pager.

▶ **A virtual view of the laundry room.** Students can access a Web site that indicates which machines are available.

▶ **Detergent and fabric softener injectables.** Students do not need to provide detergent or fabric softener. These can be purchased as part of the washing/drying service and injected directly from the machines into the student's wash.

The e-Suds.net system also eliminates a number of the maintenance headaches encountered by the owner and operator of a laundromat. With e-Suds.net, the laundromat operator can conduct virtually coin-free transactions (eliminating jammed machines and reducing vandalism), can monitor machine usage and performance online, and can service machines on as-needed basis, reducing service costs and machine down time. In addition, operators can better control costs by holding service employees accountable for cash and inventory and can boost revenue by selling injected detergent and fabric softener as part of a wash.

In the spring semester of 2002, a pilot program was run at Boston College. The students loved it. Based on that experience, IBM and USA Technologies have decided to connect about 9,000 of the machines on 40 campuses, all (so far) in the Midwest.

Sources: Weise (2002) and condensed from *usatech.com* (2003).

occurred in California over the past few years. By embedding intelligence in larger appliances, for example, air conditioners and freezers, the appliances could be notified when electricity was scarce and could modify their power consumption or shut down for short periods of time. Multiply the savings across millions of appliances, both in homes and businesses, and the power savings could be enormous.

To date, however, consumers have shown little interest in smart appliances. As a result, the manufacturers of these appliances are focusing on improving people's lives by eliminating repetitive, nonquality tasks. One example is Sunbeam's corded Home Linking Technology (HLT) products that communicate with one another using an embedded technology called Power Line Communication (PLC). This enables, for instance, an HLT alarm clock to coordinate an entire morning's routine. The heating system, the coffee maker, and the lights in the kids' rooms go on, and the electric blanket goes off.

Another example is Whirlpool's home-preparation concept (ETA Technology). This technology will automatically cook a full meal by the time a person gets home from work. Basically, it is a set of coordinate appliances—such as a slow cooker, a rice maker, and a bread maker—whose actions can be scheduled and automatically coordinated.

Whether offerings of this sort will prove any more successful than the earlier generations of smart appliances is an open question. In the near term, one of the biggest technical barriers to widespread adoption of smart appliances will continue to be the fact that most homes lack a broadband connection to the Internet.

SMART CARS

The average automobile on the road today has 20 or more microprocessors on board. The microprocessors on a car are truly invisible. They are under the hood, behind the dash, in the door panels, and on the undercarriage. They require little maintenance, continuing to operate through extreme temperature, vibration, and humidity.

The number of automobile microprocessors has been increasing steadily over the years. The increase has been driven by the need for the following: sophisticated engine controls to meet emissions and fuel-economy standards; advanced diagnostics; simplification of the manufacture and design of cars; reduction of the amount of wiring in cars; new safety features; and new comfort and convenience features.

Every car has at least one computer on board to operate the engine, regulate fuel consumption, and control exhaust emissions. Microprocessors control the radio, decide when the transmission should shift gears, remember seat positions, and adjust the temperature in the passenger cabin. They can make the suspension work better, help drivers see in the dark, and warn when a tire goes flat. In the shop, the onboard microprocessors are used to diagnose problems. Car computers often operate independently, but some swap data among themselves—a growing trend.

In 1998, the U.S. Department of Transportation (DOT) identified eight areas where microprocessors and intelligent systems could improve or impact auto safety (U.S. Department of Transportation 2002). The list included four kinds of collision avoidance, vision and vehicle stability, and two kinds of driver monitoring. The automotive industry is in the process of testing a variety of experimental systems addressing the areas identified by the DOT. For example, GM, in partnership with Delphi Automotive Systems, has developed an Automotive Collision Avoidance System that employs radar, video cameras, special sensors, and GPS to monitor traffic and driver actions in an effort to reduce collisions with other vehicles and pedestrians (Sharke 2003).

A growing trend is connecting car microprocessors to mobile networks. Emergency assistance, driving directions, and e-mail are some of the services these connections can support. GM's OnStar system (onstar.com) already supports many of these services. The OnStar system uses cellular telephone and satellite technology to connect a vehicle to a 24-hour service center. The system is controlled by a simple keypad or voice command. Some of the services provided by OnStar include:

▶ Air Bag Deployment Notification, which contacts the driver and offers assistance if the car's air bags are deployed.

▶ A voice-activated nationwide wireless calling service.

▶ Emergency services and roadside assistance that automatically locate an automobile and dispatch emergency assistance or roadside help. Or, if the driver is unable to continue, the service will contact family members or a taxi.

▶ The Personal Concierge, which plans entire trips, makes reservations, and purchases tickets to entertainment events.

▶ Route Support, which guides the driver to any destination.

▶ Stolen Vehicle Tracking, through which advisors can locate a stolen vehicle by satellite and contact the police.

▶ Remote Door Unlock, by which a driver who is locked out of the car can have the service send a signal to the car to unlock the doors.

▶ Remote Diagnostics, which runs a diagnostic test of the engine while the car is being driven.

OnStar is the forerunner of smart cars of the future. The next generation of smart cars is likely to provide even more automated services, especially in emergency situations. For instance, although OnStar will automatically signal the service center when the air bags are deployed and will immediately contact emergency services if the driver and passengers are incapacitated, what OnStar cannot provide is detailed information about a crash. Newer systems are under development that will automatically determine the speed upon impact, whether the car has rolled over, and whether the driver and passengers were wearing seat belts. Information of this sort might be used by emergency personnel to determine the severity of the accident and what types of services will be needed.

SMART "THINGS"

Barcodes

Barcodes are a familiar sight, at least the ones that appear on consumer items. This is the *Universal Product Code* (UPC). It is made up of 12 digits arranged into various groups. The first two digits show the country where the UPC was issued, the next four represent the manufacturer, and the remaining six are the product code assigned by the manufacturer. On a package, the code is represented by a series of bars and spaces of varying widths. Barcodes, like the UPC, are used at various points in the supply chain to track inventory and shipments and to identify items at the point of sale. A barcode scanner is required to support these tasks. It consists of a scanning device for reading the code and translating it into an electrical output, a decoder for converting the electrical output to data that a computer or terminal can recognize, and a cable that connects the decoder to a computer or terminal.

Barcodes have worked pretty well over the past 25 years. However, they have their limitations. First, they require line-of-sight of the scanning device. This is fine in a store but can pose substantial problems in a manufacturing plant, a warehouse, or on a shipping/receiving dock. Second, they are printed on paper, meaning that they can be ripped, soiled, or lost. Third, the barcode identifies the manufacturer and product, not the item. For example, every carton of milk of a given producer has the same barcode, regardless of when it was produced. This makes a barcode useless in determining things such as the expiration date.

Auto-ID

An alternative identification method that overcomes the limitations of barcodes is now available. This method has been promoted over the past couple of years by the **Auto Identification Center (Auto-ID)** (autoidcenter.org), a joint partnership among more than 87 global companies and three of the world's leading research universities—MIT in the United States, the University of Cambridge in the United Kingdom, and the University of Adelaide in Australia. The companies include manufacturers (e.g., Coca-Cola, Gillette, and Canon), retailers (e.g., Wal-Mart and Tesco), shippers (e.g., UPS and the U.S. Postal Service), standards bodies (e.g., Uniform Code Council), and government agencies (e.g., the U.S. Department of Defense). The mission of the center goes well beyond replacing one code with another. Its stated aim is to create an **Internet of Things**, a network that connects computers to objects—boxes of laundry detergent, pairs of jeans, airplane engines. This Internet

Auto Identification Center (Auto-ID)
Joint partnership among global companies and research universities to create an Internet of Things.

Internet of Things
A network that connects computers to objects in order to be able to track individual items as they move from factories to store shelves to recycling facilities, providing near-perfect supply chain visibility.

of Things will provide the ability to track individual items as they move from factories to store shelves to recycling facilities, providing near-perfect supply chain visibility. A network of this sort could eliminate human error from data collection, reduce inventories, keep products in-stock, reduce loss and waste, and improve safety and security.

The key technical elements of the Auto-ID system include:

- **RFID.** As discussed earlier, RFID is a generic term for technologies that use radio waves to automatically identify individual items. There are several methods of identifying objects using RFID, but the most common is to store a serial number that identifies a product, and perhaps other information, on a microchip that is attached to an antenna. (The chip and the antenna together are called a *RFID transponder* or a *RFID tag.*) The antenna enables the chip to transmit the identification information to a reader. The *RFID reader* converts the radio waves returned from the RFID tag into a form that can then be passed on to computers that can make use of it. One of the major benefits of an RFID tag is that it does not require line-of-sight to identify an object.

- **Electronic Product Code (EPC).** The Electronic Product Code (EPC) is a universal standard for product identification. Like a barcode, it is divided into numbers that identify the manufacturer, product, version, and serial number. It also includes an extra set of digits to identify unique items. The EPC is the only information stored on the RFID tag's microchip.

- **Object Name Service (ONS).** The EPC identifies only a product. To support the various links in the supply chain, other information is required. This information is provided by the Object Name Service (ONS), which points a computer to an address on the Internet where information about the product is stored. The concept is very similar to the Domain Name Service (DNS) that is used to identify the address of computers on the Internet.

- **Product Markup Language (PML).** In order to standardize the information about products, the center has proposed a new markup language, called Product Markup Language (PML). It is based on the widely accepted XML standard. The standard specifies the manner in which a product's name, category, manufacture date, expiration date, and the like will be represented in a computer. The PML can also be used to provide standards for representing special instructions for shipping, point-of-sale display, or preparation. The actual PML information for a given product will be stored on a PML server whose address is specified by the ONS.

- **Savant.** The center has created a software system, called Savant, that manages and moves information across corporate intranets and the public Internet. Savant gathers information from the RFID readers and passes it on to various business applications. Because of the tremendous numbers of items and products involved, Savant uses a distributed architecture rather than a single, centralized computer. In this way, it distributes the processing load across different computers so that existing systems are not overloaded.

Insights and Additions 10.4 (page 422) describes how these key technical elements support the supply chain process.

Cost of RFID

RFID has been around awhile. In World War II, RFIDs were used to identify friendly aircraft. Today, they are used in wireless tollbooth systems, such as the E-Z Pass used on highways throughout the Eastern United States. In Singapore, RFIDs are used in a system called Electronic Road Pricing, which charges different prices to drive on different roads at different times, encouraging drivers to stay off busy roads at busy times. Every car has an RFID tag that communicates with card readers on the major roads. The reader identifies each car and sends the information to a central computer that bills the car owner.

Until now, the problem with RFID has been the expense. Tags have cost at least 50 cents, which makes them unusable for low-priced items. A California company called Alien Technology (alientechnology.com) has invented a way to mass-produce RFID tags for less than 10 cents apiece for large production runs. In January 2003, Gillette placed an order

Electronic Product Code (EPC)
Universal standard for product identification, stored on an RFID tag.

Object Name Service (ONS)
Service that points a computer to an address on the Internet where information about a product is stored.

Product Markup Language (PML)
Proposed new markup language, based on the XML standard, that specifies how a product's name, category, manufacture date, expiration date, and the like will be represented in a computer.

Savant
Software created by the Auto-ID center that gathers information from RFID readers and passes it on to various business applications.

Insights and Additions 10.4   Auto-ID at Work

RFID, EPS, ONS, PML, and Savant are the underlying elements of the proposed Auto-ID system currently under development. Although each of these elements is important in its own right, it is the combination of these technologies that will impact the way in which goods are manufactured, distributed, delivered, and sold. The Auto-ID center has created the following example for a fictitious manufacturer, SuperCola, Inc., to illustrate how these elements will work in concert and their overall impact on supply chain. (See *autoidcenter.com* for a series of diagrams depicting the process.)

1. **Adding identity to products.** SuperCola, Inc. adds a RFID tag to every cola can it produces. Each tag is cheap (it costs about 5 cents) and contains a unique EPC. The EPC is stored in the tag's microchip which, at 400 microns square, is smaller than a grain of sand. The tag also includes a tiny radio antenna.
2. **Adding identity to cases.** The RFID tags will allow the cola cans to be identified, counted, and tracked in a completely automated, cost-effective fashion. The cans are packed into cases, which feature their own RFID tags, and loaded onto tagged pallets.
3. **Reading tags.** As the pallets of cola leave the manufacturer, an RFID reader positioned above the loading dock door hits the smart tags with radio waves, powering them. The tags "wake up" and start broadcasting their individual EPCs. Like a good kindergarten teacher, the reader allows only one tag to talk at a time. It rapidly switches them on and off in sequence, until it has read them all.
4. **Savant at work.** The RFID reader is wired into a computer system running Savant. It sends Savant the EPCs it has collected, and Savant goes to work. The system sends a query over the Internet to an ONS database, which acts like a reverse telephone directory—it receives a number and produces an address.
5. **PML at work.** This second server uses PML to store comprehensive data about manufacturers' products. It recognizes the incoming EPCs as belonging to cans of SuperCola, Inc.'s Cherry Hydro. Because it knows the location of the reader that sent the query, the system now also knows which plant produced the cola. If an incident involving a defect or tampering were to arise, this information would make it easy to track the source of the problem and to recall the products in question.
6. **Efficiency in distribution.** The pallets of cola arrive at the shipping service's distribution center. Thanks to RFID readers in the unloading area, there is no need to open packages and examine their contents. Savant provides a description of the cargo, and the cola is quickly routed to the appropriate truck.
7. **Efficiency in inventory.** The delivery of cola products arrives at SpeedyMart, which has been tracking the shipment thanks to its own Savant connection. SpeedyMart also has loading dock readers. As soon as the cola arrives, SpeedyMart's retail systems are automatically updated to include every can of Cherry Hydro that arrived. In this manner, SpeedyMart can locate its entire Cherry Hydro inventory automatically, accurately, and without incurring additional cost.
8. **Overstocking eliminated.** SpeedyMart's retail shelves also feature integrated readers. When the cans of cola are stocked, the shelves "understand" what is being put on them. Now, when a customer grabs a six-pack of Cherry Hydro, the diminished shelf will route a message to SpeedyMart's automated replenishment system, which will order more Cherry Hydro from SuperCola, Inc. With such a system, the need to maintain costly "safety volumes" of Cherry Hyrdo in remote warehouses is eliminated.
9. **Consumer convenience.** Auto-ID makes the customer's life easier, too. Rather than wait in line for a cashier, a customer can practically walk out the door with their purchases. A reader built into the door recognizes the items in the customer's cart by their individual EPCs; a swipe of their debit or credit card and the customer is out the door.

Source: Compiled from *autoidcenter.com* (2003).

with Alien Technology for 500 million RFID tags (*RFID Journal* 2002). Gillette will use the tags in a number of trial programs. In one of the early trials, Gillette will attach the tags to the Mach 3 razors they ship to Wal-Mart, whose store shelves will be equipped with special RFID readers. The overall success of RFID tags in the market place will depend on the outcome of trials such as this.

Section 10.9 ▶ REVIEW

1. Define pervasive computing.
2. List some of the major properties of pervasive computing.
3. Discuss some of the ways that pervasive computing can be used in the home.
4. Describe the OnStar system.

5. Describe some of the ways that microprocessors are being used to enhance the intelligence of appliances.

6. Discuss the key elements of Auto-ID.

10.10   INHIBITORS AND BARRIERS OF M-COMMERCE

Several limitations are slowing down the spread of m-commerce or leaving many m-commerce customers disappointed or dissatisfied. The major ones are covered in the following discussion.

THE USABILITY PROBLEM

When mobile Internet users visit mobile Internet sites, the *usability* of the site is critical to attract attention and retain user stickiness. There are three dimensions to usability, namely *effectiveness*, *efficiency*, and *satisfaction*. However, users find current mobile devices to be ineffective, particularly with respect to restricted keyboards and pocket-size screens, limiting their usability. In addition, because of the limited storage capacity and information access speed of most smartphones and PDAs, it is often difficult or impossible to download large files to these devices.

Mobile visitors to a Web site are typically paying premium rates for connections and are focused on a specific goal (e.g., conducting a stock trade). Therefore, if customers want to find exactly what they are looking for easily and quickly, they need more than text-only devices with small screens. In 2001, most WAP applications were text-based and had only simple black-and-white graphics. This made tasks such as mobile shopping difficult. Because all the transactions were essentially text-based, mobile users could not "browse" an online picture-based catalog. However, more and faster multimedia are becoming available as 3G spreads.

TECHNICAL LIMITATIONS

A number of technical limitations have slowed the spread of m-commerce, as discussed in the following sections.

Lack of a Standardized Security Protocol

As of 2003, there was no consensus on or standardization of the security methodologies that must be incorporated into all mobile-enabled Web sites and Wi-Fi hotspots. Because of this, customer confidence in the security of using their mobile phones or PDAs to make payments is low. In order for m-commerce to spread, confidence in its security must be raised.

Insufficient Bandwidth

A shortage of bandwidth limits the extent to which mobility can be viewed as a commodity (i.e., the extent to which mobility is characterized by widespread use, low cost, and little differentiation in service). This situation will continue to exist until widespread deployment and acceptance of 3G technologies. Given the decline in the telecommunications industry over the past few years, worldwide deployment of 3G will be limited in the near term.

Transmission and Power Consumption Limitations

Depending on the media used, users of mobile devices may experience multipath interference, weather and terrain problems, and distance-limited connections. In addition, reception in tunnels and certain buildings may be poor. For example, GPS may be inaccurate if the device is in a city with tall buildings. In addition, as bandwidth increases, power consumption increases. In a mobile device, this reduces battery life.

WAP Limitations

As noted earlier, WAP is the primary standard for delivering Web content to mobile devices. In today's wireless environment, WAP is underpowered. It takes too long to build a screen, and it requires too many screens to surface an application. The types of applications that can be surfed are very rudimentary when compared to standard Web applications. Overall, there are fewer than 50,000 WAP sites worldwide (mobileinfo.com 2003), compared to the millions of standard Web sites. Many of the WAP sites that do exist have minimal participation.

POTENTIAL HEALTH HAZARDS

The issue of cellular radio frequency emissions and the fear that radiation from wireless mobile devices may induce cancer has been debated for several years. As of 2002, no conclusive evidence has linked radiation from wireless devices with cancer (Rapid Interagency Committee 2001). However, drivers using mobile telephones have an increased chance of being involved in a traffic accident, even if they are using hands-free kits. In addition, the use of cell phones may interfere with sensitive medical devices, such as pacemakers. Researchers are examining these topics. Results are expected in 2003 to 2005.

Lawsuits relating to the potential health hazards of wireless devices have already been filed against major vendors (Borland 2000). In the meantime, the public is advised to adopt a precautionary approach in using mobile phones (e.g., use an earphone device that keeps the phone's antenna away from your head).

Section 10.10 ❭ REVIEW

1. Discuss the role that usability plays in the adoption of m-commerce.
2. List the technical limitations of m-commerce.
3. Describe the potential health hazards of mobile devices.

MANAGERIAL ISSUES

Some managerial issues related to this chapter are as follows.

1. **What's our timetable?** Although there has been a great deal of hype about m-commerce in the last few years, only a small number of large-scale m-commerce applications have been deployed to date. Exceptions include applications in e-banking, e-stock trading, emergency services, and some B2B tasks. This means that companies still have time to carefully craft an m-commerce strategy. This will reduce the number of failed initiatives and bankrupted companies.

2. **Which applications first?** Finding and prioritizing applications is a part of an organization's e-strategy. Although location-based advertising is logically attractive, its effectiveness may not be known for several years. Therefore, companies should be very careful in committing resources to m-commerce. For the near term, applications that enhance the efficiency and effectiveness of mobile workers are likely to have the highest payoff.

3. **Is it real or just a buzzword?** In the short run, m-commerce, and especially l-commerce, may be just buzzwords due to the many limitations they now face. However, in the long run, both concepts will fly. Management should monitor the technological developments and make plans accordingly.

4. **Which system to use?** The multiplicity of standards, devices, and supporting hardware and software can confuse a company planning to implement m-commerce. An unbiased consultant can be of great help. Checking the vendors and products carefully, as well as who is using them, is also critical. This issue is related to the issue of whether or not to use an application service provider (ASP) for m-commerce.

SUMMARY

In this chapter, you learned about the following EC issues as they relate to the learning objectives.

1. **Characteristics and attributes of m-commerce.** M-commerce is based on mobility and reach. These characteristics provide convenience, instant connectivity, product and service localization, ubiquity, and personalization.

2. **Drivers of m-commerce.** The following are the major drivers of m-commerce: large numbers of users of mobile devices, especially cell phones; no need for a PC; a developing "cell phone culture" in some areas; vendor marketing; declining prices; increasing bandwidth; and the explosion of EC in general.

3. **Supporting technologies.** M-commerce requires mobile devices (e.g., PDAs, cell phones) and other hardware, software, and wireless technologies. Commercial services and applications are still emerging. These technologies allow users to access the Internet anytime, anywhere. For l-commerce, a GPS receiver is needed.

4. **Wireless standards and technologies.** Standards are being developed by several organizations in different countries, resulting in competing systems. It is expected that over time some of these will converge.

5. **Finance, advertising, and content-providing applications.** Many EC applications in the service industries (e.g., banking, travel, and stocks) can be conducted with wireless devices. Also, shopping can be done from mobile devices. Location-based advertising and advertising via SMSs on a very large scale is expected. Mobile portals aggregate and provide content and services for mobile users.

6. **Intrabusiness applications.** Large numbers of intrabusiness applications, including inventory management, sales force automation, wireless voice, job dispatching, and more are already evident inside organizations.

7. **B2B applications.** Emerging B2B applications are being integrated with the supply chain and are facilitating cooperation between business partners.

8. **Consumer applications.** M-commerce is being used to provide applications in travel, gaming, entertainment, and delivery of medical services. Many other applications for individual consumers are being planned, especially targeted advertising.

9. **Non-Internet applications.** Most non-Internet applications involve various types of smart cards. They are used mainly in transportation, security, and shopping from vending machines and gas pumps.

10. **L-commerce.** Location-based commerce, or l-commerce, is emerging in applications such as calculating the arrival time of buses (using GPS) and providing emergency services (wireless 911). In the future, it will be used to target advertising to individuals based on their location. Other innovative applications are expected.

11. **Pervasive computing.** This is the world of invisible computing in which virtually every object has an embedded microprocessor that is connected in a wired or wireless fashion to the Internet. This Internet of Things—homes, appliances, cars, and many manufactured items—will provide a number of life-enhancing, consumer-centric, and B2B applications.

12. **Limitations of m-commerce.** The major limitations of m-commerce are small screens on mobile devices, limited bandwidth, high cost, lack of (or small) keyboards, transmission interferences, unproven security, and possible health hazards. Many of these limitations are expected to diminish over time.

KEY TERMS

1G	384	Location-based commerce (l-commerce)	410	Smartphone	385
2G	384	M-wallet (mobile wallet)	398	Subscriber Identification Module (SIM) card	390
2.5G	384	Microbrowser	389	Telematics	413
3G	384	Micropayments	397	Voice portal	396
4G	385	Mobile commerce (m-commerce, m-business)	384	Voice XML (VXML)	390
802.11b	392	Mobile portal	400	Wearable devices	400
Auto Identification Center (Auto-ID)	420	Multimedia Messaging Service (MMS)	385	Wireless 911 (e-911)	412
Automatic Crash Notification (ACN)	413	Object Name Service (ONS)	421	Wireless access point	392
Bluetooth	389	Personal Digital Assistant (PDA)	385	Wireless Application Protocol (WAP)	390
Electronic Product Code (EPC)	421	Pervasive computing	414	Wireless fidelity (Wi-Fi)	392
Enhanced Messaging Service (EMS)	385	Product Markup Language (PML)	421	Wireless Local Area Network (WLAN)	392
Geographical Information System (GIS)	411	Radio Frequency Identification (RFID)	414	Wireless Markup Language (WML)	390
Global Positioning System (GPS)	411	Savant	421	Wireless Transport Layer Security (WTLS)	394
Interactive Voice Response (IVR)	395	Screenphone	388		
Internet of Things	420	Short Message Service (SMS)	385		

DISCUSSION QUESTIONS

1. Discuss how m-commerce can solve some of the problems of the *digital divide* (the gap within a country or between countries with respect to people's ability to access the Internet). (See the 1999 report "Challenges to the Network" at itu.int.)

2. Discuss how m-commerce can expand the reach of EC.

3. Explain the role of protocols in m-commerce.

4. Discuss the impact of m-commerce on emergency medical services.

5. How do smartphones and screenphones differ? What characteristics do they share?

6. How are GIS and GPS related?

7. List three to four major advantages of wireless commerce to consumers presented in this chapter and explain what benefits they provide to consumers.

8. Location-based tools can help a driver find their car or the closest gas station. However, some people view location-based tools as an invasion of privacy. Discuss the pros and cons of location-based tools.

9. Discuss how wireless devices can help people with disabilities.

10. Discuss the benefits of IVR.

11. Discuss the benefits of telemetry-based systems.

12. Discuss the ways in which Wi-Fi is being used to support m-commerce. Describe the ways in which Wi-Fi is affecting the use of cellular phones for m-commerce.

13. Which of the following applications of pervasive computing—smart cars, homes, appliances, and things—are likely to gain the greatest market acceptance over the next few years?

14. Which of the current m-commerce limitations do you think will be minimized within 5 years? Which ones will not?

15. Describe some m-commerce B2B applications along the supply chain.

INTERNET EXERCISES

1. Learn about PDAs by visiting vendors' sites such as Palm, Handspring, HP, IBM, Phillips, NEC, Hitachi, Compaq, Casio, Brother, Texas Instruments, and others. List the m-commerce devices manufactured by these companies.

2. Access progressive.com, an insurance company, from your cell phone (use the "Go to . . ." feature). If you have a Sprint PCS wireless phone, do it via the Finance menu. If you have a Palm i705, you can download the Web-clipping application from Progressive. Report on these capabilities.

3. Research the status of 3G and the future of 4G by visiting itu.int, 4g.newstrove.com, and 3gnewsroom.com. Prepare a report on the status of 3G and 4G based on your findings.

4. Explore nokia.com. Prepare a summary of the types of mobile services and applications Nokia currently supports and plans to support in the future.

5. Enter kyocera-wireless.com. Take the smart tour and view the demos. What is a smartphone? What are its capabilities? How does it differ from a regular cell phone?

6. Enter www.i3mobile.com. Run the Pronto demo. What types of services are provided by Pronto? What types of users would be more likely to use Pronto rather than a smart phone?

7. Enter ibm.com. Search for *wireless e-business*. Research the resulting stories to determine the types of wireless capabilities and applications supported by IBM software and hardware. Describe some of the ways these applications have helped specific businesses and industries.

8. Using a search engine, try to determine whether there are any Wi-Fi hotspots in your area. Enter wardriving.com. Based on information provided at this site, what sorts of equipment and procedures could you use to locate hotspots in your area?

9. Enter mapinfo.com and look for the location-based services demos. Try all the demos. Find all of the wireless services. Summarize your findings.

10. Visit ordersup.com, astrology.com, and similar sites that capitalize on l-commerce. What features do these sites share?

11. Enter packetvideo.com and microsoft.com/mobile/pocketpc. Examine their demos and products and list their capabilities.

12. Enter internethomealliance.com and review their white papers. Based on these papers, what are the major appliances that are currently in most U.S.

homes? Which of these appliances would most home-owners be likely to connect to a centrally controlled network?

13. Enter onstar.com. What types of *fleet* services does OnStar provide? Are these any different from the services OnStar provides to individual car owners?

14. Enter autoidcenter.org. Read about the Internet of Things. What is it? What types of technologies are needed to support it? Why is it important?

15. Enter mdsi-advantex.com and review the wireless products for the enterprise. Summarize the advantages of the different products.

TEAM ASSIGNMENTS AND ROLE PLAYING

1. Each team should examine a major vendor of mobile devices (Nokia, Kyocera, Motorola, Palm, BlackBerry, etc.). Each team will research the capabilities and prices of the devices offered by each company and then make a class presentation, the objective of which is to convince the rest of the class why one should buy that company's products.

2. Each team should explore the commercial applications of m-commerce in one of the following areas: financial services, including banking, stocks, and insurance; marketing and advertising; manufacturing; travel and transportation; human resources management; public services; and health care. Each team will present a report to the class based on their findings. (Start at mobiforum.org.)

3. Each team will investigate a global organization involved in m-commerce, such as gmcforum.com and openmobilealliance.com. The teams will investigate the membership and the current projects the organization is working on and then present a report to the class based on their findings.

4. Each team will investigate a standards-setting organization and report on its procedures and progress in developing wireless standards. Start with the following: atis.org, etsi.org, and tiaonline.org.

5. Each team should take one of the following areas—homes, cars, appliances, or other consumer goods such as clothing—and investigate how embedded microprocessors are currently being used and will be used in the future to support consumer-centric services. Each team will present a report to the class based on their findings.

REAL-WORLD CASE

HERTZ GOES WIRELESS

The car rental industry is very competitive, and Hertz (*hertz.com*), the world's largest car rental company, competes against hundreds of companies in thousands of locations. Competition focuses on customer acquisition and loyalty. In the last few years, competition has intensified, and profits in the industry have been drifting downward. Hertz has been a "first mover" to information technologies since the 1970s, so it has naturally looked for new technologies to improve its competitive position. In addition to data warehousing and mining, a superb executive information system, and e-commerce, Hertz has pioneered a number of m-commerce applications:

 ▶ **Quick rentals.** Upon arrival at the airport, Hertz's curbside attendant greets the customer and transmits their name wirelessly to the renting booth. The renting-booth employee advises the curbside attendant about the location of the customer's car. All the customer needs to do is go to the slot where the car is parked and drive away. This system, which once operated over a WLAN, is now part of a national wireless network that

can check credit cards, examine a customer's rental history, determine which airline to credit loyalty mileage to, and more.

 ▶ **Instant returns.** Pioneered by Hertz in 1987, a handheld device connected to a database via a wireless system expedites the car return transaction. From the parking lot, the lot attendant uses a handheld device to calculate the cost of the rental and print a receipt for the renter. The customer can check out in less than a minute, and they do not have to enter the renting booth at all.

 ▶ **In-car cellular phones.** Starting in 1988, Hertz began renting cell phones with its cars. Today, of course, this is not as "big a deal" as it was in 1988, when it was a major innovation.

 ▶ **NeverLost Onboard.** Some cars come equipped with an onboard GPS system, which provides route guidance in the form of turn-by-turn directions to many destinations. The information is displayed on a screen with computer-generated voice prompts. An electronic mapping system (GIS) is combined with the GPS, enabling the driver to see on the map where they are and where they are going. Also, consumer information about the locations of the nearest hospitals, gas stations, restaurants, and tourist areas is provided.

- **Additional customer services.** Hertz's customers can download city guides, Hertz's location guide, emergency telephone numbers, city maps, shopping guides, and even reviews of restaurants, hotels, and entertainment into their PDAs and other wireless devices. Of course, driving directions are provided.

- **Car locations.** Hertz is experimenting with a GPS-based car-locating system. This will enable the company to know where a rental car is at any given time and even how fast it is being driven. Although the company promises to provide discounts based on driver usage pattern, this capability is seen by many as an invasion of privacy. On the other hand, some may feel safer knowing that Hertz knows where they are at all times.

Hertz has been the top car rental company and still maintains that position. It is also a very profitable company that is expanding and growing continuously. Its success is attributed to being customer-centric, as facilitated by its use of wireless technologies and EC.

Source: *hertz.com* (2003).

Questions

1. Which of these applications are intrabusiness in nature?

2. Identify any finance- and marketing-oriented applications.

3. What are the benefits to Hertz of knowing exactly where each of its cars is? As a renter, how would you feel about this capability?

REFERENCES

Amor, D. *Internet Future Strategies: How Pervasive Computing Services Will Change the World.* Upper Saddle River, NJ: Prentice Hall, 2001.

autoidcenter.com (accessed February 2003).

Axis Communications. *Mobile Access by Axis: Wireless Access Points.* 2001, axis.com/documentation/brochure/wireless/mobile_access.pdf (accessed May 2003).

Baard, M. "After the Fall: Help for Climbers." *Wired News,* December 24, 2002, wired.com/news/technology/0,1282,56146,00.html.

Becker, D. "Sega Forms Mobile Games Division." *CNET News.com,* April 2002, news.zdnet.co.uk/story/0,,t269-s2108679,00.html (accessed May 2003).

Borland, J. "Technology Tussle Underlies Wireless Web." *CNET News.com,* April 19, 2000, news.com.com/2100-1033-239482.html?legacy=cnet (accessed January 2003).

CellularOnline. "China Now Has More Than 200 Million Mobile Phone Users." cellular.co.za/news_2003/011003-china_now_has_more_than_200_mill.htm (accessed February 2003a).

CellularOnline. "Latest Global, Handset, Base Station, & Regional Cellular Statistics." cellular.co.za/stats/stats main.htm (accessed February 2003b).

Conrad, D. "Medlink to the Rescue." March 11, 2002, alaskasworld.com/news/2002/03/11_MedLink.asp (accessed February 2003).

CyberAtlas. "Mobile Users Yearning for Micropayments." March 12, 2002, cyberatlas.internet.com/markets/wireless/article/0,1323,10094_995801,00.html (accessed January 2003).

Dignan, L. and B. Charny. "Openwave Woes Bad Omen for Wireless." *CNET News.Com,* October 5, 2001, news.com.com/2100-1033-274005.html?tag-bplst, (accessed January 2003).

DPS-Promatic. "Innovative Pay-by-GSM Meter." June 2002, dpspro.com/tcs_news_park.html (accessed January 2003).

Duan, M. "Enhancing the Shopping Experience, One $2,000 Suit at a Time." *Mpulse,* November 2002, cooltown.hp.com/mpulse/1102-prada.asp (accessed January 2003).

Edgington, C. "How Internet Gateways and Smart Appliances Will Transform Our Homes." *TNTY Futures,* 2001, tnty.com/newsletter/futures/technology.html (accessed February 2003).

Eklund, B. "Wireless Advertising's Home of the Free." *Red Herring,* March 6, 2001, redherring.com/mag/issue94/650018065.html (accessed January 2003).

Eklund, R. "Mobile CRM Comes of Age." *CRM Magazine,* July 15, 2002, destinationcrm.com/articles/default.asp?ArticleID=2352 (accessed January 2003).

Evers, J. "Dutch Police Fight Cell Phone Theft with SMS Bombs." *IDG News Service,* March 27, 2001.

Fikes, B. "Unguarded Wireless Networks a Snap for 'Stumbling.'" *Californian North County Times*, nctimes.net/news/2003/20030112/53511.html (accessed January 2003).

Global Mobile Suppliers Association (GSA). "Survey of Mobile Portal Services." Quarter 4, 2002 gsacom.com/downloads/MPSQ4_2002.pdf (accessed January 2003).

Henning, T. "Wireless Imaging–Overcoming the Challenges." *The Future Image Report*, futureimage.com, 2002 (accessed January 2003).

hertz.com (accessed January 2003).

Hill, K. "Mobile CRM Software: The Race Is On." *Wireless NewsFactor Network*, December 3, 2002, crmbuyer.com/perl/story/20135.html (accessed January 2003).

Hornberger, M., and C. Kehlenbeck. "Mobile Financial Services on the Rise in Europe." Bank Systems and Technology Online. September 19, 2002, banktech.com/story/wireless/BNK20020919S0005 (accessed January 2003).

Houck, J. "For Hotel Check-in, Press 1 Now." *Wireless NewsFactor*, February 15, 2001, wirelessnewsfactor.com/perl/story/7547.html (accessed January 2003).

Kellner, M. "Is This the Year for Wireless Gear?" *Government Computer News*, gcn.com/22_2/buyers_guide/20950-1.html (accessed January 2003).

Lipset, V. "Bluefish and Zaryba Enable Mobile Bill Payment." January 21, 2003, mcommercetimes.com/Solutions/309 (accessed January 2003).

Lipset, V. "Magex Launches Mobile Payments Using SMS." December 3, 2002, mcommercetimes.com/Solutions/299 (accessed January 2003).

Ludorf, C. "U.S. Fleet Services and Wireless Networking." *Transportation and Technology Today*, August 2002, 12–15.

Mapinfo.Com. "MiAware." www.mapinfo.com/industries/mobile/miaware.cfm (accessed June 2003).

Mathieson, R. "The Future According to Spielberg: *Minority Report* and the World of Ubiquitous Computing." August 2002, *Cooltown*, cooltown.hp.com/mpulse/0802-minorityreport.asp (accessed January 2003).

Mayor, M. "Bluetooth App Slams Door on Hotel Room Keys." *Wireless NewsFactor*, April 4, 2001, wirelessnewsfactor.com/perl/story/8704.html (accessed February 2003).

McDougall, P. "Wireless Handhelds Speed Inventory." *Informationweek*, November 8, 1999, informationweek.com/760/palm.htm (accessed January 2003).

Mobileinfo.com. "Future Outlook for WAP." mobileinfo.com/WAP/future_outlook.htm (accessed January 2003).

Monteith, K. *Wireless E911: Regulatory Framework, Current Status, and Beyond*. Federal Communications Commission, January 24, 2002, nena.org/Wireless911/CIF%20Presentation%20PDFs/Kris%20Monteith.pdf (accessed February 2003).

Murphy, P. "Running Late? Take the NextBus." *Environmental News Network*, September 7, 1999, enn.com/enn-features-archive/1999/09/090799/nextbus_4692.asp (accessed January 2003).

Nelson, M. "Kemper Insurance Uses Wireless Digital Imaging to Lower Costs, Streamline Process." *InformationWeek*, September 25, 2000, informationweek.com/805/photo.htm (accessed January 2003).

Newstream.com. "PacketVideo Demonstrates Mobilemedia on Nokia Series 60 Devices." November 2002, newstream.com/us/story_pub.shtml?story_id=7810&user_ip=68.43.237.184 (accessed February 2003).

nextbus.com (accessed January 2003).

"NextBus Expands Real-Time Transit Information in the Bay Area with AC Transit." August 9, 2001, itsa.org/itsnews.nsf (accessed February 2003).

nokia.com. "Payment Solutions." nokia.com/pc_files/download.swf (accessed January 2003).

Nokia. "Nokia Brings Mobility to the Games Industry by Making Rich Games Mobile." Press release, November 4, 2002.

Palm Computing. "United Center Scores with Mobile Point-of-Sale System." palm.com/enterprise/studies/study15.html (accessed January 2003).

Pilato, F. "World's Mobile Phone Production Expands 6.5%—Short of 400 Million." September 4, 2002, mobilemag.com/content/100/102/C1277 (accessed January 2003).

Pinto, J. "The Pervasive Internet and Its Effect on Industrial Automation." November 2002, automationtechies.com/sitepagers/pid1020.php (accessed June 2003).

RFID Journal. "Gillette to Buy 500 Million EPC Tags." November 15, 2002, 216.121.131.129/articlc/articleprint/115/-1/1/ (accessed February 2003).

Raina, K., and A. Harsh. *MCommerce Security*. New York: Osborne, 2002.

Rapid Interagency Committee. "Mobile Phones, Cancer Not Linked in Two Short-Term Studies." *Microwave News*, January–February, 2001, microwavenews.com/j-f01ahf.html (accessed January 2003).

Republica IT. "Busta Paga in Pensione Lo Stipendio Arriva via SMS." March 20, 2001, repubblica.it/online/tecnologie_internet/tim/tim/tim.html (accessed January 2003).

Reuters. "Marriott Hotels to Offer Wi-Fi Access." December 18, 2002, news.com.com/2100-1033-978411.html (accessed February 2003).

SAP AG Corp. "CRM and the mySAP.com Mobile Workplace." SAP AG Brochure, 2000.

Sharke, P. "Smart Cars." *Mechanical Engineering*, 2003, www.memagazine.org/contents/current/features/smartcar/smartcar.html (accessed February 2003).

Siau, K., et al. "Mobile Commerce: Promises, Challenges, and Research Agenda." *Journal of Database Management* 12, no. 2 (2001): 4–13.

Smith Advanced Technology. "RALI Mobile." 2001, rali.com/Products/Mobile.htm (accessed January 2003).

Stanford, J. "Using Technology to Empower Assisted Living Patients." *Healthcare Review*, July 2, 2002.

Steede-Terry, K. *Integrating GIS and the Global Positioning System*. Redlands, CA: Environmental Systems Research Institute, 2000.

Taj Hotel. "Taj Hotels Introduce WiFi Facilities." *The Hindu*, July 31, 2002, thehindu.com/2002/07/31/stories/2002073102321600.htm (accessed February 2003).

Takahashi, D. "HP Partnership Will Work on Mobile Printing." *Mercury News*, October 16, 2002, bayarea.com/mld/siliconvalley/business/columnists/gmsv/4300513.htm (accessed January 2003).

usatech.com (accessed January 2003).

U.S. Department of Transportation. "Intelligent Vehicle Initiative." May 13, 2002, its.dot.gov/ivi/ivi.htm (accessed February 2003).

Varshney, U. and R. Vetter. "Recent Advances in Wireless Networking." *IEEE Computer* 33, no. 6 (2001): 100–103.

vindigo.com (accessed January 2003).

Weise, E. "Laundry Spins on the High Tech Cycle." *USA Today*, September 3, 2002, usatoday.com/tech/techreviews/products/2002-09-02-wired-washers_x.htm (accessed February 2003).

Weiser, M. "The Computer for the Twenty-First Century." *Scientific American* 265 (1991): 94–10.

XyberFlash. "Wearable Computers for the Working Class." *New York Times*, December 14, 2000, nytimes.com/2000/12/14/technology/14wear.htm (accessed February 2003).

Yankee Group. "Wireless Advertising: Still Waiting for Takeoff." November 2001, yankeegroup.com/public/products/research_note.jsp?ID=8907 (accessed January 2003).

AUCTIONS

Learning objectives

Upon completion of this chapter, you will be able to:

1. Define the various types of auctions and list their characteristics.

2. Describe the processes involved in conducting forward and reverse auctions.

3. Describe the benefits and limitations of auctions.

4. Describe some unique auction models.

5. Describe the various services that support auctions.

6. Describe the hazards of e-auction fraud and discuss possible countermeasures.

7. Describe bartering and negotiating.

8. Describe auction deployment and implementation issues.

9. Analyze future directions of mobile auctions.

Content

EBAY—THE WORLD'S LARGEST AUCTION SITE

The Opportunity

eBay is one of the most profitable e-businesses. The successful online auction house has its roots in a 50-year-old novelty item—Pez candy dispensers. Pam Omidyar, an avid collector of Pez dispensers, came up with the idea of trading them over the Internet. When she expressed this idea to her boyfriend (now her husband), Pierre Omidyar, he was instantly struck with the soon-to-be-famous e-business auction concept.

The Solution

In 1995, the Omidyars created a company called AuctionWeb. The company was renamed eBay and has since become the premier online auction house, with millions of unique auctions in progress and over 500,000 new items added each day. Today, eBay is much more than an auction house, but its initial success was in electronic auctions.

The initial business model of eBay was to provide an electronic infrastructure for conducting mostly C2C auctions. There is no auctioneer; technology manages the auctioning process.

On eBay, people can buy and sell just about anything. The company collects a submission fee upfront, plus a commission as a percentage of the sale amount. The submission fee is based on the amount of exposure the seller wants their item to receive, with a higher fee if the seller would like the item to be among the featured auctions in a specific product category, and an even higher fee if they want the item to be listed on the eBay home page under *Featured Items*. Another attention-grabbing option is to publish the product listing in a boldface font (for an additional charge).

The auction process begins when the seller fills in the appropriate registration information and posts a description of the item for sale. The seller must specify a minimum opening bid. If potential buyers feel this price is too high, the item may not receive any bids. Sellers might set the opening bid lower than the *reserve price,* a minimum acceptable bid price, to generate bidding activity.

If a successful bid is made, the seller and the buyer negotiate the payment method, shipping details, warranty, and other particulars. eBay serves as a liaison between the parties; it is the interface through which sellers and buyers can conduct business. eBay does not maintain a costly physical inventory or deal with shipping, handling, or other services that businesses such as Amazon.com and other retailers must provide. The eBay site basically serves individuals, but it also caters to small businesses.

In 2001, eBay started to auction fine art in collaboration with *icollector.com* of the United Kingdom and with the art auction house Sotheby's (*sothebys.com*), whose auction page is on eBay's main menu. Due to lack of profit, as of May 2003, eBay and Sotheby's discontinued separate online auctions and began placing emphasis on promoting Sotheby's live auctions through eBay's Live Auctions technology while they also continue to build eBay's highly successful arts and antiques categories. The *sothebys.com* Web site still exists, but now is focused on supporting Sotheby's live auction business.

In addition, eBay operates globally, permitting international trades to take place. Country-specific sites are located in over 25 countries, including the United States, Canada, France, Sweden, Brazil, the United Kingdom, Australia, Singapore, and Japan. Buyers from more than 150 other countries participate. eBay also operates a business exchange in which SMEs can buy and sell new and used merchandise in B2B or B2C modes.

eBay has over 60 local sites in the United States that enable users to easily find items located near them, to browse through items of local interest, and to meet face-to-face to conclude transactions. In addition, some eBay sites, such as eBay Motors, concentrate on specialty items. Trading can be done from anywhere, at any time. Wireless trading is also possible.

In 2002, eBay Seller Payment Protection began making it safer to sell on eBay. Now sellers are protected against bad checks and fraudulent credit card purchases. The service offers credit card chargeback protection, guaranteed electronic checks, secure processing, and privacy protection. After a few years of successful operation and tens of million of loyal members, eBay decided to leverage its large customer base and started to do e-tailing, mostly at fixed prices. This may have been in response to Amazon.com's decision to start auctions or it may have been a logical idea for a diversification. By 2003, eBay operated several specialty sites.

In addition to eBay Motors cited earlier, *half.com*, the famous discount e-tailer, is now part of eBay, and so is PayPal.com, the P2P payment company. A special feature is eBay Stores. These stores are rented to individuals and companies. The renting companies can use these stores to sell from catalogs or conduct auctions. In 2002, eBay introduced the Business Marketplace, located at *ebaybusiness.com*. This site brings together all business-related listings on eBay into one destination, making it easier for small businesses to find the equipment and supplies they need.

The Results

The impact of eBay on e-business has been profound. Its founders took a limited-access off-line business model and, by using the Internet, were able to bring it to the desktops of consumers worldwide. This business model consistently generates a profit and promotes a sense of community—a near addiction that keeps traders coming back.

eBay is the world's largest auction site, with a community of close to 50 million registered users as of fall 2002. According to company financial statements, in 2002, it transacted over $14.7 billion in sales.

As a matter of fact, the only place where people are doing more business online than off-line (and considerably more, at that) is auctions. For comparison, e-tailing is less than 2 percent of total retail sales (*emarketer.com* 2002).

Sources: Compiled from press releases at *eBay.com* (2002, 2003a, and 2003b), Cohen (2002), and Deitel et al. (2001).

WHAT WE CAN LEARN . . .

The eBay case demonstrates the success of a company that implemented an EC business model that took off very rapidly. The case presents some of the ideas of auctioning. It also demonstrates that auctions can be an online-only e-commerce channel or they can be a supplementary channel. The operations and issues of auctions, as well as their variations and economic impacts, are the subject of this chapter.

11.1 FUNDAMENTALS OF DYNAMIC PRICING AND AUCTIONS

As described in Chapter 2, an **auction** is a market mechanism by which sellers place items for buyers to make bids on (forward auction) or buyers place RFPs for specific items and sellers place bids to win the jobs (reverse auction). Auctions are characterized by the competitive and dynamic nature by which a final price is reached. Auctions, an established method of commerce for generations, deal with products and services for which conventional marketing channels are ineffective or inefficient.

The Internet provides an infrastructure for executing auctions at lower administrative costs and with many more participating sellers and buyers. **Electronic auctions (e-auctions)**, which are auctions conducted online, have been in existence for several years. Individual consumers and corporations alike can participate in this rapidly growing and very convenient form of electronic commerce. (For an elementary introduction see Rothkopf and Park 2001. For more on how to do auctions, see the tutorial at eBay.com.)

Although many consumer goods are not suitable for auctions and are best sold through conventional sales techniques (i.e., posted-price retailing), the flexibility offered by online auction trading may offer innovative market processes. For example, instead of searching for products and vendors by visiting sellers' Web sites, a buyer may solicit offers from all potential sellers. Such a buying mechanism is so innovative that it has the potential to be used for almost all types of consumer goods.

Many major manufacturers and e-tailers are using auctions to sell products and services (e.g., Dell, Amazon.com, Sam's Club, Wal-Mart) or to buy products and services (e.g., GE, GM, Boeing). Also, hundreds of intermediaries ranging from eBay.com to autions.cnet.com are active in this fast-growing, multibillion-dollar market.

As discussed in Chapter 2, the major characteristic of an auction is that it is based on dynamic pricing. **Dynamic pricing** refers to a transaction in which the price is not fixed but fluctuates based on supply-and-demand relationships. In contrast, catalog prices are fixed, as are prices in department stores, supermarkets, and many other storefronts.

There are several types of auctions, each with its own goals and procedures. As shown in Chapter 2, it is customary to classify dynamic pricing into four major categories depending on how many buyers and sellers are involved, as shown in Exhibit 11.1 (page 434) and described here. Each of the following auction types can be done online or off-line.

ONE BUYER, ONE SELLER

In the first configuration (pictured in the upper left-hand box in Exhibit 11.1), each party can use negotiation, bargaining, or bartering. The resulting price will be determined by bargaining power, supply and demand in the item's market, and possibly business-environment factors.

ONE SELLER, MANY POTENTIAL BUYERS

In the second configuration (in the bottom left-hand box of Exhibit 11.1, a seller uses a **forward auction** to offer a product to many potential bidders. There are four major types of forward auctions: English, Yankee, Dutch, and free-fall. (For additional details on these auctions, see Elliot 2000 and Prince 1999.) An example of B2C forward auctions is provided in Insights and Additions 11.1 (page 434).

auction
Market mechanism by which buyers make bids and sellers place offers; characterized by the competitive and dynamic nature by which the final price is reached.

electronic auctions (e-auctions)
Auctions conducted online.

dynamic pricing
Prices that are determined based on supply and demand relationships at any given time.

forward auction
An auction in which a seller offers a product to many potential buyers.

EXHIBIT 11.1 Types of Dynamic Pricing

	Sellers	
Buyers	**One**	**Many**
One	Negotiation, Bartering, Bargaining	Reverse auctions, RFQ, Tendering
Many	Forward (regular) auctions	Dynamic exchanges

sealed-bid auction

Auction in which each bidder bids only once; a silent auction, in which bidders do not know who is placing bids or what the prices are.

Vickrey auction

Sealed-bid auction in which the item is awarded to the highest bidder, but at the second-highest price that was bid (in the case of selling items).

Sealed-bid auctions are another example of one seller, many potential buyers auctions. In a **sealed-bid auction**, a bidder bids only once. It is a *silent auction*, and the bidders do not know who is placing bids or what the bids are. In a *first-price* sealed-bid auction, the item is awarded to the highest bidder.

In a *second-price* sealed-bid auction (also called a **Vickrey auction**), the item is awarded to the highest bidder, *but at the second-highest price that was bid.* This is done to alleviate bidders' fears of significantly exceeding the item's true market value. (Sealed-bid auctions also can be conducted in reverse auctions.)

ONE BUYER, MANY POTENTIAL SELLERS

Auctions in this category (pictured in the upper right-hand corner of Exhibit 11.1) are tenderings (biddings), in which one buyer solicits bids from many sellers or suppliers (see examples of GE and GM in Chapter 6). An item the buyer needs is placed on an RFQ (request for quote), and potential sellers bid on the item, *reducing the price sequentially.* (Refer back to Exhibit 2.5, page 52, for an illustration of this process.) These auctions are called

Insights and Additions 11.1 B2C Forward Auctions: Dell Auction

Consumers who want to buy or sell used or obsolete Dell products can go to *dellauction.com*. Buyers will find lots of information on the items they are interested in. For example, a buyer can find out if the seller is Dell (B2C) or an individual (C2C). The buyer also can check product details, such as item warranty and condition. The site also offers general services, such as escrow. Everything on the site is organized for both buyers and sellers, from shopping carts and account management features to payment and shipping services.

The site is clearly marked with icons that denote and allow for the following:

▶ Reserve price, which is the lowest price at which a seller is willing to sell an item

▶ English auction, in which items are sold to the highest bidder at the end of auction period

▶ Dutch auction, in which more than one item is up for bid at a time and all winning bidders pay the same price, which is the *lowest* winning bid on the items

▶ QuickWin auction, in which an item is sold to the first bidder who meets the threshold price (set by the seller)

▶ Classified listings, in which the buyer and seller communicate off-line to decide on a price for the item

▶ AutoMarkdown listings, which are designed to sell large quantities of items and are posted with an initial price that declines over the course of the auction until the quantities run out

▶ Fixed-price listings that offer items for sale at the price listed

▶ "Hot" listings, indicating that an item has generated a high level of bidding interest

reverse auctions because *suppliers* bid on goods or services the buyer needs. In reverse auctions, the price is reduced sequentially, and the lowest bid wins. These auctions are used mainly in B2B (both large and small businesses) or G2B.

B2B Reverse Auctions

Most of the publicity related to auctions is around the C2C and B2C markets. However, as described in Chapters 6 through 9, B2B reverse auctions are gaining popularity as an online mechanism for selling and especially for buying goods and services. Sashi and O'Leary (2002) present the opportunities, advantages, and economic benefits of B2B e-auctions.

C2C Reverse Auctions

Although most of C2C auctions are of a forward nature (usually the English type), increasingly, individuals are conducting reverse auctions. For example, if a person wants to buy a used car, they may create a *request-for-bid* (RFB, for individuals) for the car of their dreams and let those who have such cars contact them. C2C Reverse Auction Creator provides the software to do just that (see greatshop.com).

"Name-Your-Own-Price" Model

Another type of auction in the one buyer, many potential sellers category is the "name-your-own-price" model pioneered by Priceline.com. In this model, a would-be buyer specifies the price (or other terms) that they are willing to pay to any willing and able seller. This is basically a C2B model, although it is also used by some businesses (see Section 11.3). Competitors to Priceline offer similar models. A variation of the model as used by an entrepreneur is described in EC Application Case 11.1.

reverse auction
Auction in which the buyer places an item for bid (*tender*) on a request for quote (RFQ) system, potential suppliers bid on the job, with price reducing sequentially, and the lowest bid wins; used mainly in B2B and G2B e-commerce.

"name-your-own-price" model
Auction model in which would-be buyers specify the price (and other terms) they are willing to pay to any willing seller; a C2B model, pioneered by Priceline.com.

CASE 11.1
EC Application

REVERSE AUCTIONS FOR SMALL MOVERS AT DM & S

DM & S is a small trucking and moving company with less than $2 million in annual sales. During 1999, truckers were very busy, but in early 2000, the U.S. economy started to slow down and fuel prices increased. DM & S started to lose money, as did many other small truckers.

A major problem in the trucking industry is that trucks need to move cargo at certain times but they may not have a full load. Furthermore, on return trips trucks are usually not completely full or they may even be empty. Unused cargo space is lost revenue. Bret Lamperes, owner and CEO of DM & S, had an idea: create a service in which small moving companies bid on jobs of moving goods for individuals. Customers with flexible moving dates would benefit the most.

Lamperes spent $15,000 to create an auction site, *dickerabid.com*, for the new service. Once customers place notice of their job on the site, small truckers start to bid. For a trucker with a destination and travel date that matches the customers' requirement, hauling almost anything is better than going with empty space. They can earn money to help cover their fuel expenses. Simultaneously, customers can get huge discounts.

Starting with four participating truckers and increasing to 20, the auction site increased DM & S's revenues by $14,000 during the first few months of operation. Additional revenue is generated by advertisers that cater to people who are relocating, such as furniture and window-blind companies. The Web site won third place in *Inc.*'s Web innovations in 2000.

DM & S is a small, third-party auction maker, as well as a buyer of small truckers' services. (Compare it to NTE, in Chapter 2, for example, which was a large, full-fledged exchange.) Larger truckers (moving companies) also have their own auction Web site, *imove.com* (now part of SIRVA moving services, which includes Allied, Global, and North American Van Lines), which provides a considerable amount of services and information.

Sources: *Inc.* (2000) and *dickerabid.com* (2002).

Questions

1. Why is it easy, from a technology point of view, to build an inexpensive auction site such as this one?
2. What are some of the potential difficulties in operating such a site?
3. Can you think of similar applications for a small company in other industries?
4. Compare *imove.com* to *dickerabid.com*. How are they similar? How do they differ?

MANY SELLERS, MANY BUYERS

In this final configuration (the bottom right-hand box in Exhibit 11.1), buyers and their bidding prices are matched with sellers and their asking prices based on the quantities on both sides and the dynamic interaction between the buyers and sellers. Stocks and commodities markets are typical examples of this type of configuration (see also Chapter 7). Buyers and sellers can be individuals or businesses. Such auctions are called double auctions (see Section 11.6).

Section 11.1 ▶ REVIEW

1. List the four categories of auctions.
2. List the major auction models available to one seller.
3. List the auction models available to one buyer.

11.2   BENEFITS, LIMITATIONS, AND STRATEGIC USES OF AUCTIONS

As stated in Chapter 2, electronic auctions are becoming important selling and buying channels for companies and individuals. Almost perfect market information is available to both buyers and sellers about prices, products, current supply and demand, and so on. These features provide benefits to all.

BENEFITS OF E-AUCTIONS

Electronic auctions create some economic changes that benefit both sellers and buyers. The major economic impacts of auctions are summarized in Exhibit 11.2.

Benefits to Sellers

Electronic auctions provide the following benefits to sellers.

Increased revenues. By broadening the customer base and shortening the disposal cycle time, sellers can reach the most interested buyers in the most efficient way and sell more at a

EXHIBIT 11.2   Economic Impacts of Auctions

Impact	Description
Market liquidity	Increased numbers of buyers and sellers who can easily find each other online and participate. This includes global participation.
Coordination mechanism for equilibrium in prices	Efficient mechanism for setting prices based on supply, demand, and participants' requirements.
Price discovery	Both buyers and sellers can easily find existing offers and bids, as well as historical price settlements. This is especially important in rare items.
Highly visible distribution mechanism	Via special offers, attention is given to certain groups of sellers (e.g., liquidators) and buyers (e.g., bargain hunters).
Price transparency	Prices are visible to all; this allows sellers to be more realistic, and buyers to be more careful in making offers.
Volume effect	The larger the auction sites (e.g., eBay), the more of the previous impacts are felt. Thus, transaction costs are lower, more people can find what they want, and more sellers can sell quickly at reasonable prices.

price equal to buyer valuation of the product. This eliminates the need to predict demand and the risk of pricing items too high or too low.

Optimal price setting. Sellers can make use of the information about price sensitivity collected in auctions to set prices in fixed-price markets.

Removal of expensive intermediaries. Sellers can gain more customer dollars by offering items directly, rather than going through an expensive intermediary or by using an expensive physical auction. Using e-auctions via intermediaries can be more cost-effective than using a physical auction place.

Better customer relationships. Buyers and sellers have more chances and time to interact with each other, thus creating a sense of community and loyalty. Additionally, by making use of information gathered on customer interests, sellers can improve the overall e-commerce experiences of buyers and can deliver more personalized content, thus enhancing customer relationships.

Liquidation. Sellers can liquidate large quantities of obsolete or surplus items very quickly (see the Real-World Case at the end of this chapter).

Lower transaction costs. Compared to manual auctions and liquidations, e-auctions offer lower transaction costs.

Lower administrative cost. The cost of selling via e-auctions can be much lower than the costs of selling via e-retailing or via non-Internet auctions.

Benefits of E-Auctions to Buyers

Electronic auctions provide the following benefits to buyers.

Opportunities to find unique items and collectibles. Items that are hard to find in certain areas or at certain times are auctioned regularly on the Internet. Stamps, coins, Barbie dolls, and the Pez dispensers that started the idea of eBay are examples of popular collectible items on the Internet.

Chance to pay less. Instead of buying at a fixed price, buyers can use the bidding mechanism to reduce prices.

Entertainment. Participating in e-auctions can be entertaining and exciting. The competitive environment, as well as the interaction between buyers and sellers, may create goodwill and positive feelings. Buyers can interact with sellers as much or as little as they like.

Anonymity. With the help of a third party, e-auction buyers can remain anonymous if they choose to.

Convenience. Buyers can trade from anywhere, even with a cell phone (m-commerce auctions).

Benefits to E-Auctioneers

Electronic auctions provide the following benefits to e-auctioneers.

Higher repeat purchases. Jupiter Communications conducted a study in 1998 that showed comparative repeat-purchase rates across some of the top e-commerce sites (Subramaniam 2000). The findings indicated that auction sites, such as eBay and uBid, tend to garner higher repeat-purchase rates than the top e-commerce B2C sites, such as Amazon.com.

A stickier Web site. "Stickiness" (Chapter 5) refers to the tendency of customers to stay at Web sites longer and come back more. Auction sites are frequently stickier than fixed-priced sites. With sticky sites, more advertising revenue can be generated because of more impressions and longer viewing times.

Expansion of the auction business. An example of how auctioneers can expand their business can be seen in the example of Manheim Auctions (McKeown and Watson 1999). In response to the Japanese company Aucnet's efforts to penetrate the U.S. car auction business, Manheim Auctions, the world's largest conventional auction house, created Manheim Online (MOL) in 1999 to sell program cars (cars that have been previously leased or hired). This Internet-based system has tremendous potential to change the car auction business. The United States has over 80,000 used car dealers, and Manheim auctions some 6 million cars for them each year. Trying to leverage its knowledge of the automobile market to provide services to its customers, Manheim developed two other products, Manheim Market Report and AutoConnect. It also is expanding its auction business in Europe. Manheim wants to continue to add value to Manheim Online as a way of discouraging competition and of extending sales through the Internet without cannibalizing Manheim's core business. By 2003, hundreds of car auction sites had gone online. Portals such as eBay, Yahoo, Amazon.com, and MSN offer thousands of cars each year (car---auctions.com 2003).

LIMITATIONS OF E-AUCTIONS

As discussed in Chapter 2, e-auctions have several limitations, including the following.

Possibility of fraud. The fraud rate in e-auctions is very high. Auction items are in many cases unique, used, or antique. Because buyers cannot see the item, they may get a defective product. Buyers can also commit fraud. (For specific fraud techniques and how to prevent them, see Section 11.7.)

Limited participation. Some auctions are by invitation only; others are open only to dealers.

Security. Some of the C2C auctions conducted on the Internet are not secure, and some potential participants are scared away by the lack of security.

Auction software. Unfortunately, auction software is limited. Only a few off-the-shelf software solutions that can support the dynamic commerce functionality required for optimizing pricing strategies and that can be easily customized to a company or industry are available. However, this situation is improving with time.

Long cycle time. Some auctions last for days, and in some cases sellers and buyers need to meet face-to-face or with an escrow agent to complete a deal. This may take time, and buyers and sellers may not want to invest such time.

Monitoring time. Although in some cases buyers can use intelligent agents to monitor an auction and place bids, in others they have to do this time-consuming job themselves.

Equipment for buyers. Buyers need a PC to engage in electronic auctions, and they also need to pay for Internet access. These requirements have somewhat limited the number of potential auction participants. These requirements are changing as people are starting to use their cell phones for auctions; however, an Internet-connected cell phone is required.

Order fulfillment costs. Buying at an auction site means that the buyer will pay shipment and handling costs plus any extra insurance cost.

STRATEGIC USES OF AUCTIONS AND PRICING MECHANISMS

Through dynamic pricing, buyers and sellers are able to adjust pricing strategies and optimize product inventory levels very quickly. For example, by using Web-based auctions and exchanges, suppliers can quickly flush excess inventory and liquidate idle assets. Buyers may end up with the power to procure goods and services at the prices they desire. The end game is to accurately assess and exploit market supply-and-demand requirements faster and more efficiently than the competition.

Aberdeen Group (2000) showed that e-marketplaces that are using auctions extensively are reaching liquidity ("critical mass") more rapidly than those utilizing only catalog-order-based trading environments. However, businesses are still struggling to understand how to truly implement dynamic pricing models to augment existing business practices.

One suggestion of how to do so was provided by Westland (2000), who observed that e-auctions place much more power in the hands of the consumer than does e-tailing done by using catalogs. He suggested that a number of lessons from stock exchange trading can be applied to e-tailing auctions; these lessons are listed at the book's Web site.

For a summary of the impacts of electronic auctions on their participants, see Exhibit W11.1 at the book's Web site.

Section 11.2 ▶ REVIEW

1. List the major benefits of auctions to buyers.
2. List the major benefits of auctions to sellers.
3. List the benefits of auctions to auctioneers.
4. List the limitations of auctions.

11.3 THE "NAME-YOUR-OWN-PRICE" C2B MODEL

One of the most interesting e-commerce models is the *"name-your-own-price" model*. This model, which appears in several variations, is associated with Priceline.com (priceline.com). As described in Chapter 2, Priceline.com pioneered this model, which enables consumers to achieve significant savings by naming their own price for goods and services. Basically, the concept is that of a C2B reverse auction, in which vendors bid on a job by submitting offers and the lowest-priced vendor or the one that meets the buyer's requirements gets the job. Priceline and its "name-your-own-price" model is one of the most recognized e-commerce brands on the Web today.

Priceline.com either presents consumer offers to sellers who can fill as much of that guaranteed demand as they wish at price points requested by buyers, or, more likely, searches a Priceline.com database that contains vendors' minimum prices and tries to match supply against requests. Priceline.com asks customers to guarantee acceptance of the offer if it is at or below the requested price. Priceline.com guarantees this by having the buyer's credit card number. Priceline.com's "virtual" business model allows for rapid scaling, using the Internet for collecting consumer demand and trying to fill it. The approach is based on the fundamental concept of the downward-sloping demand curve in which prices vary based on demand.

However, Priceline.com and similar companies have one limitation: When a buyer names their own price for airline tickets, they are *not* told what airline they are going to fly with, how many stops are involved, or what time of the day the flight will depart until the buyer accepts the offer and pays. Then, the buyer must take the offer or lose that money that they guaranteed by a credit card. To overcome this problem, travelers can go to online travel sites, such as expedia.com, orbitz.com, travelocity.com, aa.com, or others, that provide price comparisons. By becoming familiar with the routes and flights, a buyer may be able to find what is available and then go to Priceline and bid for lower prices, knowing basically who is offering what. This way buyers will get real bargains.

Priceline.com has offered multiple products and services: travel services, personal finance services, an automotive service that offers new cars for sale, and credit cards and long-distance calling. (In 2000, Priceline.com suspended the delivery of food, gasoline, and groceries due to accumulated losses.) Some of the services are offered via partners. Priceline.com receives either a commission for referrals or royalties for use of its technology. Also in 2000, the company teamed up with Hutchison Whampoa Limited, one of Asia's largest owners of telecommunications and Internet infrastructure, to offer a range of services in Asia. Priceline.com also has offices in many other countries.

By 2002, the company offered products for sale in two categories: (1) a travel service that offers leisure airline tickets, hotel rooms, rental cars, vacation packages and cruises; and (2) a personal finance service that offers home mortgages, refinancing, and home equity loans through an independent licensee. Also in 2002, Priceline.com purchased the Internet domain names and trademarks of LowestFare.com, another Web-based travel site. Priceline.com licenses its business model to independent licensees, including pricelinemortgage.com and certain international licensees.

At one point, Priceline.com initiated a service for helping people get rid of old things that they no longer wanted. It was similar to an auction site, with heavy emphasis on second-hand goods, but with a different auction process. The site, named Perfect YardSale, was intended to let a user make an offer below the seller's asking price for an item, a system that is similar to the haggling that goes on at garage and yard sales. Perfect YardSale transactions were limited to local metropolitan areas, enabling the buyer and seller to meet face-to-face. Buyers and sellers would be able to swap goods in person, eliminating the expense of shipping. This service was discontinued in 2001 due to incurred losses. A variation of this service is the sale of previously owned items at fixed prices by half.com (now a subsidiary of eBay).

Section 11.3 ▶ REVIEW

1. What is the logic behind the "name-your-own-price" model?
2. Describe Priceline.com's business model.
3. How does Priceline.com match supply and demand?
4. Enter priceline.com and try to book a flight. Comment on your experience.

11.4 THE AUCTION PROCESS AND SOFTWARE SUPPORT

A number of software products and intelligent tools are available to help buyers and sellers find an auction site, identify what is going on there, or complete a transaction. In an auction, sellers and buyers usually complete a four-phase process: searching and comparing, getting started at an auction, actual bidding, and postauction activities (see Exhibit 11.3). Each phase has several support tools. Let's explore them by the auction phase in which they are used.

PHASE 1: SEARCHING AND COMPARING

Auctions are conducted on hundreds of sites worldwide. Therefore, sellers and buyers need to execute extensive searches and comparisons to select desirable auction locations. The following support tools may be helpful in conducting these searches and comparisons.

Finding when and where an item will be auctioned. Many Web sites offer links to hundreds of auction sites or provide search tools for specific sites. The searching utility not only helps sellers find suitable locations to list their items, but it also enables buyers to browse available auction sites efficiently. See Insights and Additions 11.2 for an example of how to find when and where an item is being auctioned.

The following are some popular auction search tools:

▶ Online Auctions Network (online-auctions.net) contains a directory of auction sites organized by categories, as well as auction news.

▶ The Internet Auction List (internetauctionlist.com) is packed with news about e-auctions worldwide and features access to innumerable specialty auctions.

▶ Yahoo's auction list (auctions.yahoo.com) contains a list of over 400 auction-related links.

▶ BidXS (bidxs.com) conducts searches across multiple auction houses for specific auction products and pricing information. It provides detailed historical information on previous sales.

▶ Turbobid (etusa.com) provides a mega-search service that helps local bidders look for items they want from a pool of e-auction sites.

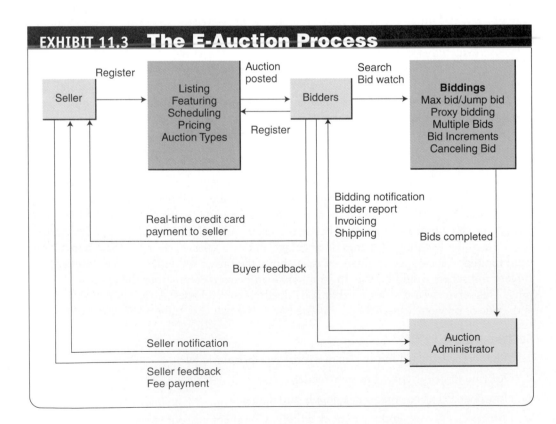

EXHIBIT 11.3   The E-Auction Process

Insights and Additions 11.2   Finding a Pool Table and More

Assume a potential buyer is interested in purchasing a pool table. The following process is one example of how that buyer might use the Internet to locate the desired pool table. To find auctions that feature pool tables, the would-be buyer performs the following two steps:

1. Enter *bidxs.com*.
2. Enter "pool table" as the key word option.

The search engine claims that it searches more than 200 auction sites. The buyer's key word search found 63 auctions, organized as shown here. The buyer can sort auctions by type of seller, item, auction site, price, current highest bid, and closing time.

To decide on a reasonable price for a pool table, the buyer can check price histories. Price histories for a pool table, however, were not available on the site, but a buyer might find a great deal of price history on other products. For example, a Barbie doll search generated price ranges at different times during the last 12 months. Assume now that the buyer has a new desire—an airplane. The buyer returns to *bidxs.com* and searches for a Boeing 777. One auction notes a Herpa Wings Emirates Boeing 777–200 for $18. This, of course, is a toy plane, rather than the real plane the buyer wants, but the buyer can register with the site's auction tracker, which promises to track any product including an airplane. This free service, provided by the auction house, will "ping" the buyer with a notification alert if any similar merchandise becomes available.

Site	Description (Click on column header to sort results)	Pic	Price	Bids	Expires
Yahoo	HOT Earnhardt **Pool Table** Cue/Rack/Brush L@@K!!	📷	$24.75	0	1 day 5 hrs 58 mins
Yahoo	Executive Size **Pool Table** - NEW	📷	$82.00	0	2 days 4 hrs 58 mins
Amazon	8 Harvard **Pool Table** Billiards, Half Price!	📷	$388.88	0	1 day 1 hr 27 mins
Amazon	Harvard Dlx Wall Rack Billiards **Pool Table**	📷	$32.99	0	1 day 0 hrs 27 mins
eBay	SOLID CHERRY **POOL**/BILLIARDS **TABLE**-*NO RESERVE	📷	$710.00	0	0 hrs 0 mins
eBay	Med-Oak **Pool**/Billiards **Table**, NEW, FREE SHIP	📷	$1225.00	0	0 hrs 0 mins

Source: Courtesy of BidXS, a division of Seet Internet Ventures, Inc., ©2003.

Auction aggregators and notification. The search to find what is being auctioned and where can be difficult; there are thousands of auction sites, some of which are very specialized. **Auction aggregators** are companies that use software agents to visit Web auction sites, find information, and deliver it to users. Leading aggregators are auctionwatch.com, bidfind.com, auctionsonthenet.com, and rubylane.com.

At these aggregation sites, buyers fill out electronic forms specifying the item they want. Then the aggregators keep tabs on various auction sites and notify buyers by e-mail when the items they wish to bid on appear. For example, CityAuction's Notify Me and eBay's Favorite Searches assist bidders at these sites.

Aggregation services are beneficial to users but may not be appreciated by the auction sites, as discussed in Insights and Additions W11.1 at the book's Web site.

The task of auction aggregation can be complex when the aggregators have to monitor several items, at several auction sites, in several auction formats. An international

auction aggregators
Companies that use software agents to visit Web auction sites, find information, and deliver it to users.

competition took place in 2000 called the Trading Agent Competition (TAC) to identify the best aggregators. See auction2.eecs.umich.edu to read about TAC 2001 and TAC 2002.

Browsing site categories. Almost all auction home pages contain a directory of categories. Buyers can browse a category and its subcategories to narrow a search. Some sites also enable users to sort items according to the time a specific auction is being conducted.

Basic and advanced searching. Buyers can use search engines to look for a single term, multiple terms, or key words. To conduct an advanced search, buyers can fill in a search form to specify search titles, item descriptions, sellers' IDs, auction item numbers, price ranges, locations, closing dates, completed auctions, and so forth.

PHASE 2: GETTING STARTED AT AN AUCTION

To participate in an auction, both sellers and buyers need to register at the selected site. After registration, sellers can list, feature, schedule, and price their items on the site. Buyers can check sellers' profiles and other details, such as the minimum bid amount, the auction policy, and the payment method allowed, and then place their bids.

Registration and profiles. Sellers and buyers must usually register their names, user IDs, and passwords before they can participate at a specific auction site. The user's page header (heading at the top of the screen) and the auction listing will display a basic description of sellers and their listings. Before submitting a bid, buyers can check a seller's profile, including the seller's membership ID and previous transactions. If the auction site provides voluntary verified-user programs such as BidSafe (auctions.com), buyers can check whether sellers are qualified auction community members as verified by a third-party security source.

Listing and promoting. Several software programs are available that can help sellers list and promote their items:

▶ Advertisement Wizard (see illumix.com) helps users create attractive auction postings. With a simple-to-use, fill-in-the-blank interface, users can create great-looking advertisements for e-auctions or for other purposes.

▶ Auction Assistant (see tucows.com) and Ad Studio (adstudio.net) can be combined to create auction listings. This combination enables users to manipulate fonts, backgrounds, and themes on their listings. It also enables users to include standard details, such as shipping policy and payment terms, and to track sales, payments, and shipping.

▶ Auctiva Mr. Poster (aucitva.com), a software program that interacts directly with eBay, makes it simple to add pictures to a listing. The program can create up to 100 ads at a time, and it supports bulk listing.

▶ Auction Wizard (auctionwizard2000.com) can upload up to 100 items simultaneously. It is an auction-posting tool that saves time spent cutting and pasting. Auction Wizard also enters user ID, password, auction title, location, opening bid, category, and auction duration.

▶ Mister Lister (ebay.com/services/buyandsell), one of eBay's tools, enables sellers to upload the listings of many items at one time. Similarly, using Bulk Loader (see Yahoo Auctions at auctions.yahoo.com), sellers can load several auctions into a spreadsheet program such as Microsoft Excel.

Pricing. To post an item for bid, sellers have to decide the minimum bid amount, the bid increment, and any *reserve price* (i.e., the lowest price for which a seller is willing to sell an item). Sellers can search for guides for setting minimum bid amounts, the bid increments, and reserve prices for comparable auctions with Web search engines such as bidfind.com, freemerchant.com, pricescan.com, and auctionwatch.com. If the auction site allows users to search completed auctions, the transacted prices of similar items can provide a benchmark for a buyer's bidding strategy or a minimum acceptable price for a seller.

PHASE 3: THE ACTUAL BIDDING

In the bidding phase, buyers can submit bids themselves or can make use of software tools that place bids on their behalf. They can also use software tools to view the bidding status and to place bids across different sites in real time.

Bid watching and multiple bids. Buyers can visit their personalized page at an e-auction Web site at any time and keep track of the status of active auctions. They can review bids and auctions they are currently winning or losing or have recently won. Tools provided in the United States by Bid Monitor (see bruceclay.com) and EasyScreen Layout (see auctionbroker.com) enable bidders to view their bids across different auction sites in an organized way. Bidders can also use the tools to place bids at multiple auction sites using a single screen without switching from one window to another.

Sniping. The act of entering a bid during the very last seconds of an auction and outbidding the highest bidder is called sniping. *Auto-sniping* involves the use of electronic tools to perform the sniping automatically.

Occasionally, sellers use sniping in a fraudulent way: When the bidding price seems to be too low, they may enter the auction and bid for their own goods or services, pretending they are buyers. In this way, they hope to inspire other bidders to join in at higher prices. (Being aware of this possible activity should help one avoid being caught up in last-minute bidding frenzy and overpaying in an online auction.)

Proxy bids. A software system can be used for proxy bidding, in which the system operates as a *proxy* (agent) to place bids on behalf of buyers. In proxy bidding, a buyer should determine their maximum bid and then place the first bid manually. The proxy will then execute the buyer's bids, trying to keep the bids as low as possible. When someone enters a new bid, the proxy will automatically raise the bid to the next level until it reaches the predetermined maximum price. This function is not applicable in a Dutch auction.

PHASE 4: POSTAUCTION FOLLOW-UP

Postauction activities take place once an auction in completed. These activities include e-mail notifications and arrangements for payment and shipping. A typical postauction tool is Easy! Auction (saveeasy.com).

Postauction notifications. Typical postauction activities include the following:

▶ **Bidding notifications.** Buyers receive e-mail, SMS messages, or beeper messages notifying them while the bidding is going on (English auctions), each time they are outbid, or when they win an auction.

▶ **End-of-auction notices.** When an auction closes, the seller receives an e-mail (or SMS) message naming the highest bidder. End-of-auction e-mails provide seller and buyer IDs; seller and winner e-mail addresses (or cell phone number); a link to the auction ad, auction title, or item name; the final price; the auction ending date and time; the total number of bids; and the starting and highest bid amounts.

▶ **Seller notices.** After an auction ends, the seller generally contacts the buyer. The seller's notice typically provides the auction number and item name, total purchase price (winning bid plus shipping), payment preferences, mailing address, and so on.

▶ **Postcards and thank-you notes.** Sites such as auctionwatch.com help sellers create a customized close-of-auction or thank-you note for winning bidders.

User communication. User-to-user online communication provides an avenue by which auction participants can share information about goods and services being offered and about the process of online auctions. User communication appears in a number of forms:

▶ **Chat groups.** Areas on e-auction sites and auction-related sites where people can post messages in real time to get quick feedback from others.

▶ **Mailing lists.** A group of people talking about a chosen topic via e-mail messages.

▶ **Message boards.** Areas on e-auction and auction-related sites where people can post messages that other users can read at their convenience. Other message board participants can post replies for all to read.

Feedback and ratings. Most e-auction sites provide a feedback and rating feature that enables auction community members to monitor each other. This feature enables users to rank sellers or bidders and to add short comments about sellers, bidders, and transactions.

Invoicing and billing. An invoicing tool (invoicing utility) can e-mail and print one or all invoices, search and arrange invoices in a number of ways, edit invoices, and delete

sniping
Entering a bid during the very last seconds of an auction and outbidding the highest bidder (in the case of selling items).

proxy bidding
Use of a software system to place bids on behalf of buyers; when another bidder places a bid, the software (the proxy) will automatically raise the bid to the next level until it reaches the predetermined maximum price.

incorrect invoices. This utility automatically calculates shipping charges and sales tax. It can also automatically calculate and charge the seller with the listing fees and/or a percentage of the sale as commission. An example of this tool is Accounting 2002 from Billboardnet International (billboardnet.com).

Payment methods. Sellers and winning bidders can arrange payment to be made by cashier's check, C.O.D. (cash on delivery), credit card, electronic transfer, or through an escrow service (see Chapter 13). A number of online services are available for electronic transfer, escrow services, and credit card payment, including the following:

▶ **Electronic transfer service.** Buyers can pay electronically via services at sites such as paybyweb.com, paypal.com, and bidpay.com. (See Chapter 13 for further discussion.)

▶ **Escrow service.** An independent third party holds a bidder's payment in trust until the buyer receives and accepts the auction item from the seller. The third party charges a fee for the escrow service, and the service is usually reserved for high-end transactions. Examples of escrow service provider sites are valicert.com and escrow.com.

▶ **Credit card payment.** PayPal (paypal.com) and CCNow (ccnow.com) facilitate person-to-person credit card transactions (see Chapter 13).

Shipping and postage. Finally, to complete the auction process, the purchased goods must be shipped from the seller to the buyer. Shipping and postage services offered include the following:

▶ **Internet shippers.** Shipping providers such as iship.com and auctionship.com help sellers by providing a one-stop integrated service for processing, shipping, and packing e-commerce goods. UPS, FedEx, the U.S. Postal Service, and other shippers move much of the purchases to their destinations.

▶ **Internet postage.** Postage service providers such as stamps.com enable users to download postage, print "stamped" envelopes and labels, and arrange shipments via the U.S. Postal Service. These providers charge sellers both fixed and transaction fees for services.

ADDITIONAL TERMS AND RULES

Each auction house has its own rules and guides. The following are some examples:

▶ **Reserve price auction.** In a reserve price auction, the seller establishes the lowest price (the *reserve price*) at which they are willing to sell an item.

vertical auction
Auction that takes place between sellers and buyers in one industry or for one commodity.

▶ **Vertical auction.** A **vertical auction** is one that takes place between sellers and buyers in one industry or for one commodity (e.g., flowers, cars, or cattle). It is considered vertical because activity goes up and down the supply chain in a single industry, rather than horizontally between members of supply chains in different industries. These specialized auctions are sometimes referred to as **auction vortals**. Vertical auctions are particularly useful in B2B. At eBay "anything goes" (i.e., almost anything can be sold), but many auction sites specialize in one area. For example, TechSmart Inc. (techsmart.com) specializes in selling used or outdated PCs in B2B auctions.

auction vortals
Another name for a vertical auction portal.

▶ **Bid retraction.** This is the cancellation of a bid by a bidder. It is used only in special circumstances. Usually a bid is considered to be a binding contract.

▶ **Featured auctions.** These are auctions that get added exposure on the auction Web site. Sellers pay extra for this service.

Section 11.4 ▶ REVIEW

1. List the activities of phase 1. What software tools or agents are available to support these activities?

2. List the activities of phase 2. What software tools or agents are available to support these activities?

3. List the activities of phase 3. What software tools or agents are available to support these activities?

4. List the activities of phase 4. What tools or agents are available to support these activities?

11.5 AUCTIONS ON PRIVATE NETWORKS

Electronic auctions that run on private networks have been in use for about 15 years. Chapter 7 introduced the flower market in the Netherlands as a B2B example of an auction on a private network. The following are additional B2B examples of auctions on private networks.

Pigs in Singapore and Taiwan. The auctioning of pigs in Singapore and Taiwan has been conducted over private networks for over 10 years (see Neo 1992). Farmers bring the pigs to one area where they are washed, weighed, and prepared for display. The pigs are auctioned (via a forward auction) one at a time while the data on each pig are displayed to approved bidders who bid by watching a displayed price. If bids are submitted, the price can be increased incrementally only by 20 cents per kilogram. The process continues until no further bids occur. The bidders' financial capability is monitored by a computer. (The computer verifies that the bidder has available funds in the prepaid account that was opened for the auction.) The process is illustrated in Exhibit 11.4 (page 446).

Livestock in Australia. ComputerAided Livestock Marketing (CALM) is an online system for trading cattle and sheep that has been in operation since 1986. In contrast with the pig-auctioning system in Singapore, livestock do not have to travel to CALM, a feature that lowers stress in the animals and reduces sellers' costs. The buyers use PCs or Vt100 terminals to connect to the auction. The system also handles payments to farmers.

Section 11.5 ▶ REVIEW

1. Describe pig auctions in Singapore.
2. Describe CALM.

11.6 DOUBLE AUCTIONS, BUNDLE TRADING, AND PRICING ISSUES

Other issues to be considered in a discussion of auctions are single versus double actions, bundling of goods or services to attract buyers, and pricing.

DOUBLE AUCTIONS

Auctions can be single or double. In a **single auction**, an item is either offered for sale and the market consists of multiple buyers making bids to buy or an item is needed by a buyer and the market consists of multiple sellers making offers to sell. In either case, one side of the market consists of a single entity.

In a **double auction**, multiple buyers and sellers may be making bids and offers simultaneously. An example of a double auction is stock trading. In double auctions, multiple units of a product may be auctioned off at the same time. The situation becomes complicated when the quantity offered is more than one and buyers and sellers bid on varying quantities.

Although most online auctions are single, double auctions are the form used for transactions such as corporate stocks and commodities (grains, metals, livestock, etc.). In a given trading period, any seller may make an offer while any buyer makes a bid. Either a seller or a buyer may accept the offer or bid at any time. The difference between the cost and price paid is the seller's profit; the difference between the price paid and valuation is the buyer's surplus. If the quantities vary, as in a stock market, a *market maker* needs to match quantities. (For details, see Choi and Whinston 2000.)

Prices in Double Auctions

According to Choi and Whinston (2000), double-auction markets tend to generate competitive outcomes. Simply put, a double auction is an interactive market in which both buyers and sellers are competitive. In contrast, in a single auction, contract prices may be much higher or much lower than in a competitive format. This conclusion may have a significant effect on the future use of double auctions in the digital economy.

Ideally, any effort to promote competitiveness should include expanding online double auctions and similar market mechanisms because they offer an opportunity to raise economic

single auction
Auction in which at least one side of the market consists of a single entity (a single buyer or a single seller).

double auction
Auction in which multiple buyers and sellers may be making bids and offers simultaneously; buyers and their bidding prices and sellers and their asking prices are matched, considering the quantities on both sides.

EXHIBIT 11.4   Auctioning Pigs in Singapore

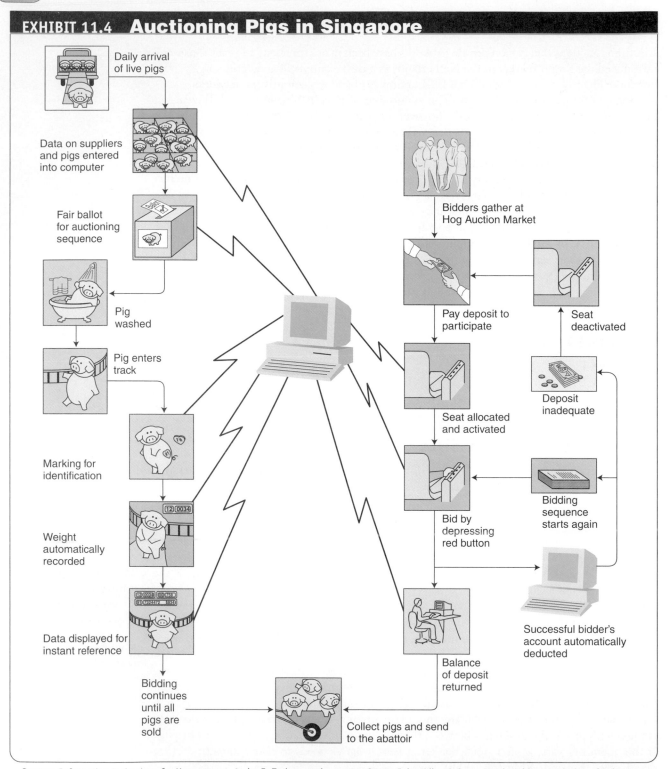

Daily arrival of live pigs

Data on suppliers and pigs entered into computer

Fair ballot for auctioning sequence

Pig washed

Pig enters track

Marking for identification

Weight automatically recorded

Data displayed for instant reference

Bidding continues until all pigs are sold

Bidders gather at Hog Auction Market

Pay deposit to participate

Seat deactivated

Seat allocated and activated

Deposit inadequate

Bid by depressing red button

Bidding sequence starts again

Balance of deposit returned

Successful bidder's account automatically deducted

Collect pigs and send to the abattoir

Source: *Information Technology for Management,* 2e by E. Turban et al., p. 163. ©2001 John Wiley & Sons. Reprinted by permission of John Wiley & Sons, Inc.

efficiencies that is unsurpassed by any physical market organization. For auctioneers, how-ever, single auctions generate substantially more revenue than double auctions.

BUNDLE TRADING

One of the major characteristics of the digital economy is the ability of businesses to person-alize and customize products and services. Many e-businesses do this by offering their cus-tomers a customized collection of complementary goods and services. **Bundle trading** involves selling (auctioning) several related products or services together. For example, airline tickets, hotel rooms, rental cars, meals, and amusement park admission tickets can be *bundled* as a packaged leisure product. Some bundled products that are vertically related (e.g., a com-puter OS and a Web browser) may be provided by different vendors. Although a purchase that involves multiple sellers may be carried out through a series of transactions or auctions, bundle trading offers an efficient alternative solution.

bundle trading
The selling of several related products and/or service together.

The management and operation of a bundle market is complex, and it differs consider-ably from those of single or double auction markets. For a discussion of the bundle market, see Choi and Whinston (2000).

PRICES IN AUCTIONS: HIGHER OR LOWER?

Compared to competitive markets, prices in auctions tend to be higher, reaching monopoly level when there is only one seller or one product, such as an old painting (Choi and Whinston 2000). In general, the auction seller is in a better position to maximize revenues than is the seller in a competitive (nonauction) market. When the auction seller is selling a product among multiple bidders, the expected price is often higher than in the competitive market.

However, in many instances, prices in auctions are lower. This may happen in cases of liquidation, where the seller's objective is to sell as quickly as possible. Alternatively, buyers go to online global markets where they can get products more cheaply than those imported by intermediaries. In general, buyers expect online prices to be lower. For example, truckers or airlines selling unused capacity at the last minute usually do so at a lower price. Also, consid-ering the fact that most C2C auctions are for used merchandise and surplus B2B auctions may include used or obsolete products, bargain prices are likely to prevail.

Finally, a more fundamental reason for lower online auction prices is that an online auc-tion is usually an alternative selling channel rather than an exclusive selling arrangement. Therefore, buyers can always revert to physical markets if online bids exceed prices posted in physical markets. In short, few people in online auctions are willing to pay what they are expected to pay in physical markets. However, if products are sold exclusively through online auctions, the average price will certainly be high.

Pricing Strategies in Online Auctions

Both sellers and buyers may develop pricing strategies for online auctions. Sellers have the option to use different auction mechanisms, such as English, Dutch, sealed-bid first price, and sealed-bid second price. Buyers need to develop a strategy regarding how much to increase a bid and when to stop bidding. These topics are relevant to off-line auctions as well and will not be dealt with here.

Section 11.6 ▶ REVIEW

1. Describe double auction operations and pricing.
2. What is bundle trading?
3. Discuss the conditions under which prices in online auctions are higher or lower than prices in physical auctions.

11.7 AUCTION FRAUD AND ITS PREVENTION

According to the National Consumers League (nclnet.org) (McKay 2003), of all e-commerce activities conducted over the Internet, fraud is most serious in e-auctions. E-auction fraud accounted for 90 percent of the e-commerce fraud that occurred in 2002 (McKay 2003). Less than 1 percent of Internet auctions are fraudulent, according to the auction sites and FBI statistics (fraud.net 2002). The U.S. Fraud Complaint Center says that the median dollar loss per auction fraud was $225 in the first half of 2001, but jumped to $489 in the second half of the year, as criminals evidently focused on high-tech, big-ticket items (Lee 2002). In 2003, auctions appear to be 35 to 40 percent worse than in 2002, judging from the reported 400 frauds at any given time, as compared to 250 in 2002 (Sullivan 2003).

TYPES OF E-AUCTION FRAUD

Fraud may be conducted by sellers or buyers. The following are some examples of fraud.

bid shielding

Having phantom bidders bid at a very high price when an auction begins; they pull out at the last minute, and the bidder who bid a much lower price wins.

Bid shielding. The use of phantom bidders to bid at a very high price when an auction begins is called bid shielding. The phantom bidders pull out at the last minute, and the bidder (friend of the phantom bidder) who bids with a very low price wins. The bogus bidders were the shields, protecting the low bid of the bidder in the stack. By bid shielding, a ring of dishonest bidders can target an item and inflate the bid value to scare off other real bidders. Then, they get it at a low price.

shilling

Placing fake bids on auction items to artificially jack up the bidding price.

Shilling. A similar type of fraud can be conducted by sellers. In this fraud, called shilling, sellers arrange to have fake bids placed on their items (either by associates or by using multiple user IDs) to artificially jack up high bids. If they see that the legitimate high bid does not meet their expectations as the end of an auction draws near, they might pop in to sell the item to themselves. This way they can put the item again for auction, attempting to get a higher price next time.

Fake photos and misleading descriptions. In reaching for bidders' attention, some sellers distort what they can truly sell. Borrowed images, ambiguous descriptions, and falsified facts are some of the tactics that sellers might employ to convey a false impression of the item.

Improper grading techniques. The grading of items is one of the most hotly debated issues among buyers and sellers. A seller might describe an item as 90 percent new, whereas the bidder, after receiving the item and paying the full amount, feels it is only 70 percent new. Condition is often in the eye of the beholder. Although many grading systems have been devised and put to use, condition is still subject to interpretation.

Selling reproductions. A seller sells something that the seller claims is original, but it turns out to be a reproduction.

Failure to pay. Buyers do not pay after a deal is agreed upon.

Failure to pay the auction house. Sometimes sellers fail to pay the auction's listing or transaction fees.

High shipping costs and handling fees. Some sellers just want to get a little more cash out of bidders. Postage and handling rates vary from seller to seller. Some charge extra to cover "handling" costs and other overhead intangibles, whereas others charge to cover the cost of packaging supplies, even though such supplies are often available for free.

Failure to ship merchandise. This is the old collect-and-run routine. Money was paid out but the merchandise never arrives.

Loss and damage claims. Buyers claim that they did not receive an item or that they received it in damaged condition and then ask for a refund. They might be trying to get a freebie. The seller sometimes cannot prove whether the item ever arrived or whether it was in perfect condition when shipped.

Switch and return. The seller has successfully auctioned an item, but when the buyer receives it, the buyer is not satisfied. The seller offers a cheerful refund. However, what the seller gets back is a mess that doesn't much resemble the item that was originally shipped. Some buyers might attempt to swap out their junk for someone else's jewels.

Other frauds. Many other types fraud are also possible, including the sale of stolen goods, the use of false identities, providing false contact information, and selling the same item to several buyers.

PROTECTING AGAINST E-AUCTION FRAUD

The largest Internet auctioneer, eBay, has introduced several measures in an effort to reduce fraud. Some are free, others are not. The company has succeeded in its goal: less than one-tenth of 1 percent of the transactions at eBay were fraudulent in 2001 (Konrad 2002). The following are some of eBay's antifraud measures.

User identity verification. eBay uses the services of Equifax to verify user identities for a $5 fee. Verified eBay User, a voluntary program, encourages users to supply eBay with information for online verification. By offering their Social Security number, driver's license number, and date of birth, users can qualify for the highest level of verification on eBay.

Authentication service. Product authentication is a way of determining whether an item is genuine and described appropriately. Authentication is very difficult to perform because it relies on the expertise of the authenticators. Because of their training and experience, experts can (for a fee) often detect counterfeits based on subtle details. However, two expert authenticators may have different opinions about the authenticity of the same item. eBay has links to companies that provide this specialized service including opinions, authentication, and grading (see the following). These companies charge a small fee.

Grading services. Grading is a way of determining the physical condition of an item, such as "poor quality" or "mint condition." The actual grading system depends on the type of item being graded. Different items have different grading systems—for example, trading cards are graded from A1 to F1, whereas coins are graded from poor to perfect uncirculated.

Feedback forum. The eBay Feedback Forum allows registered buyers and sellers to build up their online trading reputations. It provides users with the ability to comment on their experiences with other individuals.

Insurance policy. eBay offers insurance underwritten by Lloyd's of London. Users are covered up to $200, with a $25 deductible. The program is provided at no cost to eBay users. Supplementary insurance is available from companies such as WebTradeInsure.com. At other auction sites, such as amazon.com/auctions, some insurance is provided, but extra insurance may be needed.

Escrow services. For items valued at more than $200 or when either a buyer or seller feels the need for additional security, eBay recommends escrow services (for a fee). With an easy-to-access link to a third-party escrow service, both partners in a deal are protected. The buyer mails the payment to the escrow service, which verifies the payment and alerts the seller when everything checks out. At that point, the seller ships the goods to the buyer. After an agreed-upon inspection period, the buyer notifies the service, which then sends a check to the seller. (An example of a provider of online escrow services can be found at tradenable.com.)

Nonpayment punishment. eBay implemented a policy against those who do not honor their winning bids. To help protect sellers, a first-time nonpayment results in a friendly warning. A sterner warning is issued for a second-time offense, a 30-day suspension for a third offense, and indefinite suspension for a fourth offense.

Appraisal services. Appraisers use a variety of methods to appraise items, including expert assessment of authenticity and condition and reviewing what comparable items have sold for in the marketplace in recent months. An appraised value is usually accurate only at the time of appraisal. Eppraisals.com provides eBay users access to over 700 experts and a selection of online appraisal services that are located throughout eBay's categories of fine art, antiques, and collectibles, as well as on eBay Premier.

Physical inspection. Providing for a physical inspection can eliminate many problems. This is especially true for collectors' items. When the seller and buyer are in the same location, it is easy to arrange for such inspections. eBay offers inspection services on a regional basis, so buyers can arrange for nearby inspections.

Verification. One way of confirming the identity and evaluating the condition of an item is through *verification*. With verification, neutral third parties will evaluate and identify an item through a variety of means. For example, some collectors have their item "DNA tagged" for identification purposes. This provides a way of tracking an item if it changes ownership in the future. In addition to the antifraud measures discussed here, one can use the general EC fraud protection measures suggested in Chapters 12 and 17.

Section 11.7 ▶ REVIEW

1. What types of fraud can be perpetuated by sellers?
2. What types of fraud can be perpetuated by buyers?
3. What kinds of protections exist for sellers?
4. What kinds of protections exist for buyers?

11.8 BARTERING AND NEGOTIATING ONLINE

In addition to the more common types of auctions, in which money is exchanged for goods, e-auctions can also take the form of online bartering. Also, prices in e-commerce can be arrived at through a process of negotiation.

BARTERING

bartering
The *exchange* of goods and services.

As discussed in Chapter 2, **bartering** is an *exchange* of goods and services. The oldest method of trade, today, bartering is usually conducted between organizations, but some individuals exchange goods and services as well. The problem with bartering is that it is often difficult to find partners. As discussed in Chapter 2, *bartering exchanges*, in which intermediaries arrange the transactions, were created to address this problem

electronic bartering (e-bartering)
Bartering conducted online, usually by a bartering exchange.

Electronic bartering (e-bartering)—bartering conducted online, usually in a bartering exchange—can improve the matching process by inducing more customers to take part in the exchange. Items that are frequently bartered electronically include office space, storage space, factory space, idle facilities and labor, surplus products, and banner ads. E-bartering may have tax implications that need to be considered.

Bartering Web sites include intagio.com, ubarter.com, bigvine.com, and whosbartering.com (see Lorek 2000). (For more on online bartering, see fsb.com and search for "virtual bartering 101.")

NEGOTIATION AND BARGAINING

online negotiation
A back-and-forth electronic process of bargaining until the buyer and seller reach a mutually agreeable price; usually done by software (intelligent) agents.

Dynamic prices also can be determined by **online negotiation**, a back-and-forth process of bargaining until buyer and seller reach a mutually agreeable price. Negotiation is a well-known process in the off-line world, especially for expensive or specialized products such as real estate, automobiles, and jewelry. Negotiations also deal with nonpricing terms, such as shipment, warranties, payment methods, and credit. E-markets allow negotiations to be used for virtually all products and services. Three factors may facilitate negotiated prices (see Choi and Whinston 2000): (1) intelligent agents that perform searches and comparisons; (2) computer technology that facilitates the negotiation process; and (3) bundling and customization of products.

Technologies for Bargaining

According to Choi and Whinston (2000), negotiation and bargaining involve a bilateral interaction between a seller and a buyer who are engaged in the following five-step process that is necessary to complete a transaction:

1. **Search.** The buyer or seller gathers information about products and services and locates potential vendors or customers.
2. **Selection.** The buyer or seller processes and filters information in order to select a product or trading partner.
3. **Negotiation.** The two parties interact with bids and offers until an agreement is made.
4. **Continuing selection and negotiation.** The previous steps are repeated sequentially, if necessary, until an agreement is reached and a contract is written.
5. **Transaction completion.** The buyer pays for the product and the seller ships the product to the buyer.

Search. Bargaining starts with the collection of all relevant information about products and sellers or buyers. Computer-mediated markets excel in raising the search efficiency. Once information has been gathered, the next step is to process it into a usable data set that is employed for decision making. (Search tools are described in Chapters 3 and 4.)

Selection. Selection filters retrieve screened information that helps each party determine what to buy (sell) and from whom to buy (sell). This filtering process encompasses the evaluation of products and seller alternatives based on consumer-provided criteria such as price, warranty, availability, delivery time, and reputation. The screening/selection process results in a set of names of products and partners to negotiate with in the next step. Software agents, such as Pricemix (bizrate.com), and other tools can facilitate the selection (see Chapter 4).

Negotiation. The negotiation stage focuses on establishing the terms of the transaction, such as price, product characteristics, delivery, and payment terms. Negotiation varies in duration and complexity depending on the market. In online markets, all stages of negotiation can be carried out by automated programs or software agents (see Appendix D at the book's Web site).

Negotiation agents are software programs that make independent decisions to make bids within predetermined constraints or to accept or reject offers. The agents might be bound by negotiation rules or protocols that control how sellers and buyers interact. For example, price negotiation may start with a seller's list price as a starting point or it may start with any bid or offer depending on the rule. (For an overview of electronic negotiation and comparison, see Beam et al. 1999.)

The following are the major *benefits* of electronic negotiations:

▶ Buyers and sellers do not need to determine prices beforehand, and thereby do not have to engage in the difficult process of collecting relevant information. Negotiating prices transfers the burden of determining prices (i.e., market valuation) to the market itself. Insofar as the market process is efficient, the resulting negotiated prices will be fair and efficient.

▶ Intelligent agents can negotiate both price and nonprice attributes such as delivery time, return policy, and other transactions that add value. In addition, intelligent agents can deal with multiple partners (see Appendix D at the book's Web site). An example of such an application is negotiation among several freight dispatch centers of different companies to solve their vehicle routing problems.

Other applications include (1) a factory-floor-scheduling domain, where different companies in a subcontracting web negotiate over a joint scheduling problem and (2) an airport resource management domain, where negotiations take place for the servicing of airplanes between flights. (For further discussion, see Esmahi and Bernard 2000 and Strobel 2000.)

Transaction completion. After product, vendor, and price are determined, the final step is to complete the transaction. This involves online payment and product delivery in accordance with the terms determined in the negotiation phase. Other characteristics, such as customer service, warranty, and refunds, may also be implemented.

Section 11.8 ▶ REVIEW

1. What are the major reasons for e-bartering?
2. List the factors that may facilitate price negotiation.
3. Discuss the benefits of electronic negotiation.
4. What are the five steps of online negotiations?

11.9 ISSUES IN AUCTION IMPLEMENTATION

Implementing auctions may not be a simple task, and for this reason many companies use intermediaries. This section presents some issues that are relevant to auction implementation and use.

USING INTERMEDIARIES

Any seller can auction from a Web site. The question is: Will the buyers come? A similar issue was raised in Chapter 3: Should sellers sell from their own storefront, join an online mall, or use another third-party arrangement?

Large companies often choose to auction from their own Web site. If their name is well recognized, they can feel some assurance that buyers will come. Chapter 6 presented the example of GM selling obsolete equipment from its site. Governments and large corporations also are using reverse auctions from their sites for procurement purposes. Some individuals even conduct auctions from their own Web sites.

However, most individuals, SMEs, and many large companies use third-party intermediaries whose charges are fairly low compared to the charges in physical auctions and who provide many services that are critical to the success of auctions.

The following are some of the popular third-party auction sites:

▶ **General sites.** Such sites include eBay (the world's largest general auction site); auctions.amazon.com, auctions.yahoo.com, auctions.msn.com, auctions.lycos.com, and ubid.com.

▶ **Specialized sites.** Such sites are focused on a particular industry or product; examples include auctions.cnet.com (computers, electronics), baseball-cards.com, teletrad.com (coins), oldandsold.com (antiques), and erauctions.com.au.

▶ **B2B-oriented site.** Such sites are focused on B2B transactions; examples include freemarkets.com (see the Real-World Case) and bid4assets.com.

AUCTION RULES

The success of auctions depends on a large number of rules. These rules are intended to smooth the auction mechanism and to prevent fraud. Wurman (2001) divides the rules into three major categories: bidding rules, clearing rules, and information-revelation rules. These rules are shown in Online Exhibit W11.2. The rules provide definitions, restrictions, and timing constraint.

Auction rules may vary from country to country due to legal considerations. They may also vary within a country due to the nature of the items auctioned, the auctioneer's policies, and the nature of competition among the auction houses.

STRATEGIC ISSUES

When a company decides to use auctions as a selling channel, it must make several important strategic decisions such as which items (services) to auction; what type of auction to use; whether to do the auction in-house or to use an auctioneer (and which one); how long to run each auction; how to set the initial prices; how to accept a bid; what increments to allow in the bidding; and what information to disclose to the participants (e.g., the name of bidders, the current prices, etc.). For help in making such decisions, see Elliot (2000).

One of the strategic issues in B2B is the potential conflict with existing distributors and distribution channels. Therefore, some companies use auctions only to liquidate obsolete, used, refurbished, or damaged products.

AUCTIONS IN EXCHANGES

Chapter 7 mentioned that exchanges are using auctions to supplement their regular buying/selling channels. An example of such an auction is provided in EC Application Case 11.2.

BUILDING AUCTION SITES

One final issue of auction implementation is the topic of building auction sites. The process of building auction applications is complex for two reasons. First, as shown in Exhibit 11.5, the number of needed features can be very large. Second, in the case of B2B auctions, auctions must be integrated with the back-end offices and with the legacy systems of participating companies. Exhibit 11.6 (page 454) shows a sample integrated auction model. Because of these two complexities, even large companies typically outsource the construction of auction sites. For example, Dell Computer used FairMarkets.com to build its auction site.

Sections 11.9 ▶ REVIEW

1. What are the reasons for using auction intermediaries?
2. What types of intermediaries exist?
3. List some of the necessary auction rules.
4. List major strategic issues in conducting B2B auctions.

CASE 11.2
EC Application

ONLINE GRAPE AUCTION—WHERE TRADITION MEETS TECHNOLOGY

The wine industry is hundreds of years old, consisting of established associations between grape growers and wineries. Typically, vintners have multiyear buying contracts with growers. The adoption of the Internet to facilitate the trading grapes was slow, but in March 2001, 2,000 tons of grapes were traded in the first of many online auctions.

The WineryExchange (*wineryexchange.com*), based in Novato, California, conducted the first online grape auction. "In the past, most of the deals have been cut on the tailgate of a truck," said Doug Wilson, director of grower relations at Fetzer Vineyards, producer of 4 million cases of wine each year. His company was among some 30 buyers who intended to make $10 to $50 bottles of wine from the "super premium" grapes to be offered by 36 California coastal growers.

The online exchange auction helped competitors find the true market price by buying and selling grapes from computer terminals. It is expected that online grape auctions will help vintners save money on raw materials (grapes) and streamline their purchasing, just as it has in online exchanges for high-tech companies, pharmaceutical companies, and automakers. "Winemakers still will have to know their growers, visit vineyards to taste grapes, and participate in harvests," said Wilson. While he anticipates "meeting" new growers and "seeing" new vineyards at the online auction, he doesn't expect it to change the relationship-oriented business. "It's a tool. It cannot replace the human element," he said.

Sources: Compiled from Reuters (2001) and from *wineryexchange.com* (2002).

Questions

1. What drives auctions in the winery exchange?
2. Enter *wineryexchange.com* and describe any auction-related activities.

EXHIBIT 11.5 Components of a Comprehensive Auction Site

Help	Services	Basics	Buyers Guide	Sellers Guide	Rules	Safety and Protection
How to Bid	Online Communities	Registration	How to Buy	How to Sell	User Agreement	Feedback Forum
How to Sell	Tutorials	General Inquiries	Auction Types	Auction Types	Privacy Policy	Insurance
What Is Allowed	Charity	Glossary of Terms	Tips for Buyers	Tips for Sellers	GST Policy	Safe Harbor
Authentication	Suggestion Box	Bidding Basics	Proxy Bidding	Packaging and Shipping	Board Usage	Escrow
Grading	Chats	Security, Privacy	Retracting a Bid	Retracting a Sale	Trade Offenses	Defamation
	Library		Contacting Others	Closing the Deal	Selling Offenses	Fraud Prevention
	International Traders		Closing a Deal	International Trading	Identity Offenses	Authentication
	Buying and Selling Tools		Buying Abroad	Power Trading	Grading	Grading
	Reverse Auctions		My E-auction		Netiquette	Appraising
	Payments					
	Notification					
	Historical Prices					

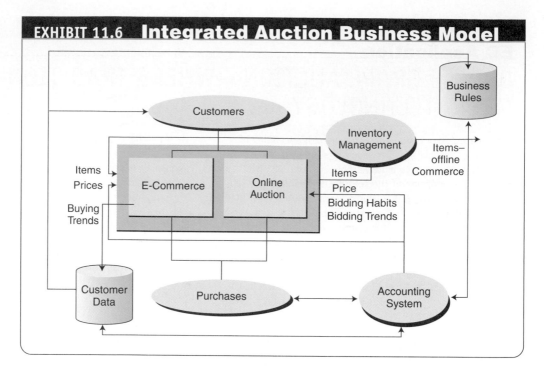

EXHIBIT 11.6   Integrated Auction Business Model

11.10   MOBILE AUCTIONS AND THE FUTURE OF AUCTIONS

Researchers estimate that 1.4 billion people will be using digital devices over mobile networks by 2004, and in the near future, the number of m-commerce users is expected to surpass the number of fixed e-commerce users worldwide (Delichte 2001). Mobile phones and other wireless devices could be the primary way for people to access the Internet, resulting in large-volume m-commerce. In response, auctions are implementing m-commerce applications.

In the United States, eBay went wireless in October 1999, and uBid and FairMarket.com followed in 2000. Yahoo and other auction sites also have been scrambling to go wireless. In the United Kingdom, BlueCycle (bluecycle.com), which conducts auctions on used cars for dealers, allows dealers to bid from anywhere by using their cell phones.

The use of cell phones for online auctions presents a number of benefits and some limitations.

BENEFITS AND LIMITATIONS OF MOBILE AUCTIONS

The benefits of mobile auctions are as follows:

▶ **Convenience and ubiquity.** People can conduct auction business on the go and from any location via a mobile phone. One can auction anything from anywhere and search for information in the middle of a discussion around a café table. Bids can be checked on the run.

▶ **Privacy.** The Internet cell phone is more private than a PC, and you can take it to a place where no one can see you. Thus, participation in an auction can take place in a secure and private environment.

▶ **Simpler and faster.** Because online auctions require a limited amount of information, it is relatively easy to adapt WAP-enabled phones to display auction information, even if they can only handle limited bandwidth and data.

The limitations of mobile auctions are as follows:

▶ **Visual quality.** The screen on Internet-enabled phones is very small. One cannot read through the same amount of information as on a computer. Also, the screen quality is not as good as on a PC monitor. One can send pictures of desired products to bidders via a cell phone, but if the images are too complicated they will appear as blurs. It also is much more difficult to send information about products via the phone than via a PC.

▶ **Memory capacity.** Internet-enabled phones have little memory capacity. In the near future, the development of new WAP services will probably press hardware producers to come up with better memory systems for mobile terminals.

▶ **Security.** Security issues particular to WAP, such as protecting personal data transmitted via wireless communications and avoiding computer viruses, are being tackled through new security standards, such as SIM Toolkit and WTLS.

See Chapter 10 for more on these and other benefits and limitations of m-commerce.

THE FUTURE OF AUCTIONS

The online auction industry is growing. The following are areas of potential growth.

Global Auctions

Many of the auction companies that sell products and services on the Web are extending their reach. One way to do so is by going global. However, companies that seek to serve the international market may face all the regular problems of selling online in foreign countries (see Chapter 15).

Selling Art Online in Real-Time Auctions

As of January 2001, collectors in the United Kingdom can bid online in live showroom auctions using an application provided by eBay and icollector.com. Icollector.com provides real-time access to 300 independent auction houses, such as the United Kingdom's Charter House Auctioneers and Valuers. Christie's has an online site, but as of winter 2002 it was not allowing online bidding for live showroom auctions. In the United States, Butterfields (butterfields.com) allows for real-time auction bidding and has a relationship with eBay (see Beer 1999). Butterfields.com has been purchased by Bonhams, auctioneers and valuers since 1793, but will continue to sell through eBay's Live Auctions feature, allowing online bidders to participate in auctions at traditional auction houses in real time. In spring 2002, eBay merged its Premier site for online fine art, antiques, and big-ticket collectibles auctions with Sothebys (sothebys.com). The new sothebys.com site is managed by eBay and will use eBay's Live Auctions technology to enable online real-time auction bidding for some auctions in New York and London (Geralds 2002). See Mirapaul (2001) to find out how individual artists use Internet auctions.

Strategic Alliances

Auctions may have a major impact on competition and on industry structure because they put sellers and buyers together more directly, cutting out intermediaries in a market. In addition, auctions may be used as a strategic tool by both online and off-line companies. An example of such a strategy is provided in EC Application Case W11.1, which describes an online auction site in Australia that enables SMEs to offer heavily discounted merchandise to consumers. It appears that this type of strategic alliance will be very popular in the future due to its win-win possibilities.

Section 11.10 ▶ REVIEW

1. Describe the benefits of wireless auctions.
2. Describe the limitations of wireless auctions.
3. Describe the future of global auctions.
4. Describe auctioning of art on the Internet.
5. Why are strategic alliances used in auctions?

MANAGERIAL ISSUES

Some managerial issues related to this chapter are as follows:

1. **Should we have our own auction site or use a third-party site?** This is a strategic issue, and there are pluses and minuses to each alternative. If you decide to auction from your site, you will need to advertise and attract visitors, which may be expensive. Also, you will need to install fraud-prevention mechanisms and provide services. Either way, you may need to consider connectivity to your back-office and logistics system.

2. **What are the costs and benefits of auctions?** A major strategic issue is whether you need to do auctions or not. Auctions do have risks, and in forward auctions you may create conflicts with your other distribution channels. In addition, auctions may change the manner in which companies sell their products. They also may change the nature of competition in certain industries, as well as price and margin levels. However, conducting a cost-benefit analysis is essential.

3. **What auction strategies would we use?** Selecting an auction mechanism, pricing, and bidding strategy can be very complex for sellers. These strategies determine the success of the auction and the ability to attract and retain visitors on the site. Management should understand and carefully assess the options.

4. **What about support services?** Auctions require support services, such as those for escrow service, payment, and delivery. Decisions about how to provide them and to what extent to use business partners are critical to the success of repeated high-volume auctions. An efficient payment mechanism is essential for auctions, especially when the buyers or sellers are individuals. Some innovative methods can solve the payment problem (see Chapter 13).

5. **What would we auction?** Both individuals and companies would like to auction everything. However, is it ethical or even legal to do it? Ask eBay, which is trying, for example, to clean up pornographic auctions by banning some items and directing some items into a "mature audiences" area. Another issue is pirated software, which is offered on about 2,000 auction sites worldwide. As a matter of fact, eBay was sued in 2000 by videogame manufacturers Nintendo, Sega, and Electronic Arts. eBay immediately began working with software companies and other owners of intellectual property to halt the sale of pirated items (Wolverton 2000). (See Beato 2000 for more on this topic.)

6. **What is the best bartering strategy?** Bartering can be an interesting strategy, especially for companies that need cash and have some surpluses. However, the valuation of what is bought or sold may be difficult, and the tax implications in some countries are not clear. Nevertheless, e-bartering can be rewarding and should be considered as an alternative to regular auctions.

7. **How can we promote our auction?** By monitoring what is going on in auctions (e.g., what people like, how much bidders are willing to pay, etc.), both sellers and auctioneers can foster selling strategy. Sometimes auctions bring very high prices to sellers. Auction houses such as eBay do analyses to determine advertising strategy for their business.

8. **Should we combine auctions with other models?** Consider combining auctions with other EC models. For example, group purchasing is often combined with a reverse auction once orders are aggregated.

SUMMARY

In this chapter, you learned about the following EC issues as they relate to the learning objectives.

1. **The various types of auctions and their characteristics.** The types of auctions are based on the numbers of buyers and sellers involved. Negotiation and bartering take place between one seller and one buyer. One seller and many buyers characterize forward auctions. One buyer and many sellers typify reverse auctions. "Name-your-own-price" auctions are a form of reverse auctions. Many buyers and many sellers participate in auctions (called double auctions) in which prices are determined dynamically, based on supply and demand.

2. **The processes of forward and reverse auctions.** In a forward auction, the seller places the item to be sold on the auction site, specifying a starting price and closing time. Bids from buyers are placed sequentially, either increasing (English mode) or decreasing (Dutch mode). At the close, the highest bidder wins. In reverse auctions, buyers place an RFQ for a product or service, and suppliers (providers) submit offers in one or several rounds. The lowest-price bidder wins.

3. **Benefits and limitations of auctions.** The major benefits for sellers are the ability to reach many buyers and to sell quickly. Also, sellers save the commissions they might otherwise pay to intermediaries. Buyers have a chance to obtain collectibles while shopping from their homes, and they can find bargains. The major limitation is the possibility of fraud.

4. **Unique auction models.** In the "name-your-own-price" reverse auction, buyers specify how much they are willing to pay for a product or service and an intermediary tries to find a supplier to fulfill the request. Also, auctions can be conducted on private networks (e.g., pigs in Singapore), can be organized as double auctions (multiple buyers and sellers bidding simultaneously), or can offer bundle trading (related products or services auctioned together).

5. **Services that support auctions.** Auction-support services exist along the entire process and include tools for (a) searching and comparing auctions for specific items, (b) registering, promoting, pricing, and so on, (c) bid watching, making multiple bids, and proxy bidding, and (d) notification, payment, and shipping.

6. **Hazards of e-auction fraud and countermeasures.** Fraud can be committed either by sellers or by buyers. Good auction sites provide protection that includes voluntary identity verification, monitoring of rule violations, escrow services, and insurance.

7. **Bartering and negotiating.** Electronic bartering can greatly facilitate the swapping of goods and services among organizations, thanks to improved search and matching capabilities.

8. **Auction deployment and implementation.** Some implementation issues are whether to use an intermediary or to run the auction oneself, various strategic issues (e.g., what rules to use and competition with regular channels), and whether to outsource construction of the auction site.

9. **Future directions and the role of mobile auctions.** B2B, C2C, G2B, and B2C auctions are all expanding rapidly. Future directions include use of wireless devices to monitor and trade at auctions, an increase in global auctioning, and strategic alliances

KEY TERMS

Auction	433	Electronic auctions (e-auctions)	433	Sealed-bid auction	434
Auction aggregators	441	Electronic bartering		Shilling	448
Auction vortals	444	(e-bartering)	450	Single auction	445
Bartering	450	Forward auction	433	Sniping	443
Bid shielding	448	"Name-your-own-price" model	435	Vertical auction	444
Bundle trading	447	Online negotiation	450	Vickrey auction	434
Double auction	445	Proxy bidding	443		
Dynamic pricing	433	Reverse auction	435		

DISCUSSION QUESTIONS

1. Discuss the advantages of dynamic pricing over fixed pricing. What are the potential disadvantages?

2. The "name-your-own-price" model is considered to be a reverse auction. However, there is no RFQ or consecutive bidding, so why is it called an auction? Is it an auction at all?

3. Find some material on why individuals like C2C auctions so much. Write a report.

4. Compare the "name-your-own-price" and RFQ approaches. Under what circumstances is each advantageous?

5. Identify three fraud practices in which a seller might engage. How can buyers protect themselves?

6. Identify three fraud practices in which a buyer might engage. How can sellers protect themselves?

7. It is said that Manheim Auction is trying to sell more online without cannibalizing its core business. Discuss this situation.

8. Discuss the need for software agents in auctions. Start by analyzing proxy bidding and auction aggregators.

9. Discuss the role of auction aggregators.

10. It is said that *individuals* prefer an English auction whereas *corporations* prefer a Dutch one. Speculate on the reasons for this.

11. Relate consumer trust to auctions.

INTERNET EXERCISES

1. Enter eBay's professional auctions (elance.com). Post a project and see how professionals will bid on this work. Summarize your experience.

2. Enter dellauction.com and click on "site terms." Examine the policies, security and encryption statement, privacy protection statement, escrow services, payment options, and other features. Register (for free) and then bid on a computer of interest to you. If you are not interested, bid very low, so that you will not get it.

   Alternatively, try to sell a computer. If you do not have one to sell, place an asking price so high that you will not get any bids. Read the FAQs. Which of the following auction mechanisms are used on the Dell site: English, Dutch (declining), reverse, etc.

   Write a report on your experiences and describe all the features available at this site. (Note: If you are outside the United States, use an auction site accessible to you.)

3. Visit ebay.com and examine all of the quality assurance measures available either for a fee or for free. Prepare a list.

4. Visit vendio.com and report on the various services offered at the site. What are the site's revenue models?

5. Enter bidfind.com and report on the various services provided. What is the site's revenue model?

6. Enter ebay.com and investigate the use of "anywhere wireless." Review the wireless devices and find out how they work.

7. Enter imandi.com and review the process by which buyers can send RFQs to merchants of their choice.

Also, evaluate the services provided in the areas of marketing, staffing, and travel. Write a report.

8. Examine the auction process used by office.com. Review its reverse auction arrangement with bigbuyer.com. Write a report.

9. Enter escrow.com and view the tutorial on how escrow services work for both buyers and sellers in electronic commerce.

10. Enter bidxs.com and find historical prices on an item of your choice. How may this information be of help to you as a seller? As a buyer?

11. Enter priceline.com and name a price to travel from where you live to a place you would like to visit. Go through the process without actually buying the ticket (do not give your credit card number). Summarize your experience.

12. Enter respond.com and send a request for a product or a service. Once you receive replies, select the best deal. You have no obligation to buy. Write a short report on your experience.

13. Enter icollector.com and review the process used to auction art. Find support services, such as currency conversion and shipping. Take the tour of the site. Prepare a report on buying collectibles online.

14. Enter ubid.com and examine the "auction exchange." What is unique about it? Compare this auction with those conducted on eBay.com. What are the major differences between the auctions on the two sites?

15. Enter autoparts.com and describe how auctions are being conducted there.

TEAM ASSIGNMENTS AND ROLE PLAYING

1. Each team is assigned an auction method (English, Dutch, etc.). Each team should convince a (hypothetical) company that wants to liquidate items that their method is the best. Items to be liquidated:

   a. Five IBM top-of-the-line mainframe systems valued at about $500,000 each

   b. 750 PCs valued at about $1,000 each

   c. A property valued at about $10 million

   Present arguments for which auction method should be used with each item.

2. Assign teams to major third-party auction sites from your country and from two other countries. Each team should present the major functionalities of the sites and the fraud protection measures they use. Convince a user that your site is the best.

REAL-WORLD CASE

FREEMARKETS

FreeMarkets (*freemarkets.com*) began in 1995 with an idea: By conducting B2B auctions online, procurement professionals could raise the quality of the direct materials and services they buy while substantially lowering the prices they pay for them.

FreeMarkets is a leader in creating B2B online auctions for buyers of industrial parts, raw materials, commodities, and services around the globe. The company has created auctions for goods and services in more than 70 industrial product categories. In 1999, FreeMarkets auctioned more than $2.7 billion worth of purchase orders and saved buyers an estimated 2 to 25 percent.

FreeMarkets operates two marketplaces. First, the company helps customers source billions of dollars worth of goods and services in hundreds of product and service categories through *Onsite Auctions*, its B2B global marketplace where reverse auctions usually take place. Second, FreeMarkets helps companies improve their asset-recovery results by getting timely market prices for surplus assets through *Asset Exchange,* which employs the forward auction process as well as other selling models.

FreeMarkets Asset Exchange, the asset-recovery business, provides a solution that addresses even the most complex transactions. It bridges the gaps in information, geography, and industry that made traditional surplus-asset markets very inefficient. Asset Exchange provides a flexible trading platform that includes an online marketplace and onsite auctions. Asset Exchange has the following solutions to help companies meet their asset-recovery goals:

▶ **FreeMarkets online markets.** An effective method for asset disposal that delivers timely, market-based pricing.

▶ **FreeMarkets online marketplace.** A self-service venue where sellers post available assets. This marketplace is useful when getting the right price is more important than a quick sale.

▶ **FreeMarkets onsite auctions.** Live auction events that are ideal for clearing a facility, time-critical sales, or selling a mix of high- and low-value assets.

FreeMarkets Onsite Auctions provide the following:

▶ **Asset disposal analysis.** Market makers work with sellers to determine the best strategy to meet asset-recovery goals.

▶ **Detailed sales offering.** The company collects and consolidates asset information into a printed or online sales offering for buyers.

▶ **Targeted market outreach.** FreeMarkets conducts targeted marketing to a global database of 500,000 buyers and suppliers.

▶ **Event coordination.** The company prepares the site, provides qualified personnel, and enforces auction rules.

▶ **Sales implementation.** FreeMarkets summarizes auction results and assists in closing sales.

Asset Recovery Success Stories

FreeMarkets has been able to help companies recover assets. A couple of these success stories follow.

New Line Cinema (*newline.com*) had unique memorabilia that the company had stored for years. In 2001, New Line decided to auction these via FreeMarket's auction marketplace. Items to be auctioned included props from the original *Austin Powers* movie, including a 1965 Corvette driven by Felicity Shagwell (sold in the auction for $121,000) and one of Austin's suits (sold for $7,500). The auction was covered in newspapers and TV, providing publicity to the sequel, *Austin Powers: The Spy Who Shagged Me.* Besides generating income and cleaning out the company's storage space, an additional benefit was that the auctions were linked to the company's online store, thus providing ongoing publicity for new projects. Though fans might not be able to buy Austin's 1965 Corvette, they may buy a new T-shirt or a poster of a new movie. Finally, the auction created a dedicated community of users. The auction site also helped the publicity of the *Lord of the Rings* trilogy.

American Power Conversion Corp. (*apcc.com*) needed a channel for end-of-life (old models) and refurbished power-protection products. These were difficult to sell in regular distribution channels. Before using auctions, the company used special liquidation sales, which were not very successful. Using its AuctionPlace technology, a part of Asset Exchange, but customizing the application, FreeMarkets deployed *auction.apcc.com*. It also helped the company determine the best auction strategies (such as starting bid price and auction running length). The site became an immediate success. American Power Conversion is considering selling some of its regular products there (only merchandise for which there would be no conflict with the company's regular distributors).

Procurement Success Story

Singapore Technologies Engineering (STE) (*stengg.com*), a large integrated global engineering group specializing in the fields of aerospace, electronics, and land and marine systems, wanted to improve its e-procurement (sourcing) through the use of reverse auctions. Specifically, STE had the following goals when it decided to use e-sourcing with the help of FreeMarkets:

1. Minimize the cost of products they needed to buy, such as board parts.
2. Identify a new global supply base for their multisourcing strategy.

3. Maximize efficiency in the procurement process.

4. Find new, quality suppliers for reliability and support.

5. Consolidate existing suppliers.

These are typical goals of business purchasers. FreeMarkets started by training STE's, corporate buyers and other staff. Then it designed an improved process that replicated the traditional negotiations with suppliers. Finally, it took a test item (printed circuit board assemblies) and prepared an RFQ, placing it for bid in the FreeMarkets Global Supply Network, the database of suppliers that are exposed to the RFQs of buyers. FreeMarkets used a five-step process that started with the RFQ and ended with supplier management (which included supplier verification and training). STE saved 35 percent on the cost of printed circuit board assemblies.

It is interesting to note that one of STE's traditional suppliers threatened to not participate in the event. The supplier claimed that its prequoted price was so competitive that it would be impossible to beat the price through online bidding. In spite of these claims, STE followed through with the auction and subsequently awarded the business to another high-quality bidder with even better pricing.

Sources: Compiled from *freemarkets.com* (2002a and b).

Questions

1. Enter *freemarkets.com* and explore the current activities of the company. Prepare a report of what activities FreeMarkets offers to its customers.

2. Look at six customer success stories (three for sourcing and three for supplying and asset recovery) at the company's Web site. What common elements can you find?

3. Identify additional services provided by the company to support procurement (sourcing).

4. If you work in a business, register with *freemarkets.com* and examine the process as a buyer and as a seller.

5. Compare the use of *freemarkets.com* with the option of building your own auction site.

6. How does surplus-asset recovery become more efficient with FreeMarkets?

7. Compare FreeMarkets auctions with those conducted on eBay.

REFERENCES

Aberdeen Group. "The Moment: Providing Pricing Flexibility for eMarkets." July 27, 2000, aberdeen.com (accessed May 2001).

Beam, C., et al. "On Negotiations and Deal Making in Electronic Markets." *Information Systems Frontiers* 1, no. 3 (1999).

Beato, G. "Online Piracy's Mother Ship." *Business2.com*, December 12, 2000.

Beer, M. "Butterfield–eBay Marriage Looks Real; Art Auction House, On-Line Auctioneer Team for Web Sales." *San Francisco Examiner*, April 13, 1999.

car---auctions.com (accessed April 2003).

Choi, S. Y., and A. B. Whinston. *The Internet Economy: Technology and Practice*. Austin, TX: SmartconPub, 2000.

Cohen, A. *The Perfect Store—Inside eBay*. Boston: Little Brown & Co., 2002.

Deitel, H. M., et al. *e-Business and e-Commerce for Managers*. Upper Saddle River, NJ: Prentice Hall, 2001.

Delichte, J. "Reinventing Commerce with Mobility." *The IT Journal*, (2001): 26–31. hp.com/solutions1/corporatebusiness/itj/first_qtr_01/pdf/re_invent.pdf.

dickerabid.com (accessed December 2002).

eBay.com. "eBay Launches eBay Business to Serve Its Growing Community of Business Buyers." eBay press release, January 28, 2002, shareholder.com/ebay/releases-2003.cfm (accessed April 2003).

eBay.com. ebay.com/help/sellerguide/safeseller.html (accessed April 2003a).

eBay.com. "Sotheby's and eBay Announce Change in Relationship." eBay press release, February 4, 2003b, shareholder.com/ebay/releases-2003.cfm (accessed April 2003).

Elliot, A. C. *Getting Started in Internet Auctions*. New York: John Wiley & Sons, 2000.

EMarketer.com. "Retail Industry Online." *eMarketer*, October 2, 2002, emarketer.com/products/report.php?retail_ind (accessed May 2003).

Esmahi, L., and J. C. Bernard. "MIAMAP: A Virtual Marketplace for Intelligent Agents." *Proceedings of the 33rd HICSS*, Maui, HI, January 2000.

fraud.net (accessed December 2002).

Freemarkets.com. "American Power Conversion Corporation Case Study." 2002a, freemarkets.com/en/freemarkets/literature.asp#casestudy (accessed May 2002).

Freemarkets.com. "FreeMarkets and Singapore Technologies Engineering Expand Relationship." Freemarkets.com press release, January 15, 2002b, freemarkets.com/en/news/press_releases/newsitem.asp?NewsID=331 (accessed May 2003).

Freemarkets.com. "Singapore Technologies Engineering Case Study." 2003, freemarkets.com/en/literature/CaseStudy_SingTech.pdf (accessed June 2003).

Freemarkets.com. "New Line Cinema Case Study." 2002c, freemarkets.com/en/freemarkets/literature.asp#case study (accessed June 2002).

Geralds, J. "Sotheby's Teams with eBay for E-Auctions." January 2, 2002, vnunet.com/News/ 1128881 (accessed April 2003).

Inc. "Web Awards 2000: Innovation—Third Place—Cross Country Savings." *Inc.*, November 15, 2000, inc.com/magazine/2000/1115/21019.html (accessed June 2003).

Konrad, R. "eBay Touts Anti-Fraud Software's Might." *News.com*, June 5, 2002, marketwatch-cnet.com.com/2100–1017– 932874.html (accessed May 2003).

Lee, B. "Web's Bloom a Garden for Sophisticated Scammers." *Chicago Tribune*, March 11, 2002, chicagotribune.com/technology/local/chi-020311crime,0,6398375.story (accessed April 2003).

Lorek, L. "Trade Ya? E-Barter Thrives." *InteractiveWeek*, August 14, 2000.

McKay, C. "Online Auctions Dominant Consumer Fraud." *National Consumers League*, March 25, 2003, nclnet.org/internetfraud02.htm (accessed May 2003).

McKeown, P. G., and R. T. Watson. "Manheim Auctions." *Communication of the AIS* 1 (1999).

Mirapaul, M. "The New Canvas: Artists Use Online Auctions for Art Projects." *New York Times*, February 5, 2001.

Neo, B. S. "The Implementation of an Electronic Market for Pig Trading in Singapore." *Journal of Strategic Information Systems* 1, no. 5 (1992).

Prince, D. L. *Auction This!: Your Complete Guide to the World of Online Auctions*. Roseville, CA: Prima Publishing, 1999.

Reuters. "Grape Auction Goes Online." *cnn.com*, March 20, 2001, cnn.com/2001/BUSINESS/03/20/wine.online.reut/ (accessed May 2003).

Rothkopf, M. H., and S. Park. "An Elementary Introduction to Auctions." *Interfaces*, November–December 2001.

Sashi, C. M., and B. O'Leary. "The Role of Internet Auctions in the Expansion of B2B Markets." *Industrial Marketing Management* 31 (2002).

Strobel, M. "On Auctions as the Negotiation Paradigm of Electronic Markets." *Electronic Markets* 10, no. 1 (2000).

Subramaniam, R. "Experience Pricing." *Business Line*, August 31, 2000, blonnet.com/businessline/2000/08/31/stories/043101ra.htm (accessed May 2003).

Sullivan, B. "Auction Fraud on the Rise Some Say." *MSNBC*, July 29, 2003, msnbc.com/news/784132.asp (accessed April 2003).

Turban, E. et al. *Introduction to Information Technology*, 2e. New York: John Wiley & Sons, 2001.

Westland, J. C. "Ten Lessons that Internet Auction Markets Can Learn from Securities Market Automation." *Journal of Global Management* 8, no. 1 (2000).

wineryexchange.com (accessed December 2002).

Wolverton, T. "Survey Finds Pirates Rule Online Auctions." *CNET News.com*, April 11, 2000, news.com.com/2100–1017–239146.html?legacy=cnet (accessed April 2003).

Wurman, P. "Dynamic Pricing in the Virtual Marketplace." *IEEE Internet Computing* (March/April 2001): 38–39, computer.org/internet/ (accessed August 2003).

E-COMMERCE SECURITY

Learning objectives

Upon completion of this chapter, you will be able to:

1. Document the rapid rise in computer and network security attacks.

2. Describe the common security practices of businesses of all sizes.

3. Understand the basic elements of EC security.

4. Explain the basic types of network security attacks.

5. Describe common mistakes that organizations make in managing security.

6. Discuss some of the major technologies for securing EC communications.

7. Detail some of the major technologies for securing EC networks components.

Content

BRUTE FORCE CREDIT CARD ATTACK

The Problem

On September 12, 2002, Spitfire Novelties fell victim to what is called a "brute force" credit card attack. On a normal day, the Los Angeles-based company generates between 5 and 30 transactions. That Thursday, Spitfire's credit card transaction processor, Online Data Corporation, processed 140,000 fake credit card charges worth $5.07 each. Of these, 62,000 were approved. The total value of the approved charges was around $300,000. Spitfire found out about the transactions only when they were called by one of the credit card owners who had been checking his statement online and had noticed the $5.07 charge.

The Solution

Brute force credit card attacks require minimal skill. Hackers simply run thousands of small charges through merchant accounts, picking numbers at random. Although the number of valid transactions is likely to be miniscule, when the perpetrator finds a valid credit card number the number can then be sold on the black market. Some modern-day black markets are actually member-only Web sites such as *carderplanet.com*, *shadowcrew.com*, and *counterfeitlibrary.com* where hackers trade illicit information such as stolen credit card numbers.

A brute force attack rests on the perpetrator's ability to pose as a merchant requesting authorization for a credit card purchase. This requires either a merchant ID, a password, or both. In the case of Online Data's credit card processing services, all a perpetrator needed was a merchant's password in order to request authorization. Online Data is a reseller of VeriSign Inc. credit card gateway services. Although VeriSign actually handles the transactions, Online Data issues passwords to its merchant customers. VeriSign blamed Online Data for the incident. Online Data blamed Spitfire for not changing their initial starter password. Spitfire reported that their password was "OnlneAp16501," which was the one Online Data had originally given them. Most likely, many of the other merchants being serviced by Online Data had also failed to change their passwords. At a minimum, Online Data ought to assign strong passwords at the start. In turn their customers need to modify those passwords frequently.

Like Online Data, other credit card processors have fallen prey to similar brute force attacks. In April 2002, hackers got into the Authorize.Net card processing system, executing 13,000 credit card transactions, of which 7,000 succeeded. A number of the merchants that had been victimized indicated that entry into the Authorize.Net system required only a log-on name, not a password. Once the hackers obtained the merchant ID, they could test as many credit cards numbers as they wanted. Several thousand merchants use Authorize.Net, performing millions of transactions per month. It is the largest gateway payment system on the Internet. The method used to access the Authorize.Net system really depends on the processes used by the resellers issuing the merchant IDs. Regardless, good security practices dictate that authorization ought to require more than a log-on ID.

Even if a merchant's log-on ID and password fall into the hands of a hacker, authorization services such as VeriSign and Authorize.Net should have built in safeguards that recognize brute force attacks. Any time a merchant issues an extraordinary number of requests, it ought to automatically trigger a more extensive authorization process. Repeated requests for small amounts emanating from the same merchant should be an automatic signal that something is amiss.

The Results

Fortunately for Spitfire, VeriSign halted the transactions before they were settled, saving the merchant $316,000 in charges. The other merchants using the Authorize.Net system were not so lucky. Although the transactions were only for pennies, these merchants were charged $0.35 for each transaction. The only ones who really made out were the criminals perpetrating the assault. The transactions that were approved gave them thousands of valid credit card numbers to sell on the black market.

Sources: Sullivan (2002a, 2002b).

WHAT WE CAN LEARN . . .

Any type of EC involves a number of players who use a variety of network and application services that provide access to a variety of data sources. The sheer numbers are what makes EC security so difficult. A perpetrator needs only a single weakness in order to attack a system. Some attacks require sophisticated techniques and technologies. Most, however, are like the brute force method used in the attack on Spitfire—simple techniques preying on poor security practices and human weaknesses. Because most attacks are not sophisticated, standard security risk management procedures can be used to minimize their probability and impact.

This chapter focuses on the basic security issues in EC, the major types of attacks that are perpetrated against EC networks and transactions, and the procedures and technologies that can be used to address these attacks. Because security is a multifaceted and highly technical problem, the complexities cannot be addressed in a single chapter. Those readers interested in a more comprehensive discussion should read Proctor and Byrnes (2002) and Garfinkel (2002).

12.1   THE ACCELERATING NEED FOR E-COMMERCE SECURITY

Evidence from a variety of security surveys continues to highlight the growing incidence of cyber attacks and cyber crimes in the world of e-commerce. The best known and most widely cited of these is the annual survey conducted by the *Computer Security Institute* (CSI) and the San Francisco Federal Bureau of Investigation's (FBI) Computer Intrusion Squad. The results from the 2002 survey were based on the responses of 538 security practitioners. Of these respondents, approximately 50 percent worked for organizations that conducted e-commerce on their Web sites. Their responses reinforced patterns that have appeared over the past 5 to 6 years. More specifically (CSI and FBI 2002):

1. Organizations continue to experience cyber attacks from inside and outside of the organization. Of the organizations surveyed, about 90 percent of the respondents indicated that they had detected security breaches over the past 12 months.

2. The types of cyber attacks that organizations experience were varied. For example, 85 percent detected computer viruses, 78 percent detected Net abuse (unauthorized uses of the Internet) by employees, and 40 percent were the victims of denial of service attacks.

3. The financial losses from a cyber attack can be substantial: 80 percent of the respondents acknowledged that they had experienced financial losses due to various cyber attacks. Of these respondents, 44 percent were willing to detail their losses. The combined loss for these respondents was approximately $455 million. As in previous years, the theft of proprietary information and financial fraud accounted for more than half of the losses.

4. It takes more than one type of technology to defend against cyber attacks. Virtually all of the respondents indicated that they employed physical security devices, firewalls, access control, and a number of other techniques and technologies to reduce or thwart cyber attacks from both the inside and outside the organization.

National Infrastructure Protection Center (NIPC)
A joint partnership, under the auspices of the FBI, among governmental and private industry; designed to prevent and protect the nation's infrastructure.

In response to the growing incidents of cyber attacks and cyber crime, the FBI has formed the National Infrastructure Protection Center (NIPC), which is located at FBI headquarters. This is a joint partnership between government and private industry and is designed to prevent and protect the nation's infrastructure—telecommunications, energy, transportation, banking and finance, and emergency and governmental operations.

The FBI has also established *Regional Computer Intrusion Squads*, which are located at different FBI offices throughout the United States. These are charged with the task of investigating violations of the Computer Fraud and Abuse Act. This Act and the Intrusion Squads' activities are focused on intrusions to public switched networks, major computer network intrusions, privacy violations, industrial espionage, pirated computer software, and other cyber crimes.

Computer Emergency Response Team (CERT)
Group of three teams at Carnegie Mellon University that monitor incidence of cyber attacks, analyze vulnerabilities, and provide guidance on protecting against attacks.

Evidence of the increase in cyber attacks is also provided by the Computer Emergency Response Team (CERT) at Carnegie Mellon University (cert.org). The CERT Coordination Center (CC) consists of three teams: the Incident Handling Team, the Vulnerability Handling Team, and the Artifact Analysis Team. The Incident Handling Team receives incident reports of cyber attacks from Internet sites and provides information and guidance to the Internet community on combating reported incidents. The Vulnerability Handling Team receives reports on suspected computer and network vulnerabilities, verifies and analyzes the reports, and works with the Internet community to understand and develop countermeasures to those vulnerabilities. The Artifact Analysis Team focuses on the code used to carry out cyber attacks (e.g., computer viruses), analyzing the code and finding ways to combat it.

According to the statistics reported to CERT/CC over the past year (CERT/CC 2002), the number of incidents skyrocketed from approximately 22,000 in 2000 to over 82,000 in 2002. This is more than a 20-fold increase from the number reported in 1998. Through the first calendar quarter of 2003 the number was already over 43,000. Similarly, the number of reported vulnerabilities went from approximately 1,000 in 2000 to almost 4,000 in 2002. Again, this is almost a 20-fold increase from 1998.

Section 12.1 ▶ REVIEW

1. What evidence exists that cyber attacks and crime are on the rise?

2. What units does the FBI have for combating cyber attacks?

3. What is CERT and what services does it provide?

12.2 SECURITY IS EVERYONE'S BUSINESS

As the technology underlying e-commerce has become more complex, the opportunities for intrusion and attack have increased. Not only are the underlying components more vulnerable, they are also harder to administer. Teenage hackers, industrial spies, corporate insiders, agents of foreign governments, and criminal elements have all taken advantage of the situation. The variety of potential perpetrators makes it hard to deter potential attacks and detect them once they have occurred.

According to International Data Corporation (IDC), worldwide spending on corporate digital security was almost $25 billion in 2002, including costs associated with people, products, and services (Darby 2002). This was up significantly from 1999 when the figure was only $6.2 billion. Although spending on security has increased significantly, the average company still spends very little of its IT budget on security and very little per employee.

A recent survey of 2,196 IT security professionals conducted by Information Security Magazine (Briney and Prince 2002) looked specifically at the security practices of organizations of various sizes. The results were surprising:

▶ Small organizations (10 to 100 computers). Small organizations tend to be divided into the "haves" and "have-nots." The "haves" are centrally organized, devote a sizeable percentage of their IT budgets to security, spend the most amount of money on security per employee, have well-established incident response plans, and base their security decisions on management approved policies. Their major problem is that they are dependent on one or two people to manage their IT security. Their success or failure depends on these individuals. In contrast to the "haves," the "have-nots" are basically clueless when it comes to IT security. This makes them extremely vulnerable to cyber attacks and intrusions. Fortunately, for most small organizations, the chance of an attack is lower than it is for other organizations, and the chance of loss is also smaller. Unfortunately, if they do suffer an attack, the results can be catastrophic.

▶ Medium organizations (100 to 1,000 computers). The systems of medium-sized organizations are more complex than those of smaller organizations. These organizations rarely rely on managerial policies in making security decisions, and they have little managerial support for their IT policies. Their budgets and staffing are comparatively less than other organizations of any size. The staff they do have is poorly educated and poorly trained. As a consequence, their overall exposure to cyber attacks and intrusion is substantially greater than smaller organizations (70 percent said they suffered damage or loss).

▶ Large organizations (1,000 to 10,000 computers). Large organizations have complex infrastructures and substantial exposure on the Internet. Although their aggregate IT security expenditures are fairly large, their security expenditures per employee are low. Where they skimp is on security head count. In general, IT security is part-time and undertrained. As a consequence, a sizeable percentage of the large organizations suffer loss or damage due to incidents. Despite these obstacles, large organizations do base their security decisions on organizational policies.

▶ Very large organizations (more than 10,000 computers). The average IT security budget of very large organizations was $6 million, which is substantially greater than those of other organizations. However, the average IT security expenditure *per employee* is the least. Organizations of this size rely on managerial policies in making IT security decisions, although only a small percentage have a well-coordinated incident response plan. The major difficulty is that these are extremely complex environments that are difficult to manage even with a larger staff.

Based on these findings, the ISM survey concluded that while there is increasing security awareness among organizations of all sizes, IT security is still trying to gain a foothold in the day-to-day activities that impact the organization. Even though spending has increased, it has not kept pace with security demands, especially in large, complex organizations. Although most organizations have management-approved security policies, these policies have little impact on the way in which organizations respond to specific security incidents.

Section 12.2 ❱ REVIEW

1. Based on the ISM survey results, what are some of the major differences in security issues facing small, medium, large, and very large organizations?

2. Does the amount of money that a organization spends on security have an impact on the chance of a organization suffering loss or damage due to cyber attacks? Explain.

12.3 BASIC SECURITY ISSUES

EC security involves more than just preventing and responding to cyber attacks and intrusion. Consider, for example, the situation in which a user connects to a Web server at a marketing site in order to obtain some product literature (Loshin 1998). In return, the user is asked to fill out a Web form providing some demographic and other personal information in order to receive the literature. In this situation, what kinds of security questions arise?

From the user's perspective:

❱ How can the user be sure that the Web server is owned and operated by a legitimate company?

❱ How does the user know that the Web page and form do not contain some malicious or dangerous code or content?

❱ How does the user know that Web server will not distribute the information the user provides to some other party?

From the company's perspective:

❱ How does the company know the user will not attempt to break into the Web server or alter the pages and content at the site?

❱ How does the company know that the user will not try to disrupt the server so that it isn't available to others?

From both parties' perspectives:

❱ How do both parties know that the network connection is free from eavesdropping by a third party "listening" on the line?

❱ How do they know that the information sent back and forth between the server and the user's browser hasn't been altered?

These questions illustrate the types of security issues that can arise in an EC transaction. For transactions involving e-payments, additional types of security issues must be confronted. The following list summarizes some of the major security issues that can occur in EC:

authentication

The process by which one entity verifies that another entity is who they claim to be.

❱ Authentication. When a person views a Web page from a Web site, how can they be sure that the site is not fraudulent? If a person files a tax return electronically, how do they know that it has been sent to the taxing authority? If a person receives an e-mail, how can they be sure that the sender is who they claim to be? The process by which one entity verifies that another entity is who they claim to be is called **authentication**. Authentication requires evidence in the form of credentials, which can take a variety of forms, including something known (e.g., a password), something possessed (e.g., a smart card), or something unique (e.g., a signature).

▶ Authorization. Once authenticated, does a person or program have the right to access particular data, programs, or system resources (e.g., files, registries, directories, etc.)? Authorization ensures that a person or program has the right to access certain resources. It is usually determined by comparing information about the person or program with access control information associated with the resource being accessed.

▶ Auditing. If a person or program accesses a Web site, various pieces of information are noted in a log file. If a person or program queries a database, the action is also noted in a log file. The process of collecting information about accessing particular resources, using particular privileges, or performing other security actions (either successfully or unsuccessfully) is known as auditing. Audits provide the means to reconstruct the specific actions that were taken and often enable IT personnel to identify the person or program that performed the actions.

▶ Confidentiality (privacy). The idea behind confidentiality is that information that is private or sensitive should not be disclosed to unauthorized individuals, entities, or computer software processes. It is intertwined with the notion of digital privacy, which is now a regulatory issue in many countries. Some examples of things that should be confidential are trade secrets, business plans, health records, credit card numbers, and even the fact that a person visited a particular Web site. Confidentiality requires that we know what data or applications we want to protect and who should have access to them. Confidentiality is usually ensured by encryption.

▶ Integrity. Data can be altered or destroyed while it is in transit or after it is stored. The ability to protect data from being altered or destroyed in an unauthorized or accidental manner is called integrity. Financial transactions are one example of data whose integrity needs to be secured. Again, encryption is one way of ensuring integrity of data while it is in transit.

▶ Availability. If a person is trying to execute a stock trade through an online service, then the service needs to be available in near-real time. An online site is *available* if a person or program can gain access to the pages, data, or services provided by the site when they are needed. Technologies such as load-balancing hardware and software are aimed at ensuring availability.

▶ Nonrepudiation. If a person orders an item through a mail-order catalog and pays by check, then it is difficult to dispute the veracity of the order. If the same item is ordered through the company's "1-800" number and the person pays by credit card, then there is always room for dispute. Similarly, if a person uses the company's Web site and pays by credit card, the person can always claim that they did not place the order. Nonrepudiation is the ability to limit parties from refuting that a legitimate transaction took place. One of the keys to nonrepudiation is a "signature" that makes it difficult for a person to dispute that they were involved in an exchange.

Exhibit 12.1 (page 468) depicts some of the major components involved in most EC applications and indicates where the above security issues come into play. It is safe to say that virtually every component in an EC application is subject to some sort of security threat.

Section 12.3 ▶ REVIEW

1. If a customer purchases an item from an online store, what are some of the security concerns that might arise?

2. What are the major security issues facing EC sites?

12.4 TYPES OF THREATS AND ATTACKS

Security experts distinguish between two types of attacks—nontechnical and technical. Nontechnical attacks are those in which a perpetrator uses chicanery or other forms of persuasion to trick people into revealing sensitive information or performing actions that can be used to compromise the security of a network. These attacks are also called *social engineering attacks*, a benign-sounding name for what is basically trickery.

authorization
The process that ensures that a person has the right to access certain resources.

auditing
The process of collecting information about attempts to access particular resources, use particular privileges, or perform other security actions.

confidentiality
Keeping private or sensitive information from being disclosed to unauthorized individuals, entities, or processes.

integrity
As applied to data, the ability to protect data from being altered or destroyed in an unauthorized or accidental manner.

nonrepudiation
The ability to limit parties from refuting that a legitimate transaction took place, usually by means of a signature.

nontechnical attack
An attack that uses chicanery to trick people into revealing sensitive information or performing actions that compromise the security of a network.

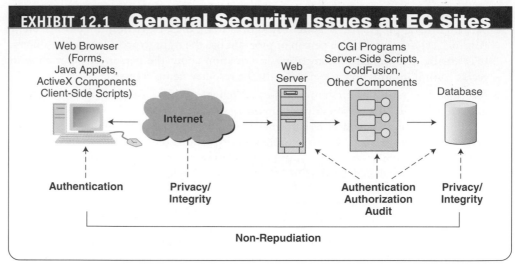

EXHIBIT 12.1   General Security Issues at EC Sites

Source: Scambray, J. et al. *Hacking Exposed 2e.* New York: McGraw-Hill, 2000. Copyright © McGraw-Hill Companies, Inc.

NONTECHNICAL ATTACKS: SOCIAL ENGINEERING

social engineering

A type of nontechnical attack that uses social pressures to trick computer users into compromising computer networks to which those individuals have access.

In **social engineering**, individual users are tricked by social pressures into providing information or carrying out actions that they feel are innocuous but that inadvertently support hackers in their attempts to attack and compromise the networks to which those individuals have access. Social engineering preys on an individual's desire to help, an individual's fear of getting into trouble, or the general trust among individuals. EC Application Case 12.1 details some of the methods used in social engineering attacks.

Because the key to successful social engineering rests with the victims, the key to combating social engineering attacks also rests with the victims. Certain positions within an organization are clearly more vulnerable than others. These are the individuals who have access to private and confidential information and interact with the public on a frequent basis. Some of the positions with this sort of access and contact are secretaries and executive assistants, database and network administrators, computer operators, call-center operators, and help-desk attendants.

A multiprong approach should be used to combat social engineering (Damle 2002):

1. Education and training. All staff, but especially those in vulnerable positions, need to be educated about the risks associated with social engineering, the social engineering techniques used by hackers, and ways and means to combat these attacks.

2. Policies and procedures. Specific policies and procedures need to be developed for securing confidential information, guiding employee behavior with respect to confidential information, and taking the steps needed to respond to and report any social engineering breaches.

3. Penetration testing. The policies, procedures, and responses of individual staff need to be tested on a regular basis by outside experts playing the role of a hacker. Because of the possibility of adverse effects on employee or staff morale, they should be debriefed after the penetration test, and any weaknesses should be corrected.

TECHNICAL ATTACKS

technical attack

An attack perpetrated using software and systems knowledge or expertise.

In contrast to nontechnical attacks, software and systems knowledge are used to perpetrate **technical attacks**. In conducting a technical attack, an expert hacker often uses a methodical approach. Several software tools are readily and freely available over the Internet that enable a hacker to expose a system's vulnerabilities. Although many of these tools require expertise, novice hackers can easily use many of the existing tools.

In 1999, Mitre Corporation (cve.mitre.org) and 15 other security-related organizations began to enumerate all publicly known **common (security) vulnerabilities and exposures**

CASE 12.1
EC Application
SOCIAL ENGINEERING

I LOVE YOU. On May 4, 2000, this message appeared in the in-boxes of an estimated 45 million Microsoft Outlook e-mail users. When the message was opened, the message was re-sent to everyone in the recipient's address book, and more seriously, it deleted every JPEG, MP3, and certain other files on the recipient's hard drive. Although this virus was spread through technical means, its impact was actually the result of social engineering: It played on the psychological curiosity of the recipients. Upon opening the message, the recipients' curiosity was more than satisfied.

IT staffs tend to concentrate on the technical side of network security—firewalls, encryption, digital signatures, and the like. However, the real Achilles heel of most networks is the humans that use them. Tricking individual users into providing information or carrying out actions that seem innocuous but are not is the process known as social engineering.

There are two categories of social engineering—human-based and computer-based.

Human-based social engineering relies on traditional methods of communication (in person or over the phone). For example, a hacker posing as IT support staff might call up an employee and simply ask the employee for their password under the guise that the IT staff needs to fix a problem with the system. Or, a hacker might turn the tables. The hacker, posing as an officer of a company, might call the IT support staff asking for a password that the hacker claims to have forgotten. Fearing that they might seem uncooperative to upper management, the IT support staff comply. Employees are also notorious for writing their passwords on sticky notes or desk pads that can be easily viewed by people walking by or that are discarded in the trash and later retrieved by a hacker.

With computer-based social engineering, various technical ploys are used to encourage individuals to provide sensitive information. For example, a hacker might simply send an e-mail requesting sensitive information or might create a Web page that surfaces a form that looks like a legitimate network log-on request for user ID and password.

Over the past couple of years, Internet chat rooms and instant messaging have also been used to perpetrate social engineering attacks. In September 2000, a hacker called AOL technical support (Granger 2001). During the hour-long conversation, the hacker mentioned that he had a car for sale. The technical support person indicated that he was interested and wanted to see a picture of the car. The hacker sent the picture through e-mail. When the technical support person opened the message, the e-mail surreptitiously installed a Trojan horse (described later) that enabled the hacker to gain access to AOL's internal network.

Kevin Mitnick, who spent 5 years in prison for breaking and entering into computers and whose exploits were documented in the best-selling book *Takedown*, was quoted as saying that more than half of his successful attacks were carried out through social engineering. Mitnick, now a computer security advisor, has recently published a book on social engineering called *The Art of Deception*. From Mitnick's perspective, the key to successful social engineering is trust: "You try to make an emotional connection with the person on the other side to create a sense of trust. That's the whole idea: to create a sense of trust and then exploit it" (quoted in Lewis 2000).

Sources: Granger (2001), Lewis (2000), Mitnick and Simon (2002), and Shimomura et al. (1996).

Questions

1. Describe the different types of social engineering.

2. Who is Kevin Mitnick?

3. What types of people are most likely to be targeted by social engineering?

(CVEs). One of the goals was to assign standard and unique names to each of the known security problems so that information could be collected and shared with the security community throughout the world. The number of known CVE's has grown from approximately 320 in 1999 to over 2,500 in 2003. Additionally, there are close to 3,100 CVE *candidates*, which are those vulnerabilities or exposures under consideration for acceptance into CVE (Mitre 2002).

For the past 2 years, the SANS Institute, in conjunction with the FBI's NIPC, has produced a document summarizing the "Ten Most Critical Internet Security Vulnerabilities" (SANS 2003). This year the list was expanded to incorporate the top 10 for those computers running Microsoft Windows and the top 10 for those computers running UNIX. The list helps organizations prioritize their security efforts, addressing the most dangerous vulnerabilities first.

Examining the list of the top 10 or 20 CVEs, one quickly realizes that all the CVEs are very technical in nature. For this reason, we will confine our discussion to two types of attacks that are well known and that have affected the lives of millions—distributed denial of service (DDoS) attacks and malicious code attacks (viruses, worms, and Trojan horses).

common (security) vulnerabilities and exposures (CVEs)
Publicly known computer security risks, which are collected, listed, and shared by a board of security-related organizations (*cve.mitre.org*).

Distributed Denial of Service Attacks

In February 2000, Amazon.com, Buy.com, CNN.com, eBay, E*TRADE, Yahoo, ZDNet, and other well-known Web sites were inundated with so many Internet requests that legitimate traffic was virtually halted (Kabay and Walsh 2000). These attacks cost businesses an estimated $1.7 billion. Similar sorts of attacks occurred throughout that year. In January 2001, a number of Microsoft's Web sites—including MSN, MSNBC, Expedia, Hotmail, Carpoint, HomeAdvisor, and the WindowsMedia entertainment guide—experienced the same type of outage. Interestingly, that same month a Canadian teenager with the moniker of "Mafiaboy" pled guilty to committing the February 2000 attacks (Harrison 2000). Technically speaking, all of these sites were the victims of DDoS attacks.

In a **denial-of-service (DoS) attack**, an attacker uses specialized software to send a flood of data packets to the target computer, with the aim of overloading its resources. Many attackers rely on software that has been created by other hackers and made available over the Internet rather than developing it themselves.

With a **distributed denial of service (DDoS) attack**, the attacker gains illegal administrative access to as many computers on the Internet as possible. Once an attacker has access to a large number of computers, they load the specialized DDoS software onto these computers. The software lays in wait, listening for a command to begin the attack. When the command is given, the distributed network of computers begins sending out requests to the target computer. The requests can be legitimate queries for information or can be very specialized computer commands designed to overwhelm specific computer resources. There are different types of DDoS attacks. In the simplest case, it is the magnitude of the requests that brings the target computer to a halt.

The machines on which the DDoS software is loaded are known as *zombies* (Heim and Ackerman 2001). Zombies are often located at university and government sites (see Exhibit 12.2). Increasingly, with the rise of cable modems and DSL modems, home computers that are connected to the Internet and left on all the time have become good zombie candidates.

DoS attacks are not new. In 1996, a New York ISP had service disrupted for over a week by a DoS attack, denying service to over 6,000 users and 1,000 companies. At the time, the attacker was considered something of an expert, with enough systems knowledge to "spoof" their Internet address, making it impossible to determine the attacker's identify. Today, the intruder population has changed. Due to the widespread availability of free intrusion tools and scripts and the overall interconnectivity on the Internet, virtually anyone with minimal computer experience (often a teenager with time on his hands) can mount a DoS attack. Unfortunately, a successful DoS attack can literally threaten the survival of an EC site, especially for SMEs.

Malicious Code: Viruses, Worms, and Trojan Horses

Sometimes referred to as **malware** (for malicious software), malicious code is classified by the way in which it is propagated. Some malicious code is rather benign, but it all has the potential to do damage.

New variants of malicious code appear quite frequently. According to annual surveys conducted by the Computer Security Association (ICSA 2002), the number of computer viruses doubled annually from 1996 to 1999. From 1999 to 2002, the rate of growth slowed to 15 percent. However, the severity of the viruses increased substantially, requiring much more time and money to recover. For example, the survey put the average recovery costs at $81,000 in 2002 compared to $69,000 in 2000. Additionally, in the last few years virtually every organization has been the victim of an e-mail virus or worm. Both this survey and the CSI survey described earlier indicated that approximately 85 percent of the respondents said that their organizations had been the victims of e-mail viruses in 2002. In the future, the frequency of computer viruses may increase as the number of users accessing the Internet with mobile devices increases. (See Section 10.2 for a discussion of security issues in mobile commerce.)

Malicious code takes a variety of forms—both pure and hybrid. The names of such code are taken from the real-world pathogens they resemble. Viruses are the best known. A whole industry has grown up around computer viruses. Companies such as Network Associates (owner of McAfee products) and Symantec (Owner of Norton products) exist for the sole

---

denial-of-service (DoS) attack
An attack on a Web site in which an attacker uses specialized software to send a flood of data packets to the target computer with the aim of overloading its resources.

distributed denial-of-service (DDoS) attack
A denial-of-service attack in which the attacker gains illegal administrative access to as many computers on the Internet as possible and uses these multiple computers to send a flood of data packets to the target computer.

malware
A generic term for malicious software.

EXHIBIT 12.2   Using Zombies in a Distributed Denial of Service Attack

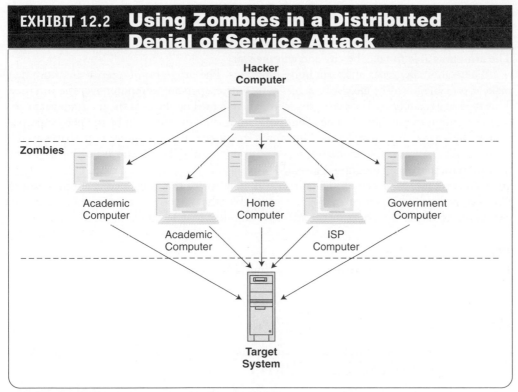

Source: Scambray, J. et al. *Hacking Exposed 2e.* New York: McGraw-Hill, 2000. Copyright © McGraw-Hill Companies, Inc.

purpose of fighting viruses. The antivirus industry is extensive and profitable. Today, it has expanded beyond viruses and now also follows and catalogs worms, macro viruses and macro worms, and Trojan horses.

Viruses. This is the best known of the malicious code categories. Although there are many definitions of a computer virus, the Request for Comment (RFC) 1135 definition is widely used: "A virus is a piece of code that inserts itself into a host, including the operating systems, to propagate. It cannot run independently. It requires that its host program be run to activate it."

A virus has two components. First, it has a propagation mechanism by which it spreads. Second, it has a payload that refers to what the virus does once it is executed. Sometimes the execution is triggered by a particular event. The Michelangelo virus, for instance, was triggered by Michelangelo's birth date. Some viruses simply infect and spread. Others do substantial damage (e.g., deleting files or corrupting the hard drive).

Worms. The major difference between a worm and a virus is that a worm propagates between systems (usually through a network), whereas a virus propagates locally. RFC 1135 defines a worm in this way: "A worm is a program that can run independently, will consume the resources of its host from within in order to maintain itself, and can propagate a complete working version of itself onto another machine."

Macro viruses and macro worms. A macro virus or macro worm is usually executed when the application object (e.g., spreadsheet, word processing document, e-mail message) containing the macro is opened or a particular procedure is executed (e.g., a file is saved). Melissa and ILOVEYOU were both examples of macro worms that were propagated through Microsoft Outlook e-mail and whose payloads were delivered as a Visual Basic for Application (VBA) programs attached to e-mail messages. When the unsuspecting recipient opened the e-mail, the VBA program looked up the entries in the recipient's Outlook address book and sent copies of itself to the contacts in the address book. If you think this is a difficult task, note that the ILOVEYOU macro was about 40 lines of code.

Trojan horses. A Trojan horse is a program that appears to have a useful function but contains a hidden function that presents a security risk (Norton and Stockman 2000). The name is derived from the Trojan horse in Greek mythology. Legend has it that during the

virus
A piece of software code that inserts itself into a host, including the operating systems, to propagate; it requires that its host program be run to activate it.

worm
A software program that runs independently, consuming the resources of its host in order to maintain itself and is capable of propagating a complete working version of itself onto another machine.

macro virus or macro worm
A virus or worm that is executed when the application object that contains the macro is opened or a particular procedure is executed.

Trojan horse
A program that appears to have a useful function but that contains a hidden function that presents a security risk.

Trojan War the city of Troy was presented with a large wooden horse as a gift to the goddess Athena. The Trojans hauled the horse into the city gates. During the night, Greek soldiers, who were hiding in the hollow horse, opened the gates of Troy and let in the Greek army. The army was able to take the city and win the war.

There are many types of Trojan horse programs. The programs of interest are those that make it possible for someone else to access and control a person's computer over the Internet. This type of Trojan horse has two parts: server and client. The server is the program that runs on the computer under attack. The client program is the program used by the person perpetrating the attack. For example, the Girlfriend Trojan is a server program that arrives in the form of a file that looks like an interesting game or program. When the unsuspecting user runs the program, the Trojan program is installed. The installed program is executed every time the attacked computer is turned on. The server simply waits for the associated client program to send a command. This particular Trojan horse enables the perpetrator to capture user IDs and passwords, to display messages on the affected computer, to delete and upload files, and so on.

Section 12.4 ▌ REVIEW

1. Describe the difference between a nontechnical and a technical cyber attack.
2. What is a CVE?
3. How are DDoS attacks perpetrated?
4. What are the major forms of malicious code?

12.5 MANAGING EC SECURITY

Although awareness of security issues has increased in recent years, organizations continue to make some fairly common mistakes in managing their security risks (McConnell 2002):

▌ **Undervalued information.** Few organizations have a clear understanding of the value of specific information assets.

▌ **Narrowly defined security boundaries.** Most organizations focus on securing their internal networks and fail to understand the security practices of their supply chain partners.

▌ **Reactive security management.** Many organizations are reactive rather than proactive, focusing on security *after* an incident or problem occurs.

▌ **Dated security management processes.** Organizations rarely update or change their security practices to meet changing needs. Similarly, they rarely update the knowledge and skills of their staff about best practices in information security.

▌ **Lack of communication about security responsibilities.** Security often is viewed as an IT problem, not an organizational one.

Given these common mistakes, it is clear that a holistic approach is required to secure an EC site. Sites must constantly evaluate and address emerging vulnerabilities and threats. End users must recognize that IT security is as important as physical security and must adopt responsible behavior. Senior management must articulate the need for IT security, play a key role in formulating organizational security policies, and actively support those policies. Those organizations with sound security practices rely on comprehensive risk management to determine their security needs (King 2001; Power 2000).

SECURITY RISK MANAGEMENT

security risk management
A systematic process for determining the likelihood of various security attacks and for identifying the actions needed to prevent or mitigate those attacks.

Security risk management is a systematic process for determining the likelihood of various security attacks and for identifying the actions needed to prevent or otherwise mitigate those attacks. It consists of four phases:

honeynet
A way to evaluate vulnerabilities of an organization by studying the types of attacks to which a site is subjected, using a network of systems called *honeypots*.

▌ **Assessment.** In this phase, organizations evaluate their security risks by determining their assets, the vulnerabilities of their system, and the potential threats to these vulnerabilities. One way to evaluate the vulnerabilities and threats facing a specific organization is to rely on the knowledge of the organization's IT personnel or to use outside consultants to make the determination. Another way is to utilize a honeynet to study the types of attacks to which a site is being actively subjected. A **honeynet** is a network of

honeypots, which are production systems (firewalls, routers, Web servers, database servers, and the like) that can be watched and studied as network intrusions occur. EC Application Case 12.2 discusses the operation and benefits of a honeynet in researching the vulnerabilities and threats faced by an organization.

▸ Planning. The goal of this phase is to arrive at a set of policies defining which threats are tolerable and which are not. A threat is deemed *tolerable* if the cost of the safeguard is too high or the risk too low. The policies also specify the general measures to be taken against those threats that are intolerable or high priority.

▸ Implementation. During implementation, particular technologies are chosen to counter high-priority threats. The selection of particular technologies is based on the general guidelines established in the planning phase. As a first step in the implementation phase, generic types of technology should be selected for each of the high priority threats. Given the generic types, particular software from particular vendors can then be selected.

honeypots

Production systems (e.g., firewalls, routers, Web servers, database servers) designed to do real work but to be watched and studied as network intrusions occur.

CASE 12.2
EC Application
HONEYNETS ATTRACT HACKERS

What motivates a hacker to carry out illegal, destructive, or unauthorized activities on the Internet? Instead of theorizing about how hackers thinks and operate, a better way to learn about them is to set a trap with a real system. When hackers attack the system, IT professionals can watch and learn what tools and techniques are used. This is what the Honeynet Project has been doing since April 1999. The Honeynet Project is a worldwide, not-for-profit research group of security professionals. The group focuses on raising awareness of security risks that confront any system connected to the Internet and teaching and informing the security community about better ways to secure and defend network resources.

As the name implies, the main tool the project uses is a honeynet. A *honeynet* is a network of honeypots designed to attract hackers like honey attracts bees. In this case, the honeypots are production systems—firewalls, routers, Web servers, database servers, and the like—that are designed to do real work. The main difference between a honeypot and a real production system is that the activities on a honeypot come from intruders attempting to compromise the system. In this way, researchers watching the honeynet can gather information about why hackers attack, when they attack, how they attack, what they do after the system is compromised, and how they communicate with one another during and after the attack.

There is nothing special about the honeypots being run by the Honeynet Project. The project makes no attempt to attract hackers. They simply connect the honeypots to the Internet and wait for attacks to occur. Given that there are millions of routers and computers on the Internet, what is the chance that an intruder will find one of the honeypots being operated by the Honeynet Project? One would think that the chance is about the same as winning a lottery. Think again.

In the first phase of the project, which ran from 1999 to 2001, the honeynet consisted of eight honeypots. The original honeypots ran standard operating systems—Windows and Linux—and were designed to mimic a typical setup on a home computer. One of the honeypots running Linux was hit within 15 minutes of being connected to the Internet. The rest of the Linux systems were attacked within 3 days of being connected. The Windows systems were just as vulnerable; the first attack was launched (and succeeded) within 24 hours. Over the course of the initial phase, these computers were repeatedly compromised.

During the first phase, many of the attacks were crude. The vulnerabilities of the specific operating systems were fairly well known by the hacking community. Yet, the various attacks were generic in nature, rather than exploiting known vulnerabilities. One surprising finding was that the attacks were generally preceded by a buildup of activity rather than a sudden strike. This means that in a real production system a system administrator might be able to predict an impending attack and take preventative actions.

In the Honeynet Project, honeypots are used for research. Honeypots also can be used in production systems to mitigate security risks. An organization does this by simply adding a honeypot to its existing networks. Although a honeypot cannot prevent an attack, it can simplify the detection and reaction to an attack. Because the only traffic on a honeypot comes from intruders, it is easier to analyze the data produced by a honeypot (e.g., log files of system activity) to determine what is happening and how to respond. Production honeypots can be built from scratch or commercial or open source versions can be used. Backofficer Friendly (*nfr.com/products/bof*), Specter (*specter.ch*), Honeyd (*citi.umich.edu/u/provos/honeyd*), and Mantrap (*recourse.com*) are some examples of commercial or open source systems.

Sources: Spitzner (2002), Honeynet Project (2000), and Piazza (2001).

Questions

1. What is a honeynet? A honeypot?
2. What are the main goals of the Honeynet Project?
3. How can a honeypot be used in a production system?

> ▶ Monitoring. This is an ongoing process that is used to determine which measures are successful, which measures are unsuccessful and need modification, whether there are any new types of threats, whether there have been advances or changes in technology, and whether there are any new business assets that need to be secured.

Section 12.5 ▶ REVIEW

1. What are some common mistakes that EC sites make in managing their security?
2. Describe the basic steps in security risk management.

12.6 SECURING EC COMMUNICATIONS

As the CERT/FBI survey indicates, most organizations rely on multiple technologies to secure their networks. The technologies can be divided into two major groups: those designed to secure communications *across* the network and those designed to protect the servers and clients *on* the network. This section considers the first of these technologies.

EC of all sorts rests on the concept of trust. The acronym PAIN (privacy, authentication, integrity, and non-repudiation) is used to represent the key issues of trust that arise in EC. More specifically, online buyers, sellers, and partners must be sure that their transactions have not been intercepted or altered and that the parties involved in the transactions are who they claim to be.

AUTHENTICATION

authentication system
System that identifies the legitimate parties to a transaction, determines the actions they are allowed to perform, and limits their actions to only those that are necessary to initiate and complete the transaction.

Information security requires that the legitimate parties to a transaction are identified, that the actions they are allowed to perform are determined, and that their actions are limited to only those that are necessary to initiate and complete the transaction. This can be accomplished with an **authentication system**. Authentication systems have five key elements (Smith 2002): (1) a person or group to be authenticated; (2) a distinguishing characteristic that differentiates the person or group from others; (3) a proprietor responsible for the system being used; (4) an authentication mechanism for verifying the presence of the differentiating characteristic; and (5) an **access control mechanism** for limiting the actions that can be performed by the authenticated person or group.

access control mechanism
Mechanism that limits the actions that can be performed by an authenticated person or group.

In an authentication system, the distinguishing characteristics can be based on something one knows (e.g., passwords), something one has (e.g., a token), or something one is (e.g., fingerprint). Traditionally, authentication systems have been based on passwords. Passwords are notoriously insecure because people have a habit of writing them down in easy to find places, of choosing values that are easily guessed, and of willingly telling people their passwords when asked (see EC Application Case 12.1).

passive tokens
Storage devices (e.g., magnetic strips) used in a two-factor authentication system that contain a secret code.

Stronger security is achieved by combining something one knows with something one has, a technique known as *two-factor authentication*. Tokens qualify as something one has. Tokens come in various shapes, forms, and sizes. **Passive tokens** are storage devices containing a secret code. The most common passive tokens are plastic cards with magnetic strips containing a hidden code. With passive tokens, the user swipes the token through a reader attached to a personal computer or workstation and then enters their password in order to gain access to the network.

active tokens
Small, stand-alone electronic devices in a two-factor authentication system that generate one-time passwords.

Active tokens are usually small stand-alone electronic devices that generate one-time passwords. In this case, the user enters a PIN into the token, the token generates a password that is only good for a single log-on, and the user then logs on to the system using the one-time password. ActivCard (activcard.com) and Cryptocard (cryptocard.com) are companies that provide active token authentication devices.

Biometric Systems

biometric systems
Authentication systems that identify a person by measurement of a biological characteristic such as a fingerprint, iris (eye) pattern, facial features, or voice.

Two-factor authentication can also be based on something one is. Fingerprint scanners, iris scanners, facial recognition systems, and voice recognition are all examples of **biometric systems** that identify a person by something they have. In the public arena, biometric systems are being deployed on a small scale in experimental trial runs (more about this later).

Fingerprint scanning is only one of a number of possible biometrics that can be used to verify an individual's identity (authentication). Biometrics come in two "flavors"—physiological and behavioral. **Physiological biometrics** are based on measurements derived directly from different parts of the body (e.g., scans of fingerprints, the iris, hand geometry, and facial characteristics). In contrast, **behavioral biometrics** are derived from various actions and indirectly from various body parts (e.g., voice scans or keystroke monitoring).

In practice, physiological biometrics are used more often than behavioral biometrics. Among the physiological biometrics, the scans of fingerprints, iris scans, hand geometry, and facial characteristics are the most popular.

To implement a biometric authentication system, the physiological or behavioral characteristics of a participant must be scanned repeatedly under different settings. The scans are then averaged to produce a template. The template is stored in a database as a series of numbers that can range from a few bytes for hand geometry to several thousand bytes for facial recognition. When a person uses a biometric system, a live scan is conducted, and the scan is converted to a series of numbers, which is then compared against the templates stored in the database. Examples of various types of biometric templates are detailed in the following text.

Fingerprint scanning. Fingerprints can be distinguished by a variety of "discontinuities that interrupt the smooth flow of ridges" (Kroeker 2002) on the bottom tips of the fingers. Ridge endings, dots (small ridges), and ponds (spaces between ridges) are examples of such discontinuities. In **fingerprint scanning**, a special algorithm is used to convert the scanned discontinuities to a set of numbers stored as a template. The chance that any two people have the same template is one in a billion.

Iris scanning. The iris is the colored part of the eye surrounding the pupil. The iris has a large number of unique spots that can be captured by a camera that is placed 3 to 10 inches from the eye. Within a second, a special algorithm can convert the iris scan to a set of numbers. The numbers can be used to construct an iris-scan template that can be used in **iris scanning**, in which a camera scans a person's iris, compares the scan to a template, and verifies the person's identity. The chance that any two people have identical iris templates is considerably smaller than the chance that they have the same fingerprint templates.

Voice scanning. Differences in the physiology of speech production from one individual to the next produce different acoustical patterns that can be converted into a template used in **voice scanning**. In most voice-scanning systems, the user talks into a microphone or telephone. The word that is spoken is usually the user's system ID or password. The next time a user wants to gain access to a system, the user simply repeats the spoken word. It takes about 4 to 6 seconds to verify a voice scan.

Keystroke monitoring. This biometric is still under development. **Keystroke monitoring** is based on the assumption that the way in which users type words at a keyboard varies from one user to the next. The pressure, speed, and rhythm with which a word is entered are converted through a special algorithm to a set of numbers to form a keystroke template. Again, the word that is employed in most of these systems is the user's system ID or password. When a user wants to gain access to a system, the user simply types in their system ID or password. The system checks the pressure, speed, and rhythm with which the word is typed against the templates in the database. The main problem with these systems is that there is still too much variability in the way an individual types from one session to the next.

Biometric systems can be used for purposes of identification or verification. Identifying an individual requires the system to match the individual's template against the various templates stored in the database until a match is found. For large populations of users, the identification process can be quite time-consuming. However, *verification* simply requires that the system determine that an individual is who they claim to be. EC Application Case 12.3 (page 476) describes the use of a biometric system for verification purposes.

PUBLIC KEY INFRASTRUCTURE

The "state of the art" in authentication rests on the **public key infrastructure (PKI)**. In this case, the something one has is not a token, but a certificate. PKI has become the cornerstone for secure e-payments. It refers to the technical components, infrastructure, and practices needed to enable the use of public key encryption, digital signatures, and digital certificates with a network application. PKI is also the foundation of a number of network applications, including SCM, VPNs, secure e-mail, and intranet applications.

physiological biometrics
Measurements derived directly from different parts of the body (e.g., fingerprints, iris, hand, facial characteristics).

behavioral biometrics
Measurements derived from various actions and indirectly from various body parts (e.g., voice scans or keystroke monitoring).

fingerprint scanning
Measurement of the discontinuities of a person's fingerprint, converted to a set of numbers that are stored as a template and used to authenticate identity.

iris scanning
Measurement of the unique spots in the iris (colored part of the eye), converted to a set of numbers that are stored as a template and used to authenticate identity.

voice scanning
Measurement of the acoustical patterns in speech production, converted to a set of numbers that are stored as a template and used to authenticate identity.

keystroke monitoring
Measurement of the pressure, speed, and rhythm with which a word is typed, converted to a set of numbers that are stored as a template and used to authenticate identity; this biometric is still under development.

public key infrastructure (PKI)
A scheme for securing e-payments using public key encryption and various technical components.

CASE 12.3
EC Application
BIOMETRIC AUTHENTICATION AT THRIFTWAY

In May 2002, West Seattle Thriftway, a privately owned supermarket, deployed biometric technology at its cash registers. Instead of using credit cards or checks, customers could pay with a fingerprint scan. To participate in the "Pay By Touch" program, customers first registered by filling out various forms; providing a credit card, debit card, or checking account number; selecting a seven-digit passcode (known only to them); and allowing their fingerprint to be scanned. Once they signed up, every time they checked out at a cash register, they simply provided the seven-digit passcode and had their fingerprint scanned. Once the system had verified their identity, the amount of their bill was automatically deducted from their credit card, debit card, or checking account.

Indivos, an Oakland, California, software company, developed the biometric system used in the "Pay By Touch" program. The cost to implement the system is between $150 and $200 per sensor. There is one sensor per cash register. The fingerprint scanning system not only speeds the checkout process, but also reduces the interchange fees that the company would pay if customers used their credit cards. Unlike the credit card companies that charge for every transaction, Indivos charges only a fee for every four transactions.

The "Pay By Touch" system is a verification system. In the system, the user makes a claim by entering a passcode number. The fingerprint template associated with that number is then checked against the actual fingerprint scan. This eliminates the need for the system to search through the database of fingerprint templates comparing the actual scan against all the scans in the database.

All biometric systems have their problems. The chance that the fingerprints of any two Thriftway customers are the same is infinitesimal. For Thriftway, this means that the probability that one person can falsely charge his or her bill to another person's account is extremely small. However, what happens if a customer has a cut on their finger, a broken finger, or oily or dry hands? These changes can preclude the use of the fingerprint device or can lead the system to reject the customer even though the system should authorize their payment.

Thriftway has a number of backups to the system. If the system does not work, the customer can pay by check, credit card, or debit card. The same is true with other biometric systems. Because there is always the possibility of a false rejection, many systems offer fallback authentication, whether to a live operator, a password, or another biometric method.

Sources: U.S. Banker (2002); Alga (2002).

Questions

1. Explain how a fingerprint-scanning system works.
2. Why would Thriftway have chosen a verification systems rather than an identification system?
3. What are some of the complications that might arise in using a fingerprint-scanning system to verify a person's identify?

---

encryption

The process of scrambling (encrypting) a message in such a way that it is difficult, expensive, or time-consuming for an unauthorized person to unscramble (decrypt) it.

plaintext

An unencrypted message in human-readable form.

ciphertext

A plaintext message after it has been encrypted into a machine-readable form.

encryption algorithm

The mathematical formula used to encrypt the plaintext into the ciphertext, and vice versa.

Private and Public Key Encryption

At the heart of PKI is **encryption**. Encryption is the process of transforming or scrambling (encrypting) data in such a way that it is difficult, expensive, or time-consuming for an unauthorized person to unscramble (decrypt) it. All encryption has four basic parts (shown in Exhibit 12.3): the **plaintext**, **ciphertext**, **encryption algorithm**, and the **key**. The simple example in Exhibit 12.3 forms the bases of an actual encryption algorithm called the "Vigenère cipher." Of course, simple algorithms and keys of this sort are useless in the networked world. More complex encryption algorithms and keys are required.

The two major classes of encryption systems are *symmetric systems*, with one secret key, and *asymmetric systems*, with two keys.

Symmetric (Private) Key System

In a **symmetric (private) key system** the same key is used to encrypt and decrypt the plaintext (see Exhibit 12.4). The sender and receiver of the text must share the same key without revealing it to anyone else—thus making it a so-called *private* system.

For years, the **Data Encryption Standard (DES)** (itl.nist.gov/fipspubs/fip46–2.htm) was the standard symmetric encryption algorithm supported by U.S. government agencies. On October 2, 2000, the National Institute of Standards and Technology (NIST) announced that DES was being replaced by **Rijndael**, the new Advanced Encryption Standard (csrc.nist.gov/encryption/aes) used to secure U.S. government communications.

EXHIBIT 12.3   Encryption Components

Component	Description	Example
Plaintext	Original message in human readable form	Credit Card Number 5342 8765 3652 9982
Encryption algorithm	Mathematical formula or process used to encrypt/decrypt the message	Add a number (the key) to each number in the card. If the number is greater than 9, wrap around the number to the beginning (i.e., modulus arithmetic). For example, add 4 to each number so that 1 becomes 5, 9 becomes 3, etc.
Key	A special number passed to the algorithm to transform the message	Number to be added to original number (e.g., 4).
Ciphertext	Plaintext message after it has been encrypted into unreadable form.	The original 5342 8765 3652 9982 becomes 9786 2109 7096 3326.

EXHIBIT 12.4   Symmetric (Private) Key Encryption

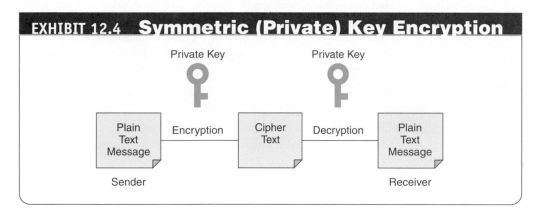

key
The secret code used to encrypt and decrypt a message.

symmetric (private) key system
An encryption system that uses the same key to encrypt and decrypt the message.

Data Encryption Standard (DES)
The standard symmetric encryption algorithm supported the NIST and used by U.S. government agencies until October 2, 2000.

Rijndael
The new Advanced Encryption Standard used to secure U.S. government communications since October 2, 2000.

public key encryption
Method of encryption that uses a pair of matched keys—a public key to encrypt a message and a private key to decrypt it, or vice versa.

public key
Encryption code that is publicly available to anyone.

private key
Encryption code that is known only to its owner.

Because the algorithms used to encrypt a message are well known, the confidentiality of a message depends on the key. It is possible to guess a key simply by having a computer try all the encryption combinations until the message is decrypted. High-speed and parallel-processing computers can try millions of guesses in a second. This is why the length of the key (in bits) is the main factor in securing a message. If a key were 4 bits long (e.g., 1011), there would be only 16 possible combinations (i.e., 2 raised to the 4th power). One would hardly need a computer to crack the key. Now consider the time it would take to try all possible encryption keys. According to Howard (2000), there are over 1 trillion possible combinations in a 40-bit key—but even this number of combinations can be broken in 8 days (using a computer that can check 1.6 million keys per second), or in just 109 seconds (at 10 million keys per second). However, a 64-bit encryption key would take *58.5 years* to be broken (at 10 million keys per second) (Howard 2000).

Public (Asymmetric) Key Encryption

Imagine trying to use one-key encryption to buy something offered on a particular Web server. If the seller's key were distributed to thousands of buyers, then the key would not remain secret for long. This is where public key (asymmetric) encryption comes into play. Public key encryption uses a pair of matched keys—a public key that is publicly available to anyone and a private key that is known only to its owner. If a message is encrypted with a public key, then the associated private key is required to decrypt the message. If, for example, a person wanted to send a purchase order to a company and have the contents remain private, they would encrypt the message with the company's public key. When the company received the order, they would decrypt it with the associated private key.

RSA
The most common public key encryption algorithm; uses keys ranging in length from 512 bits to 1,024 bits.

The most common public key encryption algorithm is **RSA** (rsa.com). RSA uses keys ranging in length from 512 bits to 1,024 bits. The main problem with public key encryption is speed. Symmetrical algorithms are significantly faster than asymmetric key algorithms. Therefore, public key encryption cannot be used effectively to encrypt and decrypt large amounts of data. In practice, a combination of symmetric and asymmetric encryption is used to encrypt messages.

Digital Signatures

In the online world, how can one be sure that a message is actually coming from the person who they think sent it? Similarly, how one be sure that a person cannot deny that they sent a particular message?

digital signature
An identifying code that can be used to authenticate the identity of the sender of a document.

One part of the answer is a **digital signature**—the electronic equivalent of a personal signature that cannot be forged. Digital signatures are based on public keys. They can be used to authenticate the identity of the sender of a message or document. They also can be used to ensure that the original content of an electronic message or document is unchanged. Digital signatures have additional benefits in the online world. They are portable, cannot be easily repudiated or imitated, and can be time-stamped.

Exhibit 12.5 shows how a digital signature works. Suppose a person wants to send the draft of a financial contract to a company with whom they plan to do business as an e-mail message. The sender wants to assure the company that the content of the draft has not been changed en route and that they really are the sender. To do so, they take the following steps:

1. The sender creates the e-mail message with the contract in it.

hash
A mathematical computation that is applied to a message, using a private key, to encrypt the message.

2. Using special software, a mathematical computation called a **hash** function is applied to the message, which results in a special summary of the message, converted into a string of digits called a **message digest**.

3. The sender uses their private key to encrypt the hash. This is their *digital signature*. No one else can replicate the sender's digital signature because it is based on their private key.

message digest
A summary of a message, converted into a string of digits, after the hash has been applied.

4. The sender encrypts both the original message and the digital signature using the recipient's public key. This is their **digital envelope**.

5. The sender e-mails the digital envelope to the receiver.

6. Upon receipt, the receiver uses their private key to decrypt the contents of the digital envelope. This produces a copy of the message and the sender's digital signature.

digital envelope
The combination of the encrypted original message and the digital signature, using the recipient's public key.

7. The receiver uses the sender's public key to decrypt the digital signature, resulting in a copy of the original message digest.

8. Using the same hash function employed in step 2, the recipient then creates a message digest from the decrypted message (as shown in Exhibit 12.6).

9. The recipient compares this digest with the original message digest

10. If the two digests match, then the recipient concludes that the message is authentic.

In this scenario, the company has evidence that the sender sent the e-mail because (theoretically) the sender is the only one with access to the private key. The recipient knows that the message has not been tampered with, because if it had been, then the two hashes would not have matched.

According to the U.S. Federal Electronic Signatures in Global and National Commerce Act that went into effect in October 2000, digital signatures in the United States now have the same legal standing as a signature written in ink on paper. Although PKI will certainly be the foundation of digital signatures, the act does not specify that any particular technology needs to be used. Several third-party companies are now exploring other methods to verify a person's legal identity, including the use of personal smart cards, PDA encryption devices, and biometric verifications.

digital certificate
Verification that the holder of a public or private key is who they claim to be.

Digital Certificates and Certificate Authorities

If one has to know someone's public key to send them a message, where does the public key come from and how can one be sure of the person's actual identity? **Digital certificates** ver-

EXHIBIT 12.5 Digital Signatures

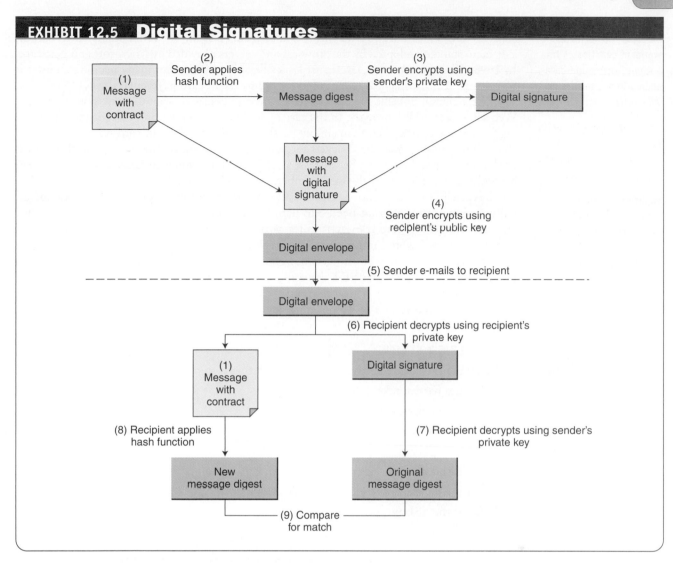

ify that the holder of a public and/or private key is who they claim to be. Third parties called **certificate authorities (CAs)** issue digital certificates. A certificate contains things such as the holder's name, validity period, public key information, and a signed hash of the certificate data (i.e., hashed contents of the certificate signed with the CA's private key). Certificates are used to authenticate Web sites (*site certificates*), individuals (*personal certificates*), and software companies (*software publisher certificates*).

There are a large number of third-party CAs. VeriSign (verisign.com) is the best known of the CAs. VeriSign issues three classes of certificates: Class 1 verifies that an e-mail actually comes from the user's address. Class 2 checks the user's identity against a commercial credit database. Class 3 requires notarized documents. Companies such as Microsoft offer systems that enable companies to issue their own private, in-house certificates.

certificate authorities (CAs)
Third parties that issue digital certificates.

SECURE SOCKET LAYER

If the average user had to figure out how to use encryption, digital certificates, digital signatures, and the like, there would be few secure transactions on the Web. Fortunately, many of these issues are handled in a transparent fashion by Web browsers and Web servers. Given that different companies, financial institutions, and governments, in many countries, are involved in e-commerce, it is necessary to have generally accepted protocols for securing e-commerce. One of the major protocols in use today is Secure Socket Layer (SSL), also known as Transport Layer Security (TLS).

Secure Socket Layer (SSL)
Protocol that utilizes standard certificates for authentication and data encryption to ensure privacy or confidentiality.

Transport Layer Security (TLS)
As of 1996, another name for the SSL protocol.

Secure Electronic Transaction (SET)
A protocol designed to provide secure online credit card transactions for both consumers and merchants; developed jointly by Netscape, Visa, MasterCard, and others.

The Secure Socket Layer (SSL) was invented by Netscape to utilize standard certificates for authentication and data encryption to ensure privacy or confidentiality. SSL became a de facto standard adopted by the browsers and servers provided by Microsoft and Netscape. In 1996, SSL was renamed Transport Layer Security (TLS), but many people still use the SSL name. It is the major standard used for online credit card payments.

SSL makes it possible to encrypt credit card numbers and other transmissions between a Web server and a Web browser. In the case of credit card transactions, there is more to making a purchase on the Web than simply passing an encrypted credit card number to a merchant. The number must be checked for validity, the consumer's bank must authorize the card, and the purchase must be processed. SSL is not designed to handle any of the steps beyond the transmission of the card number.

Secure Electronic Transaction (SET) is a cryptographic protocol that was originally designed to meet that need—to handle a complete online transaction. It provided secure online credit card transactions for both consumers and merchants. Although Visa and MasterCard were instrumental in developing SET, the initiative appears to have gained little acceptance in the commercial world. Instead, secure EC relies on SSL. Detailed information about SET can still be found at a MasterCard-supported Web site, setco.org.

For more on SSL and SET, see online material for Chapter 13 at the book's Web site.

Section 12.6 ▶ REVIEW

1. What are the basic elements of an authentication system?
2. What is a passive token? An active token?
3. Describe the basic components of encryption.
4. What are the key elements of PKI?
5. What are the basic differences between symmetric and asymmetric encryption?
6. Describe how a digital signature is created.
7. What is a digital certificate? What role does a certificate authority play?
8. What is the SSL protocol? The SET protocol?

12.7 SECURING EC NETWORKS

Several technologies exist that ensure that an organization's network boundaries are secure from cyber attack or intrusion and that if the organization's boundaries are compromised that the intrusion is detected.

FIREWALLS

firewall
A network node consisting of both hardware and software that isolates a private network from a public network.

packet-filtering routers
Firewalls that filter data and requests moving from the public Internet to a private network based on the network addresses of the computer sending or receiving the request.

The term *firewall* came into use in the 1700s to describe the gaps cut into forests so that fires could be prevented from spreading to other parts of the forest (Garfinkel 2002). The term also describes a protective shield between a car engine and the interior of the car. In the world of networked computing, a firewall is a network node consisting of both hardware and software that isolates a private network from a public network. Hazari (2000) provides a simple analogy to understand the general operation of a firewall: "We can think of firewalls as being similar to a bouncer in a nightclub. Like a bouncer in a nightclub, firewalls have a set of rules, similar to a guest list or a dress code, that determine if the data should be allowed entry. Just as the bouncer places himself at the door of the club, the firewall is located at the point of entry where data attempts to enter the computer from the Internet. But, just as different nightclubs might have different rules for entry, different firewalls have different methods of inspecting data for acceptance or rejection."

Some firewalls filter data and requests moving from the public Internet to a private network based on the network addresses of the computer sending or receiving the request. These firewalls are called packet-filtering routers. On the Internet, the data and requests sent from one computer to another are broken into segments called **packets**. Each packet contains the Internet address of the computer sending the data, as well as the Internet address of the computer receiving the data. Packets also contain other identifying information that can be used to distinguish one packet from another. **Packet filters** are rules that can accept or reject incoming packets based on source and destination addresses and the other identifying information. Some simple examples of packet filters include the following:

▸ "Block all packets sent from a given Internet address." Companies sometimes use this to block requests from computers owned by competitors.

▸ "Block any packet coming from the outside that has the address of a computer on the inside." Companies use this type of rule to block requests where an intruder is using his computer to impersonate a computer that belongs to the company.

Packet-filtering firewalls provide low-level control and are difficult to get around. However, they do have their disadvantages. In setting up the rules, an administrator might miss some important rules or incorrectly specify a rule, thus leaving a hole in the firewall. Additionally, because the content of a packet is irrelevant to a packet filter, once a packet is let through the firewall, the inside network is open to data-driven attacks. That is, the data may contain hidden instructions that cause the receiving computer to modify access control or security-related files.

Other firewalls block data and requests depending on the type of application being accessed. For instance, a firewall might permit requests for Web pages to move from the public Internet to the private network. This type of firewall is called an **application-level proxy**. In an application-level proxy there is often a special server called a **bastion gateway**. The bastion gateway server has two network cards so that data packets reaching one card are not relayed to the other card (see Exhibit 12.6 on page 482). Instead, special software programs called **proxies** run on the bastion gateway server and pass repackaged packets from one network to the other. Each Internet service that an organization wishes to support has a proxy. For instance, there is a Web (i.e., HTTP) proxy, a file transfer (FTP) proxy, and so on. Special proxies can also be established to allow business partners, for example, to access particular applications running inside the firewall. If a request is made for an unsupported proxy service, then it is blocked by the firewall.

In addition to controlling inbound traffic, the firewall and proxies control outbound traffic. All outbound traffic requests are first sent to the proxy server and then forwarded by the proxy on behalf of the computers behind the firewall. This makes all the requests look as if they were coming from a single computer rather than multiple computers. In this way, the Internet addresses of the internal computers are hidden to the outside.

One disadvantage of an application-level proxy firewall is performance degradation. It takes more processing time to tie particular packets to particular applications. Another disadvantage is that the users on the internal network must configure their machines or browsers to send their Internet requests via the proxy server.

Firewall systems can be created from scratch. However, most companies rely on commercial firewall systems. Security.Com provides a listing and reviews of a number of commercial firewall products (securitydogs.com).

PERSONAL FIREWALLS

In recent years, the number of individuals with high-speed broadband (cable modem or digital subscriber lines [DSL]) Internet connections to their homes or small businesses has increased. These "always-on" connections are much more vulnerable to attack than simple dial-up connections. With these connections, the homeowner or small business owner runs the risks of information being stolen or destroyed, of sensitive information (e.g., personal or business financial information) being accessed, and of the computer being used in a DoS attack on others.

Personal firewalls are designed to protect desktop systems by monitoring all the traffic that passes through the computer's network interface card. They operate in one of two ways.

---

packets
Segments of data and requests sent from one computer to another on the Internet; consist of the Internet addresses of the computers sending and receiving the data, plus other identifying information that distinguish one packet from another.

packet filters
Rules that can accept or reject incoming packets based on source and destination addresses and the other identifying information.

application-level proxy
A firewall that permits requests for Web pages to move from the public Internet to the private network.

bastion gateway
A special hardware server that utilizes application-level proxy software to limit the types of requests that can be passed to an organization's internal networks from the public Internet.

proxies
Special software programs that run on the gateway server and pass repackaged packets from one network to the other.

personal firewall
A network node designed to protect an individual user's desktop system from the public network by monitoring all the traffic that passes through the computer's network interface card.

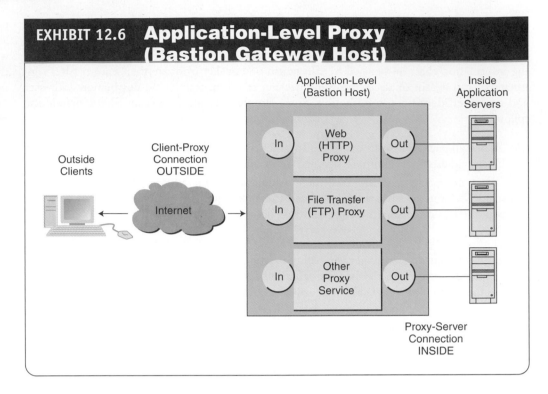

EXHIBIT 12.6   Application-Level Proxy (Bastion Gateway Host)

With the first method, the owner can create filtering rules (much like packet filtering) that are used by the firewall to permit or delete packets. With the other method, the firewall can learn, by asking the user questions, how particular traffic ought to be handled. A number of personal firewall products are on the market, including Symantec's Norton Personal Firewall (symantec.com). For a detailed comparison of a number of these products see firewallguide.com/software.htm.

virtual private network (VPN)
A network that uses the public Internet to carry information but remains private by using encryption to scramble the communications, authentication to ensure that information has not been tampered with, and access control to verify the identity of anyone using the network.

protocol tunneling
Method used to ensure confidentiality and integrity of data transmitted over the Internet, by encrypting data packets, sending them in packets across the Internet, and decrypting them at the destination address.

VPNs

Suppose a company wants to establish a B2B application, providing suppliers, partners, and others access not only to data residing on their internal Web site, but also to data contained in other files (e.g., Word documents) or in legacy systems (e.g., large relational databases). Traditionally, communications with the company would have taken place over a private leased line or through a dial-up line to a bank of modems or a remote access server (RAS) that provided direct connections to the company's LAN. With a private line, the chances of a hacker eavesdropping on the communications between the companies would be nil, but it is an expensive way to do business.

A less expensive alternative would be to use a virtual private network (VPN). A VPN uses the public Internet to carry information but remains private by using a combination of encryption to scramble the communications, authentication to ensure that the information has not been tampered with and comes from a legitimate source, and access control to verify the identity of anyone using the network. In addition, a VPN can also be used to support site-to-site communications between branch offices and corporate headquarters and the communications between mobile workers and their workplace. In all these cases, communication costs are drastically reduced. The estimate of cost savings for site-to-site networks is 20 to 40 percent for sites in the same country and much more if they are in different countries. The savings for mobile and remote workers is estimated at 60 to 80 percent (Prometheum Technolgies 2003).

The main technical challenge of a VPN is to ensure the confidentiality and integrity of the data transmitted over the Internet. This is where protocol tunneling comes into the picture. With protocol tunneling, data packets are first encrypted and then encapsulated into packets that can be transmitted across the Internet. The packets are decrypted at the destination address by a special host or router.

Three technologies can be used to create a VPN. First, many of the firewall packages—hardware and software—support VPN functionality. Second, routers (i.e., special network components for controlling communications) cannot only function as firewalls, but they can also function as VPN servers. Finally, software solutions are available that can be used to handle VPN connections. The VPN Consortium (vpnc.org/vpnc-features-chart.html) provides a comparison of a number of commercial VPN products.

Many telecommunications carriers and larger ISPs offer VPN services for Internet-based dial-up and site-to-site communications. These carriers use their own private network backbones to which they have added security features, intranet connectivity, and new dial-up capabilities for remote services. Two of the carriers providing these services are AT&T VPN Services (att.com) and Cable & Wireless IP-VPN Internet (www1.cw.com).

INTRUSION DETECTION SYSTEMS

Even if an organization has a well-formulated security policy and a number of security technologies in place, it is still vulnerable to attack. For example, in 2002, 100 percent of the respondents to the CSI/FBI survey had antivirus software, yet 85 percent reported incidents of virus contamination. This is why an organization must continually watch for attempted, as well as actual, security breaches.

In the past, *audit logs*, produced by a variety of system components and applications, were manually reviewed for excessive failed log-on attempts, failed file and database access attempts, and other application and system violations. Obviously, this manual procedure had its flaws. For example, if intrusion attempts were spread out over a long period of time, they could be easily missed. Today, a special category of software exists that can monitor activity across a network or on a host computer, watch for suspicious activity, and take automated action based on what it sees. This category of software is called intrusion detection systems (IDSs).

IDSs are either host-based or network-based (Ott 2001; Norton and Stockman 2000). A *host-based IDS* resides on the server or other host system that is being monitored. Host-based systems are particularly good at detecting whether critical or security-related files have been tampered with or whether a user has attempted to access files that they are not authorized to use. The host-based system does this by computing a special signature or check-sum for each file. The IDS checks files on a regular basis to see if the current signatures match the previous signatures. If the signatures do not match, security personnel are immediately notified. Some examples of commercial host-based systems are Axent's Intruder Alert (axent.com), Tripwire Security's Tripwire (tripwiresecurity.com), and Network Associates CyberCop Monitor (nai.com).

A *network-based IDS* uses rules to analyze suspicious activity at the perimeter of a network or at key locations in the network. It usually consists of a monitor—a software package that scans the network—and software agents that reside on various host computers and feed information back to the monitor. This type of IDS examines network traffic (i.e., packets) for known patterns of attack and automatically notifies security personnel when specific events or event thresholds occur. A network-based IDS can also perform certain actions when an attack occurs. For instance, it can terminate network connections or reconfigure network devices, such as firewalls and routers, based on security policies. Cisco Systems' NetRanger (cisco.com) and Computer Associates' Session Wall-3 (abirnet.com) are both examples of commercially available network-based IDSs.

intrusion detection systems (IDSs)
A special category of software that can monitor activity across a network or on a host computer, watch for suspicious activity, and take automated action based on what it sees.

Section 12.7 ▶ REVIEW

1. List the basic types of firewalls and briefly describe each.
2. What is a personal firewall?
3. How does a VPN work?
4. Briefly describe the major types of IDSs.

MANAGERIAL ISSUES

Some managerial issues related to this chapter are as follows.

1. **Have we budgeted enough for security?** If one asked the senior management of the *Fortune* 500 corporations whether they take network security seriously, they would certainly answer with a resounding, "Yes." Yet, in spite of this answer, most of these organizations spend only a small percentage of their budgets on network security, have fairly small staffs working on network security issues, and generally relegate network security matters to personnel on lower rungs on the organizational ladder. Because the consequences of poor network security can be severe, it is imperative that senior management have a basic understanding of best practices in network risk management.

2. **What are the business consequences of poor security?** Ineffective security opens the door to computer and network attacks that can result in damage to technical and information assets; theft of information and information services; temporary loss of a Web site and Internet access; loss of income; litigation brought on by dissatisfied organizational stakeholders; loss of customer confidence; and damaged reputation and credibility. In some cases, attacks can literally put a company out of business, especially if EC is their sole source of revenue.

3. **Which e-commerce sites are vulnerable to attack?** Suppose you decide to set up a B2B site in order to service your suppliers and partners. Because it is not a public site, the only ones who are likely to know of its existence are you, your suppliers, and your partners. You assume that there is no need to institute strong security measures. Wrong! Because of the prevalence of automated scanning tools, it will be only a matter of days before hackers discover your site. Once discovered, it will be only a matter of hours or minutes before the hackers have compromised your site and taken control if your system has known vulnerabilities. Regardless of how obscure, uninteresting, or unadvertised a site is, no EC site can afford to take security for granted. All sites should thoroughly review their security requirements and institute stringent measures to guard against high-priority threats.

4. **What is the key to establishing strong e-commerce security?** Most discussions about security focus on technology. One hears statements like "firewalls are mandatory" or "all transmissions should be encrypted." Although firewalls and encryption can be important technologies, no security solution is useful unless it solves a business problem. Determining your business requirements is the most important step in creating a security solution. Business requirements in turn determine your information requirements. Once your information requirements are known, you can begin to understand the value of those assets and the steps that should be taken to secure those that are most valuable and vulnerable.

5. **What steps should businesses follow in establishing a security plan?** Security risk management is an ongoing process involving four phases: assessment, planning, implementation, and monitoring. By actively monitoring existing security policies and measures, companies can determine which are successful or unsuccessful and, in turn, which should be modified or eliminated. However, it also is important to monitor changes in business requirements, changes in technology and the way it is used, and changes in the way people can attack the systems and networks. In this way, an organization can evolve its security policies and measures, ensuring that they continue to support the critical needs of the business.

6. **Should organizations be concerned with internal security threats?** Except for viruses and worms, breaches perpetrated by insiders are much more frequent than those perpetrated by outsiders. This is true for both B2C and B2B sites. Security policies and measures for EC sites need to address these insider threats.

SUMMARY

In this chapter, you learned about the following EC issues as they relate to the learning objectives.

1. **Increase in computer attacks.** Computer and network security attacks are on the rise. Data collected by the Computer Security Institute (CSI), the FBI, and the Computer Emergency Response Team (CERT) indicate that the number of security incidents has skyrocketed since 1998, that the overwhelming majority of firms have experienced computer security breaches from inside and outside the organization, that the financial losses from these breaches have been substantial, and that it takes a concerted effort to guard against cyber attack. In response to this growing problem, the FBI has established the National Infrastructure Protection

Center (NIPC), as well as Regional Computer Intrusion Squads throughout the United States.

2. **Security is everyone's business.** Although businesses of all sizes are impacted by cyber attacks, their security practices are varied. Some small businesses are well prepared, with devoted IT staff and well-established security plans. Other small businesses are ill prepared and very vulnerable to cyber attack and intrusion. Medium-sized organizations are also vulnerable because they lack managerial support for improved security and their staffs often lack the necessary training. In larger organizations, IT security expenditures per employee are often low, making it difficult to protect their complex systems against attack.

3. **Basic security issues.** EC sites need to be concerned with a variety of security issues: authentication, verifying the identity of the participants in a transaction; authorization, ensuring that a person or process has access rights to particular systems or data; auditing, being able to determine whether particular actions have been taken and by whom; confidentiality, ensuring that information is not disclosed to unauthorized individuals, systems, or processes; integrity, protecting data from being altered or destroyed; availability, ensuring that data and services are available when needed; and nonrepudiation, the ability to limit parties from refuting that a legitimate transaction took place.

4. **Basic types of network security attacks.** EC sites are exposed to a wide range of attacks. Attacks may be nontechnical (social engineering), in which a perpetrator tricks people into revealing information or performing actions that compromise network security. Or they may be technical, in which software and systems expertise are used to attack the network. DoS and DDoS attacks bring operations to a halt by sending floods of data to target computers or to as many computers on the Internet as possible. Malicious code attacks include viruses, worms, or some combination of both, and are often propagated by e-mail.

5. **Managing EC security.** Even with increased awareness of security issues, organizations continue to be reactive in their security practices, with little understanding of their information assets or security needs. A systematic security-risk-management approach must be adopted to address these needs. This approach involves four phases: assessment of assets, vulnerabilities, and risks; planning to establish policies for which threats are tolerable and which are not; implementation of particular technologies to address the threats; and monitoring to determine which measures are successful.

6. **Securing EC communications.** In EC, issues of trust are paramount. These issues are summarized by the acronym PAIN—privacy, authentication, integrity, and nonrepudiation. Trust starts with the authentication of the parties involved in a transaction, identifying the parties in a transaction along with the actions they can perform. Authentication can be established with something one knows (e.g., a password), something one has (e.g., a token), or something one is (e.g., a fingerprint). Biometric systems can be used to confirm a person's identity. Fingerprint scanners, iris scanners, facial recognition, and voice recognition are examples of biometric systems. Public key infrastructure (PKI), which is the cornerstone of secure e-payments, also can be used to authenticate the parties in a transaction. PKI uses encryption (private and public) to ensure privacy and integrity and digital signatures to ensure authenticity and nonrepudiation. Digital signatures are themselves authenticated through a system of digital certificates issued by certificate authorities (CAs). For the average consumer and merchant, PKI is simplified because it is built into Web browsers and services. Such tools are secure because security is based on SSL (TSL) communications.

7. **Technologies for securing networks.** At EC sites, firewalls, VPNs, and IDSs have proven extremely useful. A firewall is a combination of hardware and software that isolates a private network from a public network. Firewalls are of two general types—packet-filtering routers or application-level proxies. A packet-filtering router uses a set of rules to determine which communication packets can move from the outside network to the inside network. An application-level proxy is a firewall that accepts requests from the outside and repackages a request before sending it to the inside network, thus ensuring the security of the request. Personal firewalls are needed by individuals with broadband access. VPNs are generally used to support secure site-to-site transmissions across the Internet between B2B partners or communications between a mobile and remote worker and a LAN at a central office. Finally, IDSs are used to monitor activity across a network or on a host. The systems watch for suspicious activity and take automated actions whenever a security breach or attack occurs.

KEY TERMS

DISCUSSION QUESTIONS

1. Cyber attacks are on the rise. What are some of the reasons for the increase? Do you expect the situation to get worse or better? Explain.

2. A homeowner has just installed a cable modem. The homeowner feels that there is no need to worry about security because no one will ever know about their home computer. Why should the homeowner be worried about attacks by hackers? What are some of the steps the homeowner should take to secure their home computer?

3. A large number of B2C EC sites have experienced DDoS attacks. Why are these attacks so hard to safeguard against? What are some of the things a site can do to mitigate such attacks?

3. All EC sites share common security threats and vulnerabilities. Discuss these threats and vulnerabilities and some of the security policies that can be implemented to mitigate them. Do you think that B2C Web sites face different threats and vulnerabilities than B2B sites? Explain.

4. What type of security attack is most prevalent on the Internet? Discuss some of the major reasons for its prevalence.

5. All EC sites employ one or more security safeguards. Yet, B2C and B2B sites differ in the safeguards they use. Discuss the similarities and differences between the two types of sites.

6. A business wants to establish and run its own Web site for advertising and marketing. Some of the marketing materials will come from databases located on its LAN. What types of security components could be used to ensure that outsiders do not have direct access to those databases? What type of network configuration (e.g., bastion gateway server) will provide the most security?

7. Two businesses want to use the Internet to handle purchase orders, payments, and deliveries. They are afraid that hackers will eavesdrop on the Internet communications between them. What type of security technology could they use to safeguard against this threat?

8. You are responsible for the security at a B2C EC site and need to do an audit of your network's vulnerabilities. What type of software tool should you use to conduct the audit? What types of information will the tool provide? Once you've identified various vulnerabilities and corrected them, how can you be sure your site is safe? Explain.

INTERNET EXERCISES

1. The Computer Vulnerabilities and Exposures Board (cve.mitre.org) maintains a list of common network security vulnerabilities. Review the list. How many vulnerabilities are there? Based on that list, which system components appear to be most vulnerable to attack? What impact do these vulnerable components have on EC?

2. A number of B2C sites rely on hidden fields in their Web forms to pass information back and forth between a consumer's browser and their Web servers. Go to Google (google.com) and search for the following string: <INPUT TYPE=hidden NAME="price." What types of EC forms use this type of hidden field? Give some examples. What sort of security threat does a hidden field of this sort represent?

3. Your B2C site has just been hacked. You would like to report the incident to the Computer Emergency Response Team (cert.org) at Carnegie Mellon University so that they can alert other sites. How do you do this and what types of information do you have to provide?

4. Go to McAfee virus library (vil.nai.com/vil/default.asp). What are the general characteristics of a virus? What tips does McAfee (mcafeeb2b.com) give for avoiding or minimizing the impact of viruses?

5. The World Wide Web Consortium maintains a security FAQ (list of frequently asked questions). Based on this FAQ (w3.org/Security/Faq/www-security-faq.html#contents), what sorts of general precautions should be taken to secure a Web site?

6. SecurityDogs.com (securitydogs.com) provides access to a number of third-party reviews of commercial firewall products. Select three of the products and compare their features. Based on your comparison, which product would you select?

7. You have just installed a DSL line in your home so you will have faster Internet access. You have heard that this makes your computer susceptible to DDoS attacks and you want to install a personal firewall to guard against this threat. What sorts of commercial products are available? Which one would you choose?

TEAM ASSIGNMENTS AND ROLE PLAYING

1. Script kiddies, white hats, black hats, hacktivists, and cyberterrorists are some of the terms used to describe different types of hackers. Divide the class up into teams. Using the Web as a primary data source, have each team explore one of these types. The team should provide a general description of the hackers within this type and the methods they employ to compromise Web sites. For each type, explain how a site can detect and defend against these attacks.

2. There are several personal firewall products on the market. A list of these products can be found at fire wallguide.com/software.htm. Assign each team three products from the list. Each team should prepare a detailed review and comparison of each of the products they have been assigned.

3. Assign each team member a different B2C or B2B Web site. Have each team prepare a report summarizing the site's security assets, threats, and vulnerabilities. Prepare a brief security risk management plan for the site.

REAL-WORLD CASE

IS IT A QUESTION OF COMMON SENSE?

The Internet Security Alliance (isalliance.org) was formed in April 2001. The alliance is a collaborative endeavor of Carnegie Mellon University's Software Engineering Institute (SEI); its CERT Coordination Center (CEDRT/CC); the Electronics Industries Alliance (EIA), a federation of trade groups; and other private and public member organizations and corporations. Their goal is to provide information sharing and thought leadership on information security and to represent its members and the larger security community before legislators and regulators.

On September 9, 2002, the alliance released results from a recent security survey conducted jointly with the

National Association of Manufacturers (NAM) and RedSiren Technologies Inc. (Durkovich 2002). The survey asked 227 information security specialists from North America, Europe, the Middle East, and the Pacific Rim regions to compare their current attitudes towards information security with their attitudes prior to the 2001 terrorist attacks on the World Trade Center and the U.S. Pentagon. Overall, the results showed that information security is more of an issue now and that it is crucial to the survival of their organization or business. However, most were still inadequately prepared to meet their current security challenges, and just as importantly, most lacked senior management commitment to address these challenges.

The following are some of the specific survey findings:

▸ The overwhelming majority (91 percent) recognize the importance of information security.

▸ Most of the organizations reported at least one attack in the past year, with approximately 30 percent reporting more than six attacks.

▸ Almost half (48 percent) said that the terrorist attacks made them more concerned about information security, while an equal number (48 percent) said there had been no change in their attitudes.

▸ Forty-seven percent said that they had increased spending on information security since the attacks.

▸ Forty percent said that they had improved their physical security, electronic security, network security, and security policies since the attacks

▸ Thirty percent indicated that their companies are still inadequately prepared to deal with security attacks.

Based on the results of the survey, the alliance and its partners concluded that "it is clear that many organizations need to revise how security risks, threats and costs are identified, measured and managed" and that "information security specialists must work together to identify and implement more effective ways to communicate these pertinent issues to senior executives and also, to ensure these issues are given adequate visibility and priority in all organizations" (Durkovich 2002).

Based on the results of this and similar surveys, along with their general knowledge of the security industry, the Best Practices Working Group of the Internet Security Alliance has identified 10 of the highest priority and most frequently recommended practices necessary for implementation of a successful security process. The practices encompass policy, process, people, and technology. They include (ISAlliance 2002):

1. **General management.** Information security is a normal part of everyone's responsibilities—managers and employees alike. Managers must ensure that there are adequate resources, that security policies are well defined, and that the policies are reviewed regularly.

2. **Policy.** Security policies must address key areas such as security risk management, identification of critical assets, physical security, network security, authentication and authorization, vulnerability and incident management, privacy, and the like. Policies need to be embedded in standard procedures, practices, training, and architectures.

3. **Risk management.** The impacts of various risks need to be identified and quantified. A management plan needs to be developed to mitigate those risks with the greatest impact. The plan needs to be reviewed on a regular basis.

4. **Security architecture and design.** An enterprise-wide security architecture is required to protect critical information assets. High-risk areas (e.g., power supplies) should employ diverse and redundant solutions.

5. **User issues.** The user community includes general employees, IT staff, partners, suppliers, vendors, and other parties who have access to critical information systems. Users should be trained to understand and be held accountable for the consequences of their actions. Adequate in-house or outsourced expertise to manage and support all security technologies and policies also is needed.

6. **System and network management.** The key lines of defense include access control for all network devices and data, encrypted communications and VPNs where required, and perimeter protection (e.g., firewalls) based on security policies. Any software, files, and directories on the network should be verified on a regular basis. Procedures and mechanisms must be put in place that ensure that software patches are applied to correct existing problems; adequate levels of system logging are deployed; systems changes are analyzed from a security perspective; and vulnerability assessments are performed on a periodic basis. Software and data must also be backed up on a regular schedule.

7. **Authentication and authorization.** Strict policies must be formulated and implemented for authenticating and authorizing network access. Special attention must be given to those employees accessing the network from home and on the road and to partners, contractors, and service providers who are accessing the network remotely.

8. **Monitor and audit.** Network events and conditions must be monitored, audited, and inspected on a regular basis. Standards should be in place for responding to suspicious or unusual behavior.

9. **Physical security.** Physical access to key information assets, IT services, and resources should be controlled by two-factor authentication.

10. **Continuity planning and disaster recovery.** Business continuity and recovery plans need to be implemented and periodically tested to ensure that they are effective.

Increasingly, organizations must cope with a variety of cyber intrusions and losses. Organizations need to learn that security is not a one-time affair, but a continuous process. Information survivability is the key to an effective security process. The best practices recommended by the Internet Security Alliance indicate that there is nothing complex or highly technical about ensuring information survivability. It is more a matter of common sense that requires straightforward procedures and active involvement across the organization.

Sources: Durkovich (2002) and ISAlliance (2002).

Questions

1. How do the results of the ISAlliance survey compare with the results of the CSI/FBI survey reported in Section 12.1? Explain the similarities and differences.

2. Most of the ISAlliance recommendations seem like common sense. Why do you think that common-sense advice is required? What types of businesses do you think these standards are aimed at? Based on what you know about information security, what other recommendations would you make?

3. Given the breadth of known vulnerabilities, what sort of impact will any set of security standards have on the rise in cyber attacks?

4. For any organization, why is the involvement of senior management crucial to the success of their security information practices?

REFERENCES

Alga, N. "Increasing Security Levels." *Information Systems Control Journal* 2 (2002): 35–1.

Briney, A., and F. Prince. "2002 ISM Survey." *Information Security*, September 2002, infosecuritymag.com/2002/sep/2002survey.pdf (accessed April 2003).

CERT/CC. "CERT/CC Statistics 1988–2002." 2002, cert.org/stats/cert_stats.html (accessed April 2003).

CSI and FBI. "Computer Crime and Security Survey." 2002, gocsi.com (accessed April 2003).

Damle, P. "Social Engineering: A Tip of the Iceberg." *Information Systems Control Journal* 2 (2002).

Darby, C. "The Dollars and Cents of Security." October 2002, optimizemag.com (accessed April 2003).

Durkovich, C., et al. "Global Computer Security Survey—Results Analysis." September 9, 2002, redsiren.com/survey.html (accessed April 2003).

Garfinkel, Simson. *Web Security, Privacy and Commerce.* Sebastopol, CA: O'Reilly and Associates, 2002.

Granger, S. "Social Engineering Fundamentals, Part I: Hacker Tactics." December 18, 2001, online.securityfocus.com (accessed April 2003).

Harrison, A. "Update: Mafiaboy a Copycat, Attitudes Could Have Been Stupid." *Computerworld*, April 20, 2000, computerworld.com/news/2000/story/0,11280,43932,00.html (accessed April 2003).

Hazari, S. "Firewalls for Beginners." November 6, 2000, securityfocus.com/focus/basics/articles/fwbeg.htm (accessed April 2003).

Heim, K., and E. Ackerman. "'Zombie' Attacks Blamed in New Online Outages." *Mercury News*, January 27, 2001, 1A.

Honeynet Project. "Know Your Enemy." March 2000, project.honeynet.org (accessed April 2003).

Howard, M. *Designing Secure Web-Based Applications for Microsoft Windows 2000.* Redmond, WA: Microsoft Press, 2000.

ICSA. "Eighth Annual Computer Virus Prevelance Survey 2002." TruSecure Corporation, 2002, icsalabs.com/2002avpsurvey/index.shtml (accessed April 2003).

ISAlliance. "Common Sense Guide for Senior Managers." Internet Security Alliance, July 2002, www.isalliance.org (accessed April 2003).

Kabay, M., and L. Walsh. "The Year in Computer Crime." *Information Security Magazine,* December 2000, infosecuritymag.com/articles/december00/features.shtml (accessed April 2003).

King, C. "Protect Your Assets with This Enterprise Risk-Management Guide." *Internet Security Advisor*, February 2001.

Kroeker, K. "Graphics and Security: Exploring Visual Biometrics." *IEEE Computer Society*, 2002, computer.org/cga/homepage/2002/n4/biometrics.htm (accessed April 2003).

Lewis, R. "Mitnick Teaches Social Engineering." *ZDNet News*, July 18, 2000, zdnet.com.com/2100–11–522261.html?legacy=zdnn (accessed April 2003).

Loshin, P. *Extranet Design and Implementation.* San Francisco: Sybex Network Press, 1998.

McConnell, M. "Information Assurance in the Twenty-First Century." *IEEE Security and Privacy*, 2002, computer.org/security/supplement1/mcc/?SMSESSION=NO (accessed April 2003).

MDSI Mobile Data Solutions, Inc., 2003. mdsi-advantix.com/index.html (accessed April 2003).

Merkow, M., and J. Breithaupt. *Internet Security: The Complete Guide.* New York: Amacom, 2000.

Mitnick, K., and W. Simon. *The Art of Deception.* New York: Wiley, 2002.

Mitre. "CVE List Exceeds 5000 Security Issues." September 9, 2002, cve.mitre.org/news/ (accessed April 2003).

Norton, P., and M. Stockman. *Network Security Fundamentals.* Indianapolis, IN: SAMS, 2000.

Ott, J. "Intrusion Detection Systems Overview." *Internet Security Advisor*, February 2001.

Piazza, P. "Honeynet Attracts Hacker Attack." *Security Management*, November 2001, securitymanagement.com/library/001138.html (accessed April 2003).

Power, R. *Tangled Web.* Indianapolis, IN: Que, 2000.

Proctor, P., and F. Byrnes. *The Secured Enterprise*. Upper Saddle River, NJ: Prentice Hall, 2002.

Prometheum Technologies. "Secure Remote Access to Your Data." April 2003, promethian.com/m_vpn.htm (accessed April 2003).

SANS. "The Twenty Most Critical Internet Security Vulnerabilities." 2002, SANS Institute, sans.org/top20 (accessed April 2003).

Scambray, J. et al. *Hacking Exposed*, 2d ed. New York: McGraw-Hill, 2000.

Shimomura, T., et al. *Takedown: The Pursuit and Capture of Kevin Mitnick, America's Most Wanted Computer Outlaw, By the Man Who Did It*. New York: Warner Books, December 1996.

Smith, R. *Authentication: From Passwords to Public Keys*. New York: Addison-Wesley, 2002.

Spitzner, L. "Honeypots: Definition and Value." May 2002, enteract.com/~lspitzer (accessed April 2003).

Sullivan, B. "Hackers Just Dial Through Account Numbers Until They Find One." April 23, 2002a, msnbc.com/news (accessed April 2003).

Sullivan, B. "Massive Credit Card Heist Suspected." September 13, 2002b, msnbc.com/news (accessed April 2003).

U.S. Banker. "Biometrics Come to Life." *U.S. Banker*, June 2002, us-banker.com/usb/articles/usbjun02–3.shtml (accessed April 2003).

ELECTRONIC PAYMENT SYSTEMS

Content

Learning objectives

Upon completion of this chapter, you will be able to:

1. Understand the crucial factors that determine the success of e-payment methods.

2. Discuss the players and processes involved in using credit cards online.

3. Discuss the different categories and potential uses of smart cards.

4. Discuss various online alternatives to credit card payments and identify under what circumstances they are best used.

5. Describe the processes and parties involved in e-checking.

6. Describe payment methods in B2B EC, including payments for global trade.

7. Discuss bill presentment and payment.

8. Describe special payment methods.

LENSDOC ORGANIZES PAYMENTS ONLINE

The Problem

LensDoc (*lensdoc.com*), based in Hilton Head, South Carolina, is an online retailer of contact lenses, sun and magnifying glasses, and dental care and personal care products. As with most B2C retailers, a customer can pay for an online purchase from LensDoc in only one way—with a credit card. Over 80 percent of the B2B purchases made on the Web are done with credit cards, and over 90 percent for Web purchases made in the United States (Electronic Check Clearing House Organization 2002).

Although LensDoc relies on credit cards, they present a troubling dilemma for the retailer (Carr 2000). Credit cards make it easy for customers from all over the world to purchase items from online stores. They also make it easy for a customer to return an item and receive credit for the return. LensDoc had a problem with the return of contact lenses. People try them and return them if they are not satisfied. The problem is that U.S. regulations prohibit the return of contact lenses that have been used, forcing LensDoc to discard the lenses and to take a loss on the return. In addition, LensDoc has been the victim of a number of fraudulent charges from customers in Eastern Europe who have used other people's credit cards to buy expensive sunglasses.

The Solution

LensDoc has implemented special handling procedures for authorizing online credit card purchases. The company manually processes credit card orders and asks customers to fax a form that includes the *cardholder's address* as well as the *shipping address*. Obviously, the assumption is that if the card being used is a fraudulent one, the perpetrator is unlikely to know or use the cardholder's address

The Results

The manual processing of credit card payments is slow and solves some, but not all, of the problems. LensDoc has investigated a number of alternative *e-payment methods*, including cash cards, special card-swiping peripherals, credit card processing services, and the like. Each has its advantages and disadvantages. To date, the disadvantages of each alternative e-payment method seem to outweigh the advantages, or at least none seems more advantageous than credit cards.

Sources: Carr (2000) and *lensdoc.com* (2003).

WHAT WE CAN LEARN . . .

Most B2C purchases are paid for by credit card. However, as the LensDoc case illustrates, the potential for fraud is high when credit cards are used online. As recently as 2000, some 83 percent of online merchants surveyed said that online fraud is a serious problem (Lanford and Lanford 2000). Merchants are responsible for fraudulent charges because online credit card purchases are treated as "card-not-present" transactions. Thus, the merchant must absorb the loss and also incur a chargeback fee of $25 to $100, as well as the initial transaction fee of 2 percent (or more) levied by the credit card company (Duvall 2000; Caswell 2000). However, by 2002, e-tailers have begun to view credit card fraud as a solvable problem (see the Real-World Case at the end of the chapter).

This chapter discusses alternative e-payment methods for B2C and B2B. It also examines some related issues, such as tax payments.

13.1 ELECTRONIC PAYMENTS: A CRITICAL ELEMENT IN EC SUPPORT SERVICES

In the off-line world, consumers use cash, checks, and credit cards to make purchases. At a fast-food restaurant, people usually pay with cash. If someone purchases an appliance at a discount store, they are likely to use a credit card. When people pay their bills, most use checks. How do people pay online? Unfortunately, paying online with the same instruments that people use off-line, namely cash, credit card, debit card, or paper check may be too slow, inefficient, or expensive for online payments. When a buyer places an order, the seller wants to make sure they will pay. When a bidder wins an electronic auction, the money must be ready. Therefore, special payment methods were developed for online payments. These are referred to as e-payments (electronic payments). E-payments are payments made electronically rather than by paper (cash, checks, vouchers, etc.). For example, a person can pay their bills electronically or transfer money electronically among their accounts or to their child's college fund.

e-payments
Payments made online.

Before we present the various e-payment methods, it will be beneficial to understand the limitations of using credit cards in EC.

PAYING WITH CREDIT CARDS ONLINE

A few years ago, it was generally believed that consumers would be extremely reluctant to use their credit card numbers on the Web. The assumption was that special forms of electronic or digital cash were required for B2C to survive and thrive. Today, EC is thriving, and, as noted earlier, the overwhelming majority of Web purchases are made with credit cards, not with digital cash.

However, some statistics indicate that the picture may change in the near future. First, many of the people who will be on the Internet in 2004 have not even had their first Web experience. Many of these users will come from countries outside the United States, where the use of credit cards is not as prevalent (Gazala and Shepard 1999). A good number of these users are also likely to be younger and have less access to credit and debit cards. Many of the purchases they make will involve monetary values that are too small for credit cards (e.g., purchasing a single song or playing an online game). These small payments are called *micropayments* and will be described in more detail later in the chapter.

Second, and more importantly, according to a recent research report issued by the Gartner Group, by 2004, 95 percent of all e-commerce will be B2B transactions, with the remaining 5 percent B2C transactions (O'Donnell 2003). Credit cards are rarely used in B2B transactions. Instead, more traditional methods of payment, such as checks, are used. In the future, a sizeable percentage of these payments will be electronic. However, these electronic payments are more likely to involve EFTs or electronic checks. Third, a large amount of fraud with online credit card shopping occurs that results in chargebacks.

THE CHARGEBACK PROBLEM

A *chargeback* means that the customer refuses to pay, claiming that the purchase was made by someone else. According to First Data Group, 1.25 percent of transactions on the Internet result in a chargeback (Datastar Group 2001). This is approximately four times the percentage of catalog transaction chargebacks and nine times the percentage of brick-and-mortar chargebacks (see Angwin 2000b).

In an effort to combat this high level of online chargebacks, Visa established a list of high-risk business models. Businesses following these models are subject to high levels of credit card fraud and, as a result, are highly penalized when their chargeback rates climb above a specified percentage of the total number of transactions. This percentage generally falls between 1 and 2 percent. Opponents argue that the method is overbroad, often deterring business owners from accepting online payments. The list includes travel and direct-marketing industries (Angwin 2000a, 2000b).

Visa has also developed a list of "best practices" to be used by merchants when conducting credit card transactions. The list includes implementing a firewall, using encryption and antivirus software, and incorporating intercompany security practices. The protocols are mandatory: Merchants failing to meet the requirements may not be able to accept Visa credit cards as a method of payment.

By 2002, e-tailers saw credit card fraud as a solvable problem. Risk management techniques and fraud-prevention software were widely available. The Merchant Fraud Squad, a not-for-profit organization, was founded in September 2000 by American Express and other e-commerce leaders. It provides education about fraud prevention techniques and encourages businesses selling online to adopt best practices and antifraud technologies. The content is free to e-tailers who agree to the coalition's principles for fighting fraud, which include developing multifaceted defenses to curb credit card thieves. The resources include 10 free online services that e-commerce merchants identified as effective for analyzing customer orders and catching fraud before it happens (Merchant Fraud Squad 2002). Members access tools that help them do the following: verify the existence of an address; verify a name with an address; do a reverse look-up of phone numbers to retrieve corresponding addresses; verify phone numbers; capture a consumer's Internet protocol address; review all free e-mail domains; verify the owner of a domain; verify credit card numbers via MOD 10 (a mathematic formula used to identify correct credit card formats); report a cyber crime; and review a list of freight forwarders, which international fraudsters regularly use to pass on unsolicited goods

Another solution is a Web site called nochargeback.com, which provides merchants with a solution for preventing online credit card fraud. Site members can access the site's database of credit card numbers, e-mail addresses, and postal addresses used for purchases that resulted in a chargeback. Merchants can check for "deadbeats" at this site and then refuse to accept charges from people listed there. Combatfraud.org offers similar fraud-protection services.

To minimize or avoid the chargeback problem, it is necessary to secure the credit card payment process (see Chapter 12) as well as to develop and encourage the use of alternative e-payment methods. These alternative methods are our next topic.

E-PAYMENT METHODS

Electronic payment methods expedite payments online and reduce payment processing costs (e.g., see Shesney 2000). However, such methods must be safe and trusted by users. The basic e-payment methods are similar to off-line methods. However, some innovative methods exist only in cyberspace. The major methods that are in use and will be described in the chapter include the following:

- Electronic payment cards (credit, debit, charge)
- Virtual credit cards
- E-wallets (or e-purses)
- Smart cards
- Electronic cash (several variations)
- Wireless payments
- Stored-value card payments
- Loyalty cards
- Person-to-person payment methods
- Payments made electronically at kiosks

Other methods are used primarily for B2B payments:

- Electronic checks
- Purchasing cards
- Electronic letters of credit
- Electronic funds transfer (EFT)
- Electronic benefits transfer (EBT) (see Chapter 9)
- Other innovative methods, including e-lines of credit

What these diverse e-payment methods share in common is the ability to transfer a payment from one person or party to another person or party over a network without face-to-face interaction.

Whatever the e-payment method, five parties may be involved:

1. **Customer/payer/buyer.** The party making the e-payment in exchange for goods or services

2. **Merchant/payee/seller.** The party receiving the e-payment in exchange for goods and services

3. **Issuer.** The banks or nonbanking institutions that issue the e-payment instrument used to make the purchase

4. **Regulator.** Usually a government agency whose regulations control the e-payment process

5. **Automated Clearing House (ACH).** An electronic network that transfers money between bank accounts

Although usually behind the scenes, issuers play a key role in any online purchase for two reasons. First, customers must obtain their e-payment accounts from an issuer. Second, issuers are usually involved in authenticating a transaction and approving the amount involved (often in real time).

Because online buyers and sellers are not in the same place and cannot exchange payments and products at the same time, issues of *trust* come into play. The acronym PAIN—privacy, authentication, integrity, and nonrepudiation—has been devised to represent the key issues of trust that must be addressed by any e-payment method. (See Cornwell 2000, Keen et al. 2000, and Chapter 12.)

Automated Clearing House (ACH)
Electronic network that connects all U.S. financial institutions for the purpose of making funds transfers.

CHARACTERISTICS OF SUCCESSFUL E-PAYMENT METHODS

A crucial element in the success of an e-payment method is the "chicken-and-egg" problem: How do you get sellers to adopt a method when there are few buyers using it? And, how do you get buyers to adopt a method when there are few sellers using it? A number of factors come into play in determining whether a particular method of e-payment achieves widespread acceptance. Some of the crucial factors include the following.

Independence. Some forms of e-payment require specialized software or hardware to make the payment. Almost all forms of e-payment require the seller or merchant to install specialized software to receive and authorize a payment. Those e-payment methods that require the payer to install specialized components are less likely to succeed.

Interoperability and portability. All forms of EC run on specialized systems that are interlinked with other enterprise systems and applications. An e-payment method must mesh with these existing systems and applications and be supported by standard computing platforms.

Security. How safe is the transfer? What are the consequences of the transfer being compromised? Again, if the risk for the payer is higher than the risk for the payee, then the method is not likely to be accepted.

Anonymity. Unlike credit cards and checks, if a buyer uses cash, there is no way to trace the cash back to the buyer. Some buyers want their identities and purchase patterns to remain anonymous. To succeed, special payment methods such as e-cash (discussed later) have to maintain anonymity.

Divisibility. Most sellers accept credit cards only for purchases within a minimum and maximum range. If the cost of the item is too small—say, only a few dollars—a credit card will not do. In addition, a credit card will not work if an item or set of items costs too much—say, an airline company purchasing a new airplane. Any method that can address the lower or higher end of the price continuum or that can span one of the extremes and the middle has a chance of being widely accepted.

Ease of use. For B2C e-payments, credit cards are the standard due to their ease of use. For B2B payments, the question is whether the online e-payment methods can supplant the existing off-line methods of procurement.

Transaction fees. When a credit card is used for payment, the merchant pays a transaction fee of up to about 3 percent of the item's purchase price (above a minimum fixed fee). These fees make it prohibitive to support smaller purchases with credit cards, which leaves room for alternative forms of payment.

Critical mass. A critical mass of vendors must be willing to accept the payment method. Conversely, a critical mass of places to acquire the payment method (i.e., buy payment cards) is also necessary.

To date, the acceptance rate of various e-payment methods has been slow. Some areas—online billing and presentment (see Section 13.6 and Chapter 3)—will see e-payments make significant inroads in the near future. Several key business drivers are behind the growth of these alternatives. Using e-payment reduces transaction costs by 30 to 50 percent compared to off-line payments. Another is speed. If a person pays a bill by check, for example, it takes time to mail the bill, time to mail the check, and time to deposit and process the check. The whole process takes at least a week. If the bill is presented and paid online, it may take only seconds and in the worst case a day or two. E-payments also make it possible to conduct business across geographical and political boundaries, greatly enhancing the possibilities for international deals and transactions. Finally, e-payments are extremely important in EC not only because there is no trade without a payment, but also because a good and secured payment system increases the confidence and trust of buyers in EC in general. (For details, see Keen et al. 2000. For an overview of e-payments, see Donahue 2000.)

SECURITY FOR E-PAYMENTS

When a person uses a credit card to make a purchase on the Internet, how can they be sure that someone will not intercept the card number as it traverses the network? If a buyer contacts an EC site with the intention of making a purchase, how can they be sure that it is a legitimate site? If one company sends a bill to another company over the Internet, how can the recipient be sure that the bill has not been changed? If a customer sends a company a bad e-check and later denies that they sent it, how can the company refute the denial?

These questions illustrate the issues of trust (or PAIN) that arise with e-payment systems. A well-devised online security system provides the answer to many, but not all, of these and similar questions. Internet security is a very complex issue that was addressed in Chapter 12.

Standards for E-Payments

If the average user had to figure out how to use encryption, digital certificates, digital signatures, and the like (as discussed in Chapter 12), there would be few secure transactions, and, in turn, few purchases made on the Web. Fortunately, all of these issues are handled in a transparent fashion by Web browsers and Web servers.

Because many different companies, financial institutions, and governments, in many countries, are involved in e-payments, it is necessary to have generally accepted protocols for securing e-payments. As discussed in detail in Chapter 12, two protocols (and their variants) are in use: SSL, also known as TLS, and SET.

Other Security Measures

In addition to using PKI and encryption, one can increase the security of e-payments by using intelligent agents. For descriptions of the use of intelligent agents in securing e-payments, see Chapter 12 and Litan (2002). Also, the *biometrics* discussed in Chapter 12 can be used to improve e-payment security. Remember that both the funds that are being transferred and the consumer data must be protected. For a comprehensive white paper on the topic, see (Cybersource 2002). Also see a primer at verisign.com.

Section 13.1 ▶ REVIEW

1. Why is credit card payment so popular in EC? What are the problems with using credit cards for EC?
2. List all of the parties that may be involved in e-payment.
3. List the major e-payment methods that are good for B2B.
4. List the various factors (characteristics) that determine the acceptance of an e-payment method.

5. What are some of the benefits of e-payments?
6. Describe the various e-payment security issues.

13.2 ELECTRONIC CARDS AND SMART CARDS

Electronic cards are plastic cards that contain digitized information. This information can be used for payment purposes. Electronic cards also can be used for other purposes, such as identification or to access a secure location. Some electronic cards are considered "smart" cards because they can manipulate information. This section examines both types of electronic cards.

PAYMENT CARDS

If you are an American, you are likely to have at least one electronic **payment card**, an electronic card that contains information used for payment purposes. In the United States, there are over 700 million payment cards. They can be used at over 4 million merchants in the United States and another 11 million merchants around the world. Over the last few years, Americans paid for over $850 billion worth of purchases with their payment cards every year. About 12 billion payment card transactions are processed each year in the United States (Evans and Schmalensee 2000).

payment card
Electronic card that contains information that can be used for payment purposes.

There are three types of payment cards:

▶ **Credit cards.** A credit card provides the holder with credit to make purchases up to a limit fixed by the card issuer. Credit cards rarely have an annual fee. Instead, holders are charged high interest—the annual percentage rate—on their unpaid balances. Visa, MasterCard, and EuroPay are the predominant credit cards.

▶ **Charge cards.** The balance on a charge card is supposed to be paid in full upon receipt of the monthly statement. Technically, the holder of a charge card receives a loan for 30 to 45 days equal to the balance of their statement. Such cards usually have annual fees. American Express's Green Card is the leading charge card, followed by the Diner's card.

▶ **Debit cards.** With a debit card, the money for a purchased item comes directly out of the holder's checking account (called a demand-deposit account). The actual transfer of funds from the holder's account to the merchant's takes place within 1 to 2 days. MasterCard, Visa, and EuroPay are the predominant debit cards.

Whether a credit card payment is processed off-line or online, the processes involved are essentially the same. For example, suppose a person wants to buy music CDs from a Web site with their credit card. The buyer adds the CDs to their shopping cart and goes to the checkout page. On the checkout page, they select a method of shipping and enter their credit card information. The checkout page is usually secured; the credit card and other information are protected by SSL encryption.

When the buyer hits "Submit," the page is transmitted to the merchant. From there, the information, along with the merchant's identification number, is passed on to the merchant's *acquirer* (or third-party processor). The acquirer sends the information on to the customer's *issuing bank* for approval. The issuer sends its response (approve or disapprove) back to the acquirer, from where it is passed on to the merchant. Finally, the customer is notified. The entire process is automated and takes place in seconds.

After the transaction is complete, the issuer settles the transaction. Typically, for a $100 purchase, the merchant receives $96, the acquirer $1.34, the authorization network $0.16, and the issuer $2.50 (see Exhibit 13.1 on page 498).

It takes time, skill, money, software, and hardware to establish an online connection between the merchant's EC systems and the merchant's acquirer or third-party processor. Recognizing the difficulties associated with this task, several vendors now offer credit card gateways. A **credit card gateway** ties the merchant's systems to the back-end processing systems of the credit card issuer. A few of the vendors offering credit card gateway software are Authorize.net (authorizenet.com), First Data (firstdata.com), SurePay (surepay.com), and VeriSign (verisign.com). For additional vendors, see Carr (2000).

credit card gateway
An online connection that ties a merchant's systems to the back-end processing systems of the credit card issuer.

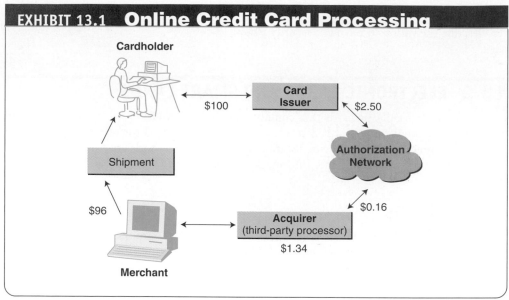

EXHIBIT 13.1   Online Credit Card Processing

Source: S. Korper and J. Ellis, *The E-Commerce Book: Building the E-Empire.* © 2000 by Academic Press, used with permission from Elsevier.

Virtual Credit Cards

virtual credit card

An e-payment system in which a credit card issuer gives a special transaction number that can be used online in place of regular credit card numbers.

One innovation in online credit cards is a **virtual credit card**. This is an e-payment system in which a credit card issuer issues a special number that can be used in place of regular credit card numbers to make online purchases. This allows users to use a credit card online without having to disclose the actual credit card number. The user gives a transaction number instead of a credit card number. Insights and Additions 13.1 has more on virtual credit cards.

Debiting Checking Accounts

An increasing number of e-vendors are offering shoppers (individuals or organizations) the option of debiting their checking accounts to pay for items ordered over the Web.

One company that provides such a service is Western Union with its MoneyZap service. The service is aimed at the over 80 million Americans who do not use credit cards as well as at those customers who prefer to pay with checks. (Remember, many people are afraid to use their credit cards online.) The MoneyZap service, which in 2002 was available only in the United States, is similar to that of a credit card transaction. The merchant sends a transaction ID electronically and indicates the amount a shopper wants to pay. MoneyZap checks the

Insights and Additions 13.1   Virtual Credit Cards

For those who are still leery of using their credit cards online, American Express has a new virtual credit card service called *Private Payment*. With this service, when a user shops online and wants to use an American Express card for a payment, they enter a user name and password, which logs the user into a special site run by American Express. Next, the user selects the particular American Express card to be used for the purchase. At this point, American Express will generate a one-time, limited-life transaction number that is good for anywhere from 30 to 67 days.

Instead of the user entering their American Express number, the shopper enters the transaction number. The transaction number is tied to the specific card. The merchant who receives the transaction number will pass it on to American Express in order to receive an authorization for the purchase. The transaction number operates just like a real credit card, except that it is good for only one purchase. If the number is stolen or intercepted, it will do little harm because it can be used only once.

Similar virtual credit card services are available through many banks (e.g., see Cyota 2000 and Orbiscom 2003).

Sources: Compiled from an advertising supplement in *CIO Magazine* (1999), *americanexpress.com* (2002), *bankrate.com* (2002), and Dell Computer (2003).

person's account balance and then sends back a confirmation that sufficient funds are available. All of this is done electronically in seconds. To use the MoneyZap service, shoppers complete a one-time registration form. After that, they can use the service by giving their user ID and password. There is no charge for the customer.

E-WALLETS AND DIGITAL IDs

Most of the time when a person makes a purchase on the Web they are required to fill out a form with their name, shipping address, billing address, and credit card information. Doing this a few times is fine, but having to do it every time one shops on the Web can be an annoyance. Some merchants solve the problem by having customers fill out a form once and then saving the information on their servers for later use. For instance, this is what Amazon.com has done with its "One-Click" shopping feature. Of course, even if every merchant provided "one-click" shopping, customers would still have to set up an account with every merchant. This would also increase the possibility that the information might fall into the hands of a merchant who wanted to use this information for some other purpose. Also, the merchant wants to be sure of the identity of the buyer.

One way to avoid the problem is to use an electronic wallet (e-wallet). An e-wallet is a software component that a user downloads to their desktop PC and in which the user stores credit card numbers and other personal information. When a user shops at a merchant who accepts the e-wallet, the user clicks the e-wallet, which automatically fills in all the necessary information.

Credit card companies such as Visa and MasterCard also offer e-wallets. So do Yahoo, AOL (Quick Checkout), Liberty, Alliance, and Microsoft (Passport) (see Kane 2002). These efforts are called digital IDs.

Digital IDs: A Universal E-Wallet

A digital identity (digital ID) refers to a set of digital information that is associated with a particular individual. This information may include user IDs, passwords, access control lists, public key certificates, and voiceprint patterns. It is used typically for security—both to confirm that a person is who they say they are and to authorize access to online applications, services, and data, including e-payments (when the digital ID is included in the e-wallet) (Costa 2002). Digital IDs are safe and secure to the extent that the computer that stores a digital ID is secure, both physically and cryptographically.

As indicated earlier, many would like to see one e-wallet that can be used for multiple purposes, and this is exactly what two popular digital IDs, *Microsoft.Net Passport* and *Project Liberty,* attempt to offer, as described in Insights and Additions 13.2 (page 500).

How E-Wallets Work As an Authenticator

An e-wallet uses a public key encryption system (see Chapter 12) in the following four steps:

1. The user contacts the merchant to place an order.

2. The authentication/registry part of the e-wallet generates a pair of keys called *session keys*. It encrypts one key with the user's public key that resides in the e-wallet. In addition, the e-wallet creates a message called a *ticket* that includes a second session key and the user's name. The ticket is then encrypted with the merchant's public key. Both the encrypted session key and the message are sent to the user.

3. The user decrypts the first session key, using their private key. The user then creates a new message, called the *authenticator*, which contains the user's name, and encrypts it with the first session key. The user then sends the authenticator and the ticket to the merchant.

4. The merchant decrypts the ticket, using its private key, retrieving the user's name and the second session key. Using the second session key, the merchant unlocks the authenticator to find the user's name. If the name matches with that in the ticket, the merchant knows that the buyer is actually who they purport to be.

After the first transaction has been completed, and from then on, that user and the merchant can carry out secure transactions using the first and second session keys to encrypt communications. The authentication process is done in seconds, and because it is fully automated, the cost is minimal.

electronic wallet (e-wallet)

A software component in which a user stores credit card numbers and other personal information; when shopping online, the user simply clicks the e-wallet to automatically fill in information needed to make a purchase.

digital identity (digital ID)

A set of digital information that is associated with a particular individual and is used to identify that individual for security purposes.

EXHIBIT 13.2 How Passport and Express Purchase Work

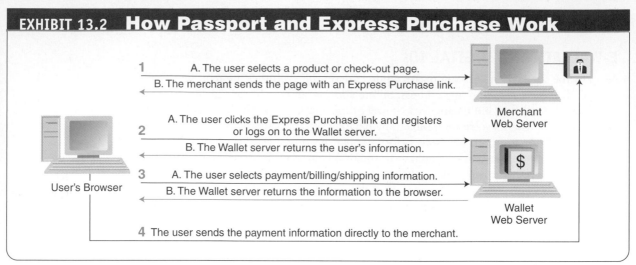

1
  A. The user selects a product or check-out page.
  B. The merchant sends the page with an Express Purchase link.

2
  A. The user clicks the Express Purchase link and registers or logs on to the Wallet server.
  B. The Wallet server returns the user's information.

3
  A. The user selects payment/billing/shipping information.
  B. The Wallet server returns the information to the browser.

4 The user sends the payment information directly to the merchant.

User's Browser

Merchant Web Server

Wallet Web Server

Source: From "Microsoft Passport Technical White Paper," July 18, 2001. © Copyright Microsoft Corporation.

The two most talked about digital ID platforms are Microsoft.Net Passport and Project Liberty.

Passport is a proprietary, consumer-identity service from Microsoft that has been in use since 1999. The process by which Passport works is shown in Exhibit 13.2.

Liberty is a *proposed* set of specifications based on the Security Association Markup Language (SAML), an open XML-based standard. It is backed by an alliance of about 100 major corporations (e.g., GM, Citigroup, Sony, Sun Microsystems). Passport is currently based on SSL, but it will support SAML as well. The process by which Liberty 1.0 will work is shown in Costa (2002), and its details are available on this book's Web site (see online Chapter 13, Exhibit W13.1).

The differences between Passport and Liberty are summarized in Exhibit 13.3.

EXHIBIT 13.3 Liberty and Passport: Head to Head

	Liberty and Passport: Head to Head	
	Liberty Version 1.0 *www.projectliberty.com*	**Microsoft .NET Passport** *www.microsoft.com/netservices/passport*
Purpose	An architecture for federated identity through account linking and single sign-on	An identity aggregator that provides single sign-on service to participating sites
Single sign-on capabilities	Works with businesses that are part of the Liberty Alliance	Works with Microsoft properties and Passport-enabled retailers
Required data	User name and password; member sites may require more info	User name and password
Underlying standards	Security Assertion Markup Language (SAML)	Secure Sockets Layer (SSL), Triple DES, WS-Security
User control	Opt-in, with limited control of profile information	Opt-in; lots of control of profile information
Profile storage	Distributed throughout member sites and linked	Centralized at Microsoft
Supporting companies	95 companies, including American Express, Fidelity Investments, GM, Novell, Sun Microsystems, United Airlines, and Visa U.S.A.	Microsoft and more than 100 other companies, including Buy.com, Costco Online, Crutch-field, eBay, Godiva, Monster, and The Sports Authority
Status	Proposed specification; service available by 2002	Currently available consumer service

Source: Costa, D. "Identity Crisis (Digital IDs)." *PC Magazine*, October 18, 2002.

SECURITY RISKS WITH CREDIT CARDS

Even though SSL is used to secure the transaction between the Web browser and Web server, there are still risks with using credit cards online. For the most part, *the merchant* bears the responsibility for the following risks:

- **Stolen cards.** If someone steals a credit card and the valid cardholder contests any charges made by the thief, the issuer will credit the cardholder's account and chargeback the merchant.

- **Reneging by the customer.** A customer can authorize a payment and later deny it. If the denial is believable to the issuer, the merchant will bear the loss. Merchants can avoid such a situation by showing evidence that the cardholder confirmed the order and received the goods. The purchase can also be handled with a digital signature, but this form of verification is expensive and cumbersome for most online credit card transactions.

- **Theft of card details stored on the merchant's computer.** Cases where hackers have electronically broken into a merchant's computer where credit card details are stored have been reported. The key to protecting this information is to isolate the computer or files storing this information so that it cannot be accessed directly from the Internet.

SMART CARDS

One of the technologies that is used to support e-payments is smart cards. A smart card looks like any plastic payment card, but it is distinguished by the presence of an embedded microchip (see Exhibit 13.4). The embedded chip can either be a microprocessor and a memory chip combined or just a memory chip with nonprogrammable logic. The microprocessor card can add, delete, and otherwise manipulate information on the card, whereas a memory-chip card is usually a "read only" card like a credit card. Although the microprocessor is capable of running programs like a computer does, it is not a stand-alone computer. The programs and data must be downloaded from some other device (such as an ATM machine).

Smart cards are used for transaction processing, authentication, and authorization, and they can be categorized by the way in which data (and applications) are downloaded and read from the card. Under this scheme there are two major types of smart cards. The first type is a contact card, a card that is inserted in a smart card reader. These cards have a small gold plate about one-half inch in diameter on the front; when the card is inserted in the reader, the plate makes electronic contact and data are passed to and from the chip.

The second type of smart card is the contactless (proximity) card. In addition to the chip, a contactless card has an embedded antenna. In this case, data (and applications) are passed to and from the card through the card's antenna to another antenna attached to a card-reader unit or other device. Contactless cards are used for those applications in which the data must be processed very quickly (e.g., mass-transit applications such as paying in buses and

smart card
An electronic card containing an embedded microchip that enables predefined operations or the addition, deletion, or manipulation of information on the card.

contact card
A smart card containing a small gold plate on the face that when inserted in a smart-card reader makes contact and so passes data to and from the embedded microchip.

contactless (proximity) card
A smart card with an embedded antenna, by means of which data and applications are passed to and from a card reader unit or other device without contact between the card and the card reader.

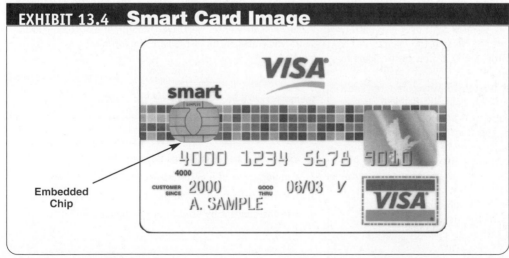

EXHIBIT 13.4 Smart Card Image

Embedded Chip

Source: Courtesy of Visa USA, Inc..

trains) or when contact is difficult (e.g., security-entering mechanisms to buildings). Proximity cards usually work at short range, just a few inches. However, one type of proximity card can be used at a distance of over 100 feet, as shown in EC Application Case 13.1.

Securing Smart Cards

Smart cards house or provide access to either valuable assets (e.g., e-cash) or to sensitive information (e.g., medical records). For this reason they must be secured against theft, fraud, or misuse.

In general, smart cards are more secure than conventional payment cards. If someone steals a payment card, the number of the card is clearly visible, as is the owner's signature. Although it may be hard to forge the signature, in many situations only the number is required to make a purchase. The only protection the cardholder has is that there are usually limits on how much they will be held liable for (e.g., in the United States it is $50). A stored-value card is a prepaid card that has monetary value loaded onto it, such as a phone card, and is usually rechargeable. If someone steals a stored-value card (or the owner loses it), the original owner is out of luck.

On the other hand, if someone steals a smart card, the thief is out of luck. Some smart cards show account numbers, but others do not. Before the card can be used, the holder may be required to enter a PIN that is matched on the card. Theoretically, it is possible to "hack" into a smart card. Most cards, however, now store the information in encrypted form. The smart cards can also encrypt and decrypt data that is downloaded or read from the card. Because of these factors, the possibility of hacking into a smart card is classified as a "class 3" attack, which means that the cost to the attacker of doing so far exceeds the benefits.

stored-value card
A card that has monetary value loaded onto it, and is usually rechargeable.

CASE 13.1
EC Application
THE HIGHWAY 91 PROJECT

Route 91 is a major eight-lane, east-west highway near Los Angeles. Traffic is especially heavy during rush hours. California Private Transportation Company (CPT) built six express toll lanes along a 10-mile stretch in the median of the existing Highway 91. The express lane system has only one entrance and one exit, and it is totally operated with EC technologies. Here is how the system works.

▶ Only prepaid subscribers can drive on the road. Subscribers receive an automatic vehicle identification (AVI) device that is placed on the rearview mirror of the car. The device, about the size of a thick credit card, includes a microchip, an antenna, and a battery. A large sign over the tollway tells drivers the current fee for cruising the express lanes. In a recent year it varied from $0.50 in slow traffic hours to $3.25 during rush hours.

▶ Sensors in the pavement let the tollway computer know that a car has entered; the car does not need to slow or stop. The AVI makes radio contact with a transceiver installed above the lane. The transceiver relays the car's identity through fiber-optic lines to the control center, where a computer calculates the fee for that day's trip. The system accesses the driver's account and the fare is automatically deducted from the driver's prepaid account. A monthly statement is sent to the subscriber's home.

▶ Surveillance cameras record the license numbers of cars without AVIs. These cars can be stopped by police at the exit or fined by mail.

▶ Video cameras along the tollway also enable managers to keep tabs on traffic, for example, sending a tow truck to help a stranded car. Also, through knowledge of the traffic volume, pricing decisions can be made. Raising the price as traffic increases ensures that the tollway will not be jammed.

The system saves commuters between 40 and 90 minutes each day, so it is in high demand.

An interesting extension of the system is the use of the same AVIs for other purposes. For example, they can be used in paid parking lots. Someday a customer may be recognized when they enter the drive-through lane of McDonald's and a voice asks them, "Mr. Smart, do you want your usual meal today?"

Source: Compiled from *91expresslanes.com* (2002).

Questions

1. Explain the benefits of this payment method.
2. Can you think of a better payment system? Explain.
3. Can this system be transferred to the Internet?
4. Can the concept be used in other applications? Explain.

Applications of Smart Cards

The growth in smart card usage is being driven by its applications (see Shelfer and Procaccino 2002 and Sorenson 2001). Today, the vast majority of smart cards are being issued in Europe, South America, and Asia. Over the next few years, their use in the United States and Canada will expand as well. At present, disposable, prepaid phone cards are the most widely used smart cards in the United States. Transit cards are quite popular in a few large metropolitan areas (New York, Chicago, Washington, D.C.).

Smart cards are making significant inroads in a number of applications. A thorough discussion of these applications can be found at the International Card Manufacturing Association Web site (icma.com/info/quick-facts.htm). The following are some of the more important applications.

Loyalty cards. Retailers are using smart cards to identify their loyal customers and reward them. Both Boots (Advantage Card) (boots.com) and Shell Company (Plus Points) (shell.com) have deployed millions of cards that allow customers to collect points that can be redeemed for rewards. Many supermarkets provide their frequent shoppers with loyalty cards as well. Loyalty cards are available for car rentals, airlines, discount stores, and many more.

Financial applications. Financial institutions, payment associations, and credit card, debit card, and charge card issuers are using smart cards to extend traditional card payment services. *Multiple applications* such as credit card, loyalty programs, digital identification, and electronic money are securely offered. In fact, in many countries, there are tens of millions of smart bankcards in use (e.g., see citicorp.com).

Information technology cards. In the future, many PCs will contain smart card readers. All major card issuers will utilize the underlying security of the smart card to extend relationships from the physical world to the virtual world. Smart cards will allow individuals to protect their privacy (people can buy them without disclosing their name), and card issuers will be able to ensure that only valid customers access services. The technology will allow individuals to accept other people's smart cards (e.g., as payments), to pay from a PC, to download money value on a physical smart card, and more.

Health and social welfare information cards. Many countries with national health care systems are evaluating or deploying smart card technology to reduce the costs associated with delivering health services and government social services. The largest deployed system is in Germany, with over 80 million cards. The program was introduced in 1993 with the primary purposes of identification, eligibility verification, and electronic claims processing. France, Italy, and the United Kingdom implemented a similar card-based system, Adicarte. Local authorities use this system to monitor and distribute social services in home-care programs, minimizing the fraud and misuse of funds that previously plagued such programs.

Transportation. The availability of low-cost, single-chip, contactless smart card technology has many mass-transit agencies implementing or evaluating the technology, especially for fare collection. One of the first large projects to deploy contactless card technology was the Seoul (Korea) Bus Association, which won the SCIA 1998 Outstanding Smart Card Application award. For details, see Turban and Brahm (2000). An interesting transportation card that can be used for other payments, such as in vending machines, restaurants, and gas stations, is Octopus in Hong Kong (see Poon and Chan 2001).

Identification. Smart cards are a natural fit in the identification market and are being used in applications such as college IDs, driver's licenses, and immigration cards. In the United States, several million smart cards are issued annually in the college market alone. Several countries are moving their national ID cards to smart cards. One advantage of smart cards is that they may contain biometrics, and therefore are extremely difficult to forge. Another advantage is that smart cards may contain a considerable amount of information.

Multipurpose Cards

For years, the trend has been to issue one card for each application—for example, credit card, debit card, cash card, loyalty card. However, in February 2001, MasterCard International and Korea's Kookmin Card Corp. issued the first multipurpose smart card in the world. It contained credit and debit card features, e-cash (from Mondex), and public transportation fares, all in one card. Today, many other banks (e.g., Citicorp) provide such cards. Visa International also supports these cards.

Section 13.2 ❱ REVIEW

1. List the common types of payment cards.
2. Describe how online credit card processing works.
3. List security issues related to payment cards.
4. Describe how a purchase card works.
5. Define smart cards and list some major applications.
6. List the advantages of smart cards.

13.3 E-CASH AND INNOVATIVE PAYMENT METHODS

It was the mid-1990s, and EC was in its infancy. At the time, most pundits and analysts were saying that consumers would be unwilling to use their credit cards on the Internet and that other digital money schemes would be needed. Up stepped DigiCash, Inc., offering a product called *eCash*, which was intended to be used as a payment medium in place of paper currency and coins. During its short life, DigiCash was able to convince only one U.S. bank, Mark Twain Bank of St. Louis, to participate. A few months later DigiCash ran out of money and filed for bankruptcy. A similar fate befell other early electronic payment and e-cash schemes and vendors.

e-cash
The digital equivalent of paper currency and coins, which enables secure and anonymous purchase of low-priced items.

Conceptually, e-cash—the digital equivalent of paper currency and coins—makes a lot of sense. It is secure and anonymous, and it can be used to support payments that cannot be economically supported with payment cards. From a practical standpoint, however, the inconvenience of opening an account and downloading software and the difficulty of obtaining a critical mass of users seems to have outweighed the benefits of e-cash.

In spite of these hurdles, though, new e-cash schemes, or at least alternatives to payment cards, appear with some regularity. These schemes can be grouped into four categories: e-cash and credit card alternatives, stored-value cards, e-loyalty and rewards programs, and person-to-person (P2P) payments. In addition, special payment arrangements must be made for global B2B payments.

E-CASH AND ALTERNATIVES TO CREDIT CARDS

Consider the following online shopping scenarios:

- ❱ A customer goes to an online music store and purchases a single CD that costs $8.95.
- ❱ A person goes online to a leading newspaper or news journal (such as *Forbes* or *Business Week*) and purchases (downloads) a copy of an archived news article for $1.50.
- ❱ A person goes to an online gaming company, selects a game, and plays it for 30 minutes. The person owes the company $3 for the playing time.
- ❱ A person goes to a Web site selling digital images and clip art. The person purchases a couple of images at a cost of $0.80.

micropayments
Small payments, usually under $10.

These are all examples of **micropayments**, which are small payments, usually under $10. Credit cards do not work well for such small payments. Vendors who accept credit cards typically must pay a minimum transaction fee that ranges from 25 cents to 35 cents, plus 2 to 3 percent of the purchase price. These fees are relatively insignificant for credit card purchases above $10, but are cost-prohibitive for smaller transactions. Also, when the purchase amount is small, consumers are unwilling to type in credit card numbers or wait for a standard credit card authorization. Micropayments are one area where e-cash and other payment card schemes come into play. Here are examples of a few innovative methods.

Wireless Payments

An ideal way to pay for certain types of micropayments is to use wireless devices (see Chapter 10 and Deitel et al. 2002). Vodafone, for example, has an "m-pay bill" system that enables wireless subscribers to use their mobile phones to make payments of $10 or less. The m-pay bill system is based on reverse billing: Users respond to a telephone number posted on a Web site by sending a text message (SMS) from their cell phones. A message is then sent back, confirming the payment arrangement and including a PIN number that acts as a password to the specific customer's account (at vodafone.com). The customer then proceeds with the transaction, and the charge shows up on their monthly Vodafone bill. Other telecommunications companies offer similar services. Wireless payments require standards, as discussed by Jin et al. (2002).

Qpass

One micropayment system that avoids some of the e-cash problems and has enjoyed some success is Qpass (qpass.com). Qpass is used primarily to purchase content from participating news services and periodicals such as the *New York Times*, *Wall Street Journal*, and *Forbes*.

A user sets up a Qpass account, creating a user name and password and specifying a credit card against which purchases will be charged. Then, when a purchase is made at a participating site, the user simply enters their Qpass user name and password and confirms the purchase. Instead of immediately billing the user's credit card account, the charges are aggregated into a single monthly statement, which is billed to the user's credit card.

STORED-VALUE CARDS AND OTHER INNOVATIONS

Stored-value smart cards have found greater usage than e-cash schemes as an alternative to credit cards. When used to store cash downloaded from a bank or credit card account, smart cards can be used to purchase items with values ranging from a few cents to hundreds of dollars. Various types of vendors worldwide accept stored-value cards: telephone companies, fast-food restaurants, convenience stores, vending machines, gas stations, transportation facilities, sundries stores, cinemas, parking garages, grocery stores, department stores, taxis, parking meters, cafeterias, and video stores. For example, people can now buy such a card at Kinko's and use it for services such as photocopying and Internet time. A leading vendor of stored-value cards is Visa.

Visa Cash

Visa Cash is a stored-value card designed to handle small purchases or micropayments. This chip-based card can be used in the physical (off-line) world or on the Internet. When a purchase is made, the cost of the purchase is deducted from the cash loaded on the card. Visa Cash can be used only at vendors having special terminals displaying the Visa Cash logo.

There are two types of Visa Cash: disposable and reloadable. *Disposable cards* are loaded with a predetermined value. These cards typically come in denominations of local currency, such as $10. When the value of the card is used, the card is discarded, and a new card may be purchased. *Reloadable cards* come without a predefined value. Cash value is reloaded onto the card at specialized terminals and at ATMs. When the value is used up, users can reload the card.

Visa Cash cards can be obtained from financial institutions, special card-dispensing machines, and kiosks. These cards are widely used outside the United States. They were initially introduced in Hong Kong in 1996, and they can now be used there at more than 1,500 merchants and reloaded at over 300 ATMs. For PCs with a Visa Cash card reader, it also is possible to make payments across the Internet. The card may be combined with a regular Visa credit card.

Visa Buxx

A prepaid card designed for teens is Visa's Buxx ("bucks"). It looks like a regular card, but it is safer because it contains only a limited stored value. Teens use it to shop online, and it is a powerful tool for teaching teens about budgeting and financial responsibility. Reloading of money can be done automatically, say, once a month, or the card can be reloaded when it is depleted. Balances and purchasing history can be checked online (see visabuxx.com).

Mondex

The Mondex microchip card is a MasterCard product similar to Visa Cash. It is administered and developed by Mondex International, a subsidiary of MasterCard. Cash is downloaded onto the card through cash dispensers, pay phones, and home phones. Payments can

Visa Cash
A stored-value card designed to handle small purchases or micropayments; sponsored by Visa.

Mondex
A stored-value card designed to handle small purchases or micropayments; sponsored by Mondex, a subsidiary of MasterCard.

be made wherever the Mondex sign is displayed. In addition, using a Mondex Wallet, two cardholders can transfer cash between their cards. A Mondex card can also be used to transfer cash from one party to the next. Unlike Visa Cash, a Mondex card can store up to five currencies at the same time. Mondex is currently being tested in the United Kingdom, Canada, the United States, Hong Kong, and New Zealand. About 250,000 Mondex cards were in use in 2002 (mondex.com 2003).

Campus Cards

Many universities offer cards that can be used on campus. The simplest card is a *library copying card*. Students purchase a card and then load it with cash at an ATM-type device. The money value is not stored on the card, but in an account equivalent to the card's ID number. When the student wants to copy material, they insert the card into a card reader on the copying machine. The reader will read the ID number and the account balance and charge the account for any copies the student makes. At some universities, students can use the same card in vending machines. These cards provide complete anonymity.

Many universities offer a multipurpose card in conjunction with Visa or a bank. Such a card is a credit card, ID card, and library card. Students can use it as a key to enter their dorm, buy from a vending machine, and much more.

E-LOYALTY AND REWARDS PROGRAMS

Some B2C sites spend dozens of dollars for acquiring each new customer. Yet, the payback comes only after the customer has made several purchases. These repeat customers are also more likely to refer other customers to a site. In the off-line retail world, companies often use *loyalty programs* to encourage repeat business. In the United Kingdom, for example, the *Airmiles program* is one of the best-known rewards programs. Airmiles can be earned at over 10,000 locations worldwide, and the Airmiles are exchanged for airline tickets and other merchandise (Cassy 2000).

electronic script
A form of electronic money (or points), issued by a third party as part of a loyalty program; can be used by consumers to make purchases at participating stores.

Loyalty programs are also appearing online. The currency used by loyalty programs is **electronic script**. This is a form of electronic money (or points) issued by a third party that can be used by consumers to make purchases at participating stores. MyPoints-CyberGold and RocketCash are two of the better-known loyalty programs. Beenz.com and Flooz were famous, but they folded in August 2001.

Beenz.com is an instructive example about what can go wrong in a loyalty program. Beenz.com was selling a quantity of loyalty points, called "beenz," to a merchant Web site. A consumer earned beenz by visiting, registering, or making purchases at participating sites. The beenz were deposited into the customer's account, maintained by Beenz.com. Later, consumers were able to redeem their beenz for products at the participating sites. Forrester analysts said that the Beenz payment system failed to create a critical mass of places to use it (usability) and a critical mass of ways to obtain it (availability) (Vigoroso 2001).

MyPoints-CyberGold (mypoints.com) is the result of the merger of two separate loyalty programs—MyPoints and CyberGold. In this program, customers earn cash by visiting, registering, or making purchases at affiliated MyPoints merchants. The cash can be used to make purchases at participating sites or can be transferred to a credit card or bank account.

Prepaid Stored-Value Cards

Another innovative loyalty program is the use of prepaid cards, such as prepaid telephone cards. These can be used both online and off-line. Obviously, if the customer has a prepaid stored-value card, they are more likely to be loyal to the card sponsor, at least until the stored value runs out (e.g., see powells.com).

Several companies attempting this approach offer cards that are sold in kiosks, supermarkets, and even the post office. Starbucks, for example, offers a prepaid stored-value card, intended to keep customers coming back for more coffee products. (The maximum amount one can load onto the card is $500, which represents a lot of prepaid coffee drinks!) One company that is offering a stored-value-card program for use online is InternetCash, whose story is described in EC Application Case W13.1.

Similarly, RocketCash (rocketcash.com) combines an online cash account with a rewards program. A user opens a RocketCash account and adds funds to the account with a money order, a credit card, or MyPoints. The cash account can then be used to make purchases at participating merchants. Purchases earn RocketCash rewards that can also be redeemed for merchandise.

P2P PAYMENTS

Person-to-person (P2P) payments are one of the newest and fastest-growing e-payment schemes. They enable the transfer of funds between two individuals for a variety of purposes, such as repaying money borrowed from a friend, paying for an item purchased at an online auction, sending money to students at college, or sending a gift to a family member. People also can use it to pay some vendors.

person-to-person (P2P) payments
E-payment schemes (such as PayPal) that enable the transfer of funds between two individuals.

One of the first companies to offer this service was PayPal (paypal.com). As of June 30, 2002, PayPal (now owned by eBay) had 17.8 million member accounts, including 3.7 million business accounts and users in 38 countries including the United States. More than $3 billion was sent through the PayPal network in the first half of 2002 (kurant.com 2003). This kind of activity has drawn the attention of a number of other companies who are trying to get in on the action. Citibank c2it (c2it.com); AOL QuickCash (aol.com), which is a private-branded version of c2it; Bank One's eMoneyMail (bankone.com/presents/emoneymail/home/); Yahoo PayDirect (paydirect.yahoo.com); and WebCertificate (webcertificate.com) are all PayPal competitors. PayPal was purchased by eBay in July 2002, however, PayPal continues to operate as an independent brand.

Virtually all of these services work the same way. Assume a person wants to send money to someone over the Internet. First, they select a service like PayPal and open an account with it. Basically, this entails creating a user name and a password, giving the service an e-mail address and providing the service with a payment card or bank account number. Next, the person adds funds to their account with a credit card or bank account.

Once the account has been funded, the money can be sent. The sender accesses the account with their user name and password. The sender then specifies the e-mail address of the person to receive the money, along with the dollar amount that they want to send. An e-mail is sent to the specified e-mail address (see Exhibit 13.5 on page 508). The e-mail will contain a link back to the service's Web site. When the recipient clicks on the link, they will be taken to the service and asked to set up an account to which the money that was sent will be credited. Recipients can then transfer the money from that account to their credit card or bank account. Other services also are available. For example, using PayPal, ATM cardholders can withdraw cash off-line or send money electronically to vendors.

Although the various services all work in similar ways, there are differences. For example, in 2002, c2it charged $2 per transaction from the receiver, offered no insurance against fraud, and required paperwork sent by snail mail if the money had to be moved into a bank account. On the other hand, PayPal does not charge individuals, but charges receiving corporations, offers insurance against fraud, and does not require any paperwork for bank transfers. P2P services have regulatory and fraud issues to deal with, and some face class-action suits because of customer service problems.

NON-INTERNET, E-COMMERCE PAYMENT SYSTEMS

An increasing number of applications involve non-Internet e-commerce payment systems. Some were cited earlier when smart cards were discussed. Here are a few other examples.

Self-Checkout

Why should customers stand in line to pay in a retail store or supermarket when they can be their own cashier and check themselves out? Consumers can use kiosks to check out, such as the ones used in Sears, Kmart, and in many supermarkets (see photo on page 509). All the customer has to do is to scan the product's ID code and then scan their credit (or debit) card (or pay using fingertip identification, as described in EC Application Case 12.3 on page 476). The kiosk generates a receipt and then the customer is on their way. Of course, such systems need security features or a person on the floor to supervise all of the checkout machines to avoid shoplifting.

EXHIBIT 13.5   Sending Money with PayPal

PayPal®   Log Out | Help

| My Account | Send Money | Request Money | Merchant Tools | Auction Tools |

Send Money   Secure Transaction 🔒

Pay anyone with an email address - even if they don't have a PayPal account!

Recipient's Email: [   ]   Try: BillPay | Pay for ebY Items

– OR – Select a recipient ▾

Amount: [   ]

Currency: U.S. Dollars ▾ [?]

Type: – Please Select Type – ▾ [?]

Subject:
(optional) [   ]

Note:
(optional) [   ]

[Continue]

Mobile | Mass Pay | Money Market | ATM/Debit Card | BillPay | Referrals

About Us | Accounts | Fees | Privacy | Security Center | User Agreement | Developers | Shops

an eBay company

Copyright © 1999-2003 PayPal. All rights reserved.

Source: These materials have been reproduced with permission of PayPal, Inc. Copyright © 2003 Paypal, Inc. All rights reserved.

Buying from Vending Machines

In addition to using a cell phone and smart cards that have money stored on them, one can use regular credit cards at PepsiCo and Coca-Cola vending machines. This solves the problem of micropayments. Coca-Cola also allows customers to swipe a customized key chain in front of a vending machine. This is based on RFID technology.

Pay with a Check Without Writing It

Customers no longer have to write checks at some leading retailers (e.g., Wal-Mart) and supermarkets. All customers have to do is present a blank check to the cashier. The check is scanned and returned to the customer with a VOID on it (so the same check cannot be used twice). The customer's bank account is debited and the merchant account is credited. With this technology, customers will write fewer checks in stores and wait less time in line while waiting for other people to write them. A greater revolution is being made with electronic checks, the subject of the next section.

Section 13.3 ▶ REVIEW

1. Describe the drivers of e-cash.
2. Define micropayments. Why are they suitable for e-cash?
3. What are stored-value cards?
4. Describe e-loyalty programs.
5. Describe P2P payment methods.
6. Describe some non-Internet payment methods.

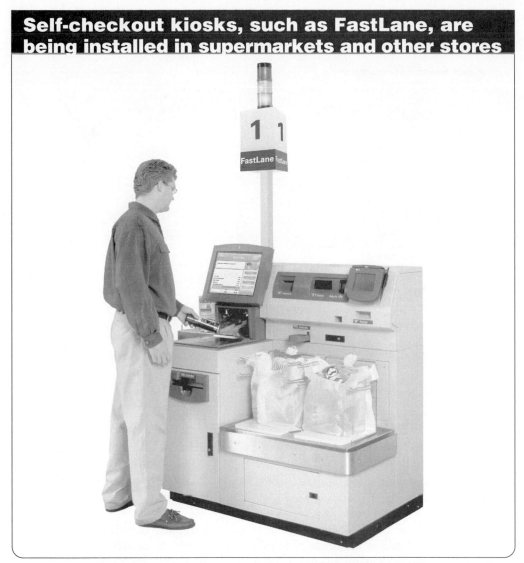

Self-checkout kiosks, such as FastLane, are being installed in supermarkets and other stores

Source: Photo of NCR Fastlane™ self-checkout system is provided courtesy of NCR Corporation.

13.4 E-CHECKING

According to U.S. government statistics, over 70 percent of all noncash payments in the United States are made by check. In 2002, U.S. consumers, businesses, and government entities wrote about 80 billion checks. It costs about 1 percent of the U.S. gross domestic product (GDP) to process these checks. This percentage does not count the costs associated with check fraud, which is estimated to be $60 billion annually (in 2002), with banks absorbing about $1.45 billion in losses and retailers and other payees about $58.5 billion. These costs are one of the driving forces behind the move to electronic checks (e-checks). According to the Electronic Check Clearing House Organization (2002), a not-for-profit clearinghouse, e-checks can yield industry-wide savings and benefits in the United States of $2 to $3 billion per year.

An **e-check** is the electronic version or representation of a paper check. E-checks contain the same information as a paper check, can be used wherever paper checks are used, and are based on the same legal framework. E-checks work essentially the same way a paper check works, but in pure electronic form, with fewer manual steps. Simply put, they are faster and cheaper, and they can be more secure.

E-checks fit within current business practices, eliminating the need for expensive process reengineering and taking advantage of the competency of the banking industry. Using state-of-the-art security techniques, e-checks can be used by all bank customers who have checking accounts, including small and midsize businesses that otherwise have little access to electronic payment systems (authorize.net 2002).

e-check
The electronic version or representation of a paper check.

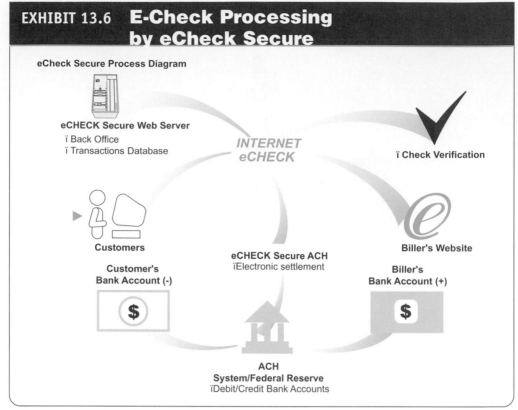

Source: Courtesy of Troy Financial Services.

eCheck Secure (from troygroup.com/financial/echecksecure/index.asp) and Checkfree (checkfree.com) provide software that enables the purchase of goods and services with an e-check. The processes that are supported, as shown in Exhibit 13.6, are fairly common, regardless of the Web site used.

In situations such as B2B e-commerce or e-government purchases, where the dollar values are likely to be in the hundreds of thousands of dollars, more secure procedures are required. Some e-check standards are being tested in pilot projects by the U.S. Treasury Department. (For further information on e-checking, see the online addition to this chapter at the book's Web site.) Other methods of B2B payments are described next.

Section 13.4 ▶ REVIEW

1. Define e-check.
2. List some of the benefits of e-checks.
3. Why are e-checks used in B2C? In B2B?

13.5   B2B ELECTRONIC PAYMENTS

B2B payments are more complex than B2C payments. In the physical world, companies use checks, wire transfers, lines of credit, and escrow systems (in addition to credit cards, which are used for small amounts). It is difficult to create B2B payment systems that tie into buyers' and sellers' internal accounting systems (see Donahue 2000).

To better understand the difficulty of automating the B2B payment process, let's look briefly at the concept of the financial supply chain.

FINANCIAL SUPPLY CHAINS

The financial supply chain (FSC) parallels the physical supply chain. It closely follows a buyer's transaction activities related to cash flow, which start with a purchase order and end in settlement with the seller. Integration of the FSC with current procurement, fulfillment, and settlement processes needs to become a critical element of buying and selling electronically.

Significant capital, information, and process improvements in accounts payable and accounts receivable can be achieved through automation and integration with the financial supply chain. Some of the areas that can be addressed are cash forecasting, real-time transaction management, faster discrepancy resolution, and receivables and payables reconciliation.

The complexity of the financial supply chain can be seen by examining the typical segments of the chain:

- **Segment 1:** Examination of catalogs, electronic order entry
- **Segment 2:** Online negotiations, culminating in a preliminary agreement
- **Segment 3:** Credit check, seller validation, payment assurance, financing
- **Segment 4:** Invoice presentment, verification of delivery, "trade service" quote, and booking
- **Segment 5:** Data matching, discrepancy resolution, final payment calculation, buyer approval, currency exchange calculation (if needed), and arrangements for automatic payment
- **Segment 6:** Payment instructions, money transfer, debit and credit notices

This process is supported by technology infrastructure that includes workflow, document management, security, data compliance, ERP, and other interfaces.

B2B PAYMENT SOLUTIONS

Several vendors are trying to capitalize on the huge potential B2B market by providing solutions that will be secure and fast. For example, Hewlett-Packard has developed a comprehensive B2B payment software, described in Insights and Additions 13.3 (page 512).

The remaining parts of this section present other B2B payment solutions.

PURCHASING CARDS FOR B2B

Though credit cards are the instrument of choice for B2C payments, this is not the case for the B2B marketplace. Traditionally, payments between companies have been handled by checks, financial EDI, letters of credit, and EFT. Credit cards are used mostly for small purchases.

The problem is that the traditional B2B payment methods may be too expensive for SMEs. Today, the major credit card players—Visa, MasterCard, and American Express—are trying to convince companies to utilize *purchasing cards* instead of checks for repetitive, low-cost purchases. Purchasing cards are special-purpose payment cards issued to a company's employees. They are to be used solely for the purpose of paying for nonstrategic materials and services (e.g., stationery, office supplies, computer supplies, repair and maintenance services, courier services, and temporary labor services) up to a limit (usually $1,000 to $2,000). According to an American Express study conducted by Ernst & Young in 1999, moving from paper checks to purchasing cards can lower the average processing cost per buying transaction from 90 cents to 22 cents. Purchasing cards are very popular in *desktop purchasing* (American Express 2003).

Purchasing cards operate essentially the same as any other charge card. They are used both for off-line and online purchases. However, the company's account with the merchant is maintained on a *nonrevolving* basis, meaning that it needs to be paid in full each month, usually within 5 days of the end of the billing period. Exhibit 13.8 (page 513) shows how a purchasing card is used.

A couple of general benefits accrue from the use of purchasing cards (Jilovec 1999):

- **Productivity gains.** Purchasing departments are freed from day-to-day procurement activities and can focus on developing and managing relationships with suppliers.
- **Bill consolidation.** Small purchases done by many cardholders in one company can be consolidated into a single invoice that can be paid electronically through EDI or EFT.

purchasing cards
Special-purpose payment cards issued to a company's employees to be used solely for purchasing nonstrategic materials and services up to a preset dollar limit.

Insights and Additions 13.3   HP Payment System for Businesses

In December 2000, Hewlett-Packard (HP) launched a B2B e-payment solution that enables financial institutions to provide their customers with a seamless electronic payment each time a B2B transaction takes place. By allowing payments to be processed, completed, and recorded online at the time of the transaction, this technology eliminates the paper-based payment inefficiencies of B2B exchanges—dramatically improving the speed and accuracy of transactions and reducing costs by as much as 80 percent.

The HP e-payment solution can be integrated with e-marketplaces, online exchanges, e-procurement hubs, and sell/buy Web sites to guarantee immediate electronic status updates for corporate transactions. For example, foreign currency payments can be integrated with user accounting systems to ensure that accounts receivable and accounts payable reflect up-to-date currency values as business is conducted online. The solution also increases efficiencies by decentralizing the processing of payments across all parties and locations and by allowing for centralized control over workflow rules and transactions.

The HP B2B e-payment solution consists of two components that are preintegrated with the complete HP Enterprise Commerce solution suite that together provide end-to-end payment automation (see attached figure). The B2B e-payment handler offers embedded payment options that establish business rules to facilitate direct-debit payment options. These options allow companies to set up buyer accounts, purchasing limits, corporate discounting, and other payment-related authentication and alert mechanisms. The solution securely connects customers' e-commerce sites enabled with the HP B2B e-payment handler to their online financial institutions. The second component is the HP financial link that connects buyers to sellers and maintains a database of payment authorization and information (see Exhibit 13.7). Combined, these components are robust enough to even handle the most complex cross-border transactions quickly and securely.

(continued)

EXHIBIT 13.7   Hewlett-Packard B2B E-Payment Solution

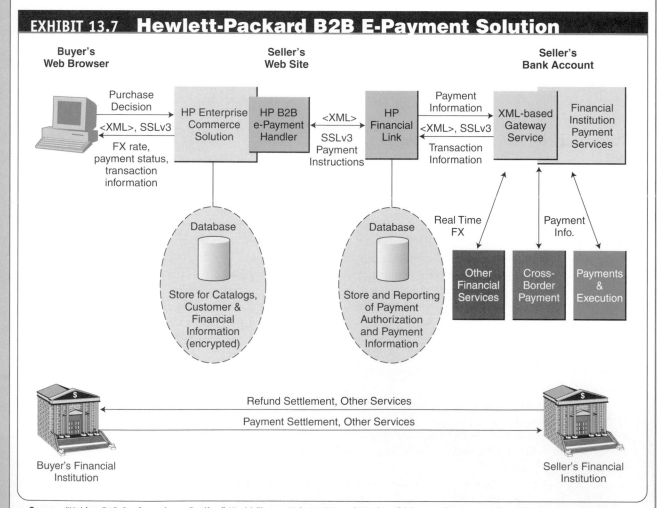

Source: "Making B2B Conferencing a Reality," *World Finance* Vol. 11, No. 1 (2001) myfsi.hp.com/magazine/wf11_1/b2b.asp. Copyright (1999–2003) Hewlett-Packard Development Company, L.P. Reproduced with Permission.

Insights and Additions 13.3 (continued)

In the new digital world, companies look for the values they have come to expect from financial services, such as low-cost, real-time transactions performed by trusted partners. With this solution, HP connects the financial world to the new economy, bringing those values to the Web environment. The HP solution closes the payment gap in the B2B Internet value chain, while driving companies' business growth and profitability by offering customers the best end-to-end online purchasing experience.

HP has integrated its B2B e-payment solution with BroadVision's Business Commerce application to create comprehensive B2B e-commerce systems that feature seamless payment processing. The integrated system also reduces the cost of order processing, contract administration, and customer service, and captures and analyzes information that allows companies to provide unique purchasing experiences for each customer, partner, and employee.

Source: Compiled from *hp.com* 2001 and from Hewlett-Packard press release, 2000–2003.

EXHIBIT 13.8 The Participants and the Process of Using a Purchasing Card

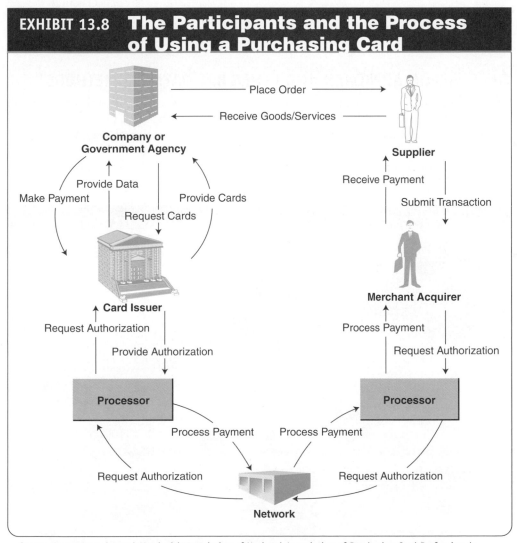

Source: *napcp.com* (2003.) Used with permission of National Association of Purchasing Card Professionals.

Specific benefits to the actual buyers, the agency where they work, and the merchant include the following:

▶ **Payment reconciliation.** Data from the card vendors can be more easily integrated with a corporation's general ledger system, making the process of payment reconciliation simpler, more efficient, and more accurate.

▶ **Expedited payments.** Settlement of accounts can occur in 5 days or less (rather than the traditional 30 days). This enables buyers to negotiate with their suppliers for more favorable prices, and sellers get paid faster.

▶ **Management reports.** The financial institutions issuing the cards provide the user organizations with detailed reports of purchasing activities (frequently online). This makes it easier for a company to analyze the spending behavior of its purchasing agents and to monitor supplier compliance with agreed-upon prices.

▶ **Control.** Companies can better control unplanned purchases by limiting the authorized amount per purchase.

Purchasing cards are used by most state governments (e.g., purchasingcard.state.fl.us) and by many public universities. Purchasing cards are used within countries; for global trade, one can use other payment instruments.

To learn more about purchasing cards, see the National Association of Purchasing Card Professionals (napcp.org), visa.com, and ge.com/capital/cardservices/corpcard/6onecard.htm.

THE CLAREON APPROACH AND OTHER B2B PAYMENT METHODS

Clareon Corp. (clareon.com) facilitates B2B transactions by providing digital payments and settlement services, which are shown in Exhibit 13.9. As can be seen, payment is digitally signed, secured, and authenticated via digital payment authentication (DPA). Unlike traditional EDI, Clareon's system is compatible with ERP software. Therefore, it can adapt electronic records for companies, banks, and each member of a given transaction. From there, the

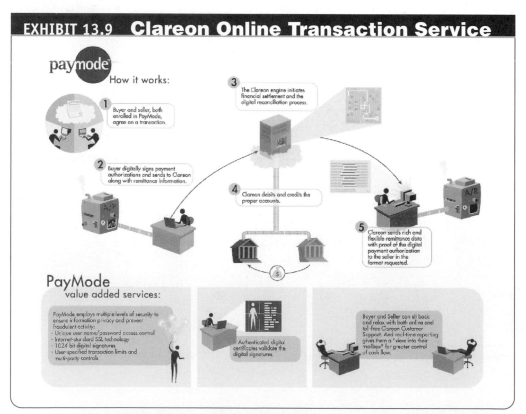

EXHIBIT 13.9 Clareon Online Transaction Service

Source: Used with permission of Clarion, a division of FleetBoston.

information is again converted; the remittance data is sent to the seller, and the DPA is forwarded to the bank. Both the buyer and the seller have access to the payment status. For small payments and B2C payments, both within the United States and globally, one can use the services of c2it.com and paypal.com.

Systems such as HP, Clareon, and TradeCard (see EC Application Case 13.2 on page 516) are attempts to automate the B2B transaction settlement processes. For large systems, especially those involving B2B exchanges, it is necessary to build payment networks. Examples of such networks are Ariba's Commerce Services Network and financial settlementmatrix.com.

GLOBAL B2B PAYMENTS

B2B payments are especially complex when global payments may need to be made. Here we describe two alternative global B2B payment methods, one that is close to a form of cash payment and another that is an innovative e-payment method that uses a payment card.

Electronic Letters of Credit

A letter of credit (LC) is a written agreement by a bank to pay to the beneficiary (the seller) on account of the applicant (the buyer) a sum of money upon presentation of certain documents. The LC gives precise instructions concerning the documents that must be produced by the beneficiary before the LC expiration date. LCs benefit both sellers and buyers.

The main benefit of LCs to the seller is that payment is highly assured if all the terms and conditions stipulated in the LC are met. In addition, credit risk is reduced because payment is accessed via the creditworthiness of the issuing bank. Finally, political/country risk is reduced if the LC is confirmed by a bank in the seller's country.

LCs also benefit buyers in various ways. For one, an LC may allow the buyer to negotiate for a lower purchase price because credit risk for the seller is reduced. Also, because certain sellers are willing to supply goods only under LC arrangements, the buyer may expand its sources of supply and bargaining power. Finally, funds will be withdrawn from the buyer's account only after the documents have been inspected by the issuing bank, thus giving the buyer a bit more time to hold its money than might otherwise be the case.

LC arrangements usually involve five steps: issuance, credit advising, confirmation, transfer, and negotiation. These five steps can be conducted online much faster than they can be done off-line. For example, Royal Bank of Canada issues electronic LCs from its International Business Centre (rbcroyalbank.com/trade/tradeview). RoyalBank's TradeView enables the preparation of a credit application on your computer, and electronically transmits it to Royal Bank for review and processing. Credit can be issued in as few as 24 hours. It also enables the reception of export letters of credit electronically and the ability to review them directly from your personal computer. This reduces the time spent having letters of credit refaxed in order to view them clearly. For a comprehensive example of electronic banking, see ANZ (anz.com/international).

Electronic LCs also are used in auctions such as those at ebay.com. Payments are guaranteed in minutes. One problem with online LCs is that their cost is too high for many SMEs. For these, global trading cards are a possible solution.

TradeCard Payments in B2B Global Trading

Letters of credit may be too expensive or too complicated, especially for SMEs. An alternative solution, introduced by MasterCard and TradeCard, Inc., allows businesses to effectively and efficiently complete B2B transactions, whether large or small, domestic or cross-border, or in multiple currencies. Buyers and sellers become TradeCard members, a process that entails evaluation of their creditworthiness and a check (by Thomas Cook Corp.) that they have not been involved in money-laundering activities. The buyers and sellers then interact with each other via the TradeCard system, which checks purchase orders for both parties, waits for a confirmation from a logistics company that deliveries have been made and received, and authorizes payment to complete the financial transaction between the buyer and seller.

letter of credit (LC)
A written agreement by a bank to pay the seller, on account of the buyer, a sum of money upon presentation of certain documents.

CASE 13.2

EC Application

TAL APPAREL TAKES ONLINE GOODS TO THE NEXT STAGE WITH TRADECARD

TAL Apparel (*tap.com*) has built its reputation mainly by manufacturing shirts, blouses, trousers, men's tailored suits, and outerwear in its Asian factories for delivery to markets in the United States and Europe. The company produces 40 million garments a year, generating revenues of US $600 million. The company's customers include Brooks Brothers, Calvin Klein, JCPenney, Liz Claiborne, and Ralph Lauren.

TAL Apparel Ltd. has adopted the TradeCard online global trade transaction management system to increase the operational efficiency of its buying and selling operations. The system processes payments as well as ordering and other transactions. Data transmission on the new system has proven to be 100 percent reliable, with no lost data and no system downtime.

TAL Apparel began using TradeCard in the middle of 2002, initially to process orders sent to suppliers, and soon began to use it also with its buyers. Transactions are taken online and automated right through to financial settlement.

Buyers and sellers negotiate online to agree on the purchase order. The same data then are used to create all related documents, including invoice and statements, shipping documents, insurance, and inspection. Letters of credit can be replaced by a payment protection system provided by TradeCard partners, coupled with a patented online compliance process. The system also supports open account trading.

TAL emphasizes technology in its trade operations. The company was an early adopter of e-mail and a pioneer in electronic document interchange (EDI). By 1995, TAL was using e-commerce technologies in the supply chain; it currently is focusing on electronically issuing shipping documents and payments. TradeCard's use of Web technology is radically increasing retail efficiency and lowering costs, especially since no paper documents are used.

By substituting TradeCard's online compliance engine for letters of credit, the time taken to process these payment agreements has been reduced. With TradeCard, the charge for issuing a letter of credit (L/C) is also much lower than for paper copies of such documents purchased through banks. In addition, TradeCard's purchase and payments system can serve both large and small transactions. Faster payments are the key. Ruth Kan, financial controller for TAL, says, "Using bank L/C payment takes 4 weeks, but TradeCard payments take 2 weeks. For SMEs (small- and medium-sized enterprises) and small suppliers, it is very important to get paid quickly and to turn the money around faster. Most of our largest suppliers have adopted TradeCard and are benefiting. If our buyers adopt the system, we get paid faster, too."

TradeCard provides more than electronic payments; it also provides communication with suppliers and customers and with government agencies for export declarations. TradeCard has enabled TAL to communicate with its buyers more effectively, especially in case of problems or delays. Electronic documents can be searched and reported within seconds, unlike paper documents that are slow to process and in which errors are difficult to detect.

"Our suppliers are happy to get paid punctually, and also happy that, whatever country they are in, they have instant visibility of the transaction progress. Using paper documents, we would hear arguments like: 'We did not receive your fax,' but now all parties can see and understand each transaction," says Ms. Kan. As retail customers adopt TradeCard, supplier-managed inventory is facilitated and customer relations improved.

Source: Condensed from TradeCard 2003.

Questions

1. Describe the benefits of TradeCard to TAL's buyers and suppliers.
2. What are the benefits of combining the payment system with other processes?
3. The system is good both for local and global trade. What are the particular benefits for global trade?

The service can be integrated with B2B exchanges or company-centric market-places, which currently have no similar comprehensive online payment solution for handling different sizes and types of transactions. Businesses can pay for spot transactions or they can track larger, more complicated corporate purchase orders through their transaction cycle and then pay for them when the contract terms have been satisfied. Companies are able to receive integrated payment information, including transaction-level detail, via secure Web access.

For more information, see tradecard.com (see the Global Trading Program). A video of "World Business Review" dealing with the program also is available from tradecard.com.

1. List the major B2B e-payment methods.
2. Describe purchasing cards and list their benefits.
3. Describe an electronic letter of credit and its use.
4. Describe TradeCard and its advantages.

13.6 ELECTRONIC BILL PRESENTMENT AND PAYMENT

In Chapter 3, we introduced the topic of paying bills online, basically as a B2C service. This section shows the topic from a corporate view and also considers it as a payment mechanism.

E-BILLING

For a number of years, banks and companies such as Intuit (intuit.com) have made it possible for customers to pay their bills online. However, the vast majority of all bills are still paid the traditional way. That is, on a regular basis a billing company calculates, prints, and mails the customer a paper bill. In turn, the customer sends back a paper check that is processed by the billing company in order to receive funds. It can take a week or more to complete the whole process.

Slowly but surely, electronic billing (e-billing) is making some headway against traditional billing. By one report, bills paid online are about 3 percent of the 15 *billion* bills sent each year. Online payments are expected to grow to more than 15 percent of 19 billion bills by 2011 (CIO Forum 2002). By another estimate, e-billing will represent 34 percent of all billing by 2005 (Borths and Young 2000).

E-billing is also called electronic bill presentment and payment (EBPP). E-billing enables the presentment, payment, and posting of bills via the Internet. **Presentment** involves taking the information that is typically printed on a bill and hosting it on a bill-presentment Web server. (See Exhibit 13.10 on page 518, for an example.) Once the bill is available on the Web server, a customer can access the bill with a browser, review it, and pay it electronically. After the payment is received, it must be posted against the biller's accounts receivable system. Payments are generally transferred from the customer's checking account via the ACH. In e-billing, the customers can be either individuals or companies.

E-bills can be presented in a variety of ways. Two models are common-biller direct and third-party consolidators. With *biller direct*, the customer is presented with a bill from a single billing merchant. For example, a customer could access the Web site of a utility company in order to pay their bill. In contrast, a *third-party consolidator* presents bills from multiple merchants. The steps involved with each model are essentially the same.

Individual biller. The customer signs up to receive and pay bills via the biller's Web site (service initiation). Exhibit 13.11 (page 518) shows the general steps in the e-billing process of a single biller. The biller makes the billing information available to the customer (presentment) on their Web site or the site of a billing hosting service (step 1). Once the customer views the bill (step 2), they authorize and initiate payment at the site (step 3). The payment can be made with a credit/debit card or an ACH debit. The biller then initiates a payment transaction (step 4) that moves funds through the payment system (payment), crediting the biller and debiting the customer (step 5).

Billing consolidator. Exhibit 13.12 (page 519) shows the steps in the process used by bill consolidators. The customer enrolls to receive and pay bills for multiple billers (service initiation). The customer's enrollment information is forwarded to every biller that the customer wishes to activate (service initiation). For each billing cycle, the biller sends a bill summary or bill detail to the consolidator (presentment). The bill summary, which links to the bill detail stored with the biller or consolidator, is forwarded to the aggregator and made available to the customer (presentment). The customer views the bill and initiates payment instructions (payment). The customer service provider (CSP) or aggregator initiates a credit

presentment
The presentation and hosting on a specialized Web server of information that is typically printed on a bill.

EXHIBIT 13.10 E-Bill Presentment

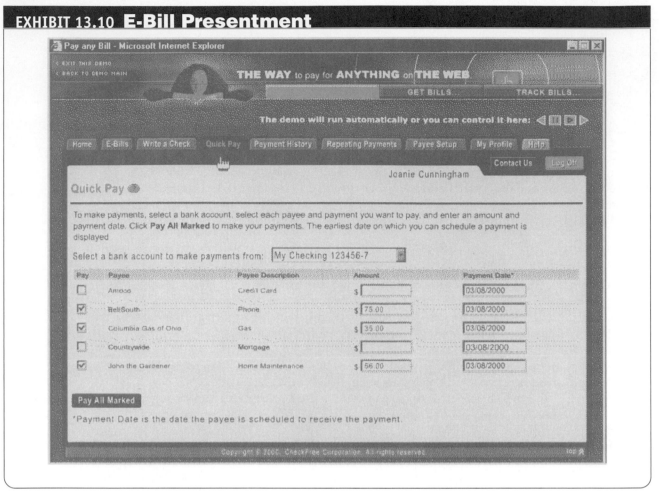

EXHIBIT 13.11 E-Billing Process for Single Biller

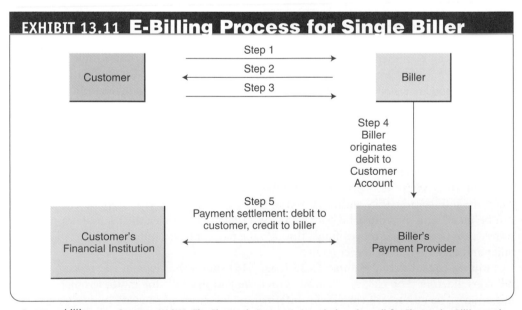

EXHIBIT 13.12 E-Billing Processes for Bill Consolidator

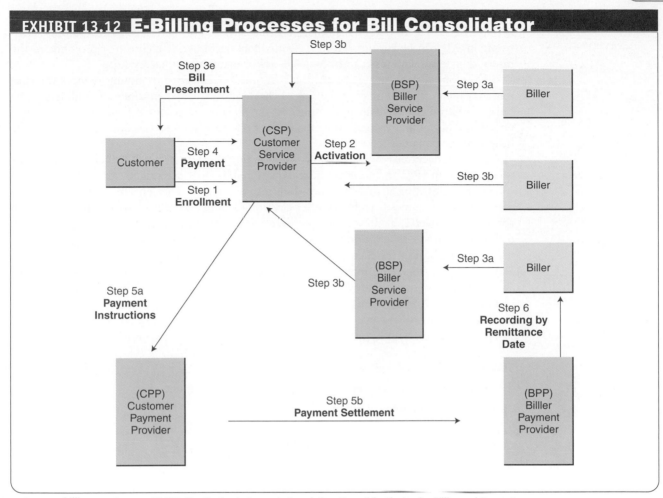

Source: *ebilling.org.* Courtesy NACHA–The Electronic Payments Association, Council for Electronics Billing and Payment.

payment transaction that moves funds through the payment system to the biller (payment). Remittance data are provided to the biller, who posts this information to its own accounts receivable system (posting).

Paying Bills at ATMs

In some countries (e.g., Hong Kong, Singapore), customers can pay bills at regular ATMs. The bills are sent by mail or can be viewed online. When a customer receives the bill, they can go to any ATM, slide in their bank card, enter a password, and go to "bill payments" on the menu. All they then need to do is insert the account number of the biller and the amount to be paid. The customer then gets a printed receipt showing that the payment has been made. In addition to utility bills that can be paid this way, customers can pay for purchases (e.g., airline tickets). Merchants appreciate the system, and some even give a discount for payments by ATM because they do not have to pay 3 percent to Visa or MasterCard.

Advantages of E-Billing

From the perspective of the billing firm, e-billing has several advantages. The most obvious benefit is the reduction in expenses related to billing and processing payments. The estimate is that paper bills cost between $0.75 and $2.70 per bill. E-billing costs between $0.25 and $0.30 per bill. One recent industry source is quoting an average cost savings of $1.00 to $5.00 per e-bill (ebilling.org 2003). E-billing also enables better customer service. Not only can customer service representatives see the same presentment that the customer is seeing, but the presentment can also provide access to frequently asked questions and help boxes.

Another advantage relates to advertising. A paper bill can include advertising and marketing inserts. Usually, every customer gets the same ads or materials. With e-billing, electronic inserts can be customized to the individual customer. If a customer responds to the insert, then it is much easier to trace which ads or materials are successful.

There are also advantages from the customer's perspective. E-billing reduces the customer's expenses by eliminating the cost of checks, postage, and envelopes. E-billing simplifies and centralizes payment processing and provides better record keeping. Customers can review and pay bills at virtually any time. In this way, the customer has direct control over the timing of the payment.

By far, Checkfree (checkfree.com) is the leading third-party e-billing vendor. Checkfree was founded in 1981 and is currently headquartered in Atlanta, Georgia. Checkfree is a consolidator, aggregating all of a customer's bills into a single presentment. It can also set up payments with companies that do not offer electronic billing. Checkfree serves about 6 million consumers in over 1,000 businesses and over 350 financial institutions (including most U.S. banks and Yahoo). In addition to these services, Checkfree also provides portfolio management, reconciliation products and services, check conversion, e-billing and payment and e-statement delivery, consumer e-commerce, and for years has been a leading processor of ACH payments. Today, more than two-thirds of the nation's 8 billion ACH payments (valued at more than $22 trillion) are processed by Checkfree. Checkfree alerts users if there is a problem with any of the payments. Users can export the transaction records to Quicken or Microsoft Money. See checkfree.com for a demo.

Section 13.6 ❱ REVIEW

1. Describe the process of online bill presentment and payment.

2. Describe the benefits of EBPP.

13.7 SPECIAL PAYMENT-RELATED ISSUES

This section will discuss a few of the many payment-related issues, specifically, tax calculation and collection services, comprehensive payment-related services, and other financial services for B2B.

TAX CALCULATION SERVICES FOR BUSINESSES

E-tailers face a bewildering patchwork of tax rules both nationally and internationally. The United States alone has over 30,000 taxing jurisdictions (Netcaucus.org 1998). In some cases, food and clothing are exempt from sales taxes. In others, one or the other, or both, are taxed or are taxed only up to some level. In Massachusetts, for example, articles of clothing are free from sales tax up to the first $175, but the value over $175 is taxed at 5 percent. In many states, there is a statewide sales tax plus local (city and/or county) sales taxes that range dramatically from one jurisdiction to another. For example, sales taxes in the Denver area vary from under 4 percent to over 8 percent. Global EC sales add significantly to the sales tax confusion. Currently, a temporary sales tax moratorium on Internet sales is in effect in the United States (see Chapter 17), but it applies only if the seller has no physical presence (a store, a factory, or a distribution center) in the state of the buyer. Noncompliance with sales tax collection regulations can lead to fines and penalties. To further complicate matters, the tax rules are dynamic, and most companies are not equipped to keep up with the hundreds of changes that can happen monthly.

In B2B, one also must differentiate between a tax on final products and a tax on raw materials or semifinished products. In many countries, such a distinction is made with a VAT (value-added tax).

To ease the problem of calculating taxes, both in B2B and in B2C, a business can use tax services (see the Real-World Case at the end of the chapter). Here are some sample services:

> ❱ **DPC.** This company (at salestax.com) licenses software that makes it simple to collect and report sales taxes. DPC promises that its software, which is updated monthly, reduces errors and puts its clients in compliance with the law. The company provides assistance with the integration of its databases into its client's systems, if necessary.

▶ **Sales Tax Clearinghouse (STC).** The STC has a free online sales tax calculator for the United States and Canada at thestc.com/ratecalc.stm. Its licensed software module allows a merchant's NT- or UNIX-based business system to connect to their server to calculate sales taxes and post transactions online in real time.

▶ **Taxware International.** This company (taxware.com) produces software that operates seamlessly with leading financial and accounting packages on multiple hardware platforms to accurately automate tax compliance. Its Sales/Use Tax System has a Product Taxability Matrix to ensure accurate tax calculation for all products sold on the Internet in all U.S. and Canadian tax jurisdictions. It also calculates European VAT and other tax rates around the world. This software can be integrated with the VERAZIP system, which matches state, zip code, city, and county information, to ensure that an address is correct so that the Sales/Use System is able to locate the correct taxing jurisdiction and tax rate.

Implementing Tax Collection in the United States

In 2001, four U.S. states (Kansas, Michigan, North Carolina, and Wisconsin) tested an Internet-based tax calculation and remission system using software and services from several vendors as a cost-effective way to manage the complexities of the evolving tax code. This Streamlined Sales Tax Project (SSTP) was designed to create uniformity in the way states administer sales and use taxes. The SSTP project involved tax collection and management software from Taxware.com, Vertex.com, and Esalestax.com that is being integrated by Pitney Bowes and HP. Merchants use the Internet to send sales transaction data in real time to any participating system.

The SSTP system works as follows: After a consumer initiates an online purchase, the e-business uses the Internet to access a trusted third-party tax service provider that calculates the tax on the purchase based on the locations of the buyer and the seller, as well as applicable state and local tax laws. The third party provides custom links, typically with XML, between its system and a commonly used ERP or EC platform, making it easier for retailers to connect to the system through the Internet.

For each client (business), the third party makes a single monthly or quarterly tax payment to each relevant government tax authority. The tax authority then securely accesses a database, managed by the third party over the Web, to examine the transaction data for tax compliance. The multistate approach—in which one or more third parties gets certified to manage tax compliance for businesses that choose to use the service rather than handle tax compliance alone—ultimately makes sense. Online merchants also save money because the service provider monitors changes in tax rules and updates its compliance database accordingly. See Tillett (2001) for additional information.

COMPREHENSIVE PAYMENT-RELATED SERVICES

Payment schemes are often supplemented by other services including verification, fraud prevention, and consulting. Insights and Additions 13.4 (page 522) discusses a variety of these comprehensive services available at CyberSource.

FINANCIAL SERVICES FOR B2B

B2B transactions may require additional financial services other than those for payments. Here are some examples of such services:

▶ **Credit reporting.** Companies such as Equifax have long served as independent sources of unbiased financial data. In the Internet economy, these firms deliver their data in machine-readable XML formats and tie them directly to digital certificates, as Dun & Bradstreet is doing with its alliance with VeriSign (Dun & Bradstreet 2003). In addition, eCredit.com offers a variety of services to business, including verification checks of customer data, automated credit analysis, and more.

▶ **Risk analysis and financial matching.** With many B2B transactions including a credit component, firms such as eCredit.com play a key role in the real-time selection of short-term financing. Using up-to-the-second data streams from information brokers, these new credit intermediaries connect sellers to institutions that will guarantee against financial loss.

Insights and Additions 13.4   CyberSource: A Comprehensive Payment Provider

CyberSource (*cybersource.com*) offers comprehensive e-payments and related services in the following categories:

▶ **Electronic payments.** Designed to enable both credit card and electronic check payments, CyberSource electronic payment solutions work effectively across multiple sales channels—including the Web, call center services, IVR systems, and POS scanners. CyberSources's business customers can manage payment processing systems in-house or outsource it, depending on their business needs. Complementary services include gift/prepaid certificates, tax calculation, payer authentication, and fraud screening.

▶ **Credit card fraud management.** CyberSource provides modular credit card fraud management solutions that effectively detect fraud and optimize operating efficiency in "card-not-present" sales operations; that is, those that take place over the Web, by call center, or via IVR. This modular approach allows users to implement a comprehensive risk management system or to start small with individual components. A unique relationship with Visa enhances fraud detection accuracy.

▶ **Verification and compliance services.** CyberSouce provides verification and compliance services that enable businesses to verify specific customer data during non-face-to-face transactions, use additional data points for fraud detection, and comply with government policies (regulatory compliance).

In addition, the company provides consultation and professional services. For details on these services and others, see *cybersource.com*.

Source: *cybersource.com* (2002).

▶ **Exchange insurance.** In any given vertical industry, only a few exchanges are likely to survive. To increase liquidity and help ensure their own survival, leading exchanges are beginning to offer complete transaction guarantees to their members by purchasing insurance from underwriters and absorbing the costs in their transaction fees.

Several other B2B financial services exist, one of which is shown in Insights and Additions 13.5.

Section 13.7 ▶ REVIEW

1. Describe the EC tax-calculation problem.
2. Describe possible solutions to the tax-collection problem.
3. Describe non-payment-related financial support services used in B2B.

Insights and Additions 13.5   Transaction-Based Financing at eRevenue.com

One company, eRevenue (*eRevenue.com*), provides a key service at a critical point in the procurement process—a transaction-based finance (TBF) solution for e-marketplaces. This solution enables sellers to make the decision to receive payment at the time of the transaction, without having to convince buyers to alter their payment cycles.

The service offered by eRevenue.com focuses on shortening cycle times in procuring goods and services. Financial incentives (more money in hand sooner) exist for buyers to shorten cycle times.

The company combines both front- and back-office operations, with credit administration delivered as a hosted service by ASPs. Getting away from the traditional batched-invoice financing model, eRevenue.com enables suppliers to exchange their invoices for funds at the time an online transaction occurs. Basically, eRevenue.com transmits to the selling company the funds from the transaction (less a commission) and takes on the collection of the funds and the financing of the aging invoices (those not paid within the month). As a result, eRevenue.com's solution integrates financing for accounts receivable directly into the buy/sell transaction process. The process is illustrated in Exhibit 13.13. For details, see Rosall and Alschuler (2000).

(continued)

Insights and Additions 13.5   (*continued*)

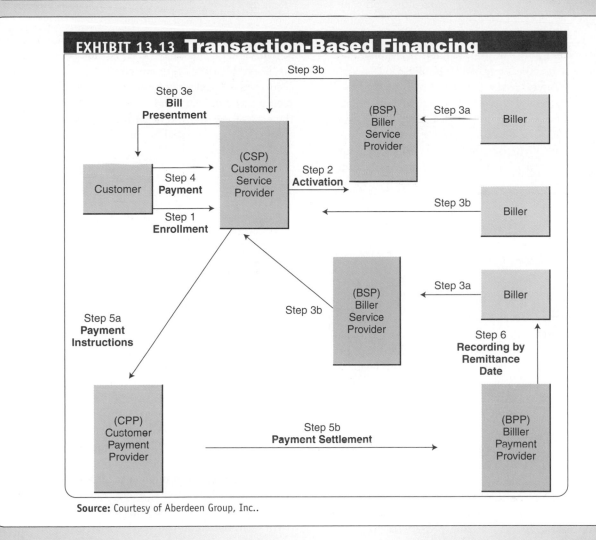

EXHIBIT 13.13 Transaction-Based Financing

Source: Courtesy of Aberdeen Group, Inc..

MANAGERIAL ISSUES

Some managerial issues related to this chapter are as follows.

1. **What B2C payment methods should we use?** Companies that only accept credit cards rule out a number of potential segments of buyers. Teenagers, non-U.S. customers, and customers who do not want to use credit cards online are examples of market segments that are unable or unwilling to use credit cards to make online purchases. E-cash, virtual credit cards, and stored-value cards are possible alternatives to credit cards. Also, when the purchase price is less than $10, credit cards are not a viable solution. Again, e-cash and stored-value cards are possibilities. Third-party companies such as PayPal also can handle payment transactions via secure e-mail. In all of these cases, merchants and other sellers need to be aware of

the volatility of the alternatives they are adopting and their true costs. Because the various alternatives do not yet enjoy widespread use, it is always possible that they will not exist tomorrow.

2. **What B2B payment methods should we use?** Keep an open mind about online alternatives. When it comes to paying suppliers or accepting payments from partners, most large businesses have opted to stick with the tried-and-true method of EFT over a financial EDI or with nonelectronic payments (e.g., checks). For MROs, consider using purchasing cards. For global trade, electronic letters of credit are popular. The use of e-checks is another area where costs savings

can accrue. Finally, innovative methods such as TradeCard can be very effective. With all of these methods, a key factor is determining how well they work with existing accounting and ordering systems and with business partners.

3. **Should we use an in-house payment mechanism or outsource it?** It takes time, skill, money, software, and hardware to integrate the payment systems of all the parties involved in processing any sort of e-payment. For this reason, even a business that runs its own EC site should consider outsourcing the e-payment component. Many third-party vendors provide payment gateways designed to handle the interactions among the various financial institutions that operate in the background of an e-payment system. Also, if a Web site is hosted by a third party (e.g., at Yahoo Store), an e-payment service will be provided.

4. **How secure are e-payments?** Security continues to be a major issue in making and accepting e-payments of all kinds. Measures that are employed to ensure the security of e-payments have to be part of a broader security scheme that weighs risks against issues such as the ease of use and the fit within the overall business context. Generally speaking, most e-payment systems are sufficiently secure.

SUMMARY

In this chapter, you learned about the following EC issues as they relate to the learning objectives.

1. **Crucial factors determining the success of an e-payment method.** For success, an e-payment method should require little specialized hardware or software, integrate well with existing EC and legacy systems, offer security, maintain the anonymity of the buyer and seller, support products and services with varying prices, be easy to use, and cost little for both the buyer and seller to use.

2. **Online credit card players and processes.** Credit cards dominate the online B2C world in the United States and a few other countries. The players in online credit cards are the same as they are in the off-line world: cardholders, merchants, card issuers (institutions that establish the cardholder's account, e.g., Visa), regulators, and the ACH. The process is done all online.

3. **Categories and potential uses of smart cards.** Smart cards look like credit cards but contain embedded chips for manipulating data and large memory capacity. Cards that contain microprocessor chips can be programmed to handle a wide variety of tasks. Other cards have memory chips to which data can be written and from which data can be read. Most memory cards are disposable, but others—smart cards—can hold large amounts of data and are rechargeable. Smart cards have been and will be used for a number of purposes, including generating loyalty among shoppers (loyalty cards), holding e-cash, ensuring secure payment card usage, maintaining health and social welfare records, paying for mass transit services, and identifying the cardholder (e.g., holding driver's licenses and immigration status).

4. **Online alternatives to credit card payments.** When an item or service being sold costs less than $10, credit cards are too costly. In such micropayment situations, various other payment methods can come into play: e-cash loaded to stored-value cards (smart cards with e-cash), specialized electronic script, or e-rewards such as MyPoints. These alternatives can also serve certain market segments (e.g., teenagers) that do not have their own credit cards but still want to make online purchases. Some buyers simply do not trust using their credit cards online. In this instance, special systems allow a consumer to set up accounts that assign a special name and number that can be used in place of the consumer's own credit card number. Finally, in some cases, sellers and buyers cannot process credit cards or smart cards. A number of alternatives for such situations, such as PayPal, have been established to handle P2P transactions and transactions between parties without credit cards.

5. **E-check processes and involved parties.** E-checks are the electronic equivalent of paper checks. E-checks are employed in situations where consumers do not want to use their credit cards, in B2B EC, and in cases when the payments are too large for credit cards. E-checks are handled in much the same way as paper checks, but are processed electronically in 2 days or less. When e-checks are used by a business to pay suppliers, more stringent security is required because of the size of the payments and the sensitivity of the information. The eCheck Consortium has been working on establishing standards for these larger payments. These standards are currently being tested by professional organizations and the U.S. Treasury.

6. **Payment methods in B2B, including global trade.** Purchasing cards are special-purpose charge cards issued to employees solely for purchasing low-cost, nonstrategic goods and services up to a certain limit. Use of these cards substantially reduces the paperwork and cycle time associated with such purchases. They are used off-line and online. Large payments are made by e-checks, EFT,

or letters of credit. For SMEs, special mechanisms such as those offered by TradeCard are gaining acceptance.

7. **Bill presentment and payment.** Paying bills online is becoming more popular, saving time for busy people and money for the billers. A bill is presented to the customer, who reviews the bill and approves payment. Bills can be paid one at a time or several can be paid at once (through a bill consolidator). In some places, bills can be paid from ATMs as well. Advertising can be attached to online bill presentments.

8. **Special payment methods.** One of the many topics related to electronic payment methods is the issue of taxation. In some cases, EC transactions are not taxed, however, in other cases there may be a tax. Several companies provide help to vendors in calculating the appropriate tax for the taxing jurisdiction(s) involved. Also important are financial services that support e-payments (e.g., verification, compliance, credit ratings, and transaction insurance). Some of these are critical for global trade.

KEY TERMS

Automated Clearing House (ACH)	495	E-payments	493	Person-to-person (P2P) payments 507
Contact card	501	Electronic script	506	Presentment	517
Contactless (proximity) card	501	Electronic wallet (e-wallet)	499	Purchasing card	511
Credit card gateway	497	Letter of credit (LC)	515	Smart card	501
Digital identity (digital ID)	499	Micropayments	504	Stored-value card	502
E-cash	504	Mondex	505	Virtual credit card	498
E-check	509	Payment card	497	Visa Cash	505

DISCUSSION QUESTIONS

1. Credit cards were able to overcome the "chicken-and-egg" problem with regard to online payments. However, to date, various e-cash methods have failed. What are some of the reasons for their failures? What does an e-cash company need to do to break the barrier?

2. A small business owner wants to sell handcrafted jewelry to teenagers on the Web. What methods of e-payment would you recommend that the owner accept and why?

3. Recently, a merchant who accepts online credit card payments has experienced a wave of fraudulent purchases. What sorts of security measures can the merchant impose without hindering legitimate customers?

4. You receive an online e-check. What security methods can be used to ensure the identity of the sender? (Consult Chapter 12 for information on PKI.)

5. You invite a group of friends to lunch. At the end of lunch, you pick up the check and your friends agree to repay you later. How could they pay you online?

6. Compare solutions such as PayPal to InternetCash.

7. How would you suggest a furniture company pay its online office-supply vendor? What about the supplier of wood? Also, the company exports products to several countries using an online ordering system. How should overseas buyers pay?

8. Discuss the workflow of B2B payments. Visit surepay.com for hints. Relate this workflow to e-procurement.

INTERNET EXERCISES

1. Visit verisign.com and take the guided tour of e-payment processing solutions. While at VeriSign, sign up for a digital ID that can be used with e-mail. Use the ID to encrypt and e-mail a message to your instructor.

2. Go to checkfree.com and run the e-billing demo. Check the "Pay Everyone" and other services. What features and functions does CheckFree provide? Would you use the service? Why or why not?

3. Go to the RocketCash site (rocket cash.com). What is RocketCash? What is RocketFuel? Approximately how many stores accept RocketCash? What types of stores are they and to whom do they cater?

4. Visit the following Web sites: toysrus.com, kbkids.com, amazon.com, lego.com, and dogtoys.com. Find out

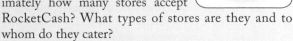

what payment options are offered by each company. Then examine payment options offered by starbucks.com and carsdirect.com. Prepare a report based on your findings.

5. Enter tradecard.com. Review a demo or a video Webcast about the process. Summarize the process and the benefits of the service to a small exporter.

6. Enter projectliberty.com and passport.net/Consumer. Compare the two products (also see Costa 2002). Write a report.

7. Enter paypal.com and c2it.com and compare their modes of operations. What do you like and dislike about each service?

8. Enter gemplus.com and identify the smart-card-based applications. Prepare a list of applications not cited in the text.

9. Visit qpass.com and identify the services offered by the company.

10. Visit firstdata.com. Identify all the services they provide for B2B payments. Examine the nature of their partners. Write a report. Compare its services to those offered by surepay.com.

11. Enter checkagain.com. Review the services offered. Use a calculator to calculate savings in a scenario that you create.

TEAM ASSIGNMENTS AND ROLE PLAYING

1. Select some B2C sites that cater to teens (e.g., alloy.com) and some that cater to older consumers (e.g., seniorcitizens.com and snow-bird.net). Have team members visit these sites. What types of e-payment methods do they provide? Are there any differences among the methods used on different types of sites? What other types of e-payment would you recommend for the various sites and why?

2. Organize teams to explore successful smart card applications by application area and/or country. Prepare a report.

3. Have one team represent Mondex and another represent Visa Cash. The task of each team is to convince a company that their product is superior.

4. Have each team member interview three to five people who have made a purchase or sold an item at auction over the Internet. Find out how they paid. What security and privacy concerns did they have regarding the payment? Is there an ideal payment method?

REAL-WORLD CASE

GUESS OVERCOMES ONLINE FRAUD

GUESS? is a well-recognized fashion brand name. The company decided in 1999 to bring its jeans, apparel, and fashion accessories to customers via the Internet. At first, the launch of GUESS.com (*guess.com*) was a big success. However, the online store soon caught the attention of cyber thieves, and GUESS, Inc. became a victim of online fraud. The thieves used stolen credit card numbers to order goods. As indicated earlier in the chapter, the loss in such cases is that of the merchant. The number of fraudulent orders increased rapidly, causing the company to experience heavy losses.

The solution was found in CyberSource's Internet Fraud Screen (IFS), which is combined with Visa screens of EC transactions. Here is how the system works:

▷ When a customer places an order, the request for a credit card authorization is securely transmitted, in real time, from GUESS's server to CyberSource's data center via the Internet.

▷ From there the request is routed to the appropriate payment processor (bank) and an authorization (or decline) is returned within a few seconds to GUESS.com's server.

▷ At the same time, CyberSource's IFS examines 150 different factors and calculates the risk of fraud in the requested purchase. The 150 factors include unique Internet order variables and other transaction characteristics, leveraging Visa's fraud modeling expertise and CyberSource's Internet fraud reduction experience and historical transaction database.

▷ Each transaction receives a score that assesses the likelihood of fraud (risk factor).

▷ GUESS's decision support system (DSS) then makes a decision: to approve or reject the customer's request.

In a short time GUESS was able to reduce the incidence of fraudulent transactions dramatically. Both GUESS and its customers were happy. In addition to fraud reduction, GUESS enjoys other payment support services from CyberSource. For example:

- A calculator enables multicurrency payments in real time with conversion to 170 currencies worldwide. This enables GUESS to sell online in the international market. Since the introduction of the multicurrency systems, global sales have mushroomed.

- A tax-calculation service supports the thousands of ever-changing tax jurisdictions in 18 countries. The calculations are performed in real time as well, so buyers know exactly what price, including the value-added tax, they will pay.

- The Policy Compliance services help Guess.com to comply with foreign government regulations and with policies of corporate business partners and service providers worldwide. Using intelligent systems, the Web site validates buyers' information in foreign countries in seconds.

- High-volume transactions are processed in seconds with a reliability of 99.98 percent uptime. Response time takes only up to 3 seconds—even during peak sales periods.

The biggest advantage of such financial services is recognized during peak demand, especially during the holiday season.

Sources: Compiled from *cybersource.com* (1999) and *guess.com* (press releases 2000–2002).

Questions

1. This system is used for online credit card payments. Can it be used for other e-payment methods? Explain.

2. What are the advantages of such a system for GUESS?

3. Review the benefits for international export.

4. Relate this case to the opening case of this chapter. Do you think that this solution could be applied to LensDoc's problem? Why or why not?

REFERENCES

91expresslanes.com, 2002 (accessed June 2003).

americanexpress.com (accessed June 2003).

American Express. "Corporate Purchasing Solutions." americanexpress.com/taiwan/corporateservices/en/purchasing/default.asp (accessed April 2003).

Angwin, J. "And How Will You Pay For That?" Special e-commerce report, *Wall Street Journal Europe*, October 23, 2000a, fininter.net/payments/pmnt_systems.htm (accessed June 2003).

Angwin, J. "Credit-Card Scams Bedevil E-Stores." *Wall Street Journal*, September 19, 2000b.

Authorizenet. "eCheck.net." authorizenet.com/solutions/echeck.php (accessed June 2003).

Bankrate.com. "Comparing Virtual Credit Cards." bankrate.com/brm/news/cc/20021011b.asp (accessed December 2002).

Borths, R., and D. Young. "E-Billing, Today and Beyond." *Information Strategy: The Executive's Journal* (Winter 2000).

Carr, J. "The Problem with Plastic." *eCommerce Business*, December 2000.

Cassy, J. "No Just Rewards in E-Heaven." *Business 2.0*, November 2000.

Caswell, S. "Credit Card Fraud Crippling Online Merchants." *E-Commerce Times*, March 2000.

CIO Magazine. Advertising supplement. *CIO Magazine*, July 1999.

CIO Forum. "CIO Forum Financial Services 2003 e-letter." no. 59, June 19, 2002, cioforum.com/newsletter/cnews59.asp (accessed April 2003).

clareon.com, 2002 (accessed April 2003).

Cornwell, A. "Commerce Service Providers and Future Internet Payment Methods." *World Market Series Business Briefings*, 2000, wmrc.com (accessed May 2001).

Costa, D. "Identity Crisis (Digital IDs)." *PC Magazine*, October 18, 2002.

Cybersource. "An Electronic Citadel." White paper, 2002, cybersource.com/resources/collateral/pdf/ecitadel.pdf (accessed May 2003).

Cybersource.com. "GUESS? Gives Internet Credit Card Fraud the Boot." September 23, 1999, cybersource.com/news_and_events/archive/view.xml?page_id=145 (accessed June 2003).

Cyota. "Cyota's SecureClick Allows Customers to Shop Without Revealing Their Credit Card Number." Press release May 16, 2000, cyota.com/viewReleases.cfm?id=30 (accessed May 2003).

Datastar Group. "Project 3: Online Fraud Protection." Fall 2001, 129.118.49.94/Fall2001/6341/datastar/project3.htm (accessed April 2003).

Deitel, H., et al. *Wireless Internet and Mobile Business.* Upper Saddle River, NJ: Prentice Hall, 2002.

Dell Computer. "Services Portfolio Summary." dell.com/us/en/esg/services/service_servicesportfolio.htm (accessed May 2003).

Donahue, S. "Paper Chase." *Business 2.com*, November 14, 2000.

dot.ca.gov/fastrack/ (April 2002).

Dun & Bradstreet. "D & B and VeriSign: The Alliance Today." dnb.com/US/alliances/verisign/index.asp?link=verisign (accessed April 2003).

Duvall, M. "Retailers Predict Increased Credit Card Theft." *Interactive Week*, November 2000.

Ebilling.org. "Building the EBPP Business Case." ebilling.org/EBPP/20 (accessed May 2003).

echecksecure.com (accessed September 2002).

Electronic Check Clearing House Organization. "Managing Value in the Transition to Electronic Payments: Executive Summary." April 11, 2002, eccho.com/eccho_vision.html (accessed May 2003).

Evans, D., and R. Schmalensee. *Playing with Plastic: The Digital Revolution in Buying and Borrowing*. Cambridge, MA: MIT Press, 2000.

Gazala, M., and A. Shepard. "Credit Card Security Fears Wane." Forrester Research, September 1999, forrester.com (accessed August 2001).

guess.com, press releases 2000–2002 (accessed June 2003).

Hewlett-Packard. "Making B2B E-Commerce a Reality." myfsi.hp.com/magazine/wf11_1/b2b.asp (accessed April 2003).

Hp.com. "HP Closes the Payment Gap in B2B e-Commerce." November 28, 2000, hp.com/hpinfo/newsroom/press/2000/001128a.html (accessed June 2003).

Jilovec, N. *E-Business: Thriving in the Electronic Marketplace*. Loveland, CO: 29th Street Press, 1999.

Jin, L., et al. "Research on WAP Clients Supports SET Payment Protocol." *IEEE Wireless Communications* 9, no. 1, February (2002).

Kane, M. "E-Wallets Get a Boost from Amazon." *CNET News.com*, August 28, 2002, news.com.com/2100-1017-955420.html (accessed May 2003).

Keen, P., et al. *Electronic Commerce Relationships: Trust by Design*. Upper Saddle River, NJ: Prentice Hall, 2000.

Korper, S., and J. Ellis. *The E-Commerce Book: Building the Empire*. New York: Academic Press, 2000.

Kurant.com. "PayPal," kurant.com/partner/channel-technology.shtml (accessed May 2003).

Lanford, A. and J. Lanford. Internet ScamBusters, #40. web.trytel.com/at_work/press/press_scamb.php3 (accessed June 2003).

lensdoc.com (accessed June 2003).

Litan, A. "E-Payment 2004: Empowered E-Agents." Research note, *Gartner Interactive*, June 27, 2002.

Merchant Fraud Squad. "MerchantFraudSquad.com Releases Free Fraud Prevention Tools, New Research." Press release, April 9, 2002, merchantfraudsquad.com/pages/release_040902.html (accessed April 2003).

mondexphil.com/worldwide/asia.html (accessed June 2003).

National Association of Purchasing Card Professionals. napcp.org/napcp.nsf/NavigationAll/P-Card+Basics+-+Participants?OpenDocument Page (accessed May 2003).

NetCaucus.org. "Internet Taxation: Can More Than 30,000 Taxing Jurisdictions Impose Taxes on the Internet?" March 27, 1998, netcaucus.org/events/1998/taxation (accessed April 2003).

O'Donnell, M. "What You Really Need to Know About B2B." *Workz.com*, workz.com/cgi-bin/gt/tpl_page.html,template=1&content=1415&nav1=1& (accessed May 2003).

orbiscom.com (accessed April 2003).

paypal.com (accessed May 2003).

Poon, S., and P. Y. K. Chan. "Octopus: The Growing e-Payment System in Hong Kong." *Electronic Markets* 11, no. 2 (2001).

Reda, S. "Online Check Service Expands Internet Payment Options." *Stores*, February 2002.

Rosall, J., and D. Alschuler. "eRevenue, Inc.: The Case for Supplier Financing e-Services." Aberdeen Group, November 2000, aberdeen.com/ab%5Fabstracts/2000/12/12002083.htm (accessed May 2003).

Rosenbaum, D. "Passport Purchasing." *PC Magazine* January 29, 2002.

Shelfer, K. M., and J. D. Procaccino. "Smart Card Evolution." *Communications of the ACM* 45, no. 7, July (2002).

Shesney, G. "Process Online Payments Quickly and Effectively." *e-Business Advisor*, June 2000.

Sorenson, D. "Smart-Card Devices and Applications." 2001, dell.com/downloads/global/vectors/smartcards.pdf (accessed May 2003).

Tillett, S. "States Test Systems for E-Comm Taxation." *InternetWeek*, January 16, 2001, internetweek.com/newslead01/lead011601.htm (accessed May 2003).

TradeCard. "Financial Supply Chain Automation: The Missing Link in Supply Chain Management." White paper, 2001.

TradeCard. "TAL Apparel Takes Online Goods to the Next Stage with Tradecard." Tradecard.com, 2003, tradecard.com/resources/pressReleases/tal.html (accessed August 2003).

troygroup.com/financial/echecksecure/products/makingitwork.asp (accessed May 2003).

Turban, E., and J. Brahm. "Smart Card-Based Electronic Card Payment Systems in the Transportation Industry." *Journal of Organizational Computing and Electronic Commerce* 10, no. 4 (2000).

Vigoroso, M. W. "Beenz.com Closes Internet Currency Business." *Ecommerce Times*, August 17, 2001, ecommercetimes.com/perl/story/12892.html (accessed May 2003).

CHAPTER 14

ORDER FULFILLMENT, CONTENT MANAGEMENT, AND OTHER SUPPORT SERVICES

Content

Learning objectives

Upon completion of this chapter, you will be able to:

1. Describe the role of support services in EC.
2. Define EC order fulfillment and describe its process.
3. Describe the major problems of EC order fulfillment.
4. Describe various solutions to EC order fulfillment problems.
5. Describe content issues and management of EC sites.
6. Describe other EC support services.
7. Discuss the drivers of outsourcing support services and the use of ASPs.

HOW BIKEWORLD FULFILLS ORDERS

The Problem

BikeWorld, based in San Antonio, Texas, is known for its high-quality bicycles and components, expert advice, and personalized service. The company opened its Web site (*bikeworld.com*) in February 1996, hoping it would keep customers from using out-of-state mail-order houses. The Web represented a 24-hour global retail space where small companies such as BikeWorld, with its 16 employees, had the same reach and potential for success as much larger ones.

BikeWorld encountered one of the Internet retailing's biggest problems: fulfillment and after-sale customer service. Sales of its high-value bike accessories over the Internet steadily increased, including in global markets, but the time spent processing orders, manually shipping packages, and responding to customers' order status inquiries were overwhelming for the small company.

The Solution

BikeWorld decided to outsource its order fulfillment to FedEx. FedEx offered reasonably priced quality express delivery, exceeding customer expectations while automating the fulfillment process. "To go from a complete unknown to a reputable worldwide retailer was going to require more than a fair price. We set out to absolutely amaze our customers with unprecedented customer service. FedEx gave us the blinding speed we needed," says Whit Snell, BikeWorld's founder.

Exhibit 14.1 (page 531) shows the five steps in BikeWorld's order fulfillment process.

The Results

Four years after venturing online, BikeWorld's sales volume has more than quadrupled, and the company was on track to surpass $6 million in 2000. The company is consistently profitable. It has a fully automated and scalable fulfillment system; access to real-time order status, enhancing customer service and leading to greater customer retention; and is able to service customers around the globe.

Source: Compiled from FedEx (2000).

WHAT WE CAN LEARN . . .

Like many other e-tailers, BikeWorld had neither the experience nor the resources to fulfill the orders it generated online. Its solution was to outsource the job to FedEx, a major EC logistics company. Outsourcing and order fulfillment options are presented in this chapter. Order fulfillment is only one support service required in e-commerce, others are payment (already discussed in Chapter 13), content management, consulting services, and several others discussed in this chapter.

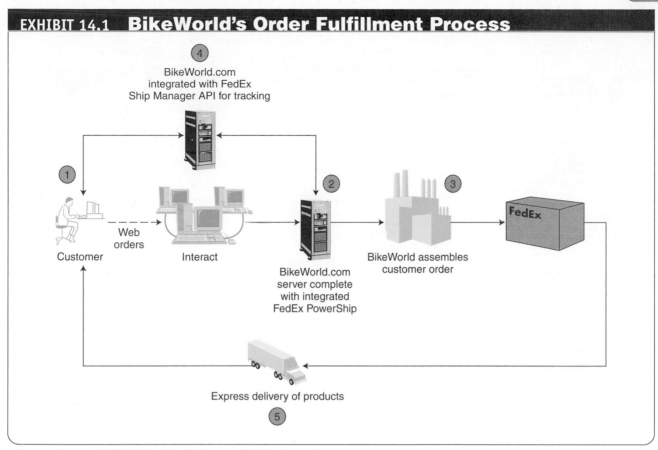

EXHIBIT 14.1   BikeWorld's Order Fulfillment Process

14.1 ORDER FULFILLMENT AND LOGISTICS— AN OVERVIEW

The implementation of most EC applications requires the use of support services. The most obvious support services are payments (Chapter 13), security (Chapter 12), infrastructure and technology (Online Chapter 18), and order fulfillment and logistics (this chapter). Most of the services described in these later chapters are relevant for both B2C and B2B. The major services described in these chapters are summarized in Exhibit 14.2 (page 532) which organizes services into the following categories suggested by the Delphi Group (delphigroup.com): e-infrastructure, e-process, e-markets, e-content, e-communities, and e-services. The exhibit shows representative topics in each category. This section of the chapter gives an overview of order fulfillment and logistics.

Taking orders over the Internet could well be the easy part of B2C. Fulfillment and delivery to customers' doors are the sticky parts (e.g., see Lee and Whang 2001; Bhise et al. 2000). As a matter of fact, many e-tailers have experienced fulfillment problems since they started EC. Amazon.com, for example, which initially operated as a totally virtual company, added physical warehouses with thousands of employees in order to expedite deliveries and reduce order fulfillment costs.

Several factors can be responsible for delays in deliveries. They range from an inability to accurately forecast demand to ineffective e-tailing supply chains. Several such problems also exist in off-line businesses. One factor typical to EC is that EC is based on the concept of "pull" operations that begin with an order, frequently a customized one. This is in contrast with traditional retailing, which usually begins with a production to inventory that is then "pushed" to customers (see Exhibit 2A.1 on page 79). In the pull case, it is more difficult to forecast demand because of lack of experience and changing consumer tastes. Another delay factor is that in a B2C pull model, many small orders needed to be delivered to the customer's

EXHIBIT 14.2   E-Commerce Services

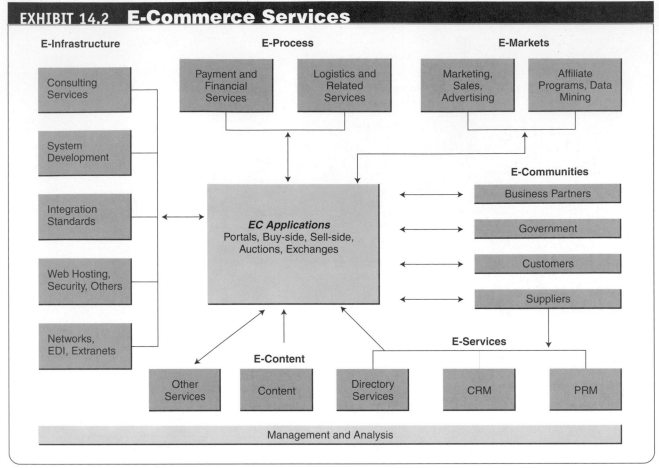

Source: Adapted from Choi et al. (1997), p. 18.

order fulfillment
All the activities needed to provide customers with ordered goods and services, including related customer services.

back-office operations
The activities that support fulfillment of sales, such as accounting and logistics.

front-office operations
The business processes, such as sales and advertising, that are visible to customers.

logistics
The operations involved in the efficient and effective flow and storage of goods, services, and related information from point of origin to point of consumption.

door, whereas in brick-and-mortar retailing, the goods are shipped in large quantities to retail stores where they are picked up by customers.

Before we analyze the order fulfillment problems and describe some solutions, we need to introduce some basic concepts relating to order fulfillment and logistics.

OVERVIEW OF ORDER FULFILLMENT

Order fulfillment refers not only to providing customers with what they ordered and doing it on time, but also to providing all related customer services. For example, a customer must receive assembly and operation instructions with a new appliance. This can be done by including a paper document with the product or by providing the instructions on the Web. (A nice example of this is available at livemanuals.com.) In addition, if the customer is not happy with a product, an exchange or return must be arranged.

Order fulfillment is basically a part of the back-office operations, which are the activities that support the fulfillment of orders, such as accounting, inventory management, and shipping. It is also strongly related to the front-office operations, which are activities, such as sales and advertising, that are visible to customers. Order fulfillment is a part of the logistics system (see Bayles 2001).

OVERVIEW OF LOGISTICS

Logistics is defined by the Council of Logistics Management as "the process of planning, implementing, and controlling the efficient and effective flow and storage of goods, services, and related information from point of origin to point of consumption for the purpose of conforming to customer requirements" (Council of Logistics Management 2003). Note that this definition includes inbound, outbound, internal, and external movement and return of materials and goods.

It also includes *order fulfillment*. However, the distinction between logistics and order fulfillment is not always clear, and the terms are sometimes used interchangeably, as we do in this text.

Obviously, the key aspects of order fulfillment are delivery of materials or services at the right time, to the right place, and at the right cost.

THE EC ORDER FULFILLMENT PROCESS

In order to understand why there are problems in order fulfillment, it is beneficial to look at a typical EC fulfillment process, as shown in Exhibit 14.3. The process starts on the left when an order is received. Several activities take place, some of which can be done simultaneously; others must be done in sequence. These activities include the following:

1. **Making sure the customer will pay.** Depending on the payment method and prior arrangements, the validity of each payment must be determined. This activity may be done in B2B by the company's finance department or financial institution (i.e., a bank or a credit card issuer such as Visa). Any holdup may cause a shipment to be delayed, resulting in a loss of goodwill or a customer.

2. **Checking for in-stock availability.** Regardless of whether the vendor is a manufacturer or a retailer, as soon as an order is received, an inquiry needs to be made regarding stock availability. Several scenarios are possible here that may involve the material management and production departments, as well as outside suppliers and warehouse facilities. In this step, the order information needs to be connected to the information about in-stock inventory availability.

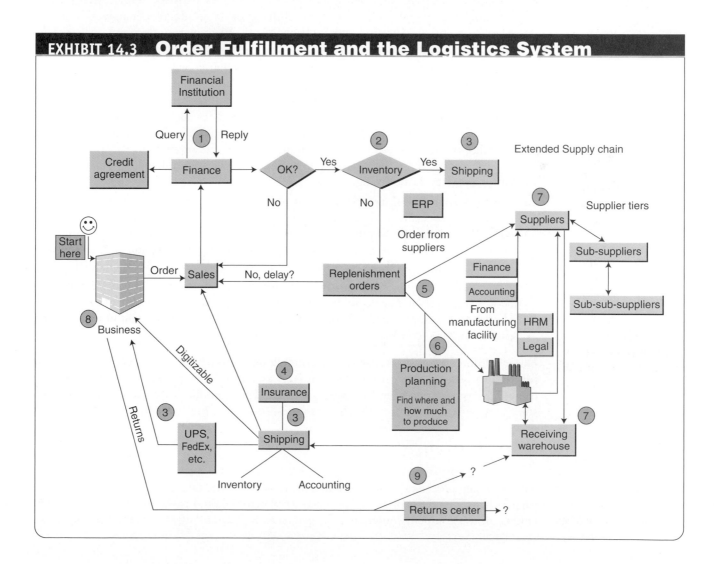

EXHIBIT 14.3 Order Fulfillment and the Logistics System

3. **Arranging shipments.** If the product is available, it can be shipped to the customer (otherwise, go to step 5). Products can be digital or physical. If the item is physical and it is readily available, packaging and shipment arrangements need to be made. Both the packaging/shipping department and internal shippers or outside transporters may be involved. Digital items are usually available because their "inventory" is not depleted. However, a digital product, such as software, may be under revision, and thus unavailable for delivery at certain times. In either case, information needs to flow among several partners.

4. **Insurance.** Sometimes the contents of a shipment need to be insured. Both the finance department and an insurance company could be involved, and again, information needs to flow frequently not only inside the company, but also to and from the customer and insurance agent.

5. **Production.** Customized orders will always trigger a need for some manufacturing or assembly operation. Similarly, if standard items are out of stock, they need to be produced or procured. Production can be done in-house or by contractors. In-house production needs to be planned. Production planning involves people, machines, financial resources, and possibly suppliers and subcontractors. Manufacturing involves the acquisition of materials and components. The suppliers may have their own suppliers. The actual production facilities may be in a different country from where the company's headquarters or retailers are. This may further complicate the flow of information and communication.

6. **Plant services.** In the case of assembly and/or manufacturing, several plant services may be needed, including possible collaboration with business partners. Services may include scheduling of people and equipment, shifting other products' plans, working with engineering on modifications, getting equipment, and content preparation.

7. **Purchasing and warehousing.** If the seller is a retailer, such as in the case of amazon.com or walmart.com, the retailer must purchase products from manufacturers. Several scenarios may exist. Purchased items can be stocked in warehouses, which is what Amazon.com does with its best-selling books. However, Amazon.com does not stock books for which only a few orders are received. In such cases, special deliveries from the publishers or intermediaries must be made. This also requires appropriate receiving and quality assurance of incoming materials and products.

   Once production (step 5) or purchasing (step 7) is completed, shipments to the customers (step 3) are arranged.

8. **Contacts with customers.** Sales representatives need to keep in constant touch with customers, especially in B2B, starting with notification of orders received and ending with notification of a shipment or change in delivery date. These contacts are usually done via e-mail, and are frequently generated automatically. Customer service includes many of the activities described in Chapter 4 and in Insights and Additions 14.1.

9. **Returns.** In some cases, customers want to exchange or return items. Such returns can be a major problem, as up to 30 percent of all items purchased electronically in the United States are returned to vendors (see Bayles 2001). The movement of returns from customers back to vendors is called reverse logistics.

reverse logistics
The movement of returns from customers to vendors.

Order fulfillment processes may vary, depending on the product and the vendor. The order fulfillment process also differs between B2B and B2C activities, between the delivery of goods and of services, and between small and large products. Furthermore, additional steps may be required in certain circumstances, such as in the case of perishable materials or foods.

Order Fulfillment and the Supply Chain

The nine-step processes of order fulfillment, as well as order taking, are integral parts of the supply chain. The flows of orders, payments, and materials and parts need to be coordinated among all the company's internal participants, as well as among the external partners (see

Insights and Additions 14.1   What Services Do Customers Need?

Bayles (2001) provides the following insights on online customer services, which are based on Forrester Research studies (1999–2001):

▶ **Customer preferences.** Customers tend not to do much self-service in terms of getting information from companies (e.g., only 19 percent use FAQs), so they require attention. As more companies offer online self-service, though, this situation is changing. When contacting companies for information, customers use e-mail more than the telephone (71 percent vs. 51 percent).

▶ **Types of service.** Four types of service exist, based on where the customer is in the purchase experience: *during shopping* (search products, compare, find product attributes); *during buying* (questions on warranties, billing, receipt, payment); *after the order is placed* (checking status in processing and in shipment); and *after the item is received* (checking return procedures, how to use the items).

▶ **Problem resolution.** Customers expect problems to be solved quickly and to their satisfaction. Easy returns and order tracking are desirable.

▶ **Shipping options.** Several shipping options are needed.

▶ **Fraud protection.** Customers need to make sure that they are not going to be cheated by the sellers or others.

▶ **Order status tracking, order status, and updates.** Customers want to have some way to check on the status of their order, either by phone or online. These services are highly desired, including order notification and a clear return policy.

▶ **Developing customer relationships.** This includes building trust, providing security, and ensuring privacy protection (see Chapters 4, 12, and 17).

For details on these and more services see Bayles (2001) and *bayles.com*.

Bayles 2001). The principles of SCM (Online Tutorial T3 and Handfield et al. 2002) must be considered when planning and managing the order fulfillment process.

Traditional Versus EC Logistics

EC logistics, or e-logistics, refers to the logistics of EC systems. The major difference between e-logistics and traditional logistics is that the latter deals with movement of large amounts of materials to a few destinations (e.g., to retail stores). E-logistics shipments typically are small parcels sent to many customers' homes. Other differences are shown in Exhibit 14.4.

e-logistics
The logistics of EC systems, typically involving small parcels sent to many customers' homes.

EXHIBIT 14.4   How E-Logistics Differs from Traditional Logistics

Characteristic	Traditional Logistics	EC Logistics
Type	Bulk, large volume	Small, parcel
Destinations	Few, concentrated in one area	Large number, highly dispersed
Demand type	Push	Pull
Value of shipment	Very large, usually more than $1,000	Very small, frequently less than $100
Nature of demand	Stable, consistent	Seasonal (holiday season), fragmented
Customers	Business partners (in B2B), usually regular (B2C), not many	Usually unknown B2C, many
Inventory order flow	Usually unidirectional	Usually bidirectional
Accountability	One link	Through the entire supply chain
Transporter	Frequently the company, sometimes outsourced	Usually outsourced, sometimes the company
Warehouse	Common	Only very large shippers (e.g., *amazon.com*) or moving companies (UPS, FedEx)

Section 14.1 ▶ REVIEW

1. Define order fulfillment and logistics.
2. List the nine steps of the order fulfillment process.
3. Compare logistics with reverse logistics.
4. Compare traditional logistics with e-logistics.

14.2 PROBLEMS IN ORDER FULFILLMENT

During the 1999 holiday season, the B2C e-tailers, especially those that sold toys, were plagued with logistics problems. Price wars boosted demand, and neither the e-tailers nor the manufacturers were ready for it. As a result, supplies were late in coming from manufacturers. Toys R Us, for example, had to stop taking orders around December 14. The manufacturers, warehouses, and distribution channels were not in sync with the e-tailers. As a result, many customers did not get their holiday gifts on time. (For more on the order fulfillment troubles experienced by Toys R Us, see Chapter 3 and Insights and Additions W14.1 at the book's Web site.)

TYPICAL SUPPLY CHAIN PROBLEMS

The inability to deliver products on time is a typical problem in both off-line and online commerce. Several other problems have been observed along the supply chain: Some companies grapple with high inventory costs; quality problems exist due to misunderstandings; shipments of wrong products, materials, and parts occur frequently; and the cost to expedite operations or shipments is high. The chance that such problems will occur in EC is even higher due to the lack of appropriate infrastructure and e-tailing experience, as well as the special characteristics of EC. For example, most manufacturers or distributors' warehouses are designed to ship large quantities to several stores; they cannot optimally pack and ship many small packages to many customers' doors. Improper inventory levels are typical in EC, as are poor delivery scheduling and mixed-up warehousing.

Another major activity related to the supply chain problem is the difficulties in *demand forecasting*. In the case of noncustomized items, such as toys, a demand forecast must be done in order to determine appropriate inventories of finished goods at various points in the supply chain. Such a forecast is difficult in the fast-growing field of ordering online. In the case of customized products, it is necessary to forecast the demand for the components and materials required for fulfilling customized orders. Demand forecasting must be done with business partners along the supply chain, as was described in Chapter 8. Supply chain problems jeopardize order fulfillment.

Why Supply Chains Problems Exist

Many problems along the EC supply chain stem from *uncertainties* and from the need to *coordinate* several activities, internal units, and business partners.

A major source of the uncertainties in EC, as noted earlier, is the demand forecast. Demand is influenced by factors such as consumer behavior, economic conditions, competition, prices, weather conditions, technological developments, consumer confidence, and more. Any one of these factors may change quickly. The demand forecast should be conducted frequently, in conjunction with collaborating business partners along the supply chain, in order to correctly gauge demand and make plans to meet it. As was shown in Chapter 8, companies attempt to achieve accurate demand forecasts by methods such as information sharing in collaborative commerce.

Other uncertainties that lead to supply chain and order fulfillment problems are variable delivery times, which depend on many factors ranging from machine failures to road conditions; quality problems of materials and parts, which may create production time delays; and labor troubles (such as strikes), which may interfere with shipments.

Pure EC companies are likely to have more problems because they do not have a logistics infrastructure already in place and thus are forced to use external logistics services rather than in-house departments for these functions. These external logistics services are often called **third-party logistics (3PL) suppliers** or *logistics service providers*. Outsourcing such services can be expensive, and it requires more coordination and dependence on outsiders who may not be reliable. For this reason, large virtual retailers such as Amazon.com are developing their own physical warehouses and logistics systems. Other virtual retailers are creating strategic alliances with logistics companies or with experienced mail-order companies that have their own logistics systems.

In addition to uncertainties, EC supply chain/fulfillment problems are also created by lack of coordination and inability or refusal to share information among business partners. One of the most persistent order fulfillment problems is the bullwhip effect (see Chapter 8).

EC (and IT) can provide solutions to these order fulfillment problems, as will be shown in the next section.

**third-party logistics
(3PL) suppliers**
External, rather than in-house, providers of logistics services.

Section 14.2 ▶ REVIEW

1. Describe the order fulfillment problem of the 1999 holiday season.
2. List some problems along the EC supply chain.
3. Explain how uncertainties create order fulfillment problems. List some of these problems

14.3 SOLUTIONS TO ORDER FULFILLMENT PROBLEMS

Many EC logistics problems are generic; they can be found in the non-Internet world as well. Therefore, many of the solutions that have been developed for these problems in brick-and-mortar companies also work for e-tailers. Most of these solutions are facilitated by IT and by EC technologies, as was shown in Chapter 8. In this section, we will discuss some of the specific solutions to the EC order fulfillment problems (see Rao et al. 1999).

IMPROVEMENTS IN THE ORDER-TAKING PROCESS

One way to improve order fulfillment is to improve the order-taking process and its links to fulfillment and logistics. Order taking can be done via EDI, EDI/Internet, Internet, or an extranet, and it may be fully automated. For example, in B2B, orders are generated and transmitted automatically to suppliers when inventory levels fall below certain threshold. The result is a fast, inexpensive, and more accurate (no need to rekey data) order-taking process. In B2C, Web-based ordering, using electronic forms, expedites the process, makes the process more accurate (e.g., intelligent agents can check the input data and provide instant feedback) and reduces processing costs for sellers. When EC order taking can interface with a company's back-office system, such an interface, or even integration, it shortens cycle times and eliminates errors.

Order-taking improvements can also take place *within* an organization, for example, when manufacturers order parts from a warehouse. Whenever delivery of such parts runs smoothly, disruptions to the manufacturing process are minimized, reducing losses from downtime. For example, as detailed in the Real-World Case at the end of the chapter, Dell has improved the flow of parts in its PC repair operations, resulting in greater efficiency and cost savings.

Implementing linkages between order-taking and payment systems can also be helpful in improving order fulfillment. Electronic payments can expedite both the order fulfillment cycle and the payment delivery period. With such systems, payment processing can be significantly less expensive and fraud can be better controlled.

INVENTORY MANAGEMENT IMPROVEMENTS

Inventories can be minimized by introducing a make-to-order (pull) production process and by providing fast and accurate demand information to suppliers. By allowing business partners to electronically track and monitor orders and production activities, inventory management can be improved, and inventory levels, as well as the administrative expenses of inventory management, can be minimized. In some instances, the ultimate inventory improvement is to have no inventory at all; for products that can be digitized (e.g., software), order fulfillment can be instantaneous and the need for inventory can be eliminated.

Automated Warehouses

Large-volume EC fulfillment requires automated warehouses. Regular warehouses are built to deliver large quantities to a small number of stores and plants. In B2C, however, businesses need to send small quantities to a very large number of individuals. Automation of warehouses can minimize the order fulfillment problems that arise from this need.

Automated warehouses may include robots and other devices that expedite the pick-up of products. An example of a company that built such a warehouse is Amazon.com (Cone 1999). The largest EC/mail-order warehouse in the United States was operated by a mail-order company, Fingerhut. This company handles its own order fulfillment process for mail orders and online orders, as well as orders for Wal-Mart, Macy's, KbKids, and many others. The order fulfillment process at the Fingerhut warehouse involved eight steps (Duvall 1999):

1. Retailers contracted with Fingerhut to stock products and deliver orders they received from their Web sites, by phone, or by fax.

2. Retailers' merchandise was stored by SKU at Fingerhut's warehouse.

3. Incoming orders were transferred to Fingerhut's mainframe computer.

4. To optimize the work of pickers, a special computer program consolidated the orders from all vendors (including Fingerhut's catalog) and organized them into "picking waves." These waves were organized so that pickers did not have to run from one end of the warehouse to another to prepare an order. Some picking was done by robots.

5. The "picked" items were moved by conveyors to the packing area. The computer configured the size and type of box (or envelope) needed for packaging and typed special packaging and delivery instructions.

6. Packages passed on a conveyor belt through a scanning station where they were weighed. (The actual weight had to match the SKU-projected weight.)

7. The bar-code scanner identified the destination, and at an appropriate time, each package was pushed onto one of 26 destination conveyer belts that carried the package directly to a waiting truck.

8. Once trucks were full, they departed for local postal offices in 26 major cities, dramatically cutting shipping costs.

Fingerhut was sold to Federated Department Stores in 1999. With the purchase, Federated hoped to create a fulfillment giant, but unexpectedly large numbers of deadbeat customers and a less-than-perfect IT system resulted in a financial loss for Federated on its investment (Burke 2001). In the spring of 2002, the Fingerhut warehouse was revived (Haeg 2002). Discounter/wholesaler Tom Petters and former Fingerhut CEO Ted Deikel bought the Minnetonka, Minnesota-based catalog and direct mail retailer from Federated on June 11, 2002. As of December 2002, the St. Cloud distribution center reopened and business began again in earnest (Workday Minnesota 2002).

Other companies (e.g., submitorder.com and rubyglen.com/s/h2.htm) provide similar order fulfillment services. The keys to successful inventory management, in terms of order fulfillment, are efficiency and speed.

SPEEDING DELIVERIES

In 1973, a tiny company initiated the concept of "next-day delivery." It was a revolution in door-to-door logistics. A few years later, that company, FedEx, introduced the "next-morning delivery" service. Today, FedEx is moving over 3.3 million packages a day, all over the globe, using several hundred airplanes and several thousand vans. Incidentally, by one report (Pickering 2000), 70 percent of these packages are the result of EC.

Same Day, Even Same Hour, Delivery

In the digital age, however, even the next morning may not fast enough. Today we talk about *same-day delivery*, and even delivery within an hour. Deliveries of urgent material to and from hospitals are an example of such a service. Two of the newcomers to this area are the Web sites efulfillmentservice.com and owd.com. These companies have created networks for the rapid distribution of products, mostly EC-related ones. They offer a national distribution system across the United States in collaboration with shipping companies such as FedEx and UPS.

Delivering groceries is another area where speed is important, as discussed in Chapter 3. Quick pizza deliveries have been available for a long time (e.g., Domino's Pizza). Today, many pizza orders can be placed online. Also, many restaurants deliver food to customers who order online, a service called "dine online." Examples of this service can be found at food.com, gourmetdinnerservice.com.au, and anniesdinners.com. Some companies even offer aggregating services, processing orders from several restaurants and making deliveries (e.g., dialadinner.com.hk in Hong Kong).

Supermarket Deliveries

Supermarket deliveries are done the same or next day, and they may be difficult, especially when fresh food is to be transported, as discussed in Chapter 3. Buyers need to be home at certain times to accept the deliveries. Therefore, the distribution systems for such enterprises are critical. For an example of an effective distribution system, see EC Application Case W14.1 about Woolworths of Australia at the book's Web site.

One of the most comprehensive delivery systems is that of GroceryWorks (now a subsidiary of Safeway U.K.). The system is illustrated in Exhibit 14.5 (page 540). Note that the delivery trucks can pick up other items (such as rented videos and dry cleaning).

Failed Delivery Companies

As described in Chapters 1 and 3, one of the most publicized dot-coms was Webvan, an express-delivery company that lost $1.2 billion (the largest of any dot-com loss). Another well-publicized failure was that of Kozmo.com, described in EC Application Case 14.1 (page 541).

PARTNERING EFFORTS AND OUTSOURCING LOGISTICS

An effective way to solve order fulfillment problems is for an organization to partner with other companies. For example, several EC companies partner with UPS or FedEx, which may own part of the EC company.

One such unsuccessful partnering was demonstrated by the joint venture of MailBoxes Etc. with a fulfillment services company, Innotrac Corp., and with a logistics firm, AccuShip.com. The three companies developed a comprehensive logistics system that used software that connected e-tailers and order management systems to an intelligent system. The system determined whether a customer who wanted to make a return could do so and if they were entitled to a refund. If allowed to make a return, customers had the option of doing so using the kiosks in MailBoxes Etc.'s physical franchises. This partnership failed, and many of the MailBoxes Etc. stores have now been taken over by UPS and renamed "The UPS Store."

Logistics-related partnerships can take many forms. For example, another partnering example is a marketplace managed by relysoftware.com that helps companies with goods find "forwarders"—the intermediaries that prepare goods for shipping. The company also helps forwarders find the best prices on air carriers and the carriers bid to fill the space with forwarders goods that need to be shipped.

SkyMall (skymall.com, now a subsidiary of Gem-Star TV Guide International) is a retailer that sells from catalogs on airplanes, over the Internet, and by mail order. It relies on its catalog partners to fill the orders. For small vendors that do not handle their own shipments and for international shipments, SkyMall contracts distribution centers owned by fulfillment outsourcer Sykes Enterprise. To coordinate the logistics of sending orders to thousands of customers, SkyMall uses an EC order management integrator called Order Trust. As orders come in, SkyMall conveys the data to Order Trust, which disseminates it to the appropriate vendor or to a Sykes distribution center. A report is then sent to SkyMall, and SkyMall pays Order Trust a transaction fee. This arrangement has allowed SkyMall to increase its online business by about 3 percent annually (Kenneally 1999).

EXHIBIT 14.5   Order Fulfillment at GroceryWorks

1. Each customer order is placed 6.5 to 9 hours ahead of delivery time.

2. Suppliers pick goods off their own shelves and package them for pickup, with orders sorted by customer and placed in coded bags.

3. GroceryWorks vans pick up the goods from suppliers.

4. Fresh goods from suppliers are sent along a conveyor belt; dry goods are picked from GroceryWorks warehouse shelves.

5. GroceryWorks vans head to customers' homes, stopping by suppliers on their return trip to the local warehouse to pick up the next round of customer orders.

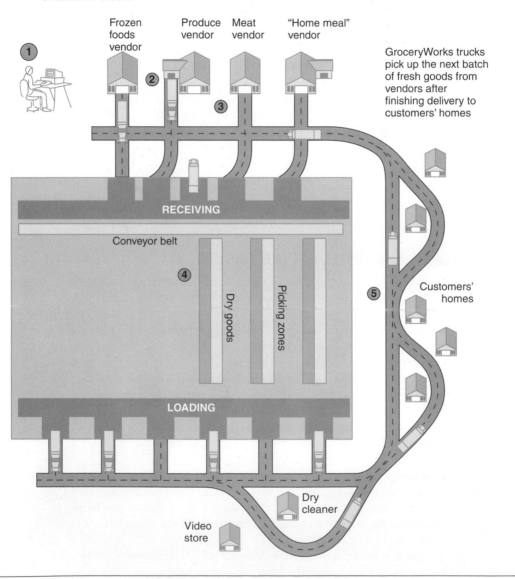

Source: As seen in *Interactive Week,* © 2003 XPLANATIONS™ by Xplane.com®.

CASE 14.1
EC Application
THE RISE AND FALL OF KOZMO.COM

The idea sounded logical: Create an express delivery system for online orders and deliver within an hour. The idea is not new. Domino's Pizza built its fortune on this idea, and today pizzas are delivered by many companies, door-to-door, in less than an hour.

Kozmo.com's business model was based on this idea. But instead of pizzas, Kozmo.com envisioned delivery of food items, rented videos, electronic games, and convenience products. Also, the model targeted large cities, especially New York and Boston, where people use public transportation that may not be in operation at certain times. Items were delivered by "Kozmonauts"—employees with vans, bikes, or scooters. Orders were placed on the Internet, but telephone and fax orders were also accepted. The products were delivered from Kozmo.com's distribution centers.

The first logistics problem faced by Kozmo.com was the *return* of the rented videos. It was uneconomical to send the Kozmonauts to collect them. So Kozmo.com built drop-in boxes (like the FedEx boxes), initially in New York. Many of these boxes were vandalized. In an attempt to solve the problem, Kozmo.com partnered with Starbucks and moved the boxes to Starbucks cafes, some of which are open 24 hours a day. In exchange, Starbucks became an investor in Kozmo.com. Kozmo.com started to deliver coffee products to Starbucks' customers, and Starbucks printed Kozmo.com's logo on their coffee cups.

With a venture capital investment of over $250 million, the company expanded rapidly to 10 cities. During the initial period, delivery was free, and no minimum dollar amount of order was required. This strategy attracted many customers, but resulted in heavy losses, especially on small-value items. The company's growth was rapid: By the end of 2000 it had 1,100 employees, and an IPO was launched.

Soon after, problems started to surface. As with other B2C dot-coms, the more Kozmo.com sold, the larger the losses grew. In response, Kozmo.com closed operations in San Diego and Houston, imposed minimum charges, and added more expensive items (such as rented DVD players) to its offerings. This helped to generate profits in New York and San Francisco. However, with hundreds of dot-coms going out of business in late 2000 and early 2001, a major financial backer withdrew its support. Kozmo.com eventually ran out of cash and as a result had to close its doors on April 11, 2001.

Sources: Compiled from *kozmo.com* (2002) and Blair (2000, 2001).

Questions

1. Draw the supply chains for food and rented items at Kozmo. What logistics problems did these supply chains present?

2. Compare Kozmo.com with Domino's Pizza. Why did Domino's do so well while Kozmo failed? Analyze the situation from an order fulfillment point of view.

3. The partnership with Starbucks was said to be extremely innovative, but it was cancelled by Kozmo.com when its financial problems began. (Kozmo.com had paid money to Starbucks for the permission to place the drop-in boxes.) Analyze this partnership.

4. Later in this chapter, you will learn about "returns." After you have read that discussion, come back to this case and answer the following question: What advice could you have given Kozmo.com regarding the return of rented items?

Comprehensive Logistics Services

Comprehensive logistic services are offered by major shippers, notably UPS and FedEx. These services are for B2C, B2B, G2B, and other types of EC. See EC Application Case 14.2 (page 542) for a description of the broad EC services offered by UPS.

Outsourcing Logistics

Instead of a joint venture or equity ownership with partners, most companies simply outsource logistics (see Bayles 2001). One advantage of this is that it is easy to change the logistics provider, as can be seen in the case of National Semiconductor Corp. described in EC Application Case W14.2.

HANDLING RETURNS

Allowing for the return of unwanted merchandise and providing for product exchanges are necessary to maintain customers' trust and loyalty. The Boston Consulting Group (2001) found that the "absence of a good return mechanism" was the number two reason shoppers cited for refusing to buy on the Web frequently. According to Bayles (2001), a good return policy is a must in EC.

CASE 14.2
EC Application
UPS PROVIDES BROAD EC SERVICES

UPS is not only a leading transporter of goods sold on the Internet, but it is also a provider of several other EC support services, ranging from supply chain activities such as inventory management to electronic bill payment.

UPS has a massive infrastructure to support these efforts. For example, it has an over 120-terabyte (10^{12} byte) database that contains customer information and shipping records. Here are some of the EC applications offered by UPS:

▸ Electronic tracking of packages.
▸ Electronic supply chain services for corporate customers, by industry. This includes a portal page with industry-related information and statistics.
▸ Calculators for computing shipping fees.
▸ Helping customers manage their electronic supply chains (e.g., expediting billing and speeding up accounts receivable).
▸ Improved inventory management, warehousing, and delivery.
▸ A shipping management system that integrates tracking systems, address validation, service selection, and time-in-transit tools with Oracle's ERP application suite (similar integration with SAP and PeopleSoft exists).
▸ Notification of customers by e-mail about the status and expected arrival time of incoming packages.

Representative Tools

UPS's online tools—a set of seven transportation and logistics applications—lets customers do everything from track packages to analyze their shipping history using customized criteria to calculate exact time-in-transit for shipments between any two postal codes in the continental United States.

The tools, which customers can download to their Web sites, lets customers query UPS systems to get proof that specific packages were delivered on schedule. For example, if a company is buying supplies online and wants them delivered on a certain day, a UPS customer can use an optimal-routing feature to ensure delivery on that day, as well as to automatically record proof of the delivery into its accounting system.

UPS is offering logistics services tailored for certain industries. For example, UPS Logistics Group provides supply chain reengineering, transportation network management, and service parts logistics to vehicle manufacturers, suppliers, and parts distributors in the auto industry worldwide. UPS Autogistics improves automakers' vehicle delivery networks. For example, Ford reduced the time to deliver vehicles from plants to dealers in North America from an average of 14 days to about 6. UPS Logistics Group offers similar supply chain and delivery tracking services to other kinds of manufacturers.

UPS is also expanding into another area important to e-business—delivery of digital documents. The company was the first conventional package shipper to enter this market in 1998 when it launched UPS Document Exchange. This service monitors delivery of digitally delivered documents and provides instant receipt notification, encryption, and password-only access.

UPS offers many other EC-related services. These include the ability to enter the UPS system from wireless devices, helping customers configure and customize services, and providing for electronic bill presentation and payment (for B2B), EFT, and processing of COD payments.

Sources: Compiled from Violino (2000), Farber (2003), and United Parcel Service (2003).

Questions

1. Why would a shipper such as UPS expand to other logistic services?
2. Why would shippers want to handle payments?
3. Why does UPS provide software tools to customers?
4. What B2B services does UPS provide? (*Note:* Check *ups.com* to make sure that your answers are up-to-date.)

Dealing with returns is a major logistics problem for EC merchants. Several options for handling returns exist (see Bayles 2001, Rogers and Tibben-Lembke 1998, and Trager 2000):

▸ **Return the item to the place where it was purchased.** This is easy to do with a purchase from a brick-and-mortar store, but not a virtual one. To return a product to a virtual store a customer needs to get authorization, pack everything up, pay to ship it back, insure it, and wait up to two billing cycles for a credit to show up on their statement. The buyer is not happy, and neither is the seller, who must unpack, check the paperwork, and resell the item, usually at a loss. This solution is workable only if the number of returns is small.

▸ **Separate the logistics of returns from the logistics of delivery.** In this option, returns are shipped to an independent returns unit and are handled separately. This solution may be more efficient from the seller's point of view, but it does not ease the returns process for the buyer.

▶ **Completely outsource returns.** Several outsourcers, including UPS and FedEx, provide logistics services for returns (as described in Bayles 2001). The services deal not only with delivery and returns, but also with the entire logistics process. FedEx, for example, offers several options for returning goods.

▶ **Allow the customer to physically drop the returned item at a collection station.** Offer customers locations (such as a convenience store or at MailBoxes Etc.) where they can drop off returns. In Asia and Australia, returns are accepted in convenience stores and at gas stations. For example, BP Australia Ltd. (gasoline service stations) teamed up with wishlist.com.au, and Caltex Australia is accepting returns at the convenience stores connected to its gasoline stations. The accepting stores may offer in-store computers for ordering and may also offer payment options, as at Japanese 7-Eleven's (7dream.com). Click-and-mortar stores usually allow customers to return merchandise that was ordered from the online outlet to their physical stores (e.g., toysrus.com and eddiebauer.com).

For strategy and guidelines on returns, see Bayles (2001).

ORDER FULFILLMENT IN B2B

Most of the discussion in this section has centered around B2C order fulfillment. Some of the discussion pertains to B2B fulfillment as well. The B2B fulfillment options are shown in Exhibit 14.6. The exhibit shows how the buy options (green lines) are related to shipping options (blue lines). (For another overview of B2B fulfillment, see *Business Week* 2000.)

B2B fulfillment may be more complex than that of B2C because it has at least six dimensions of complexity (versus two in B2C): shipment size, multiple distribution channels, more variety of shipment frequency, uneven breadth of carrier services, fewer carrier EC offerings, and complex EC transaction paths.

Some representative B2B fulfillment players and challenges are listed in Exhibit 14.7 (page 544).

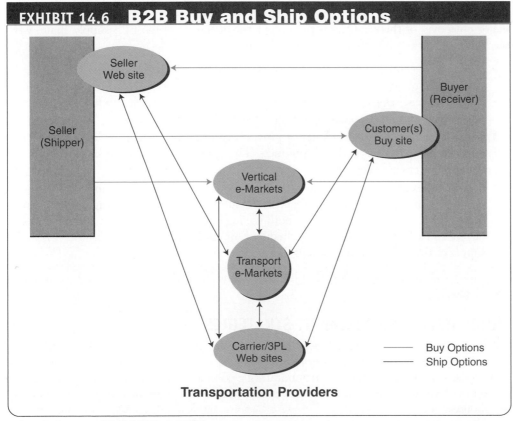

EXHIBIT 14.6 B2B Buy and Ship Options

Buyer (Receiver)

Seller (Shipper)

- Seller Web site
- Customer(s) Buy site
- Vertical e-Markets
- Transport e-Markets
- Carrier/3PL Web sites

—— Buy Options
—— Ship Options

Transportation Providers

Source: Courtesy of Norbridge Inc., © 2003.

EXHIBIT 14.7 Players and Challenges in B2B Fulfillment

Players	Challenges
Shippers (sellers)	Mix of channels, choice of logistics partners, solo or use aggregation, what to outsource, integration of strategic/tactical/operational decisions
Receivers (buyers)	Solo and/or consortia buy sites, supply chain collaboration, total delivered costs, when to buy
Carriers	Self-service Web sites, links to verticals and transportation marketplaces, institutional drag
Third-party logistics providers	Cooperation from carriers, breadth of modes/services, IT resources, customer acquisition
Warehouse companies	Location, operational intensity, capital investment, mode of automation, choice of builders
Vertical e-marketplaces	Where's the "ship-it" button? Who's behind it? What services are offered?
Transportation e-marketplaces	Moving beyond spot transactions to ASPs and value-added services, neutrality vs. alignment, market mechanisms (e.g., bidding)
Logistics software application vendors	Comprehensive solutions, e-marketplace involvement, strategic partnerships, integration with existing software

Using E-Marketplaces and Exchanges to Ease Order Fulfillment Problems in B2B

In Chapters 6 and 7, we introduced a variety of e-marketplaces and exchanges. One of the major objectives of these entities is to improve the operation of the B2B supply chain. Let's see how this works with different business models.

▶ A company-centric marketplace can solve several supply chain problems. For example, CSX Technology developed an extranet-based EC system for tracking cross-country train shipments as part of its supply chain initiative and was able to effectively identify bottlenecks and more accurately forecast demand.

▶ Using an extranet, Toshiba America provides an ordering system for its dealers to buy replacement parts for Toshiba's products. The system smoothes the supply chain and delivers better customer service.

▶ A vertical exchange, such as that of Covisint.com in the automotive industry, connects thousands of suppliers with automakers. Hundreds of vertical exchanges exist all over the world; many of them deal with both buying and selling. The direct contact between buyers and sellers in such exchanges reduces communication and search problems in the supply chain and helps with order fulfillment.

For additional discussion on how fulfillment is done in B2B, see fedex.com, ups.com, and Bayles (2001).

INNOVATIVE E-FULFILLMENT STRATEGIES

merge-in-transit
Logistics model in which components for a product may come from two different physical locations and are shipped directly to customer's location.

Lee and Whang (2001) proposed several innovative e-fulfillment strategies. They call one of these innovations *logistics postponement*. Supply chain partners can move information flows and hold off shipping actual physical goods until a point at which they can make more-direct shipments. Two examples of logistics postponement are (1) merge-in-transit and (2) rolling warehouses.

Merge-in-transit is a model in which components for a product may come from two different physical locations. For example, in shipping a PC, the monitor may come from the east coast of the United States and the CPU from the west coast. Instead of shipping the components to a central location and then shipping both together to the customer, the components are shipped directly to the customer, reducing unnecessary transportation.

A **rolling warehouse** is a method in which products on the delivery truck are not pre-assigned to a destination, but the decision about the quantity to unload at each destination is made at the time of unloading. Thus, the latest order information can be taken into account, assisting in inventory control and lowering logistics costs (by avoiding repeat delivery trips). The rolling warehouse method also works in the ocean shipping industry, where it is called *floating warehouses*.

Another example of innovative e-fulfillment strategies proposed by Lee and Whang (2001) is *leveraged shipments*. By this, they mean planning shipments based on a combination of size (or value) of the order and geographical location. The size of the orders shipped by most e-tailers is small. The cost of delivery is justified only if there is a high concentration of orders from customers located in close proximity or if the value of the order is large enough. *Delivery-value density* is a decision support tool that helps determine whether it is economical to deliver goods to a neighborhood area in one trip. (The density is computed by dividing average total dollar volume of the shipment per trip by the average travel distance per trip.) The larger the density value, the better. One example of leveraging shipments is to deliver to specific geographical areas on specific days of the week and to install delivery receptacles at the destination so drivers do not have to return to or wait at the site for a customer to arrive. A second example of leveraging shipments is when a 3PL hires "dealers" that are familiar with the physical region of the delivery. The 3PL provides the dealers with the products, and the dealers deliver to the final destination.

For more discussion of the innovative e-fulfillment strategies proposed by Lee and Whang (2001), see Insights and Additions W14.2 at the book's Web site. For other innovative applications, see EC Application Case W14.3 about Ingram Micro, also at the book's Web site.

rolling warehouse
Logistics method in which products on the delivery truck are not preassigned to a destination, but the decision about quantity to unload at each destination is made at the time of unloading.

Section 14.3 ❯ REVIEW

1. List the various order-taking solutions.
2. List solutions for improved delivery.
3. Describe same-day shipments.
4. Describe some innovative e-strategies for order fulfillment.
5. Describe how the return of items can be effectively managed.
6. Describe issues in B2B fulfillment.

14.4 CONTENT GENERATION, SYNDICATION, DELIVERY, AND MANAGEMENT

The three most important support services are payments, order fulfillment, and content. The first two of these services were covered in Chapter 13 and at the beginning of this chapter. We now turn our attention to various aspects of content—its generation, delivery, and management.

Content providers and distributors are, as their name implies, those who provide and distribute content online. These services are offered by several specialized companies (e.g., akamai.com, sandpiper.net, and mirror-image.com), as well as by news services such as the Associated Press and ABC News. For more about content providers and distributors, see Chapter 9 in this book.

Providing content to EC sites may be a complex job because of the variety and quantity of sources from which content is acquired and the fact that the content must frequently be updated (see Chapter 10 in Coupey 2001). Also, B2B content, especially in online catalogs, must include pictures, diagrams, and even sound. The major content categories are information about the company, products, services, customers, investor relations, press releases, and so on; detailed product information provided in electronic catalogs, which are sometimes personalized for major customers; customers' personalized Web pages; and information provided to the B2B community, such as industry news. One of the difficulties in Web content management is that content needs to be kept up-to-date. This means that it needs to be changed continually. This is referred to as dynamic Web content.

dynamic Web content
Content at a Web site that needs to be changed continually to keep it up to date.

For each type of content, companies may use a different approach for content creation and delivery. Exhibit 14.8 shows the content life cycle. Once content is created, it may appear in different sources (e.g., text, video, music). Then, it is moved to a content syndicator. The syndicator moves the content to a portal or news site. From there, a hosting service moves the content, possibly via an optimizer (such as akamai.com). The optimizer delivers the content to its final consumer. We will discuss this process and its elements in more detail a bit later.

MEASURING CONTENT QUALITY

How does a company know if the content on their Web site is meeting their e-commerce goals? How does a company know if they are delivering what their customers need? According to Barnes (2001b), companies need metrics to control the quality of their online content. In addition, content must meet privacy requirements, copyright and other legal requirements, language translation needs, and much more. Guidelines for knowledge management may be used as well. Metrics are available from W3C (w3c.org/PICS) and periodically at e-businessadvisor.com. Measuring the quality of content also requires appropriate Web traffic measurement tools (see Online Chapter 18). For specific suggestions on how to effectively use metrics to measure content quality, see Barnes (2001a), Radoff (2000), and Sterne (2002).

PITFALLS OF CONTENT MANAGEMENT

According to Byrne (2002), companies face various content management pitfalls. The top six content management pitfalls, and the best practices for avoiding them, are presented in Exhibit 14.9.

SYNDICATION

Chapter 2 introduced the concept of *syndication*. The basic idea behind syndication is that knowledge creators can use syndicators to distribute the creator's content to a large number of delivery companies who then provide it to the end customer (see yellowbrix.com). For example, the financial industry often uses syndicated content. The syndication approach is appropriate for community-type content.

Thousands of consumer-oriented Web sites provide free dynamic content to their visitors. This content may be daily news, sports, weather, or stock quotes or it may be specialized information, such as the snow reports from various ski resorts. The content may be text, graphics, or sound (e.g., music or streaming audio). It may be in the public domain or may be

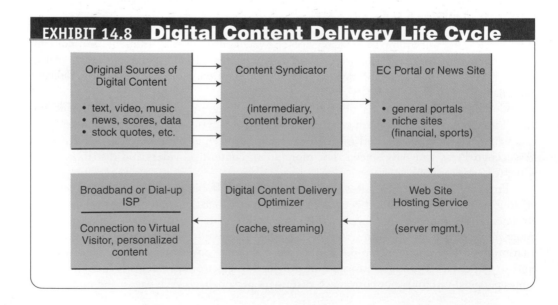

EXHIBIT 14.8 Digital Content Delivery Life Cycle

Original Sources of Digital Content
- text, video, music
- news, scores, data
- stock quotes, etc.

Content Syndicator
(intermediary, content broker)

EC Portal or News Site
- general portals
- niche sites (financial, sports)

Web Site Hosting Service
(server mgmt.)

Digital Content Delivery Optimizer
(cache, streaming)

Broadband or Dial-up ISP
Connection to Virtual Visitor, personalized content

EXHIBIT 14.9   Content Management Pitfalls and Their Solutions

Problem or Pitfall	Solution
Picking content management software before developing solid requirements and business case	Convert some of the resources currently being expended on software evaluations to a deeper examination of company's own content and business needs.
Not getting a clear mandate from the top to proceed	Get business leaders onboard; you will need their strategic direction and a mandate for change.
Underestimating integration and professional service needs	Budget two to four times the cost of software license for consulting, customization, and integration.
Hiring inexperienced developers to integrate and extend the software	Hire good developers with content management software experience to implement mediocre software. This is always preferable to excellent software in the hands of novice integrators.
Depending entirely on an outside company to make changes to the system	Involve your own technical people closely in the initial development, even if you are outsourcing the integration. Do not skimp on training.
Thinking your migration will be painless despite what the content management system provider tells you	Start to prepare yourself for a content management system by cleaning up your HTML code and organizing your content. This takes longer than you think!

Source: Compiled from Byrne (2002).

proprietary in nature (e.g., information about the company and its products and services). The sites at which content is offered may be general-purpose consumer portals, such as Yahoo or Lycos. Or they may be specialized portals designed to appeal to a specific audience, such as espn.com or ski.com.

Up-to-the-minute dynamic content is what attracts new and returning customers ("eyeballs") and makes them stay longer ("stickiness"). Therefore, dynamic content contributes to customer loyalty. For banner-ad-supported Web sites, the dynamic content may be the primary draw for a site. For transactional sites (e.g., one selling ski equipment), the dynamic content may be the distinguishing factor bringing certain customers back repeatedly.

WEB CONTENT MANAGEMENT

Web content management is the process of collecting, publishing, revising, and removing content from a Web site to keep content fresh, accurate, compelling, and credible. The focus is on content creation and integration, security, and visitor approval. *Web content* management differs from *Web site* management, which focuses on easy navigation, availability, performance, scalability, and security (see Online Chapter 18). Web content management makes sure that a site eliminates clutter and does not waste visitors' time. For an overview of Web content management, see Gupta et al. (2001); for a list of content management vendors, see Clyman (2002).

Web content management
The process of collecting, publishing, revising, and removing content from a Web site to keep content fresh, accurate, compelling, and credible.

CONTENT DELIVERY NETWORKS

Content delivery is a service that is sometimes offered by hosting companies to help customers manage their content. Using *content delivery networks (CDNs)*, companies can update content, improve the quality of the site, increase consistency, control content, and decrease the time needed to create or maintain a site. CDNs are provided by Allaire.com, Mediasurface.com, and Akamai. The case of Akamai is discussed later in this section.

In B2B, the information contained in electronic catalogs is of extreme importance. Companies can create and maintain the content in-house or they can outsource such tasks.

CATALOG CONTENT AND ITS MANAGEMENT

Much of the content in B2B and B2C sites is catalog-based content. Chapter 2 discussed the benefits of electronic catalogs. Although there are many positive aspects of electronic catalogs, poorly organized ones may deter buyers (e.g., see Kapp 2001). Companies need to make sure that their catalog content is well managed.

For buyers who aggregate suppliers' catalogs on their own Web site, content management begins with engaging suppliers and then collecting, standardizing, classifying, hosting, and continually updating their catalog data. That is no small task, considering that most large buying organizations have hundreds of suppliers, each using different data formats and nomenclature to describe their catalog items.

An Example: Bloomsburg Carpet

An example of a successful e-catalog is that of Bloomsburg Carpet (bloomsburgcarpet.com) described by Kapp (2001). At Bloomsburg Carpet, e-technology has solved the long-standing problem of shipping and using bulky carpet-sample books by creating an e-catalog searchable by color, weave, and brand. Sales representatives and potential customers enter the searchable database to quickly find a variety of colors and weaves with the click of a mouse. Potential clients view the samples online and make decisions concerning colors without the assistance of sales representatives. The site has streamlined the business functions for the company.

The success of Bloomsburg Carpet's Web site is due to the attention paid to the critical steps of understanding and simplifying the system before implementing the e-technology—the principles of understanding, simplifying, and automating. This process takes place in three steps: Step 1—understanding—includes "walking the process" (introducing the process, maybe by a demo), conducting a *work breakdown structure* (WBS) analysis, and a *fishbone analysis* (a systematic way of looking at effects and the causes that create or contribute to those effects) that examines problems in regard to people, materials, methods, and technology found in the walk-through and WBS. Step 2—simplifying—combines multiple procedural steps for increased productivity, eliminates duplicated steps in the systems, rearranges information for ease in collecting the data, and increases the number of systems to streamline daily activities. Step 3—automating—implements the e-technology. The system, in this case, Bloomsburg Carpet's e-catalog, supports the organization, it does not control it.

Catalog Content Management Options

Companies have five basic options to manage catalog content.

1. **Do it yourself.** This option is satisfactory for small buyers with few suppliers or large buyers that buy from few suppliers. The per line item is about $30. The cost for a catalog containing a large number of products can easily be $1 million or more for the first year.

2. **Let the suppliers do it.** Most suppliers do not like to modify their catalogs to meet the buyers' format. A few suppliers may agree to do so. This solution is not feasible when many suppliers are involved.

3. **Buy the content from an aggregator.** Some companies standardize and aggregate content across industries. The result may be in a standard format that large buyers want. The buyers then host the content on their servers. For smaller companies that can host and manage content, this is a viable option. The problem is that the content is not customized to the buyer's needs. Furthermore, the buyer is expected to keep the catalogs up-to-date. Also, updating through aggregators can be expensive.

4. **Subscribe to a vertical exchange.** Vertical exchanges can be an excellent solution for occasional spot buys and for one or a few commodities. The problem here is that one buyer may need to visit many exchanges to find everything they need. Finally, most vertical exchanges do not usually offer customized views or negotiated prices, nor do they enable integration with a buying organization's e-procurement applications.

5. **Outsource to a full-service Internet exchange.** A full-service exchange connects many suppliers with many buyers and offers comprehensive catalog services. These services may include: cleansed, standardized, and categorized supplier catalog content; online content maintenance and update tools; robust search capabilities, including quick searches, category browsing, and advanced attribute-based searches; buyer-specific "virtual private catalogs" with negotiated pricing information; and seamless integration with ERP and other Internet procurement systems or Web portals using a single sign-on. However, this option may be expensive, and it may be difficult to find an exchange that will meet all the special needs of every buyer.

CONTENT TRANSLATION TO OTHER LANGUAGES

In the global marketplace, content created in one language often needs to be translated to another in order to reach customers in other countries. Furthermore, in some cases an effective Web site may need to be specifically designed and targeted to the market that it is trying to reach. Language translation is less of a problem in B2B, due to the ability of many business people to speak English. It is a big problem in B2C, though, especially in countries such as China, Japan, and Korea, where relatively few people understand enough English to trade online. The language barrier between countries and regions presents an interesting and complicated challenge (see worldlingo.com).

The primary problems with language customization are cost and speed. It currently takes a human translator about a week to translate a medium-size Web site into just one language. For larger sites the cost ranges from $30,000 to $500,000, depending on the complexity of the site and languages of translation.

WorldPoint (worldpoint.com) presents a creative solution to these translation issues with its WorldPoint Passport multilingual software tool. The WorldPoint Passport solution allows Web developers to create a Web site in one language and to deploy it in several other languages. Cost of translation using the software is estimated at 24 to 26 cents per word. In a 1999 demonstration of the software's power, WorldPoint translated Japan's primary telephone company's (NTT) Web site into 10 different Asian languages in only 3 days.

However, automatic translation can be inaccurate. Therefore, many experts advocate manual translation with the help of the computer as a productivity booster. As time passes, though, automatic translation is becoming better (see Sullivan 2001).

For more on automatic language translation, including some existing tools for translation, see Insights and Additions 14.2 (page 550).

REPRESENTATIVE CONTENT-RELATED VENDORS

A large number of vendors support content creation and management that facilitates sharing of an organization's digital assets. Representative vendors are described here:

- Documentum (documentum.com) offers robust content management products. It is especially well known for its support of the pharmaceutical and aerospace industries, where massive amounts of paper information are digitized and made available to multiple parties, including government agencies.
- Microsoft (microsoft.com) offers a Content Management Server that features applications that can interoperate with the Microsoft Office suite and CommerceServer. Also, it fits companies using the .Net system. The software is also integrated with Microsoft's SharePoint portal server for complete enterprise content management.
- Vignette (vignette.com) is a dot-com survivor that specializes in personalization, content syndication, and portal functions. Of special interest are its add-on analytical tools that help, for example, better predict customer behavior in order to create appropriate content.
- Interwoven (interwoven.com), another dot-com survivor, delivers content to the Web. Its MetaTagger categorization technology creates automatic taxonomies for content.
- Opentext (opentext.com) is known for its Livelink. Livelink is a browser-based system that allows companies to search for and retrieve documents. It also enables workers to collaborate in real time via the Livelink MessageZone applications.
- Akamai (akamai.com) specializes in content delivery maximization, as illustrated in the next section.

Many other companies such as Oracle, Digital Island, and IBM are also involved in content management activities.

Thus far, we have discussed the role of intermediaries and other third-party B2B providers in channeling digital content to the sites that display that content to consumers. Discussion will now turn to the next step in the content delivery chain, the task of optimizing and delivering digital content to customers.

Insights and Additions 14.2   Automatic Web Page Translation

Many companies, research institutions, and content providers are busy with automatic language translation. Here are some examples.

▶ Alis Technologies (*alis.com*) and Netscape (*netscape.com*) developed *AutoTranslate,* which is offered in Netscape's browser. Available in the "View" menu (click on "translate"), users can see a translation of a Web site from English to 1 of 10 available languages. A similar feature is being offered at *mozilla.com*.

▶ Google (*google.com*) offers a service, called BETA, that translates the content of Web pages published in French, German, Italian, Spanish, Portuguese, and more to English. All the user has to do is click on "Translate this Page," which appears after a title in a foreign language.

▶ The U.S. Air Force Research Lab (*rl.af.mil/div/IFB/techtrans/datasheets/ASLT.html*) developed automatic spoken language translation for purposes of training service personnel and intelligence work. The project now includes Web translation as well.

▶ Uniscape.com, now TRADOS.com (*trados.com*), offers multilingual translation of both documents and Web pages. The company's technology accelerates the human translation process, both for the individual translator and across the enterprise. Its technology enables product documentation, Web sites, marketing collaterals, and software interfaces to be translated into many different languages quickly and cost-effectively. The company's site (*translationzone.com*) is a portal for translation professionals worldwide. Professional translators can purchase the latest releases of TRADOS software as well as create online professional profiles through which they can market themselves to potential clients. The portal currently has more than 12,000 registered users.

▶ *Rikai.com* is an online character translator that allows people to enjoy Japanese Web pages.

According to Sullivan (2001), the best way to assess machine translation is to use the following criteria: (1) Intelligibility—how well can a reader get the gist of a translated document? (2) Accuracy—how many errors occur during a translation? (3) Speed—how many words per second are translated?

Those who do not believe in automatic translation or who have to translate critical material can use manual translation. It is slow and expensive, but the quality is superior (if the translators are good). For example, Cone (2001) reports that Glides Corp. uses the following process: First, a company's Web content is captured, separated into text and graphics, and given XML tags before being stored in the company's UniSite database. Content is then translated by human translators. The translation process can be reviewed and managed remotely through browser-based tools. Next, content is "localized," that is, checked with speakers of the local language to make sure it conforms to local customs and regulations. Finally, the translated content is published on the company's Web site and stored in the UniSite database for future use.

At this point in time, combining manual and machine translation may be the best bet.

CONTENT MAXIMIZATION AND STREAMING SERVICES

Many companies provide media-rich content, such as video clips, music, or flash media, in an effort to reach their target audience with an appealing marketing message. For example, automakers want to provide a virtual driving experience as seen from the car's interior, realtors want to provide 360-degree views of their properties, and music sellers want to provide easily downloadable samples of their songs. Public portals and others are using considerable amounts of media-rich information as well. Finally, B2B e-catalogs may include thousands of photos.

These and other content providers are concerned about the download time from the user's perspective. Impatient or fickle Web surfers may click "Stop" before the multimedia has had a chance to be fully downloaded. Remember that B2C and B2B customers not only want their news stories, music, video clips, reference information, financial information, and sports scores delivered to them over the Web, but they also want them to be delivered fast and effortlessly. Therefore, it is important that content providers and marketers use technical delivery solutions that will not cause "traffic jams" during the download process. Several technical solutions are available from vendors who are referred to as *content maximizers* or *streaming services*. One such vendor is Akamai, described in EC Application Case 14.3.

Section 14.4 ▶ REVIEW

1. Describe content creation and management.
2. Describe catalog content and the options for its management.

CASE 14.3
EC Application
AKAMAI CORPORATION

An Internet company decided to name itself after the Hawaiian word meaning "intelligent, clever, or cool"—Akamai (AH-kuh-my). And indeed, the company has created a clever product. Let's explain.

As user interest in high-speed Internet connections has grown, demand for bandwidth-heavy applications and media has also begun to surge. Paul Kagen Associates estimated that revenues from streaming media services will total $1.5 billion by 2002 and $21 billion by 2008 (as reported at *threesquared.com* 2000). In addition, the interactive broadcast video market will reach $4.2 billion by 2005 (DFC Intelligence 1999) Finally, according to a DFC Intelligence study (reported in Saunders 2001), streaming video is estimated to grow to over $1 billion by 2005.

However, user connection speeds are only part of the streaming media picture. How will the networks themselves handle the influx of bandwidth-chewing material? With a growing number of users and an abundance of rich media, the Internet is becoming extremely congested. Network traffic control now is needed. Akamai and its competitors (Digital Island, Ibeam, and Mirror Image) are stepping in to manage Internet traffic.

Akamai products act as Internet traffic cops by using complicated mathematical algorithms to speed Web pages from the closest Akamai-owned server to a customer's location—thereby passing through fewer router hops. This process also helps to eliminate Internet gridlock. Today, caching and content distribution are the only practical way to reduce network delay.

How does it work? To provide the service, Akamai maintains a global network of thousands of servers and leases space on them to giant portals such as Yahoo and CNN. These sites use the servers to store graphic-rich information closer to Internet users' computers and circumvent Web traffic jams. Akamai allows customer data to move to and from big Web sites through its global network for a fee. (In 2001, the fee was $2,500 for setup and $5,500/month per data center.)

With the use of Akamai services, delivery time to the users is reduced by 20 to 30 percent. When a user visits a Web site, all the site's multimedia objects must be downloaded from a Web server. If a company's Web server is located in Germany and a user in the United States visits the Web site, the multimedia content of the site has to be transmitted halfway around the globe. Akamai's FreeFlow technology speeds the delivery of images, multimedia, and other Web content by placing that content on servers worldwide. Using the FreeFlow Launcher, Web site designers "Akamaize" their site by marking content to be delivered using the Akamai network. FreeFlow takes this content and stores it on Akamai Web servers around the world. When a user visits a Web site that has been "Akamaized," the images and multimedia content are downloaded from an Akamai server near the user for faster content delivery.

Unfortunately, the service is not 100 percent reliable.

The speed for the end user depends upon how many people are using the user's LAN at any given point in time, and also on the speed of the server downloading any given Web site. A number of competing technologies are trying to provide the same solutions, and only a limited number of large companies that use lots of rich media are willing to pay for the service.

In 2001, Akamai started to diversify, offering a comprehensive suite of content delivery, streaming audio and video, traffic management, and other services, such as dynamic page view, bundled in a package called EdgeAdvantage. Akamai and its competitors were losing money in early 2001, but their revenues were increasing rapidly. By April 2003 the company had 13,000 servers in 60 countries storing data for its worldwide clientele (Junnarkar 2003).

Sources: Compiled from Mulqueen (2001), Korzeniowski (2002), *Business 2.0* (2002), and Akamai (2003).

Questions

1. What services are provided by Akamai?
2. What is the company's revenue model?
3. What are the service's limitations?

3. Discuss the issue of Web site language translation.
4. Explain how content maximization works.

14.5 OTHER EC SUPPORT SERVICES

Depending on the magnitude of the EC project, a company may require several other support services.

CONSULTING SERVICES

How does a firm learn how to do something that it has never done before? Many firms, both start-ups and established companies, are turning to consultants that have established themselves as experts in guiding their clients through the maze of legal, technical, strategic, and operational problems and decisions that must be addressed in order to ensure success in this new business environment. Some of these firms have established a reputation in one area of expertise, whereas others are generalists. Some consultants even take equity (ownership) positions in the firms they advise. Some consultants will build, test, and deliver a working Web site, and may even host it and maintain it for their clients. There are three broad categories of consulting firms.

The first type of consulting firm includes those that provide expertise in the area of EC, but not in traditional business. Some of the consultants that provide general EC expertise are Agency.com, Answerthink, BreakAway Creative, Cysive, Digital Lighthouse, Digitas, Virtusa.com, Sun.com, Inforte, SBI & Company, Organic, Sapient, Verity, WebTrends, and WebMethods.

Also included in the first category of consulting firms are those that provide very specialized expertise. There are thousands of these smaller, more specialized consulting firms. Some fill a unique niche in this growing field. Matching these consultants with clients can be done via service companies such as EXP.com, eLance.com, SoloGig.com, and FirmFinder. FirmFinder (from designshops.com) features a robust search system, enabling firms to showcase their services to prospective clients.

See EC Application Case W14.4 at the book's Web site for an overview of the EC consulting services offered by one firm, Sapient.

The second type of consulting firm is a traditional consulting company that maintains divisions that focus on EC. These include the so-called "Big 4" U.S. accounting firms and the large established U.S. national consulting firms. These firms leverage their existing relationship with their corporate clients and offer EC value-added services. Representative companies are Accenture (formerly Andersen Consulting); Computer Services Corp.; Cambridge Technology Partners; Boston Consulting Group; Booz-Allen & Hamilton; Deloitte & Touche; Ernst and Young; EDS; KPMG; McKinsey; and PricewaterhouseCoopers. Also, most large technology companies have extensive management-oriented consulting services (e.g., IBM, Microsoft, Sun Microsysetms, Oracle, SAP, and Intel).

The third category of consulting firms is EC hardware and software vendors that provide technology-consulting services. These include SAP, IBM, Oracle, Sun Microsystems, and many more.

It is imperative that any firm seeking help in devising a successful online strategy select not only an experienced and competent consulting firm, but also one with sufficient synergies with the client firm. For a discussion of vendor selection and management, see Online Chapter 18.

DIRECTORY SERVICES, NEWSLETTERS, AND SEARCH ENGINES

The EC landscape is huge, with hundreds of thousands of companies online. How can a buyer find all suitable sellers? How can a seller find all suitable buyers? In B2B, vertical exchanges can help with this matching process, but even vertical exchanges include only a limited number of potential partners, usually located in one country. To overcome the problem of finding buyers or sellers online, a company may use directory services.

Directory Services

There are several types of directory services. Some simply list companies by categories; others provide links to companies. In many cases, the data are classified in several different ways for easy search purposes. In others, special search engines are provided. Finally, value-added services such as matching buyers and sellers are available. Here are some popular directories.

▶ B2Business.net is a major resource for B2B professionals. It includes listings of business resources in about 30 functional areas, company research resources (e.g., credit checks, customs research, and financial reviews), information on start-ups (business plans, domain names, recruiting, patents, incubators, and even a graveyard), general EC information (e.g., books, articles, reports, events, and research), e-marketplace directories (e.g., enablers and builders, services, support services, and major markets), and infrastructure resources (e.g., security, connectivity, catalogues, content, portal builders, and ASPs).

▶ B2BToday.com is a directory that contains listings of B2B services organized by type of service (e.g., Web site creation, B2B marketing, and B2B software) and product category (e.g., automotive and books). Each part of the directory highlights several companies at the start of the list that pay extra fees to be listed on the top; after the premium slots, the directory is organized in alphabetical order. The directory listings are hyperlinked to the companies' Web sites. Many of the sites are involved in B2C.

▶ Communityb2b.com offers many B2B community services, such as news, a library, events calendar, job market, resource directory, and more.

▶ A2ZofB2B.com is a directory of B2B companies organized in alphabetical order or industry order. It specifies the type and nature of the company, the venture capital sponsor of the B2B, and the stock market ticker (if the company's stock is listed on a publicly traded stock exchange).

▶ I-stores.co.uk is a United Kingdom-based directory that targets online stores. The company provides validation of secure Web sites.

▶ Websteronline.com is a large business directory organized by location and by product or service. In addition, it provides listings by industry and subindustry (according to SIC and NAICS codes).

▶ The Thomas Register (thomasregister.com) provides a directory of more than 150,000 manufacturers of industrial products and services.

▶ Bocal.com is a comprehensive B2B site for marketers, marketplaces, directories, news, auctions, and much more.

▶ B2BYahoo (smallbusiness.yahoo.com/marketplace.html) provides business directories and has over 300,000 listed companies (dir.yahoo.com/Business_and_Economy/Directories/Companies) (in 2003).

Newsletters

There are many B2B newsletters to choose from. Several are e-mailed to individuals free of charge. Examples of B2B newsletters are emarketer.com/newsletters (look for B2B Weekly) and line56.com. For information about the ASP industry (Chapter 18), see aspnews.com. Many companies (e.g., Ariba, Intel) issue corporate newsletters and e-mail them to people who request them. Also, companies can use software from onlinepressreleases.com to send online press releases to thousands of editors.

Directories and newsletters are helpful, but they may not be sufficient. Therefore, one may need specialized search engines.

Search Engines and News Aggregators

Several search engines can be used to discover information about B2B. Some of these are embedded in the directories. Some examples are listed here.

▶ Moreover.com is a search engine that not only locates information, but aggregates B2B (and other business) news.

▶ Google offers a directory of components for B2B and B2C Web sites. These range from currency exchange calculators to server performance monitors (see directory.google.com).

▶ iEntry.com provides B2B search engines, targeted "niche engines," and several industry-focused newsletters. iEntry operates a network of Web sites and e-mail newsletters that reaches over 2 million unique opt-in subscribers. Newsletters are available in each of the following categories: Web Developers, Advice, Technology, Professional, Sports & Entertainment, Leisure & Lifestyles, and Web Entrepreneurs. Click on a newsletter to get a brief description and a sample of content.

SOME MORE EC SUPPORT SERVICES

Many other service providers support e-commerce in different ways. Each service provider adds a unique value-added service. This section describes representative examples.

Trust services. Chapter 4 introduced the role of trust in B2C. Trust is also important in B2B because one cannot touch the seller's products and because buyers may not be known to sellers. Trust-support services such as TRUSTe, BBBOnline, and Ernst & Young's trust service are used both in B2C and B2B. For more discussion of these trust services, see Chapter 17.

Trademark and domain names. A number of domain name services are available. Examples are mydomain.com, register.com, easyspace.com, and virtualavenue.com.

Digital photos. Companies such as iPIX (ipix.com) provide innovative pictures for Web sites.

Global business communities. The eCommerce Portal from WizNet (wiznet.net) is a global, Web-based "business community" that supports the unique requirements of buying organizations, including cross-catalogue searches, RFQ development and distribution, and decision support, while simultaneously enabling suppliers to dictate the content and presentation of their own product catalogues.

Access to commercial databases. Subscribers to Thomson Dialog (dialog.com) can access about 1,000 databases, including those containing patents, trademarks, government reports, and news articles.

Online consulting. Find/SVP (findsvp.com) sells instant consulting. For an ad hoc fee starting at $500 or an annual fee of up to $10,000 (in 2003) (Entrepreneur.com 2003), clients can reach over 70 consultants for phone- or Web-based queries. Answers to business questions are produced within 24 hours, with backup documents. Experts give advice on product launches, market segmentation, and potential competitors' moves. A Web-only service to SMEs is available for only $400 a year (in 2002).

Knowledge management. Lotus Domino, a major knowledge management and collaboration company, offers the capability to manage Web content in its Domino product (see Chapter 8).

Client matching. Techrepublic.com matches business clients with firms that provide a wide variety of IT services. It works like a matchmaking service. Clients define what it is they want, and Techrepublic.com performs the searching and screening, checking against some general parameters and criteria. This reduces the risk of clients making bad choices. Buyers also save time and have greater exposure to a larger number of IT service providers.

E-business rating sites. A number of services are available for businesses to research rankings of potential partners and suppliers. Bizrate.com, Forrester.com, Gomez.com, and Consumersearch.com all provide business ratings.

Encryption sites. VeriSign provides valuable encryption tools for all types of EC organizations.

Web research services. A number of Web research providers help companies learn more about technologies, trends, and potential business partners and suppliers. Some of these are MMXI, WebTrack, IDG, ZDNet, and Forrester.

Coupon-generating sites. A number of vendors help companies generate online coupons. Some of these are Q-pon.com, CentsOff.com, LifeMinders.com, and TheFreeSite.com.

Additional services available for B2B operations are given in Exhibit 14.10.

Section 14.5 ▶ REVIEW

1. Describe the role of EC consultants and list their major types.

2. Describe the value offered by directory services. Provide three examples of what value they add.

3. Explain why specialized search engines are needed.

4. List some other EC support services.

14.6 OUTSOURCING EC SUPPORT SERVICES

Most companies do not maintain in-house support services. Instead, they outsource many of these services.

WHY OUTSOURCE EC SERVICES?

Historically, early businesses were vertically integrated—they owned or controlled their own sources of materials, manufactured components, performed final assembly, and managed the distribution and sale of their products to consumers. Later, nearly all firms began to contract

EXHIBIT 14.10 Other B2B Services

Category	Description	Examples
Marketplace Concentrator (aggregator)	Aggregates information about products and services from multiple providers at one central point. Purchasers can search, compare, shop, and sometimes complete the sales transaction.	InternetMall, DealerNet, InsureMarket, Industrial Marketplace
Information Brokers (infomediaries)	Provide product, pricing, and availability information. Some facilitate transactions, but their main value is the information they provide.	PartNet, Travelocity, Auto-by-Tel
Transaction Brokers	Buyers can view rates and terms, but the primary business activity is to complete the transaction.	E*Trade, Ameritrade
Digital Product Delivery	Sells and delivers software, multimedia, and other digital products over the Internet.	Build-a-Card, PhotoDisc, SonicNet
Content Provider	Creates revenue by providing content. The customer may pay to access the content, or revenue may be generated by selling advertising space or by having advertisers pay for placement in an organized listing in a searchable database.	*Wall Street Journal* Interactive, *Quote.com*, Tripod
Online Service Provider	Provides service and support for hardware and software users.	Cyber Media, *TuneUp.com*

with other firms to execute various activities along the supply chain, from manufacturing to distribution and sale, in order to concentrate their activities in their *core competency*. This practice is known as *outsourcing*.

When EC emerged, it became obvious that it would be necessary to outsource some of the support services involved in its deployment. The major reasons why many companies prefer to do this include the following:

▶ A desire to concentrate on the core business
▶ The need to have services up and running rapidly
▶ Lack of expertise (experience and resources) for many of the required support services
▶ The inability to have the economy of scale enjoyed by outsourcers, which often results in high costs for in-house options
▶ Inability to keep up with rapidly fluctuating demands if an in-house option is used
▶ The number of required services, which usually are simply too many for one company to handle

To show the importance of outsourcing, we will look at the typical process of developing and managing EC applications (the e-infrastructure), a topic we address in detail in Online Chapter 18. The process includes the following major steps:

1. EC strategy formulation
2. Application design
3. Building (or buying) the application
4. Hosting, operating, and maintaining the EC site

Each of these steps may include several activities, as shown in Exhibit 14.11 (page 556). A firm may execute all the activities of this process internally or it may outsource some or all of them. In addition to design and maintenance of technical systems, many other system design issues and business functions related to using a Web site also must be addressed. For example, a firm doing EC must design and operate its order fulfillment system and outbound logistics (delivery) functions; it must provide dynamic content on the site; and it must also provide services to its customers and partners.

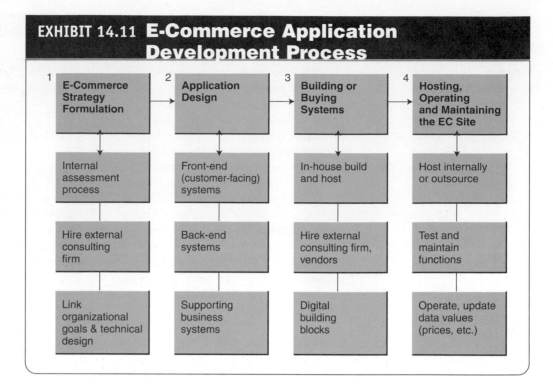

EXHIBIT 14.11 E-Commerce Application Development Process

IT OUTSOURCING AND APPLICATION SERVICE PROVIDERS

Of all business outsourcing, IT outsourcing is done more often than any other area. Most enterprises engaged in EC practice a very large degree of outsourcing. While concentrating on core competencies, they develop strategic alliances with partner firms in order to provide activities such as payment processing, order fulfillment, outbound logistics, Web site hosting, and customer service.

SMEs with few IT staff and smaller budgets are best served by outside contractors. Outside contractors also have proven to be a good choice for large companies wanting to experiment with EC without a great deal of up-front investment. In addition, outsourcing allows them to protect their own internal networks or to rely on experts to establish sites over which they will later assume control. Some of the best-known B2C sites on the Web (e.g., Eddie Bauer and 1-800-FLOWERS) are run by third-party vendors.

Several types of providers offer services for creating and operating electronic storefronts:

▶ **Internet malls.** There are several thousand malls on the Web. Like a real-world mall, an Internet mall consists of a single entry displaying a collection of electronic storefronts. A well-run mall offers cross-selling from one store to another and provides a common payment structure where buyers can use a single credit card purchase to buy products from multiple stores. Theoretically, a mall has wider marketing reach than a stand-alone site and, as a consequence, generates more traffic. The downside is that income must be shared with the mall owner. For additional details, see Chapter 3.

▶ **ISPs.** In addition to providing Internet access to companies and individual users, a large number of ISPs offer hosting services for EC. For the most part, ISPs are focused on operating a secure transaction environment and not on store content. This means that merchants using the services of an ISP must still design their own pages. Of course, this task can be outsourced to a different third party. A listing of top site designers can be found at internetworld.com.

▶ **Telecommunication companies.** Increasingly, the large telecommunications companies are expanding their hosting services to include the full range of EC solutions. MCI, for example, offers Convergence Networking for a flat monthly fee. Web Commerce runs on Microsoft Commerce Server technologies. Similarly, AT&T provides a number of EC services, including the AT&T eCommerce Suite for under $1,000 per month.

- ▶ **Software houses.** Many software companies, such as IBM and Ariba, offer a range of outsourcing services for developing, operating, and maintaining EC applications.
- ▶ **Outsourcers and others.** IT outsourcers, such as EDS, offer a variety of EC services. Also, the large CPA companies and management consultants offer such services.

One of the most interesting types of EC outsourcing is the use of application service providers.

Application Service Providers

An **application service provider (ASP)** is an agent or vendor who assembles the functions needed by enterprises and packages them with outsourced development, operation, maintenance, and other services (see Kern and Kreijger 2001). The essential difference between an ASP and an outsourcer is that an ASP will manage application servers in a centrally controlled location, rather than on a customer's site. Applications are accessed via the Internet or VANs through a standard Web browser interface.

In such an arrangement, applications can be scaled, upgrades and maintenance can be centralized, physical security over the applications and servers can be guaranteed, and the necessary critical mass of human resources can be efficiently utilized. In general, monthly fees, which include fees for the application software, hardware, service and support, maintenance, and upgrades, are paid by the end-user businesses. The fee can be fixed or based on use. According to Scott McNealy, Sun Microsystems CEO, by 2005, "if you're a CIO with a head for business, you won't buy software or computers anymore. You'll rent all your resources from a service provider" (Bonnerjee 2000).

Leasing from an ASP is a particularly desirable option for SMEs, for whom in-house development and operation of EC applications can be time-consuming and expensive. Leasing from ASPs not only saves various expenses (such as labor costs) in the initial development stage, it also helps reduce the software maintenance and upgrading and user training costs in the long run. A company can always select another software from the ASP to meet its changing needs and does not have to invest further in upgrading the existing one. In this way, overall business competitiveness can be strengthened through reducing the time-to-market and enhancing the ability to adapt to changing market conditions. This is particularly true of EC applications for which timing and flexibility are crucial. A detailed list of benefits and risks are provided in Exhibit W14.1.

Leasing from ASPs does have its disadvantages. Many companies are concerned with the adequacy of the protection offered by ASPs against hackers, theft of confidential information, and virus attacks. Also, leased software often does not provide the perfect fit for the desired application. It also is important to ensure that the speed of the Internet connection is compatible with that of the application in order to avoid distortions in its performance. For example, it is not advisable to run heavy-duty applications on a modem link below a T1 line or a high-speed DSL.

ASPs are especially active in enterprise computing and EC applications, which may be too complex to build and too cumbersome to modify and maintain (e.g., see Ward 2000). Therefore, the major providers of ERP software, such as SAP and Oracle, also offer ASP options. An example can be seen at mysap.com. IBM, Microsoft, and Computer Associates also offer ASP services. Similarly, major EC vendors, such as Ariba, offer ASP services.

For an analysis of ASPs in EC, including its advantages and pitfalls, see Segev and Gebauer 2001.

application service provider (ASP)
An agent or vendor who assembles the functions needed by enterprises and packages them with outsourced development, operation, maintenance, and other services.

Section 14.6 ▶ REVIEW

1. List the major reasons why companies outsource EC support services.
2. Which types of services are outsourced the most?
3. Describe the benefits of using ASPs.
4. Comment on the risks of using ASPs.

MANAGERIAL ISSUES

Some managerial issues related to this chapter are as follows.

1. **Have we planned for order fulfillment?** Order fulfillment is a critical task, especially for virtual EC vendors. Even for brick-and-mortar retailers with physical warehouses, delivery to customers' doors is not always easy. The problem is not just the physical shipment, but also the efficient execution of the entire order fulfillment process, which may be complex along a long supply chain.

2. **How should we handle returns?** Dealing with returns can be a complex issue. A company should estimate its percentage of returns and design and plan the process of receiving and handling them. Some companies completely separate the logistics of returns from that of order fulfillment and outsource its execution.

3. **Do we want alliances in order fulfillment?** Partnerships and alliances can improve logistics and alleviate supply chain problems. Many possibilities and models exist. Some are along the supply chain, whereas others are not related to it.

4. **What EC logistics applications would be useful?** One should think not only about how to create logistical systems for EC, but also how to use EC applications to improve the supply chain.

5. **What is the best e-content strategy?** Given the legal implications and the risk of providing strategic information on the Web site, content management should be taken seriously. Unfortunately, this is not usually the case because it is difficult to show tangible benefits. Hiring a consultant to tell you what to do is not a bad idea. Outsourcing content creation and implementation is fairly popular. Remember that content is part of a company's branding and advertising.

6. **Should we provide content translation?** Given that some browsers provide translation, why bother? To begin with, the most popular browser, Internet Explorer, does not provide translation. Translation is related to localization on a large scale. This is why automatic translation may not be sufficient, and at least a combination of manual and automatic should be considered.

7. **EC consultants are expensive. Should we use them?** It depends. If the company lacks expertise or time, consultants may be the best solution. However, first consider using publicly available information on the Internet. Some publicly available information is quite valuable.

8. **Should we outsource EC services?** Outsourcing is a viable option that must be considered. Even large IT companies do so. Again, if a company lacks time or expertise, selective outsourcing may be the best course of action.

SUMMARY

In this chapter, you learned about the following EC issues as they relate to the learning objectives.

1. **The order fulfillment process.** Large numbers of support services are needed for EC implementation. Most important are payment mechanisms and order fulfillment. On-time delivery of products to customers may be a difficult task, especially in B2C. Fulfilling an order requires several activities ranging from credit and inventory checks to shipments. Most of these activities are part of back-office operations and are related to logistics. The order fulfillment process varies from business to business and also depends on the product. Generally speaking, however, the following steps are recognized: payment verification, inventory checking, shipping arrangement, insurance, production (or assembly), plant services, purchasing, customer contacts, and return of products.

2. **Problems in order fulfillment.** It is difficult to fulfill B2C orders due to uncertainties in demand and potential delays in supply and deliveries. Problems also result from lack of coordination and information sharing among business partners.

3. **Solutions to order fulfillment problems.** Automating order taking (e.g., by using forms over the Internet) and smoothing the supply chain are two ways to solve order fulfillment problems. Several other innovative solutions exist, most of which are supported by software that facilitates correct inventories, coordination along the supply chain, and appropriate planning and decision making.

4. **EC content issues and management.** Content creation for EC Web pages is critical for branding and advertising. The major content issues are the use of vendors (content creators, syndicators, etc.), translation to other languages, maintenance (keeping it up-to-date), and maximization and streamlining of its delivery.

5. **Other support services.** EC support services include consulting services, directory services, infrastructure providers, and many more. One cannot practice EC without some of them. These support services need to be coordinated and integrated. Some of them can be done in-house, others must be outsourced.

6. **Outsourcing EC services and using ASPs.** Selective outsourcing of EC services is usually a must. Lack of time and expertise forces companies to outsource, despite the risks of doing so. Using ASPs is a viable alternative, but they are not inexpensive nor risk-free.

KEY TERMS

DISCUSSION QUESTIONS

1. Discuss the problems of reverse logistics in EC. What types of companies may suffer the most?

2. Explain why UPS defines itself as a "technology company with trucks," rather than a "trucking company with technology."

3. Chart the supply chain portion of returns to a virtual store. Check with an e-tailer to see how it handles returns. Prepare a report based on your findings.

4. Chart the supply chain of BikeWorld (in the opening case). Discuss how FedEx services improved the supply chain.

5. Under what situations might the outsourcing of EC services not be desirable?

6. Why does it make sense to use a consultant to develop an e-strategy?

7. Discuss the advantages of EC content syndication.

8. UPS and other logistic companies also provide financial services. Discuss the logic behind this.

9. Discuss the strategy of automatic Web page language translation.

10. Differentiate order fulfillment in B2C from that of B2B.

11. Discuss the benefits and risks of outsourcing e-content.

12. Discuss the pros and cons of using ASPs.

INTERNET EXERCISES

1. The U.S. Postal Service also is in the EC logistics field. Examine its services and tracking systems at usps.com/shipping. What are the potential advantages of these systems for EC shippers?

2. Enter rawmart.com and find what information the site provides that supports logistics. Also find what shipment services they provide online.

3. Visit ups.com and find its recent EC initiatives. Compare them with those of fedex.com. Then go to onlinestore.ups.com and simulate a purchase. Report your experiences.

4. Visit freight-online.com and the sites of one or two other online freight companies. Compare the features offered by these companies for online delivery.

5. Enter efulfillmentservice.com. Review the products you find there. How does the company organize the network? How is it related to companies such as FedEx? How does this company make money?

6. Enter akamai.com and examine its latest content-maximization solutions. Examine customers' stories.

What kinds of customers are most likely to use the service? For what purpose?

7. Enter categoric.com and find information about products that can facilitate order fulfillment. Write a report.

8. Enter kewill.com. Find the innovations offered there that facilitate order fulfillment. Compare it to shipsmo.com. Write a report.

9. Enter unitechnetworks.com and find out how they redirect content.

10. Enter rikai.com. Find any Japanese Web site that deals with a topic of your choice and try to get the English translation. Report your results.

11. Enter b2byellowpages.com and a2zofb2b.com. Compare the information provided on each site. What

features do all both sites share? How do the sites differ?

12. Visit b2btoday.com. Go to the B2B Communities area and identify the major vendors there. Then select three vendors and examine the services they provide to the B2B community. Also enter communityb2b.com and examine the information provided and the usefulness of joining the site.

13. Enter emarket.com, google.com, and cnnfn.com and find recent information about Akamai. Summarize recent information on Akamai.

14. Enter ahls.com and find out what they offer. Comment on the uniqueness of the services.

TEAM ASSIGNMENTS AND ROLE PLAYING

1. Each team should investigate the order fulfillment process offered at an e-tailer's site, such as amazon.com, staples.com, or landsend.com. Contact the company, if necessary, and examine any related business partnerships. Based on the content of this chapter, prepare a report with suggestions for how the company can improve its order fulfillment process. Each group's findings will be discussed in class. Based on the class's findings, draw some conclusions about how order fulfillment can be improved.

2. FedEx, UPS, the U.S. Postal Service, and others are competing in the EC logistics market. Each team should examine one such company and investigate the services it provides. Contact the company, if necessary, and aggregate the findings into a report that will convince classmates or readers that the company in question is the best. (What are its best features?)

3. Assign each team to a content management company. Have each team research their company and present its capabilities and shortcomings.

REAL-WORLD CASE

HOW DELL COMPUTER FULFILLS CUSTOMER REPAIR ORDERS

One of Dell Computer's success factors is its superb logistics and order fulfillment systems. Customer orders, which are received mostly online, are automatically transferred to the production area, where configuration is done to determine which components and parts are needed to create the customized computer that the customer wants.

Once configuration is complete, the problem becomes how to get all the needed components so that a computer can be ready for shipment the next day. As part of the solution, Dell created a network of dedicated suppliers for just-in-time deliveries, as well as a sophisticated computerized global network of components and parts invento-

ries. The global network is also used for *product services* (e.g., repairs, upgrades, demanufacturing, etc.).

Let's examine how Dell provides service when a computer that is in the customer's possession needs to be repaired. Dell is trying to achieve for repairs, upgrades, and other services the next-day shipment that it uses for new computers. For repair activities, Dell needs parts and subassemblies to be delivered to hundreds of repair stations, worldwide, from internal warehouses or external vendors. The search for the parts and their delivery must be done very quickly.

To facilitate this search for parts, Dell is using an online intelligent inventory optimization system from

LPA software (*xelus.com*). The system can reconcile the demand for parts with the action needed (e.g., repair, upgrade, transfer, or demanufacture). For example, the system allows Dell to factor the yield on reusable parts into its supply projection. This allows Dell to use repairable parts to compress time and reduce costs, enabling a team of about 10 employees to successfully process more than 6,000 service orders every day.

The online system generates timely information about demand forecast, the cost of needed inventory, and "days of supply of inventory." It compares actual with forecasted demand. This enables Dell to communicate critical information to external and internal customers, reducing order fulfillment delays.

Producing or acquiring the required parts through component substitution, upgrades, and engineering-change orders must be effective in order to provide superb customer service at a low inventory cost. The system also provides an online standard body of knowledge about parts and planning strategies.

Sources: Compiled from an advertising supplement in *CIO Magazine* (1999), Xelus, Inc.(1999), and Dell (2002).

Questions

1. What portions of order fulfillment are improved by this process?

2. Enter *xelus.com* and find information about its inventory optimization and other SCM-related products. List the major capabilities of the products it offers.

3. Enter *dell.com* and find information about how Dell conducts repair (warranty) customer service.

4. Relate this case to the discussion of "returns" in this chapter.

5. What competitive advantage is provided by this Dell system?

REFERENCES

Akamai. "Akamai and Engage Form Strategic Alliance to Enhance the Targeting and Delivery of Rich Content and Streaming Media Across the Web." Akamai press release, May 8, 2000, akamai.com/en/html/about/press/press116.html (accessed August 2001).

Akamai. "Thomson Financial Contracts Akamai's Industry-Leading EdgeSuite Service for Guaranteed Uptime of Web Operations." Akamai press release, April 8, 2003, akamai.com/en/html/about/press/press391.html (accessed April 2003).

Barnes, H. "Implement Strategic Content Management." *e-Business Advisor*, April 2001a.

Barnes, H. "Three Steps to Effective Web Content Measurement." *e-Business Advisor*, June 2001b.

bayles.com (accessed June 2003)

Bayles, D. L. *E-Commerce Logistics and Fulfillment.* Upper Saddle River, NJ: Prentice Hall, 2001.

Bhise, H., et al. "The Duel for the Doorstep." *The McKinsey Quarterly*, April–June (2000).

Blair, J. "Behind Kozmo's Demise." *New York Times*, April 13, 2001.

Blair, J. "Online Delivery Sites Finding that Manhattan Can be a Hard Place to Make It." *New York Times*, October 2000.

Bonnerjee, A. "ASPs: Exploring the Buzzword." *Network Computing*, August 8, 2000, zdnetindia.com/biztech/ebusiness/asp/stories/550.html (accessed May 2003).

Boston Consulting Group. "Winning the Online Consumer: The Challenge of Raised Expectations." 2001, bcg.com/publications/search_view_ofas.asp?pubID=632 (accessed September 2002).

Burke, M. "Federated Poised to Survive Retail Malaise." *Forbes*, August 6, 2001, forbes.com/2001/08/06/0806federated_2.html (accessed June 2003).

Business 2.0. staff. "The Who's Who of E-Business." *Business2.0*, January 2002, business2.com/articles/mag/0,1640,35691|5,FF.html (accessed August 2002).

Business Week. Special Advertising Section, *Business Week*. June 26, 2000.

Business Week. "What Led to Kosmo's Final Delivery." April 16, 2001, businessweek.com/bwdaily/dnflash/apr2001/nf20010416_207.htm (accessed June 2003).

Byrne, T. "Top Six Content Management Pitfalls." *PC Magazine*, September 17, 2002.

Chio, S. Y., et al. *The Economics of Electronic Commerce.* Indianapolis, IN: Macmillan Technical Publishing, 1997.

CIO Magazine. Advertising supplement, October 1, 1999.

Clyman, J. "From Chaos to Control (Content Management)." *PC Magazine*, September 17, 2002.

Cone, E. "E-Com Meets Logistical Web." *Interactive Week*, July 26, 1999.

Cone, E. "Translation Please: Think Globally, Act Locally." *Interactive Week*, April 23, 2001.

Council of Logistics Management. clm1.org (accessed January 2003).

Coupey, E. *Marketing and the Internet.* Upper Saddle River, NJ: Prentice Hall, 2001.

Dell. dell.com/us/en/gen/services/service_servicesportfolio.htm (accessed May 2002).

DFC Intelligence. "Interactive Broadcast Video Market to Reach $4.2 Billion by 2005." DFC Intelligence news release, November 16, 1999, dfcint.com/news/pr111699.html (accessed May 2003).

Duvall, M. "Santa's Helpers Get Their Feet Webbed." *Interactive Week*, September 13, 1999.

Entrepreneur.com. "Where Do I Find One?" entrepreneur.com/mag/article/0,1539,2303763----,00.html (accessed April 2003).

Farber, D. "UPS Takes Wireless to the Next Level." ZDNet.com, April 28, 2003, techupdate.zdnet.com/techupdate/stories/main/0,14179,2913461,00.html (accessed May 2003).

FedEx. "BikeWorld Goes Global Using FedEx Technologies and Shipping." FedEx case study, August 2000, fedex.com/us/ebusiness/ecommerce/bikeworld.pdf?link=4 (accessed October 2002).

Gupta, V. K., et al. "Overview of Content Management Approaches and Strategies." *Electronic Markets* 11, no. 4 (2001).

Haeg, A. "The Turnaround Artists." *MPR News,* March 5, 2002, news.mpr.org/features/200203/05_haega_fingerhut/ (accessed May 2003).

Handfield, R. B., et al. *Supply Chain Redesign: Transforming Supply Chains into Integrated Value Systems.* Upper Saddle River, NJ: Prentice Hall, 2002.

Junnarkar, S. "Akamai Ends Al-Jazeera Server Support." CNET News, April 4, 2003, news.com.com/1200-1035-995546.html (accessed May 2003).

Kapp, K. M. "A Framework for Successful E-Technology Implementation: Understand, Simplify, Automate." *Journal of Organizational Excellence,* October-December (2001).

Kenneally, C. "It's a Bird, It's a Plane—It's SkyMall!" *Salon.com*, December 21, 1999, salon.com/travel/feature/1999/12/21/skymall/print.html (accessed April 2003).

Kern, T., and J. Kreijger. "An Exploration of the ASP Ousourcing Option." *Proceedings of the 34th HICSS,* Maui, HI, January 2001.

Korzeniowski, P. "ESI Does It." *eWeek*, April 1, 2002.

Lee, H. L., and S. Whang. "Winning the Last Mile of E-Commerce." *MIT Sloan Management Review* (Summer 2001).

Mulqueen, J. T. "Akamai: Taking Content Delivery to the Edge." *Interactive Edge,* July 9, 2001.

Pickering, C. "New Power Centers—FedEx Hub." *Business 2.0,* January 2000.

Radoff, J. "Smart Content Management." *e-Business Advisor,* June 2000.

Rao, B., et al. "Building a World-Class Logistics, Distribution, and EC Infrastructure." *Electronic Markets* 9, no. 3 (1999).

Rogers, D. S., and R. S. Tibben-Lembke. *Going Backward: Reverse Logistics.* Reno, NV: University of Nevada, Center of Logistics Management, 1998.

Saunders, C. "Study: Streaming Media Marketing to Rake in $3.1 Billion in 2005." *Internetnews.com*, June 18, 2001, internetnews.com/IAR/article.php/12_786611 (accessed April 2003).

Segev, A., and J. Gebauer. "B2B Procurement and Marketplace Transformation." *Information Technology and Management* 2, no. 3 (2001).

Steinert-Threlkeld, T. "GroceryWorks: The Low-Touch Alternative." *Interactive Week*, January 31, 2000.

Sterne, J. *Web Metrics.* New York: John Wiley & Sons, 2002.

Sullivan, D. "Machine Translation: Is It Good Enough?" *e-Business Advisor,* June 2001.

Three Squared, Inc. "Three Squared First to Market as One-Stop-Shop for Streaming Media Services." *threesquared.com*, 2000, threesquared.com/download/market.pdf (accessed May 2003).

Trager, L. "Not So Many Happy Returns." *Interactive Week*, March 20, 2000.

United Parcel Service. "UPS E-Logistics Gives Power Boost to Back-End Fulfillment Solution." May 22, 2001, pressroom.ups.com/pressreleases/archives/archive/0,1363,3866,00.html (accessed May 2003).

United Parcel Service. "E-Logistics: Your Inventory Is Worth More Than Money." ec.ups.com/ecommerce/clicks/e_Logistics.html (accessed May 2003).

Varshney, U., and R. Vetter. "Recent Advances in Wireless Networking." *IEEE Computer,* June 2000.

Violino, B. "Supply Chain Management and E-Commerce." *Internet Week,* May 4, 2000.

Ward, L. "How ASPs Can Accelerate Your E-Business." *e-Business Advisor,* March 2000.

Workday Minnesota. "Negotiations to Start at Re-opened St. Cloud Distribution Center." December 5, 2002, workdayminnesota.org/view_article.php?id=22a53ef621f3f2cdb6a8a1b867da7a5d (accessed May 2003).

Xelus, Inc. "Case Study: Dell." 1999, xelus.com/CaseStudies/cs_dell.asp (accessed May 2003).

CHAPTER 15

E-COMMERCE STRATEGY AND GLOBAL EC

Content

Lonely Planet Travels from Place to Space

Learning objectives

Upon completion of this chapter, you will be able to:

1. Describe the strategic planning process.

2. Understand how e-commerce impacts the strategic planning process.

3. Understand how EC applications are formulated, justified, and prioritized.

4. Describe strategy implementation and assessment, including the use of metrics.

5. Understand the causes of EC failures and lessons for success.

6. Evaluate the issues involved in global EC.

7. Analyze the impact of EC on small businesses.

LONELY PLANET TRAVELS FROM PLACE TO SPACE

The Problem

Scan the luggage of independent travelers anywhere in the world and you will find that most of them have something in common—they depend on a Lonely Planet guidebook to tell them how to get to their destination, where to sleep, the best places to eat, and what to see and do, all at a price they can afford. The Lonely Planet (LP) library includes more than 500 book titles as well as maps, travel videos, and a television series. Lonely Planet's principal assets are its global brand name; the dedication of its writers and editorial staff; its vast library of text, maps, photos, and images; and the community of global travelers who buy LP products and contribute to the company's knowledge base.

Lonely Planet faces many of the dilemmas that confront businesses that have been successful in the physical marketplace and are now migrating to the electronic marketspace. These opportunities and threats are especially challenging for companies in the information industry, those that sell newspapers, music, magazines, pictures, software, and books. How can Lonely Planet apply electronic technologies to its vast library of travel information to reinvent the travel guide? How can LP sell its content electronically and not create channel conflict with its traditional outlets, the bookstores? What changes should Lonely Planet make in the way it collects information, stores it, and uses it to publish travel guides?

The Solution

The Lonely Planet EC strategy must consider the combination of business models that make up LP's current value proposition and revenue model. These models include the following:

- **Content provider.** Lonely Planet creates branded and unbranded travel content that is distributed through a number of distributors, including bookstores, travel sites (e.g., Travelocity), and publishers of in-flight magazines. Although a significant portion of this content carries the LP brand, only rarely does LP have a relationship with the purchaser or reader; instead, that relationship is owned by the bookstore, travel site, or publisher.

- **Virtual community.** The LP brand and Web site create a virtual community of independent travelers that LP management recognizes as a key asset. This community, when traveling or preparing to travel, has information and communication needs that LP can use in formulating its online strategy.

- **Direct to consumer.** Lonely Planet has traditionally sold its products through bookstores and other intermediaries. The Internet enables LP to add the direct-to-consumer business model to its e-strategy. However, LP must be cautious with this approach because of the opportunities and threats presented.

In moving online, Lonely Planet has launched the following initiatives:

- Lonely Planet Online (*lonelyplanet.com*) includes an online store (LP shop), access to brief destination overviews (WorldGuide, Theme Guides), free updates to currently published guides (Upgrades), various forms of travel news (Scoop, Postcards), a traveler's bulletin board (Thorn Tree), and links to related sites (SubWWWay). Collectively, these features represent the primary imple-

mentation of LP's direct-to-consumer business model. All products sold online are priced at the recommended retail price so as to not undercut bookstore sales and alienate what is still the company's most important sales outlet. A key to leveraging the virtual community business model is Thorn Tree, an electronic bulletin board for travelers to share up-to-the-minute travel information with other travelers or provide feedback to LP.

- eKno (*ekno.lonelyplanet.com*) is a joint venture with eKit.com to provide an interactive communications service for international travelers, including an e-mail account, a voice mail account, and inexpensive long-distance calls. The eKno initiative generates revenue but, more critically, offers LP a platform for promoting and selling other products because it provides a means for regular contact with its customer database (i.e., direct-to-consumer business model).

- CitySyn (*citysync.com*) is branded "the personal digital guide to urban adventure." It allows owners of handheld computers to load their devices with LP city guides; in these electronic versions, the information is searchable, hyperlinked, and can be annotated and sorted by the traveler. CitySyn can be purchased and downloaded from the LP Web site (i.e., direct-to-consumer model) or bought on a CD-ROM from retail outlets (i.e., content provider model).

- Knowledge Bank is an internal knowledge management project that aims to transfer all of LP's intellectual property into a standardized and centralized digital database. The Knowledge Bank will enable LP to more easily maintain and update current information, to tailor information for specific products (i.e., content provider), and to eliminate duplicate research and storage.

The Results

According to electronic publishing manager Rob Flynn, Lonely Planet seeks nothing less than to use the Internet to "reinvent the travel guide." So far, its steps toward this strategic vision have been cautionary and in line with its core competencies in gathering and distributing travel-related information. When it

has stepped outside its core competencies, it has done so with strategic partners (e.g., eKit.com to provide communication services for eKno).

Perhaps the principal success story of LP's initiatives thus far is its award-winning Web site, which offers a successful sales and information distribution channel to its customer base. The site is also the most visible presence of its virtual community. LP now must consider how to successfully use this strategic asset, and its 2 million visitors per month, to generate revenue and further promote its branded products, but at the same time avoid channel conflict and ally anxiety.

Another asset with huge strategic potential is the Knowledge Bank. Not only does it promise increased internal efficiencies in information handling, it also offers numerous

long-term business possibilities, including the ability to license and syndicate content to outside organizations. It also will be key to the strategic vision of reinventing the travel guide, such as personalized travel guides that allow travelers to make selective choices about the information they need.

Sources: Compiled from Weill and Vitale (2001) and from *lonelyplanet.com* (2003).

WHAT WE CAN LEARN . . .

The opening case raises some interesting issues related to strategic planning for EC. The Lonely Planet approach exemplifies the marketplace-to-marketspace strategies that brick-and-mortar firms need to consider.

A strategic vision—to reinvent the travel guide—takes the company's core business and envisions its future in Cyberspace. All of Lonely Planet's current initiatives would score high for development on the Internet portfolio map discussed in Section 15.4. Lonely Planet has avoided schemes outside its scope and the temptation of the IPO rush that has lured other companies into unprofitable ventures and bankruptcies.

LP's current initiatives have been incremental steps into the marketspace, created by a skunk works (a small, informal, in-house team created to develop new ideas and products outside the usual bureaucratic structure), and strategic experiments that have not distracted the company from its core business of producing information independent travelers need. In addition, leadership from the top is essential in making the LP e-commerce strategy a reality. As CEO Steve Hibbard says, "My role in supporting new initiatives can be critical. Although others do 99 percent of the work, my 1 percent can make a difference" (Weill and Vitale 2001). Finally, Lonely Planet has been successful at avoiding the channel conflict and ally alienation that has plagued other move-to-the-Net companies.

How to create an EC strategy, as Lonely Planet has done, is the subject of this chapter. The chapter will also present the related topics of global EC and EC in SMEs.

15.1 ORGANIZATIONAL STRATEGY: CONCEPTS AND OVERVIEW

A strategy for EC deployment can be very useful to companies, providing them with competitive advantage (Lumpkin 2002). A **strategy** is a broad-based formula for how a business is going to compete, what its goals should be, and what plans and policies will be needed to carry out those goals (Porter 1980). An organization's strategy addresses fundamental questions about the current position of a company and its future directions, such as:

▶ What is our organization about?

▶ What current and anticipated events are affecting our business?

▶ How will our organization have to change to be ready for these events?

▶ How do we make those changes happen?

Is strategy merely a determination of what a company should do next? No, strategy is also about making tough decisions about what *not* to do. Strategic positioning is about making decisions about trade-offs, recognizing that a company must abandon or not pursue some products, services, and activities in order to excel at others. How are these trade-offs determined? Not merely with a focus on growth and increases in revenue, but on profitability and increases in shareholder value over the long run. How is this profitability and economic value determined? By establishing a unique *value proposition* and the configuration of a tailored *value chain* that enables a company to offer unique value to its customers. Therefore, strategy has been, and remains, focused on questions about organizational fit, trade-offs, profitability, and value (Porter 1996; 2001).

Any contemporary strategy-setting process now includes the Internet. Michael Dell, founder of Dell Computer, says, "The Internet is like a weapon sitting on a table, ready to be picked up by either you or your competitors" (Dell 1999). Another perspective is offered by strategy guru Michael Porter who views the Internet not as a source of competitive advantage,

strategy

A broad-based formula for how a business is going to compete, what its goals should be, and what plans and policies will be needed to carry out those goals.

e-commerce strategy (e-strategy)
The formulation and execution of a vision of how a new or existing company intends to do business electronically.

but as a complement to traditional ways of competing (Porter 2001). Whether used as a weapon or as a complement in strategic positioning, many businesses are taking a focused look at the impact of the Internet and EC on their future. For these firms, an **e-commerce strategy**, or **e-strategy**, is the formulation and execution of a vision of how a new or existing company intends to do business electronically. E-commerce strategy is explored in more detail in the next few sections. First, though, we continue our overview of organizational strategy.

THE STRATEGIC PLANNING PROCESS

A strategy is important, but the *process* of developing a strategy is even more important. (See Insights and Additions W15.1 at the book's Web site for some "words of wisdom" about the importance of planning.) No matter how large or how small the organization, the strategic planning process forces the corporate executives or the company's general manager or the small business owner to assess the current position of the company, where it should be, and how to get from here to there. The process also involves primary stakeholders, including the board of directors, employees, and strategic partners. This involvement ensures that stakeholders buy into the strategy and reinforces stakeholder commitment to the future of the organization.

Strategy development will differ depending on the type of strategy, the implementation method, the size of the firm, and the approach that is taken. Nevertheless, any strategic planning process has four major phases, as shown in Exhibit 15.1. (Note that the phases in Exhibit 15.1 correspond to section numbers in this chapter.) The major phases of the strategic planning process, and some identifiable activities and outcomes associated with each phase, are discussed briefly in the following text. The phases are then discussed more extensively as part of the e-commerce strategic planning process in Sections 15.3 through 15.6 of this chapter.

STRATEGY INITIATION

strategy initiation
The initial phase of strategic planning in which the organization examines itself and its environment.

In the **strategy initiation** phase, the organization examines itself and its environment. The principal activities include setting the organization's mission and goals, examining organizational strengths and weaknesses, assessing environmental factors impacting the business, and conducting a competitor analysis. For purposes of EC planning, this includes an examination of the potential contribution that the Internet and other emerging technologies can make to the business.

Specific outcomes from this phase include:

▶ **Company analysis.** The company analysis includes the vision, purpose, value proposition, capabilities, constraints, strengths, and weaknesses of the company. Questions typically asked in a company analysis are: What business are we already in? Who are our future customers? Do our mission statement and our goals adequately describe our

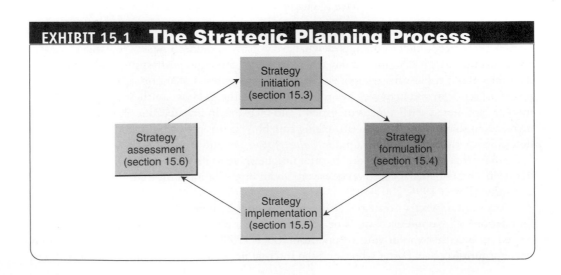

EXHIBIT 15.1 **The Strategic Planning Process**

intended future? What opportunities, and threats, do our business and our industry face? One key outcome from this analysis should be a clear statement of the company's **value proposition**—the benefit that a company's products or services provide to customers or the consumer need that is being fulfilled. Chief-level executives must understand what customer needs their company is satisfying. It is only by knowing the value they provide to customers that they can truly understand "what business they are in" and who their potential competitors are (Harmon et al. 2001).

> ▶ **Core competencies.** A core competency refers to the unique combination of the resources and experiences of a particular firm. It takes time to build these core competencies, and they are difficult to imitate (Rowe et al. 1994). For example, a core competency of Amazon.com is its ability to efficiently ship books and other goods to any location in the world.

> ▶ **Forecasts.** Forecasting means identifying business, technological, political, economic, and other relevant trends that are currently affecting the business or have the potential to do so.

> ▶ **Competitor (industry) analysis.** Competitor analysis involves scanning the business environment to collect and interpret relevant information about direct competitors, indirect competitors, and potential competitors. Several methodologies are available to conduct such an analysis, including a SWOT analysis and competitor analysis grid.

value proposition
The benefit that a company's products or services provide to customers; the consumer need that is being fulfilled.

STRATEGY FORMULATION

Strategy formulation is the development of strategies to exploit opportunities and manage threats in the business environment in light of corporate strengths and weaknesses. In an EC strategy, the end result is likely to be a list of EC applications or projects to be implemented.

Specific activities and outcomes from this phase include:

> ▶ **Business opportunities.** If the strategy initiation has been done well, a number of scenarios for future development of the business will be obvious. How well these scenarios fit with the future direction of the company are assessed. Similarly, the first phase may also have identified some current activities that are no longer relevant to the company's future and are candidates for divestiture, outsourcing, or elimination.

> ▶ **Cost-benefit analysis.** Each proposed opportunity must be assessed in terms of the potential costs and benefits to the company in light of its mission and goals. These costs and benefits can be financial or nonfinancial, tangible or intangible, and short term or long term.

> ▶ **Risk analysis, assessment, and management.** The risks each proposed opportunity represents must be analyzed and assessed. If a significant risk is evident, then a risk management plan is required. Of particular importance in an EC strategy are business risk factors such as transition risk and partner risk, which are discussed in more detail in Section 15.4.

strategy formulation
The development of strategies to exploit opportunities and manage threats in the business environment in light of corporate strengths and weaknesses.

STRATEGY IMPLEMENTATION

In this phase, the emphasis shifts from "what do we do?" to "how do we do it?" In the **strategy implementation** phase, detailed, short-term plans are developed for carrying out the projects agreed on in strategy formulation. Specifically, decision makers evaluate options, establish specific milestones, allocate resources, and manage the projects.

Specific activities and outcomes from this phase include:

> ▶ **Business planning.** Business planning refers to the plan of how to get from the current position to the desired one. Business planning includes setting specific project objectives, creating a project schedule with milestones, and setting measurable performance targets. Normally, a project plan would be set for each project and application.

> ▶ **Resource allocation.** Organizational resources are those owned, available to, and controlled by a company. They can be human, financial, technological, managerial, or knowledge based.

> ▶ **Project management.** This is the process of making the selected applications and projects a reality—staff is hired; equipment is purchased; software is licensed, purchased, or written, and so on.

strategy implementation
The development of detailed, short-term plans for carrying out the projects agreed on in strategy formulation.

STRATEGY ASSESSMENT

strategy assessment
The continuous evaluation of progress toward the organization's strategic goals, resulting in corrective action and, if necessary, strategy reformulation.

Just as soon as implementation is complete, assessment begins. Strategy assessment is the continuous evaluation of progress toward the organization's strategic goals, resulting in corrective action and, if necessary, strategy reformulation. In strategy assessment, specific measures called *metrics* (discussed in Section 15.6) are used to assess the progress of the strategy. In some cases, data gathered in the first phase can be used as baseline data at project implementation. If not, this information will have to be gathered.

What happens with the results from strategy assessment? As shown in Exhibit 15.1, the strategic planning process starts over again, immediately. Early descriptions of the strategic planning process described strategy development as a linear process that terminated at implementation. However, a linear approach simply is not viable in the modern, fast-paced world of competitive business activity. Instead, a cyclical approach is required—a strategic planning process that requires constant reassessment of today's strategy while preparing a new strategy for tomorrow.

Online Tutorial T1 (An E-Business Plan Tutorial) at the book's Web site provides guidance on how to carry out many of the steps in the strategic planning process (e.g., write a mission statement, competitor analysis, business planning).

STRATEGIC PLANNING TOOLS

Strategists have devised a number of strategic planning tools and techniques that can be used in strategic planning. A partial list of these tools is shown in Exhibit 15.2. A few of the most popular tools are briefly described in this section. A strategic management textbook or handbook can provide more information about these and other strategic planning tools.

SWOT analysis
A methodology that surveys external opportunities and threats and relates them to internal strengths and weaknesses.

SWOT analysis is a methodology that surveys the opportunities (O) and threats (T) in the external environment and relates them to the organization's internal strengths (S) and weaknesses (W). For example, Lonely Planet's vast library of travel information is a strength that creates opportunities such as personalized travel guides, making the Knowledge Bank project a key initiative in LP's e-commerce strategy.

EXHIBIT 15.2 Strategic Planning Tools

Tools Used in Strategy Initiation	
SWOT analysis	Analyze external opportunities and threats and relate them to internal strengths and weaknesses (discussed in later text).
Competitor analysis grid	Seek points of differentiation between competitors and the target firm (discussed in later text).
Strategy canvas	Plot a strategic profile based on competition factors (see Kim and Mauborgne 2002).
Tools Used in Strategy Formulation	
Scenario planning	Generate, and prepare for, several plausible alternative futures (discussed in later text).
Return on investment (ROI)	A quantitative, financial measure of costs and benefits (discussed in later text).
BCG growth-share matrix	Compare projects on potential market growth and market share to determine the best projects to adopt, sell, redesign, or abandon (discussed in Section 15.4).
Tools Used in Strategy Implementation	
Project management	A planned effort to accomplish a specific effort of defined scope, resources, and duration.
Business process reengineering (BPR)	Redesign an enterprise's processes to accommodate a new application (discussed in Section 15.5).

A **competitor analysis grid** is a table with the company's most significant competitors entered in the columns and the key factors for comparison entered in the rows. Factors might include mission statements, strategic partners, sources of competitive advantage (e.g., cost leadership, global reach), customer relationship strategies, and financial resources. Sources of information for a competitor analysis grid include the competitor's Web site, publicly available financial documents (e.g., from sec.gov/edgar.shtml), Web-based discussion groups, and corporate research companies (e.g., Dun & Bradstreet). An additional column includes the company's data on each factor so that significant similarities and differences (i.e., points of differentiation) will be obvious.

Scenario planning offers an alternative to traditional planning approaches that rely on straight-line projections of current trends. These approaches fail when low-probability events occur, radically altering current trends. The aim of scenario analysis is to generate several plausible alternative futures, giving decision makers the opportunity to identify actions that can be taken today to ensure success under varying future conditions (see Levinson 1999/2000).

Return on investment (ROI) is a ratio of required costs and perceived benefits of a project or application. Because it is a quantitative financial tool, all costs and benefits must be expressed in financial numbers. The tricky part of ROI is expressing in financial terms costs such as short-term business disruptions and financial *benefits* such as streamlined business processes.

Balanced scorecard is an adaptive tool that assesses organizational progress toward strategic goals by measuring performance in a number of different areas. Originally proposed by Kaplan and Norton (1996) as an alternative to narrowly focused financial assessments, the balanced scorecard seeks more balance by measuring organizational performance in four areas: finance, customers' assessments, internal business processes, and learning and growth.

Section 15.1 ▶ REVIEW

1. What is strategy? What is e-commerce strategy?
2. Which is more important, a plan or the planning process? Why?
3. Describe the four phases of strategic planning.
4. Why is a cyclic approach to strategic planning required?
5. Describe five tools that can be used for strategic planning.

competitor analysis grid
A strategic planning tool that highlights points of differentiation between competitors and the target firm.

scenario planning
A strategic planning methodology that generates plausible alternative futures to help decision makers identify actions that can be taken today to ensure success in the future.

return on investment (ROI)
A ratio of required costs and perceived benefits of a project or an application.

balanced scorecard
An adaptive tool that assesses organizational progress toward strategic goals by measuring performance in a number of different areas.

15.2 EC STRATEGY: CONCEPTS AND OVERVIEW

Earlier an *e-commerce strategy*, or *e-strategy*, was defined as the formulation and execution of a vision of how a new or existing company intends to do business electronically. This section introduces some fundamental considerations in building an e-strategy before the process is explained in more detail later in the chapter.

THE E-DIFFERENCE

The outcomes of a strategic planning process change, sometimes dramatically, when the impact of electronic commerce is considered. Why is this so? Electronic technologies make an "e-difference" in strategy development. The following are just a few of the many differences an e-strategy must consider:

▶ **Reach and richness are possible.** In the old economy, companies had to trade off reach (number of people receiving information) and richness (the customization and interactivity of the information). For example, a newspaper ad has high reach with low richness, but a sales presentation has low reach with high richness. Using Internet tools such as collaborative filtering, personalized e-mail newsletters, and colorful graphics, companies can reach millions of people with rich information (Evans and Wurster 2000).

▶ **Barriers to entry are reduced.** Setting up a Web site is relatively easy and inexpensive, and doing so reduces the need for a sales force and brick-and-mortar stores. Companies have to view this as both a threat (e.g., where will our next competitor come from?) and as an opportunity (e.g., can we use our core competencies in new areas of business?).

▶ **Virtual partnerships multiply.** With access to a World Wide Web of expertise and the ability to share production and sales information easily, the ability of a firm to create a virtual team to exploit an EC opportunity increases dramatically. The Internet is especially good at reducing **interaction costs**, the time and money expended when people and companies exchange goods, services, and ideas (e.g., meetings, sales presentations, telephone calls) (Hagel and Singer 1999).

▶ **Market niches abound.** The market niche strategy is as old as the study of competitive advantage. What has changed is that without the limits imposed by physical storefronts, the number of business opportunities is as large as the Web. The challenge strategists face is to discover and reap the benefits from profitable niches before the competition does so.

Many more e-differences exist in the areas of intermediation (e.g., disintermediation, re-intermediation), alliances (e.g., reduced bargaining power of suppliers), customer service (e.g., mass customization, personalization, CRM), technology (e.g., the ubiquity of the Internet, technology as a competitive imperative), and the market (e.g., competition over who can offer the best price, global reach). Clearly, no strategy plan is complete without considering the impact of the Internet on the company's future.

THE ORGANIZATIONAL DIFFERENCE

The dot-com era of the 1990s witnessed the emergence of *born-on-the-Net* businesses such as Amazon.com, eBay, Priceline.com, and Yahoo. These emergent companies conduct business with innovative business models and without physical storefronts. In the early years of the twenty-first century, the focus has shifted to existing companies with a brick-and-mortar presence that are integrating electronic commerce into their business practices. These firms are variously called *brick-and-click*, *click-and-mortar*, or *move-to-the-Net* businesses.

Born-on-the-Net and move-to-the-Net firms both start with substantial assets and liabilities that influence their ability to formulate and execute an e-commerce strategy (see Exhibit 15.3). The difference between success and failure is rarely the assets and liabilities on the company's strategy balance sheet, but in the company's ability to utilize its strengths effectively. For example, the customer, product, and market knowledge in the move-to-the-Net firm is worthless unless processes and systems are in place to acquire, store, and distribute this knowledge to where it is needed, and innovative management direction is required to recognize its use for competitive advantage in the marketplace. Similarly, whereas the lack of a logistics channel and value chain partnerships is a born-on-the-Net liability, it is easier to build a brand-new, Web-based value chain than to change an established one that is flawed in its practices and processes. In the case that opened this chapter, Lonely Planet illustrates many of these points for the move-to-the-Net firm.

Section 15.2 ▶ REVIEW

1. What factors make the "e-difference" in EC strategic planning?

2. What assets and liabilities do born-on-the-Net organizations have in developing an e-strategy?

3. What assets and liabilities do move-to-the-Net organizations have in developing an e-strategy?

15.3 E-STRATEGY INITIATION

In the *strategy initiation* phase, the organization prepares information about itself, its competitors, and its environment. Information that describes the contribution that EC can make to the business is of special importance here. The steps in strategy initiation are to review the

---

interaction costs
The time and money expended when people and companies exchange goods, services, and ideas.

EXHIBIT 15.3   An EC Strategy Balance Sheet for Born-on-the-Net and Move-to-the-Net Firms

Assets of the Born-on-the-Net Firm	Assets of the Move-to-the-Net Firm
• Executive management tends to be young and entrepreneurial, willing to take risks and make commitments for the long term. • The organizational structure is flat and flexible, with wide spans of control, so the organization responds rapidly to change when asked to. • Information systems are new, allowing rapid implementation of fast, Web-based services that customers demand. • The company as a whole is agile, flexible, hungry for success, and looking to topple the market leader from its perch.	• A customer base, and decades of knowledge about customers and their requirements, is available. This knowledge base can be mined to anticipate customer needs and demands. • Years of experience in the product marketplace are available to the company, which knows what its customers buy, how they buy, and why they buy. • An established brand, a marketplace reputation, and a physical presence gives customers reassurance in terms of trust, long-term viability, and convenience (e.g., for returns). • The initiation of an EC application or project can be funded from existing or redirected resources. A long-term commitment to funding an EC application is possible.
Liabilities of the Born-on-the-Net Firm	**Liabilities of the Move-to-the-Net Firm**
• The customer base on day one is zero, and each new customer must be acquired from an existing firm within a competitive marketplace. • Product knowledge, logistics channels, and value chain partnerships must be built from scratch. • The lack of a brand, reputation, and physical presence raises issues of quality uncertainty among customers. Assets such as brand and reputation must be built, at considerable cost. • The born-on-the-Net business must be built from scratch, using limited venture capital funds or bank loans. If results, and revenues, do not appear fast, the company will go under.	• Executive management tends to be focused on the short-term, looking after satisfactory next quarter results rather than the long-term viability of the company. • The organizational infrastructure is old and lethargic, with layers of management that make responding to change difficult. • Legacy information systems make implementation of strategic EC applications difficult. • The company as a whole is rigid, satisfied with the established way of doing things, and, if it is an industry leader, complacent in its market prominence.

Source: Adapted from Plant (2000), pp. 13, 38, 78–79.

organization's vision and mission, to analyze its industry, company, and competitive position, and to consider various initiation issues.

ISSUES IN E-STRATEGY INITIATION

With company, competitor, and trend data in hand, the company faces a number of questions about its approach to and operation of its EC strategy, as discussed next.

Be a First Mover or a Follower?

Is there a real advantage to being the first mover in an industry or market segment? In e-commerce, does "the early bird get the worm"? Or does the old saying about pioneers—"they are the ones with arrows in their backs"—apply to EC? The answers to these questions are far from clear.

The business, IT, and e-commerce worlds all have examples of companies that succeeded with first-mover advantage, companies that failed in spite of first-mover advantage, and late movers who are now success stories. Generally, the advantages of being first include an opportunity to make a first and lasting impression on customers, to establish strong brand recognition, to lock in strategic partners, and to create switching costs for customers. The risks of being a first-mover include the high cost of developing EC initiatives, making mistakes followers into the market can avoid, the chance that a second wave of competitors will eliminate a first-mover's lead through innovation, and the risk that the move will be too early, before the market is ready (e.g., home banking systems in the early 1990s). Although the importance of a speedy market entry cannot be dismissed, some research suggests that over the long run first movers are substantially less profitable than followers (Boulding and Christen 2001) and that switching costs and network effects are not as substantial as claimed (Porter 2001).

So what determines whether a first mover succeeds or fails? In their examination of "the first-mover advantage misconception," Rangan and Adner (2001) suggest the following factors:

▶ **Size of the opportunity.** The company must be big enough for the opportunity, and the opportunity must be big enough for just one company. If the first-mover company is too small or underfunded to fill the market, there will be an opportunity for a late mover. The same applies if the opportunity is too large for any one company (e.g., the food grocery market).

▶ **Commodity products.** The product or service should be simple enough that the offerings are hard to differentiate (e.g., books, airline seats). If later entrants can differentiate themselves by offering better products and services (e.g., clothes, restaurants), buyers will be encouraged to switch to late movers.

▶ **Be the best.** Time and time again, first-mover advantage has been lost because the company failed to capitalize on its first-mover position or, more precisely, a late mover offered a better and more innovative product or service. Usually it is *best*-mover advantage, not first-mover advantage, that will determine the market leader.

For a sampler of successes and failures among first movers, see Insights and Additions 15.1.

Insights and Additions 15.1   First-Mover and Best-Mover Success Stories

Companies that "got there first" and leveraged their first-mover advantage for success

eBay	eBay was a first mover into the online auction market. Listening to the customer and constantly adding new features and services has kept eBay on top.
Yahoo	The world's first Internet directory remains the world's most popular Internet directory. Innovations such as My Yahoo (*my.yahoo.com*), Yahoo Groups (*groups.yahoo.com*), and Web-page hosting (*geocities.yahoo.com*) have helped Yahoo morph into a profitable Internet portal.
Apple Computer	Being first with a Windows desktop, mouse, hard floppy disk, floppyless laptops, and wireless technology has given Apple a frontier-pushing reputation that keeps it in the personal computer operating system market, while others (e.g., IBM's OS/2) have floundered in the face of the Microsoft Windows juggernaut.

Companies that had first mover advantage, but lost the marketplace battle to late movers

Citibank	The company that invented automatic teller machines has lost the ATM protocol race to Cirrus.
Sony	Being first and having the technically superior beta videotape format did not save Sony from being beaten by Matsushiata's VHS format.
Chemdex	The original B2B digital exchange closed down when revenue growth slowed and the owners decided to change to a different business model.
Netscape	The world's first Internet browser company saw its dominance of the browser market diminish as Microsoft bundled Internet Explorer into the Windows operating system.

Companies that were late movers, but gained success over first movers by being best movers

Intel	Intel didn't invent the microchip, but its alliance with Microsoft ("Wintel") and its world-best research and development efforts have made Intel the world's leading microchip manufacturer.
America Online	Innovative marketing (e.g., mass distribution of free installation disks) and provision of online information people could use moved AOL to the top of the ISP market while first movers (e.g., Compuserv, Prodigy) failed.
Google	While other search engines battled for supremacy in the "keyword ranking" battleground, Google invented "link popularity" and soared to the top in the search engine market.

Go Global?

The decision whether or not to go global is important enough to be part of the strategy initiation process. For example, Lego of Denmark elected to go global selectively (i.e., in a few countries with a few products). The issues involved in deciding whether or not to go global are discussed in Section 15.8.

Have a Separate Online Company?

Separating a company's online operations into a new company makes sense when: (a) the volume of anticipated e-business is large, (b) a new business model needs development apart from the constraints of current operations, (c) the subsidiary can be created without dependence on current operations and legacy systems, and (d) the online company is given the freedom to form new alliances, attract new talent, and raise additional funding (Venkatraman 2000). Barnes and Noble, Nordstrom Shoes, Halifax in the United Kingdom, and the ASB Bank in New Zealand (see EC Application Case 15.1) are a few examples of companies that have established separate companies or subsidiaries for online operations.

The advantages of creating a separate company are reduction or elimination of internal conflicts; more freedom for the online company's management in pricing, advertising, and other decisions; the ability to create a new brand quickly (see next section); the opportunity to build new, efficient information systems that are not burdened by the legacy systems of the old company; and an influx of outside funding if the market likes the e-business idea and buys the IPO of stock. The disadvantages of creating an independent division are that it may be very costly and/or risky; expertise vital to the existing company may be lost to the new firm; and the new company will not benefit from the expertise and spare capacity in the business functions (marketing, finance, distribution) unless it gets superb collaboration from the parent company.

CASE 15.1
EC Application

BANKDIRECT: NEW ZEALAND'S VIRTUAL BANK

For four decades, ASB Bank (formerly Auckland Savings Bank) has had a reputation as a technologically savvy bank that knows how to use information technology for competitive advantage. In the mid-1960s, ASB Bank was a first mover into real-time processing of banking transactions. In the 1970s, ASB Bank replaced its account-oriented database software with a customer-oriented data model. This enabled ASB Bank to be New Zealand's first bank to introduce a comprehensive customer-account product in 1986, a competitive advantage that took other banks more than 2 years to counter.

Despite this reputation, ASB Bank's launch of its virtual bank, BankDirect (*bankdirect.co.nz*), in 1997 took the Australasian banking world by surprise. Initiated by CEO (and former CIO) Ralph Norris as a skunk works project several months earlier, BankDirect was launched as a flexible, innovative bank in an increasingly competitive banking market. Norris's IT background contributed to the BankDirect vision. As a virtual bank, BankDirect has no bank tellers and no bank facilities. Instead, the bank uses the Internet, a telephone call center, ATMs, and mobile mortgage managers to conduct business. The target market is the online customer who is willing to forgo face-to-face bank transactions and receive cost savings and innovative services in return. For example, BankDirect consistently offers one of the lowest interest rates for home loans. Despite the lack of face-to-face contact, an

October 2002 survey by the Consumers Institute of New Zealand ranked BankDirect third in customer satisfaction, ahead of all "Big 5" New Zealand banks, including ASB Bank.

BankDirect remains ASB Bank's "virtual bank brand." It competes directly against ASB Bank's Fastnet and Fastphone services. However, any ASB Bank customers who have been lost to BankDirect have been more than compensated for by the BankDirect customers who have switched from one of ASB Bank's competitors. By launching a separate company and a new brand to fill an obvious gap in the banking market, ASB Bank has been able to increase its customer base and further enhance its reputation as New Zealand's leading technology bank.

Sources: Compiled from Barton and Peters (1992), *bankdirect.co.nz* (2003), *asbbank.co.nz* (2003), and *consumers.co.nz* (2003).

Questions

1. Why did ASB Bank launch BankDirect as a separate company rather than within ASB Bank itself?

2. Describe BankDirect's value proposition to its customers.

3. How has ASB Bank benefited from creating a separate online company as its virtual bank brand?

Creating a separate company versus in-house development are not the only two approaches that are available to a brick-and-mortar firm looking to enhance its EC future. These are two options at the ends of a continuum that also includes strategic partnerships (e.g., Rite Aid bought an equity stake in Drugstore.com) and joint ventures (e.g., KB Toys joined forces with BrainPlay.com to create Kbkids.com). These options, and other permutations along the integration continuum, enable an aspiring click-and-mortar company to strike an effective balance between the freedom and flexibility that come with separation and the marketing leverage and access to organizational knowledge that is inherent with in-house development (Gulati and Garino 2000).

Have a Separate Online Brand?

A company faces a similar decision when deciding whether to create a separate brand for its online offerings.

Generally, companies with strong, mature, international brands will want to retain and promote that brand online. For example, when BMW (**bmw.com**) went online, it adopted an e-strategy of brand reinforcement intended to build strong relationships with existing and prospective customers. This strategy flowed through the company's entire plan, even down to Web site design, as a BMW executive explains: "We wanted to design a site that said to those people who are BMW enthusiasts; BMW really knows who I am. . . . We wanted to make sure that it added value to the ownership relationship of having a BMW. *We wanted to make sure that it navigated and felt like a BMW*" (Plant 2000, p. 181; emphasis added).

However, existing firms with a weak brand or a brand that does not reflect the intent of the online effort may decide to create a new brand. For example, Axon Computertime (**axon.co.nz**) has a high-value, low-cost reputation in the highly competitive computer sales and configuration market. An analysis from an e-commerce strategic planning effort identified an opportunity to deliver premium quality, ISO 9002–compliant service in the computer services marketplace. To capitalize on this opportunity and retain the current Axon reputation, the company created a new division and launched a new brand, Quality Direct, to distinguish this effort within the parent company.

Section 15.3 ❱ REVIEW

1. Describe the advantages, risks, and success factors that first movers face.

2. What are the advantages and disadvantages of creating a separate online company?

3. Why would an existing company want to create a new brand for its e-commerce initiative?

15.4 E-STRATEGY FORMULATION

Based on the results of the company and competitive analyses, the company is ready to evaluate potential EC strategies and select a small number for implementation. *Strategy formulation* activities include evaluating specific EC opportunities and conducting cost-benefit and risk analyses associated with those opportunities. Specific outcomes include a list of approved EC projects or applications, risk management plans, and pricing strategies that will be used in the next phase of strategy implementation.

SELECTING EC OPPORTUNITIES

The principal outcome of the strategy initiation phase should have been a number of potential EC initiatives that exploit opportunities and manage threats in the business environment in light of corporate strengths and weaknesses. In the strategy formulation phase, the firm must decide which initiatives to implement and in what order.

As is the case with many business decisions, there are correct approaches to EC-strategy selection and incorrect ones. According to Tjan (2001), companies often make one of the following three mistakes in selecting EC projects:

1. **Let a thousand flowers bloom.** In this context, this phrase means that an organization funds many projects indiscriminately, hoping that the majority will succeed. Unfortunately, organizational financial resources, time, and attention cannot support multiple initiatives, and widespread success seldom happens.

2. **Bet it all.** In contrast, sometimes the company bets everything on a single high-stakes initiative. This strategy is very risky: If you wager it all, you can lose it all.

3. **Trend-surf.** The company follows the crowd toward the next "big thing," the most fashionable new idea. With this strategy, too much capital ends up pursuing too few opportunities or too much competition is created.

We would add to this list the following additional mistake:

4. **Being fear- or greed-driven.** Sometimes companies are either so scared that if they do not practice EC they will be big losers or they think that they can make lots of money by rushing into EC. In such cases, afraid that they will "miss the boat," companies frequently jump into inappropriate ventures.

Some companies have found that compelling internal or external forces can drive the strategy selection process in an ad hoc, crisis-driven, decision-making process. For example, the following approaches have propelled strategy formulation:

▶ **Problem driven.** When an organization has a specific problem (such as excess inventory or delays in deliveries), an EC application may solve the problem. An example is General Motors, whose problem of disposing of old equipment was solved by implementing forward e-auctions.

▶ **Technology driven.** In this case, the company wants to put certain existing technology to use. IBM, for example, is one of the world's largest holders of U.S. patents. Not only does IBM license and sell its proprietary technology to others (a form of e-strategy in itself), but IBM applies these technologies for use inside the company as well. First movers and industry leaders, such as IBM, usually use the technology-driven approach. In taking this approach, the company may stumble over problems that no one knew existed; solving them may bring a big reward.

▶ **Market driven.** In this approach, the company waits to see what the competitors in the industry do. When one or more competitors start to use EC, and it seems that they are doing well, then the company decides it is time to follow suit. ToysRUs.com followed eToys, Barnesandnoble.com followed Amazon.com, and Merrill Lynch's online operations followed E*TRADE and Ameritrade. As noted earlier, this late-mover strategy can be effective if the company can use the brand, technology, superior customer service, or innovative products and strategies to overcome any lost first-mover advantage.

The E-Business Maturity Model

The consulting company PricewaterhouseCoopers (PWC) developed, with Carnegie Mellon University, an *e-business maturity model* (known by the acronym emm@). The model evaluates online initiatives within the context of established business criteria. Described as both a diagnostic and a prescriptive tool for assessing a company's e-business capability, the model is designed to help companies think of what's necessary to implement an e-business solution.

For example, suppose a company wants to offer e-business transactions over the Web in three countries. Using emm@, this company is prompted to provide information that is then used to craft an assessment. In the case of establishing an international Web presence, clients might be prompted to examine tax and legal implications as well as their marketing and logistics efforts. The feedback emm@ provides is contingent on the objectives selected by clients.

Most times, however, businesses are best served by a systematic methodology to determine an appropriate EC application profile that determines which initiatives to pursue and when. Such an approach is described in the next section.

DETERMINING AN APPROPRIATE EC APPLICATION PORTFOLIO

For years, companies have tried to find the most appropriate portfolio (group) of projects among which an organization should share its limited resources. The classical portfolio strategy attempts to balance investments with different characteristics. For example, the company would combine long-term speculative investments in new, potentially high-growth businesses with short-term investments in existing, profit-making businesses.

One well-known framework of this strategy is Boston Consulting Group's market growth/market share matrix (*BCG growth share matrix*) with its "star," "cash cow," "wild card," and "dog" opportunities (Stern and Stalk 1998).

An Internet Portfolio Map for Selecting Applications

Tjan (2001) adopted the Boston Consulting Group's approach to create what he calls an "Internet portfolio map." However, instead of trading off market potential and market share, the Internet portfolio map is based on *company fit* and *project viability*, both of which can be either low or high. *Viability* can be assessed by various criteria such as market value potential, time to positive cash flow, time to implementation, and funding requirements. Similarly, *fit* can be evaluated by metrics such as alignment with core capabilities, alignment with other company initiatives, fit with organizational structure, and ease of technical implementation. Together, these create an *Internet portfolio map* (see Exhibit 15.4).

Each company will want to determine for itself the criteria used to assess viability and fit. Each proposed EC initiative (e.g., a B2B procurement site, a B2C store, an enterprise portal) is evaluated by senior managers and outside experts on each of these criteria, typically on a quantitative (e.g., 1 to 100) or qualitative (e.g., high, medium, low) scale. If some criteria are more important than others, these can be weighted appropriately. The scores are combined, and average fit and viability scores are calculated for each initiative. Initiatives in which there is high agreement on rankings by the experts can be considered with more confiden   ce.

The various initiatives are then mapped onto the Internet portfolio map. If both viability and fit are low, the project is *rejected*. If both are high, the project is *adopted*. If fit is high but viability is low, the project is *redesigned*. Finally, if the fit is low but the viability is high, the project is *sold*. Senior management must also consider factors such as cost-benefit and risk in making the final decision about what initiatives get funded and in what order. However, the Internet portfolio map can be an invaluable guide for navigating an e-commerce strategy through uncharted waters.

MAKING A BUSINESS CASE

Executives need to be sure that EC initiatives can truly enhance their company's ability to generate revenues and reduce costs, thereby increasing competitiveness and profits. This is the principal objective of the business case.

As defined in Chapter 1, the **business case** is a written document that is used by managers to garner funding for specific applications or projects by providing a justification for the investment of resources. The business case provides the bridge between planning and execution. Specifically, the business case helps clarify how the organization will use its resources by identifying the strategic justification ("Where are we going?"), operational justification

business case
A written document that is used by managers to garner funding for specific applications or projects by providing justification for investment of resources.

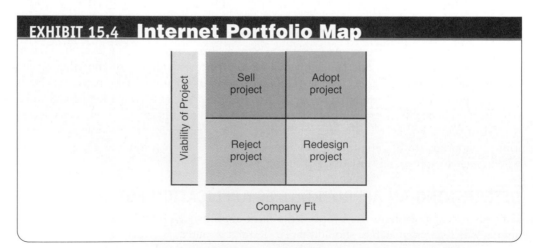

EXHIBIT 15.4 Internet Portfolio Map

("How will we get there?"), technical justification ("When will we get there?"), and financial justification ("Why will we win?") (Kalakota and Robinson 2001).

A business case usually is done for each EC project in an existing firm. The case typically follows the format of a traditional business plan, with a few significant differences. (See Online Tutorial T1 for more information about how to prepare a business case.)

COST-BENEFIT ANALYSIS

Like any other investment, an EC project must undergo the scrutiny of a cost-benefit analysis and justification. A cost-benefit analysis is not only a valuable planning tool, it also assists in the development of metric measures that later will be used in strategy assessment. Various methods of performing a cost-benefit analysis, principally a ROI (explained earlier), can be used. Exactly how costs and benefits are calculated are beyond the scope of this discussion but are available in Turban et al. (2004), Alter (2002), or Boardman et al. (2000). Instead, this section briefly addresses the difficult problems strategists face in estimating costs and benefits in an EC project.

Many of the costs of an EC project can be clearly identified and estimated. For example, the costs of hardware, software, new staff, and facilities can be quantified in dollars, euros, yen, or yuan. Other costs are intangible and more difficult to measure. What will be the short-term cost of disruption in business? How many staff days, expressed in salary costs, will be lost in training?

Most benefits of an EC project are quite intangible. Increased sales from an expanded customer base, savings from streamlined purchasing procedures, and reduced telecommunications costs are easy to identify, but they may be difficult to estimate. More difficult both to identify and to quantify are benefits such as increased productivity from staff, better customer service, and improved staff morale.

One of the most difficult factors in accurate benefit estimation, especially for start-up companies, is to properly plan the revenue model. Many of the EC failures in 2000 and 2001 can be attributed to an incorrect revenue model. For example, many portals expected large revenues from advertising, but these revenues did not materialize. These companies overestimated the amount of advertising revenue they could obtain or just failed to find the ad revenue that might have been available. In addition, many revenue models based on sales depended on large and rapid customer acquisition. In many cases, the expenses for customer acquisition greatly exceeded revenues from sales, resulting in large losses. A lesson from the bursting of the dot-com bubble is that a realistic assessment of the revenue model is essential for EC opportunity selection.

RISK ANALYSIS AND MANAGEMENT

Risk is inherent in all business activities, and especially when organizations are moving into new territory, as an e-commerce strategy inevitably implies. Managing that risk is a process of analyzing the risk factors and then taking the steps necessary to reduce the threat to the business from that risk. Adapting a definition of IT risk from Markus (2000), **e-commerce (EC) risk** is the likelihood that a negative outcome will occur in the course of developing and operating an e-commerce strategy.

Mention e-commerce risk and most business professionals think of information security—the threat posed by hackers and negligent loss of data. This is the most obvious, but not the most threatening aspect of EC risk. *The most dangerous risk to a company engaged in e-commerce is business risk*—the possibility that developing and operating an e-commerce strategy could negatively impact the well-being of the organization itself. Chapter 12 focuses on information security; the emphasis here is on business risk.

The first step in any risk assessment is risk analysis—identifying and evaluating the sources of risk. Microsoft, for example, has an exemplary program of risk analysis that is based on 12 primary sources of risk: business partners, competitive, customer, distribution, financial, operations, people, political, regulatory and legislative, reputational, strategic, and technological (Teach 1997).

e-commerce (EC) risk
The likelihood that a negative outcome will occur in the course of developing and operating an electronic commerce strategy.

Four sources of business risk in an e-commerce strategy (Viehland 2001), with pertinent questions, are:

1. **Competitive risk.** Can a strategy intended to introduce competitive advantage have negative, unanticipated consequences? What is the competitive threat posed by new entrants?

2. **Transition risk.** What are the consequences for current customers, distribution channels, and business processes if an organization adopts e-commerce as a new growth strategy?

3. **Customer-induced risk.** How can an organization manage customer relations in an online world that is different from the traditional marketplace?

4. **Business partner risk.** How can increasing dependence on business partnerships be managed?

Once sources of risk have been identified, the next step is *risk management*—to put in place a plan that reduces the threat posed by the risk. Risk management principally is taking steps to reduce the probability that the threat will occur, minimizing the consequences if it occurs anyway, or both. Many risk management strategies in the off-line world of business apply to e-commerce risk management. For example, minimizing transition risk is mostly about successful change management. In other risk areas, new and innovative risk management strategies are necessary. For example, putting trust-generating policies and procedures in place can minimize customer-induced risk.

Various methods can be used to conduct risk assessment (e.g., see Wheelen and Hunger 2002; Vose 2000). A number of sources offer specific advice about analyzing and managing e-commerce risk (e.g., Deise et al. 2000; Hiles 2001; Viehland 2001).

ISSUES IN STRATEGY FORMULATION

A variety of issues exist in strategy formulation, depending on the company, industry, nature of applications, and so forth. Some representative issues are discussed in this section.

How to Handle Channel Conflict

As discussed in Chapter 3, channel conflict may arise when an existing company creates an additional distribution channel online. Several options exist for handling channel conflict. These include the following:

▶ Let the established distributors handle e-business fulfillment, as the auto industry is doing. Ordering can be done online or directions to distributors can be provided online.

▶ Provide online services to intermediaries (e.g., by building portals for them) and encourage them to reintermediate themselves in other ways.

▶ Sell some products only online, such as lego.com is doing. Other products may be advertised online but sold exclusively off-line.

▶ Avoid channel conflict entirely by not selling online. Of course, in such a case, a company could still have an EC presence by offering promotion and customer service online, as BMW (bmw.com) is doing.

How to Handle Conflict Between the Off-Line and Online Businesses

In a click-and-mortar business, the allocation of resources between off-line and online activities can create difficulties. Especially in sell-side projects, the two activities can come to be viewed as competitors. In this case, personnel in charge of off-line and online activities may behave as competitors. This conflict may cause problems when the off-line side needs to handle the logistics of the online side or when prices need to be determined. For example, when Schwab started e-Schwab, it experimented with different prices for online and off-line customers, making off-line customers angry. When the company subsequently merged its online and off-line services, it set one price for all stock trades (Pottruck and Pearce 2000).

Corporate culture, the ability of top management to introduce change properly, and the use of innovative processes that support collaboration will all determine the degree of collaboration between off-line and online activities in a business. Clear support by top management for both the off-line and online operations and a clear strategy of "what and how" each unit will operate are essential.

Pricing Strategy

Traditional methods for determining price are the cost-plus and competitor models. *Cost-plus* means adding up all the costs involved—material, labor, rent, overheads, and so forth—and adding a percentage mark-up as profit. The *competitor model* determines price based on what competitors are charging for similar products in the marketplace.

Pricing products and services for online sales changes these pricing strategies in subtle ways:

> **Price comparison is easier.** In traditional markets, either the buyer or, more often, the seller has more information than the other party, and this situation is exploited in determining a product's price. By facilitating price comparison, the Internet helps create what economists call a *perfect market*—one in which both the buyer and the seller have ubiquitous and equal access to information, usually in the buyer's favor. On the Internet, search engines, price comparison sites (e.g., mysimon.com, comparenet.com), infomediaries, and intelligent agents make it easy for customers to find who offers the best product at the best price.

> **Buyers sometimes set the price.** Name-your-own-price models such as Priceline.com and auction sites such as onsale.com mean that buyers do not necessarily just take the price; sometimes they *make* the price.

> **Online and off-line goods are priced differently.** Pricing strategy may be especially difficult for a click-and-mortar company. Setting prices lower than those offered by the off-line business may lead to internal conflict, whereas setting prices at the same level will hurt competitiveness.

> **Differentiated pricing can be a pricing strategy.** For decades, airline companies have maximized revenues with yield management—charging different prices for the same product. In the B2C EC marketplace, one-on-one marketing can extend yield management from class of customer (e.g., buying an airline seat early or later) to individual customers. In the B2B EC marketplace, extranets with customized pricing pages present different prices to different customers based on purchasing contracts, the customer's buying history, and other factors. **Versioning**, which is selling the same good but with different selection and delivery characteristics (Shapiro and Varian 1999), is especially effective in selling digital information goods. For example, time-critical information such as stock market prices can be sold at a higher price if delivered immediately. As with all forms of differentiated pricing, versioning information is based on the fact that some buyers are willing to pay more to receive some additional advantage.

versioning
Selling the same good, but with different selection and delivery characteristics.

The overall impact of these changes is good news for the consumer. Internet technologies tend to provide consumers with easier access to pricing information, which increases their bargaining power. To remain competitive and profitable, sellers will have to adopt smarter pricing strategies. Specifically, businesses will have to look at ways of using the Internet to optimize prices, principally through greater precision in setting prices, more adaptability in changing prices, and new ways of customer segmentation for differentiated pricing (see Exhibit 15.5 on page 580).

Dewan et al. (2000) and Prasad and Harker (2000) have developed quantitative economic models for making pricing decisions. Watson et al. (2000) discuss pricing-setting strategy in conjunction with marketing strategy.

Section 15.4 ▶ REVIEW

1. Describe how a company should not select EC applications.
2. Explain Tjan's Internet portfolio map.
3. Describe some of the difficulties in cost-benefit analysis in an EC application.

EXHIBIT 15.5			
Three Strategies for Smarter Pricing on the Internet			
Pricing Strategy	**Source of Value from the Internet**	**B2C Examples**	**B2B Examples**
Precision: Determine the highest price that has little or no impact on purchase decisions (i.e., price at the top of the zone of price indifference).	Prices can be tested continually, in real time, leading to better understanding of the zone of price indifference.	Commodity products such as toys, books, and CDs.	Maintenance, repair, and operation (MRO) products.
Adaptability: Change prices frequently, in response to market conditions, inventory levels, or competitor pricing.	Prices can be changed fast and frequently, and in response to Internet-monitored conditions.	Consumer goods with short product life cycles (e.g., electronics); goods with fluctuating demand (e.g., luxury cars).	Perishable goods (e.g., chemicals) or goods with fluctuating demand and availability (e.g., raw materials).
Segmentation: Divide customers into different classes and offer different prices based on customer segments.	Easily identify which segment a buyer belongs to and create barriers between segments.	Products in which customer profitability varies widely (e.g., credit cards, mortgages) or goods purchased in response to special offers (e.g., automobiles).	"Fill-in" customers (purchasing in emergency) will pay more than regular customers (e.g., industrial components, business services).

Source: Reprinted by permission of *Harvard Business Review*. From "Price Smarter on the Net" by Baker et al., *Harvard Business Review, 2001*. Copyright © 2001 by the Harvard Business School Publishing Corporation; all rights reserved.

4. List four sources of business risk in EC. What questions exemplify each source of risk?

5. Discuss three strategies for smarter pricing online.

15.5 E-STRATEGY IMPLEMENTATION

The execution of the strategic plan takes place in the *strategy implementation* phase, in which detailed, short-term plans are developed for carrying out the projects agreed on in strategy formulation. Decision makers evaluate options, establish specific milestones, allocate resources, and manage the projects.

Typically, the first step in strategy implementation is to establish a Web team, which then initiates the execution of the plan. As EC implementation continues, the team is likely to introduce changes in the organization. During the implementation phase, it also becomes necessary to develop an effective change management program, including the possibility of business process reengineering.

In this section, we deal with some of the topics related to this implementation process. Chapter 16 continues the implementation discussion with an overview of many of the practical considerations involved in launching an online business.

CREATING A WEB TEAM

In creating a Web (project) team, the organization should carefully define the roles and responsibilities of the team leader, team members, Web master, and technical staff. The purpose of the Web team is to align business goals and technology goals to implement a sound EC plan with available resources. A Web team needs individuals who are knowledgeable about the technology that is required, as well as employees who are familiar with business information and data and how they should be structured and delivered.

Every Web project, and every Web team, also requires a project champion. In his study of EC strategy in 43 companies, Plant (2000) found, "In every successful e-commerce project studied for this book, a strong project champion was present in the form of a senior executive or someone in a position to demonstrate to a senior executive the potential added value such a project could bring to the organization" (pp. 34–35). Similarly, "top management championship" was identified as a critical factor for organizational assimilation of Web technologies

(Chatterjee et al. 2002). The **project champion** is the person who ensures that the project gets the time, attention, and resources required, as well as defends the project from detractors at all times. The project champion might be the Web team leader or a more senior executive, as shown in EC Application Case 15.2.

project champion
The person who ensures the EC project gets the time, attention, and resources required, as well as defending the project from detractors at all times.

STARTING WITH A PILOT PROJECT

Implementing EC often requires significant investments in infrastructure. Therefore, a good way to start is to undertake one or a few small EC pilot projects. Pilot projects help uncover problems early, when the plan can be easily modified before significant investments are made.

General Motors' pilot program (GM BuyPower) is an example of the successful use of a pilot project. On its Web site, gmbuypower.com, shoppers can choose car options, check local dealer inventory, schedule test drives, and get best-price quotes by e-mail or telephone. GM BuyPower started as a pilot project in four western U.S. states before expanding to all states. Similarly, when Home Depot decided to go online in 2000, it started in six stores in Las Vegas, then moved to four other cities in the western United States, and eventually went nationwide.

ALLOCATING RESOURCES

The resources required for the EC projects depend on the information requirements and the capabilities of each project. Some resources—software, computers, warehouse capacity, staff—will be new and unique to the project or application. Even more critical for the project's success is effective allocation of infrastructure resources that are shared by many applications, such as databases, the intranet, and possibly an extranet.

A variety of tools can assist in resource allocation. Project management tools such as Microsoft Project assist with determining project tasks, milestones, and resource requirements. Standard system design tools can help in executing the resource-requirement plan.

CASE 15.2
EC Application

MR. SEEGERS PUTS GE ON THE E-BUSINESS TRACK

General Electric (GE) is the world's largest company, and it suffers from many of the problems that plague large, established, old-economy companies in the Internet Age. GE should have been on the e-business track from the very beginning. The GE Information Services (GEIS) division was one of the world's premier users of EDI to support one of the world's largest electronic buying networks. However, in the late 1990s when companies such as Ariba and Commerce One began to produce Internet-based software for B2B e-commerce, GEIS saw the Web only as a cheap on-ramp into its vast EDI network. Suggestions to change current systems were met with burdensome executive and board approval processes, an intolerance for any short-term losses due to development and conversion costs, and concerns about cannibalizing the profitable proprietary data business (GEIS itself).

Harvey Seegers joined GEIS in 1996 and began to agitate for a larger role for GEIS, at first without much success. However, in late 1998, GE's CEO Jack Welch watched his family do their Christmas shopping online, and in early 1999, he issued his famous edict that e-business would be every division's "priority one, two, three, and four." After leading GEIS through the Y2K crisis, Mr. Seegers pitched his e-strategy. He proposed splitting GEIS into two parts: GE Systems Services

to continue the EDI network and GE Global eXchange Services (GXS) to develop Internet marketplaces. An hour and a half later, Jack Welch said, "Go for it." Mr. Seegers decided to lead the much smaller GXS, and he became its executive champion.

The rest, as they say, is history. Today GE's big divisions all run their own e-marketplaces for internal and external buying and selling. Mr. Seeger's boss, Jack Welch, went on to become an e-business icon for turning GE into an e-business. However, much of the credit rightfully belongs to Harvey Seegers, who today, as GXS Chief Executive, heads the main part of GE's e-business activities.

Source: *The Economist* (2001).

Questions

1. Describe GE's position as a move-to-the-Net business. What specific assets and liabilities did it have on its e-strategy balance sheet?

2. In what ways did Harvey Seegers reflect the characteristics of a project champion?

Checklists such as IBM's Internet Implementation Planner (at **advisor.internet.ibm.com**) help ensure that nothing is overlooked in the project management process.

STRATEGY IMPLEMENTATION ISSUES

There are many strategy implementation issues, depending on the circumstances. Here we describe some common ones.

Application Development

Implementation of an EC application requires access to the Web, construction of the Web site, and integration of the site with the existing corporate information systems (e.g., front end for order taking, back end for order processing). At this point, the company is faced with a number of decisions of whether to build, buy, or outsource various construction aspects of the application implementation process. Some of these decisions include the following:

- Should site development be done internally, externally, or by a combination of internal and external development?
- Should the software application be built or will commercially available software be satisfactory?
- If a commercial package will suit, should it be purchased from the vendor or rented from an ASP?
- Will the company or an external ISP host the Web site?
- If hosted externally, who will be responsible for monitoring and maintaining the information and system?

Each option has its strengths and weaknesses, and the correct decisions will depend on factors such as the strategic nature of the application, the skills of the company's technology group, and the necessity to move fast or not. Many of these options—build or buy, in-house or outsource, host externally or internally—are discussed in more detail in Chapter 16 and especially in Chapter 18 on the book's Web site.

Partners' Strategy

Another important issue is that many EC applications involve business partners—ASPs, ERP vendors and consultants, ISPs, and virtual corporations—with different organizational cultures and their own EC strategies and profit motives. A key criterion in choosing an EC partner is finding one whose strategy aligns with or complements the company's own.

When negotiating a partnership, one must recognize that the partner's principal goal is to make a profit, and it is the negotiator's responsibility to make sure that is not being done at the expense of the company's bottom line. One popular EC partner strategy is **outsourcing**, which is the use of an external vendor to provide all or part of the products and services that could be provided internally. An outsourcer's promise to manage the IT function with world-class service at lower long-term, stable costs has great appeal to a CEO and CFO. However, one must question how an outsourcer can do this and still make a profit. If it is too good to be true, it probably is.

As discussed in Chapter 14, a new and Internet-savvy case of outsourcing is the *application service provider (ASP)*, an outsourcer that sells access to software applications. By distributing the cost to purchase, operate, and maintain expensive applications such as an ERP system, the savings offered by an ASP can be very real. The bottom line here is that partnerships can be an effective way to develop and implement an EC strategy, but they require a realistic evaluation of the potential risks and rewards.

Virtual Corporations

The highest level of business partnering in strategy implementation is the formation of a **virtual corporation (VC)**, an organization composed of several business partners sharing costs and resources for the production or utilization of a product or service. A virtual corporation typically includes several partners, each with a physical presence and each creating a portion of the product or service in an area in which it has special advantage, such as expertise or low

outsourcing
The use of a third-party vendor to provide all or part of the products and services that could be provided internally.

virtual corporation (VC)
An organization composed of several business partners sharing costs and resources for the production or utilization of a product or service.

cost. VCs may be *permanent* (designed to create or assemble a broad range of productive resources on an ongoing basis) or *temporary* (created for a specific purpose and existing only for a short time).

The major attributes of a VC are:

- **Excellence.** Each partner contributes its core competency, creating an all-star winning team.
- **Utilization.** Resources of the individual business partners are frequently underutilized. A VC can utilize them more profitably.
- **Trust.** Business partners in a VC are more reliant on each other than in traditional partnerships and this requires more trust than usual.
- **Lack of borders.** It is difficult to identify the boundaries of a virtual corporation—it redefines traditional boundaries.
- **Opportunism.** A VC can find and meet a market opportunity better than an individual company.
- **Adaptability to change.** The VC can adapt quickly to environmental changes because its structure is relatively simple.
- **Technology.** Information technology makes the VC possible. Connected, integrated information systems are a requirement.

The important critical success factor for VCs is the need for superb collaboration, which is provided by B2B technologies and collaborative commerce.

Alliances in E-Commerce

Both the partners' strategy and VCs involve the formation of *e-alliances*, an EC-related partnership in which the goal is to launch an EC company or a large-scale EC application. The partners are in different locations, and they communicate and collaborate online. Strategic e-alliances become an important feature of EC when the EC initiatives are just too large and complex for one company to undertake. Typically, alliances were popular in B2B exchanges where many support services are needed. Logistics companies such as UPS and FedEx participate in many alliances, and so do telecommunications and other technology companies, especially those providing network solutions. According to Reda (2002), a strategic partner in an alliance should be one that has the ability to deliver and is willing to collaborate to provide a service. An example of a successful e-alliance is the one between 1-800-Flowers.com, a major e-tailer, and AT&T, which hosts the Web site.

Ernest et al. (2001) examined the viability of e-alliances in light of the dot-com failures of 2000–2001. Their conclusion is that e-alliances are now more essential than ever because EC implementation requires a diversity of support services, which a single organization can seldom provide by itself. An e-alliance provides synergy when companies bring complementary contributions.

Working with partners may not be a simple task; partnerships can be risky and difficult to manage. Dyer (2001) and Adobor and McMullen (2002) offer guidelines on how to make strategic alliances work.

Redesigning Business Processes

An internal issue many firms face at the implementation stage is the need to change business processes to accommodate the changes an EC strategy brings. Sometimes these changes are incremental and can be managed as part of the project implementation process. Sometimes the changes are so dramatic that they affect the manner in which the entire organization operates. In other words, old-economy organizations sometimes must change to meet the requirements of the new economy. When such a change is necessary, this process of changing an organization to a new mode of operation may be referred to as an *organizational transformation.*

One of the major issues faced by many companies is how to conduct a transformation to an e-business. As will be shown in the Real-World Case at the end of this chapter, this transformation may be fairly lengthy, complex, and expensive. For example, it took more

business process reengineering (BPR)
A methodology for conducting a comprehensive redesign of an enterprise's processes.

than 4 years for Siemens AG to transform itself to an e-business at a cost of over $1 billion (see Schultz 2002 and EC Application Case W15.1 at this book's Web site). Several factors are involved in such transformations, such as determining the correct e-business structure (Chen 2001).

Business process reengineering (BPR) is a methodology for conducting a comprehensive redesign of an enterprise's processes. BPR may be needed for the following reasons:

▶ To fix poorly designed processes (e.g., processes are not flexible or scalable), rather than just automate them

▶ To change processes so that they will fit commercially available software (e.g., ERP, e-procurement)

▶ To produce a fit between systems and processes of different companies that are partnering in e-commerce (e.g., e-marketplaces, ASPs)

▶ To align procedures and processes with e-services such as logistics, payments, or security

BPR may be very complex and expensive, especially when many business partners are involved. A major tool used in conjunction with redesign is workflow technology (see Chapter 8). For more on restructuring, see El Sawy (2001).

Section 15.5 ▶ REVIEW

1. Describe a Web (project) team and its purpose.
2. What is the role of a project champion?
3. What is the purpose of a pilot project?
4. Discuss the major strategy implementation issues of application construction, partners' strategy, virtual corporations, alliances, and BPR.

15.6 E-STRATEGY AND PROJECT ASSESSMENT

The last phase of e-strategy begins as soon as the implementation of the EC application or project is complete. *Strategy assessment* includes both the continual assessment of EC metrics and the periodic formal evaluation of progress toward the organization's strategic goals. Based on the results, corrective actions are taken and, if necessary, the strategy is reformulated.

THE OBJECTIVES OF ASSESSMENT

Strategic assessment has several objectives. The most important ones are:

▶ Measure the extent to which the EC strategy and ensuing projects are delivering what they were supposed to deliver. If they are not delivering, apply corrective actions to ensure that the projects are able to meet their objectives.

▶ Determine if the EC strategy and projects are still viable in the current environment.

▶ Reassess the initial strategy in order to learn from mistakes and improve future planning.

▶ Identify failing projects as soon as possible and determine why they failed to avoid the same problems on subsequent projects.

Web applications grow in unexpected ways, often expanding beyond their initial plan. For example, Genentec Inc., a biotechnology giant, wanted merely to replace a homegrown bulletin-board system. It started the project with a small budget, but soon found that the intranet had grown rapidly and become very popular in a short span of time, encompassing many applications. Another example is Lockheed Martin, which initially planned to put its corporate phone directory and information about training programs on the intranet. Within a short time, many of its human resources documents were placed on the intranet as well, and soon thereafter, the use of the Web for internal information expanded from administrative purposes to collaborative commerce and PRM applications.

MEASURING RESULTS AND USING METRICS

Each company measures success or failure by a different set of standards. Some companies may find that their goals were unrealistic, that their Web server was inadequate to handle demand, or that expected cost savings were not realized. Others may experience so much success that they have to respond to numerous application requests from various functional areas in the company.

Assessing EC is difficult because of the many configurations and impact variables involved and the sometimes intangible nature of what is being measured. However, a review of the requirements and design documents should help answer many of the questions raised during the assessment. It is important that the Web team develop a thorough checklist to address both the evaluation of project performance and the assessment of a changing environment. One way to measure a project's performance is to use metrics.

EC Metrics

A **metric** is a specific, measurable standard against which actual performance is compared. Metrics can produce very positive results in organizations by driving behavior in a number of ways. According to Rayport and Jaworski (2002), metrics can:

metric
A specific, measurable standard against which actual performance is compared.

- Define the value proposition of the business model
- Communicate the strategy to the workforce through performance targets
- Increase accountability when metrics are linked to performance-appraisal programs
- Align the objectives of individuals, departments, and divisions to the enterprise's strategic objectives

An example of EC metrics implementation can be found in a white paper that analyzed the impact of a new online service on the profitability of Axon Computertime, a small computer services business in New Zealand (Green 2002). Axon found the following results were obtained from the implementation of this service as part of their EC strategy:

- **Revenue growth.** Product revenue increased over 40 percent in the first 12 months of operation.
- **Cost reduction.** Selling costs were reduced by 40 percent for each dollar of margin generated.
- **Cost reduction.** Expenditures on brochure design and production were reduced by 45 percent.
- **Cost avoidance.** Obsolete stock write-offs as percentage of revenue were reduced by 93 percent.
- **Customer fulfillment.** Average days to delivery were reduced by 20 percent over 2 years.
- **Customer service.** Customer satisfaction with the delivery process is consistently in excess of 80 percent.
- **Customer communications.** Customer response to e-mail communications is five times the response rate to postal mail.

The last few metrics in this list highlight the importance of including nonfinancial measures in the measurement of strategy performance. As discussed earlier, the *balanced scorecard* approach is a popular strategy assessment methodology that encourages measuring organizational performance in a number of areas. Taking a balanced scorecard approach, Plant (2000) suggests seven areas for assessment in an e-commerce strategy: financial impact, competitive leadership, brand, service, market, technology, and internal site metrics. Similarly, Zhu and Kraemer (2002) suggest four metric areas—information, transaction, interaction and customization, and supplier connection—that manufacturing firms should use for assessing performance of their e-commerce strategy. Finally, Rayport and Jaworski (2002) propose five categories of financial and nonfinancial metrics to assess strategy in a five-step process they call the *performance dashboard* (see Exhibit 15.6 on page 586).

For an overview of EC metrics, including many examples and suggested metrics, see Sterne (2002). For an extensive discussion on metrics and management, see Straub et al. (2002a, 2002b).

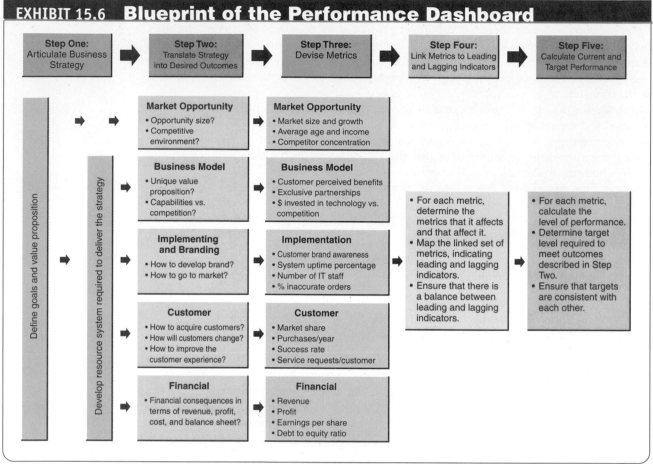

EXHIBIT 15.6 Blueprint of the Performance Dashboard

Source: Rayport, J., and B. J. Jaworski. *Introduction to E-Commerce.* Boston: McGraw-Hill, 2002. Copyright © McGraw-Hill Companies, Inc.

STRATEGY ASSESSMENT FUTURES

The tools, methodologies, activities, and processes in EC strategy initiation, formulation, and implementation are rather well defined. The "brave new world" of strategy development seems to be in the strategy assessment phase, in which the methodologies are mostly new and still emerging. In part, this is because strategy assessment has been largely ignored in traditional strategic planning (e.g., the balanced scorecard approach emerged only in 1996). This is largely because much of the assessment in EC strategy is so new and different, such as Web site e-metrics (Watchfire 2001; Palmer 2002) and CRM (Voss 2000; Chen and Hitt 2002). The growing number of assessment approaches (e.g., Plant 2000; Rayport and Jaworski 2002), emerging theory (e.g., Wheeler 2002), and online resources (e.g., metricnet.com) make this an interesting area for study, research, and new applications.

Section 15.6 ▶ REVIEW

1. Describe the need for assessment.

2. Define metrics and their contribution to strategic planning.

3. Describe the performance dashboard approach to strategy assessment.

15.7 KEYS TO EC SUCCESS

At this point in the chapter, we turn our attention away from the strategic planning process per se to focus on some topics that are related to, or an outcome of, the EC strategy process. The first of these issues is the much-hyped topic of EC failure and success, with an emphasis on keys to EC success.

E-COMMERCE FAILURES

By their nature, EC initiatives and EC companies are likely to fail. Why? Three economic reasons suggest why this is the case.

1. At a macro-economic level, technological revolutions such as the railroad and the automobile each had a boom-and-bust-and-consolidation cycle. For example, between 1904 and 1908, more than 240 companies entered the then-new automobile business in the United States. In 1910 a shakeout began. Today, there are only three U.S. automakers, but the size of the auto industry has grown by several hundredfold. The technological revolution posed by the Internet should be expected to go through a similar process.

2. At a mid-economic level, the bursting of the dot-com bubble in mid-2000 is consistent with economic downturns that have occurred in property, precious metals, currency, and stock markets.

3. At a micro-economic level, the "Web rush" reflected an overallocation of scarce resources—venture capital, technical personnel, and, in many advertising-driven business models, visitors' eyeballs.

Most economic commentators view the high failure rate of start-up, dot-com companies in a positive light, as a step toward industry consolidation with increased prospects for profitability and success for the firms that remain.

Some of the reasons for failure in B2C EC were provided in Chapter 3: lack of profitability, excessive risk exposure, the high cost of branding, poor performance, and static Web site design. Two additional financial reasons are lack of funding and incorrect revenue models.

▶ **Lack of funding.** It takes a few years to acquire a large enough customer base to support an e-tail venture. Most of the failed companies "burned" (used up) all the cash they had before they had enough customers. Additional funding became very difficult to obtain in 2000 and 2001 when investors were no longer willing to wait a long time for profits, figuring that the risk was too high. Typical examples of company sites that ran out of funds are boo.com, garden.com, and living.com. Numerous other examples of failed B2C ventures can be found at startupfailures.com and disobey.com.

▶ **Incorrect revenue model.** In the late 1990s, many companies used a business model in which the company would spend as much as it could on customer acquisition. The idea was that if a site had millions of visitors per month, advertisers would rush to the site. This model failed when the competition for advertising money grew rapidly and the price of advertisements fell dramatically. With big expenses but little revenue from sales and outside advertisers, companies reached bankruptcy quickly.

In the B2B market, the EC community was shocked in late 2000 when Chemdex, the "granddaddy" of the third-party exchanges, closed down. The reasons for failure provided by Ventro.com, its parent company, were that the revenue growth was too slow and that it wanted to move to a new business model, that of selling B2B software. It is predicted that as many as 90 percent of all exchanges will collapse (Ulph et al. 2001). The major reason for this is the difficulty in obtaining enough buyers and sellers fast enough before the cash disappears. Critical success factors necessary for digital exchanges to reduce their chance of failure were provided in Chapter 7.

In both the B2C and B2B markets, other anecdotal reasons for failure include misdirected energies, a lack of understanding of market needs, poor business planning, greed, and a mismatch of innovative youth, inexperience, and overeager sponsors (Yap 2002). The reasons for past failures are only important in that they provide insight for avoiding such failures in the future, which is the focus of the next section.

E-COMMERCE SUCCESS

EC success stories abound, primarily in specialty and niche markets. One example is puritan.com, a successful vitamin and natural health-care product store. Another is campusfood.com, which serves take-out food to college students. Also doing very well are the employment site monster.com and alloy.com, a successful shopping and entertainment portal for young adults. For a comparison of how these and other thriving online businesses have

EXHIBIT 15.7 Critical Success Factors for EC

CSFs in the Old Economy	CSFs for EC Success
Vertically integrate or do it yourself	Create new partnerships and alliances, stay with core competency
Deliver high-value products	Deliver high-value service offerings that encompass products
Build market share to establish economies of scale	Optimize natural scale and scope of business, look at mass customization
Analyze carefully to avoid missteps	Approach with urgency to avoid being locked out; use proactive strategies
Leverage physical assets	Leverage intangible assets, capabilities, and relationships—unleash dormant assets
Compete to sell product	Compete to control access and relationships with customers; compete with Web sites

translated critical success factors (CSFs) from the old economy into EC success, see Exhibit 15.7.

Reasons for Success

Here are some of the reasons for EC success and suggestions on how to succeed from EC experts and consultants.

First, thousands of brick-and-mortar companies are adding online channels, with great success. Examples are uniglobe.com, staples.com, homedepot.com, clearcommerce.com, 1-800-FLOWERS (800flowers.com), and Southwest Airlines (iflyswa.com). Weill and Vitale (2001) provide clear guidance about how existing firms can use organizational knowledge, brand, infrastructure, and other strategic assets to migrate from the off-line marketplace to the online marketspace.

In response to the bursting of the dot-com bubble, firms are adopting a variety of "morphing strategies" to survive. These strategies include moving to higher quality customers (e.g., B2C to B2B), changing products or services in their existing market, and establishing an off-line presence (e.g., moving from pure-play dot-com to click-and-mortar) (Kauffman et al. 2002).

Another take on reasons for EC success comes from a group of Asian CEOs, who recommend the following CSFs: select robust business models, anticipate the dot-com future, foster e-innovation, carefully evaluate a spin-off strategy, co-brand, employ ex-dot-com staffers, and focus on the e-generation as alloy.com and bolt.com have done (Phillips 2000).

Other experts and researchers have blended a variety of factors into their own recipes for EC success. Agrawal et al. (2001) suggest that companies should match a value proposition with customer segments, control extensions of product lines and business models, and avoid expensive technology. Huff and Wade (2000) suggest the following EC CSFs: add value, focus on a niche and then extend that niche, maintain flexibility, get the technology right, manage critical perceptions, provide excellent customer service, create effective connectedness, and understand Internet culture. Barua et al. (2001) provide a systematic approach for driving EC excellence, including guidelines for selecting appropriate business models and assuring sufficient ROI. Useem (2000) uncovered "12 truths" about how the Internet really works by analyzing the dot-com crash. You can find these "truths" on the book's Web site. In addition, many, many more keys (e.g., Yap 2002), rules (e.g., Paul and Franco 2001), and steps (e.g., Hayes 2000) to EC success have been proposed by experts and consultants.

A research study of 30 organizations identified the following factors that contributed to the successful implementation of B2C and B2B EC projects (Esichaikul and Chavananon 2001):

▶ The top three factors for successful B2C e-commerce were effective marketing management, an attractive Web site, and building strong connections to the customers.

▶ The top three factors for successful B2B e-commerce were the readiness of trading partners, information integration inside the company and in the supply chain, and the completeness of the application.

▶ The top three factors for overall, successful e-business were a proper business model, readiness of the firm to become an e-business, and internal enterprise integration.

At this still-early stage of the EC revolution, success cannot be assured, and failure rates will remain high. However, if companies learn from the mistakes of the past and follow the guidelines offered by experts and researchers, the chances for success are greatly enhanced.

Section 15.7 ▶ REVIEW

1. Why are EC failures so likely?
2. List some reasons why B2C (e-tailing) companies fail.
3. What are some EC CSFs?

15.8 GOING GLOBAL

A global electronic marketplace is an attractive thrust for an EC strategy. "Going global" means access to larger markets, mobility (e.g., to minimize taxes), and flexibility to employ workers anywhere using a worldwide telecommuting workforce. However, going global is a complex and strategic decision process due to a multiplicity of issues. Geographical distance is the most obvious dimension of conducting business globally, but frequently, it is not the most important dimension. Instead cultural, administrative, and economic dimensions of distance are equally likely to threaten a firm's international ambitions (Ghemawat 2001). This section briefly examines the opportunities, problems, and solutions for companies using e-commerce to go global.

BENEFITS AND EXTENT OF OPERATIONS

Global electronic activities have existed for more than 25 years, mainly EFT and EDI in support of B2B financial and other repetitive, standardized transactions. However, these activities required expensive and inflexible private telecommunications lines and, therefore, were limited mostly to large corporations. The emergence of the Internet and technologies such as extranets and XML has resulted in an inexpensive and flexible infrastructure that can greatly facilitate global trade.

The major advantage of EC is the ability to do business at any time, from anywhere, and at a reasonable cost. These are the drivers behind global EC and there have been some incredible success stories in this area. For example:

▶ One can use E*TRADE or boom.com to buy and sell stocks in several countries.

▶ Exchanges such as e-Steel and ChemConnect have members in dozens of countries.

▶ Amazon.com sells books to individuals and organizations in over 190 countries.

▶ Small companies, such as ZD Wines (zdwines.com), sell to hundreds of customers worldwide. Hothothot (hothothot.com) reported its first international trade only after it went online; within 2 years global sales accounted for 25 percent of its total sales.

▶ Major corporations, such as GE and Boeing, reported an increasing number of out-of-the-country vendors participating in their electronic RFQs. These electronic bids resulted in a 10 to 15 percent cost reduction and an over 50 percent reduction in cycle time.

▶ Many international corporations considerably increased their success in recruiting employees for foreign locations when online recruiting was utilized.

▶ Several global trading exchanges have been created in the last few years.

BARRIERS TO GLOBAL EC

Despite the benefits and opportunities offered by globalization, there are many barriers to global EC. Some are barriers that face any EC venture but become more difficult when international impacts are considered. These barriers include authentication of buyers and sellers (Chapter 12), generating and retaining trust (Chapter 4), order fulfillment and delivery

(Chapter 14), security (Chapter 12), and domain names (Chapter 16). Others are unique to global EC. We will use the CAGE (culture, administration, geography, economics) distance framework proposed by Ghemawat (2001) to identify areas in which natural or man-made barriers hinder global EC. Each of the four factors represents a different type of distance (difference) between two companies.

Cultural Issues

The Internet is a multifaceted marketplace made up of users from many cultures. The multi-cultural nature of global EC is important because cultural attributes determine how people interact with companies, agencies, and each other based on social norms, local standards, religious beliefs, and language (Ghemawat 2001). Doing business globally requires *cultural marketing*, a strategy for meeting the needs of a culturally diverse population (DePalma 2000).

Cultural and related differences include languages (e.g., English vs. other languages), spelling differences (e.g., American vs. British spelling), information formatting (e.g., dates can be mm/dd/yy or dd/mm/yy), graphics and icons (e.g., mailbox shapes differ from country to country), measurement standards (e.g., metric vs. imperial system), the use of color (e.g., white is a funeral color in some countries), protection of intellectual property (e.g., Chinese tolerance of copyright infringement has Confucian roots), time standards (e.g., local time zones vs. Greenwich Mean Time), and information requests (e.g., requiring a "zip" code in an order form can lead to abandoned shopping carts in countries without postal codes). Even the way individuals access the Web—at home, work, or an Internet cafe—varies from country to country, with implications for the use of graphics and personalization strategies.

Administrative Issues

One of the most contentious areas of global EC is the resolution of international legal issues. A number of national governments and international organizations are working together to find ways to avoid uncoordinated actions and encourage uniform legal standards.

An ambitious effort to reduce differences in international law governing EC is the United Nations Commission on International Trade Law (UNCITRAL) Model Law on Electronic Commerce. Its purpose is to "offer national legislators a set of internationally acceptable rules which detail how a number of legal obstacles to the development of e-commerce may be removed, and how a more secure legal environment may be created" (*e-Business World* 2000). The Model Law has been adopted in some form in many countries and legal jurisdictions including Singapore, Australia, Canada, Hong Kong, and the U.S. state of Illinois.

International trade organizations such as the World Trade Organization (WTO) and the Asia-Pacific Economic Cooperation (APEC) forum have working groups that are attempting to reduce EC trade barriers in areas such as pricing regulations, customs, import/export restrictions, tax issues, and product specification regulations.

An emerging issue in the administrative distance dimension is consumer privacy protection. The European Union (EU) has enacted a set of regulations collectively known as the EU Data Protection Directive. The most controversial part of that legislation prohibits the export of personal data from EU members to countries that lack adequate protection of personal data. This could include some U.S. states, restricting trans-Atlantic EC trade (Sheldon and Strader 2002). Negotiations to resolve this impasse are continuing.

Geographical Issues

The geographical issues of shipping goods and services across international borders are well known. Barriers posed by geography differ based on transportation infrastructure between and within countries and the type of product or service being delivered. For example, geographical distance is almost irrelevant in online software sales.

Companies launching a worldwide EC strategy need to evaluate bandwidth requirements and availability in the principal target countries. A country's market-access infrastructure is key to accommodating all users and all types of data. Monitoring and complying with technical standards will also minimize the possibility of incompatible technologies between the company and the international user.

Economic Issues

Economic and financial issues encompassing global EC include government tariffs, customs, and taxation. In areas subject to government regulation, tax and regulatory agencies have attempted to apply the rules used in traditional commerce to electronic commerce, with considerable success. Exceptions include areas such as international tariff duties and taxation. Software shipped in a box would be taxed for duties and tariffs when it arrives in the country. However, software downloaded online relies on self-reporting and voluntary payment of tax by the purchaser, something which does not happen very often.

A major tax issue in the United States is attempts by states and local authorities to impose sales taxes on goods purchased by their residents from out-of-state EC companies. According to research sponsored by the Institute for State Studies (Bruce and Fox 2001), state governments could lose as much as US$45 billion in revenue by 2006 if they are not able to collect taxes from online sales. However, the imposition of interstate sales taxes would raise the cost of EC goods and sharply increase operational overheads of firms doing business online because there may be as many as 15,000 different tax rates for various governments and products.

The key financial barrier to global EC is electronic payment systems. To sell effectively online, EC firms must have flexible payment methods that match the ways different groups of people pay for their online purchases. Although credit cards are widely used in the United States, many European and Asian customers prefer to complete online transactions with off-line payments. Even within the category of off-line payments, companies must offer different options depending on the country. For example, French consumers prefer to pay with a check, Swiss consumers expect an invoice by mail, Germans commonly pay for products upon delivery, and Swedes are accustomed to paying online with debit cards.

Pricing is another economic issue. A vendor may want to price the same product at different prices in different countries in consideration of local prices and competition. However, if a company has one Web site, differential pricing will be difficult or impossible. Similarly, what currency will be used for pricing? What currency will be used for payment?

BREAKING DOWN THE BARRIERS TO GLOBAL EC

A number of international organizations (e.g., OECD 2001) have written reports, and experts (e.g., Josephson 2001; Sheldon and Strader 2002) have offered suggestions on how to break down the barriers to global EC. Some of these suggestions include the following:

- **Be strategic.** Identify a starting point and lay out a globalization strategy. Remember that Web globalization is a business-building process. Consider what languages and countries it makes sense for the company to target and how the company will support the site for each target audience.

- **Know your audience.** Carefully consider the target audience. Be fully informed of the cultural preferences and legal issues that matter to customers in a particular part of the world.

- **Localize.** As much as practical and necessary, offer Web sites in national languages; offer different sites in different countries (e.g., "Yahoo Japan" is at yahoo.co.jp); price products in local currencies; and base terms, conditions, and business practices on local laws and cultural practices. Chapter 4 includes a brief discussion of localization in advertising, and comprehensive discussions on localization can be found in Fessenden and Dwyer (2000) and at tradecompass.com.

- **Think globally, act consistently.** An international company with country Web sites managed by local offices must make sure areas such as brand management, pricing, corporate information, and content management are consistent with company strategy (DePalma 2001).

- **Value the human touch.** Trust the translation of the Web site content only to human translators, not automatic translation programs. Involve language and technical editors in the quality assurance process. One slight mistranslation or one out-of-place graphic might turn off customers forever.

- **Clarify, document, explain.** Pricing, privacy policies, shipping restrictions, contact information, and business practices should be well documented and located on the Web site and visible to the customer. To help protect against foreign litigation, identify where the company is located and the jurisdiction for all contract or sales disputes.

▸ **Offer services that reduce barriers.** It is not feasible to offer prices and payments in all currencies, so link to a currency exchange service (e.g., xe.com) for the customer's convenience. In B2B e-commerce, be prepared to integrate the EC transaction with the accounting/finance internal information system of the buyer.

We close our discussion of global e-commerce with an example of how, with proper planning, a small business went global with low costs and high success (see EC Application Case 15.3). Indeed, although going global introduces new risks into the small-business environment (Hornby et al. 2000), the global marketspace erases national borders and gives even the smallest companies worldwide reach. These small- and medium-sized enterprises are the focus of the next section.

Section 15.8 ▸ REVIEW

1. Describe globalization in EC and the advantages it presents.
2. Describe the major barriers to global EC in each dimension of the CAGE framework.
3. What can companies do to overcome the barriers to global EC?

15.9 EC IN SMALL- AND MEDIUM-SIZED ENTERPRISES

Some of the first companies to take advantage of Web-based electronic commerce were small- and medium-sized enterprises (SMEs). While larger, established, tradition-bound companies hesitated, SMEs moved onto the Web because they realized there were opportunities in marketing, business expansion, business launches, cost cutting, and tighter partner alliances. Prime examples are virtualvine.com, hothothot.com, and happypuppy.com. However, many SMEs have found it difficult to formulate or implement an EC strategy, principally because of low use of EC and IT by customers and suppliers, lack of knowledge or IT expertise in the SME, and limited awareness of the opportunities and risks (OECD 2001). A more complete list of major advantages and disadvantages of EC for SMEs is provided in Exhibit 15.8.

CASE 15.3
EC Application
A SMALL BUSINESS GOES GLOBAL

Cardiac Science of Irvine, California, which makes cardiac medical devices, had been trying to break into the international market for years. Within 2 years after the company started using the Internet for online sales, it was shipping its products to 46 countries. Today, 85 percent of the company's revenue is international, and much of this is executed over its Web site (*cardiacscience.com*). The company answers inquiries within 24 hours, linking product information to promising sales leads.

Small businesses need a great deal of advice in going global. Cardiac found the following Web sites to be useful:

▸ Universal Business Exchange (*unibex.com*) offers trade leads with the added capability of matching buyers and sellers automatically.

▸ Several government agencies provide online information for nominal fees (e.g., National Trade Data Bank, Economic

Bulletin Board, and Globus; all can be accessed from *stat-usa.gov*).

The global Web business is not as simple as some may think. It takes a lot more commitment than putting up a snazzy Web site and waiting for customers to show up. The Internet is important for introductions, but one must follow up on it.

Source: *cardiacscience.com* (2003).

Questions

1. What are Cardiac's critical success factors?
2. Visit the sources of data suggested in the case and describe their usefulness.

EXHIBIT 15.8   Advantages and Disadvantages of EC for Small- and Medium-Sized Businesses

Advantages/Benefits	Disadvantages/Risks
• Inexpensive sources of information. A Scandinavian study found over 90 percent of SMEs use the Internet for information search (OECD 2001). • Inexpensive ways of advertising and conducting market research. Banner exchanges, newsletters, chat rooms, etc., are nearly zero-cost ways to reach customers. • Competitor analysis is easier. The Scandinavian study found Finnish firms rated competitor analysis third in their use of the Internet, after information search and marketing. • Inexpensive ways to build (or rent) a storefront. Creating and maintaining a Web site is relatively easy and cheap (see Chapter 16). • SMEs are less locked into legacy technologies and existing relationships with traditional retail channels. • Image and public recognition can be generated quickly. A Web presence makes it easier for a small business to compete against larger firms. • An opportunity to reach worldwide customers. No other medium is as efficient at global marketing, sales, and customer support. • Other advantages for SMEs include increased speed of customer payments, closer ties with business partners, reduced errors in information transfer, lower operating costs, and other benefits that apply to all businesses.	• Lack of financial resources to fully exploit the Web. A transactional Web site may entail relatively high up-front, fixed costs in terms of cash flow for an SME. • Lack of technical staff or insufficient expertise in legal issues, advertising, etc. These human resources may be unavailable or prohibitively expensive to an SME. • Less risk tolerance than a large company. If initial sales are low or the unexpected happens, the typical SME does not have a large reserve of resources to fall back on. • When the product isn't suitable or difficult for online sales (e.g., commodities such as CDs, perishable products such as certain foods) the Web opportunity is not as great. • Reduced personal contact with customers represents the dilution of what is normally a strong point for a small business. • Inability to afford entry to or purchase enough volume to take advantage of digital exchanges.

CRITICAL SUCCESS FACTORS FOR SMEs

EC success for small businesses is not a just matter of chance. Considerable research has been done to identify the critical success factors that help determine whether a small business will succeed in EC. Many of the small businesses that have succeeded on the Internet, either as click-and-mortar or virtual businesses, have the following strategies in common:

▶ **Product is critical.** The most effective product strategy for SMEs has been niche or specialty items. It is difficult to compete against online bookstores such as Amazon.com, unless one specializes, as powells.com does in the technical book market. Other strategies are to sell a wide variety of low volume products that regular stores do not stock (e.g., dogtoys.com), international products not readily available in neighborhood stores (e.g., russianfoods.com), goods that appeal to hobbyists or a community's special interests (e.g., diecastmodelcars.com), regional products (e.g., newyorkartworld.com), or local information (e.g., baliadventuretours.com).

▶ **Payment methods must be flexible.** Some customers prefer to mail or fax in a form or talk to a person rather than transmit a credit card number over the Internet.

▶ **Electronic payments must be secure.** Fortunately, ISPs and banks can easily provide this security.

▶ **Capital investment should be kept to a minimum.** Doing so enables the company to keep its overhead and risk low. For example, SMEs typically outsource Web hosting.

▶ **Inventory control is crucial.** Carrying too much stock ties up valuable capital. Too little stock on hand results in unfilled orders and disappointed customers. Contingency plans for scaling up inventory fast are recommended.

▶ **Logistical services must be quick and reliable.** Many small businesses have successfully subcontracted out their logistical services to shipping firms such as FedEx or DHL.

▶ **High visibility on the Internet.** The Web site should be submitted to directories such as Yahoo and search engines such as Google, MSN Search, and Lycos and optimized for prominent search engine placement, as described in Chapter 16.

▶ **Join an online community.** The company may want to become a member of an online service or mall, such as AOL or ViaWeb's Viamall. Other partnership strategies that bring in customers include affiliate programs (see affiliatematch.com) and Web rings (see webring.com).

▶ **A Web site should provide all the services needed by consumers.** In addition, the Web site should look professional enough to compete with larger competitors and be updated on a continual basis to maintain consumer interest. Chapter 16 covers this topic in more detail.

SUPPORTING SMEs

SMEs have a variety of support options. Almost every country in the world has a government agency devoted to helping SMEs become more aware of and able to participate in electronic commerce (e.g., sba.gov, business.gov.au).

Vendors realized the opportunity represented by thousands of business going online, and many have set up a variety of service centers that typically offer a combination of free information and fee-based support. Examples are IBM's Small Business Center (ibm.com/businesscenter) and Microsoft's bCentral (bcentral.com). Other small business support centers are sponsored by professional associations, Web resource services (e.g., smallbusiness.yahoo.com, workz.com), and small businesses that are in the business of helping other small businesses go online (e.g., bellzinc.ca).

Section 15.9 ▶ REVIEW

1. What are the advantages/benefits of EC for small businesses?
2. What are the disadvantages/risks of EC for small businesses?
3. What are the CSFs for small businesses online?

MANAGERIAL ISSUES

Some managerial issues related to this chapter are as follows.

1. **What is the strategic value of EC to the organization?** Management needs to understand how EC can improve marketing and promotions, customer service, and sales. More significantly, the greatest potential of EC is realized when management views EC from a strategic perspective, not merely as a technological advancement.

2. **What are the benefits and risks of EC?** Strategic moves have to be carefully weighed against potential risks. Identifying CSFs for EC and doing a cost-benefit analysis should not be neglected. Benefits are often hard to quantify, especially because gains tend to be strategic. In such an analysis, risks should be addressed with contingency planning (deciding what to do if problems arise).

3. **What metrics should we use?** The use of metrics is very popular, but the problem is that one must compare "apples with apples." Companies first must choose appropriate metrics for the situation and then

must exercise caution in deriving conclusions whenever gaps between the metrics and actual performance are seen.

4. **What staffing is required?** Forming a Web team is critical for EC project success. The team's leadership, the balance between technical and business staff, getting the best staff representation on the team, and having a project champion are essential for success.

5. **How can we go global?** Going global is a very appealing proposition, but it may be difficult to do, especially on a large scale. In B2B, one may create collaborative projects with partners in other countries. Once such partners are discovered, exchanges and third-party marketplaces that promote global trade may lose business.

6. **Can we learn to love smallness?** Small can be beautiful to some; to others it may be ugly. Competing on commodity-type products with the big guys is very difficult, and is even more so in cyberspace. Finding a

niche market is advisable, but it will usually be limited in scope. More opportunity exists in providing specialized support services than in selling goods and services.

7. **Is e-business is always beneficial?** According to Coltman et al. (2002), e-business may not fit some businesses. It may be too expensive to justify benefits or it may result in internal conflicts. Many businesses simply do not need e-business. Therefore, a careful analysis of fitness must be conducted (see Wilson and Abel 2002).

SUMMARY

In this chapter, you learned about the following EC issues as they relate to the learning objectives.

1. **The strategic planning process.** This process is composed of four major phases: initiation, formulation, implementation, and assessment. A variety of tools are available to carry out this process.

2. **The EC strategic process.** Considering electronic commerce in strategy development does not radically change the process, but it does impact on the outcomes. Move-on-the-Net firms must approach the process differently than born-to-the-Net firms, but both types of firms must recognize the way electronic technologies such as the Internet make an e-difference. Because of the comprehensiveness of EC, formal strategic planning is a must.

3. **E-strategy initiation and formulation.** The strategy initiation phase involves understanding the company, the industry, and the competition. Companies must consider questions such as "Should we be a first mover?" "Should we go global?" "Should we create a separate company or brand?" In strategy formulation, specific opportunities are selected for implementation based on project viability, company fit, cost-benefit, risk, and pricing.

4. **E-strategy implementation and assessment.** Creating an effective Web team and ensuring that sufficient resources are available initiate the implementa-

tion phase. Other important implementation issues are whether or not to outsource various aspects of development and the need to redesign existing business processes. Immediately after implementation, assessment begins. Metrics provide feedback, and management acts by taking corrective action and reformulating strategy, if necessary.

5. **Understanding failures and learning from them.** Many EC initiatives and companies failed in 2000 and 2001. The causes of failure, and factors for success, provide guidance to remaining firms about how to survive and thrive.

6. **Issues in global EC.** Going global with EC can be done quickly and with a relatively small investment. However, businesses must deal with a number of different issues in the cultural, administrative, geographical, and economic dimensions of global trading.

7. **Small businesses and EC.** Depending on the circumstances, innovative small companies have a tremendous opportunity to adopt EC with little cost and to expand rapidly. Being in a niche market provides the best chance for small business success, and a variety of Web-based resources that small business owners can use to help ensure success are available.

KEY TERMS

Term	Page	Term	Page	Term	Page
Balanced scorecard	569	Interaction costs	570	Strategy assessment	568
Business case	576	Metric	585	Strategy formulation	567
Business process reengineering (BPR)	584	Outsourcing	582	Strategy implementation	567
		Project champion	581	Strategy initiation	566
Competitor analysis grid	569	Return on investment (ROI)	569	SWOT analysis	568
E-commerce (EC) risk	577			Value proposition	567
E-commerce strategy (e-strategy)	566	Scenario planning	569	Versioning	579
		Strategy	565	Virtual corporation (VC)	582

DISCUSSION QUESTIONS

1. How would you identify competitors for a small business that wants to launch an EC project?

2. How would you apply the SWOT approach to a small, local bank evaluating its e-banking services?

3. Explain the logic of Tjan's Internet portfolio map.

4. Amazon.com decided not to open physical stores, whereas First Network Security Bank (FNSB), which was the first online bank, opened its first physical bank in 1999. Compare and discuss the two strategies.

5. Discuss the pros and cons of going global with a physical product.

6. Find some SME EC success stories and identify the common elements in them.

INTERNET EXERCISES

1. Survey several online travel agencies (e.g., travelocity.com, orbitz.com, cheaptickets.com, priceline.com, expedia.com, bestfares.com, and so on) and compare their business strategies. How do they compete against physical travel agencies?

2. Enter digitalenterprise.org and find Web metrics. Read the material on metrics and prepare a report on the use of metrics for measuring advertising success.

3. Check the music CD companies on the Internet (e.g., cdnow.com). Do any focus on specialized niche markets as a strategy?

4. Enter ibm.com/procurement and go to the e-procurement section. Read IBM's e-procurement strategy and the "Consultant's Report—Best Practices." Prepare a report on the best lessons you learned.

5. Compare the following recording industry associations: aria.com.au (Australia), bpi.co.uk (United Kingdom), and riaa.com (United States). Consider the services offered: functionality of the site, use of multimedia, search capabilities, timeliness, range, links, customization (languages), product information, EC activities, and so forth. Prepare a report based on your findings.

6. One of the most global companies is Amazon.com (amazon.com). Find stories about its global strategies and activities (try fortune.com, forbes.com, and smallbusiness.com). What are the most important lessons you learned?

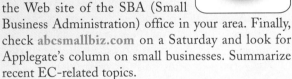

7. Visit abcsmallbiz.com and find some of the EC opportunities available to small businesses. Also, visit the Web site of the SBA (Small Business Administration) office in your area. Finally, check abcsmallbiz.com on a Saturday and look for Applegate's column on small businesses. Summarize recent EC-related topics.

8. Enter alloy.com and bolt.com. Compare the sites on functionality, ease of use, message boards, homepage layout, and so on. Prepare a report based on your findings.

9. Find out how Web sites such as tradecard.com facilitate the conduct of international trade over the Internet. Prepare a report based on your findings.

10. Use a currency conversion table (e.g., xe.com/ucc) to find out the exchange rate of $100 (U.S.) with the currencies of Brazil, Canada, China, India, Sweden, the European Union, and South Africa.

11. Conduct research on small businesses and their use of the Internet for EC. Visit sites such as success.com, webcom.com, and uschamber.org. Also, enter google.com or yahoo.com and type "small businesses + electronic commerce." Use your findings to write a report on current small business EC issues.

TEAM ASSIGNMENTS AND ROLE PLAYING

1. Have three teams represent the following units of one click-and-mortar company: (1) an off-line division, (2) an online division, and (3) top management. Each team member represents a different functional area within the division. The teams will develop a strategy in a specific industry (a group of three teams will represent a company in one industry). Teams will present their strategies to the class.

2. The relationship between manufacturers and their distributors regarding sales on the Web can be very strained. Direct sales may cut into the distributors'

business. Review some of the strategies available to handle such channel conflicts. Each team member should be assigned to a company in a different industry. Study the strategies, compare and contrast them, and derive a proposed generic strategy.

3. Each team must find the latest information on one global EC issue (e.g., cultural, administrative, geo-

graphical, economical). Each team will offer a report based on their findings.

4. Survey **google.com**, **electronicmarkets.org**, and **isworld.org** to find out about EC efforts in different countries. Assign a country or two to each team. Relate the developments to each country's level of economic development and to its culture.

REAL-WORLD CASE

IBM'S E-BUSINESS STRATEGY

IBM has been a huge presence in the computer industry since its inception in the 1940s. In the face of increased competition over the years, IBM has continually revamped its business strategy. Even more important, though, is IBM's need to capture new business opportunities and technologies, such as EC, and to develop a business strategy for that purpose. Since 1999, IBM's declared strategy has been to transform itself into an e-business in order to provide business value to the corporation and its shareholders.

To ensure successful implementation of its e-business strategy, IBM formed an independent division, called Enterprise Web Management, that has the following four goals:

1. To lead IBM's strategy to transform itself into an e-business and to act as a catalyst to help facilitate that transformation.
2. To help IBM's business units become more effective in their use of the Internet, both internally and with their customers.
3. To establish a strategy for the corporate Internet site. This includes a definition of how it should look, feel, and be navigated—in short, to create an online environment most conducive to customers doing business with IBM.
4. To leverage the wealth of e-business information accumulated in case studies to highlight the potential of e-business to customers.

Like many other companies, IBM first used the Internet as a static digital brochure, basically a tool for posting information. IBM is now moving towards comprehensive e-business, carrying out business transactions of all kinds over the Internet, intranets, and extranets between IBM and its suppliers, among members of its Business Partner Network, among its employees, and so on. IBM wants to become truly e-business-oriented and to focus on how it can use powerful networking technology to fulfill the diverse needs of its customers and partners.

One of the major issues in moving to e-business was the redesign of many of its core business processes on the Internet—including sales, procurement, customer care, and knowledge management. Implementing EC frequently requires such a redesign. IBM adopted a strategy of streamlining its core business processes by simplifying its internal business processes (using BPR), eliminating redundant IT applications (reduced from 16,000 to

8,000), simplifying IT infrastructure (reducing the number of data centers from 131 to 16), introducing standardization, creating one global network (instead of 31), and more.

The company targeted EC projects at those areas in which IBM could earn the biggest ROI. It focused its activities initially around eight key initiatives:

1. Selling more goods over the Web—*e-commerce*
2. Providing customer support online, from technical support to marketing backup—*e-care for customers*
3. Support for IBM's business partners over the Web—*e-care for business partners*
4. Dedicated services providing faster, better information for IT analysts and consultants, financial analysts, media, and stakeholders—*e-care for influencers*
5. Improving the effectiveness of "IBMers" by making needed information and services available to them—*e-care for employees*
6. Working closely with customers and suppliers to improve the tendering process and to better administer the huge number of transactions involved—*e-procurement*
7. Using the Internet to better communicate IBM's marketing stance—*e-marketing communications*
8. Creating a visible and usable portal by modifying the old Web site—*enterprise portal*

The company later added two more initiatives:

9. Using Lotus Notes and Domino, the company created many knowledge management applications—*knowledge management*
10. Moving close to 50 percent of all training to the Web by 2003—*e-learning*

Some of these initiatives have already borne fruit. For example, the e-procurement system that spans IBM globally saved the company more than $6 billion in 1999–2002, reducing the maverick (unplanned) buying from 33 percent to 2 percent. Online sales were close to $20 billion in 2002.

However, there is more to e-business than just how many dollars per day IBM sells or saves on the Web. In the procurement area, for example, IBM is invoicing electronically to reduce the millions of paper invoices it sends out and to enable fast, competitive tendering from its suppliers. IBM has evaluated every step of the procurement process to determine where the use of the Web can add value. This has resulted in the identification of more than 20 initiatives—including collaboration with suppliers, online purchasing, and knowledge-management-based applications—in which the company is already reducing cost and improving purchasing. (For more information, see Bonnett 2000.) As a matter of fact, a new corporate culture has been created: People are sharing and collaborating and are happier in doing their jobs.

Sources: Compiled from Bonnett (2000) and IBM (2003).

Questions

1. Why it was necessary to simplify business processes before doing EC?
2. Relate this case to strategy initiation, formulation, and implementation.
3. Review Section 15.7. Which factors contributed to IBM's success?
4. Do you think that IBM is becoming an e-business? Why or why not?

REFERENCES

Adobor, H., and R. McMullen. "Strategic Partnering in E-Commerce: Guidelines for Managing Alliances." *Business Horizons* 45, no. 2 (2002): 67–76.

Agrawal, V. L., et al. "E-Performance: The Path to Rational Exuberance." *The McKinsey Quarterly* 1 (2001).

Alter, S. *Information Systems: Foundations of E-Business.* Upper Saddle River, NJ: Prentice Hall, 2002.

asbbank.co.nz (accessed April 2003).

Baker, W., et al. "Price Smarter on the Net." *Harvard Business Review* (February 2001): 122–127.

bankdirect.co.nz (accessed April 2003).

Barton, P. S., and D. Peters. "The ASB Bank: An IT Case Study in Sustained Competitive Advantage." *Journal of Strategic Information Systems* (June 1992): 155–160.

Barua, A., et al. "Driving E-Business Excellence." *MIT Sloan Management Review* 43, no. 1 (2001): 36–44.

Boardman, A. D., et al. *Cost-Benefit Analysis: Concepts and Practice,* 2d ed. Upper Saddle River, NJ: Prentice Hall, 2000.

Bonnett, K. R. *An IBM Guide to Doing Business on the Internet.* New York: McGraw-Hill, 2000.

Boulding, W., and M. Christen. "First-Mover Disadvantage." *Harvard Business Review* (October 2001): 20–21.

Bruce, D., and W. F. Fox. *State and Local States Tax Revenue Losses from E-Commerce: Updated Estimates.* Knoxville, TN: Center for Business and Economic Research, University of Tennessee, 2001.

cardiacscience.com (accessed January 2003).

Chatterjee, D., et al. "Shaping Up for E-Commerce: Institutional Enablers for the Organizational Assimilation of Web Technologies." *MIS Quarterly* (June 2002).

Chen, B. "Do You Have the Right E-Business Structure?" *e-Business Advisor,* June 2001.

Chen, P., and L. M. Hitt. "Measuring Switching Costs and the Determinants of Customer Retention in Internet-Enabled Businesses: A Study of the Online Brokerage Industry." *Information Systems Research* (September 2002): 255–274.

Coltman, T., et al. "Keeping E-Business in Perspective." *Communications of the ACM* 45, no. 8 (August 2002): 69.

consumers.co.nz (accessed April 2003).

Deise, M. V., et al. *Executive's Guide to E-Business—From Tactics to Strategy.* New York: Wiley, 2000.

Dell, M. Keynote Address at the DirectConnect Conference, Austin, TX, August 25, 1999.

DePalma, D. "Meet Your Customers' Needs Through Cultural Marketing." *e-Business Advisor,* August 2000.

DePalma, D. "Think Globally, Act Consistently." *e-Business Advisor,* June 2001, 24–26.

Dewan, R., et al. "Adoption of Internet-Based Product Customization and Pricing Strategies." *Proceedings of the 33rd HICSS,* Maui, HI, January 2000.

Dyer, J. "The Impact of IT on Relationship Marketing." *Chartered Accountants Journal of New Zealand* 80, no. 11 (2001): 57–58.

e-Business World. "Global Imperative . . . and the Pitfalls of Regionalism." *e-Business World,* January–February 2000, 8–10.

El Sawy, O. *Redesigning Enterprise Processes for E-Business.* New York: McGraw-Hill, 2001.

Ernest D., et al. "A Future for E-Alliances." *The McKinsey Quarterly* (April–June 2001).

Esichaikul, V., and S. Chavananon. "Electronic Commerce and Electronic Business Implementation Success Factors." *Proceedings of the 14th Bled Electronic Commerce Conference,* Bled, Slovenia, June 25–26, 2001, pp. 259–275.

Evans, P., and T. Wurster. *Blown to Bits: How the New Economics of Information Transforms Strategy.* Boston: Harvard Business School Press, 2000.

Fessenden, K., and T. Dwyer. "Going Global with E-Business." Aberdeen Group, September 2000, **aberdeen.com** (accessed March 2003).

Ghemawat, P. "Distance Still Matters: The Hard Reality of Global Expansion." *Harvard Business Review* (September 2001): 137–147.

Green, S. *Profit on the Web*. Auckland, New Zealand: Axon Computertime, 2002.

Gulati, R., and J. Garino. "Get the Right Mix of Bricks and Clicks." *Harvard Business Review* (May–June 2000): 107–114.

Hagel J., III, and M. Singer. "Unbundling the Corporation." *Harvard Business Review* (March–April 1999): 133–141.

Harmon, P., et al. *Developing E-Business Systems and Architectures: A Manager's Guide*. San Francisco: Morgan Kaufmann Publishers, 2001.

Hayes, I. S. "Seven Steps to E-Business Success." *Software Magazine*, February 2000, **softwaremag.com/L.cfm?Doc=archive/2000feb/SevenSteps.html** (accessed June 2003).

Hiles, A. "E-Commerce: Managing the Risks." *MyITAdvisor*, Winter 2001.

Hornby, G., et al. "Export Through E-Business: Cultural Issues Faced by SMEs." *Proceedings, PACIS* 2000, Hong Kong, May 2000.

Huff, S., and M. Wade. "Critical Success Factors for Electronic Commerce." In Huff, et al. (ed.), *Cases in Electronic Commerce*. New York: Irwin/McGraw-Hill, 2000, 450–461.

IBM. **ibm.com/e-business/doc/content/casestudy/46406.html** (accessed January 2003).

Josephson, M. "Why a Content Management System Won't Take You Global." September 2001, **diominc.com/us/solutions/gls_doc/GLS_september2001.pdf** (accessed April 2003).

Kalakota, R., and M. Robinson. *E-Business 2.0-Roadmap for Success*. Reading, MA: Addison-Wesley, 2001.

Kaplan, R. S., and D. P. Norton. *The Balanced Scorecard: Translating Strategy into Action*. Boston: Harvard Business School Press, 1996.

Kauffman, R. J., et al. "When Internet Companies Morph: Understanding Organizational Strategy Changes in the 'New' New Economy." *First Monday*, July 2002, **firstmonday.dk/issues/issue7_7/kauffman** (accessed February 2003).

Kim, W. C., and R. Mauborgne. "Charting Your Company's Future." *Harvard Business Review* (June 2002): 77–83.

Levinson, M. "Don't Stop Thinking about Tomorrow." *CIO Magazine*, December 1999–January 2000.

lonelyplanet.com (accessed May 2003).

Lumpkin, G. T. "Achieving Sustainable Competitive Advantage and Avoiding Pitfalls." *Organizational Dynamics* (Spring 2002).

Markus, L. "Toward an Integrated Theory of IT-Related Risk Control." In Baskerville, R., et al. (eds.), *The Social and Organizational Perspective on Information Technology*. London: Chapman & Hall, 2000, 11–27.

OECD (Organization for Economic Cooperation and Development). *Enhancing SME Competitiveness: The OECD Bologna, Italy, Ministerial Conference*. 2001.

Palmer, J. "Web Site Usability, Design, and Performance Metrics." *Information Systems Research* (June 2002): 151–167.

Paul, L., and A. Franco. "Twelve Rules to Avoid." *Business Online*, August 2001.

Phillips, M. "Seven Steps to Your New E-Business." *Business Online*, August 2000.

Plant, R. T. *E-Commerce: Formulation of Strategy*. Upper Saddle River, NJ: Prentice Hall, 2000.

Porter, M. E. *Competitive Strategy: Techniques for Analyzing Industries and Competitors*. New York: The Free Press, 1980.

Porter, M. E. "What Is Strategy?" *Harvard Business Review* (November–December 1996): 61–78.

Porter, M. E. "Strategy and the Internet." *Harvard Business Review* (March 2001): 63–78.

Pottruck, D., and T. Pearce. *Clicks and Mortar*. San Francisco: Jossey-Bass, 2000.

Prasad, B., and P. Harker. "Pricing Online Banking Services Amid Network Externalities." *Proceedings of the 33rd HICSS*, Maui, HI, January 2000.

Rangan, S., and R. Adner. "Profits and the Internet: Seven Misconceptions." *Sloan Management Review* (2001): 44–53.

Rayport, J., and B. J. Jaworski. *Introduction to E-Commerce*. Boston: McGraw-Hill, 2002.

Reda, S. "Online Check Service Expands Internet Payment Options." *Stores*, February 2002.

Rowe, A. J., et al. *Strategic Management: A Methodological Approach*. Boston: Addison-Wesley, 1994.

Schultz, G. "Siemens: 100% e-Business." *APICS Magazine*, April 2002.

Shapiro, C., and H. Varian. *Information Rules: A Strategic Guide to the Network Economy*. Boston: Harvard Business School Press, 1999.

Sheldon, L. A., and T. J. Strader. "Managerial Issues for Expanding into International Web-Based Electronic Commerce." *SAM Advanced Management Journal* (Summer 2002): 22–30.

Stern, C. W., and G. Stalk. *Perspectives on Strategy from the Boston Consulting Group*. New York: John Wiley & Sons, 1998.

Sterne, J. *Web Metrics: Proven Methods for Measuring Web Site Success*. New York: John Wiley & Sons, 2002.

Straub, D. W., et al. "Measuring E-Commerce in Net-Enabled Organizations: An Introduction to the Special Issue." *Information Systems Research* (June 2002a): 115–124.

Straub, D. W., et al. "Toward New Metrics for Net-Enhanced Organizations." *Information Systems Research* (September 2002b): 227–238.

Teach, E. "Microsoft's Universe of Risk." *CFO*, March 1997, 69–72, cfo.com/html/Articles/CFO/1997/97MR micr.html (accessed April 2003).

The Economist. "While Welch Waited." *The Economist*, May 19, 2001, 75–76.

Tjan, A. K. "Finally, a Way to Put Your Internet Portfolio in Order." *Harvard Business Review* (February 2001): 76–85.

Turban, E., et al. *Information Technology for Management.* 4th ed. New York: John Wiley & Sons, 2004.

Ulph, R., et al. "Integrated Marketing Needs Hubs." *Tech Strategy Report*, December 2001, forrester.com/ER/Research/Report/Summary/0,1338,13712,00.html (accessed March 2003).

Useem, J. "Dot-Coms: What Have We Learned?" *Fortune*, October 2000.

Venkatraman, N. "Five Steps to a Dot-Com Strategy: How to Find Your Footing on the Web." *Sloan Management Review* (Spring 2000): 15–28.

Viehland, D. "Managing Business Risk in Electronic Commerce." *Proceedings of the 2001 Americas Conference on Information Systems*, Boston, MA, August 3, 2001.

Vose, D. *Risk Analysis: A Quantitative Guide*, 2d ed. New York: John Wiley and Sons, 2000.

Voss, C. "Developing an eService Strategy." *Business Strategy Review* (Spring 2000).

Watchfire. *You Can't Manage What You Don't Measure: Improving Website ROI Through E-Metrics and Website Management.* Kanata, Ontario: Watchfire Corporation, 2001.

Watson, R. P., et al. *Electronic Commerce: The Strategic Perspective.* Fort Worth, TX: Dryden Press, 2000.

Weill, P., and M. R. Vitale. *Place to Space: Migrating to eBusiness Models.* Boston: Harvard Business School Press, 2001.

Wheelen, T., and J. Hunger. *Strategic Management and Business Policy*, 8th ed. Reading, MA: Addison-Wesley, 2002.

Wheeler, B. "The Net-Enabled Business Innovation Cycle: A Dynamic Capabilities Theory for Assessing Net-Enablement." *Information Systems Research* (May 2002): 125–146.

Wilson, S. G., and I. Abel. "So You Want to Get Involved in E-Commerce." *Industrial Marketing Management* 31 (January–February 2002).

Yap, E. "Seven Keys to Successful e-Business." *MIS Asia*, March 2002, 45–53.

Zhu, K., and K. Kraemer. "E-Commerce Metrics for Net-Enhanced Organizations: Assessing the Value of E-Commerce to Firm Performance in the Manufacturing Sector." *Information Systems Research* (September 2002): 275–295.

CHAPTER 16

LAUNCHING A SUCCESSFUL ONLINE BUSINESS

Content

Learning objectives

Upon completion of this chapter, you will be able to:

1. Understand the fundamental requirements for initiating an online business.

2. Describe the funding options available to start-up businesses.

3. Evaluate the options for hosting Web sites.

4. Understand the processes and business decisions associated with managing Web site development.

5. Understand the importance of providing content that meets the needs and expectations of the intended audience.

6. Evaluate Web sites on design criteria such as appearance, navigation, consistency, and performance.

7. Know the techniques of search engine optimization to obtain high placement in search engines.

8. Understand the benefits of customer relationship management through customer self-service, listening to customers, and increasing trust.

OBO SETS ITS GOALS FOR SUCCESS

The Problem

OBO sells protective gear for field hockey goalkeepers. The leg guards, helmets, gloves, and other products are designed to protect goalies from the hard hockey ball while not inhibiting the goalie's need to move quickly and easily. OBO's protective foam has a tighter and more consistent cell structure than competitors' products to provide maximum, long-wearing protection, and OBO's unique three-dimensional thermo-bonding manufacturing process produces equipment that is shaped to reflect the way the body moves. By manufacturing a quality product and listening to the customer, OBO has become the market leader in most of the 20 countries in which its products are sold. In the 2000 Olympics, all of the medal-winning teams were wearing OBO gear.

OBO is based in Palmerston North, a small provincial town in New Zealand that is a very long way from its principal markets in Europe and the Americas. OBO sells a niche product that is best sold thorough agents or stores to ensure a proper fit. How does OBO use its Web site to market an experiential product to a global market from New Zealand?

The Solution

The goals of the *obo.co.nz* Web site are community building, product sales, and research and development. As the "About OBO" page proudly boasts "OBO loves the Web because it lets us have contact with the people we exist to serve."

Community building happens through online discussion forums, sponsored players, and an image gallery. OBO's company director Simon Barnett says: "We sponsor goalkeepers. We e-mail out to 900–1,000 people biweekly and give them the opportunity to ask an expert about the game and the equipment, join a database, link to other hockey sites, and seek readers' opinions. We try to get people involved by having their photo on the Web site. If we can get people involved, they'll love the brand name and the image and the feelings that go with it" (New Zealand Ministry of Economic Development [MED] 2000, p. 12).

OBO also sells goalie equipment through the Web site. However, the principal marketing and sales goal of the Web site is to convince the visitor of the value of the product and direct the customer to a store or agent to make the purchase. Barnett calls the Web site "a support mechanism for the brand and the sale of equipment through the agents, and we will pick up the odd sale here and there" (New Zealand MED 2000, p. 12).

The research and development goal is met through online surveys, solicitation of players' opinions of the products, and focus groups. According to Barnett: "We use the Web site for research and development through focus groups. We give a topic such as goalkeeping shoes—Is there a need for them? What features should they have? What pricing? The focus group is carefully selected off the database, given the brief (the purpose of the questions), and asked to respond by the end of the week with their opinions" (New Zealand MED 2000, p. 12).

The Results

The OBO Web site is most successful at community building. In 2000, over 100,000 people visited the Web site, many of them first-time OBO equipment buyers who must register their product warranty online. Many become registered team players and contribute to discussion forums as well as create their own "favorites" section and online address book. The site also builds community by promoting a goalie-friendly approach to OBO's customers. Simon Barrett signs his introduction letter as "Team Captain" and says, "the most special thing about OBO are its people. The people who bring you the OBO product are dedicated, honest, and earnest about our work" (*obo.co.nz* 2003).

Online product sales have been modest, approximately NZ$150,000 in 2000. This is in line with the company's expectation that the Web site supports, not competes, with OBO's agent network. For example, prices at the Web site are slightly higher than in retail stores. However, online sales are expected to grow because OBO has introduced a new line of clothes designed specifically for goalies that is sold exclusively through the Web site.

The focus groups deliver high-value feedback at almost no cost, and the discussion forums contribute to both community building and a constant stream of feedback about OBO's product in the marketplace.

Sources: New Zealand Ministry of Economic Development (2000) and *obo.co.nz* (2003).

WHAT WE CAN LEARN . . .

OBO's use of the Web matches many of the expectations that online business owners have for their Web site. A small company with a great product is using its Web site to reach its target markets in distant countries. Like many successful online businesses, OBO is using the site to support business goals, as well as to meet the needs and expectations of its target audience. The Web site is simple and well designed, includes "attractors" that encourage customer interaction and keep customers coming back, contains content that promotes cross selling, and effectively promotes sustainable customer relationships. OBO is one of tens of thousands of small businesses successfully using the Web for e-commerce. The purpose of this chapter is to describe the requirements for creating and maintaining a successful e-business in the online marketplace. This chapter builds on the conceptual material offered in previous chapters to provide a practical understanding of what it takes to be successful in the competitive world of electronic commerce.

16.1 DOING BUSINESS ONLINE: GETTING STARTED

Success in the online marketplace is never an assured outcome. As in the brick-and-mortar marketplace, the failure rate of online companies is high (Kauffman et al. 2002; Saracevic 2000). Why do a few online companies succeed while many others fail? What does the "ontrepreneur"—online entrepreneur—need to know to launch a profitable online business?

BUSINESS FORMATION

Most new businesses—brick-and-mortar, purely online, or brick-and-click begin in a similar way. The process can be briefly described as follows:

▶ **Identify a consumer or business need in the marketplace.** Many businesses simply start with a good idea. Perhaps a magazine article, a personal observation, an unsolved problem, a small irritation, or a friend's suggestion triggers the idea, and the prospective business owner sees a gap between what people want and what is available. For example, both Amazon.com (see EC Application Case 16.1) and eBay began this way.

▶ **Investigate the opportunity.** Just because a person perceives that an opportunity exists does not mean that it is real. Perhaps the number of individuals interested in purchasing the product or service is too small. Perhaps the cost of manufacturing, marketing, and

---

CASE 16.1
EC Application

A BRILLIANT IDEA

Call it fate or call it the right person being in the right head space at the right time. Whatever you call it, the idea behind Amazon.com and its founder, Jeff Bezos, seemed destined for each other.

Jeff Bezos was born in January 1964 in Albuquerque, New Mexico. Even as a boy his cleverness, intelligence, and entrepreneurial skills were obvious. At the age of 12, Bezos built a motorized mirrored Infinity Cube because he couldn't afford the $20 to buy one. A few years later he graduated valedictorian of his Florida high school. As a young entrepreneur, he created a summer camp for middle school students, promoting that it "emphasizes the use of new ways of thinking in old areas," which was in many ways a prediction of his future success.

Bezos graduated from Princeton University with a degree in Computer Science, and his first employment was in electronic commerce, building an EDI network for settling cross-border equity transactions. A few jobs later he was a senior vice president at hedge fund firm D. E. Shaw, responsible for exploring new business opportunities on the Internet. It was then that his intelligence, entrepreneurial talents, computing education, and e-commerce experience all came together in a brilliant idea: The most logical thing to sell over the Internet was books!

Why books? Behind the thousands of brick-and-mortar bookstores are just two large book distributors, with an extensive list of books already online in the distributors' database. Jeff Bezos was willing to bet that book buyers would be willing to give up the cozy, coffee-shop, browsing environment of the local bookstore if he could offer them the "earth's biggest bookstore," fantastic customer service, and features that no physical bookstore could match—customer book reviews, author interviews, personalized book recommendations, and more.

The other driving force behind his idea was what Jeff Bezos called his "regret-minimization framework." "When I am 80," he asked himself, "am I going to regret leaving Wall Street? No. Will I regret missing a chance to be there at the start of the Internet? Yes" (Bayers 1999).

The rest of the story is the stuff of legend. Bezos left his six-figure Wall Street salary and wrote the Amazon.com business plan during a cross-country move to Seattle, Washington. The Amazon.com Web site was built in a cramped, poorly insulated garage. When Amazon.com launched in July 1995, a bell would ring every time the server recorded a sale. Within a few weeks the constant bell ringing became unbearable, and they turned it off.

In the late 1990s, Amazon.com invested millions of dollars in infrastructure and expansion opportunities. This was in line with Bezos' vision for Amazon.com as "broader than books and music." After years of large losses, Amazon.com announced its first small profit in the 2001 fourth quarter. It all began with a smart entrepreneur whose life experiences gave him a brilliant idea that led to the founding of a legendary e-commerce company.

Sources: Compiled from Bayers (1999) and Spector (2000).

Questions

1. What was the gap in the consumer market that inspired Jeff Bezos to create Amazon.com?

2. What factors, at both personal and business levels, led Jeff Bezos to his brilliant idea?

distributing the product or providing the service is too large. The revenue model may be wrong, others may have tried already and failed, satisfactory substitute products may be available, and so on. For example, online grocery shopping would seem to be a wonderful opportunity—relieving busy professionals of the time-consuming and tiresome task of regular visits to a grocery store. Many large- and small-scale online grocery ventures have been tried (e.g., NetGrocer, Peapod, HomeGrocer, Webvan), but most have failed or continue to lose money because they misjudged the logistical problems associated with grocery warehousing and delivery (Bakshi and Deighton 1999). One of the purposes of a business plan, described shortly, is to determine the feasibility of a business opportunity in the marketplace.

> **Determine the business owner's ability to meet the need.** Assuming that a realistic business opportunity exists, does the prospective business owner have the ability to convert the opportunity into success? Some personal qualities are important: Is the business in an industry the prospective business owner knows well? Is it something the entrepreneur loves doing? Are family and friends supportive? Business skills in staff recruitment, management, negotiation, marketing, and financial management are required, as well as entrepreneurial attitudes such as innovation, risk taking, and being proactive. Many good ideas and realistic initiatives have failed in the execution stage because the owners or principals of the business lacked sufficient business skills to make it a reality. Boo.com, for example, seemingly had a great concept (retailing ultra-modern, designer-wear clothing) and superior software, but it failed because of the inability of management to organize the business and manage the projects necessary to bring Boo.com online before it burned through $120 million of start-up capital (Cukier 2000).

Beyond these general platitudes about what it takes to start a prosperous business, the owner of an online business must consider some requirements that reflect the online nature of the business. The first of these is the need to understand Internet culture. Activities such as spam, extensive use of graphics, forced visitor registration, and intrusive pop-up browser windows are counter to the accepted norms of behavior on the Internet (Huff et al. 2000). Similarly, business owners new to the Net need to realize that, contrary to expectations, textual exchanges of information are "media rich" (Markus 1994; Huang et al. 1996), customers are active in how they absorb and use information, and the Internet is a personal, helping, and sharing place for most users. Businesses that ignore the cultural and behavioral norms of the Internet do so at their peril.

A second requirement that the owner of an online business must consider is the nature of appropriate products and services. Although virtually anything is available for sale on the Internet, the degree of sales success is somewhat dependent on the type of item or service being offered. For example, products that can be digitized (e.g., information, music, software) sell well and are easily delivered. Similarly, services (e.g., stock brokering, ticket sales) and commodities (e.g., books, CDs) also have been quite successful. In contrast, experiential products such as clothes and perfume do not sell well, except as a second purchase of the same product. However, one of the greatest opportunities the Internet offers is in niche marketing. Rare and quirky sales ideas such as antique Coke bottles (antiquebottles.com), gadgets for left-handed individuals (anythingleft-handed.co.uk), Swedish gourmet food (wikstromsgourmet.com), and gift items from Belize (belizenet.com) would rarely succeed in a physical storefront, but the Internet offers the owners of these sites an opportunity to pursue their business idea and be successful. The Internet's worldwide reach makes it easy for people with a common interest to find each other and conduct business together.

E-BUSINESS PLANNING

business plan
A written document that identifies a company's goals and outlines how the company intends to achieve the goals.

Every online business needs a business plan. As defined in Chapter 1, a **business plan** is a written document that identifies a company's goals and outlines how the company intends to achieve those goals. A business plan includes both *strategic* elements (e.g., mission statement, value proposition, competitive positioning statement) and *operational* elements (e.g., operations plan, financial statements) of how a new business intends to do business.

The principal reason an entrepreneur writes a business plan is to acquire funding—from a bank, an angel investor, a venture capitalist, or the financial markets. A business plan also is important as a tool to recruit senior management and to convince business partners to make a commitment to the business. A business plan helps ensure a thriving business by encouraging an entrepreneur to set goals, anticipate problems, set measures for success, and keep the business on track after it is started. A business plan forces the entrepreneur to be realistic about the business's prospects. Indeed, sometimes the most successful outcome of a business plan is a decision not to proceed.

A business plan for an online business—an "e-business plan"—differs only subtly from a traditional, off-line business plan. After all, a business is a business and a plan is a plan, so most of what one finds in a business plan is also in an e-business plan. Many of the differences between the two types of plans are obvious and can be readily accounted for—an online business never closes, the market is global not local, and e-commerce is conducted at "Internet speed."

The biggest difference in e-business planning is for the entrepreneur to recognize that the Internet is unlike any other sales channel. As discussed in previous chapters, the Internet allows companies to interact with consumers with both reach and richness (Evans and Wurster 2000), to introduce new and innovative business models, and to distribute information at the speed of light at almost zero cost. The Internet also changes business assumptions, such as creating more bargaining power for the customer and less bargaining power for the supplier (Porter 2001), creating a more perfect information market to the customer's benefit, and making it easier for competitors to invade a company's marketplace and vice versa. Finally, the Internet creates greater opportunities for focusing on the customer through personalization of content, one-to-one marketing, and customer self-service. Because the Web allows these and other customer service features, online businesses must make them part of their business plan, and before their competitors do so, too. These differences, and more, make the "e-difference" in e-business planning.

The E-Business Plan Tutorial at the book's Web site explores this topic in further depth and offers a detailed explanation of how to prepare a business plan.

An existing brick-and-mortar business looking to move online also needs a plan, or more specifically, a **business case**—a document that is used to justify the investment of internal, organizational resources in a specific application or project. A business case for a large, resource-intensive project resembles a business plan. The similarities and differences in writing such a business case are included in the E-Business Plan Tutorial at the book's Web site. For a small- or medium-sized project, the business case can be much simpler. Insights and Additions 16.1 (page 606) presents a business case template that can be used to justify an online application or project such as a new Web site, adding transactional processing to an existing Web site, an e-newsletter, an extranet, or participation in a digital exchange.

business case
A document that is used to justify the investment of internal, organizational resources in a specific application or project.

FUNDING THE ONLINE BUSINESS

Launching an online business can be expensive. The brave entrepreneur is usually willing to invest personal funds from savings, personal lines of credit, or a house mortgage, but these sources of "bootstrap funding" are unlikely to be enough. The new venture involves significant risk, so some traditional sources of debt financing such as a bank loan are difficult or impossible to get. What are other sources of funding for a start-up business?

One major source of funding during the dot-com boom was venture capital. **Venture capital (VC)** is money invested in a business by an individual or a group of individuals (venture capitalists) in exchange for equity in the business. Venture capitalists tend to invest in companies that have identified what seems to be an outstanding business opportunity, have taken some action to make the opportunity happen (e.g., written a new software application, secured a patent, built a Web site), and need an infusion of funds and management expertise to launch the business. Venture capitalists usually invest large sums of money and expect, in return, some management control and a profit on their investment within 3 to 5 years when the successful start-up goes public (an IPO) or is merged with or acquired by a larger company. The start-up company receives the funds and experienced management guidance it needs during its launch and expansion stages.

venture capital (VC)
Money invested in a business by an individual or a group of individuals (venture capitalists) in exchange for equity in the business.

Insights and Additions 16.1   A Business Case Template

This template is best used to justify the expenditure of resources on a specific online project or initiative in an existing business. If the business is considering a number of different initiatives, a separate business case should be prepared for each one. If the initiative is for a new business, a more comprehensive business plan will be required.

▶ **Goals.** Begin with a specific description of what the business intends to achieve through the initiative—increased sales, reinforcement of the brand or corporate image, improved customer support, reduction in communications and marketing costs, and so forth. A useful approach is to define the problem, propose a solution, and describe the expected outcomes or impacts. Conclude this section with *goals*—one or more statements that succinctly describe a desired future condition toward which efforts will be directed.

▶ **Cost savings.** If one or more goals include reduction of existing expenditures, then calculate the following: (1) an itemized and quantified list of existing costs that will be affected by the project and (2) the estimated levels of savings that the project will generate (e.g., reduce long-distance telephone costs by 45 percent). When costs and saving levels are multiplied together, the expected reduction of expenditures will be known. These savings should be estimated for a short-term time frame, perhaps the first 3 years of the project's operation.

▶ **New revenue.** If one or more of the goals suggests an increased revenue stream, then calculate: (1) an itemized and quantified list of existing net income (revenue from sales minus cost of sales) that will be affected by the application or project and (2) the estimated levels of new sales that are expected (e.g., increase product sales by 12 percent). When net income and increased sales levels are multiplied together, the expected amount of increased revenue will be revealed. Do this for the same multiyear time frame as used in the cost-savings calculation.

▶ **Extra benefits.** List and, if possible, quantify any additional fiscal benefits that are associated with the project (e.g., improved staff productivity, faster collection of outstanding debts). If these are difficult to estimate accurately, it is best to list them but not quantify them nor add them to the benefits identified previously. This approach will produce an overall more conservative estimate of benefits, building in an extra cushion for project success should not all quantified benefits be realized.

▶ **Cost of the solution.** This is an itemized and quantified list of costs associated with the online project. Both direct costs (e.g., amortized cost of Web site development, Web site hosting) and indirect costs (e.g., staff training) should be estimated for the period.

▶ **Net benefits.** Add together all benefits (i.e., cost savings, new revenue, extra benefits) and subtract the costs. The result should be a specific amount of expected monetary gains (or losses) resulting from successful implementation of the project in each year of the period being examined.

▶ **Recommendation.** Summarize the decision that is being recommended in light of the foregoing analysis. If the net benefit result is strongly positive, then a decision to proceed is likely, and the next steps (e.g., a risk analysis, customer survey, staff hiring) can be started. If the results are slightly positive or negative in one or all years of operation, the decision to proceed may still be justified on the basis of seeing the online initiative as a long-term strategy, a competitive imperative, or simply the cost of staying in business. If the bottom line is strongly negative, then the most likely outcome will be a decision that there is no justification for this project, saving the business a lot of time and money. Even that can be viewed as a positive outcome of a business case.

The downside for the start-up business is minimal, losing some control over the business in return for funds it is unlikely to acquire from any other source. The more difficult problem is *finding* venture capital. Due to the many dot-com failures in 2000 onwards, many VC sources have disappeared, and competition for venture capital is extremely difficult

The downside for the venture capitalist is if the business fails or even if it is a mediocre success. Then the promised return on equity from going public, merging, or being bought out does not happen. This occurrence is common, and venture capitalists plan on one wildly successful investment to make up the losses from other less-than-successful ventures. Some well-known venture capital companies are vFinance Capital (vfinance.com), The Capital Network (thecapitalnetwork.com), and Garage Technology Ventures (garage.com), which was founded by personal computing guru Guy Kawasaki. Rayport and Jaworski (2002) offer a more comprehensive discussion of venture capital markets and other sources of equity financing such as holding companies and corporate ventures.

Because venture capitalists tend to come in only after the business is started and just before its launch, who funds initial product or business development? If the ontrepreneur's personal investment is insufficient, an angel investor may be able to help. An **angel investor** is a wealthy individual who contributes personal funds and expertise at the earliest stage of business development.

A typical angel investor scenario begins with a young software developer who has identified a niche in the market for a new software application, but who has insufficient funding to get started. An angel investor will provide the developer with an office, hardware, software, salary, and access to the human and financial resources required to write the software application. The angel investor typically also provides guidance and/or access to management expertise. In addition to sometimes-altruistic goals, the angel investor is looking for a reasonable return on the investment when the business is ready to launch. In other words, the angel investor is almost always a pre-VC funding source and is usually paid out from the infusion of venture capital funds. As with venture capital, an angel investor is an excellent source of funding for the ontrepreneur, but angel funding is equally scarce and difficult to find.

Another important source of support, if not funding, for pre-VC firms is an incubator. An **incubator** is a company, university, or not-for-profit organization that supports businesses in their initial stages of development. A few incubators offer start-up funding, but the primary purpose of most incubators is to offer a variety of support services—office space, accounting services, group purchasing schemes, reception services, coaching, information technology consulting—at little or no cost. In return, the incubator receives a modest fee, start-up equity in the company, or both.

angel investor
A wealthy individual who contributes personal funds and expertise at the earliest stage of business development.

incubator
A company, university, or not-for-profit organization that supports businesses in their initial stages of development.

Section 16.1 ▶ REVIEW

1. Describe the formation process of a typical business.

2. What special requirements must an online business consider in its formation? In e-business planning?

3. What is a business plan and how does it contribute to business success? What is a business case and how does it contribute to business success?

4. Describe three funding options available to a start-up business.

16.2 DOING BUSINESS ONLINE: BUILDING THE WEB SITE

Every online business needs a Web site. A Web site is the primary way any firm doing business on the Internet advertises its products or services and attracts customers. Many Web sites also sell products and services, and businesses with digital products usually deliver their products via the Web site as well.

CLASSIFICATION OF WEB SITES

Web sites exist in all kinds, shapes, and sizes. One of the major distinctions made in Web site classification is the level of functionality inherent in the site. An **informational Web site** does little more than provide information about the business and its products and services. For many brick-and-mortar businesses such as a New England weathervane shop (vtweatherworks.com), a Cook Islands beach house (varas.co.ck), or a B2B secure storage facility (safestoreusa.com), an informational "brochureware" Web site is perfectly satisfactory.

An **interactive Web site** provides opportunities for the customers and the business to communicate and share information. An interactive site will contain all the information about products and services that an informational site does, but it also will deliver informational features intended to encourage interaction between the business and customers or between customers, such as an e-newsletter, product demonstrations, and customer discussion forums. An interactive Web site will strongly encourage feedback by including contact e-mail addresses, providing feedback forms, and encouraging completion of online surveys. Navigation can be made more interactive with features such as the ability to search the site, a well-designed site map, and mouseovers (clickable buttons that change shape or color when a visitor passes a mouse cursor over the button). Interactivity can be enhanced with value-added tools such as currency converters, calendars, and various types of calculators (e.g., a mortgage calculator on a bank's Web site).

informational Web site
A Web site that does little more than provide information about the business and its products and services.

interactive Web site
A Web site that provides opportunities for the customers and the business to communicate and share information.

attractors
Web site features that attract and interact with visitors in the target stakeholder group.

transactional Web site
A Web site that sells products and services.

At the highest level of interactivity are **attractors**—Web site features that attract and interact with site visitors (Watson et al. 2000). Attractors such as games, puzzles, prize give-aways, contests, and electronic postcards encourage customers to find the Web site, visit again, and recommend the site to their friends. For example, Ragu's Web site does not sell spaghetti sauce or other Ragu products, but the recipes, customer interaction ("talk to mama"), unforgettable domain name (eat.com), and other features make this an attractor-loaded site that increases brand awareness and sells Ragu's products in the customer's next trip to the grocery store.

A **transactional Web site** sells products and services. These Web sites typically include information and interactivity features but also have sell-side features such as a shopping cart, a product catalog, shipping calculator, and the ability to accept a credit card number to complete the sale.

BUILDING THE WEB SITE

Assuming a business has completed the preparatory work of business formation, writing a business plan, and acquiring initial funding, as outlined in Section 16.1, the process of building a Web site is as follows:

1. **Select a Web host.** One of the first decisions that an online business will face is where the Web site will be located on the Internet. The Web site might be included in a virtual shopping mall such as activeplaza.com or hosted in a collection of independent storefronts as at Yahoo (store.yahoo.com). However, most small businesses and all medium-sized and large businesses will decide to build a standalone Web site either with an independent hosting service or through self-hosting arrangements.

2. **Register a domain name.** Nearly concurrent with the selection of a Web host will be the domain name decision. In a mall or Web storefront, the business's name may be an extension of the host's name (e.g., store.yahoo.com/mybusiness). A standalone Web site will have a standalone domain name (e.g., mybusiness.com), and decisions will have to be made about which top-level domain name to use and whether the domain name includes the business name or some aspect of branding.

3. **Create and manage content.** The Web site also needs content—the text, images, sound, and video that deliver the information that site visitors need and expect. Content can come from a variety of sources, but getting the right content in place, making it easy to find, delivering it effectively, and managing content so it remains accurate and up-to-date are crucial to the success of the online business. Exhibit 16.1 lists the primary criteria Web site visitors use to evaluate the content of a Web site.

4. **Design the Web site.** This is the critically important and creative part of the process that determines what the site will look like (e.g., color schemes, graphics, typography) and how visitors will use it (e.g., information architecture, navigation design). Mall or storefront businesses may have limited options, but there are nearly unlimited opportunities in Web design for the standalone site. Exhibit 16.1 also lists the primary criteria Web site visitors use to evaluate the design of a Web site.

5. **Construct the Web site and test.** Businesses must also decide whether to design and construct the Web site internally, contract this out to a Web design firm, or some proportion of both. When the business owners are satisfied with the Web site, it is transferred to the Web site host. At this point, the Web site is open for business, but final testing is required to ensure all links work and processes function as expected (e.g., acceptance of credit card numbers).

6. **Market and promote the Web site.** At this stage, the location or URL of the Web site is widely promoted by the business on products, business cards, letters, and promotional material. Many of the advertising strategies discussed in Chapter 6—banner exchanges, chat rooms, viral marketing—can be used. Another key strategy for attracting customers is increased visibility by search engine optimization.

Each of these steps and processes are discussed in the following sections.

EXHIBIT 16.1 Web Site Evaluation Criteria

How Web Site Visitors Evaluate Content

Criteria (and related "subcriteria")	Explanation
Relevance (applicable, related, clear)	Concerned with issues such as relevancy, clearness, and "goodness" of the information.
Timeliness (current, continuously updated)	Concerned with the currency of the information.
Reliability (believable, accurate, consistent)	Concerned with the degree of accuracy, dependability, and consistency of the information.
Scope (sufficient, complete, covers a wide range, detailed)	Evaluates the extent of information, range of information, and level of detail provided by the Web site.
Perceived usefulness (informative, valuable, instrumental)	Visitor's assessment of the likelihood that the information will enhance their purchasing decision.

How Web Site Visitors Evaluate Web Site Design

Criteria (and related "subcriteria")	Explanation
Access (responsive, loads quickly)	Refers to the speed of access and the availability of the Web site at all times.
Usability (simple layout, easy to use, well organized, visually attractive, fun, clear design)	Concerned with the extent to which the Web site is visually appealing, consistent, fun, and easy to use.
Navigation	Evaluates the links to needed information.
Interactivity (customized product; search engine; ability to create list of items, change list of items, and find related items)	Evaluates the search engine and the personal features (e.g., shopping cart) of the Web site.

Source: McKinney et al., "The Measurement of Web-Customer Satisfaction: An Expectation and Disconfirmation Approach," *Information Systems Research* 13, no. 3. September 2002, pp. 296–315. Courtesy of Blackwell Publishing.

Section 16.2 ▶ REVIEW

1. Distinguish between informational, interactive, and transactional Web sites.
2. List the six steps necessary to build a Web site.
3. Describe five criteria that Web site visitors use to evaluate Web site content. Describe four criteria that visitors use to evaluate Web site design.

16.3 WEB SITE HOSTING

Every brick-and-mortar business has a storefront from which it sells goods and services. The business either owns or rents the storefront in a mall or independent location. Every online business has a storefront, too, its Web site. The decisions about whether to own (self-host) or rent, where to host the Web site (storebuilder service, ISP, Web hosting service), and the site's domain name are some of the first important decisions an online business owner has to make. This section discusses the considerations in making these decisions.

WEB HOSTING OPTIONS

A **storebuilder service** (also called design-and-host service) provides disk space and services to help small and micro businesses build a Web site quickly and cheaply. A storebuilder service such as Yahoo Store (store.yahoo.com) provides a series of templates and tools to easily build the site, disk space to store Web pages, a Web site address (e.g., a URL such as store.yahoo.com/mybusiness), and management, security, and maintenance of the Internet connection that makes the Web site available to the world. Storebuilder services offer a variety of hosting options, but the most basic storebuilder process is that in which a business registers at the site, selects one of the templates, and enters business and product information.

The principal advantage of a storebuilder service is that it is a quick, easy, and inexpensive way to build the Web site. The disadvantages are the lack of a strong online identity, limited functionality (e.g., accepting credit cards may not be possible), dependence on the service

storebuilder service
A hosting service that provides disk space and services to help small and micro businesses build a Web site quickly and cheaply.

ISP hosting service

A hosting service that provides an independent, standalone Web site for small- and medium-sized businesses.

Web hosting service

A dedicated Web site hosting company that offers a wide range of hosting services and functionality to businesses of all sizes.

mirror site

An exact duplicate of the original Web site, but it is physically located on a Web server on another continent.

co-location

A Web server owned and maintained by the business is placed in a Web hosting service that manages the server's connection to the Internet.

self-hosting

When a business acquires the hardware, software, staff, and dedicated telecommunications services necessary to set up and manage its own Web site.

for proper management of connectivity to the site, and some lack of differentiation (the Web site tends to look like other sites because everyone is using the same set of templates).

The same company that delivers e-mail and Web access to a business is also likely to be able to host the company's Web site. An **ISP hosting service** provides an independent, standalone Web site for small- and medium-sized businesses. The ISP is likely to provide additional hosting services (e.g., more storage space, simple site statistics, credit card gateway software) at the same or slightly higher cost than the storebuilder service.

The major difference between a storebuilder and an ISP hosting service is that the time-consuming and sometimes expensive task of designing and constructing the Web site becomes the responsibility of the business in the ISP hosting service. The business owners, usually with a contracted Web designer, must use a Web site construction tool (e.g., Website Builder at ownspot.com, ibuilt.net at ibuilt.net) or a Web page editor (e.g. Dreamweaver at macromedia.com or FrontPage at microsoft.com) to create the Web site. This is not necessarily a bad thing. Compared to the storebuilder template, the business gets increased flexibility in terms of what it can do with the site, and the site will be distinctive, able to stand out from the competition. The site also now has a branded domain name (e.g., www.mybusiness.com). One disadvantage to using an ISP is that most providers have limited functionality (e.g., an ISP may be unwilling to host a back-office database). Another consideration is the commitment of the ISP to maintain quality service and keep its hosting services up-to-date. This is a concern because the principal business of an ISP is providing Internet service, not hosting Web sites.

A **Web hosting service** is a dedicated Web site hosting company that offers a wide range of hosting services and functionality to businesses of all sizes. Companies such as Hostway (hostway.com) and DellHost (dellhost.com) offer more and better services than an ISP because Web site hosting is their core business. Almost all Web hosting companies have internal Web design departments, so the cooperation between the designer and host is assured. Also, functionality such as database integration, shipping and tax calculators, sufficient bandwidth to support multimedia files, shopping carts, site search engines, and comprehensive site statistics are likely to be readily available.

A Web hosting service is also the best option for an online business that needs one or more mirror sites. A **mirror site** is an exact duplicate of the original Web site, but it is physically located on a Web server on another continent. A business may decide a mirror site is needed when large numbers of customers are geographically a long distance from the original site. A mirror site reduces telecommunications costs and improves speed of customer access because the distance between the Web server and the customer's browser is sharply reduced. Typically, customers do not know, or care, that they are accessing a mirror site.

A variation of the Web hosting service is **co-location**. In this arrangement, a Web server owned and maintained by the business is placed in a Web hosting service that manages the server's connection to the Internet. This allows the business maximum control over site content and functionality, as in self-hosting (described next), but without the need for specialized staff or other requirements for 24/7 network management.

The highest level of hosting options is **self-hosting**. With this option, the business acquires the hardware, software, staff, and dedicated telecommunications services necessary to set up and manage its own Web site. Self-hosting is considered necessary when a business has special requirements such as maximum data security, protection of intellectual property, or, most likely, when the business intends to have a significant Web presence.

The principal disadvantage of self-hosting is the cost. The other Web-hosting options allow the hosting company to amortize the set-up and running costs of site hosting across hundreds or thousands of customers. A business that hosts its own Web site will have to bear these costs alone, not to mention concerns about security and full-time Web site management. These costs must be weighed against the benefits of better control over site performance and increased flexibility in site design, improvement, and functionality.

CONTRACTING THE WEB HOST

When the online business owners have a firm idea about the type of hosting service that best suits their needs, the next step is to find and negotiate a contract with the Web host. The process outlined in this section assumes a small- or medium-sized business has identified an

ISP as best able to meet both the Web hosting and Internet service provision requirements. The process would not be much different if a Web hosting service were chosen.

Typically, the search for an ISP host begins by contacting local ISPs for information, asking others in the business community for recommendations, and consulting with local telecommunications and computer user groups. Most businesses will want to use a local ISP because face-to-face contact is helpful if there are problems with customer access to the Web site or the business's ability to update it. However, a business may decide to host the site in another location for cost-saving or customer-location purposes. If so, lists of ISPs can be found at The List of ISPs (thelist.internet.com), Providers of Commercial Internet Access (celestin.com/pocia), and Yahoo's lists of ISPs.

When a short list of potential ISPs has been compiled, a RFQ can be used to ensure that complete and consistent bids for provision of service are submitted. (An illustrative RFQ for Web site hosting and Internet service provision for a small business is provided on the book's Web site). Companies looking for Web hosting services should look closely at service quality measures such as the type of servers and connections the ISP operates, guaranteed uptime, number of clients, current traffic rates, software support (e.g., CGI scripts, Java, database connectivity, storefront features), security, site traffic analysis, technical support services, and costs. It makes sense to purchase an Internet connection from the same company that hosts the Web site, but this is not a requirement.

REGISTERING A DOMAIN NAME

Selecting a domain name is an important marketing and branding consideration for any business. The domain name will be the business's online address, and it provides an opportunity to create an identity for the business.

A **domain name** is a name-based address that identifies an Internet-connected server. The domain name is an easy-to-remember name (e.g., congress.gov) that the *domain name system (DNS)* maps to a corresponding IP (Internet Protocol) address (e.g., 140.147.248.209). Each domain name starts with a *top-level domain (TLD)* at the far right. This is either a general top-level domain (e.g., .com or .biz for commercial businesses, .org for not-for-profit businesses, .name for individuals), or it is a country-code top-level domain (ccTLD) (e.g., .au for Australia, .za for South Africa, .jp for Japan). Most ccTLDs also have a *second-level domain name* that indicates the type of organization (e.g., redcross.org.au, yahoo.co.jp). At the left side of the domain name is the organization's name (e.g., dell.com), a brand name (e.g., coke.com for Coca-Cola), or a generic name (e.g., plumber.com).

Domain name assignment is under the authority of the Internet Corporation for Assigned Names and Numbers (ICANN) (icann.org). ICANN has delegated responsibility for domain name registration procedures and database administration in the general TLDs to top-level domain administrators such as Afilias (for .info), Public Interest Registry (for .org), and VeriSign Global Registry Services (for .com and .net). Similarly, regional Internet registries administer the ccTLDs (e.g., Nominet for the .uk domain, Japan Registry Service for .jp).

Actual registration of domain names is carried out by numerous ICANN-accredited registrars. These are located in various countries, but are principally in the United States. A list of these registrars is available at icann.org/registrars/accredited-list.html. A **domain name registrar** is a business that assists prospective Web site owners with finding and registering a domain name of their choice.

The first step for a prospective Web site owner is to visit a domain name registrar such as AllDomains (alldomains.com) or directNIC (directnic.com). Typically, the owner will use the domain name lookup service at the registrar's Web site to determine if the desired domain name is available. If it is, the visitor is invited to register it through the registrar for a small fee. The registrar submits the domain name and the owner's details to the appropriate domain name database and the name then becomes unavailable to anyone else. If the domain name is not available, most registrars automatically offer a list of alternatives that are available.

If the desired domain name is already taken, sometimes it can be purchased from the current owner. The Better Whois database of registered domain names (betterwhois.com) contains the name, postal address, e-mail address, and telephone number of the domain name owner. A business with an established Web site will be reluctant to give up a domain

domain name
A name-based address that identifies an Internet-connected server.

domain name registrar
A business that assists prospective Web site owners with finding and registering a domain name of their choice.

name, but if the domain name is reserved, but not in use, the owner may be willing to sell it for a reasonable price.

Once the name is registered with a registrar it can be held by the registrar until the hosting service is in place. Then management of the domain name can be transferred from the registrar or previous owner to the host for establishment of the Web site.

Some suggestions for selecting a good domain name are shown in the following list (Kienan 2001; O'Keefe 2002):

> ▶ Make it memorable. Use the company's name, a product name, a brand name, or a generic word that describes the product or service.

> ▶ Make it easy to spell. Spelling should be simple, easy, and straightforward. Trick spellings should be avoided because they may well trick potential visitors into not finding the site. Consider acquiring "near names," too. Near names are domain names that are similar enough that customers might mistype or misspell them and go elsewhere or nowhere. For example, gogle.com is owned by Google; Web users who miss an "o" in Google are automatically directed to google.com.

> ▶ Avoid numbers and special characters such as hyphens and underscores unless there is a special reason, such as putting an existing brand online (e.g., 7-eleven.com, 1800Flowers.com).

> ▶ Keep the domain name short while maintaining a good, sensible name. A domain name should be eight letters or less, not including the .com or other suffix, because short domain names are easier to remember and type. Avoid acronyms unless the acronym is well-branded as part of the company name (e.g., cnn.com).

> ▶ Be flexible. If the perfect domain name is already taken, then consider creative variations. For example, Ryder Rental Trucks is located at yellowtruck.com, named after their distinctive yellow trucks.

> ▶ Think about the future; do not let the name be too limiting. For example, the original mission of classmates.com was to reunite classmates from U.S. high schools. However, the business quickly found a market in colleges and universities as well, and then the military and the workplace. CEO Michael Schutzer acknowledges that he would choose another name had he started the business today. "Our business is more than high school reunions," he says. "It is a personal network for reconnecting people" (Taulli 2002). Similarly, Jeff Bezos selected Amazon.com as a nondescriptive name (e.g., not "books forsale.com") because he envisioned that Amazon.com would also sell CDs, videos, clothes, and many more products, not just books.

> ▶ Give products their own name. If the business sells more than one product or service, consider buying a domain name for each of them. Procter& Gamble, for example, has many sites for its many products—Tide laundry powder (tide.com) and Crest toothpaste (crest.com) are two examples.

> ▶ Investigate the competition. Look at competitor domain names to create both a distinctive name and one that complies with any inherent industry standard.

> ▶ Avoid trademarked names, or otherwise plan to end up in court.

> ▶ Consider registering in more than one top-level domain (e.g., register the same name in the .com, .org, .biz, and .info top-level domains).

A useful resource for learning more about domain names and the registration process is About Domains (aboutdomains.com), which offers "guides and resources for successful Internet presence" including a domain name glossary, a registration FAQ file, and "horror stories" from domain name owners who have had bad experiences with registrars.

Section 16.3 ▶ REVIEW

1. What are the advantages and disadvantages offered by the different Web hosting options?

2. What is a mirror site? Why would a company use a mirror site?

3. What criteria should an online business consider in choosing a Web hosting service?

4. What is a domain name? Why is selecting a domain name an important step for going online?

5. List 10 suggestions for selecting a good domain name.

16.4 CONTENT CREATION AND MANAGEMENT

Content is the text, images, sound, and video that make up a Web page. Creating and managing content is critical to Web site success because content is what a visitor comes looking for at a Web site, and content is what the Web site owners use to sell the site, the product or service, and the company that stands behind the site. Not all sites do this well; almost every Web user has been to Web pages that confuse, are overly verbose, or simply do not deliver the message.

Successful Internet presence has always been about effective delivery of the information the visitor wants. "Content is king!" is a rallying cry that has been around almost as long as the World Wide Web, and content's critical importance to Web site success continues to be supported by contemporary research (e.g., Agarwal and Venkatesh 2002). This section describes the role content plays in successful online business operations and the key aspects of creating and managing content on new and developing Web sites.

Although every Web site has content, Web sites differ according to the criticality of content to their business goals. Some sites offer **commodity content**, which is information that is widely available and generally free to access on the Web (Tomsen 2000). Portals such as MSN.com and content aggregators such as Nua Internet Surveys (nua.ie) collect information published elsewhere on the Net and make it available to visitors. The value added is the *aggregation* of the content, not the content itself.

Web sites such as Amazon.com are content rich because they offer unique content such as book reviews and author interviews. At most Web sites, publishing quality content is a strategy to achieve the real purpose of the site, which is to sell the product or service.

Web sites such as nytimes.com and cnn.com sit at the top of the content ladder. These sites are content driven because delivering **premium content**—content not available elsewhere on the Web—is their mission, their reason for being (Tomsen 2000). A few content-driven sites are successful enough at delivering premium content that they can charge for it (e.g., thestreet.com).

CONTENT CREATION AND ACQUISITION

Creating effective content begins with examining business goals. The principal purpose of content is to contribute to the Web site's goals of product sales, company promotion, branding, and customer service. For example, content is one of the most effective ways for a Web site to differentiate itself from its competitors, and content can create an identity that is consistent with the branding strategy. To fulfill these goals, the content should be complete, accurate, and timely and should project the image that a business intends to portray in its online presence.

Content pages should contain more than information about the product itself (the *primary content*). A Web site also should include *secondary content* that offers many opportunities for achieving business goals, such as:

▶ **Cross selling.** Using content for **cross selling** means offering similar or related products and services to increase sales. In the off-line world, cross selling is exemplified by the McDonald's question, "Would you like fries with that?" In the online world, Amazon.com offers book buyers options such as "customers who bought this book also bought . . ." and "look for similar books by subject." Accessories, add-on products, extended warranties, and gift-wrapping are other examples of cross-selling opportunities that can be offered to buyers on the product pages or in the purchase process.

▶ **Up selling.** Creating content for **up selling** means offering an upgraded version of the product in order to boost sales and profit. McDonald's practices up selling every time a sales clerk asks a combo-meal buyer "Would you like to super-size that?" Amazon.com offers "great buy" book combinations (buy two complementary books for slightly more than the price of one). (It also practices "down selling" by offering visitors cheaper, used

content
The text, images, sound, and video that make up a Web page.

commodity content
Information that is widely available and generally free to access on the Web.

premium content
Content not available elsewhere on the Web.

cross selling
Offering similar or related products and services to increase sales.

up selling
Offering an upgraded version of the product in order to boost sales and profit.

copies of a book directly under the new book price.) Up selling activities usually include offering products with a different design, color, fabric, or size.

▶ **Promotion.** A coupon, rebate, discount, or special service is secondary content that can increase sales or improve customer service. Amazon.com frequently offers reduced or free shipping charges, and this offer is promoted on each product page.

▶ **Comment.** Reviews, testimonials, expert advice, or further explanation about the product can be offered after introducing the product. Amazon.com book pages always have editorial and customer reviews of the book, and sometimes book contents can be previewed online with the "look inside this book" feature.

Creating effective content also means fulfilling the information needs and experiential expectations of the visitor. For the most part, the information needs of the visitor are consistent with the goals of the business—the visitor comes looking for information about a product to buy, and the company provides product information to entice a sale. To meet the customer's needs, the Web site owner must provide the information the visitor is looking for and in a way that visitors anticipate and will appreciate. Content relevance, timeliness, reliability, scope, and usefulness are important (as per Exhibit 16.1), but so are writing style, information structure, and the use of graphics and color. This is part Web design, discussed in the next section, and part content creation and management, discussed in the rest of this section.

Creating Content

Where does content come from? Content on most sites is created by the site's owners and developers. Typically, it begins by collecting all the content that is currently available (e.g., product information, company information, logos). Then the value of additional content—content such as an e-newsletter, discussion forum, customer personalization, FAQ page, and external links—is assessed for inclusion in the Web site. This assessment determines what is critical, important, or merely desirable by carefully considering how each bit of content will serve the site's goals and whether customers will want it or expect it. The assessment leads to a content development plan that may, for example, call for launching the site with all of the critical information and the most affordable important content (e.g., external links, FAQ) in place. As time and resources permit, the rest of the important content (e.g., personalization) can be added.

Content also can be generated by customers—through product reviews, testimonials, discussion forums, and other ways. Content can be provided by companies downstream in the supply chain (e.g., a chemical industry digital exchange would not need to duplicate product information but could simply source it from the chemical manufacturers). Original content can also be created by freelance researchers, compilers, and writers.

Buying Content

Content can be purchased or licensed. Lonely Planet, the Australian travel guide company, and the popular Mobile Travel Guide both sell travel information to Web sites such as Travelocity. *Content syndicators* such as Content Outfitter (contentoutfitter.com), NewsEdge (newsedge.com), and Content Finder (electroniccontent.com/conFinder.cfm) serve as intermediaries that link content creators with businesses interested in acquiring content. Finally, some individuals and businesses, such as Mike Valentine's WebSite 101 (website101.com/freecontent.html), provide free content and ask only for proper attribution in return.

Content that is acquired from outside sources should be supplemental content, not primary content. If primary content is being purchased, without adding any additional value, visitors will go to the originating site and not return.

Personalizing Content

personalized content
Web content that is prepared to match the needs and expectations of the individual visitor.

Personalized content is content that visitors value highly. **Personalized content** is Web content that is prepared to match the needs and expectations of the individual visitor. Doing so enables visitors to find the information they need faster than at traditional sites.

The process begins by tracking the visitor's behavior on the Web site via cookies (bits of text stored on the visitor's computer that identify the visitor to the Web site). This information is provided to server software that generates dynamic Web pages that contain content the visitor can use. Amazon.com's Web site is the king of personalized content, offering content such as recommendations for products based on previous purchases, recently viewed items, and even a personalized "Welcome Back" message for repeat visitors. The downside of personalization is that it is expensive and can slow down performance. Special programming and powerful computers are required to control and manage the customer information and dynamic page creation process.

Delivering Content by E-Newsletter

One of the most effective strategies for delivering content of interest to potential customers is an e-mail newsletter. An **e-newsletter** is a collection of short, informative articles sent at regular intervals by e-mail to individuals who have an interest in the newsletter's topic. An e-newsletter can be used to support the business and the product. In some cases, the newsletter is the online business (see the Real-World Case at the end of this chapter).

e-newsletter
A collection of short, informative articles sent at regular intervals by e-mail to individuals who have an interest in the newsletter's topic.

Simply e-mailing a newsletter to a private group in an e-mail program such as Outlook is unsatisfactory because the size of the list will soon grow very large and become unwieldy. Also, there is the risk that the e-mail addresses of subscribers will be revealed to each other. Instead, e-mail list software such as Listserv, Listproc, and Majordomo, owned by the Web site host, can be used to compile and maintain a list of subscribers. The software sends each newsletter individually, so no subscriber knows who else is on the mailing list.

Soliciting new subscribers to an e-newsletter is easy. Usually a sign-up box on the homepage invites the site visitor to "subscribe to our newsletter" (underline indicates a hyperlink) with a link to a page that provides details about the benefits of subscribing, privacy policies, frequency of the newsletter, and sample issues. Similarly, a "send me your newsletter" tick box can be included at the end of the order form. This process allows a Web site visitor or customer to "opt in" to a subscription. A more aggressive method of obtaining subscribers is to automatically join customers to the e-newsletter mailing list with an option to unsubscribe or "opt out." Most customers consider opt out to be a form of spam, therefore, this approach is not recommended.

Over time, subscribers' interests or e-mail addresses change. Therefore, e-newsletters usually include an e-mail address or Web site link for subscribers who want to unsubscribe from the e-newsletter. It may seem counterintuitive to make it easy for subscribers to unsubscribe, but they will appreciate it, and a visible and automatic unsubscribe process minimizes management overhead.

Subscribers do not subscribe to e-newsletters just because they like getting e-mail, and they certainly do not subscribe to satisfy the business's goals of marketing the product or service. Instead, past and future customers subscribe because they believe they will receive content that will be of value to them. An e-newsletter offers a value-for-value exchange, where each party gets what it expects, as long as valuable information is provided to the subscriber.

What is valuable information for the e-newsletter subscriber? The content of an e-newsletter needs to include information—news, tips, announcements—that the subscriber can use. A business selling snowboards will soon lose most subscribers if the e-newsletter contains nothing but product information and hype about the company's snowboards. A more effective newsletter will contain articles about snowboarding as an Olympic sport, snowboard safety, and a list of regional snowboarding contests. News about products can be included, but infrequently and in small proportion to the overall content.

The content of e-newsletters can come from Web sites, print sources, or even other newsletters as long as sources are properly cited or appropriate permissions are obtained. Brief summaries of news articles or press releases can include a link to the originating Web site, and the site owners usually will appreciate the free promotion. Web sites such as Webwire (webwire.com), PR Web (prweb.com), and Business Wire (businesswire.com) all collect press releases published on the Web; these are a rich source of information for e-newsletters. An e-newsletter can also solicit subscribers to send in ideas, stories, and tips, with proper attribution to the contributor. The business benefits by receiving relevant content, and most people are thrilled to see their name in print.

Writing Effective Content

Delivering effective content is not only what is said, but how it is said. Some of the rules Web wordsmiths use when creating Web content include the following:

▶ Write scannable text. Web site visitors do not read pages, they scan pages to find the information they are looking for (Morkes and Nielsen 1997). Headings, graphics, links, lists, and tables will catch the visitor's eyes, while large, uninterrupted blocks of text will be ignored.

▶ If long sections of text are required, break the text into sections with clearly noted headings, use small paragraphs, and insert relevant graphics to break up the text. If there are more than two or three screens of text, create separate pages and lead the reader through it with a <u>More. . . .</u> or <u>Next</u> link. Above all else, always write concisely, using perhaps half the word count of conventional writing or less (Morkes and Nielsen 1997).

▶ Begin each page or section of text with a sentence or short paragraph that grabs the reader's attention and compels them to continue reading. This leading sentence may ask a question, propose a provocative thought, or introduce a startling statistic while telling the reader what they will discover by reading what follows.

▶ Write in a tone and with language that reflects the purpose of the material. Promotional material may be written lightly with many adjectives that highlight the features of the product or service. Privacy, security, and disclaimer policies should be written in a more formal language to show that the business takes these seriously. Product support information will be written clearly, simply, and factually so that the reader will easily understand it and be able to act on the advice that is given.

▶ Consistency in site content can be achieved using a style guide that specifies, for example, whether the style "e-mail" or "email" will be used throughout the site.

▶ If proper appearance of the text is absolutely necessary (e.g., a form to be filled out, a poster to be posted) or to reduce the possibility of losing intellectual property (e.g., a research report), make the material available in a .pdf (Adobe Acrobat) file.

▶ Create compelling links that encourage a reader to click. Avoid the infamous "click here." Instead provide short descriptions that tell the reader why to click and include adjectives to enhance the benefit. For example, "to order <u>click here</u>" is poor, "fill out an <u>order form</u>" is better, but "to get your copy now, use our <u>quick and easy order process</u>" is best.

▶ External links can offer good content for visitors and, after all, no Web site is an island. However, be sure external links do not funnel the user out too quickly (e.g., consider carefully any external links on the homepage). Also, set external links to open in a new window so the path to the originating Web site is not lost.

▶ Do not use phrases that date fast, such as "soon," "currently," "next Christmas," or "last month." For example, a Web page that describes a new service that was launched "last month" will be wrong in 30 days or less, but a page that describes that service as being launched in June 2003 will always be correct.

▶ Avoid material that is not highly valued by customers. An employee list is unnecessary and becomes out-of-date fast. Instead, list only key individuals (e.g., chief executives, customer support manager, press contact) by name and phone number on appropriate pages. Similarly, visitor counters and when the page was last updated have fallen out of favor in recent years. First, this is almost always strictly optional, nonessential information for visitors. Second, if the page is updated infrequently or receives few visitors, the information sends a negative message about the Web site, and the business behind it.

CONTENT MANAGEMENT

content management
The process of adding, revising, and removing content from a Web site to keep content fresh, accurate, compelling, and credible.

Content management is the process of collecting, publishing, revising, and removing content from a Web site to keep content fresh, accurate, compelling, and credible. Almost all sites begin with a high level of relevant content, but over time material becomes dated, irrelevant, or incorrect. Content management makes sure a site remains relevant and accurate long after the initial push to launch the site is over. Content management applies quality assurance processes and content development to promote the reliability and integrity of the site (Awad 2002).

Content Testing

The most obvious task in content management is testing the content. Web managers need to make extensive and frequent checks of material for accuracy, clarity, typos, poor punctuation, misspelled words, and inconsistencies. Employees knowledgeable about the content should read site material to test it for accuracy; customer focus groups and professional editors should read it to check for clarity; and everyone should read new content to find mistakes. For ongoing testing, new employees might be asked to read the Web site content to learn about the company and to look for improvements with a "fresh eye."

Content Removal

An important task within content management is removing old, out-of-date pages from the Web server. Even if all references to the page in the Web site have been removed, the page is still visible to search engines, searches on the site itself, and links from other Web pages. Expired pages should be deleted or moved to an off-line location that can serve as an archive.

Content Management Software

Content management software allows nontechnical staff to create, edit, and delete content on the company's Web site. The driving forces behind *content management software (CMS)* include the desire for companies to empower content owners to manage their own content and the inability of the computing services staff to keep up with demands for new or changed content on the Web site.

Content management systems generally include workflow systems for monitoring content creation, review, approval, distribution, posting, and evaluation processes. Most contain tools that allow nontechnical personnel to publish content without specialized training. Other features might include content expiration schedules, backup and archive management, security, and enterprise application integration functions. For a partial list of content management software vendors, see Chapter 14.

Despite the strong driving forces and the promise of CMS to create and maintain content with great efficiency, most systems have failed to live up to expectations. A Jupiter Research (2003) study reported that "over-complicated, end-to-end packages can as much as quintuple Web site operational costs over human alternatives. In fact, 61 percent of companies who have already deployed Web content management software still rely on manual processes to update their sites." Companies embarking on a CMS purchase should consider following these steps (Arnold 2003):

1. Do a thorough needs analysis.

2. Document requirements and discuss them with at least two other companies that have purchased a CMS.

3. Start small and with content management software that has a trial version or low entry cost.

4. Assess the system after 30 days to determine what is right, wrong, needed, and unnecessary.

5. Repeat the assessment process regularly, increasing functionality as requirements and resources permit.

Section 16.4 ▶ REVIEW

1. What is content? Commodity content? Premium content? Personalized content?
2. How can content be used for cross selling? For up selling? For promotion?
3. What are the two key requirements for creating effective content?
4. Where does content come from? Identify four sources of Web site content.
5. What e-newsletter content does a subscriber value most?
6. List 7 to 10 suggestions for writing effective content.
7. What is the purpose of content management?
8. What are the driving forces behind the growth of content management software?

16.5 WEB SITE DESIGN

The goal of any Web site is to deliver quality content to its intended audience and to do so with an elegant design. With the Web site's content in hand, the Web site owner's next task is Web site design, including information architecture, navigation design, colors and graphics, and maximizing site performance. The purpose of this section is not to make the owner a Web site designer, but to enable the owner to contribute to the design of the Web site when working with professionals.

Successful Web site design is about meeting customer expectations. Design starts with identifying customer needs, expectations, and problems. Then a site is designed that meets those needs and expectations or that solves the customer's problems. A list of important Web site design criteria, with relevant questions, is shown in Exhibit 16.2. Some of these criteria, such as interactivity, scalability, and security, are discussed elsewhere in this and other chapters. The focus of this section is on the fundamental design criteria of navigation, consistency, performance, appearance, and quality assurance.

INFORMATION ARCHITECTURE

information architecture
How the site and its Web pages are organized, labeled, and navigated to support browsing and searching throughout the Web site.

A Web site's **information architecture** determines how the site and its Web pages are organized, labeled, and navigated to support browsing and searching throughout the Web site (Rosenfeld and Morville 1998). Information architecture begins with designing the site's structure. The most common site structure is hierarchical. A typical hierarchical structure for an online store is shown in Exhibit 16.3. Most hierarchical Web sites are built wide and shallow, putting 3 to 10 sections in the second level and limiting most sections to two or three levels. If the hierarchy is narrow (few second-level sections) and deep (many levels),

EXHIBIT 16.2	**Web Site Design Criteria**
Navigation	Is it easy for visitors to find their way around the site?
	Does the site comply with the three-click rule?
Consistency	Are design elements, especially look and feel, consistent from page to page?
	Will the Web site and contents appear the same on all visitors' screens?
Performance	How long does it take for the page to appear?
	Does the site comply with the 12-second rule? With the 4-second rule?
Appearance	Is the site aesthetically pleasing?
	Does the site's look and feel express the company's desired image?
	Is the site easy to read, easy to navigate, and easy to understand?
Quality assurance	Do the site's calculators, navigation links, visitor registration processes, search tools, etc., work properly?
	Are all dead links fixed promptly?
	Is the site available for full service 24 hours a day, 7 days a week?
Interactivity	Does the site encourage the visitor to play an active role in learning about the business's products or services?
	Are all appropriate contact details available on the Web site so that visitors can submit feedback and ask questions?
Security	Is customer information protected?
	Does the customer feel safe in actions such as submitting credit card information?
Scalability	Does the site design provide a seamless path for enhancements or upgrades in the future?
	Will site growth and increased usage protect the initial investment in site construction?

Source: Adapted from Awad (2002), pp. 145–146.

visitors become frustrated by being forced to click through numerous levels to find the information they need.

Other, less frequently used structures are circular and linear ones. A circular structure is useful when presenting training materials. A linear structure is useful when telling a story or presenting a tutorial. For example, Exhibit 16.4 (page 620) presents an abbreviated version of the linear structure of the E-Business Plan Tutorial at the book's Web site. Note that the linear structure is reinforced because external links that take the visitor outside the tutorial open a new, secondary window, whereas internal links between the lessons (e.g., mission statement) or file downloads (e.g., competitor analysis grid) keep the visitor inside the primary window.

A Web site typically includes a *homepage* that welcomes a visitor and introduces the site; *help* pages that assist the visitor to use or navigate through the site; *company* pages that inform the visitor about the online business; *transaction* pages that lead the customer through the purchase process; and *content* pages that deliver information about products and services at all stages of the purchase process, from information search to postpurchase service and evaluation.

Getting the homepage right is especially critical because it is the Web site's front door; it is the first page that visitors see if they enter the company's URL (e.g., www.company.com) into a Web browser. The purpose of the homepage is not to sell products or the business, but to sell the Web site. It does so by describing what is available or new at the site, helping the visitor to move around the site, and establishing a look and feel—the site's "personality"—that reflects the branding strategy and continues throughout the site. All pages within the site should link back to the homepage. Search engines or external links may bring visitors into the Web site's interior pages—an action known as **deep linking**—but the site owner will want the new visitor to be able to easily find the homepage.

deep linking
Entry into a Web site via the site's interior pages, not the homepage, typically through search engines or external links.

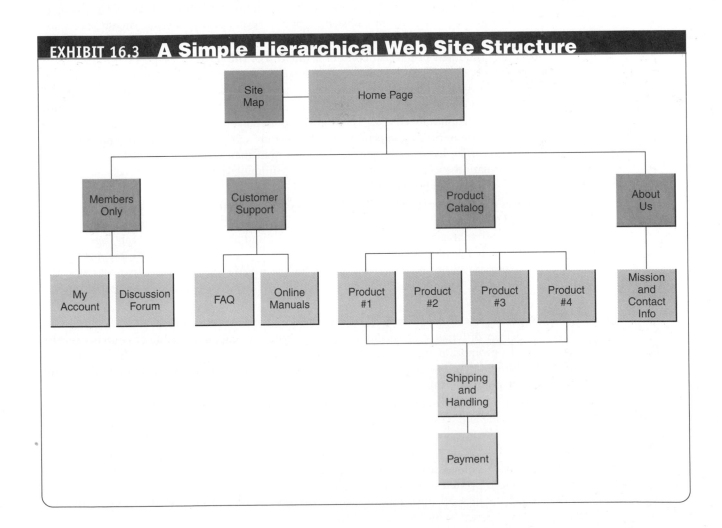

EXHIBIT 16.3 A Simple Hierarchical Web Site Structure

EXHIBIT 16.4   A Simple Linear Web Site Structure

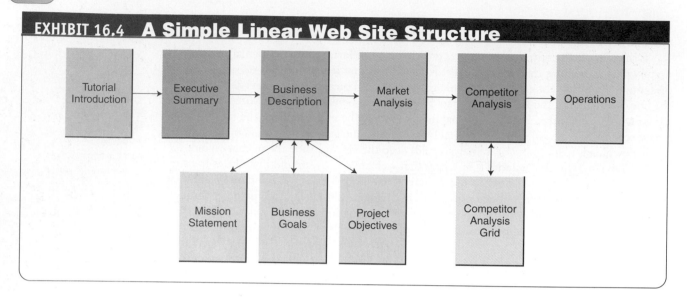

Some suggestions for organizing and labeling the site and its Web pages to support browsing and searching are:

▶ **Obey the three-click rule.** Visitors should be able to find what they are looking for within three clicks from the homepage. The exception to the three-click rule is getting to the homepage. Here the one-click rule applies—every page on the site should have a link that takes the user back to the homepage.

▶ **Place the most important content at the top of the page.** Newspaper editors put the most important information—the premier story, an eye-catching picture—"above the fold" of the front page. They do this because they know that many readers make a decision to buy the newspaper based on the information they see at first glance. The same principle applies to Web pages: Visitors should be able to find the information they are looking for in the first screen. Put product pictures, prices, navigation aids, mission statements, and a list of FAQ questions at the top of their respective pages. Less significant information such as product specifications, shipping details, external links, and contact information can be placed "below the fold."

▶ **Keep pages short.** Most pages should be two or, at most, three computer screens in length. Long pages are confusing to the reader and take a long time to download. If necessary, break long pages into several pages and at the bottom of each page provide links that lead the visitor forward to the next page and back to the previous page. Alternatively, on naturally long pages, such as a FAQ page, outline the material at the top of the page and use internal page links to move the visitor to the material quickly and easily.

▶ **Keep page layouts simple.** Consider dividing the page into columns or a grid pattern to deliver different types of information consistently (e.g., a site table of contents on the left, promotion and advertising material on the right, page content in the center). Use different sizes of graphics (but rarely large) and short blocks of text to draw the eye to the main offerings on the page.

▶ **Do not create barriers.** A "splash page" as the homepage usually has a large welcome graphic and requires the visitor to click "enter" to access the site. A splash page is a barrier to information visitors came to get, so do not use it. Similarly, well-designed sites do not force visitors to register in order to tour the site or browse the product selections.

▶ **Follow commonsense publishing rules.** Most of the same design principles that work well in printed text also work well on Web pages. For example, use text effects such as bold, italics, all caps, and underline sparingly in order to increase their impact and use white space to increase readability.

- ▶ **Make the primary content easy to find.** Links to the primary content of the Web site—a product catalog, list of services, directory of information—should appear in the navigation bar on each page and in appropriately placed links in page content.
- ▶ **Show the products in many ways.** Make it easy to search for and display items based on price, size, model, alphabetically, and so on.

SITE NAVIGATION

The purpose of Web **site navigation** is to help visitors quickly and easily find the information they need. Among the questions to be considered in site navigation are: How will visitors enter a site? How will visitors use the site? How will they find what is available at the site? How will they get from one page to another and from one section to another? How will visitors find what they are looking for? Site navigation has to help visitors find information quickly because visitors do not want to take the time to figure out how to move around on a site. Site navigation has to be easy because visitors want moving around the site to be predictable, consistent, and intuitive enough that they do not have to think about it.

Web designers execute successful site navigation through consistency (described later) and through navigation aids such as a navigation bar, navigation column, site map, and searchable Web site.

The simplest navigation aid is a *navigation bar* (see example in Exhibit 16.5). A navigation bar provides the visitor an opportunity to link to likely destinations (e.g., homepage, "about us") and major sections of the Web site (e.g., product catalog, customer support). Generally, the items in the bar should decrease in importance from left to right, beginning with the homepage at the far left. A navigation bar can be built using text, clickable buttons, or menu tabs.

A navigation bar almost always appears at the top of the page where it will load first in the browser window and be visible "above the fold." However, if the page contains banner ads, then the navigation bar should be placed prominently below the ads. Why? Frequent Web users develop "banner ad blindness" in which they ignore banner ads and everything above them.

A second navigation bar should also appear at the bottom of every page. Then visitors who have read the page and not found what they were looking for can be easily guided to where they need to go next. An effective navigation scheme is to offer a simple, attractive, graphical navigation bar at the top of the page and a longer, text navigation bar at the bottom of each page.

If the site's contents need more options than what can fit on a navigation bar, subsections can be placed in each section of the navigation bar (e.g., customer support might include subsections such as customer service FAQ, product information, status of your order). The subsections can appear on the navigation bar via a pull-down menu or a mouseover (when a visitor passes a mouse cursor over the button a submenu will pop up).

A Web site that has a lot to offer needs a navigation column on the left side of the browser window. This concept arose with the introduction of browser frames in the mid-1990s. A **frame** is an HTML element that divides the browser window into two or more separate windows. For the most part, frames are no longer used, but the idea of a navigation column as a site's "table of contents" remains as a familiar, comfortable, and easy navigation aid.

Large- and medium-sized sites should include a site map page so that the visitor who is unsure of where to go can be presented with all the options available. The site map should be easily accessible, reflect the information structure of the Web site, and be simply presented with easy-to-understand text links.

site navigation
Aids that help visitors find the information they need quickly and easily.

frame
An HTML element that divides the browser window into two or more separate windows.

EXHIBIT 16.5   A Generic Navigation Bar

Home | Products | Support | Community | Guided Tour | About Us

A large- or medium-sized site also should be searchable. A "search this site" box should appear near the top of the homepage and on navigation-oriented pages such as the site map. The Web site hosting service can assist with this, which involves computer scripts and indexing tools.

Many of the information architecture and navigation concepts discussed here are illustrated in Exhibit 16.6.

Other suggestions for designing successful Web site navigation are:

- **Use small lists and menus.** In designing navigation aids such as a navigation column or a site map, group items together in groups of five or less. The human brain handles multiple small lists better than a single long list. So, for example, six lists of 5 options each is better navigation design than a list of 30 options.

- **Do not rely entirely on graphical images for navigation.** Using graphics for navigation can look very stylish, but graphics take time to load, will not appear on browsers with graphics turned off, and are high-maintenance items to alter as the Web site changes and grows. If a graphical navigation aid is included, make sure an alternative text-only aid is available as well.

- **Make the homepage easy to find.** Include a link to the homepage in the most prominent position in a navigation bar or navigation column. This is helpful for visitors who are lost in the site and critical for visitors who land in subpages of the site from search engines or external links.

- **Integrate navigation into content.** In addition to standard navigation aids, do not miss opportunities to put navigation suggestions in the content itself. For example, in addition to "contact us" in the navigation bar, include "contact our staff in the USA, Canada, or UK" in product information and similar pages.

- **Avoid frames.** Frames can be useful for navigating large sites, but they create numerous usability problems. Pages created with frames are difficult to bookmark and print, search engines cannot identify them, and they are difficult for the browser back button to handle well. Most Web designers agree: Do not use frames unless absolutely necessary, especially when alternatives such as a navigation column achieves the same result with fewer problems.

- **Follow accessibility guidelines.** Design the site to be accessible to all users, regardless of physical ability or the way they use the Internet. The World Wide Web Consortium (w3.org) has created a series of guidelines for individuals with visual, audio, neurological, and physical disabilities. A side benefit is that by designing a site for these users, the site also becomes more usable for visitors who are accessing the site with mobile tele-

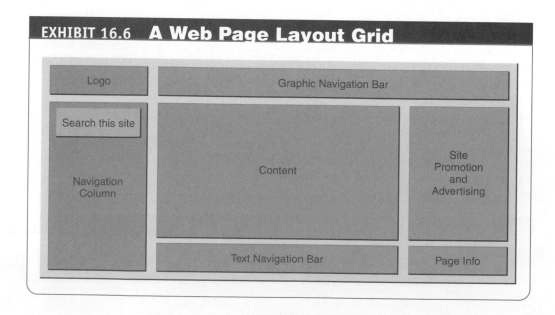

EXHIBIT 16.6   A Web Page Layout Grid

phones, low-bandwidth modems, in a noisy environment, or with different learning styles (Peck 2002).

CONSISTENCY

Closely linked to both information architecture and site navigation is consistency in a Web site's design. First and foremost, consistency means that there is a common look and feel to the Web site's pages. A site's **look and feel** consists of the elements that visually distinguish a site from any other, including layout, typeface, colors, graphics, and navigation aids. Visitors will become confused if different layouts, colors, and navigation bars are used on different pages. Web page construction aids such as cascading style sheets help insure a consistent look and feel on a Web site.

Consistency begins with clear and uniform navigation. Every page should have navigation aids, and the aids should be of the same format, style, and in approximately the same location on each page.

Certain elements of page content also should be consistent. The company's logo should appear on every Web page. Contact information should be included on every page, both a "contact us" link in the navigation bar or navigation column and a contact e-mail address on most pages. For example, "direct any further questions to support@company.com" should be on all customer support pages, and "for more information write to info@company.com" can be on the homepage and on all FAQ, "about us," and privacy policy pages. Writing out e-mail addresses as shown, instead of "e-mail us" with a HTML e-mail link, also helps visitors who might print a page and give it to a friend. Similarly, the Web page's URL or the homepage URL, should appear on every page in case the page is printed and distributed. Readers should always be able to find the site from a printout of the page.

A short, descriptive title should appear on every page. Titles are important because they tell the visitor the page content when viewed in the browser window, in printed copy, in a search engine results page, and in a favorites or bookmark list. Avoid using words such as "the" or "welcome" as the first word in a title because in an alphabetized favorites list these all get bunched together.

A second aspect of consistency is whether the Web site appears the same on all visitors' screens. The visitor's view of the Web site depends on the Web browser being used. Many Web designers design Web pages for the current version of Internet Explorer (IE) for Windows. Even if IE dominates the market, millions of users also use Netscape, Opera, Safari, Cyberdog, OmniWeb, Mozilla, and many others on Lynx, Macintosh, and Unix operating systems, not to mention older versions of these browsers and different screen resolutions. When all the permutations are considered, over 100 different browsers are being used.

The solution is not to try to design a Web site for all of these browsers, but to use designated World Wide Web Consortium standards, currently HTML 4.01 (for more information, see w3.org/TR/html401). Unless there is a compelling reason and the site's target audience is ready for it, avoid leading-edge browser technology. The visitor's browsing experience should not be dependent on HTML features that cannot be seen with older and different browsers. It is counterproductive to use leading-edge technology that will not work on a large portion of the world's browsers.

Browsers also differ in how they handle forms, text size, and file names. For example, Internet Explorer will read a file with a space in a file name, such as "about us.html," but Netscape will not (use "aboutus.html" instead). An experienced Web designer will know these problems and be able to design the site to meet different browser requirements or put browser-specific features where they will cause the least trouble to the visitor.

PERFORMANCE

Speed ranks at or near the top of every list of essential design considerations, for good reason. Visitors who have to wait more than a few seconds for a Web page to load are likely to hit the "stop" or "back" button and go somewhere else.

A number of factors affect the speed at which the page is transferred from the Web server to the client's browser. Factors out of the control of the Web designer and site owner are the visitor's modem speed, the bandwidth available at the customer's ISP, and, to some

look and feel
The elements that visually distinguish a site from any other, including layout, typeface, colors, graphics, and navigation aids.

degree, the current bandwidth available at the Web host where the server is located. The critical factor that is under the control of the Web designer is the content and design of the page. A competent Web designer will know what can be done to improve a page's download speed or at least give it the appearance of loading fast.

The most widely recognized cause of long download times is a large graphic or a large number of small graphics on a single page. Graphic images should be created at the lowest possible resolution so that the visitor can clearly see the picture, art, or icon but so that the graphic file is only a few kilobytes in size. If a large, high-resolution graphic image is important, thumbnail images can be put on the page and linked to full-size, higher-resolution images available at the visitor's discretion.

Other design traps that also affect a page's loading time are page personalization features that require information from a back-office database for dynamic page creation, Java applets, sound files, animated banner ads, and complex table structures, especially the page-in-a-table that requires the entire table/page to load before any of it displays. To decrease page download time, these features should be avoided or used sparingly.

A good benchmark by which to judge speed and responsiveness of the Web site is the 12-second rule: Every page on the Web site should appear within 12 seconds; if visitors have to wait longer than that for a page to appear, they will likely stop the transfer and move on to the competition. The 12-second rule should be speed-tested for the lowest common denominator in the site's target audience. A site that appeals to young gamers with fast connectivity can have a higher level of graphic content than one designed for rural farmers who are unlikely to have high bandwidth connections. Again, the fundamental rule of Web design is to design the site for the intended audience.

A variation of the 12-second rule is the 4-second rule, which says that something should appear in the visitor's browser in 4 seconds or less. Even if downloading the whole page takes slightly longer than 12 seconds, if visitors can see something is happening they will be unlikely to halt the download and move on. So, for example, a large graphic or image map can be divided into composite smaller images that begin to appear immediately.

COLORS AND GRAPHICS

The World Wide Web is a colorful and graphic world, and colors, pictures, artwork, and video can be used to good effect if they are used correctly.

The key to effective use of color and graphics is to design the site to match the expectations of the target audience. Financial services sites tend to use formal colors (e.g., green, blue) with simple charts to illustrate the text but not many pictures. Sites directed at a female audience tend to feature lighter colors, usually pastels, with many pictures and an open design featuring lots of white space. Game sites are one type of site that can get away with in-your-face colors, Flash effects, and highly animated graphics.

Other rules that guide the use of color and graphics on Web sites are:

- **Use standard colors.** All colors should be one of the 216 Web-safe colors that can be specified by hexadecimal notation (e.g., #FFFF99 for pale yellow).

- **Follow color standards.** Most visitors expect dark text and blue, red, or purple links because those tend to be the browser standards. If this color scheme is changed, do not pick a scheme that will confuse the visitor. For example, if colored text is important, avoid blue, because visitors may interpret this as an unfollowed hyperlink. For the same reason, minimize the use of underlined text.

- **Use complementary colors.** Never mix the primary colors of red, green, and blue in text and background. Generally dark text (not necessarily black) on a light background (but not white) is the easiest to read.

- **Specify the background color.** If the background color is left to the browser's default color, it will not distinguish the site. The BGCOLOR tag allows a designer to control the color in most browsers, except when the visitor has specified a preferred background color. When selecting a background color, the operative word is "background." The color should be unobtrusive and complementary to the colors in the logo, text, and graphics in the site.

▶ **Use bandwidth-intensive features selectively.** Animation, video, and audio clips are useful for demonstrations or promoting entertainment events, but because they require a lot of bandwidth to download and processor speed to display, they should be used sparingly, at the visitor's discretion, in low resolution, and with streaming technology if possible. Every graphic, animation, audio clip, and video should be carefully considered and used only if they are quick to download and worth the wait.

▶ **Design for visually or hearing-impaired visitors.** Make a text version of any visual or audio content available from the Web site for visitors with visual or hearing difficulties.

▶ **Use the ALT tag.** To speed up Web access, 20 to 30 percent of Web users surf with graphics turned off. This means the browser downloads the text, but not the graphic images unless specifically requested, so information embedded in graphics is lost. The ALT tag overcomes this problem by telling the visitor what the image is (e.g., logo, Merlina's picture) or what it represents (e.g., site search, navigation bar). With this information the no-graphics visitor can use the site without frustration. The ALT tag also helps visually impaired visitors because the graphic label can be picked up and read through the computer's soundboard.

▶ **Avoid distracting features.** Wild colors, overactive animation, blinking text, and similar features can irritate the visitor or distract their attention away from content. Use these only when necessary and never as a gimmick. Similarly, avoid excessive use of different fonts and colors on the page, because these will make the page difficult to read and unattractive.

Are these Web design rules followed in practice? To test the application of theory on practice, usability gurus Jakob Nielsen and Marie Tahir tested homepages from 50 of the world's most popular Web sites, such as eBay, Microsoft, and Victoria's Secret (Nielsen and Tahir 2002). Their analysis of compliance with design and navigation standards, using our classification of the good, the bad, and the ugly, is shown in Exhibit 16.7 (page 626). A similar study that tested 62 Web sites in the United Kingdom on 12 design tests found that most companies are committing fundamental errors when presenting themselves online (BBC Training and Development 2002).

QUALITY ASSURANCE

Quality assurance is about making sure the Web site design is properly tested before it is launched and ensuring that it continues to perform up to expectations after launch. This is a critically important part of Web design because the Web is constantly changing—content goes out-of-date, external links go dead or become meaningless, new browsers and Web standards come out.

A lesson most Web designers can learn from total quality management (TQM) principles is to design the site for easy maintenance. Keeping the page layout neat and simple not only makes it easier for the visitor to find the information, but also makes ongoing maintenance simpler. Using text instead of graphics also increases flexibility in maintenance because it is much easier to change a bit of text than a graphical icon.

Quality Web sites have responsible owners who test all features of the site personally and do not leave maintenance to the technical staff. Quality Web sites also have responsive owners who know that successful sites are never done. It is a never-ending task to weed out dead links, identify and fix broken graphics, add new pages, update old pages, and constantly review the site's look and feel for improvements.

Quality Web sites are tested regularly. Take a tip from fire departments that encourage fire alarms be tested when clocks are set forward or backward for daylight savings time. Set a similar time (e.g., when first and third quarter reports are due or just before the peak selling season and 6 months later) for a comprehensive "site test" to review all current content, eliminate or consolidate infrequently accessed pages, check the content development plan for new content that may be required, update the FAQ file, and test all links to be sure they are working and still reflect the intended purpose. Link-test software such as SiteInspector (linkexchange.com) can help determine dead links, but only a human scan can determine if the content of the external link is still relevant.

EXHIBIT 16.7   Homepage Usability: Lessons from Practice

The Good

- The median homepage was 1,018 pixels high, or about two full screens. This is consistent with recommended design practice.
- All homepages had a logo, and 84 percent placed the logo in the upper-left corner. This is very nearly a standard, and all Web sites should adopt this practice.
- All sites had navigation aids, frequently more than one. At the top of the page, 30 percent used a left-hand navigation column, 30 percent used a navigation bar with tabs, and 18 percent used a navigation bar with links. At the bottom of the page, 80 percent included a navigation bar with a median of 7.5 links.
- Only 4 percent of homepages used frames, consistent with most designers' recommendations to avoid this design element.
- Nine out of 10 homepages provided a way for visitors to easily find contact information, 60 percent of the time through a "Contact Us" link on the homepage and 22 percent of the time through the "About Us" page.
- Only three of the pages had a splash page, a site feature that Nielsen and Tahir (2002) call "a curse on the Web."
- Only two of the pages offered music automatically, another practice criticized by most Web designers.
- The median number of graphics on the homepage was three, and only 8 percent had a significant portion of the page devoted to graphics. The lesson is clear: Top sites use few or no graphics.
- None of the sites had a mandatory registration procedure for visitors to browse the site. Fifty-two percent offered registered users a sign-in box on the homepage to access special features, personalized information, or user-supplied content.
- White was the set background color on 84 percent of the sites. Black text was used by 72 percent of the sites (8 percent used blue text and 8 percent used gray text).
- When a text font was set, 96 percent used a sans-serif font such as Helvetica or Arial. These contemporary fonts look good on low-resolution computer screens.

The Bad

- Average download time was 26 seconds. Only 28 percent of the homepages downloaded in 10 seconds, and 26 percent took more than 30 seconds.
- Only 48 percent of these top sites provided a site map.
- Fourteen percent of the homepages did not have a "search this site" feature, a percentage Neilson and Tahir called "unbelievable." Nielsen and Tahir recommend a white (97 percent) search box (81 percent) that is 25 to 30 characters wide in the upper-left (31 percent) or upper-right (35 percent) corner with a "search" (42 percent) or "go" (40 percent) button. (These percentages indicate the proportion of homepages that follow this recommendation.)
- Eighty-four percent of the homepages had an "About Us" link. Nielsen and Tahir think that this should be 100 percent.
- Eighty-six percent of the top homepages had a link to the company's privacy policy. Again, Neilson and Tahir believe that this should be at or near 100 percent for sites that collect information from visitors or customers.
- The median number of ads from external companies was three, the "absolute upper limit from a usability perspective" according to Nielsen and Tahir. Almost half (46 percent) carried advertising promoting products from other companies.

The Ugly

- Only 18 percent of the homepages used a liquid layout that automatically adapts the page's content to fill the browser window. The other 82 percent of pages used a frozen layout that risked having text cut off or a large amount of white space on the right side of the screen.
- Only 42 percent of the pages with graphics used the ALT text tag that benefits visually impaired users and those users who browse with graphics turned off. The authors call this "a disgrace" because it makes pages inaccessible to visually impaired users.

Source: Compiled from Nielsen and Tahir (2002).

Web site performance is also an ongoing concern. The 12–second rule should continue to be tested under a number of different scenarios, including a typical customer using a dial-up modem in another country at the Web host's peak traffic period. The look, speed, and feel of the site should be tested on a number of hardware and software options. Services such as Net Mechanic (netmechanic.com) and Trimak (trimak.com) offer tools and services that speed up download time, identify dead links, optimize graphics, and assess browser compatibility.

Section 16.5 ▶ REVIEW

1. Describe eight criteria used to judge Web site design.

2. What is deep linking? Why is it a problem for site designers? What should they do about it?

3. What is the three-click rule? What are its implications for information architecture?

4. Describe four site navigation aids.

5. Why is performance a key design criterion? What causes slow performance? What can be done to decrease download time?

6. List eight suggestions for proper use of color and graphics on a Web site.

7. What are some actions Web site owners should take to ensure a quality Web site?

16.6 WEB SITE CONSTRUCTION

Creating content and designing the Web site are the creative aspects of building a Web site. Determining how the Web site will be built and by whom are the business parts of Web site construction. Web site construction is really about three options—internal development, outsourcing, and partnering—spread over two time periods—start-up construction and ongoing maintenance.

WHO BUILDS THE WEB SITE?

Early in the Web site development process, the online business owner has to decide whether to build the Web site with internal staff, an outside contractor, or a combination of these two options. This involves managerial considerations such as control, speed, and desired organizational competencies, as generally described in information technology textbooks (e.g., Turban et al. 2004; Post and Anderson 2003; especially McNurlin and Sprague 2002). This section will cover some of the most important of these managerial considerations as they apply specifically to Web site construction.

Internal Web site development is the do-it-yourself option of building and maintaining the Web site with company staff. Factors that lead companies to develop their own Web site include:

> **internal Web site development**
> The process of building and/or maintaining the Web site with company staff.

- ▶ **Use of existing in-house expertise.** Having an experienced Web designer or Webmaster on the company's payroll is a good first reason for internal development.

- ▶ **Desire to build in-house expertise.** A closely related reason is that a company may not have existing expertise on the staff, but wishes to add Web site development to the company's skill set. In this case, new employees are hired or existing staff members are trained in order to build and maintain the site.

- ▶ **Protection of proprietary technologies.** If new software or an internally developed Web-based application is critical to the company's EC value proposition, then a business is likely to use its own staff to protect that intellectual property and advance its ongoing development.

- ▶ **Tighter control and responsiveness.** Especially in the maintenance stage, a company is likely to find that problem resolution, content management, and ongoing development of the site will be faster, less expensive, and more responsive if internal staff members are responsible for the Web site.

External Web site development, or outsourcing, takes place when the business hires another firm to build and/or maintain the Web site. Factors that tend to favor external development include:

> **external Web site development**
> When the business hires another firm to build and/or maintain the Web site.

- ▶ **Speed to market.** If getting online fast is critical to the company's start-up success, it is likely that companies that specialize in Web site construction will have the resources necessary to build the site quickly. Generally, but not always, internal development takes more time.

▶ **Not a core competency.** Frequently, companies decide that Web site development and maintenance should not be one of their core competencies. Outsourcing Web development allows an online business to focus more on promoting the product, increasing sales, building business relationships, and other business activities.

▶ **Access to special expertise.** Especially in initial site construction, a Web design firm is more likely to have access to all the expertise and development tools site construction requires. For example, a business may have competent HTML writers, but database integration or specialized programming expertise may be missing. This expertise could be hired in on an individual contract basis, but it will be expensive and time-consuming.

partnering Web site development
When a mixture of internal and external development is used to build and/or maintain a Web site.

This last point suggests that the internal-or-external decision does not need to be all one way or the other. Instead, some form of **partnering Web site development** may be the best option. Depending on the nature of the site and the skills required, a mixture of internal and external development to build or maintain the Web site is possible and may be desirable. The principal downside to partnering is the additional overhead of contract and relationship management—managing a partnership can sometimes be more difficult than doing it all internally or externally.

WEB SITE CONSTRUCTION AND MAINTENANCE

Developing a Web site occurs over two time periods, and both periods impose different considerations on Web site development.

Web site construction
The initial content creation, design, programming, and installation phases of a Web site's development.

Web site construction consists of the initial content creation, design, programming, and installation phases of a Web site's development. As suggested earlier, this is likely to require a variety of expert skills that are only rarely available inside the company (e.g., information architects, Web page designers, database integration expertise, and programmers). Unless the Web site is small and offers limited functionality or one of the factors favoring internal development is especially compelling, most businesses decide on external development or partnering as the best option for Web site construction.

Web site maintenance
The on-going process of keeping the Web site open for business, managing content, fixing problems, and making incremental additions to the site.

Web site maintenance begins when construction ends. This phase consists of the ongoing process of keeping the Web site open for business, managing content, fixing problems, and making incremental additions to the site. Building a Web site is one process, maintaining it is another. Once the initial Web site has been constructed, the ongoing development and maintenance usually can be managed internally or externally.

MANAGING WEB SITE CONSTRUCTION

The Web site construction team and online business owner are in a partnership to achieve the same goal: a well-designed, functional Web site that works. However, each partner also comes into the construction process with different incentives, especially in keeping the cost of a Web site reasonable. Some suggestions for the business owner to successfully manage this partnership include the following:

▶ **Start with a plan.** Before interviewing Web designers, know what the goals of the site are, prepare a list of prioritized content, visit some Web sites to acquire some preferences for the overall design, and have a budget figure in mind. Having a plan will make it easier for the designer to quickly learn what is expected and give an accurate bid.

▶ **Set goals early and stick to them.** What the site intends to accomplish is the driving force behind the design. If the Web designer begins by talking about page layout, interesting graphics, and site architecture, go find a designer who starts with a discussion of goals and content. Then stick those goals in a prominent place and justify every feature and every page by the contribution they make to achieving those goals.

▶ **Use a fixed-price contract.** A Web designer may want to be paid by the hour because then the designer is assured payment for each hour worked. However, the buyer does not have any certainty about what the final cost will be, and there is little incentive for the designer to keep the hours to a minimum. The result is likely to be higher costs and delayed implementation. Using fixed pricing, either for the entire site or per page, requires more preproduction planning, but Web sites should be designed and constructed with plenty of advanced planning.

▶ **Justify graphics and features.** Pictures, art, sound, and video all represent escalating costs in terms of production, page design, disk space, and bandwidth. Some graphics (e.g., a logo, products), features (e.g., shopping cart), and visual effects (e.g., mouse-overs) are required or desirable for functionality or aesthetics reasons. However, each of these should be justified in the context of the site's goals, not at the whim of the designer. In other words, avoid "feature creep"—the adding-in of features that were not in the original plan.

ACCEPTING CREDIT CARDS

You can't do business if you can't get paid! This truism means that every online business has to face decisions about electronic payment systems, the most dominant of which is accepting credit cards over the Internet.

The process for accepting credit card payments was briefly described in Chapter 13. As noted there, processing credit card payments on the Internet differs only slightly from the process in traditional, face-to-face transactions. What are these differences from a merchant's perspective? What are the basic requirements for an online business to be able to accept credit cards for payment?

First, in the online process, the credit card reader in the store is replaced with credit card processing software (a credit card gateway) that is capable of accepting input from a Web page and submitting it into the credit card system (the merchant's bank, the customer's bank, and the credit card interchange such as Visa or MasterCard).

Second, with online transactions, a signature and verification of the signature by the merchant is not required, resulting in what is known as a **card-not-present (CNP) transaction**. This situation removes a considerable amount of certainty and security from the process. In response to this increased risk, banks are more selective about who gets an online merchant account, and they require that the entire process be as secure as possible (e.g., checking that the shipping address provided by the customer matches the billing address on file at the customer's bank). In addition, banks charge higher transaction fees for CNP transactions to offset the increased risks.

card-not-present (CNP) transaction
When there is no signature and no verification of the credit card signature by the merchant.

An online business that wants to accept credit cards for payment generally has to do the following (Kienan 2001):

▶ **Open a merchant account.** It is likely that the business's current bank will be happy to extend banking privileges for the business to accept credit cards online. However, some small, regional banks may not offer this service; other banks may establish thresholds that are too high for the business to qualify (i.e., banks are more selective about CNP merchant accounts). Opening a merchant account means acquiring bank approval, making an application and signing a contract with one or more credit card companies, and paying the bank and card companies a set-up fee. Ongoing costs for a merchant account include a percentage-based transaction fee and additional charges for other services, such as if a customer credit is issued.

▶ **Purchase credit card processing software.** Credit card gateway companies such as CyberCash and CyberSource provide credit card processing software and services that accept credit card numbers and manage their transfer into and back from the credit card system. Factors to consider in deciding which gateway company to use include companies that the site developer has worked with before and what software the organization hosting the Web site will accept. A business typically pays the credit card gateway a set-up fee and a per-transaction fee.

▶ **Integrate the credit card processing software into the transaction system.** To work effectively, the software must be able to manage the flow of data between the transaction and customer databases and the credit card systems. The site developer writes scripts that enable the different components in the credit card transaction to share data they require.

1. Define the three options for Web site construction.
2. What factors favor internal development of a Web site? What factors favor external development?
3. When is internal development most likely to be used in the Web site development process? When are external development or partnering most likely to be used?
4. Describe the process required for an online business to accept credit cards over the Internet.

16.7 WEB SITE PROMOTION

Every successful online business needs a highly visible Web site. External Web site promotion through advertising (e.g., banner ads, pop-up ads) and marketing strategies (e.g., banner swapping, chat room sponsorship) was discussed in Chapter 5. This section focuses on internal Web site promotion (selling the Web site on the site) and search engine optimization (getting the Web site to the top of the search engine listings).

INTERNAL WEB SITE PROMOTION

Internal Web site promotion begins by including content that establishes the site as a useful site for customers to remember so that they return and make a purchase. To do this, the Web site should become not only a place to buy something, but also an indispensable resource with compelling content, useful links to other Web sites, and features that will make customers want to return.

Promoting the Web site internally often includes a page of testimonials from satisfied customers. If the site or the business has received any awards, those should be drawn to the attention of the visitor. If the business owner's background or credentials are related to the business, then list any degrees, professional affiliations, and awards that relate to the online business.

signature file
A simple text message an e-mail program automatically adds to outgoing messages.

Site promotion continues with a marketing plan that includes the URL on every product, business card, letterhead, package, and e-mail message that leaves the business. A **signature file** is a simple text message that an e-mail program automatically adds to outgoing messages. A typical signature file includes the person's name, title, contact details, and name and URL of the business. A promotional signature file also includes something that encourages the reader to visit the Web site. For example, a diet center includes this teaser on all outgoing messages: "Are you the right weight for your shape? The answer might surprise you. Take our body shape quiz and find out for yourself."

SEARCH ENGINE OPTIMIZATION

search engine optimization (SEO)
The application of strategies intended to position a Web site at the top of Web search engines.

How does a Web site get found in the vast world of cyberspace? How does a new online business get noticed ahead of its more well-established competitors? In addition to promotional and advertising strategies discussed in this and other chapters, perhaps the most important and cost-effective way to attract new customers is search engine optimization. **Search engine optimization (SEO)** is the application of strategies intended to position a Web site at the top of Web search engines such as Google, AllTheWeb, and Teoma. Search engines are the primary way many Web users find relevant Web sites; an online business cannot ignore SEO strategies.

Although SEO is discussed near the end of this chapter, it does not occur late in the Web site development process. The strategies to maximize a Web site's ranking in search engines should be part of content creation, Web site design, and site construction. Optimizing search engine rankings through keyword placement and link building is much easier, less time-consuming, and less expensive if it is integrated into the Web site development process.

How does SEO work? At the center of any search engine is a database of Web pages that have been indexed on criteria such as keyword occurrence and link popularity. These Web pages have been collected by aptly named software called *spiders* that "crawl" the Web, finding new Web pages and sending them back to the search engine for placement in the database. When a search engine user "searches the Web" the results actually come from the archived database.

Search engines differ according to the behavior of the spiders (e.g., how many levels of the site are visited, how much information is collected), how many pages are in the database, the amount and type of information the searcher receives, whether pay-for-placement links are included or not, and, critically for SEO, the search engine algorithm used to rank pages. More specific discussions of how search engines work can be found at searchenginewatch.com and searchengineshowdown.com.

The key to SEO is understanding the algorithms the search engines use to determine the ranking of the results returned to the searcher. All search engines rely on keyword occurrence in some way. Early search engines used keywords as the principal or sole criteria for ranking search results. In a simplified example, if a keyword entered into a search engine appeared in the page's title, meta tags, headings, and numerous times on the page, then that page would rank high in the results returned to the searcher. This led to *search engine spamming* strategies; for example, including a long list of keywords in text the same color as the background color so that the site visitor would see only blank space but the spider would find numerous keywords.

In 1998, Google initiated a fundamental change in search engine ranking strategies when it introduced link popularity into its algorithm. In addition to keyword analysis, Google counts the number of sites that link to a target site (i.e., incoming links). Presumably the most relevant or credible sites will have a larger number of incoming links, and those sites merit higher placement in the Google results. Today, link popularity figures prominently in the results-placement algorithm used by most search engines.

Because every Web search begins with one or more keywords that a user submits to a search engine, choosing the right keywords and putting them in the right locations is critical to SEO. The following are some strategies for keyword creation and placement (Wong 2002; bCentral 2003):

- **Create keywords the target audience is most likely to use.** Focus groups of prospective customers should be asked what keywords they would use if looking for the site. Also, because the site is seeking a higher ranking against competitors, investigate what keywords competitors include in their titles and meta tags.

- **Use specific phrases, not general keywords.** General keywords such as vacation, stereo, and computer occur so frequently that they will not contribute much toward a high ranking in a search engine. Instead, use phrases such as African safari, micro-stereo, and Pentium laptop computer.

- **Optimize the title.** The page's title is the single most important place to improve keyword SEO. Not only do search engine algorithms place a higher value on keywords in a title, but the title also is the dominant item in most search results. Even if a page does not get the number one placement on a Google search, being high in the rankings with an alluring title will guarantee visitors.

- **Use meta tags.** A **meta tag** is a HTML element that describes the contents of a Web page. A *description meta tag* provides a brief description of the Web site that some search engines include in their results, so be sure that the site's premier keywords are used in the description. A *keyword meta tag* tells spiders what keywords the site owner thinks best describes the page's content. Keyword meta tags are also useful places to put common misspellings or alternative spellings of a keyword (e.g., potatoe, colour, organisation).

- **Use keywords early and often in page content.** Obviously, the content of the page must be readable to human visitors, but keyword-loaded copy helps increase search engine rankings. Use keywords in headings and in hyperlinks. Some search engine algorithms give higher weight to these keywords, assuming that they are more important in describing page content than normal text. Keywords should be placed high on the page because spiders from search engines such as Google crawl only the first 110k of a page. Other spiders ignore pages with very little content; a recommended page length for maximizing SEO is 300 to 750 words. Finally, spiders sometimes visit only pages in the first and second level of a site, another reason to build a wide and shallow site structure.

meta tag
An HTML element that describes the contents of a Web page.

➧ **Include keywords in ALT tags.** An *ALT tag* should describe the image, but with keywords if possible. So instead of "tiger.gif" use "a tiger on a Vacationtime African safari" in an ALT tag.

➧ **Avoid spider-hostile features.** Search engine spiders and algorithms have a difficult time with frames, dynamic URLs, Flash, image maps, and JavaScript. Use these features only if a compelling design or content consideration requires them.

➧ **Do not spam search engines.** Search engine designers know most of the tactics used to spam search engines, so be honest and do not try to trick them. Spamming strategies such as duplicate pages, excessive repetition of a keyword in a meta tag, tiny text, and same-color text can be detected by a search engine, and the site will be blacklisted from inclusion in the search engine.

After the Web site and pages are optimized for keyword occurrence and placement, the second major step in search engine optimization is to increase a Web site's link popularity. Getting other sites to link to the target Web site promotes the site in two ways. First, surfers will find the link at other Web sites, click through to visit, and hopefully become a customer. Second, increasing the number of incoming links increases the site's ranking in search engines. Some strategies for maximizing link popularity are:

➧ **Create content that promotes linking.** A site that simply sells product and promotes itself is unlikely to be a site others want to link to. Instead, create linkable content such as product reviews, tips and hints for using the products, free downloads, and informative articles. This content will not only promote the site to its visitors, but also encourage other sites to link to it.

➧ **Seek reciprocal links.** In the mutual quest for link popularity, it is likely that business partners, suppliers, business associations, and major customers will be happy to provide reciprocal links. At a more general level, Web sites such as linkpartners.com list Web sites interested in reciprocal links. However, be careful to select and place these links cautiously so as not to devalue the key business and customer links on the site.

➧ **Determine what sites already link to the target site.** An existing site may already have incoming links that are unknown to the owner. Software such as MarketLeap's Link Popularity Analysis Tool (marketleap.com/publinkpop) can reveal incoming links. The reverse link search feature of the search engines themselves (enter *link:URL* in the search box) will show similar results. Once incoming links are known, seek links from similar sites as appropriate.

➧ **Visit competitors.** Linking to competitors is not advised, but a visit to a competitor's site may reveal outgoing links that will work equally well on your site. Search for incoming links on a competitor's site, too, using the software mentioned earlier. When link partners with competitors are known, seek reciprocal links as appropriate.

➧ **Seek highly placed links.** When asking for reciprocal links, encourage link partners to place the link in the first and second levels of the site so spiders will find it.

➧ **Seek links from well-known sites.** Not all links are created equal; a link from Yahoo or CNN will be much more valuable than a link from a friend's homepage.

➧ **Do not use free-for-all (FFA) or link farms.** These sites sell or give away links, but search engines ignore them because they represent a form of spamming.

Online libraries of articles about enhancing a Web site's link popularity can be found at marketleap.com, linking101.com, and ericward.com.

When all keyword and link popularity strategies have been executed, the site should be registered at Web search engines (e.g., Google, AllTheWeb) and at Web directories (e.g., Yahoo, Virtual Library, Open Directory Project). Registering the site invites spiders to visit the site, rather than waiting for the site to be found. Search engine registration services such as Wpromote (wpromote.com), Addme (addme.com), and SiteAnnounce (siteannounce.com) will do this for little or no cost, but all search engines also have a "submit URL" box.

Several SEO services (e.g., webposition.com, searchsummit.com) are available that will supervise the entire SEO process for a Web site. However, SEO requires constant monitoring to be effective, and decisions such as which companies are acceptable linking partners are management decisions that should not be left to neutral parties. SEO services can assist, but successful SEO requires site owner supervision and involvement.

Section 16.7 ❱ REVIEW

1. List four types of Web site content that can promote the Web site internally.
2. What is search engine optimization? Why is it important?
3. What is the key factor for understanding search engine optimization?
4. List strategies for optimizing keyword occurrence and placement.
5. List strategies for optimizing link popularity.

16.8 CUSTOMER RELATIONSHIP MANAGEMENT

As defined in Chapter 4, **customer relationship management (CRM)** is a customer service approach that focuses on building long-term and sustainable customer relationships that add value for the customer and the company. Entire books have been written about delivering effective CRM (e.g., Brown and Gulycz 2002; Cunningham 2002; Dyche 2001), and that material cannot be duplicated or even summarized here. This section focuses on what every start-up online business needs to know in order to initiate a program of effective CRM. After getting these fundamentals right, successful online firms will be ready to move into more advanced CRM techniques such as contact management, data mining, and personalization.

customer relationship management (CRM) A customer service approach that focuses on building long-term and sustainable customer relationships that add value for the customer and the company.

USING CONTENT TO BUILD CUSTOMER RELATIONSHIPS

The first step to building customer relationships is to give customers good reasons to visit and return to the Web site. In other words, create a site that is rich in information, hopefully with more content than a visitor can absorb in a single visit. The site should include not just product information, but also should have value-added content, from which visitors can get valuable information and services for free. Exhibit 16.8 lists some ways in which online businesses can build customer relationships through content.

EXHIBIT 16.8 Building CRM Through Content

Content Strategy	Description	CRM Benefits
Provide membership	Offer registration at the site to gain access to premium content and services	Community building, targeted marketing, paid subscription opportunity
Personalize the user experience	Present content that the site visitor has indicated an interest in through previous browsing or member profiles	Community building, targeted commerce offers, customer and site loyalty
Support users	Provide responsive and convenient customer service	Community building, customer and site loyalty, repeat purchases
Communicate via the community	Allow visitors to communicate with each other and the publisher through the site	Community building, customer and site loyalty
Reward visitors	Provide visitors with rewards for visiting and using the Web site	Customer and site loyalty, promotional product up-sell and cross-sell opportunities
Market effectively	Promote the site's content and products without alienating current and potential customers	Customer and site loyalty, promotional product up-sell and cross-sell opportunity
Set up smart affiliate relationships	Establish affiliate relationships with both private (consumer) and commercial Web publishers	Customer and site loyalty, new revenue stream

Source: *Killer Content Strategies for Web Content and E-Commerce* by Tomsen. © Reprinted by permission of Pearson Education, Inc. Upper Saddle River, NJ.

CUSTOMER SELF-SERVICE THROUGH AN FAQ PAGE

FAQ page
A Web site page that lists questions that are frequently asked by customers and the answers to those questions.

Every Web site needs a FAQ page that helps customers help themselves. A **FAQ page** lists questions that are frequently asked by customers and the answers to those questions. By making a FAQ page available, customers can quickly and easily find answers to their questions, saving time and effort for both the owner and the customer. An effective FAQ page has the following characteristics:

▶ **The FAQ page is easy to find.** The FAQ page should be available from a navigation bar or navigation column, even if it is on a pull-down menu. Alternatively, include a prominently placed link on the homepage and on every page offering customer service.

▶ **The FAQ page loads fast.** The FAQ page should deliver answers to questions a customer might have, and do so fast. Both purposes are best met with text; only rarely will diagrams, pictures, or art be justified. If the number of questions or the length of the answers increase page size enough to negatively impact loading time, then the FAQ page should be divided into a number of smaller pages by category (e.g., product FAQ, customer support FAQ, shipping FAQ). Alternatively, create a FAQ index page with all the questions and link to individual pages with answers.

▶ **The questions are easy to find.** Do not force visitors to page down through screens of questions and answers to find the question they want to ask. List all questions at the top of the page and use an internal hyperlink to take the visitor to the repeated question with an answer further down the page. After each answer, include a "back to top" link to assist visitors who have additional questions. Questions should be grouped by category, with headings, and in a logical order (e.g., questions about placing an order should precede questions about shipping).

▶ **The answers are written from a customer's perspective.** Answers should be written in a simple and straightforward manner with a focus on telling the customer what to do and how to do it. Limit the use of technical terms and clearly explain any that are used. If the Web site serves two or more distinctive markets, more than one FAQ page may be needed to serve each type of customer.

▶ **The answers do not repeat information offered elsewhere.** Writing duplicate information is a waste of FAQ space and creates problems when the original information is updated and the FAQ page is not. For example, the answer to the question, "Is my credit card information safe?" should include a one-word answer—yes—with a link to the privacy policies page. Similarly, do not be afraid to refer the answers to complex questions to user manuals or technical documents, especially if they are available online. Finally, if the answer to a question is best provided by an external Web site, create a link to that page, but in a new window so that the customer can easily return to the original Web site.

▶ **Offer an opportunity to ask a question not on the FAQ.** Because no FAQ page can answer every question a visitor might ask, every FAQ page should also have an e-mail address, telephone number, a "search this site" box, and a prominently placed "ask your question here" box.

▶ **The FAQ page is never done.** Customer service representatives should always be looking for new questions customers are asking that need to be added to the FAQ page. Be open-minded in this process; many people may be asking the same question in different ways. By definition, a FAQ page is not intended to answer every question that is asked or submitted, but someone should be responsible for looking for truly frequently asked questions. Similarly, at least twice each year each question should be reviewed by relevant staff to ensure that the question is still justified and that the answer is correct. Perhaps every new staff person should be required to read the FAQ page and suggest additions, deletions, and changes.

LISTENING TO CUSTOMERS

Web sites that practice successful CRM listen to customers through a variety of methods. Customers may provide information overtly through surveys or contests in which they indicate customer preferences. Customers also provide valuable business information through the e-mail messages they send. A business can listen to customers by following these suggestions:

▶ **Mine e-mail for information.** E-mail messages should not be deleted until they have been mined for valuable information about product performance, frequently asked questions, and necessary improvements in the business's processes and operations.

▶ **Survey customers quickly and frequently.** Customer surveys are an easy feedback tool for an online business. A survey form can be easily created online and results can be readily imported into a spreadsheet or database for analysis. Unsolicited surveys can provide rich feedback, but the results can be skewed because only individuals who have time or a complaint may complete an online survey. One successful strategy to get more complete and accurate results is to invite a certain proportion (e.g., every tenth customer) to complete a survey, perhaps with a small incentive (e.g., $3 off their next purchase). All surveys, solicited or not, should be short, requiring, at most, 5 minutes of the customer's time. Include easy-to-answer and easy-to-analyze multiple choice and Likert scale (e.g., a five-point scale ranging from very satisfied to very unsatisfied) questions. Include only a few open-ended questions but offer numerous opportunities for respondents to make comments. Try to ask the most important questions first, just in case the survey is submitted incomplete, and minimize the amount of personal information that is asked.

▶ **Create an e-mail list.** An e-mail discussion list is a group of people who share a common interest and who communicate with each other via e-mail messages managed by e-mail list software. Basically, visitors to the Web site sign up for an e-mail list sponsored by the site. Then a list member with a question or a comment sends an e-mail message to the e-mail list software, which sends it to all members on the list. The list should be moderated by an individual who reads and approves all messages before being sent to the group. The moderator should not be censoring communications, but inappropriate or off-topic messages can be intercepted and discarded before being forwarded to the e-mail list.

▶ **Create a discussion forum.** An electronic discussion e-forum is a portion of the Web site where visitors can post questions, comments, and answers. An e-forum has a similar purpose as an e-mail list, except the messages are posted on the business's Web site, not distributed through e-mail. Most message boards are moderated. The principal disadvantage of a message board is that the participants must make an effort to visit the site and read the messages, whereas messages from an e-mail discussion group are delivered directly to the recipient's mailbox.

▶ **Create a chat group.** A chat group is a portion of the Web site where visitors can communicate synchronously. Basically, participants read and respond to messages in real time as they are typed. Few online businesses have enough Web site traffic to support chat groups, not to mention the cost and staffing requirements to maintain them.

From the business's perspective, all three types of electronic discussion groups—e-mail lists, discussion forums, and chat groups—offer an opportunity for the business to keep track of industry news and customer concerns, to implicitly promote the firm's products, and to gain visibility among people who are in some way interested in what the business is selling. However, these positive benefits can be undermined if the business promotes its products too blatantly, if the discussion gets off track or is spammed (thus the need for a moderator), or if there is only a small amount of significant discussion. This last point is an important one. There should be evidence of a sizable audience, willingness to participate, and compelling topics to talk about before launching an electronic discussion group. If a business sets up an e-mail list or discussion forum and only a few customers join and even fewer participate, this can be viewed as an embarrassment for the business.

INCREASING TRUST

A key part of CRM is establishing trust. As defined in Chapter 4, trust is a psychological state of mind when two or more parties are willing to pursue further interactions to achieve a planned goal. CRM helps establish trust by reassuring the customer about the nature of the relationship being established by the business.

---

e-mail discussion list
A group of people who share a common interest and who communicate with each other via e-mail messages managed by e-mail list software.

electronic discussion (e-forum)
A portion of the Web site where visitors can post questions, comments, and answers.

chat group
A portion of the Web site where visitors can communicate synchronously.

trust
A psychological state-of-mind when two or more parties are willing to pursue further interactions to achieve a planned goal.

Some ways that online businesses can use the Web site to increase trust are:

▶ **Tell the customer about the company.** Include an "about us" link on every page, either in the navigation bar or navigation column. This link directs the visitor to a page that describes the business and identifies the key people who own or manage the business, with contact details. A history of the company, the founder's motivations for creating the company, and other aspects of the business and its people that do not necessarily relate to making money can add a human touch in a sometimes-sterile Web environment. Pictures of managers, customer support personnel, and the building where the business is located will help assure the visitor that the business is real. A British company called Anything Left-Handed builds trust in all these ways and more (see anythingleft-handed.co.uk/about.html).

▶ **Include testimonials from loyal, satisfied customers.** Especially effective are testimonials from customers who were dissatisfied for some reason but have been turned into happy customers through excellent customer service.

▶ **Provide numerous opportunities for feedback.** Start by including a "contact us" on every page. Another useful feature is a feedback box so a customer can quickly type in a question or comment, include their e-mail address, and then click the send button.

▶ **Answer customer e-mails promptly.** If a complete answer will take some time or research, respond promptly with a message acknowledging receipt of the inquiry. In e-mail messages and all communications with customers, be careful about commitments or inappropriate content because e-mail messages can be considered part of a binding, legal contract.

▶ **Provide information to the customer about an order.** First, acknowledge the receipt of the order upon arrival and include an estimated shipping date. Second, notify the customer when the order has been shipped and include the expected delivery date or promptly notify them of any delays in shipment. Third, a few days after the order was expected to arrive, send a final thank-you-for-your-order message and seek confirmation that the order arrived and is satisfactory.

Section 16.8 ▶ REVIEW

1. List ways Web sites can use content to manage customer relationships.
2. What are some of the characteristics of an effective FAQ page?
3. Describe three electronic discussion groups with an emphasis on their similarities and differences.
4. List ways Web sites can increase trust to build a sustained relationship with a customer.

MANAGERIAL ISSUES

Some managerial issues related to this chapter are as follows.

1. **What does it take to create a successful online business?** The ability of a business idea to survive, and thrive, in the marketplace depends on the strength of the business concept, the capabilities of the entrepreneur, and successful execution of the business plan. Creativity, entrepreneurial attitudes, and management skills represent a human capital investment that every potentially successful business needs.

2. **Is creating a Web site a technical task or a management task?** It is both. Although somewhat expensive, the technical skills required to build a Web site are readily available in the marketplace. The prerequisite managerial skills are somewhat more difficult to find. Online business owners need to possess traditional business skills as well as understand the technical aspects of building a Web site to be able to hire and work with information architects, Web designers, and Web site hosting services.

3. **How do we attract visitors to the Web site?** Search engine optimization is important, but the key to attracting visitors, getting them to return, and encouraging them to tell others about the site is to offer credible content that fulfills a value exchange proposition. That is, both the site owner and the customer must receive value from the visit. What the site says (content) is important, but so is *how* it is said. Web design delivers content in a compelling manner that enhances the readability of the content and the quality of the customer experience.

4. **How do we turn visitors into buyers?** Getting people to come to the Web site is only half the battle. Visitors become buyers when a Web site offers products and services that customers need, with promotions and a price that entice visitors to buy there rather than go somewhere else, and in an environment that promotes trust.

SUMMARY

In this chapter, you learned about the following EC issues as they relate to the learning objectives.

1. **Fundamental requirements for initiating an online business.** A good idea becomes a successful online business when owners with the required skills, attitudes, and understanding of Internet culture execute a powerful business plan.

2. **Funding options for a start-up online business.** Incubators provide support services whereas angel investors and venture capitalists provide funds for a prospective online business. The business and business owners usually benefit greatly from these arrangements, but the funding sources are scare and competition is stiff.

3. **Web site hosting options for an online business.** Storebuilder services, ISPs, dedicated Web site hosting services, and self-hosting give online business owners a range of options in deciding how and where to host the Web site. A well-chosen domain name is an "address for success," a way of making the site easy to find and remember. Choosing a domain name is an important step in setting up the hosting site.

4. **Web site construction options for an online business.** Internal development, external contracting, and partnerships give business owners a range of options in deciding who builds the Web site.

5. **Provide content that attracts and keeps Web site visitors.** Content is king! Content can be created, purchased, or acquired for free and used for site promotion, sales, and building customer relationships.

Successful Web sites offer content that the site's target audience wants and expects.

6. **Design a visitor-friendly site.** Although text is content rich and inexpensive, a text-only site is also a barren and unmemorable site. Graphics and colors should be selected with the site's business goals and visitors' needs in mind. Web site owners and designers should never overestimate the attention span of the site visitor, so it is best to include small graphics that are few in number so the end result is an attractive page but one that also will load fast. The key to visitor-friendly navigation is to project a visitor's mental map on the Web site: where they are, where they have been, where they should go next, and how to get to where they want to be.

7. **High placement in search engines is key.** Keyword occurrence and placement on the site and promoting link popularity are the fundamental strategies for search engine optimization. High placement on search engine keyword searches will guarantee visitors, the essential first step toward online business success.

8. **Customer relationship management can contribute to success.** CRM is not just about sophisticated contact management techniques and expensive software. Effective management of long-term and sustainable customer relationships begins with helping customers help themselves, listening to customers, and creating trust.

KEY TERMS

DISCUSSION QUESTIONS

1. Compare and contrast setting up a traditional, brick-and-mortar business and an online business. Consider factors such as entrepreneurial skills, facilities and equipment, and business processes.

2. Compare and contrast the creation of a new online business and the establishment of an online initiative in an existing company. Consider factors such as resource acquisition, start-up processes, and competitor analysis.

3. How is an e-business plan different from a traditional business plan?

4. How would you decide which Web site hosting option an online business should use? List and briefly explain factors to include in your decision.

5. What is the relationship between information architecture, site navigation, and consistency in Web site design?

6. What are the trade-offs in giving the customer everything possible (e.g., personalized content, high-resolution graphics, a feature-full site) and the fundamental rules of Web design?

7. Who should be on a Web site development team for a small business? For a large business?

8. Should a small business build its own Web site? Why or why not? Should a large business build its own Web site? Why or why not?

9. Should a small business maintain its own Web site? Why or why not? Should a large business maintain its own Web site? Why or why not?

10. How do the CRM techniques discussed in Section 16.8 add value for the customer and the company?

11. Several times in this chapter online business owners are advised to gather competitive intelligence from competitors (e.g., in SEO, what sites link to competitor sites). Is this ethical? Why or why not?

INTERNET EXERCISES

1. Go to the vFinance Capital (**vfinance.com**) and National Venture Capital Association (**nvca.com**) sites and identify any trends or opportunities in acquiring start-up funding.

2. Go to a Yahoo category such as tourist agencies or insurance companies and pick 10 sites. Classify them as informational, interactive, or transactional Web sites. Make a list of any informational, interactive, or transactional features.

3. Many individuals attempt to make a living simply by buying and selling goods on eBay. Visit **ebay.com** and make a list of the ways in which these entrepreneurs use cross selling and up selling in their sales activities.

4. Visit Webmaster Forums (**webmaster-forums.net**), register (for free), and visit the Web site critique area. Compare the design rules offered in this chapter with some of the Web sites being offered for critique at the site. Offer at least one design suggestion to a Webmaster who is soliciting feedback.

5. Visit the "Sixty Ticks for a Good Website" (**waller.co.uk/eval.htm**) or "Web Site Scorecard" (**newentrepreneur.com/Resources Articles/Rate_a_Web_Site/rate_a_web_site.html**). Then go to a Web site you visit regularly and critique its design according to these tools.

6. Visit "Safe Web Colors for Color-Deficient Vision" (**more.btexact.com/people/rigdence/colours**) to learn what colors work and do not work for people with color blindness. Visit at least five Web sites and rate them on their use of colors for Web users with color blindness.

7. Explore the Web to find five dedicated Web site hosting services. Compare them on the criteria listed in this chapter. Write a report based on your findings.

8. Select five firms from an industry such as banking, stock trading, or ISPs. Go to **google.com** and enter *link:URL* for each of the five firms where URL is the firm's homepage. Which firms have higher numbers of incoming links? Examine their Web sites and try to determine why this is so.

TEAM ASSIGNMENTS AND ROLE PLAYING

1. Pretend your team has been asked to make a 20-minute presentation to a local business group about how to launch an online business. Prepare the presentation by highlighting the most important considerations you learned in this chapter.

2. Write a RFQ for a fictitious company following the example provided on the book's Web site (at Chapter 16). Submit the RFQ to several local ISPs. (Be honest and tell them this is a student assignment; most ISPs will be happy to assist if you volunteer to send them a copy of your report.) Write a report that compares the responses, selects a winning ISP, and justifies your decision.

3. Assume that a commercial or not-for-profit organization in your community has asked for your assistance in selecting and registering a domain name. Write a report that identifies several appropriate available domain names, explain the pros and cons of each name, make a recommendation, and justify your recommendation.

4. Form two teams, the client team and the Web design team. After suitable preparation, both teams meet for their first Web site planning meeting. Afterwards, both teams critique their own and the other team's performance in the meeting.

5. Form two debating teams. One team supports the proposition that using a number of images and colors on a Web site is okay because "soon everyone will have a high-speed connection to the Internet." The other team disagrees with this statement and its justification.

REAL-WORLD CASE

MAKING E-NEWSLETTERS PAY

Electronic newsletters are a standard feature of hundreds, perhaps thousands of Web sites. Almost all Web site owners consider these newsletters to be a promotion cost; that is, a price to be paid for capturing and holding the visitor's attention. A rare exception is Fred Langa, whose *LangaList Plus* newsletter not only pays for itself, but has subscriber renewal rates that would make any print publisher green with envy.

The year was 1998. The business world was abuzz with talk about computers, electronic commerce, and the Internet. Fred Langa, a computer journalist and editor, decided to leave the corporate publishing world and become a freelance writer. Central to his career change was *LangaList* (*langa.com*), a free newsletter that was to promote his writing business, pay for itself with advertising, and enable him to give something back to the computing community that had supported his publishing career. In his words, *LangaList*'s original purpose was "for the e-mails to contain useful tips, tricks, and other information about using computer hardware and software" (Hartsock 2001). The *LangaList* revenue model was ad fees from advertisers who would want to reach the newsletter's computer-savvy subscriber base.

From the start, both advertising and subscription numbers grew, and *LangaList* was a modest success. Then the dot-com boom went bust. By late 2000, advertising revenue was dropping fast, while expenses grew as the subscriber list passed 150,000. The problem was how to leverage the *LangaList* success into a new business model.

Langa's solution was to create *LangaList Plus*, a premium content newsletter that generated revenue through subscriptions and was marketed as an up-sell version of *LangaList*. The "plus" in *LangaList Plus* was original content that Fred felt subscribers would be willing to pay for, plus no advertising, plus a reader's choice of versions (HTML, plain text, or digest). *LangaList Plus* was marketed as costing only 11 cents per issue for the twice-weekly newsletter. Within weeks of its launch in January 2001, 10,000 *LangaList* readers had paid $10 each to subscribe to *LangaList Plus*. By the end of its first year of publication, *LangaList Plus* had almost 20,000 paid subscribers.

With a successful launch and start, the next hurdle was getting *LangaList Plus* subscribers to renew. Many e-newsletters and e-zines such as *Salon* have found that getting subscribers to take a risk on a publication is difficult, but keeping them through the first renewal is nearly impossible. Yet at the end of his first round of renewals in March 2002, *LangaList Plus* had an 80 percent renewal rate. According to MarketingSherpa.com (2003), "In the print newsletter world this would be considered a very high response for B2B and almost unbelievable for B2C."

What can e-newsletter editors learn from Fred Langa's success? He cites these factors as critical to his success:

▶ An e-newsletter should not be just a tease. The articles and newsletters themselves should contain enough "meat" to be worth reading in their own right.

▶ The e-newsletter should have a personal tone, more like a letter from a friend than a generic magazine article.

▶ Labor-intensive newsletter and site features are minimized. For example, of the approximately 150 e-mail responses per issue, the vast majority are answered with a form letter on a FAQ topic.

▶ Everything is made "dead easy" for the subscribers. Subscriptions can be paid in a number of ways, including postal check, online credit card, fax, and PayPal. When the Excite@home ISP went under, hundreds of subscriber e-mail addresses became invalid. In response, Langa gave them tools on the *LangaList* Web site to easily switch their subscription address, which not only impressed readers but avoided his having to manually process the changes.

A series of friendly renewal letters emphasized the value *LangaList Plus* subscribers receive, including downloadable archives, a private Web site, 18 special issues, donations to charity, and "almost 100 *LangaList Plus* issues comprising over 325,000 words." (MarketingSherpa.com 2003). Fred Langa sees e-newsletters evolving into three groups. First are the truly free newsletters that are either supported by volunteer labor-of-love or sponsored as part of an ongoing Web site promotion. Second are those that insert advertising in between content. Third are the very

few that are directly supported by readers in some way. Langa has these words of advice for aspiring e-newsletter editors: "The prevailing thinking is that 'people won't pay for content.' But some people will pay for some content: Manage that equation carefully, and you've got a viable business" (Hartsock 2001).

Sources: Hartsock (2001), *MarketingSherpa.com* (2003), *langa.com* (2003).

Questions

1. What distinguishes *LangaList Plus* from *LangaList*? How do these differences add value so that subscribers are willing to pay for *LangaList Plus*?

2. How has Fred Langa used interactive features to attract and retain newsletter readers?

3. Do you agree that "some people will pay for some content"? Explain.

REFERENCES

Agarwal, R., and V. Venkatesh. "Assessing a Firm's Web Presence: A Heuristic Evaluation Procedure for the Measurement of Usability." *Information Systems Research* 13, no. 2 (2002): 168–186.

Arnold, S. E. "Content Management's New Realities." *OnLine Magazine* 27, no. 1 (2003), **onlinemag.net/Jan03/arnold.htm** (accessed March 2003).

Awad, E. M. *Electronic Commerce: From Vision to Fulfillment.* Upper Saddle River, NJ: Prentice Hall, 2002.

Bakshi, K., and J. Deighton. *Webvan: Groceries on the Internet.* Boston: Harvard Business School Press, 1999.

Bayers, C. "The Inner Bezos." *Wired* 7, no. 3 (1999): 115–121, 172–187.

bCentral. *Search Engine Optimization Tips.* **submit-it.com/subopt_print.htm** (accessed February 2003).

BBC Training and Development. *The 12 Deadly Sins of Site Design.* October 2002.

Brown, S. A., and M. Gulycz. *Performance-Driven CRM: How to Make Your Customer Relationship Management Vision a Reality.* New York: John Wiley & Sons, 2002.

Cukier, K. N. "Boo's Blues." *Red Herring,* May 4, 2000, **redherring.com/vc/2000/0504/vc-boo050400.html** (accessed February 2003).

Cunningham, M. J. *Customer Relationship Management.* New York: Capstone Publishing/John Wiley, 2002.

Dyche, J. *The CRM Handbook: A Business Guide to Customer Relationship Management.* Reading, MA: Addison-Wesley Information Technology, 2001.

Evans, P., and T. Wurster. *Blown to Bits: How the New Economics of Information Transforms Strategy.* Boston: Harvard Business School Press, 2000.

Hartsock, N. "Interview: Fred Langa." *ibiz Interviews.com,* March 2001, **ibizinerviews.com/fred11.htm** (accessed March 2003).

Huang, W., et al. "Transforming a Lean CMC Medium into a Rich One: An Empirical Investigation in Small Groups." *Proceedings of the 17th International Conference on Information Systems,* December 1996, Cleveland, OH, 265–277.

Huff, S., et al. *Cases in Electronic Commerce.* Boston: Irwin McGraw-Hill, 2000.

Jupiter Research. *Web Content Management: Covering the Essentials, Avoiding Overspending.* February 2003, **jupiterresearch.com** (accessed March 2003).

Kauffman, R. J., et al. "When Internet Companies Morph: Understanding Organizational Strategy Changes in the 'New' New Economy." *First Monday,* July 2002, **firstmonday.dk/issues/issue7_7/kauffman** (accessed February 2003).

Kienan, B. *Managing Your E-Commerce Business.* Redmond, WA: Microsoft Press, 2001.

langa.com (accessed February 2003).

MarketingSherpa.com. "Newsletter Gets 80% Paid Renewal Rate with a Four-Part Email Campaign." 2003, **marketingsherpa.com/sample.cfm?contentID=2001** (accessed March 2003).

Markus, L. "Electronic Mail as the Medium of Managerial Choice." *Organizational Science* 5 (1994): 502–527.

McKinney, V., et al. "The Measurement of Web-Customer Satisfaction: An Expectation and Disconfirmation Approach." *Information Systems Research* 13, no. 3 (2002): 296–315.

McNurlin, B. C., and P. Sprague. *Information Systems: Management in Practice*, 5th ed. Upper Saddle River, NJ: Prentice Hall, 2002.

Morkes, J., and J. Nielsen. *Concise, Scannable, and Objective: How to Write for the Web.* 1997, useit.com/papers/webwriting/writing.html (accessed March 2003).

New Zealand Ministry of Economic Development (MED). *E-Commerce: A Guide for New Zealand Business.* Wellington, New Zealand: New Zealand Ministry of Economic Development, 2000.

Nielsen, J., and M. Tahir. *Homepage Usability: 50 Websites Deconstructed.* Indianapolis, IN: New Riders Publishing, 2002.

OBO. obo.co.nz, 2003 (accessed March 2003).

O'Keefe, P. "Buy the Ultimate Domain Name." webmasterbase.com/article.php?aid=865&pid=0 (accessed September 2002).

Peck, N. "An Introduction to Accessible Web Design." webmasterbase.com/article.php?aid=952&pid=0 (accessed December 2002).

Porter, M. E. "Strategy and the Internet." *Harvard Business Review* (March 2001): 63–78.

Post, G. V., and D. L. Anderson. *Management Information Systems: Solving Business Problems with Information Technology.* Boston: McGraw-Hill, 2003.

Rayport, J., and B. J. Jaworski. *Introduction to E-Commerce.* Boston: McGraw-Hill, 2002.

Rosenfeld, L., and P. Morville. *Information Architecture for the World Wide Web.* Cambridge, MA: O'Reilly, 1998.

Saraccvic, A. T. "Vulture Capitalists." *Business 2.0*, November 2000, 158–169.

Spector, R. *Amazon.com—Get Big Fast: Inside the Revolutionary Business Model That Changed the World.* New York: HarperBusiness, 2000.

Taulli, T. "Dot-com Content that Works?" News.com, April 18, 2002, news.com.com/2010–1076–885735.html (accessed April 2003).

Tomsen, M. *Killer Content: Strategies for Web Content and E-Commerce.* Boston: Addison-Wesley, 2000.

Turban, E., et al. *Information Technology for Management*, 4th ed. New York: John Wiley & Sons, 2004.

Watson, R. T., et al. *Electronic Commerce: The Strategic Perspective.* Fort Worth, TX: Dryden Press, 2000.

Wong, M. *The Thirty-One Steps to SEO.* Promotionbase.com, promotionbase.com/article.php?aid=715&pid=0 (accessed April 2002).

CHAPTER 17

LEGAL, ETHICAL, AND SOCIETAL IMPACTS OF EC

Learning objectives

Upon completion of this chapter, you will be able to:

1. Describe the differences between legal and ethical issues in EC.
2. Understand the difficulties of protecting privacy in EC.
3. Discuss issues of intellectual property rights in EC.
4. Understand the conflict between free speech and censorship on the Internet.
5. Describe major legal issues in EC.
6. Describe the types of fraud on the Internet and how to protect against them.
7. Describe representative societal issues in EC.
8. Describe the role and impact of virtual communities on EC.
9. Describe the future of EC.

Content

MP3.COM, NAPSTER, AND INTELLECTUAL PROPERTY RIGHTS

The Problem

Before the advent of the Web, people made audiotape copies of music and videos. They either gave these copies to friends and family or used them for their own personal enjoyment. Few individuals had either the interest or the means to create and distribute copies to larger populations. For the most part, these activities were ignored by the producers, distributors, and artists who had the legal rights to the content (Spaulding 2000).

Then came the Web and a variety of enterprising sites such as MP3.com and Napster (*napster.com*). MP3.com enabled users to listen to music from any computer with an Internet connection without paying royalties. Using peer-to-peer (P2P) technology, Napster supported the distribution of music and other digitized content among millions of users. When asked whether they were doing anything illegal, MP3.com and Napster claimed that they were simply supporting what had been done for years and, like most private individuals, were not charging for their services. Other companies extended the concept to other digitizable media such as videos and movies. The popularity of MP3.com and P2P services was too great for the content creators and owners to ignore. Music sales declined (and are still declining as of 2003). To the creators and owners, the Web was becoming a vast copying machine for pirated software, CDs, movies, and the like. If left undeterred, MP3.com's and Napster's services could result in the destruction of many thousands of jobs and millions of dollars in revenue.

The Solution

In December 2000, EMusic (*emusic.com*) filed a copyright infringement lawsuit against MP3.com. They claimed ownership of the digital rights to some of the music made available at MP3.com. Warner Brothers Music Group, EMI Group PLC, BMG Entertainment, and Sony Music Entertainment followed suit. A year later, Napster faced similar legal claims, lost the legal battle, and was forced to pay royalties for each piece of music it supported. This resulted in its collapse. As described in previous chapters, some P2P companies moved to other countries, but the legal problems follow them.

Copyright laws and copyright infringement cases have been in existence for decades. By the year 2000, the EC laws should have been clear. However, the legal system can be picky and slow to resolve legal difficulties and close loopholes. First, existing copyright laws were written for physical, not digital, content. Second, the Copyright Infringement Act states, "the defendant must have willfully infringed the copyright and gained financially." With respect to the second point, a MIT student named David LaMacchia was sued for offering free copies of Excel, Word, and other software titles on the Internet. The suit was settled in his favor because there was no financial gain. This loophole in the Act was later closed.

The Results

In 1997, the U.S. Electronic Theft Act (NET) was passed, making it a crime for anyone, including individuals, to reproduce and distribute copyrighted works. The act further clarified that it applied to reproduction or distribution accomplished by electronic means. It also stated that even if copyrighted products are distributed without charge, financial harm is experienced by the authors or creators of a copyrighted work.

Given the precedents and laws, MP3.com and Napster had little recourse but to capitulate. MP3.com suspended operations in April 2000 and settled the lawsuit against itself, paying the litigants $20 million each. Napster suspended service and settled its lawsuits for $26 million. With the backing of the record company Bertelsmann AG's BMG, Napster tried—with little success—to resurrect itself as an online music subscription service. Napster eventually filed for bankruptcy in June 2002. Its assets were purchased by Roxio (*roxio.com*). Roxio is planning to revive Napster, in a royalty-paying framework, in early 2004.

Sources: Spaulding (2000), *roxio.com* (2002), and Olavsrud (2000).

WHAT WE CAN LEARN . . .

All commerce involves a number of legal, ethical, and regulatory issues. Copyright, trademark, and patent infringement, freedom of thought and speech, theft of property, and fraud are not new issues in the world of commerce. However, as this opening case illustrates, EC adds to the scope and scale of these issues. It also raises a number of questions about what constitutes illegal behavior versus unethical, intrusive, or undesirable behavior. This chapter examines some of the legal and ethical issues arising from EC and various legal and technical remedies and safeguards. The chapter also examines some social impacts of EC and, finally, assesses the future of EC.

17.1 LEGAL ISSUES VERSUS ETHICAL ISSUES

Using the Internet in general and EC in particular raises large numbers of legal and ethical issues, some of which will be explored in this chapter. First, let's distinguish between legal issues and ethical ones.

In theory, one can quickly distinguish between legal issues and ethical issues. Laws are enacted by governments and developed through case precedents (common law). Laws are strict legal rules governing the acts of all citizens within their jurisdictions. If a person breaks the law, they have done something illegal and can be held liable for punishment by the legal system.

In contrast, **ethics** is a branch of philosophy that deals with what is considered to be right and wrong. Over the years, philosophers have proposed many ethical guidelines, yet what is unethical is not necessarily illegal. Ethics are supported by common agreement in a society as to what is right and wrong, but they are not subject to legal sanctions (except when they overlap with activities that are also illegal). A framework for ethical issues is shown in Exhibit W17.1 at the book's Web site.

EC opens up a new spectrum of unregulated activity, where the definitions of right and wrong are not always clear (e.g., see Hamelink 2001). Business people engaging in e-commerce need guidelines as to what behaviors are reasonable under any given set of circumstances. Consider the following scenarios:

▶ A Web site collects information from potential customers and sells it to its advertisers. Some of the profiles are inaccurate; consequently, people receive numerous pieces of inappropriate and intrusive e-mail. Should junk e-mail of this sort be allowed? Should it come with a warning label?

▶ A company allows its employees to use the Web for limited personal use. Unknown to the employees, the IT staff not only monitors employees' messages, but also examines the content. If the monitors find objectionable content, should the company be allowed to fire the offending employees?

Whether these actions are considered unethical (or even illegal) depends on the regulatory and value systems of the country in which they occur. What is unethical in one culture may be perfectly acceptable in another. Many Western countries, for example, have a much higher concern for individuals and their rights to privacy than do some Asian countries. In Asia, more emphasis is placed on the benefits to society rather than on the rights of individuals. Some countries, such as Sweden and Canada, have very strict privacy laws; others have none. This situation may obstruct the flow of information among countries. Indeed, the European Community Commission issued guidelines in 1998 to all its member countries regarding the rights of individuals to access information about them and to correct errors. These guidelines may cause problems for companies outside Europe that do business there.

EC ETHICAL ISSUES

There are many EC- and Internet-related ethical issues. (For a list and framework, see Spinello and Tavani 2001; the special issue of *Ethics and Information Technology* 2001; and Stead and Gilbert 2001). Examples of ethical issues discussed elsewhere in this book are channel conflict (Chapter 3), internal conflict (Chapter 3), disintermediation (Chapters 2, 3, and 7), and trust (Chapter 4). Two additional EC-related ethical issues are non-work-related use of the Internet and code of ethics.

Non-Work-Related Use of the Internet

Employees are tempted to use e-mail and the Web for non-work-related purposes. In some companies, this use is tremendously out of proportion with its work-related use (see Anandarajan 2002). The problem has several dimensions. For example, e-mail can be used to harass other employees or pose a legal threat to a company. It also can be used for illegal gambling activity (e.g., betting on results of a football game). Some employees may use the com-

---

ethics
The branch of philosophy that deals with what is considered to be right and wrong.

pany e-mail to advertise their own businesses. Using other corporate computing facilities for private purposes may be a problem, too. Last, but not least, is the time employees waste while surfing non-work-related Web sites during working hours.

Code of Ethics

A practical approach to limiting non-work-related Internet surfing is to develop an Internet usage policy and make it known to the employees (Siau et al. 2002). Without a formal policy, it is much more difficult to enforce desired behavior and deal with violators. Some companies send monthly reminders on the intranet about the usage policy. Others tell employees that their movement may be monitored and that their e-mail may even be read. Such notification can be a part of a code of ethics.

Corporate *codes of ethics* express the formalization of rules and expected behavior and action. Typically, the ethics code should address offensive content and graphics, as well as proprietary information. It should encourage employees to think about who should and who should not have access to information before they post it on the Web site. The code should specify whether the company allows employees to set up their own Web pages on the company intranet and about private e-mail usage and non-work-related surfing during working hours. A company should formulate a general idea of the role it wants Web sites to play. This should guide the company in developing a policy and providing employees with a rationale for that policy. Finally, do not be surprised if the code of ethics looks a lot like simple rules of etiquette; it should.

The following are some useful guidelines for corporate Web policy:

▶ Issue written policy guidelines about employee use of the Internet.
▶ Make it clear to employees that they cannot use copyrighted trademarked material without permission.
▶ Post disclaimers concerning content, such as sample code, that the company does not support.
▶ Post disclaimers of responsibility concerning content of online forums and chat sessions.
▶ Make sure that Web content and activity comply with the laws in other countries, such as those governing contests.
▶ Make sure that the company's Web content policy is consistent with other company policies.
▶ Appoint someone to monitor Internet legal and liability issues.
▶ Have attorneys review Web content to make sure that there is nothing unethical, or illegal, on the company's Web site.

Urbaczewski and Jessup (2002) explored the utility of monitoring employee usage, calling it "one of the most controversial EC issues" (see Team Assignment 4).

THE MAJOR ETHICAL/LEGAL ISSUES DISCUSSED IN THIS CHAPTER

Of the many ethical and legal issues related to e-commerce, the following will be discussed in this chapter:

▶ **Privacy.** Internet users in many countries rate privacy as their first or second top concern.
▶ **Intellectual property rights.** Rights to intellectual property are easy to violate on the Internet, resulting in billions of dollars of losses to the owners of the rights.
▶ **Free speech versus censorship.** The issue of attempting to control offensive, illegal, and potentially dangerous information on the Net is controversial. This collides with rights of free speech.
▶ **Consumer and merchant protection against fraud.** It is easy to reach millions on the Internet and to conduct different types of EC-related fraud. The success of EC depends on the protection provided to consumers and merchants.

Section 17.1 ▶ REVIEW

1. Define ethics and distinguish it from the law.
2. Give an example of an EC activity that is unethical but legal.
3. List major EC ethical issues (consult online Exhibit W17.1).
4. List the major EC ethical/legal issues presented in this chapter.

17.2 PRIVACY

privacy
The right to be left alone and the right to be free of unreasonable personal intrusions.

Privacy means different things to different people. In general, **privacy** is the right to be left alone and the right to be free of unreasonable personal intrusions. (For other definitions of privacy and for its relationships to EC, see Rykere et al. 2002.) Privacy has long been a legal, ethical, and social issue in many countries.

The right to privacy is recognized today in virtually all U.S. states and by the federal government, either by statute or by common law. The definition of privacy can be interpreted quite broadly. However, the following two rules have been followed fairly closely in past U.S. court decisions: (1) The right of privacy is not absolute. Privacy must be balanced against the needs of society. (2) The public's right to know is superior to the individual's right of privacy. These two rules show why it is difficult, in some cases, to determine and enforce privacy regulations (see Buchholz and Rosenthal 2002).

COLLECTING INFORMATION ABOUT INDIVIDUALS

In the past, the complexity of collecting, sorting, filing, and accessing information manually from several different government agencies was, in many cases, a built-in protection against misuse of private information. It was simply too expensive, cumbersome, and complex to invade a person's privacy. The Internet, in combination with large-scale databases, has created an entirely new dimension of accessing and using data. The inherent power in systems that can access vast amounts of data can be used for the good of society. For example, by matching records with the aid of a computer, it is possible to eliminate or reduce fraud, crime, government mismanagement, tax evasion, welfare cheats, family support filchers, employment of illegal aliens, and so on. The question is: What price must every individual pay in terms of loss of privacy so that the government can better apprehend these types of criminals?

The Internet offers a number of opportunities to collect private information about individuals. Here are some of the ways that the Internet can be used to find information about an individual:

▶ By reading an individual's newsgroup postings
▶ By looking up an individual's name and identity in an Internet directory
▶ By reading an individual's e-mail
▶ By conducting surveillance on employees (Steinberg 2001)
▶ By wiretapping wireline and wireless communication lines and listening to employees (Ghosh and Swaminatha 2001)
▶ By asking an individual to complete a Web site registration
▶ By recording an individual's actions as they navigate the Web with a browser, usually using cookies

Of these, the last two are the most common ways of gathering information on the Internet.

Web Site Registration

Americans are a little schizophrenic when it comes to privacy and the Internet. In a 2000 poll conducted by the Pew Internet and American Life Project, 86 percent of the respondents said they were worried about online privacy (as reported by Hawkins 2000). Yet, in another poll conducted by Jupiter Media Matrix, 50 percent said they would disclose personal information on a Web site for the chance to win a sweepstakes (Graves et al. 2000).

Virtually all B2C and marketing Web sites ask visitors to fill out registration forms. During the process, customers voluntarily provide their names, addresses, phone numbers, e-mail addresses, sometimes their hobbies and likes or dislikes, and so forth in return for information, for the chance to win a lottery, or for some other item of exchange. There are few restraints on the ways in which the site can use this information. The site might use it to improve customer service or its own business. Or, the site could just as easily sell the information to another company, which could use it in an inappropriate or intrusive manner.

Cookies

Another way that a Web site can gather information about an individual is by using cookies. As described in Chapter 4, in Internet terminology, a **cookie** is a small piece of data that is passed back and forth between a Web site and an end user's browser as the user navigates the site. Cookies enable sites to keep track of which users are which without having to constantly ask the users to identify themselves. Similar methods are Web bugs and spyware, described in Section 4.4.

    Originally, cookies were designed to help with personalization and CRM, as described in Chapter 4. However, cookies also can be used to invade an individual's privacy. Cookies allow Web sites to collect detailed information about a user's preferences, interests, and surfing patterns. The personal profiles created by cookies are often more accurate than self-registration because users have a tendency to falsify information in a registration form.

    The personal information collected via cookies has the potential to be used in illegal and unethical ways. EC Application Case 17.1 details the resistance faced by online advertiser DoubleClick when it attempted to use cookies to better target its advertising. Although the use of cookies is still debated, concerns about cookies reached a pinnacle in 1997 at the U.S.

cookie
A small piece of data that is passed back and forth between a Web site and an end user's browser as the user navigates the site; enables sites to keep track of users' activities without asking for identification.

CASE 17.1
EC Application
PRIVACY ADVOCATES TAKE ON DOUBLECLICK

DoubleClick is one of the leading providers of online advertising. Like other online advertisers, DoubleClick uses cookies to personalize ads based on consumers' interests (see EC Application Case 5.1 in Chapter 5). Although privacy advocates have long criticized the use of cookies, they have generally tolerated the practice because there was no way to tie the data collected by cookies to a consumer's identity. All this changed in January 1999 when DoubleClick bought catalog marketer Abacus Direct and announced plans to merge Abacus's off-line database with DoubleClick's online data.

    Following the announcement, several class-action lawsuits were brought against DoubleClick, claiming that the company was "tracking Internet users and obtaining personal and financial information such as names, ages, addresses, and shopping patterns, without their knowledge" (Dembeck and Conlin 2000). Many of these suits were consolidated into a single suit brought in DoubleClick's home state of New York. A short time later, the Electronic Privacy Information Center (EPIC) filed a complaint with the Federal Trade Commission (FTC) alleging that DoubleClick was using unfair and deceptive trading practices. The Attorney General of Michigan also claimed that DoubleClick was in violation of the state's Consumer Protection Act and asked it to stop placing cookies on consumers' computers without their permission.

    In January 2001, the FTC ruled that DoubleClick had not violated FTC policies. In March 2002, DoubleClick reached a preliminary settlement, clearing up a number of the class-action suits brought by the states. As a consequence, DoubleClick agreed to enhance its privacy measures and to

pay legal fees and costs up to $18 million. One of the key provisions of the settlement requires DoubleClick to "obtain permission from consumers before combining any personally identifiable data with Web surfing history" (Olsen 2002).

    Prior to the settlement, DoubleClick had already appointed a chief privacy officer and substantially strengthened its privacy policies. (For a detailed listing of the policies, see *doubleclick.com/us/corporate/privacy*.) In spite of these changes and the proposed settlement, EPIC was still not satisfied. As Marc Rotenberg, EPIC's executive director, stated, "You have to keep in mind DoubleClick's unique position—its consumer profiles are collected from Web sites it supplies advertising to. For this reason, we should expect a much higher standard for privacy protection" (Olsen 2002).

Sources: Compiled from Dembeck and Conlin (2000), Olsen (2002), and *doubleclick.com* (2003).

Questions

1. What are some of the ways in which DoubleClick's use of cookies might infringe on an individual's privacy rights?

2. What are some of the key elements in DoubleClick's new privacy policies?

3. In its complaint, EPIC proposed a number of ways to curb DoubleClick's practices. What were some of EPIC's suggestions, and does the recent ruling enforce any of the proposed limitations?

Federal Trade Commission hearings regarding online privacy. Following those hearings, Netscape and Microsoft introduced options enabling users to block the use of cookies. Since that time, the furor has abated, and most users willingly accept cookies.

Users can protect themselves against cookies: They can delete them from their computers or they can use anticookie software such as Pretty Good Privacy's (pgp.com) Cookie Cutter or Luckman's Anonymous Cookie. Anticookie software disables all cookies and allows the user to surf the Web anonymously. The problem with deleting or disabling cookies is that the user will be forced to keep reentering information and in some instances may be blocked from viewing particular pages.

Today, a Microsoft product called *Passport* is beginning to raise some of the same concerns as cookies. Passport is an Internet strategy that lets consumers permanently enter a profile of information along with a password and use this information and password repeatedly to access services at multiple sites. (See the discussion on e-wallets in Chapter 13 for details.) Critics say that Passport affords the same opportunities as cookies to invade an individual's privacy. Critics also feel that the product gives Microsoft an unfair competitive edge in EC.

Privacy of Employees

In addition to privacy of customers there is the issue of employees' privacy, as reflected in monitoring of employees' e-mail and Web activities. In addition to wasting time, employees may disclose trade secrets and possibly make employers liable for defamation by what others do on a corporate Web site. In response to these concerns, according to Lewis (2002), 77 percent of companies monitor their employees' communications.

PROTECTION OF PRIVACY

The ethical principles commonly used when it comes to the collection and use of personal information also apply to information collected in e-commerce. These principles include the following:

> **Notice/awareness.** Consumers must be given notice of an entity's information practices prior to collection of personal information. Consumers must be able to make informed decisions about the type and extent of their disclosures based on the intentions of the party collecting the information.

> **Choice/consent.** Consumers must be made aware of their options as to how their personal information may be used, as well as any potential secondary uses of the information. Consent may be granted through **opt-out clauses**, which require steps to *prevent* collection of information. In other words, no action equals consent. Or, consumers may grant consent through **opt-in clauses**, which require steps to *allow* the collection of information.

> **Access/participation.** Consumers must be able to access their personal information and challenge the validity of the data.

> **Integrity/security.** Consumers must be assured that their personal data are secure and accurate. It is necessary for those collecting the data to take whatever precautions are required to ensure that data are protected from loss, unauthorized access, destruction, and fraudulent use, and to take reasonable steps to gain information from reputable and reliable sources.

> **Enforcement/redress.** A method of enforcement and remedy must be available. Otherwise, there is no real deterrent or enforceability for privacy issues.

opt-out clauses
Agreement that requires computer users to take specific steps to *prevent* collection of information.

opt-in clauses
Agreement that requires computer users to take specific steps to *allow* collection of information.

In the United States, these principles are supported by specific pieces of legislation (see Nickell 2001). For example, the *Federal Internet Privacy Protection Act* prohibits federal agencies from disclosing personal records or making identifying records about an individual's medical, financial, or employment history. Probably the broadest in scope is the *Consumer Empowerment Act,* which requires (for instance) the FTC to enforce online privacy rights in EC, including the collection and use of personal data.

For existing U.S. Federal privacy legislation, see online Exhibit W17.2. In addition to existing legislation, there are several pending laws, both in the United States and in other countries. Numerous privacy legislation bills are in various committees and subcommittees of the House and Senate, as they have been since 2001, including H.R. 237 Consumer Internet Privacy

Enhancement Act of 2001, H.R.48 Global Internet Freedom Act, H.R.69 Online Privacy Protection Act of 2003, and H.R.71 Wireless Privacy Protection Act of 2003, (see epic.org/privacy/bill_track.html. For the status of pending legislation in the United States, visit cdt.org.

The American Civil Liberties Union, the Electronic Freedom Foundation, and other organizations have grave concerns over the most important act passed since 2001—the Uniting and Strengthening America by Providing Appropriate Tools Required to Intercept and Obstruct Terrorism (USA Patriot Act), introduced October 2, 1001, and passed October 4, 2001. Their chief concerns include: (1) expanded surveillance with reduced checks and balances, (2) overbreadth with a lack of focus on terrorism, and (3) rules that would allow Americans to be more easily spied upon by U.S. foreign intelligence agencies. Between October 2001 and September 2002, federal agencies used this act for many federal cases not pertaining to terrorist activities (see house.gov/judiciary/patriolet051303.pdf). For more information, see eff.org/Privacy/Surveillance/Terrorism_militias//20011031_eff_usa_patriot_analysis.php, and infowars.com.

In 1998, the European Union passed a privacy directive (EU Data Protection Directive) reaffirming the principles of personal data protection in the Internet age. Member countries are required to put this directive into effect by introducing new laws or modifying existing laws in their respective countries. The directive aims to regulate the activities of any person or company that controls the collecting, holding, processing, or use of personal data on the Internet.

In many countries, the debate continues about the rights of the individual versus the rights of society (see Buchholz and Rosenthal 2002). Some feel that the ISPs should be the regulators; others feel that self-regulation is the best alternative. However, some empirical data suggest that self-regulation does not work. For instance, in 1998, the U.S. FTC audited 1,400 commercial Web sites in the United States to measure the effectiveness of self-regulation (Federal Trade Commission 1998). They found that privacy protection at these sites was poor. Additionally, few sites provided end users with the following privacy protections: details about the site's information-gathering and dissemination policies; choice over how their personal information is used; control over personal information; verification and oversight of claims made by the site; and recourse for resolving user complaints.

Fortunately, users can take steps to improve their online privacy. Tynan (2002) provides 34 tips for how to do so. (Also, see pcworld.com/26702 for more suggestions.)

Section 17.2 ▶ REVIEW

1. Define privacy.

2. List some of the ways that the Internet can be used to collect information about individuals.

3. What are cookies and what do they have to do with online privacy?

4. List four common ethical principles related to the gathering of personal information.

17.3 INTELLECTUAL PROPERTY RIGHTS

According to the World Intellectual Property Organization (WIPO; wipo.org), **intellectual property** refers to "creations of the mind: inventions, literary and artistic works, and symbols, names, images, and designs used in commerce." Whereas privacy protection is the major concern for individuals, intellectual property protection is the major concern of those who own intellectual property. Intellectual property rights are one of the foundations of modern society. Without these rights, the movie, music, software, publishing, pharmaceutical, and biotech industries would collapse (Claburn 2001). There are four main types of intellectual property in EC: copyrights, trademarks, domain names, and patents.

COPYRIGHTS

A **copyright** is an exclusive grant from the government that confers on its owner an essentially exclusive right to: (1) reproduce a work, in whole or in part, and (2) distribute, perform, or display it to the public in any form or manner, including the Internet. In general, the owner has an exclusive right to export the copyrighted work to another country (Delgado-Martinez 2002).

intellectual property
Creations of the mind, such as inventions, literary and artistic works, and symbols, names, images, and designs used in commerce.

copyright
An exclusive grant from the government that allows the owner to reproduce a work, in whole or in part, and to distribute, perform, or display it to the public in any form or manner, including the Internet.

Copyrights usually exist in the following works:

- Literary works (e.g., books and computer software)
- Musical works (e.g., compositions)
- Dramatic works (e.g., plays)
- Artistic works (e.g., drawings, paintings)
- Sound recordings, films, broadcasts, cable programs

On the Web, copyrights also can be used to protect images, photos, logos, text, HTML, JavaScript, and other materials.

The greatest threat to intellectual property is wide-scale individual theft. Tens of millions of individuals are using the Internet to illegally download music, videos, games, software, and other digital products (see discussion on P2P in Chapter 9). However, the theft of even an obscure piece of research in which only a few are interested is still theft.

Various international treaties provide global copyright protection. Of these, the Berne Union for the Protection of Literary and Artistic Property (Berne Convention) is one of the most important. The Berne Convention dates to 1886. It is administered by the WIPO and is supported by over 90 percent of the world's countries.

A copyright owner may seek a court injunction to prevent or stop any infringement and to claim damages. Certain kinds of copyright infringements also incur criminal liabilities. These include: commercial production of infringing works, selling or dealing in infringing works, possessing infringing works for trade or business, and manufacturing and selling technology for defeating copyright protection systems.

A copyright does not last forever; it is good for a fixed number of years after the death of the author or creator (e.g., 50 in the United Kingdom). In the United States copyright was extended to 70 years after the death of the author, by the 1998 "Sonny Bono Copyright Extension Act" (U.S. Congress 1998). After that time, the copyright of the work reverts to the public domain.

Copyright Protection Approaches

In the United States, congressional legislation has been proposed that will make it "unlawful to manufacture, import, offer to the public, provide, or otherwise traffic in any interactive device that does not include and utilize certified security technology" (Nickell 2001). If this measure becomes law, the implication is that virtually any digital device—PC, MP3 player, digital camera, and so on—must include government-approved copy protection that makes it impossible to reproduce copyrighted material.

It is possible to use software to produce digital content that cannot be copied. Two approaches are used to design effective electronic copyright management systems (see Piva et al. 2001):

- Preventing copyright violations by using cryptography (e.g., IBM's Cryptolope at domino.research.ibm.com/comm/wwwr_thinkresearch.nsf/pages/packinginfo396.html)
- Tracking copyright violations (e.g., see imprimatur.net)

digital watermarks
Unique identifiers imbedded in digital content that make it possible to identify pirated works.

One other successful method is digital watermarks. Similar to watermarks on fine paper, which indicate the maker of the paper, **digital watermarks** are unique identifiers that are imbedded in the digital content. Although they do not prevent an individual from making illegal copies, they do make it possible to identify pirated works. If a pirated copy is placed on the Internet, then sophisticated search programs, such as Digimarc's MarSpider, can be used to locate the illegal copies and notify the rightful owner. (For details on copyright protection methods, see Piva et al. 2001 and Cherry 2002.)

trademark
A symbol used by businesses to identify their goods and services; government registration of the trademark confers exclusive legal right to its use.

TRADEMARKS

A **trademark** is a symbol used by businesses to identify their goods and services. The symbol can be composed of words, designs, letters, numbers, shapes, a combination of colors, or other such identifiers. Trademarks need to be registered in a country in order to be protected by law. To be eligible for registration, a trademark must be distinctive, original, and not deceptive. Once registered, a trademark lasts forever, as long as a periodic registration fee is paid.

The owner of a registered trademark has exclusive rights to:

▶ Use the trademark on goods and services for which the trademark is registered

▶ Take legal action to prevent anyone else from using the trademark without consent on goods and services (identical or similar) for which the trademark is registered

On the Internet, fake brand names and products can be sold or auctioned from anywhere. In the United States, the Federal Dilution Act of 1995 protects famous trademarks from dilution (trademarks preempt domain names). Trademark infringement carries criminal liabilities. In particular, it is a crime for anyone to fraudulently use a registered trademark, including the selling and importing of goods bearing an infringing trademark, and to use or possess equipment for forging registered trademarks. For example, in 1998, Playboy was able to shut down an adult Web site that was using the Playboy trademark.

Domain Names

A variation of a trademark is a domain name. As explained in Chapter 16, a *domain name* refers to the upper category of an Internet address (URL), such as prenhall.com or oecd.org. Two controversies surround domain names. One is whether additional (new) top-level domain names (similar to .com, .org, and .gov) should be added. The other is the use of trademarked names that belong to other companies as domain names. In November 2000, the Internet's governing body on Web site names approved the following top-level names: .biz, .info, .name, .pro, .museum, .aero, and .coop. (For an overview, see Froomkin 2001.)

Network Solutions, Inc. At the heart of the controversies is Network Solutions, Inc. (NSI), a subsidiary of VeriSign, which has been contracted by the U.S. government to assign domain addresses. Until 1998, NSI exclusively assigned domain names for several top levels: .com, .net, .gov, .edu, and .org. The United States, as well as the rest of the world, had been subject to NSI for domain names, and critics in Europe and elsewhere were ready to relieve the United States of that responsibility. Europe was weary of the United States assuming the right to direct Internet governance, effectively subjecting the Internet to U.S. law.

On June 1, 1998, the monopoly of NSI over domain names ended. NSI created a registration system that it shares with several other competing companies. The new registration system is handled by ICANN, an international nonprofit corporation. Instilling competition in the registration system has caused the price of registration to drop.

The Council of Registrars (CORE), a European private-sector group, and the Global Internet Project, a U.S. private-sector group, want to increase the number of top-level names. One of the objectives is to create an adult-only top-level name that will prevent pornographic material from getting into the hands of children.

Domain name disputes and resolutions. Both CORE and the Global Internet Project also want to repair the disputes over domain names. Companies are using trade names of other companies as their domain address to help attract traffic to their Web site. For example, DC Comics is suing Brainiac Services, Inc. for using one of its comic book names, Brainiac. Private-sector groups will have to resolve this issue in the future before more lawsuits begin to surface. Major disputes are international in scope, because the same corporate name may be used in different countries by different corporations. (A guide to domain names, by the U.S. Patent and Trademark Office, is available at uspto.gov/web/offices/tac/notices/guide299.htm.)

In order to avoid legal battles, the Internet community created a speedy way to resolve domain name disputes using *arbitration*. A new domain name dispute resolution procedure was adopted on January 1, 2000, for domain name addresses ending in .com, .net, and .org. Three arbitration organizations have been given the authority to make determinations regarding domain name disputes. They are Disputes.org Consortium, the National Arbitration Forum, and the WIPO. If one of these organizations makes a determination regarding a domain name dispute, NSI/ICANN will respect the decision and will transfer the registration of the disputed domain name in accordance with the arbitration determination. One advantage of this new procedure is speed; it takes less than 45 days, compared to the months it used to take to resolve disputes through legal action. A core set of policies, rules, and procedures for dispute resolution under the three organizations is set forth in a document entitled "Rules for Uniform Domain Name Dispute Resolution Policy," which can be found through ICANN at icann.org/dndr/udrp/uniform-rules.htm.

Two interesting arbitration rulings follow:

▶ The World Wrestling Federation won the first ever ruling, against a California resident who filed for the name worldwreslingfederation.com.

▶ Penguin Books was denied the name penguin.org. The name (which is not now in use) was given instead to a person who was known by the nickname Mr. Penguin.

In addition to the resolution of disputes by submission to arbitration, a legal action can also be initiated in various jurisdictions. Legal action provides a more potent protection, because in addition to an organization's winning the right to use a certain domain name, courts can also grant monetary damages and enforce specific *anticybersquatting* legislation, discussed next. For more on domain names and resolutions, visit verisign.com.

cybersquatting

The practice of registering domain names in order to sell them later at a higher price.

Cybersquatting. Cybersquatting refers to the practice of registering domain names in order to sell them later at a higher price. The Consumer Protection Act of 1999 is aimed at cybersquatters who register Internet domain names of famous companies or people and hold them hostage for "ransom" payments from the person or company. Companies such as Christian Dior, Nike, Deutsche Bank, and even Microsoft had to fight or pay to get the domain name that corresponds to their company's name. In the case of tom.com, the original owner of the tom.com domain name received about $8 million for the name from a large media company in Hong Kong that changed its name to Tom.com to correspond to the URL. In this case, the sale was judged both ethical and legal. However, in other cases, cybersquatting can be either illegal, or at least unethical (e.g., see Stead and Gilbert 2001). (For an overview of cybersquatting, see Rupp and Parrish 2002.)

In the past, several private individuals were given the right by the governing bodies of the Internet to use Web site (domain) names that involved trademarked names. For example, in 1998 a New Jersey dealer named Russell Boyd applied for and was given the rights to 50 domain names, including juliaroberts.com and alpacino.com. He then proceeded to auction the names on eBay. In that same year, Julia Roberts complained to WIPO. In the summer of 2000, WIPO's Complaint and Arbitration Center, which coordinates international patents, copyrights, and trademarks, upheld the actress's claim. It ruled that Boyd had no rights to the domain name juliaroberts.com even though the actress by that name was not using it at that time. The same is true for madonna.com. The Anticybersquatting Consumer Protection Act of 1999 lets trademark owners sue for statutory damages.

PATENTS

patent

A document that grants the holder exclusive rights on an invention for a fixed number of years.

A **patent** is a document that grants the holder exclusive rights on an invention for a fixed number of years (e.g., 17 years in the United States and 20 years in the United Kingdom). Patents serve to protect tangible technological inventions, especially in traditional industrial areas. They are not designed to protect artistic or literary creativity. Patents confer monopoly rights to an idea or an invention, regardless of how it may be expressed. An invention may be in the form of a physical device or a method or process for making a physical device.

Thousands of IT-related patents have been granted over the years. Examples of EC patents given to Open Market Corp., for example, are Internet Server Access Control and Monitoring (patent 5708780), Network Sales Systems (5715314), and Digital Active Advertising (5724424). Juno Online Services received an interactive ad patent (5809242). IBM has many patents, including 5870717, a system for ordering from electronic catalogs, and 5926798, a system for using intelligent agents to perform online commerce.

Certain patents granted in the United States deviate from established practices in Europe. For example, Amazon.com has successfully obtained a U.S. patent on its One-Click ordering procedure. Using this patent, Amazon.com sued Barnes and Noble in 1999 and in 2000, alleging that its rival had copied its patented technology. Barnes and Noble was enjoined by the courts from using the procedure. Similarly, in 1999, Priceline.com filed a suit against Expedia.com alleging that Expedia was using Priceline's patented reverse auction business model. The suit was settled on January 9, 2001, when Expedia.com agreed to pay Priceline.com royalties for use of the model. However, in Europe and many Asian, African, and South American countries, it is almost impossible to obtain patents on business methods or computer processes. For more on the relationship between copyrights and patents, see Burk (2001).

FAN AND HATE SITES

Fan and hate Web sites are part of the Internet self-publishing phenomena that includes *blogging* (see Chapter 9). Fan sites may interfere with intellectual property. For example, some people get advanced copies of new movies or TV programs and create sites that compete with the formal sites of the movie or TV producer. Although the producers can get a court order to close such sites, new sites can appear the next day. Although the intention of the fans may be good, they may cause damage to the creators of the intellectual property.

Hate Web sites can cause problems for corporations as well. Many hate sites are directed against large corporations (e.g., Wal-Mart, Microsoft, Nike). Associated with hate sites is the idea of **cyberbashing**, or *cybergriping*, which is the registration of a domain name that criticizes an organization or person (e.g., chasebanksucks.com, sucks500.com, or even bushsucks.com). As long as the sites contain only legitimate gripes that are not libelous, defaming, or threatening, they are allowed to operate (see Rupp and Parrish 2002 for details). (Note that the freedom of expression guaranteed in the U.S. Constitution has, thus far, allowed sites such as the third one cited here.)

cyberbashing
The registration of a domain name that criticizes an organization or person.

According to Kopp and Suter (2001), material published on fan sites, hate sites, and newsgroups may violate the copyrights of the creators or distributors of intellectual property. This issue shows the potential collision between protection of intellectual property and free speech.

Section 17.3 ▶ REVIEW

1. List three types of intellectual property.
2. List the legal rights covered by a copyright.
3. What is the purpose of a digital watermark?
4. List the legal rights of a trademark owner.
5. Describe domain name issues and solutions.
6. Define patents.
7. Distinguish between cybersquatting and cyberbashing.

17.4 FREE SPEECH VERSUS CENSORSHIP AND OTHER LEGAL ISSUES

Several surveys indicate that the issue of censorship is one of the most important to Web surfers. Censorship usually ranks as the number one or number two concern in Europe and the United States; privacy is the other main issue (e.g., see the GVU User Surveys at gvu.gatech.edu/user_surveys/). On the Internet, *censorship* refers to government's attempt to control, in one way or another, material that is broadcasted.

At a symposium on free speech in the information age, Parker Donham (1994) defined his own edict, entitled "Donham's First Law of Censorship." This semiserious precept states: "Most citizens are implacably opposed to censorship in any form—except censorship of whatever they personally happen to find offensive" (Virginia Tech 1997).

Take, for example, the question, "How much access should children have to Web sites, newsgroups, and chat rooms containing 'inappropriate' or 'offensive' materials, and who should control this access?" This is one of the most hotly debated issues between the advocates of censorship and the proponents of free speech. The proponents of free speech contend that there should be no government restrictions on Internet content and that parents should be responsible for monitoring and controlling their children's travels on the Web. The advocates of censorship feel that government legislation is required to protect children from offensive material.

The Children's Online Protection Act (COPA) exemplifies the protection approach. Passed in 1998, this law required, among other things, that companies verify a viewer's age before showing online material that is deemed "harmful to minors" and that parental consent is required before personal information can be collected from a minor. The fact that the Act was ruled unconstitutional illustrates how hard it is to craft legislation that abridges freedom of speech in the United States. The fate of a modified Children's Internet Protection Act, which was ruled unconstitutional in Pennsylvania in 2001, is now in the hands of the U.S. Supreme Court.

In addition to concern for children, there is also a concern about hate sites (e.g., see Kopp and Suter 2001), about defamation of character, and about other offensive material. On December 10, 2002, in a landmark case, Australia's highest court gave a businessman the right to sue in Australia for defamation over an article published in the United States and posted on the Internet. This reasoning basically equates the Net to any other published material. The publisher, Dow Jones & Co., said that it will defend those sued in a jurisdiction (Australia) that is far removed from the country in which the article was prepared (the United States).

The advocates of censorship also believe that it is the responsibility of ISPs to control the content of the data and information that flow across their networks and computers. The difficulty is that ISPs have no easy way of monitoring the content or determining the age of the person viewing the content. The only way to control "offensive" content is to block it from children and adults alike. This is the approach that AOL has taken, for instance, in blocking sites pandering to hate crime and serial killer enthusiasts.

CONTROLLING SPAM

spamming

The practice of indiscriminately broadcasting messages over the Internet (e.g., junk mail).

As discussed elsewhere in this book, **spamming** refers to the practice of indiscriminately broadcasting messages over the Internet (e.g., junk mail and pop-up screens). One major piece of U.S. legislation addressing marketing practices in EC is the Electronic Mailbox Protection Act, passed in 1997. The primary thrust of this law is that commercial speech is subject to government regulation, and secondly, that spamming, which can cause significant harm, expense, and annoyance, should be controlled.

At some of the largest ISPs, spam now comprises 25 to 50 percent of all e-mail (Black 2002). This volume significantly impairs an already-limited bandwidth, slowing down the Internet in general and, in some cases, shutting down ISPs completely. The Electronic Mailbox Protection Act requires those sending spam to identify it as advertising, to indicate the name of the sender prominently, and to include valid routing information. Recipients may waive the right to receive such information. Also, ISPs are required to offer spam-blocking software, and recipients of spam have the right to request termination of future spam from the same sender and to bring civil action if necessary.

Chapter 5 discussed the issue of spamming and provided an example of how spamming is controlled in Korea with very strict legislation. Similar legislation is pending in several other countries at the time of the writing of this book. For example, a bill is pending in the U.S. House of Representatives that seeks to control spamming.

OTHER LEGAL ISSUES

Privacy, intellectual property, and censorship receive a great deal of publicity because consumers easily understand them. However, there are numerous other legal issues related to EC and the Internet. These usually arise as new situations come up, and they must be worked out in courts of law and in legislatures—a time-consuming process. One such issue, for example, is whether a company can link into a Web site without permission. See the story of Ticketmaster versus Microsoft provided online in EC Application Case W17.1.

Some of these EC legal issues are summarized in Exhibit 17.1 (page 656). A few of them will be discussed in more detail here.

Electronic Contracts

A legally binding contract requires a few basic elements: offer, acceptance, and consideration. However, these requirements are difficult to establish when the human element in the processing of the transaction is removed and the contracting is performed electronically. For example, Web site development agreements can be very complex.

The Uniform Electronic Transactions Act of 1999 seeks to extend existing provisions for contract law to cyberlaw by establishing uniform and consistent definitions for electronic records, digital signatures, and other electronic communications. This Act is a procedural one that provides the means to effect transactions accomplished through an electronic medium. The language purposefully refrains from addressing questions of substantive law, leaving this to the scope of the Uniform Commercial Code (UCC).

The UCC is a comprehensive body of law regarding business conduct. An amendment to the UCC is Article 2B, which is designed to build upon existing law by providing a government code that supports existing and future electronic technologies in the exchange of goods or services. This law was approved in 1999 and enacted in 2000. It is one of the more significant EC legal developments.

Shrink-wrap agreements or *box-top licenses* appear in or on a package that contains software. The user is bound to the license by opening the package, even though the user has not yet used the product or even read the agreement. This has been a point of contention for some time. The U.S. Court of Appeals for the Seventh Circuit (in ruling No. 96-1139) felt that providing information such as warranties or handling instructions *inside* the package would provide more benefit to the consumer, given the limited space available on the exterior of the package. The *ProCD v. Zeidenberg* case (June 1996) supported the validity of shrink-wrap agreements when the court ruled in favor of the plaintiff, ProCD.

Click-wrap contracts are an extension of this ruling. These are contracts derived entirely over the Internet. The software vendor offers to sell or license the use of the software according to the terms accompanying the software. The buyer agrees to be bound by the terms based on certain conduct; usually that conduct is retaining the product for a sufficient time to review the terms and return of the software if unacceptable.

In fall 2000, the Electronic Signatures in Global and National Commerce Act was approved. This federal law gives contracts signed online the same legal status as a contract signed with pen on paper. Similar laws have been enacted in several European and Asian countries.

Intelligent agents and contracts. Article 2B of the Uniform Computer Information Transactions Act passed in October 2000, makes clear that contracts can be formed even when no human involvement is present. It states that a contract is formed if the interaction of electronic agents results in operations that confirm the existence of a contract or indicate agreement. Further, such a contract can be made by interaction between an individual and an electronic agent, or even between two electronic agents, even if no individual was aware of or reviewed the actions. The Act recognizes that counteroffers are ineffectual against electronic agents (which is one limitation of e-commerce), and so it provides that a contract is formed if an individual takes action that causes an electronic agent to perform or promise benefits to the individual. The basic idea is that if an individual sets electronic agents to work, the contract is valid, and (of course) that individual is responsible for the outcome.

The Uniform Electronic Transactions Act (UETA) includes the following two provisions: (1) that electronic records do satisfy the requirement for a contract and (2) that an electronic signature is enforceably equal to a written signature on a paper contract.

Gambling

Methods of wagering can be found all over the Internet. For example, the World Sports Exchange (wsex.com) advertises, "If you can use a mouse, you can place a wager." Ostensibly located in Antigua, where gaming is legal, not only has this site shown the ease of wagering,

EXHIBIT 17.1 Other EC Legal Issues

Issue	Description
E-filings in court	Litigation means a large quantity of paper. Electronic filing of such documents is allowed in some courts (e.g., Manhattan Bankruptcy Court, New York).
Evidence	Some electronic documents can be used as evidence in court. The State of New York, for example, allows e-mails to be used as evidence.
Jurisdiction	Ability to sue in other states or countries. Whose jurisdiction prevails when litigants are in different states or countries? Who can sue for Internet postings done in other countries?
Liability	The use of multiple networks and trading partners makes the documentation of responsibility difficult. How can liability for errors, malfunctions, or fraudulent use of data be determined?
Defamation	Is the ISP liable for material published on the Internet in services they provide or support? (usually not)
Identity fraud	The Identity, Theft, and Assumption Deference Act of 1998 makes identity fraud a federal felony (3- to 25-year prison sentence).
Computer crime	The Information Infrastructure Protection Act (IIP Act, 1996) protects information in all computers.
Digital signature	Digital signatures are now recognized as legal in the United States and some other countries, but not in all countries (see Chapter 12).
Regulation of consumer databases	The United States allows compilation and selling of customer databases; the European Union Directive on Data Protection prohibits this practice.
Encryption technology	Export of U.S. encryption technology was made legal in 1999 (countries restricted from export are Iran, Iraq, Syria, Sudan, North Korea, and Cuba).
Time and place	An electronic document signed in Japan on January 5 may have the date January 4 in Los Angeles. Which date is considered legal if disputes arise?
Location of files and data	Much of the law hinges on the physical location of files and data. With distributed and replicated databases, it is difficult to say exactly where data are stored at any given time.
Electronic contracts	If all of the elements to establish a contract are present, an electronic contract is valid and enforceable.
E-communications privacy	Electronic Communications Privacy Act (ECPA) makes it illegal to access stored e-mail as well as e-mail in transmission.
IPOs online	Web sites posted with the necessary information about the securities offerings are considered a legal channel for selling stock in a corporation.
Antitrust	*U.S. vs. Microsoft* found (1) Microsoft used predatory and anticompetitive conduct to illegally maintain the monopoly in Windows OS; (2) Microsoft illegally attempted to monopolize the market for Internet browsing software; and, (3) Microsoft illegally bundled its Web browser with Windows OS, engaging in a tying arrangement in violation of the Sherman Act.
Taxation	Taxation of sales transactions by states is on hold in the United States and some (not all) countries, but the issue will be revived. An additional issue is whether (and how) taxes can be collected from online gamblers' winnings.
Money laundering	How can money laundering be prevented when the value of the money is in the form of a smart card? (Japan limits the value of money on a smart card to about $5,000; other countries such as Singapore and Hong Kong set even lower limits.)
Corporate reporting	Online corporate reports are difficult to audit because they can be changed frequently, and auditors may not have time to perform with due diligence. How should auditing of online reports be conducted? What legal value does it have?

Sources: Compiled from Alberts et al. (1998), Burnett (2001), Cheeseman (2001), Guernsey (2001), and Mykytyn (2002).

it has made it their slogan. At the site, an account can be established by wiring or electronically transferring funds; even sending a check will establish an electronic gaming account. This account is used to fund a variety of available wagers on all types of sporting events that can be viewed and transacted online. The issue is that anyone that travels physically to Antigua can play there legally. But what about electronic travel from places where gambling is illegal?

In the United Sates, gaming commissions have had a tough time regulating gambling laws in Nevada, on Indian reservations, in offshore casinos, in sports bars, and other places where gambling is legal. Technology makes this effort all the more difficult to monitor and enforce because the individuals abusing the rules have at least the same level of sophistication available as the law enforcement officials; in many cases, they are even better equipped. The ease and risk of online wagering is evidenced by many recent cases of individuals losing their life savings without understanding the implications of what they are doing on their home PCs.

Online casinos have all of the inherent dangers of physical gaming houses, with the added risk of accessibility by minors or individuals of diminished capacity who may financially injure themselves without the constraints otherwise found in a physical environment. As is the case with most issues in cyberspace, self-regulation may be the best policy.

However, given the sometimes-addictive nature of gambling, legal steps have also been taken. The Internet Gambling Prohibition Act of 1999 was established to make online wagering illegal except for minimal amounts. The Act provides criminal and civil remedies against individuals making online bets or wagers and those in the business of offering online betting or wagering venues. Additionally, it gives U.S. district courts original and exclusive jurisdiction to prevent and restrain violations, and it subjects ISPs to the duties of common carriers (telecommunications carriers such as AT&T, Verizon, etc.). The impact of this legislation is to make ISPs "somewhat" liable for illegal currency movements and for reportable transactions requiring documentation by the carriers.

According to the Australian Internet Industry Association (AIIA; 2001), the Communication Ministry is looking favorably on imposing a total ban on interactive gambling in Australia through the use of filtering technology. The attempt is to block Australian Internet users from accessing gaming sites. At present (2003), there is a moratorium on *new* interactive gaming only. Although the AIIA campaigns against the ban, many politicians support it. Civil liberties groups in Australia, as in many other countries, oppose any Internet filtering.

Related to the control of gambling is the tax on winners' profits. Because it is now illegal to charge sales tax on Internet transactions, should sales taxes (or VAT taxes) be paid on electronic winnings? If so, to whom would they be paid? How would they be collected? Despite all of the legal issues, online gambling is mushrooming (King 2003).

TAXING BUSINESS ON THE INTERNET

As just mentioned, another controversial issue in EC is taxation. This issue is extremely important because it is related to global EC as well as to fairness in competition when EC competes with off-line marketing channels and conventional mail order, which requires the collection of taxes. It also is an important issue due to the large volume of online trade that is forecast for the next decade. EC transactions are multiplying at an exponential rate, and the $2.64 trillion forecasted for 2004 (Keenan 2000) means lots of potential sales tax. Cities, states, and countries all want a piece of the pie. (For an overview of Internet taxation, see Vijayasarathy 2001.)

The Taxation Exemption Debate

The Internet Tax Freedom Act passed the U.S. Senate on October 8, 1998. This Act sought to promote e-commerce through tax incentives, by barring any new state or local sales taxes on Internet transactions until October 2001. (Note that this law dealt only with *sales* tax, and *not* with federal or state *income* taxes that Internet companies must pay.) Similar acts exist in several other countries, including Hong Kong. This Act also carried an amendment known as the Children's Online Privacy Protection Act, which was added in an effort to prevent extension of tax benefits to pornographers. The Act also created a special commission to study Internet taxation issues and recommend new policies. In April 2000, the special commission recommended the following to the U.S. Congress:

- Eliminate the 3 percent federal excise tax on telecommunications services.
- Extend the current moratorium on multiple or discriminatory taxation of EC through 2006.
- Prohibit taxation of digitized goods sold over the Internet.
- Make permanent the current moratorium on Internet access taxes.
- Establish nexus standards for U.S. businesses engaged in interstate commerce—rules that would spell out whether the use of a Web server in Indiana, for example, gives an Internet company based in New Jersey "nexus" in Indiana, where residents are subject to sales taxes.
- Place the burden on states to simplify their own telecommunications, sales, and use tax systems.
- Clarify state authority to use federal welfare money to give poor people more Internet access.
- Provide tax incentives and federal matching funds to states to encourage public–private partnerships to get low-income families online.
- Respect and protect consumer privacy.
- Continue to press for a moratorium on international tariffs on electronic transmissions over the Internet.

The U.S. Congress extended the tax moratorium until 2006, giving it time to digest the contents of the report and hash out contentious tax issues. State and local governments (which depend on sales tax revenues) and traditional brick-and-mortar retailers (which compete against e-tailers) generally want to tax EC. Internet companies, antitax advocates, and many politicians champion keeping the Internet tax free.

The taxation issues, which involve 30,000 state and local jurisdictions in the United States, in addition to the innumerable international jurisdictions, will add numerous volumes to an already complex tax code. Applying existing law to this new medium of exchange is far more difficult than ever imagined. The global nature of business today suggests that cyberspace be considered a *distinct tax zone* unto itself, with unique rules and considerations befitting the stature of the online environment.

This is, in fact, what has occurred. The moratorium on taxation of Internet transactions is a fine temporary solution where no precedent exists; however, longer-range strategies must be developed quickly. Some complicating factors must be considered. For example, several tax jurisdictions may be involved in a single transaction, not only on a domestic level but internationally. The implications of such involvement are tremendous; the identity of the parties involved and transaction verification is frequently a problem. The probabilities for tax evasion also are potentially large. Tax havens and offshore banking facilities will become more accessible. Singapore has passed a law to establish itself as a legal and financial safe haven for the rest of the world for the EC industry, similar to Swiss banks' role in the off-line financial industry.

Arguments continue to rage over tax-free policies. Some say that tax-free policies give online businesses an unfair advantage. For instance, some argue that Internet phone services should be exempt from paying access charges to local telephone companies for use of their networks. In their effort to avoid sales taxes, Internet merchants like to point to the difficulty of tracking who should be paid what. The opposition argues that the same is true for telephone transactions, so existing laws should suffice. The same opposition asks, "Should EC business be allowed to operate without taxing consumers, while regular telephone companies cannot?"

Non-EC industries feel that Internet businesses must pay their fair share of the tax bill for the nation's social and physical infrastructure. They feel that the Internet industries are not pulling their own weight. These companies are screaming that the same situation exists in the mail-order business, for which some sales tax laws *have* been established, and that there are sufficient parallels to warrant similar legal considerations. In fact, in many states,

EC has already been treated the same as mail-order businesses. Others suggest simply applying the established sales tax laws. "You've got a tax structure in place—it's called sales tax," said Bill McKiernan, chairman and CEO of Cybersource.com, "Just apply that to Internet transactions" (Nelson 1998).

Proposed Taxation Solutions in the United States

The National Governors' Association, the National League of Cities, and the U.S. Conference of Mayors fought the Tax Free Bill for the Internet. The National Governors' Association estimates that by 2003, state and local governments will lose between $10 and $20 billion in tax revenues on difficult-to-control, mail-order sales to out-of-state merchants and customers (Gordon-Murnane 2000). They figure that more is lost through EC sales and are suggesting that the IRS might "come to the rescue" with a single and simplified national sales tax. That would reduce 30,000 different tax codes to "no more than 50." Internet sales would be taxed at the same rate as mail-order or Main Street transactions. Although states could set their own rate, each sale could be taxed only once. The details of Internet taxation would be settled by a panel of industry and government officials.

For discussion of services that compute sales tax, see Chapter 13. To calculate international tax levies on European Union sales, see europa.eu.int.

Section 17.4 ▶ REVIEW

1. Describe the conflict between free speech and the right to present offensive material on the Internet.
2. What is spamming?
3. Describe the Electronic Mailbox Protection Act.
4. Describe the issues related to electronic contracting.
5. Why is it difficult to control online gambling?
6. Discuss the issues relating to Internet taxation.

17.5 EC FRAUD AND CONSUMER AND SELLER PROTECTION

When buyers and sellers cannot see each other and may even be in different countries, chances are high that dishonest people might commit all types of fraud and other crimes over the Internet. During the first few years of EC, many types of crime came to light, ranging from manipulation of stocks on the Internet to the creation of a virtual bank that disappeared together with the investors' deposits. This section is divided into the following parts: Internet fraud, consumer protection (including automatic authentication), and seller's protection.

FRAUD ON THE INTERNET

Internet fraud and its sophistication have grown even faster than the Internet itself. The following examples demonstrate the scope of the problem.

Online auction fraud. Internet auction fraud accounts for 87 percent of all incidents of online crime, according to eMarketer (reported by Saliba 2001). (See Chapter 11 for discussion of the problem and remedies.)

Internet stock fraud. In fall 1998, the U.S. Securities and Exchange Commission (SEC) brought charges against 44 companies and individuals who illegally promoted stocks on computer bulletin boards, online newsletters, and investment Web sites. Details on both settled and pending cases can be found at sec.gov (1998). In most cases, stock promoters spread false positive rumors about the prospects of the companies they touted. In other cases, the information provided might have been true, but the promoters did not disclose that they were paid to talk up the companies. Stock promoters specifically target small investors who are lured to the promise of fast profit.

The following is a typical example. In November 1996, a federal judge agreed to freeze the assets of the chairman of a small company called SEXI (Systems of Excellence) and the proprietors of an Internet electronic newsletter called SGA Goldstar. The latter illegally received SEXI stocks in exchange for promoting the stock to unwary investors. As a result, SEXI stock jumped from $0.25 to $4.75, at which time the proprietors dumped the shares (called a "pump-and-dump" scheme). Cases like this, as well as ones involving nonregistered securities, are likely to increase because of the popularity of the Internet.

Other financial fraud. Stocks are only one of many areas where swindlers are active. Other areas include the sale of bogus investments, phantom business opportunities, and other schemes (see Bloomberg News 2001). With the use of the Internet, financial criminals now have access to far more people, mainly due to the availability of e-mail. An example of a multi-billion-dollar international financial fraud is provided in EC Application Case 17.2. In addition, foreign currency trading scams are increasing on the Internet because most online currency-exchange shops are not licensed (see Commodity Futures Trading Commission 2001).

Other fraud in EC. Many nonfinancial types of fraud also exist on the Internet. For example, customers may receive poor-quality products and services, may not get products in time, may be asked to pay for things they assume will be paid for by sellers, and much more.

Buyers can protect against EC fraud in several ways. The major methods are described next.

CONSUMER PROTECTION

Buyer protection is critical to the success of any commerce, especially electronic, where buyers do not see sellers. The FTC enforces consumer protection laws in the United States (see ftc.gov). The FTC provides a list of 12 scams labeled the "dirty dozen" (the name of a famous movie) that are most likely to arrive by bulk e-mail (see ftc.gov/bcp/conline/pubs/alerts/doznalrt.htm). In addition, the European Union and the United States are attempting to develop joint consumer protection policies. For details, see tacd.org/about/about.htm. For more about the FTC and Internet scams, see Teodoro (2001).

CASE 17.2
EC Application
FINANCIAL FRAUD ON THE INTERNET

David Lee, a 41-year-old Hong Kong resident, replied to an advertisement in a respected business magazine that offered him free investment advice. When he replied, he received impressive brochures and a telephone sales speech. Then he was directed to the Web site of Equity Mutual Trust (Equity), from which he was able to track the impressive daily performance of a fund that listed offices in London, Switzerland, and Belize. From that Web site, he was linked to sister funds and business partners. He monitored what he believed were independent Web sites that provided high ratings on the funds. Finally, he was directed to read about Equity and its funds in the respected *International Herald Tribune*'s Internet edition; the article appeared to be a news items but was actually an advertisement.

Convinced that he would receive good short-term gains, Lee mailed US$16,000, instructing Equity to invest in the Grand Financial Fund. Soon he grew suspicious when letters from Equity came from different countries, telephone calls and e-mails were not answered on time, and the daily Internet listings dried up.

When Lee wanted to sell, he was advised to increase his investment and shift to a Canadian company, Mit-Tec,

allegedly a Y2K-bug troubleshooter. The Web site he was directed to looked fantastic. However, this time Lee was more careful. He contacted the financial authorities in the Turks and Caicos Islands—where Equity was based at that time—and was referred to the British police.

Soon he learned that chances were slim that he would ever see his money again. Furthermore, he learned that several thousand victims had paid billions of dollars to Equity. Most of the victims live in Hong Kong, Singapore, and other Asian countries. Several said that the most convincing information came from the Web sites, including the seemingly "independent" Web sites that rated Equity and its funds.

Source: *South China Morning Post* (1999).

Questions

1. How can such a large-scale crime go undetected for months? Speculate on the reasons.

2. What advice would you give to people looking for investment opportunities on the Internet?

Tips for safe electronic shopping include the following:

▶ Users should make sure that they enter the real Web site of well-known companies such as Wal-Mart Online, Disney Online, and Amazon.com (by going directly to the site, rather than through a link) and shop for reliable brand names at those sites.

▶ Search any unfamiliar site for an address and telephone and fax numbers. Call and quiz a person about the seller.

▶ Check out the seller with the local chamber of commerce, Better Business Bureau (bbbonline.org), or TRUSTe (described later).

▶ Investigate how secure the seller's site is and how well it is organized.

▶ Examine the money-back guarantees, warranties, and service agreements before making a purchase.

▶ Compare prices online to those in regular stores—too-low prices may be too good to be true.

▶ Ask friends what they know. Find testimonials and endorsements.

▶ Find out what redress is available in case of a dispute.

▶ Consult the National Fraud Information Center (fraud.org).

▶ Check the resources available at consumerworld.org.

In addition to these tips, consumers also have shopper's rights on the Internet, as described in see Insights and Additions 17.1 (page 662).

For information on consumer protection in the European Union, see McDonald (2000).

Third-Party Assurance Services

Several public organizations and private companies attempt to protect consumers. The following are just a few examples.

TRUSTe's "Trustmark." TRUSTe (truste.org) is a nonprofit group whose mission is to build users' trust and confidence in the Internet by promoting the policies of disclosure and informed consent. Sellers who become members of TRUSTe can add value and increase consumer confidence in online transactions by displaying the TRUSTe Advertising Affiliate "Trustmark" (a seal of quality). This mark identifies sites that have agreed to comply with responsible information-gathering guidelines. In addition, the TRUSTe Web site provides for its members a "privacy policy wizard," which is aimed at helping companies create their own privacy policies. The site offers four types of seals: privacy, children, e-health, and safe harbor (in May 2003).

The TRUSTe program is voluntary. The licensing fee for use of the Trustmark ranges from $500 to $5,000, depending on the size of the online organization and the sensitivity of the information it is collecting. By the end of 2002, more than 1,500 Web sites were certified as TRUSTe participants, including AT&T, CyberCash, Excite, IBM, America Online, Buena Vista Internet Group, CNET, GeoCities, Infoseek, Lycos, Netscape, the *New York Times*, and Yahoo (TRUSTe 2003). However, there still seems to be fear that signing with TRUSTe could expose firms to litigation from third parties if they fail to live up to the letter of the TRUSTe pact, and that fear is likely to deter some companies from signing up.

How well can TRUSTe and others protect your privacy? According to Rafter (2000), there are continuous violations of privacy by companies carrying the TRUSTe seal.

Better Business Bureau. The Better Business Bureau (BBB), a private nonprofit organization supported largely by membership, provides reports on business firms that are helpful to consumers before making a purchase. The BBB responds to millions of such inquiries each year. Its BBBOnLine program (bbbonline.com) is similar to TRUSTe's Trustmark. The goal of the program is to promote confidence on the Internet through two different seals. Companies that meet the BBBOnLine standards for the Reliability Seal are members of the local BBB and have good truth-in-advertising and consumer service practices. Those that exhibit the BBBOnLine Privacy Seal on their Web sites have an online privacy protection policy and standards for handling personal information of consumers. In addition, consumers are able to click on the BBBOnLine seals and instantly get a BBB report on the participating company.

Insights and Additions 17.1   Internet Shopping Rights

Although the Web offers new ways to shop, users can still benefit from legal protections developed for shopping by telephone, mail, and other means. The two most important consumer protection laws for online shopping come from the U.S. government: the Mail/Telephone Order Rule and the Fair Credit Billing Act.

Mail/Telephone (E-Mail) Order Rule

Sellers must deliver goods within a certain time period or face penalties from the FTC. If the seller advertises or tells a buyer a delivery date before a purchase, the item must be delivered by that date. If the seller does not give the buyer a delivery date, the seller must deliver the item within 30 days after receiving the order.

If the seller cannot deliver by the required date, it must give the buyer notice before that date, so that the buyer can either choose to cancel the order and receive a full and prompt refund or permit the seller to deliver at a later date. If delivery problems continue, consumers should see the resources at the end of this feature for additional rights and how to make a complaint.

Fair Credit Billing Act

Using a credit card on the Web is like using it at a store. The Fair Credit Billing Act gives buyers certain rights if there is an error or dispute relating to a bill. If there is an error on a consumer's statement, the consumer can withhold payment for the disputed amount while they notify the creditor. The consumer also can withhold payment when a bill contains a charge for the wrong amount, for items that were returned or not accepted, or for items not delivered as agreed.

Creditors should be notified of errors promptly, no later than 60 days after the first bill on which the error appeared. All correspondence should be in writing. The consumer should describe the error clearly and include their name, address, and credit card number. After sending the notice, the creditor must give written acknowledgment that the notice was received within 30 days and must resolve the error within 90 days.

New Payment Methods

A word of caution: Although consumer protections for traditional credit cards are well established, the protections for those who use new forms of "digital payment"—such as digital cash and the like—are unclear. Some of the forms of payment resemble credit cards; others resemble ATM cards; still others are brand-new forms of payment. Check the resources at the end of this feature for the latest information on new regulations that may help protect consumers using these payment methods.

Resources for Further Information

▶ U.S. FTC (*ftc.gov*), click on "complaint form"
▶ Abusive e-mail should be forwarded to *uce@fte.gov*
▶ National Fraud Information Center (*fraud.org*)
▶ Consumer Information Center (*pueblo.gsa.gov*)
▶ U.S. Department of Justice (*usdoj.gov*)
▶ Direct Market Association (*the-dma.org*, telephone 202–347–1222 for advice)
▶ Internet Fraud Complaint Center (*ifccfbi.gov/index.asp*), this FBI unit registers complaints online from consumers

Disclaimer: This is general information on consumer rights. It is not legal advice on how any particular individual should proceed. If you want legal advice, consult an attorney.

Source: Based on Rose (1997), p. 104.

WHICHonline. Supported by the EuropeanUnion, WHICHonline(which.net) gives consumers protection by ensuring that online traders under its Which?Web Trader Scheme abide by a code of proactive guidelines. These guidelines outline issues such as product information, advertising, ordering methods, prices, delivery of goods, consumer privacy, receipting, dispute resolution, and security.

Web Trust seal and others. Web Trust seal is a program similar to that offered by TRUSTe. It is sponsored by the American Institute of Certified Public Accountants (cpawebtrust.org). Another program, Gomez.com (gomez.com), monitors customer complaints and provides merchant certification.

Online Privacy Alliance. The Online Privacy Alliance is a diverse group of corporations and associations that lead and support self-regulatory initiatives which create an environment of trust and foster the protection of individuals' privacy online. They have guidelines for privacy policies, enforcement of self-regulation, and children's online activities. Major members are AT&T, Bell Atlantic, Compaq, Dell, IBM, Microsoft, NETCOM, AOL-Time Warner, and Yahoo. The Online Privacy Alliance supports third-party enforcement programs, such as the TRUSTe and BBB programs, because the symbol awarded by these programs signifies to consumers the use of a privacy policy that includes the elements articulated by the Online Privacy Alliance.

Evaluation by Consumers

A large number of sites include product and vendor evaluations offered by consumers. For example, Deja.com, now part of Google, is the home of many communities of interest whose members trade comments about products at groups.google.com/. In addition, epubliceye.com allows consumers to give feedback on reliability, privacy, and customer satisfaction. It makes available a company profile that measures a number of elements, including payment options.

Authentication and Biometric Controls

In cyberspace, buyers and sellers do not see each other. Even when videoconferencing is used, the authenticity of the person on the other end must be verified, unless the person has been dealt with before. However, if one can be assured of the identity of the person on the other end of the line, one can imagine improved and new EC applications: Students will be able to take exams online from any place, at any time, without the need for proctors. Fraud among recipients of government entitlements and transfer payments will be reduced to a bare minimum. Buyers will be assured who the sellers are, and sellers will know who the buyers are, with a very high degree of confidence. Arrangements can be made so that only authorized people in companies can place (or receive) purchasing orders. Interviews for employment and other matching applications will be accurate, because it will be almost impossible for imposters to represent other people. Overall, trust in online transactions and in EC in general will increase significantly.

As discussed in Chapter 12, the solution for such *authentication* is provided by information technologies known as *biometric controls*. Biometric controls provide access procedures that match every valid user with a *unique user identifier (UID)*. They also provide an authentication method that verifies that users requesting access to the computer system are really who they claim to be. Authentication and biometric controls are valid for both consumer and merchant protection.

SELLERS' PROTECTION

The Internet makes fraud by customers easier because of the ease of anonymity. Sellers must be protected against:

- Customers who deny that they placed an order
- Customers who download copyrighted software and/or knowledge and sell it to others
- Customers who give false payment (credit card) information in payment for products and services provided
- Use of their name by others
- Use of their unique words and phrases, names and slogans, and their Web address (trademark protection)

What Can Sellers Do?

As discussed in Chapter 13, the Web site nochargeback.com was a database of credit card numbers that had chargeback orders recorded against them. Sellers who are merchants and had access to the database could use this information to decide whether to proceed with a sale. In the future, the credit card industry is planning to use biometrics to deal with electronic shoplifting. Also, sellers can use PKI and digital certificates, especially the SET protocol, to help prevent fraud (see Chapter 12).

Other possible solutions include the following:

▶ Use intelligent software to identify possibly questionable customers (or doing this identification manually in small companies). One technique in such identification, for example, involves comparing credit card billing and requested shipping addresses.
▶ Identify warning signals for possibly fraudulent transactions. After writing off $4.1 million of uncollectible accounts receivable in May 2000, Expedia.com developed a list of such warning signals for its own use (Angwin 2000).
▶ Ask customers whose billing address is different from the shipping address to call their bank and have the alternate address added to their bank account. Retailers agree to ship the goods to the alternate address only if this is done.

For further discussion of what merchants can do to protect themselves from fraud, see Swisher (1998) and combatfraud.org. Also, third-party escrow and trust companies help to prevent fraud against both buyers and sellers.

Section 17.5 ▶ REVIEW

1. Why is there so much fraud on the Internet?
2. What types of fraud are most common?
3. Describe consumer protection measures.
4. Describe assurance services.

17.6 SOCIETAL ISSUES

At this point in the chapter, our attention turns to societal issues of EC. The first topic is one of concern to many—the digital divide.

THE DIGITAL DIVIDE

digital divide
The gap between those who have and those who do not have the ability to access electronic technology in general, and the Internet and EC in particular.

Despite the factors and trends that contribute to future EC growth, since the inception of technology in general and the Internet and e-commerce in particular, we have witnessed a gap between those who have and those who do not have the ability to use the technology (e.g., see Adams 2001; Venkat 2002). This gap is referred to as the **digital divide**. In 2000, about 9 out of 10 of all Internet hosts were located in developed countries, where only less than a fifth of the world's population resides (United Nations 2001). In 2001, the city of New York, for example, had more Internet hosts than the whole continent of Africa (Hoffman 2000).

The gap exists both *within* and *between* countries. The U.S. federal and state governments are attempting to close this gap (see ecommerce.gov) within the country by encouraging training and supporting education and infrastructure. The gap among countries, however, may be widening rather than narrowing. Many government and international organizations are trying to close the digital divide. (For more on the digital divide, see Compaine 2001; for strategies on how to close the divide, see Iyer et al. 2002.)

OTHER SOCIETAL ISSUES

Many other societal issues can be related to EC. Three are mentioned here in which EC has had a generally positive impact: education, public safety, and health. For more details on societal issues, see Mowshowitz (2002), Raghavan (2002), and Lubbe and Van Heerden (2003).

Education

E-commerce has had a major impact on education and learning, as described in Chapter 9. Virtual universities are helping to reduce the digital divide. Companies can use the Internet to retrain employees much more easily, enabling them to defer retirement if they so choose.

Home-bound individuals can get degrees from good institutions, and many vocational professions can be learned from home.

Public Safety and Criminal Justice

With increased concerns about public safety after September 11, many organizations and individuals have started to look at technologies that will help to deter, prevent, or detect early criminal activities of various types. Various e-commerce tools can help increase our safety at home and in public. These include the e-911 systems (described in Chapter 10 and by Fujimoto 2002); collaborative commerce (for collaboration among national and international law enforcement units); e-procurement (of unique equipment to fight crime); e-government efforts at coordinating, information sharing, and expediting legal work and cases; intelligent homes, offices, and public buildings; and e-training of law enforcement officers.

Health Aspects

Is EC a health risk? Generally speaking, it is probably safer and healthier to shop from home than to shop in a physical store. However, some believe that exposure to cellular mobile communication radiation may cause health problems (e.g., Lin 2001). It may take years before the truth of this claim is known. Even if communication radiation does cause health problems, the damage could be insignificant due to the small amount of time most people spend on wireless shopping and other wireless activities. However, given the concern of some about this issue, protective devices may soon be available that will solve this problem.

EC technologies such as collaborative commerce can help improve health care. For example, using the Internet, the approval process of new drugs has been shortened, saving lives and reducing suffering. Pervasive computing helps in the delivery of health care. Intelligent systems facilitate medical diagnoses. Health-care advice can be provided from a distance. Finally, intelligent hospitals (Weiss 2002), doctors (Landro 2002), and other health-care facilities use some of the tools of EC.

Section 17.6 ▶ REVIEW

1. Define the digital divide.
2. Describe how EC can improve education.
3. Describe how EC can improve safety and security.
4. Describe the impacts of EC on health services.

17.7 VIRTUAL (INTERNET) COMMUNITIES

A topic somewhat related to the societal impact of EC is Internet communities. A *community* is a group of people with some interest in common who interact with one another. A **virtual (Internet) community** is one in which the interaction takes place by using the Internet. Virtual communities parallel typical physical communities such as neighborhoods, clubs, or associations, but people do not meet face-to-face. Instead, they meet online. Virtual communities offer several ways for members to interact, collaborate, and trade (see Exhibit 17.2 on page 666). Similar to the click-and-mortar model, many *physical communities* have a Web site for Internet-related activities.

virtual (Internet) community
A group of people with similar interests who interact with one another using the Internet.

CHARACTERISTICS OF COMMUNITIES

Pure-play Internet communities may have thousands or even millions of members. This is one major difference from purely physical communities, which are usually smaller. Another difference is that off-line communities are frequently confined to one geographical location, whereas only a few online communities are geographically confined.

Many thousands of communities exist on the Internet. Several communities are independent and are growing rapidly. For instance, GeoCities grew to 10 million members in less than 2 years and had over 45 million members in 2002 (Geocities 2003). GeoCities members can set up personal homepages on the site, and advertisers buy ad space targeted to community

EXHIBIT 17.2 Elements of Interaction in a Virtual Community

Category	Element
Communication	Bulletin boards (discussion groups)
	Chat rooms/threaded discussions (string Q&A)
	E-mail and instant messaging
	Private mailboxes
	Newsletters, "netzines" (electronic magazines)
	Blogging
	Web postings
	Voting
Information	Directories and yellow pages
	Search engine
	Member-generated content
	Links to information sources
	Expert advice
EC element	Electronic catalogs and shopping carts
	Advertisements
	Auctions of all types
	Classified ads
	Bartering online

members. A number of examples of online communities are presented in Insights and Additions 17.2.

Virtual communities can be classified in several ways. One possibility is to classify members as *traders*, *players*, *just friends*, *enthusiasts*, or *friends in need*. The most common classification is the one proposed by Armstrong and Hagel (1996) and Hagel and Armstrong (1997). This classification recognizes the four types of Internet communities shown in Exhibit 17.3. (For a different, more complete classification, see that proposed by Schubert and Ginsburg 2000.)

Rheingold (1993) thinks that the Web is being transformed from just a communication and information-transfer tool into a social Web of communities. He thinks that every Web site should incorporate a place for people to chat. A community site should be an interesting place to visit, a kind of virtual community center. He believes that it should be a place where discussions may range over many controversial topics. Many issues are related to the operation of communities. For example, Mowbray (2001) raised the issue of freedom of speech and its control in a community. Mahlhotra (2002) raised the issue of knowledge exchange among community members.

Virtual communities also are closely related to EC. For example, Champy et al. (1996) and Zetlin and Pfleging (2002) describe online, consumer-driven markets in which most of the consumers' needs, ranging from finding a mortgage to job hunting, are arranged from a community Web site. This gathering of needs in one place enables vendors to sell more and community members to get discounts. Internet communities will eventually have a massive impact on almost every company that produces consumer goods or services, and they could change the nature of corporate advertising and community sponsorship strategies and the manner in which business is done. Although this process of change is slow, some of the initial commercial development changes can be observed.

COMMERCIAL ASPECTS OF COMMUNITIES

Forrester Research conducted a survey in 1998 that found the following expected payback for organizations that sponsor online communities (in descending order of importance): increases in customer loyalty, sales, customer participation and feedback, repeat traffic to the site, and new traffic to the site (WebMasterTechniques 2000).

Insights and Additions 17.2   Examples of Communities

The following are examples of online communities.

▶ **Associations.** Many associations have a Web presence. These range from PTAs (parent-teacher associations) to professional associations. An example of this type of community is the Australian Record Industry Association (*aria.com.au*).

▶ **Ethnic communities.** Many communities are country or language specific. An example of such a site is *elsitio.com*, which provides content for the Spanish- and Portuguese-speaking audiences mainly in Latin America and the United States. A number of sites, including *china.com*, *hongkong.com*, *sina.com*, and *sohu.com*, cater to the world's large Chinese-speaking community.

▶ **Gender communities.** *Women.com* and *ivillage.com*, the two largest female-oriented community sites, merged in 2001 in an effort to cut losses and to become profitable.

▶ **Affinity portals.** These are communities organized by interest, such as hobbies, vocations, political parties, unions (*working families.com*), and many, many more.

▶ **Catering to young people (teens and people in their early 20s).** Many companies see unusual opportunities here. Three community sites of particular interest are *alloy.com*, *bolt.com*, and *blueskyfrog.com*. Alloy.com is based in the United Kingdom and claims to have over 10 million members. Bolt.com claims to have 4 million members and operates from the United States. Blueskyfrog.com operates from Australia, concentrating on cell phone users, and claims to have more than 1 million devoted members.

▶ **Mega communities.** Mega-communities combine numerous smaller communities under one "umbrella" (under one name) GeoCities is one example of a mega community, divided into many subcommunities. Owned by Yahoo, it is by far the largest online community.

▶ **B2B online communities.** Chapter 7 introduced many-to-many B2B exchanges. These are referred to by some as communities (e.g., Raisch 2000 and *commerceone.com* 2002). B2B exchanges support community programs such as technical discussion forums, interactive Webcasts, user-created product reviews, virtual conferences and meetings, experts' seminars, and user-managed profile pages. Classified ads can help members to find jobs or employers to find employees. Many also include industry news, directories, links to government and professional associations, and more.

EXHIBIT 17.3   Types of Virtual Communities

Community Type	Description
Transaction	Facilitates buying and selling (e.g., *ausfish.com.au*; see Real-World Case). Combines information portal with infrastructure for trading. Members are buyers, sellers, intermediaries, etc. Focused on a specific commercial area (e.g., fishing).
Purpose or interest	No trading, just exchange of information on a topic of mutual interest. Examples: Investors consult The Motley Fool (*fool.com*) for investment advice; rugby fans congregate at the Fans Room at *nrl.com.au*; music lovers go to *mp3.com*; *city411.com* is a directory of cities and their entertainment. *Geocities.yahoo.com* is a collection of several areas of interest in one place.
Relations or practice	Members are organized around certain life experiences. Examples: *ivillage.com* caters to women, *seniornet.com* to senior citizens, and Chinadotcom at *corp.china.com* caters to Chinese-speaking people. Professional communities also belong to this category. Examples: *isworld.org* for information systems faculty, students, and professionals; *energycentral.com* for energy-industry traders.
Fantasy	Members share imaginary environments. Examples: sport fantasy teams at *espn.com*; Geocities members can pretend to be medieval barons at *dir.yahoo.com/Recreation/Games/Role_Playing_Games/Titles/*. See *games.yahoo.com* for many more fantasy communities.

Sources: Compiled from Armstrong and Hagel (1996) and Hagel and Armstrong (1997).

A logical step as a community site grows in number of members and influence may be to turn it into a commercial site. Examples of such community-commercial sites include ivillage.com and geocities.yahoo.com. The following are suggestions on how to make the transformation from a community site to a commercial one:

▶ Understand a particular niche industry, its information needs, and the step-by-step process by which it does the research needed to do business and try to match the industry with a potential or existing community.

▶ Build a site that provides that information, either through partnerships with existing information providers or by gathering it independently, or identify a community that can be sponsored.

▶ Set up the site to mirror the steps a user goes through in the information-gathering and decision-making process (e.g., how a chip designer whittles down the list of possible chips that will fit a particular product).

▶ Build a community that relies on the site for decision support (or modify an existing one).

▶ Start selling products and services that fit into the decision-support process (such as selling sample chips to engineers who are members of the community).

Electronic communities can create value in several ways. This value-creation process is summarized in Exhibit 17.4. Members input useful information to the community in the form of comments and feedback, elaborating on their attitudes and beliefs and information needs. This information can then be retrieved and used by other members or by marketers. The community organizers may also supply their own content to communities, as AOL does.

Also, some communities charge members content fees for downloading certain articles, music, or pictures, thus producing sales revenue for the site. Finally, because many commu-

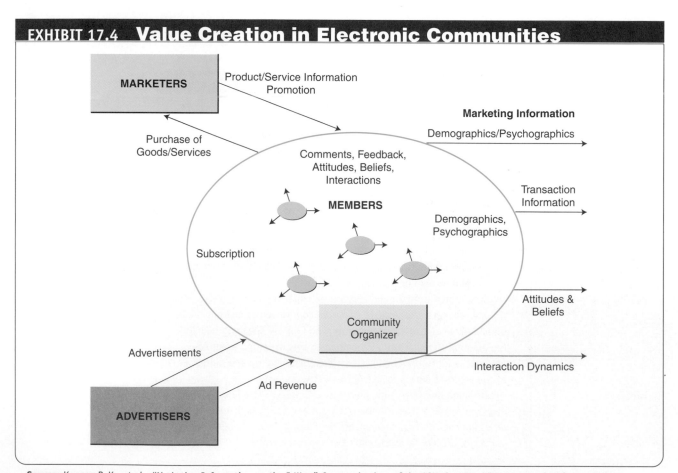

EXHIBIT 17.4 Value Creation in Electronic Communities

Source: Kannen P. K., et al., "Marketing Information on the I-Way," *Communications of the ACM.* © 1998, ACM, Inc. Used with permission.

nity members create their own homepages, it is easy to learn about them and reach them with targeted advertising and marketing. For more on this topic, see Lechner et al. (2001).

Financial Viability of Communities

The revenue model of communities can be based on sponsorship, membership fees, sales commissions, and advertising, or some combination of these. The operating expenses for communities are very high due to the need to provide fresh content and free services. In addition, most communities initially provide free membership. The objective is to have as many registered members as possible and to build a strong brand in order to attract advertisers (see McWilliam 2000 and Zetlin and Pfleging 2002).

The model of self-financing communities (i.e., those without a sponsor) has not worked very well. Several communities that were organized for profit, such as ivillage.com, china.com, and elsitio.com, sustained heavy losses. Several other communities ceased operations in 2000 and 2001 (e.g., esociety.com and renren.com). The trend toward mergers and acquisitions among communities, started in 2001, is expected to improve the financial viability of some communities.

KEY STRATEGIES FOR SUCCESSFUL ONLINE COMMUNITIES

The management consulting company Accenture outlined the following eight critical factors for community success (see details in Duffy 1999):

1. Increase traffic and participation in the community.
2. Focus on the needs of the members; use facilitators and coordinators.
3. Encourage free sharing of opinions and information—no controls.
4. Obtain financial sponsorship. This factor is a must. Significant investment is required.
5. Consider the cultural environment.
6. Provide several tools and activities for member use; communities are not just discussion groups.
7. Involve community members in activities and recruiting.
8. Guide discussions, provoke controversy, and raise sticky issues. This keeps interest high.

Examples of some communities that use one or more of these principles of success include the following: earthweb.com, icollector.com, webmd.com, terra.es, eslcafe.com, tradingdirect.com, icq.com, letsbuyit.com, barclays.co.uk, paltalk.com, radiolinja.fi, and projectconnections.com. (For more details and discussion of communities, see Raisch 2000; Preece 2000; and McWilliam 2000.)

Section 17.7 ▶ REVIEW

1. Define virtual (Internet) communities and describe their characteristics.
2. List the major categories of communities.
3. Describe the commercial aspects of communities.
4. Describe the CSFs for communities.

17.8 THE FUTURE OF EC

Generally speaking, the consensus regarding the future of EC is that it is bright. EC will become an increasingly important method of reaching customers, providing services, and improving operations of organizations. Analysts differ in their predictions about the anticipated growth rate of EC and how long it will take for it to be a substantial portion of the economy, as well as in the identification of industry segments that will grow the fastest. However, based on the following factors and trends, there is general optimism about the future of EC.

NON-TECHNOLOGICAL SUCCESS FACTORS

The rosy scenario for the future of EC is based partially on the following non-technological factors and trends.

Internet usage. The number of Internet users is increasing rapidly. With the integration of computers and television, Internet access via mobile devices, increased availability of access kiosks, increased publicity about the Internet, and availability of inexpensive computers (such as the *simputer*, short for simple computer), the number of Internet surfers will continue to increase. As younger people (who have grown up with computers) grow older, usage will grow even faster. There is no question that sooner or later there will be a billion people who surf the Internet. By 2002, the number of worldwide Internet users was estimated to be 450 million, including more than half of the U.S. population (Ipsos-Reid 2000).

Opportunities for buying. The number of products and services available online is increasing rapidly with improved trading mechanisms, search engines, online shopping aids, intermediary services, presentations in multiple languages, and the willingness of more sellers and buyers to give EC a try. It is logical to expect significantly more purchasing opportunities. Annual sales increased an average of 41 percent in 2001 (Boston Consulting Group 2002).

M-commerce. With over 1.2 billion people using cell phones in 2003 (Charney 2003), the ease with which one can connect from them to the Internet, and the introduction of 3G capabilities, it is clear that m-commerce will play a major role in EC. Forrester Research predicts that as many as 50 percent of these wireless users will be online by 2007 (Golvin 2002). The fact that one does not need a computer to go online will bring more and more people to the Web. M-commerce, as discussed in Chapter 10, has special capabilities that will result in new applications, as well as in more people using traditional applications.

Purchasing incentives. The buyers' advantages described in Chapter 1 are likely to increase. Prices will go down, and the purchasing process will be streamlined. Many innovative options will be available, and electronic shopping may even become a social trend. Also, for many organizations, e-procurement is becoming an attractive EC initiative.

Increased security and trust. One of the major inhibitors of growth of B2C and B2B EC is the perception of poor security and privacy and a lack of trust. As time passes, significant improvements in these areas are expected.

Efficient information handling. More information will become accessible from anywhere, at any time. Using data warehouses, data mining, and intelligent agents, companies can constantly learn about their customers, steering marketing and service activities accordingly. The notion of *real-time marketing* might not be so far away. This will facilitate the use of EC.

Innovative organizations. Organizations are being restructured and reengineered with the help of IT (Turban et al. 2004; El Sawy 2001; Hammer and Stanton 1995). Using different types of empowered teams, some of which are virtual, organizations become innovative, flexible, and responsive. The trend for process reengineering is increasing, as is organizational creativity. Innovative organizations will probably be more inclined to use EC.

Virtual communities. Virtual communities of all kinds are spreading rapidly, with some already reaching several million members. Virtual communities can enhance commercial activities online. Also, some communities are organized around professional areas of interest and can facilitate B2B and B2C EC.

Payment systems. The ability to use e-cash or person-to-person (P2P) payments and to make micropayments online is spreading quickly. When these systems are implemented on a large scale, many EC activities will flourish. B2B payment systems also have matured, and attractive options are available. As international standards become the norm, electronic payments will extend globally, facilitating global EC.

B2B EC. Figures about the growth of B2B are revised frequently. In some cases, industry-type extranets are forcing many buyers and sellers to participate in B2B EC (e.g., Covisint, see Chapter 7). B2B will continue to dominate the EC field (in terms of volume traded) for the intermediate future. More sellers, more buyers, and more services will continue to appear; the rapid growth will continue. The success of B2B will depend upon the success of integrating EC technology with business processes and with conventional information systems.

B2B exchanges. In 2000, the number of B2B exchanges exploded, but many subsequently collapsed in 2001 and 2002. The few that have remained are maturing, providing the infrastructure for $12.8 trillion of B2B trade forecasted by 2006 (Sharrard 2001). However, company-centric (private) marketplaces will account for the majority of the B2B trade.

Auctions. The popularity of auctions and reverse auctions is increasing rapidly in B2B, B2C, G2B, and C2C. This is an effective and efficient EC business model. eBay is probably the most successful large dot-com.

Going global. One of the most appealing benefits of EC is the ability to go global. However, many barriers exist to global EC. With time, these are expected to be reduced, but at a fairly slow pace.

E-government. Starting in 1999, many governments launched comprehensive G2C, G2B, G2G, and G2E projects. By 2002, over 120 countries had established some form of e-government program.

Intrabusiness EC. Many companies are starting to discover opportunities for using EC in-house, particularly in improving the internal supply chain and communications with among employees.

E-learning. The fastest-growing area in EC in 2002 was e-learning. Large numbers of companies have installed e-learning programs, and many universities are experimenting with distance-learning programs. E-learning should grow even faster in the near future.

EC legislation. The legislative process is slow, especially when multiple countries are involved. However, with passage of time, the necessary EC framework will be in place.

EC TECHNOLOGY TRENDS

The trend in EC technologies generally points toward significant cost reduction coupled with improvements in capabilities, ease of use, increased availability of software, ease of site development, and improved security and accessibility. Specific technology trends include the following.

Clients. PCs of all types are getting cheaper, smaller, and more capable. The concept of a network computer (NC), also known as a *thin client*, which moves processing and storage off the desktop and onto centrally located servers running Java-based software on UNIX (Windows on Microsoft's version), and the simputer (simputer.com) could bring the price of a PC to that of a television.

Embedded clients. Another major trend is the movement toward *embedded clients*. A client, in such a case, can be a car or a washing machine with an embedded microchip. In many cases, an expert system is embedded with rules that make the client "smarter" or more responsive to changes in the environment. It is a typical device in pervasive computing.

Pervasive computing. The Gartner Group calls pervasive computing the next "big thing" in IT (Fenn and Linden 2001). Pervasive computing (Chapter 10) is starting to impact EC positively. Pervasive computing is facilitated by improvements in wireless communication and wearable devices.

Wireless communications and m-commerce. For countries without fiber-optic cables, wireless communication can save considerable installation time and money. In 1998, wireless access reached T1 speed (about 1.5 mbps), with cost savings of over 80 percent. However, wireless networks may be too slow for some futuristic digitized products (see Chapter 10). An exception is the Wi-Fi WLANs, which are growing rapidly. According to Kenny and Marshall (2000), wireless communications is expected to change the nature of e-commerce from content to context, reaching customers whenever and wherever they are ready to buy.

Wearable devices. With advances in pervasive computing and artificial intelligence, the number of wearable computing devices (Chapter 10) will increase. Wearable devices will enhance collaborative commerce, B2E, and intrabusiness EC.

Servers and operating systems. A major trend is to use Windows XP and NT as the enterprise operating system. Among NT's capabilities is *clustering*. Clustering servers can add processing power in much smaller increments than was previously possible. Clustering servers is also very economical, resulting in cost reductions. Special EC servers are offered by Microsoft and others (see online Chapter 18).

Networks. The use of EC frequently requires rich multimedia (such as color catalogs or samples of movies or music). A large bandwidth is required to deliver this rich multimedia. Several broadband technologies (such as XDSL) will increase bandwidth many-fold. This could help in replacing expensive WANs or VANs with the inexpensive Internet. Security on the Internet can be enhanced by the use of VPNs.

EC software and services. The availability of all types of EC software will make it easier to establish stores on the Internet and to conduct all types of trades. Already, hundreds of sites offer pages for inexpensive rent for a variety of activities ranging from conducting auctions to selling in a foreign language. Other support services, such as escrow companies that support auctions and multiple types of certifications, also are developing rapidly. In addition, a large number of consultants are being trained to assist in specialty areas.

Search engines. Search engines are getting smarter and better. Use of this improved technology will enable consumers and organizational buyers to find and compare products and services easier and faster.

Peer-to-peer technology. P2P technology is developing rapidly and is expected to have a major impact on knowledge sharing, communication, and collaboration by making these activities better, faster, less expensive, and more convenient.

Integration. The forthcoming integration of the computer and the TV and of the computer and the telephone will increase Internet accessibility (e.g., see Silberman 1999). Web Services (see next item) also will facilitate integration.

Web Services. Web Services (see Chapters 8 and online 18) are being developed rapidly, solving major problems in EC systems development and integration, especially in complex B2B systems and exchanges. Web Services will enable companies to build EC applications more efficiently, cheaply, and more quickly.

Software agents. Users will be able to dispatch intelligent software agents to search, match, negotiate, and conduct many other tasks that will facilitate EC activities.

Interactive TV. Although it has shown few signs of success, some believe that in the future interactive TV may outshine the Net for e-commerce (see Williamson 2001).

Tomorrow's Internet. Many research institutions around the world are working on tomorrow's Internet. Although projects such as Internet2 are slow to progress, sooner or later these efforts will greatly advance EC applications (Boyles 2000 and internet2.org).

INTEGRATING THE MARKETPLACE WITH THE MARKETSPACE

Throughout this book we have commented on the relationship between the physical marketplace and the marketspace. We pointed out conflicts in certain areas, as well as successful applications and cooperation. The fact is that from the point of view of the consumer, as well as of most organizations, these two entities exist, and will continue to exist, together.

Probably the most noticeable integration of the two concepts is in the click-and-mortar organization. For the foreseeable future, the click-and-mortar organization will be the most prevalent model (e.g., see Otto and Chung 2000), though it may take different shapes and formats. Some organizations will use EC as just another selling channel, as most large retailers do today. Others will use EC for only some products and services, while they sell other products and services the conventional way (e.g., Lego and GM). As experience is gained on how to excel at such a strategy, more and more organizations, private and public, will move to this dual mode of operation.

A major problem in the click-and-mortar approach is how the two outlets can cooperate in planning, advertising, logistics, resource allocation, and so on, and how to align the strategic plans of the marketspace and marketplace. Another major issue is the conflict with existing distribution channels (i.e., wholesalers, retailers).

Another area of coexistence is in many B2C ordering systems, where customers have the option to order the new way or the old way. For example, consumers can do their banking both online and off-line. People can trade stocks via the computer, by placing a call to their broker, or just by walking into a brokerage firm and talking to a trader. In the areas of B2B and G2B, the option to choose the old way or the new way may not be available much longer; some organizations may discontinue the old-economy option as the number of off-line users declines below a certain threshold. However, in most B2C activities, the option will remain, at least for the foreseeable future.

In conclusion, many people believe that the impact of EC on our lives will be as much as, and possibly more profound than, that of the Industrial Revolution. No other phenomenon since the Industrial Revolution has been classified in this category. It is our hope that this book will help you move successfully into this exciting and challenging digital revolution.

1. Describe non-technological EC trends.
2. Describe technological trends for EC.
3. Discuss the integration of marketplaces and marketspaces.

MANAGERIAL ISSUES

1. **What sorts of legal and ethical issues should be of major concern to an EC enterprise?** There is no set list of ethical and legal issues that are paramount in EC. However, some of the key issues to consider include the following: (1) What type of proprietary information should we allow on our site? (2) Who will have access to information that is posted by visitors to our site? (3) Do the content and activities on our site comply with the laws in other countries? (4) Do we need to post disclaimers concerning the content of our Web site? (5) Are we inadvertently using trademarked or copyrighted materials without permission? Regardless of the specific issues, an attorney should periodically review the content on the site, and someone should be responsible for monitoring legal and liability issues.

2. **What are the most critical ethical issues?** Issues of privacy, ethics, and so on may seem tangential to running a business, but ignoring them may hinder the operation of many organizations. Privacy protection can cut into profits, especially in B2C in which sellers need to learn more about customers and their behaviors but cannot do so (Hildebrand 1996).

3. **Should we obtain patents?** Some people claim that patents should not be awarded to business or computer processes related to EC (as is the case in Europe). Therefore, investing large amounts of money in developing or buying patents may be financially unwise in cases where patents may not hold.

4. **What impacts on business is EC expected to make?** The impacts of EC and the Internet can be so strong that the entire manner in which companies do business will be changed, with significant impacts on procedures, people, organizational structure, management, and business processes. (Read "The Economic and Social Impact of Electronic Commerce" at oecd.org/subject/e_commerce.)

5. **Do we have a community?** Although sponsoring a community may sound like a good idea, it may not be simple to execute. Community members need services, and these cost money to provide. The most difficult task is to find a community that matches your business.

SUMMARY

1. **Differences between legal and ethical issues.** The legal framework for EC—both statutory and common law—is just beginning to solidify. To date, the major legal issues in EC have involved rights of privacy, intellectual property, freedom of speech and censorship, and fraud. In the absence of legal constraints, ethical codes help to fill the gap. The problem is that ethics are subjective and vary widely from one culture to the next.

2. **Protecting privacy in EC.** B2C companies require customer information in order to improve products and services and sell them via one-to-one marketing. Registration and cookies are two of the ways used to collect this information. The key privacy issues are who controls this information and how private it should remain. Although legal measures are being developed to protect the privacy of individuals, it is basically up to the EC companies to regulate themselves. If they fail to do so to the satisfaction of consumers, they may face bad publicity from consumer- and privacy-oriented organizations.

3. **Intellectual property rights in EC.** It is extremely easy and inexpensive to copy or steal intellectual works on the Internet (e.g., music, photos, graphics, and the like) and to distribute or sell them without the permission of the owners—violating or infringing on copyrights, trademarks, and patents. Although the legal aspects are now fairly clear, monitoring and catching violators is sometimes difficult.

4. **Conflict between free speech and censorship.** There is an ongoing debate about censorship on the Internet. The proponents of censorship feel that it is up to the government and various ISPs and Web sites to control inappropriate or offensive content. Others oppose any form of censorship; they believe that control is up to the individual. In the United States, most legal attempts to censor content on the Internet have been

found unconstitutional. The debate is not likely to subside in the near term.

5. **Legal issues.** Doing business electronically requires a supportive legal environment. Of special importance are electronic contracts (including digital signatures), the control of offshore gambling, and what taxes should be paid to whom on interstate and international transactions. Although the trend is not to have a sales tax or a value-added tax, this may not be the case for too much longer.

6. **Protecting buyers and sellers online.** Protection is needed because there is no face-to-face contact, because there is a great possibility for fraud, because there are insufficient legal constraints, and because new issues and scams appear constantly. Several organizations, private and public, are attempting to provide the protection that is needed to build the trust that is essential for the success of widespread EC.

7. **Societal issues and EC.** EC has impacted society in several different ways. Some of these impacts are very positive, such as improvements in education, public safety and criminal justice, and health care. On the negative side is the creation of the digital divide.

8. **The role of virtual communities.** Virtual communities create new types of business opportunities—people with similar interests that are congregated in one Web site are a natural target for advertisers and marketers. Using chat rooms, members can exchange opinions about certain products and services. Of special interest are communities of transactions, whose interest is the promotion of commercial buying and selling. Virtual communities can foster customer loyalty, increase sales of related vendors, and increase customers' feedback for improved service and business.

9. **The future of EC.** EC will continue to expand fairly rapidly for a number of reasons. To begin with, its infrastructure is becoming better and less expensive with time. Consumers will become more experienced and will try different products and services and tell their friends about them. Security, privacy protection, and trust will be much higher, and more support services will simplify the transaction process. Legal issues will be formally legislated and clarified, and more and more products and services will be online at reduced prices. The fastest growing area is B2B EC. Company-centric systems (especially e-procurement) and auctions will also continue to spread rapidly. The development of exchanges and other many-to-many e-marketplaces will be much slower..The most promising technology for facilitating integration is Web Services. Finally, a technology that will facilitate EC in general is wireless (especially Wi-Fi).

KEY TERMS

DISCUSSION QUESTIONS

1. Provide two privacy examples in EC in which the situation is legal but unethical.

2. Distinguish between self-registration and cookies in EC. Why do you think Internet users are concerned about cookies?

3. What are some of the things that EC Web sites can do to ensure that personal information is safeguarded?

4. On the Internet, why is it difficult to protect intellectual property? Do you think that sites such as MP3.com and Kazaa should be able to operate without restrictions? Justify your answer.

5. Who should control minors' access to "offensive" material on the Internet—parents, the government, or ISPs? Why?

6. Should spamming be illegal? Explain why or why not.

7. Discuss the relationship between virtual communities and doing business on the Internet.

8. Discuss the issue of the digital divide and how to deal with the problem. (See ecommerce.gov and google.com.)

9. Discuss the conflict between freedom of speech and control of offending Web sites.

10. Discuss the insufficient protection of opt-in and opt-out options. What would you be happy with?

11. The IRS buys demographic market research data from private companies. These data contain income statistics that could be compared to tax returns. Many U.S. citizens feel that their rights within the realm of the Privacy Act are being violated; others say that this is an unethical behavior on the part of the government. Discuss.

12. Clerks at 7-Eleven stores enter data regarding customers (gender, approximate age, and so on) into the computer. These data are then processed for improved decision making. Customers are not informed about this, nor are they being asked for permission. (Names are not keyed in.) Are the clerks' actions ethical? Compare this with the case of cookies.

13. Many hospitals, health maintenance organizations, and federal agencies are converting, or plan to convert, all patient medical records from paper to electronic storage (using imaging technology). Once completed, electronic storage will enable quick access to most records. However, the availability of these records in a database and on networks or smart cards may allow people, some of whom are unauthorized, to view another person's private medical data. To protect privacy fully may cost too much money or may considerably slow accessibility to the records. What policies could health-care administrators use to prevent unauthorized access? Discuss.

14. Why do many companies and professional organizations develop their own codes of ethics?

15. Cyber Promotions Inc. attempted to use the First Amendment in defense of their flooding of AOL subscribers with junk e-mail. AOL tried to block the junk mail. A federal judge agreed with AOL that unsolicited mail that is annoying, a costly waste of Internet time, and often inappropriate should not be sent. Discuss some of the issues involved, such as freedom of speech, how to distinguish between junk and nonjunk mail, and the analogy with regular mail.

16. Digital Equipment paid over $3 million for the AltaVista name and Tom.com paid $8 million for its domain name. Why are companies willing to pay millions of dollars for domain names?

17. The Communication Decency Act, which was intended to protect children and others from pornography and other offensive material online, was approved by the U.S. Congress but then was ruled unconstitutional by the courts. Discuss the importance and implications of this incident.

18. Why does the government warn customers to be careful with their payments for EC products and services?

19. Some say that it is much easier to commit a fraud online than off-line. Do you agree?

INTERNET EXERCISES

1. Two commonly used Internet terms are *flaming* and *spamming*. Surf the Web to find out more about these terms. How are they similar? How are they different?

2. You want to set up a personal Web site. Using legal sites such as cyberlaw.com, prepare a report summarizing the types of materials you can and cannot use (e.g., logos, graphics, etc.) without breaking copyright law.

3. Use google.com to prepare a list of industry and trade organizations involved in various computer privacy initiatives. One of these groups is the World Wide Web Consortium (W3C). Describe its Privacy Preferences Project (w3.org/TR/2001/WD-P3P-20010928).

4. Enter the Web site of an Internet community (e.g., tripod.com or geocities.yahoo.com). Build a homepage free of charge. You can add a chat room and a message board to your site using the free tools provided.

5. Investigate the community services provided by Yahoo to its members (groups.yahoo.com). List all the services available and assess their potential commercial benefits to Yahoo.

6. Enter pgp.com. Review the services offered. Use the free software to encrypt a message.

7. Enter calastrology.com. What kind of community is this? Check the revenue model. Then enter astrocenter.com. What kind of site is this? Compare and comment on the two sites.

8. Enter nolo.com. Click on free law centers. Try to find information about various EC legal issues. Find information about international EC issues. Then go to lawstreet.com. Try to find information about international legal aspects of EC. Locate additional information on EC legal issues with a visit to google.com or a search on Yahoo. Prepare a report on the international legal aspects of EC.

9. Find the status of the latest copyright legislation. Try fairuse.stanford.edu. Is there anything regarding the international aspects of copyright legislation?

10. Enter ftc.gov and identify some of the typical types of fraud and scams on the Internet.

11. Enter the Internet Service Providers' Web site (**ispc.org**) and identify the various initiatives they have undertaken regarding topics discussed in this chapter.

12. Check the latest on domain names by visiting sites such as **internic.net**. Prepare a report.

13. Private companies such as **thepubliceye.com** and **investigator.com** act as third-party investigators of the honesty of your business. What do these companies do? Why are the services of these companies necessary given the services of TRUSTe and BBBOnLine? (That is, are the services of TRUSTe and BBBOnLine somehow insufficient?)

14. Visit **consumers.com**. What protection can this group give that is not provided by BBBOnLine?

15. Find the status of fingerprint identification systems. Try **omin.com**, **bergdata.com**, and **morpho.com**. Prepare a report based on your findings.

16. Download freeware from **junkbuster.com** and learn how to prohibit unsolicited e-mail. Describe how your privacy is protected.

17. Enter **scambusters.com** and identify and list their antifraud and antiscam activities.

TEAM ASSIGNMENTS AND ROLE PLAYING

1. Over the past few years, the number of lawsuits in the United States and elsewhere involving EC has been increasing. Have each team prepare a list of five or more such cases on each topic in this chapter (e.g., privacy, defamation, domain names). What have been the outcomes of these cases? If there has not yet been an outcome in certain cases, what is likely to happen and why?

2. Each team member is assigned to a different type of community, per Exhibit 17.3. Identify the services offered by that type of community. Have each team compare the services offered by each type of community. Prepare a report.

3. Have a debate between two teams. One team is for complete freedom of speech on the Internet, the other team advocates the censoring of offensive and pornographic material. Other class members will act as judges.

4. It is legal to monitor employees' movements on the Internet and read their e-mail. But is it ethical? Should it be practiced? About 50 percent think it is ethical, 50 percent disagree. Have two teams debate this issue.

REAL-WORLD CASE

THE AUSTRALIAN FISHING COMMUNITY

Recreational fishing in Australia is popular both with residents and with international visitors. Over 700,000 Australians fish regularly. The Australian Fishing Shop (AFS) (*ausfish.com.au*) is a small e-tailer that was founded in 1994. At that time, the goal of the site was to provide information for the recreational fisherperson. Over the last few years, the site has featured a fishing portal that has formed a devoted community.

A visit to the site will show immediately that the site is not a regular storefront, but actually provides considerable information to the recreational fishing community. In addition to the sale of products (rods, reels, clothing, and boats and fishing-related books, software, and CD-ROMs) and services (fishing charters and holiday packages), the site provides the following information:

▷ Hints and tips for fishing

▷ What's new?

▷ A photo gallery of visitors' prize catches

▷ Chat boards—general and specialized

▷ Directions from boat builders, tackle manufacturers, etc.

▷ Recipes for cooking fish

▷ Information about discussion groups and mailing lists

▷ Free giveaways and competitions

▷ Links to fishing-related government bodies, other fishing organizations (around the globe and in Australia), and daily weather maps and tide reports

▷ General information site and FAQs

▷ List of fishing sites around the globe

▷ Contact details by phone, post, and e-mail

▷ Free e-mail and Web page hosting

In addition, an auction mechanism for fishing equipment is provided and answers are provided for customer inquiries.

The company is fairly small (gross income of about AU$600,000 a year). How can such a small company survive? The answer can be found in its strategy of providing value-added services to the recreational fishing community. These services attract over 4.5 million visitors each month, from all over the world, of which about 1 percent make a purchase. Also, several advertisers sponsor the site. This generates sufficient revenue to survive. Aiming at the global market is another interesting strategy. Most of the total income is derived from customers in the United States and Canada who buy holiday and fishing packages.

The company acts basically as a referral service for vendors. Therefore, it does not have to carry an inventory. However, the company is also an e-tailer. AFS does business with a small number of suppliers; thus they are able to aggregate orders from suppliers and then pack and send them to customers. Some orders are shipped directly from vendors to the customers.

Source: *ausfish.com.au* (2002).

Questions

1. Why is this site considered a community site?
2. Which of the services offered are typical of online communities?
3. List the CSFs of the company.

REFERENCES

Adams, A. R. "Introduction: Beyond Numbers and Demographics: 'Experience-Near' Explorations of the Digital Divide." *Computers and Society* 31, no. 3 (2001).

Alberts, R. J., et al. "The Threat of Long-Arm Jurisdiction to Electronic Commerce." *Communications of the ACM* 41, no. 12 (1998).

Anandarajan, M. "Internet Abuse in the Workplace." *Communications of the ACM* 45, no. 1 (2002).

Angwin, J. "Credit-Card Fraud Has Become a Nightmare for E-Merchants." *Wall Street Journal Interactive Edition*, September 19, 2000, mcnees.org/mainpages/misc/security/sec_subpages/wsj_cc_fraud_919.htm (accessed May 2003).

Armstrong, A. G., and J. Hagel. "The Real Value of Online Communities." *Harvard Business Review* (May–June 1996).

ausfish.com.au (accessed February 2002).

Australian Internet Industry Association (AIIA). Interactive Gambling Bill 2001. *Submission to the Environment, Communications, Information Technology and the Arts Legislation Committee*, April 24, 2001, iia.net.au/news/senate_submission2.html (accessed January 2003).

Black, J. "The High Price of Spam." *BusinessWeek Online*, March 1, 2002, businessweek.com/technology/content/mar2002/tc2002031_8613.htm (accessed May 2003).

Bloomberg News. "The S.E.C. Accuses 23 of Internet Fraud." *New York Times*, March 2, 2001, lynchlawfirm.net/pdf/news_WSJ_SEC%2003022001.pdf (accessed May 2003).

Boston Consulting Group. "Online Sales in 2001 Generated Profits for more than Half of All U.S. Retailers Selling Online." *bcg.com*, June 12, 2002, bcg.com/media_center/media_press_release_subpage69.asp (accessed May 2003).

Boyles, H. "Internet2: Fostering Tomorrow's Internet." *Global Electronic Commerce* (2000).

Buchholz, R. A., and S. B. Rosenthal. "Internet Privacy: Individual Rights and the Common Good." *SAM Advanced Management Journal* 67, no. 1, Winter (2002).

Burk, D. L. "Copyrightable Functions and Patentable Speech." *Communications of the ACM* 44, no. 2 (2001).

Burnett, R. "Legal Aspects of E-commerce." *Computing & Control Engineering Journal* (2001).

Champy, J., et al. "The Rise of Electronic Community." *InformationWeek*, June 10, 1996.

Charny, B. "Microsoft: Security Fix Due for Phone OS." CNET News.com, January 17, 2003, news.com.com/2100-1033-981244.html?tag=fd_top (accessed May 2003).

Cheeseman, H. R. *Business Law*, 4th ed. Upper Saddle River, NJ: Prentice Hall, 2001.

Cherry, S. M. "Getting Copyright Right." *IEEE Spectrum* (February 2002).

Claburn, T. "Intellectual Property: Harder to Protect than Ever." *Smart Business*, December 1, 2001.

commerceone.com (accessed May 2002).

Commodity Futures Trading Commission (CFTC). "CFTC Issues Two Advisories Addressing the Offering of Foreign Currency (FOREX) Trading Opportunities to the Retail Public." CFTC News Release 4489-01,

February 8, 2001, cftc.gov/opa/ enf01/opa4489-01.htm (accessed May 2003).

Compaine, B. M. *The Digital Divide: Facing a Crisis or Creating a Myth*. Cambridge, MA: MIT Press, 2001.

Delgado-Martinez, R. "What Is Copyright Protection?" whatiscopyright.org (accessed June 2002).

Dembeck, C., and R. Conlin. "Beleaguered DoubleClick Appoints Privacy Board." *E-Commerce Times*, May 17, 2000, ecommercetimes.com/perl/story/3348.html# storystart (accessed May 2003).

Donham, P. "An Unshackled Internet: If Joe Howe Were Designing Cyberspace." *Proceedings of the Symposium on Free Speech and Privacy in the Information Age*, University of Waterloo, November 26, 1994, efc.ca/pages/don ham2.html (accessed January 2003).

doubleclick.com (accessed June 2003).

Duffy, D. "It Takes an E-Village." *CIO Magazine*, October 25, 1999.

ei.cs.vt.edu/~wwbtb/book/chap5/opine1.html (accessed July 1997).

El Sawy, O. *Redesigning Enterprise Processes for E-Business*. New York: McGraw-Hill, 2001.

Ethics and Information Technology, Special Issue, 3 (2001): 89–246.

Federal Trade Commission. "FTC Names Its Dirty Dozen: 12 Scams Most Likely to Arrive Via Bulk Email." ftc.gov/bcp/conline/pubs/alerts/doznalrt.htm (accessed May 2003).

Federal Trade Commission. "Privacy Online: A Report to the Congress." ftc.gov/reports/privacy3, June 1998 (accessed May 2003).

Fenn, J., and A. Linden. "Wearing It Out: The Growth of the Wireless Wearable World." *Gartner Group Research*, April 17, 2001, security1.gartner.com/story.php.id. 134.s.1.jsp (accessed May 2003).

Froomkin, A. M. "The Collision of Trademarks Domain Names, and Due Process in Cyberspace." *Communications of the ACM* 44 (2001).

Fujimoto, L. "Police Can Track Emergency-Call Location." *Maui News*, December 14, 2002.

Geocities. geocities.yahoo.com (accessed February 2003).

Ghosh, A. K., and T. M. Swaminatha. "Software Security and Privacy Risks in Mobile E-Commerce." *Communications of the ACM* 44, no. 2 (2001).

Golvin, C. S., et al. "Mobile Applications that Drive Revenue." *Forrester Research*, October 2002, forrester.com/ ER/Research/Report/Summary/0,1338,15068,00.html (accessed May 2003).

Gordon-Murnane, L. "E-Commerce and Internet Taxation: Issues, Organizations, and Findings." *Searcher*, June 2000, infotoday.com/searcher/jun00/gordon-murnane.htm (accessed January 2001).

Graves, L., et al. "Online Commerce: Building Consumer Confidence." *Jupiter Media Metrix*, June 28, 2000.

Guernsey, L. "Welcome to the World Wide Web. Passport, Please?" *New York Times*, March 15, 2001.

Hagel, J., and A. Armstrong. *Net Gain*. Boston: Harvard Business School Press, 1997.

Hamelink, C. J. *The Ethics of Cyberspace*. Thousand Oaks, CA: Sage Publishers, 2001.

Hammer, M., and S. A. Stanton. *The Reengineering Revolution: A Handbook*. New York: HarperCollins, 1995.

Hawkins, D. "More Web Users Wage a Guerrilla War on Nosy Sites." *USNEWS.com*, August 28, 2000, usnews.com/ usnews/nycu/tech/articles/000828/nycu/privacy2.htm (accessed May 2003).

Hildebrand, C. "Privacy vs. Profit." *CIO Magazine*, February 15, 1996.

Hoffman, T. "Education Called Key to Bridging Digital Divide." *Computerworld*, September 7, 2000, computerworld.com/news/2000/story/0,11280,49728, 00.html (accessed May 2003).

Ipsos-Reid. "Face of the Web Study Pegs Global Internet Population at More than 300 Million." Ipsos-Reid press release, March 21, 2000, ipsos-reid.com/media/dsp_dis playpr_cdn.cfm?id_to_view=1001 (accessed May 2003).

Iyer, L. S., et al. "Global E-Commerce: Rationale, Digital Divide, and Strategies to Bridge the Divide." *Journal of Global Information Technology Management* 5, no. 1 (2002).

Kannen, P. K., et al. "Marketing Information on the I-Way." *Communications of the ACM* 41, no. 3 (1998): 35–40.

Keenan, V. "Internet Exchange 2000: B2X Emerges as New Industry to Service Exchange Transactions." Keenan Vision Inc., April 24, 2000, eyefortransport.com/archive/ keenanvision17.pdf (accessed February 2003).

Kenny, D., and J. F. Marshall. "Contextual Marketing: The Real Business of the Internet." *Harvard Business Review* (November–December 2000).

King, R. "Online Gambling's Mr. Big." *Business 2.0*, April 2003.

Kopp, S. W., and T. A. Suter. "Fan Sites and Hate Sites on the World Wide Web." *Quarterly Journal of Electronic Commerce* 2, no. 4 (2001).

Landro, L. "Is There a Doctor in the House?" *Wall Street Journal Europe*, June 14–16, 2002.

Lewis, J. B. "I Know What You E-Mailed Last Summer." *Security Management*, January (2002).

Lechner, U., et al. (eds). "Communities and Platforms." Special issue of *Electronic Markets* 10, no. 4 (2001).

Lin, J. C. "Specific Absorption Rates Induced in Head Tissues by Microwave Radiation from Cell Phones." *IEEE Microwave Magazine* 2, no. 1 (2001).

Lubbe, S., and J. M. Van Heerden (eds.). *The Economic and Social Impacts of E-Commerce*. Hershey, PA: The Idea Group, 2003.

Malhotra, Y. "Enabling Knowledge Exchanges for E-Business Communities." *Information Strategy: The Executive's Journal* 18, no. 3, Spring (2002).

McDonald, F. "Consumer Protection Policy in the European Union." *European Business Journal* 12 (2000).

McWilliam, G. "Building Stronger Brands Through Online Communities." *Sloan Management Review,* Spring (2000).

Mowbray, M. "Philosophically Based Limitations to Freedom of Speech in Virtual Communities." *Information Systems Frontiers* 3, no. 1 (2001).

Mowshowitz, A. *Virtual Organization: Toward a Theory of Societal Transformation Stimulated by Information Technology.* Westport, CT: Greenwood Publishing Group, 2002.

Mykytyn, P. P., Jr. "Some Internet and E-Commerce Legal Perspectives Impacting the End User." *Journal of End User Computing* 14, no. 1 (2002).

Nelson, M. "U.S. Governors Support Tax on Internet Commerce." *InfoWorld Electric,* February 26, 1998, idg.net/new_docids/internet/many/government/governors/commerce/keeping/vendors/online/new_docid_9-37716.html (accessed January 2003).

Nickell, J. "Legislation: Privacy, Telecom, Copyrights, and Taxes." *Smart Business,* December 1, 2001.

OECD. oecd.org/subject/e_commerce (accessed February 2003).

Olavsrud, T. "Bertelsmann, Napster Create Membership-based Service." Internetnews. October 31, 2000, internetnews.com/ec-news/article.php/499541 (accessed July 2003).

Olsen, S. "DoubleClick Nearing Privacy Settlements." CNET News.com, March 29, 2002, news.com.com/2100-1023-871654.html (accessed March 2002).

Otto, J. R., and O. B. Chung. "A Framework for Cyber-Enhanced Retailing: Integrating EC Retailing with Brick-and-Mortar Retailing." *Electronic Markets* 10, no. 3 (2000).

Piva, A., et al. "A New Decoder for the Optimum Recovery of Non-Additive Watermarks." *IEEE Transactions on Image Processing* 10, no. 5 (2001).

Piva, A., et al. "Managing Copyright in Open Networks." *IEEE Internet Computing* 6, no. 3 (2002).

Preece, J. *Online Communities.* Chichester, UK: John Wiley & Sons, 2000.

Rafter, M. V. "Trust or Bust?" *The Standard,* March 6, 2000.

Raghaven, P. "Social Networks: From the Web to the Enterprise." *IEEE Internet Computing,* January/February (2002).

Raisch, W. D. *The eMarketplace:Strategies for Succeeding in B2BE-Commerce.* New York: McGraw-Hill, 2000.

Rheingold, H. *The Virtual Community: Homesteading on the Electronic Frontier.* Reading, MA: Addison-Wesley, 1993.

Rose, L. "Know Your Online Shopping Rights." *Internet Shopper* 1, no. 1, 1997, 104.

Roxio.com. "Roxio to Acquire Assets of Napster." November 15, 2002, roxio.com/en/company/news/archive/prelease021115.jhtml (accessed July 2003).

Rupp, W. T., and N. J. Parrish. "Help! I've Been Cybersquatted On!" *Business Horizons,* March–April 2002.

Rykere, R., et al. "Online Privacy Policies: An Assessment." *Journal of Computer Information Systems* (Summer 2002).

Saliba, C. "Study: Auction Fraud Still Top Cybercrime." *E-Commerce Times,* January 10, 2001, ecommercetimes.com/perl/story/6590.html (accessed January 2003).

Schubert, P., and M. Ginsburg. "Virtual Communities of Transaction: The Role of Personalization in E-Commerce." *Electronic Markets* 10, no. 1 (2000).

sec.gov. "SEC Charges 44 Stock Promoters in First Internet Securities Fraud Sweep." SEC news release, October 28, 1998, sec.gov/news/headlines/netfraud.htm (accessed May 2003).

Sharrard, J., et al. "Global Online Trading will Climb to 18% of Sales." *Forrester Research,* December 26, 2001, forrester.com/ER/Research/Brief/Excerpt/0,1317,13720,00.html (accessed January 2003).

Siau, K., et al. "Acceptable Internet Use Policy." *Communications of the ACM* 45, no. 1 (2002).

Silberman, S. "Just Say Nokia Wired." *Wired,* September 1999, wired.com/wired/archive/7.09/nokia_pr.html (accessed May 2003).

South China Morning Post (1999).

Spaulding, M. "The ABC's of MP3: A Crash Course in the Digital Music Phenomenon." In *Signal or Noise? The Future of Music on the Net.* Berkman Center for Internet & Society at Harvard Law School and the Electronic Frontier Foundation, August 23, 2000, cyber.law.harvard.edu/events/netmusic_brbook.html#_Toc475699191 (accessed May 2003).

Spinello, R. A., and H. T. Tavani. "The Internet, Ethical Values, and Conceptual Frameworks: An Introduction to CyberEthics." *Computers and Society,* June (2001).

Stead, B. A., and J. Gilbert. "Ethical Issues in Electronic Commerce." *Journal of Business Ethics,* no. 34, November (2001).

Steinberg, D. "Privacy: Surveillance vs. Freedom." *Smart Business,* December 1, 2001.

Swisher, K. "Seller Beware." *Wall Street Journal,* December 7, 1998.

Teodoro, B. "Internet Scams 101: How You Can Protect Yourself." CNNFN, June 6, 2001, money.cnn.com/2001/06/06/news/q_scams/ (accessed May 2003).

TRUSTe. "TRUSTe 2002 Annual Report." TRUSTe, March 2003, truste.org/truste_annual_report.pdf (accessed May 2003).

Turban, E., et al. *Information Technology for Management,* 4th ed. New York: John Wiley & Sons, 2004.

Tynan, D. "How to Take Back Your Privacy: Keep Spammers and Online Snoops at Bay." *PCWorld,* June 2002.

United Nations. "In Interconnected World All People Must Have Access to Internet Says Secretary-General, in World Telecommunication Day Message." UN.org press release, May 17, 2001, un.Org/News/Press/Docs/2001/Sgsm7791.Doc.Htm (accessed May 2003).

Urbaczewski, A., and L. M. Jessup. "Does Electronic Monitoring of Employee Internet Usage Work?" *Communications of the ACM* (January 2002).

U. S. Congress. "Sonny Bono Copyright Extension Act." *Congressional Legislation*, October 27, 1998, copyright.gov/legislation/s505.pdf (accessed May 2003).

Venkat, K. "Delving into the Digital Divide." *IEEE Spectrum*, February (2002).

Vijayasarathy, L. R. "Internet Taxation, Privacy and Security." *Quarterly Journal of Electronic Commerce*, March (2001).

WebMasterTechniques. "Multichannel Customer Service Increases Online Consumer Demand." August 25, 2000, webmastertechniques.com/News2000/August2000/082500.html (accessed May 2003).

Weiss, G. "Welcome to the (Almost) Digital Hospital." *IEEE*, March (2002).

Williamson, R. "Changing Channels." *Interactive Week*, April 2, 2001.

Wipo.org. wipo.org/about-ip/en/overview.html (accessed May 2003).

Zetlin, M., and B. Pfleging. "The Cult of Community." *Smart Business Magazine*, June 2002.

GLOSSARY

1G. The first generation of wireless technology, which was analog-based.

2G. The second generation of digital wireless technology; accommodates mainly text.

2.5G. Interim wireless technology that can accommodate limited graphics.

3G. The third generation of digital wireless technology; supports rich media such as video clips.

4G. The expected next generation of wireless technology.

802.11b. Standard, developed by the IEEE, on which most of today's WLANs run; WLANs employing this standard have communication speeds of 11 mbps.

access control mechanism. Mechanism that limits the actions that can be performed by an authenticated person or group.

active tokens. Small, stand-alone electronic devices in a two-factor authentication system that generate one-time passwords.

ad management. Methodology and software that enable organizations to perform a variety of activities involved in Web advertising (e.g., tracking viewers, rotating ads).

ad views. The number of times users call up a page that has a banner on it during a specific time period; known as *impressions* or *page views*.

admediaries. Third-party vendors that conduct promotions, especially large scale ones.

advanced planning and scheduling (APS) systems. Programs that use algorithms to identify optimal solutions to complex planning problems that are bound by constraints.

advertising networks. Specialized firms that offer customized Web advertising, such as brokering ads and helping target ads to selected groups of consumers.

advertorial. An advertisement "disguised" to look like an editorial or general information.

affiliate marketing. An arrangement whereby a marketing partner (a business, an organization, or even an individual) refers consumers to the selling company's Web site.

angel investor. A wealthy individual who contributes personal funds and expertise at the earliest stage of business development.

application service provider (ASP). An agent or vendor who assembles the functions needed by enterprises and packages them with outsourced development, operation, maintenance, and other services.

application-level proxy. A firewall that permits requests for Web pages to move from the public Internet to the private network.

associated ad display (text links). An advertising strategy that displays a banner ad related to a term entered in a search engine.

attractors. Web site features that attract and interact with visitors in the target stakeholder group.

auction. A market mechanism by which a seller places an offer to sell a product and buyers make bids sequentially and competitively until a final price is reached.

auction aggregators. Companies that use software agents to visit Web auction sites, find information, and deliver it to users.

auction vortals. Another name for a vertical auction portal.

auditing. The process of collecting information about attempts to access particular resources, use particular privileges, or perform other security actions.

authentication. The process by which one entity verifies that another entity is who they claim to be.

authentication system. System that identifies the legitimate parties to a transaction, determines the actions they are allowed to perform, and limits their actions to only those that are necessary to initiate and complete the transaction.

authorization. The process that ensures that a person has the right to access certain resources.

Auto Identification Center (Auto-ID). Joint partnership among global companies and research universities to create an Internet of Things.

Automated Clearing House (ACH). Electronic network that connects all U.S. financial institutions for the purpose of making funds transfers.

automatic crash notification (ACN). Device that automatically sends the police the location of a vehicle that has been involved in a crash.

autoresponders. Automated e-mail reply systems (text files returned via e-mail), which provide answers to commonly asked questions.

avatars. Animated computer characters that exhibit human-like movements and behaviors.

B2B portals. Information portals for businesses.

back end. The activities that support online order-taking. It includes fulfillment, inventory management, purchasing from suppliers, payment processing, packaging, and delivery.

back-office operations. The activities that support fulfillment of sales, such as accounting and logistics.

balanced scorecard. An adaptive tool that assesses organizational progress toward strategic goals by measuring performance in a number of different areas.

banner. On a Web page, a graphic advertising display linked to the advertiser's Web page.

banner exchanges. Markets in which companies can trade or exchange placement of banner ads on each other's Web sites.

banner swapping. An agreement between two companies to each display the other's banner ad on its Web site.

bartering The exchange of goods and services.

bartering exchange. An intermediary that links parties in a barter; a company submits its surplus to the exchange and receives points of credit, which can be used to buy the items that the company needs from other exchange participants.

bastion gateway. A special hardware server that utilizes application-level proxy software to limit the types of requests that can be passed to an organization's internal networks from the public Internet.

behavioral biometrics. Measurements derived from various actions and indirectly from various body parts (e.g., voice scans or keystroke monitoring).

bid shielding. Having phantom bidders bid at a very high price when an auction begins; they pull out at the last minute, and the bidder who bid a much lower price wins.

biometric systems. Authentication systems that identify a person by measurement of a biological characteristic such as a fingerprint, iris (eye) pattern, facial features, or voice.

blog. A personal Web site that is open to the public.

Bluetooth. Chip technology that enables voice and data communications between many wireless devices through low-power, short-range, digital two-way radio frequencies.

brick-and-mortar organizations. Old-economy organizations (corporations) that perform most of their business off-line, selling physical products by means of physical agents.

brick-and-mortar retailers. Retailers who do business in the non-Internet, physical world in traditional brick-and-mortar stores.

build-to-order. Production system in which manufacturing or assembly will start only after an order is received.

bullwhip effect. Erratic shifts in orders up and down supply chains.

bundle trading. The selling of several related products and/or services together.

business case. A written document that is used by managers to garner funding for specific applications or projects by providing justification for investment of resources.

business intelligence. Activities that not only collect and process data, but also make possible analysis that results in useful—intelligent—solutions to business problems.

business model. A method of doing business by which a company can generate revenue to sustain itself.

business plan. A written document that identifies a company's goals and outlines how the company intends to achieve the goals.

business process reengineering (BPR). A methodology for conducting a comprehensive redesign of an enterprise's processes.

business-to-business (B2B). E-commerce model in which all of the participants are businesses or other organizations.

business-to-business e-commerce (B2B EC). Transactions between businesses conducted electronically over the Internet, extranets, intranets, or private networks; also known as *eB2B* (*electronic B2B*) or just *B2B*.

business-to-business-to-consumer (B2B2C). E-commerce model in which a business provides some product or service to a client business that maintains its own customers.

business-to-consumer (B2C). E-commerce model in which businesses sell to individual shoppers.

business-to-employees (B2E). E-commerce model in which an organization delivers services, information, or products to its individual employees.

buy-side e-marketplace. A corporate-based acquisition site that uses reverse auctions, negotiations, group purchasing, or any other e-procurement method from invited suppliers.

card-not-present (CNP) transaction. When there is no signature and no verification of the credit card signature by the merchant.

certificate authorities (CAs). Third parties that issue digital certificates.

channel conflict. Situation in which an online marketing channel upsets the traditional channels due to real or perceived damage from competition.

chat group. A portion of the Web site where visitors can communicate synchronously.

chatterbots. Animation characters that can talk (chat).

ciphertext. A plaintext message after it has been encrypted into a machine-readable form.

click (click-through or ad click). A count made each time a visitor clicks on an advertising banner to access the advertiser's Web site.

click ratio. The ratio between the number of clicks on a banner ad and the number of times it is seen by viewers; measures the success of a banner in attracting visitors to click on the ad.

click-and-mortar organizations. Organizations that conduct some e-commerce activities, but do their primary business in the physical world.

click-and-mortar retailers. Brick-and-mortar retailers with a transactional Web site from which to conduct business.

clickstream behavior. Customer movements on the Internet; and, what the customer is doing there.

collaborative commerce (c-commerce). The use of digital technologies that enable companies to collaboratively plan, design, develop, manage, and research products, services, and innovative EC applications.

collaborative filtering. A personalization method that uses customer data to predict, based on formulas derived from behavioral sciences, what other products or services a customer may enjoy; predictions can be extended to other customers with similar profiles.

collaborative planning, forecasting, and replenishment (CPFR). Project in which suppliers and retailers collaborate in their planning and demand forecasting to optimize flow of materials along the supply chain.

collaborative portals. Portals that allow collaboration.

co-location. A Web server owned and maintained by the business is placed in a Web hosting service that manages the server's connection to the Internet.

commodity content. Information that is widely available and generally free to access on the Web.

common (security) vulnerabilities and exposures (CVEs). Publicly known computer security risks, which are collected, listed, and shared by a board of security-related organizations (cve.mitre.org).

company-centric EC. E-commerce that focuses on a single company's buying needs (many-to-one or buy-side) or selling needs (one-to-many or sell-side).

competitive forces model. Model, devised by Michael Porter, that says that five major forces of competition determine industry structure and how economic value is divided among the industry players in the industry; analysis of these forces helps companies develop their competitive strategy.

competitor analysis grid. A strategic planning tool that highlights points of differentiation between competitors and the target firm.

Computer Emergency Response Team (CERT). Group of three teams at Carnegie Mellon University that monitor incidence of cyber attacks, analyze vulnerabilities, and provide guidance on protecting against attacks.

confidentiality. Keeping private or sensitive information from being disclosed to unauthorized individuals, entities, or processes.

consortia. E-marketplaces owned by a small group of large vendors, usually in a single industry.

consortium trading exchange (CTE). An exchange formed and operated by a group of major companies to provide industrywide transaction services.

consumer-to-business (C2B). E-commerce model in which individuals use the Internet to sell products or services to organizations or individuals seek sellers to bid on products or services they need.

consumer-to-consumer (C2C). E-commerce model in which consumers sell directly to other consumers. *See also* customer-to-customer.

contact card. A smart card containing a small gold plate on the face that when inserted in a smart-card reader makes contact and so passes data to and from the embedded microchip.

contactless (proximity) card. A smart card with an embedded antenna, by means of which data and applications are passed to and from a card reader unit or other device without contact between the card and the card reader.

content. The text, images, sound, and video that make up a Web page.

content management. The process of adding, revising, and removing content from a Web site to keep content fresh, accurate, compelling, and credible.

cookie. A data file that is placed on a user's hard drive by a Web server, frequently without disclosure or the user's consent, that collects information about the user's activities at a site.

copyright. An exclusive grant from the government that allows the owner to reproduce a work, in whole or in part, and to distribute, perform, or display it to the public in any form or manner, including the Internet.

corporate (enterprise) portal. A gateway for entering a corporate Web site, enabling communication, collaboration, and access to company information.

CPM (cost per thousand impressions). The fee an advertiser pays for each 1,000 times a page with a banner ad is shown.

credit card gateway. An online connection that ties a merchant's systems to the back-end processing systems of the credit card issuer.

cross selling. Offering similar or related products and services to increase sales.

customer interaction center (CIC). A comprehensive service entity in which EC vendors address customer-service issues communicated through various contact channels.

customer relationship management (CRM). A customer service approach that focuses on building long-term and sustainable customer relationships that add value both for the customer and the company.

customer-to-customer (C2C). E-commerce in which both the buyer and the seller are individuals (not businesses); involves activities such as auctions and classified ads. *See also* consumer-to-consumer.

customization. Creation of a product or service according to the buyer's specifications.

cyberbashing. The registration of a domain name that criticizes an organization or person.

cybermediation (electronic intermediation). The use of software (intelligent) agents to facilitate intermediation.

cybersquatting. The practice of registering domain names in order to sell them later at a higher price.

cycle time reduction. Shortening the time it takes for a business to complete a productive activity from its beginning to end.

data conferencing. Virtual meeting in which geographically dispersed groups work on documents together and to exchange computer files during videoconferences.

Data Encryption Standard (DES). The standard symmetric encryption algorithm supported the National Institute of Standards and Technology and used by U.S. government agencies until October 2, 2000. It was replaced by Rijndael, the new Advanced Encryption Standard.

data mart. A small data warehouse designed for a strategic business unit (SBU) or a department.

data mining. The process of searching a large database to discover previously unknown patterns; automates the process of finding predictive information.

data warehouse (DW). A single, server-based data repository that allows centralized analysis, security, and control over the data.

deep linking. Entry into a Web site via the site's interior pages, not the homepage, typically through search engines or external links.

denial-of-service (DoS) attack. An attack on a Web site in which an attacker uses specialized software to send a flood of data packets to the target computer with the aim of overloading its resources.

desktop purchasing. Direct purchasing from internal marketplaces without the approval of supervisors and without intervention of a procurement department.

desktop purchasing systems. Software that automates and support purchasing operations for nonpurchasing professionals and casual end users.

differentiation. Providing a product or service that is unique.

digital certificate. Verification that the holder of a public or private key is who they claim to be.

digital divide. The gap between those who have and those who do not have the ability to access electronic technology in general, and the Internet and EC in particular.

digital economy. An economy that is based on digital technologies, including digital communication networks, computers, software, and other related information technologies; also called the *Internet economy*, the *new economy*, or the *Web economy*.

digital envelope. The combination of the encrypted original message and the digital signature, using the recipient's public key.

digital identity (digital ID). A set of digital information that is associated with a particular individual and is used to identify that individual for security purposes.

digital products. Goods that can be transformed to digital format and delivered over the Internet.

digital signature. An identifying code that can be used to authenticate the identity of the sender of a document.

digital watermarks. Unique identifiers embedded in digital content that make it possible to identify pirated works.

direct marketing. Broadly, marketing that takes place without intermediaries between manufacturers and buyers; in the context of this book, marketing done online between any seller and buyer.

direct materials. Materials used in the production of a product (e.g., steel in a car or paper in a book).

disintermediation. Elimination of intermediaries between sellers and buyers.

distance learning. Formal education that takes place off campus, usually, but not always, through online resources.

distributed denial-of-service (DDoS) attack. A denial-of-service attack in which the attacker gains illegal administrative access to as many computers on the Internet as possible and uses these multiple computers to send a flood of data packets to the target computer.

domain name. A name-based address that identifies an Internet-connected server.

domain name registrar. A business that assists prospective Web site owners with finding and registering a domain name of their choice.

double auction. Auction in which multiple buyers and their bidding prices are matched with multiple sellers and their asking prices, considering the quantities on both sides.

dynamic pricing. Prices that are determined based on supply and demand relationships at any given time.

dynamic trading. Exchange trading that occurs in situations when prices are being determined by supply and demand (e.g., in auctions).

dynamic Web content. Content at a Web site that needs to be changed continually to keep it up to date.

early liquidity. Achieving a critical mass of buyers and sellers as fast as possible, before a start-up company's cash disappears.

e-bartering. *See* electronic bartering.

e-book. A book in digital form that can be read on a computer screen or on a special device.

e-business. A broader definition of EC, which includes not just the buying and selling of goods and services, but also servicing customers, collaborating with business partners, and conducting electronic transactions within an organization.

e-cash. The digital equivalent of paper currency and coins, which enables secure and anonymous purchase of low-priced items.

e-check. The electronic version or representation of a paper check.

e-commerce risk. The likelihood that a negative outcome will occur in the course of developing and operating an electronic commerce strategy.

e-commerce strategy (e-strategy). The formulation and execution of a vision on how a new or existing company intends to do business electronically.

e-co-ops. Another name for online group purchasing organizations.

eCRM. Customer relationship management conducted electronically.

e-distributor. An e-commerce intermediary that connects manufacturers (suppliers) with buyers by aggregating the catalogs of many suppliers in one place—the intermediary's Web site.

edutainment. The combination of education and entertainment, often through games.

e-government. E-commerce model is which a government entity buys or provides goods, services, or information to businesses or individual citizens.

e-grocer. A grocer that will take orders online and provide deliveries on a daily or other regular schedule or will deliver items within a very short period of time.

elasticity. The measure of the incremental spending by buyers as a result of the savings generated.

e-learning. The online delivery of information for purposes of education, training, or knowledge management.

electronic auctions (e-auctions). Auctions conducted online.

electronic banking (e-banking). Various banking activities conducted from home or the road using an Internet connection; also known as *cyberbanking*, *virtual banking*, *online banking*, and *home banking*.

electronic bartering (e-bartering). Bartering conducted online, usually by a bartering exchange.

electronic catalogs. The presentation of product information in an electronic form; the backbone of most e-selling sites.

electronic commerce (EC). The process of buying, selling, or exchanging products, services, and information via computer networks.

electronic data interchange (EDI). The electronic transfer of specially formatted standard business documents, such as bills, orders, and confirmations sent between business partners.

electronic discussion forum. A portion of the Web site where visitors can post questions, comments, and answers.

electronic market (e-marketplace). An online marketplace where buyers and sellers meet to exchange goods, services, money, or information.

Electronic Product Code (EPC). Universal standard for product identification, stored on an Radio Frequency Identification (RFID) tag.

electronic retailing (e-tailing). Retailing conducted online, over the Internet.

electronic script. A form of electronic money (or points), issued by a third party as part of a loyalty program; can be used by consumers to make purchases at participating stores.

electronic shopping cart. An order-processing technology that allows customers to accumulate items they wish to buy while they continue to shop.

electronic wallet (e-wallet). A software component in which a user stores credit card numbers and other personal information; when shopping online; the user simply clicks the e-wallet to automatically fill in information needed to make a purchase.

e-logistics. The logistics of EC systems, typically involving small parcels sent to many customers' homes.

e-loyalty. Customer loyalty to an e-tailer.

e-mail discussion list. A group of people who share a common interest and who communicate with each other via e-mail messages managed by e-mail list software.

e-mall (online mall). An online shopping center where many stores are located.

e-marketplace. *See* electronic marketplace.

encryption. The process of scrambling (encrypting) a message in such a way that it is difficult, expensive, or time-consuming for an unauthorized person to unscramble (decrypt) it.

encryption algorithm. The mathematical formula used to encrypt the plaintext into the ciphertext, and vice versa.

e-newsletter. A collection of short, informative articles sent at regular intervals by e-mail to individuals who have an interest in the newsletter's topic.

Enhanced Messaging Service (EMS). An extension of SMS capable of simple animation, tiny pictures, and short tunes.

e-payments. Payments made online.

e-procurement. The electronic acquisition of goods and services for organizations.

e-supply chain. A supply chain that is managed electronically, usually with Web technologies.

e-supply chain management (e-SCM). The collaborative use of technology to improve the operations of supply chain activities as well as the management of supply chains.

e-tailers. Those who conduct retail business over the internet.

e-tailing. *See* electronic retailing.

ethics. The branch of philosophy that deals with what is considered to be right and wrong.

exchange (electronic). A public electronic market with many buyers and sellers, usually owned and run by a third party or a consortium, in which many buyers and many sellers meet electronically to trade with each other; also called *e-marketplaces, e-markets, trading communities,* and *trading exchanges.*

exchange-to-exchange (E2E). E-commerce model in which electronic exchanges formally connect to one another for the purpose of exchanging information.

external. Web site development; when the business hires another firm to build and/or maintain the Web site.

extranet. A network that uses a Virtual Printer Network (VPN) to link intranets in different locations over the Internet; an "extended intranet."

e-zines. Electronic magazines.

FAQ page. A Web site page that lists questions that are frequently asked by customers and also contains the answers to those questions.

fingerprint scanning. Measurement of the discontinuities of a person's fingerprint, converted to a set of numbers that are stored as a template and used to authenticate identity.

firewall. A network node consisting of both hardware and software that isolates a private network from a public network.

forward auction. An auction in which a seller entertains bids for a product from potential buyers.

frame. An HTML element that divides the browser window into two or more separate windows.

front end. The portion of an e-tailer's business processes through which customers interact, including the seller's portal, electronic catalogs, a shopping cart, a search engine, and a payment gateway.

front-office operations. The business processes, such as sales and advertising, that are visible to customers.

geographical information system (GIS). System that integrates GPS data onto digitized map displays.

global positioning system (GPS). A wireless system that uses satellites to enable users to determine their position anywhere on the earth.

government-to-business (G2B). E-government category that includes interactions between governments and businesses (government selling to businesses and providing them with services and businesses selling products and services to government).

government-to-citizens (G2C). E-government category that includes all the interactions between a government and its citizens.

government-to-employees (G2E). E-government category that includes activities and services between government units and their employees.

government-to-government (G2G). E-government category that includes activities within government units and those between governments.

group decision support system (GDSS). An interactive computer-based system that facilitates the solution of semistructured and unstructured problems by a group of decision makers.

group purchasing. The aggregation of orders from several buyers into volume purchases so that better prices can be negotiated.

groupware. Software products that support collaboration, over networks, among groups of people who share a common task or goal.

hash. A mathematical computation that is applied to a message, using a private key, to encrypt the message.

hit. A request for data from a Web page or file.

honeynet. A way to evaluate vulnerabilities of an organization by studying the types of attacks to which a site is subjected, using a network of systems called *honeypots*.

honeypots. Production systems (e.g., firewalls, routers, Web servers, database servers) designed to do real work but to be watched and studied as network intrusions occur.

horizontal exchanges. Exchanges that handle materials used by companies in different industries.

horizontal marketplaces. Markets that concentrate on a service, materials, or a product that is used in all types of industries (e.g., office supplies, PCs).

hypermediation. Extensive use of both human and electronic intermediation to provide assistance in all phases of an e-commerce venture.

incubator. A company, university, or not-for-profit organization that supports businesses in their initial stages of development.

indirect materials. Materials used to support production (e.g., office supplies or light bulbs).

infomediaries. Electronic intermediaries that control information flow in cyberspace, often aggregating information and selling it to others.

information architecture. How the site and its Web pages are organized, labeled, and navigated to support browsing and searching throughout the Web site.

information portal. A single point of access through a Web browser to business information inside and/or outside an organization; portals that store data and enable users to navigate and query these data.

information systems. Communication systems that enable e-commerce activities to go on *within* individual organizations.

informational Web site. A Web site that does little more than provide information about the business and its products and services.

integrity. As applied to data, the ability to protect data from being altered or destroyed in an unauthorized or accidental manner.

intellectual property. Creations of the mind, such as inventions, literary and artistic works, and symbols, names, images, and designs used in commerce.

interaction costs. The time and money expended when people and companies exchange goods, services, and ideas.

interactive marketing. Online marketing, enabled by the Internet, in which advertisers can interact directly with customers and consumers can interact with advertisers/vendors.

interactive voice response (IVR). A computer voice system that enables users to request and receive information and to enter and change data through regular telephone lines or through 1G cell phones.

interactive Web site. A Web site that provides opportunities for the customers and the business to communicate and share information.

intermediary. A third party that operates between sellers and buyers.

internal marketplace. A marketplace that is internal to one organization; it includes the aggregated catalogs of all approved suppliers combined into a single internal electronic catalog.

internal Web site development. The process of building and/or maintaining the Web site with company staff.

Internet. A public, global communications network that provides direct connectivity to anyone over a LAN via an ISP or directly via an ISP.

Internet ecosystem. The business model of the Internet economy.

Internet radio. A Web site that provides music, talk, and other entertainment, both live and stored, from a variety of radio stations.

Internet of Things. A network that connects computers to objects in order to be able to track individual items as they move from factories to store shelves to recycling facilities, providing near-perfect supply chain visibility.

Internet-based (Web) EDI. EDI that runs on the Internet and is widely accessible to most companies, including SMEs.

interorganizational information systems (IOSs). Communications systems that allows routine transaction processing and information flow between two or more organizations.

interstitial. An initial Web page or a portion of it that is used to capture the user's attention for a short time while other content is loading.

intrabusiness EC. E-commerce activities conducted *within* an organization.

intranet. A corporate LAN or WAN that uses Internet technology such as Web browsers and is secured behind a company's firewalls.

intrusion detection systems (IDSs). A special category of software that can monitor activity across a network or on a host computer, watch for suspicious activity, and take automated action based on what it sees.

iris scanning. Measurement of the unique spots in the iris (colored part of the eye), converted to a set of numbers that are stored as a template and used to authenticate identity.

ISP hosting service. A hosting service that provides an independent, standalone Web site for small and medium-sized businesses.

key. The secret code used to encrypt and decrypt a message.

keystroke monitoring. Measurement of the pressure, speed, and rhythm with which a word is typed, converted to a set of numbers that are stored as a template and used to authenticate identity; this biometric is still under development.

keyword banners. Banner ads that appear when a predetermined word is queried from a search engine.

knowledge discovery in databases (KDD)/knowledge discovery (KD). The process of extracting useful knowledge from volumes of data.

knowledge management (KM). The process of creating or capturing knowledge, storing and protecting it, updating and maintaining it, and using it.

knowledge portal. A single point of access software system intended to provide timely access to information and to support communities of knowledge workers.

letter of credit (LC). A written agreement by a bank to pay the seller, on account of the buyer, a sum of money upon presentation of certain documents.

liquidity. The result of having a sufficient number of participants in the marketplace as well as a sufficient transaction volume.

localization. The process of converting media products developed in one country to a form culturally and linguistically acceptable in countries outside the original target market.

location-based commerce (l-commerce). Mobile commerce transactions targeted to individuals in specific locations, at specific times.

logistics. The operations involved in the efficient and effective flow and storage of goods, services, and related information from point of origin to point of consumption.

look and feel. The elements that visually distinguish a site from any other, including layout, typeface, colors, graphics, and navigation aids.

macro virus or **macro worm.** A virus or worm that is executed when the application object that contains the macro is opened or a particular procedure is executed.

maintenance, repair, and operation items (MROs). Indirect materials used in activities that support production that are usually not under regular contract with suppliers.

malware. A generic term for malicious software.

market maker. The third party that operates an exchange (and in many cases, also owns the exchange).

market segmentation. The process of dividing a consumer market into logical groups for conducting marketing research, advertising, and sales.

marketspace. A marketplace in which sellers and buyers exchange goods and services for money (or for other goods and services), but do so electronically.

mass customization. Production of large quantities of customized items.

maverick buying. Unplanned purchases of items needed quickly, often at non-pre-negotiated, higher prices.

m-business. The broadest definition of m-commerce, in which e-business is conducted in a wireless environment.

merchant brokering. Deciding from whom (from what merchant) to buy a product.

merge-in-transit. Logistics model in which components for a product may come from two different physical locations and are shipped directly to customer's location.

message digest. A summary of a message, converted into a string of digits, after the hash has been applied.

meta tag. An HTML element that describes the contents of a Web page.

metadata. Data about data, including software programs about data, rules for organizing data, and data summaries.

metric. A specific, measurable standard against which actual performance is compared; may be quantitative or qualitative.

microbrowser. Wireless software designed with limited bandwidth and limited memory requirements.

micropayments. Electronic payments for small-purchase amounts (generally less than $10).

microproduct. A small digital product costing a few cents.

mirror site. An exact duplicate of the original Web site, but it is physically located on a Web server on another continent.

mobile commerce (m-commerce). E-commerce transactions and activities conducted in a wireless environment.

mobile computing. Permits real-time access to information, applications, and tools that, until recently, were accessible only from a desktop computer.

mobile portal. A customer interaction channel that aggregates content and services for mobile users; a portal accessible via mobile devises such as cell phones and PDAs.

Mondex. A stored-value card designed to handle small purchases or micropayments; sponsored by Mondex, a subsidiary of MasterCard.

multichannel business model. Describes a company that sells in multiple marketing channels simultaneously (e.g., both physical and online stores).

Multimedia Messaging Service (MMS). The next generation of wireless messaging; will be able to deliver rich media.

m-wallet (mobile wallet). A wireless wallet that enables cardholders to make purchases with a single click from their wireless device.

"name-your-own-price" model. Auction model in which a would-be buyer specifies the price (and other terms) they are willing to pay to any willing and able seller. It is a C2B model, pioneered by Priceline.com.

National Infrastructure Protection Center (NIPC). A joint partnership, under the auspices of the FBI, among governmental and private industry; designed to prevent and protect the nation's infrastructure.

Netizen. Any person surfing the Internet.

nonrepudiation. The ability to limit parties from refuting that a legitimate transaction took place, usually by means of a signature.

nontechnical attack. An attack that uses chicanery to trick people into revealing sensitive information or performing actions that compromise the security of a network.

Object Name Service (ONS). Service that points a computer to an address on the Internet where information about a product is stored.

on-demand delivery service. Express delivery made fairly quickly after an online order is received.

one-to-one marketing. Marketing that treats each customer in a unique way.

online analytical processing (OLAP). End-user analytical activities, such as DSS modeling using spreadsheets and graphics, that are done online.

online intermediary. An online third party that brokers a transaction online between a buyer and a seller; can be virtual or click-and-mortar.

online negotiation. A back-and-forth electronic process of bargaining until the buyer and seller reach a mutually agreeable price; usually done by software (intelligent) agents.

online publishing. The electronic delivery of newspapers, magazines, books, news, music, videos, and other digitizable information over the Internet.

operational data store. A database for use in transaction processing (operational) systems that uses data warehouse concepts to provide clean data.

opt-in clause. Agreement that requires computer users to take specific steps to *allow* collection of information.

opt-out clause. Agreement that requires computer users to take specific steps to *prevent* collection of information.

order fulfillment. All the activities needed to provide customers with ordered goods and services, including related customer services.

organizational knowledge base. The repository for an enterprise's accumulated knowledge.

outsourcing. The use of a third-party vendor to provide all or part of the products and services that could be provided internally.

packet filters. Rules that can accept or reject incoming packets based on source and destination addresses and the other identifying information.

packet-filtering routers. Firewalls that filter data and requests moving from the public Internet to a private network based on the network addresses of the computer sending or receiving the request.

packets. Segments of data and requests sent from one computer to another on the Internet; consist of the Internet addresses of the computers sending and receiving the data, plus other identifying information that distinguish one packet from another.

partner relationship management (PRM). Business strategy that focuses on providing comprehensive quality service to business partners.

partnering Web site development. When a mixture of internal and external development is used to build and/or maintain a Web site.

passive tokens. Storage devices (e.g., magnetic strips) used in a two-factor authentication system that contain a secret code.

patent. A document that grants the holder exclusive rights on an invention for a fixed number of years.

payment card. Electronic card that contains information that can be used for payment purposes.

peer-to-peer (P2P). A network architecture in which workstations (or PCs) share data and processing with each other directly rather than through a central server; can be used in C2C, B2B, and B2C e-commerce.

permission advertising (permission marketing). Advertising (marketing) strategy in which customers agree to accept advertising and marketing materials.

personal digital assistant (PDA). A handheld wireless computer.

personal firewall. A network node designed to protect an individual user's desktop system from the public network by monitoring all the traffic that passes through the computer's network interface card.

personalization. The ability to tailor a product, service, or Web content to specific user preferences.

personalized content. Web content that is prepared to match the needs and expectations of the individual visitor.

person-to-person (P2P) payments. E-payment schemes (such as PayPal) that enable the transfer of funds between two individuals.

pervasive computing. Invisible, everywhere computing that is embedded in the objects around us.

physiological biometrics. Measurements derived directly from different parts of the body (e.g., fingerprints, iris, hand, facial characteristics).

plaintext. An unencrypted message in human-readable form.

pop-under ad. An ad that appears underneath the current browser window, so when the user closes the active window, they see the ad.

pop-up ad. An ad that appears before, after, or during Internet surfing or when reading e-mail.

premium content. Content not available elsewhere on the Web.

presentment. The presentation and hosting on a specialized Web server of information that is typically printed on a bill.

privacy. The right to be left alone and the right to be free of unreasonable personal intrusions.

private e-marketplaces. Online markets owned by a single company; can be either sell-side or buy-side marketplaces.

private exchanges. E-marketplaces that are owned and operated by one company. Also known as *company-centric marketplaces*.

private key. Encryption code that is known only to its owner.

procurement management. The coordination of all the activities relating to purchasing goods and services needed to accomplish the mission of an organization.

product brokering. Deciding what product to buy.

product lifecycle management (PLM). Business strategy that enables manufacturers to control and share product-related data as part of product design and development efforts.

Product Markup Language (PML). Proposed new markup language, based on the XML standard, that specifies how a product's name, category, manufacture date, expiration date, and the like will be represented in a computer.

project champion. The person who ensures the EC project gets the time, attention, and resources required, as well as defending the project from detractors at all times.

protocol tunneling. Method used to ensure confidentiality and integrity of data transmitted over the Internet, by encrypting data packets, sending them in packets across the Internet, and decrypting them at the destination address.

proxies. Special software programs that run on the gateway server and pass repackaged packets from one network to the other.

proxy bidding. Use of a software system to place bids on behalf of buyers; when another bidder places a bid, the software (the proxy) will automatically raise the bid to the next level until it reaches the predetermined maximum price.

public e-marketplaces (public exchanges). B2B markets, usually owned and/or managed by an independent third party, that include many sellers and many buyers; also known as *exchanges*.

public key. Encryption code that is publicly available to anyone.

public key encryption. Method of encryption that uses a pair of matched keys—a public key to encrypt a message and a private key to decrypt it, or vice versa.

public key infrastructure (PKI). A scheme for securing e-payments using public key encryption and various technical components.

purchasing cards. Special-purpose payment cards issued to a company's employees to be used solely for purchasing nonstrategic materials and services up to a preset dollar limit.

quality uncertainty. The uncertainty of online buyers about the quality of non-commodity type products that they have never seen, especially from an unknown vendor.

radio frequency identification (RFID). Generic term for technologies that use radio waves to automatically identify individual items.

random banners. Banner ads that appear at random, not as the result of the viewer's action.

reintermediation. Establishment of new intermediary roles for traditional intermediaries that were disintermediated.

request for quote (RFQ). The "invitation" to participate in a tendering (bidding) system.

return on investment (ROI). A ratio of required costs and perceived benefits of a project or an application.

revenue model. Description of how the company or an EC project will earn revenue.

reverse auction (bidding or **tendering system).** Auction in which the buyer places an item for bid (*tender*) on a request for quote (RFQ) system, potential suppliers bid on the job, with price reducing sequentially, and the lowest bid wins; primarily a B2B or G2B mechanism.

reverse logistics. The movement of returns from customers to vendors.

Rijndael. The new Advanced Encryption Standard used to secure U.S. government communications since October 2, 2000.

rolling warehouse. Logistics method in which products on the delivery truck are not preassigned to a destination, but the decision about quantity to unload at each destination is made at the time of unloading.

RSA. The most common public key encryption algorithm; uses keys ranging in length from 512 bits to 1,024 bits.

sales force automation (SFA). Software that automates the tasks performed by sales people in the field, such as data collection and its transmission.

Savant. Software created by the Auto-ID center that gathers information from RFID readers and passes it on to various business applications.

scenario planning. A strategic planning methodology that generates plausible alternative futures to help decision makers identify actions that can be taken today to ensure success in the future.

screen sharing. Software that enables group members, even in different locations, to work on the same document, which is shown on the PC screen of each participant.

screenphone. A telephone equipped with a color screen, possibly a keyboard, e-mail, and Internet capabilities.

sealed-bid auction. Auction in which each bidder bids only once; a silent auction, in which bidders do not know who is placing bids or what the prices are.

search engine. A computer program that can access a database of Internet resources, search for specific information or keywords, and report the results.

search engine optimization (SEO). The application of strategies intended to position a Web site at the top of Web search engines.

Secure Electronic Transaction (SET). A protocol designed to provide secure online credit card transactions for both consumers and merchants; developed jointly by Netscape, Visa, MasterCard, and others.

Secure Socket Layer (SSL). Protocol that utilizes standard certificates for authentication and data encryption to ensure privacy or confidentiality.

security risk management. A systematic process for determining the likelihood of various security attacks and for identifying the actions needed to prevent or mitigate those attacks.

self-hosting. When a business acquires the hardware, software, staff, and dedicated telecommunications services necessary to set up and manage its own Web site.

sell-side e-marketplace. A Web-based private e-market in which a company sells either standard or customized products to qualified companies via e-catalogs or auctions, usually over an extranet.

shilling. Placing fake bids on auction items to artificially jack up the bidding price.

shopping portals. Gateways to storefronts and malls; may be comprehensive or niche-oriented.

shopping robots (also shopping agents or shopbots). Tools that scout the Web on behalf of consumers who specify search criteria.

Short Message Service (SMS). Technology that allows for sending of short text messages on some cell phones.

signature file. A simple text message an e-mail program automatically adds to outgoing messages.

single auction. Auction in which at least one side of the market consists of a single entity (a single buyer or a single seller).

site navigation. Aids that help visitors find the information they need quickly and easily.

smart card. An electronic card containing an embedded microchip that enables predefined operations or the addition, deletion, or manipulation of information on the card.

smartphone. Internet-enabled cell phones that can support mobile applications.

SMEs. Small to medium enterprises.

sniping. Entering a bid during the very last seconds of an auction and outbidding the highest bidder (in the case of selling items).

social computing. An approach aimed at making the human–computer interface more natural.

social engineering. A type of nontechnical attack that uses social pressures to trick computer users into compromising computer networks to which those individuals have access.

software (intelligent) agent. Software that can perform routine tasks that require intelligence.

spamming. The practice of indiscriminately broadcasting messages over the Internet (e.g., junk mail).

spot buying. The purchase of goods and services as they are needed, usually at prevailing market prices.

spot sourcing. Unplanned purchases made as the need arises.

spyware. Software that gathers user information, through an Internet connection, without the user's knowledge.

stickiness. Characteristic that influences the average length of time a visitor stays in a site.

storebuilder service. A hosting service that provides disk space and services to help small and micro businesses build a Web site quickly and cheaply.

stored-value card. A card that has monetary value loaded onto it, and is usually rechargeable.

storefront. A single company's Web site where products and services are sold.

strategic sourcing. Purchases involving long-term contracts that are usually based on private negotiations between sellers and buyers.

strategy. A broad-based formula for how a business is going to compete, what its goals should be, and what plans and policies will be needed to carry out those goals.

strategy assessment. The continuous evaluation of progress toward the organization's strategic goals, resulting in corrective action and, if necessary, strategy reformulation.

strategy formulation. The development of strategies to exploit opportunities and manage threats in the business environment in light of corporate strengths and weaknesses.

strategy implementation. The development of detailed, short-term plans for carrying out the projects agreed on in strategy formulation.

strategy initiation. The initial phase of strategic planning in which the organization examines itself and its environment.

Subscriber Identification Module (SIM) card. An extractable storage card used for identification, transaction processing, and the like.

supply chain. The flow of materials, information, money, and services from raw material suppliers through factories and warehouses to the end customers.

SWOT analysis. A methodology that surveys external opportunities and threats and relates them to internal strengths and weaknesses.

symmetric (private) key system. An encryption system that uses the same key to encrypt and decrypt the message.

syndication. The sale of the same good (e.g., digital content) to many customers, who then integrate it with other offerings and resell it or give it away free.

systematic sourcing. Purchasing done in long-term supplier–buyer relationships.

technical attack. An attack perpetrated using software and systems knowledge or expertise.

teleconferencing. The use of electronic communication that allows two or more people at different locations to have a simultaneous conference.

telematics. The integration of computers and wireless communications to improve information flow using the principles of telemetry.

telewebs. Call centers that combine Web channels with portal-like self-service.

tendering. Model in which a buyer requests would-be sellers to submit bids and the lowest bidder wins.

text mining. The application of data mining to nonstructured or less-structured text files.

third-party logistics (3PL) suppliers. External, rather than in-house, providers of logistics services.

trademark. A symbol used by businesses to identify their goods and services; government registration of the trademark confers exclusive legal right to its use.

transaction log. A record of user activities at a company's Web site.

transactional Web site. A Web site that sells products and services.

Transport Layer Security (TLS). As of 1996, another name for the SSL protocol.

Trojan horse. A program that appears to have a useful function but contains a hidden function that presents a security risk.

trust. The psychological state-of-mind of involved parties who are willing to pursue further interaction to achieve a planned goal.

unique visit. A count of the number of visitors to a site, regardless of how many pages are viewed per visit.

up selling. Offering an upgraded version of the product in order to boost sales and profit.

user profile. The requirements, preferences, behaviors, and demographic traits of a particular customer.

value proposition. The benefit that a company's products or services provide to customers using EC; the consumer need that is being fulfilled.

value-added networks (VANs). Private, third–party-managed networks that add communications services and security to existing common carriers; used to implement traditional EDI systems.

venture capital (VC). Money invested in a business by an individual or a group of individuals (venture capitalists) in exchange for equity in the business.

versioning. Selling the same good, but with different selection and delivery characteristics.

vertical auction. Auction that takes place between sellers and buyers in one industry or for one commodity.

vertical exchange. An exchange whose members are in one industry or industry segment.

vertical marketplaces. Markets that deal with one industry or industry segment (e.g., steel, chemicals).

Vickrey auction. Sealed-bid auction in which the item is awarded to the highest bidder, but at the second-highest price that was bid (in the case of selling items).

video teleconference. Virtual meeting in which participants in one location can see participants at other locations on a large screen or a desktop computer.

viral marketing. Word-of-mouth marketing by which customers promote a product or service by telling others about it.

virtual (Internet) community. A group of people with similar interests who interact with one another using the Internet.

virtual corporation. An organization composed of several business partners sharing costs and resources for the production or utilization of a product or service.

virtual credit card. An e-payment system in which a credit card issuer gives a special transaction number that can be used online in place of regular credit card numbers.

virtual (pure-play) e-tailers. Firms that sell directly to consumers over the Internet without maintaining a physical sales channel.

virtual meetings. Online meetings whose members are indifferent locations, frequently in different countries.

virtual (pure-play) organizations. Organizations that conduct their business activities solely online.

virtual private network (VPN). A network that creates tunnels of secured data flows, using cryptography and authorization algorithms, to provide secure transport of private communications over the public Internet.

virtual reality (VR). System that delivers interactive computer-generated three-dimensional graphics to a user through a head-mounted display.

virtual university. An online university from which students take classes from home or other off-site locations usually via the Internet.

virus. A piece of software code that inserts itself into a host, including the operating systems, to propagate; it requires that its host program be run to activate it.

Visa Cash. A stored-value card designed to handle small purchases or micropayments; sponsored by Visa.

visit. A series of requests during one navigation of a Web site; a pause of request for a certain length of time ends a visit.

voice portal. A portal accessed by telephone or cell phone

voice scanning. Measurement of the acoustical patterns in speech production, converted to a set of numbers that are stored as a template and used to authenticate identity.

Voice XML (VXML). An extension of XML designed to accommodate voice.

vortals. B2B portals that focus on a single industry or industry segment; "vertical portals."

wearable devices. Mobile wireless computing devices for employees who work on buildings and other difficult-to-climb places.

Web bugs. Tiny graphics files embedded on e-mail messages and in Web sites that transmit information about the user and their movements to a Web server.

Web content management. The process of collecting, publishing, revising, and removing content from a Web site to keep content fresh, accurate, compelling, and credible.

Web hosting service. A dedicated Web site hosting company that offers a wide range of hosting services and functionality to businesses of all sizes.

Web mining. The application of data mining techniques to discover meaningful patterns, profiles, and trends from both the content and usage of Web sites.

Web self-service. Activities conducted by users on the Web to provide answers to their questions (e.g., tracking) or for product configuration.

Web services. An architecture enabling assembly of distributed applications from software services and tying them together.

Web site construction. The initial content creation, design, programming, and installation phases of a Web site's development.

Web site maintenance. The ongoing process of keeping the Web site open for business, managing content, fixing problems, and making incremental additions to the site.

Webcasting. A free Internet news service that broadcasts personalized news and information in categories selected by the user.

Webinars. Seminars on the Web (Web-based seminars).

Weblogging (blogging). Technology for personal publishing on the Internet.

wireless 911 (e-911). Calls from cellular phones to providers of emergency services.

wireless access point. An antenna connecting a mobile device (laptop or PDA) to a wired LAN.

Wireless Application Protocol (WAP). A set of communications protocols designed to enable different kinds of wireless devices to talk to a server installed on a mobile network so users can access the Internet.

wireless fidelity (Wi-Fi). Another name for the 802.11b standard on which most WLANs run.

wireless LAN (WLAN). LAN without the cables; used to transmit and receive data over the airwaves.

Wireless Markup Language (WML). Scripting language used for creating content in the wireless Web environment; based on XML, minus unnecessary content to increase speed.

Wireless Transport Layer Security (WTLS). Communication protocols that enable encrypted communications between a mobile device and the WAP gateway and support the key elements of electronic payment systems.

workflow. The movement of information as it flows through the sequence of steps that make up an organization's work procedures.

workflow management. The automation of workflows, so that documents, information, and tasks are passed from one participant to the next in the steps of an organization's business process.

workflow systems. Business process automation tools that place system controls in the hands of user departments to automate information-processing tasks.

worm. A software program that runs independently, consuming the resources of its host in order to maintain itself and propagating a complete working version of itself onto another machine.

XML (eXtensible Markup Language). Standard (and its variants) used to improve compatibility between the disparate systems of business partners by defining the meaning of data in business documents.

Index

A

Access control mechanism, defined, 474

Ace Hardware Corporation, 314

ACN. *See* Automatic crash notification

Active tokens, defined, 474

Activity-based filtering, 139

Adaptec, Inc., 310–311

Ad click, defined, 181

Ad-hoc query, 175

Ad management, defined, 199

Admediation, defined, 195

Administrative workflow, 325

Ads as a commodity, 193

Ad server networks, defined, 184

Ad spawning, 188

Adult services online, 374–375

Advanced planning and scheduling (APS) systems, defined, 315

Advertising
in B2B, 162–164
e-commerce impact on, 66
wireless, 399–400
See also Online advertising

Advertising fees, in exchanges, 265

Advertising fees revenue model, 12, 13

Advertising networks, defined, 184

Advertorial, defined, 192

Ad views, defined, 181

Advise, online, 367–369

Advocacy marketing, 193

Affiliate fees revenue model, 12, 13

Affiliate marketing
business model
defined, 14
syndication and, 45
in online advertising, 192–193

Affiliate programs (B2B), 164
advertising and, 197

Affiliateworld.com, 14

Agency costs, in electronic market-places, 61

Aggregation
buyer model, 271, 272
external (purchasing, 243–244
internal (purchasing), 243
of supplier catalogs, 240–241
supplier model, 270–271

Akamai Corporation, 551

Akamai Technologies, Inc., 195

Alibaba.com, 268–269

Alta Vista, 48

Amadeus Global Travel Distribution, 91

Amazon.com, 4, 15
affiliate marketing, 14
alliance of virtual and traditional retailers, 114–115
B2C and B2B, 82–83
change with changing market conditions, 16
differentiation, personalization, and customer service by, 63
e-tailing example, 81
history of, 603

American Airlines, 53

American Express, 498

America Online (AOL), 7, 48
change with changing market conditions, 16

AMR Research, 10

Amway, 335–336

Analytical customer relationship management (CRM), 23

Analytical processing
data marts, 173
data warehouses (DW), 171–173, 174
operational data stores, 174

Angel investor, defined, 607

Anticybersquatting Consumer Protection Act (1999), 652

AOL Time Warner. *See* America Online

Application-level proxy
defined, 481
exhibit, 482

Application middleware, 390

Application server provider (ASP), 582
defined, 557

Application service providers (ASPs), 199

APS. *See* Advanced planning and scheduling (APS) systems

Arena.com, 38

Asia-Pacific Economic Cooperation (APEC), 590

Asite.com, 284–285

AskJeeves, 48

Assessment. *See* Strategy assessment

Associated ad display, defined, 192

Atomic e-business models, 12

Attacks on e-commerce security, 467
nontechnical (social engineering), 468, 469
technical, 469
common (security) vulnerabilities and exposures (CVEs), 468–469
defined, 468
denial-of-service (DoS) attack, 470
distributed denial-of-service (DDoS) attacks, 470, 471

zombies, 470
See also Malware

Attractors, 608

Auction aggregators, defined, 441

Auctions, 671
auction aggregators, 441
auction vortals, 444
auto-sniping, 443
B2B forward auctions (Dell), 434
B2B reverse auctions, 435
bartering, 450
benefits
to buyers, 437
to e-auctioneers, 437–438
to sellers, 436–437
bid retraction, 444
bundle trading, 447
C2C reverse auctions, 435
characteristics, 50
customer-to-customer (C2C), 369
defined, 50, 433
double, 52, 445, 447
dynamic pricing, 51
B2B reverse auctions, 435
C2C reverse auctions, 435
many sellers, many buyers, 436
name-your-own-price model, 435
one buyer, many potential sellers, 434–435
one buyer, one seller, 433
one seller, many potential buyers, 433–434
reverse auctions, 435
types of (exhibit), 434
in dynamic trading, 277
economic impacts of (exhibit), 436
featured, 444
first-price sealed bid, 434
forward, 51, 216, 348, 433, 434
fraud in, 447, 659
protecting against, 448–449
types of, 448
future of, 455
global, 455
implementation issues
auction rules, 452
auctions in exchanges, 452
building auction sites, 453
strategic issues, 452
using intermediaries, 451–452
limitations of, 438
limitations of traditional off-line, 50
many sellers, many buyers, 52
mobile, 454–455
name-your-own-price model, 435, 439

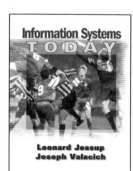

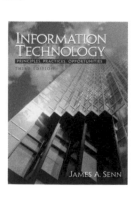
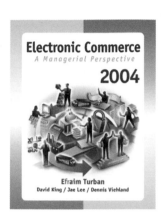

Systems Analysis and Design:

George/Batra/Valacich/ Hoffer, *Object-Oriented Systems Analysis and Design*

Hoffer/George/Valacich, *Modern Systems Analysis and Design 3/e*

Kendall & Kendall, *Systems Analysis and Design 5/e*

Valacich/George/Hoffer, *Essentials of Systems Analysis and Design 2/e*

Telecommunications, Networking and Business Data Communications:

Stamper & Case, *Business Data Communications 6/e*

Panko, *Business Data Networks and Telecommunications 4/e*

Security:

Panko, *Corporate Computer and Network Security*

Volonino & Robinson, *Principles and Practice of Information Security*

Other Titles:

Awad & Ghaziri, *Knowledge Management*

Becerra-Fernandez et al., *Knowledge Management*

Crews, *Programming Right from the Start with VB .Net*

George, *Computers in Society*

Marakas, *Decision Support Systems in the 21st Century 2/e*

Marakas, *Modern Data Warehousing, Mining, and Visualization: Core Concepts*

Turban & Aronson, *Decision Support Systems and Intelligent Systems 6/e*

Wagner & Zubey, *Customer Relationship Management Applications*